ASP.NET Core in Action

THIRD EDITION

ANDREW LOCK

MANNING

SHELTER ISLAND

For online information and ordering of this and other Manning books, please visit
www.manning.com. The publisher offers discounts on this book when ordered in quantity.
For more information, please contact

Special Sales Department
Manning Publications Co.
20 Baldwin Road
PO Box 761
Shelter Island, NY 11964
Email: orders@manning.com

Manning Publications Co.
20 Baldwin Road
PO Box 761
Shelter Island, NY 11964

Development editor: Marina Michaels
Technical editor: Filip Wojcieszyn
Review editor: Adriana Sabo
Production editor: Kathleen Rossland
Copy editor: Keir Simpson
Proofreader: Jason Everett
Technical proofreader: Tanya Wilke
Typesetter: Gordan Salinovic
Cover designer: Marija Tudor

ISBN 9781633438620
Printed and bound by CPI Group (UK) Ltd, Croydon, CR0 4YY

brief contents

contents

preface

ASP.NET has a long history; Microsoft released the first version in 2002 as part of the original .NET Framework 1.0. Since then, it's been through multiple iterations, each version bringing added features and extensibility. Each iteration, however, was built on the same underlying framework provided by System.Web.dll. This library is part of the .NET Framework, so it comes preinstalled in all versions of Windows.

This brings mixed blessings. On one hand, the ASP.NET 4.X framework today is a reliable, battle-tested platform for building modern applications on Windows. On the other hand, it is limited by this reliance; changes to the underlying System.Web.dll are far-reaching and consequently slow to roll out, and it fundamentally excludes the many developers who are building and deploying to Linux or macOS.

When I began looking into ASP.NET Core, I was one of those developers. A Windows user at heart, I was issued a Mac by my employer, so I was stuck working in a virtual machine all day. ASP.NET Core promised to change all that, allowing me to develop natively on both my Windows machine and my Mac.

I was relatively late to the party in many respects, taking an active interest only just before the RC2 release of ASP.NET Core. By this point there had already been eight (!) beta releases, many of which contained significant breaking changes. By not diving in fully until RC2, I was spared the pain of dodgy tooling and changing APIs.

What I saw at that point really impressed me. ASP.NET Core let developers use their existing knowledge of the .NET Framework, and of ASP.NET MVC applications in particular, while baking in current best practices such as dependency injection, strongly typed configuration, and logging. On top of that, you could build and deploy cross-platform. I was sold.

This book came about largely due to my approach to learning about ASP.NET Core. Rather than simply reading documentation and blog posts, I decided to try something new and start writing about what I learned. Each week I would dedicate some time to exploring a new aspect of ASP.NET Core, and I'd write a blog post about it. When the possibility of writing a book came about, I jumped at the chance—another excuse to dive further into the framework!

Since I started this book, a lot has changed, both with the book and ASP.NET Core. The first major release of the framework in June 2016 still had many rough edges, in particular around the tooling experience. With the release of .NET 7 in November 2022, ASP.NET Core has really come into its own, with the APIs and tooling reaching mature levels.

Updates to the framework in .NET 6 and .NET 7 significantly simplified the getting-started experience for newcomers with the introduction of minimal hosting and minimal APIs, which provide a terser, simpler approach to writing APIs, much closer to the experience in other languages. You can get straight into building your app's functionality without having to understand architecture first.

For some experienced ASP.NET Core developers, these changes can feel regressive and unstructured, but if you're one of them, I encourage you to give them a chance and to build your own structure and patterns. For brevity and clarity of the examples in this book, I often put the whole code for your app in one file, but don't think that's how you need to write your real applications. You're free to create helper methods, classes, and any structure that helps keep your applications maintainable while taking advantage of the performance benefits of minimal APIs.

This book covers everything you need to get started with ASP.NET Core, whether you're new to web development or an existing ASP.NET developer. It focuses on the framework itself, so I don't go into details about client-side frameworks such as Angular and React or technologies like Docker. I also don't cover all the new features in .NET 7, such as Blazor and gRPC; instead, I provide links where you can find more information.

In this edition, I have significantly expanded and rearranged many chapters compared with previous editions of the book; some chapters have been split into more manageable sizes. The early chapters feature a lot of new content focusing on minimal APIs and minimal hosting introduced in .NET 6.

I find it a joy to work with ASP.NET Core apps compared with apps using the previous version of ASP.NET, and I hope that my passion comes through in this book!

acknowledgments

Although there is only one name on the cover of this book, a plethora of people contributed to both its writing and production. In this section I'd like to thank everyone who encouraged me, contributed, and put up with me for the past year.

First, and most important, I'd like to thank my girlfriend, Becky. Your continual support and encouragement means the world to me and has kept me going through such a busy time. You've taken the brunt of my stress and pressure, and I'm eternally grateful. I love you always.

I'd also like to thank my whole family for their support, in particular my parents, Jan and Bob, for putting up with my ranting; my sister, Amanda, for your always upbeat chats; and of course, Goose, for diligently ensuring that I take regular breaks for walks and tummy tickles.

On a professional level, I'd like to thank Manning for giving me this opportunity. Brian Sawyer "discovered" me for the first version of this book and encouraged me to tackle the subsequent versions. Marina Michaels served as my development editor for the third time running and again proved to be alternately meticulous, critical, encouraging, and enthusiastic. The book is undoubtedly better thanks to your involvement.

Thank you to my review editor, Adriana Sabo, and to all the reviewers: Alen Adanić, Ben McNamara, Bela Istók, Darrin Bishop, Dennis Liabenow, Al Pezewski, Emmanouil Chardalas, Foster Haines, Onofrei George, John Guthrie, Jean-François Morin, Pedro Seromenho, Joe Cuevas, José Antonio Martinez Perez, Joe Suchy, Luis Moux, Milan Šarenac, Milorad Imbra, Nik Rimington, Nitin Ainani, Oliver Korten, Raushan Jha, Richard Young, Rick Beerendonk, Ron Lease, Ruben Vandeginste,

Sumit K. Singh, Towhidul Bashar, Daniel Vásquez, and Will Lopez. Your suggestions helped make this a better book.

My thanks go to the technical editor for this book, Filip Wojcieszyn, who is a founder and maintainer of several popular open-source projects, frequent conference speaker, and a Microsoft MVP. Filip provided invaluable feedback, highlighting my incorrect assumptions and technical biases, and ensuring technical correctness in everything I wrote.

I also wish to thank Tanya Wilke, who served as technical proofreader. Tanya verified that the code I wrote actually ran and made sense, working through the chapters with formidable efficiency.

To everyone at Manning who helped get this book published and marketed, a heartfelt thanks. I'd also like to thank all the MEAP readers for their comments, which helped improve the book in numerous ways.

I would have never been in a position to write this book if not for the excellent content produced by members of the .NET community and those I follow on social media.

Finally, thanks to all those friends who encouraged and supported me, and showed interest generally. We may not have been able to meet up as much as we'd like, but I look forward to getting together for a drink as soon as it's possible.

about this book

This book is about the ASP.NET Core framework, what it is, and how you can use it to build web applications. Although some of this content is already available online, it's scattered around the internet in disparate documents and blog posts. This book guides you through building your first applications, introducing additional complexity as you cement previous concepts.

I present each topic using relatively small examples rather than building on a single example application through the book. There are merits to both approaches, but I wanted to ensure that the focus remained on the specific topics being taught, without the mental overhead of navigating an increasingly large project.

By the end of the book, you should have a solid understanding of how to build apps with ASP.NET Core, its strengths and weaknesses, and how to use its features to build apps securely. I don't spend a lot of time on application architecture, but I make sure to point out best practices, especially where I cover architecture only superficially for the sake of brevity.

Who should read this book

This book is for C# developers who are interested in learning a cross-platform web framework. It doesn't assume that you have any experience building web applications. You may be a mobile or desktop developer, for example, though experience with ASP.NET or another web framework is undoubtedly beneficial.

I assume that in addition to a working knowledge of C# and .NET, you have some knowledge of common object-oriented practices and a basic understanding of relational databases in general. I assume passing familiarity with HTML and CSS and of JavaScript's place as a client-side scripting language. You don't need to know any JavaScript or CSS frameworks for this book, though ASP.NET Core works well with both if that is your forte.

Web frameworks naturally touch on a wide range of topics, from the database and network to visual design and client-side scripting. I provide as much context as possible, and I include links to sites and books where you can learn more.

How this book is organized

This book is divided into 5 parts, 36 chapters, and 2 appendices. Ideally, you will read the book cover to cover and then use it as a reference, but I realize that this approach won't suit everyone. Although I use small sample apps to demonstrate a topic, some chapters build on the work of previous ones, so the content will make more sense when read sequentially.

I strongly suggest reading the chapters in part 1 in sequence, as each chapter builds on topics introduced in the previous chapters and provides a basis for the rest of the book. Part 2 is also best read sequentially, though most of the chapters are independent if you wish to jump around. Part 3, again, is best read sequentially. You'll get the best experience by reading the chapters in parts 4 and 5 sequentially, but many of the topics are independent, so you can read them out of order if you prefer. But I recommend only doing so after you've covered parts 1 to 3.

Part 1 provides a general introduction to ASP.NET Core, focusing on building small JSON APIs by using the latest features introduced in .NET 7. After we cover the basics, we look at building minimal API applications that provide the simplest programming model for ASP.NET Core web applications.

- Chapter 1 introduces ASP.NET Core and its place in the web development landscape. It describes the type of applications you can build, some of the reasons to choose ASP.NET Core, and the basics of web requests in an ASP.NET Core application.
- Chapter 2 looks at why you should consider using any web framework, why ASP.NET Core was created, and the different application paradigms you can use with ASP.NET Core. Finally, it looks at the situations when you should and shouldn't choose ASP.NET Core.
- Chapter 3 walks through all the components of a basic ASP.NET Core minimal API application, discussing their role and how they combine to generate a response to a web request.
- Chapter 4 describes the middleware pipeline, the main application pipeline in ASP.NET Core, which defines how incoming requests are processed and how a response should be generated.

- Chapter 5 shows how to use minimal API endpoints to create a JavaScript Object Notation (JSON) HTTP API that can be called by client-side apps, server-side apps, or mobile devices.
- Chapter 6 describes the ASP.NET Core routing system. Routing is the process of mapping incoming request URLs to a specific handler method, which executes to generate a response.
- Chapter 7 looks at model binding in minimal APIs, the process of mapping form data and URL parameters passed in a request to concrete C# objects.

Part 2 covers important topics for building fully-featured web applications after you understand the basics:

- Chapter 8 introduces the concept of dependency injection (DI) and describes the DI container built into ASP.NET Core.
- Chapter 9 builds on chapter 8 by describing how to register your own services with the DI container, the patterns you can use, and how to understand the lifetime of services the DI container creates.
- Chapter 10 discusses how to read settings and secrets in ASP.NET Core, and how to map them to strongly typed objects.
- Chapter 11 describes how to document your APIs using the OpenAPI standard and how this helps with testing scenarios and for automatically generating clients to call your APIs.
- Chapter 12 introduces Entity Framework Core (EF Core) for saving data in a relational database.

Part 3 moves away from minimal APIs and looks at how to build server-rendered page-based HTML applications using Razor Pages and the Model-View-Controller (MVC) architecture:

- Chapter 13 shows how to use Razor Pages to build page-based web sites. Razor Pages are the recommended way to build server-rendered applications in ASP.NET Core and are designed for page-based applications.
- Chapter 14 describes the Razor Pages routing system and how it differs from minimal APIs.
- Chapter 15 looks at page handlers in Razor Pages, which are responsible for choosing how to respond to a request and selecting what response to generate.
- Chapter 16 looks at model binding in Razor Pages, how it differs from minimal APIs, and the importance of validating your models.
- Chapter 17 shows how to generate HTML web pages using the Razor template language.
- Chapter 18 builds on chapter 17 by introducing Tag Helpers, which can greatly reduce the amount of code required to build forms and web pages.
- Chapter 19 introduces MVC controllers as an alternative approach to building both server-rendered HTML applications and API applications.

- Chapter 20 describes how to use MVC controllers to build APIs that can be called by client-side apps as an alternative to minimal APIs.
- Chapter 21 introduces the MVC and Razor Pages filter pipeline, shows how it works, and describes some of the filters built into the framework.
- Chapter 22 builds on chapter 21 by showing how to create custom filters to reduce some of the duplication in your MVC and Razor Pages applications.

The chapters that make up part 4 cover important cross-cutting aspects of ASP.NET Core development:

- Chapter 23 describes how to add user profiles and authentication to your application by using ASP.NET Core Identity.
- Chapter 24 builds on the previous chapter by introducing authorization for users so you can restrict which pages a signed-in user can access.
- Chapter 25 discusses authentication and authorization for API applications, how this differs from authentication in HTML applications, and how to get started with authentication in ASP.NET Core APIs.
- Chapter 26 shows how to configure logging in your application and how to write log messages to multiple locations.
- Chapter 27 looks at how to publish your app and configure it for a production environment.
- Chapter 28 discusses the reason for adding HTTPS to your application, how to use HTTPS when developing locally and in production, and how to force HTTPS for your whole application.
- Chapter 29 explores some other security considerations you should make when developing your application and how to stay safe with ASP.NET Core.

Part 5 looks at various topics that help you take your ASP.NET Core applications further, including nonweb applications, custom configuration and components, and testing:

- Chapter 30 discusses an alternative bootstrapping approach for ASP.NET Core apps, using the generic host and a `Startup` class.
- Chapter 31 describes how to build and use a variety of custom components, such as custom middleware, and how to handle complex configuration requirements.
- Chapter 32 expands on chapter 31, showing how to build custom Razor Page components such as custom Tag Helpers and custom validation attributes.
- Chapter 33 discusses the `IHttpClientFactory` service and how to use it to create `HttpClient` instances for calling remote APIs.
- Chapter 34 explores the generic `IHost` abstraction, which you can use to create Windows Services and Linux daemons. You'll also learn to run tasks in the background of your applications.
- Chapter 35 shows how to test an ASP.NET Core application with the xUnit testing framework.

- Chapter 36 follows on from chapter 35, showing how to test ASP.NET Core applications specifically. It covers both unit tests and integration tests using the Test Host.

The two appendices provide supplementary information:

- Appendix A describes how to configure your development environment, whether you're in Windows, Linux, or macOS.
- Appendix B contains links that I've found useful in learning about ASP.NET Core.

About the code

Source code is provided for all chapters except chapters 1, 2, 21, and 27, which don't have any code. You can view the source code for each chapter in my GitHub repository at https://github.com/andrewlock/asp-dot-net-core-in-action-3e. A zip file containing all the source code is also available on the publisher's website at https://www.manning.com/books/asp-net-core-in-action-third-edition. You can get executable snippets of code from the liveBook (online) version of this book at https://livebook.manning.com/book/asp-net-core-in-action-third-edition.

All the code examples in this book use .NET 7 and were built using both Visual Studio and Visual Studio Code. To build and run the examples, you need to install the .NET software development kit (SDK), as described in appendix A.

This book contains many examples of source code, both in numbered listings and inline with normal text. In both cases, source code is formatted in a `fixed-width font like this` to separate it from ordinary text. Sometimes code is also **in bold** to highlight changes from previous steps in the chapter, such as when a new feature adds to an existing line of code.

In many cases, the original source code has been reformatted; we've added line breaks and reworked indentation to accommodate the available page space in the book. In rare cases, even this was not enough, and some listings include line-continuation markers (➥). Additionally, comments in the source code have been removed from the listings when the code is described in the text. Code annotations accompany many of the listings, highlighting important concepts.

liveBook discussion forum

Purchase of *ASP.NET Core in Action, Third Edition*, includes free access to liveBook, Manning's online reading platform. Using liveBook's exclusive discussion features, you can attach comments to the book globally or to specific sections or paragraphs. It's a snap to make notes for yourself, ask and answer technical questions, and receive help from the author and other users. To access the forum, go to https://livebook.manning.com/book/asp-net-core-in-action-third-edition/discussion. You can also learn more about Manning's forums and the rules of conduct at https://livebook.manning.com/discussion.

Manning's commitment to our readers is to provide a venue where a meaningful dialogue between individual readers and between readers and the author can take place. It is not a commitment to any specific amount of participation on the part of the author, whose contribution to the forum remains voluntary (and unpaid). We suggest that you try asking the author some challenging questions lest his interest stray! The forum and the archives of previous discussions will be accessible on the publisher's website as long as the book is in print.

about the author

ANDREW LOCK is a .NET developer and Microsoft MVP. He graduated with an engineering degree from Cambridge University, specializing in software engineering, and went on to obtain a PhD in digital image processing. He has been developing professionally with .NET since 2010, using a wide range of technologies, including Win-Forms, ASP.NET WebForms, ASP.NET MVC, ASP.NET Webpages, and most recently ASP.NET Core. Andrew has put many ASP.NET Core applications into production since version 1 was released in 2016. He has an active blog at https://andrewlock.net dedicated to ASP.NET Core. This blog has frequently been featured in the community spotlight by the ASP.NET team at Microsoft, on the .NET blog, and in the weekly community standups.

about the cover illustration

The caption for the illustration on the cover of *ASP.NET Core in Action, Third Edition,* is "The Captain Pasha. Kapudan pasha, admiral of the Turkish navy," taken from a collection published in 1802 by William Miller.

In those days, it was easy to identify where people lived and what their trade or station in life was by their dress alone. Manning celebrates the inventiveness and initiative of the computer business with book covers based on the rich diversity of regional culture centuries ago, brought back to life by pictures from collections such as this one.

Getting started with ASP.NET Core

This chapter covers

- What is ASP.NET Core?
- Things you can build with ASP.NET Core
- How ASP.NET Core works

Choosing to learn and develop with a new framework is a big investment, so it's important to establish early on whether it's right for you. In this chapter, I provide some background on ASP.NET Core: what it is, how it works, and why you should consider it for building your web applications.

By the end of this chapter, you should have a good overview of the benefits of ASP.NET Core, the role of .NET 7, and the basic mechanics of how ASP.NET Core works. So without further ado, let's dive in!

1.1 What is ASP.NET Core?

ASP.NET Core is a cross-platform, open-source application framework that you can use to build dynamic web applications quickly. You can use ASP.NET Core to build server-rendered web applications, backend server applications, HTTP APIs that can

1

be consumed by mobile applications, and much more. ASP.NET Core runs on .NET 7, which is the latest version of .NET Core—a high-performance, cross-platform, open-source runtime.

ASP.NET Core provides structure, helper functions, and a framework for building applications, which saves you from having to write a lot of this code yourself. Then the ASP.NET Core framework code calls in to your handlers, which in turn call methods in your application's business logic, as shown in figure 1.1. This business logic is the core of your application. You can interact with other services here, such as databases or remote APIs, but your business logic typically doesn't depend *directly* on ASP.NET Core.

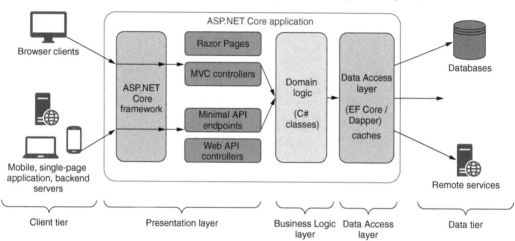

Figure 1.1   A typical ASP.NET Core application consists of several layers. The ASP.NET Core framework code handles requests from a client, dealing with the complex networking code. Then the framework calls in to handlers (Razor Pages and Web API controllers, for example) that you write using primitives provided by the framework. Finally, these handlers call in to your application's domain logic—typically, C# classes and objects without any dependencies that are specific to ASP.NET Core.

1.2   *What types of applications can you build?*

ASP.NET Core provides a generalized web framework that you can use to build a wide variety of applications. ASP.NET Core includes APIs that support many paradigms:

- *Minimal APIs*—Simple HTTP APIs that can be consumed by mobile applications or browser-based single-page applications.
- *Web APIs*—An alternative approach to building HTTP APIs that adds more structure and features than minimal APIs.
- *gRPC APIs*—Used to build efficient binary APIs for server-to-server communication using the gRPC protocol.

- *Razor Pages*—Used to build page-based server-rendered applications.
- *MVC controllers*—Similar to Razor Pages. Model-View-Controller (MVC) controller applications are for server-based applications but without the page-based paradigm.
- *Blazor WebAssembly*—A browser-based single-page application framework that uses the WebAssembly standard, similar to JavaScript frameworks such as Angular, React, and Vue.
- *Blazor Server*—Used to build stateful applications, rendered on the server, that send UI events and page updates over WebSockets to provide the feel of a client-side single-page application, but with the ease of development of a server-rendered application.

All these paradigms are based on the same building blocks of ASP.NET Core, such as the configuration and logging libraries, and then place extra functionality on top. The best paradigm for your application depends on multiple factors, including your API requirements, the details of existing applications you need to interact with, the details of your customers' browsers and operating environment, and scalability and uptime requirements. You don't need to choose only one of these paradigms; ASP.NET Core can combine multiple paradigms within a single application.

1.3 Choosing ASP.NET Core

I hope that now you have a general grasp of what ASP.NET Core is and the type of applications you can build with it. But one question remains: should you use it? Microsoft recommends that all new .NET web development use ASP.NET Core, but switching to or learning a new web stack is a big ask for any developer or company.

If you're new to .NET development and are considering ASP.NET Core, welcome! Microsoft is pushing ASP.NET Core as an attractive option for web development beginners, but taking .NET cross-platform means that it's competing with many other frameworks on their own turf. ASP.NET Core has many selling points compared with other cross-platform web frameworks:

- It's a modern, high-performance, open-source web framework.
- It uses familiar design patterns and paradigms.
- C# is a great language (but you can use VB.NET or F# if you prefer).
- You can build and run on any platform.

ASP.NET Core is a reimagining of the ASP.NET framework, built with modern software design principles on top of the new .NET platform. Although it's new in one sense, .NET (previously called *.NET Core*) has had widespread production use since 2016 and has drawn significantly from the mature, stable, and reliable .NET Framework, which has been used for more than two decades. You can rest easy knowing that by choosing ASP.NET Core and .NET 7, you're getting a dependable platform as well as a full-featured web framework.

One major selling point of ASP.NET Core and .NET 7 is the ability to develop and run on any platform. Whether you're using a Mac, Windows, or Linux computer, you can run the same ASP.NET Core apps and develop across multiple environments. A wide range of distributions are supported for Linux users: RHEL, Ubuntu, Debian, CentOS, Fedora, and openSUSE, to name a few. ASP.NET Core even runs on the tiny Alpine distribution, for truly compact deployments to containers, so you can be confident that your operating system of choice will be a viable option.

If you're already a .NET developer, the choice of whether to invest in ASP.NET Core for new applications was largely a question of timing. Early versions of .NET Core lacked some features that made it hard to adopt, but that problem no longer exists in the latest versions of .NET. Now Microsoft explicitly advises that all new .NET applications should use .NET 7 (or newer).

Microsoft has pledged to provide bug and security fixes for the older ASP.NET framework, but it won't provide any more feature updates. .NET Framework isn't being removed, so your old applications will continue to work, but you shouldn't use it for new development.

The main benefits of ASP.NET Core over the previous ASP.NET framework are

- Cross-platform development and deployment
- Focus on performance as a feature
- A simplified hosting model
- Regular releases with a shorter release cycle
- Open-source
- Modular features
- More application paradigm options
- The option to package .NET with an app when publishing for standalone deployments

As an existing .NET developer who's moving to ASP.NET Core, your ability to build and deploy cross-platform opens the door to a whole new avenue of applications, such as taking advantage of cheaper Linux virtual machine hosting in the cloud, using Docker containers for repeatable continuous integration, or writing .NET code on your Mac without needing to run a Windows virtual machine. ASP.NET Core, in combination with .NET 7, makes all this possible.

That's not to say that your experience deploying ASP.NET applications to Windows and Internet Information Services (IIS) is wasted. On the contrary, ASP.NET Core uses many of the same concepts as the previous ASP.NET framework, and you can still run your ASP.NET Core applications in IIS, so moving to ASP.NET Core doesn't mean starting from scratch.

1.4   *How does ASP.NET Core work?*

I've covered the basics of what ASP.NET Core is, what you can use it for, and why you should consider using it. In this section, you'll see how an application built with

ASP.NET Core works, from a user request for a URL to the display of a page in the browser. To get there, first you'll see how an HTTP request works for any web server; then you'll see how ASP.NET Core extends the process to create dynamic web pages.

1.4.1 How does an HTTP web request work?

As you know now, ASP.NET Core is a framework for building web applications that serve data from a server. One of the most common scenarios for web developers is building a web app that you can view in a web browser. Figure 1.2 shows the high-level process you can expect from any web server.

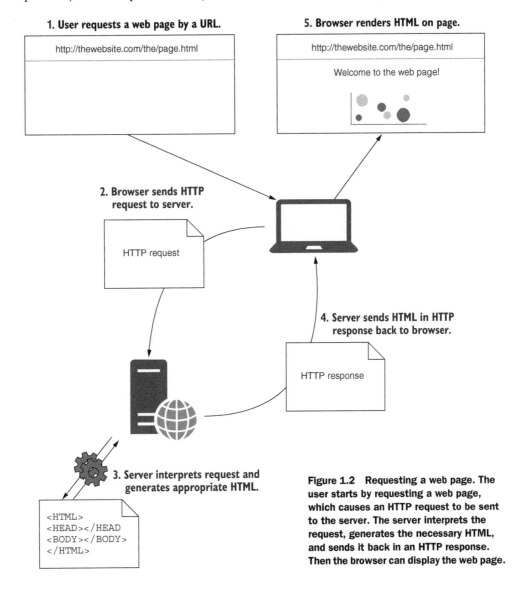

Figure 1.2 Requesting a web page. The user starts by requesting a web page, which causes an HTTP request to be sent to the server. The server interprets the request, generates the necessary HTML, and sends it back in an HTTP response. Then the browser can display the web page.

The process begins when a user navigates to a website or types a URL in their browser. The URL or web address consists of a *hostname* and a *path* to some resource on the web app. Navigating to the address in the browser sends a request from the user's computer to the server on which the web app is hosted, using the HTTP protocol.

> **DEFINITION**   The *hostname* of a website uniquely identifies its location on the internet by mapping via the Domain Name Service (DNS) to an IP address. Examples include microsoft.com, www.google.co.uk, and facebook.com.

A brief primer on HTTP

Hypertext Transfer Protocol (HTTP) is the application-level protocol that powers the web. It's a stateless request-response protocol whereby a client machine sends a *request* to a server, which sends a *response* in turn.

Every HTTP request consists of a *verb* indicating the type of the request and a *path* indicating the resource to interact with. A request typically also includes *headers*, which are key-value pairs, and in some cases a *body*, such as the contents of a form, when sending data to the server.

An HTTP response contains a *status code*, indicating whether the request was successful, and optionally *headers* and a *body*.

For a more detailed look at the HTTP protocol itself, as well as more examples, see section 1.3 ("A quick introduction to HTTP") of *Go Web Programming*, by Sau Sheong Chang (Manning, 2016), at http://mng.bz/x4mB. You can also read the raw RFC specification at https://www.rfc-editor.org/rfc/rfc9110.txt if dense text is your thing!

The request passes through the internet, potentially to the other side of the world, until it finally makes its way to the server associated with the given hostname, on which the web app is running. The request is potentially received and rebroadcast at multiple routers along the way, but only when it reaches the server associated with the hostname is the request processed.

When the server receives the request, it processes that request and generates an HTTP response. Depending on the request, this response could be a web page, an image, a JavaScript file, a simple acknowledgment, or practically any other file. For this example, I'll assume that the user has reached the home page of a web app, so the server responds with some HTML. The HTML is added to the HTTP response, which is sent back across the internet to the browser that made the request.

As soon as the user's browser begins receiving the HTTP response, it can start displaying content on the screen, but the HTML page may also reference other pages and links on the server. To display the complete web page instead of a static, colorless, raw HTML file, the browser must repeat the request process, fetching every referenced file. HTML, images, Cascading Style Sheets (CSS) for styling, and JavaScript files for extra behavior are all fetched using exactly the same HTTP request process.

Pretty much all interactions that take place on the internet are a facade over this basic process. A basic web page may require only a few simple requests to render fully, whereas a large modern web page may take hundreds. At this writing, the Amazon .com home page (https://www.amazon.com) makes 410 requests, including requests for 4 CSS files, 12 JavaScript files, and 299 image files!

Now that you have a feel for the process, let's see how ASP.NET Core dynamically generates the response on the server.

1.4.2 How does ASP.NET Core process a request?

When you build a web application with ASP.NET Core, browsers will still be using the same HTTP protocol as before to communicate with your application. ASP.NET Core itself encompasses everything that takes place on the server to handle a request, including verifying that the request is valid, handling login details, and generating HTML.

As with the generic web page example, the request process starts when a user's browser sends an HTTP request to the server, as shown in figure 1.3.

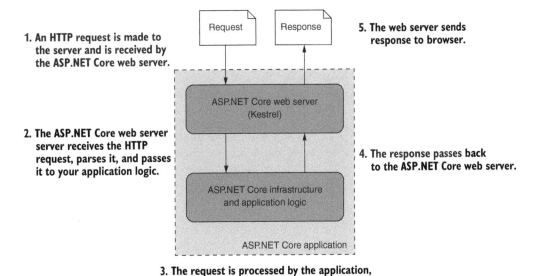

Figure 1.3 How an ASP.NET Core application processes a request. A request is received by the ASP.NET Core application, which runs a self-hosted web server. The web server processes the request and passes it to the body of the application, which generates a response and returns it to the web server. The web server sends this response to the browser.

The request is received from the network by your ASP.NET Core application. Every ASP.NET Core application has a built-in web server—Kestrel, by default—that is responsible for receiving raw requests and constructing an internal representation of the data, an HttpContext object, which the rest of the application can use.

Your application can use the details stored in `HttpContext` to generate an appropriate response to the request, which may be to generate some HTML, to return an "access denied" message, or to send an email, all depending on your application's requirements.

When the application finishes processing the request, it returns the response to the web server. The ASP.NET Core web server converts the representation to a raw HTTP response and sends it to the network, which forwards it to the user's browser.

To the user, this process appears to be the same as for the generic HTTP request shown in figure 1.2: the user sent an HTTP request and received an HTTP response. All the differences are server-side, within your application.

You've seen how requests and responses find their way to and from an ASP.NET Core application, but I haven't yet touched on how the response is generated. Throughout this book, we'll look at the components that make up a typical ASP.NET Core application and how they fit together. A lot goes into generating a response in ASP.NET Core, typically within a fraction of a second, but over the course of the book we'll step through an application slowly, covering each of the components in detail.

1.5   *What you'll learn in this book*

This book takes you on an in-depth tour of the ASP.NET Core framework. To benefit from the book, you should be familiar with C# or a similar object-oriented language. Basic familiarity with web concepts such as HTML and JavaScript will also be beneficial. You'll learn the following:

- How to build HTTP API applications using minimal APIs
- How to create page-based applications with Razor Pages
- Key ASP.NET Core concepts such as model-binding, validation, and routing
- How to generate HTML for web pages by using Razor syntax and Tag Helpers
- How to use features such as dependency injection, configuration, and logging as your applications grow more complex
- How to protect your application by using security best practices

Throughout the book we'll use a variety of examples to learn and explore concepts. The examples are generally small and self-contained so that we can focus on a single feature at a time.

I'll be using Visual Studio for most of the examples in this book, but you'll be able to follow along using your favorite editor or integrated development environment (IDE). Appendix A includes details on setting up your editor or IDE and installing the .NET 7 software development kit (SDK). Even though the examples in this book show Windows tools, everything you see can be achieved equally well on the Linux or Mac platform.

> **TIP** You can install .NET 7 from https://dotnet.microsoft.com/download. Appendix A contains further details on configuring your development environment to work with ASP.NET Core and .NET 7.

In chapter 2, we'll look in greater depth at the types of applications you can create with ASP.NET Core. We'll also explore its advantages over the older ASP.NET and .NET Framework platforms.

Summary

- ASP.NET Core is a cross-platform, open-source, high-performance web framework.
- ASP.NET Core runs on .NET, previously called .NET Core.
- You can use Razor Pages or MVC controllers to build server-rendered, page-based web applications.
- You can use minimal APIs or web APIs to build RESTful or HTTP APIs.
- You can use gRPC to build highly efficient server-to-server RPC applications.
- You can use Blazor WebAssembly to build client-side applications that run in the browser and Blazor Server to build stateful, server-rendered applications that send UI updates via a WebSocket connection.
- Microsoft recommends ASP.NET Core and .NET 7 or later for all new web development over the legacy ASP.NET and .NET Framework platforms.
- Fetching a web page involves sending an HTTP request and receiving an HTTP response.
- ASP.NET Core allows you to build responses to a given request dynamically.
- An ASP.NET Core application contains a web server, which serves as the entry point for a request.

Part 1

Getting started with minimal APIs

Web applications are everywhere these days, from social media web apps and news sites to the apps on your phone. Behind the scenes, there's almost always a server running a web application or an HTTP API. Web applications are expected to be infinitely scalable, deployed to the cloud, and highly performant. Getting started can be overwhelming at the best of times, and doing so with such high expectations can be even more of a challenge.

The good news for you as a reader is that ASP.NET Core was designed to meet those requirements. Whether you need a simple website, a complex e-commerce web app, or a distributed web of microservices, you can use your knowledge of ASP.NET Core to build lean web apps that fit your needs. ASP.NET Core lets you build and run web apps in Windows, Linux, or macOS. It's highly modular, so you use only the components you need, keeping your app as compact and performant as possible.

In part 1 you'll go from a standing start all the way to building your first API applications. Chapter 2 gives you a high-level overview of ASP.NET Core, which you'll find especially useful if you're new to web development in general. You'll get your first glimpse of a full ASP.NET Core application in chapter 3; we'll look at each component of the app in turn and see how they work together to generate a response.

Chapter 4 looks in detail at the middleware pipeline, which defines how incoming web requests are processed and how a response is generated. We'll look at several standard pieces of middleware and see how they can be combined to create your application's pipeline.

Chapters 5 through 7 focus on building ASP.NET Core apps with minimal API endpoints, which are the new simplified approach to building JSON APIs in ASP.NET Core apps. In chapter 5 you'll learn how to create endpoints that generate JSON, how to use filters to extract common behavior, and how to use route groups to organize your APIs. In chapter 6 you'll learn about routing, the process of mapping URLs to endpoints. And in chapter 7 you'll learn about model binding and validation.

There's a lot of content in part 1, but by the end you'll be well on your way to building simple APIs with ASP.NET Core. Inevitably, I'll gloss over some of the more complex configuration aspects of the framework, but you should get a good understanding of minimal APIs and how you can use them to build simple APIs. In later parts of this book, you'll learn how to configure your application and add extra features, such as user profiles and database interaction. We'll also look at how to build other types of applications, such as server-rendered web apps with Razor Pages.

Understanding ASP.NET Core

2

This chapter covers

- Why ASP.NET Core was created
- The many application paradigms of ASP.NET Core
- Approaches to migrating an existing application to ASP.NET Core

In this chapter, I provide some background on ASP.NET Core: why web frameworks are useful, why ASP.NET Core was created, and how to choose when to use ASP.NET Core. If you're new to .NET development, this chapter will help you understand the .NET landscape. If you're already a .NET developer, I provide guidance on whether now is the right time to consider moving your focus to .NET Core and .NET 7, as well as on the advantages ASP.NET Core can offer over previous versions of ASP.NET.

2.1 Using a web framework

If you're new to web development, it can be daunting to move into an area with so many buzzwords and a plethora of ever-changing products. You may be wondering whether all those products are necessary. How hard can it be to return a file from a server?

Well, it's perfectly possible to build a static web application without the use of a web framework, but its capabilities will be limited. As soon as you want to provide any kind of security or dynamism, you'll likely run into difficulties, and the original simplicity that enticed you will fade before your eyes.

Just as desktop or mobile development frameworks can help you build native applications, ASP.NET Core makes writing web applications faster, easier, and more secure than trying to build everything from scratch. It contains libraries for common things like

- Creating dynamically changing web pages
- Letting users log in to your web app
- Letting users use their Facebook accounts to log in to your web app
- Providing a common structure for building maintainable applications
- Reading configuration files
- Serving image files
- Logging requests made to your web app

The key to any modern web application is the ability to generate dynamic web pages. A *dynamic web page* may display different data depending on the current logged-in user, or it could display content submitted by users. Without a dynamic framework, it wouldn't be possible to log in to websites or to display any sort of personalized data on a page. In short, websites like Amazon, eBay, and Stack Overflow (shown in figure 2.1) wouldn't be possible. Web frameworks for creating dynamic web pages are almost as old as the web itself, and Microsoft has created several over the years, so why create a new one?

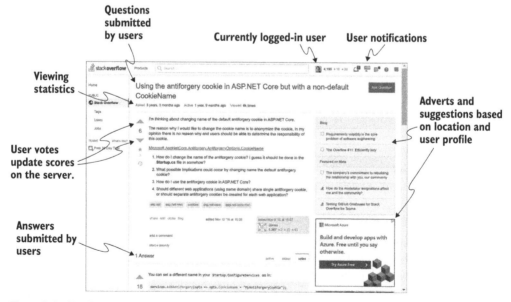

Figure 2.1   The Stack Overflow website (https://stackoverflow.com) is built with ASP.NET and has almost entirely dynamic content.

2.2   Why ASP.NET Core was created

Microsoft's development of ASP.NET Core was motivated by the desire to create a web framework with five main goals:

- To be run and developed cross-platform
- To have a modular architecture for easier maintenance
- To be developed completely as open-source software
- To adhere to web standards
- To be applicable to current trends in web development, such as client-side applications and deployment to cloud environments

To achieve all these goals, Microsoft needed a platform that could provide underlying libraries for creating basic objects such as lists and dictionaries, and for performing tasks such as simple file operations. Up to this point, ASP.NET development had always been focused—and dependent—on the Windows-only .NET Framework. For ASP.NET Core, Microsoft created a lightweight platform that runs on Windows, Linux, and macOS called .NET Core (subsequently .NET), as shown in figure 2.2.

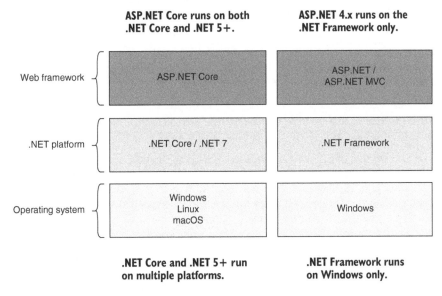

Figure 2.2   The relationships among ASP.NET Core, ASP.NET, .NET Core/.NET 5+, and .NET Framework. ASP.NET Core runs on .NET Core and .NET 5+, so it can run cross-platform. Conversely, ASP.NET runs on .NET Framework only, so it's tied to the Windows OS.

DEFINITION   .NET 5 was the next version of .NET Core after 3.1, followed by .NET 6 and .NET 7. It represents a unification of .NET Core and other .NET platforms in a single runtime and framework. It was considered to be the future of .NET, which is why Microsoft chose to drop the "Core" from its name. For consistency with Microsoft's language, I use the term *.NET 5+* to refer to .NET 5, .NET 6, and .NET 7, and the term *.NET Core* to refer to previous versions.

.NET Core (and its successor, .NET 5+) employs many of the same APIs as .NET Framework but is more modular. It implements a different set of features from those in .NET Framework, with the goal of providing a simpler programming model and modern APIs. It's a separate platform rather than a fork of .NET Framework, though it uses similar code for many of its APIs.

> **NOTE**   If you'd like to learn more about the .NET ecosystem, you can read two posts on my blog: "Understanding the .NET ecosystem: The evolution of .NET into .NET 7" (http://mng.bz/Ao0W) and "Understanding the .NET ecosystem: The introduction of .NET Standard" (http://mng.bz/ZqPZ).

The benefits and limitations of ASP.NET

ASP.NET Core is the latest evolution of Microsoft's popular ASP.NET web framework, released in June 2016. Previous versions of ASP.NET had many incremental updates, focusing on high developer productivity and prioritizing backward compatibility. ASP.NET Core bucks that trend by making significant architectural changes that rethink the way the web framework is designed and built.

ASP.NET Core owes a lot to its ASP.NET heritage, and many features have been carried forward from before, but ASP.NET Core is a new framework. The whole technology stack has been rewritten, including both the web framework and the underlying platform.

At the heart of the changes is the philosophy that ASP.NET should be able to hold its head high when measured against other modern frameworks, but existing .NET developers should continue to have a sense of familiarity.

To understand why Microsoft decided to build a new framework, it's important to understand the benefits and limitations of the legacy ASP.NET web framework.

The first version of ASP.NET was released in 2002 as part of .NET Framework 1.0. The ASP.NET Web Forms paradigm that it introduced differed significantly from the conventional scripting environments of classic ASP and PHP. ASP.NET Web Forms allowed developers to create web applications rapidly by using a graphical designer and a simple event model that mirrored desktop application-building techniques.

The ASP.NET framework allowed developers to create new applications quickly, but over time the web development ecosystem changed. It became apparent that ASP.NET Web Forms suffered from many problems, especially in building larger applications. In particular, a lack of testability, a complex stateful model, and limited influence on the generated HTML (making client-side development difficult) led developers to evaluate other options.

In response, Microsoft released the first version of ASP.NET MVC in 2009, based on the Model-View-Controller (MVC) pattern, a common web pattern used in frameworks such as Ruby on Rails, Django, and Java Spring. This framework allowed developers to separate UI elements from application logic, made testing easier, and provided tighter control of the HTML-generation process.

ASP.NET MVC has been through four more iterations since its first release, but all these iterations were built on the same underlying framework provided by the System .Web.dll file. This library is part of .NET Framework, so it comes preinstalled with all versions of Windows. It contains all the core code that ASP.NET uses when you build a web application.

This dependency brings both advantages and disadvantages. On one hand, the ASP.NET framework is a reliable, battle-tested platform that's fine for building web applications in Windows. It provides a wide range of features that have been in production for many years, and it's well known by virtually all Windows web developers.

On the other hand, this reliance is limiting. Changes to the underlying System.Web.dll file are far-reaching and, consequently, slow to roll out, which limits the extent to which ASP.NET is free to evolve and results in release cycles happening only every few years. There's also an explicit coupling with the Windows web host, Internet Information Services (IIS), which precludes its use on non-Windows platforms.

More recently, Microsoft declared .NET Framework to be "done." It won't be removed or replaced, but it also won't receive any new features. Consequently, ASP.NET based on System.Web.dll won't receive new features or updates either.

In recent years, many web developers have started looking at cross-platform web frameworks that can run on Windows as well as Linux and macOS. Microsoft felt the time had come to create a framework that was no longer tied to its Windows legacy; thus, ASP.NET Core was born.

With .NET 7, it's possible to build console applications that run cross-platform. Microsoft created ASP.NET Core to be an additional layer on top of console applications so that converting to a web application involves adding and composing libraries, as shown in figure 2.3.

When you add an ASP.NET Core web server to your .NET 7 app, your console application can run as a web application. ASP.NET Core contains a huge number of APIs, but you'll rarely need all the features available to you. Some of the features are built in and will appear in virtually every application you create, such as the ones for reading configuration files or performing logging. Other features are provided by separate libraries and built on top of these base capabilities to provide application-specific functionality, such as third-party logins via Facebook or Google.

Most of the libraries and APIs you'll use in ASP.NET Core are available on GitHub, in the Microsoft .NET organization repositories at https://github.com/dotnet/aspnetcore. You can find the core APIs there, including the authentication and logging APIs, as well as many peripheral libraries, such as the third-party authentication libraries.

All ASP.NET Core applications follow a similar design for basic configuration, but in general the framework is flexible, leaving you free to create your own code conventions. These common APIs, the extension libraries that build on them, and the design conventions they promote are covered by the somewhat-nebulous term ASP.NET Core.

You write a .NET 7 console app
that starts up an instance of an
ASP.NET Core web server.

Microsoft provides a cross-platform
web server called Kestrel by default.

Your web application logic is run by
Kestrel. You'll use various libraries to
enable features such as logging and
HTML generation as required.

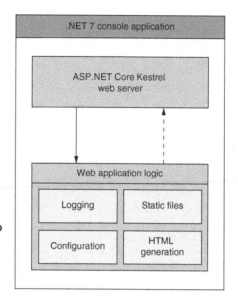

Figure 2.3 ASP.NET Core application model. The .NET 7 platform provides a base console application model for running command-line apps. Adding a web server library converts this model to an ASP.NET Core web app. You can add other features, such as configuration and logging, using various libraries.

2.3   *Understanding the many paradigms of ASP.NET Core*

In chapter 1 you learned that ASP.NET Core provides a generalized web framework that can be used to build a wide variety of applications. As you may recall from section 1.2, the main paradigms are

- *Minimal APIs*—Simple HTTP APIs that can be consumed by mobile applications or browser-based single-page applications (SPAs)
- *Web APIs*—An alternative approach for building HTTP APIs that adds more structure and features than minimal APIs
- *gRPC APIs*—Used to build efficient binary APIs for server-to-server communication using the gRPC protocol
- *Razor Pages*—Used to build page-based server-rendered applications
- *MVC controllers*—Similar to Razor Pages; used for server-based applications but without the page-based paradigm
- *Blazor WebAssembly*—A browser-based SPA framework using the WebAssembly standard, similar to JavaScript frameworks such as Angular, React, and Vue
- *Blazor Server*—Used to build stateful applications, rendered on the server, that send UI events and page updates over WebSockets to provide the feel of a client-side SPA but with the ease of development of a server-rendered application

All these paradigms use the core functionality of ASP.NET Core and layer the additional functionality on top. Each paradigm is suited to a different style of web application or API, so some may fit better than others, depending on what sort of application you're building.

Traditional page-based, server-side-rendered web applications are the bread and butter of ASP.NET development, both in the previous version of ASP.NET and now in ASP.NET Core. The Razor Pages and MVC controller paradigms provide two slightly different styles for building these types of applications but have many of the same concepts, as you'll see in part 2. These paradigms can be useful for building rich, dynamic websites, whether they're e-commerce sites, content management systems (CMSes), or large n-tier applications. Both the open-source CMS Orchard Core[1] (figure 2.4) and cloudscribe[2] CMS project, for example, are built with ASP.NET Core.

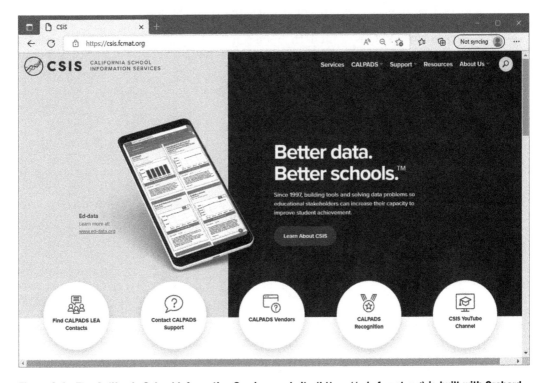

Figure 2.4 The California School Information Services website (https://csis.fcmat.org) is built with Orchard Core and ASP.NET Core.

In addition to server-rendered applications, ASP.NET core is ideally suited to building a REST or HTTP API server. Whether you're building a mobile app, a JavaScript SPA using Angular, React, Vue, or some other client-side framework, it's easy to create an ASP.NET Core application to act as the server-side API by using both the minimal API

---

[1] Orchard Core (https://orchardcore.net). Source code at https://github.com/OrchardCMS/OrchardCore.
[2] The cloudscribe project (https://www.cloudscribe.com). Source code at https://github.com/cloudscribe.

and web API paradigms built into ASP.NET Core. You'll learn about minimal APIs in part 1 and about web APIs in chapter 20.

> **DEFINITION** *REST* stands for *representational state transfer*. RESTful applications typically use lightweight and stateless HTTP calls to read, post (create/update), and delete data.

ASP.NET Core isn't restricted to creating RESTful services. It's easy to create a web service or remote procedure call (RPC)-style service for your application, using gRPC for example, as shown in figure 2.5. In the simplest case, your application might expose only a single endpoint! ASP.NET Core is perfectly designed for building simple services, thanks to its cross-platform support and lightweight design.

> **DEFINITION** gRPC is a modern open-source, high-performance RPC framework. You can read more at https://grpc.io.

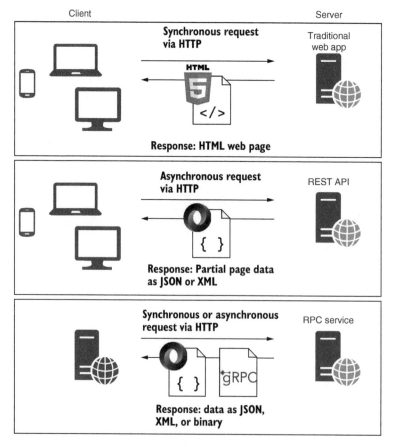

Figure 2.5   ASP.NET Core can act as the server-side application for a variety of clients: it can serve HTML pages for traditional web applications, act as a REST API for client-side SPA applications, or act as an ad hoc RPC service for client applications.

As well as server-rendered web apps, APIs, and gRPC endpoints, ASP.NET Core includes the Blazor framework, which can be used to build two very different styles of application. Blazor WebAssembly (WASM) apps run directly in your browser, in the same way as traditional JavaScript SPA frameworks such as Angular and React. Your .NET code is compiled to WebAssembly (https://webassembly.org) or executes on a .NET runtime compiled for WASM, and the browser downloads and runs it as it would a JavaScript app. This way you can build highly interactive client-side applications while using C# and all the .NET APIs and libraries you already know.

By contrast, Blazor Server applications run on the server. Each mouse click or keyboard event is sent to the server via WebSockets. Then the server calculates the changes that should be made to the UI and sends the required changes back to the client, which updates the page in the browser. The result is a "stateful" application that runs server-side but can be used to build highly interactive SPAs. The main downside of Blazor Server is that it requires a constant internet connection.

> **NOTE** In this book I focus on building traditional page-based, server-side-rendered web applications and RESTful web APIs. I also show how to create background worker services in chapter 34. For more information on Blazor, I recommend *Blazor in Action*, by Chris Sainty (Manning, 2022).

With the ability to call on all these paradigms, you can use ASP.NET Core to build a wide variety of applications, but it's still worth considering whether ASP.NET Core is right for your specific application. That decision will likely be affected by both your experience with .NET and the application you want to build.

2.4   *When to choose ASP.NET Core*

In this section I'll describe some of the points to consider when deciding whether to use ASP.NET Core and .NET 7 instead of legacy .NET Framework ASP.NET. In most cases the decision will be to use ASP.NET Core, but you should consider some important caveats.

When choosing a platform, you should consider multiple factors, not all of which are technical. One such factor is the level of support you can expect to receive from its creators. For some organizations, limited support can be one of the main obstacles to adopting open-source software. Luckily, Microsoft has pledged to provide full support for Long Term Support (LTS) versions of .NET and ASP.NET Core for at least three years from the time of their release. And as all development takes place in the open, sometimes you can get answers to your questions from the general community as well as from Microsoft directly.

> **NOTE** You can view Microsoft's official support policy at http://mng.bz/RxXP.

When deciding whether to use ASP.NET Core, you have two primary dimensions to consider: whether you're already a .NET developer and whether you're creating a new application or looking to convert an existing one.

2.4.1   *If you're new to .NET development*

If you're new to .NET development, you're joining at a great time! Many of the growing pains associated with a new framework have been worked out, and the result is a stable, high-performance, cross-platform application framework.

The primary language of .NET development, and of ASP.NET Core in particular, is C#. This language has a huge following, for good reason! As an object-oriented C-based language, it provides a sense of familiarity to those who are used to C, Java, and many other languages. In addition, it has many powerful features, such as Language Integrated Query (LINQ), closures, and asynchronous programming constructs. The C# language is also designed in the open on GitHub, as is Microsoft's C# compiler, code-named Roslyn (https://github.com/dotnet/roslyn).

> **NOTE** I use C# throughout this book and will highlight some of the newer features it provides, but I won't be teaching the language from scratch. If you want to learn C#, I recommend *C# in Depth*, 4th ed., by Jon Skeet (Manning, 2019), and *Code Like a Pro in C#*, by Jort Rodenburg (Manning, 2021).

One big advantage of ASP.NET Core and .NET 7 over .NET Framework is that they enable you to develop and run on any platform. With .NET 7 you can build and run the same application on Mac, Windows, and Linux, and even deploy to the cloud using tiny container deployments.

> **Built with containers in mind**
>
> Traditionally, web applications were deployed directly to a server or, more recently, to a virtual machine. Virtual machines allow operating systems to be installed in a layer of virtual hardware, abstracting away the underlying hardware. This approach has several advantages over direct installation, such as easy maintenance, deployment, and recovery. Unfortunately, virtual machines are also heavy, in terms of both file size and resource use.
>
> This is where containers come in. Containers are far more lightweight and don't have the overhead of virtual machines. They're built in a series of layers and don't require you to boot a new operating system when starting a new one, so they're quick to start and great for quick provisioning. Containers (Docker in particular) are quickly becoming the go-to platform for building large, scalable systems.
>
> Containers have never been a particularly attractive option for ASP.NET applications, but with ASP.NET Core, .NET 7, and Docker for Windows, all that is changing. A lightweight ASP.NET Core application running on the cross-platform .NET 7 framework is perfect for thin container deployments. You can learn more about your deployment options in chapter 27.

In addition to running on each platform, one of the selling points of .NET is your ability to write and compile only once. Your application is compiled to Intermediate Language (IL) code, which is a platform-independent format. If a target system has the .NET 7 runtime installed, you can run compiled IL from any platform. You can develop on a Mac or a Windows machine, for example, and deploy *exactly the same files* to your production Linux machines. This compile-once, run-anywhere promise has finally been realized with ASP.NET Core and .NET 7.

> **TIP** You can go one step further and package the .NET runtime with your app in a so-called *self-contained deployment* (SCD). This way, you can deploy cross-platform, and the target machine doesn't even need .NET installed. With SCDs, the generated deployment files are customized for the target machine, so you're no longer deploying the same files everywhere in this case.

Many of the web frameworks available today use similar well-established *design patterns*, and ASP.NET Core is no different. Ruby on Rails, for example, is known for its use of the MVC pattern; Node.js is known for the way it processes requests using small discrete modules (called a *pipeline*); and dependency injection is available in a wide variety of frameworks. If these techniques are familiar to you, you should find it easy to transfer them to ASP.NET Core; if they're new to you, you can look forward to using industry best practices!

> **NOTE** *Design patterns* are solutions to common software design problems. You'll encounter a pipeline in chapter 4, dependency injection in chapters 8 and 9, and MVC in chapter 19.

Whether you're new to web development generally or only with .NET, ASP.NET Core provides a rich set of features with which you can build applications but doesn't overwhelm you with concepts, as the legacy ASP.NET framework did. On the other hand, if you're familiar with .NET, it's worth considering whether now is the time to take a look at ASP.NET Core.

2.4.2 *If you're a .NET Framework developer creating a new application*

If you're already a .NET Framework developer, you've likely been aware of .NET Core and ASP.NET Core, but perhaps you were wary about jumping in too soon or didn't want to hit the inevitable "version 1" problems. The good news is that ASP.NET Core and .NET are now mature, stable platforms, and it's absolutely time to consider using .NET 7 for your new apps.

As a .NET developer, if you aren't using any Windows-specific constructs such as the Registry, the ability to build and deploy cross-platform opens the possibility for cheaper Linux hosting in the cloud, or for developing natively in macOS without the need for a virtual machine.

.NET Core and .NET 7 are inherently cross-platform, but you can still use platform-specific features if you need to. Windows-specific features such as the Registry and Directory Services, for example, can be enabled with a Compatibility Pack that makes these APIs available in .NET 5+. They're available only when running .NET 5+ in Windows, not Linux or macOS, so you need to take care that such applications run only in a Windows environment or account for the potential missing APIs.

TIP   The Windows Compatibility Pack is designed to help port code from .NET Framework to .NET Core/.NET 5+. See http://mng.bz/2DeX.

The hosting model for the previous ASP.NET framework was a relatively complex one, relying on Windows IIS to provide the web-server hosting. In a cross-platform environment, this kind of symbiotic relationship isn't possible, so an alternative hosting model has been adopted—one that separates web applications from the underlying host. This opportunity has led to the development of Kestrel, a fast, cross-platform HTTP server on which ASP.NET Core can run.

Instead of the previous design, whereby IIS calls into specific points of your application, ASP.NET Core applications are console applications that self-host a web server and handle requests directly, as shown in figure 2.6. This hosting model is conceptually much simpler and allows you to test and debug your applications from the command line, though it doesn't necessarily remove the need to run IIS (or the equivalent) in production.

> ### ASP.NET Core and reverse proxies
>
> You can expose ASP.NET Core applications directly to the internet so that Kestrel receives requests directly from the network. That approach is fully supported. It's more common, however, to use a reverse proxy between the raw network and your application. In Windows, the reverse-proxy server typically is IIS; in Linux or macOS, it might be NGINX, HAProxy, or Apache. There's even an ASP.NET Core-based reverse proxy library called YARP (https://microsoft.github.io/reverse-proxy) that you can use to build your own reverse proxy.
>
> A *reverse proxy* is software responsible for receiving requests and forwarding them to the appropriate web server. The reverse proxy is exposed directly to the internet, whereas the underlying web server is exposed only to the proxy. This setup has several benefits, primarily security and performance for the web servers.
>
> You may think that having a reverse proxy *and* a web server is somewhat redundant. Why not have one or the other? Well, one benefit is the decoupling of your application from the underlying operating system. The same ASP.NET Core web server, Kestrel, can be cross-platform and used behind a variety of proxies without putting any constraints on a particular implementation. Alternatively, if you wrote a new ASP.NET Core web server, you could use it in place of Kestrel without needing to change anything else about your application.
>
> Another benefit of a reverse proxy is that it can be hardened against potential threats from the public internet. Reverse proxies are often responsible for additional aspects, such as restarting a process that has crashed. Kestrel can remain a simple HTTP server, not having to worry about these extra features, when it's used behind a reverse proxy. You can think of this approach as being a simple separation of concerns: Kestrel is concerned with generating HTTP responses, whereas the reverse proxy is concerned with handling the connection to the internet.

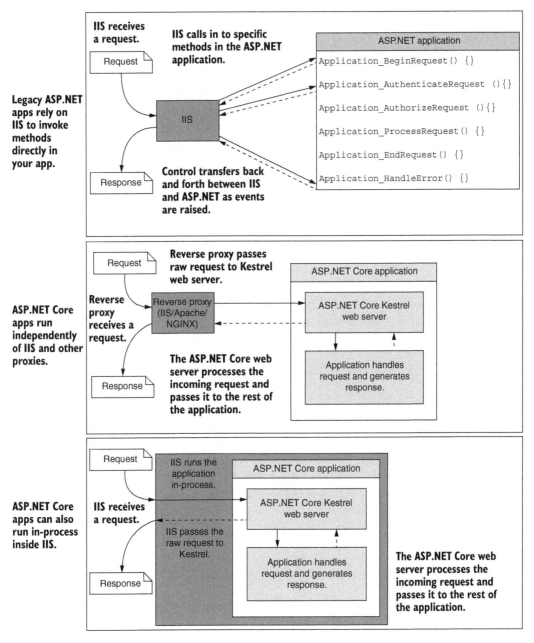

Figure 2.6   The difference between hosting models in ASP.NET (top) and ASP.NET Core (bottom). In the previous version of ASP.NET, IIS is tightly coupled with the application. The hosting model in ASP.NET Core is simpler; IIS hands off the request to a self-hosted web server in the ASP.NET Core application and receives the response but has no deeper knowledge of the application.

NOTE By default, when running in Windows, ASP.NET Core runs *inside* IIS, as shown in figure 2.6, which can provide better performance than the reverse-proxy version. This is primarily a deployment detail and doesn't change the way you build ASP.NET Core applications.

Changing the hosting model to use a built-in HTTP web server has created another opportunity. Performance has been something of a sore point for ASP.NET applications in the past. It's certainly possible to build high-performing applications—Stack Overflow (https://stackoverflow.com) is a testament to that fact—but the web framework itself isn't designed with performance as a priority, so it can end up being an obstacle.

To make the product competitive cross-platform, the ASP.NET team focused on making the Kestrel HTTP server as fast as possible. TechEmpower (https://www.techempower.com/benchmarks) has been running benchmarks on a wide range of web frameworks from various languages for several years now. In round 20 of the plain-text benchmarks, TechEmpower announced that ASP.NET Core with Kestrel was among the 10 fastest of more than 400 frameworks tested![3]

> ### Web servers: Naming things is hard
>
> One difficult aspect of programming for the web is the confusing array of often-conflicting terminology. If you've used IIS, for example, you may have described it as a web server or possibly a web host. Conversely, if you've ever built an application with Node.js, you may have also referred to that application as a web server. Or you may have called the physical machine on which your application runs a web server. Similarly, you may have built an application for the internet and called it a website or a web application, probably somewhat arbitrarily based on the level of dynamism it displayed.
>
> In this book, when I say *web server* in the context of ASP.NET Core, I'm referring to the HTTP server that runs as part of your ASP.NET Core application. By default, this server is the Kestrel web server, but that's not a requirement. It's possible to write a replacement web server for Kestrel if you so desire.
>
> The web server is responsible for receiving HTTP requests and generating responses. In the previous version of ASP.NET, IIS took this role, but in ASP.NET Core, Kestrel is the web server.
>
> I'll use the term *web application* in this book to describe ASP.NET Core applications, regardless of whether they contain only static content or are dynamic. Either way, these applications are accessed via the web, so that name seems to be the most appropriate.

Many of the performance improvements made to Kestrel came not from the ASP.NET team members themselves, but from contributors to the open-source project on GitHub (https://github.com/dotnet/aspnetcore). Developing in the open means that you typically see fixes and features make their way to production faster than you would

---

[3] As always in web development, technology is in a constant state of flux, so these benchmarks will evolve over time. Although ASP.NET Core may not maintain its top-10 slot, you can be sure that performance is one of the key focal points of the ASP.NET Core team.

for the previous version of ASP.NET, which was dependent on .NET Framework and Windows and, as such, had long release cycles.

By contrast, .NET 5+ and hence ASP.NET Core are designed to be released in small increments. Major versions will be released on a predictable cadence, with a new version every year and a new LTS version released every two years (http://mng.bz/1qrg). In addition, bug fixes and minor updates can be released as and when they're needed. Additional functionality is provided in NuGet packages independent of the underlying .NET 5+ platform.

> **NOTE** NuGet is a package manager for .NET that enables you to import libraries into your projects. It's equivalent to Ruby Gems, npm for JavaScript, or Maven for Java.

To enable this approach to releases, ASP.NET Core is highly modular, with as little coupling to other features as possible. This modularity lends itself to a pay-for-play approach to dependencies, where you start with a bare-bones application and add only the libraries you require, as opposed to the kitchen-sink approach of previous ASP.NET applications. Even MVC is an optional package! But don't worry—this approach doesn't mean that ASP.NET Core is lacking in features, only that you need to opt into them. Some of the key infrastructure improvements include

- Middleware pipeline for defining your application's behavior
- Built-in support for dependency injection
- Combined UI (MVC) and API (web API) infrastructure
- Highly extensible configuration system
- Standardized, extensible logging system
- Uses asynchronous programming by default for built-in scalability on cloud platforms

Each of these features was possible in the previous version of ASP.NET but required a fair amount of additional work to set up. With ASP.NET Core, they're all there, ready and waiting to be connected.

Microsoft fully supports ASP.NET Core, so if you want to build a new system, there's no significant reason not to use it. The largest obstacle you're likely to come across is wanting to use programming models that are no longer supported in ASP.NET Core, such as Web Forms or WCF Server, as I'll discuss in the next section.

I hope that this section whetted your appetite to use ASP.NET Core for building new applications. But if you're an existing ASP.NET developer considering whether to convert an existing ASP.NET application to ASP.NET Core, that's another question entirely.

2.4.3 Converting an existing ASP.NET application to ASP.NET Core

By contrast with new applications, an existing application presumably already provides value, so there should always be a tangible benefit to performing what may amount to a significant rewrite in converting from ASP.NET to ASP.NET Core. The advantages of adopting ASP.NET Core are much the same as those for new applications: cross-platform deployment, modular features, and a focus on performance. Whether the benefits are sufficient will depend largely on the particulars of your application, but some characteristics make conversion more difficult:

- Your application uses ASP.NET Web Forms.
- Your application is built with WCF.
- Your application is large, with many advanced MVC features.

If you have an ASP.NET Web Forms application, attempting to convert it directly to ASP.NET Core isn't advisable. Web Forms is inextricably tied to System.Web.dll and IIS, so it will likely never be available in ASP.NET Core. Converting an application to ASP.NET Core effectively involves rewriting the application from scratch, not only shifting frameworks, but also potentially shifting design paradigms.

All is not lost, however. Blazor server provides a stateful, component-based application that's *similar* to the Web Forms application model. You may be able to gradually migrate your Web Forms application page by page to an ASP.NET Core Blazor server application.[4] Alternatively, you could slowly introduce web API concepts into your Web Forms application, reducing the reliance on legacy Web Forms constructs such as View-State, with the goal of ultimately moving to an ASP.NET Core web API application.

Windows Communication Foundation (WCF) is only partially supported in ASP.NET Core. It's possible to build client-side WCF services using the libraries provided by ASP.NET Core (https://github.com/dotnet/wcf) and to build server-side WCF services by using the Microsoft-supported community-driven project CoreWCF.[5] These libraries don't support all the APIs available in .NET Framework WCF (distributed transactions and some message security formats, for example), so if you absolutely need those APIs, it may be best to avoid ASP.NET Core for now.

> **TIP** If you like WCF's contract-based RPC-style of programming but don't have a hard requirement for WCF itself, consider using gRPC instead. gRPC is a modern RPC framework with many concepts that are similar to WCF, and it's supported by ASP.NET Core out of the box (http://mng.bz/wv9Q).

If your existing application is complex and makes extensive use of the previous MVC or web API extensibility points or message handlers, porting your application to ASP.NET Core may be more difficult. ASP.NET Core is built with many features similar to the previous version of ASP.NET MVC, but the underlying architecture is different. Several of the previous features don't have direct replacements, so they'll require rethinking.

The larger the application is, the greater the difficulty you're likely to have converting your application to ASP.NET Core. Microsoft itself suggests that porting an application from ASP.NET MVC to ASP.NET Core is at least as big a rewrite as porting

---

[4] There is a community-driven effort to create Blazor versions of common WebForms components (http://mng.bz/PzPP). Also see an e-book for Blazor for Web Forms developers at http://mng.bz/JgDv.

[5] You can find the CoreWCF libraries at https://github.com/corewcf/corewcf and details on upgrading a WCF service to .NET 5+ at http://mng.bz/mVg2.

from ASP.NET Web Forms to ASP.NET MVC. If that suggestion doesn't scare you, nothing will!

If an application is rarely used, isn't part of your core business, or won't need significant development in the near term, I suggest that you *don't* try to convert it to ASP.NET Core. Microsoft will support .NET Framework for the foreseeable future (Windows itself depends on it!), and the payoff in converting these fringe applications is unlikely to be worth the effort.

So when *should* you port an application to ASP.NET Core? As I've already mentioned, the best opportunity to get started is on small new greenfield projects instead of existing applications. That said, if the existing application in question is small or will need significant future development, porting may be a good option.

It's always best to work in small iterations if possible when porting an application, rather than attempt to convert the entire application at the same time. Luckily, Microsoft provides tools for that purpose. A set of System.Web adapters, a .NET-based reverse proxy called YARP (Yet Another Reverse Proxy; http://mng.bz/qr92), and tooling built into Visual Studio can help you implement the strangler fig pattern (http://mng.bz/rW6J). This tooling allows you to migrate your application one page/API at a time, reducing the risk associated with porting an ASP.NET application to ASP.NET Core.

In this chapter, we walked through some of the historical context of ASP.NET Core, as well as some of the advantages of adopting it. In chapter 3, you'll create your first application from a template and run it. We'll walk through each of the main components that make up your application and see how they work together to render a web page.

Summary

- Web frameworks provide a way to build dynamic web applications easily.
- ASP.NET Core is a web framework built with modern software architecture practices and modularization as its focus.
- ASP.NET Core runs on the cross-platform .NET 7 platform. You can access Windows-specific features such as the Windows Registry by using the Windows Compatibility Pack.
- .NET 5, .NET 6, and .NET 7 are the next versions of .NET Core after .NET Core 3.1.
- ASP.NET Core is best used for new greenfield projects.
- Legacy technologies such as WCF Server and Web Forms can't be used directly with ASP.NET Core, but they have analogues and supporting libraries that can help with porting ASP.NET applications to ASP.NET Core.
- You can convert an existing ASP.NET application to ASP.NET Core gradually by using the strangler fig pattern, using tooling and libraries provided by Microsoft.
- ASP.NET Core apps are often protected from the internet by a reverse-proxy server, which forwards requests to the application.

Your first application 3

This chapter covers

- Creating your first ASP.NET Core web application
- Running your application
- Understanding the components of your application

In the previous chapters, I gave you an overview of how ASP.NET Core applications work and when you should use them. Now you should set up a development environment to use for building applications.

> **TIP** See appendix A for guidance on installing the .NET 7 software development kit (SDK) and choosing an editor/integrated development environment (IDE) for building ASP.NET Core apps.

In this chapter, you'll dive right in by creating your first web app. You'll get to kick the tires and poke around a little to get a feel for how it works. In later chapters, I'll show you how to go about customizing and building your own applications.

As you work through this chapter, you should begin to get a grasp of the various components that make up an ASP.NET Core application, as well as an understanding of the general application-building process. Most applications you create will start from a similar template, so it's a good idea to get familiar with the setup as soon as possible.

> **DEFINITION** A *template* provides the basic code required to build an application. You can use a template as the starting point for building your own apps.

I'll start by showing you how to create a basic ASP.NET Core application using one of the Visual Studio templates. If you're using other tooling, such as the .NET command-line interface (CLI), you'll have similar templates available. I use Visual Studio 2022 and ASP.NET Core 7 with .NET 7 in this chapter, but I also provide tips for working with the .NET CLI.

> **TIP** You can view the application code for this chapter in the GitHub repository for the book at http://mng.bz/5wj1.

After you've created your application, I'll show you how to restore all the necessary dependencies, compile your application, and run it to see the output. The application will be simple, containing the bare bones of an ASP.NET Core application that responds with "Hello World!"

Having run your application, your next step is understanding what's going on! We'll take a journey through the ASP.NET Core application, looking at each file in the template in turn. You'll get a feel for how an ASP.NET Core application is laid out and see what the C# code for the smallest possible app looks like.

As a final twist, you'll see how to extend your application to handle requests for static files, as well as how to create a simple API that returns data in standard JavaScript Object Notation (JSON) format.

At this stage, don't worry if you find parts of the project confusing or complicated; you'll be exploring each section in detail as you move through the book. By the end of the chapter, you should have a basic understanding of how ASP.NET Core applications are put together, from when your application is first run to when a response is generated. Before we begin, though, we'll review how ASP.NET Core applications handle requests.

3.1 A brief overview of an ASP.NET Core application

In chapter 1, I described how a browser makes an HTTP request to a server and receives a response, which it uses to render HTML on the page. ASP.NET Core allows you to generate that HTML dynamically depending on the particulars of the request, so that (for example) you can display different data depending on the current logged-in user.

Suppose that you want to create a web app to display information about your company. You could create a simple ASP.NET Core app to achieve this goal; later, you could add dynamic features to your app. Figure 3.1 shows how the application would handle a request for a page in your application.

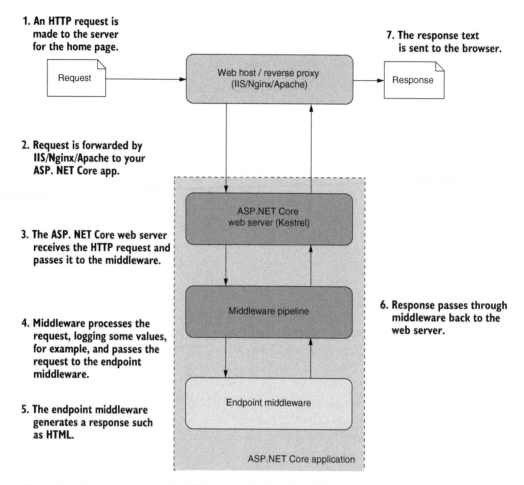

1. An HTTP request is made to the server for the home page.

7. The response text is sent to the browser.

Request

Web host / reverse proxy
(IIS/Nginx/Apache)

Response

2. Request is forwarded by IIS/Nginx/Apache to your ASP. NET Core app.

ASP.NET Core
web server (Kestrel)

3. The ASP. NET Core web server receives the HTTP request and passes it to the middleware.

Middleware pipeline

6. Response passes through middleware back to the web server.

4. Middleware processes the request, logging some values, for example, and passes the request to the endpoint middleware.

Endpoint middleware

5. The endpoint middleware generates a response such as HTML.

ASP.NET Core application

Figure 3.1 An overview of an ASP.NET Core application. The ASP.NET Core application receives an incoming HTTP request from the browser. Every request passes to the middleware pipeline, which potentially modifies it and then passes it to the endpoint middleware at the end of the pipeline to generate a response. The response passes back through the middleware to the server and finally out to the browser.

Much of this diagram should be familiar to you from figure 1.3 in chapter 1; the request and response and the ASP.NET Core web server are still there. But you'll notice that I've added a reverse proxy to show a common deployment pattern for ASP.NET Core applications. I've also expanded the ASP.NET Core application itself to show the middleware pipeline and the endpoint middleware—the main custom part of your app that goes into generating the response from a request.

The first port of call after the reverse proxy forwards a request is the ASP.NET Core web server, which is the default cross-platform Kestrel server. Kestrel takes the raw incoming network request and uses it to generate an HttpContext object that the rest of the application can use.

> **The HttpContext object**
>
> The `HttpContext` constructed by the ASP.NET Core web server is used by the application as a sort of storage box for a single request. Anything that's specific to this particular request and the subsequent response can be associated with it and stored in it, such as properties of the request, request-specific services, data that's been loaded, or errors that have occurred. The web server fills the initial `HttpContext` with details of the original HTTP request and other configuration details and then passes it on to the rest of the application.

NOTE Kestrel isn't the only HTTP server available in ASP.NET Core, but it's the most performant and is cross-platform. I'll refer only to Kestrel throughout the book. A different web server, IIS HTTP Server, is used when running in-process in *Internet Information Services* (IIS). The main alternative, HTTP.sys, runs only in Windows and can't be used with IIS.[1]

Kestrel is responsible for receiving the request data and constructing a .NET representation of the request, but it doesn't attempt to generate a response directly. For that task, Kestrel hands the `HttpContext` to the middleware pipeline in every ASP.NET Core application. This pipeline is a series of components that process the incoming request to perform common operations such as logging, handling exceptions, and serving static files.

NOTE You'll learn about the middleware pipeline in detail in chapter 4.

At the end of the middleware pipeline is the *endpoint* middleware, which is responsible for calling the code that generates the final response. In most applications that code will be a Model-View-Controller (MVC), Razor Pages, or minimal API endpoint.

Most ASP.NET Core applications follow this basic architecture, and the example in this chapter is no different. First, you'll see how to create and run your application; then you'll look at how the code corresponds to the outline in figure 3.1. Without further ado, let's create an application!

3.2 *Creating your first ASP.NET Core application*

In this section you're going to create a minimal API application that returns `"Hello World!"` when you call the HTTP API. This application is about the simplest ASP.NET Core application you can create, but it demonstrates many of the fundamental concepts of building and running applications with .NET.

You can start building applications with ASP.NET Core in many ways, depending on the tools and operating system you're using. Each set of tools has slightly different templates, but the templates have many similarities. The example used throughout

---

[1] If you want to learn more about Kestrel, IIS HTTP Server, and HTTP.sys, this documentation describes the differences among them: http://mng.bz/6DgD.

this chapter is based on a Visual Studio 2022 template, but you can easily follow along with templates from the .NET CLI or Visual Studio for Mac.

> **NOTE**   As a reminder, I use Visual Studio 2022 and ASP.NET Core with .NET 7 throughout the book.

Getting an application up and running locally typically involves four basic steps, which we'll work through in this chapter:

1 *Generate*—Create the base application from a template to get started.
2 *Restore*—Restore all the packages and dependencies to the local project folder using NuGet.
3 *Build*—Compile the application, and generate all the necessary artifacts.
4 *Run*—Run the compiled application.

Visual Studio and the .NET CLI include many ASP.NET Core templates for building different types of applications, such as

- *Minimal API applications*—HTTP API applications that return data in JSON format, which can be consumed by single-page applications (SPAs) and mobile apps. They're typically used in conjunction with client-side applications such as Angular and React.js or mobile applications.
- *Razor Pages web applications*—Razor Pages applications generate HTML on the server and are designed to be viewed by users in a web browser directly.
- *MVC applications*—MVC applications are similar to Razor Pages apps in that they generate HTML on the server and are designed to be viewed by users directly in a web browser. They use traditional MVC controllers instead of Razor Pages.
- *Web API applications*—Web API applications are similar to minimal API apps, in that they are typically consumed by SPAs and mobile apps. Web API apps provide additional functionality compared to minimal APIs, at the expense of some performance and convenience.

We'll look at each of these application types in this book, but in part 1 we focus on minimal APIs, so in section 3.2.1 we start by looking at the simplest ASP.NET Core app you can create.

3.2.1 *Using a template to get started*

In this section you'll use a template to create your first ASP.NET Core minimal API application. Using a template can get you up and running with an application quickly, automatically configuring many of the fundamental pieces. Both Visual Studio and the .NET CLI come with standard templates for building web applications, console applications, and class libraries.

> **TIP**   In .NET, a *project* is a unit of deployment, which will be compiled into a .dll file or an executable, for example. Each separate app is a separate project. Multiple projects can be built and developed at the same time in a *solution*.

To create your first web application, open Visual Studio, and perform the following steps:

1 Choose **Create a New Project** from the splash screen, or choose **File > New > Project** from the main Visual Studio screen.
2 From the list of templates, choose **ASP.NET Core Empty**; select the C# language template, as shown in figure 3.2; and then choose **Next**.

Figure 3.2 The Create a New Project dialog box. Select the C# ASP.NET Core Empty template in the list on the right side. When you next create a new project, you can choose a template from the Recent Project Templates list on the left side.

3 On the next screen, enter a project name, location, and solution name, and choose **Create**, as shown in figure 3.3. You might use WebApplication1 as both the project and solution name, for example.

Figure 3.3 The Configure Your New Project dialog box. Enter a project name, location, and solution name, and choose Next.

4   On the following screen (figure 3.4), do the following:

    d   Select **.NET 7.0**. If this option isn't available, ensure that you have .NET 7 installed. See appendix A for details on configuring your environment.

    e   Ensure that **Configure for HTTPS** is checked.

    f   Ensure that **Enable Docker** is not checked.

    g   Ensure that **Do not use top-level statements** is not checked. (I explain top-level statements in section 3.6.)

    h   Choose **Create**.

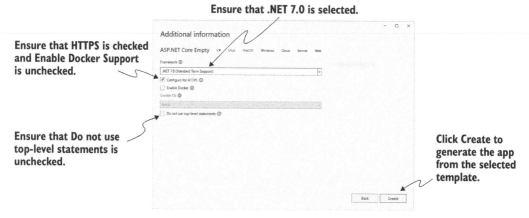

Figure 3.4   The Additional Information dialog box follows the Configure Your New Project dialog box and lets you customize the template that will generate your application. For this starter project, you'll create an empty .NET 7 application that uses top-level statements.

5   Wait for Visual Studio to generate the application from the template. When Visual Studio finishes, an introductory page about ASP.NET Core appears; you should see that Visual Studio has created and added some files to your project, as shown in figure 3.5.

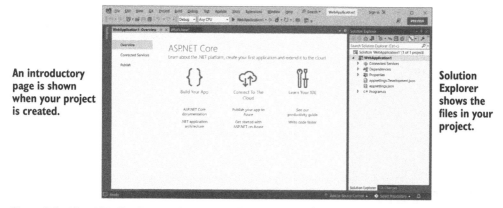

Figure 3.5   Visual Studio after creating a new ASP.NET Core application from a template. The Solution Explorer shows your newly created project. The introductory page has helpful links for learning about ASP.NET Core.

If you're not using Visual Studio, you can create a similar template by using the .NET CLI. Create a folder to hold your new project. Open a PowerShell or cmd prompt in the folder (Windows) or a terminal session (Linux or macOS), and run the commands in the following listing.

Listing 3.1 Creating a new minimal API application with the .NET CLI

```
  dotnet new sln -n WebApplication1    ⟵──────┐  Creates a solution file called WebApplication1
  dotnet new web -o WebApplication1  ⟵──────┐ │  in the current folder
┌─▷ dotnet sln add WebApplication1          │ │
│                                           │ │  Creates an empty ASP.NET Core project
│ Adds the new project to the solution file │    in a subfolder, WebApplication1
```

NOTE Visual Studio uses the concept of a solution to work with multiple projects. The example solution consists of a single project, which is listed in the .sln file. If you use a CLI template to create your project, you won't have a .sln file unless you generate it explicitly by using additional .NET CLI templates (listing 3.1).

Whether you use Visual Studio or the .NET CLI, now you have the basic files required to build and run your first ASP.NET Core application.

3.2.2 Building the application

At this point, you have most of the files necessary to run your application, but you've got two steps left. First, you need to ensure all the dependencies used by your project are downloaded to your machine, and second, you need to compile your application so that it can be run.

The first step isn't strictly necessary, as both Visual Studio and the .NET CLI automatically restore packages when they create your project, but it's good to know what's going on. In earlier versions of the .NET CLI, before 2.0, you needed to restore packages manually by using `dotnet restore`.

You can compile your application by choosing Build > Build Solution, pressing the shortcut Ctrl-Shift-B, or running `dotnet build` from the command line. If you build from Visual Studio, the output window shows the progress of the build, and assuming that everything is hunky-dory, Visual Studio compiles your application, ready for running. You can also run the `dotnet build` console commands from the Package Manager Console in Visual Studio.

TIP Visual Studio and the .NET CLI tools build your application automatically when you run it if they detect that a file has changed, so you generally won't need to perform this step explicitly yourself.

NuGet packages and the .NET CLI

One of the foundational components of .NET 7 cross-platform development is the .NET CLI, which provides several basic commands for creating, building, and running .NET 7 applications. Visual Studio effectively calls these commands automatically, but you can also invoke them directly from the command line if you're using a different editor. The most common commands used during development are

- dotnet restore
- dotnet build
- dotnet run

Each of these commands should be run inside your project folder and will act on that project alone. Except where explicitly noted, this is the case for all .NET CLI commands.

Most ASP.NET Core applications have dependencies on various external libraries, which are managed through the NuGet package manager. These dependencies are listed in the project, but the files of the libraries themselves aren't included. Before you can build and run your application, you need to ensure that there are local copies of each dependency on your machine. The first command, dotnet restore, ensures that your application's NuGet dependencies are downloaded and the files are referenced correctly by your project.

ASP.NET Core projects list their dependencies in the project's .csproj file, an XML file that lists each dependency as a PackageReference node. When you run dotnet restore, it uses this file to establish which NuGet packages to download. Any dependencies listed are available for use in your application.

The restore process typically happens implicitly when you build or run your application, as shown in the following figure, but it can be useful sometimes to run it explicitly, such as in continuous-integration build pipelines.

dotnet restore fetches and restores any referenced NuGet packages.   **dotnet build both restores and compiles by default.**   **dotnet run restores, builds, and then runs your app by default.**

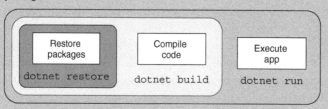

You can skip the previous steps with the –no-restore and –no-build flags.

The dotnet build **command runs** dotnet restore **implicitly. Similarly,** dotnet run **runs** dotnet build **and** dotnet restore**. If you don't want to run the previous steps automatically, you can use the** --no-restore **and** --no-build **flags, as in** dotnet build --no-restore**.**

You can compile your application by using `dotnet build`, which checks for any errors in your application and, if it finds no problems, produces output binaries that can be run with `dotnet run`.

Each command contains switches that can modify its behavior. To see the full list of available commands, run

```
dotnet --help
```

To see the options available for a particular command, such as `new`, run

```
dotnet new --help
```

3.3 Running the web application

You're ready to run your first application, and you have several ways to go about it. In Visual Studio, you can click the green arrow on the toolbar next to WebApplication1 or press the F5 shortcut. Visual Studio will automatically open a web browser window for you with the appropriate URL, and after a second or two, you should see the basic `"Hello World!"` response, as shown in figure 3.6.

Alternatively, instead of using Visual Studio, you can run the application from the command line with the .NET CLI tools by using `dotnet run`. Then you can open the URL in a web browser manually, using the address provided on the command line. Depending on whether you created your application with Visual Studio, you may see an http:// or https:// URL.

Figure 3.6   The output of your new ASP.NET Core application. The template chooses a random port to use for your application's URL, which will be opened in the browser automatically when you run from Visual Studio.

TIP   The first time you run the application from Visual Studio, you may be prompted to install the development certificate. Doing so ensures that your browser doesn't display warnings about an invalid certificate.[2] See chapter 28 for more about HTTPS certificates.

---

[2] You can install the development certificate in Windows and macOS. For instructions on trusting the certificate on Linux, see your distribution's instructions. Not all browsers (Mozilla Firefox, for example) use the certificate store, so follow your browser's guidelines for trusting the certificate. If you still have difficulties, see the troubleshooting tips at http://mng.bz/o1pr.

This basic application has a single endpoint that returns the plain-text response when you request the path /, as you saw in figure 3.6. There isn't anything more you can do with this simple app, so let's look at some code!

3.4 *Understanding the project layout*

When you're new to a framework, creating an application from a template can be a mixed blessing. On one hand, you can get an application up and running quickly, with little input required on your part. Conversely, the number of files can be over-whelming, leaving you scratching your head working out where to start. The basic web application template doesn't contain a huge number of files and folders, as shown in figure 3.7, but I'll run through the major ones to get you oriented.

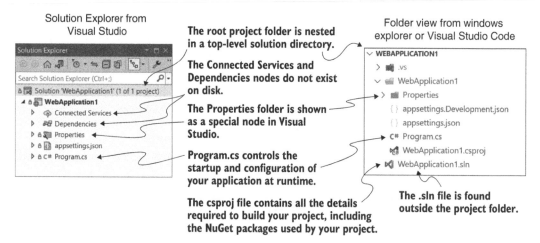

Figure 3.7   Solution Explorer and folder on disk for a new ASP.NET Core application. Solution Explorer also displays the Connected Services and Dependencies nodes, which list NuGet and other dependencies, though the folders themselves don't exist on disk.

The first thing to notice is that the main project, WebApplication1, is nested in a top-level directory with the name of the solution, which is also WebApplication1 in this case. Within this top-level folder you'll also find the solution (.sln) file used by Visual Studio, though this is hidden in Visual Studio's Solution Explorer view.

Inside the solution folder you'll find your project folder, which contains the most important file in your project: WebApplication1.csproj. This file describes how to build your project and lists any additional NuGet packages that it requires. Visual Studio doesn't show the .csproj file explicitly, but you can edit it if you double-click the project name in Solution Explorer or right-click and choose Properties from the contextual menu. We'll take a closer look at this project file in the next section.

Your project folder contains a subfolder called Properties, which contains a single file: launchSettings.json. This file controls how Visual Studio will run and debug the application. Visual Studio shows the file as a special node in Solution Explorer, out of alphabetical order, near the top of your project. You've got two more special nodes in the project, Dependencies and Connected Services, but they don't have corresponding folders on disk. Instead, they show a collection of all the dependencies, such as NuGet packages, and remote services that the project relies on.

In the root of your project folder, you'll find two JSON files: appsettings.json and appsettings.Development.json. These files provide configuration settings that are used at runtime to control the behavior of your app.

Finally, Visual Studio shows one C# file in the project folder: Program.cs. In section 3.6 you'll see how this file configures and runs your application.

3.5 The .csproj project file: Declaring your dependencies

The .csproj file is the project file for .NET applications and contains the details required for the .NET tooling to build your project. It defines the type of project being built (web app, console app, or library), which platform the project targets (.NET Core 3.1, .NET 7 and so on), and which NuGet packages the project depends on.

The project file has been a mainstay of .NET applications, but in ASP.NET Core it has had a facelift to make it easier to read and edit. These changes include

- *No GUIDs*—Previously, globally unique identifiers (GUIDs) were used for many things, but now they're rarely used in the project file.
- *Implicit file includes*—Previously, every file in the project had to be listed in the .csproj file to be included in the build. Now files are compiled automatically.
- *No paths to NuGet package .dll files*—Previously, you had to include the path to the .dll files contained in NuGet packages in the .csproj, as well as list the dependencies in a packages.config file. Now you can reference the NuGet package directly in your .csproj, and you don't need to specify the path on disk.

All these changes combine to make the project file far more compact than you'll be used to from previous .NET projects. The following listing shows the entire .csproj file for your sample app.

Listing 3.2   The .csproj project file, showing SDK, target framework, and references

```
<Project Sdk="Microsoft.NET.Sdk.Web">      ⊲ ⎯  The SDK attribute specifies the
  <PropertyGroup>                               type of project you're building.
    <TargetFramework>net7.0</TargetFramework>      ⊲ ⎯  The TargetFramework is the framework
    <Nullable>enable</Nullable>                          you'll run on—in this case, .NET 7.
    <ImplicitUsings>enable</ImplicitUsings>   ⊲
  </PropertyGroup>                               Enables the C# 10 feature
</Project>                                       "implicit using statements"
```

Enables the C# 8 feature
"nullable reference types"

For simple applications, you probably won't need to change the project file much. The `Sdk` attribute on the `Project` element includes default settings that describe how to build your project, whereas the `TargetFramework` element describes the framework your application will run on. For .NET 6.0 projects, this element will have the `net6.0` value; if you're running on .NET 7, this will be `net7.0`. You can also enable and disable various features of the compiler, such as the C# 8 feature nullable reference types or the C# 10 feature implicit using statements.[3]

> **TIP** With the new csproj style, Visual Studio users can double-click a project in Solution Explorer to edit the .csproj file without having to close the project first.

The most common changes you'll make to the project file are to add more NuGet packages by using the `PackageReference` element. By default, your app doesn't reference any NuGet packages at all.

Using NuGet libraries in your project

Even though all apps are unique in some way, they also have common requirements. Most apps need to access a database, for example, or manipulate JSON- or XML-formatted data. Rather than having to reinvent that code in every project, you should use existing reusable libraries.

NuGet is the library package manager for .NET, where libraries are packaged in *NuGet packages* and published to https://www.nuget.org. You can use these packages in your project by referencing the unique package name in your .csproj file, making the package's namespace and classes available in your code files. You can publish (and host) NuGet packages to repositories other than nuget.org; see https://learn.micro soft.com/en-us/nuget for details.

You can add a NuGet reference to your project by running `dotnet add package <packagename>` from inside the project folder. This command updates your project file with a `<PackageReference>` node and restores the NuGet package for your project. To install the popular Newtonsoft.Json library, for example, you would run

```
dotnet add package Newtonsoft.Json
```

This command adds a reference to the latest version of the library to your project file, as shown next, and makes the Newtonsoft.Json namespace available in your source-code files:

```
<Project Sdk="Microsoft.NET.Sdk.Web">
  <PropertyGroup>
    <TargetFramework>net7.0</TargetFramework>
    <Nullable>enable</Nullable>
    <ImplicitUsings>enable</ImplicitUsings>
  </PropertyGroup>
  <ItemGroup>
    <PackageReference Include="NewtonSoft.Json" Version="13.0.1" />
  </ItemGroup>
</Project>
```

---

[3] You can read about the new C# features included in .NET 7 and C# 11 at http://mng.bz/nWMg.

> If you're using Visual Studio, you can manage packages with the NuGet Package Manager by right-clicking the solution name or a project and choosing Manage NuGet Packages from the contextual menu.
>
> As a point of interest, there's no officially agreed-on pronunciation for NuGet. Feel free to use the popular "noo-get" or "nugget" style, or if you're feeling especially posh, try "noo-jay"!

The simplified project file format is much easier to edit by hand than previous versions, which is great if you're developing cross-platform. But if you're using Visual Studio, don't feel that you have to take this route. You can still use the GUI to add project references, exclude files, manage NuGet packages, and so on. Visual Studio will update the project file itself, as it always has.

> **TIP** For further details on the changes to the csproj format, see the documentation at http://mng.bz/vnzJ.

The project file defines everything Visual Studio and the .NET CLI need to build your app—everything, that is, except the code! In the next section we'll look at the file that defines your whole ASP.NET Core application: the Program.cs file.

3.6 Program.cs file: Defining your application

All ASP.NET Core applications start life as a .NET Console application. As of .NET 6, that typically means a program written with *top-level statements*, in which the startup code for your application is written directly in a file instead of inside a `static void Main` function.

> **Top-level statements**
>
> Before C# 9, every .NET program had to include a `static void Main` function (it could also return `int`, `Task`, or `Task<int>`), typically declared in a class called `Program`. This function, which must exist, defines the entry point for your program. This code runs when you start your application, as in this example:
>
> ```
> using System;
> namespace MyApp
> {
>     public class Program
>     {
>         public static void Main(string[] args)
>         {
>             Console.WriteLine("Hello World!");
>         }
>     }
> }
> ```
>
> With top-level statements you can write the body of this method directly in the file, and the compiler generates the `Main` method for you.

(continued)

When combined with C# 10 features such as implicit using statements, this dramatically simplifies the entry-point code of your app to

```
Console.WriteLine("Hello World!");
```

When you use the explicit `Main` function you can access the command-line arguments provided when the app was run using the `args` parameter. With top-level statements the `args` variable is also available as a `string[]`, even though it's not declared explicitly. You could echo each argument provided by using

```
foreach(string arg in args)
{
    Console.WriteLine(arg);
}
```

In .NET 7 all the default templates use top-level statements, and I use them throughout this book. Most of the templates include an option to use the explicit `Main` function if you prefer (using the `--use-program-main` option if you're using the CLI). For more information on top-level statements and their limitations, see http://mng.bz/4DZa. If you decide to switch approaches later, you can always add or remove the `Main` function manually as required.

In .NET 7 ASP.NET Core applications the top-level statements build and run a `WebApplication` instance, as shown in the following listing, which shows the default Program.cs file. The `WebApplication` is the core of your ASP.NET Core application, containing the application configuration and the Kestrel server that listens for requests and sends responses.

Listing 3.3 **The default Program.cs file that configures and runs a `WebApplication`**

```
WebApplicationBuilder builder = WebApplication.CreateBuilder(args);    ◁──┐
WebApplication app = builder.Build();  ◁──┐                                │
                                           │    Creates a WebApplicationBuilder
                                           │    using the CreateBuilder method
app.MapGet("/", () => "Hello World!");  ◁──┤
                                           │    Builds and returns an instance of WebApplication
    ┌─▷ app.Run();                          │    from the WebApplicationBuilder
    │  Runs the WebApplication to start listening
    │  for requests and generating responses   Defines an endpoint for your application, which
                                               returns Hello World! when the path "/" is called
```

These four lines contain all the initialization code you need to create a web server and start listening for requests. It uses a `WebApplicationBuilder`, created by the call to `CreateBuilder`, to define how the `WebApplication` is configured, before instantiating the `WebApplication` with a call to `Build()`.

> **NOTE** You'll find this pattern of using a builder object to configure a complex object repeated throughout the ASP.NET Core framework. This technique is useful for allowing users to configure an object, delaying its creation

until all configuration has finished. It's also one of the patterns described in the "Gang of Four" book *Design Patterns: Elements of Reusable Object-Oriented Software*, by Erich Gamma, Richard Helm, Ralph Johnson, and John Vlissides (Addison-Wesley, 1994).

In this simple application we don't make any changes to `WebApplicationBuilder` before calling `Build()`, but `WebApplicationBuilder` configures a lot of things by default, including

- *Configuration*—Your app loads values from JSON files and environment variables that you can use to control the app's runtime behavior, such as loading connection strings for a database. You'll learn more about the configuration system in chapter 10.
- *Logging*—ASP.NET Core includes an extensible logging system for observability and debugging. I cover the logging system in detail in chapter 26.
- *Services*—Any classes that your application depends on for providing functionality—both those used by the framework and those specific to your application—must be registered so that they can be instantiated correctly at runtime. The `WebApplicationBuilder` configures the minimal set of services needed for an ASP.NET Core app. Chapters 8 and 9 look at service configuration in detail.
- *Hosting*—ASP.NET Core uses the Kestrel web server by default to handle requests.

After configuring the `WebApplicationBuilder` you call `Build()` to create a `WebApplication` instance. The `WebApplication` instance is where you define how your application handles and responds to requests, using two building blocks:

- *Middleware*—These small components execute in sequence when the application receives an HTTP request. They can perform a whole host of functions, such as logging, identifying the current user for a request, serving static files, and handling errors. We'll look in detail at the middleware pipeline in chapter 4.
- *Endpoints*—Endpoints define how the response should be generated for a specific request to a URL in your app.

For the application in listing 3.3, we didn't add any middleware, but we defined a single endpoint using a call to `MapGet`:

```
app.MapGet("/", () => "Hello World!");
```

You use the `MapGet` function to define how to handle a request that uses the GET *HTTP verb*. There are other `Map*` functions for other HTTP verbs, such as `MapPost`.

> **DEFINITION** Every HTTP request includes a *verb* that indicates the type of the request. When you're browsing a website, the default verb is GET, which *fetches* a resource from the server so you can view it. The second-most-common verb is POST, which is used to *send* data to the server, such as when you're completing a form.

The first argument passed to MapGet defines which URL path to respond to, and the second argument defines *how* to generate the response as a delegate that returns a string. In this simple case, the arguments say "When a request is made to the path / using the GET *HTTP verb*, respond with the plain-text value Hello World!".

> **DEFINITION** A *path* is the remainder of the request URL after the domain has been removed. For a request to www.example.org/accout/manage, the path is /account/manage.

While you're configuring the WebApplication and WebApplicationBuilder the application isn't handling HTTP requests. Only after the call to Run() does the HTTP server start listening for requests. At this point, your application is fully operational and can respond to its first request from a remote browser.

> **NOTE** The WebApplication and WebApplicationBuilder classes were introduced in .NET 6. The initialization code in previous versions of ASP.NET Core was more verbose but gave you more control of your application's behavior. Configuration was typically split between two classes—Program and Startup—and used different configuration types—IHostBuilder and IHost, which have fewer defaults than WebApplication. In chapter 30 I describe some of these differences in more detail and show how to configure your application by using the generic IHost instead of WebApplication.

So far in this chapter, we've looked at the simplest ASP.NET core application you can build: a Hello World minimal API application. For the remainder of this chapter, we're going to build on this app to introduce some fundamental concepts of ASP.NET Core.

3.7   *Adding functionality to your application*

The application setup you've seen so far in Program.cs consists of only four lines of code but still shows the overall *structure* of a typical ASP.NET Core app entry point, which typically consists of six steps:

1 Create a WebApplicationBuilder instance.
2 Register the required services and configuration with the WebApplicationBuilder.
3 Call Build() on the builder instance to create a WebApplication instance.
4 Add middleware to the WebApplication to create a pipeline.
5 Map the endpoints in your application.
6 Call Run() on the WebApplication to start the server and handle requests.

The basic minimal API app shown previously in listing 3.3 was simple enough that it didn't need steps 2 and 4, but otherwise it followed this sequence in its Program.cs file. The following listing extends the default application to add more functionality, and in doing so it uses all six steps.

Listing 3.4   The Program.cs file for a more complex example minimal API

```
using Microsoft.AspNetCore.HttpLogging;

WebApplicationBuilder builder = WebApplication.CreateBuilder(args);

builder.Services.AddHttpLogging(opts =>
    opts.LoggingFields = HttpLoggingFields.RequestProperties);

builder.Logging.AddFilter(
    "Microsoft.AspNetCore.HttpLogging", LogLevel.Information);

WebApplication app = builder.Build();

if (app.Environment.IsDevelopment())
{
    app.UseHttpLogging();
}

app.MapGet("/", () => "Hello World!");
app.MapGet("/person", () => new Person("Andrew", "Lock"));

app.Run();

public record Person(string FirstName, string LastName);
```

You can customize features by adding or customizing the services of the application.

Ensures that logs added by the HTTP logging middleware are visible in the log output

You can add middleware conditionally, depending on the runtime environment.

The HTTP logging middleware logs each request to your application in the log output.

Creates a new endpoint that returns the C# object serialized as JSON

Creates a record type

The application in listing 3.4 configures two new features:

- When running in the Development environment, details about each request are logged using the `HttpLoggingMiddleware`.[4]
- Creates a new endpoint at /person that creates an instance of the C# record called `Person` and serializes it in the response as JSON.

When you run the application and send requests via a web browser, you see details about the request displayed in the console, as shown in figure 3.8. If you call the /person endpoint you'll see the JSON representation of the `Person` record you created in the endpoint.

> **NOTE** You can view the application only on the same computer that's running it at the moment; your application isn't exposed to the internet yet. You'll learn how to publish and deploy your application in chapter 27.

Configuring services, logging, middleware, and endpoints is fundamental to building ASP.NET Core applications, so the rest of section 3.7 walks you through each of these concepts to give you a taste of how they're used. I won't explain them in detail (we have the rest of the book for that!), but you should keep in mind how they follow on from each other and how they contribute to the application's configuration as a whole.

---

[4] You can read in more detail about HTTP logging in the documentation at http://mng.bz/QPmw.

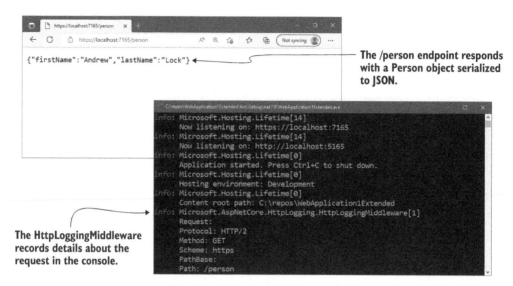

The /person endpoint responds with a Person object serialized to JSON.

The HttpLoggingMiddleware records details about the request in the console.

Figure 3.8   Calling the `/person` endpoint returns a JSON-serialized version of the `Person` record instance. Details about each request are logged to the console by the `HttpLoggingMiddleware`.

3.7.1   Adding and configuring services

ASP.NET Core uses small modular components for each distinct feature. This approach allows individual features to evolve separately, with only a loose coupling to others, and it's generally considered to be good design practice. The downside to this approach is that it places the burden on the consumer of a feature to instantiate it correctly. Within your application, these modular components are exposed as one or more *services* that are used by the application.

> **DEFINITION**   Within the context of ASP.Net Core, *service* refers to any class that provides functionality to an application. Services could be classes exposed by a library or code you've written for your application.

In an e-commerce app, for example, you might have a `TaxCalculator` that calculates the tax due on a particular product, taking into account the user's location in the world. Or you might have a `ShippingCostService` that calculates the cost of shipping to a user's location. A third service, `OrderTotalCalculator`, might use both of these services to work out the total price the user must pay for an order. Each service provides a small piece of independent functionality, but you can combine them to create a complete application. This design methodology scenario is known as the *single-responsibility principle*.

> **DEFINITION**   The *single-responsibility principle* (SRP) states that every class should be responsible for only a single piece of functionality; it should need to change only if that required functionality changes. SRP is one of the five main design principles promoted by Robert C. Martin in *Agile Software Development, Principles, Patterns, and Practices* (Pearson, 2013).

`OrderTotalCalculator` needs access to an instance of `ShippingCostService` and `TaxCalculator`. A naive approach to this problem is to use the `new` keyword and create an instance of a service whenever you need it. Unfortunately, this approach tightly couples your code to the specific implementation you're using and can undo all the good you achieved by modularizing the features in the first place. In some cases, it may break the SRP by making you perform initialization code in addition to using the service you created.

One solution to this problem is to make it somebody else's problem. When writing a service, you can declare your dependencies and let another class fill those dependencies for you. Then your service can focus on the functionality for which it was designed instead of trying to work out how to build its dependencies.

This technique is called *dependency injection* or the *Inversion of Control* (IoC) principle, a well-recognized design pattern that is used extensively. Typically, you'll register the dependencies of your application into a *container*, which you can use to create any service. You can use the container to create both your own custom application services and the framework services used by ASP.NET Core. You must register each service with the container before using it in your application.

> **NOTE** I describe the dependency inversion principle and the IoC container used in ASP.NET Core in detail in chapters 8 and 9.

In an ASP.NET Core application, this registration is performed by using the `Services` property of `WebApplicationBuilder`. Whenever you use a new ASP.NET Core feature in your application, you need to come back to Program.cs and add the necessary services. This task isn't always as arduous as it sounds, typically requiring only a line or two of code to configure your applications.

In listing 3.4 we configured an optional service for the HTTP logging middleware by using the line

```
builder.Services.AddHttpLogging(opts =>
    opts.LoggingFields = HttpLoggingFields.RequestProperties);
```

Calling `AddHttpLogging()` adds the necessary services for the HTTP logging middleware to the IoC container and customizes the options used by the middleware for what to display. `AddHttpLogging` isn't exposed directly on the `Services` property; it's an extension method that provides a convenient way to encapsulate all the code required to set up HTTP logging. This pattern of encapsulating setup behind extension methods is common in ASP.NET Core.

As well as registering framework-related services, the `Services` property is where you'd register any custom services you have in your application, such as the example `TaxCalculator` discussed previously. The `Services` property is an `IServiceCollection`, which is a list of every known service that your application will need to use. By adding a new service to it, you ensure that whenever a class declares a dependency on your service, the IoC container will know how to provide it.

As well as configuring services, WebApplicationBuilder is where you customize other cross-cutting concerns, such as logging. In listing 3.4, I showed how you can add a logging filter to ensure that the logs generated by the HttpLoggingMiddleware are written to the console:

```
builder.Logging.AddFilter(
    "Microsoft.AspNetCore.HttpLogging", LogLevel.Information);
```

This line ensures that logs of severity Information or greater created in the Microsoft .AspNetCore.HttpLogging namespace will be included in the log output.

> **NOTE** I show configuring log filters in code here for convenience, but this isn't the idiomatic approach for configuring filters in ASP.NET Core. Typically, you control which levels are shown by adding values to appsettings.json instead, as shown in the source code accompanying this chapter. You'll learn more about logging and log filtering in chapter 26.

After you call Build() on the WebApplicationBuilder instance, you can't register any more services or change your logging configuration; the services defined for the WebApplication instance are set in stone. The next step is defining how your application responds to HTTP requests.

3.7.2 *Defining how requests are handled with middleware and endpoints*

After registering your services with the IoC container on WebApplicationBuilder and doing any further customization, you create a WebApplication instance. You can do three main things with the WebApplication instance:

- Add middleware to the pipeline.
- Map endpoints that generate a response for a request.
- Run the application by calling Run().

As I described previously, middleware consists of small components that execute in sequence when the application receives an HTTP request. They can perform a host of functions, such as logging, identifying the current user for a request, serving static files, and handling errors. Middleware is typically added to WebApplication by calling Use* extension methods. In listing 3.4, I showed an example of adding the HttpLogging-Middleware to the middleware pipeline conditionally by calling UseHttpLogging():

```
if (app.Environment.IsDevelopment())
{
    app.UseHttpLogging();
}
```

We added only a single piece of middleware to the pipeline in this example, but when you're adding multiple pieces of middleware, the order of the Use* calls is important: the order in which they're added to the builder is the order in which they'll execute in the final pipeline. Middleware can use only objects created by previous middleware in the pipeline; it can't access objects created by later middleware.

> **WARNING** It's important to consider the order of middleware when adding it to the pipeline, as middleware can use only objects created earlier in the pipeline.

You should also note that listing 3.4 uses the `WebApplication.Environment` property (an instance of `IWebHostEnvironment`) to provide different behavior when you're in a development environment. The `HttpLoggingMiddleware` is added to the pipeline only when you're running in development; when you're running in production (or, rather, when `EnvironmentName` is *not* set to `"Development"`), the `HttpLoggingMiddleware` will not be added.

> **NOTE** You'll learn about hosting environments and how to change the current environment in chapter 10.

The `WebApplicationBuilder` builds an `IWebHostEnvironment` object and sets it on the `Environment` property. `IWebHostEnvironment` exposes several environment-related properties, such as

- `ContentRootPath`—Location of the working directory for the app, typically the folder in which the application is running
- `WebRootPath`—Location of the wwwroot folder that contains static files
- `EnvironmentName`—Whether the current environment is a development or production environment

`IWebHostEnvironment` is already set by the time the `WebApplication` instance is created. `EnvironmentName` is typically set externally by using an environment variable when your application starts.

Listing 3.4 added only a single piece of middleware to the pipeline, but `WebApplication` *automatically* adds more middleware, including two of the most important and substantial pieces of middleware in the pipeline: the *routing* middleware and the *endpoint* middleware. The routing middleware is added automatically to the *start* of the pipeline, before any of the additional middleware added in Program.cs (so before the `HttpLoggingMiddleware`). The endpoint middleware is added to the *end* of the pipeline, after all the other middleware added in Program.cs.

> **NOTE** `WebApplication` adds several more pieces of middleware to the pipeline by default. It automatically adds error-handling middleware when you're running in the development environment, for example. I discuss some of this autoadded middleware in detail in chapter 4.

Together, this pair of middleware is responsible for interpreting the request to determine which endpoint to invoke, for reading parameters from the request, and for generating the final response. For each request, the *routing* middleware uses the request's URL to determine which endpoint to invoke. Then the rest of the middle-ware pipeline executes until the request reaches the endpoint middleware, at which point the endpoint middleware executes the endpoint to generate the final response.

The routing and endpoint middleware work in tandem, using the set of endpoints defined for your application. In listing 3.4 we defined two endpoints:

```
app.MapGet("/", () => "Hello World!");
app.MapGet("/person", () => new Person("Andrew", "Lock"));
```

You've already seen the default `"Hello World!"` endpoint. When you send a GET request to /, the routing middleware selects the `"Hello World!"` endpoint. The request continues down the middleware pipeline until it reaches the endpoint middleware, which executes the lambda and returns the `string` value in the response body.

The other endpoint defines a lambda to run for GET requests to the /person path, but it returns a C# record instead of a `string`. When you return a C# object from a minimal API endpoint, the object is serialized to JSON automatically and returned in the response body, as you saw in figure 3.8. In chapter 6 you'll learn how to customize this response, as well as return other types of responses.

And there you have it. You've finished the tour of your first ASP.NET Core application! Before we move on, let's take one last look at how our application handles a request. Figure 3.9 shows a request to the /person path being handled by the sample application. You've seen everything here already, so the process of handling a request should be familiar. The figure shows how the request passes through the middleware pipeline before being handled by the endpoint middleware. The endpoint executes the lambda method and generates the JSON response, which passes back through the middleware to the ASP.NET Core web server before being sent to the user's browser.

The trip has been pretty intense, but now you have a good overview of how an entire application is configured and how it handles a request by using minimal APIs. In chapter 4, you'll take a closer look at the middleware pipeline that exists in all ASP.NET Core applications. You'll learn how it's composed, how you can use it to add functionality to your application, and how you can use it to create simple HTTP services.

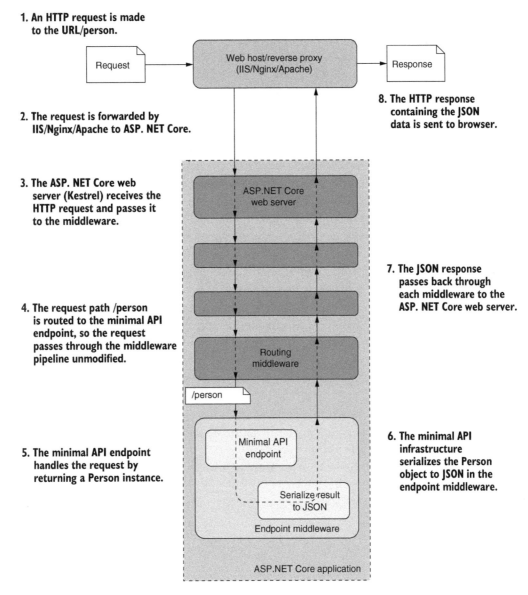

1. An HTTP request is made to the URL/person.

Request → Web host/reverse proxy (IIS/Nginx/Apache) → Response

2. The request is forwarded by IIS/Nginx/Apache to ASP. NET Core.

8. The HTTP response containing the JSON data is sent to browser.

3. The ASP. NET Core web server (Kestrel) receives the HTTP request and passes it to the middleware.

ASP.NET Core web server

7. The JSON response passes back through each middleware to the ASP. NET Core web server.

4. The request path /person is routed to the minimal API endpoint, so the request passes through the middleware pipeline unmodified.

Routing middleware

/person

5. The minimal API endpoint handles the request by returning a Person instance.

Minimal API endpoint

6. The minimal API infrastructure serializes the Person object to JSON in the endpoint middleware.

Serialize result to JSON

Endpoint middleware

ASP.NET Core application

Figure 3.9 An overview of a request to the /person URL for the extended ASP.NET Core minimal API application. The routing middleware routes the request to the correct lambda method. The endpoint generates a JSON response by executing the method and passes the response back through the middleware pipeline to the browser.

Summary

- The .csproj file contains the details of how to build your project, including which NuGet packages it depends on. Visual Studio and the .NET CLI use this file to build your application.
- Restoring the NuGet packages for an ASP.NET Core application downloads all your project's dependencies so that it can be built and run.
- Program.cs is where you define the code that runs when your app starts. You can create a `WebApplicationBuilder` by using `WebApplication.CreateBuilder()` and call methods on the builder to create your application.
- All services, both framework and custom application services, must be registered with the `WebApplicationBuilder` by means of the `Services` property, to be accessed later in your application.
- After your services are configured you call `Build()` on the `WebApplicationBuilder` instance to create a `WebApplication` instance. You use `WebApplication` to configure your app's middleware pipeline, to register the endpoints, and to start the server listening for requests.
- Middleware defines how your application responds to requests. The order in which middleware is registered defines the final order of the middleware pipeline for the application.
- The `WebApplication` instance automatically adds `RoutingMiddleware` to the start of the middleware pipeline and `EndpointMiddleware` as the last middleware in the pipeline.
- Endpoints define how a response should be generated for a given request and are typically tied to a request's path. With minimal APIs, a simple function is used to generate a response.
- You can start the web server and begin accepting HTTP requests by calling `Run` on the `WebApplication` instance.

Handling requests with the middleware pipeline

This chapter covers

- Understanding middleware
- Serving static files using middleware
- Adding functionality using middleware
- Combining middleware to form a pipeline
- Handling exceptions and errors with middleware

In chapter 3 you had a whistle-stop tour of a complete ASP.NET Core application to see how the components come together to create a web application. In this chapter, we'll focus on one small subsection: the middleware pipeline.

In ASP.NET Core, *middleware* consists of C# classes or functions that handle an HTTP request or response. Middleware is chained together, with the output of one acting as the input to the next to form a pipeline.

The middleware pipeline is one of the most important parts of configuration for defining how your application behaves and how it responds to requests. Understanding how to build and compose middleware is key to adding functionality to your applications.

In this chapter you'll learn what middleware is and how to use it to create a pipeline. You'll see how you can chain multiple middleware components together, with each component adding a discrete piece of functionality. The examples in this chapter are limited to using existing middleware components, showing how to arrange them in the correct way for your application. In chapter 31 you'll learn how to build your own middleware components and incorporate them into the pipeline.

We'll begin by looking at the concept of middleware, all the things you can achieve with it, and how a middleware component often maps to a cross-cutting concern. These functions of an application cut across multiple different layers. Logging, error handling, and security are classic cross-cutting concerns that are required by many parts of your application. Because all requests pass through the middleware pipeline, it's the preferred location to configure and handle this functionality.

In section 4.2 I'll explain how you can compose individual middleware components into a pipeline. You'll start out small, with a web app that displays only a holding page. From there, you'll learn how to build a simple static-file server that returns requested files from a folder on disk.

Next, you'll move on to a more complex pipeline containing multiple middleware. In this example you'll explore the importance of ordering in the middleware pipeline, and you'll see how requests are handled when your pipeline contains multiple middleware.

In section 4.3 you'll learn how you can use middleware to deal with an important aspect of any application: error handling. Errors are a fact of life for all applications, so it's important that you account for them when building your app.

You can handle errors in a few ways. Errors are among the classic cross-cutting concerns, and middleware is well placed to provide the required functionality. In section 4.3 I'll show how you can handle exceptions with middleware provided by Microsoft. In particular, you'll learn about two different components:

- `DeveloperExceptionPageMiddleware`—Provides quick error feedback when building an application
- `ExceptionHandlerMiddleware`—Provides a generic error page in production so that you don't leak any sensitive details

You won't see how to build your own middleware in this chapter; instead, you'll see that you can go a long way by using the components provided as part of ASP.NET Core. When you understand the middleware pipeline and its behavior, you'll find it much easier to understand when and why custom middleware is required. With that in mind, let's dive in!

4.1 Defining middleware

The word *middleware* is used in a variety of contexts in software development and IT, but it's not a particularly descriptive word.

In ASP.NET Core, *middleware* is a C# class[1] that can handle an HTTP request or response. Middleware can

---

[1] Technically, middleware needs to be a *function*, as you'll see in chapter 31, but it's common to implement middleware as a C# class with a single method.

- Handle an incoming HTTP *request* by generating an HTTP *response*
- Process an incoming HTTP *request*, modify it, and pass it on to another piece of middleware
- Process an outgoing HTTP *response*, modify it, and pass it on to another piece of middleware or to the ASP.NET Core web server

You can use middleware in a multitude of ways in your own applications. A piece of logging middleware, for example, might note when a request arrived and then pass it on to another piece of middleware. Meanwhile, a static-file middleware component might spot an incoming request for an image with a specific name, load the image from disk, and send it back to the user without passing it on.

The most important piece of middleware in most ASP.NET Core applications is the `EndpointMiddleware` class. This class normally generates all your HTML and JavaScript Object Notation (JSON) responses, and is the focus of most of this book. Like image-resizing middleware, it typically receives a request, generates a response, and then sends it back to the user (figure 4.1).

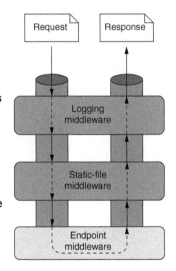

1. ASP. NET Core web server passes the request to the middleware pipeline.

2. The logging middleware notes the time the request arrived and passes the request on to the next middleware.

3. If the request is for a known file, the static-file middleware will handle it. If not, the request is passed on to the next middleware.

6. The response is returned to ASP. NET Core web server.

5. The response passes through each middleware that ran previously in the pipeline.

4. If the request makes it through the pipeline to the endpoint middleware, it will handle the request and generate a response.

Figure 4.1 Example of a middleware pipeline. Each middleware component handles the request and passes it on to the next middleware component in the pipeline. After a middleware component generates a response, it passes the response back through the pipeline. When it reaches the ASP.NET Core web server, the response is sent to the user's browser.

DEFINITION This arrangement—whereby a piece of middleware can call another piece of middleware, which in turn can call another, and so on—is referred to as a *pipeline*. You can think of each piece of middleware as being like a section of pipe; when you connect all the sections, a request flows through one piece and into the next.

One of the most common use cases for middleware is for the cross-cutting concerns of your application. These aspects of your application need to occur for every request, regardless of the specific path in the request or the resource requested, including

- Logging each request
- Adding standard security headers to the response
- Associating a request with the relevant user
- Setting the language for the current request

In each of these examples, the middleware receives a request, modifies it, and then passes the request on to the next piece of middleware in the pipeline. Subsequent middleware could use the details added by the earlier middleware to handle the request in some way. In figure 4.2, for example, the authentication middleware associates the request with a user. Then the authorization middleware uses this detail to verify whether the user has permission to make that specific request to the application.

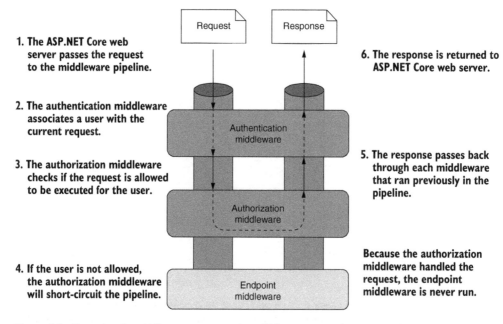

Figure 4.2   Example of a middleware component modifying a request for use later in the pipeline. Middleware can also short-circuit the pipeline, returning a response before the request reaches later middleware.

If the user has permission, the authorization middleware passes the request on to the endpoint middleware to allow it to generate a response. If the user doesn't have permission, the authorization middleware can short-circuit the pipeline, generating a response directly; it returns the response to the previous middleware, and the endpoint middleware never sees the request. This scenario is an example of the *chain-of-responsibility* design pattern.

DEFINITION   When a middleware component short-circuits the pipeline and returns a response, it's called *terminal middleware*.

A key point to glean from this example is that the pipeline is *bidirectional*. The request passes through the pipeline in one direction until a piece of middleware generates a response, at which point the response passes *back* through the pipeline, passing through each piece of middleware a *second* time, in reverse order, until it gets back to the first piece of middleware. Finally, the first/last piece of middleware passes the response back to the ASP.NET Core web server.

The `HttpContext` object

I mentioned the `HttpContext` in chapter 3, and it's sitting behind the scenes here, too. The ASP.NET Core web server constructs an `HttpContext` for each request, which the ASP.NET Core application uses as a sort of storage box for a single request. Anything that's specific to this particular request and the subsequent response can be associated with and stored in it. Examples are properties of the request, request-specific services, data that's been loaded, or errors that have occurred. The web server fills the initial `HttpContext` with details of the original HTTP request and other configuration details, and then passes it on to the middleware pipeline and the rest of the application.

All middleware has access to the `HttpContext` for a request. It can use this object to determine whether the request contains any user credentials, to identify which page the request is attempting to access, and to fetch any posted data, for example. Then it can use these details to determine how to handle the request.

When the application finishes processing the request, it updates the `HttpContext` with an appropriate response and returns it through the middleware pipeline to the web server. Then the ASP.NET Core web server converts the representation to a raw HTTP response and sends it back to the reverse proxy, which forwards it to the user's browser.

As you saw in chapter 3, you define the middleware pipeline in code as part of your initial application configuration in Program.cs. You can tailor the middleware pipeline specifically to your needs; simple apps may need only a short pipeline, whereas large apps with a variety of features may use much more middleware. Middleware is the fundamental source of behavior in your application. Ultimately, the middleware pipeline is responsible for responding to any HTTP requests it receives.

Requests are passed to the middleware pipeline as `HttpContext` objects. As you saw in chapter 3, the ASP.NET Core web server builds an `HttpContext` object from an incoming request, which passes up and down the middleware pipeline. When you're using existing middleware to build a pipeline, this detail is one that you'll rarely have to deal with. But as you'll see in the final section of this chapter, its presence behind the scenes provides a route to exerting extra control over your middleware pipeline.

You can also think of your middleware pipeline as being a series of concentric components, similar to a traditional matryoshka (Russian) doll, as shown in figure 4.3.

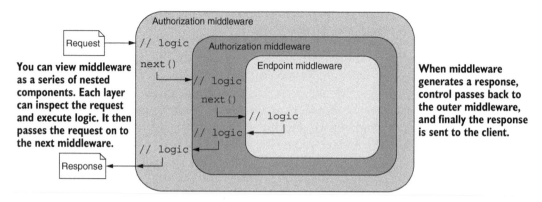

You can view middleware as a series of nested components. Each layer can inspect the request and execute logic. It then passes the request on to the next middleware.

When middleware generates a response, control passes back to the outer middleware, and finally the response is sent to the client.

Figure 4.3   You can also think of middleware as being a series of nested components; a request is sent deeper into the middleware, and the response resurfaces from it. Each middleware component can execute logic before passing the response on to the next middleware component and can execute logic after the response has been created, on the way back out of the stack.

A request progresses through the pipeline by heading deeper into the stack of middleware until a response is returned. Then the response returns through the middleware, passing through the components in reverse order from the request.

Middleware vs. HTTP modules and HTTP handlers

In the previous version of ASP.NET, the concept of a middleware pipeline isn't used. Instead, you have HTTP modules and HTTP handlers.

An *HTTP handler* is a process that runs in response to a request and generates the response. The ASP.NET page handler, for example, runs in response to requests for .aspx pages. Alternatively, you could write a custom handler that returns resized images when an image is requested.

HTTP modules handle the cross-cutting concerns of applications, such as security, logging, and session management. They run in response to the life-cycle events that a request progresses through when it's received by the server. Examples of events include `BeginRequest`, `AcquireRequestState`, and `PostAcquireRequestState`.

This approach works, but sometimes it's tricky to reason about which modules will run at which points. Implementing a module requires relatively detailed understanding of the state of the request at each individual life-cycle event.

The middleware pipeline makes understanding your application far simpler. The pipeline is defined completely in code, specifying which components should run and in which order. Behind the scenes, the middleware pipeline in ASP.NET Core is simply a chain of method calls, with each middleware function calling the next in the pipeline.

That's pretty much all there is to the concept of middleware. In the next section, I'll discuss ways you can combine middleware components to create an application and how to use middleware to separate the concerns of your application.

4.2 Combining middleware in a pipeline

Generally speaking, each middleware component has a single primary concern; it handles only one aspect of a request. Logging middleware deals only with logging the request, authentication middleware is concerned only with identifying the current user, and static-file middleware is concerned only with returning static files.

Each of these concerns is highly focused, which makes the components themselves small and easy to reason about. This approach also gives your app added flexibility. Adding static-file middleware, for example, doesn't mean you're forced to have image-resizing behavior or authentication; each of these features is an additional piece of middleware.

To build a complete application, you compose multiple middleware components into a pipeline, as shown in section 4.1. Each middleware component has access to the original request, as well as any changes made to the HttpContext by middleware earlier in the pipeline. When a response has been generated, each middleware component can inspect and/or modify the response as it passes back through the pipeline before it's sent to the user. This feature allows you to build complex application behaviors from small, focused components.

In the rest of this section, you'll see how to create a middleware pipeline by combining various middleware components. Using standard middleware components, you'll learn to create a holding page and to serve static files from a folder on disk. Finally, you'll take a look at a more complex pipeline such as you'd get in a minimal API application with multiple middleware, routing, and endpoints.

4.2.1 Simple pipeline scenario 1: A holding page

For your first app in this chapter and your first middleware pipeline, you'll learn how to create an app consisting of a holding page. Adding a holding page can be useful occasionally when you're setting up your application to ensure that it's processing requests without errors.

> **TIP** Remember that you can view the application code for this book in the GitHub repository at http://mng.bz/Y1qN.

In previous chapters, I mentioned that the ASP.NET Core framework is composed of many small individual libraries. You typically add a piece of middleware by referencing a package in your application's .csproj project file and configuring the middleware in Program.cs. Microsoft ships many standard middleware components with ASP.NET Core for you to choose among; you can also use third-party components from NuGet and GitHub, or you can build your own custom middleware. You can find the list of built-in middleware at http://mng.bz/Gyxq.

> **NOTE** I discuss building custom middleware in chapter 31.

In this section, you'll see how to create one of the simplest middleware pipelines, consisting only of WelcomePageMiddleware. WelcomePageMiddleware is designed to provide a sample HTML page quickly when you're first developing an application, as you can see in figure 4.4. You wouldn't use it in a production app, as you can't customize the output, but it's a single, self-contained middleware component you can use to ensure that your application is running correctly.

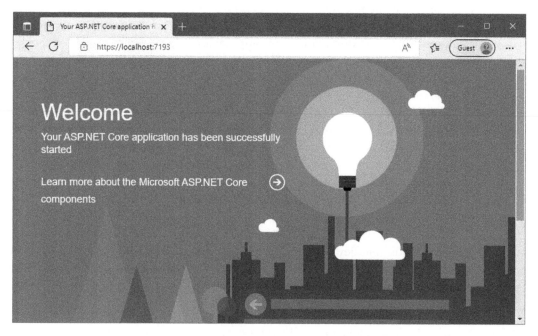

Figure 4.4   The Welcome-page middleware response. Every request to the application, at any path, will return the same Welcome-page response.

> **TIP** WelcomePageMiddleware is included as part of the base ASP.NET Core framework, so you don't need to add a reference to any additional NuGet packages.

Even though this application is simple, the same process you've seen before occurs when the application receives an HTTP request, as shown in figure 4.5.

The request passes to the ASP.NET Core web server, which builds a representation of the request and passes it to the middleware pipeline. As it's the first (only!) middleware in the pipeline, WelcomePageMiddleware receives the request and must decide how to handle it. The middleware responds by generating an HTML response, no matter what request it receives. This response passes back to the ASP.NET Core web server, which forwards it to the reverse proxy and then to the user to display in their browser.

As with all ASP.NET Core applications, you define the middleware pipeline in Program.cs by calling Use* methods on the WebApplication instance. To create your first middleware pipeline, which consists of a single middleware component, you need a

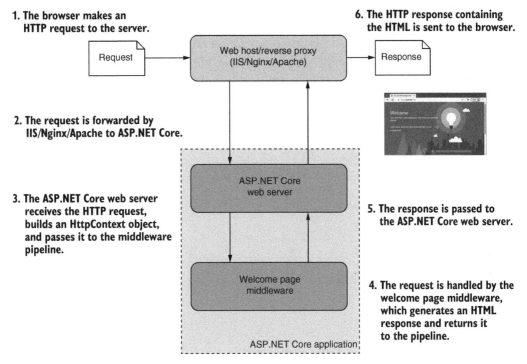

1. The browser makes an HTTP request to the server.

6. The HTTP response containing the HTML is sent to the browser.

2. The request is forwarded by IIS/Nginx/Apache to ASP.NET Core.

3. The ASP.NET Core web server receives the HTTP request, builds an HttpContext object, and passes it to the middleware pipeline.

5. The response is passed to the ASP.NET Core web server.

4. The request is handled by the welcome page middleware, which generates an HTML response and returns it to the pipeline.

Figure 4.5 `WelcomePageMiddleware` handles a request. The request passes from the reverse proxy to the ASP.NET Core web server and finally to the middleware pipeline, which generates an HTML response.

single method call. The application doesn't need any extra configuration or services, so your whole application consists of the four lines in the following listing.

> **Listing 4.1 Program.cs for a Welcome-page middleware pipeline**

```
WebApplicationBuilder builder = WebApplication.CreateBuilder(args);
WebApplication app = builder.Build();
```
Uses the default WebApplication configuration

`app.UseWelcomePage();` ◁——— **The only custom middleware in the pipeline**

`app.Run();` ◁——— **Runs the application to handle requests**

You build up the middleware pipeline in ASP.NET Core by calling methods on Web-Application (which implements IApplicationBuilder). WebApplication doesn't define methods like UseWelcomePage itself; instead, these are *extension* methods.

Using extension methods allows you to add functionality to the WebApplication class, while keeping the implementation isolated from it. Under the hood, the methods typically call *another* extension method to add the middleware to the pipeline. Behind the scenes, for example, the UseWelcomePage method adds the WelcomePage-Middleware to the pipeline by calling

```
UseMiddleware<WelcomePageMiddleware>();
```

This convention of creating an extension method for each piece of middleware and starting the method name with Use is designed to improve discoverability when you add middleware to your application.[2] ASP.NET Core includes a lot of middleware as part of the core framework, so you can use IntelliSense in Visual Studio and other integrated development environments (IDEs) to view all the middleware that's available, as shown in figure 4.6.

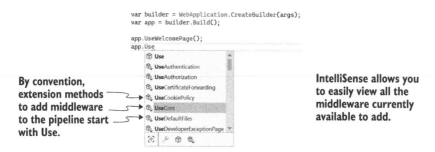

Figure 4.6   IntelliSense makes it easy to view all the available middleware to add to your middleware pipeline.

Calling the UseWelcomePage method adds the WelcomePageMiddleware as the next middleware in the pipeline. Although you're using only a single middleware component here, it's important to remember that the order in which you make calls to IApplication-Builder in Configure defines the order in which the middleware will run in the pipeline.

> **WARNING**   When you're adding middleware to the pipeline, always take care to consider the order in which it will run. A component can access only data created by middleware that comes before it in the pipeline.

This application is the most basic kind, returning the same response no matter which URL you navigate to, but it shows how easy it is to define your application behavior with middleware. Next, we'll make things a little more interesting by returning different responses when you make requests to different paths.

4.2.2   *Simple pipeline scenario 2: Handling static files*

In this section, I'll show you how to create one of the simplest middleware pipelines you can use for a full application: a static-file application. Most web applications, including those with dynamic content, serve some pages by using static files. Images, JavaScript, and CSS stylesheets are normally saved to disk during development and are served up when requested from the special wwwroot folder of your project, normally as part of a full HTML page request.

---

[2] The downside to this approach is that it can hide exactly which middleware is being added to the pipeline. When the answer isn't clear, I typically search for the source code of the extension method directly in GitHub (https://github.com/aspnet/aspnetcore).

DEFINITION By default, the wwwroot folder is the only folder in your application that ASP.NET Core will serve files from. It doesn't serve files from other folders for security reasons. The wwwroot folder in an ASP.NET Core project is typically deployed as is to production, including all the files and folders it contains.

You can use StaticFileMiddleware to serve static files from the wwwroot folder when requested, as shown in figure 4.7. In this example, an image called moon.jpg exists in the wwwroot folder. When you request the file using the /moon.jpg path, it's loaded and returned as the response to the request.

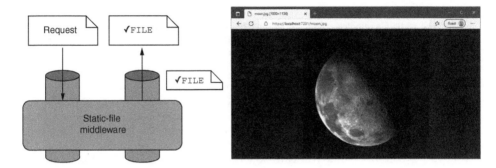

1. The static-file middleware handles the request by returning the file requested.

2. The file stream is sent back through the middleware pipeline and out to the browser.

3. The browser displays the file returned in the response.

Figure 4.7 Serving a static image file using the static-file middleware

If the user requests a file that doesn't exist in the wwwroot folder, such as missing.jpg, the static-file middleware won't serve a file. Instead, a 404 HTTP error code response will be sent to the user's browser, which displays its default "File Not Found" page, as shown in figure 4.8.

NOTE How this page looks depends on your browser. In some browsers, you may see a blank page.

Building the middleware pipeline for this simple static-file application is easy. The pipeline consists of a single piece of middleware, StaticFileMiddleware, as you can see in the following listing. You don't need any services, so configuring the middleware pipeline with UseStaticFiles is all that's required.

Listing 4.2 Program.cs for a static-file middleware pipeline

```
WebApplicationBuilder builder = WebApplication.CreateBuilder(args);
WebApplication app = builder.Build();

app.UseStaticFiles();   ⟵—— Adds the StaticFileMiddleware to the pipeline

app.Run();
```

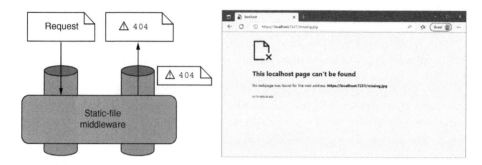

1. The static-file middleware handles the request by trying to return the requested file, but as it doesn't exist, it returns a raw 404 response.

2. The 404 HTTP error code is sent back through the middleware pipeline to the user.

3. The browser displays its default "File Not Found" error page.

Figure 4.8   Returning a 404 to the browser when a file doesn't exist. The requested file didn't exist in the wwwroot folder, so the ASP.NET Core application returned a 404 response. Then the browser (Microsoft Edge, in this case) shows the user a default "File Not Found" error page.

> **TIP**   Remember that you can view the application code for this book in the GitHub repository at http://mng.bz/Y1qN.

When the application receives a request, the ASP.NET Core web server handles it and passes it to the middleware pipeline. StaticFileMiddleware receives the request and determines whether it can handle it. If the requested file exists, the middleware handles the request and returns the file as the response, as shown in figure 4.9.

If the file doesn't exist, the request effectively passes *through* the static-file middleware unchanged. But wait—you added only one piece of middleware, right? Surely you can't pass the request through to the next middleware component if there *isn't* another one.

ASP.NET Core automatically adds a dummy piece of middleware to the end of the pipeline. This middleware always returns a 404 response if it's called.

> **TIP**   If no middleware generates a response for a request, the pipeline automatically returns a simple 404 error response to the browser.

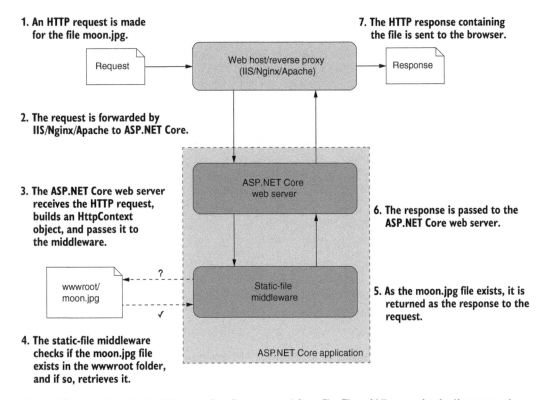

1. **An HTTP request is made for the file moon.jpg.**

2. **The request is forwarded by IIS/Nginx/Apache to ASP.NET Core.**

3. **The ASP.NET Core web server receives the HTTP request, builds an HttpContext object, and passes it to the middleware.**

4. **The static-file middleware checks if the moon.jpg file exists in the wwwroot folder, and if so, retrieves it.**

7. **The HTTP response containing the file is sent to the browser.**

6. **The response is passed to the ASP.NET Core web server.**

5. **As the moon.jpg file exists, it is returned as the response to the request.**

Figure 4.9 `StaticFileMiddleware` **handles a request for a file. The middleware checks the wwwroot folder to see if whether requested moon.jpg file exists. The file exists, so the middleware retrieves it and returns it as the response to the web server and, ultimately, to the browser.**

HTTP response status codes

Every HTTP response contains a *status code* and, optionally, a *reason phrase* describing the status code. Status codes are fundamental to the HTTP protocol and are a standardized way of indicating common results. A 200 response, for example, means that the request was successfully answered, whereas a 404 response indicates that the resource requested couldn't be found. You can see the full list of standardized status codes at https://www.rfc-editor.org/rfc/rfc9110#name-status-codes.

Status codes are always three digits long and are grouped in five classes, based on the first digit:

- *1xx*—Information. This code is not often used; it provides a general acknowledgment.
- *2xx*—Success. The request was successfully handled and processed.
- *3xx*—Redirection. The browser must follow the provided link to allow the user to log in, for example.

(continued)

- *4xx*—Client error. A problem occurred with the request. The request sent invalid data, for example, or the user isn't authorized to perform the request.
- *5xx*—Server error. A problem on the server caused the request to fail.

These status codes typically drive the behavior of a user's browser. The browser will handle a 301 response automatically, for example, by redirecting to the provided new link and making a second request, all without the user's interaction.

Error codes are in the 4xx and 5xx classes. Common codes include a 404 response when a file couldn't be found, a 400 error when a client sends invalid data (such as an invalid email address), and a 500 error when an error occurs on the server. HTTP responses for error codes may include a response body, which is content to display when the client receives the response.

This basic ASP.NET Core application makes it easy to see the behavior of the ASP.NET Core middleware pipeline and the static-file middleware in particular, but it's unlikely that your applications will be this simple. It's more likely that static files will form one part of your middleware pipeline. In the next section you'll see how to combine multiple middleware components as we look at a simple minimal API application.

4.2.3 *Simple pipeline scenario 3: A minimal API application*

By this point, you should have a decent grasp of the middleware pipeline, insofar as you understand that it defines your application's behavior. In this section you'll see how to combine several standard middleware components to form a pipeline. As before, you do this in Program.cs by adding middleware to the `WebApplication` object.

You'll begin by creating a basic middleware pipeline that you'd find in a typical ASP.NET Core minimal APIs template and then extend it by adding middleware. Figure 4.10 shows the output you see when you navigate to the home page of the application—identical to the sample application in chapter 3.

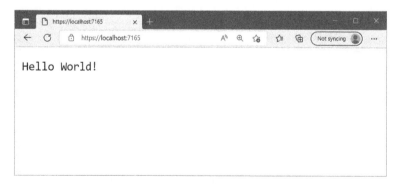

Figure 4.10 **A simple minimal API application. The application uses only four pieces of middleware: routing middleware to choose the endpoint to run, endpoint middleware to generate the response from a Razor Page, static-file middleware to serve image files, and exception-handler middleware to capture any errors.**

Creating this application requires only four pieces of middleware: routing middleware to choose a minimal API endpoint to execute, endpoint middleware to generate the response, static-file middleware to serve any image files from the wwwroot folder, and exception-handler middleware to handle any errors that might occur. Even though this example is still a Hello World! example, this architecture is much closer to a realistic example. The following listing shows an example of such an application.

Listing 4.3 A basic middleware pipeline for a minimal APIs application

```
WebApplicationBuilder builder = WebApplication.CreateBuilder(args);
WebApplication app = builder.Build();
                                          This call isn't strictly necessary, as it's already
app.UseDeveloperExceptionPage();  ◁────    added by WebApplication by default.
app.UseStaticFiles();
app.UseRouting();       ◁────── Adds the RoutingMiddleware to the pipeline

app.MapGet("/", () => "Hello World!");  ◁──┐ Defines an endpoint
                                            │ for the application
app.Run();
```
Adds the StaticFileMiddleware to the pipeline

The addition of middleware to WebApplication to form the pipeline should be familiar to you now, but several points are worth noting in this example:

- Middleware is added with Use*() methods.
- MapGet defines an *endpoint*, not middleware. It defines the endpoints that the routing and endpoint middleware can use.
- WebApplication automatically adds some middleware to the pipeline, such as the EndpointMiddleware.
- The order of the Use*() method calls is important and defines the order of the middleware pipeline.

First, all the methods for adding middleware start with Use. As I mentioned earlier, this is thanks to the convention of using extension methods to extend the functionality of WebApplication; prefixing the methods with Use should make them easier to discover.

Second, it's important to understand that the MapGet method does *not* add middleware to the pipeline; it defines an *endpoint* in your application. These endpoints are used by the routing and endpoint middleware. You'll learn more about endpoints and routing in chapter 5.

> **TIP** You can define the endpoints for your app by using MapGet() anywhere in Program.cs before the call to app.Run(), but the calls are typically placed after the middleware pipeline definition.

In chapter 3, I mentioned that WebApplication automatically adds middleware to your app. You can see this process in action in listing 4.3 automatically adding the EndpointMiddleware to the end of the middleware pipeline. WebApplication also automatically adds the developer exception page middleware to the *start* of the middleware pipeline when you're running in development. As a result, you can omit the call to `UseDeveloperExceptionPage()` from listing 4.3, and your middleware pipeline will be essentially the same.

WebApplication and autoadded middleware

`WebApplication` and `WebApplicationBuilder` were introduced in .NET 6 to try to reduce the amount of boilerplate code required for a `Hello World!` ASP.NET Core application. As part of this initiative, Microsoft chose to have `WebApplication` *automatically* add various middleware to the pipeline. This decision alleviates some of the common getting-started pain points of middleware ordering by ensuring that, for example, `UseRouting()` is always called before `UseAuthorization()`.

Everything has trade-offs, of course, and for `WebApplication` the trade-off is that it's harder to understand exactly what's in your middleware pipeline without having deep knowledge of the framework code itself.

Luckily, you don't need to worry about the middleware that `WebApplication` adds for the most part. If you're new to ASP.NET Core, generally you can accept that `WebApplication` will add the middleware only when it's necessary and safe to do so.

Nevertheless, in some cases it may pay to know exactly what's in your pipeline, especially if you're familiar with ASP.NET Core. In .NET 7, `WebApplication` automatically adds some or all of the following middleware to the start of the middleware pipeline:

- `HostFilteringMiddleware`—This middleware is security-related. You can read more about why it's useful and how to configure it at http://mng.bz/zXxa.
- `ForwardedHeadersMiddleware`—This middleware controls how forwarded headers are handled. You can read more about it in chapter 27.
- `DeveloperExceptionPageMiddleware`—As already discussed, this middleware is added when you run in a development environment.
- `RoutingMiddleware`—If you add any endpoints to your application, `UseRouting()` runs before you add any custom middleware to your application.
- `AuthenticationMiddleware`—If you configure authentication, this middleware authenticates a user for the request. Chapter 23 discusses authentication in detail.
- `AuthorizationMiddleware`—The authorization middleware runs after authentication and determines whether a user is permitted to execute an endpoint. If the user doesn't have permission, the request is short-circuited. I discuss authorization in detail in chapter 24.
- `EndpointMiddleware`—This middleware pairs with the `RoutingMiddleware` to *execute* an endpoint. Unlike the other middleware described here, the `EndpointMiddleware` is added to the *end* of the middleware pipeline, after any other middleware you configure in Program.cs.

Depending on your Program.cs configuration, `WebApplication` may not add all this middleware. Also, if you don't want some of this automatic middleware to be at the start of your middleware pipeline, generally you can override the location. In listing 4.3, for example, we override the automatic `RoutingMiddleware` location by calling `UseRouting()` explicitly, ensuring that routing occurs exactly where we need it.

Another important point about listing 4.3 is that the order in which you add the middleware to the `WebApplication` object is the order in which the middleware is added to the pipeline. The order of the calls in listing 4.3 creates a pipeline similar to that shown in figure 4.11.

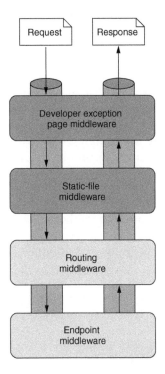

The developer exception page middleware was added first, so it is the first (and last) middleware to process the request.

The static-file middleware is the second middleware in the pipeline. It handles requests for static files before they get to the endpoint middleware.

The routing middleware attempts to find an endpoint that will handle the request.

The endpoint middleware is the last in the pipeline. If there is no endpoint to handle the request, the pipeline returns a 404 response.

Figure 4.11   The middleware pipeline for the example application in listing 4.3. The order in which you add the middleware to `WebApplication` defines the order of the middleware in the pipeline.

The ASP.NET Core web server passes the incoming request to the developer exception page middleware first. This exception-handler middleware ignores the request initially; its purpose is to catch any exceptions thrown by later middleware in the pipeline, as you'll see in section 4.3. It's important for this middleware to be placed early in the pipeline so that it can catch errors produced by later middleware.

The developer exception page middleware passes the request on to the static-file middleware. The static-file handler generates a response if the request corresponds to a file; otherwise, it passes the request on to the routing middleware. The routing middleware selects a minimal API endpoint based on the endpoints defined and the request URL, and the endpoint middleware executes the selected minimal API endpoint. If no endpoint can handle the requested URL, the automatic dummy middleware returns a 404 response.

In chapter 3, I mentioned that `WebApplication` adds the `RoutingMiddleware` to the start of the middleware pipeline automatically. So you may be wondering why I explicitly added it to the pipeline in listing 4.3 using `UseRouting()`.

The answer, again, is related to the order of the middleware. Adding an explicit call to UseRouting() tells WebApplication *not* to add the RoutingMiddleware automatically before the middleware defined in Program.cs. This allows us to "move" the Routing-Middleware to be placed *after* the StaticFileMiddleware. Although this step isn't strictly necessary in this case, it's good practice. The StaticFileMiddleware doesn't use routing, so it's preferable to let this middleware check whether the incoming request is for a static file; if so, it can short-circuit the pipeline and avoid the unnecessary call to the RoutingMiddleware.

> **NOTE**   In versions 1.x and 2.x of ASP.NET Core, the routing and endpoint middleware were combined in a single Model-View-Controller (MVC) middleware component. Splitting the responsibilities for routing from execution makes it possible to insert middleware *between* the routing and endpoint middleware. I discuss routing further in chapters 6 and 14.

The impact of ordering is most obvious when you have two pieces of middleware that are listening for the same path. The endpoint middleware in the example pipeline currently responds to a request to the home page of the application (with the / path) by returning the string "Hello World!", as shown in figure 4.10. Figure 4.12 shows what happens if you reintroduce a piece of middleware that you saw previously, WelcomePage-Middleware, and configure it to respond to the / path as well.

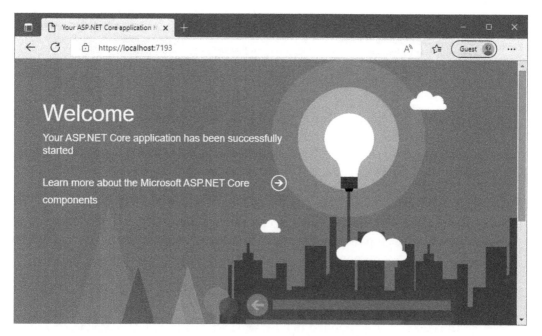

Figure 4.12   The Welcome-page middleware response. The Welcome-page middleware comes before the endpoint middleware, so a request to the home page returns the Welcome-page middleware instead of the minimal API response.

As you saw in section 4.2.1, `WelcomePageMiddleware` is designed to return a fixed HTML response, so you wouldn't use it in a production app, but it illustrates the point nicely. In the following listing, it's added to the start of the middleware pipeline and configured to respond only to the `"/"` path.

Listing 4.4 Adding `WelcomePageMiddleware` to the pipeline

```
WebApplicationBuilder builder = WebApplication.CreateBuilder(args);
WebApplication app = builder.Build();

app.UseWelcomePage("/");       ◁
app.UseDeveloperExceptionPage();
app.UseStaticFiles();
app.UseRouting();

app.MapGet("/", () => "Hello World!");

app.Run();
```

WelcomePageMiddleware handles all requests to the "/" path and returns a sample HTML response.

Requests to "/" will never reach the endpoint middleware, so this endpoint won't be called.

Even though you know that the endpoint middleware can *also* handle the `"/"` path, `WelcomePageMiddleware` is earlier in the pipeline, so it returns a response when it receives the request to `"/"`, short-circuiting the pipeline, as shown in figure 4.13. None of the other middleware in the pipeline runs for the request, so none has an opportunity to generate a response.

As `WebApplication` automatically adds `EndpointMiddleware` to the *end* of the middleware pipeline, the `WelcomePageMiddleware` will *always* be ahead of it, so it always generates a response before the endpoint can execute in this example.

> **TIP** You should always consider the order of middleware when adding it to `WebApplication`. Middleware added earlier in the pipeline will run (and potentially return a response) before middleware added later.

All the examples shown so far try to handle an incoming request and generate a response, but it's important to remember that the middleware pipeline is bidirectional. Each middleware component gets an opportunity to handle both the incoming request and the outgoing response. The order of middleware is most important for those components that create or modify the outgoing response.

In listing 4.3, I included `DeveloperExceptionPageMiddleware` at the start of the application's middleware pipeline, but it didn't seem to do anything. Error-handling middleware characteristically ignores the incoming request as it arrives in the pipeline; instead, it inspects the outgoing response, modifying it only when an error has occurred. In the next section, I discuss the types of error-handling middleware that are available to use with your application and when to use them.

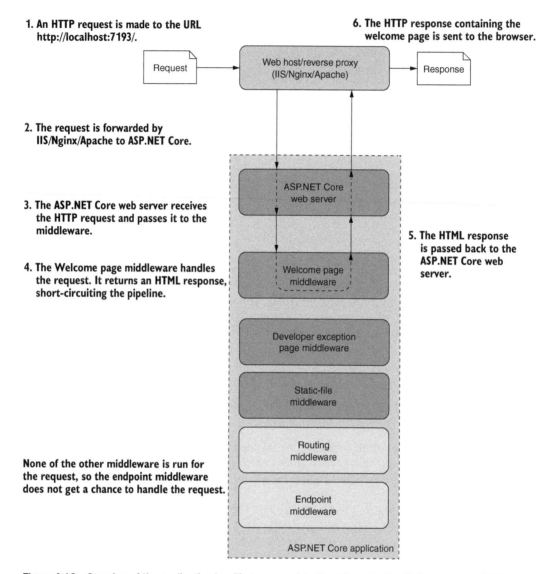

1. An HTTP request is made to the URL http://localhost:7193/.

6. The HTTP response containing the welcome page is sent to the browser.

2. The request is forwarded by IIS/Nginx/Apache to ASP.NET Core.

3. The ASP.NET Core web server receives the HTTP request and passes it to the middleware.

5. The HTML response is passed back to the ASP.NET Core web server.

4. The Welcome page middleware handles the request. It returns an HTML response, short-circuiting the pipeline.

None of the other middleware is run for the request, so the endpoint middleware does not get a chance to handle the request.

Figure 4.13 Overview of the application handling a request to the " / " path. The Welcome-page middleware is first in the middleware pipeline, so it receives the request before any other middleware. It generates an HTML response, short-circuiting the pipeline. No other middleware runs for the request.

4.3 Handling errors using middleware

Errors are a fact of life when you're developing applications. Even if you write perfect code, as soon as you release and deploy your application, users will find a way to break it, by accident or intentionally! The important thing is that your application handles these errors gracefully, providing a suitable response to the user and not causing your whole application to fail.

The design philosophy for ASP.NET Core is that every feature is opt-in. So because error handling is a feature, you need to enable it explicitly in your application. Many types of errors could occur in your application, and you have many ways to handle them, but in this section I focus on a single type of error: exceptions.

Exceptions typically occur whenever you find an unexpected circumstance. A typical (and highly frustrating) exception you'll no doubt have experienced before is `NullReferenceException`, which is thrown when you attempt to access a variable that hasn't been initialized.[3] If an exception occurs in a middleware component, it propagates up the pipeline, as shown in figure 4.14. If the pipeline doesn't handle the exception, the web server returns a 500 status code to the user.

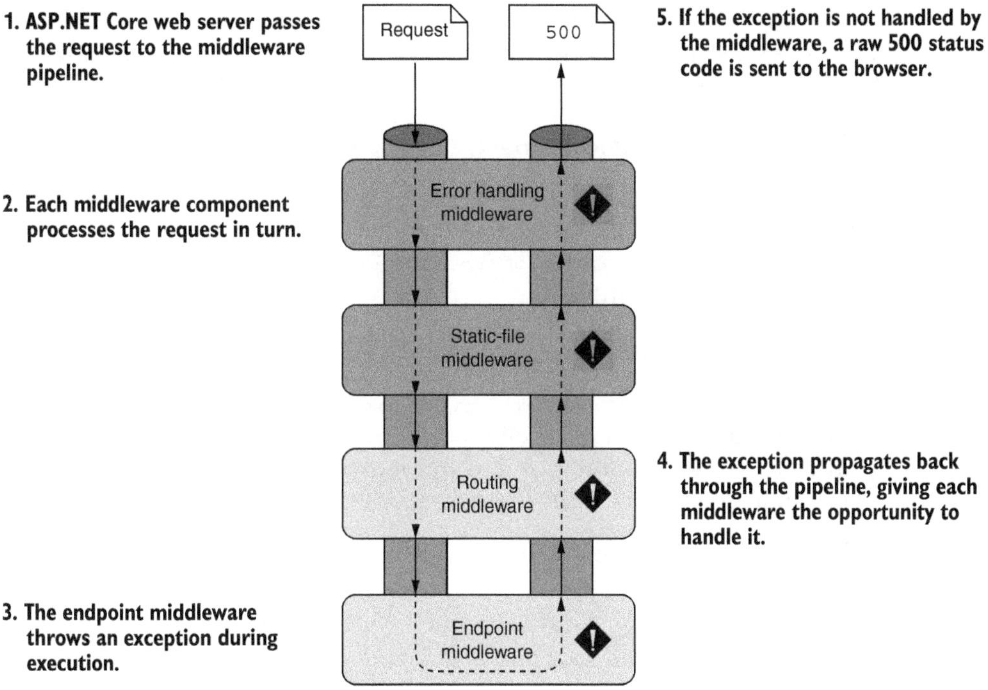

1. ASP.NET Core web server passes the request to the middleware pipeline.

2. Each middleware component processes the request in turn.

3. The endpoint middleware throws an exception during execution.

Request   500

Error handling middleware

Static-file middleware

Routing middleware

Endpoint middleware

5. If the exception is not handled by the middleware, a raw 500 status code is sent to the browser.

4. The exception propagates back through the pipeline, giving each middleware the opportunity to handle it.

Figure 4.14   An exception in the endpoint middleware propagates through the pipeline. If the exception isn't caught by middleware earlier in the pipeline, a 500 "Server error" status code is sent to the user's browser.

In some situations, an error won't cause an exception. Instead, middleware might generate an error status code. One such case occurs when a requested path isn't handled. In that situation, the pipeline returns a 404 error.

---

[3] C# 8.0 introduced non-nullable reference types, which provide a way to handle null values more clearly, with the promise of finally ridding .NET of `NullReferenceExceptions`! The ASP.NET Core framework libraries in .NET 7 have fully embraced nullable reference types. See the documentation to learn more: http://mng.bz/7V0g.

For APIs, which typically are consumed by apps (as opposed to end users), that result probably is fine. But for apps that typically generate HTML, such as Razor Pages apps, returning a 404 typically results in a generic, unfriendly page being shown to the user, as you saw in figure 4.8. Although this behavior is correct, it doesn't provide a great experience for users of these types of applications.

Error-handling middleware attempts to address these problems by modifying the response before the app returns it to the user. Typically, error-handling middleware returns either details on the error that occurred or a generic but friendly HTML page to the user. You'll learn how to handle this use case in chapter 13 when you learn about generating responses with Razor Pages.

The remainder of this section looks at the two main types of exception-handling middleware that's available for use in your application. Both are available as part of the base ASP.NET Core framework, so you don't need to reference any additional NuGet packages to use them.

4.3.1 *Viewing exceptions in development: DeveloperExceptionPage*

When you're developing an application, you typically want access to as much information as possible when an error occurs somewhere in your app. For that reason, Microsoft provides `DeveloperExceptionPageMiddleware`, which you can add to your middleware pipeline by using

```
app.UseDeveloperExceptionPage();
```

> **NOTE** As shown previously, `WebApplication` automatically adds this middleware to your middleware pipeline when you're running in the `Development` environment, so you don't need to add it explicitly. You'll learn more about environments in chapter 10.

When an exception is thrown and propagates up the pipeline to this middleware, it's captured. Then the middleware generates a friendly HTML page, which it returns with a 500 status code, as shown in figure 4.15. This page contains a variety of details about the request and the exception, including the exception stack trace; the source code at the line the exception occurred; and details on the request, such as any cookies or headers that were sent.

Having these details available when an error occurs is invaluable for debugging a problem, but they also represent a security risk if used incorrectly. You should never return more details about your application to users than absolutely necessary, so you should use `DeveloperExceptionPage` only when developing your application. The clue is in the name!

> **WARNING** Never use the developer exception page when running in production. Doing so is a security risk, as it could publicly reveal details about your application's code, making you an easy target for attackers. `WebApplication` uses the correct behavior by default and adds the middleware only when running in development.

Title indicating the problem

Detail of the exception that occured

Location in the code where exception occured

Buttons to click that reveal further details about the request that caused the exception

Code that caused the exception. You can click the "+" symbol to expand the code around the exception.

Full stack trace for the exception

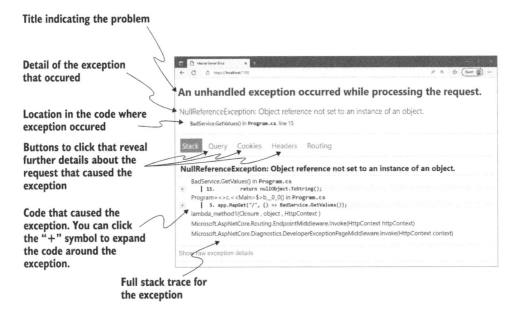

Figure 4.15 The developer exception page shows details about the exception when it occurs during the process of a request. The location in the code that caused the exception, the source code line itself, and the stack trace are all shown by default. You can also click the Query, Cookies, Headers, and Routing buttons to reveal further details about the request that caused the exception.

If the developer exception page isn't appropriate for production use, what should you use instead? Luckily, you can use another type of general-purpose error-handling middleware in production: ExceptionHandlerMiddleware.

4.3.2 Handling exceptions in production: ExceptionHandlerMiddleware

The developer exception page is handy when you're developing your applications, but you shouldn't use it in production, as it can leak information about your app to potential attackers. You still want to catch errors, though; otherwise, users will see unfriendly error pages or blank pages, depending on the browser they're using.

You can solve this problem by using ExceptionHandlerMiddleware. If an error occurs in your application, the user will see a custom error response that's consistent with the rest of the application but provides only necessary details about the error. For a minimal API application, that response could be JSON or plain text, as shown in figure 4.16.

For Razor Pages apps, you can create a custom error response, such as the one shown in figure 4.17. You maintain the look and feel of the application by using the same header, displaying the currently logged-in user, and displaying an appropriate message to the user instead of full details on the exception.

Given the differing requirements for error handlers in development and production, most ASP.NET Core apps add their error-handler middleware conditionally,

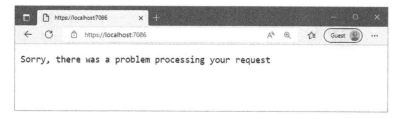

Figure 4.16   Using the `ExceptionHandlerMiddleware`, you can return a generic error message when an exception occurs, ensuring that you don't leak any sensitive details about your application in production.

Dynamic details such as the current user can be shown on the error page.

Menu bar consistent with the rest of your application

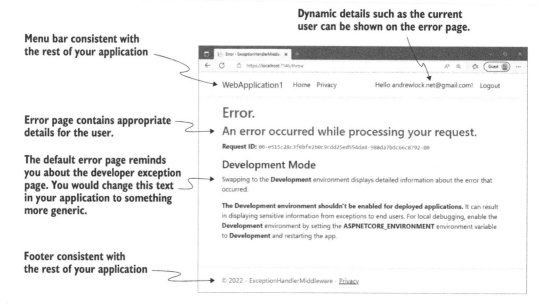

Error page contains appropriate details for the user.

The default error page reminds you about the developer exception page. You would change this text in your application to something more generic.

Footer consistent with the rest of your application

Figure 4.17   A custom error page created by `ExceptionHandlerMiddleware`. The custom error page can have the same look and feel as the rest of the application by reusing elements such as the header and footer. More important, you can easily control the error details displayed to users.

based on the hosting environment. `WebApplication` automatically adds the developer exception page when running in the development hosting environment, so you typically add `ExceptionHandlerMiddleware` when you're *not* in the development environment, as shown in the following listing.

Listing 4.5   Adding exception-handler middleware when in production

```
WebApplicationBuilder builder = WebApplication.CreateBuilder(args);
WebApplication app = builder.Build();

if (!app.Environment.IsDevelopment())
{
```

In development, WebApplication automatically adds the developer exception page middleware.

Configures a different pipeline when not running in development

```
        app.UseExceptionHandler("/error");   ◁─┐   The ExceptionHandlerMiddleware won't leak
}                                              │   sensitive details when running in production.

// additional middleware configuration
app.MapGet("/error", () => "Sorry, an error occurred");
```
This error endpoint will be executed when an exception is handled.

As well as demonstrating how to add `ExceptionHandlerMiddleware` to your middleware pipeline, this listing shows that it's perfectly acceptable to configure different middleware pipelines depending on the environment when the application starts. You could also vary your pipeline based on other values, such as settings loaded from configuration.

> **NOTE** You'll see how to use configuration values to customize the middleware pipeline in chapter 10.

When adding `ExceptionHandlerMiddleware` to your application, you typically provide a path to the custom error page that will be displayed to the user. In the example in listing 4.5, you used an error handling path of `"/error"`:

```
app.UseExceptionHandler("/error");
```

`ExceptionHandlerMiddleware` invokes this path after it captures an exception to generate the final response. The ability to generate a response dynamically is a key feature of `ExceptionHandlerMiddleware`; it allows you to reexecute a middleware pipeline to generate the response sent to the user.

Figure 4.18 shows what happens when `ExceptionHandlerMiddleware` handles an exception. It shows the flow of events when the minimal API endpoint for the `"/"` path generates an exception. The final response returns an error status code but also provides an error string, using the `"/error"` endpoint.

The sequence of events when an unhandled exception occurs somewhere in the middleware pipeline (or in an endpoint) after `ExceptionHandlerMiddleware` is as follows:

1   A piece of middleware throws an exception.
2   `ExceptionHandlerMiddleware` catches the exception.
3   Any partial response that has been defined is cleared.
4   The `ExceptionHandlerMiddleware` overwrites the request path with the provided error-handling path.
5   The middleware sends the request back down the pipeline, as though the original request had been for the error-handling path.
6   The middleware pipeline generates a new response as normal.
7   When the response gets back to `ExceptionHandlerMiddleware`, it modifies the status code to a 500 error and continues to pass the response up the pipeline to the web server.

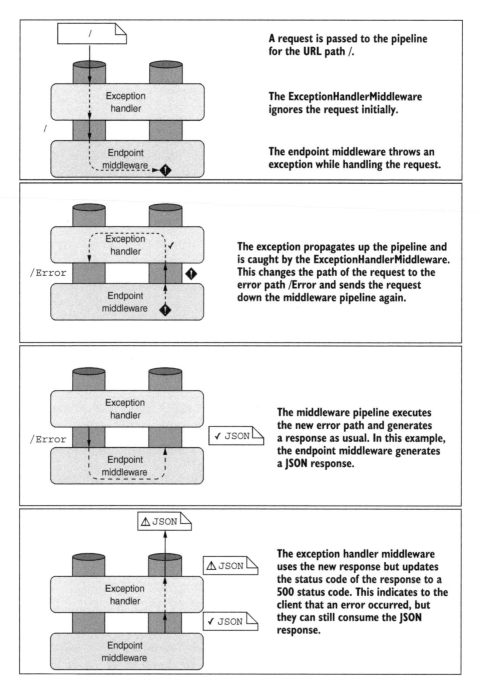

A request is passed to the pipeline for the URL path /.

The ExceptionHandlerMiddleware ignores the request initially.

The endpoint middleware throws an exception while handling the request.

The exception propagates up the pipeline and is caught by the ExceptionHandlerMiddleware. This changes the path of the request to the error path /Error and sends the request down the middleware pipeline again.

The middleware pipeline executes the new error path and generates a response as usual. In this example, the endpoint middleware generates a JSON response.

The exception handler middleware uses the new response but updates the status code of the response to a 500 status code. This indicates to the client that an error occurred, but they can still consume the JSON response.

Figure 4.18 `ExceptionHandlerMiddleware` handling an exception to generate a JSON response. A request to the / path generates an exception, which is handled by the middleware. The pipeline is reexecuted, using the /error path to generate the JSON response.

One of the main advantages of reexecuting the pipeline for Razor Page apps is the ability to have your error messages integrated into your normal site layout, as shown in figure 4.17. It's certainly possible to return a fixed response when an error occurs without reexecuting the pipeline, but you wouldn't be able to have a menu bar with dynamically generated links or display the current user's name in the menu, for example. By reexecuting the pipeline, you ensure that all the dynamic areas of your application are integrated correctly, as though the page were a standard page of your site.

> **NOTE** You don't need to do anything other than add `ExceptionHandler-Middleware` to your application and configure a valid error-handling path to enable reexecuting the pipeline, as shown in figure 4.18. The middleware will catch the exception and reexecute the pipeline for you. Subsequent middleware will treat the reexecution as a new request, but previous middleware in the pipeline won't be aware that anything unusual happened.

Reexecuting the middleware pipeline is a great way to keep consistency in your web application for error pages, but you should be aware of some gotchas. First, middleware can modify a response generated farther down the pipeline only if the response *hasn't yet been sent to the client.* This situation can be a problem if, for example, an error occurs while ASP.NET Core is sending a static file to a client. In that case, ASP.NET Core may start streaming bytes to the client immediately for performance reasons. When that happens, the error-handling middleware won't be able to run, as it can't reset the response. Generally speaking, you can't do much about this problem, but it's something to be aware of.

A more common problem occurs when the error-handling path throws an error during the reexecution of the pipeline. Imagine that there's a bug in the code that generates the menu at the top of the page in a Razor Pages app:

1 When the user reaches your home page, the code for generating the menu bar throws an exception.
2 The exception propagates up the middleware pipeline.
3 When reached, `ExceptionHandlerMiddleware` captures it, and the pipe is reexecuted, using the error-handling path.
4 When the error page executes, it attempts to generate the menu bar for your app, which again throws an exception.
5 The exception propagates up the middleware pipeline.
6 `ExceptionHandlerMiddleware` has already tried to intercept a request, so it lets the error propagate all the way to the top of the middleware pipeline.
7 The web server returns a raw 500 error, as though there were no error-handling middleware at all.

Thanks to this problem, it's often good practice to make your error-handling pages as simple as possible to reduce the possibility that errors will occur.

WARNING If your error-handling path generates an error, the user will see a generic browser error. It's often better to use a static error page that always works than a dynamic page that risks throwing more errors. You can see an alternative approach using a custom error handling function in this post: http://mng.bz/0Kmx.

Another consideration when building minimal API applications is that you generally don't want to return HTML. Returning an HTML page to an application that's expecting JSON could easily break it. Instead, the HTTP 500 status code and a JSON body describing the error are more useful to a consuming application. Luckily, ASP.NET Core allows you to do exactly this when you create minimal APIs and web API controllers.

NOTE I discuss how to add this functionality with minimal APIs in chapter 5 and with web APIs in chapter 20.

That brings us to the end of middleware in ASP.NET Core for now. You've seen how to use and compose middleware to form a pipeline, as well as how to handle exceptions in your application. This information will get you a long way when you start building your first ASP.NET Core applications. Later, you'll learn how to build your own custom middleware, as well as how to perform complex operations on the middleware pipeline, such as forking it in response to specific requests. In chapter 5, you'll look in depth at minimal APIs and at how they can be used to build JSON APIs.

Summary

- Middleware has a similar role to HTTP modules and handlers in ASP.NET but is easier to reason about.
- Middleware is composed in a pipeline, with the output of one middleware passing to the input of the next.
- The middleware pipeline is two-way: requests pass through each middleware on the way in, and responses pass back through in reverse order on the way out.
- Middleware can short-circuit the pipeline by handling a request and returning a response, or it can pass the request on to the next middleware in the pipeline.
- Middleware can modify a request by adding data to or changing the `HttpContext` object.
- If an earlier middleware short-circuits the pipeline, not all middleware will execute for all requests.
- If a request isn't handled, the middleware pipeline returns a 404 status code.
- The order in which middleware is added to `WebApplication` defines the order in which middleware will execute in the pipeline.
- The middleware pipeline can be reexecuted as long as a response's headers haven't been sent.

- When it's added to a middleware pipeline, `StaticFileMiddleware` serves any requested files found in the wwwroot folder of your application.
- `DeveloperExceptionPageMiddleware` provides a lot of information about errors during development, but it should never be used in production.
- `ExceptionHandlerMiddleware` lets you provide user-friendly custom error-handling messages when an exception occurs in the pipeline. It's safe for use in production, as it doesn't expose sensitive details about your application.
- Microsoft provides some common middleware, and many third-party options are available on NuGet and GitHub.

Creating a JSON API with minimal APIs

So far in this book you've seen several examples of minimal API applications that return simple Hello World! responses. These examples are great for getting started, but you can also use minimal APIs to build full-featured HTTP API applications. In this chapter you'll learn about HTTP APIs, see how they differ from a server-rendered application, and find out when to use them.

Section 5.2 starts by expanding on the minimal API applications you've already seen. You'll explore some basic routing concepts and show how values can be extracted from the URL automatically. Then you'll learn how to handle additional HTTP verbs such as POST and PUT, and explore various ways to define your APIs.

In section 5.3 you'll learn about the different return types you can use with minimal APIs. You'll see how to use the `Results` and `TypedResults` helper classes to easily create HTTP responses that use status codes like `201 Created` and `404 Not Found`. You'll also learn how to follow web standards for describing your errors by using the built-in support for Problem Details.

Section 5.4 introduces one of the big features added to minimal APIs in .NET 7: filters. You can use filters to build a mini pipeline (similar to the middleware pipeline from chapter 4) for each of your endpoints. Like middleware, filters are great for extracting common code from your endpoint handlers, making your handlers easier to read.

You'll learn about the other big .NET 7 feature for minimal APIs in section 5.5: *route groups.* You can use route groups to reduce the duplication in your minimal APIs, extracting common routing prefixes and filters, making your APIs easier to read, and reducing boilerplate. In conjunction with filters, route groups address many of the common complaints raised against minimal APIs when they were released in .NET 6.

One great aspect of ASP.NET Core is the variety of applications you can create with it. The ability to easily build a generalized HTTP API presents the possibility of using ASP.NET Core in a greater range of situations than can be achieved with traditional web apps alone. But *should* you build an HTTP API, and if so, why? In the first section of this chapter, I'll go over some of the reasons why you may—or may not—want to create a web API.

5.1 What is an HTTP API, and when should you use one?

Traditional web applications handle requests by returning HTML, which is displayed to the user in a web browser. You can easily build applications like that by using Razor Pages to generate HTML with Razor templates, as you'll learn in part 2 of this book. This approach is common and well understood, but the modern application developer has other possibilities to consider (figure 5.1), as you first saw in chapter 2.

Client-side single-page applications (SPAs) have become popular in recent years with the development of frameworks such as Angular, React, and Vue. These frameworks typically use JavaScript running in a web browser to generate the HTML that users see and interact with. The server sends this initial JavaScript to the browser when the user first reaches the app. The user's browser loads the JavaScript and initializes the SPA before loading any application data from the server.

NOTE Blazor WebAssembly is an exciting new SPA framework. Blazor lets you write an SPA that runs in the browser like other SPAs, but it uses C# and Razor templates instead of JavaScript by using the new web standard, WebAssembly. I don't cover Blazor in this book, so to find out more, I recommend *Blazor in Action*, by Chris Sainty (Manning, 2022).

Once the SPA is loaded in the browser, communication with a server still occurs over HTTP, but instead of sending HTML directly to the browser in response to requests,

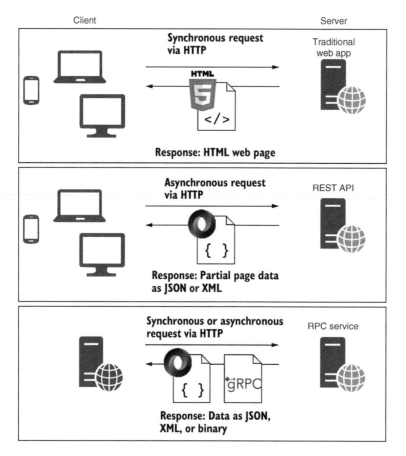

Figure 5.1   Modern developers have to consider several consumers of their applications. As well as traditional users with web browsers, these users could be single-page applications, mobile applications, or other apps.

the server-side application sends data—normally, in the ubiquitous JavaScript Object Notation (JSON) format—to the client-side application. Then the SPA parses the data and generates the appropriate HTML to show to a user, as shown in figure 5.2. The server-side application endpoint that the client communicates with is sometimes called an *HTTP API*, a *JSON API*, or a *REST API*, depending on the specifics of the API's design.

> **DEFINITION**   An *HTTP API* exposes multiple URLs via HTTP that can be used to access or change data on a server. It typically returns data using the JSON format. HTTP APIs are sometimes called web APIs, but as *web API* refers to a specific technology in ASP.NET Core, in this book I use *HTTP API* to refer to the generic concept.

These days, mobile applications are common and, from the server application's point of view, similar to client-side SPAs. A mobile application typically communicates with a

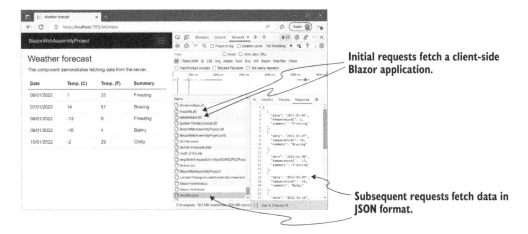

Figure 5.2   A sample client-side SPA using Blazor WebAssembly. The initial requests load the SPA files into the browser, and subsequent requests fetch data from a web API, formatted as JSON.

server application by using an HTTP API, receiving data in JSON format, just like an SPA. Then it modifies the application's UI depending on the data it receives.

One final use case for an HTTP API is where your application is designed to be partially or solely consumed by other backend services. Imagine that you've built a web application to send emails. By creating an HTTP API, you can allow other application developers to use your email service by sending you an email address and a message. Virtually all languages and platforms have access to an HTTP library they could use to access your service from code.

That's all there is to an HTTP API: it exposes endpoints (URLs) that client applications can send requests to and retrieve data from. These endpoints are used to power the behavior of the client apps, as well as to provide all the data the client apps need to display the correct interface to a user.

> **NOTE** You have even more options when it comes to creating APIs in ASP.NET Core. You can create remote procedure call APIs using gRPC, for example, or provide an alternative style of HTTP API using the GraphQL standard. I don't cover those technologies in this book, but you can read about gRPC at https:// docs.microsoft.com/aspnet/core/grpc and find out about GraphQL in *Building Web APIs with ASP.NET Core,* by Valerio De Sanctis (Manning, 2023).

Whether you need or want to create an HTTP API for your ASP.NET Core application depends on the type of application you want to build. Perhaps you're familiar with client-side frameworks, or maybe you need to develop a mobile application, or you already have an SPA build pipeline configured. In each case, you'll most likely want to add HTTP APIs for the client apps to access your application.

One selling point for using an HTTP API is that it can serve as a generalized backend for all your client applications. You could start by building a client-side application that uses an HTTP API. Later, you could add a mobile app that uses the same HTTP API, making little or no modification to your ASP.NET Core code.

If you're new to web development, HTTP APIs can also be easier to understand initially, as they typically return only JSON. Part 1 of this book focuses on minimal APIs so that you can focus on the mechanics of ASP.NET Core without needing to write HTML or CSS.

In part 3, you'll learn how to use Razor Pages to create server-rendered applications instead of minimal APIs. Server-rendered applications can be highly productive. They're generally recommended when you have no need to call your application from outside a web browser or when you don't want or need to make the effort of configuring a client-side application.

> **NOTE**   Although there's been an industry shift toward client-side frameworks, server-side rendering using Razor is still relevant. Which approach you choose depends largely on your preference for building HTML applications in the traditional manner versus using JavaScript (or Blazor!) on the client.

Having said that, whether to use HTTP APIs in your application isn't something you necessarily have to worry about ahead of time. You can always add them to an ASP.NET Core app later in development, as the need arises.

SPAs with ASP.NET Core

The cross-platform, lightweight design of ASP.NET Core means that it lends itself well to acting as a backend for your SPA framework of choice. Given the focus of this book and the broad scope of SPAs in general, I won't be looking at Angular, React, or other SPAs here. Instead, I suggest checking out the resources appropriate to your chosen SPA. Books are available from Manning for all the common client-side JavaScript frameworks, as well as Blazor:

- *React in Action*, by Mark Tielens Thomas (Manning, 2018)
- *Angular in Action*, by Jeremy Wilken (Manning, 2018)
- *Vue.js in Action*, by Erik Hanchett with Benjamin Listwon (Manning, 2018)
- *Blazor in Action*, by Chris Sainty (Manning, 2022)

After you've established that you need an HTTP API for your application, creating one is easy, as it's the default application type in ASP.NET Core! In the next section we look at various ways you can create minimal API endpoints and ways to handle multiple HTTP verbs.

5.2   *Defining minimal API endpoints*

Chapters 3 and 4 gave you an introduction to basic minimal API endpoints. In this section, we'll build on those basic apps to show how you can handle multiple HTTP verbs and explore various ways to write your endpoint handlers.

5.2.1 *Extracting values from the URL with routing*

You've seen several minimal API applications in this book, but so far, all the examples have used fixed paths to define the APIs, as in this example:

```
app.MapGet("/", () => "Hello World!");
app.MapGet("/person", () => new Person("Andrew", "Lock"));
```

These two APIs correspond to the paths / and /person, respectively. This basic functionality is useful, but typically you need some of your APIs to be more dynamic. It's unlikely, for example, that the /person API would be useful in practice, as it always returns the same Person object. What might be more useful is an API to which you can provide the user's first name, and the API returns all the users with that name.

You can achieve this goal by using *parameterized routes* for your API definitions. You can create a parameter in a minimal API route using the expression {someValue}, where someValue is any name you choose. The value will be extracted from the request URL's path and can be used in the lambda function endpoint.

> **NOTE** I introduce only the basics of extracting values from routes in this chapter. You'll learn a lot more about routing in chapter 6, including why we use routing and how it fits into the ASP.NET Core pipeline, as well as the syntax you can use.

If you create an API using the route template /person/{name}, for example, and send a request to the path /person/Andrew, the name parameter will have the value "Andrew". You can use this feature to build more useful APIs, such as the one shown in the following listing.

Listing 5.1 A minimal API that uses a value from the URL

```
WebApplicationBuilder builder = WebApplication.CreateBuilder(args);
WebApplication app = builder.Build();

var people = new List<Person>
{
    new("Tom", "Hanks"),              Creates a list
    new("Denzel", "Washington"),      of people as the
    new("Leondardo", "DiCaprio"),     data for the API
    new("Al", "Pacino"),
    new("Morgan", "Freeman"),
};                                              The route is parameterized
                                                to extract the name from
                                                the URL.
app.MapGet("/person/{name}", (string name) =>
    people.Where(p => p.FirstName.StartsWith(name)));    The extracted value
                                                         can be injected into
app.Run();                                               the lambda handler.
```

If you send a request to /person/Al for the app defined in listing 5.1, the name parameter will have the value "Al", and the API will return the following JSON:

```
[{"firstName":"Al","lastName":"Pacino"}]
```

> **NOTE** By default, minimal APIs serialize C# objects to JSON. You'll see how to return other types of results in section 5.3.

The ASP.NET Core routing system is quite powerful, and we'll explore it in more detail in chapter 6. But with this simple capability, you can already build more complex applications.

5.2.2 *Mapping verbs to endpoints*

So far in this book we've defined all our minimal API endpoints by using the MapGet() function. This function matches requests that use the GET HTTP verb. GET is the most-used verb; it's what a browser uses when you enter a URL in the address bar of your browser or follow a link on a web page.

You should use GET only to *get* data from the server, however. You should never use it to *send* data or to *change* data on the server. Instead, you should use an HTTP verb such as POST or DELETE. You generally can't use these verbs by navigating web pages in the browser, but they're easy to send from a client-side SPA or mobile app.

> **TIP** If you're new to web programming or are looking for a refresher, Mozilla Developer Network (MDN), maker of the Firefox web browser, has a good introduction to HTTP at http://mng.bz/KeMK.

In theory, each of the HTTP verbs has a well-defined purpose, but in practice, you may see apps that only ever use POST and GET. This is often fine for server-rendered applications like Razor Pages, as it's typically simpler, but if you're creating an API, I recommend that you use the HTTP verbs with the appropriate semantics wherever possible.

You can define endpoints for other verbs with minimal APIs by using the appropriate Map* functions. To map a POST endpoint, for example, you'd use MapPost(). Table 5.1 shows the minimal API Map* methods available, the corresponding HTTP verbs, and the typical semantic expectations of each verb on the types of operations that the API performs.

Table 5.1 The minimal API map endpoints and the corresponding HTML verbs

Method	HTTP verb	Expected operation
MapGet(path, handler)	GET	Fetch data only; no modification of state. May be safe to cache.
MapPost(path, handler)	POST	Create a new resource.
MapPut(path, handler)	PUT	Create or replace an existing resource.

Table 5.1 The minimal API map endpoints and the corresponding HTML verbs *(continued)*

Method	HTTP verb	Expected operation
`MapDelete(path, handler)`	DELETE	Delete the given resource.
`MapPatch(path, handler)`	PATCH	Modify the given resource.
`MapMethods(path, methods, handler)`	Multiple verbs	Multiple operations.
`Map(path, handler)`	All verbs	Multiple operations.
`MapFallback(handler)`	All verbs	Useful for SPA fallback routes.

RESTful applications (as described in chapter 2) typically stick close to these verb uses where possible, but some of the actual implementations can differ, and people can easily get caught up in pedantry. Generally, if you stick to the expected operations described in table 5.1, you'll create a more understandable interface for consumers of the API.

> **NOTE** You may notice that if you use the `MapMethods()` and `Map()` methods listed in table 5.1, your API probably doesn't correspond to the expected operations of the HTTP verbs it supports, so I avoid these methods where possible. `MapFallback()` doesn't have a path and is called *only* if no other endpoint matches. Fallback routes can be useful when you have a SPA that uses client-side routing. See http://mng.bz/9DMl for a description of the problem and an alternative solution.

As I mentioned at the start of section 5.2.2, testing APIs that use verbs other than GET is tricky in the browser. You need to use a tool that allows sending arbitrary requests such as Postman (https://www.postman.com) or the HTTP Client plugin in JetBrains Rider. In chapter 11 you'll learn how to use a tool called Swagger UI to visualize and test your APIs.

> **TIP** The HTTP client plugin in JetBrains Rider makes it easy to craft HTTP requests from inside your API, and even discovers all the endpoints in your application automatically, making them easier to test. You can read more about it at https://www.jetbrains.com/help/rider/Http_client_in__product__code_editor.html.

As a final note before we move on, it's worth mentioning the behavior you get when you call a method with the *wrong* HTTP verb. If you define an API like the one in listing 5.1

```
app.MapGet("/person/{name}", (string name) =>
  people.Where(p => p.FirstName.StartsWith(name)));
```

and call it by using a POST request to /person/Al instead of a GET request, the handler won't run, and the response you get will have status code `405 Method Not Allowed`.

TIP You should never see this response when you're calling the API correctly, so if you receive a 405 response, make sure to check that you're using the right HTTP verb and the right path. Often when I see a 405, I've used the correct verb but made a typo in the URL!

In all the examples in this book so far, you provide a lambda function as the handler for an endpoint. But in section 5.2.3, you'll see that there are many ways to define the handler.

5.2.3 *Defining route handlers with functions*

For basic examples, using a lambda function as the handler for an endpoint is often the simplest approach, but you can take many approaches, as shown in the following listing. This listing also demonstrates creating a simple CRUD (Create, Read, Update, Delete) API using different HTTP verbs, as discussed in section 5.2.1.

Listing 5.2 Creating route handlers for a simple CRUD API

```
WebApplicationBuilder builder = WebApplication.CreateBuilder(args);
WebApplication app = builder.Build();

app.MapGet("/fruit", () => Fruit.All);          ◄─── Lambda expressions are the simplest but
                                                     least descriptive way to create a handler.

var getFruit = (string id) => Fruit.All[id];    │ Storing the lambda expression as a variable
app.MapGet("/fruit/{id}", getFruit);            │ means you can name it—getFruit in this case.

app.MapPost("/fruit/{id}", Handlers.AddFruit);  ◄───    Handlers can be static
                                                        methods in any class.
Handlers handlers = new();
app.MapPut("/fruit/{id}", handlers.ReplaceFruit);
                                                        Handlers can also be
app.MapDelete("/fruit/{id}", DeleteFruit);  ◄───        instance methods.

app.Run();                                              You can also use local
                                                        functions, introduced in C#
                                                        7.0, as handler methods.
void DeleteFruit(string id)                     ◄───
{
    Fruit.All.Remove(id);
}

record Fruit(string Name, int Stock)
{
    public static readonly Dictionary<string, Fruit> All = new();
};

class Handlers
{                                                       Handlers can also be
    public void ReplaceFruit(string id, Fruit fruit)  ◄─── instance methods.
    {
        Fruit.All[id] = fruit;
    }
```

```
    public static void AddFruit(string id, Fruit fruit)    ◁─┐   Converts the response
    {                                                         │   to a JsonObject
        Fruit.All.Add(id, fruit);
    }
}
```

Listing 5.2 demonstrates the various ways you can pass handlers to an endpoint by simulating a simple API for interacting with a collection of Fruit items:

- A lambda expression, as in the `MapGet("/fruit")` endpoint
- A `Func<T, TResult>` variable, as in the `MapGet("/fruit/{id}")` endpoint
- A static method, as in the `MapPost` endpoint
- A method on an instance variable, as in the `MapPut` endpoint
- A local function, as in the `MapDelete` endpoint

All these approaches are functionally identical, so you can use whichever pattern works best for you.

Each `Fruit` record in listing 5.2 has a `Name` and a `Stock` level and is stored in a dictionary with an `id`. You call the API by using different HTTP verbs to perform the CRUD operations against the dictionary.

> **WARNING** This API is simple. It isn't thread-safe, doesn't validate user input, and doesn't handle edge cases. We'll remedy some of those deficiencies in section 5.3.

The handlers for the POST and PUT endpoints in listing 5.2 accept both an `id` parameter and a `Fruit` parameter, showing another important feature of minimal APIs. *Complex types*—that is, types that can't be extracted from the URL by means of route parameters—are created by deserializing the JSON body of a request.

> **NOTE** By contrast with APIs built using ASP.NET and ASP.NET Core web API controllers (which we cover in chapter 20), minimal APIs can bind only to JSON bodies and always use the System.Text.Json library for JSON deserialization.

Figure 5.3 shows an example of a POST request sent with Postman. Postman sends the request body as JSON, which the minimal API automatically deserializes into a `Fruit` instance before calling the endpoint handler. You can bind only a single object in your endpoint handler to the request body in this way. I cover model binding in detail in chapter 7.

Minimal APIs leave you free to organize your endpoints any way you choose. That flexibility is often cited as a reason to *not* use them, due to the fear that developers will keep all the functionality in a single file, as in most examples (such as listing 5.2). In practice, you'll likely want to extract your endpoints to separate files so as to modularize them and make them easier to understand. Embrace that urge; that's the way they were intended to be used!

Select an HTTP verb.   **Enter the URL for the request.**   **Choose Send to send the request.**

Select the raw radio button, choose JSON from the drop-down, and enter the body as JSON.

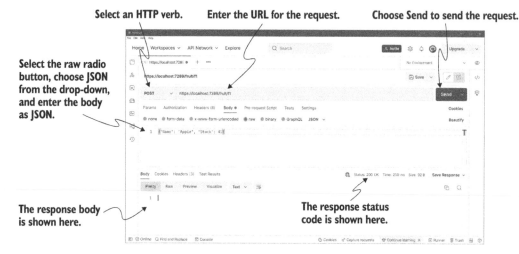

The response body is shown here.

The response status code is shown here.

Figure 5.3   Sending a POST request with Postman. The minimal API automatically deserializes the JSON in the request body to a Fruit instance before calling the endpoint handler.

Now you have a simple API, but if you try it out, you'll quickly run into scenarios in which your API seems to break. In section 5.3 you learn how to handle some of these scenarios by returning status codes.

5.3   Generating responses with IResult

You've seen the basics of minimal APIs, but so far, we've looked only at the happy path, where you can handle the request successfully and return a response. In this section we look at how to handle bad requests and other errors by returning different status codes from your API.

The API in listing 5.2 works well as long as you perform only operations that are valid for the current state of the application. If you send a GET request to /fruit, for example, you'll always get a 200 success response, but if you send a GET request to /fruit/f1 *before* you create a Fruit with the id f1, you'll get an exception and a 500 Internal Server Error response, as shown in figure 5.4.

Throwing an exception whenever a user requests an id that doesn't exist clearly makes for a poor experience all round. A better approach is to return a status code indicating the problem, such as 404 Not Found or 400 Bad Request. The most declarative way to do this with minimal APIs is to return an IResult instance.

All the endpoint handlers you've seen so far in this book have returned void, a string, or a plain old CLR object (POCO) such as Person or Fruit. There is one other type of object you can return from an endpoint: an IResult implementation.

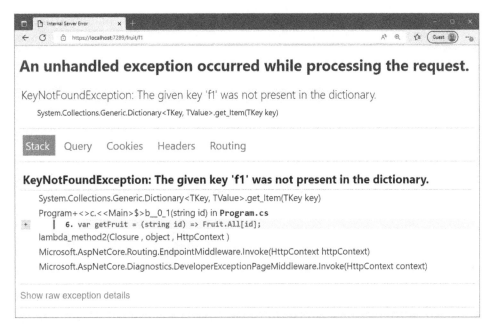

Figure 5.4   If you try to retrieve a fruit by using a nonexistent id **for the simplistic API in listing 5.2, the endpoint throws an exception. This exception is handled by the** DeveloperExceptionPage- Middleware **but provides a poor experience.**

In summary, the endpoint middleware handles each return type as follows:

- void or Task—The endpoint returns a 200 response with no body.
- string or Task<string>—The endpoint returns a 200 response with the string serialized to the body as text/plain.
- IResult or Task<IResult>—The endpoint executes the IResult.ExecuteAsync method. Depending on the implementation, this type can customize the response, returning any status code.
- T or Task<T>—All other types (such as POCO objects) are serialized to JSON and returned in the body of a 200 response as application/json.

The IResult implementations provide much of the flexibility in minimal APIs, as you'll see in section 5.3.1.

5.3.1   *Returning status codes with Results and TypedResults*

A well-designed API uses status codes to indicate to a client what went wrong when a request failed, as well as potentially provide more descriptive codes when a request is successful. You should anticipate common problems that may occur when clients call your API and return appropriate status codes to indicate the causes to users.

ASP.NET Core exposes the simple static helper types Results and TypedResults in the namespace Microsoft.AspNetCore.Http. You can use these helpers to create a response with common status codes, optionally including a JSON body. Each of the methods on `Results` and `TypedResults` returns an implementation of `IResult`, which the endpoint middleware executes to generate the final response.

> **NOTE** `Results` and `TypedResults` perform the same function, as helpers for generating common status codes. The only difference is that the `Results` methods return an `IResult`, whereas `TypedResults` return a concrete generic type, such as `Ok<T>`. There's no difference in terms of functionality, but the generic types are easier to use in unit tests and in OpenAPI documentation, as you'll see in chapters 36 and 11. `TypedResults` were added in .NET 7.

The following listing shows an updated version of listing 5.2, in which we address some of the deficiencies in the API and use `Results` and `TypedResults` to return different status codes to clients.

Listing 5.3   Using `Results` and `TypedResults` in a minimal API

```
using System.Collections.Concurrent;

WebApplicationBuilder builder = WebApplication.CreateBuilder(args);
WebApplication app = builder.Build();

var _fruit = new ConcurrentDictionary<string, Fruit>();

app.MapGet("/fruit", () => _fruit);

app.MapGet("/fruit/{id}", (string id) =>
    _fruit.TryGetValue(id, out var fruit)
        ? TypedResults.Ok(fruit)
        : Results.NotFound());

app.MapPost("/fruit/{id}", (string id, Fruit fruit) =>
    _fruit.TryAdd(id, fruit)
        ? TypedResults.Created($"/fruit/{id}", fruit)
        : Results.BadRequest(new
            { id = "A fruit with this id already exists" }));

app.MapPut("/fruit/{id}", (string id, Fruit fruit) =>
{
    _fruit[id] = fruit;
    return Results.NoContent();
});

app.MapDelete("/fruit/{id}", (string id) =>
{
    _fruit.TryRemove(id, out _);
    return Results.NoContent();
});

app.Run();
record Fruit(string Name, int stock);
```

Annotations:
- Uses a concurrent dictionary to make the API thread-safe
- Tries to get the fruit from the dictionary. If the ID exists in the dictionary, this returns true . . .
- . . . and we return a 200 OK response, serializing the fruit in the body as JSON.
- If the ID doesn't exist, returns a 404 Not Found response
- Tries to add the fruit to the dictionary. If the ID hasn't been added yet, this returns true . . .
- . . . and we return a 201 response with a JSON body and set the Location header to the given path.
- If the ID already exists, returns a 400 Bad Request response with an error message
- After adding or replacing the fruit, returns a 204 No Content response
- After deleting the fruit, always returns a 204 No Content response

Listing 5.3 demonstrates several status codes, some of which you may not be familiar with:

- `200 OK`—The standard successful response. It often includes content in the body of the response but doesn't have to.
- `201 Created`—Often returned when you successfully created an entity on the server. The `Created` result in listing 5.3 also includes a `Location` header to describe the URL where the entity can be found, as well as the JSON entity itself in the body of the response.
- `204 No Content`—Similar to a 200 response but without any content in the response body.
- `400 Bad Request`—Indicates that the request was invalid in some way; often used to indicate data validation failures.
- `404 Not Found`—Indicates that the requested entity could not be found.

These status codes more accurately describe your API and can make an API easier to use. That said, if you use only `200 OK` responses for all your successful responses, few people will mind or think less of you! You can see a summary of all the possible status codes and their expected uses at http://mng.bz/jP4x.

> **NOTE** The `404` status code in particular causes endless debate in online forums. Should it be *only* used if the request didn't match an endpoint? Is it OK to use `404` to indicate a missing entity (as in the previous example)? There are endless proponents in both camps, so take your pick!

`Results` and `TypedResults` include methods for all the common status code results you could need, but if you don't want to use them for some reason, you can always set the status code yourself directly on the `HttpResponse`, as in listing 5.4. In fact, the listing shows how to define the entire response manually, including the status code, the content type, and the response body. You won't need to take this manual approach often, but it can be useful in some situations.

Listing 5.4 Writing the response manually using `HttpResponse`

```
using System.Net.Mime
WebApplicationBuilder builder = WebApplication.CreateBuilder(args);
WebApplication app = builder.Build();

app.MapGet("/teapot", (HttpResponse response) =>      Accesses the HttpResponse by
{                                                      including it as a parameter in
    response.StatusCode = 418;                         your endpoint handler
    response.ContentType = MediaTypeNames.Text.Plain;  Defines the content type that
    return response.WriteAsync("I'm a teapot!");       will be sent in the response
});                                                    You can write data to the
                                                       response stream manually.
app.Run();
```
You can set the status code directly on the response.

`HttpResponse` represents the response that will be sent to the client and is one of the special types that minimal APIs know to inject into your endpoint handlers (instead of trying to create it by deserializing from the request body). You'll learn about the other types you can use in your endpoint handlers in chapter 7.

5.3.2   *Returning useful errors with Problem Details*

In the `MapPost` endpoint of listing 5.3, we checked to see whether an entity with the given `id` already existed. If it did, we returned a `400` response with a description of the error. The problem with this approach is that the client—typically, a mobile app or SPA—must know how to read and parse that response. If each of your APIs has a different format for errors, that arrangement can make for a confusing API. Luckily, a web standard called Problem Details describes a consistent format to use.

> **DEFINITION**   Problem Details is a web specification (https://www.rfc-editor.org/rfc/rfc7807.html) for providing machine-readable errors for HTTP APIs. It defines the required and optional fields that should be in the JSON body for errors.

ASP.NET Core includes two helper methods for generating Problem Details responses from minimal APIs: `Results.Problem()` and `Results.ValidationProblem()` (plus their `TypedResults` counterparts). Both of these methods return Problem Details JSON. The only difference is that `Problem()` defaults to a `500` status code, whereas `ValidationProblem()` defaults to a `400` status and requires you to pass in a `Dictionary` of validation errors, as shown in the following listing.

Listing 5.5   Returning Problem Details using `Results.Problem`

```
using System.Collections.Concurrent;

WebApplicationBuilder builder = WebApplication.CreateBuilder(args);
WebApplication app = builder.Build();

var _fruit = new ConcurrentDictionary<string, Fruit>();

app.MapGet("/fruit", () => _fruit);

app.MapGet("/fruit/{id}", (string id) =>
    _fruit.TryGetValue(id, out var fruit)
        ? TypedResults.Ok(fruit)
        : Results.Problem(statusCode: 404));

app.MapPost("/fruit/{id}", (string id, Fruit fruit) =>
    _fruit.TryAdd(id, fruit)
        ? TypedResults.Created($"/fruit/{id}", fruit)
        : Results.ValidationProblem(new Dictionary<string, string[]>
          {
              {"id", new[] {"A fruit with this id already exists"}}
          }));
```

Returns a Problem Details object with a 404 status code

Returns a Problem Details object with a 400 status code and includes the validation errors

The `ProblemHttpResult` returned by these methods takes care of including the correct title and description based on the status code, and generates the appropriate JSON, as shown in figure 5.5. You can override the default title and description by passing additional arguments to the `Problem()` and `ValidationProblem()` methods.

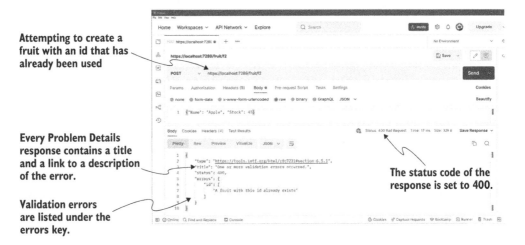

Attempting to create a fruit with an id that has already been used

Every Problem Details response contains a title and a link to a description of the error.

The status code of the response is set to 400.

Validation errors are listed under the errors key.

Figure 5.5   You can return a Problem Details response by using the `Problem` and `ValidationProblem` methods. The `ValidationProblem` response shown here includes a description of the error, along with the validation errors in a standard format. This example shows the response when you try to create a fruit with an `id` that has already been used.

Deciding on an error format is an important step whenever you create an API, and as Problem Details is already a web standard, it should be your go-to approach, especially for validation errors. Next, you'll learn how to ensure that all your error responses are Problem Details.

5.3.3   Converting all your responses to Problem Details

In section 5.3.2 you saw how to use the `Results.Problem()` and `Results.Validation-Problem()` methods in your minimal API endpoints to return Problem Details JSON. The only catch is that your minimal API endpoints aren't the *only* thing that could generate errors. In this section you'll learn how to make sure that all your errors return Problem Details JSON, keeping the error responses consistent across your application.

A minimal API application could generate an error response in several ways:

- Returning an error status code from an endpoint handler
- Throwing an exception in an endpoint handler, which is caught by the `ExceptionHandlerMiddleware` or the `DeveloperExceptionPageMiddleware` and converted to an error response
- The middleware pipeline returning a `404` response because a request isn't handled by an endpoint

- A middleware component in the pipeline throwing an exception
- A middleware component returning an error response because a request requires authentication, and no credentials were provided

There are essentially two classes of errors, which are handled differently: exceptions and error status code responses. To create a consistent API for consumers, we need to make sure that both error types return Problem Details JSON in the response.

CONVERTING EXCEPTIONS TO PROBLEM DETAILS

In chapter 4 you learned how to handle exceptions with the `ExceptionHandlerMiddleware`. You saw that the middleware catches any exceptions from later middleware and generates an error response by executing an error-handling path. You could add the middleware to your pipeline with an error-handling path of `"/error"`:

```
app.UseExceptionHandler("/error");
```

`ExceptionHandlerMiddleware` invokes this path after it captures an exception to generate the final response. The trouble with this approach for minimal APIs is that you need a dedicated error endpoint, the sole purpose of which is to generate a Problem Details response.

Luckily, in .NET 7, you can configure the `ExceptionHandlerMiddleware` (and `DeveloperExceptionPageMiddleware`) to convert an exception to a Problem Details response automatically. In .NET 7, you can add the new `IProblemDetailsService` to your app by calling `AddProblemDetails()` on `WebApplicationBuilder.Services`. When the `ExceptionHandlerMiddleware` is configured *without* an error-handling path, it automatically uses the `IProblemDetailsService` to generate the response, as shown in figure 5.6.

> **WARNING** Calling `AddProblemDetails()` registers the `IProblemDetailsService` service in the dependency injection container so that other services and middleware can use it. If you configure `ExceptionHandlerMiddleware` without an error-handling path but forget to call `AddProblemDetails()`, you'll get an exception when your app starts. You'll learn more about dependency injection in chapters 8 and 9.

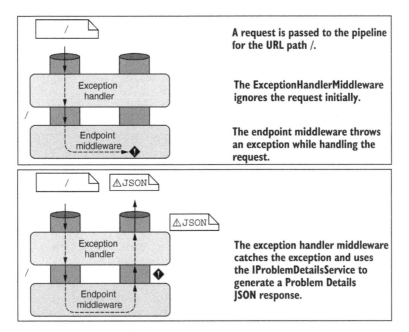

Figure 5.6 The `ExceptionHandlerMiddleware` **catches exceptions that occur later in the middleware pipeline. If the middleware isn't configured to reexecute the pipeline, it generates a Problem Details response by using the** `IProblemDetailsService`.

Listing 5.6 shows how to configure Problem Details generation in your exception handlers. Add the required `IProblemDetailsService` service to your app, and call `UseExceptionHandler()` without providing an error-handling path, and the middleware will generate a Problem Details response automatically when it catches an exception.

Listing 5.6   Configuring `ExceptionHandlerMiddleware` **to use Problem Details**

```
WebApplicationBuilder builder = WebApplication.CreateBuilder(args);
builder.Services.AddProblemDetails();        ⟵┐
                                               │  Adds the IProblemDetailsService implementation
WebApplication app = builder.Build();

                                                  Configures the
if (!app.Environment.IsDevelopment())             ExceptionHandlerMiddleware
{                                                 without a path so that it uses
    app.UseExceptionHandler();      ⟵───────────  the IProblemDetailsService
}

app.MapGet("/", void () => throw new Exception());  ⟵┐  Throws an exception to
                                                      │  demonstrate the behavior
app.Run();
```

As discussed in chapter 4, `WebApplication` automatically adds the `DeveloperException-PageMiddleware` to your app in the development environment. This middleware similarly supports returning Problem Details when two conditions are satisfied:

- You've registered an `IProblemDetailsService` with the app (by calling `AddProblem-Details()` in Program.cs).
- The request indicates that it doesn't support HTML. If the client supports HTML, middleware uses the HTML developer exception page from chapter 4 instead.

The `ExceptionHandlerMiddleware` and `DeveloperExceptionPageMiddleware` take care of converting all your exceptions to Problem Details responses, but you still need to think about nonexception errors, such as the automatic 404 response generated when a request doesn't match any endpoints.

CONVERTING ERROR STATUS CODES TO PROBLEM DETAILS

Returning error status codes is the common way to communicate errors to a client with minimal APIs. To ensure a consistent API for consumers, you should return a Problem Details response whenever you return an error. Unfortunately, as already mentioned, you don't control all the places where an error code may be created. The middleware pipeline automatically returns a 404 response when an unmatched request reaches the end of the pipeline, for example.

Instead of generating a Problem Details response in your endpoint handlers, you can add middleware to convert responses to Problem Details automatically by using the `StatusCodePagesMiddleware`, as shown in figure 5.7. Any response that reaches the middleware with an error status code and doesn't already have a body has a Problem

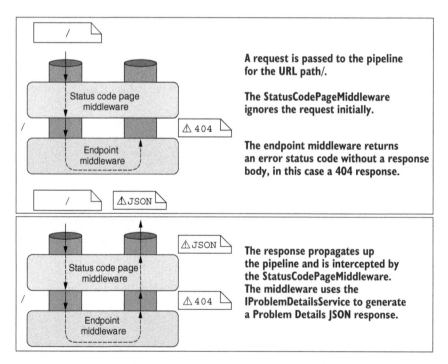

Figure 5.7 The `StatusCodePagesMiddleware` **intercepts responses with an error status code that have no response body and adds a Problem Details response body.**

Details body added by the middleware. The middleware converts all error responses automatically, regardless of whether they were generated by an endpoint or from other middleware.

> **NOTE** You can also use the `StatusCodePagesMiddleware` to reexecute the middleware pipeline with an error handling path, as you can with the `Exception-HandlerMiddleware` (chapter 4). This technique is most useful for Razor Pages applications when you want to have a different error page for specific status codes, as you'll see in chapter 15.

Add the `StatusCodePagesMiddleware` to your app by using the `UseStatusCodePages()` extension method, as shown in the following listing. Ensure that you also add the `IProblemDetailsService` to your app by using `AddProblemDetails()`.

Listing 5.7 Using `StatusCodePagesMiddleware` to return Problem Details

```
WebApplicationBuilder builder = WebApplication.CreateBuilder(args);
builder.Services.AddProblemDetails();      ⊲──┐
                                              │  Adds the IProblemDetailsService
WebApplication app = builder.Build();         │  implementation

if (!app.Environment.IsDevelopment())
{
    app.UseExceptionHandler();
}

app.UseStatusCodePages();      ⊲──── Adds the StatusCodePagesMiddleware

app.MapGet("/", () => Results.NotFound());  ⊲──┐
                                               │  The StatusCodePagesMiddleware
app.Run();                                     │  automatically adds a Problem
                                               │  Details body to the 404 response.
```

The `StatusCodePagesMiddleware`, coupled with exception-handling middleware, ensures that your API returns a Problem Details response for all error responses.

> **TIP** You can also customize how the Problem Details response is generated by passing parameters to the `AddProblemDetails()` method or by implementing your own `IProblemDetailsService`.

So far in section 5.3, I've described returning objects as JSON, returning a `string` as text, and returning custom status codes and Problem Details by using `Results`. Sometimes, however, you need to return something bigger, such as a file or a binary. Luckily, you can use the convenient `Results` class for that task too.

5.3.4 *Returning other data types*

The methods on `Results` and `TypedResults` are convenient ways of returning common responses, so it's only natural that they include helpers for other common scenarios, such as returning a file or binary data:

- `Results.File()`—Pass in the path of the file to return, and ASP.NET Core takes care of streaming it to the client.
- `Results.Byte()`—For returning binary data, you can pass this method a `byte[]` to return.
- `Results.Stream()`—You can send data to the client asynchronously by using a `Stream`.

In each of these cases, you can provide a content type for the data, and a filename to be used by the client. Browsers offer to save binary data files using the suggested filename. The `File` and `Byte` methods even support range requests by specifying `enableRangeProcessing` as `true`.

> **DEFINITION**   Clients can create range requests using the `Range` header to request a specific range of bytes from the server instead of the whole file, reducing the bandwidth required for a request. When range requests are enabled for `Results.File()` or `Results.Byte()`, ASP.NET Core automatically handles generating an appropriate response. You can read more about range requests at http://mng.bz/Wzd0.

If the built-in `Results` helpers don't provide the functionality you need, you can always fall back to creating a response manually, as in listing 5.4. If you find yourself creating the same manual response several times, you could consider creating a custom `IResult` type to encapsulate this logic. I show how to create a custom `IResult` that returns XML and registers it as an extension in this blog post: http://mng.bz/8rNP.

5.4   Running common code with endpoint filters

In section 5.3 you learned how to use `Results` to return different responses when the request isn't valid. We'll look at validation in more detail in chapter 7, but in this section, you'll learn how to use filters to extract common code that executes before (or after) an endpoint executes.

Let's start by adding some extra validation to the `fruit` API from listing 5.5. The following listing adds an additional check to the `MapGet` endpoint to ensure that the provided `id` isn't empty and that it starts with the letter `f`.

> **Listing 5.8   Adding basic validation to minimal API endpoints**

```
using System.Collections.Concurrent;
WebApplicationBuilder builder = WebApplication.CreateBuilder(args);
WebApplication app = builder.Build();

var _fruit = new ConcurrentDictionary<string, Fruit>();

app.MapGet("/fruit/{id}", (string id) =>
{
    if (string.IsNullOrEmpty(id) || !id.StartsWith('f'))       ◁───  Adds extra validation that the provided id has the required format
    {
        return Results.ValidationProblem(new Dictionary<string, string[]>
```

```
        {
            {"id", new[] {"Invalid format. Id must start with 'f'"}}
        });
    }

    return _fruit.TryGetValue(id, out var fruit)
            ? TypedResults.Ok(fruit)
            : Results.Problem(statusCode: 404);
});
```

```
app.Run()
```

Even though this check is basic, it starts to clutter our endpoint handler, making it harder to read what the endpoint is doing. One improvement would be to move the validation code to a helper function. But you're still inevitably going to clutter your endpoint handlers with calls to methods that are tangential to the main function of your endpoint.

NOTE Chapter 7 discusses additional validation patterns in detail.

It's common to perform various cross-cutting activities for every endpoint. I've already mentioned validation; other cross-cutting activities include logging, authorization, and auditing. ASP.NET Core has built-in support for some of these features, such as authorization (chapter 24), but you're likely to have some common code that doesn't fit into the specific pigeonholes of validation or authorization.

Luckily, ASP.NET Core includes a feature in minimal APIs for running these tangential concerns: endpoint filters. You can specify a filter for an endpoint by calling `AddEndpointFilter()` on the result of a call to `MapGet` (or similar) and passing in a function to execute. You can even add multiple calls to `AddEndpointFilter()`, which builds up an *endpoint filter pipeline,* analogous to the middleware pipeline. Figure 5.8 shows that the pipeline is functionally identical to the middleware pipeline in figure 4.3.

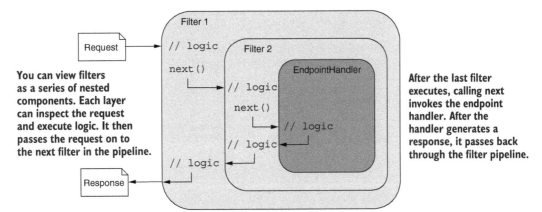

You can view filters as a series of nested components. Each layer can inspect the request and execute logic. It then passes the request on to the next filter in the pipeline.

After the last filter executes, calling next invokes the endpoint handler. After the handler generates a response, it passes back through the filter pipeline.

Figure 5.8 **The endpoint filter pipeline. Filters execute code and then call** `next(context)` **to invoke the next filter in the pipeline. If there are no more filters in the pipeline, the endpoint handler is invoked. After the handler has executed, the filters may run further code.**

Each endpoint filter has two parameters: a `context` parameter, which provides details about the selected endpoint handler, and the `next` parameter, which represents the filter pipeline. When you invoke the methodlike `next` parameter by calling `next(context)`, you invoke the remainder of the filter pipeline. If there are no more filters in the pipeline, you invoke the endpoint handler, as shown in figure 5.8.

Listing 5.9 shows how to run the same validation logic you saw in listing 5.8 in an endpoint filter. The filter function accesses the endpoint method arguments by using the `context.GetArgument<T>()` function, passing in a position; `0` is the first argument of your endpoint handler, `1` is the second argument, and so on. If the argument isn't valid, the filter function returns an `IResult` object response. If the argument is valid, the filter calls `await next(context)` instead, executing the endpoint handler.

Listing 5.9   Using `AddEndpointFilter` to extract common code

```
WebApplicationBuilder builder = WebApplication.CreateBuilder(args);
WebApplication app = builder.Build();
var _fruit = new ConcurrentDictionary<string, Fruit>();

app.MapGet("/fruit/{id}", (string id) =>
    _fruit.TryGetValue(id, out var fruit)
        ? TypedResults.Ok(fruit)
        : Results.Problem(statusCode: 404))       ← Adds the filter to
    .AddEndpointFilter(ValidationHelper.ValidateId);     the endpoint using
                                                         AddEndpointFilter
app.Run();

class ValidationHelper                        context exposes the
{                                             endpoint method
    internal static async ValueTask<object?> ValidateId(   arguments and the
        EndpointFilterInvocationContext context,   ←       HttpContext.
        EndpointFilterDelegate next)
    {
        var id = context.GetArgument<string>(0);   ←
        if (string.IsNullOrEmpty(id) || !id.StartsWith('f'))   You can retrieve the
        {                                                      method arguments
            return Results.ValidationProblem(                  from the context.
                new Dictionary<string, string[]>
                {
                    {"id", new[]{"Invalid format. Id must start with 'f'"}}
                });
        }
        return await next(context);   ←   Calling next executes the remaining
    }                                     filters in the pipeline.
}
```

The method must return a ValueTask. *(annotation for `internal static async ValueTask<object?> ValidateId(` and `EndpointFilterDelegate next)`)*

next represents the filter method (or endpoint) that will be called next. *(annotation)*

NOTE   The `EndpointFilterDelegate` is a named delegate type. It's effectively a `Func<EndpointFilterInvocationContext, ValueTask<object?>>`.

There are many parallels between the middleware pipeline and the filter endpoint pipeline, and we'll explore them in section 5.4.1.

5.4.1 Adding multiple filters to an endpoint

The middleware pipeline is typically the best place for handling cross-cutting concerns such as logging, authentication, and authorization, as these functions apply to all requests. Nevertheless, it can be common to have additional cross-cutting concerns that are endpoint-specific, as we've already discussed. If you need many endpoint-specific operations, you might consider using multiple endpoint filters.

As you saw in figure 5.8, adding multiple filters to an endpoint builds up a pipeline. Like the middleware pipeline, the endpoint filter pipeline can execute code both before and after the rest of the pipeline executes. Similarly, the filter pipeline can short-circuit in the same way as the middleware pipeline by returning a result and not calling next.

> **NOTE** You've already seen an example of a short circuit in the filter pipeline. In listing 5.9 we short-circuit the pipeline if the id is invalid by returning a Problem Details object instead of calling next(context).

As with middleware, the order in which you add filters to the endpoint filter pipeline is important. The filters you add first are called first in the pipeline, and filters you add last are called last. On the return journey through the pipeline, after the endpoint handler is invoked, the filters are called in reverse order, as with the middleware pipeline. As an example, consider the following listing, which adds an extra filter to the endpoint shown in listing 5.9.

Listing 5.10 Adding multiple filters to the endpoint filter pipeline

```
WebApplicationBuilder builder = WebApplication.CreateBuilder(args);
WebApplication app = builder.Build();
var _fruit = new ConcurrentDictionary<string, Fruit>();

app.MapGet("/fruit/{id}", (string id) =>
    _fruit.TryGetValue(id, out var fruit)
        ? TypedResults.Ok(fruit)
        : Results.Problem(statusCode: 404))
    .AddEndpointFilter(ValidationHelper.ValidateId)
    .AddEndpointFilter(async (context, next) =>
    {
        app.Logger.LogInformation("Executing filter...");
        object? result = await next(context);
        app.Logger.LogInformation($"Handler result: {result}");
        return result;
    });

app.Run();
```

Annotations:
- **Adds a new filter using a lambda function** → `.AddEndpointFilter(async (context, next) =>`
- **Adds the validation filter as before** → `.AddEndpointFilter(ValidationHelper.ValidateId)`
- **Logs a message before executing the rest of the pipeline** → `app.Logger.LogInformation("Executing filter...");`
- **Executes the remainder of the pipeline and the endpoint handler** → `object? result = await next(context);`
- **Logs the result returned by the rest of the pipeline** → `app.Logger.LogInformation($"Handler result: {result}");`
- **Returns the result unmodified** → `return result;`

The extra filter is implemented as a lambda function and simply writes a log message when it executes. Then it runs the rest of the filter pipeline (which contains only the endpoint handler in this example) and logs the result returned by the pipeline. Chapter 26 covers logging in detail. For this example, we'll look at the logs written to the console.

Figure 5.9 shows the log messages written when we send two requests to the API in listing 5.10. The first request is for an entry that exists, so it returns a 200 OK result. The second request uses an invalid id format, so the first filter rejects it. Figure 5.9 shows that neither the second filter nor the endpoint handler runs in this case; the filter pipeline has been short-circuited.

The first request is valid so the logging filter also executes.

The minimal API returns a JSON response with a 200 OK status code.

The second request is invalid, so the logging filter does not execute.

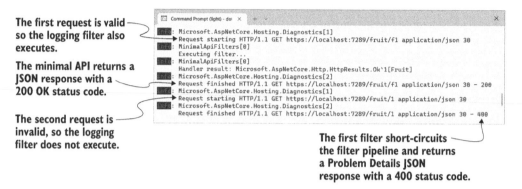

The first filter short-circuits the filter pipeline and returns a Problem Details JSON response with a 400 status code.

Figure 5.9   Sending two requests to the API from listing 5.10. The first request is valid, so both filters execute. An invalid id is provided in the second request, so the first filter short-circuits the requests, and the second filter doesn't execute.

By adding calls to AddEndpointFilter, you can create arbitrarily large endpoint filter pipelines, but the fact that you can doesn't mean you should. Moving code to filters can reduce clutter in your endpoints, but it makes the flow of your application harder to understand. I suggest that you avoid using filters unless you find duplicated code in multiple endpoints, and then favor a filter over a simple method call only if it significantly simplifies the code required.

5.4.2   Filters or middleware: Which should you choose?

The endpoint filter pipeline is similar to the middleware pipeline in many ways, but you should consider several subtle differences when deciding which approach to use. The similarities include three main parallels:

- *Requests pass through a middleware component on the way in, and responses pass through again on the way out.* Similarly, endpoint filters can run code before calling the next filter in the pipeline and can run code after the response is generated, as shown in figure 5.8.
- *Middleware can short-circuit a request by returning a response instead of passing it on to later middleware.* Filters can also short-circuit the filter pipeline by returning a response.
- *Middleware is often used for cross-cutting application concerns, such as logging, performance profiling, and exception handling.* Filters also lend themselves to cross-cutting concerns.

By contrast, there are three main differences between middleware and filters:

- Middleware can run for all requests; filters will run only for requests that reach the `EndpointMiddleware` and execute the associated endpoint.
- Filters have access to additional details about the endpoint that will execute, such as the return value of the endpoint, for example an `IResult`. Middleware in general won't see these intermediate steps, so it sees only the generated response.
- Filters can easily be restricted to a subset of requests, such as a single endpoint or a group of endpoints. Middleware generally applies to all requests (though you can achieve something similar with custom middleware components).

That's all well and good, but how should we interpret these differences? When should we choose one over the other?

I like to think of middleware versus filters as a question of specificity. Middleware is the more general concept, operating on lower-level primitives such as `HttpContext`, so it has wider reach. If the functionality you need has no endpoint-specific requirements, you should use a middleware component. Exception handling is a great example; exceptions could happen anywhere in your application, and you need to handle them, so using exception-handling middleware makes sense.

On the other hand, if you *do* need access to endpoint details, or if you want to behave differently for some requests, you should consider using a filter. Validation is a good example. Not all requests need the same validation. Requests for static files, for example, don't need parameter validation, the way requests to an API endpoint do. Applying validation to the endpoints via filters makes sense in this case.

> **TIP** Where possible, consider using middleware for cross-cutting concerns. Use filters when you need different behavior for different endpoints or where the functionality relies on endpoint concepts such as `IResult` objects.

So far, the filters we've looked at have been specific to a single endpoint. In section 5.4.3 we look at creating generic filters that you can apply to multiple endpoints.

5.4.3 *Generalizing your endpoint filters*

One common problem with filters is that they end up closely tied to the *implementation* of your endpoint handlers. Listing 5.9, for example, assumes that the `id` parameter is the first parameter in the method. In this section you'll learn how to create generalized versions of filters that work with *multiple* endpoint handlers.

The `fruit` API we've been working with in this chapter contains several endpoint handlers that take multiple parameters. The `MapPost` handler, for example, takes a `string id` parameter and a `Fruit fruit` parameter:

```
app.MapPost("/fruit/{id}", (string id, Fruit fruit) => { /* */ });
```

In this example, the `id` parameter is listed first, but there's no requirement for that to be the case. The parameters to the handler could be reversed, and the endpoint would be functionally identical:

```
app.MapPost("/fruit/{id}", (Fruit fruit, string id) => { /* */ });
```

Unfortunately, with this order, the `ValidateId` filter described in listing 5.9 won't work. The `ValidateId` filter assumes that the first parameter to the handler is `id`, which isn't the case in our revised `MapPost` implementation.

ASP.NET Core provides a solution that uses a factory pattern for filters. You can register a filter factory by using the `AddEndpointFilterFactory()` method. A *filter factory* is a method that returns a *filter function*. ASP.NET Core executes the filter factory when it's building your app and incorporates the returned filter into the filter pipeline for the app, as shown in figure 5.10. You can use the same filter-factory function to emit a different filter for each endpoint, with each filter tailored to the endpoint's parameters.

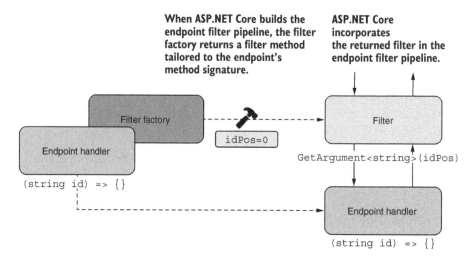

Figure 5.10   A filter factory is a generalized way to add endpoint filters. The factory reads details about the endpoint, such as its method signature, and builds a filter function. This function is incorporated into the final filter pipeline for the endpoint. The build step means that a single filter factory can create filters for multiple endpoints with different method signatures.

Listing 5.11 shows an example of the factory pattern in practice. The filter factory is applied to multiple endpoints. For each endpoint, the factory first checks for a parameter called `id`; if it doesn't exist, the factory returns `next` and doesn't add a filter to the pipeline. If the `id` parameter exists, the factory returns a filter function, which is virtually identical to the filter function in listing 5.9; the main difference is that this filter handles a variable location of the `id` parameter.

Listing 5.11 Using a filter factory to create an endpoint filter

```
WebApplicationBuilder builder = WebApplication.CreateBuilder(args);
WebApplication app = builder.Build();
var _fruit = new ConcurrentDictionary<string, Fruit>();

app.MapGet("/fruit/{id}", (string id) =>
    _fruit.TryGetValue(id, out var fruit)
        ? TypedResults.Ok(fruit)
        : Results.Problem(statusCode: 404))
    .AddEndpointFilterFactory(ValidationHelper.ValidateIdFactory);

app.MapPost("/fruit/{id}", (Fruit fruit, string id) =>
    _fruit.TryAdd(id, fruit)
        ? TypedResults.Created($"/fruit/{id}", fruit)
        : Results.ValidationProblem(new Dictionary<string, string[]>
        {
            { "id", new[] { "A fruit with this id already exists" } }
        }))
    .AddEndpointFilterFactory(ValidationHelper.ValidateIdFactory);

app.Run();

class ValidationHelper
{
    internal static EndpointFilterDelegate ValidateIdFactory(
        EndpointFilterFactoryContext context,
        EndpointFilterDelegate next)
    {
        ParameterInfo[] parameters =
            context.MethodInfo.GetParameters();
        int? idPosition = null;
        for (int i = 0; i < parameters.Length; i++)
        {
            if (parameters[i].Name == "id" &&
                parameters[i].ParameterType == typeof(string))
            {
                idPosition = i;
                break;
            }
        }

        if (!idPosition.HasValue)
        {
            return next;
        }

        return async (invocationContext) =>
        {
            var id = invocationContext
                .GetArgument<string>(idPosition.Value);
            if (string.IsNullOrEmpty(id) || !id.StartsWith('f'))
            {
                return Results.ValidationProblem(
                    new Dictionary<string, string[]>
```

The filter factory can handle endpoints with different method signatures.

The context parameter provides details about the endpoint handler method.

GetParameters() provides details about the parameters of the handler being called.

Loops through the parameters to find the string id parameter and record its position

If the id parameter exists, returns a filter function (the filter executed for the endpoint)

If the id parameter isn't not found, doesn't add a filter, but returns the remainder of the pipeline

If the id isn't valid, returns a Problem Details result

If the id is valid, executes the next filter in the pipeline

```
                     {{ "id", new[] { "Id must start with 'f'" }}});
        }
```

If the id isn't valid, returns a Problem Details result

```
        return await next(invocationContext);
    };
  }
}
```

The code in listing 5.11 is more complex than anything else we've seen so far, as it has an extra layer of abstraction. The endpoint middleware passes an `EndpointFilter-FactoryContext` object to the factory function, which contains extra details about the endpoint in comparison to the context passed to a normal filter function. Specifically, it includes a `MethodInfo` property and an `EndpointMetadata` property.

NOTE   You'll learn about endpoint metadata in chapter 6.

The `MethodInfo` property can be used to control how the filter is created based on the definition of the endpoint handler. Listing 5.11 shows how you can loop through the parameters to check for the details you need—a `string id` parameter, in this case—and customize the filter function you return.

   If you find all these method signatures to be confusing, I don't blame you. Remembering the difference between an `EndpointFilterFactoryContext` and `EndpointFilter-InvocationContext` and then trying to satisfy the compiler with your lambda methods can be annoying. Sometimes, you yearn for a good ol' interface to implement. Let's do that now.

5.4.4   *Implementing the IEndpointFilter interface*

Creating a lambda method for `AddEndpointFilter()` that satisfies the compiler can be a frustrating experience, depending on the level of support your integrated development environment (IDE) provides. In this section you'll learn how to sidestep the issue by defining a class that implements `IEndpointFilter` instead.

   You can implement `IEndpointFilter` by defining a class with an `InvokeAsync()` that has the same signature as the lambda defined in listing 5.9. The advantage of using `IEndpointFilter` is that you get IntelliSense and autocompletion for the method signature. The following listing shows how to implement an `IEndpointFilter` class that's equivalent to listing 5.9.

Listing 5.12   Implementing `IEndpointFilter`

```
WebApplicationBuilder builder = WebApplication.CreateBuilder(args);
WebApplication app = builder.Build();
var _fruit = new ConcurrentDictionary<string, Fruit>();

app.MapGet("/fruit/{id}", (string id) =>
    _fruit.TryGetValue(id, out var fruit)
        ? TypedResults.Ok(fruit)
        : Results.Problem(statusCode: 404))
```

```
    .AddEndpointFilter<IdValidationFilter>();
                                                        Adds the filter using the generic
app.Run();                                              AddEndpointFilter method

class IdValidationFilter : IEndpointFilter             The filter must implement
{                                                      IEndpointFilter . . .
    public async ValueTask<object?> InvokeAsync(
        EndpointFilterInvocationContext context,        . . . which requires
        EndpointFilterDelegate next)                    implementing a single method.
    {
        var id = context.GetArgument<string>(0);
        if (string.IsNullOrEmpty(id) || !id.StartsWith('f'))
        {
            return Results.ValidationProblem(
                new Dictionary<string, string[]>
                {
                    {"id", new[]{"Invalid format. Id must start with 'f'"}}
                });
        }

        return await next(context);
    }
}
```

Implementing IEndpointFilter is a good option when your filters become more complex, but note that there's no equivalent interface for the filter-factory pattern shown in section 5.4.3. If you want to generalize your filters with a filter factory, you'll have to stick to the lambda (or helper-method) approach shown in listing 5.11.

5.5   *Organizing your APIs with route groups*

One criticism levied against minimal APIs in .NET 6 was that they were necessarily quite verbose, required a lot of duplicated code, and often led to large endpoint handler methods. .NET 7 introduced two new mechanisms to address these critiques:

- *Filters*—Introduced in section 5.4, filters help separate validation checks and cross-cutting functions such as logging from the important logic in your endpoint handler functions.
- *Route groups*—Described in this section, route groups help reduce duplication by applying filters and routing to multiple handlers at the same time.

When designing APIs, it's important to maintain consistency in the routes you use for your endpoints, which often means duplicating part of the route pattern across multiple APIs. As an example, all the endpoints in the fruit API described throughout this chapter (such as in listing 5.3) start with the route prefix /fruit:

- MapGet("/fruit", () => {/* */})
- MapGet("/fruit/{id}", (string id) => {/* */})
- MapPost("/fruit/{id}", (Fruit fruit, string id) => {/* */})
- MapPut("/fruit/{id}", (Fruit fruit, string id) => {/* */})
- MapDelete("/fruit/{id}", (string id) => {/* */})

Additionally, the last four endpoints need to validate the `id` parameter. This validation can be extracted to a helper method and applied as a filter, but you still need to *remember* to apply the filter when you add a new endpoint.

All this duplication can be removed by using route groups. You can use route groups to extract common path segments or filters to a single location, reducing the duplication in your endpoint definitions. You create a route group by calling `MapGroup("/fruit")` on the `WebApplication` instance, providing a route prefix for the group (`"/fruit"`, in this case), and `MapGroup()` returns a `RouteGroupBuilder`.

When you have a `RouteGroupBuilder`, you can call the same `Map*` extension methods on `RouteGroupBuilder` as you do on `WebApplication`. The only difference is that all the endpoints you define on the group will have the prefix `"/fruit"` applied to each endpoint you define, as shown in figure 5.11. Similarly, you can call `AddEndpointFilter()` on a route group, and all the endpoints on the group will also use the filter.

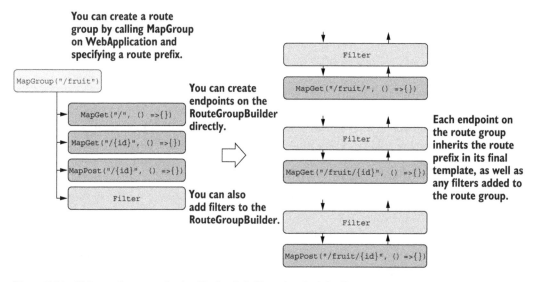

Figure 5.11   Using route groups to simplify the definition of endpoints. You can create a route group by calling MapGroup() and providing a prefix. Any endpoints created on the route group inherit the route template prefix, as well as any filters added to the group.

You can even create nested groups by calling `MapGroup()` on a group. The prefixes are applied to your endpoints in order, so the first `MapGroup()` call defines the prefix used at the start of the route. `app.MapGroup("/fruit").MapGroup("/citrus")`, for example, would have the prefix `"/fruit/citrus"`.

> **TIP**   If you don't want to add a prefix but still want to use the route group for applying filters, you can pass the prefix `"/"` to `MapGroup()`.

Listing 5.13 shows an example of rewriting the `fruit` API to use route groups. It creates a top-level `fruitApi`, which applies the `"/fruit"` prefix, and creates a nested route group called `fruitApiWithValidation` for the endpoints that require a filter. You can find the complete example comparing the versions with and without route groups in the source code for this chapter.

Listing 5.13 Reducing duplication with route groups

```
using System.Collections.Concurrent;

WebApplicationBuilder builder = WebApplication.CreateBuilder(args);
WebApplication app = builder.Build();

var _fruit = new ConcurrentDictionary<string, Fruit>();

RouteGroupBuilder fruitApi = app.MapGroup("/fruit");

fruitApi.MapGet("/", () => _fruit);

RouteGroupBuilder fruitApiWithValidation = fruitApi.MapGroup("/")
    .AddEndpointFilter(ValidationHelper.ValidateIdFactory);

fruitApiWithValidation.MapGet("/{id}", (string id) =>
    _fruit.TryGetValue(id, out var fruit)
        ? TypedResults.Ok(fruit)
        : Results.Problem(statusCode: 404));

fruitApiWithValidation.MapPost("/{id}", (Fruit fruit, string id) =>
    _fruit.TryAdd(id, fruit)
        ? TypedResults.Created($"/fruit/{id}", fruit)
        : Results.ValidationProblem(new Dictionary<string, string[]>
          {
              { "id", new[] { "A fruit with this id already exists" } }
          }));

fruitApiWithValidation.MapPut("/{id}", (string id, Fruit fruit) =>
{
    _fruit[id] = fruit;
    return Results.NoContent();
});

fruitApiWithValidation.MapDelete("/fruit/{id}", (string id) =>
{
    _fruit.TryRemove(id, out _);
    return Results.NoContent();
});

app.Run();
```

Annotations:
- Creates a route group by calling MapGroup and providing a prefix → `RouteGroupBuilder fruitApi = app.MapGroup("/fruit");`
- Endpoints defined on the route group will have the group prefix prepended to the route. → `fruitApi.MapGet("/", () => _fruit);`
- You can create nested route groups with multiple prefixes.
- You can add filters to the route group . . .
- . . . and the filter will be applied to all the endpoints defined on the route group.

In .NET 6, minimal APIs were a bit too verbose to be generally recommended, but with the addition of route groups and filters, minimal APIs have come into their own. In chapter 6 you'll learn more about routing and route template syntax, as well as how to generate links to other endpoints.

Summary

- HTTP verbs define the semantic expectation for a request. GET is used to fetch data, POST creates a resource, PUT creates or replaces a resource, and DELETE removes a resource. Following these conventions will make your API easier to consume.

- Each HTTP response includes a status code. Common codes include 200 OK, 201 Created, 400 Bad Request, and 404 Not Found. It's important to use the correct status code, as clients use these status codes to infer the behavior of your API.

- An HTTP API exposes methods or endpoints that you can use to access or change data on a server using the HTTP protocol. An HTTP API is typically called by mobile or client-side web applications.

- You define minimal API endpoints by calling Map* functions on the WebApplication instance, passing in a route pattern to match and a handler function. The handler functions runs in response to matching requests.

- There are different extension methods for each HTTP verb. MapGet handles GET requests, for example, and MapPost maps POST requests. You use these extension methods to define how your app handles a given route and HTTP verb.

- You can define your endpoint handlers as lambda expressions, Func<T, TResult> and Action<T> variables, local functions, instance methods, or static methods. The best approach depends on how complex your handler is, as well as personal preference.

- Returning void from your endpoint handler generates a 200 response with no body by default. Returning a string generates a text/plain response. Returning an IResult instance can generate any response. Any other object returned from your endpoint handler is serialized to JSON. This convention helps keep your endpoint handlers succinct.

- You can customize the response by injecting an HttpResponse object into your endpoint handler and then setting the status code and response body. This approach can be useful if you have complex requirements for an endpoint.

- The Results and TypedResults helpers contain static methods for generating common responses, such as a 404 Not Found response using Results.NotFound(). These helpers simplifying returning common status codes.

- You can return a standard Problem Details object by using Results.Problem() and Results.ValiationProblem(). Problem() generates a 500 response by default (which can be changed), and ValidationProblem() generates a 400 response, with a list of validation errors. These methods make returning Problem Details objects more concise than generating the response manually.

- You can use helper methods to generate other common result types on Results, such as File() for returning a file from disk, Bytes() for returning arbitrary binary data, and Stream() for returning an arbitrary stream.

- You can extract common or tangential code from your endpoint handlers by using endpoint filters, which can keep your endpoint handlers easy to read.
- Add a filter to an endpoint by calling `AddEndpointFilter()` and providing the lambda function to run (or use a static/instance method). You can also implement `IEndpointFilter` and call `AddEndpointFilter<T>()`, where `T` is the name of your implementing class.
- You can generalize your filter functions by creating a factory, using the overload of `AddEndpointFilter()` that takes an `EndpointFilterFactoryContext`. You can use this approach to support endpoint handlers with various method signatures.
- You can reduce duplication in your endpoint routes and filter configuration by using route groups. Call `MapGroup()` on `WebApplication`, and provide a prefix. All endpoints created on the returned `RouteGroupBuilder` will use the prefix in their route templates.
- You can also call `AddEndpointFilter()` on route groups. Any endpoints defined on the group will also have the filter, as though you defined them on the endpoint directly, removing the need to duplicate the call on each endpoint.

Mapping URLs to endpoints using routing

This chapter covers

- Mapping URLs to endpoint handlers
- Using constraints and default values to match URLs
- Generating URLs from route parameters

In chapter 5 you learned how to define minimal APIs, how to return responses, and how to work with filters and route groups. One crucial aspect of minimal APIs that we touched on only lightly is how ASP.NET Core selects a specific endpoint from all the handlers defined, based on the incoming request URL. This process, called *routing*, is the focus of this chapter.

This chapter begins by identifying the need for routing and why it's useful. You'll learn about the endpoint routing system introduced in ASP.NET Core 3.0 and why it was introduced, and explore the flexibility routing can bring to the URLs you expose.

The bulk of this chapter focuses on the route template syntax and how it can be used with minimal APIs. You'll learn about features such as optional parameters, default parameters, and constraints, as well as how to extract values from the URL automatically. Although we're focusing on minimal APIs in this chapter, the same routing system is used with Razor Pages and Model-View-Controller (MVC), as you'll see in chapter 14.

In section 6.4 I describe how to use the routing system to *generate* URLs, which you can use to create links and redirect requests for your application. One benefit of using a routing system is that it decouples your handlers from the underlying URLs they're associated with. You can use URL generation to avoid littering your code with hard-coded URLs like `/product/view/3`. Instead, you can generate the URLs at runtime, based on the routing system. This approach makes changing the URL for a given endpoint easier: instead of your having to hunt down every place where you used the endpoint's URL, the URLs are updated for you automatically, with no other changes required.

By the end of this chapter, you should have a much clearer understanding of how an ASP.NET Core application works. You can think of routing as being the glue that ties the middleware pipeline to endpoints. With middleware, endpoints, and routing under your belt, you'll be writing web apps in no time!

6.1   What is routing?

Routing is the process of mapping an incoming request to a method that will handle it. You can use routing to control the URLs you expose in your application. You can also use routing to enable powerful features such as mapping multiple URLs to the same handler and automatically extracting data from a request's URL.

In chapter 4 you saw that an ASP.NET Core application contains a middleware pipeline, which defines the behavior of your application. Middleware is well suited to handling both cross-cutting concerns, such as logging and error handling, and narrowly focused requests, such as requests for images and CSS files.

To handle more complex application logic, you'll typically use the `EndpointMiddleware` at the end of your middleware pipeline. This middleware can handle an appropriate request by invoking a method known as a handler and using the result to generate a response. Previous chapters described using minimal API endpoint handlers, but there are other types of handlers, such as MVC action methods and Razor Pages, as you'll learn in part 2 of this book.

One aspect that I've glossed over so far is *how* the `EndpointMiddleware` selects which handler executes when you receive a request. What makes a request appropriate for a given handler? The process of mapping a request to a handler is *routing*.

> **DEFINITION** *Routing* in ASP.NET Core is the process of selecting a specific handler for an incoming HTTP request. In minimal APIs, the handler is the endpoint handler associated with a route. In Razor Pages, the handler is a page handler method defined in a Razor Page. In MVC, the handler is an action method in a controller.

In chapters 3 to 5, you saw several simple applications built with minimal APIs. In chapter 5, you learned the basics of routing for minimal APIs, but it's worth exploring *why* routing is useful as well as how to use it. Even a simple URL path such as /person uses routing to determine which handler should be executed, as shown in figure 6.1.

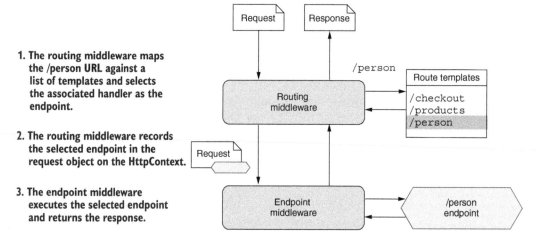

1. The routing middleware maps the /person URL against a list of templates and selects the associated handler as the endpoint.

2. The routing middleware records the selected endpoint in the request object on the HttpContext.

3. The endpoint middleware executes the selected endpoint and returns the response.

Figure 6.1   The router compares the request URL with a list of configured route templates to determine which handler to execute.

On the face of it, that seems pretty simple. You may wonder why I need a whole chapter to explain that obvious mapping. The simplicity of the mapping in this case belies how powerful routing can be. If this approach, using a direct comparison with static strings, were the only one available, you'd be severely limited in the applications you could feasibly build.

Consider an e-commerce application that sells multiple products. Each product needs to have its own URL, so if you were using a purely static routing system, you'd have only two options:

- *Use a different handler for every product in your product range.* That approach would be unfeasible for almost any realistically sized product range.
- *Use a single handler, and use the query string to differentiate among products.* This approach is much more practical, but you'd end up with somewhat-ugly URLs, such as "/product?name=big-widget" or "/product?id=12".

DEFINITION   The *query string* is part of a URL containing additional data that doesn't fit in the path. It isn't used by the routing infrastructure to identify which handler to execute, but ASP.NET Core can extract values from the query string automatically in a process called *model binding*, as you'll see in chapter 7. The query string in the preceding example is id=12.

With routing, you can have a *single* endpoint handler that can handle *multiple* URLs without having to resort to ugly query strings. From the point of the view of the endpoint handler, the query string and routing approaches are similar; the handler returns the results for the correct product dynamically as appropriate. The difference is that with routing, you can completely customize the URLs, as shown in figure 6.2. This feature gives you much more flexibility and can be important in real-life applications for search engine optimization (SEO).

NOTE With the flexibility of routing, you can encode the hierarchy of your site properly in your URLs, as described in Google's SEO starter guide at http://mng.bz/EQ2J.

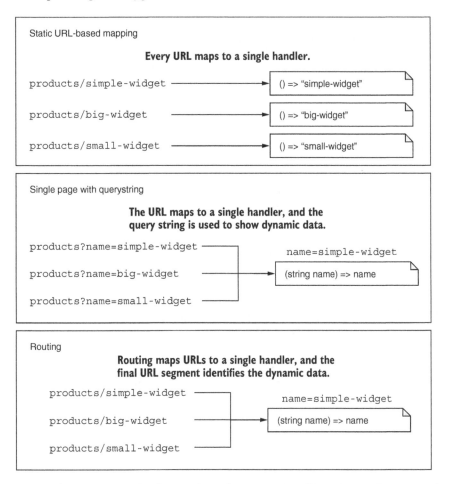

Figure 6.2   If you use static URL-based mapping, you need a different handler for every product in your product range. With a query string, you can use a single handler, and the query string contains the data. With routing, multiple URLs map to a single handler, and a dynamic parameter captures the difference in the URL.

As well as enabling dynamic URLs, routing fundamentally decouples the URLs in your application from the definition of your handlers.

> **File-system based routing**
>
> In one alternative to routing, the location of a handler on disk dictates the URL you use to invoke it. The downside of this approach is that if you want to change an exposed URL, you also need to change the location of the handler on disk.
>
> This file-based approach may sound like a strange choice, but it has many advantages for some apps, primarily in terms of simplicity. As you'll see in part 2, Razor Pages is partially file-based but also uses routing to get the best of both worlds!

With routing it's easy to modify your exposed URLs without changing any filenames or locations. You can also use routing to create friendlier URLs for users, which can improve discovery and "hackability." All of the following routes could point to the same handler:

- `/rates/view/1`
- `/rates/view/USD`
- `/rates/current-exchange-rate/USD`
- `/current-exchange-rate-for-USD`

This level of customization isn't often necessary, but it's quite useful to have the capability to customize your app's URLs when you need it. In the next section we'll look at how routing works in practice in ASP.NET Core.

6.2   *Endpoint routing in ASP.NET Core*

In this section I describe how endpoint routing works in ASP.NET Core, specifically with respect to minimal APIs and the middleware pipeline. In chapter 14 you'll learn how routing is used with Razor Pages and the ASP.NET Core MVC framework.

Routing has been part of ASP.NET Core since its inception, but it has been through some big changes. In ASP.NET Core 2.0 and 2.1, routing was restricted to Razor Pages and the ASP.NET Core MVC framework. There was no dedicated routing middleware in the middleware pipeline; routing happened only within Razor Pages or MVC components.

Unfortunately, restricting routing to the MVC and Razor Pages infrastructure made some things a bit messy. Some cross-cutting concerns, such as authorization, were restricted to the MVC infrastructure and were hard to use from other middleware in your application. That restriction caused inevitable duplication, which wasn't ideal.

ASP.NET Core 3.0 introduced a new routing system: *endpoint routing*. Endpoint routing makes the routing system a more fundamental feature of ASP.NET Core and no longer ties it to the MVC infrastructure. Now Razor Pages, MVC, and other middleware can all use the same routing system. .NET 7 continues to use the same endpoint routing system, which is integral to the minimal API functionality that was introduced in .NET 6.

Endpoint routing is fundamental to all but the simplest ASP.NET Core apps. It's implemented with two pieces of middleware, which you've already seen:

- `EndpointRoutingMiddleware`—This middleware chooses which registered endpoints execute for a given request at runtime. To make it easier to distinguish between the two types of middleware, I'll be referring to this middleware as the `RoutingMiddleware` throughout this book.
- `EndpointMiddleware`—This middleware is typically placed at the end of your middleware pipeline. The middleware *executes* the endpoint selected by the `RoutingMiddleware` at runtime.

You register the endpoints in your application by calling `Map*` functions on an `IEndpointRouteBuilder` instance. In .NET 7 apps, this instance typically is a `WebApplication` instance but doesn't have to be, as you'll see in chapter 30.

> **DEFINITION**   An *endpoint* in ASP.NET Core is a handler that returns a response. Each endpoint is associated with a URL pattern. Depending on the type of application you're building, minimal API handlers, Razor Page handlers, or MVC controller action methods typically make up the bulk of the endpoints in an application. You can also use simple middleware as an endpoint or you could use a health-check endpoint, for example.

`WebApplication` implements `IEndpointRouteBuilder`, so you can register endpoints on it directly. Listing 6.1 shows how you'd register several endpoints:

- A minimal API handler using `MapGet()`, as you've seen in previous chapters.
- A health-check endpoint using `MapHealthChecks()`. You can read more about health checks at http://mng.bz/N2YD.
- All Razor Pages endpoints in the application using `MapRazorPages()`. You'll learn more about routing with Razor Pages in chapter 14.

Listing 6.1   Registering multiple endpoints with `WebApplication`

```
WebApplicationBuilder builder = WebApplication.CreateBuilder(args);

builder.Services.AddHealthChecks();        Adds the services required by the health-
builder.Services.AddRazorPages();          check middleware and Razor Pages

WebApplication app = builder.Build();
                                                   Registers a minimal API endpoint that
app.MapGet("/test", () => "Hello world!");  ⟵──┘  returns "Hello World!" at the route /test
app.MapHealthChecks("/healthz");  ⟵──
app.MapRazorPages();                    Registers a health-check
                                        endpoint at the route /healthz
app.Run();

Registers all the Razor Pages in
your application as endpoints
```

Each endpoint is associated with a *route template* that defines which URLs the endpoint should match. You can see two route templates, `"/healthz"` and `"/test"`, in listing 6.1.

> **DEFINITION**   A *route template* is a URL pattern that is used to match against request URLs, which are strings of fixed values, such as `"/test"` in the previous listing. They can also contain placeholders for variables, as you'll see in section 6.3.

The `WebApplication` stores the registered routes and endpoints in a dictionary that's shared by the `RoutingMiddleware` and the `EndpointMiddleware`.

> **TIP** By default, `WebApplication` automatically adds the `RoutingMiddleware` to the *start* of the middleware and `EndpointMiddleware` to the *end* of the middleware pipeline, though you can override the location in the pipeline by calling `UseRouting()` or `UseEndpoints()`. See section 4.2.3 for more details about automatically added middleware.

At runtime, the `RoutingMiddleware` compares an incoming request with the routes registered in the dictionary. If the `RoutingMiddleware` finds a matching endpoint, it makes a note of which endpoint was selected and attaches that to the request's `HttpContext` object. Then it calls the next middleware in the pipeline. When the request reaches the `EndpointMiddleware`, the middleware checks to see which endpoint was selected and executes the endpoint (and any associated endpoint filters), as shown in figure 6.3.

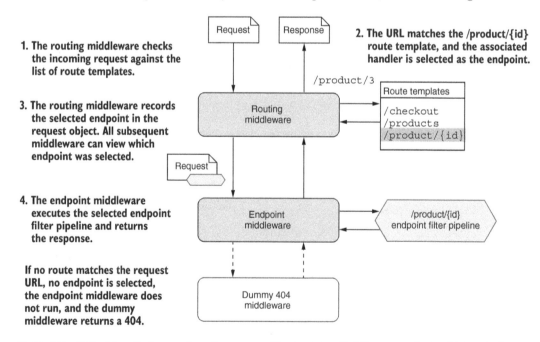

1. The routing middleware checks the incoming request against the list of route templates.

2. The URL matches the /product/{id} route template, and the associated handler is selected as the endpoint.

3. The routing middleware records the selected endpoint in the request object. All subsequent middleware can view which endpoint was selected.

4. The endpoint middleware executes the selected endpoint filter pipeline and returns the response.

If no route matches the request URL, no endpoint is selected, the endpoint middleware does not run, and the dummy middleware returns a 404.

Figure 6.3   Endpoint routing uses a two-step process. The `RoutingMiddleware` selects which endpoint to execute, and the `EndpointMiddleware` executes it. If the request URL doesn't match a route template, the endpoint middleware won't generate a response.

If the request URL *doesn't* match a route template, the RoutingMiddleware doesn't select an endpoint, but the request still continues down the middleware pipeline. As no endpoint is selected, the EndpointMiddleware silently ignores the request and passes it to the next middleware in the pipeline. The EndpointMiddleware is typically the final middleware in the pipeline, so the "next" middleware is normally the dummy middleware that always returns a 404 Not Found response, as you saw in chapter 4.

> **TIP** If the request URL doesn't match a route template, no endpoint is selected or executed. The whole middleware pipeline is still executed, but typically a 404 response is returned when the request reaches the dummy 404 middleware.

The advantage of having two separate pieces of middleware to handle this process may not be obvious at first blush. Figure 6.3 hinted at the main benefit: all middleware placed after the RoutingMiddleware can see which endpoint is *going* to be executed before it is.

> **NOTE** Only middleware placed after the RoutingMiddleware can detect which endpoint is going to be executed.

Figure 6.4 shows a more realistic middleware pipeline in which middleware is placed both *before* the RoutingMiddleware and *between* the RoutingMiddleware and the EndpointMiddleware.

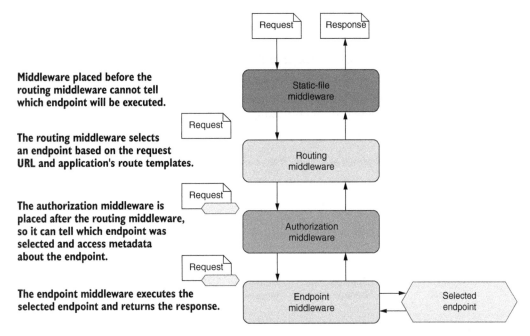

Figure 6.4 Middleware placed before the routing middleware doesn't know which endpoint the routing middleware will select. Middleware placed between the routing middleware and the endpoint middleware can see the selected endpoint.

The `StaticFileMiddleware` in figure 6.4 is placed before the `RoutingMiddleware`, so it executes before an endpoint is selected. Conversely, the `AuthorizationMiddleware` is placed after the `RoutingMiddleware`, so it can tell which minimal API endpoint will be executed eventually. In addition, it can access certain metadata about the endpoint, such as its name and the permissions required to access it.

> **TIP** The `AuthorizationMiddleware` needs to know which endpoint will be executed, so it must be placed after the `RoutingMiddleware` and before the `EndpointMiddleware` in your middleware pipeline. I discuss authorization in more detail in chapter 24.

It's important to remember the different roles of the two types of routing middleware when building your application. If you have a piece of middleware that needs to know which endpoint (if any) a given request will execute, you need to make sure to place it after the `RoutingMiddleware` and before the `EndpointMiddleware`.

> **TIP** If you want to place middleware before the `RoutingMiddleware`, such as the `StaticFileMiddleware` in figure 6.4, you need to override the automatic middleware added by `WebApplication` by calling `UseRouting()` at the appropriate point in your middleware pipeline. See listing 4.3 in chapter 4 for an example.

I've covered how the `RoutingMiddleware` and `EndpointMiddleware` interact to provide routing capabilities in ASP.NET Core, but we've looked at only simple route templates so far. In the next section we'll look at some of the many features available with route templates.

6.3   *Exploring the route template syntax*

So far in this book we've looked at simple route templates consisting of fixed values, such as /person and /test, as well as using a basic route parameter such as /fruit/{id}. In this section we explore the full range of features available in route templates, such as default values, optional segments, and constraints.

6.3.1   *Working with parameters and literal segments*

Route templates have a rich, flexible syntax. Figure 6.5, however, shows a simple example, similar to ones you've already seen.

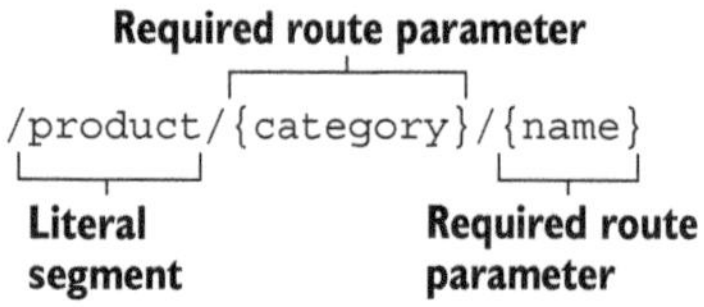

Figure 6.5   A simple route template showing a literal segment and two required route parameters

The routing middleware parses a route template by splitting it into *segments*. A segment is typically separated by the / character, but it can be any valid character.

DEFINITION Segments that use a character other than / are called *complex segments*. I generally recommend that you avoid them and stick to using / as a separator. Complex segments have some peculiarities that make them hard to use, so be sure to check the documentation at http://mng.bz/D4RE before you use them.

Each segment is either

- *A literal value* such as product in figure 6.5
- *A route parameter* such as {category} and {name} in figure 6.5

The request URL must match literal values exactly (ignoring case). If you need to match a particular URL exactly, you can use a template consisting only of literals.

TIP Literal segments in ASP.NET Core aren't case-sensitive.

Imagine that you have a minimal API in your application defined using

```
app.MapGet("/About/Contact", () => {/* */})
```

This route template, "/About/Contact", consists only of literal values, so it matches only the exact URL (ignoring case). None of the following URLs would match this route template:

- /about
- /about-us/contact
- /about/contact/email
- /about/contact-us

Route parameters are sections of a URL that may vary but are still a match for the template. You define them by giving them a name and placing them in braces, such as {category} or {name}. When used in this way, the parameters are required, so the request URL must have a segment that they correspond to, but the value can vary.

The ability to use route parameters gives you great flexibility. The simple route template "/{category}/{name}" could be used to match all the product-page URLs in an e-commerce application:

- /bags/rucksack-a—Where category=bags and name=rucksack-a
- /shoes/black-size9—Where category=shoes and name=black-size9

But note that this template would *not* map the following URLs:

- /socks/—No name parameter specified
- /trousers/mens/formal—Extra URL segment, formal, not found in route template

When a route template defines a route parameter and the route matches a URL, the value associated with the parameter is captured and stored in a dictionary of values associated with the request. These *route values* typically drive other behavior in the endpoint and can be injected into the handlers (as you saw briefly in chapter 5) in a process called *model binding*.

> **DEFINITION**   *Route values* are the values extracted from a URL based on a given route template. Each route parameter in a template has an associated route value, and the values are stored as a string pair in a dictionary. They can be used during model binding, as you'll see in chapter 7.

Literal segments and route parameters are the two cornerstones of ASP.NET Core route templates. With these two concepts, it's possible to build all manner of URLs for your application. In the remainder of section 6.3 we'll look at additional features that let you have optional URL segments, provide default values when a segment isn't specified, and place additional constraints on the values that are valid for a given route parameter.

6.3.2   *Using optional and default values*

In section 6.3.1 you saw a simple route template with a literal segment and two required routing parameters. Figure 6.6 shows a more complex route that uses several additional features.

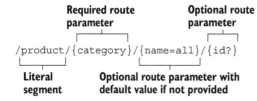

Figure 6.6   A more complex route template showing literal segments, named route parameters, optional parameters, and default values.

The literal `product` segment and the required `{category}` parameter are the same as those in in figure 6.6. The `{name}` parameter looks similar, but it has a default value specified for it by `=all`. If the URL doesn't contain a segment corresponding to the `{name}` parameter, the router will use the `all` value instead.

The final segment of figure 6.6, `{id?}`, defines an optional route parameter called `id`. This segment of the URL is optional. If this segment is present, the router captures the value for the `{id}` parameter; if the segment isn't there, the router doesn't create a route value for `id`.

You can specify any number of route parameters in your templates, and these values will be available to you for model binding. The complex route template shown in figure 6.6 allows you to match a greater variety of URLs by making `{name}` and `{id}` optional and by providing a default for `{name}`. Table 6.1 shows some of the URLs that this template would match and the corresponding route values that the router would set.

Note that there's no way to specify a value for the optional `{id}` parameter without also specifying the `{category}` and `{name}` parameters. You can put an optional parameter (that doesn't have a default) only at the end of a route template.

Table 6.1   URLs that would match the template of figure 6.7 and their corresponding route values

URL	Route values
`/product/shoes/formal/3`	`category=shoes, name=formal, id=3`
`/product/shoes/formal`	`category=shoes, name=formal`
`/product/shoes`	`category=shoes, name=all`
`/product/bags/satchels`	`category=bags, name=satchels`
`/product/phones`	`category=phones, name=all`
`/product/computers/laptops/ABC-123`	`category=computers, name=laptops, id=ABC-123`

Using default values allows you to have multiple ways to call the same URL, which may be desirable in some cases. Given the route template in figure 6.6, the following two URLs are equivalent:

- `/product/shoes`
- `/product/shoes/all`

Both URLs will execute the same endpoint handler, with the same route values of `category=shoes` and `name=all`. Using default values allows you to use shorter, more memorable URLs in your application for common URLs but still gives you the flexibility to match a variety of routes in a single template.

6.3.3   *Adding additional constraints to route parameters*

By defining whether a route parameter is required or optional and whether it has a default value, you can match a broad range of URLs with terse template syntax. Unfortunately, in some cases this approach ends up being a little too broad. Routing only matches URL segments to route parameters; it doesn't know anything about the data you're expecting those route parameters to contain. If you consider a template similar to the one in figure 6.6, `"/{category}/{name=all}/{id?}"`, all of the following URLs would match:

- `/shoes/sneakers/test`
- `/shoes/sneakers/123`
- `/Account/ChangePassword`
- `/ShoppingCart/Checkout/Start`
- `/1/2/3`

These URLs are perfectly valid given the template's syntax, but some might cause problems for your application. These URLs have two or three segments, so the router happily assigns route values and matches the template when you might not want it to! These are the route values assigned:

- `/shoes/sneakers/test` has route values `category=shoes, name=sneakers,` and `id=test.`

- `/shoes/sneakers/123` has route values `category=shoes, name=sneakers,` and `id=123.`

- `/Account/ChangePassword` has route values `category=Account,` and `name=Change-Password.`

- `/Cart/Checkout/Start` has route values `category=Cart, name=Checkout,` and `id=Start.`

- `/1/2/3` has route values `category=1, name=2,` and `id=3.`

Typically, the router passes route values to handlers through model binding, which you saw briefly in chapter 5 (and which chapter 7 discusses in detail). A minimal API endpoint defined as

```
app.MapGet("/fruit/{id}", (int id) => "Hello world!");
```

would obtain the `id` argument from the `id` route value. If the `id` route parameter ends up assigned a *noninteger* value from the URL, you'll get an exception when it's bound to the *integer* `id` parameter.

To avoid this problem, it's possible to add more *constraints* to a route template that must be satisfied for a URL to be considered a match. You can define constraints in a route template for a given route parameter by using : (colon). `{id:int}`, for example, would add the `IntRouteConstraint` to the `id` parameter. For a given URL to be considered a match, the value assigned to the `id` route value must be convertible to an integer.

You can apply a large number of route constraints to route templates to ensure that route values are convertible to appropriate types. You can also check more advanced constraints, such as that an integer value has a particular minimum value, that a string value has a maximum length, or that a value matches a given regular expression. Table 6.2 describes some of the available constraints. You can find a more complete list online in Microsoft's documentation at http://mng.bz/BmRJ.

Table 6.2   A few route constraints and their behavior when applied

Constraint	Example	Description	Match examples
`int`	`{qty:int}`	Matches any `integer`	`123, -123, 0`
`Guid`	`{id:guid}`	Matches any Guid	`d071b70c-a812-4b54-87d2-7769528e2814`
`decimal`	`{cost:decimal}`	Matches any decimal value	`29.99, 52, -1.01`
`min(value)`	`{age:min(18)}`	Matches `integer` values of **18** or greater	`18, 20`
`length(value)`	`{name:length(6)}`	Matches `string` values with a length of 6	`Andrew, 123456`

Table 6.2   A few route constraints and their behavior when applied *(continued)*

Constraint	Example	Description	Match examples
optional int	{qty:int?}	Optionally matches any integer	123, -123, 0, null
optional int max(value)	{qty:int:max(10)?}	Optionally matches any integer of 10 or less	3, -123, 0, null

> **TIP**   As you can see from table 6.2, you can also combine multiple constraints by separating the constraints with colons.

Using constraints allows you to narrow down the URLs that a given route template will match. When the routing middleware matches a URL to a route template, it interrogates the constraints to check that they're all valid. If they aren't valid, the route template isn't considered a match, and the endpoint won't be executed.

> **WARNING**   Don't use route constraints to validate general input, such as to check that an email address is valid. Doing so will result in 404 "Page not found" errors, which will be confusing for the user. You should also be aware that all these built-in constraints assume invariant culture, which may prove to be problematic if your application uses URLs localized for other languages.

Constraints are best used sparingly, but they can be useful when you have strict requirements on the URLs used by the application, as they can allow you to work around some otherwise-tricky combinations. You can even create custom constraints, as described in the documentation at http://mng.bz/d14Q.

Constraints and overlapping routes

If you have a well-designed set of URLs for your application, you'll probably find that you don't need to use route constraints. Route constraints are most useful when you have overlapping route templates.

Suppose that you have an endpoint with the route template "/{number}/{name}" and another with the template "/{product}/{id}". When a request with the URL /shoes/123 arrives, which template is chosen? Both match, so the routing middleware panics and throws an exception—not ideal.

Using constraints can fix this problem. If you update the first template to "/{number:int}/{name}", the integer constraint means that the URL is no longer a match, and the routing middleware can choose correctly. Note, however, that the URL /123/shoes still matches both route templates, so you're not out of the woods.

Generally, you should avoid overlapping route templates like these, as they're often confusing and more trouble than they're worth. If your route templates are well defined so that each URL maps to a single template, ASP.NET Core routing will work without any difficulties. Sticking to the built-in conventions as far as possible is the best way to stay on the happy path!

We're coming to the end of our look at route templates, but before we move on, there's one more type of parameter to think about: the catch-all parameter.

6.3.4   *Matching arbitrary URLs with the catch-all parameter*

You've seen how route templates take URL segments and attempt to match them to parameters or literal strings. These segments normally split around the slash character, /, so the route parameters themselves won't contain a slash. What do you do if you need them to contain a slash or don't know how many segments you're going to have?

Imagine that you're building a currency-converter application that shows the exchange rate from one currency to one or more other currencies. You're told that the URLs for this page should contain all the currencies as separate segments. Here are some examples:

- /USD/convert/GBP—Show USD with exchange rate to GBP.
- /USD/convert/GBP/EUR—Show USD with exchange rates to GBP and EUR.
- /USD/convert/GBP/EUR/CAD—Show USD with exchange rates for GBP, EUR, and CAD.

If you want to support showing any number of currencies, as these URLs do, you need a way to capture everything after the convert segment. You could achieve this goal by using a catch-all parameter in the route template, as shown in figure 6.7.

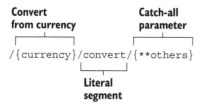

Figure 6.7   You can use catch-all parameters to match the remainder of a URL. Catch-all parameters may include the / character or may be an empty string.

You can declare catch-all parameters by using either one or two asterisks inside the parameter definition, as in {*others} and {**others}. These parameters match the remaining unmatched portion of a URL, including any slashes or other characters that aren't part of earlier parameters. They can also match an empty string. For the USD/convert/GBP/EUR URL, the value of the route value others would be the single string "GBP/EUR".

> **TIP**   Catch-all parameters are greedy and will capture the whole unmatched portion of a URL. Where possible, to avoid confusion, avoid defining route templates with catch-all parameters that overlap other route templates.

The one- and two-asterisk versions of the catch-all parameter behave identically when routing an incoming request to an endpoint. The difference occurs only when you're *generating* URLs (which we'll cover in the next section): the one-asterisk version URL encodes forward slashes, and the two-asterisk version doesn't. Typically, the round-trip behavior of the two-asterisk version is what you want.

NOTE For examples and a comparison between the one and two-asterisk catch-all versions, see the documentation at http://mng.bz/rWyX.

You read that last paragraph correctly: mapping URLs to endpoints is only half of the responsibilities of the routing system in ASP.NET Core. It's also used to generate URLs so that you can reference your endpoints easily from other parts of your application.

6.4 Generating URLs from route parameters

In this section we'll look at the other half of routing: generating URLs. You'll learn how to generate a URL as a string you can use in your code and how to send redirect URLs automatically as a response from your endpoints.

One of the benefits and byproducts of using the routing infrastructure in ASP.NET Core is that your URLs can be somewhat fluid. You can change route templates however you like in your application—by renaming /cart to /basket, for example—and won't get any compilation errors.

Endpoints aren't isolated, of course; inevitably, you'll want to include a link to one endpoint in another. Trying to manage these links within your app manually would be a recipe for heartache, broken links, and 404 errors. If your URLs were hardcoded, you'd have to remember to do a find-and-replace operation with every rename!

Luckily, you can use the routing infrastructure to generate appropriate URLs dynamically at runtime instead, freeing you from the burden. Conceptually, this process is almost the exact reverse of the process of mapping a URL to an endpoint, as shown in figure 6.8. In the routing case, the routing middleware takes a URL, matches it to a route template, and splits it into route values. In the URL generation case, the generator takes in the route values and combines them with a route template to build a URL.

You can use the LinkGenerator class to generate URLs for your minimal APIs. You can use it in any part of your application, so you can use it in middleware and any other services too. LinkGenerator has various methods for generating URLs, such as GetPathByPage and GetPathByAction, which are used specifically for routing to Razor Pages and MVC actions, so we'll look at those in chapter 14. We're interested in the methods related to named routes.

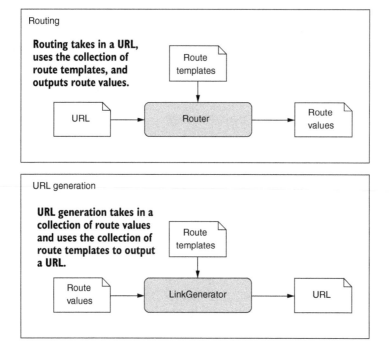

Figure 6.8   A comparison between routing and URL generation. Routing takes in a URL and generates route values, but URL generation uses route values to generate a URL.

6.4.1   *Generating URLs for a minimal API endpoint with LinkGenerator*

You'll need to generate URLs in various places in your application, and one common location is your minimal API endpoints. The following listing shows how you could generate a link to one endpoint from another by annotating the target endpoint with a name and using the LinkGenerator class.

Listing 6.2   Generating a URL LinkGenerator and a named endpoint

The endpoint echoes the name it receives in the route template.

```
app.MapGet("/product/{name}", (string name) => $"The product is {name}")
    .WithName("product");
```
Gives the endpoint a name by adding metadata to it

```
app.MapGet("/links", (LinkGenerator links) =>
{
    string link = links.GetPathByName("product",
        new { name = "big-widget"});
    return $"View the product at {link}";
});
```
References the LinkGenerator class in the endpoint handler

Creates a link using the route name "product" and provides a value for the route parameter

Returns the value "View the product at /product/big-widget"

The `WithName()` method adds metadata to your endpoints so that they can be referenced by other parts of your application. In this case, we're adding a name to the endpoint so we can refer to it later. You'll learn more about metadata in chapter 11.

> **NOTE** Endpoint names are case-sensitive (unlike the route templates themselves) and must be globally unique. Duplicate names cause exceptions at runtime.

The `LinkGenerator` is a service available anywhere in ASP.NET Core. You can access it from your endpoints by including it as a parameter in the handler.

> **NOTE** You can reference the `LinkGenerator` in your handler because it's registered with the dependency injection container automatically. You'll learn about dependency injection in chapters 8 and 9.

The `GetPathByName()` method takes the name of a route and, optionally, route data. The route data is packaged as key-value pairs into a single C# anonymous object. If you need to pass more than one route value, you can add more properties to the anonymous object. Then the helper will generate a path based on the referenced endpoint's route template.

Listing 6.2 shows how to generate a path. But you can also generate a complete URL by using the `GetUriByName()` method and providing values for the host and scheme, as in this example:

```
links.GetUriByName("product", new { Name = "super-fancy-widget"},
    "https", new HostString("localhost"));
```

Also, some methods available on `LinkGenerator` take an `HttpContext`. These methods are often easier to use in an endpoint handler, as they extract ambient values such as the scheme and hostname from the incoming request and reuse them for URL generation.

> **WARNING** Be careful when using the `GetUriByName` method. It's possible to expose vulnerabilities in your app if you use unvalidated host values. For more information on host filtering and why it's important, see this post: http://mng.bz/V1d5.

In listing 6.2, as well as providing the route name, I passed in an anonymous object to `GetPathByName`:

```
string link = links.GetPathByName("product", new { name = "big-widget"});
```

This object provides additional route values when generating the URL, in this case setting the `name` parameter to `"big-widget"`.

If a selected route explicitly includes the defined route value in its definition, such as in the `"/product/{name}"` route template, the route value will be used in the URL path, resulting in `/product/big-widget`. If a route doesn't contain the route value explicitly, as in the `"/product"` template, the route value is appended to the query string as additional data. as in `/product?name=big-widget`.

6.4.2 *Generating URLs with IResults*

Generating URLs that link to other endpoints is common when you're creating a REST API, for example. But you don't always need to display URLs. Sometimes, you want to redirect a user to a URL automatically. In that situation you can use `Results.RedirectToRoute()` to handle the URL generation instead.

> **NOTE** Redirects are more common with server-rendered applications such as Razor Pages, but they're perfectly valid for API applications too.

Listing 6.3 shows how you can return a response from an endpoint that automatically redirects a user to a different named endpoint. The `RedirectToRoute()` method takes the name of the endpoint and any required route parameters, and generates a URL in a similar way to `LinkGenerator`. The minimal API framework automatically sends the generated URL as the response, so you never see the URL in your code. Then the user's browser reads the URL from the response and automatically redirects to the new page.

Listing 6.3   Generating a redirect URL using Results.`RedirectToRoute()`

```
app.MapGet("/test", () => "Hello world!")        │ Annotates the route with the name "hello"
    .WithName("hello");                       ◄──┘

app.MapGet("/redirect-me",                          │ Generates a response that sends a
    () => Results.RedirectToRoute("hello"))  ◄──┘ redirect to the "hello" endpoint
```

By default, `RedirectToRoute()` generates a `302 Found` response and includes the generated URL in the Location response header. You can control the status code used by setting the optional parameters `preserveMethod` and `permanent` as follows:

- `permanent=false, preserveMethod=false`—`302 Found`
- `permanent=true, preserveMethod=false`—`301 Moved Permanently`
- `permanent=false, preserveMethod=true`—`307 Temporary Redirect`
- `permanent=true, preserveMethod=true`—`308 Permanent Redirect`

> **NOTE** Each of the redirect status codes has a slightly different semantic meaning, though in practice, many sites simply use `302`. Be careful with the permanent move status codes; they'll cause browsers to never call the original URL, always favoring the redirect location. For a good explanation of these codes (and the useful `303 See Other` status code), see the Mozilla documentation at http://mng.bz/x4GB.

As well as redirecting to a specific endpoint, you can redirect to an arbitrary URL by using the `Results.Redirect()` method. This method works in the same way as `RedirectToRoute()` but takes a URL instead of a route name and can be useful for redirecting to external URLs.

Whether you're generating URLs by using `LinkGenerator` or `RedirectToRoute()`, you need to be careful in these route generation methods. Make sure to provide the correct endpoint name and any necessary route parameters. If you get something wrong—if you have a typo in your endpoint name or forget to include a required route parameter, for example—the URL generated will be `null`. Sometimes it's worth checking the generated URL for `null` explicitly to make sure that there are no problems.

6.4.3 Controlling your generated URLs with RouteOptions

Your endpoint routes are the public surface of your APIs, so you may well have opinions on how they should look. By default, `LinkGenerator` does its best to generate routes the same way you define them; if you define an endpoint with the route template `/MyRoute`, `LinkGenerator` generates the path `/MyRoute`. But what if that path isn't what you want? What if you'd rather have `LinkGenerator` produce prettier paths, such as `/myroute` or `/myroute/`? In this section you'll learn how to configure URL generation both globally and on a case-by-case basis.

> **NOTE** Whether to add a trailing slash to your URLs is largely a question of taste, but the choice has some implications in terms of both usability and search results. I typically choose to add trailing slashes for Razor Pages applications but not for APIs. For details, see http://mng.bz/Ao1W.

When ASP.NET Core matches an incoming URL against your route templates by using routing, it uses a case-insensitive comparison, as you saw in chapter 5. So if you have a route template `/MyRoute`, requests to `/myroute`, `/MYROUTE`, and even `/myROUTE` match. But when generating URLs, `LinkGenerator` needs to choose a single version to use. By default, it uses the same casing that you defined in your route templates. So if you write

```
app.MapGet("/MyRoute", () => "Hello world!").WithName("route1");
```

`LinkGenerator.GetPathByName("route1")` returns `/MyRoute`.

Although that's a good default, you'd probably prefer that all the links generated by your app be consistent. I like all my links to be lowercase, regardless of whether I accidentally failed to make my route template lowercase.

You can control the route generation rules by using `RouteOptions`. You configure the `RouteOptions` for your app using the `Configure<T>` extension method on `WebApplicationBuilder.Services`, which updates the `RouteOptions` instance for the app using the configuration system.

> **NOTE** You'll learn all about the configuration system and the `Configure<T>` method in chapter 10.

`RouteOptions` contains several configuration options, as shown in listing 6.4. These settings control whether the URLs your app generates are forced to be lowercase, whether the query string should also be lowercase, and whether a trailing slash (`/`)

should be appended to the final URLs. In the listing, I set the URL to be lowercased, for the trailing slash to be added, and for the query string to remain unchanged.

> **NOTE** In listing 6.4 the whole path is lowercased, including any route parameter segments such as {name}. Only the query string retains its original casing.

Listing 6.4   Configuring link generation using RouteOptions

```
WebApplicationBuilder builder = WebApplication.CreateBuilder(args);
builder.Services.Configure<RouteOptions>(o =>
{                                                  Configures the
                                                   RouteOptions used
    o.LowercaseUrls = true;                        for link generation
    o.AppendTrailingSlash = true;
    o.LowercaseQueryStrings = false;    <────
});                                                All the settings default to false.


WebApplication app = builder.Build();

app.MapGet("/HealthCheck", () => Results.Ok()).WithName("healthcheck");
app.MapGet("/{name}", (string name) => name).WithName("product");

app.MapGet("/", (LinkGenerator links) =>
new []
{                                                  Returns /healthcheck/
    links.GetPathByName("healthcheck"),    <────
    links.GetPathByName("product",
        new { Name = "Big-Widget", Q = "Test"})    Returns /big-widget/?Q=Test
});

app.Run();
```

Whatever default options you choose, you should try to use them throughout your whole app, but in some cases that may not be possible. You might have a legacy API that you need to emulate, for example, and can't use lowercase URLs. In these cases, you can override the defaults by passing an optional LinkOptions parameter to Link-Generator methods. The values you set in LinkOptions override the default values set in RouteOptions. Generating a link for the app in listing 6.4 by using

```
links.GetPathByName("healthcheck",
    options: new LinkOptions
    {
        LowercaseUrls = false,
        AppendTrailingSlash = false,
    });
```

would return the value /HealthCheck. Without the LinkOptions parameter, GetPathByName would return /healthcheck/.

Congratulations—you've made it all the way through this detailed discussion of routing! Routing is one of those topics that people often get stuck on when they come to building an application, which can be frustrating. We'll revisit routing when we look at Razor Pages in chapter 14 and web API controllers in chapter 20, but rest assured that this chapter has covered all the tricky details!

In chapter 7 we'll dive into model binding. You'll see how the route values generated during routing are bound to your endpoint handler parameters and, perhaps more important, how to validate the values you're provided.

Summary

- Routing is the process of mapping an incoming request URL to an endpoint that executes to generate a response. Routing provides flexibility to your API implementations, enabling you to map multiple URLs to a single endpoint, for example.

- ASP.NET Core uses two pieces of middleware for routing. The EndpointRouting-Middleware and the EndpointMiddleware. WebApplication adds both pieces of middleware to your pipeline by default, so typically, you don't add them to your application manually.

- The EndpointRoutingMiddleware selects which endpoint should be executed by using routing to match the request URL. The EndpointMiddleware executes the endpoint. Having two separate middleware components means that middleware placed between them can react based on the endpoint that will execute when it reaches the end of the pipeline.

- Route templates define the structure of known URLs in your application. They're strings with placeholders for variables that can contain optional values and map to endpoint handlers. You should think about your routes carefully, as they're the public surface of your application.

- Route parameters are variable values extracted from a request's URL. You can use route parameters to map multiple URLs to the same endpoint and to extract the variable value from the URL automatically.

- Route parameters can be optional and can use default values when a value is missing. You should use optional and default parameters sparingly, as they can make your APIs harder to understand, but they can be useful in some cases. Optional parameters must be the last segment of a route.

- Route parameters can have constraints that restrict the possible values allowed. If a route parameter doesn't match its constraints, the route isn't considered to be a match. This approach can help you disambiguate between two similar routes, but you shouldn't use constraints for validation.

- Use a catch-all parameter to capture the remainder of a URL into a route value. Unlike standard route parameters, catch-all parameters can include slashes (/) in the captured values.

- You can use the routing infrastructure to generate URLs for your application. This approach ensures that all your links remain correct if you change your endpoint's route templates.

- The LinkGenerator can be used to generate URLs from minimal API endpoints. Provide the name of the endpoint to link to and any required route values to generate an appropriate URL.
- You can use the RedirectToRoute method to generate URLs while also generating a redirect response. This approach is useful when you don't need to reference the URL in code.
- By default, URLs are generated using the same casing as the route template and any supplied route parameters. Instead, you can force lowercase URLs, lowercase query strings, and trailing slashes by customizing RouteOptions, calling builder.Services.Configure<RouteOptions>().
- You can change the settings for a single URL generation by passing a LinkOptions object to the LinkGenerator methods. These methods can be useful when you need to differ from the defaults for a single endpoint, such as when you're trying to match an existing legacy route.

Model binding and validation in minimal APIs

7

This chapter covers

- Using request values to create binding models
- Customizing the model-binding process
- Validating user input using DataAnnotations attributes

In chapter 6 I showed you how to define a route with parameters—perhaps for the unique ID for a product API. But say a client sends a request to the product API. What then? How do you access the values provided in the request and read the JavaScript Object Notation (JSON) in the request body?

For most of this chapter, in sections 7.1-7.9, we'll look at model binding and how it simplifies reading data from a request in minimal APIs. You'll see how to take the data posted in the request body or in the URL and bind it to C# objects, which are then passed to your endpoint handler methods as arguments. When your handler executes, it can use these values to do something useful—return a product's details or change a product's name, for example.

When your code is executing in an endpoint handler method, you might be forgiven for thinking that you can happily use the binding model without any further thought. Hold on, though. Where did that data come from? From a user—and you know users can't be trusted! Section 7.10 focuses on how to make sure that the user-provided values are valid and make sense for your app.

Model binding is the process of taking the user's raw HTTP request and making it available to your code by populating plain old CLR objects (POCOs), providing the input to your endpoint handlers. We start by looking at which values in the request are available for binding and where model binding fits in your running app.

7.1 *Extracting values from a request with model binding*

In chapters 5 and 6 you learned that route parameters can be extracted from the request's path and used to execute minimal API handlers. In this section we look in more detail at the process of extracting route parameters and the concept of model binding.

By now, you should be familiar with how ASP.NET Core handles a request by executing an endpoint handler. You've also already seen several handlers, similar to

```
app.MapPost("/square/{num}", (int num) => num * num);
```

Endpoint handlers are normal C# methods, so the ASP.NET Core framework needs to be able to call them in the usual way. When handlers accept parameters as part of their method signature, such as num in the preceding example, the framework needs a way to generate those objects. Where do they come from, exactly, and how are they created?

I've already hinted that in most cases, these values come from the request itself. But the HTTP request that the server receives is a series of strings. How does ASP.NET Core turn that into a .NET object? This is where model binding comes in.

> **DEFINITION**   *Model binding* extracts values from a request and uses them to create .NET objects. These objects are passed as method parameters to the endpoint handler being executed.

The model binder is responsible for looking through the request that comes in and finding values to use. Then it creates objects of the appropriate type and assigns these values to your model in a process called *binding*.

> **NOTE**   Model binding in minimal APIs (and in Razor Pages and Model-View-Controller [MVC]) is a one-way population of objects from the request, not the two-way data binding that desktop or mobile development sometimes uses.

ASP.NET Core automatically creates the arguments that are passed to your handler by using the request's properties, such as the request URL, any headers sent in the HTTP request, any data explicitly POSTed in the request body, and so on.

Model binding happens before the filter pipeline and your endpoint handler execute, in the EndpointMiddleware, as shown in figure 7.1. The RoutingMiddleware is responsible for matching an incoming request to an endpoint and for extracting the route parameter values, but all the values at that point are `strings`. It's only in the `EndpointMiddleware` that the `string` values are converted to the real argument types (such as `int`) needed to execute the endpoint handler.

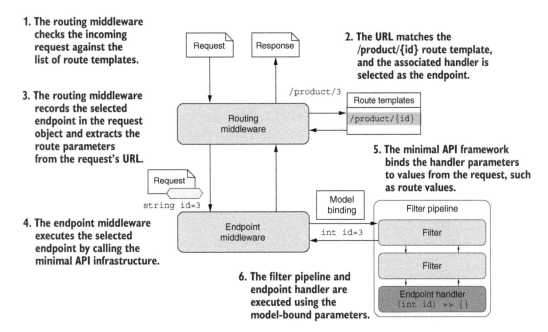

1. The routing middleware checks the incoming request against the list of route templates.

3. The routing middleware records the selected endpoint in the request object and extracts the route parameters from the request's URL.

4. The endpoint middleware executes the selected endpoint by calling the minimal API infrastructure.

2. The URL matches the /product/{id} route template, and the associated handler is selected as the endpoint.

5. The minimal API framework binds the handler parameters to values from the request, such as route values.

6. The filter pipeline and endpoint handler are executed using the model-bound parameters.

Figure 7.1 The `RoutingMiddleware` **matches the incoming request to an endpoint and extracts the route parameters as** `strings`. **When the** `EndpointMiddleware` **executes the endpoint, the minimal API infrastructure uses model binding to create the arguments required to execute the endpoint handler, converting the** `string` **route values to real argument types such as** `int`.

For every parameter in your minimal API endpoint handler, ASP.NET core must decide how to create the corresponding arguments. Minimal APIs can use six different binding sources to create the handler arguments:

- *Route values*—These values are obtained from URL segments or through default values after matching a route, as you saw in chapter 5.
- *Query string values*—These values are passed at the end of the URL, not used during routing.
- *Header values*—Header values are provided in the HTTP request.
- *Body JSON*—A single parameter may be bound to the JSON body of a request.
- *Dependency injected services*—Services available through dependency injection can be used as endpoint handler arguments. We look at dependency injection in chapters 8 and 9.
- *Custom binding*—ASP.NET Core exposes methods for you to customize how a type is bound by providing access to the `HttpRequest` object.

> **WARNING**   Unlike MVC controllers and Razor Pages, minimal APIs do *not* auto-
> matically bind to the body of requests sent as forms, using the application/
> x-www-form-urlencoded mime type. Minimal APIs will bind only to a JSON
> request body. If you need to work with form data in a minimal API endpoint, you
> can access it on HttpRequest.Form, but you won't benefit from automatic binding.

We'll look at the exact algorithm ASP.NET Core uses to choose which binding source
to use in section 7.8, but we'll start by looking at how ASP.NET Core binds simple
types such as int and double.

7.2   *Binding simple types to a request*

When you're building minimal API handlers, you'll often want to extract a simple
value from the request. If you're loading a list of products in a category, for example,
you'll likely need the category's ID, and in the calculator example at the start of section 7.1, you'll need the number to square.

When you create an endpoint handler that contains simple types such as int,
string, and double, ASP.NET Core automatically tries to bind the value to a route
parameter, or a query string value:

- If the name of the handler parameter matches the name of a route parameter
  in the route template, ASP.NET Core binds to the associated route value.
- If the name of the handler parameter doesn't match any parameters in the
  route template, ASP.NET Core tries to bind to a query string value.

If you make a request to /products/123, for example, this will match the following
endpoint:

```
app.MapGet("/products/{id}", (int id) => $"Received {id}");
```

ASP.NET Core binds the id handler argument to the {id} route parameter, so the
handler function is called with id=123. Conversely, if you make a request to
/products?id=456, this will match the following endpoint instead:

```
app.MapGet("/products", (int id) => $"Received {id}");
```

In this case, there's no id parameter in the route template, so ASP.NET Core binds to
the query string instead, and the handler function is called with id=456.

In addition to this "automatic" inference, you can force ASP.NET Core to bind
from a specific source by adding attributes to the parameters. [FromRoute] explicitly
binds to route parameters, [FromQuery] to the query string, and [FromHeader] to
header values, as shown in figure 7.2.

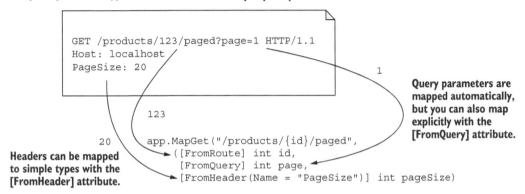

Figure 7.2 **Model binding an HTTP get request to an endpoint. The** `[FromRoute]`, `[FromQuery]`, **and** `[FromHeader]` **attributes force the endpoint parameters to bind to specific parts of the request. Only the** `[FromHeader]` **attribute is required in this case; the route parameter and query string would be inferred automatically.**

The `[From*]` attributes override ASP.NET Core's default logic and forces the parameters to load from a specific binding source. Listing 7.1 demonstrates three possible `[From*]` attributes:

- `[FromQuery]`—As you've already seen, this attribute forces a parameter to bind to the query string.
- `[FromRoute]`—This attribute forces the parameter to bind a route parameter value. Note that if a parameter of the required name doesn't exist in the route template, you'll get an exception at runtime.
- `[FromHeader]`—This attribute binds a parameter to a header value in the request.

Listing 7.1 Binding simple values using `[From]` **attributes**

```
using Microsoft.AspNetCore.Mvc;        ⟵──┤ All the [From*] attributes
                                            are in this namespace.
WebApplicationBuilder builder = WebApplication.CreateBuilder(args);
WebApplication app = builder.Build();       [FromRoute] forces the argument
                                            to bind to the route value.
app.MapGet("/products/{id}/paged",
    ([FromRoute] int id,            ⟵──┘
     [FromQuery] int page,          ⟵──    [FromQuery] forces the argument
                                           to bind to the query string.
     [FromHeader(Name = "PageSize")] int pageSize)    ⟵─────    [FromHeader]
    => $"Received id {id}, page {page}, pageSize {pageSize}");    binds the
                                                                 argument to the
                                                                 specified header.
app.Run();
```

Later, you'll see other attributes, such as [FromBody] and [FromServices], but the preceding three attributes are the only [From*] attributes that operate on simple types such as int and double. I prefer to avoid using [FromQuery] and [FromRoute] wherever possible and rely on the default binding conventions instead, as I find that they clutter the method signatures, and it's generally obvious whether a simple type is going to bind to the query string or a route value.

> **TIP**   ASP.NET Core binds to route parameters and query string values based on convention, but the only way to bind to a header value is with the [FromHeader] attribute.

You may be wondering what would happen if you try to bind a type to an incompatible value. What if you try to bind an int to the string value "two", for example? In that case ASP.NET Core throws a BadHttpRequestException and returns a 400 Bad Request response.

> **NOTE**   When the minimal API infrastructure fails to bind a handler parameter due to an incompatible format, it throws a BadHttpRequestException and returns a 400 Bad Request response.

I've mentioned several times in this section that you can bind route values, query string values, and headers to simple types, but what *is* a simple type? A *simple type* is defined as any type that contains either of the following TryParse methods, where T is the implementing type:

```
public static bool TryParse(string value, out T result);
public static bool TryParse(
    string value, IFormatProvider provider, out T result);
```

Types such as int and bool contain one (or both) these methods. But it's also worth noting that you can create your own types that implement one of these methods, and they'll be treated as simple types, capable of binding from route values, query string values, and headers.

Figure 7.3 shows an example of implementing a simple strongly-typed ID[1] that's treated as a simple type thanks to the TryParse method it exposes. When you send a request to /product/p123, ASP.NET Core sees that the ProductId type used in the endpoint handler contains a TryParse method and that the name of the id parameter has a matching route parameter name. It creates the id argument by calling ProductId.TryParse() and passes in the route value, p123.

Listing 7.2 shows how you could implement the TryParse method for ProductId. This method creates a ProductId from strings that consist of an integer prefixed with 'p' (p123 or p456, for example). If the input string matches the required format, it

---

[1] I have a series discussing strongly-typed IDs and their benefits on my blog at http://mng.bz/a1Kz.

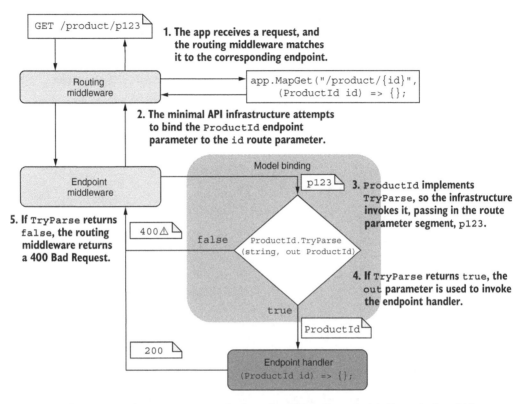

Figure 7.3 The routing middleware matches the incoming URL to the endpoint. The endpoint middleware attempts to bind the route parameter `id` to the endpoint parameter. The endpoint parameter type `ProductId` implements `TryParse`. If parsing is successful, the parsed parameter is used to call the endpoint handler. If parsing fails, the endpoint middleware returns a `400 Bad Request` response.

creates a `ProductId` instance and returns `true`. If the format is invalid, it returns `false`, binding fails, and a `400 Bad Request` is returned.

Listing 7.2 Implementing `TryParse` in a custom type to allow parsing from route values

```
WebApplicationBuilder builder = WebApplication.CreateBuilder(args);
WebApplication app = builder.Build();

app.MapGet("/product/{id}", (ProductId id) => $"Received {id}");
app.Run();

readonly record struct ProductId(int Id)
{
    public static bool TryParse(string? s, out ProductId result)
    {
        if(s is not null
            && s.StartsWith('p')
            && int.TryParse(
```

> **ProductId automatically binds to route values as it implements TryParse.**

> **ProductId is a C# 10 record struct.**

> **It implements TryParse, so it's treated as a simple type by minimal APIs.**

> **Checks that the string is not null and that the first character in the string is 'p' ...**

> **and if it is, tries to parse the remaining characters as an integer**

Efficiently skips the first character by treating the string as a ReadOnlySpan

```
          s.AsSpan().Slice(1),
            out int id))
        {
          result = new ProductId(id);
          return true;
        }

      result = default;
      return false;
    }
}
```

If the string was parsed successfully, id contains the parsed value.

Everything parsed successfully, so creates a new ProductId and returns true

Something went wrong, so returns false and assigns a default value to the (unused) result

---

Using modern C# and .NET features

Listing 7.2 included some C# and .NET features that you may not have seen before, depending on your background:

- *Pattern matching for null values*—`s is not null`. Pattern matching features have been introduced gradually into C# since C# 7. The `is not null` pattern, introduced in C# 9, has some minor advantages over the common `!= null` expression. You can read all about pattern matching at http://mng.bz/gBxl.

- *Records and struct records*—`readonly record struct`. Records are syntactical sugar over normal `class` and `struct` declarations, which make declaring new types more succinct and provide convenience methods for working with immutable types. Record structs were introduced in C# 10. You can read more at http://mng.bz/5wWz.

- `Span<T>` *for performance*—`s.AsSpan()`. `Span<T>` and `ReadOnlySpan<T>` were introduced in .NET Core 2.1 and are particularly useful for reducing allocations when working with `string` values. You can read more about them at http://mng.bz/6DNy.

- `ValueTask<T>`—It's not shown in listing 7.2, but many of the APIs in ASP.NET Core use `ValueTask` instead of the more common `Task` for APIs that normally complete asynchronously but *may* complete asynchronously. You can read about why they were introduced and when to use them at http://mng.bz/o1GM.

Don't worry if you're not familiar with these constructs. C# is a fast-moving language, so keeping up can be tricky, but there's generally no reason you need to use the new features. Nevertheless, it's useful to be able to recognize them so that you can read and understand code that uses them.

If you're keen to embrace new features, you might consider implementing the `IParsable` interface when you implement `TryParse`. This interface uses the `static abstract interfaces` feature, which was introduced in C# 11, and requires implementing both a `TryParse` and `Parse` method. You can read more about the `IParsable` interface in the announcement post at http://mng.bz/nW2K.

Now we've looked extensively at binding simple types to route values, query strings, and headers. In section 7.3 we'll learn about binding to the body of a request by deserializing JSON to complex types.

7.3   Binding complex types to the JSON body

Model binding in minimal APIs relies on certain conventions to simplify the code you need to write. One such convention, which you've already seen, is about binding to route parameters and query string values. Another important convention is that minimal API endpoints assume that requests will be sent using JSON.

Minimal APIs can bind the body of a request to a single complex type in your endpoint handler by deserializing the request from JSON. That means that if you have an endpoint such as the one in the following listing, ASP.NET Core will automatically deserialize the request for you from JSON, creating the `Product` argument.

Listing 7.3   Automatically deserializing a JSON request from the body

```
WebApplicationBuilder builder = WebApplication.CreateBuilder(args);
WebApplication app = builder.Build();

app.MapPost("/product", (Product product) => $"Received {product}");   ⟵

app.Run();
```
Product is a complex type, so it's bound to the JSON body of the request.

```
record Product(int Id, string Name, int Stock);
```
Product doesn't implement TryParse, so it's a complex type.

If you send a POST request to /product for the app in listing 7.3, you need to provide valid JSON in the request body, such as

```
{ "id": 1, "Name": "Shoes", "Stock": 12 }
```

ASP.NET Core uses the built-in System.Text.Json library to deserialize the JSON into a `Product` instance and uses it as the `product` argument in the handler.

Configuring JSON binding with System.Text.Json

The System.Text.Json library, introduced in .NET Core 3.0, provides a high-performance, low-allocation JSON serialization library. It was designed to be something of a successor to the ubiquitous Newtonsoft.Json library, but it trades flexibility for performance.

Minimal APIs use System.Text.Json for both JSON deserialization (when binding to a request's body) and serialization (when writing results, as you saw in chapter 6). Unlike for MVC and Razor Pages, you can't replace the JSON serialization library used by minimal APIs, so there's no way to use Newtonsoft.Json instead. But you can customize some of the library's serialization behavior for your minimal APIs.

You can set System.Text.Json, for example, to relax some of its strictness to allow trailing commas in the JSON and control how property names are serialized with code like the following example:

```
(continued)
WebApplicationBuilder builder = WebApplication.CreateBuilder(args);
builder.Services.ConfigureRouteHandlerJsonOptions(o => {
    o.SerializerOptions.AllowTrailingCommas = true;
    o.SerializerOptions.PropertyNamingPolicy =
            JsonNamingPolicy.CamelCase;
    o.SerializerOptions.PropertyNameCaseInsensitive = true;
});
```

Typically, the automatic binding for JSON requests is convenient, as most APIs these days are built around JSON requests and responses. The built-in binding uses the most performant approach and eliminates a lot of boilerplate that you'd otherwise need to write yourself. Nevertheless, bear several things in mind when you're binding to the request body:

- You can bind only a single handler parameter to the JSON body. If more than one complex parameter is eligible to bind to the body, you'll get an exception at runtime when the app receives its first request.
- If the request body isn't JSON, the endpoint handler won't run, and the EndpointMiddleware will return a 415 Unsupported Media Type response.
- If you try to bind to the body for an HTTP verb that usually doesn't send a body (GET, HEAD, OPTIONS, DELETE, TRACE, and CONNECT), you'll get an exception at runtime. If you change the endpoint in listing 7.3 to MapGet instead of MapPost, for example, you'll get an exception on your first request, as shown in figure 7.4.
- If you're sure that you want to bind the body of these requests, you can override the preceding behavior by applying the [FromBody] attribute to the handler parameter. I strongly advise against this approach, though: sending a body with GET requests is unusual, could confuse the consumers of your API, and is discouraged in the HTTP specification (https://www.rfc-editor.org/rfc/rfc9110#name-get).
- It's uncommon to see, but you can also apply [FromBody] to a simple type parameter to force it to bind to the request body instead of to the route/query string. As for complex types, the body is deserialized from JSON into your parameter.

We've discussed binding of both simple types and complex types. Unfortunately, now it's time to admit to a gray area: arrays, which can be simple types *or* complex types.

Attempting to read the
body of a GET request
causes an exception.

The exception indicates
which parameter caused
the exception and the
binding source used.

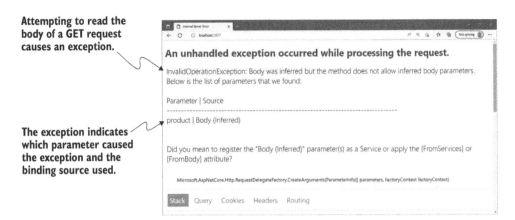

Figure 7.4   If you try to bind the body to a parameter for a GET request, you'll get an exception when your app receives its first request.

7.4   Arrays: Simple types or complex types?

It's a little-known fact that entries in the query string of a URL don't have to be unique. The following URL is valid, for example, even though it includes a duplicate id parameter:

```
/products?id=123&id=456
```

So how do you access these query string values with minimal APIs? If you create an endpoint like

```
app.MapGet("/products", (int id) => $"Received {id}");
```

a request to /products?id=123 would bind the id parameter to the query string, as you'd expect. But a request that includes two id values in the query string, such as /products?id=123&id=456, will cause a runtime error, as shown in figure 7.5. ASP.NET Core returns a 400 Bad Request response without the handler or filter pipeline running at all.

   If you want to handle query strings like this one, so that users can optionally pass multiple possible values for a parameter, you need to use arrays. The following listing shows an example of an endpoint that accepts multiple id values from the query string and binds them to an array.

Listing 7.4   Binding multiple values for a parameter in a query string to an array

```
WebApplicationBuilder builder = WebApplication.CreateBuilder(args);
WebApplication app = builder.Build();

app.MapGet("/products/search",
    (int[] id) => $"Received {id.Length} ids");

app.Run();
```

The array will bind to
multiple instances of
id in the query string.

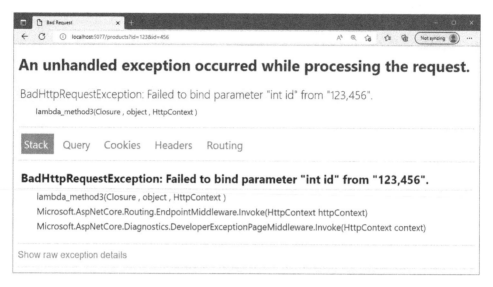

Figure 7.5   Attempting to bind a handler with a signature such as `(int id)` **to a query string that contains** `?id=123&id=456` **causes an exception at runtime and a** `400 Bad Request` **response.**

If you're anything like me, the fact that the `int[]` handler parameter in listing 7.4 is called `id` and not `ids` will really bug you. Unfortunately, you have to use `id` here so that the parameter binds correctly to a query string like `?id=123&id=456`. If you renamed it `ids`, the query string would need to be `?ids=123&ids=456`.

Luckily, you have another option. You can control the name of the target that a handler parameter binds to by using the `[FromQuery]` and `[FromRoute]` attributes, similar to the way you use `[FromHeader]`. For this example, you can have the best of both worlds by renaming the handler parameter `ids` and adding the `[FromQuery]` attribute:

```
app.MapGet("/products/search",
    ([FromQuery(Name = "id")] int[] ids) => $"Received {ids.Length} ids");
```

Now you can sleep easy. The handler parameter has a better name, but it still binds to the query string `?id=123&id=456` correctly.

> **TIP** You can bind array parameters to multiple header values in the same way that you do for as query string values, using the `[FromHeader]` attribute.

The example in listing 7.4 binds an `int[]`, but you can bind an array of any simple type, including custom types with a `TryParse` method (listing 7.2), as well as `string[]` and `StringValues`.

> **NOTE** `StringValues` is a helper type in the `Microsoft.Extensions.Primitives` namespace that represents zero, one, or many `string`s in an efficient way.

So where is that gray area I mentioned? Well, arrays work as I've described only if

- You're using an HTTP verb that typically doesn't include a request body, such as GET, HEAD, or DELETE.
- The array is an array of simple types (or string[] or StringValues).

If either of these statements is *not* true, ASP.NET Core will attempt to bind the array to the JSON body of the request instead. For POST requests (or other verbs that typically have a request body), this process works without problems: the JSON body is deserialized to the parameter array. For GET requests (and other verbs without a body), it causes the same unhandled exception you saw in figure 7.4 when a body binding is detected in one of these verbs.

> **NOTE** As before, when binding body parameters, you can work around this situation for GET requests by adding an explicit [FromBody] to the handler parameter, but you shouldn't!

We've covered binding both simple types and complex types, from the URL and the body, and we've even looked at some cases in which a mismatch between what you expect and what you receive causes errors. But what if a value you expect isn't there? In section 7.5 we look at how you can choose what happens.

7.5 *Making parameters optional with nullables*

We've described lots of ways to bind parameters to minimal API endpoints. If you've been experimenting with the code samples and sending requests, you may have noticed that if the endpoint *can't* bind a parameter at runtime, you get an error and a 400 Bad Request response. If you have an endpoint that binds a parameter to the query string, such as

```
app.MapGet("/products", (int id) => $"Received {id}");
```

but you send a request without a query string or with the wrong name in the query string, such as a request to /products?p=3, the EndpointMiddleware throws an exception, as shown in figure 7.6. The id parameter is required, so if it can't bind, you'll get an error message and a 400 Bad Request response, and the endpoint handler won't run.

All parameters are required regardless of which binding source they use, whether that's from a route value, a query string value, a header, or the request body. But what if you want a handler parameter to be optional? If you have an endpoint like this one,

```
app.MapGet("/stock/{id?}", (int id) => $"Received {id}");
```

given that the route parameter is marked optional, requests to both /stock/123 and /stock will invoke the handler. But in the latter case, there'll be no id route value, and you'll get an error like the one shown in figure 7.6.

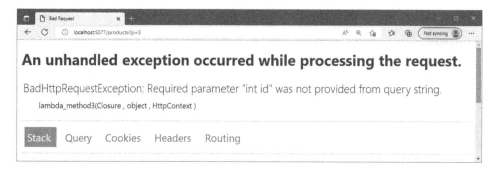

Figure 7.6   If a parameter can't be bound because a value is missing, the `EndpointMiddleware`
throws an exception and returns a `400 Bad Request` **response. The endpoint handler doesn't run.**

The way around this problem is to mark the *handler parameter* as optional by making it
nullable. Just as ? signifies optional in route templates, it signifies optional in the handler
parameters. You can update the handler to use int? instead of int, as shown in the following listing, and the endpoint will handle both /stock/123 and /stock without errors.

Listing 7.5   Using optional parameters in endpoint handlers

```
WebApplicationBuilder builder = WebApplication.CreateBuilder(args);
WebApplication app = builder.Build();

app.MapGet("/stock/{id?}", (int? id) => $"Received {id}");

app.MapGet("/stock2", (int? id) => $"Received {id}");

app.MapPost("/stock", (Product? product) => $"Received {product}");

app.Run();
```

Uses a nullable simple
type to indicate that the
value is optional, so id is
null when calling /stock

A nullable complex type binds
to the body if it's available;
otherwise, it's null.

This example binds to the query string.
Id will be null for the request /stock2.

If no corresponding route value or query string contains the required value and the
handler parameter is optional, the `EndpointHandler` uses `null` as the argument when
invoking the endpoint handler. Similarly, for complex types that bind to the request
body, if the request doesn't contain anything in the body and the parameter is
optional, the handler will have a `null` argument.

> **WARNING**   If the request body contains the literal JSON value `null` and the
> handler parameter is marked optional, the handler argument will also be
> `null`. If the parameter isn't marked optional, you get the same error as
> though the request didn't have a body.

It's worth noting that you mark complex types binding to the request body as optional
by using a *nullable reference type* (NRT) annotation: ?. NRTs, introduced in C# 8, are an
attempt to reduce the scourge of null-reference exceptions in C#, colloquially known
as "the billion-dollar mistake." See http://mng.bz/vneM.

ASP.NET Core in .NET 7 is built with the assumption that NRTs are enabled for your project (and they're enabled by default in all the templates), so it's worth using them wherever you can. If you choose to disable NRTs explicitly, you may find that some of your types are unexpectedly marked optional, which can lead to some hard-to-debug errors.

> **TIP** Keep NRTs enabled for your minimal API endpoints wherever possible. If you can't use them for your whole project, consider enabling them selectively in Program.cs (or wherever you add your endpoints) by adding `#nullable enable` to the top of the file.

The good news is that ASP.NET Core includes several analyzers built into the compiler to catch configuration problems like the ones described in this section. If you have an optional route parameter but forget to mark the corresponding handler parameter as optional, for example, integrated development environments (IDEs) such as Visual Studio will show a hint, as shown in figure 7.7, and you'll get a build warning. You can read more about the built-in analyzers at http://mng.bz/4DMV.

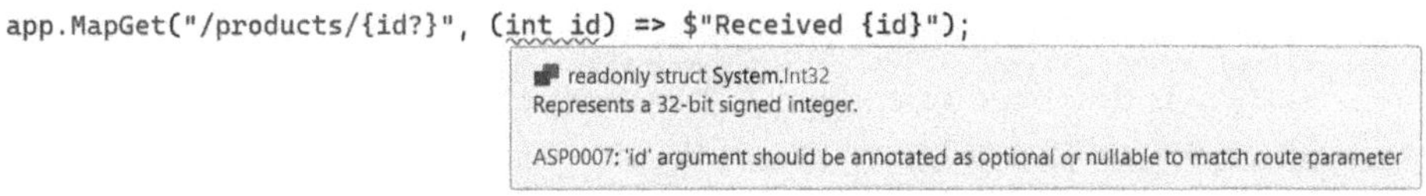

```
app.MapGet("/products/{id?}", (int id) => $"Received {id}");
```

readonly struct System.Int32
Represents a 32-bit signed integer.

ASP0007: 'id' argument should be annotated as optional or nullable to match route parameter

Figure 7.7 Visual Studio and other IDEs use analyzers to detect potential problems with mismatched optionality.

Making your handler parameters optional is one of the approaches you can take, whether they're bound to route parameters, headers, or the query string. Alternatively, you can provide a default value for the parameter as part of the method signature. You can't provide default values for parameters in lambda functions in C# 11,[2] so the following listing shows how to use a local function instead.

Listing 7.6 Using default values for parameters in endpoint handlers

```
WebApplicationBuilder builder = WebApplication.CreateBuilder(args);
WebApplication app = builder.Build();

app.MapGet("/stock", StockWithDefaultValue);

app.Run();

string StockWithDefaultValue(int id = 0) => $"Received {id}";
```

> The local function StockWithDefaultValue is the endpoint handler.

> The id parameter binds to the query string value if it's available; otherwise, it has the value 0.

We've thoroughly covered the differences between simple types and complex types and how they bind. In section 7.6 we look at some special types that don't follow these rules.

---

[2] C# 12, which will be released with .NET 8, should include support for default values in lambda expressions. For more details, see http://mng.bz/AoRg.

7.6   *Binding services and special types*

In this section you'll learn how to use some of the special types that you can bind to in your endpoint handlers. By *special*, I mean types that ASP.NET Core is hardcoded to understand or that aren't created from the details of the request, by contrast with the binding you've seen so far. The section looks at three types of parameters:

- Well-known types—that is, hard-coded types that ASP.NET Core knows about, such as `HttpContext` and `HttpRequest`
- `IFormFileCollection` and `IFormFile` for working with file uploads
- Application services registered in `WebApplicationBuilder.Services`

We start by looking at the well-known types you can bind to.

7.6.1   *Injecting well-known types*

Throughout this book you've seen examples of several well-known types that you can inject into your endpoint handlers, the most notable one being `HttpContext`. The remaining well-known types provide shortcuts for accessing various properties of the `HttpContext` object.

> **NOTE**   As described in chapter 3, `HttpContext` acts as a storage box for everything related to a single a request. It contains access to all the low-level details about the request and the response, plus any application services and features you might need.

You can use a well-known type in your endpoint handler by including a parameter of the appropriate type. To access the `HttpContext` in your handler, for example, you could use

```
app.MapGet("/", (HttpContext context) => "Hello world!");
```

You can use the following well-known types in your minimal API endpoint handlers:

- `HttpContext`—This type contains all the details on both the request and the response. You can access everything you need from here, but often, an easier way to access the common properties is to use one of the other well-known types.
- `HttpRequest`—Equivalent to the property `HttpContext.Request`, this type contains all the details about the request only.
- `HttpResponse`—Equivalent to the property `HttpContext.Response`, this type contains all the details about the response only.
- `CancellationToken`—Equivalent to the property `HttpContext.RequestAborted`, this token is canceled if the client aborts the request. It's useful if you need to cancel a long-running task, as described in my post at http://mng.bz/QP2j.

- `ClaimsPrincipal`—Equivalent to the property `HttpContext.User`, this type contains authentication information about the user. You'll learn more about authentication in chapter 23.
- `Stream`—Equivalent to the property `HttpRequest.Body`, this parameter is a reference to the `Stream` object of the request. This parameter can be useful for scenarios in which you need to process large amounts of data from a request efficiently, without holding it all in memory at the same time.
- `PipeReader`—Equivalent to the property `HttpContext.BodyReader`, `PipeReader` provides a higher-level API compared with `Stream`, but it's useful in similar scenarios. You can read more about PipeReader and the System.IO.Pipelines namespace at http://mng.bz/XNY6.

You can access each of the latter well-known types by navigating via an injected `Http-Context` object if you prefer. But injecting the exact object you need generally makes for code that's easier to read.

7.6.2 Injecting services

I've mentioned several times in this book that you need to configure various core services to work with ASP.NET Core. Many services are registered automatically, but often, you must add more to use extra features, such as when you called `AddHttpLogging()` in chapter 3 to add request logging to your pipeline.

> **NOTE** Adding services to your application involves registering them with a dependency injection (DI) container. You'll learn all about DI and registering services in chapters 8 and 9.

You can automatically use any registered service in your endpoint handlers, and ASP.NET Core will inject an instance of the service from the DI container. You saw an example in chapter 6 when you used the `LinkGenerator` service in an endpoint handler. `LinkGenerator` is one of the core services registered by `WebApplicationBuilder`, so it's always available, as shown in the following listing.

Listing 7.7 Using the `LinkGenerator` service in an endpoint handler

```
app.MapGet("/links", (LinkGenerator links) =>
{
    string link = links.GetPathByName("products");
    return $"View the product at {link}";
});
```

The LinkGenerator can be used as a parameter because it's available in the DI container.

Minimal APIs can automatically detect when a service is available in the DI container, but if you want to be explicit, you can also decorate your parameters with the `[From-Services]` attribute:

```
app.MapGet("/links", ([FromServices] LinkGenerator links) =>
```

[FromServices] may be necessary in some rare cases if you're using a custom DI container that doesn't support the APIs used by minimal APIs. But generally, I find that I can keep endpoints readable by avoiding the [From*] attributes wherever possible and relying on minimal APIs to do the right thing automatically.

7.6.3   *Binding file uploads with IFormFile and IFormFileCollection*

A common feature of many websites is the ability to upload files. This activity could be relatively infrequent, such as a user's uploading a profile picture to their Stack Overflow profile, or it may be integral to the application, such as uploading photos to Facebook.

Letting users upload files to your application

Uploading files to websites is a common activity, but you should consider carefully whether your application *needs* that ability. Whenever users can upload files, the situation is fraught with danger.

You should be careful to treat the incoming files as potentially malicious. Don't trust the filename provided, take care of large files being uploaded, and don't allow the files to be executed on your server.

Files also raise questions about where the data should be stored: in a database, in the filesystem, or in some other storage? None of these questions has a straightforward answer, and you should think hard about the implications of choosing one over the other. Better, don't let users upload files if you don't have to!

ASP.NET Core supports uploading files by exposing the IFormFile interface. You can use this interface in your endpoint handlers, and it will be populated with the details of the file upload:

```
app.MapGet("/upload", (IFormFile file) => {});
```

You can also use an IFormFileCollection if you need to accept multiple files:

```
app.MapGet("/upload", (IFormFileCollection files) =>
{
    foreach (IFormFile file in files)
    {
    }
});
```

The IFormFile object exposes several properties and utility methods for reading the contents of the uploaded file, some of which are shown here:

```
public interface IFormFile
{
    string ContentType { get; }
    long Length { get; }
    string FileName { get; }
    Stream OpenReadStream();
}
```

As you can see, this interface exposes a `FileName` property, which returns the filename that the file was uploaded with. But you know not to trust users, right? You should *never* use the filename directly in your code; users can use it to attack your website and access files that they shouldn't. Always generate a new name for the file before you save it anywhere.

> **WARNING** There are lots of potential threats to consider when accepting file uploads from users. For more information, see http://mng.bz/yQ9q.

The `IFormFile` approach is fine if users are going to be uploading only small files. When your method accepts an `IFormFile` instance, the whole content of the file is buffered in memory and on disk before you receive it. Then you can use the `OpenReadStream` method to read the data out.

If users post large files to your website, you may start to run out of space in memory or on disk as ASP.NET Core buffers each of the files. In that case, you may need to stream the files directly to avoid saving all the data at the same time. Unfortunately, unlike the model-binding approach, streaming large files can be complex and error-prone, so it's outside the scope of this book. For details, see Microsoft's documentation at http://mng.bz/MBgn.

> **TIP** Don't use the `IFormFile` interface to handle large file uploads, as you may see performance problem. Be aware that you can't rely on users *not* to upload large files, so avoid file uploads when you can!

For the vast majority of minimal API endpoints, the default configuration of model binding for simple and complex types works perfectly well. But you may find some situations in which you need to take a bit more control.

7.7 Custom binding with BindAsync

The model binding you get out of the box with minimal APIs covers most of the common situations that you'll run into when building HTTP APIs, but there are always a few edge cases in which you can't use it.

You've already seen that you can inject `HttpContext` into your endpoint handlers, so you have direct access to the request details in your handler, but often, you still want to encapsulate the logic for extracting the data you need. You can get the best of both worlds in minimal APIs by implementing `BindAsync` in your endpoint handler parameter types and taking advantage of completely custom model binding. To add custom binding for a parameter type, you must implement one of the following two `static` `BindAsync` methods in your type `T`:

```
public static ValueTask<T?> BindAsync(HttpContext context);
public static ValueTask<T?> BindAsync(
HttpContext context, ParameterInfo parameter);
```

Both methods accept an `HttpContext`, so you can extract anything you need from the request. But the latter case also provides reflection details about the parameter you're binding. In most cases the simpler signature should be sufficient, but you never know!

Listing 7.8 shows an example of using `BindAsync` to bind a record to the request body by using a custom format. The implementation shown in the listing assumes that the body contains two `double` values, with a line break between them, and if so, it successfully parses the `SizeDetails` object. If there are any problems along the way, it returns `null`.

Listing 7.8 Using `BindAsync` for custom model binding

```
WebApplicationBuilder builder = WebApplication.CreateBuilder(args);
WebApplication app = builder.Build();

app.MapPost("/sizes", (SizeDetails size) => $"Received {size}");      ◄──
                                                                          No extra attributes are needed for the SizeDetails
app.Run();                                                                parameter, as it has a BindAsync method.

public record SizeDetails(double height, double width)               SizeDetails
{                                                                    implements the static
              public static async ValueTask<SizeDetails?> BindAsync( BindAsync method.
Creates a         HttpContext context)
StreamReader
to read the   {
request body      using var sr = new StreamReader(context.Request.Body);

Reads a line      string? line1 = await sr.ReadLineAsync(context.RequestAborted);
of text from      if (line1 is null) { return null; }                     ◄──
the body          string? line2 = await sr.ReadLineAsync(context.RequestAborted);
                  if (line2 is null) { return null; }                     ◄──
                                                                   If either line is null,
Tries to parse the   return double.TryParse(line1, out double height)    indicating no content,
two lines as doubles     && double.TryParse(line2, out double width)     stops processing
                  ? new SizeDetails(height, width)  ◄──
                  : null;  ◄──                                   If the parsing is successful, creates the
    }                          ... otherwise,                    SizeDetails model and returns it ...
}                              returns null
```

In listing 7.8 we return `null` if parsing fails. The endpoint shown will cause the `EndpointMiddleware` to throw a `BadHttpRequestException` and return a `400` error, because the size parameter in the endpoint is required (not marked optional). You could have thrown an exception in `BindAsync`, but it wouldn't have been caught by the `EndpointMiddleware` and would have resulted in a `500` response.

7.8 Choosing a binding source

Phew! We've finally covered all the ways you can bind a request to parameters in minimal APIs. In many cases, things should work as you expect. Simple types such as `int` and `string` bind to route values and query string values by default, and complex types bind to the request body. But it can get confusing when you add attributes, `BindAsync`, and `TryParse` to the mix!

When the minimal API infrastructure tries to bind a parameter, it checks all the following binding sources in order. The first binding source that matches is the one it uses:

1 If the parameter defines an explicit binding source using attributes such as `[FromRoute]`, `[FromQuery]`, or `[FromBody]`, the parameter binds to that part of the request.

2 If the parameter is a well-known type such as `HttpContext`, `HttpRequest`, `Stream`, or `IFormFile`, the parameter is bound to the corresponding value.

3 If the parameter type has a `BindAsync()` method, use that method for binding.

4 If the parameter is a `string` or has an appropriate `TryParse()` method (so is a simple type):

   a If the name of the parameter matches a route parameter name, bind to the route value.

   b Otherwise, bind to the query string.

5 If the parameter is an array of simple types, a `string[]`, or `StringValues`, and the request is a `GET` or similar HTTP verb that normally doesn't have a request body, bind to the query string.

6 If the parameter is a known service type from the dependency injection container, bind by injecting the service from the container.

7 Finally, bind to the body by deserializing from JSON.

The minimal API infrastructure follows this sequence for every parameter in a handler and stops at the first matching binding source.

> **WARNING** If binding fails for the entry, and the parameter isn't optional, the request fails with a `400 Bad Request` response. The minimal API doesn't try another binding source after one source fails.

Remembering this sequence of binding sources is one of the hardest things about minimal APIs to get your head around. If you're struggling to work out why a request isn't working as you expect, be sure to come back and check this sequence. I once had a parameter that wasn't binding to a route parameter, despite its having a `TryParse` method. When I checked the sequence, I realized that it also had a `BindAsync` method that was taking precedence!

7.9 Simplifying handlers with AsParameters

Before we move on, we'll take a quick look at a .NET 7 feature for minimal APIs that can simplify some endpoint handlers: the `[AsParameters]` attribute. Consider the following `GET` endpoint, which binds to a route value, a header value, and some query values:

```
app.MapGet("/category/{id}", (int id, int page, [FromHeader(Name = "sort")]
➥ bool? sortAsc, [FromQuery(Name = "q")] string search) => { });
```

I think you'll agree that the handler parameters for this method are somewhat hard to read. The parameters define the expected shape of the request, which isn't ideal. The [AsParameters] attribute lets you wrap all these arguments into a single class or struct, simplifying the method signature and making everything more readable.

Listing 7.9 shows an example of converting this endpoint to use [AsParameters] by replacing it with a record struct. You could also use a class, record, or struct, and you can use properties instead of constructor parameters if you prefer. See the documentation for all the permutations available at http://mng.bz/a1KB.

Listing 7.9   Using [AsParameters] to simplify endpoint handler parameters

```
WebApplicationBuilder builder = WebApplication.CreateBuilder(args);
WebApplication app = builder.Build();

app.MapGet("/category/{id}",
    ([AsParameters] SearchModel model) => $"Received {model}");

app.Run();

record struct SearchModel(
    int id,
    int page,
    [FromHeader(Name = "sort")] bool? sortAsc,
    [FromQuery(Name = "q")] string search);
```

[AsParameters] indicates that the constructor or properties of the type should be bound, not the type itself.

Each parameter is bound as though it were written in the endpoint handler.

The same attributes and rules apply for binding an [AsParameters] type's constructor parameters and binding endpoint handler parameters, so you can use [From*] attributes, inject services and well-known types, and read from the body. This approach can make your endpoints more readable if you find that they're getting a bit unwieldy.

> **TIP**   In chapter 16 you'll learn about model binding in MVC and Razor Pages. You'll be pleased to know that in those cases, the [AsParameters] approach works out of the box without the need for an extra attribute.

That brings us to the end of this section on model binding. If all went well, your endpoint handler's arguments are created, and the handler is ready to execute its logic. It's time to handle the request, right? Nothing to worry about.

Not so fast! How do you know that the data you received was valid? How do you know that you haven't been sent malicious data attempting a SQL injection attack or a phone number full of letters? The binder is relatively blindly assigning values sent in a request, which you're happily going to plug into your own methods. What stops nefarious little Jimmy from sending malicious values to your application? Except for basic safeguards, nothing is stopping him, which is why it's important that you *always* validate the input coming in. ASP.NET Core provides a way to do this in a declarative manner out of the box, which is the focus of section 7.10.

7.10 *Handling user input with model validation*

In this section, I discuss the following topics:

- What validation is and why you need it
- How to use `DataAnnotations` attributes to describe the data you expect
- How to validate your endpoint handler parameters

Validation in general is a big topic, one that you'll need to consider in every app you build. Minimal APIs don't include validation by default, instead opting to provide nonprescriptive hooks via the filters you learned about in chapter 5. This design gives you multiple options for adding validation to your app; be sure that you do add some!

7.10.1 *The need for validation*

Data can come from many sources in your web application. You could load data from files, read it from a database, or accept values that are sent in a request. Although you may be inclined to trust that the data already on your server is valid (though this assumption is sometimes dangerous!), you *definitely* shouldn't trust the data sent as part of a request.

> **TIP** You can read more about the goals of validation, implementation approaches, and potential attacks at http://mng.bz/gBxE.

You should validate your endpoint handler parameters before you use them to do anything that touches your domain, anything that touches your infrastructure, or anything that could leak information to an attacker. Note that this warning is intentionally vague, as there's no defined point in minimal APIs where validation should occur. I advise that you do it as soon as possible in the minimal API filter pipeline.

Always validate data provided by users before you use it in your methods. You have no idea what the browser may have sent you. The classic example of little Bobby Tables (https://xkcd.com/327) highlights the need to always validate data sent by a user.

Validation isn't used only to check for security threats, though. It's also needed to check for nonmalicious errors:

- *Data should be formatted correctly.* Email fields have a valid email format, for example.
- *Numbers may need to be in a particular range.* You can't buy -1 copies of this book!
- *Some values may be required, but others are optional.* Name may be required for a profile, but phone number is optional.
- *Values must conform to your business requirements.* You can't convert a currency to itself; it needs to be converted to a different currency.

As mentioned earlier, the minimal API framework doesn't include anything specific to help you with these requirements, but you can use filters to implement validation, as you'll see in section 7.10.3. .NET 7 also includes a set of attributes that you can use to simplify your validation code significantly.

7.10.2 *Using DataAnnotations attributes for validation*

Validation attributes—more precisely, `DataAnnotations` attributes—allow you to specify the rules that your parameters should conform to. They provide metadata about a parameter type by describing the *sort* of data the binding model should contain, as opposed to the data itself.

You can apply `DataAnnotations` attributes directly to your parameter types to indicate the type of data that's acceptable. This approach allows you to check that required fields have been provided, that numbers are in the correct range, and that email fields are valid email addresses, for example.

Consider the checkout page for a currency-converter application. You need to collect details about the user—their name, email, and (optionally) phone number—so you create an API to capture these details. The following listing shows the outline of that API, which takes a `UserModel` parameter. The `UserModel` type is decorated with validation attributes that represent the validation rules for the model.

Listing 7.10 Adding `DataAnnotations` to a type to provide metadata

```
using System.ComponentModel.DataAnnotations;          ◁──┐  Adds this using statement to
                                                         │  use the validation attributes

WebApplicationBuilder builder = WebApplication.CreateBuilder(args);
WebApplication app = builder.Build();

app.MapPost("/users", (UserModel user) => user.ToString());   ◁──┐  The API takes
                                                                  │  a UserModel
app.Run();                                                        │  parameter and
                                                                  │  binds it to the
public record UserModel        Values marked                      │  request body.
{                              Required must
    [Required]            ◁──  be provided.    The StringLengthAttribute
    [StringLength(100)]                 ◁────  sets the maximum length
    [Display(Name = "Your name")]    ◁──       for the property.
    public string FirstName { get; set; }   Customizes the name used
                                            to describe the property
    [Required]
    [StringLength(100)]
    [Display(Name = "Last name")]
    public string LastName { get; set; }

    [Required]                        Validates that the value of Email
    [EmailAddress]             ◁────  may be a valid email address
    public string Email { get; set; }
                                      Validates that the value of PhoneNumber
    [Phone]                    ◁────  has a valid telephone number format
    [Display(Name = "Phone number")]
    public string PhoneNumber { get; set; }
}
```

Suddenly, your parameter type, which was sparse on details, contains a wealth of information. You've specified that the `FirstName` property should always be provided; that it should have a maximum length of 100 characters; and that when it's referred to (in error messages, for example), it should be called `"Your name"` instead of `"FirstName"`.

The great thing about these attributes is that they clearly declare the *expected* state of an instance of the type. By looking at these attributes, you know what the properties will contain, or at least *should* contain. Then you can then write code after model binding to confirm that the bound parameter is valid, as you'll see in section 7.10.3.

You've got a plethora of attributes to choose among when you apply `DataAnnotations` to your types. I've listed some of the common ones here, but you can find more in the `System.ComponentModel.DataAnnotations` namespace. For a more complete list, I recommend using IntelliSense in your IDE or checking the documentation at http://mng.bz/e1Mv.

- `[CreditCard]`—Validates that a property has a valid credit card format
- `[EmailAddress]`—Validates that a property has a valid email address format
- `[StringLength(max)]`—Validates that a string has at most max number of characters
- `[MinLength(min)]`—Validates that a collection has at least the min number of items
- `[Phone]`—Validates that a property has a valid phone number format
- `[Range(min, max)]`—Validates that a property has a value between min and max
- `[RegularExpression(regex)]`—Validates that a property conforms to the regex regular expression pattern
- `[Url]`—Validates that a property has a valid URL format
- `[Required]`—Indicates that the property must not be null
- `[Compare]`—Allows you to confirm that two properties have the same value (such as `Email` and `ConfirmEmail`)

> **WARNING** The `[EmailAddress]` and `[Phone]` attributes validate only that the *format* of the value is potentially correct. They don't validate that the email address or phone number exists. For an example of how to do more rigorous phone number validation, see this post on the Twilio blog: http://mng.bz/xmZe.

The `DataAnnotations` attributes aren't new; they've been part of the .NET Framework since version 3.5, and their use in ASP.NET Core is almost the same as in the previous version of ASP.NET. They're also used for purposes other than validation. Entity Framework Core (among others) uses `DataAnnotations` to define the types of columns and rules to use when creating database tables from C# classes. You can read more about Entity Framework Core in chapter 12 and in *Entity Framework Core in Action*, 2nd ed., by Jon P. Smith (Manning, 2021).

If the `DataAnnotation` attributes provided out of the box don't cover everything you need, it's possible to write custom attributes by deriving from the base `Validation-Attribute`. You'll see how to create a custom validation attribute in chapter 32.

One common limitation with `DataAnnotation` attributes is that it's hard to validate properties that depend on the values of other properties. Maybe the `UserModel` type from listing 7.10 requires you to provide either an email address or a phone number but not both, which is hard to achieve with attributes. In this type of situation, you can implement `IValidatableObject` in your models instead of, or in addition to, using attributes. In listing 7.11, a validation rule is added to `UserModel` whether the email or phone number is provided. If it isn't, `Validate()` returns a `ValidationResult` describing the problem.

Listing 7.11 Implementing `IValidatableObject`

```
using System.ComponentModel.DataAnnotations;

public record CreateUserModel : IValidatableObject          ← Implements the
{                                                             IValidatableObject interface
    [EmailAddress]                                ←
    public string Email { get; set; }              The DataAnnotation attributes
                                                   continue to validate basic
    [Phone]                                    ←   format requirements.
    public string PhoneNumber { get; set; }

    public IEnumerable<ValidationResult> Validate(      Validate is the only function to
        ValidationContext validationContext)            implement in IValidatableObject.
    {
        if(string.IsNullOrEmpty(Email)
            && string.IsNullOrEmpty(PhoneNumber))
        {
            yield return new ValidationResult(                   ... and if not,
                "You must provide an Email or a PhoneNumber",    returns a result
                New[] { nameof(Email), nameof(PhoneNumber) });   describing the error
        }
    }
}
```

Checks whether the object is valid . . . (annotation pointing to the `if` block)

`IValidatableObject` helps cover some of the cases that attributes alone can't handle, but it's not always the best option. The `Validate` function doesn't give easy access to your app's services, and the function executes only if all the `DataAnnotation` attribute conditions are met.

> **TIP** `DataAnnotations` are good for input validation of properties in isolation but not so good for validating complex business rules. You'll most likely need to perform this validation outside the `DataAnnotations` framework.

Alternatively, if you're not a fan of the `DataAnnotation` attribute-based-plus-`IValidatableObject` approach, you could use the popular FluentValidation library (https://github.com/JeremySkinner/FluentValidation) in your minimal APIs instead. Minimal APIs are completely flexible, so you can use whichever approach you prefer.

`DataAnnotations` attributes provide the basic metadata for validation, but no part of listing 7.10 or listing 7.11 uses the validation attributes you added. You still need to add code to read the parameter type's metadata, check whether the data is valid, and return an error response if it's invalid. ASP.NET Core doesn't include a dedicated validation API for that task in minimal APIs, but you can easily add it with a small NuGet package.

7.10.3   *Adding a validation filter to your minimal APIs*

Microsoft decided not to include any dedicated validation APIs in minimal APIs. By contrast, validation is a built-in core feature of Razor Pages and MVC. Microsoft's reasoning was that the company wanted to provide flexibility and choice for users to add validation in the way that works best for them, but didn't want to affect performance for those who didn't want to use their implementation.

Consequently, validation in minimal APIs typically relies on the filter pipeline. As a classic cross-cutting concern, validation is a good fit for a filter. The only downside is that typically, you need to write your own filter rather than use an existing API. The positive side is that validation gives you complete flexibility, including the ability to use an alternative validation library (such as FluentValidation) if you prefer.

Luckily, Damian Edwards, a project manager architect on the ASP.NET Core team at Microsoft, has a NuGet package called MinimalApis.Extensions that provides the filter for you. Using a simple validation system that hooks into the `DataAnnotations` on your models, this NuGet package provides an extension method called `WithParameter-Validation()` that you can add to your endpoints. To add the package, search for MinimalApis.Extensions from the NuGet Package Manager in your IDE (be sure to include prerelease versions), or run the following, using the .NET command-line interface:

```
dotnet add package MinimalApis.Extensions
```

After you've added the package, you can add validation to any of your endpoints by adding a filter using `WithParameterValidation()`, as shown in listing 7.12. After the `UserModel` is bound to the JSON body of the request, the validation filter executes as part of the filter pipeline. If the `user` parameter is valid, execution passes to the endpoint handler. If the parameter is invalid, a `400 Bad Request` Problem Details response is returned containing a description of the errors, as shown in figure 7.8.

Listing 7.12   Adding validation to minimal APIs using MinimalApis.Extensions

```
using System.ComponentModel.DataAnnotations;

WebApplicationBuilder builder = WebApplication.CreateBuilder(args);
WebApplication app = builder.Build();

app.MapPost("/users", (UserModel user) => user.ToString())
    .WithParameterValidation();        ◁──── Adds the validation filter to the endpoint

app.Run();

public record UserModel        ◁────   The UserModel defines its
{                                       validation requirements using
    [Required]                          DataAnnotations attributes.
```

```
[StringLength(100)]
[Display(Name = "Your name")]
public string Name { get; set; }

[Required]
[EmailAddress]
public string Email { get; set; }
}
```

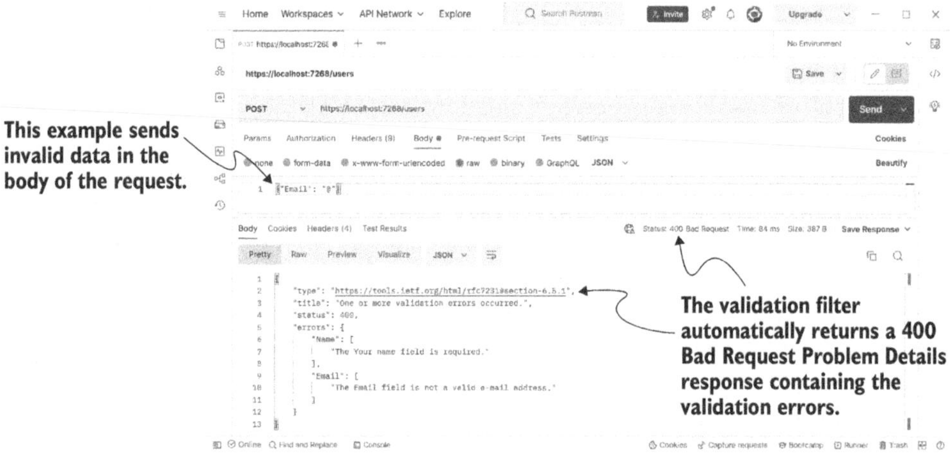

This example sends invalid data in the body of the request.

The validation filter automatically returns a 400 Bad Request Problem Details response containing the validation errors.

Figure 7.8   If the data sent in the request body is not valid, the validation filter automatically returns a 400 Bad Request response, containing the validation errors, and the endpoint handler doesn't execute.

Listing 7.12 shows how you can validate a complex type, but in some cases, you may want to validate simple types. You may want to validate that the id value in the following handler should be between 1 and 100:

```
app.MapGet("/user/{id}", (int id) => $"Received {id}")
    .WithParameterValidation();
```

Unfortunately, that's not easy to do with DataAnnotations attributes. The validation filter will check the int type, see that it's not a type that has any DataAnnotations on its properties, and won't validate it.

> **WARNING**   Adding attributes to the handler, as in ([Range(1, 100)] int id), doesn't work. The attributes here are added to the *parameter*, not to properties of the int type, so the validator won't find them.

There are several ways around this problem, but the simplest is to use the [AsParameters] attribute you saw in section 7.9 and apply annotations to the model. The following listing shows how.

Listing 7.13 Adding validation to minimal APIs using MinimalApis.Extensions

```
using System.ComponentModel.DataAnnotations;

WebApplicationBuilder builder = WebApplication.CreateBuilder(args);
WebApplication app = builder.Build();

app.MapPost("/user/{id}",
    ([AsParameters] GetUserModel model) => $"Received {model.Id}")
    .WithParameterValidation();

app.Run();

struct GetUserModel
{
    [Range(1, 10)]
    Public int Id { get; set; }
}
```

Uses [AsParameters] to create a type than can be validated

Adds the validation filter to the endpoint

Adds validation attributes to your simple types

That concludes this look at model binding in minimal APIs. You saw how the ASP.NET Core framework uses model binding to simplify the process of extracting values from a request and turning them into normal .NET objects you can work with quickly. The many ways to bind may be making your head spin, but normally, you can stick to the basics and fall back to the more complex types as and when you need them.

Although the discussion is short, the most important aspect of this chapter is its focus on validation—a common concern for all web applications. Whether you choose to use DataAnnotations or a different validation approach, you must make sure to validate any data you receive in all your endpoints.

In chapter 8 we leave minimal APIs behind to look at dependency injection in ASP.NET Core and see how it helps create loosely coupled applications. You'll learn how to register the ASP.NET Core framework services with a container, add your own services, and manage service lifetimes.

Summary

- Model binding is the process of creating the arguments for endpoint handlers from the details of an HTTP request. Model binding takes care of extracting and parsing the strings in the request so that you don't have to.
- Simple values such as int, string, and double can bind to route values, query string values, and headers. These values are common and easy to extract from the request without any manual parsing.
- If a simple value fails to bind because the value in the request is incompatible with the handler parameter, a BadHttpRequestException is thrown, and a 400 Bad Request response is returned.
- You can turn a custom type into a simple type by adding a TryParse method with the signature bool TryParse(string value, out T result). If you return false from this method, minimal APIs will return a 400 Bad Request response.

- Complex types bind to the request body by default by deserializing from JSON. Minimal APIs can bind only to JSON bodies; you can't use model binding to access form values.

- By default, you can't bind the body of GET requests, as that goes against the expectations for GET requests. Doing so will cause an exception at runtime.

- Arrays of simple types bind by default to query string values for GET requests and to the request body for POST requests. This difference can cause confusion, so always consider whether an array is the best option.

- All the parameters of a handler must bind correctly. If a parameter tries to bind to a missing value, you'll get a BadHttpRequestException and a 400 Bad Request response.

- You can use well-known types such as HttpContext and any services from the dependency injection container in your endpoint handlers. Minimal APIs check whether each complex type in your handler is registered as a service in the DI container; if not, they treat it as a complex type to bind to the request body instead.

- You can read files sent in the request by using the IFormFile and IFormFile-Collection interfaces in your endpoint handlers. Take care accepting file uploads with these interfaces, as they can open your application to attacks from users.

- You can completely customize how a type binds by using custom binding. Create a static function with the signature public static ValueTask<T?> Bind-Async(HttpContext context), and return the bound property. This approach can be useful for handling complex scenarios, such as arbitrary JSON uploads.

- You can override the default binding source for a parameter by applying [From*] attributes to your handler parameters, such as [FromHeader], [FromQuery], [FromBody], and [FromServices]. These parameters take precedence over convention-based assumptions.

- You can encapsulate an endpoint handler's parameters by creating a type containing all the parameters as properties or a constructor argument and decorate the parameter with the [AsParameters] attribute. This approach can help you simplify your endpoint's method signature.

- Validation is necessary to check for security threats. Check that data is formatted correctly, confirm that it conforms to expected values and verify that it meets your business rules.

- Minimal APIs don't have built-in validation APIs, so you typically apply validation via a minimal API filter. This approach provides flexibility, as you can implement validation in the way that suits you best, though it typically means that you need to use a third-party package.

- The MinimalApis.Extensions NuGet package provides a validation filter that uses DataAnnotations attributes to declaratively define the expected values. You can add the filter with the extension method WithParameterValidation().

- To add custom validation of simple types with MinimalApis.Extensions, you must create a containing type and use the [AsParameters] attribute.

Part 2

Building complete applications

We covered a lot of ground in part 1. We saw how an ASP.NET Core application is composed of middleware, and we focused heavily on minimal API endpoints. We saw how to use them to build JSON APIs, how to extract common code by using filters and route groups, and how to validate input data.

In part 2 we'll dive deeper into the framework, looking at a variety of components that we'll inevitably need to build more complex apps. By the end of this part, you'll be able to build dynamic applications and deploy them to multiple environments, each with a different configuration, saving data to a database.

ASP.NET Core uses dependency injection (DI) throughout its libraries, so it's important that you understand how this design pattern works. In chapter 8 I introduce DI and discuss why it's used. In chapter 9 you'll learn how to configure the services in your applications to use DI.

Chapter 10 looks at the ASP.NET Core configuration system, which lets you pass configuration values to your app from a range of sources: JSON files, environment variables, and many more. You'll learn how to configure your app to use different values depending on the environment in which it's running and how to bind strongly typed objects to your configuration to reduce runtime errors.

In chapter 11 you'll learn how to document your minimal APIs applications by using the OpenAPI specification. Adding an OpenAPI document to your application makes it easier for others to interact with your app, but it has other benefits too. You'll learn how to use Swagger UI to test your app from the browser and code generation to automatically generate strongly typed libraries for interacting with your API.

Most web applications require some sort of data storage, so in chapter 12 I'll introduce Entity Framework Core (EF Core). This cross-platform library makes it easier to connect your app to a database. EF Core is worthy of a book in and of itself, so I'll provide only a brief introduction and point you to Jon P. Smith's excellent book *Entity Framework Core in Action*, 2nd ed. (Manning, 2021). I'll also show you how to create a database and how to insert, update, and query simple data.

An introduction to
dependency injection

8

This chapter covers

- Understanding the benefits of dependency injection
- Seeing how ASP.NET Core uses dependency injection
- Retrieving services from the DI container

In part 1 of this book you saw the bare bones of how to build applications with ASP.NET Core. You learned how to compose middleware to create your application and how to create minimal API endpoints to handle HTTP requests. This part gave you the tools to start building simple API applications.

In this chapter you'll see how to use *dependency injection* (DI)—a design pattern that helps you develop loosely coupled code—in your ASP.NET Core applications. ASP.NET Core uses the pattern extensively, both internally in the framework and in the applications you build, so you'll need to use it in all but the most trivial applications.

You may have heard of DI and possibly even used it in your own applications. If so, this chapter shouldn't hold many surprises for you. If you haven't used DI, never fear; I'll make sure you're up to speed by the time the chapter is done!

173

This chapter introduces DI in general, the principles it drives, and why you should care about it. You'll see how ASP.NET Core has embraced DI throughout its implementation and why you should do the same when writing your own applications. Finally, you'll learn how to retrieve services from DI in your app.

When you finish this chapter, you'll have a solid understanding of the DI concept. In chapter 9 you'll see how to apply DI to your own classes. You'll learn how to configure your app so that the ASP.NET Core framework can create your classes for you, removing the pain of having to create new objects in your code manually. You'll learn how to control how long your objects are used and some of the pitfalls to be aware of when you write your own applications. In chapter 31 we'll look at some advanced ways to use DI, including how to wire up a third-party DI container.

For now, though, let's get back to basics. What is DI, and why should you care about it?

8.1   *Understanding the benefits of dependency injection*

This section aims to give you a basic understanding of what DI is and why you should care about it. The topic itself extends far beyond the reach of this single chapter. If you want a deeper background, I highly recommend checking out Martin Fowler's articles online. This article from 2004, for example, is a classic: http://mng.bz/pPJ8.

> **TIP** For a more directly applicable read with many examples in C#, I recommend picking up *Dependency Injection Principles, Practices, and Patterns*, by Steven van Deursen and Mark Seemann (Manning, 2019).

The ASP.NET Core framework has been designed from the ground up to be modular and to adhere to good software engineering practices. As with anything in software, what is considered to be best practice varies over time, but for object-oriented programming, the SOLID principles have held up well.

> **DEFINITION** *SOLID* is a mnemonic for "single responsibility principle, open-closed, Liskov substitution, interface segregation, and dependency inversion." This course by Steve Smith introduces the principles using C#: http://mng.bz/Ox1R.

On that basis, ASP.NET Core has DI (sometimes called *dependency inversion* or *inversion of control [IoC]*) baked into the heart of the framework. Regardless of whether you want to use DI within your own application code, the framework libraries themselves depend on it as a concept.

> **NOTE** Although related, dependency injection and dependency inversion are two different things. I cover both in a general sense in this chapter, but for a good explanation of the differences, see this post by Derick Bailey, titled "Dependency Injection Is NOT the Same As the Dependency Inversion Principle": http://mng.bz/5jvB.

When you started programming, chances are that you didn't use a DI framework immediately. That's not surprising or even a bad thing; DI adds a certain amount of extra wiring that's often not warranted in simple applications or when you're getting started. But when things start to get more complex, DI comes into its own as a great tool to help keep that complexity under control.

Let's consider a simple example, written without any sort of DI. Suppose that a user has registered on your web app, and you want to send them an email. This listing shows how you might approach this task initially, using a minimal API endpoint handler.

Listing 8.1   Sending an email without DI when there are no dependencies

```
var builder = WebApplication.CreateBuilder(args);
var app = builder.Build();

app.MapGet("/register/{username}", RegisterUser);    ◀── The endpoint is called when
                                                         a new user is created.
app.Run();                                 The RegisterUser function is
                                           the handler for the endpoint.
string RegisterUser(string username)    ◀──
{                                            Creates a new instance
    var emailSender = new EmailSender();  ◀── of EmailSender
    emailSender.SendEmail(username);   ◀──
    return $"Email sent to {username}!";      Uses the new instance to send the email
}
```

In this example, the `RegisterUser` handler executes when a new user registers on your app, creating a new instance of an `EmailSender` class and calling `SendEmail()` to send the email. The `EmailSender` class is the class that actually sends the email. For the purposes of this example, you can imagine that it looks something like this:

```
public class EmailSender
{
    public void SendEmail(string username)
    {
        Console.WriteLine($"Email sent to {username}!");
    }
}
```

`Console.WriteLine` stands in here for the real process of sending the email.

> **NOTE**   Although I'm using sending email as a simple example, in practice you may want to move this code out of your handler method. This type of asynchronous task is well suited to using message queues and a background process. For more details, see http://mng.bz/Y1AB.

If the `EmailSender` class is as simple as the previous example and has no dependencies, you may not see any need to adopt a different approach to creating objects. And to an extent, you'd be right. But what if you later update your implementation of `EmailSender` so that some of the email-sending logic is implemented by a different class?

Currently, `EmailSender` would need to do many things to send an email. It would need to

- Create an email message.
- Configure the settings of the email server.
- Send the email to the email server.

Doing all that in one class would go against the single-responsibility principle (SRP), so you'd likely end up with `EmailSender` depending on other services. Figure 8.1 shows how this web of dependencies might look. `RegisterUser` wants to send an email using `EmailSender`, but to do so, it also needs to create the `MessageFactory`, `NetworkClient`, and `EmailServerSettings` objects that `EmailSender` depends on.

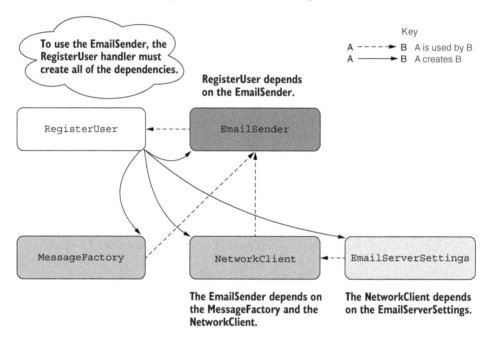

Figure 8.1   Dependency diagram without dependency injection. `RegisterUser` **indirectly depends on all the other classes, so it must create them all.**

Each class has several dependencies, so the "root" caller—in this case, the `Register-User` handler—needs to know how to create every class it depends on, as well as every class its *dependencies* depend on. This is sometimes called the *dependency graph*.

> **DEFINITION**   The *dependency graph* is the set of objects that must be created to create a specific requested "root" object.

`EmailSender` depends on the `MessageFactory` and `NetworkClient` objects, so they're provided via the constructor, as shown in the following listing.

Listing 8.2   A service with multiple dependencies

```
public class EmailSender
{
    private readonly NetworkClient _client;              Now the EmailSender depends
    private readonly MessageFactory _factory;            on two other classes.
    public EmailSender(MessageFactory factory, NetworkClient client)
    {                                                    Instances of the
        _factory = factory;                              dependencies
        _client = client;                                are provided in
    }                                                    the constructor.
    public void SendEmail(string username)
    {                                                    The EmailSender coordinates the
        var email = _factory.Create(username);           dependencies to create and send an email.
        _client.SendEmail(email);
        Console.WriteLine($"Email sent to {username}!");
    }
}
```

On top of that, the `NetworkClient` class that `EmailSender` depends on also has a dependency on an `EmailServerSettings` object:

```
public class NetworkClient
{
    private readonly EmailServerSettings _settings;
    public NetworkClient(EmailServerSettings settings)
    {
        _settings = settings;
    }
}
```

This example might feel a little contrived, but it's common to find this sort of chain of dependencies. In fact, if you *don't* have it in your code, it's probably a sign that your classes are too big and aren't following the SRP.

So how does this affect the code in `RegisterUser`? The following listing shows how you now have to send an email if you stick to `newing` up objects in the handler.

Listing 8.3   Sending email without DI when you create dependencies manually

```
string RegisterUser(string username)
{                                                    To create EmailSender, you must
    var emailSender = new EmailSender(               create all its dependencies.
        new MessageFactory(),
        new NetworkClient(                           You need a new MessageFactory.
            new EmailServerSettings
            (                                         You're already two layers
                Host: "smtp.server.com",             deep, but there could
                Port: 25                             feasibly be more.
            ))
        );
    emailSender.SendEmail(username);                 Finally, you can send the email.
    return $"Email sent to {username}!";
}
```

The NetworkClient also has dependencies.

This code is turning into something gnarly. Improving the design of `EmailSender` to separate out the responsibilities has made calling it from `RegisterUser` a real chore. This code has several problems:

- *Not obeying the SRP*—Now our code is responsible for both creating an `EmailSender` object and using it to send an email.
- *Considerable ceremony*—*Ceremony* refers to code that you have to write but that isn't adding value directly. Of the 11 lines of code in the `RegisterUser` method, only the last two are doing anything useful, which makes it harder to read and harder to understand the intent of the methods.
- *Tied to the implementation*—If you decide to refactor `EmailSender` and add another dependency, you'd need to update every place it's used. Likewise, if any dependencies are refactored, you would need to update this code too.
- *Hard to reuse instance*—In the example code we created new instances of all the objects. But what if creating a new `NetworkClient` is computationally expensive and we'd like to reuse instances? We'd have to add extra code to handle that task, further increasing the amount of boilerplate code.

`RegisterUser` has an *implicit* dependency on the `EmailSender` class, as it creates the object manually itself. The only way to know that `RegisterUser` uses `EmailSender` is to look at its source code. By contrast, `EmailSender` has *explicit* dependencies on `NetworkClient` and `MessageFactory`, which must be provided in the constructor. Similarly, `NetworkClient` has an *explicit* dependency on the `EmailServerSettings` class.

> **TIP** Generally speaking, any dependencies in your code should be explicit, not implicit. Implicit dependencies are hard to reason about and difficult to test, so you should avoid them wherever you can. DI is useful for guiding you along this path.

DI aims to solve the problem of building a dependency graph by inverting the chain of dependencies. Instead of the `RegisterUser` handler creating its dependencies manually, deep inside the implementation details of the code, an already-created instance of `EmailSender` is passed as an argument to the `RegisterUser` method.

Now, obviously *something* needs to create the object, so the code to do that has to live somewhere. The service responsible for providing the instance is called a *DI container* or an *IoC container,* as shown in figure 8.2.

> **DEFINITION** The *DI container* or *IoC container* is responsible for creating instances of services. It knows how to construct an instance of a service by creating all its dependencies and passing them to the constructor. I'll refer to it as a *DI container* throughout this book.

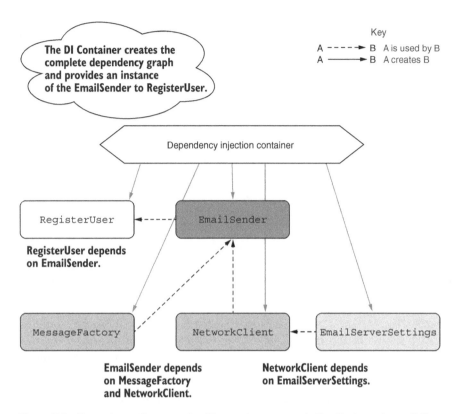

Figure 8.2 Dependency diagram using DI . `RegisterUser` **indirectly depends on all the other classes but doesn't need to know how to create them. The** `RegisterUser` **handler declares that it requires** `EmailSender`**, and the container provides it.**

The term *DI* is often used interchangeably with *IoC*. But DI is a specific version of the more general principle of IoC. In the context of ASP.NET Core,

- Without IoC, you'd write the code to listen for requests, check which handler to invoke, and then invoke it. With IoC, the control flow is the other way around. You register your handlers with the framework, but it's up to the framework to invoke your handler. Your handler is still responsible for creating its dependencies.
- DI takes IoC one step further. As well as invoking your handler, with DI, the framework creates all your handler's dependencies.

So when you use dependency injection, your `RegisterUser` handler is no longer responsible for controlling how to create an `EmailSender` instance. Instead, the framework provides an `EmailSender` to the handler directly.

NOTE Many DI containers are available for .NET, including Autofac, Lamar, Unity, Ninject, and Simple Injector, and the list goes on! In chapter 31 you'll see how to replace the default ASP.NET Core container with one of these alternatives.

The advantage of adopting this pattern becomes apparent when you see how much it simplifies using dependencies. Listing 8.4 shows how the RegisterUser handler would look if you used DI to create EmailSender instead of creating it manually. All the new noise has gone, and you can focus purely on what the endpoint handler is doing: calling EmailSender and returning a string message.

> ### Listing 8.4   Sending an email using DI to inject dependencies

```
string RegisterUser(string username, EmailSender emailSender)    ⊲──┐ Instead of
{                                                                       creating the
    emailSender.SendEmail(username);          The handler is easy to read   dependencies
    return $"Email sent to {username}!";      and understand again.     implicitly, injects
}                                                                        them directly
```

One advantage of a DI container is that it has a single responsibility: creating objects or services. The minimal API infrastructure asks the DI container for an instance of a service, and the container takes care of figuring out how to create the dependency graph, based on how you configure it.

> **NOTE** It's common to refer to services when talking about DI containers, which is slightly unfortunate, as *services* is one of the most overloaded terms in software engineering! In this context, a *service* refers to any class or interface that the DI container creates when required.

The beauty of this approach is that by using explicit dependencies, you never have to write the mess of code you saw in listing 8.3. The DI container can inspect your service's constructor and work out how to write much of the code itself. DI containers are always configurable, so if you *want* to describe how to create an instance of a service manually, you can, but by default you shouldn't need to.

> **TIP** ASP.NET Core supports constructor injection and injection into endpoint handler methods out of the box. Technically, you can inject dependencies into a service in other ways, such as by using property injection, but these techniques aren't supported by the built-in DI container.

I hope that this example made the advantages of using DI in your code apparent, but in many ways these benefits are secondary to the main benefit of using DI. In particular, DI helps keep your code loosely coupled by coding to interfaces.

8.2   *Creating loosely coupled code*

Coupling is an important concept in object-oriented programming, referring to how a given class depends on other classes to perform its function. Loosely coupled code doesn't need to know a lot of details about a particular component to use it.

The initial example of RegisterUser and EmailSender was an example of tight coupling; you were creating the EmailSender object directly and needed to know exactly how to wire it up. On top of that, the code was difficult to test. Any attempts to test RegisterUser would result in an email being sent. If you were testing the controller with a suite of unit tests, that approach would be a surefire way to get your email server blacklisted for spam!

Taking EmailSender as a parameter and removing the responsibility of creating the object helps reduce the coupling in the system. If the EmailSender implementation changes so that it has another dependency, you no longer have to update RegisterUser at the same time.

One problem that remains is that RegisterUser is still tied to an *implementation* rather than an *abstraction*. Coding to abstractions (often interfaces) is a common design pattern that helps further reduce the coupling of a system, as you're not tied to a single implementation. This pattern is particularly useful for making classes testable, as you can create stub or mock implementations of your dependencies for testing purposes, as shown in figure 8.3.

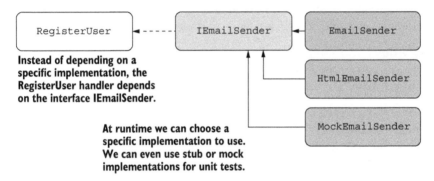

Figure 8.3 By coding to interfaces instead of an explicit implementation, you can use different IEmailSender implementations in different scenarios, such as a MockEmailSender in unit tests.

> **TIP** You can choose among many mocking frameworks. I'm most familiar with Moq, but NSubstitute and FakeItEasy are also popular options.

As an example, you might create an IEmailSender interface, which EmailSender would implement:

```
public interface IEmailSender
{
    public void SendEmail(string username);
}
```

Then RegisterUser could depend on this interface instead of the specific EmailSender implementation, as shown in the following listing, allowing you to use a different implementation during unit tests, such as a DummyEmailSender.

Listing 8.5   Using interfaces with dependency injection

```
string RegisterUser(string username, IEmailSender emailSender)
{
    emailSender.SendEmail(username);
    return $"Email sent to {username}!";
}
```

Now you depend on IEmailSender
instead of the specific EmailSender
implementation.

You don't care what the implementation is
as long as it implements IEmailSender.

The key point here is that the consuming code, RegisterUser, doesn't care how the dependency is implemented—only that it implements the IEmailSender interface and exposes a SendEmail method. Now the application code is independent of the implementation.

I hope that the principles behind DI seem to be sound. Having loosely coupled code makes it easy to change or swap out implementations. But this still leaves a question: how does the application know to use EmailSender in production instead of DummyEmailSender? The process of telling your DI container "When you need IEmailSender, use EmailSender" is called *registration*.

> **DEFINITION** You *register* services with a DI container so that it knows which implementation to use for each requested service. This registration typically takes the form "For interface X, use implementation Y."

Exactly how you register your interfaces and types with a DI container can vary depending on the specific DI container implementation, but the principles are generally the same. ASP.NET Core includes a simple DI container out of the box, so let's look at how it's used during a typical request.

8.3   *Using dependency injection in ASP.NET Core*

ASP.NET Core was designed from the outset to be modular and composable, with an almost plugin-style architecture, which is generally complemented by DI. Consequently, ASP.NET Core includes a simple DI container that all the framework libraries use to register themselves and their dependencies.

This container is used, for example, to register the minimal API infrastructure—the formatters, the Kestrel web server, and so on. It's a basic container, so it exposes only a few methods for registering services, but you have the option to replace it with a third-party DI container that gives you extra capabilities, such as autoregistration and setter injection. The DI container is built into the ASP.NET Core hosting model, as shown in figure 8.4.

The hosting model pulls dependencies from the DI container when they're needed. If the framework determines that it must invoke RegisterHandler due to the incoming URL/route, the RequestDelegateFactory responsible for creating minimal APIs asks the DI container for an IEmailSender implementation.

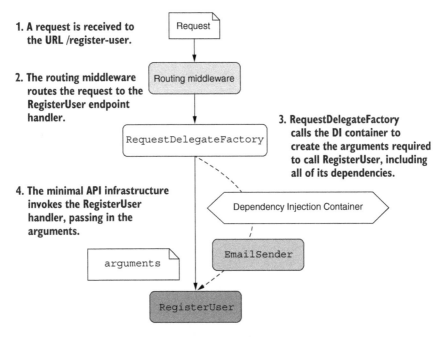

1. A request is received to the URL /register-user.

Request

2. The routing middleware routes the request to the RegisterUser endpoint handler.

Routing middleware

RequestDelegateFactory

3. RequestDelegateFactory calls the DI container to create the arguments required to call RegisterUser, including all of its dependencies.

Dependency Injection Container

4. The minimal API infrastructure invokes the RegisterUser handler, passing in the arguments.

EmailSender

arguments

RegisterUser

Figure 8.4   The ASP.NET Core hosting model uses the DI container to fulfill dependencies when creating minimal API endpoint handlers.

> **NOTE** `RequestDelegateFactory` is part of the minimal API framework that's responsible for invoking your minimal API handlers. You won't use or interact with it directly, but it's behind the scenes interacting with the DI container. I have a detailed series exploring this type on my blog at http://mng.bz/Gy6v. But be warned: this post goes into far more detail than most developers will ever need (or want)!

The DI container needs to know what to create when asked for `IEmailSender`, so you must have registered an implementation, such as `EmailSender`, with the container. When an implementation is registered, the DI container can inject it anywhere, which means that you can inject framework-related services (such as `LinkGenerator` from chapter 6) into your own custom services. It also means that you can register alternative versions of framework services and have the framework automatically use those versions in place of the defaults.

Other ASP.NET Core infrastructure, such as the Model-View-Controller (MVC) and Razor Pages frameworks (which you learn about in part 3), uses dependency injection in a similar way to minimal APIs. These frameworks use the DI container to create the dependencies required by their own handlers, such as for a Razor Page (figure 8.5).

The flexibility to choose exactly how and which components you combine in your applications is one of the selling points of DI. In section 8.4 you'll learn how to configure DI in your own ASP.NET Core application, using the default, built-in container.

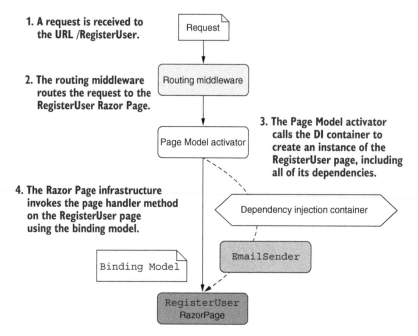

1. A request is received to the URL /RegisterUser.

Request

2. The routing middleware routes the request to the RegisterUser Razor Page.

Routing middleware

Page Model activator

3. The Page Model activator calls the DI container to create an instance of the RegisterUser page, including all of its dependencies.

4. The Razor Page infrastructure invokes the page handler method on the RegisterUser page using the binding model.

Dependency injection container

Binding Model

EmailSender

RegisterUser
RazorPage

Figure 8.5   The ASP.NET Core hosting model uses the DI container to fulfill dependencies when creating Razor Pages.

8.4   *Adding ASP.NET Core framework services to the container*

Before ASP.NET Core, using DI was optional. By contrast, to build all but the most trivial ASP.NET Core apps, some degree of DI is required. As I've mentioned, the underlying framework depends on it, so features such as Razor Pages and authentication require you to configure the required services. In this section you'll see how to register these framework services with the built-in container. In chapter 9 you'll learn how to register your *own* services with the DI container.

ASP.NET Core uses DI to configure both its internal components, such as the Kestrel web server, and extra features, such as Razor Pages. To use these components at runtime, the DI container needs to know about all the classes it will need. You register these services with the Services property on the WebApplicationBuilder instance in Program.cs.

> **NOTE** The Services property of WebApplicationBuilder is of type IService-Collection. This is where you register the collection of services that the DI container knows about.

If you're thinking "Wait—I have to configure all the internal components myself?", don't panic. Most of the core services are registered automatically by WebApplication-Builder, and you don't need to do anything else. To use other features, such as Razor Pages or authentication, you *do* need to register the components explicitly with the container in your app, but that's not as hard as it sounds. All the common libraries you use expose handy extension methods to take care of the nitty-gritty details. These extension methods configure everything you need in one fell swoop instead of leaving you to wire everything up manually.

The Razor Pages framework exposes the `AddRazorPages()` extension method, for example, which adds all the necessary framework services to your app. Invoke the extension method on the `Services` property of `WebApplicationBuilder` in Program.cs, as shown in the following listing.

> **Listing 8.6 Registering the Razor Pages services with the DI container**

```
WebApplicationBuilder builder = WebApplication.CreateBuilder(args);
builder.Services.AddRazorPages();          ◁──┐
                                              The AddRazorPages extension method adds all
                                              necessary services to the IServiceCollection.
WebApplication app = builder.Build();
app.MapRazorPages();          ◁──┐
app.Run();                        Registers all the Razor Pages in your application as endpoints
```

It's as simple as that. Under the hood, this call is registering multiple components with the DI container, using the same APIs you'll see in chapter 9 for registering your own services.

> **NOTE** Don't worry about the Razor Pages aspect of this code; you'll learn how Razor Pages work in part 3. The important point of listing 8.6 is to show how to register and enable various features in ASP.NET Core.

Most nontrivial libraries that you add to your application will have services that you need to add to the DI container. By convention, each library that has necessary services should expose an `Add*()` extension method that you can call on `WebApplication-Builder.Services`.

There's no way of knowing exactly which libraries will require you to add services to the container; it's generally a case of checking the documentation for any libraries you use. If you forget to add them, you may find that the functionality doesn't work, or you might get a handy exception in your logs, like the one shown in figure 8.6. Keep an eye out for these exceptions, and be sure to register any services you need.

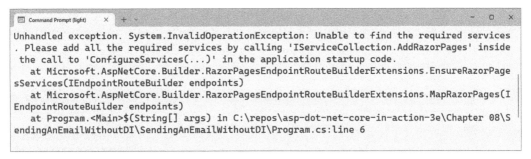

```
Unhandled exception. System.InvalidOperationException: Unable to find the required services
. Please add all the required services by calling 'IServiceCollection.AddRazorPages' inside
 the call to 'ConfigureServices(...)' in the application startup code.
   at Microsoft.AspNetCore.Builder.RazorPagesEndpointRouteBuilderExtensions.EnsureRazorPage
sServices(IEndpointRouteBuilder endpoints)
   at Microsoft.AspNetCore.Builder.RazorPagesEndpointRouteBuilderExtensions.MapRazorPages(I
EndpointRouteBuilder endpoints)
   at Program.<Main>$(String[] args) in C:\repos\asp-dot-net-core-in-action-3e\Chapter 08\S
endingAnEmailWithoutDI\SendingAnEmailWithoutDI\Program.cs:line 6
```

Figure 8.6 If you fail to call `AddRazorPages()` **in an application the uses Razor Pages, you'll get an exception when your app tries to start.**

It's also worth noting that some of the `Add*()` extension methods allow you to specify additional options when you call them, often by way of a lambda expression. You can think of these options as configuring the installation of a service into your application. The `AddRazorPages` method, for example, provides a wealth of options for fine-tuning its behavior if you want to get your hands dirty, as shown by the IntelliSense snippet in figure 8.7.

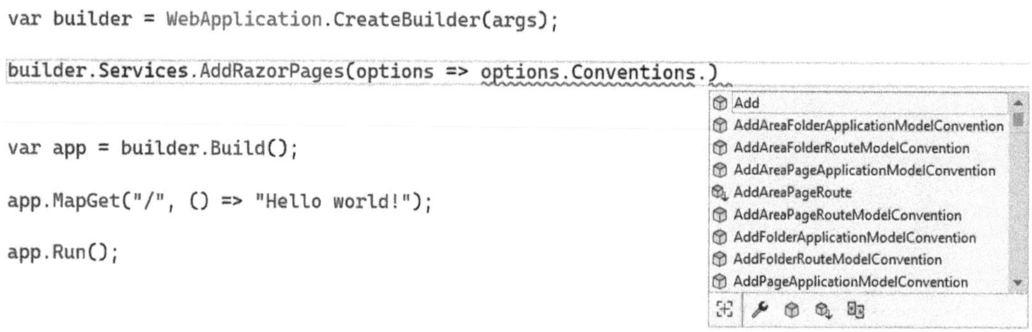

```
var builder = WebApplication.CreateBuilder(args);

builder.Services.AddRazorPages(options => options.Conventions.)
```

```
var app = builder.Build();

app.MapGet("/", () => "Hello world!");

app.Run();
```

Figure 8.7   Configuring services when adding them to the service collection. The `AddRazorPages()` function allows you to configure a wealth of the internals of the framework.

It's all very well registering services with the DI container, but the important question is how to use the container to get an instance of a registered service. In section 8.5 we look at two possible ways to access these services and discuss when you should choose one over the other.

8.5   Using services from the DI container

In a minimal API application, you have two main ways to access services from the DI container:

- Inject services into an endpoint handler.
- Access the DI container directly in Program.cs.

The first approach—injecting services into an endpoint handler—is the most common way to access the root of a dependency graph. You should use this approach in almost all cases in your minimal API applications. You can inject a service into an endpoint handler by adding it as a parameter to your endpoint handler method, as you saw in chapters 6 and 7 when you injected a `LinkGenerator` instance into your handler.

Listing 8.7   Injecting the `LinkGenerator` service in an endpoint handler

```
app.MapGet("/links", (LinkGenerator links) =>          ◁──┐   The DI container creates a
{                                                          LinkGenerator instance and
    string link = links.GetPathByName("products");         passes it as the argument to
    return $"View the product at {link}";                   the handler.
});
```

The minimal API infrastructure sees that you need an instance of the `LinkGenerator`, which is a service registered in the container, and asks the DI container to provide an instance of the service. The DI container creates a new instance of `LinkGenerator` (or reuses an existing one) and returns it to the minimal API infrastructure. Then the `Link-Generator` is passed as an argument to invoke the endpoint handler.

> **NOTE** Whether the DI container creates a new instance or reuses an existing instance depends on the lifetime used to register the service. You'll learn about lifetimes in chapter 9.

As already mentioned, the DI container creates an entire dependency graph. The `LinkGenerator` implementation registered with the DI container declares the dependencies *it* requires by having parameters in its constructor, just as the `EmailSender` type from section 8.1 declared its dependencies. When the DI container creates the `Link-Generator`, it first creates all the service's dependencies and uses them to create the final `LinkGenerator` instance.

Injecting services into your handlers is the canonical DI approach for minimal API endpoint handlers, but sometimes you need to access a service outside the context of a request. You may have lots of reasons to do this, but some of the most common relate to working with a database or logging. You may want to run some code when your app is starting to update a database's schema before the app starts handling requests, for example. If you need to access services in Program.cs outside the context of a request, you can retrieve services from the DI container directly by using the `WebApplication` `.Services` property, which exposes the container as an `IServiceProvider`.

> **NOTE** You *register* services with the `IServiceCollection` exposed on `WebApplication-cationBuilder.Services`. You *request* services with the `IServiceProvider` exposed on `WebApplication.Services`.

The `IServiceProvider` acts as a service locator, so you can request services from it directly by using `GetService()` and `GetRequiredService()`:

- `GetService<T>()`—Returns the requested service `T` if it is available in the DI container; otherwise, returns `null`
- `GetRequiredService<T>()`—Returns the requested service `T` if it is available in the DI container; otherwise, throws an `InvalidOperationException`

I generally favor `GetRequiredService` over `GetService`, as it immediately tells you whether you have a configuration problem with your DI container by throwing an exception, and you don't have to handle `null`s.

You can use either of these methods in Program.cs to retrieve a service from DI. The following listing shows how to retrieve a `LinkGenerator` from the DI container, but you can access any service registered in the DI container here.

> **Listing 8.8   Retrieving a service from the DI container using `WebApplication.Services`**

```
WebApplicationBuilder builder = WebApplication.CreateBuilder(args);
WebApplication app = builder.Build();

app.MapGet("/", () => "Hello World!");

LinkGenerator links =
    app.Services.GetRequiredService<LinkGenerator>();

app.Run();
```

Retrieves a service from the DI container using the GetRequiredService<T>() extension method

You must access services before app.Run(), as this call blocks until your app exits.

This approach, in which you call the DI container directly to ask for a class, is called the *service locator* pattern. Generally speaking, you should try to avoid this pattern in your code; include your dependencies as constructor or endpoint handler arguments directly, and let the DI container provide them for you. This pattern is the only way to access DI services in the main loop of your application in Program.cs, however, so don't worry about using it here. Still, you should absolutely avoid accessing `WebApplication.Services` from inside your endpoint handlers or other types whenever possible.

> **NOTE**   You can read about the service locator antipattern in *Dependency Injection Principles, Practices, and Patterns,* by Steven van Deursen and Mark Seemann (Manning, 2019).

In this chapter we covered some of the reasons to use DI in your applications, how to enable optional ASP.NET Core features by adding services to the DI container, and how to access services from the DI container by using injection into your endpoint handlers. In chapter 9 you'll learn about service lifetimes and how to register your own services with the DI container.

Summary

- DI is baked into the ASP.NET Core framework. You need to ensure that your application adds all the framework's dependencies for optional features in Program.cs; otherwise, you'll get exceptions at runtime when the DI container can't find the required services.
- The dependency graph is the set of objects that must be created to create a specific requested root object. The DI container creates all these dependencies for you.
- You should aim to use explicit dependencies instead of implicit dependencies in most cases. ASP.NET Core uses constructor arguments and endpoint handler arguments to declare explicit dependencies.
- When discussing DI, the term *service* is used to describe any class or interface registered with the container.

- You register services with the DI container so that the container knows which implementation to use for each requested service. This registration typically takes the form "For interface X, use implementation Y."
- You must register services with the container by calling `Add*` extension methods on the `IServiceCollection` exposed as `WebApplicationBuilder.Services` in Program.cs. If you forget to register a service that's used by the framework or in your own code, you'll get an `InvalidOperationException` at runtime.
- You can retrieve services from the DI container in your endpoint handlers by adding a parameter of the required type.
- You can retrieve services from the DI container in Program.cs via the service locator pattern by calling `GetService<T>()` or `GetRequiredService<T>()` on the `IServiceProvider` exposed as `WebApplication.Services`. Service location is generally considered to be an antipattern; generally, you shouldn't use it inside your handler methods, but it's fine to use it directly inside Program.cs.
- `GetService<T>()` returns `null` if the requested service isn't registered with the DI container. By contrast, `GetRequiredService<T>()` throws an `InvalidOperationException`.

Registering services with dependency injection

This chapter covers

- Configuring your services to work with dependency injection
- Choosing the correct lifetime for your services

In chapter 8 you learned about dependency injection (DI) in general, why it's useful as a pattern for developing loosely coupled code, and its central place in ASP.NET Core. In this chapter you'll build on that knowledge to apply DI to your own classes.

You'll start by learning how to configure your app so that the ASP.NET Core framework can create your classes for you, removing the pain of having to create new objects manually in your code. We look at the various patterns you can use to register your services and some of the limitations of the built-in DI container.

Next, you'll learn how to handle multiple implementations of a service. You'll learn how to inject multiple versions of a service, how to override a default service registration, and how to register a service conditionally if you don't know whether it's already registered.

In section 9.4 we look at how you can control for how long your objects are used—that is, their lifetime. We explore the differences among the three lifetime options and some of the pitfalls to be aware of when you come to write your own applications. Finally, in section 9.5 you'll learn why lifetimes are important when resolving services outside the context of an HTTP request.

We'll start by revisiting the EmailSender service from chapter 8 to see how you could register the dependency graph in your DI container.

9.1   Registering custom services with the DI container

In this section you'll learn how to register your own services with the DI container. We'll explore the difference between a service and an implementation, and learn how to register the EmailSender hierarchy introduced in chapter 8.

In chapter 8 I described a system for sending emails when a new user registers in your application. Initially, the minimal API endpoint handler RegisterUser created an instance of EmailSender manually, using code similar to the following listing (which you saw in chapter 8).

> **Listing 9.1   Creating an `EmailSender` instance without dependency injection**

```
WebApplicationBuilder builder = WebApplication.CreateBuilder(args);
WebApplication app = builder.Build();

app.MapGet("/register/{username}", RegisterUser);        ⟵ The endpoint is called when
                                                            a new user is created.
app.Run();

string RegisterUser(string username)                        To create EmailSender,
{                                                           you must create all its
    IEmailSender emailSender = new EmailSender(      ⟵     dependencies.
        new MessageFactory(),              ⟵
        new NetworkClient(                      You need a new MessageFactory.
            new EmailServerSettings
            (                                   You're already two layers
                Host: "smtp.server.com",        deep, but there could
                Port: 25                        feasibly be more.
            ))
        );
    emailSender.SendEmail(username);     ⟵ Finally, you can send the email.
    return $"Email sent to {username}!";
}
```

The NetworkClient also has dependencies.

We subsequently refactored this code to inject an instance of IEmailSender into the handler instead, as shown in listing 9.2. The IEmailSender interface decouples the endpoint handler from the EmailSender implementation, making it easier to change the implementation of EmailSender (or replace it) without having to rewrite RegisterUser.

Listing 9.2   Using `IEmailSender` with dependency injection in an endpoint handler

```
WebApplicationBuilder builder = WebApplication.CreateBuilder(args);
WebApplication app = builder.Build();

app.MapGet("/register/{username}", RegisterUser);
```
⟵ **The endpoint is called when a new user is created.**

```
app.Run();
```

```
string RegisterUser(string username, IEmailSender emailSender)
{
    emailSender.SendEmail(username);
    return $"Email sent to {username}!";
}
```
⟵ **The IEmailSender is injected into the handler using DI.**

`emailSender.SendEmail(username);` ⟵ **The handler uses the IEmailSender instance.**

The final step in making the refactoring work is configuring your services with the DI container. This configuration lets the DI container know what to use when it needs to fulfill the `IEmailSender` dependency. If you don't register your services, you'll get an exception at runtime, like the one in figure 9.1. This exception describes a model-binding problem; the minimal API infrastructure tries to bind the `emailSender` parameter to the request body because `IEmailSender` isn't a known service in the DI container.

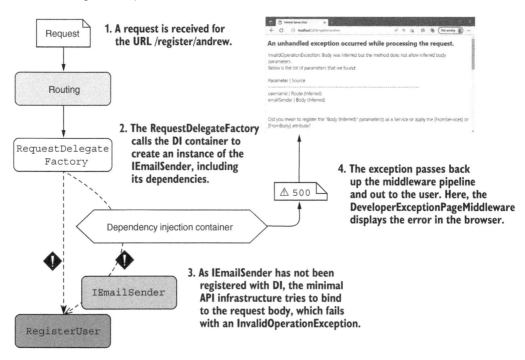

Figure 9.1   If you don't register all your required dependencies with the DI container, you'll get an exception at runtime, telling you which service wasn't registered.

To configure the application completely, you need to register an IEmailSender imple-mentation and all its dependencies with the DI container, as shown in figure 9.2.

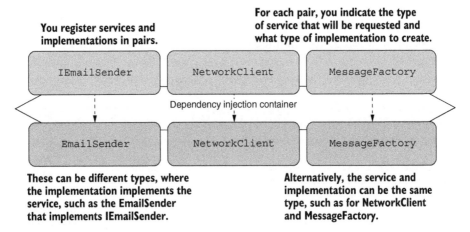

You register services and implementations in pairs.

For each pair, you indicate the type of service that will be requested and what type of implementation to create.

IEmailSender   NetworkClient   MessageFactory

Dependency injection container

EmailSender   NetworkClient   MessageFactory

These can be different types, where the implementation implements the service, such as the EmailSender that implements IEmailSender.

Alternatively, the service and implementation can be the same type, such as for NetworkClient and MessageFactory.

Figure 9.2   Configuring the DI container in your application involves telling it what type to use when a given service is requested, such as "Use EmailSender when IEmailSender is required."

Configuring DI consists of making a series of statements about the services in your app, such as the following:

- When a service requires IEmailSender, use an instance of EmailSender.
- When a service requires NetworkClient, use an instance of NetworkClient.
- When a service requires MessageFactory, use an instance of MessageFactory.

NOTE   You'll also need to register the EmailServerSettings object with the DI container. We'll do that slightly differently in section 9.2.

These statements are made by calling various Add* methods on the IServiceCollection exposed as the WebApplicationBuilder.Services property. Each Add* method provides three pieces of information to the DI container:

- *Service type*—TService. This class or interface will be requested as a dependency. It's often an interface, such as IEmailSender, but sometimes a concrete type, such as NetworkClient or MessageFactory.
- *Implementation type*—TService or TImplementation. The container should create this class to fulfill the dependency. It must be a concrete type, such as EmailSender. It may be the same as the service type, as for NetworkClient and MessageFactory.
- *Lifetime—transient, singleton, or scoped.* The lifetime defines how long an instance of the service should be used by the DI container. I discuss lifetimes in detail in section 9.4.

> **DEFINITION**   A *concrete type* is a type that can be created, such as a standard `class` or `struct`. It contrasts with a type such as an `interface` or an `abstract class`, which can't be created directly.

Listing 9.3 shows how you can configure `EmailSender` and its dependencies in your application by using three methods: `AddScoped<TService>`, `AddSingleton<TService>`, and `AddScoped<TService, TImplementation>`. This code tells the DI container how to create each of the `TService` instances when they're required and which lifetime to use.

Listing 9.3   Registering services with the DI container

```
WebApplicationBuilder builder = WebApplication.CreateBuilder(args);

builder.Services.AddScoped<IEmailSender, EmailSender>();      ◁——  Whenever you require
builder.Services.AddScoped<NetworkClient>();     ◁——                an IEmailSender, use
builder.Services.AddSingleton<MessageFactory>();  ◁——               EmailSender.

WebApplication app = builder.Build();                              Whenever you require
                                                                  a NetworkClient, use
app.MapGet("/register/{username}", RegisterUser);                 NetworkClient.

app.Run();                                                        Whenever you require
                                                                  a MessageFactory, use
string RegisterUser(string username, IEmailSender emailSender)    MessageFactory.
{
    emailSender.SendEmail(username);
    return $"Email sent to {username}!";
}
```

That's all there is to DI! It may seem a little bit like magic, but you're simply giving the container instructions for making all the parts. You give it a recipe for cooking the chili, shredding the lettuce, and grating the cheese, so when you ask for a burrito, it can put all the parts together and hand you your meal!

> **NOTE**   Under the hood, the built-in ASP.NET Core DI container uses optimized reflection to create dependencies, but different DI containers may use other approaches. The `Add*` APIs are the only way to register dependencies with the built-in container; there's no support for using external configuration files to configure the container, for example.

The service type and implementation type are the same for `NetworkClient` and `MessageFactory`, so there's no need to specify the same type twice in the `AddScoped` method—hence, the slightly simpler signature.

> **NOTE**   The `EmailSender` instance is registered only as an `IEmailSender`, so you can't resolve it by requesting the specific `EmailSender` implementation; you must use the `IEmailSender` interface.

These generic methods aren't the only ways to register services with the container. You can also provide objects directly or by using lambdas, as you'll see in section 9.2.

9.2 Registering services using objects and lambdas

As I mentioned in section 9.1, I didn't quite register all the services required by `EmailSender`. In the previous examples, `NetworkClient` depends on `EmailServer-Settings`, which you'll also need to register with the DI container for your project to run without exceptions.

I avoided registering this object in the preceding example because you have to take a slightly different approach. The preceding `Add*` methods use generics to specify the `Type` of the class to register, but they don't give any indication of *how* to construct an instance of that type. Instead, the container makes several assumptions that you have to adhere to:

- The class must be a concrete type.
- The class must have only a single relevant constructor that the container can use.
- For a constructor to be relevant, all constructor arguments must be registered with the container or must be arguments with a default value.

> **NOTE** These limitations apply to the simple built-in DI container. If you choose to use a third-party container in your app, it may have a different set of limitations.

The `EmailServerSettings` record doesn't meet these requirements, as it requires you to provide a `Host` and `Port` in the constructor, which are a `string` and `int`, respectively, without default values:

```
public record EmailServerSettings(string Host, int Port);
```

You can't register these primitive types in the container. It would be weird to say "For every `string` constructor argument, in any type, use the `"smtp.server.com"` value."

Instead, you can create an instance of the `EmailServerSettings` object yourself and provide that to the container, as shown in the following listing. The container uses the preconstructed object whenever an instance of the `EmailServerSettings` object is required.

Listing 9.4   Providing an object instance when registering services

```
WebApplicationBuilder builder = WebApplication.CreateBuilder(args);

builder.Services.AddScoped<IEmailSender, EmailSender>();
builder.Services.AddScoped<NetworkClient>();
builder.Services.AddSingleton<MessageFactory>();
builder.Services.AddSingleton(
```

```
new EmailServerSettings
(
        Host: "smtp.server.com",
        Port: 25
));
```

| This instance of EmailServerSettings will be used whenever an instance is required.

```
WebApplication app = builder.Build();

app.MapGet("/register/{username}", RegisterUser);

app.Run();
```

This code works fine if you want to have only a single instance of `EmailServerSettings` in your application; the same object will be shared everywhere. But what if you want to create a *new* object each time one is requested?

> **NOTE** When the same object is used whenever it's requested, it's known as a *singleton*. If you create an object and pass it to the container, it's always registered as a singleton. You can also register any class using the `AddSingleton<T>()` method, and the container will use only one instance throughout your application. I discuss singletons and other lifetimes in detail in section 9.4. The lifetime is how long the DI container should use a given object to fulfill a service's dependencies.

Instead of providing a single instance that the container will always use, you can provide a function that the container invokes when it needs an instance of the type, as shown in figure 9.3.

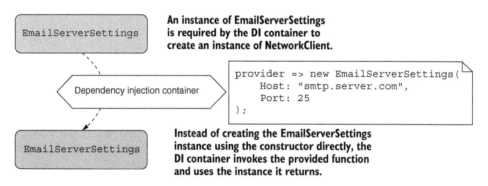

Figure 9.3 You can register a function with the DI container that will be invoked whenever a new instance of a service is required.

> **NOTE** Figure 9.3 is an example of the factory pattern, in which you define how a type is created. Note that the factory functions must be synchronous; you can't create types asynchronously by (for example) using `async`.

The easiest way to register a service using the factory pattern is with a lambda function (an anonymous delegate), in which the container creates a new `EmailServerSettings` object whenever it's needed, as shown in the following listing.

Listing 9.5   Using a lambda factory function to register a dependency

```
WebApplicationBuilder builder = WebApplication.CreateBuilder(args);

builder.Services.AddScoped<IEmailSender, EmailSender>();
builder.Services.AddScoped<NetworkClient>();
builder.Services.AddSingleton<MessageFactory>();
builder.Services.AddScoped(
    provider =>
        new EmailServerSettings
        (
            Host: "smtp.server.com",
            Port: 25
        ));

WebApplication app = builder.Build();

app.MapGet("/register/{username}", RegisterUser);

app.Run();
```

Because you're providing a function to create the object, you aren't restricted to a singleton.

The lambda is provided an instance of IServiceProvider.

The constructor is called every time an EmailServerSettings object is required instead of only once.

In this example, I changed the lifetime of the created `EmailServerSettings` object to scoped instead of singleton and provided a factory lambda function that returns a new `EmailServerSettings` object. Every time the container requires a new `EmailServer-Settings`, it executes the function and uses the new object it returns.

When you use a lambda to register your services, you're given an `IServiceProvider` instance at runtime, called `provider` in listing 9.5. This instance is the public API of the DI container itself, which exposes the `GetService<T>()` and `GetRequiredService<T>()` extension methods you saw in chapter 8. If you need to obtain dependencies to create an instance of your service, you can reach into the container at runtime in this way, but you should avoid doing so if possible.

> **TIP** Avoid calling `GetService<T>()` and `GetRequiredService<T>()` in your factory functions if possible. Instead, favor constructor injection; it's more performant and simpler to reason about.

Open generics and dependency injection

As already mentioned, you couldn't use the generic registration methods with `EmailServerSettings` because it uses primitive dependencies (in this case, `string` and `int`) in its constructor. Neither can you use the generic registration methods to register open generics.

> **(continued)**
>
> *Open generics* are types that contain a generic type parameter, such as `Repository <T>`. You normally use this sort of type to define a base behavior that you can use with multiple generic types. In the `Repository<T>` example, you might inject `IRepository <Customer>` into your services, which should inject an instance of `DbRepository <Customer>`, for example.
>
> To register these types, you must use a different overload of the `Add*` methods, as in this example:
>
> `builder.Services.AddScoped(typeof(IRespository<>), typeof(DbRepository<>));`
>
> This code ensures that whenever a service constructor requires `IRespository<T>`, the container injects an instance of `DbRepository<T>`.

At this point, all your dependencies are registered. But your Program.cs is starting to look a little messy, isn't it? The choice is entirely down to personal preference, but I like to group my services into logical collections and create extension methods for them, as in listing 9.6. This approach creates an equivalent to the framework's `AddRazorPages()` extension method—a nice, simple registration API. As you add more features to your app, I think you'll appreciate it too.

Listing 9.6 Creating an extension method to tidy up adding multiple services

```
public static class EmailSenderServiceCollectionExtensions      Creates an
{                                                                extension method on
    public static IServiceCollection AddEmailSender(            IServiceCollection by
        this IServiceCollection services)         ◁──────────  using the "this" keyword
    {
        services.AddScoped<IEmailSender, EmailSender>();
        services.AddSingleton<NetworkClient>();
        services.AddScoped<MessageFactory>();
        services.AddSingleton(                                   Cuts and pastes your
            new EmailServerSettings                              registration code from
            (                                                    Program.cs
                host: "smtp.server.com",
                port: 25
            ));
        return services;      ◁────  By convention, returns the
    }                                IServiceCollection to allow method chaining
}
```

With the preceding extension method created, the following listing shows that your startup code is much easier to grok!

Listing 9.7 Using an extension method to register your services

```
WebApplicationBuilder builder = WebApplication.CreateBuilder(args);

builder.Services.AddEmailSender();     ◁────  The extension method registers all the
                                              services associated with the EmailSender.
```

```
WebApplication app = builder.Build();

app.MapGet("/register/{username}", RegisterUser);

app.Run();
```

So far, you've seen how to register the simple DI cases in which you have a single implementation of a service. In some scenarios, you may have multiple implementations of an interface. In section 9.3 you'll see how to register these with the container to match your requirements.

9.3 Registering a service in the container multiple times

One advantage of coding to interfaces is that you can create multiple implementations of a service. Suppose that you want to create a more generalized version of IEmailSender so that you can send messages via Short Message Service (SMS) or Facebook, as well as by email. You create the interface for it as follows,

```
public interface IMessageSender
{
    public void SendMessage(string message);
}
```

as well as several implementations: EmailSender, SmsSender, and FacebookSender. But how do you register these implementations in the container? And how can you inject these implementations into your RegisterUser handler? The answers vary slightly, depending on whether you want to use all the implementations in your consumer or only one.

9.3.1 Injecting multiple implementations of an interface

Suppose that you want to send a message using each of the IMessageSender implementations whenever a new user registers so that they get an email, an SMS text, and a Facebook message, as shown in figure 9.4.

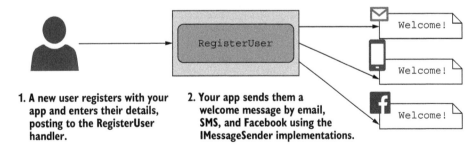

1. A new user registers with your app and enters their details, posting to the RegisterUser handler.

2. Your app sends them a welcome message by email, SMS, and Facebook using the IMessageSender implementations.

Figure 9.4   When a user registers with your application, they call the RegisterUser handler. This handler sends them an email, an SMS text, and a Facebook message using the IMessageSender classes.

The easiest way to achieve this goal is to register all the service implementations in your DI container and have it inject one of each type into the `RegisterUser` endpoint handler. Then `RegisterUser` can use a simple `foreach` loop to call `SendMessage()` on each implementation, as shown in figure 9.5.

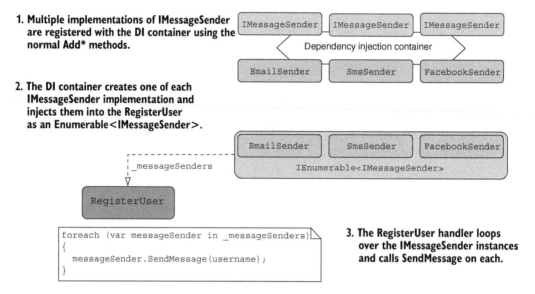

1. Multiple implementations of IMessageSender are registered with the DI container using the normal Add* methods.

2. The DI container creates one of each IMessageSender implementation and injects them into the RegisterUser as an Enumerable<IMessageSender>.

3. The RegisterUser handler loops over the IMessageSender instances and calls SendMessage on each.

```
foreach (var messageSender in _messageSenders)
{
    messageSender.SendMessage(username);
}
```

Figure 9.5   You can register multiple implementations of a service with the DI container, such as `IEmailSender` in this example. You can retrieve an instance of each of these implementations by requiring `IEnumerable<IMessageSender>` in the `RegisterUser` handler.

You register multiple implementations of the same service with a DI container in exactly the same way as for single implementations, using the `Add*` extension methods as in this example:

```
WebApplicationBuilder builder = WebApplication.CreateBuilder(args);
builder.Services.AddScoped<IMessageSender, EmailSender>();
builder.Services.AddScoped<IMessageSender, SmsSender>();
builder.Services.AddScoped<IMessageSender, FacebookSender>();
```

Then you can inject `IEnumerable<IMessageSender>` into `RegisterUser`, as shown in listing 9.8. The container injects an array of `IMessageSender` containing one of each of the implementations you have registered, in the same order as you registered them. Then you can use a standard `foreach` loop and call `SendMessage` on each implementation.

Listing 9.8   Injecting multiple implementations of a service into an endpoint

```
string RegisterUser(
    string username,
    IEnumerable<IMessageSender> senders)      Requests an IEnumerable injects
{                                             an array of IMessageSender
```

```
    foreach(var sender in senders)
    {
        Sender.SendMessage($"Hello {username}!");
    }

    return $"Welcome message sent to {username}";
}
```

> **Each IMessageSender in the IEnumerable is a different implementation.**

> **WARNING** You must use `IEnumerable<T>` as the handler parameter type to inject all the registered types of a service, `T`. Even though this parameter will be injected as a `T[]` array, you can't use `T[]` or `ICollection<T>` as your constructor argument. Doing so will cause an `InvalidOperationException`, similar to that in figure 9.1.

It's simple enough to inject all the registered implementations of a service, but what if you need only one? How does the container know which one to use?

9.3.2 Injecting a single implementation when multiple services are registered

Suppose that you've already registered all the `IMessageSender` implementations. What happens if you have a service that requires only one of them? Consider this example:

```
public class SingleMessageSender
{
    private readonly IMessageSender _messageSender;
    public SingleMessageSender(IMessageSender messageSender)
    {
        _messageSender = messageSender;
    }
}
```

Of the three implementations available, the container needs to pick a single `IMessage-Sender` to inject into this service. It does this by using the last registered implementation: `FacebookSender` from the previous example.

> **NOTE** The DI container will use the last registered implementation of a service when resolving a single instance of the service.

This feature can be particularly useful for replacing built-in DI registrations with your own services. If you have a custom implementation of a service that you know is registered within a library's `Add*` extension method, you can override that registration by registering your own implementation afterward. The DI container will use your implementation whenever a single instance of the service is requested.

The main disadvantage of this approach is that you still end up with multiple implementations registered; you can inject an `IEnumerable<T>` as before. Sometimes you want to register a service conditionally so that you always have only a single registered implementation.

9.3.3 Conditionally registering services using TryAdd

Sometimes you want to add an implementation of a service only if one hasn't already been added. This approach is particularly useful for library authors; they can create a default implementation of an interface and register it only if the user hasn't already registered their own implementation.

You can find several extension methods for conditional registration in the `Micro-soft.Extensions.DependencyInjection.Extensions` namespace, such as `TryAddScoped`. This method checks whether a service has been registered with the container before calling `AddScoped` on the implementation. Listing 9.9 shows how you can add `SmsSender` conditionally if there are no existing `IMessageSender` implementations. As you initially register `EmailSender`, the container ignores the `SmsSender` registration, so it isn't available in your app.

> **Listing 9.9   Conditionally adding a service using `TryAddScoped`**

```
WebApplicationBuilder builder = WebApplication.CreateBuilder(args);    EmailSender is
                                                                       registered with
builder.Services.AddScoped<IMessageSender, EmailSender>();    ◁───     the container.
builder.Services.TryAddScoped<IMessageSender, SmsSender>();
```
There's already an IMessageSender implementation,
so SmsSender isn't registered.

Code like this doesn't often make a lot of sense at the application level, but it can be useful if you're building libraries for use in multiple apps. The ASP.NET Core framework, for example, uses `TryAdd*` in many places, which lets you easily register alternative implementations of internal components in your own application if you want.

You can also replace a previously registered implementation by using the `Replace()` extension method. Unfortunately, the API for this method isn't as friendly as the `TryAdd` methods. To replace a previously registered `IMessageSender` with `SmsSender`, you'd use

```
builder.Services.Replace(new ServiceDescriptor(
    typeof(IMessageSender), typeof(SmsSender), ServiceLifetime.Scoped
));
```

> **TIP**   When using `Replace`, you must provide the same lifetime that was used to register the service that's being replaced.

We've pretty much covered registering dependencies but touched only vaguely on one important aspect: lifetimes. Understanding lifetimes is crucial in working with DI containers, so it's important to pay close attention to them when registering your services with the container.

9.4   *Understanding lifetimes: When are services created?*

Whenever the DI container is asked for a particular registered service, such as an instance of `IMessageSender`, it can do either of two things to fulfill the request:

- Create and return a new instance of the service.
- Return an existing instance of the service.

The *lifetime* of a service controls the behavior of the DI container with respect to these two options. You define the lifetime of a service during DI service registration. The lifetime dictates when a DI container reuses an existing instance of the service to fulfill service dependencies and when it creates a new one.

> **DEFINITION**   The *lifetime* of a service is how long an instance of a service should live in a container before the container creates a new instance.

It's important to get your head around the implications for the different lifetimes used in ASP.NET Core, so this section looks at each lifetime option and when you should use it. In particular, you'll see how the lifetime affects how often the DI container creates new objects. In section 9.4.4 I'll show you an antipattern of lifetimes to watch out for, in which a short-lifetime dependency is captured by a long-lifetime dependency. This antipattern can cause some hard-to-debug issues, so it's important to bear in mind when configuring your app.

In ASP.NET Core, you can specify one of three lifetimes when registering a service with the built-in container:

- *Transient*—Every time a service is requested, a new instance is created. Potentially, you can have different instances of the same class within the same dependency graph.
- *Scoped*—Within a scope, all requests for a service give you the same object. For different scopes, you get different objects. In ASP.NET Core, each web request gets its own scope.
- *Singleton*—You always get the same instance of the service, regardless of scope.

> **NOTE**   These concepts align well with most other DI containers, but the terminology may differ. If you're familiar with a third-party DI container, be sure you understand how the lifetime concepts align with the built-in ASP.NET Core DI container.

To illustrate the behavior of each lifetime, I use a simple example in this section. Suppose that you have DataContext, which has a connection to a database, as shown in listing 9.10. It has a single property, RowCount, which represents the number of rows in the Users table of a database. For the purposes of this example, we emulate calling the database by setting the number of rows randomly when the DataContext object is created, so you always get the same value every time you call RowCount on a given DataContext instance. Different instances of DataContext return different RowCount values.

Listing 9.10   `DataContext` generating a random `RowCount` on creation

```
class DataContext
{
    public int RowCount { get; }                    ⬅ The property is read-only, so it
        = Random.Shared.Next(1, 1_000_000_000);       always returns the same value.
}
```
Generates a random number between 1 and 1,000,000,000

You also have a `Repository` class that has a dependency on the `DataContext`, as shown in the next listing. It also exposes a `RowCount` property, but this property delegates the call to its instance of `DataContext`. Whatever value `DataContext` was created with, the `Repository` displays the same value.

> **Listing 9.11   Repository service that depends on an instance of `DataContext`**

```
public class Repository
{
    private readonly DataContext _dataContext;
    public Repository(DataContext dataContext)
    {
        _dataContext = dataContext;
    }
    public int RowCount => _dataContext.RowCount;
}
```

An instance of DataContext is provided using DI.

RowCount returns the same value as the current instance of DataContext.

Finally, you have your endpoint handler, `RowCounts`, which takes a dependency on both `Repository` and on `DataContext` directly. When the minimal API infrastructure creates the arguments needed to call `RowCounts`, the DI container injects an instance of `DataContext` and an instance of `Repository`. To create `Repository`, it must create a second instance of `DataContext`. Over the course of two requests, four instances of `DataContext` will be required, as shown in figure 9.6.

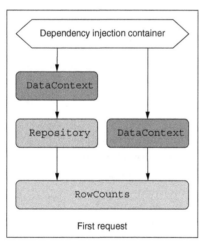
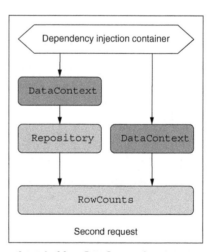

For each request, two instances of
DataContext are required to call
the RowCounts handler.

A total of four DataContext instances
are required for two requests.

Figure 9.6   The DI container uses two instances of `DataContext` for each request. Depending on the lifetime with which the `DataContext` type is registered, the container might create one, two, or four instances of `DataContext`.

The RowCounts handler retrieves the value of RowCount returned from both Repository and DataContext and then returns them as a string, similar to the code in listing 9.12. The sample code associated with this book also records and displays the values from previous requests so you can easily track how the values change with each request.

> **Listing 9.12 The RowCounts handler depends on DataContext and Repository**

```
static string RowCounts(          DataContext and
    DataContext db,               Repository are
    Repository repository)        created using DI.
{
    int dbCount = db.RowCount;
    int repositoryCount = repository.RowCount;

    return: $"DataContext: {dbCount}, Repository: {repositoryCount}";
}
```

When invoked, the page handler retrieves and records RowCount from both dependencies.

The counts are returned in the response.

The purpose of this example is to explore the relationships among the four DataContext instances, depending on the lifetimes you use to register the services with the container. I'm generating a random number in DataContext as a way of uniquely identifying a DataContext instance, but you can think of this example as being a point-in-time snapshot of, say, the number of users logged on to your site or the amount of stock in a warehouse.

I'll start with the shortest-lived lifetime (transient), move on to the common scoped lifetime, and then take a look at singletons. Finally, I'll show an important trap you should be on the lookout for when registering services in your own apps.

9.4.1 *Transient: Everyone is unique*

In the ASP.NET Core DI container, transient services are always created new whenever they're needed to fulfill a dependency. You can register your services using the AddTransient extension methods:

```
builder.Services.AddTransient<DataContext>();
builder.Services.AddTransient<Repository>();
```

When you register services this way, every time a dependency is required, the container creates a new one. This behavior of the container for transient services applies both between requests and within requests; the DataContext injected into the Repository will be a different instance from the one injected into the RowCounts handler.

> **NOTE** Transient dependencies can result in different instances of the same type within a single dependency graph.

Figure 9.7 shows the results you get from calling the API repeatedly when you use the transient lifetime for both services. You can see that every value is different, both within a request and between requests. Note that figure 9.7 was generated using the source code for this chapter, which is based on the listings in this chapter, but also displays the results from previous requests to make the behavior easier to observe.

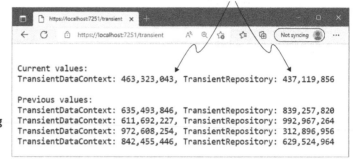

The RowCount is different within a single request, indicating that two different DataContexts are created.

The RowCount changes with each request, indicating that new DataContexts are created for every request.

Figure 9.7   When registered using the transient lifetime, all `DataContext` objects are different, as you see by the fact that all the values are different within and between requests.

Transient lifetimes can result in the creation of a lot of objects, so they make the most sense for lightweight services with little or no state. Using the transient lifetime is equivalent to calling `new` every time you need a new object, so bear that in mind when using it. You probably won't use the transient lifetime often; the majority of your services will probably be scoped instead.

9.4.2   *Scoped: Let's stick together*

The *scoped* lifetime states that a single instance of an object will be used within a given scope, but a different instance will be used between different scopes. In ASP.NET Core, a scope maps to a request, so within a single request, the container will use the same object to fulfill all dependencies.

In the row-count example, within a single request (a single scope) the same `Data-Context` is used throughout the dependency graph. The `DataContext` injected into the `Repository` is the same instance as the one injected into the `RowCounts` handler.

In the next request, you're in a different scope, so the container creates a new instance of `DataContext`, as shown in figure 9.8. A different instance means a different `RowCount` for each request, as you can see. As before, figure 9.8 also shows the counts for previous requests.

You can register dependencies as scoped by using the `AddScoped` extension methods. In this example, I registered `DataContext` as scoped and left `Repository` as transient, but you'd get the same results in this case if both were scoped:

```
builder.Services.AddScoped<DataContext>();
```

Due to the nature of web requests, you'll often find services registered as scoped dependencies in ASP.NET Core. Database contexts and authentication services are common examples of services that should be scoped to a request—anything that you

The RowCount is the same
within a single request, indicating
that a single DataContext is
used in the dependency graph.

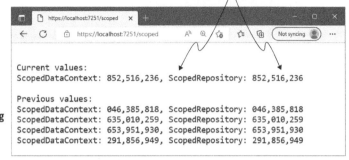

The RowCount changes
with each request, indicating
that a new DataContext is
created for every request.

Figure 9.8   Scoped dependencies use the same instance of `DataContext` **within a single request but a new instance for a separate request. Consequently, the** `RowCounts` **are identical within a request.**

want to share across your services within a single request but that needs to change between requests.

> **NOTE** If your scoped or transient services implement IDisposable, the DI container automatically disposes them when the scope ends.

Generally speaking, you'll find a lot of services registered using the scoped lifetime—especially anything that uses a database, anything that's dependent on details of the HTTP request, or anything that uses a scoped service. But some services don't need to change between requests, such as a service that calculates the area of a circle or returns the current time in different time zones. For these services, a singleton lifetime might be more appropriate.

9.4.3   Singleton: There can be only one

The *singleton* is a pattern that came before DI; the DI container provides a robust and easy-to-use implementation of it. The singleton is conceptually simple: an instance of the service is created when it's first needed (or during registration, as in section 9.2), and that's it. You'll always get the same instance injected into your services.

The singleton pattern is particularly useful for objects that are expensive to create, contain data that must be shared across requests, or don't hold state. The latter two points are important: any service registered as a singleton should be thread-safe.

> **WARNING** Singleton services must be thread-safe in a web application, as they'll typically be used by multiple threads during concurrent requests.

Let's consider what using singletons means for the row-count example. We can update the registration of `DataContext` to be a singleton:

```
builder.Services.AddSingleton<DataContext>();
```

Then we can call the RowCounts handler and observe the results in figure 9.9. We can see that every instance has returned the same value, indicating that the same instance of DataContext is used in every request, both when injected directly into the endpoint handler and when referenced transitively by Repository.

The RowCount is the same within a single request, indicating that a single DataContext is used in the dependency graph.

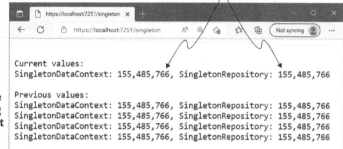

The RowCount is the same for all requests, indicating that the same DataContext is used for every request.

```
Current values:
SingletonDataContext: 155,485,766, SingletonRepository: 155,485,766

Previous values:
SingletonDataContext: 155,485,766, SingletonRepository: 155,485,766
SingletonDataContext: 155,485,766, SingletonRepository: 155,485,766
SingletonDataContext: 155,485,766, SingletonRepository: 155,485,766
SingletonDataContext: 155,485,766, SingletonRepository: 155,485,766
```

Figure 9.9   Any service registered as a singleton always returns the same instance. Consequently, all the calls to the RowCounts handler return the same value, both within a request and between requests.

Singletons are convenient for objects that need to be shared or that are immutable and expensive to create. A caching service should be a singleton, as all requests need to share the service. It must be thread-safe, though. Similarly, you might register a settings object loaded from a remote server as a singleton if you load the settings once at startup and reuse them through the lifetime of your app.

On the face of it, choosing a lifetime for a service may not seem to be too tricky. But an important gotcha can come back to bite you in subtle ways, as you'll see in section 9.4.4.

9.4.4   *Keeping an eye out for captive dependencies*

Suppose that you're configuring the lifetime for the DataContext and Repository examples. You think about the suggestions I've provided and decide on the following lifetimes:

- DataContext—Scoped, as it should be shared for a single request
- Repository—Singleton, as it has no state of its own and is thread-safe, so why not?

WARNING   This lifetime configuration is to explore a bug. Don't use it in your code; if you do, you'll experience a similar problem!

Unfortunately, you've created a captive dependency because you're injecting a scoped object, DataContext, into a singleton, Repository. As it's a singleton, the same Repository instance is used throughout the lifetime of the app, so the `DataContext` that was injected into it will also hang around, even though a new one should be used with every request. Figure 9.10 shows this scenario, in which a new instance of `DataContext` is created for each scope but the instance inside `Repository` hangs around for the lifetime of the app.

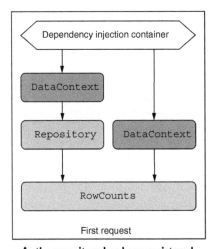
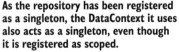
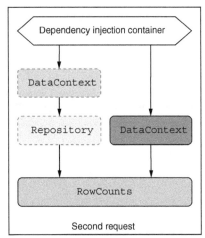

As the repository has been registered as a singleton, the DataContext it uses also acts as a singleton, even though it is registered as scoped.

The DataContext dependency has been captured by the repository, breaking the scoped lifetime.

Figure 9.10 `DataContext` **is registered as a scoped dependency, but** `Repository` **is a singleton. Even though you expect a new** `DataContext` **for every request,** `Repository` **captures the injected** `DataContext` **and causes it to be reused for the lifetime of the app.**

Captive dependencies can cause subtle bugs that are hard to root out, so you should always keep an eye out for them. These captive dependencies are relatively easy to introduce, so always think carefully when registering a singleton service.

> **WARNING**   A service should use only dependencies that have a lifetime longer than or equal to the service's lifetime. A service registered as a singleton can safely use only singleton dependencies. A service registered as scoped can safely use scoped or singleton dependencies. A transient service can use dependencies with any lifetime.

At this point, I should mention one glimmer of hope in this cautionary tale: ASP.NET Core automatically checks for these kinds of captive dependencies and throws an exception on application startup if it detects them, or on first use of a captive dependency, as shown in figure 9.11.

This scope validation check has a performance cost, so by default it's enabled only when your app is running in a development environment, but it should help you catch most problems of this kind. You can enable or disable this check regardless of

In a development environment, your app throws an Exception when the DI container detects a captured dependency.

The exception message describes which service was captured...

...and which service captured the dependency.

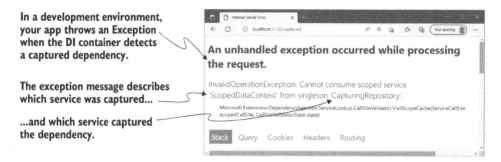

Figure 9.11 When `ValidateScopes` is enabled, the DI container throws an exception when it creates a service with a captive dependency. By default, this check is enabled only for development environments.

environment by configuring the `ValidateScopes` option on your `WebApplicationBuilder` in Program.cs by using the `Host` property, as shown in the following listing.

Listing 9.13   Setting the `ValidateScopes` property to always validate scopes

```
WebApplicationBuilder builder = WebApplication.CreateBuilder(args);

builder.Host.UseDefaultServiceProvider(o =>
{
    o.ValidateScopes = true;
    o.ValidateOnBuild = true;
});
```

The default builder sets ValidateScopes to validate only in development environments.

You can override the validation check with the UseDefaultServiceProvider extension.

Setting this to true will validate scopes in all environments, which has performance implications.

ValidateOnBuild checks that every registered service has all its dependencies registered.

Listing 9.13 shows another setting you can enable, `ValidateOnBuild`, which goes one step further. When the setting is enabled, the DI container checks on application startup that it has dependencies registered for every service it needs to build. If it doesn't, it throws an exception and shuts down the app, as shown in figure 9.12, letting you know about the misconfiguration. This setting also has a performance cost, so it's enabled only in development environments by default, but it's useful for pointing out any missed service registrations.

> **WARNING** Unfortunately, the container can't catch everything. For a list of caveats and exceptions, see this post from my blog: http://mng.bz/QmwG.

We've almost covered everything about dependency injection now, and there's only one more thing to consider: how to resolve scoped services on app startup in Program.cs.

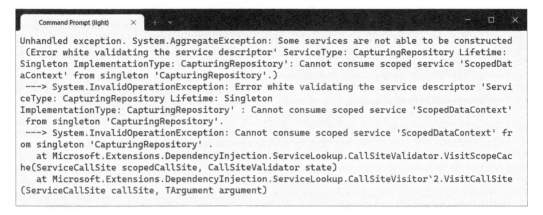

Figure 9.12 When `ValidateOnBuild` is enabled, the DI container checks on app startup that it can create all the registered services. If it finds a service it can't create, it throws an exception. By default, this check is enabled only for development environments.

9.5 Resolving scoped services outside a request

In chapter 8 I said that there are two main ways to resolve services from the DI container for minimal API applications:

- Injecting services into an endpoint handler
- Accessing the DI container directly in Program.cs

You've seen the first of those approaches several times now in this chapter. In chapter 8 you saw that you can access services in Program.cs by calling `GetRequiredService<T>()` on `WebApplication.Services`:

```
WebApplicationBuilder builder = WebApplication.CreateBuilder(args);
WebApplication app = builder.Build();
var settings = app.Services.GetRequiredService<EmailServerSettings>();
```

It's important, however, that you resolve only singleton services this way. The `IServiceProvider` exposed as `WebApplication.Services` is the root DI container for your app. Services resolved this way live for the lifetime of your app, which is fine for singleton services but typically isn't the behavior you want for scoped or transient services.

> **WARNING** Don't resolve scoped or transient services directly from `WebApplication.Services`. This approach can lead to leaking of memory, as the objects are kept alive till the app exits and aren't garbage-collected.

Instead, you should only resolve scoped and transient services from an active scope. A new scope is created automatically for every HTTP request, but when you're resolving services from the DI container directly in Program.cs (or anywhere else that's outside the context of an HTTP request), you need to create (and dispose of) a scope manually.

You can create a new scope by calling `CreateScope()` or `CreateAsyncScope()` on `IServiceProvider`, which returns a disposable `IServiceScope` object, as shown in figure

9.13. `IServiceScope` also exposes an `IServiceProvider` property, but any services resolved from this provider are disposed of automatically when you dispose the `IServiceScope`, ensuring that all the resources held by the scoped and transient services are released correctly.

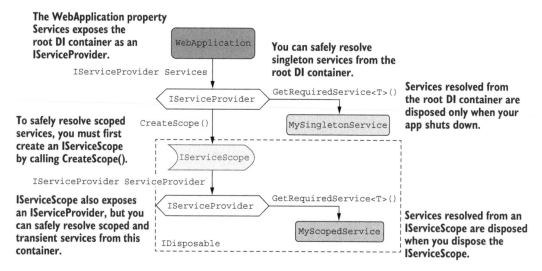

The WebApplication property Services exposes the root DI container as an IServiceProvider.

You can safely resolve singleton services from the root DI container.

To safely resolve scoped services, you must first create an IServiceScope by calling CreateScope().

Services resolved from the root DI container are disposed only when your app shuts down.

IServiceScope also exposes an IServiceProvider, but you can safely resolve scoped and transient services from this container.

Services resolved from an IServiceScope are disposed when you dispose the IServiceScope.

Figure 9.13   **To resolve scoped or transient services manually, you must create an `IServiceScope` object by calling `CreateScope()` on `WebApplication.Services`. Any scoped or transient services resolved from the DI container exposed as `IServiceScope.ServiceProvider` are disposed of automatically when you dispose of the `IServiceScope` object.**

The following listing shows how you can resolve a scoped service in Program.cs using the pattern in figure 9.13. This pattern ensures that the scoped `DataContext` object is disposed of correctly before the call to `app.Run()`.

Listing 9.14   **Resolving a scoped service using `IServiceScope` in Program.cs**

```
WebApplicationBuilder builder = WebApplication.CreateBuilder(args);

builder.Services.AddScoped<DataContext>();      ⟵┐  DataContext is registered as scoped,
                                                   │  so it shouldn't be resolved directly
WebApplication app = builder.Build();              │  from app.Services.

                                                              ┌─  Creates an
await using (var scope = app.Services.CreateAsyncScope())   ⟵┘  IServiceScope
{
    var dbContext =
        scope.ServiceProvider.GetRequiredService<DataContext>();    ┐  Resolves
    Console.WriteLine($"Retrieved scope: {dbContext.RowCount}");    │  the scoped
}   ⟵┐                                                              │  service from
      │   When the IServiceScope is disposed, all                   │  the scoped
app.Run();  │   resolved services are also disposed.                │  container
```

This example uses the async form `CreateAsyncScope()` instead of `CreateScope()`, which you generally should favor whenever possible. `CreateAsyncScope` was introduced in .NET 6 to fix an edge case related to `IAsyncDisposable` (introduced in .NET Core 3.0). You can read more about this scenario on my blog at http://mng.bz/zXGB.

With that, you've reached the end of this introduction to DI in ASP.NET Core. Now you know how to register your own services with the DI container, and ideally, you have a good understanding of the three service lifetimes used in .NET. DI appears everywhere in .NET, so it's important to try to get your head around it.

In chapter 10 we'll look at the ASP.NET Core configuration model. You'll see how to load settings from a file at runtime, store sensitive settings safely, and make your application behave differently depending on which machine it's running on. We'll even use a bit of DI; it gets everywhere in ASP.NET Core!

Summary

- When registering your services, you describe three things: the service type, the implementation type, and the lifetime. The service type defines which class or interface will be requested as a dependency. The implementation type is the class the container should create to fulfill the dependency. The lifetime is how long an instance of the service should be used for.

- You can register a service by using generic methods if the class is concrete and all its constructor arguments are registered with the container or have default values.

- You can provide an instance of a service during registration, which will register that instance as a singleton. This approach can be useful when you already have an instance of the service available.

- You can provide a lambda factory function that describes how to create an instance of a service with any lifetime you choose. You can take this approach when your services depend on other services that are accessible only when your application is running.

- Avoid calling `GetService()` or `GetRequiredService()` in your factory functions if possible. Instead, favor constructor injection; it's more performant and simpler to reason about.

- You can register multiple implementations for a service. Then you can inject `IEnumerable<T>` to get access to all the implementations at runtime.

- If you inject a single instance of a multiple-registered service, the container injects the last implementation registered.

- You can use the `TryAdd*` extension methods to ensure that an implementation is registered only if no other implementation of the service has been registered. This approach can be useful for library authors to add default services while still allowing consumers to override the registered services.

- You define the lifetime of a service during DI service registration to dictate when a DI container will reuse an existing instance of the service to fulfill service dependencies and when it will create a new one.
- A transient lifetime means that every time a service is requested, a new instance is created.
- A scoped lifetime means that within a scope, all requests for a service will give you the same object. For different scopes, you'll get different objects. In ASP.NET Core, each web request gets its own scope.
- You'll always get the same instance of a singleton service, regardless of scope.
- A service should use only dependencies with a lifetime longer than or equal to the lifetime of the service. By default, ASP.NET Core performs scope validation to check for errors like this one and throws an exception when it finds them, but this feature is enabled only in development environments, as it has a performance cost.
- To access scoped services in Program.cs, you must first create an `IServiceScope` object by calling `CreateScope()` or `CreateAsyncScope()` on `WebApplication.Services`. You can resolve services from the `IServiceScope.ServiceProvider` property. When you dispose `IServiceScope`, any scoped or transient services resolved from the scope are also disposed.

Configuring an ASP.NET Core application

This chapter covers

- Loading settings from multiple configuration providers
- Storing sensitive settings safely
- Using strongly typed settings objects
- Using different settings in different hosting environments

In part 1 of this book, you learned the basics of getting an ASP.NET Core app up and running, and how to use minimal API endpoints to create an HTTP API. When you start building real applications, you'll quickly find that you want to tweak various settings at deploy time without necessarily having to recompile your application. This chapter looks at how you can achieve this task in ASP.NET Core by using configuration.

I know. Configuration sounds boring, right? But I have to confess that the configuration model is one of my favorite parts of ASP.NET Core; it's so easy to use and so much more elegant than some approaches in old versions of .NET Framework. In section 10.2 you'll learn how to load values from a plethora of sources—JavaScript Object Notation (JSON) files, environment variables, and command-line arguments—and combine them into a unified configuration object.

On top of that, ASP.NET Core makes it easy to bind this configuration to strongly typed options objects—simple plain old CLR object (POCO) classes that are populated from the configuration object, which you can inject into your services, as you'll see in section 10.3. Binding to strongly typed options objects lets you nicely encapsulate settings for different features in your app.

In the final section of this chapter, you'll learn about the ASP.NET Core hosting environments. You often want your app to run differently in different situations, such as running it on your developer machine compared with deploying it to a production server. These situations are known as *environments*. When the app knows the environment in which it's running, it can load a different configuration and vary its behavior accordingly.

Before we get to that topic, let's cover the basics. What is configuration, why do we need it, and how does ASP.NET Core handle these requirements?

10.1 *Introducing the ASP.NET Core configuration model*

In this section I provide a brief description of configuration and what you can use it for in ASP.NET Core applications. *Configuration* is the set of external parameters provided to an application that controls the application's behavior in some way. It typically consists of a mixture of settings and secrets that the application loads at runtime.

> **DEFINITION** A *setting* is any value that changes the behavior of your application. A *secret* is a special type of setting that contains sensitive data, such as a password, an API key for a third-party service, or a connection string.

The obvious things to consider before we get started are why we need app configuration and what sort of things we need to configure. Normally, you move anything that you can consider to be a setting or a secret out of your application code. That way, you can change these values at deploy time easily without having to recompile your application.

You might have an application that shows the locations of your bricks-and-mortar stores. You could have a setting for the connection string to the database in which you store the details on the stores, but also settings such as the default location to display on a map, the default zoom level to use, and the API key for accessing the Google Maps API (figure 10.1). Storing these settings and secrets outside your compiled code is good practice, as it makes it easy to tweak them without having to recompile your code.

There's also a security aspect: you don't want to hardcode secret values such as API keys or passwords into your code, where they could be committed to source control and made publicly available. Even values embedded in your compiled application can be extracted, so it's best to externalize them whenever possible.

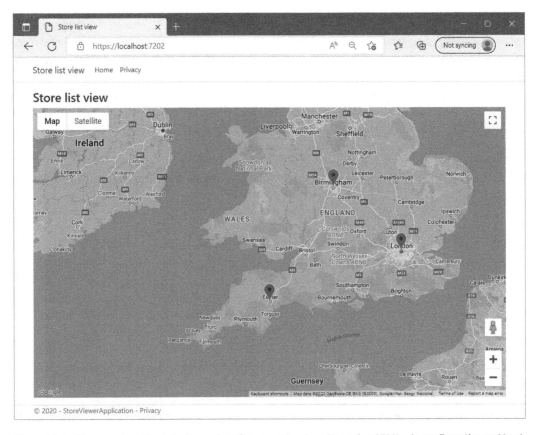

Figure 10.1   You can store the default map location, zoom level, and mapping API Key in configuration and load them at runtime. It's important to keep secrets such as API keys in configuration out of your code.

Virtually every web framework provides a mechanism for loading configuration, and the old .NET Framework version of ASP.NET was no different. It used the `<appsettings>` element in a web.config file to store key-value configuration pairs. At runtime you'd use the static (*wince*) `ConfigurationManager` to load the value for a given key from the file. You could do more advanced things using custom configuration sections, but doing so was painful and so was rarely used, in my experience.

ASP.NET Core gives you a totally revamped experience. At the most basic level, you're still specifying key-value pairs as strings, but instead of getting those values from a single file, now you can load them from multiple sources. You can load values from files, but now they can be in any format you like: JSON, XML, YAML, and so on. Further, you can load values from environment variables, from command-line arguments, from a database, or from a remote service. Or you can create your own custom configuration provider.

DEFINITION   ASP.NET Core uses *configuration providers* to load key-value pairs from a variety of sources. Applications can use multiple configuration providers.

The ASP.NET Core configuration model also has the concept of overriding settings. Each configuration provider can define its own settings, or it can overwrite settings from a previous provider. You'll see this incredibly useful feature in action in section 10.2.

ASP.NET Core makes it simple to bind these key-value pairs, which are defined as `strings`, to POCO-setting classes that you define in your code. This model of strongly typed configuration, described in section 10.3, makes it easy to group settings logically around a given feature and lends itself well to unit testing.

Before we get to strongly typed settings, we'll look at how you load the settings and secrets for your app, whether they're stored in JSON files, environment variables, or command-line arguments.

10.2   *Building a configuration object for your app*

In this section we'll get into the meat of the configuration system. You'll learn how to load settings from multiple sources, how they're stored internally in ASP.NET Core, and how settings can override other values to produce layers of configuration. You'll also learn how to store secrets securely while ensuring that they're still available when you run your app.

ASP.NET Core's configuration model has been essentially the same since .NET Core 1.0, but in .NET 6, ASP.NET Core introduced the `ConfigurationManager` class. `ConfigurationManager` simplifies common patterns for working with configuration by implementing both of the two main configuration-related interfaces: `IConfiguration-Builder` and `IConfigurationRoot`.

NOTE   `IConfigurationBuilder` describes how to construct the final configuration representation for your app, and `IConfigurationRoot` holds the configuration values themselves.

You describe your configuration by adding `IConfigurationProviders` to the `ConfigurationManager`. Configuration providers describe how to load the key-value pairs from a particular source, such as a JSON file or environment variables (figure 10.2). When you add a provider, the `ConfigurationManager` queries it and adds all the values returned to the `IConfigurationRoot` implementation.

NOTE   Adding a provider to the `ConfigurationManager` adds the configuration values to the `IConfigurationRoot` instance, which implements `IConfiguration`. You'll generally work with the `IConfiguration` interface in your code.

ASP.NET Core ships with configuration providers for loading data from common locations:

- JSON files
- Extensible Markup Language (XML) files
- Environment variables
- Command-line arguments
- Initialization (INI) files

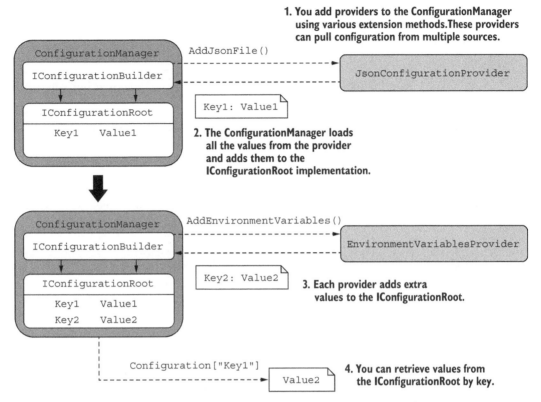

Figure 10.2 Using `ConfigurationManager` to populate `IConfiguration`. Configuration providers are added to the `ConfigurationManager` with extension methods. The manager queries the provider and adds all the returned values to the `IConfigurationRoot`, which implements `IConfiguration`.

If these providers don't fit your requirements, you can find a host of alternatives on GitHub and NuGet, and it's not difficult to create your own custom provider. You could use the official Microsoft Azure Key Vault provider NuGet package or the YAML file provider I wrote.

> **NOTE** The Azure Key Vault provider is available on NuGet at http://mng.bz/0KrN, and you can find my YAML provider on GitHub at http://mng.bz/Yqdj.

In many cases, the default providers are sufficient. In particular, most templates start with an appsettings.json file, which contains a variety of settings depending on the template you choose. The following listing shows the default file generated by the ASP.NET Core 7.0 Empty template without authentication.

Listing 10.1   Default appsettings.json file created by an ASP.NET Core Empty template

```
{
  "Logging": {
    "LogLevel": {
      "Default": "Information",
```

```
        "Microsoft.AspNetCore": "Warning"
      }
    },
    "AllowedHosts": "*"
}
```

As you can see, this file contains mostly settings to control logging, but you can add extra configuration for your app here too.

> **WARNING** Don't store sensitive values—such as passwords, API keys, and connection strings—in this file. You'll see how to store these values securely in section 10.2.3.

Adding your own configuration values involves adding a key-value pair to the JSON. It's a good idea to namespace your settings by creating a base object for related settings, as in the MapSettings object shown in the following listing.

Listing 10.2   Adding configuration values to an appsettings.json file

```
{
  "Logging": {
    "LogLevel": {
      "Default": "Information",
      "Microsoft": "Warning",
      "Microsoft.Hosting.Lifetime": "Information"
    }
  },
  "AllowedHosts": "*",
  "MapSettings": {
    "DefaultZoomLevel": 9,
    "DefaultLocation": {
      "latitude": 50.500,
      "longitude": -4.000
    }
  }
}
```

Values can be numbers in the JSON file, but they'll be converted to strings when they're read.

Nest all the configuration under the MapSettings key.

You can create deeply nested structures to organize your configuration values better.

I've nested the new configuration inside the MapSettings parent key to create a *section* that will be useful later for binding values to a POCO object. I also nested the latitude and longitude keys under the DefaultLocation key. You can create any structure of values you like; the configuration provider will read them fine. Also, you can store the values as any data type—numbers, in this case—but be aware that the provider will read and store them internally as strings.

> **TIP** The configuration keys are *not* case-sensitive in your app, so bear that fact in mind when loading from providers in which the keys are case-sensitive. If you have a YAML file with keys name and NAME, for example, only one will appear in the final IConfiguration.

Now that you have a configuration file, it's time for your app to load it into the ConfigurationManager.

10.2.1 Adding a configuration provider in Program.cs

As you've seen throughout this book, ASP.NET Core (from .NET 6 onward) uses the WebApplicationBuilder class to bootstrap your application. As part of the bootstrap process, WebApplicationBuilder creates a ConfigurationManager instance and exposes it as the property Configuration.

> **TIP** You can access the ConfigurationManager directly on WebApplicationBuilder .Configuration and WebApplication.Configuration. Both properties reference the same ConfigurationManager instance.

WebApplicationBuilder adds several default configuration providers to the ConfigurationManager, which we'll look at in more detail throughout this chapter:

- *JSON file provider*—Loads settings from an optional JSON file called appsettings.json. It also loads settings from an optional environment-specific JSON file called appsettings.*ENVIRONMENT*.json. I show how to use environment-specific files in section 10.4.
- *User Secrets*—Loads secrets that are stored safely during development.
- *Environment variables*—Loads environment variables as configuration variables, which are great for storing secrets in production.
- *Command-line arguments*—Uses values passed as arguments when you run your app.

The ConfigurationManager is configured with all these sources automatically, but you can easily add more providers. You can also start from scratch and clear the default providers as shown in the following listing, which completely customizes where configuration is loaded from.

Listing 10.3   Loading appsettings.json by clearing the configuration sources

```
WebApplicationBuilder builder = WebApplication.CreateBuilder(args);

builder.Configuration.Sources.Clear();                           ⟵ Clears the providers configured by
                                                                   default in WebApplicationBuilder
builder.Configuration.AddJsonFile("appsettings.json", optional: true);   ⟵

WebApplication app = builder.Build();                            Adds a JSON
                                                                 configuration provider,
app.MapGet("/", () => app.Configuration.AsEnumerable());         providing the name of
                                                                 the configuration file
app.Run();
```
Returns all the configuration key-value pairs for display purposes

---

This example added a single JSON configuration provider by calling the AddJson-File() extension method and providing a filename. It also set the value of optional to true, telling the configuration provider to skip files that it can't find at runtime instead of throwing FileNotFoundException. When the provider is added, the ConfigurationManager requests all the available values from the provider and adds them to the IConfiguration implementation.

ConfigurationBuilder vs. ConfigurationManager

Before .NET 6 and the introduction of `ConfigurationManager`, configuration in ASP.NET Core was implemented with `ConfigurationBuilder`. You'd add configuration providers to the builder type the same way you do with `ConfigurationManager`, but the configuration values weren't loaded until you called `Build()`, which created the final `IConfigurationRoot` object.

By contrast, in .NET 6 and .NET 7 `ConfigurationManager` acts as both the builder and the final `IConfigurationRoot`. When you add a new configuration provider, the configuration values are added to the `IConfigurationRoot` immediately, without the need to call `Build()` first.

The `ConfigurationBuilder` approach using the builder pattern is cleaner in some ways, as it has a clearer separation of concerns, but the common use patterns for configuration mean that the new `ConfigurationManager` approach is often easier to use.

If you prefer, you can still use the builder pattern by accessing `WebApplicationBuilder.Host.ConfigureAppConfiguration`. You can read about some of these patterns and the differences between the two approaches on my blog at http://mng.bz/Ke4j.

You can access the `IConfiguration` object directly in Program.cs, as in listing 10.3, but the `ConfigurationManager` is also registered as `IConfiguration` in the dependency injection (DI) container, so you can inject it into your classes and endpoint handlers. You could rewrite the endpoint handler in listing 10.3 as the following, and the `IConfiguration` object would be injected into the handler using DI:

```
app.MapGet("/", (IConfiguration config) => config.AsEnumerable());
```

> **NOTE** The `ConfigurationManager` implements `IConfigurationRoot`, which also implements `IConfiguration`. The `ConfigurationManager` is registered in the DI container as an `IConfiguration`, not an `IConfigurationRoot`.

You've seen how to add values to the `ConfigurationManager` by using providers such as the JSON file provider, and listing 10.3 showed an example of iterating over every configuration value, but normally you want to retrieve a specific configuration value.

`IConfiguration` stores configuration as a set of key-value `string` pairs. You can access any value by its key, using standard dictionary syntax. You could use

```
var zoomLevel = builder.Configuration["MapSettings:DefaultZoomLevel"];
```

to retrieve the configured zoom level for your application (using the settings shown in listing 10.2). Note that I used a colon (:) to designate a separate section. Similarly, to retrieve the `latitude` key, you could use

```
var lat = builder.Configuration["MapSettings:DefaultLocation:Latitude"];
```

NOTE If the requested configuration key doesn't exist, you get a `null` value.

You can also grab a whole section of the configuration by using the `GetSection` `(section)` method, which returns an `IConfigurationSection`, which also implements `IConfiguration`. This method grabs a chunk of the configuration and resets the namespace. Another way to get the latitude key is

```
var lat = builder.Configuration
    .GetSection("MapSettings")["DefaultLocation:Latitude"];
```

Accessing setting values this way is useful in Program.cs when you're defining your application. When you're setting up your application to connect to a database, for example, you'll often load a connection string from the `IConfiguration` object. You'll see a concrete example in chapter 12, which looks at Entity Framework Core.

If you need to access the configuration object in places other than Program.cs, you can use DI to inject it as a dependency into your service's constructor. But accessing configuration by using `string` keys this way isn't particularly convenient; you should try to use strongly typed configuration instead, as you'll see in section 10.3.

So far, this process probably feels a bit too convoluted and run-of-the-mill to load settings from a JSON file, and I'll grant you that it is. Where the ASP.NET Core configuration system shines is when you have multiple providers.

10.2.2 Using multiple providers to override configuration values

You've seen how to add a configuration provider to the `ConfigurationManager` and retrieve the configuration values, but so far, you've configured only a single provider. When you add providers, it's important to consider the order in which you add them, as that defines the order in which the configuration values will be added to the underlying dictionary. Configuration values from later providers overwrite values with the same key from earlier providers.

NOTE This sentence bears repeating: the order in which you add configuration providers to `ConfigurationManager` is important. Later configuration providers can overwrite the values of earlier providers.

Think of the configuration providers as adding layers of configuration values to a stack, where each layer may overlap some or all of the layers below, as shown in figure 10.3. If the new provider contains any keys that are already known to the `Configuration-Manager`, they overwrite the old values to create the final set of configuration values stored in `IConfiguration`.

TIP Instead of thinking in layers, you can think of the `ConfigurationManager` as a simple dictionary. When you add a provider, you're setting some key-value pairs. When you add a second provider, the provider can add new keys or overwrite the value of existing keys.

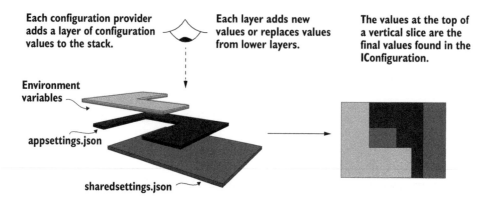

Figure 10.3   Each configuration provider adds a layer of values to `ConfigurationBuilder`**. Calling** `Build()` **collapses that configuration. Later providers overwrite configuration values with the same keys from earlier providers.**

Update your code to load configuration from three different configuration providers—two JSON providers and an environment variable provider—by adding them to `ConfigurationManager` as shown in the following listing.

Listing 10.4   Loading from multiple providers in Program.cs

Loads configuration from a different JSON
configuration file before the appsettings.json file

```
WebApplicationBuilder builder = WebApplication.CreateBuilder(args);

builder.Configuration.Sources.Clear();
builder.Configuration
    .AddJsonFile("sharedSettings.json", optional: true);
builder.Configuration.AddJsonFile("appsettings.json", optional: true);
builder.Configuration.AddEnvironmentVariables();

WebApplication app = builder.Build();

app.MapGet("/", () => app.Configuration.AsEnumerable());

app.Run();
```

Adds the machine's
environment variables as
a configuration provider

This layered design can be useful for several things. Fundamentally, it allows you to aggregate configuration values from multiple sources into a single, cohesive object. To cement this design in place, consider the configuration values in figure 10.4.

Most of the settings in each provider are unique and are added to the final `IConfiguration`. But the `"MyAppConnString"` key appears both in appsettings.json and as an environment variable. Because the environment variable provider is added after the JSON providers, the environment variable configuration value is used in `IConfiguration`.

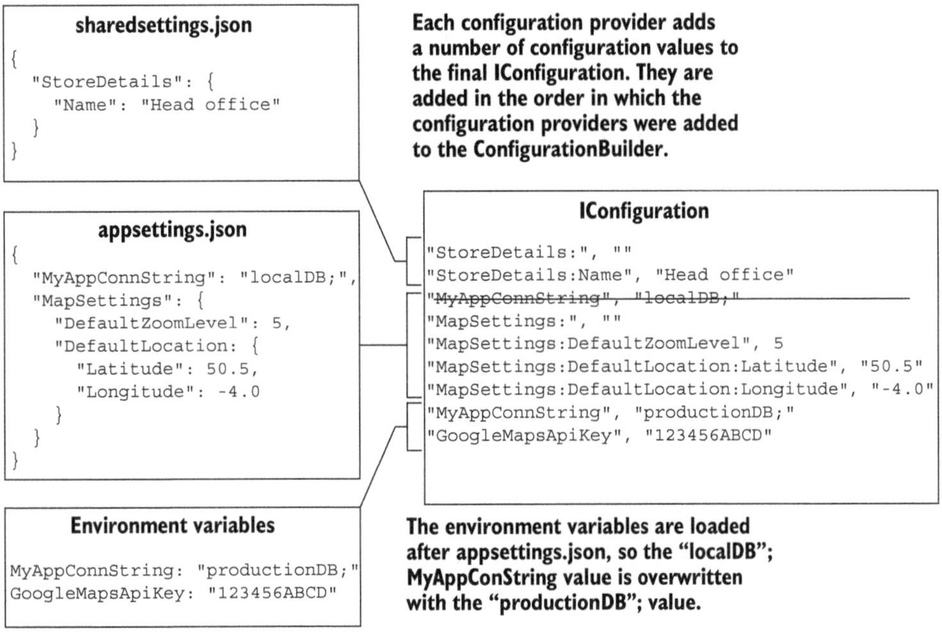

```
                                    Each configuration provider adds
  sharedsettings.json               a number of configuration values to
{                                   the final IConfiguration. They are
  "StoreDetails": {                 added in the order in which the
    "Name": "Head office"           configuration providers were added
  }                                 to the ConfigurationBuilder.
}
```

```
                                    IConfiguration
  appsettings.json          "StoreDetails:", ""
{                           "StoreDetails:Name", "Head office"
  "MyAppConnString": "localDB;",   "MyAppConnString", "localDB;"
  "MapSettings": {          "MapSettings:", ""
    "DefaultZoomLevel": 5,  "MapSettings:DefaultZoomLevel", 5
    "DefaultLocation: {     "MapSettings:DefaultLocation:Latitude", "50.5"
      "Latitude": 50.5,     "MapSettings:DefaultLocation:Longitude", "-4.0"
      "Longitude": -4.0     "MyAppConnString", "productionDB;"
    }                       "GoogleMapsApiKey", "123456ABCD"
  }
}
```

```
  Environment variables                The environment variables are loaded
                                       after appsettings.json, so the "localDB";
MyAppConnString: "productionDB;"       MyAppConString value is overwritten
GoogleMapsApiKey: "123456ABCD"         with the "productionDB"; value.
```

Figure 10.4 The final `IConfiguration` **includes the values from each of the providers. Both appsettings.json and the environment variables include the** `MyAppConnString` **key. As the environment variables are added later, that configuration value is used.**

The ability to collate configuration from multiple providers is handy on its own, but this design is especially useful for handling sensitive configuration values, such as connection strings and passwords. Section 10.2.3 shows how to deal with this problem, both locally on your development machine and on production servers.

10.2.3 Storing configuration secrets safely

As soon as you build a nontrivial app, you'll find that you need to store some sort of sensitive data as a setting somewhere. This data could be a password, a connection string, or an API key for a remote service, for example.

Storing these values in appsettings.json is generally a bad idea, as you should never commit secrets to source control; the number of secret API keys people have committed to GitHub is scary! Instead, it's much better to store these values outside your project folder, where they won't get committed accidentally.

You can do this in a few ways, but the easiest and most common approaches are to use environment variables for secrets on your production server and User Secrets locally. Neither approach is truly secure, in that neither stores values in an encrypted format. If your machine is compromised, attackers will be able to read the stored values because they're stored in plain text. These approaches are intended mainly to help you avoid committing secrets to source control.

TIP Azure Key Vault is a secure alternative, in that it stores the values encrypted in Azure, but you still need to use User Secrets and environment variables to store the Azure Key Vault connection details. See the documentation for instructions on using Azure Key Vault in your apps http://mng.bz/BR7v. Another popular option is Vault by Hashicorp (www.vaultproject.io), which can be run on-premises or in the cloud.

Whichever approach you use to store your application secrets, make sure that you aren't storing them in source control. Even private repositories may not stay private forever, so it's best to err on the side of caution.

STORING SECRETS IN ENVIRONMENT VARIABLES IN PRODUCTION

You can add the environment variable configuration provider by using the `AddEnvironmentVariables` extension method, as you saw in listing 10.4. This method adds all the environment variables on your machine as key-value pairs to `ConfigurationManager`.

NOTE The `WebApplicationBuilder` adds the environment variable provider to the `ConfigurationManager` by default.

You can create the same hierarchical sections in environment variables that you typically see in JSON files by using a colon (`:`) or a double underscore (`__`) to demarcate a section, as in `MapSettings:MaxNumberOfPoints` or `MapSettings__MaxNumberOfPoints`.

TIP Some environments, such as Linux, don't allow the colon in environment variables. You must use the double-underscore approach in these environments instead. A double underscore in an environment variable is converted to a colon when it's imported into the `IConfiguration` object. You should always use the colon when retrieving values from an `IConfiguration` in your app.

The environment-variable approach is particularly useful when you're publishing your app to a self-contained environment, such as a dedicated server, Azure, or a Docker container. You can set environment variables on your production machine or on your Docker container, and the provider reads them at runtime, overriding the defaults specified in your appsettings.json files.

TIP For instructions on setting environment variables for your operating system, see Microsoft's "Use multiple environments in ASP.NET Core" documentation at http://mng.bz/d4OD.

For a development machine, environment variables are less useful, as all your apps would use the same values. If you set the `ConnectionStrings__DefaultConnection` environment variable, for example, that variable would be added to *every* app you run locally, which sounds like more of a hassle than a benefit!

TIP To avoid collisions, you can add only environment variables that have a given prefix, such as `AddEnvironmentVariables("SomePrefix")`. The prefix is removed from the key before it's added to the `ConfigurationManager`, so the variable `SomePrefix_MyValue` is added to configuration as `MyValue`.

For development scenarios, you can use the User Secrets Manager, which effectively adds per-app environment variables, so you can have different settings for each app but store them in a different location from the app itself.

STORING SECRETS WITH THE USER SECRETS MANAGER IN DEVELOPMENT

The idea behind User Secrets is to simplify storing per-app secrets outside your app's project tree. This approach is similar to environment variables, but you use a unique key for each app to keep the secrets segregated.

> **WARNING** The secrets aren't encrypted, so don't consider them to be secure. Nevertheless, it's an improvement on storing them in your project folder.

Setting up User Secrets takes a bit more effort than using environment variables, as you need to configure a tool to read and write them, add the User Secrets configuration provider, and define a unique key for your application. To add User Secrets to your app, follow these steps:

1 `WebApplicationBuilder` adds the User Secrets provider by default. The .NET SDK includes a global tool for working with secrets from the command line.

2 If you're using Visual Studio, right-click your project and choose **Manage User Secrets** from the contextual menu. This command opens an editor for a secrets.json file in which you can store your key-value pairs as though it were an appsettings.json file, as shown in figure 10.5.

Figure 10.5 Choose Manage User Secrets to open an editor for the User Secrets app. You can use this file to store secrets when developing your app locally. These secrets are stored outside your project folder, so they won't be committed to source control accidentally.

3 Add a unique identifier to your .csproj file. Visual Studio does this automatically when you choose Manage User Secrets, but if you're using the command line, you'll need to add it yourself. Typically, you'd use a unique ID, such as a globally unique identifier (GUID):

```
<PropertyGroup>
  <UserSecretsId>96eb2a39-1ef9-4d8e-8b20-8e8bd14038aa</UserSecretsId>
</PropertyGroup>
```

You can also generate the `UserSecretsId` property with a random value using the .NET command-line interface (CLI) by running the following command from your project folder:

```
dotnet user-secrets init
```

4 Add User Secrets by using the command line

```
dotnet user-secrets set "MapSettings:GoogleMapsApiKey" F5RJT9GFHKR7
```

or edit the secret.json file directly by using your favorite editor. The exact location of this file depends on your operating system and may vary. Check the documentation for details at http://mng.bz/ryAg.

> **NOTE** The Secret Manager tool is included in the .NET CLI, but you can also use the CLI to install additional .NET tools. You can find more about .NET tools in general in Microsoft's "How to manage .NET tools" documentation: http://mng.bz/VdmX.

Phew! That's a lot of setup, and if you're adding providers to `ConfigurationManager` manually, you're not done yet! You need to update your app to load the User Secrets at runtime by using the `AddUserSecrets` extension method:

```
if (builder.Environment.IsDevelopment())
{
    builder.Configuration.AddUserSecrets<Program>();
}
```

> **NOTE** You should use the User Secrets provider only in development, not in production, so in the preceding snippet you add the provider conditionally to `ConfigurationManager`. In production you should use environment variables or Azure Key Vault, as discussed earlier. All this is configured correctly by default when you use the default `WebApplicationBuilder`.

The `AddUserSecrets` method has several overloads, but the simplest is a generic method that you can call by passing your application's `Program` class as a generic argument, as shown in the preceding example. The User Secrets provider needs to read the `UserSecretsId` property that you (or Visual Studio) added to the .csproj file. The `Program` class acts as a simple marker to indicate which assembly contains this property.

> **NOTE** If you're interested, the .NET SDK uses the `UserSecretsId` property in your .csproj file to generate an assembly-level `UserSecretsIdAttribute`. Then the provider reads this attribute at runtime to determine the `UserSecretsId` of the app and generates the path to the secrets.json file.

And there you have it—safe storage of your secrets outside your project folder during development. This cautious approach may seem like overkill, but if you have anything you consider to be remotely sensitive that you need to load into configuration, I strongly urge you to use environment variables or User Secrets.

It's almost time to leave configuration providers behind, but before we do, I'd like to show you the ASP.NET Core configuration system's party trick: reloading files on the fly.

10.2.4 Reloading configuration values when they change

Besides security, not having to recompile your application every time you want to tweak a value is one of the advantages of using configuration and settings. In the previous version of ASP.NET, changing a setting by editing web.config would cause your app to restart. This feature beats having to recompile, but waiting for the app to start up before it could serve requests was a bit of a drag.

In ASP.NET Core, you finally get the ability to edit a file and have the configuration of your application update automatically, without your having to recompile *or* restart. An often-cited scenario in which you might find this ability useful is when you're trying to debug an app you have in production. You typically configure logging to one of several levels:

- Error
- Warning
- Information
- Debug

Each of these settings is more verbose than the last, but it also provides more context. By default, you might configure your app to log only warning and error-level logs in production so that you don't generate too many superfluous log entries. Conversely, if you're trying to debug a problem, you want as much information as possible, so you may want to use the debug log level.

Being able to change configuration at runtime means that you can easily switch on extra logs when you encounter a problem and switch them back afterward by editing your appsettings.json file.

> **NOTE** Reloading is generally available only for file-based configuration providers, such as the JSON provider, as opposed to the environment variable provider, for example.

You can enable the reloading of configuration files when you add any of the file-based providers to your `ConfigurationManager`. The `Add*File` extension methods include an overload with a `reloadOnChange` parameter. If this parameter is set to `true`, the app

monitors the filesystem for changes to the file and triggers a complete rebuild of the
IConfiguration, if needs be. The following listing shows how to add configuration
reloading to the appsettings.json file added manually to the ConfigurationManager.

Listing 10.5   Reloading appsettings.json when the file changes

```
WebApplicationBuilder builder = WebApplication.CreateBuilder(args);

builder.Configuration.Sources.Clear();
builder.Configuration
    .AddJsonFile(
        "appsettings.json",
        optional: true,                    IConfiguration will be rebuilt if
        reloadOnChange: true);      ◁──┘   the appsettings.json file changes.

WebApplication app = builder.Build();

app.MapGet("/", () => app.Configuration.AsEnumerable());

app.Run();
```

Throughout section 10.2, you've seen how to customize the ConfigurationManager providers by clearing the default sources and adding your own, but in most cases, that
won't be necessary. As described in section 10.2.1, the default providers added by
WebApplicationBuilder are normally good enough unless you want to add a new provider, such as Azure Key Vault. As a bonus, WebApplicationBuilder configures the
appsettings.json with reloadOnChange:true by default. It's worth sticking with the
defaults initially and clear the sources and start again only if you really need to.

> **WARNING**   Adding a file configuration source using reloadOnChange:true isn't
> entirely free, as ASP.NET Core sets up a file watcher in the background. Nor-
> mally, this situation isn't problematic, but if you set up a configuration watch-
> ing thousands of files, you could run into difficulties!

In listing 10.5, any changes you make to the file will be mirrored in the IConfiguration.
But as I said at the start of this chapter, IConfiguration isn't the preferred way to pass
settings around in your application. Instead, as you'll see in section 10.3, you should
favor strongly typed objects.

10.3   *Using strongly typed settings with the options pattern*

In this section you'll learn about strongly typed configuration and the options pattern,
the preferred way of accessing configuration in ASP.NET Core. By using strongly
typed configuration, you can avoid problems with typos when accessing configuration.
It also makes classes easier to test, as you can use simple POCO objects for configuration instead of relying on the IConfiguration abstraction.

Most of the examples I've shown so far have been about how to get values *into*
IConfiguration, as opposed to how to *use* them. You've seen that you can access a key

by using the `builder.Configuration["key"]` dictionary syntax, but using `string` keys this way feels messy and prone to typos, and the value retrieved is always a `string`, so you often need to convert it to another type. Instead, ASP.NET Core promotes the use of strongly typed settings—POCO objects that you define and create and that represent a small collection of settings, scoped to a single feature in your app.

The following listing shows the map settings for your store locator component and display settings to customize the home page of the app. They're separated into two different objects with `"MapSettings"` and `"AppDisplaySettings"` keys, corresponding to the different areas of the app that they affect.

Listing 10.6   Separating settings into different objects in appsettings.json

```
{
  "MapSettings": {
    "DefaultZoomLevel": 6,          Settings related to
    "DefaultLocation": {            the store locator
      "latitude": 50.500,          section of the app
      "longitude": -4.000
    }
  },
  "AppDisplaySettings": {           General settings related
    "Title":  "Acme Store Locator",  to displaying the app
    "ShowCopyright": true
  }
}
```

The simplest approach to exposing the home-page settings in an endpoint handler is to inject `IConfiguration` into the endpoint handler and access the values by using the dictionary syntax:

```
app.MapGet("/display-settings", (Iconfiguration config) =>
{
    string title = config["AppDisplaySettings:Title"];
    bool showCopyright = bool.Parse(
            config["AppDisplaySettings:ShowCopyright"]);

    return new { title, showCopyright };
});
```

But you don't want to do this; there are too many strings for my liking! And that `bool.Parse`? Yuck! Instead, you can use custom strongly typed objects, with all the type safety and IntelliSense goodness that brings, as shown in the following listing.

Listing 10.7   Injecting strongly typed options into a handler using `IOptions<T>`

```
app.MapGet("/display-settings",
    (IOptions<AppDisplaySettings> options) =>     You can inject a strongly
{                                                 typed options class using the
                                                  IOptions< > wrapper interface.
```

```
        AppDisplaySettings settings = options.Value;
        string title = settings.Title;
        bool showCopyright = settings.ShowCopyright;

        return new { title, showCopyright };
});
```

The Value property exposes the POCO settings object.

The binder can also convert string values directly to built-in types.

The settings object contains properties that are bound to configuration values at runtime.

The ASP.NET Core configuration system includes a *binder*, which can take a collection of configuration values and bind them to a strongly typed object, called an *options class*. This binding is similar to the concept of JSON deserialization for creating types from chapter 6 and the model binding used by Model-View-Controller (MVC) and Razor Pages, which you'll learn about in part 3.

Section 10.3.1 shows how to set up the binding of configuration values to a POCO options class, and section 10.3.2 shows how to make sure that it reloads when the underlying configuration values change. We'll look at the different sorts of objects you can bind in section 10.3.3.

10.3.1 *Introducing the IOptions interface*

ASP.NET Core introduced strongly typed settings as a way of letting configuration code adhere to the single-responsibility principle (SRP) and to allow the injection of configuration classes as explicit dependencies. Such settings also make testing easier; instead of having to create an instance of IConfiguration to test a service, you can create an instance of the POCO options class.

The AppDisplaySettings class shown in the previous example could be simple, exposing only the values related to the home page:

```
public class AppDisplaySettings
{
    public string Title { get; set; }
    public bool ShowCopyright { get; set; }
}
```

Your options classes need to be nonabstract and have a public parameterless constructor to be eligible for binding. The binder sets any public properties that match configuration values, as you'll see in section 10.3.3.

> **TIP** You're not restricted to built-in types such as string and bool; you can use nested complex types too. The options system binds sections to complex properties. See the associated source code for examples.

To help facilitate the binding of configuration values to your custom POCO options classes, ASP.NET Core introduces the IOptions<T> interface, a simple interface with a single property, Value, that contains your configured POCO options class at runtime.

Options classes are configured as services in Program.cs , as shown in the following listing.

Listing 10.8 Configuring the options classes using `Configure<T>` in Startup.cs

```
WebApplicationBuilder builder = WebApplication.CreateBuilder(args);

builder.Services.Configure<MapSettings>(
    builder.Configuration.GetSection("MapSettings"));
builder.Services.Configure<AppDisplaySettings>(
    builder.Configuration.GetSection("AppDisplaySettings"));
```

Binds the MapSettings section to the POCO options class MapSettings

Binds the AppDisplaySettings section to the POCO options class AppDisplaySettings

> **TIP** You don't have to use the same name for both the section and class, as I do in listing 10.8; it's simply a convention I like to follow. With this convention, you can also use the `nameof()` operator to further reduce the chance of typos, such as by calling `GetSection(nameof(MapSettings))`.

Each call to `Configure<T>` sets up the following series of actions internally:

1. Creates an instance of `ConfigureOptions<T>`, which indicates that `IOptions<T>` should be configured based on configuration.

   If `Configure<T>` is called multiple times, multiple `ConfigureOptions<T>` objects will be used, all of which can be applied to create the final object in much the same way that `IConfiguration` is built from multiple layers.

2. Each `ConfigureOptions<T>` instance binds a section of `IConfiguration` to an instance of the `T` POCO class, setting any public properties on the options class based on the keys in the provided `ConfigurationSection`.

   Remember that the section name (`"MapSettings"` in listing 10.8) can have any value; it doesn't have to match the name of your options class.

3. The `IOptions<T>` interface is registered in the DI container as a singleton, with the final bound POCO object in the `Value` property.

This last step lets you inject your options classes into handlers and services by injecting `IOptions<T>`, as you saw in listing 10.7, giving you encapsulated, strongly typed access to your configuration values. No more magic strings. Woo-hoo!

> **WARNING** If you forget to call `Configure<T>` and inject `IOptions<T>` into your services, you won't see any errors, but the `T` options class won't be bound to anything and will have only default values in its properties.

The binding of the `T` options class to `ConfigurationSection` happens when you first request `IOptions<T>`. The object is registered in the DI container as a singleton, so it's bound only once.

This setup has one catch: you can't use the `reloadOnChange` parameter I described in section 10.2.4 to reload your strongly typed options classes when using `IOptions<T>`.

IConfiguration will still be reloaded if you edit your appsettings.json files, but it won't propagate to your options class.

If that fact seems like a step backward or even a deal-breaker, don't worry. IOptions<T> has a cousin, IOptionsSnapshot<T>, for such an occasion.

10.3.2 *Reloading strongly typed options with IOptionsSnapshot*

In section 10.3.1, you used IOptions<T> to provide strongly typed access to configuration. Using IOptions<T> to provide strongly typed access to configuration provided a nice encapsulation of the settings for a particular service, but with a specific drawback: the options class never changes, even if you modify the underlying configuration file from which it was loaded, such as appsettings.json.

This situation isn't always a problem (you generally shouldn't be modifying files on live production servers anyway), but if you need this functionality, you can use the IOptionsSnapshot<T> interface. Conceptually, IOptionsSnaphot<T> is identical to IOptions<T> in that it's a strongly typed representation of a section of configuration. The difference is when and how often the POCO options objects are created when they're used:

- IOptions<T>—The instance is created once, when first needed. It always contains the configuration from when the object instance was first created.
- IOptionsSnapshot<T>—A new instance is created, when needed, if the underlying configuration has changed since the last instance was created.

> **WARNING** IOptionsSnapshot<T> is registered as a scoped service, so you can't inject it into singleton services; if you do, you'll have a captive dependency, as discussed in chapter 9. If you need a singleton version of IOptionsSnapshot<T>, you can use a similar interface, IOptionsMonitor<T>. See this blog post for details: http://mng.bz/9Da7.

IOptionsSnaphot<T> is set up for your options classes automatically at the same time as IOptions<T>, so you can use it in your services in exactly the same way. The following listing shows how you could update your display-settings API so that you always get the latest configuration values in your strongly typed AppDisplaySettings options class.

Listing 10.9 Injecting reloadable options using `IOptionsSnapshot<T>`

```
app.MapGet("/display-settings",
    (IOptionsSnapshot<AppDisplaySettings> options) =>      ◁── IOptionsSnapshot<T>
{                                                             updates automatically if the
                                                              underlying configuration
    AppDisplaySettings settings = options.Value;    ◁──      values change.

    return new
    {                                                  The Value property exposes the
        title = settings.Title,                        POCO settings object, the same
        showCopyright = settings.ShowCopyright,        as for IOptions<T>.
    };                     The settings match the configuration values
});                        at that point in time instead of at first run.
```

As `IOptionsSnapshot<AppDisplaySettings>` is registered as a scoped service, it's re-created at every request. If you edit the settings file and cause `IConfiguration` to reload, `IOptionsSnapshot<AppDisplaySettings>` shows the new values on the next request. A new `AppDisplaySettings` object is created with the new configuration values and is used for all future DI—until you edit the file again, of course!

Reloading your settings automatically is as simple as that: update your code to use `IOptionsSnapshot<T>` instead of `IOptions<T>` wherever you need it. But be aware that this change isn't free. You're rebinding and reconfiguring your options object with every request, which may have performance implications. In practice, reloading settings isn't common in production, so you may decide that the developer convenience isn't worth the performance impact.

An important consideration in using the options pattern is the design of your POCO options classes themselves. These classes typically are simple collections of properties, but there are a few things to bear in mind so that you don't get stuck debugging why the binding seemingly hasn't worked.

10.3.3   Designing your options classes for automatic binding

I've already touched on some of the requirements for POCO classes to work with the `IOptions<T>` binder, but there are a few rules to remember. The first key point is that the binder creates instances of your options classes by using reflection, so your POCO options classes need to

- Be nonabstract
- Have a default (`public` parameterless) constructor

If your classes satisfy these two points, the binder will loop through all the properties on your class and bind any that it can. In the broadest sense, the binder can bind any property that

- Is public
- Has a getter (the binder won't write set-only properties)
- Has a setter or, for complex types, a non-`null` value
- Isn't an indexer

Listing 10.10 shows two extensive options class with a host of different types of properties. All the properties on `BindableOptions` are valid to bind, and all the properties on `UnbindableOptions` are not.

> **Listing 10.10   An options class containing binding and nonbinding properties**

```
public class BindableOptions
{
    public string String { get; set; }
    public int Integer { get; set; }
    public SubClass Object { get; set; }
    public SubClass ReadOnly { get; } = new SubClass();
```

The binder can bind simple and complex object types, and read-only properties with a default.

```
    public Dictionary<string, SubClass> Dictionary { get; set; }
    public List<SubClass> List { get; set; }
    public IDictionary<string, SubClass> IDictionary { get; set; }
    public IEnumerable<SubClass> IEnumerable { get; set; }
    public ICollection<SubClass> ReadOnlyCollection { get; }
        = new List<SubClass>();

    public class SubClass                      The binder will also bind collections,
    {                                                   including interfaces.
        public string Value { get; set; }
    }
}

public class UnbindableOptions                  The binder can't bind nonpublic,
{                                                 set-only, null-read-only, or
    internal string NotPublic { get; set; }           indexer properties.
    public SubClass SetOnly { set => _setOnly = value; }
    public SubClass NullReadOnly { get; } = null;
    public SubClass NullPrivateSetter { get; private set; } = null;
    public SubClass this[int i] {
        get => _indexerList[i];
        set => _indexerList[i] = value;
    }
    public List<SubClass> NullList { get; }
    public Dictionary<int, SubClass> IntegerKeys { get; set; }    These collection
    public IEnumerable<SubClass> ReadOnlyEnumerable { get; }      properties can't
        = new List<SubClass>();                                   be bound.

    public SubClass _setOnly = null;               The backing fields for implementing
    private readonly List<SubClass> _indexerList   SetOnly and Indexer properties—
        = new List<SubClass>();                    not bound directly

    public class SubClass
    {
        public string Value { get; set; }
    }
}
```

As shown in the listing, the binder generally supports collections—both implementations and interfaces. If the collection property is already initialized, the binder uses the initialized value; otherwise, the binder may be able to create the collection instance automatically. If your property implements any of the following interfaces, the binder creates a List<> of the appropriate type as the backing object:

- IReadOnlyList<>
- IReadOnlyCollection<>
- ICollection<>
- IEnumerable<>

WARNING You can't bind to an IEnumerable<> property that has already been initialized, as this interface doesn't expose an Add function, and the binder won't replace the backing value. You can bind to an IEnumerable<> if you leave its initial value null.

Similarly, the binder creates a `Dictionary<,>` as the backing field for properties with dictionary interfaces as long as they use `string`, `enum`, or `integer` (`int`, `short`, `byte`, and so on) keys:

- `IDictionary<,>`
- `IReadOnlyDictionary<,>`

WARNING   You can't bind dictionaries that use non-`string` or non-integer keys, such as custom classes or `double`. For examples of binding collection types, see the associated source code for this book.

Clearly, there are quite a few nuances here, but if you stick to the simple cases from the preceding example, you'll be fine. Be sure to check for typos in your JSON files! You could also consider using explicit options validation, as described in this post: http://mng.bz/jPjr.

TIP   The options pattern is most commonly used to bind POCO classes to configuration, but you can also configure your strongly typed settings classes in code by providing a lambda to the `Configure` function, as in `services .Configure<TestOptions>(opt => opt.Value = true)`.

The Options pattern is used throughout ASP.NET Core, but not everyone is a fan. In section 10.3.4 you'll see how to use strongly typed settings and the configuration binder without the Options pattern.

10.3.4 *Binding strongly typed settings without the IOptions interface*

The `IOptions` interface is canonical in ASP.NET Core; it's used by the core ASP.NET Core libraries and has various convenience functions for binding strongly typed settings, as you've already seen. In many cases, however, the `IOptions` interface doesn't give many benefits for *consumers* of the strongly typed settings objects. Services must take a dependency on the `IOptions` interface but then immediately extract the real object by calling `IOptions<T>.Value`. This situation can be especially annoying if you're building a reusable library that isn't inherently tied to ASP.NET Core, as you must expose the `IOptions<T>` interface in all your public APIs.

Luckily, the configuration binder that maps `IConfiguration` objects to strongly typed settings objects isn't inherently tied to `IOptions`. Listing 10.11 shows how you can bind a strongly typed settings object to a configuration section manually, register it with the DI container, and inject the `MapSettings` object directly into a handler or service without the additional ceremony required to use `IOptions<MapSettings>`.

> **Listing 10.11   Configuring strongly typed settings without `IOptions` in Program.cs**

```
WebApplicationBuilder builder = WebApplication.CreateBuilder(args);

var settings = new MapSettings ();
builder.Configuration.GetSection("MapSettings").Bind(settings);
builder.Services.AddSingleton(settings);
```

Creates a new instance of the MapSettings object

Binds the MapSettings section in IConfiguration to the settings object

Registers the settings object as a singleton

```
WebApplication app = builder.Build();

app.MapGet("/", (MapSettings mapSettings) => mapSettings);        Injects the MapSettings
                                                                  object directly using DI

app.Run();
```

Alternatively, you can register the `IOptions` type in the DI container but then use a lambda to additionally register `MapSettings` as a singleton so it can be directly injected, as shown in listing 10.12.

Listing 10.12   Configuring strongly typed settings for direct injection

```
WebApplicationBuilder builder = WebApplication.CreateBuilder(args);

builder.Services.Configure<MapSettings>(                        Configures the
    builder.Configuration.GetSection("MapSettings"));          IOptions as normal
builder.Services.AddSingleton(provider =>
    provider.GetRequiredService<IOptions<MapSettings>>().Value);

WebApplication app = builder.Build();     Registers the MapSettings object in DI by
                                          delegating to the IOptions registration

app.MapGet("/", (MapSettings mapSettings) => mapSettings);
                                                          Injects the MapSettings
app.Run();                                                object directly DI
```

If you use either of these approaches, you won't benefit from the ability to reload strongly typed settings without further work or from some of the more advanced uses of `IOptions`, but in most cases, that's not a big problem. I'm a fan of these approaches generally, but as always, consider what you're losing before adopting them wholeheartedly.

> **TIP** In chapter 31 I show one such advanced scenario in which you configure an `IOptions` object using services in your DI container. For other scenarios, see Microsoft's "Options pattern in ASP.NET Core" documentation at http://mng.bz/DR7y, or see the various `IOptions` posts on my blog, such as this one: http://mng.bz/l1Aj.

That brings us to the end of this section on strongly typed settings. In section 10.4 we'll look at how you can change your settings dynamically at runtime, based on the environment in which your app is running.

10.4   *Configuring an application for multiple environments*

In this section you'll learn about hosting environments in ASP.NET Core. You'll learn how to set and determine which environment an application is running in and how to change which configuration values are used, based on the environment. Using environments lets you switch easily among different sets of configuration values in production compared with development, for example.

Any application that makes it to production will likely have to run in multiple environments. If you're building an application with database access, for example, you'll probably have a small database running on your machine that you use for development. In production, you'll have a completely different database running on a server somewhere else.

Another common requirement is to have different amounts of logging depending on where your app is running. In development, it's great to generate lots of logs, which help with debugging, but when you get to production, too many logs can be overwhelming. You'll want to log warnings, errors, and maybe information-level logs, but definitely not debug-level logs!

To handle these requirements, you need to make sure that your app loads different configuration values depending on the environment it's running in: load the production database connection string when in production, and so on. You need to consider three aspects:

- How your app identifies the environment it's running in
- How you load different configuration values based on the current environment
- How to change the environment for a particular machine

This section tackles these aspects in turn so that you can easily tell your development machine apart from your production servers and act accordingly.

10.4.1 Identifying the hosting environment

When you create a `WebApplicationBuilder` instance in Program.cs, it automatically sets up the hosting environment for your application. By default, `WebApplicationBuilder` uses, perhaps unsurprisingly, an environment variable to identify the current environment. The `WebApplicationBuilder` looks for a magic environment variable called `ASPNETCORE_ENVIRONMENT`, uses it to create an `IHostEnvironment` object, and exposes it as `WebApplicationBuilder.Environment`.

> **NOTE** You can use either the `DOTNET_ENVIRONMENT` or `ASPNETCORE_ENVIRONMENT` environment variable. The `ASPNETCORE_` value overrides the `DOTNET_` value if both are set. I use the `ASPNETCORE_` version throughout this book.

The `IHostEnvironment` interface exposes several useful properties about the running context of your app. The `ContentRootPath` property, for example, tells the application in which directory it can find any configuration files, such as appsettings.json. This folder is typically the one in which the application is running.

> **TIP** `ContentRootPath` is *not* where you store static files that the browser can access directly; that's the `WebRootPath`, typically wwwroot. `WebRootPath` is also exposed on the `Environment` property via the `IWebHostEnvironment` interface.

The `IHostEnvironment.EnvironmentName` property is what interests us in this section. It's set to the value of the `ASPNETCORE_ENVIRONMENT` environment variable, so it can be any value, but you should stick to three commonly used values in most cases:

- `"Development"`
- `"Staging"`
- `"Production"`

ASP.NET Core includes several helper methods for working with these three values, so you'll have an easier time if you stick to them. In particular, whenever you're testing whether your app is running in a particular environment, you should use one of the following extension methods:

- `IHostEnvironment.IsDevelopment()`
- `IHostEnvironment.IsStaging()`
- `IHostEnvironment.IsProduction()`
- `IHostEnvironment.IsEnvironment(string environmentName)`

All these methods make sure that they do case-insensitive checks of the environment variable, so you won't get any wonky errors at runtime if you don't capitalize the environment variable value.

> **TIP** Where possible, use the `IHostEnvironment` extension methods instead of direct string comparison with `EnvironmentName`, as the methods provide case-insensitive matching.

`IHostEnvironment` doesn't do anything other than expose the details of your current environment, but you can use it in various ways. In chapter 4 you saw that `WebApplication` adds the `DeveloperExceptionMiddleware` to your middleware pipeline only in the development environment. Now you know where `WebApplication` was getting its information about the environment: `IHostEnvironment`.

You can use a similar approach to customize which configuration values you load at runtime by loading different files when running in development versus production. This approach is common; it's included out of the box in most ASP.NET Core templates and by default when you use the default `ConfigurationManager` included with `WebApplicationBuilder`.

10.4.2 *Loading environment-specific configuration files*

The `EnvironmentName` value is determined early in the process of bootstrapping your application, before the default `ConfigurationManager` is fully populated by `WebApplicationBuilder`. As a result, you can dynamically change which configuration providers are added to the builder and, hence, which configuration values are loaded when the `IConfiguration` is built.

A common pattern is to have an optional, environment-specific appsettings .ENVIRONMENT.json file that's loaded after the default appsettings.json file. The following listing shows how you could achieve this task if you're customizing the `ConfigurationManager` in Program.cs, but it's also effectively what `WebApplicationBuilder` does by default.

Listing 10.13   Adding environment-specific appsettings.json files

```
WebApplicationBuilder builder = WebApplication.CreateBuilder(args);

IHostEnvironment env = builder.Environment;
builder.Configuration.Sources.Clear();
builder.Configuration
    .AddJsonFile(
        "appsettings.json",
        optional: false)
    .AddJsonFile(
        $"appsettings.{env.EnvironmentName}.json",
        Optional: true);

WebApplication app = builder.Build();

app.MapGet("/", () =>"Hello world!");

app.Run();
```

> The current **IHostEnvironment** is available on **WebApplicationBuilder**.

> It's common to make the base appsettings.json compulsory.

> Adds an optional environment-specific JSON file where the filename varies with the environment

With this pattern, a global appsettings.json file contains settings applicable to most environments. Additional optional JSON files called appsettings.Development.json, appsettings.Staging.json, and appsettings.Production.json are subsequently added to ConfigurationManager, depending on the current EnvironmentName.

Any settings in these files will overwrite values from the global appsettings.json if they have the same key, as you've seen previously. Using environment-specific settings files lets you do things like set the logging to be verbose only in the development environment and switch to more selective logs in production.

Another common pattern is to add or remove configuration providers depending on the environment. You might use the User Secrets provider when developing locally, for example, but Azure Key Vault in production. Listing 10.14 shows how you can use IHostEnvironment to include the User Secrets provider conditionally only in development. Again, WebApplicationBuilder uses this pattern by default.

Listing 10.14   Conditionally including the User Secrets configuration provider

```
WebApplicationBuilder builder = WebApplication.CreateBuilder(args);

IHostEnvironment env = builder.Environment;

builder.Configuration.Sources.Clear();
builder.Configuration
    .AddJsonFile(
        "appsettings.json",
        optional: false)
    .AddJsonFile(
        $"appsettings.{env}.json",
        Optional: true);

if(env.IsDevelopment())
```

> Extension methods make checking the environment simple and explicit.

```
{
    builder.Configuration.AddUserSecrets<Program>();
}

WebApplication app = builder.Build();

app.MapGet("/", () =>"Hello world!");

app.Run();
```

In Staging and Production, the User Secrets provider won't be used.

As already mentioned, it's also common to customize your application's middleware pipeline based on the environment. In chapter 4 you learned that `WebApplication` adds the `DeveloperExceptionPageMiddleware` conditionally when developing locally. The following listing shows how you can use `IHostEnvironment` to control your pipeline in this way so that when you're in staging or production, your app uses `Exception-HandlerMiddleware` instead.

Listing 10.15 Using the hosting environment to customize your middleware pipeline

```
WebApplicationBuilder builder = WebApplication.CreateBuilder(args);

builder.AddProblemDetails();

WebApplication app = builder.Build();

if (!builder.Environment.IsDevelopment())
{
    app.UseExceptionHandler();
}

app.MapGet("/", () =>"Hello world!");

app.Run();
```

Adds the problem details service to the DI container for use by the ExceptionHandlerMiddleware

When not in development, the pipeline uses ExceptionHandlerMiddleware.

> **NOTE** In listing 10.15 you added the Problem Details services to the DI container so that the `ExceptionHandlerMiddleware` can generate a Problem Details response automatically. As you're adding the extra middleware only in Staging and Production, you could add the services conditionally to the DI container too instead of always adding them as we did here.

You can inject `IHostEnvironment` anywhere in your app, but I advise against using it in your own services outside Program.cs. It's far better to use the configuration providers to customize strongly typed settings based on the current hosting environment and inject these settings into your application instead.

As useful as it is, setting `IHostEnvironment` with an environment variable can be a little cumbersome if you want to switch back and forth among different environments during testing. Personally, I'm always forgetting how to set environment variables on the various operating systems I use. The final skill I'd like to teach you is how to set the hosting environment when you're developing locally.

10.4.3 *Setting the hosting environment*

In this section I show you a couple of ways to set the hosting environment when you're developing. These techniques make it easy to test a specific app's behavior in different environments without having to change the environment for all the apps on your machine.

If your ASP.NET Core application can't find an ASPNETCORE_ENVIRONMENT environment variable when it starts up, it defaults to a production environment, as shown in figure 10.6. So when you deploy to production, you'll be using the correct environment by default.

If the WebApplicationBuilder can't find the ASPNETCORE_ENVIRONMENT variable at runtime, it defaults to Production.

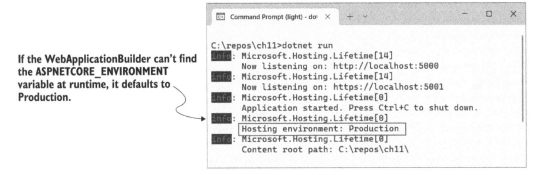

Figure 10.6   By default, ASP.NET Core applications run in the production hosting environment. You can override this default by setting the ASPNETCORE_ENVIRONMENT variable.

> **TIP** By default, the current hosting environment is logged to the console at startup, which can be useful for checking that the environment variable has been picked up correctly.

Another option is to use a launchSettings.json file to control the environment. All the default ASP.NET Core applications include this file in the Properties folder. Launch-Settings.json defines profiles for running your application.

> **TIP** You can use *profiles* to run your application with different environment variables. You can also use profiles to emulate running on Windows behind *Internet Information Services* (IIS) by using the IIS Express profile. I rarely use this profile, even in Windows, and always choose the http or https profile.

Listing 10.16 shows a typical launchSettings.json file that defines three profiles: http, https, and IIS Express. The first two profiles are equivalent to using dotnet run to run the project. The http profile listens only for http:// requests, whereas https listens for both http:// and https://. The IIS Express profile can be used only in Windows and uses IIS Express to run your application.

Listing 10.16   A typical launchSettings.json file defining three profiles

```json
{
  "iisSettings": {
    "windowsAuthentication": false,
    "anonymousAuthentication": true,
    "iisExpress": {
      "applicationUrl": "http://localhost:53846",
      "sslPort": 44399
    }
  },
  "profiles": {
    "http": {
      "commandName": "Project",
      "dotnetRunMessages": true,
      "launchBrowser": true,
      "applicationUrl": "http://localhost:5063",
      "environmentVariables": {
        "ASPNETCORE_ENVIRONMENT": "Development"
      }
    },
    "https": {
      "commandName": "Project",
      "dotnetRunMessages": true,
      "launchBrowser": true,
      "applicationUrl": "https://localhost:7202;http://localhost:5063",
      "environmentVariables": {
        "ASPNETCORE_ENVIRONMENT": "Development"
      }
    },
    "IIS Express": {
      "commandName": "IISExpress",
      "launchBrowser": true,
      "environmentVariables": {
        "ASPNETCORE_ENVIRONMENT": "Development"
      }
    }
  }
}
```

Defines settings for running behind IIS or using the IIS Express profile

The "http" profile is used by default in macOS.

The "project" command is equivalent to calling dotnet run on the project.

If true, gives feedback when dotnet run is executing a build or restore

If true, launches the browser when you run the application

Defines the URLs the application will listen on in this profile

Defines custom environment variables for the profile and sets the environment to Development

The https profile is used by default in Visual Studio in Windows.

Runs the application behind IIS Express (Windows only)

The https profile listens on both http:// and https:// URLs.

Each profile can have different environment variables.

The advantage of using the launchSettings.json file locally is that it allows you to set local environment variables for a project. In listing 10.16 the environment is set to the development environment, for example. Setting environment variables with launch-Settings.json means you can use different environment variables for each project and even for each profile, and store them in source control.

You can choose a profile to use in Visual Studio by choosing it from the drop-down menu next to the Debug button on the toolbar, as shown in figure 10.7. You can choose a profile to run from the command line by using `dotnet run --launch-profile <Profile Name>`. If you don't specify a profile, the first profile listed in launchSettings .json is used. If you don't want to use any profile, you must explicitly ignore the launchSettings.json file by using `dotnet run --no-launch-profile`.

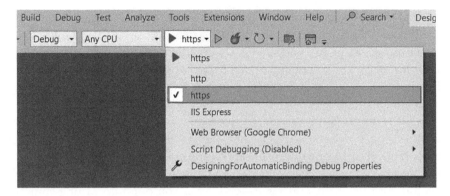

Figure 10.7   You can select the profile to use from Visual Studio by choosing it from the Debug drop-down menu. Visual Studio defaults to using the `https` profile.

If you're using Visual Studio, you can edit the launchSettings.json file visually: double-click the **Properties** node, choose the **Debug** tab, and choose **Open debug launch profiles UI**. You can see in figure 10.8 that the ASPNETCORE_ENVIRONMENT is set to Development; any changes made on this tab are mirrored in launchSettings.json.

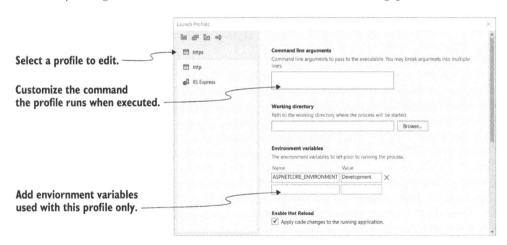

Figure 10.8   You can use Visual Studio to edit the launchSettings.json file, if you prefer. Changes will be mirrored between the launchSettings.json file and the Properties dialog box.

The launchSettings.json file is intended for local development only; by default, the file isn't deployed to production servers. Although you can deploy and use the file in production, doing so generally isn't worth the hassle. Environment variables are a better fit.

One final trick I've used to set the environment in production is to use command-line arguments. You could set the environment to staging like this:

```
dotnet run --no-launch-profile --environment Staging
```

Note that you also have to pass `--no-launch-profile` if there's a launchSettings.json file; otherwise, the values in the file take precedence.

That brings us to the end of this chapter on configuration. Configuration isn't glamorous, but it's an essential part of all apps. The ASP.NET Core configuration provider model handles a wide range of scenarios, letting you store settings and secrets in a variety of locations.

Simple settings can be stored in appsettings.json, where they're easy to tweak and modify during development, and they can be overwritten by using environment-specific JSON files. Meanwhile, your secrets and sensitive settings can be stored outside the project file in the User Secrets manager or as environment variables. This approach gives you both flexibility and safety—as long as you don't go writing your secrets to appsettings.json!

In chapter 11 we take a look at the OpenAPI specification and how you can use it for documenting your APIs, testing your endpoints, and generating strongly typed clients.

Summary

- Anything that could be considered to be a setting or a secret is normally stored as a configuration value. Externalizing these values means that you can change them without recompiling your app.

- ASP.NET Core uses configuration providers to load key-value pairs from a variety of sources. Applications can use many configuration providers.

- You can add configuration providers to an instance of `ConfigurationManager` by using extension methods such as `AddJsonFile()`.

- The order in which you add providers to `ConfigurationManager` is important; subsequent providers replace the values of the same settings defined in earlier providers while preserving unique settings.

- ASP.NET Core includes built-in providers for JSON files, XML files, environment files, and command-line arguments, among others. NuGet packages exist for many other providers, such as YAML files and Azure Key Vault.

- `ConfigurationManager` implements `IConfiguration` as well as `IConfiguration-Builder`, so you can retrieve configuration values from it directly.

- Configuration keys aren't case-sensitive, so you must take care not to lose values when loading settings from case-sensitive sources such as YAML.

- You can retrieve settings from `IConfiguration` directly by using the indexer syntax, such as `Configuration["MySettings:Value"]`. This technique is often useful for accessing configuration values in Program.cs.

- `WebApplicationBuilder` automatically configures a `ConfigurationManager` with JSON, environment variables, command-line arguments, and User Secret providers. This combination provides in-repository storage in JSON files, secret storage in both development and production, and the ability to override settings easily at runtime.

- In production, store secrets in environment variables to reduce the chance of incorrectly exposing the secrets in your code repository. These secrets can be loaded after your file-based settings in the configuration builder.

- On development machines, the User Secrets Manager is a more convenient tool than using environment variables. It stores secrets in your operating system's user profile, outside the project folder, reducing the risk of accidentally exposing secrets in your code repository.

- Be aware that neither environment variables nor the User Secrets Manager tool encrypts secrets. They merely store them in locations that are less likely to be made public, as they're outside your project folder.

- File-based providers such as the JSON provider can reload configuration values automatically when the file changes, allowing you to update configuration values in real time without restarting your app.

- Use strongly typed POCO options classes to access configuration in your app. Using strongly typed options reduces coupling in your app and ensures that classes are dependent only on the configuration values they use.

- Use the `Configure<T>()` extension method in `ConfigureServices` to bind your POCO options objects to `ConfigurationSection`. Alternatively, you can configure `IOptions<T>` objects in code instead of using configuration values by passing a lambda to the `Configure()` method.

- You can inject the `IOptions<T>` interface into your services by using DI. You can access the strongly typed options object on the `Value` property. `IOptions<T>` values are registered in DI as singletons, so they remain the same even if the underlying configuration changes.

- If you want to reload your POCO options objects when your configuration changes, use the `IOptionsSnapshot<T>` interface instead. These instances are registered in DI with a scoped lifetime, so they're re-created for every request. Using the `IOptionsSnapshot<T>` interface has performance implications due to binding to the options object repeatedly, so use it only when that cost is acceptable.

- Applications running in different environments, such as development versus production, often require different configuration values. ASP.NET Core determines the current hosting environment by using the `ASPNETCORE_ENVIRONMENT` environment variable. If this variable isn't set, the environment is assumed to be production.

- You can set the hosting environment locally by using the launchSettings.json file, which allows you to scope environment variables to a specific project.

- The current hosting environment is exposed as an `IHostEnvironment` interface. You can check for specific environments by using `IsDevelopment()`, `IsStaging()`, and `IsProduction()`. Then you can use the `IHostEnvironment` object to load files specific to the current environment, such as appsettings.Production.json.

Documenting APIs with OpenAPI

This chapter covers

- Understanding OpenAPI and seeing why it's useful
- Adding an OpenAPI description to your app
- Improving your OpenAPI descriptions by adding metadata to endpoints
- Generating a C# client from your OpenAPI description

In this chapter I introduce the OpenAPI specification for describing RESTful APIs, demonstrate how to use OpenAPI to describe a minimal API application, and discuss some of the reasons you might want to do so.

In section 11.1 you'll learn about the OpenAPI specification itself and where it fits in to an ASP.NET Core application. You'll learn about the libraries you can use to enable OpenAPI documentation generation in your app and how to expose the document using middleware.

Once you have an OpenAPI document, you'll see how to do something useful with it in section 11.2, where we add Swagger UI to your app. Swagger UI uses your app's OpenAPI document to generate a UI for testing and inspecting the endpoints in your app, which can be especially useful for local testing.

After seeing your app described in Swagger UI, it's time to head back to the code in section 11.3. OpenAPI and Swagger UI need rich metadata about your endpoints to provide the best functionality, so we look at some of the basic metadata you can add to your endpoints.

In section 11.4 you'll learn about one of the best tooling features that comes from creating an OpenAPI description of your app: automatically generated clients. Using a third-party library called NSwag, you'll learn how to automatically generate C# code and classes for interacting with your API based on the OpenAPI description you added in the previous sections. You'll learn how to generate your client, customize the generated code, and rebuild the client when your app's OpenAPI description changes.

Finally, in section 11.5, you'll learn more ways to add metadata to your endpoints to give the best experience for your generated clients. You'll learn how to add summaries and descriptions to your endpoints by using method calls and attributes and by extracting the XML documentation comments from your C# code.

Before we consider those advanced scenarios, we'll look at the OpenAPI specification, what it is, and how you can add an OpenAPI document to your app.

11.1 Adding an OpenAPI description to your app

OpenAPI (previously called Swagger) is a language-agnostic specification for describing RESTful APIs. At its core, OpenAPI describes the schema of a JavaScript Object Notation (JSON) document which in turn describes the URLs available in your application, how to invoke them, and the data types they return. In this section you'll learn how to generate an OpenAPI document for your minimal API application.

Providing an OpenAPI document for your application makes it possible to add various types of automation for your app. You can do the following things, for example:

- Explore your app using Swagger UI (section 11.2).
- Generate strongly-typed clients for interacting with your app (section 11.4).
- Automatically integrate into third-party services such as Azure API Management.

NOTE If you're familiar with SOAP from the old ASP.NET days, you can think of OpenAPI as being the HTTP/REST equivalent of Web Service Description Language (WSDL). Just as a .wsdl file described your XML SOAP services, so the OpenAPI document describes your REST API.

ASP.NET Core includes some support for OpenAPI documents out of the box, but to take advantage of them you'll need to use a third-party library. The two best-known libraries to use are called NSwag and Swashbuckle. In this chapter I use Swashbuckle to add an OpenAPI document to an ASP.NET Core app. You can read how to use NSwag instead at http://mng.bz/6Dmy.

> **NOTE** NSwag and Swashbuckle provide similar functionality for generating OpenAPI documents, though you'll find slight differences in how to use them and in the features they support. NSwag also supports client generation, as you'll see in section 11.4.

Add the Swashbuckle.AspNetCore NuGet package to your project by using the NuGet Package Manager in Visual Studio, or use the .NET CLI by running

```
dotnet add package Swashbuckle.AspNetCore
```

from your project's folder. Swashbuckle uses ASP.NET Core metadata services to retrieve information about all the endpoints in your application and to generate an OpenAPI document. Then this document is served by middleware provided by Swashbuckle, as shown in figure 11.1. Swashbuckle also includes middleware for visualizing your OpenAPI document, as you'll see in section 11.2.

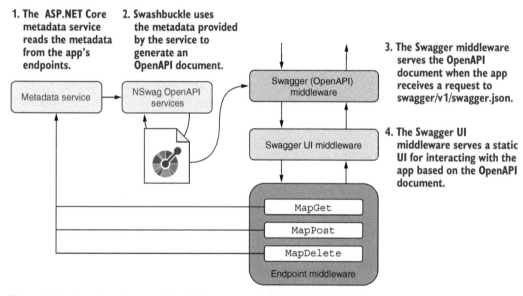

1. The ASP.NET Core metadata service reads the metadata from the app's endpoints.

2. Swashbuckle uses the metadata provided by the service to generate an OpenAPI document.

3. The Swagger middleware serves the OpenAPI document when the app receives a request to swagger/v1/swagger.json.

4. The Swagger UI middleware serves a static UI for interacting with the app based on the OpenAPI document.

Figure 11.1   Swashbuckle uses ASP.NET Core metadata services to retrieve information about the endpoints in your application and builds an OpenAPI document. The OpenAPI middleware serves this document when requested. Swashbuckle also includes optional middleware for visualizing the OpenAPI document using Swagger UI.

After installing Swashbuckle, configure your application to generate an OpenAPI document as shown in listing 11.1. This listing shows a reduced version of the `fruit` API from chapter 5, with only the GET and POST methods included for simplicity. The OpenAPI-related additions are in bold.

> **NOTE** Swashbuckle uses the old Swagger nomenclature rather than OpenAPI in its method names. You should think of OpenAPI as the name of the specification and Swagger as the name of the tooling related to OpenAPI, as described in this post: http://mng.bz/o18M.

> **Listing 11.1 Adding OpenAPI support to a minimal API app using Swashbuckle**

```
using System.Collections.Concurrent;

WebApplicationBuilder builder = WebApplication.CreateBuilder(args);

builder.Services.AddEndpointsApiExplorer();     ←┐  Adds the endpoint-discovery features of
builder.Services.AddSwaggerGen();     ←          │  ASP.NET Core that Swashbuckle requires
                                      └─────────┐
WebApplication app = builder.Build();          │  Adds the Swashbuckle services required
                                                  for creating OpenApi Documents

var _fruit = new ConcurrentDictionary<string, Fruit>();

app.UseSwagger();     ←─────┐
app.UseSwaggerUI();          │  Adds middleware to expose the
                             │  OpenAPI document for your app

app.MapGet("/fruit/{id}", (string id) =>
    _fruit.TryGetValue(id, out var fruit)
    ? TypedResults.Ok(fruit)
    : Results.Problem(statusCode: 404));

app.MapPost("/fruit/{id}", (string id, Fruit fruit) =>
    _fruit.TryAdd(id, fruit)
        ? TypedResults.Created($"/fruit/{id}", fruit)
        : Results.ValidationProblem(new Dictionary<string, string[]>
          {
              { "id", new[] { "A fruit with this id already exists" } }
          }));

app.Run();
record Fruit(string Name, int Stock);
```

Adds middleware that serves the Swagger UI (annotation pointing to `app.MapGet`)

With the changes in this listing, your application exposes an OpenAPI description of its endpoints. If you run the app and navigate to /swagger/v1/swagger.json, you'll find a large JSON file, similar to the one shown in figure 11.2. This file is the OpenAPI Document description of your application.

The OpenAPI document includes a general description of your app, such as a title and version, as well as specific details about each of the endpoints. In figure 11.2, for example, the /fruit/{id} endpoint describes the fact that it needs a GET verb and takes an id parameter in the path.

You can change some of the document values, such as the title, by adding configuration to the AddSwaggerGen() method. You can set the title of the app to "Fruitify" and add a description for the document:

```
builder.Services.AddSwaggerGen(x =>
    x.SwaggerDoc("v1", new OpenApiInfo()
    {
        Title = "Fruitify",
        Description = "An API for interacting with fruit stock",
        Version = "1.0"
    }));
```

Figure 11.2   The OpenAPI Document for the app described in listing 11.1, generated with NSwag

You can also change settings such as the path used to expose the document and various minutia about how Swashbuckle generates the final JSON. See the documentation for details: http://mng.bz/OxQR.

All that is clever, but if you're shrugging and asking "So what?", where OpenAPI *really* shines is the hooks it provides for other tooling. And you've already added one such piece of tooling to your app: Swagger UI.

11.2 Testing your APIs with Swagger UI

In this section you'll learn about Swagger UI (https://swagger.io/tools/swagger-ui), an open-source web UI that makes it easy to visualize and test your OpenAPI apps. In some ways you can think of Swagger UI as being a light version of Postman, which I used in previous chapters to interact with minimal API applications. Swagger UI provides an easy way to view all the endpoints in your application and send requests to them. Postman provides many extra features, such as creating collections and sharing them with your team, but if all you're trying to do is test your application locally, Swagger UI is a great option.

You can add Swagger UI to your ASP.NET Core application using Swashbuckle by calling

```
app.UseSwaggerUI()
```

to add the Swagger UI middleware, as you saw in listing 11.1. The Swagger UI middleware automatically integrates with the OpenAPI document middleware and exposes the Swagger UI web UI in your app at the path /swagger by default. Navigate to /swagger in your app, and you see a page like the one in figure 11.3.

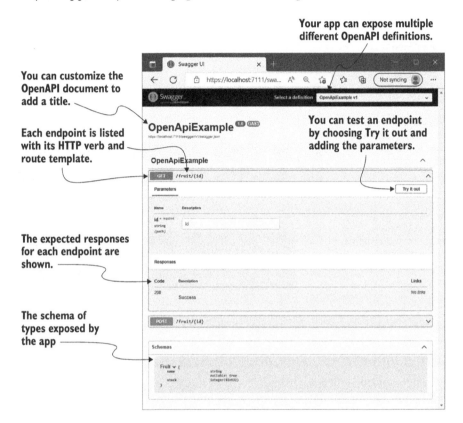

Figure 11.3 The Swagger UI endpoint for the app. With this UI you can view all the endpoints in your app, the schema of objects that are sent and returned, and even test the APIs by providing parameters and sending requests.

Swagger UI lists all the endpoints described in the OpenAPI document, the schema of objects that are sent to and received from each API, and all the possible responses that each endpoint can return. You can even test an API from the UI by choosing **Try it out**, entering a value for the parameter, and choosing **Execute**. Swagger UI shows the command executed, the response headers, and the response body (figure 11.4).

Swagger UI is a useful tool for exploring your APIs and can replace a tool like Postman in some cases. But the examples we've shown so far reveal a problem with our API: the responses described for the GET endpoint in figure 11.3 mentioned a 200 response, but our execution in figure 11.4 reveals that it can also return a 404. To solve that documentation problem, we need to add extra metadata to our APIs.

Add the required
parameters to
send a request.

Choose Execute to
send the request
to your app.

Swagger UI describes
how you can send the
same request from the
command line.

The response code
received is shown,
along with the response
body and headers.

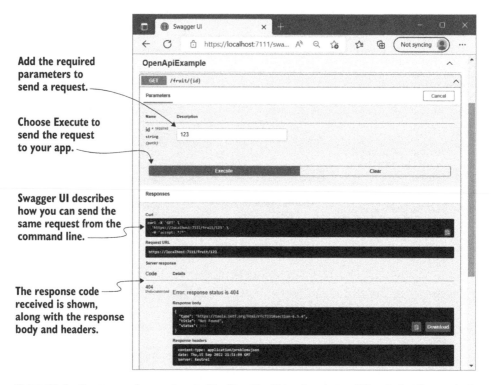

Figure 11.4   You can send requests using the Swagger UI by choosing an API, entering the required parameters, and choosing Execute. Swagger UI shows the response received.

11.3   *Adding metadata to your minimal APIs*

Metadata is information about an API that doesn't change the execution of the API itself. You used metadata in chapter 5 when you added names to your endpoints, using `WithName()`, so that you could reference them by using `LinkGenerator`. The name doesn't change anything about how the endpoint executes, but it provides information for other features to hook into.

Currently, you can add three broad categories of metadata to minimal API endpoints:

- *Routing metadata*—As you've already seen, the `WithName()` methods adds a globally unique name to an endpoint that's used for URL generation.
- *Metadata for other middleware*—Several pieces of middleware can be customized on a per-request basis by adding metadata to an endpoint. When the middleware runs, it checks the selected endpoint's metadata and acts accordingly. Examples include authorization, hostname filtering, and output caching.
- *OpenAPI metadata*—OpenAPI document generation is driven by the metadata exposed by endpoints, which in turn controls the UI exposed by Swagger UI.

We look at how to add authorization metadata to your endpoints in chapter 25, so for now we'll focus on improving the OpenAPI description of your app using metadata. You can provide a lot of details to document your APIs, some of which Swashbuckle uses during OpenAPI generation and some of which it doesn't. The following listing shows how to add a tag for each API and how to explicitly describe the responses that are returned, using `Produces()`.

Listing 11.2   Adding OpenAPI metadata to improve endpoint documentation

```
using System.Collections.Concurrent;

WebApplicationBuilder builder = WebApplication.CreateBuilder(args);

builder.Services.AddEndpointsApiExplorer();
builder.Services.AddSwaggerGen();

WebApplication app = builder.Build();

var _fruit = new ConcurrentDictionary<string, Fruit>();

app.UseSwagger();
app.UseSwaggerUI();

app.MapGet("/fruit/{id}", (string id) =>
    _fruit.TryGetValue(id, out var fruit)
        ? TypedResults.Ok(fruit)
        : Results.Problem(statusCode: 404))
    .WithTags("fruit")
    .Produces<Fruit>()
    .ProducesProblem(404);

app.MapPost("/fruit/{id}", (string id, Fruit fruit) =>
    _fruit.TryAdd(id, fruit)
        ? TypedResults.Created($"/fruit/{id}", fruit)
        : Results.ValidationProblem(new Dictionary<string, string[]>
        {
            { "id", new[] { "A fruit with this id already exists" } }
        }))
    .WithTags("fruit")
    .Produces<Fruit>(201)
    .ProducesValidationProblem();

app.Run();
record Fruit(string Name, int stock);
```

Adding a tag groups the endpoints in Swagger UI. Each endpoint can have multiple tags.

The endpoint can return a Fruit object. When not specified, a 200 response is assumed.

If the id isn't found, the endpoint returns a 404 Problem Details response.

Adding a tag groups the endpoints in Swagger UI. Each endpoint can have multiple tags.

This endpoint also returns a Fruit object but uses a 201 response instead of 200.

If the ID already exists, it returns a 400 Problem Details response with validation errors.

With these changes, Swagger UI shows the correct responses for each endpoint, as shown in figure 11.5. It also groups the endpoints under the tag `"fruit"` instead of the default tag inferred from the project name when no tags are provided.

If adding all this extra metadata feels like a bit of a chore, don't worry. Adding the extra OpenAPI metadata is optional, necessary only if you plan to expose your

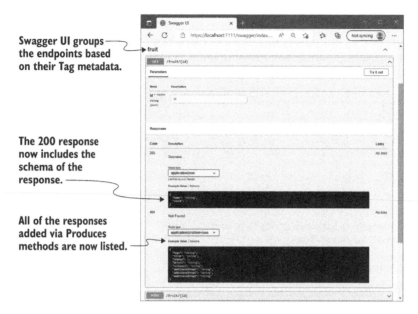

Swagger UI groups the endpoints based on their Tag metadata.

The 200 response now includes the schema of the response.

All of the responses added via Produces methods are now listed.

Figure 11.5   Swagger UI groups the endpoints in your application based on the `Tag` metadata attached to them. The UI uses the metadata added by calling `Produces()` to document the expected return types and status codes for each endpoint.

OpenAPI document for others to consume. If all you want is an easy way to test your minimal APIs, you can go a long way without many of these extra method calls.

> **TIP**   Remember that you can also use route groups (described in chapter 5) to apply metadata to multiple APIs at the same time.

One of the strongest arguments for making your OpenAPI descriptions as rich as possible is that it makes the tooling around your API easier to use. Swagger UI is one example. But an arguably even more useful tool lets you automatically generate C# clients for interacting with your APIs.

11.4   *Generating strongly typed clients with NSwag*

In this section you'll learn how to use your OpenAPI description to automatically generate a client class that you can use to call your API from another C# project. You'll create a console application, use a .NET tool to generate a C# client for interacting with your API, and finally customize the generated types. The generated code includes automatic serialization and deserialization of request types, and makes interacting with your API from another C# project much easier than the alternative method of crafting HTTP requests manually.

> **NOTE**   Generating a strongly typed client is optional. It makes it easier to consume your APIs from C#, but if you don't need this functionality, you can still test your APIs by using Postman or another HTTP client.

You could use any of several tools to automatically generate a C# client from an OpenAPI description, such as OpenAPI Generator (http://mng.bz/Y1wB), but in this chapter I use NSwag. You may remember from section 11.1 that NSwag can be used instead of Swashbuckle to generate an OpenAPI description for your API. But unlike Swashbuckle, NSwag also contains a *client* generator. NSwag is also the default library used by both Visual Studio and the Microsoft .NET OpenAPI global tool to generate C# client code.

Code generation based on an OpenAPI description works via the process shown in figure 11.6. First, Visual Studio or the .NET tool downloads the OpenAPI description JSON file so that it's available locally. The code generation tool reads the OpenAPI description, identifies all the endpoints and schemas described by the document, and generates a C# client class that you can use to call the API described in the document. The code generation tool hooks into the build process so that any time the local OpenAPI description file changes, the code generator runs to regenerate the client.

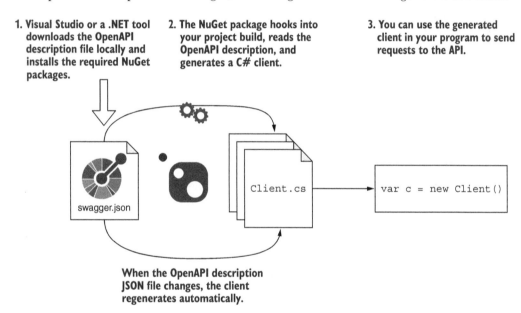

1. Visual Studio or a .NET tool downloads the OpenAPI description file locally and installs the required NuGet packages.

2. The NuGet package hooks into your project build, reads the OpenAPI description, and generates a C# client.

3. You can use the generated client in your program to send requests to the API.

swagger.json

Client.cs

var c = new Client()

When the OpenAPI description JSON file changes, the client regenerates automatically.

Figure 11.6   Visual Studio or a .NET tool downloads the OpenAPI description locally and installs the code-generation tool from NuGet. When your project builds, the generation tool reads the OpenAPI description and generates a C# class for interacting with the API.

You can generate clients by using Visual Studio, as shown in section 11.4.1, or a .NET tool, as shown in section 11.4.2. Both approaches produce the same result, so your choice is a matter of personal preference.

11.4.1 Generating a client using Visual Studio

In this section I show how to generate a client by using Visual Studio's built-in support. For this section I assume that you have a simple .NET 7 console app that needs to interact with your minimal API app.

NOTE   In the sample code for this chapter, both applications are in the same solution for simplicity, but they don't need to be. You don't even need the source code for the API; as long as you have the OpenAPI description of an API, you can generate a client for it.

To generate the client, follow these steps:

1   Ensure that the API application is running and that the OpenAPI description JSON file is accessible. Note the URL at which the JSON file is exposed. If you're following along with the source code for the book, run the OpenApiExample project.

2   In the client project, right-click the project file and then choose **Add > Service Reference** from the contextual menu, as shown in figure 11.7. This command opens the Add Service Reference dialog box.

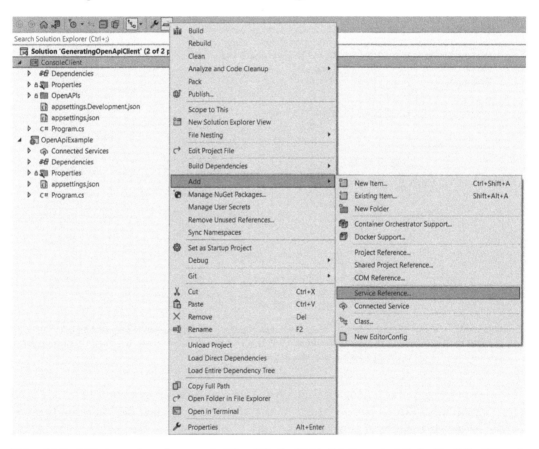

Figure 11.7   Adding a service reference using Visual Studio. Right-click the project that will call the API, and choose Add > Service Reference.

3 In the Add Service Reference dialog box, select **OpenAPI** and then choose
Next. On the Add New OpenAPI Service Reference page, enter the URL where
the OpenAPI document is located. Enter a namespace for the generated code
and a name for the generated client class, as shown in figure 11.8, and then
choose **Finish**.

The Service Reference Configuration Progress screen shows the changes
Visual Studio makes to your application, such as installing various NuGet packages and downloading the OpenAPI document.

TIP   If you're running the sample code with Visual Studio, you can find the
OpenAPI document at https://localhost:7186/swagger/v1/swagger.json. This
location is also displayed in the Swagger UI.

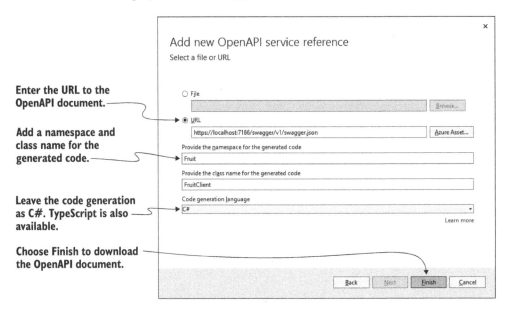

**Figure 11.8   Adding an OpenAPI service reference using Visual Studio. Add the link to the OpenAPI
document, the code generation parameters, and click Finish. Visual Studio downloads the OpenAPI
document and saves it to the project to use for code generation.**

After performing these steps, look at the csproj file of your console app. You'll see that
several NuGet package references were added, as well as a new `<OpenApiReference>` element, as shown in listing 11.3.

Listing 11.3   Adding a service reference for OpenAPI client generation with Visual Studio

```
<Project Sdk="Microsoft.NET.Sdk">

  <PropertyGroup>
    <OutputType>Exe</OutputType>
    <TargetFramework>net7.0</TargetFramework>
```

```
    <ImplicitUsings>enable</ImplicitUsings>
    <Nullable>enable</Nullable>
  </PropertyGroup>
  <ItemGroup>
  <OpenApiReference
        Include="OpenAPIs\swagger.json"
        CodeGenerator="NSwagCSharp"
        Namespace="Fruit"
        ClassName="FruitClient">
      <SourceUri>https://localhost:7186/swagger/v1/swagger.json</SourceUri>
    </OpenApiReference>
  </ItemGroup>

  <ItemGroup>
  <PackageReference
      Include="Microsoft.Extensions.ApiDescription.Client"
      Version="3.0.0">
        <PrivateAssets>all</PrivateAssets>
        <IncludeAssets>runtime; build; native; contentfiles; analyzers;
          buildtransitive</IncludeAssets>
    </PackageReference>
    <PackageReference Include="Newtonsoft.Json" Version="13.0.1" />
    <PackageReference Include="NSwag.ApiDescription.Client"
      Version="13.0.5">
        <PrivateAssets>all</PrivateAssets>
        <IncludeAssets>runtime; build; native; contentfiles; analyzers;
          buildtransitive</IncludeAssets>
    </PackageReference>
  </ItemGroup>

</Project>
```

Defines where the OpenAPI description was loaded from and code generation settings — annotation pointing to `<OpenApiReference`

Extra NuGet packages are required by the code generator. — annotation pointing to `<PackageReference`

Theoretically, this code should be everything you need to generate the client. Unfortunately, Visual Studio adds some out-of-date packages that you'll need to update before your project will build, as follows:

1 Update NSwag.ApiDescription.Client to the latest version (currently, 13.18.2). This package does the code generation based on the OpenAPI description.

2 Update Microsoft.Extensions.ApiDescription.Client to the latest version (7.0.0 at the time of the .NET 7 release). This package is referenced transitively by NSwag.ApiDescription.Client anyway, so you don't have to reference it directly, but doing so ensures that you have the latest version of the package.

NOTE   By default, the generated client uses Newtonsoft.Json to serializes the requests and responses. In section 11.4.4 you'll see how to replace it with the built-in System.Text.Json.

After you make these changes, your project should look similar to the following listing.

Listing 11.4 Updating package versions for OpenAPI generation

```
<Project Sdk="Microsoft.NET.Sdk">

  <PropertyGroup>
    <OutputType>Exe</OutputType>
    <TargetFramework>net7.0</TargetFramework>
    <ImplicitUsings>enable</ImplicitUsings>
    <Nullable>enable</Nullable>
  </PropertyGroup>
  <ItemGroup>
    <OpenApiReference
        Include="OpenAPIs\swagger.json"
        CodeGenerator="NSwagCSharp"
        Namespace="Fruit"
        ClassName="FruitClient">
      <SourceUri>https://localhost:7186/swagger/v1/swagger.json</SourceUri>
    </OpenApiReference>
  </ItemGroup>
```

Updates to the latest version ⟶
```
  <ItemGroup>
    <PackageReference
        Include="Microsoft.Extensions.ApiDescription.Client"
        Version="7.0.0">
        <PrivateAssets>all</PrivateAssets>
        <IncludeAssets>runtime; build; native; contentfiles; analyzers;
          buildtransitive</IncludeAssets>
```

Updates to the latest version ⟶
```
    </PackageReference>
    <PackageReference Include="Newtonsoft.Json" Version="13.0.1" />
    <PackageReference Include="NSwag.ApiDescription.Client"
        Version="13.18.2">
        <PrivateAssets>all</PrivateAssets>
        <IncludeAssets>runtime; build; native; contentfiles; analyzers;
          buildtransitive</IncludeAssets>
    </PackageReference>
  </ItemGroup>

</Project>
```

With the packages updated, you can build your project and generate the `FruitClient`. In section 11.4.3 you'll see how to use this client to call your API, but first we'll look at how to generate the client with a .NET global tool if you're not using Visual Studio.

11.4.2 Generating a client using the .NET Global tool

In this section you'll learn how to generate a client from an OpenAPI definition by using a .NET global tool instead of Visual Studio. The result is essentially the same, so if you've followed the steps in section 11.4.1 in Visual Studio, you can skip this section.

> **NOTE** You don't have to use Visual Studio or a .NET tool. Ultimately ,you need a csproj file that looks like listing 11.4 and an OpenAPI definition JSON file in your project, so if you're happy editing the project file and downloading the definition manually, you can take that approach. Visual Studio and the .NET tool simplify and automate some of these steps.

As in section 11.4.1, the instructions in 11.4.2 assume that you have a console app that needs to call your API, that the API is accessible, and that it has an OpenAPI description. To generate a client by using NSwag, follow these steps:

1 Ensure that the API application is running and that the OpenAPI description JSON file is accessible. Note the URL at which the JSON file is exposed. In the source code associated with the book, run the OpenApiExample project.

2 Install the .NET OpenAPI tool (http://mng.bz/GyOv) globally by running

```
dotnet tool install -g Microsoft.dotnet-openapi
```

3 From the project folder of your console app, add an OpenAPI reference by using the following command, substituting the path to the OpenAPI document and the location to download the JSON file to:

```
dotnet openapi add url http://localhost:5062/swagger/v1/swagger.json
➥ --output-file OpenAPIs\fruit.json
```

TIP If you're running the sample code by using `dotnet run`, you can find the OpenAPI document at the preceding URL. This location is also displayed in the Swagger UI.

4 Update the packages added to your project by running the following commands from the project folder:

```
dotnet add package NSwag.ApiDescription.Client
dotnet add package Microsoft.Extensions.ApiDescription.Client
dotnet add package Newtonsoft.Json
```

After you run all these steps, your OpenAPI description file should have been downloaded to OpenAPIs\fruit.json, and your project file should look similar to the following listing (elements added by the tool highlighted in bold).

Listing 11.5 Adding an OpenAPI reference using the .NET OpenAPI tool

```
<Project Sdk="Microsoft.NET.Sdk">

  <PropertyGroup>
    <OutputType>Exe</OutputType>
    <TargetFramework>net7.0</TargetFramework>
    <ImplicitUsings>enable</ImplicitUsings>
    <Nullable>enable</Nullable>
  </PropertyGroup>

  <ItemGroup>
    <PackageReference
      Include="Microsoft.Extensions.ApiDescription.Client"
      Version="7.0.0">
        <IncludeAssets>runtime; build; native; contentfiles; analyzers;
```

```
        buildtransitive</IncludeAssets>
      <PrivateAssets>all</PrivateAssets>
    </PackageReference>
    <PackageReference Include="Newtonsoft.Json" Version="13.0.1" />
    <PackageReference Include="NSwag.ApiDescription.Client"
      Version="13.18.2">
        <IncludeAssets>runtime; build; native; contentfiles; analyzers;
          buildtransitive</IncludeAssets>
      <PrivateAssets>all</PrivateAssets>
    </PackageReference>
  </ItemGroup>

  <ItemGroup>
  <OpenApiReference Include="OpenAPIs\fruit.json"
      SourceUrl="http://localhost:5062/swagger/v1/swagger.json" />
  </ItemGroup>
</Project>
```

Other than minor ordering differences, the main difference between the Visual Studio approach and the .NET tool approach is that Visual Studio lets you specify the class name and namespace for your new client, whereas the .NET Tool uses the default values. For consistency, add the ClassName and Namespace attributes to the <OpenApiReference> element added by the tool:

```
<OpenApiReference Include="OpenAPIs\fruit.json"
  SourceUrl="http://localhost:5062/swagger/v1/swagger.json"
  Namespace="Fruit"
  ClassName="FruitClient" />
```

In section 11.4.4 you'll learn how to customize the generated code further, but before we get to that topic, let's look at the generated FruitClient and how to use it.

11.4.3   Using a generated client to call your API

So far, you've been taking my word for it that a client is magically generated for your application, so in this section you get to try it out. The NSwag.ApiDescription.Client package added to your project works with the Microsoft.Extensions.ApiDescription.Client package to read the OpenAPI description file in your project. From this description it can work out what APIs you have and what types you need to serialize to and from. Finally, it outputs a C# class with the class name and namespace you specified in the OpenApiReference element.

> **NOTE**   The generated file is typically saved to your project's obj folder. After building your project, you can find the fruitClient.cs file in this folder. Alternatively, use Visual Studio's Go To Definition (F12) functionality on an instance of FruitClient to navigate to the code in your integrated development environment (IDE).

To use the FruitClient to call your API, you must create an instance of it, passing in the base address of your API and an HttpClient instance. Then you can send HTTP requests to the discovered endpoints. A client generated from the OpenAPI description of the simple minimal API in listing 11.2, for example, would have methods called `FruitPOSTAsync()` and `FruitGETASync()`, corresponding to the two exposed methods, as shown in the following listing.

> **Listing 11.6   Calling the API from listing 11.2 using a generated client**

```
using Fruit;    ◄─────  The code is generated in the Fruit namespace.

var client = new FruitClient(      ◄───────┐  Uses the generated FruitClient
    "https://localhost:7186",      ◄──────  Specifies the base address of the API
    new HttpClient());      ◄──────┐
                                    └─  The provided HttpClient is used to call the API.
Fruit.Fruit created = await client.FruitPOSTAsync("123",
    new Fruit.Fruit { Name = "Banana", Stock = 100 });  ◄─┤  The Fruit type is generated
Console.WriteLine($"Created {created.Name}");              │  automatically by NSwag.

Fruit.Fruit fetched = await client.FruitGETAsync("123");  ◄─┐
Console.WriteLine($"Fetched {fetched.Name}");               │  Calls the MapGet
                                                            │  endpoint of the API
```

Calls the MapPost endpoint of the API (annotation pointing to the `Fruit.Fruit created` line)

This code is simultaneously impressive and somewhat horrible:

- It's impressive that you're able to generate all the boilerplate code for interacting with the API. You don't have to do any string interpolation to calculate the path. You don't have to serialize the request body or deserialize the response. You don't have to check for error status codes. The generated code takes care of all those tasks.
- Those `FruitPOSTAsync` and `FruitGETAsync` methods have really ugly names!

Luckily, you can fix the ugly method names: improve your API's OpenAPI definition by adding `WithName()` to every API. The name you provide for your endpoint is used as the OperationID in the OpenAPI description; then NSwag uses it to generate the client methods. This scenario is a prime example of adding more metadata to your OpenAPI, making the tooling better for your consumers.

As well as improve your OpenAPI description, you can customize the code generation directly, as you'll see in the next section.

11.4.4 *Customizing the generated code*

In this section you'll learn about some of the customization options available with the NSwag generator and why you might want to use them. I look at three customization options in this section:

- Using System.Text.Json instead of Newtonsoft.Json for JSON serialization
- Generating an interface for the generated client implementation
- Not requiring an explicit `BaseAddress` parameter in the constructor

By default, NSwag uses Newtonsoft.Json to serialize requests and deserialize responses. Newtonsoft.Json is a popular, battle-hardened JSON library, but .NET 7 has a built-in

JSON library, System.Text.Json, that ASP.NET Core uses by default for JSON serialization. Instead of using two JSON libraries, you may want to replace the serialization used in your client to use System.Text.Json.

When NSwag generates a client, it marks the class as `partial`, which means that you can define your own `partial class FruitClient` (for example) and add any methods that you think are useful to the client. The generated client also provides partial methods that act as hooks just before a request is sent or received.

DEFINITION Partial methods in C# (http://mng.bz/zXEB) are `void`-returning methods that don't have an implementation. You can define the implementation of the method in a separate partial class file. If you don't define the implementation, the method is removed at compile time, so you use partial methods as highly performant event handlers.

Extending your generated clients is useful, but during testing it's common to also want to substitute your generated client by using interfaces. Interfaces let you substitute fake or mock versions of a service so that your tests aren't calling the API for real, as you learned in chapter 8. NSwag can help with this process by automatically generating an `IFruitClient` interface that the `FruitClient` implements.

Finally, providing a base address where the API is hosted makes sense on the face of it. But as we discussed in chapter 9, primitive constructor arguments such as `string` and `int` don't play well with dependency injection. Given that `HttpClient` contains a `BaseAddress` property, you can configure NSwag to *not* require that the base address be passed as a constructor argument and instead set it on the `HttpClient` type directly. This approach helps in dependency injection (DI) scenarios, as you'll see when we discuss `IHttpClientFactory` in chapter 33.

These three seemingly unrelated options are all configured in NSwag in the same way: by adding an `Options` element to the `<OpenApiReference>` element in your project file. The options are provided as command-line switches and must be provided on one line, without line breaks. The switches for the three settings described are

- `/UseBaseUrl:false`—When `false`, NSwag removes the `baseUrl` parameter from the generated client's constructor and instead relies on `HttpClient` to have the correct base address. It defaults to `true`.

- `/GenerateClientInterfaces:true`—When `true`, NSwag generates an interface for the client, containing all the endpoints. The generated client implements this interface. It defaults to `false`.

- `/JsonLibrary:SystemTextJson`—This switch specifies the JSON serialization library to use. It defaults to using Newtonsoft.Json.

TIP A vast number of configuration options is available for NSwag. I find that the best documentation is available in the NSwag .NET tool. You can install the tool by using `dotnet tool install -g NSwag.ConsoleCore`, and you can view the available options by running `nswag help openapi2csclient`.

You can set all three of these options by adding an `<Options>` element to the `<Open-ApiReference>` element, as shown in the following listing. Make sure that you open and close both elements correctly so the XML stays valid; it's an easy mistake to make when editing by hand!

Listing 11.7   Customizing NSwag generator options

```
<OpenApiReference Include="OpenAPIs\fruit.json"
  SourceUrl="http://localhost:5062/swagger/v1/swagger.json"
  Namespace="Fruit"
  ClassName="FruitClient" >
  <Options>/UseBaseUrl:false /GenerateClientInterfaces:true          ⟵  Customizes the
  ➥ /JsonLibrary:SystemTextJson</Options>        ◁                       options NSwag uses
⌐▷ </OpenApiReference>                                                    for code generation
```
**Make sure to close the outer XML
element to keep the XML valid.**

You'd be forgiven for thinking that after making these changes, NSwag would update the generated code next time you build. Unfortunately, it's not necessarily that simple. NSwag watches for changes to the OpenAPI description JSON file saved in your project and will regenerate the code any time the file changes, but it won't necessarily update when you change options in your csproj file. Even worse, doing a clean or rebuild similarly has no effect. If you find yourself in this situation, it's best to delete the obj folder for your project to ensure that everything regenerates correctly.

> **TIP** Another option is to make a tiny change in the OpenAPI document so that NSwag updates the generated code when you build your project. Then you can revert the OpenAPI document change.

After you've persuaded NSwag to regenerate the client, you should update your code to use the new features. You can remove the Newtonsoft.Json reference from your csproj file and update your Program.cs as shown in the following listing.

Listing 11.8   Using the updated NSwag client

```
using Fruit;                        FruitClient now
                               implements IFruitClient.
                                                              Sets the base address on
IFruitClient client = new FruitClient( ⟵                      HttpClient instead of passing
    new HttpClient() { BaseAddress =                          as a constructor argument
        new Uri("https://localhost:7186") });

Fruit.Fruit created = await client.FruitPOSTAsync("123",
    new Fruit.Fruit { Name = "Banana", Stock = 100 });
Console.WriteLine($"Created {created.Name}");

Fruit.Fruit fetched = await client.FruitGETAsync("123");
Console.WriteLine($"Fetched {fetched.Name}");
```

If you updated the operation IDs for your API endpoints using `WithName()`, you may be a little surprised to see that you still have the ugly `FruitPOSTAsync` and `FruitGETAsync` methods, even though you regenerated the client. That's because the OpenAPI description saved to your project is downloaded only once, when you initially add it. Let's look at how to update the local OpenAPI document to reflect the changes to your remote API.

11.4.5 *Refreshing the OpenAPI description*

In this section you'll learn how to update the OpenAPI description document saved to your project that's used for generation. This document doesn't update automatically, so the client generated by NSwag may not reflect the latest OpenAPI description for your API.

Whether you used Visual Studio (as in section 11.4.1) or the .NET OpenAPI tool (as in section 11.4.2), the OpenAPI description saved as a JSON file to your project is a point-in-time snapshot of the API. If you add more metadata to your API, you need to download the OpenAPI description to your project again.

> **TIP** My preferred approach is low-tech: I simply navigate to the OpenAPI description in the browser, copy the JSON contents, and paste it into the JSON file in my project.

If you don't want to update the OpenAPI description manually, you can use Visual Studio or the .NET OpenAPI tool to refresh the saved document for you.

> **WARNING** If you originally used Visual Studio, you can't refresh the document by using the OpenAPI tool and vice versa. The reason is that Visual Studio uses the `SourceUri` attribute on the `OpenApiReference` element and the .NET tool uses the `SourceUrl` attribute. And yes, that situation is arbitrary and annoying!

To update your OpenAPI description by using Visual Studio, follow these steps:

1 Ensure that your API is running and that the OpenAPI description document is available.
2 Navigate to the connected services page for your project by choosing **Project > Connected Services > Manage Connected Services**.
3 Select the overflow button next to your OpenAPI reference and choose **Refresh**, as shown in figure 11.9. Then choose **Yes** in the dialog box to update your OpenAPI document.

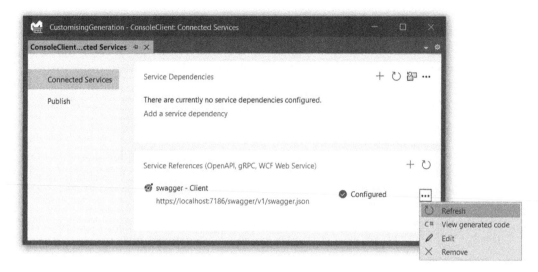

Figure 11.9 Updating the OpenAPI description for an API. Choose Refresh to download the OpenAPI description again and save it to your project. Then NSwag will generate an updated client on the next build.

To update your OpenAPI description by using the .NET OpenAPI tool, follow these steps:

1 Ensure that your API is running and that the OpenAPI description document is available.
2 From your project folder, run the following command, using the same URL you used to add the OpenAPI description originally:

```
dotnet openapi refresh http://localhost:5062/swagger/v1/swagger.json
```

After updating your OpenAPI description by using either Visual Studio or the .NET tool, build your application to trigger NSwag to regenerate your client. Any changes you made to your OpenAPI description (such as adding operation IDs) will be reflected in the generated code.

I think that client generation is the killer app for OpenAPI descriptions, but it works best when you use metadata to add extensive documentation to your APIs. In section 11.5 you'll learn how to go one step further by adding summaries and descriptions to your endpoints.

11.5 *Adding descriptions and summaries to your endpoints*

In this section you'll learn how to add extra descriptions and summaries to your OpenAPI description document. Tools such as Swagger UI and NSwag use these extra descriptions and summaries to provide a better developer experience working with your API. You'll also learn about alternative ways to add metadata to your minimal API endpoints.

11.5.1 *Using fluent methods to add descriptions*

Whilst working with your minimal API endpoints and calling methods such as With-Name() and WithTags(), you may have noticed the methods WithSummary() and WithDescription(). These methods add metadata to your endpoint in exactly the same way as the other With* methods, but unfortunately, they don't update your OpenAPI description without some extra changes.

To make use of the summary and description metadata, you must add an extra NuGet package, Microsoft.AspNetCore.OpenApi, and call WithOpenApi() on your endpoint. This method ensures that the summary and description metadata are added correctly to the OpenAPI description when Swashbuckle generates the document. Add this package via the NuGet package manager or the .NET CLI by calling

```
dotnet add package Microsoft.AspNetCore.OpenApi
```

from the project folder. Then update your endpoints to add summaries and/or descriptions, making sure to call WithOpenApi(), as shown in the following listing.

Listing 11.9 Adding summaries and descriptions to endpoints using `WithOpenApi()`

```
using System.Collections.Concurrent;

WebApplicationBuilder builder = WebApplication.CreateBuilder(args);

builder.Services.AddEndpointsApiExplorer();
builder.Services.AddSwaggerGen();

WebApplication app = builder.Build();

app.UseSwagger();
app.UseSwaggerUI();

var _fruit = new ConcurrentDictionary<string, Fruit>();

app.MapGet("/fruit/{id}", (string id) =>
    _fruit.TryGetValue(id, out var fruit)
        ? TypedResults.Ok(fruit)
        : Results.Problem(statusCode: 404))
    .WithName("GetFruit")
    .WithTags("fruit")
    .Produces<Fruit>()
    .ProducesProblem(404)
    .WithSummary("Fetches a fruit")
    .WithDescription("Fetches a fruit by id, or returns 404" +
      " if no fruit with the ID exists")
    .WithOpenApi();

app.Run();
record Fruit(string Name, int Stock);
```

Adds a summary to the endpoint → `.WithSummary("Fetches a fruit")`

`.WithDescription(...)` → **Adds a description to the endpoint**

`.WithOpenApi();` ← **Exposes the metadata added by summary and description to the OpenAPI description**

With these changes, Swagger UI reflects the extra metadata, as shown in figure 11.10. NSwag also uses the summary as a documentation comment when it generates the

You can add a summary
to the endpoint by calling
WithSummary().

The description for the
endpoint, added by
calling WithDescription()

The id parameter
does not have a
description.

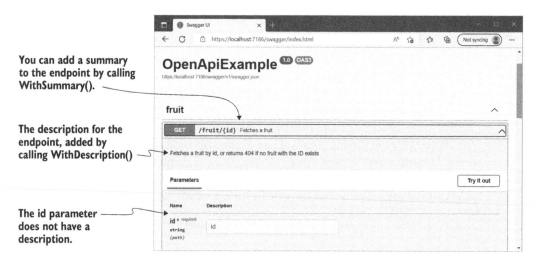

Figure 11.10   The summary and description metadata displayed in the Swagger UI. Note that no description is displayed for the id parameter.

endpoints on the client. You can see in figure 11.10, however, that one piece of documentation is missing: a description of the parameter id.

Unfortunately, you don't have a particularly elegant way to add documentation for your parameters. The suggested approach is to use an overload of the WithOpenApi() method, which takes a lambda method where you can add a description for the parameter:

```
.WithOpenApi(o =>
{
    o.Parameters[0].Description = "The id of the fruit to fetch";
    o.Summary = "Fetches a fruit";
    return o;
});
```

This example shows that you can use the WithOpenApi() method to set any of the OpenAPI metadata for the endpoint, so you can use this single method to set (for example) the summary and tags instead of using the dedicated WithSummary() or WithTags() method.

Adding all this metadata undoubtedly documents your API in more detail and makes your generated code easier to understand. But if you're anything like me, the sheer number of methods you have to call makes it hard to see where your endpoint ends and the metadata begins! In section 11.5.2 we'll look at an alternative approach that involves using attributes.

11.5.2 *Using attributes to add metadata*

I'm a fan of fluent interfaces in many cases, as I feel that they make code easier to understand. But the endpoint metadata extensions, such as those shown in listing 11.9, go to extremes. It's hard to understand what the endpoint is doing with all the noise from the metadata methods! Ever since version 1.0, C# has had a canonical way to add metadata to code—attributes—and you can replace your endpoint extension methods with dedicated attributes if you prefer.

Almost all the extension methods that you add to your endpoint have an equivalent attribute you can use instead. These attributes should be applied directly to the handler method (the lambda function, if that's what you're using). Listing 11.10 shows the equivalent of listing 11.9, using attributes instead of fluent methods where possible. The `WithOpenApi()` method is the only call that can't be replaced; it must be included so that Swashbuckle reads the OpenAPI metadata correctly.

> **Listing 11.10 Using attributes to describe your API**

```
using System.Collections.Concurrent;

WebApplicationBuilder builder = WebApplication.CreateBuilder(args);

builder.Services.AddEndpointsApiExplorer();
builder.Services.AddSwaggerGen();

WebApplication app = builder.Build();

app.UseSwagger();
app.UseSwaggerUI();

var _fruit = new ConcurrentDictionary<string, Fruit>();

app.MapGet("/fruit/{id}",
    [EndpointName("GetFruit")]
    [EndpointSummary("Fetches a fruit")]
    [EndpointDescription("Fetches a fruit by id, or returns 404" +
        " if no fruit with the ID exists")]
    [ProducesResponseType(typeof(Fruit), 200)]
    [ProducesResponseType(typeof(HttpValidationProblemDetails), 404,
        "application/problem+json")]
    [Tags("fruit")]
    (string id) =>
        _fruit.TryGetValue(id, out var fruit)
            ? TypedResults.Ok(fruit)
            : Results.Problem(statusCode: 404))
    .WithOpenApi(o =>
    {
        o.Parameters[0].Description = "The id of the fruit to fetch";
        return o;
    });

app.Run();
record Fruit(string Name, int Stock);
```

You can use attributes instead of fluent method calls.

Whether you think listing 11.10 is better than listing 11.9 is largely a matter of taste, but the reality is that neither is particularly elegant. In both cases the metadata significantly obscures the intent of the API, so it's important to consider which metadata is worth adding and which is unnecessary noise. That balance may shift depending on who your audience is (internal or external customers), how mature your API is, and how much you can extract to helper functions.

11.5.3 *Using XML documentation comments to add metadata*

One understandable complaint about both the attribute and method approaches for attaching OpenAPI metadata is that the summary and parameter descriptions are divorced from the endpoint handler to which they apply. In this section you'll see how an alternative approach that uses Extensible Markup Language (XML) documentation comments.

Every C# developer user will be used to the handy descriptions about methods and parameters you get in your IDE from IntelliSense. You can add these descriptions to your own methods by using XML documentation comments, for example:

```
/// <summary>
/// Adds one to the provided value and returns it
/// </summary>
/// <param name="value">The value to increment</param>
public int Increment(int value) => value + 1;
```

In your IDE—whether that's Visual Studio, JetBrains Rider, or Visual Studio Code—this description appears when you try to invoke the method. Wouldn't it be nice to use the same syntax to define the summary and parameter descriptions for our OpenAPI endpoints? Well, the good news is that we can!

> **WARNING** The use of XML documentation comments is only partially supported in .NET 7. These comments work only when you have static or instance method endpoint handlers, not lambda methods or local functions. You can find the issue tracking full support for XML comments at https://github.com/dotnet/aspnetcore/issues/39927.

Swashbuckle can use the XML comments you add to your endpoint handlers as the descriptions for your OpenAPI description. When enabled, the .NET SDK generates an XML file containing all your documentation comments. Swashbuckle can read this file on startup and use it to generate the OpenAPI descriptions, as shown in figure 11.11.

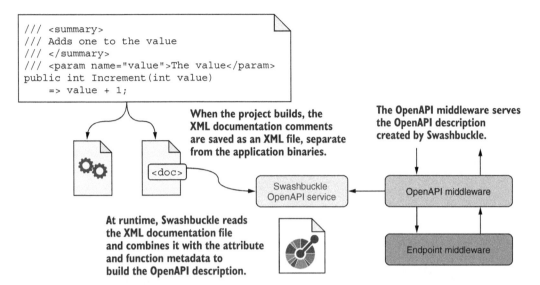

Figure 11.11 You can configure a .NET application to export documentation comments to a dedicated XML file when it builds. Swashbuckle reads this documentation file at runtime, combining it with the attribute and fluent method metadata for an endpoint to generate the final OpenAPI description.

To enable XML documentation comment extraction for your OpenAPI description document you must do three things:

1. Enable documentation generation for your project. Add the `<GenerateDocumentationFile>` inside a `<PropertyGroup>` in your csproj file, and set it to `true`:

```
<PropertyGroup>
  <GenerateDocumentationFile>true</GenerateDocumentationFile>
</PropertyGroup>
```

2. Configure Swashbuckle to read the generated XML document in `SwaggerGen()`:

```
builder.Services.AddSwaggerGen(opts =>
{
    var file = $"{Assembly.GetExecutingAssembly().GetName().Name}.xml";
    opts.IncludeXmlComments(
    Path.Combine(AppContext.BaseDirectory, file));
});
```

3. Use a static or instance method handler and add the XML comments, as shown in the following listing.

Listing 11.11 Adding documentation comments to an endpoint handler

```
using Microsoft.AspNetCore.Mvc;
using System.Collections.Concurrent;
using System.Reflection;
```

```
WebApplicationBuilder builder = WebApplication.CreateBuilder(args);

builder.Services.AddEndpointsApiExplorer();        Enables XML comments for
builder.Services.AddSwaggerGen(opts =>      ⟵       your OpenAPI descriptions
{
    var file = $"{Assembly.GetExecutingAssembly().GetName().Name}.xml";
    opts.IncludeXmlComments(Path.Combine(AppContext.BaseDirectory, file));
});

WebApplication app = builder.Build();

app.UseSwagger();
app.UseSwaggerUI();

var _fruit = new ConcurrentDictionary<string, Fruit>();

var handler = new FruitHandler(fruit);          You must use static or instance
app.MapGet("/fruit/{id}", handler.GetFruit)     handlers, not lambda methods.
    .WithName("GetFruit");        ⟵
                                        You can add extra metadata by using methods.
app.Run();
record Fruit(string Name, int Stock);

internal class FruitHandler
{
    private readonly ConcurrentDictionary<string, Fruit> _fruit;
    public FruitHandler(ConcurrentDictionary<string, Fruit> fruit)
    {
        _fruit = fruit;                         The XML comments are used in
    }                                           the OpenAPI description.

    /// <summary>
    /// Fetches a fruit by id, or returns 404 if it does not exist
    /// </summary>
    /// <param name="id" >The ID of the fruit to fetch</param>
    /// <response code="200">Returns the fruit if it exists</response>
    /// <response code="404">If the fruit doesn't exist</response>
    [ProducesResponseType(typeof(Fruit), 200)]
    [ProducesResponseType(typeof(HttpValidationProblemDetails),
        404, "application/problem+json")]
    [Tags("fruit")]
    public IResult GetFruit(string id)
        => _fruit.TryGetValue(id, out var fruit)        You can also add extra
            ? TypedResults.Ok(fruit)                     metadata by using
            : Results.Problem(statusCode: 404);           attributes on the
}                                                        handler method.
```

I like the XML comment approach, as it feels much more natural for C# and the comments are often deemphasized in IDEs, reducing visual clutter. You'll still need to use attributes and/or fluent methods to fully describe your endpoints for OpenAPI, but every little bit helps!

As I've mentioned several times, how far you go with your OpenAPI description is up to you and how much value you get from it. If you want to use OpenAPI only for local testing with Swagger UI, it doesn't make sense to clutter your code with lots of extra metadata. In fact, in those cases it would be best to add the swagger services and middleware conditionally only when you're in development, as in this example:

```
WebApplicationBuilder builder = WebApplication.CreateBuilder(args);

if(builder.Environment.IsDevelopment())
{
    builder.Services.AddEndpointsApiExplorer();
    builder.Services.AddSwaggerGen();
}

WebApplication app = builder.Build();
if(app.Environment.IsDevelopment())
{
    app.UseSwagger();
    app.UseSwaggerUI();
}

app.Run();
```

On the other hand, if you're generating C# clients for calling your API or exposing your API for public consumption, the more metadata you add, the better! It's also worth noting that you can add OpenAPI descriptions for all the endpoints in your application, not only your minimal API endpoints. When you create web API controllers in chapter 20, you can include them, too.

11.6 Knowing the limitations of OpenAPI

In this chapter I've described the benefits of OpenAPI, both for simple testing with Swagger UI and for code generation. But like most things in software, it's not all sweetness and light. OpenAPI and Swagger have limitations that you may run into, particularly as your APIs increase in complexity. In this section I describe some of the challenges to watch out for.

11.6.1 Not all APIs can be described by OpenAPI

The OpenAPI specification is meant to describe your API so that any client knows how to call it. Unfortunately, OpenAPI can't describe all APIs, which isn't an accident. The OpenAPI specification says "Not all services can be described by OpenAPI—this specification is not intended to cover every possible style of REST APIs." So, the important question is which APIs *can't* it describe?

One classic example is an API that follows the REST design known as Hypertext As the Engine of Application State (HATEOAS). In this design, each request to an API endpoint includes a list of links describing the actions you can take and the paths to use for each action, enabling clients to discover which actions are available for a given resource. The server can add or remove links dynamically, depending on the state of the resource and which user is making the request.

> **TIP** Martin Fowler has a great description of the REST maturity models, in which HATEOAS is the highest level of maturity, at http://mng.bz/0K1N.

HATEOAS generally introduces more complexity than is worthwhile for small projects, but it's a great way to decouple your client-side applications from your server APIs so that they can evolve separately. This approach can be invaluable when you have large or independent teams. The problem for OpenAPI is that it wasn't designed for these kinds of dynamic APIs. OpenAPI wants to know up front what the responses are for each of your endpoints, which isn't information that you can give it if you're following HATEOAS.

In a different scenario, you may have multiple backend APIs, each with its own OpenAPI specification. You expose a single, unified API gateway app, with which all your clients interact. Unfortunately, even though each backend API has an OpenAPI specification, there's no easy way to combine the APIs into a single unified document that you can expose in your API gateway and which clients can use for testing and code generation.

Another common problem centers on securing your APIs with authentication and authorization. The OpenAPI specification contains a section about describing your authentication requirements, and Swagger UI supports them. Where things fall down is if you're using any extensions to the common authentication protocols or advanced features. Although some of these workflows are possible, in some cases Swagger UI simply may not support your workflow, rendering Swagger UI unusable.

11.6.2 *Generated code is opinionated*

At the end of section 11.4 I said that code generation is the killer feature for Open API documents, and in many cases it is. That statement, however, assumes that you *like* the generated code. If the tooling you use—whether that's NSwag or some other code generator—doesn't generate the code you want, you may find yourself spending a lot of effort customizing and tweaking the output. At some point and for some APIs, it may be simpler and easier to write your own client!

> **NOTE** A classic complaint (with which I sympathize) is the use of exceptions for process flow whenever an error or unexpected status code is returned. Not all errors are exceptional, throwing exceptions is relatively expensive computationally, and it often means that every call made with a client needs custom exception handling. This design sometimes makes code generation seem more like a burden than a benefit.

Another, subtler issue arises when you use code generation with two separate but related OpenAPI documents, such as a products API and a cart API. If you use the techniques in this chapter to generate the clients and then try to follow this simple sequence, you'll run into trouble:

1 Retrieve a `Product` instance from the products API by using `ProductsClient.Get()`.
2 Send the retrieved `Product` to the cart API by using `CartClient.Add(Product)`.

Unfortunately, the generated `Product` type retrieved from the products API is a different type from the generated `Product` type that the `CartClient` requires, so this code won't compile. Even if the type has the same properties and is serialized to the same JSON when it's sent to the client, *C# considers the objects to be different types* and won't let them swap places. You must copy the values manually from the first `Product` instance to a new instance. These complaints are mostly small niggles and paper cuts, but they can add up when you run into them often.

11.6.3 *Tooling often lags the specification*

Another factor to consider is the many groups that are involved in generating an OpenAPI document and generating a client:

- The Open API specification is a community-driven project written by the OpenAPI Initiative group.
- Microsoft provides the tooling built into ASP.NET Core for supplying the metadata about your API endpoints.
- Swashbuckle is an open-source project that uses the ASP.NET Core metadata to generate an OpenAPI-compatible document.
- NSwag is an open-source project that takes an OpenAPI-compatible document and generates clients (and has many other features!).
- Swagger UI is an open-source project for interacting with APIs based on the OpenAPI document.

Some of these projects have direct dependencies on others (everything depends on the OpenAPI specification, for example), but they may evolve at difference paces. If Swashbuckle doesn't support some new feature of the OpenAPI specification, it won't appear in your documents, and NSwag won't be able to use it.

Most of the tools provide ways to override the behavior to work around these rough edges, but the reality is that if you're using newer or less popular features, you may have more difficulty persuading all the tools in your tool chain to play together nicely.

Overall, the important thing to remember is that OpenAPI documents *may* work well if you have simple requirements or want to use Swagger UI only for testing. In these cases, there's little investment required to add OpenAPI support, and it can improve your workflow, so you might find it worthwhile to try.

If you have more complex requirements, are creating an API that OpenAPI can't easily describe or aren't a fan of the code generation, it may not be worth your time to invest heavily in OpenAPI for your documents.

TIP If you're a fan of code generation but prefer more of a remote procedure call (RPC) style of programming, it's worthwhile to look at gRPC. Code generation for gRPC is robust, supported across multiple languages, and has great support in .NET. You can read more in the documentation at https://learn.microsoft.com/aspnet/core/grpc.

In chapter 12 we'll take a brief look at the new object-relational mapper that fits well with ASP.NET Core: Entity Framework Core. You'll get only a taste of it in this book, but you'll learn how to load and save data, build a database from your code, and migrate the database as your code evolves.

Summary

- OpenAPI is a specification for describing HTTP APIs in a machine-readable format, as a JSON document. You can use this document to drive other tooling, such as code generators or API testers.

- You can add OpenAPI document generation to an ASP.NET Core app by using the NSwag or Swashbuckle NuGet package. These packages work with ASP.NET Core services to read metadata about all the endpoints in your application to build an OpenAPI document.

- The Swashbuckle Swagger middleware exposes the OpenAPI Document for your application at the path `/swagger/v1/swagger.json` by default. Exposing the document in this way makes it easy for other tools to understand the endpoints in your application.

- You can explore and test your API by using Swagger UI. The Swashbuckle Swagger UI middleware exposes the UI at the path `/swagger` by default. You can use Swagger UI to explore your API, send test requests to your endpoints, and check how well your API is documented.

- You can customize the OpenAPI description of your endpoints by adding metadata. You can provide tags, for example, by calling `WithTags()` on an endpoint and specify that an endpoint returns a type `T` with a `201` status code using `Produces<T>(201)`. Adding metadata improves your API's OpenAPI description, which in turn improves tooling such as Swagger UI.

- You can use NSwag to generate a C# client from an OpenAPI description. This approach takes care of using the correct paths to call the API, substituting parameters in the path, and serializing and deserializing requests to the API, removing much of the boilerplate associated with interacting with an API.

- You can add code generation to your project by using Visual Studio or the .NET API tool or by making manual changes to your project. Visual Studio and the .NET tool automate downloading the OpenAPI description to your local project and adding the necessary NuGet packages. You should update the NuGet packages to the latest versions to ensure that you have the latest bug or security fixes.

- NSwag automatically generates a C# method name on the main client class for each endpoint in the OpenAPI description. If the endpoint's OperationID is missing, NSwag generates a name, which may not be optimal. You can specify the OperationID to use for an endpoint in your OpenAPI description by calling `WithName()` on the endpoint.

- You can customize the client NSwag generates by adding an `<Options>` element inside the `<OpenApiReference>` in your .csproj file. These options are specified as command-line switches such as `/JsonLibrary:SystemTextJson`. You can change many things about the generated code with these switches, such as the serialization library to use and whether to generate an interface for the client.

- If the OpenAPI description for a remote API changes, you need to download the document to your project again for the generated client to reflect these changes. If you originally added the OpenAPI reference by using Visual Studio, you should use Visual Studio to refresh the document, and the same applies to the .NET API tool. NSwag automatically updates the generated code when the downloaded OpenAPI document changes.

- You can add an OpenAPI summary and description to an endpoint by installing the Microsoft.AspNetCore.OpenApi package, calling `WithOpenApi()` on the endpoint, and adding calls to `WithSummary()` or `WithDescription()`. This metadata is shown in Swagger UI, and NSwag uses the summary to generate documentation comments in the C# client.

- You can use attributes instead of fluent methods to add OpenAPI metadata if you prefer. This approach sometimes helps improve readability of your endpoints. You must still call `WithOpenApi()` on the endpoint to read the metadata attributes.

- You can use XML documentation comments to document your OpenAPIs to reduce the clutter of extra method calls and attributes. To use this approach, you must enable documentation generation for the project, configure Swashbuckle to read the XML documentation file on startup, and use static or instance handler methods instead of lambda methods.

- Not all APIs can be described by the OpenAPI specification. Some styles, such as HATEOAS, are naturally dynamic and don't lend themselves to the static design of OpenAPI. You may also have difficulty with complex authentication requirements, as well as combining OpenAPI documents. In these cases, you may find that OpenAPI brings little value to your application.

Saving data with
Entity Framework Core

This chapter covers

- Understanding what Entity Framework Core is and why you should use it
- Adding Entity Framework Core to an ASP.NET Core application
- Building a data model and using it to create a database
- Querying, creating, and updating data with Entity Framework Core

Most applications that you'll build with ASP.NET Core require storing and loading some kind of data. Even the examples so far in this book have assumed that you have some sort of data store—storing exchange rates, user shopping carts, or the locations of physical stores. I've glossed over this topic for the most part, but typically you'll store this data in a database.

Working with databases can be a rather cumbersome process. You have to manage connections to the database, translate data from your application to a format the database can understand, and handle a plethora of other subtle problems. You can manage this complexity in a variety of ways, but I'm going to focus on using a library built for modern .NET: Entity Framework Core (EF Core). EF Core is a library that lets you quickly and easily build database access code for your ASP.NET Core applications. It's modeled on the popular Entity Framework 6.x library, but it has significant changes that make it stand alone in its own right as more than an upgrade.

The aim of this chapter is to provide a quick overview of EF Core and show how you can use it in your applications to query and save to a database quickly. You'll learn enough to connect your app to a database and manage schema changes to the database, but I won't be going into great depth on any topics.

> **NOTE** For an in-depth look at EF Core, I recommend *Entity Framework Core in Action*, 2nd ed., by Jon P. Smith (Manning, 2021). Alternatively, you can read about EF Core on the Microsoft documentation website at https://docs.microsoft .com/ef/core.

Section 12.1 introduces EF Core and explains why you may want to use it in your applications. You'll learn how the design of EF Core helps you iterate quickly on your database structure and reduce the friction of interacting with a database.

In section 12.2 you'll learn how to add EF Core to an ASP.NET Core app and configure it by using the ASP.NET Core configuration system. You'll see how to build a model for your app that represents the data you'll store in the database and how to hook it into the ASP.NET Core DI container.

> **NOTE** For this chapter I use SQLite, a small, fast, cross-platform database engine, but none of the code shown in this chapter is specific to SQLite. The code sample for the book also includes a version using SQL Server Express's LocalDB feature. This version is installed as part of Visual Studio 2022 (when you choose the ASP.NET and Web Development workload), and it provides a lightweight SQL Server engine. You can read more about LocalDB at http://mng.bz/5jEa.

No matter how carefully you design your original data model, the time will come when you need to change it. In section 12.3 I show how you can easily update your model and apply these changes to the database itself, using EF Core for all the heavy lifting.

When you have EF Core configured and a database created, section 12.4 shows how to use it in your application code. You'll see how to *create, read, update, and delete* (CRUD) records, and you'll learn about some of the patterns to use when designing your data access.

In section 12.5 I highlight a few of the problems you'll want to take into consideration when using EF Core in a production app. A single chapter on EF Core can offer only a brief introduction to all the related concepts, so if you choose to use EF Core in your own applications—especially if you're using such a data access library for the first time—I strongly recommend reading more after you have the basics from this chapter.

Before we get into any code, let's look at what EF Core is, what problems it solves, and when you may want to use it.

12.1 *Introducing Entity Framework Core*

Database access code is ubiquitous across web applications. Whether you're building an e-commerce app, a blog, or the Next Big Thing™, chances are that you'll need to interact with a database.

Unfortunately, interacting with databases from app code is often a messy affair, and you can take many approaches. A task as simple as reading data from a database, for example, requires handling network connections, writing SQL statements, and handling variable result data. The .NET ecosystem has a whole array of libraries you can use for this task, ranging from the low-level ADO.NET libraries to higher-level abstractions such as EF Core.

In this section, I describe what EF Core is and the problem it's designed to solve. I cover the motivation for using an abstraction such as EF Core and how it helps bridge the gap between your app code and your database. As part of that discussion, I present some of the tradeoffs you'll make by using EF Core in your apps, which should help you decide whether it's right for your purposes. Finally, we'll take a look at an example EF Core mapping, from app code to database, to get a feel for EF Core's main concepts.

12.1.1 *What is EF Core?*

EF Core is a library that provides an object-oriented way to access databases. It acts as an *object-relational mapper* (ORM), communicating with the database for you and mapping database responses to .NET classes and objects, as shown in figure 12.1.

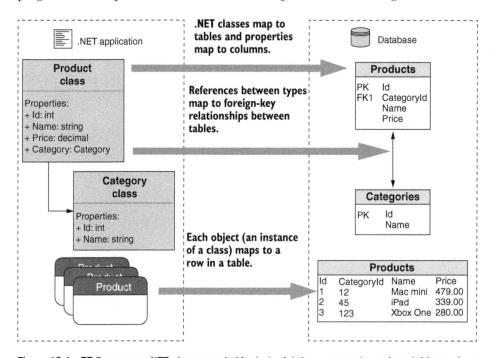

Figure 12.1   EF Core maps .NET classes and objects to database concepts such as tables and rows.

DEFINITION With an *object-relational mapper* (ORM), you can manipulate a database with object-oriented concepts such as classes and objects by mapping them to database concepts such as tables and columns.

EF Core is based on, but distinct from, the existing Entity Framework libraries (currently up to version 6.x). It was built as part of the .NET Core push to work cross-platform, but with additional goals in mind. In particular, the EF Core team wanted to make a highly performant library that could be used with a wide range of databases.

There are many types of databases, but probably the most commonly used family is *relational* databases, accessed via Structured Query Language (SQL). This is the bread and butter of EF Core; it can map Microsoft SQL Server, SQLite, MySQL, Postgres, and many other relational databases. It even has a cool in-memory feature you can use when testing to create a temporary database. EF Core uses a provider model, so support for other relational databases can be plugged in later as they become available.

NOTE As of .NET Core 3.0, EF Core also works with nonrelational, NoSQL, or document databases like Cosmos DB, too. I'm going to consider mapping only to relational databases in this book, however, as that's the most common requirement in my experience. Historically, most data access, especially in the .NET ecosystem, has used relational databases, so it generally remains the most popular approach.

That discussion covers what EF Core is but doesn't dig into why you'd want to use it. Why not access the database directly by using the traditional ADO.NET libraries? Most of the arguments for using EF Core can be applied to ORMs in general, so what are the advantages of an ORM?

12.1.2 Why use an object-relational mapper?

One of the biggest advantages of an ORM is the speed with which it allows you to develop an application. You can stay in the familiar territory of object-oriented .NET, often without needing to manipulate a database directly or write custom SQL.

Suppose that you have an e-commerce site, and you want to load the details of a product from the database. Using low-level database access code, you'd have to open a connection to the database; write the necessary SQL with the correct table and column names; read the data over the connection; create a plain old CLR object (POCO) to hold the data; and set the properties on the object, converting the data to the correct format manually as you go. Sounds painful, right?

An ORM such as EF Core takes care of most of this work for you. It handles the connection to the database, generates the SQL, and maps data back to your POCO objects. All you need to provide is a *LINQ query* describing the data you want to retrieve.

ORMs serve as high-level abstractions over databases, so they can significantly reduce the amount of plumbing code you need to write to interact with a database. At the most basic level, they take care of mapping SQL statements to objects, and vice versa, but most ORMs take this process a step further and provide additional features.

ORMs like EF Core keep track of which properties have changed on any objects they retrieve from the database, which lets you load an object from the database by mapping it from a database table, modify it in .NET code, and then ask the ORM to update the associated record in the database. The ORM works out which properties have changed and issues update statements for the appropriate columns, saving you a bunch of work.

As is so often the case in software development, using an ORM has its drawbacks. One of the biggest advantages of ORMs is also their Achilles' heel: they hide the database from you. Sometimes this high level of abstraction can lead to problematic database query patterns in your apps. A classic example is the *N*+1 problem, in which what should be a single database request turns into separate requests for every single row in a database table.

Another commonly cited drawback is performance. ORMs are abstractions over several concepts, so they inherently do more work than if you were to handcraft every piece of data access in your app. Most ORMs, EF Core included, trade some degree of performance for ease of development.

That said, if you're aware of the pitfalls of ORMs, you can often drastically simplify the code required to interact with a database. As with anything, if the abstraction works for you, use it; otherwise, don't. If you have only minimal database access requirements or need the best performance you can get, an ORM such as EF Core may not be the right fit.

An alternative is to get the best of both worlds: use an ORM for the quick development of the bulk of your application, and fall back to lower-level APIs such as ADO.NET for those few areas that prove to be bottlenecks. That way, you can get good-enough performance with EF Core, trading performance for development time, and optimize only those areas that need it.

> **NOTE**   These days, the performance aspect is one of the weaker arguments against ORMs. EF Core uses many database tricks and crafts clean SQL queries, so unless you're a database expert, you may find that it outperforms even your handcrafted ADO.NET queries!

Even if you decide to use an ORM in your app, many ORMs are available for .NET, of which EF Core is one. Whether EF Core is right for you depends on the features you need and the tradeoffs you're willing to make to get them. Section 12.1.3 compares EF Core with Microsoft's other offering, Entity Framework, but you could consider many other alternatives, such as Dapper and NHibernate, each of which has its own set of tradeoffs.

12.1.3   *When should you choose EF Core?*

Microsoft designed EF Core as a reimagining of the mature Entity Framework 6.x (EF 6.x) ORM, which it released in 2008. With many years of development behind it, EF 6.x was a stable and feature-rich ORM, but it's no longer under active development.

EF Core, released in 2016, is a comparatively new project. The APIs of EF Core are designed to be close to those of EF 6.x—though they aren't identical—but the core components have been completely rewritten. You should consider EF Core to be distinct from EF 6.x; upgrading directly from EF 6.x to EF Core is nontrivial.

Although Microsoft supports both EF Core and EF 6.x, EF 6.x isn't recommended for new .NET applications. There's little reason to start a new application with EF 6.x these days, but the exact tradeoffs will depend largely on your specific app. If you decide to choose EF 6.x instead of EF Core, make sure that you understand what you're sacrificing. Also make sure that you keep an eye on the guidance and feature comparison from the EF team at http://mng.bz/GxgA.

If you decide to use an ORM for your app, EF Core is a great contender. It's also supported out of the box by various other subsystems of ASP.NET Core. In chapter 23 you'll see how to use EF Core with the ASP.NET Core Identity authentication system for managing users in your apps.

Before I get into the nitty-gritty of using EF Core in your app, I'll describe the application we're going to be using as the case study for this chapter. I'll go over the application and database details and discuss how to use EF Core to communicate between the two.

12.1.4 Mapping a database to your application code

EF Core focuses on the communication between an application and a database, so to show it off, you need an application. This chapter uses the example of a simple cooking app API that lists recipes and lets you retrieve a recipe's ingredients, as shown in figure 12.2. Users can list all recipes, add new ones, edit recipes, and delete old ones.

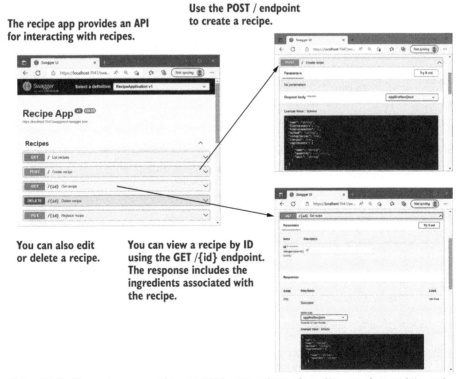

Figure 12.2   The recipe app provides an API for managing recipes. You can view, update, and delete recipes, as well as create new ones.

This API is obviously a simple one, but it contains all the database interactions you need with its two *entities*: Recipe and Ingredient.

> **DEFINITION**   An *entity* is a .NET class that's mapped by EF Core to the database. These are classes you define, typically as POCO classes, that can be saved and loaded by mapping to database tables using EF Core.

When you interact with EF Core, you'll be using primarily POCO entities and a database context that inherits from the DbContext EF Core class. The entity classes are the object-oriented representations of the tables in your database; they represent the data you want to store in the database. You use the DbContext in your application both to configure EF Core and access the database at runtime.

> **NOTE**   You can potentially have multiple DbContexts in your application and even configure them to integrate with different databases.

When your application first uses EF Core, EF Core creates an internal representation of the database based on the DbSet<T> properties on your application's DbContext and the entity classes themselves, as shown in figure 12.3.

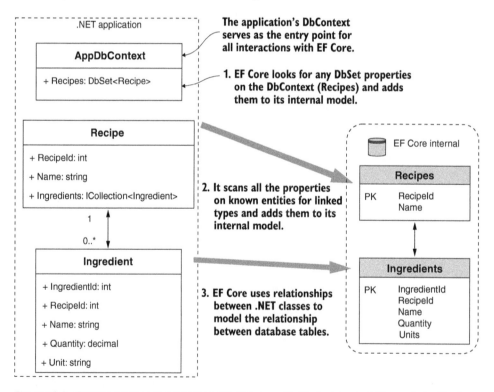

Figure 12.3   EF Core creates an internal model of your application's data model by exploring the types in your code. It adds all the types referenced in the DbSet<> properties on your app's DbContext and any linked types.

For the recipe app, EF Core builds a model of the `Recipe` class because it's exposed on the `AppDbContext` as a `DbSet<Recipe>`. Furthermore, EF Core loops through all the properties of `Recipe`, looking for types it doesn't know about, and adds them to its internal model. In the app, the `Ingredients` collection on `Recipe` exposes the `Ingredient` entity as an `ICollection<Ingredient>`, so EF Core models the entity appropriately.

EF Core maps each entity to a table in the database, but it also maps the relationships between the entities. Each recipe can have many ingredients, but each ingredient (which has a name, quantity, and unit) belongs to one recipe, so this is a many-to-one relationship. EF Core uses that knowledge to correctly model the equivalent many-to-one database structure.

> **NOTE** Two different recipes, such as fish pie and lemon chicken, may use an ingredient that has both the same name and quantity, such as the juice of one lemon, but they're fundamentally two different instances. If you update the lemon chicken recipe to use two lemons, you wouldn't want this change to automatically update the fish pie recipe to use two lemons, too!

EF Core uses the internal model it builds when interacting with the database to ensure that it builds the correct SQL to create, read, update, and delete entities.

Right—it's about time for some code! In section 12.2, you'll start building the recipe app. You'll see how to add EF Core to an ASP.NET Core application, configure a database provider, and design your application's data model.

12.2 Adding EF Core to an application

In this section we focus on getting EF Core installed and configured in your ASP.NET Core recipe API app. You'll learn how to install the required NuGet packages and build the data model for your application. As we're talking about EF Core in this chapter, I'm not going to go into how to create the application in general. I created a simple minimal API app as the basis—nothing fancy.

> **TIP** The sample code for this chapter shows the state of the application at three points in this chapter: at the end of section 12.2, at the end of section 12.3, and at the end of the chapter. It also includes examples using both LocalDB and SQLite providers.

Interaction with EF Core in the example app occurs in a service layer that encapsulates all the data access outside your minimal API endpoint handlers, as shown in figure 12.4. This design keeps your concerns separated and makes your services testable.

Adding EF Core to an application is a multistep process:

1 Choose a database provider, such as Postgres, SQLite, or MS SQL Server.
2 Install the EF Core NuGet packages.
3 Design your app's `DbContext` and entities that make up your data model.
4 Register your app's `DbContext` with the ASP.NET Core DI container.
5 Use EF Core to generate a migration describing your data model.
6 Apply the migration to the database to update the database's schema.

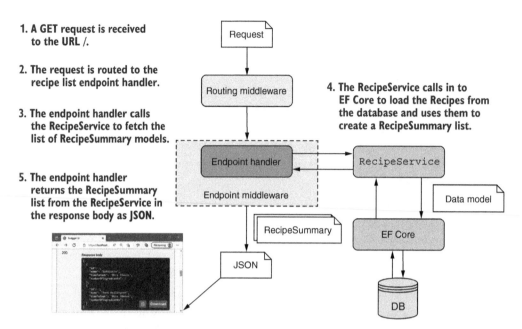

1. A GET request is received to the URL /.

2. The request is routed to the recipe list endpoint handler.

3. The endpoint handler calls the RecipeService to fetch the list of RecipeSummary models.

4. The RecipeService calls in to EF Core to load the Recipes from the database and uses them to create a RecipeSummary list.

5. The endpoint handler returns the RecipeSummary list from the RecipeService in the response body as JSON.

Figure 12.4   Handling a request by loading data from a database using EF Core. Interaction with EF Core is restricted to `RecipeService`; the endpoint doesn't access EF Core directly.

This process may seem a little daunting already, but I'll walk through steps 1–4 in sections 12.2.1–12.2.3 and steps 5–6 in section 12.3, so it won't take long. Given the space constraints of this chapter, I stick to the default conventions of EF Core in the code I show you. EF Core is far more customizable than it may initially appear to be, but I encourage you to stick to the defaults wherever possible, which will make your life easier in the long run.

The first step in setting up EF Core is deciding which database you'd like to interact with. It's likely that a client or your company's policy will dictate this decision, but giving some thought to it is still worthwhile.

12.2.1 Choosing a database provider and installing EF Core

EF Core supports a range of databases by using a provider model. The modular nature of EF Core means that you can use the same high-level API to program against different underlying databases; EF Core knows how to generate the necessary implementation-specific code and SQL statements.

You'll probably have a database in mind when you start your application, and you'll be pleased to know that EF Core has most of the popular ones covered. Adding support for a given database involves adding the correct NuGet package to your .csproj file, such as the following:

- *PostgreSQL*—Npgsql.EntityFrameworkCore.PostgreSQL
- *Microsoft SQL Server*—Microsoft.EntityFrameworkCore.SqlServer
- *MySQL*—MySql.Data.EntityFrameworkCore
- *SQLite*—Microsoft.EntityFrameworkCore.SQLite

Some of the database provider packages are maintained by Microsoft, some are maintained by the open-source community, and some (such as the Oracle provider) require a paid license, so be sure to check your requirements. You can find a list of providers at https://docs.microsoft.com/ef/core/providers.

You install a database provider in your application in the same way as any other library: by adding a NuGet package to your project's .csproj file and running `dotnet restore` from the command line (or letting Visual Studio automatically restore for you).

EF Core is inherently modular, so you'll need to install multiple packages. I'm using the SQLite database provider, so I'll be using the SQLite packages:

- *Microsoft.EntityFrameworkCore.SQLite*—This package is the main database provider package for using EF Core at runtime. It also contains a reference to the main EF Core NuGet package.
- *Microsoft.EntityFrameworkCore.Design*—This package contains shared build-time components for EF Core, required for building the EF Core data model for your app.

TIP You'll also want to install tooling to help create and update your database. I show how to install these tools in section 12.3.1.

Listing 12.1 shows the recipe app's .csproj file after adding the EF Core packages. Remember, you add NuGet packages as `PackageReference` elements.

> **Listing 12.1 Installing EF Core in an ASP.NET Core application**

```
<Project Sdk="Microsoft.NET.Sdk.Web">

  <PropertyGroup>
    <TargetFramework>net7.0</TargetFramework>    ◁——— The app targets .NET 7.0.
    <Nullable>enable</Nullable>
    <ImplicitUsings>enable</ImplicitUsings>
  </PropertyGroup>

  <ItemGroup>
    <PackageReference
      Include="Microsoft.EntityFrameworkCore.SQLite"        Installs the appropriate NuGet
      Version="7.0.0" />                                    package for your selected DB
    <PackageReference
      Include="Microsoft.EntityFrameworkCore.Design"        Contains shared design-time
      Version="7.0.0" >                                     components for EF Core
        <IncludeAssets>runtime; build; native; contentfiles;    Added automatically
          Analyzers; buildtransitive</IncludeAssets>            by NuGet
        <PrivateAssets>all</PrivateAssets>
    </PackageReference>
  </ItemGroup>
</Project>
```

With these packages installed and restored, you have everything you need to start building the data model for your application. In section 12.2.2 we'll create the entity classes and the `DbContext` for your recipe app.

12.2.2   *Building a data model*

In section 12.1.4 I showed an overview of how EF Core builds up its internal model of your database from the DbContext and entity models. Apart from this discovery mechanism, EF Core is flexible in letting you define your entities the way you want to, as POCO classes.

Some ORMs require your entities to inherit from a specific base class or require you to decorate your models with attributes that describe how to map them. EF Core heavily favors a convention over configuration approach, as you can see in listing 12.2, which shows the Recipe and Ingredient entity classes for your app.

> **TIP** The required keyword, used on several properties in listing 12.2, was introduced in C# 11. It's used here to prevent warnings about uninitialized non-nullable values. You can read more about how EF Core interacts with non-nullable types in the documentation at http://mng.bz/Keoj.

Listing 12.2   Defining the EF Core entity classes

```
public class Recipe
{
    public int RecipeId { get; set; }
    public required string Name { get; set; }          A Recipe can have many
    public TimeSpan TimeToCook { get; set; }           Ingredients, represented
    public bool IsDeleted { get; set; }                by ICollection.
    public required string Method { get; set; }
    public required ICollection<Ingredient> Ingredients { get; set; }   <──
}
public class Ingredient
{
    public int IngredientId { get; set; }
    public int RecipeId { get; set; }
    public required string Name { get; set; }
    public decimal Quantity { get; set; }
    public required string Unit { get; set; }
}
```

These classes conform to certain default conventions that EF Core uses to build up a picture of the database it's mapping. The Recipe class, for example, has a RecipeId property, and the Ingredient class has an IngredientId property. EF Core identifies this pattern of an Id suffix as indicating the *primary key* of the table.

> **DEFINITION** The *primary key* of a table is a value that uniquely identifies the row among all the others in the table. It's often an int or a Guid.

Another convention visible here is the RecipeId property on the Ingredient class. EF Core interprets this property to be a *foreign key* pointing to the Recipe class. When considered with ICollection<Ingredient> on the Recipe class, this property represents a many-to-one relationship, in which each recipe has many ingredients but each ingredient belongs to a single recipe (figure 12.5).

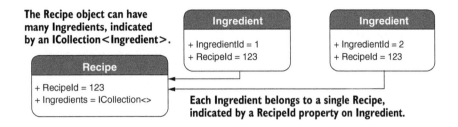

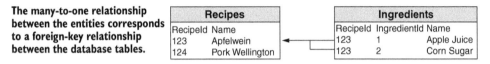

Figure 12.5 Many-to-one relationships in code are translated to foreign key relationships between tables.

DEFINITION A *foreign key* on a table points to the primary key of a different table, forming a link between the two rows.

Many other conventions are at play here, such as the names EF Core will assume for the database tables and columns or the database column types it will use for each property, but I'm not going to discuss them here. The EF Core documentation contains details about all these conventions, as well as how to customize them for your application; see https://docs.microsoft.com/ef/core/modeling.

TIP You can also use `DataAnnotations` attributes to decorate your entity classes, controlling things like column naming and `string` length. EF Core will use these attributes to override the default conventions.

As well as defining the entities, you define the `DbContext` for your application. The `DbContext` is the heart of EF Core in your application, used for all your database calls. Create a custom `DbContext`, in this case called `AppDbContext`, and derive from the `DbContext` base class, as shown in listing 12.3. This class exposes the `DbSet<Recipe>` so that EF Core can discover and map the `Recipe` entity. You can expose multiple instances of `DbSet<>` in this way for each of the top-level entities in your application.

Listing 12.3 Defining the application `DbContext`

```
public class AppDbContext : DbContext         The constructor options object, containing
{                                             details such as the connection string
    public AppDbContext(DbContextOptions<AppDbContext> options)
        : base(options) { }
    public DbSet<Recipe> Recipes { get; set; }   ◁─  You'll use the Recipes property
}                                                    to query the database.
```

The `AppDbContext` for your app is simple, containing a list of your root entities, but you can do a lot more with it in a more complex application. If you wanted to, you could customize how EF Core maps entities to the database, but for this app you're going to use the defaults.

> **NOTE**   You didn't list `Ingredient` on `AppDbContext`, but EF Core models it correctly as it's exposed on the `Recipe`. You can still access the `Ingredient` objects in the database, but you must navigate via the `Recipe` entity's `Ingredients` property to do so, as you'll see in section 12.4.

For this simple example, your data model consists of these three classes: `AppDbContext`, `Recipe`, and `Ingredient`. The two entities are mapped to tables and their columns to properties, and you use the `AppDbContext` to access them.

> **NOTE**   This *code-first* approach is typical, but if you have an existing database, you can automatically generate the EF entities and `DbContext` instead. (You can find more information in Microsoft's "reverse engineering" article at http://mng.bz/mgd4.)

The data model is complete, but you're not quite ready to use it: your ASP.NET Core app doesn't know how to create your `AppDbContext`, and your `AppDbContext` needs a connection string so that it can talk to the database. In section 12.2.3 we tackle both of these problems, and we finish setting up EF Core in your ASP.NET Core app.

12.2.3   *Registering a data context*

As with any other service in ASP.Net Core, you should register your `AppDbContext` with the dependency injection (DI) container. When registering your context, you also configure the database provider and set the connection string so that EF Core knows how to talk with the database.

You register the `AppDbContext` with the `WebApplicationBuilder` in Program.cs. EF Core provides a generic `AddDbContext<T>` extension method for this purpose; the method takes a configuration function for a `DbContextOptionsBuilder` instance. This builder can set a host of internal properties of EF Core and lets you replace all the internal services of EF Core if you want.

The configuration for your app is, again, nice and simple, as you can see in the following listing. You set the database provider with the `UseSqlite` extension method, made available by the Microsoft.EntityFrameworkCore.SQLite package, and pass it a connection string.

Listing 12.4   Registering a `DbContext` with the DI container

```
using Microsoft.EntityFrameworkCore;
WebApplicationBuillder builder = WebApplication.CreateBuilder(args);
var connString = builder.Configuration
        .GetConnectionString("DefaultConnection");
```
The connection string is taken from configuration, from the ConnectionStrings section.

```
Builder.Services.AddDbContext<AppDbContext>(        ◁─┐   Registers your app's
      options => options.UseSqlite(connString));       │   DbContext by using
                                                        │   it as the generic
WebApplication app = builder.Build();                   │   parameter
app.Run();
```
**Specifies the database provider in the
customization options for the DbContext.**

> **NOTE**   If you're using a different database provider, such as a provider for
> SQL Server, you need to call the appropriate `Use*` method on the `options`
> object when registering your `AppDbContext`.

The connection string is a typical secret, as I discussed in chapter 10, so loading it
from configuration makes sense. At runtime the correct configuration string for your
current environment is used, so you can use different databases when developing
locally and in production.

> **TIP**   You can configure your `AppDbContext`'s connection string in other ways,
> such as with the `OnConfiguring` method, but I recommend the method shown
> here for ASP.NET Core websites.

Now you have a `DbContext`, named `AppDbContext`, registered as a scoped service with the
DI container (typical for database-related services), and a data model corresponding
to your database. Codewise, you're ready to start using EF Core, but the one thing you
don't have is a database! In section 12.3 you'll see how you can easily use the .NET CLI
to ensure that your database stays up to date with your EF Core data model.

12.3   Managing changes with migrations

In this section you'll learn how to generate SQL statements to keep your database's
schema in sync with your application's data model, using migrations. You'll learn how
to create an initial migration and use it to create the database. Then you'll update
your data model, create a second migration, and use it to update the database schema.

Managing schema changes for databases, such as when you need to add a new
table or a new column, is notoriously difficult. Your application code is explicitly tied
to a particular version of a database, and you need to make sure that the two are
always in sync.

> **DEFINITION**   *Schema* refers to how the data is organized in a database, includ-
> ing the tables, columns, and relationships among them.

When you deploy an app, normally you can delete the old code/executable and
replace it with the new code. Job done. If you need to roll back a change, delete that
new code, and deploy an old version of the app.

The difficulty with databases is that they contain data, so blowing it away and creating a new database with every deployment isn't possible. A common best practice is to
version a database's schema explicitly along with your application's code. You can do
this in many ways, but typically you need to store the SQL script that takes the database

from the previous schema to the new schema. Then you can use a library such as DbUp (https://github.com/DbUp/DbUp) or FluentMigrator (https://github.com/fluentmigrator/fluentmigrator) to keep track of which scripts have been applied and ensure that your database schema is up to date. Alternatively, you can use external tools to manage this task.

EF Core provides its own version of schema management called *migrations*. Migrations provide a way to manage changes to a database schema when your EF Core data model changes.

> **DEFINITION** A *migration* is a C# code file in your application that defines how the data model changed—which columns were added, new entities, and so on. Migrations provide a record over time of how your database schema evolved as part of your application, so the schema is always in sync with your app's data model.

You can use command-line tools to create a new database from the migrations or to update an existing database by applying new migrations to it. You can even roll back a migration, which updates a database to a previous schema.

> **WARNING** Applying migrations modifies the database, so you must always be aware of data loss. If you remove a table from the database using a migration and then roll back the migration, the table will be re-created, but the data it previously contained will be gone forever!

In this section, you'll see how to create your first migration and use it to create a database. Then you'll update your data model, create a second migration, and use it to update the database schema.

12.3.1 Creating your first migration

Before you can create migrations, you need to install the necessary tooling. You have two primary ways to do this:

- *Package manager console*—You can use PowerShell cmdlets inside Visual Studio's Package Manager Console (PMC). You can install them directly from the PMC or by adding the Microsoft.EntityFrameworkCore.Tools package to your project.
- *.NET tool*—You can use cross-platform, command-line tooling that extends the .NET SDK. You can install the EF Core .NET tool globally for your machine by running `dotnet tool install --global dotnet-ef`.

In this book I use the cross-platform .NET tools, but if you're familiar with EF 6.x or prefer to use the Visual Studio PMC, there are equivalent commands for the steps you're going to take (http://mng.bz/9DK7). You can check that the .NET tool installed correctly by running `dotnet ef`, which should produce a help screen like the one shown in figure 12.6.

Figure 12.6 **Running the** `dotnet ef` **command to check that the .NET EF Core tools are installed correctly**

> **TIP** If you get the `No executable found matching command 'dotnet-ef'` message when running the preceding command, make sure that you installed the global tool by using `dotnet tool install --global dotnet-ef`. In general, you need to run the `dotnet ef` tools from the project folder in which you registered your `AppDbContext`—not from the solution-folder level.

With the tools installed and your database context configured, you can create your first migration by running the following command from inside your web project folder and providing a name for the migration (in this case, `InitialSchema`):

```
dotnet ef migrations add InitialSchema
```

This command creates three files in the Migrations folder in your project:

- *Migration file*—This file, with the Timestamp_MigrationName.cs format, describes the actions to take on the database, such as creating a table or adding a column. Note that the commands generated here are database-provider-specific, based on the database provider configured in your project.
- *Migration designer.cs file*—This file describes EF Core's internal model of your data model at the point in time when the migration was generated.
- *AppDbContextModelSnapshot.cs*—This file describes EF Core's current internal model. This file is updated when you add another migration, so it should always be the same as the current (latest) migration. EF Core can use AppDbContext-ModelSnapshot.cs to determine a database's previous state when creating a new migration without interacting with the database directly.

These three files encapsulate the migration process, but adding a migration doesn't update anything in the database itself. For that task, you must run a different command to apply the migration to the database.

> **TIP** You can, and should, look inside the migration file EF Core generates to check what it will do to your database before running the following commands. Better safe than sorry!

You can apply migrations in any of four ways:

- Using the .NET tool
- Using the Visual Studio PowerShell cmdlets
- In code, by obtaining an instance of your `AppDbContext` from the DI container and calling `context.Database.Migrate()`
- By generating a migration bundle application (see http://mng.bz/jPyr)

Which method is best for you depends on how you designed your application, how you'll update your production database, and what your personal preference is. I'll use the .NET tool for now, but I discuss some of these considerations in section 12.5. You can apply migrations to a database by running

```
dotnet ef database update
```

from the project folder of your application. I won't go into the details on how this command works, but it performs four steps:

1 Builds your application
2 Loads the services configured in your app's Program.cs, including `AppDbContext`
3 Checks whether the database in the `AppDbContext` connection string exists and if not, creates it
4 Updates the database by applying any unapplied migrations

If everything is configured correctly, as in section 12.2, running this command sets you up with a shiny new database like the one shown in figure 12.7.

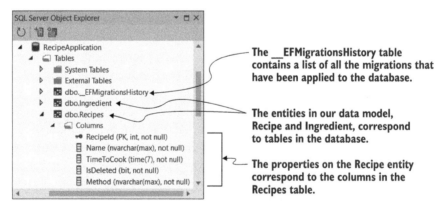

Figure 12.7   Applying migrations to a database creates the database if it doesn't exist and updates the database to match EF Core's internal data model. The list of applied migrations is stored in the __EFMigrationsHistory table.

NOTE   If you get an error message saying `No project was found` when running these commands, check that you're running them in your application's project folder, not the top-level solution folder.

When you apply the migrations to the database, EF Core creates the necessary tables in the database and adds the appropriate columns and keys. You may have also noticed the __EFMigrationsHistory table, which EF Core uses to store the names of migrations that it's applied to the database. Next time you run `dotnet ef database update`, EF Core can compare this table with the list of migrations in your app and apply only the new ones to your database.

In section 12.3.2 we'll look at how migrations make it easy to change your data model and update the database schema without having to re-create the database from scratch.

12.3.2 Adding a second migration

Most applications inevitably evolve due to increased scope or simple maintenance. Adding properties to your entities, adding new entities , and removing obsolete classes are all likely.

EF Core migrations make this evolution simple. Suppose that you decide to highlight vegetarian and vegan dishes in your recipe app by exposing `IsVegetarian` and `IsVegan` properties on the `Recipe` entity (listing 12.5). Change your entities to your desired state, generate a migration, and apply it to the database, as shown in figure 12.8.

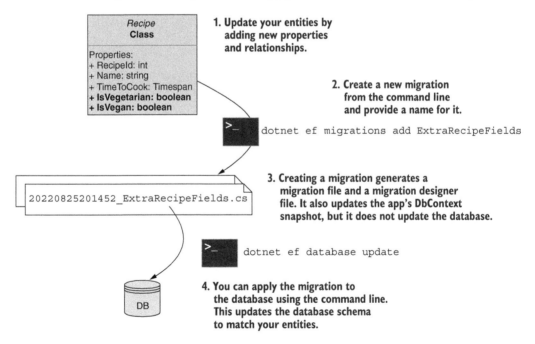

Figure 12.8　Creating a second migration and applying it to the database using the command-line tools

Listing 12.5　Adding properties to the `Recipe` entity

```
public class Recipe
{
    public int RecipeId { get; set; }
    public required string Name { get; set; }
```

```
        public TimeSpan TimeToCook { get; set; }
        public bool IsDeleted { get; set; }
        public required string Method { get; set; }
        public bool IsVegetarian { get; set; }
        public bool IsVegan { get; set; }
        public required ICollection<Ingredient> Ingredients { get; set; }
}
```

As shown in figure 12.8, after changing your entities, you need to update EF Core's internal representation of your data model. You perform this update exactly the same way that you did for the first migration, by calling `dotnet ef migrations add` and providing a name for the migration:

```
dotnet ef migrations add ExtraRecipeFields
```

This command creates a second migration in your project by adding the migration file and its .designer.cs snapshot file; it also updates AppDbContextModelSnapshot.cs (figure 12.9).

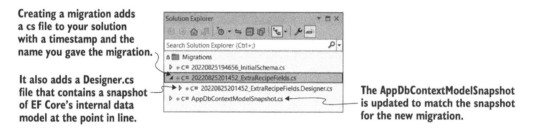

Creating a migration adds a cs file to your solution with a timestamp and the name you gave the migration.

It also adds a Designer.cs file that contains a snapshot of EF Core's internal data model at the point in line.

The AppDbContextModelSnapshot is updated to match the snapshot for the new migration.

Figure 12.9   Adding a second migration adds a new migration file and a migration Designer.cs file. It also updates AppDbContextModelSnapshot to match the new migration's Designer.cs file.

As before, this command creates the migration's files but doesn't modify the database. You can apply the migration and update the database by running

```
dotnet ef database update
```

This command compares the migrations in your application with the __EFMigrationsHistory table in your database to see which migrations are outstanding; then it runs them. EF Core runs the 20220825201452_ExtraRecipeFields migration, adding the `IsVegetarian` and `IsVegan` fields to the database, as shown in figure 12.10.

Using migrations is a great way to ensure that your database is versioned along with your app code in source control. You can easily check out your app's source code for a historical point in time and re-create the database schema your application used at that point.

Migrations are easy to use when you're working alone or deploying to a single web server, but even in these cases, you have important things to consider when deciding

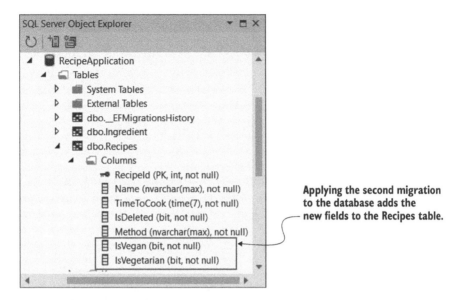

Figure 12.10   Applying the ExtraRecipeFields migration to the database adds the `IsVegetarian` and `IsVegan` fields to the Recipes table.

how to manage your databases. For apps with multiple web servers using a shared database or for containerized applications, you have even more things to think about.

This book is about ASP.NET Core, not EF Core, so I don't want to dwell on database management much. But section 12.5 points out some of the things you need to bear in mind when using migrations in production.

In section 12.4 we'll get back to the meaty stuff: defining our business logic and performing CRUD operations on the database.

12.4   Querying data from and saving data to the database

Let's review where you are in creating the recipe application:

- You created a simple data model consisting of recipes and ingredients.
- You generated migrations for the data model to update EF Core's internal model of your entities.
- You applied the migrations to the database so that its schema matches EF Core's model.

In this section you'll build the business logic for your application by creating a `Recipe-Service`. This service handles querying the database for recipes, creating new recipes, and modifying existing ones. As this app has a simple domain, I'll be using `RecipeService` to handle all the requirements, but in your own apps you may have multiple services that cooperate to provide the business logic.

NOTE For simple apps, you may be tempted to move this logic into your endpoint handlers or Razor Pages. This approach may be fine for tiny apps, but I encourage you to resist the urge generally; extracting your business logic to other services decouples the HTTP-centric nature of your handlers from the underlying business logic, whichoften makes your business logic easier to test and more reusable.

Our database doesn't have any data in it yet, so we'd better start by creating a recipe.

12.4.1 Creating a record

In this section you're going to build functionality to let users create a recipe by using the API. Clients send all the details of the recipe in the body of a POST request to an endpoint in your app. The endpoint uses model binding and validation attributes to confirm that the request is valid, as you learned in chapter 7.

If the request is valid, the endpoint handler calls RecipeService to create the new Recipe object in the database. As EF Core is the topic of this chapter, I'm going to focus on this service alone, but you can always check out the source code for this book if you want to see how everything fits together in a minimal API application.

The business logic for creating a recipe in this application is simple: there is no logic! Copy the properties from the command binding model provided in the endpoint handler to a Recipe entity and its Ingredients, add the Recipe object to AppDbContext, and save it in the database, as shown in figure 12.11.

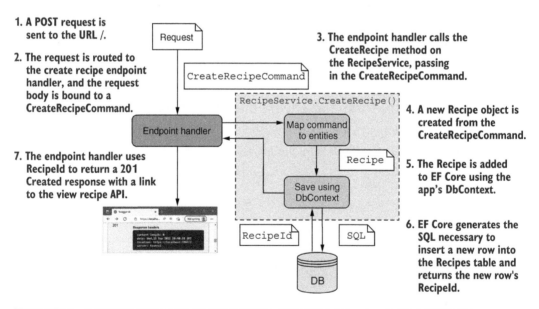

1. A POST request is sent to the URL /.

2. The request is routed to the create recipe endpoint handler, and the request body is bound to a CreateRecipeCommand.

7. The endpoint handler uses RecipeId to return a 201 Created response with a link to the view recipe API.

3. The endpoint handler calls the CreateRecipe method on the RecipeService, passing in the CreateRecipeCommand.

4. A new Recipe object is created from the CreateRecipeCommand.

5. The Recipe is added to EF Core using the app's DbContext.

6. EF Core generates the SQL necessary to insert a new row into the Recipes table and returns the new row's RecipeId.

Figure 12.11 Calling the POST endpoint and creating a new entity. A Recipe is created from the CreateRecipeCommand model and is added to the DbContext. EF Core generates the SQL to add a new row to the Recipes table in the database.

WARNING   Many simple, equivalent sample applications using EF or EF Core allow you to bind directly to the Recipe entity as the model in your endpoint. Unfortunately, this approach exposes a security vulnerability known as *overposting*, which is bad practice. If you want to avoid the boilerplate mapping code in your applications, consider using a library such as AutoMapper (http://automapper.org). For more details on overposting, see my blog post on the subject at http://mng.bz/d48O.

Creating an entity in EF Core involves adding a new row to the mapped table. For your application, whenever you create a new Recipe, you also add the linked Ingredient entities. EF Core takes care of linking all these entities correctly by creating the correct RecipeId for each Ingredient in the database.

All interactions with EF Core and the database start with an instance of AppDb-Context, which typically is DI-injected via the constructor. Creating a new entity requires three steps:

1 Create the Recipe and Ingredient entities.
2 Add the entities to EF Core's list of tracked entities using _context.Add(entity).
3 Execute the SQL INSERT statements against the database, adding the necessary rows to the Recipe and Ingredient tables, by calling _context.SaveChangesAsync().

TIP   There are *sync* and *async* versions of most of the EF Core commands that involve interacting with the database, such as SaveChanges() and SaveChanges-Async(). In general, the async versions will allow your app to handle more concurrent connections, so I tend to favor them whenever I can use them.

Listing 12.6 shows these three steps in practice. The bulk of the code in this example involves copying properties from CreateRecipeCommand to the Recipe entity. The interaction with the AppDbContext consists of only two methods: Add() and SaveChanges-Async().

Listing 12.6   Creating a Recipe entity in the database in RecipeService

An instance of the AppDbContext is injected in the class constructor using DI.

```
readonly AppDbContext _context;      ⤶
public async Task<int> CreateRecipe(CreateRecipeCommand cmd)      ⤶
{
    var recipe = new Recipe
    {
        Name = cmd.Name,
        TimeToCook = new TimeSpan(
            cmd.TimeToCookHrs, cmd.TimeToCookMins, 0),
        Method = cmd.Method,
        IsVegetarian = cmd.IsVegetarian,
        IsVegan = cmd.IsVegan,
        Ingredients = cmd.Ingredients.Select(i =>
```

CreateRecipeCommand is passed in from the endpoint handler.

Creates a Recipe by mapping from the command object to the Recipe entity

```
                 new Ingredient
                 {
                     Name = i.Name,
                     Quantity = i.Quantity,
                     Unit = i.Unit,
                 }).ToList()
            };
         _context.Add(recipe);
         await _context.SaveChangesAsync();
         return recipe.RecipeId;
    }
```

Tells EF Core to track the new entities

Maps each CreateIngredientCommand onto an Ingredient entity

Tells EF Core to write the entities to the database; uses the async version of the command

EF Core populates the RecipeId field on your new Recipe when it's saved.

If a problem occurs when EF Core tries to interact with your database—you haven't run the migrations to update the database schema, for example—this code throws an exception. I haven't shown it here, but it's important to handle these exceptions in your application so you don't present an ugly error message to user when things   go wrong.

Assuming that all goes well, EF Core updates all the autogenerated IDs of your entities (`RecipeId` on `Recipe`, and both `RecipeId` and `IngredientId` on `Ingredient`). Return the recipe ID to the endpoint handler so the handler can use it—to return the ID in the API response, for example.

> **TIP** The `DbContext` type is an implementation of both the unit-of-work and repository patterns, so you generally don't need to implement these patterns manually in your apps. You can read more about these patterns at https://martinfowler.com/eaaCatalog.

And there you have it. You've created your first entity with EF Core. In section 12.4.2 we'll look at loading these entities from the database so you can fetch them all in a list.

12.4.2 Loading a list of records

Now that you can create recipes, you need to write the code to view them. Luckily, loading data is simple in EF Core, relying heavily on LINQ methods to control the fields you need. For your app, you'll create a method on `RecipeService` that returns a summary view of a recipe, consisting of `RecipeId`, `Name`, and `TimeToCook` as a `RecipeSummaryView-Model`, as shown in figure 12.12.

> **NOTE** Creating a view model is technically a UI concern rather than a business-logic concern. I'm returning a view model directly from `RecipeService` here mostly to hammer home the fact that you shouldn't be using EF Core entities directly in your endpoint's public API. Alternatively, you might return the `Recipe` entity directly from the `RecipeService` and then build and return the `RecipeSummaryViewModel` inside your endpoint handler code.

The `GetRecipes` method in `RecipeService` is conceptually simple and follows a common pattern for querying an EF Core database, as shown in figure 12.13. EF Core uses a fluent chain of LINQ commands to define the query to return on the database. The `DbSet<Recipe>` property on `AppDataContext` is an `IQueryable`, so you can use all the usual

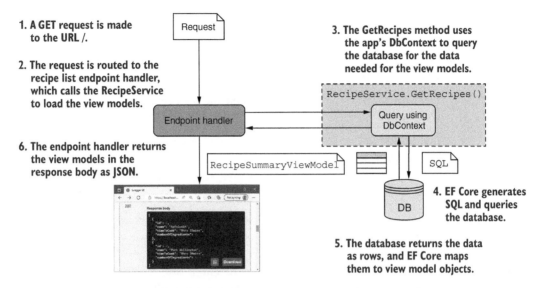

1. A GET request is made to the URL /.

2. The request is routed to the recipe list endpoint handler, which calls the RecipeService to load the view models.

6. The endpoint handler returns the view models in the response body as JSON.

3. The GetRecipes method uses the app's DbContext to query the database for the data needed for the view models.

4. EF Core generates SQL and queries the database.

5. The database returns the data as rows, and EF Core maps them to view model objects.

Figure 12.12 Calling the GET **list endpoint and querying the database to retrieve a list of** RecipeSummaryViewModels. **EF Core generates the SQL to retrieve the necessary fields from the database and maps them to view model objects.**

Select() and Where() clauses that you would with other IQueryable providers. EF Core converts these LINQ methods into a SQL statement to query the database when you call an execute function such as ToListAsync(), ToArrayAsync(), or SingleAsync(), or their non-async brethren.

You can also use the Select() extension method to map to objects other than your entities as part of the SQL query. You can use this technique to query the database efficiently by fetching only the columns you need.

`_context.Recipes.Where(r => !r.IsDeleted).ToListAsync()`

AppDbContext DbSet Property access

LINQ commands to modify data returned

Execute query command

Figure 12.13 The three parts of an EF Core database query

Listing 12.7 shows the code to fetch a list of RecipeSummaryViewModels, following the same basic pattern as figure 12.12. It uses a Where LINQ expression to filter out recipes marked as deleted and a Select clause to map to the view models. The ToListAsync() command instructs EF Core to generate the SQL query, execute it on the database, and build RecipeSummaryViewModels from the data returned.

Listing 12.7 Loading a list of items using EF Core in RecipeService

```
public async Task<ICollection<RecipeSummaryViewModel>> GetRecipes()
{
    return await _context.Recipes        ⟵── A query starts from a DbSet property.
        .Where(r => !r.IsDeleted)
```

```
        .Select(r => new RecipeSummaryViewModel
        {
            Id = r.RecipeId,
            Name = r.Name,
            TimeToCook = $"{r.TimeToCook.TotalMinutes}mins"
        })
        .ToListAsync();
    }
```

EF Core queries only the Recipe columns it needs to map the view model correctly.

Executes the SQL query and creates the final view models

Notice that in the `Select` method you convert the `TimeToCook` property from a `TimeSpan` to a `string` by using string interpolation:

```
TimeToCook = $"{r.TimeToCook.TotalMinutes}mins"
```

I said before that EF Core converts the series of LINQ expressions to SQL, but that statement is a half-truth: EF Core can't or doesn't know how to convert some expressions to SQL. In those cases, such as this example, EF Core finds the fields from the DB that it needs to run the expression on the client side, selects them from the database, and then runs the expression in C#. This approach lets you combine the power and performance of database-side evaluation without compromising the functionality of C#.

> **WARNING** Client-side evaluation is both powerful and useful but has the potential to cause problems. In general, recent versions of EF Core throw an exception if a query requires dangerous client-side evaluation, ensuring (for example) that you can't accidentally return all records to the client before filtering. For more examples, including ways to avoid these problems, see the documentation at http://mng.bz/zxP6.

At this point, you have a list of records displaying a summary of the recipe's data, so the obvious next step is loading the detail for a single record.

12.4.3 Loading a single record

For most intents and purposes, loading a single record is the same as loading a list of records. Both approaches have the same common structure you saw in figure 12.13, but when you're loading a single record, you typically use a `Where` clause that restricts the data to a single entity.

Listing 12.8 shows the code to fetch a recipe by ID, following the same basic pattern as before (figure 12.12). It uses a `Where()` LINQ expression to restrict the query to a single recipe, where `RecipeId == id`, and a `Select` clause to map to `RecipeDetailViewModel`. The `SingleOrDefaultAsync()` clause causes EF Core to generate the SQL query, execute it on the database, and build the view model.

> **NOTE** `SingleOrDefaultAsync()` throws an exception if the previous `Where` clause returns more than one record.

Listing 12.8   Loading a single item using EF Core in `RecipeService`

```
public async Task<RecipeDetailViewModel> GetRecipeDetail(int id)          ◁── The id of the
{                                                                              recipe to load
    return await _context.Recipes           ◁──┤ As before, a query starts     is passed as a
              .Where(x => x.RecipeId == id)     │ from a DbSet property.        parameter.
              .Select(x => new RecipeDetailViewModel
              {
                  Id = x.RecipeId,                                Maps the Recipe to a
                  Name = x.Name,                                  RecipeDetailViewModel
                  Method = x.Method,
                  Ingredients = x.Ingredients
                    .Select(item => new RecipeDetailViewModel.Item   Loads and maps
                    {                                                 linked Ingredients
                        Name = item.Name,                            as part of the
                        Quantity = $"{item.Quantity} {item.Unit}"    same query
                    })
              })
              .SingleOrDefaultAsync();
}
```

Labels (left margin): "Limits the query to the recipe with the provided id" (points to `.Where`); "Executes the query and maps the data to the view model" (points to `.SingleOrDefaultAsync()`).

Notice that as well as mapping the `Recipe` to a `RecipeDetailViewModel`, you map the related `Ingredients` for a `Recipe`, as though you're working with the objects directly in memory. One advantage of using an ORM is that you can easily map child objects and let EF Core decide how best to build the underlying queries to fetch the data.

NOTE   EF Core logs all the SQL statements it runs as `LogLevel.Information` events by default, so you can easily see what queries are running against the database.

Your app is definitely shaping up. You can create new recipes, view them all in a list, and drill down to view individual recipes with their ingredients and method. Soon, though, someone's going to introduce a typo and want to change their data, so you'll have to implement the *U* in *CRUD*: *update*.

12.4.4   Updating a model with changes

Updating entities when they've changed generally is the hardest part of CRUD operations, as there are so many variables. Figure 12.14 shows an overview of this process as it applies to your recipe app.

I'm not going to handle the relationship aspect in this book because that problem generally is complex, and how you tackle it depends on the specifics of your data model. Instead, I'll focus on updating properties on the `Recipe` entity itself.

NOTE   For a detailed discussion of handling relationship updates in EF Core, see *Entity Framework Core in Action*, 2nd ed., by Jon P. Smith (Manning, 2021; http://mng.bz/w9D2).

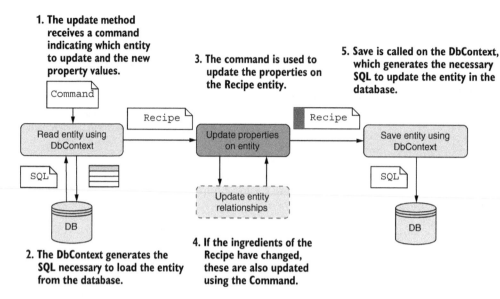

1. The update method receives a command indicating which entity to update and the new property values.

3. The command is used to update the properties on the Recipe entity.

5. Save is called on the DbContext, which generates the necessary SQL to update the entity in the database.

2. The DbContext generates the SQL necessary to load the entity from the database.

4. If the ingredients of the Recipe have changed, these are also updated using the Command.

Figure 12.14   Updating an entity involves three steps: read the entity using EF Core, update the properties of the entity, and call SaveChangesAsync() on the DbContext to generate the SQL to update the correct rows in the database.

For web applications, when you update an entity you typically follow the steps outlined in figure 12.14:

1   Read the entity from the database.
2   Modify the entity's properties.
3   Save the changes to the database.

You'll encapsulate these three steps in a method on RecipeService called UpdateRecipe. This method takes an UpdateRecipeCommand parameter and contains the code to change the Recipe entity.

> **NOTE**   As with the Create command, you don't modify the entities directly in the minimal API endpoint handler, ensuring that you keep the UI/API concern separate from the business logic.

Listing 12.9 shows the RecipeService.UpdateRecipe method, which updates the Recipe entity. It performs the three steps we defined previously to read, modify, and save the entity. I've extracted the code to update the recipe with the new values to a helper method for clarity.

Listing 12.9   Updating an existing entity with EF Core in RecipeService

```
public async Task UpdateRecipe(UpdateRecipeCommand cmd)
{
    var recipe = await _context.Recipes.FindAsync(cmd.Id);
```
Find is exposed directly by Recipes and simplifies reading an entity by id.

Sets the new values on the Recipe entity

If an invalid id is provided, recipe will be null.

```
    if(recipe is null) {
        throw new Exception("Unable to find the recipe");
    }
    UpdateRecipe(recipe, cmd);
    await _context.SaveChangesAsync();
}
```

Executes the SQL to save the changes to the database

```
static void UpdateRecipe(Recipe recipe, UpdateRecipeCommand cmd)
{
    recipe.Name = cmd.Name;
    recipe.TimeToCook =
        new TimeSpan(cmd.TimeToCookHrs, cmd.TimeToCookMins, 0);
    recipe.Method = cmd.Method;
    recipe.IsVegetarian = cmd.IsVegetarian;
    recipe.IsVegan = cmd.IsVegan;
}
```

A helper method for setting the new properties on the Recipe entity

In this example I read the `Recipe` entity using the `FindAsync(id)` method exposed by `DbSet`. This simple helper method loads an entity by its ID—in this case, `RecipeId`. I could have written a similar query with LINQ:

```
_context.Recipes.Where(r=>r.RecipeId == cmd.Id).FirstOrDefault();
```

Using `FindAsync()` or `Find()` is a little more declarative and concise, however.

> **TIP** `Find` is a bit more complicated. `Find` first checks to see whether the entity is already being tracked in EF Core's `DbContext`. If so (because the entity was previously loaded in this request), the entity is returned immediately without calling the database. Using `Find` can obviously be faster if the entity *is* tracked, but it can be slower if you know that the entity isn't being tracked yet.

You may wonder how EF Core knows which columns to update when you call `SaveChangesAsync()`. The simplest approach would be to update every column. If the field hasn't changed, it doesn't matter if you write the same value again. But EF Core is cleverer than that.

EF Core internally tracks the *state* of any entities it loads from the database and creates a snapshot of all the entity's property values so that it can track which ones have changed. When you call `SaveChanges()`, EF Core compares the state of any tracked entities (in this case, the `Recipe` entity) with the tracking snapshot. Any properties that have been changed are included in the UPDATE statement sent to the database, and unchanged properties are ignored.

> **NOTE** EF Core provides other mechanisms to track changes, as well as options to disable change tracking. See the documentation or chapter 3 of Jon P. Smith's *Entity Framework Core in Action*, 2nd ed., (Manning, 2021; http://mng.bz/q9PJ) for details. You can view which details the `DbContext` is tracking by accessing `DbContext.ChangeTracer.DebugView`, as described in the documentation at http://mng.bz/8rlz.

With the ability to update recipes, you're almost done with your recipe app. "But wait!" I hear you cry. "We haven't handled the *D* in *CRUD: delete!*" That's true, but in reality, I've found only a few occasions to delete data. Let's consider the requirements for deleting a recipe from the application:

- You need to provide an API that deletes a recipe.
- After a recipe is deleted, it must not appear in the recipe list and can't be retrieved.

You could achieve these requirements by deleting the recipe from the database, but the problem with data is that when it's gone, it's gone! What if a user accidentally deletes a record? Also, deleting a row from a relational database typically has implications on other entities. You can't delete a row from the `Recipe` table in your application, for example, without also deleting all the `Ingredient` rows that reference it, thanks to the foreign-key constraint on `Ingredient.RecipeId`.

EF Core can easily handle these true deletion scenarios for you with the `DbContext .Remove(entity)` command, but often what you mean when you find a need to delete data is to archive it or hide it from the UI. A common approach to handling this scenario is to include some sort of "Is this entity deleted?" flag on your entity, such as the `IsDeleted` flag I included on the `Recipe` entity:

```
public bool IsDeleted { get; set; }
```

If you take this approach, deleting data suddenly becomes simpler, as it's nothing more than an update to the entity—no more problems of lost data and no more referential-integrity problems.

> **NOTE**   The main exception I've found to this pattern is when you're storing your users' personally identifying information. In these cases, you may be duty-bound (and potentially legally bound) to scrub their information from your database on request.

With this approach, you can create a delete method on `RecipeService` that updates the `IsDeleted` flag, as shown in listing 12.10. In addition, make sure that you have `Where()` clauses in all the other methods in your `RecipeService` to ensure you can't return a deleted `Recipe`, as you saw in listing 12.9 for the `GetRecipes()` method.

Listing 12.10   Marking entities as deleted in EF Core

```
public async Task DeleteRecipe(int recipeId)                          Fetches the Recipe
{                                                                     entity by id
    var recipe = await _context.Recipes.FindAsync(recipeId);  ◁─┘
    if(recipe is null) {                                             If an invalid id is provided,
        throw new Exception("Unable to find the recipe");           recipe will be null.
    }
    recipe.IsDeleted = true;
    await _context.SaveChangesAsync();   ◁─  Executes the SQL to save the
}                                            changes to the database
```

Marks the Recipe as deleted

This approach satisfies the requirements—it removes the recipe from exposure by the API—but it simplifies several things. This soft-delete approach won't work for all scenarios, but I've found it to be a common pattern in projects I've worked on.

> **TIP** EF Core has a handy feature called *global query filters*. These filters allow you to specify a `Where` clause at the model level. You could ensure, for example, that EF Core never loads `Recipes` for which `IsDeleted` is `true`. This feature is also useful for segregating data in a multitenant environment. See the documentation for details: http://mng.bz/EQxd.

We're almost at the end of this chapter on EF Core. We've covered the basics of adding EF Core to your project and using it to simplify data access, but you'll likely need to learn more about EF Core as your apps become more complex. In the final section of this chapter, I'd like to pinpoint a few things you need to take into consideration before using EF Core in your own applications so that you'll be familiar with some of the problems you'll face as your apps grow.

12.5 Using EF Core in production applications

This book is about ASP.NET Core, not EF Core, so I didn't want to spend too much time exploring EF Core. This chapter should've given you enough information to get up and running, but you definitely need to learn more before you even think about putting EF Core into production. As I've said several times, I recommend reading *Entity Framework Core in Action,* 2nd ed., by Jon P. Smith (Manning, 2021), or exploring the EF Core documentation site at https://docs.microsoft.com/ef/core.

The following topics aren't essential for getting started with EF Core, but you'll quickly run up against them if you build a production-ready app. This section isn't a prescriptive guide to tackling each of these items, but more a set of things to consider before you dive into production:

- *Scaffolding of columns*—EF Core uses conservative values for things like `string` columns by allowing strings of large or unlimited length. In practice, you may want to restrict these and other data types to sensible values.
- *Validation*—You can decorate your entities with `DataAnnotations` validation attributes, but EF Core won't validate the values automatically before saving to the database. This behavior differs from EF 6.x behavior, in which validation was automatic.
- *Handling concurrency*—EF Core provides a few ways to handle *concurrency,* which occurs when multiple users attempt to update an entity at the same time. One partial solution is to use `Timestamp` columns on your entities.
- *Handling errors*—Databases and networks are inherently flaky, so you'll always have to account for transient errors. EF Core includes various features to maintain connection resiliency by retrying on network failures.
- *Synchronous vs. asynchronous*—EF Core provides both synchronous and asynchronous commands for interacting with the database. Often, async is better for web apps, but this argument has nuances that make it impossible to recommend one approach over the other in all situations.

EF Core is a great tool for being productive in writing data-access code, but some aspects of working with a database are unavoidably awkward. Database management is one of the thorniest problems to tackle. Most web applications use some sort of database, so the following problems are likely to affect ASP.NET Core developers at some point:

- *Automatic migrations*—If you deploy your app to production automatically as part of some sort of DevOps pipeline, you'll inevitably need some way to apply migrations to a database automatically. You can tackle this situation in several ways, such as scripting the .NET tool, applying migrations in your app's startup code, using EF Core bundles, or using a custom tool. Each approach has its pros and cons.
- *Multiple web hosts*—One specific consideration is whether you have multiple web servers hosting your app, all pointing to the same database. If so, applying migrations in your app's startup code becomes harder, as you must ensure that only one app can migrate the database at a time.
- *Making backward-compatible schema changes*—A corollary of the multiple-web-host approach is that you'll often be in a situation in which your app accesses a database that has a newer schema than the app thinks. Normally, you should endeavor to make schema changes backward-compatible wherever possible.
- *Storing migrations in a different assembly*—In this chapter I included all my logic in a single project, but in larger apps, data access is often in a different project from the web app. For apps with this structure, you must use slightly different commands when using .NET CLI or PowerShell cmdlets.
- *Seeding data*—When you first create a database, you often want it to have some initial seed data, such as a default user. EF 6.x had a mechanism for seeding data built in, whereas EF Core requires you to seed your database explicitly yourself.

How you choose to handle each of these problems depends on the infrastructure and the deployment approach you take with your app. None is particularly fun to tackle, but all are unfortunate necessities. Take heart, though; all these problems can be solved one way or another!

That brings us to the end of this chapter on EF Core and part 2 of the book. In part 3 we move away from minimal APIs to look at building server-rendered page-based applications with Razor Pages.

Summary

- EF Core is an ORM that lets you interact with a database by manipulating standard POCO classes called entities in your application, reducing the amount of SQL and database knowledge you need to be productive.
- EF Core maps entity classes to tables, properties on the entity to columns in the tables, and instances of entity objects to rows in these tables. Even if you use EF Core to avoid working with a database directly, you need to keep this mapping in mind.

- EF Core uses a database-provider model that lets you change the underlying database without changing any of your object manipulation code. EF Core has database providers for Microsoft SQL Server, SQLite, PostgreSQL, MySQL, and many others.

- EF Core is cross-platform and has good performance for an ORM, but it has a different feature set from EF 6.x. Nevertheless, EF Core is recommended for all new applications after EF 6.x.

- EF Core stores an internal representation of the entities in your application and how they map to the database, based on the `DbSet<T>` properties on your application's `DbContext`. EF Core builds a model based on the entity classes themselves and any other entities they reference.

- You add EF Core to your app by adding a NuGet database provider package. You should also install the design packages for EF Core, which works in conjunction with the .NET tools to generate and apply migrations to a database.

- EF Core includes many conventions for how entities are defined, such as primary keys and foreign keys. You can customize how entities are defined declaratively, by using `DataAnnotations`, or by using a fluent API.

- Your application uses a `DbContext` to interact with EF Core and the database. You register it with a DI container using `AddDbContext<T>`, defining the database provider and providing a connection string. This approach makes your `DbContext` available in the DI container throughout your app.

- EF Core uses migrations to track changes to your entity definitions. They're used to ensure that your entity definitions, EF Core's internal model, and the database schema match.

- After changing an entity, you can create a migration using either the .NET tool or Visual Studio PowerShell cmdlets. To create a new migration with the .NET command-line interface, run `dotnet ef migrations add NAME` in your project folder, where `NAME` is the name you want to give the migration. This command compares your current `DbContext` snapshot with the previous version and generates the necessary SQL statements to update your database.

- You can apply the migration to the database by using `dotnet ef database update`. This command creates the database if it doesn't already exist and applies any outstanding migrations.

- EF Core doesn't interact with the database when it creates migrations—only when you update the database explicitly—so you can still create migrations when you're offline.

- You can add entities to an EF Core database by creating a new entity, `e`, calling `_context.Add(e)` on an instance of your application's data context, `_context`, and calling `_context.SaveChangesAsync()`. This technique generates the necessary SQL `INSERT` statements to add the new rows to the database.

- You can load records from a database by using the DbSet<T> properties on your app's DbContext. These properties expose the IQueryable interface so you can use LINQ statements to filter and transform the data in the database before it's returned.

- Updating an entity consists of three steps: reading the entity from the database, modifying the entity, and saving the changes to the database. EF Core keeps track of which properties have changed so that it can optimize the SQL it generates.

- You can delete entities in EF Core by using the Remove method, but you should consider carefully whether you need this function. Often, a soft delete using an IsDeleted flag on entities is safer and easier to implement.

- This chapter covers only a subset of the problems you must consider when using EF Core in your applications. Before using it in a production app, you should consider (among other things) the data types generated for fields, validation, handling concurrency, the seeding of initial data, handling migrations on a running application, and handling migrations in a web-farm scenario.

Generating HTML with Razor Pages and MVC

In parts 1 and 2 we looked in detail at how to create JavaScript Object Notation (JSON) API applications using minimal APIs. You learned how to configure your app from multiple sources, how to use dependency injection to reduce coupling in your app, and how to document your APIs with OpenAPI.

API apps are everywhere these days. Mobile apps use them; client-side single-page applications (SPAs) like Angular, React, and Blazor use them; even other apps use them for server-to-server communication. But in many cases you don't need separate server-side and client-side apps. You could create a server-rendered app instead.

With server-rendering, your application generates the HTML on the server and the browser displays this HTML directly in the browser; no extra client-side framework is required. You can still add dynamic client-side behavior by using JavaScript, but fundamentally each page in your app is a standalone request and response, creating a simpler developer experience.

In part 3 you'll learn about the Razor Pages and Model-View-Controller (MVC) frameworks that ASP.NET Core uses to create server-rendered apps. In chapters 13 through 16 we'll examine the behavior of the Razor Pages framework itself, along with routing and model binding. In chapters 17 and 18 we'll look at how you can build the UI for your application by using the Razor syntax and Tag Helpers so that users can navigate and interact with your app.

In chapter 19 you'll learn how to use the Model-View-Controller (MVC) framework directly instead of Razor Pages. You'll learn how to use MVC controllers to build server-rendered apps and when to choose MVC controllers instead of Razor Pages. In chapter 20 you'll learn to how to use MVC controllers to build API applications, as an alternative to minimal APIs. Finally, in chapters 21 and 22 you'll learn how to refactor your apps to extract common code out of your Razor Pages and API controllers using filters.

Creating a website
with Razor Pages

This chapter covers

- Getting started with Razor Pages
- Introducing Razor Pages and the Model-View-Controller (MVC) design pattern
- Using Razor Pages in ASP.NET Core

So far in this book you've built one type of ASP.NET Core application: minimal API apps that return JavaScript Object Notation (JSON). In this chapter you'll learn how to build server-rendered, page-based applications using Razor Pages. Most ASP.NET Core apps fall into one of three categories:

- *An API designed for consumption by another machine or in code*—Web apps often serve as an API to backend server processes, to a mobile app, or to a client framework for building single-page applications (SPAs). In this case your application serves data in machine-readable formats such as JSON or Extensible Markup Language (XML) instead of the human-focused HTML output.

315

- *An HTML web application designed for direct use by users*—If the application is consumed directly by users, as in a traditional web application, Razor Pages is responsible for generating the web pages that the user interacts with. It handles requests for URLs, receives data posted via forms, and generates the HTML that enables users to view and navigate your app.
- *Both an HTML web application and an API*—It's also possible to have applications that serve both needs, which can let you cater to a wider range of clients while sharing logic in your application.

In this chapter you'll learn how ASP.NET Core uses Razor Pages to handle the second of these options: creating server-side rendered HTML pages. We'll get started quickly, using a template to create a simple Razor Pages application and comparing the features of a Razor Pages app with the minimal API apps you've seen so far. In section 13.2 we look at a more complex example of a Razor Page.

Next, we take a step back in section 13.3 to look at the MVC design pattern. I discuss some of the benefits of using this pattern, and you'll learn why it's been adopted by so many web frameworks as a model for building maintainable applications.

In section 13.4 you'll learn how the MVC design pattern applies to ASP.NET Core. The MVC pattern is a broad concept that can be applied in a variety of situations, but the use case in ASP.NET Core is specifically as a UI abstraction. You'll see how Razor Pages implements the MVC design pattern and builds on top of the ASP.NET Core MVC framework.

In this chapter I'll try to prepare you for each of the upcoming topics, but you may find that some of the behavior feels a bit like magic at this stage. Try not to become too concerned about exactly how all the Razor Pages pieces tie together yet; focus on the specific concepts being addressed and how they tie into concepts you've already met. We'll start by creating a Razor Pages app to explore.

13.1 *Your first Razor Pages application*

In this section you'll get started with Razor Pages by creating a new application from a template. After you've created the app and had a look around, we'll look at some of the similarities and differences compared with a minimal API application. You'll learn about the extra middleware added in the default template, look at how HTML is generated by Razor Pages, and take a look at the Razor Page equivalent of minimal API endpoint handlers: page handlers.

13.1.1 *Using the Web Application template*

Using a template is a quick way to get an application running, so we'll take that approach using the ASP.NET Core Web App template. To create a Razor Pages application in Visual Studio, perform the following steps:

1 Choose **Create a New Project** from the splash screen or choose **File > New > Project** from the main Visual Studio screen.

2 From the list of templates, choose **ASP.NET Core Web App**, ensuring you select the C# language template.

3 On the next screen, enter a project name, location, and solution name, and click **Next**. You might use WebApplication1 as both the project and solution name, for example.

4 On the following screen (figure 13.1), do the following:
   – Select **.NET 7.0**. If this option isn't available, ensure that you have .NET 7 installed. See appendix A for details on configuring your environment.
   – Ensure that **Configure for HTTPS** is checked.
   – Ensure that **Enable Docker** is unchecked.
   – Ensure that **Do Not Use Top-level Statements** is unchecked.
   – Choose **Create**.

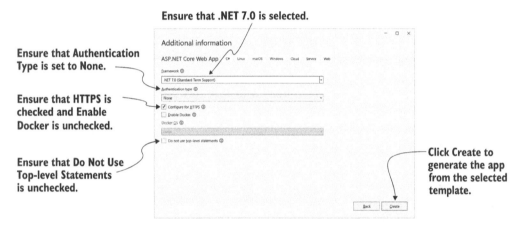

Figure 13.1 The additional information screen. This screen follows the Configure Your New Project dialog box and lets you customize the template that generates your application.

If you're not using Visual Studio, you can create a similar template using the .NET command-line interface (CLI). Create a folder to hold your new project. Open a PowerShell or cmd prompt in the folder (on Windows) or a terminal session (on Linux or macOS), and run the commands in the following listing.

Listing 13.1 Creating a new Razor Page application with the .NET CLI

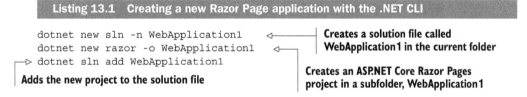

Whether you use Visual Studio or the .NET CLI, now you can build and run your application. Press F5 to run your app using Visual Studio, or use `dotnet run` in the project folder. This command opens the appropriate URL in a web browser and displays the basic Welcome page, shown in figure 13.2.

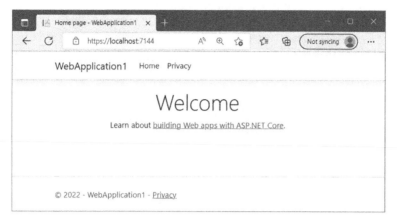

Figure 13.2   The output of your new Razor Pages application. The template chooses a random port to use for your application's URL, which is opened automatically in the browser when you run the app.

By default, this page shows a simple Welcome banner and a link to the official Microsoft documentation for ASP.NET Core. At the top of the page are two links: Home and Privacy. The Home link is the page you're currently on. Clicking Privacy takes you to a new page, shown in figure 13.3. As you'll see in section 13.1.3, you can use Razor Pages in your application to define these two pages and build the HTML they display.

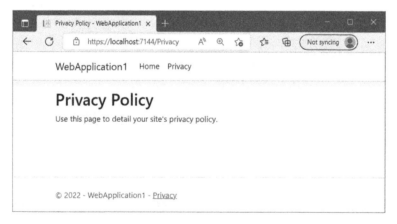

Figure 13.3   The Privacy page of your application. You can navigate between the two pages of the application using the Home and Privacy links in the application's header. The app generates the content of the pages using Razor Pages.

At this point, you should notice a couple of things:

- The header containing the links and the application title, WebApplication1, is the same on both pages.

- The title of the page, as shown in the tab of the browser, changes to match the current page. You'll see how to achieve these features in chapter 17, when we discuss the rendering of HTML using Razor templates.

There isn't any more to the user experience of the application at this stage. Click around a little, and when you're happy with the behavior of the application, return to your editor, and look at the files included in the template.

This Razor Pages app has much the same structure as the minimal API applications you've created throughout this book, as shown in figure 13.4. The overall structure is identical apart from two extra folders you haven't seen before:

- *Pages folder*—This folder contains the Razor Pages files that define the various pages in your web app, including the Home and Privacy pages you've already seen.
- *wwwroot folder*—This folder is special in that it's the only folder in your application that browsers are allowed to access directly when browsing your web app. You can store your Cascading Style Sheets (CSS), JavaScript, images, or static HTML files here, and the static file middleware will serve them to browsers when requested. The template creates subfolders inside wwwroot, but you don't have to use them; you can structure your static files however you want inside wwwroot.

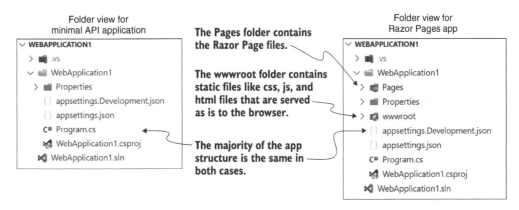

Figure 13.4 Comparing the project structure of a minimal API app with a Razor Pages app. The Razor Pages app contains all the same files and folders, as well as the Pages folder for the Razor Page definitions and the wwwroot file for static files that are served directly to the browser.

Aside from these extra files, the only other difference between a Razor Pages app and a minimal API app is the Program.cs file. In section 13.1.2 you'll see that the Razor Pages app uses the same basic structure in Program.cs but adds the extra services and middleware used in a typical Razor Pages app.

13.1.2 Adding and configuring services

One of the nice things about working with ASP.NET Core applications is that the setup code is quite similar even for completely different application models. No matter whether you're creating a Razor Pages application or using minimal APIs, your Program.cs contains the same six steps:

1   Create a `WebApplicationBuilder` instance.
2   Register the required services with the `WebApplicationBuilder`.
3   Call `Build()` on the builder instance to create a `WebApplication` instance.
4   Add middleware to the `WebApplication` to create a pipeline.
5   Map the endpoints in your application.
6   Call `Run()` on the `WebApplication` to start the server and handle requests.

The following listing shows the Program.cs file for the Razor Pages app. This file uses a lot more middleware than you've seen previously, but the overall structure should be familiar.

Listing 13.2   The Program.cs file for a Razor Pages app

```
WebApplicationBuilder builder = WebApplication.CreateBuilder(args);

builder.Services.AddRazorPages();      ◁──┐ Registers the required services
                                            to use the Razor Pages feature
WebApplication app = builder.Build();

if (!app.Environment.IsDevelopment())
{                                           Conditionally adds
    app.UseExceptionHandler("/Error");      middleware depending on
    app.UseHsts()                           the runtime environment
}

app.UseHttpsRedirection();
app.UseStaticFiles();                   Additional middleware
app.UseRouting();                       can be added to the
app.UseAuthorization();                 middleware pipeline.

app.MapRazorPages();    ◁──┐ Registers each Razor Page as an
                             endpoint in your application
app.Run();
```

In chapter 4 you learned about middleware and the importance of ordering when adding middleware to the pipeline. This example adds six pieces of middleware to the pipeline, two of which are added only when *not* running in development:

- `ExceptionHandlerMiddleware`—You learned about this middleware in chapters 4 and 5. This middleware catches exceptions thrown by middleware later in the pipeline and generates a friendly error page.
- `HstsMiddleware`—This middleware sets security headers in your response, in line with industry best practices. See chapter 28 for details about it and other security-related middleware.

- `HttpsRedirectionMiddleware`—This middleware ensures that your application responds only to secure (HTTPS) requests and is an industry best practice. We'll look at HTTPS in chapter 28.

- `StaticFileMiddleware`—As you saw in chapter 4, this middleware serves requests for static files (such as .css and .js files) from the wwwroot folder in your app.

- `RoutingMiddleware`—The routing middleware is responsible for selecting the endpoint for an incoming request. `WebApplication` adds it by default, but as discussed in chapter 4, adding it explicitly ensures that it runs after the `StaticFileMiddleware`.

- `AuthorizationMiddleware`—This middleware controls whether an endpoint is allowed to run based on the user making the request, but requires you also to configure authentication for your application. You'll learn more about authentication in chapter 23 and authorization in chapter 24.

In addition to the middleware added explicitly, `WebApplication` automatically adds some extra middleware (as discussed in chapter 4), such as the `EndpointMiddleware`, which is automatically added to the *end* of the middleware pipeline. As with minimal APIs, the `RoutingMiddleware` selects which endpoint handler to execute, and the `EndpointMiddleware` executes the handler to generate a response.

Together, this pair of middleware is responsible for interpreting the request to determine which Razor Page to invoke, for reading parameters from the request, and for generating the final HTML. Little configuration is required; you need only add the middleware to the pipeline and specify that you want to use Razor Page endpoints by calling `MapRazorPages`. For each request, the routing middleware uses the request's URL to determine which Razor Page to invoke. Then the endpoint middleware executes the Razor Page to generate the HTML response.

When the application is configured, it can start handling requests. But *how* does it handle them? In section 13.1.3 you'll get a glimpse at Razor Pages and how they generate HTML.

13.1.3 Generating HTML with Razor Pages

When an ASP.NET Core application receives a request, it progresses through the middleware pipeline until a middleware component handles it. Normally, the routing middleware matches a request URL's path to a configured route, which defines which Razor Page to invoke, and the endpoint middleware invokes it.

Razor Pages are stored in .cshtml files (a portmanteau of .cs and .html) within the Pages folder of your project. In general, the routing middleware maps request URL paths to a single Razor Page by looking in the Pages folder of your project for a Razor Page with the same path. If you look back at figure 13.3, for example, you see that the Privacy page of your app corresponds to the path `/Privacy` in the browser's address bar. If you look inside the Pages folder of your project, you'll find the Privacy.cshtml file, shown in the following listing.

Listing 13.3   The Privacy.cshtml Razor Page

```
@page                     ◁─── Indicates that this is a Razor Page
@model PrivacyModel ◁─┐
@{                        └── Links the Razor Page to a specific PageModel
    ViewData["Title"] = "Privacy Policy";   ◁─┐
}                                             └── C# code that doesn't write to the response
<h1>@ViewData["Title"]</h1>   ◁─── HTML with dynamic C# values written to the response

<p>Use this page to detail your site's privacy policy.</p>
```

Standalone, static HTML

Razor Pages use a templating syntax called *Razor* that combines static HTML with dynamic C# code and HTML generation. The @page directive on the first line of the Razor Page is the most important. This directive must always be placed on the first line of the file, as it tells ASP.NET Core that the .cshtml file is a Razor Page. Without it, you won't be able to view your page correctly.

The next line of the Razor Page defines which PageModel in your project the Razor Page is associated with:

```
@model PrivacyModel
```

In this case the PageModel is called PrivacyModel, and it follows the standard convention for naming Razor Page models. You can find this class in the Privacy.cshtml.cs file in the Pages folder of your project, as shown in figure 13.5. Visual Studio nests these files underneath the Razor Page .cshtml files in Solution Explorer. We'll look at the page model in section 13.1.4.

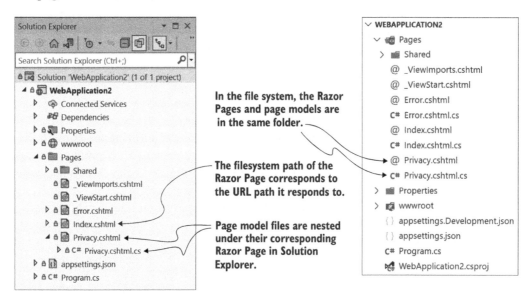

Figure 13.5   By convention, page models for Razor Pages are placed in a file with the same name as the Razor Page, with a .cs suffix appended. Visual Studio nests these files below the Razor Page in Solution Explorer.

In addition to the @page and @model directives, static HTML is always valid in a Razor Page and will be rendered as is in the response:

```
<p>Use this page to detail your site's privacy policy.</p>
```

You can also write ordinary C# code in Razor templates by using this construct:

```
@{ /* C# code here */ }
```

Any code between the curly braces will be executed but won't be written to the response. In the listing, you're setting the title of the page by writing a key to the ViewData dictionary, but you aren't writing anything to the response at this point:

```
@{
    ViewData["Title"] = "Privacy Policy";
}
```

Another feature shown in this template is that you can dynamically write C# variables and expressions to the HTML stream using the @ symbol. This ability to combine dynamic and static markup is what gives Razor Pages their power. In the example, you're fetching the "Title" value from the ViewData dictionary and writing the value to the response inside an <h1> tag:

```
<h1>@ViewData["Title"]</h1>
```

At this point, you might be a little confused by the template in listing 13.3 when it's compared with the output shown in figure 13.3. The title and the static HTML content appear in both the listing and figure, but some parts of the final web page don't appear in the template. How can that be?

Razor Pages have the concept of layouts, which are base templates that define the common elements of your application, such as headers and footers. The HTML of the layout combines with the Razor Page template to produce the final HTML that's sent to the browser. Layouts prevent you from having to duplicate code for the header and footer in every page, and mean that if you need to tweak something, you'll need to do it in only one place.

> **NOTE** I cover Razor templates, including layouts, in detail in chapter 17. You can find layouts in the Pages/Shared folder of your project.

As you've already seen, you can include C# code in your Razor Pages by using curly braces @{ }, but generally speaking, you'll want to limit the code in your .cshtml file to presentational concerns only. Complex logic, code to access services such as a database, and data manipulation should be handled in the PageModel instead.

13.1.4 *Handling request logic with page models and handlers*

As you've already seen, the @page directive in a .cshtml file marks the page as a Razor Page, but most Razor Pages also have an associated *page model*. By convention, this page model is placed in a file commonly known as a *code-behind file* that has a .cs extension, as you saw in figure 13.5. Page models should derive from the PageModel base class, and they typically contain one or more methods called *page handlers* that define how to handle requests to the Razor Page.

> **DEFINITION** A *page handler* is the Razor Pages equivalent of a minimal API endpoint handler; it's a method that runs in response to a request. Razor Page models must be derived from the PageModel class. They can contain multiple page handlers, though typically they contain only one or two.

The following listing shows the page model for the Privacy.cshtml Razor Page, located in the file Privacy.cshtml.cs.

Listing 13.4 The PrivacyModel in Privacy.cshtml.cs: A Razor Page page model

```
public class PrivacyModel: PageModel      ◁——— Razor Pages must inherit from PageModel.
{
    private readonly ILogger<PrivacyModel> _logger;        You can use
    public PrivacyModel(ILogger<PrivacyModel> logger)      dependency injection
    {                                                       to provide services
        _logger = logger;                                  in the constructor.
    }

    public void OnGet()    ◁——┐ The default page handler is OnGet. Returning
    {                          │ void indicates HTML should be generated.
    }
}
```

This page model is extremely simple, but it demonstrates a couple of important points:

- Page handlers are driven by convention.
- Page models can use dependency injection (DI) to interact with other services.

Page handlers are typically named by convention, based on the HTTP verb they respond to. They return either void, indicating that the Razor Page's template should be rendered, or an IActionResult that contains other instructions for generating the response, such as redirecting the user to a different page.

The PrivacyModel contains a single handler, OnGet, which indicates that it should run in response to GET requests for the page. As the method returns void, executing the handler executes the associated Razor template for the page to generate the HTML.

NOTE Razor Pages are focused on building page-based apps, so you typically want to return HTML rather than JSON or XML. You can also use an IActionResult to return any sort of data, to redirect users to a new page, or to send an error. You'll learn more about IActionResults in chapter 15.

DI is used to inject an ILogger<PrivacyModel> instance into the constructor of the page model the same way you would inject a service into a minimal API endpoint handler. The service is unused in this example, but you'll learn all about ILogger in chapter 26.

Clearly, the PrivacyModel page model doesn't do much in this case, and you may be wondering why it's worth having. If all page models do is tell the Razor Page to generate HTML, why do we need them at all?

The key thing to remember here is that now you have a framework for performing arbitrarily complex functions in response to a request. You could easily update the handler method to load data from the database, send an email, add a product to a basket, or create an invoice—all in response to a simple HTTP request. This extensibility is where a lot of the power in Razor Pages (and the MVC pattern in general) lies.

The other important point is that you've separated the execution of these methods from the generation of the HTML. If the logic changes, and you need to add behavior to a page handler, you don't need to touch the HTML generation code, so you're less likely to introduce bugs. Conversely, if you need to change the UI slightly (change the color of the title, for example), your handler method logic is safe.

And there you have it—a complete ASP.NET Core Razor Pages application! Before we move on, let's take one last look at how your application handles a request. Figure 13.6 shows a request to the /Privacy path being handled by the sample application. You've seen everything here already, so the process of handling a request should be familiar. The figure shows how the request passes through the middleware pipeline before being handled by the endpoint middleware. The Privacy.cshtml Razor Page executes the OnGet handler and generates the HTML response, which passes back through the middleware to the ASP.NET Core web server before being sent to the user's browser.

We've reached the end of this section working through the template, so you have a good overview of how an entire Razor Pages application is configured and how it handles a request using Razor Pages. In section 13.2 we take the basic Razor Pages in the default template a bit further, looking at a more complex example.

1. An HTTP request is made to the URL/Privacy.

2. The request is forwarded by IIS/Nginx/Apache to ASP. NET Core.

3. ASP. NET Core web server receives the HTTP request and passes it to the middleware.

4. The request path /Privacy is routed to the Privacy.cshtml Razor Page, so it passes through the middleware pipeline unmodified.

5. The Privacy.cshtml.cs Razor Page handles the request by executing the OnGet page handler.

8. The HTTP response containing HTML for the Privacy page is sent to the browser.

7. The HTML response passes back through each middleware to the ASP. NET Core web server.

6. The OnGet handler returns void, indicating that the Razor Page should generate an HTML response from its Razor template in Privacy.cshtml.

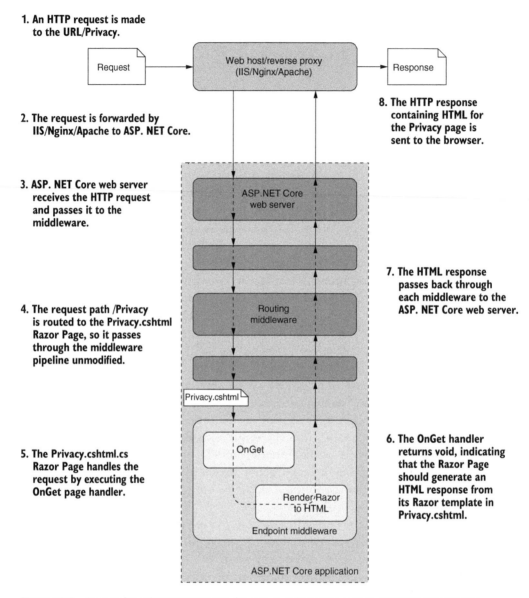

Figure 13.6   An overview of a request to the /Privacy URL for the sample ASP.NET Razor Pages application. The routing middleware routes the request to the OnGet handler of the Privacy.cshtml.cs Razor Page. The Razor Page generates an HTML response by executing the Razor template in Privacy.cshtml and passes the response back through the middleware pipeline to the browser.

13.2   *Exploring a typical Razor Page*

The Razor Pages programming model was introduced in ASP.NET Core 2.0 as a way to build server-side rendered page-based websites. It builds on top of the ASP.NET Core infrastructure to provide a streamlined experience, using conventions where possible to reduce the amount of boilerplate code and configuration required. In this section we'll look at a more complex page model to better understand the overall design of Razor Pages.

In listing 13.4 you saw a simple Razor Page that didn't contain any logic; instead, it only rendered the associated Razor view. This pattern may be common if you're building a content-heavy marketing website, for example, but more commonly your Razor Pages will contain some logic, load data from a database, or use forms to allow users to submit information.

To give you more of a flavor of how typical Razor Pages work, in this section we look briefly at a slightly more complex Razor Page. This page is taken from a to-do list application and is used to display all the to-do items for a given category. We're not focusing on the HTML generation at this point, so the following listing shows only the `PageModel` code-behind file for the Razor Page.

Listing 13.5   A Razor Page for viewing all to-do items in a given category

```
public class CategoryModel : PageModel
{
    private readonly ToDoService _service;
    public CategoryModel(ToDoService service)
    {
        _service = service;
    }

    public ActionResult OnGet(string category)
    {
        Items = _service.GetItemsForCategory(category);
        return Page();
    }
    public List<ToDoListModel> Items { get; set; }
}
```

The ToDoService is provided in the model constructor using DI.

The OnGet handler takes a parameter, category.

The handler calls out to the ToDoService to retrieve data and sets the Items property.

Returns a PageResult indicating the Razor view should be rendered

The Razor View can access the Items property when it's rendered.

This example is still relatively simple, but it demonstrates a variety of features compared with the basic example from listing 13.4:

- The page handler, `OnGet`, accepts a method parameter, `category`. This parameter is automatically populated using values from the incoming request via model binding, similar to the way binding works with minimal APIs. I discuss Razor Pages model binding in detail in chapter 16.

- The handler doesn't interact with the database directly. Instead, it uses the `category` value provided to interact with the `ToDoService`, which is injected as a constructor argument using DI.

- The handler returns `Page()` at the end of the method to indicate that the associated Razor view should be rendered. The `return` statement is optional in this case; by convention, if the page handler is a `void` method, the Razor view will still be rendered, behaving as though you called `return Page()` at the end of the method.

- The Razor View has access to the `CategoryModel` instance, so it can access the `Items` property that's set by the handler. It uses these items to build the HTML that is ultimately sent to the user.

The pattern of interactions in the Razor Page of listing 13.5 shows a common pattern. The page handler is the central controller for the Razor Page. It receives an input from the user (the `category` method parameter); calls out to the "brains" of the application (the `ToDoService`); and passes data (by exposing the `Items` property) to the Razor view, which generates the HTML response. If you squint, this pattern looks like the MVC design pattern.

Depending on your background in software development, you may have come across the MVC pattern in some form. In web development, MVC is a common paradigm, used in frameworks such as Django, Rails, and Spring MVC. But as it's such a broad concept, you can find MVC in everything from mobile apps to rich-client desktop applications. I hope that indicates the benefits of the pattern when it's used correctly! In section 13.3 we'll look at the MVC pattern in general and how ASP.NET Core uses it.

13.3   *Understanding the MVC design pattern*

The MVC design pattern is a common pattern for designing apps that have UIs. The MVC pattern has many interpretations, each of which focuses on a slightly different aspect of the pattern. The original MVC design pattern was specified with rich-client graphical user interface (GUI) apps in mind, rather than web applications, so it uses terminology and paradigms associated with a GUI environment. Fundamentally, though, the pattern aims to separate the management and manipulation of data from its visual representation.

Before I dive too far into the design pattern itself, let's consider a typical Razor Pages request. Imagine that a user requests the Razor Page from listing 13.5 that displays a to-do list category. Figure 13.7 shows how a Razor Page handles different aspects of a request, all of which combine to generate the final response.

In general, three components make up the MVC design pattern:

- *Model*—The data that needs to be displayed—the global state of the application. It's accessed via the `ToDoService` in listing 13.5.
- *View*—The template that displays the data provided by the model.
- *Controller*—Updates the model and provides the data for display to the view. This role is taken by the page handler in Razor Pages—the `OnGet` method in listing 13.5.

Each component of the MVC design pattern is responsible for a single aspect of the overall system, which, when combined, generates a UI. The to-do list example considers MVC in terms of a web application using Razor Pages, but a generalized request could be equivalent to the click of a button in a desktop GUI application.

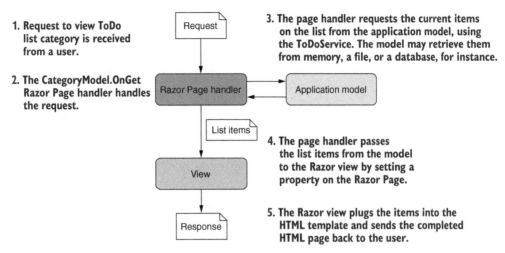

1. **Request to view ToDo list category is received from a user.**

2. **The CategoryModel.OnGet Razor Page handler handles the request.**

3. **The page handler requests the current items on the list from the application model, using the ToDoService. The model may retrieve them from memory, a file, or a database, for instance.**

4. **The page handler passes the list items from the model to the Razor view by setting a property on the Razor Page.**

5. **The Razor view plugs the items into the HTML template and sends the completed HTML page back to the user.**

Figure 13.7   Requesting a to-do list page for a Razor Pages application. A different component handles each aspect of the request.

In general, the order of events when an application responds to a user interaction or request is as follows:

1 The controller (the Razor Page handler) receives the request.
2 Depending on the request, the controller either fetches the requested data from the application model using injected services or updates the data that makes up the model.
3 The controller selects a view to display and passes a representation of the model (the view model) to it.
4 The view uses the data contained in the model to generate the UI.

When we describe MVC in this format, the controller (the Razor Page handler) serves as the entry point for the interaction. The user communicates with the controller to instigate an interaction. In web applications, this interaction takes the form of an HTTP request, so when a request to a URL is received, the controller handles it.

Depending on the nature of the request, the controller may take a variety of actions, but the key point is that the actions are undertaken using the application model. The model here contains all the business logic for the application, so it's able to provide requested data or perform actions.

> **NOTE**   In this description of MVC, the model is considered to be a complex beast, containing all the logic for how to perform an action, as well as any internal state. The Razor Page `PageModel` class is *not* the model we're talking about! Unfortunately, as in all software development, naming things is hard.

Consider a request to view a product page for an e-commerce application. The controller would receive the request and know how to contact some product service that's part of the application model. This service might fetch the details of the requested product from a database and return them to the controller.

Alternatively, imagine that a controller receives a request to add a product to the user's shopping cart. The controller would receive the request and most likely would invoke a method on the model to request that the product be added. Then the model would update its internal representation of the user's cart, by adding (for example) a new row to a database table holding the user's data.

> **TIP** You can think of each Razor Page handler as being a mini controller focused on a single page. Every web request is another independent call to a controller that orchestrates the response. Although there are many controllers, all the handlers interact with the same application model.

After the model has been updated, the controller needs to decide what response to generate. One of the advantages of using the MVC design pattern is that the model representing the application's data is decoupled from the final representation of that data, called the *view*. The controller is responsible for deciding whether the response should generate an HTML view, whether it should send the user to a new page, or whether it should return an error page.

One of the advantages of the model's being independent of the view is that it improves testability. UI code is classically hard to test, as it's dependent on the environment; anyone who has written UI tests simulating a user clicking buttons and typing in forms knows that it's typically fragile. By keeping the model independent of the view, you can ensure that the model stays easily testable, without any dependencies on UI constructs. As the model often contains your application's business logic, this is clearly a good thing!

The view can use the data passed to it by the controller to generate the appropriate HTML response. The view is responsible only for generating the final representation of the data; it's not involved in any of the business logic.

This is all there is to the MVC design pattern in relation to web applications. Much of the confusion related to MVC seems to stem from slightly different uses of the term for slightly different frameworks and types of applications. In section 13.4 I'll show how the ASP.NET Core framework uses the MVC pattern with Razor Pages, along with more examples of the pattern in action.

13.4 *Applying the MVC design pattern to Razor Pages*

In section 13.3 I discussed the MVC pattern as it's typically used in web applications; Razor Pages use this pattern. But ASP.NET Core also includes a *framework* called ASP.NET Core MVC. This framework (unsurprisingly) closely mirrors the MVC design pattern, using *controllers* containing *action methods* in place of Razor Pages and page handlers. Razor Pages builds directly on top of the underlying ASP.NET Core MVC framework, using the MVC framework under the hood for their behavior.

If you prefer, you can avoid Razor Pages and work with the MVC framework directly in ASP.NET Core. This option was the only one in early versions of ASP.NET Core and the previous version of ASP.NET.

TIP I look in greater depth at choosing between Razor Pages and the MVC framework in chapter 19.

In this section we look in greater depth at how the MVC design pattern applies to Razor Pages in ASP.NET Core. This section will also help clarify the role of various features of Razor Pages.

> **Do Razor Pages use MVC or MVVM?**
>
> Occasionally, I've seen people describe Razor Pages as using the Model-View-View Model (MVVM) design pattern rather than the MVC design pattern. I don't agree, but it's worth being aware of the differences.
>
> MVVM is a UI pattern that is often used in mobile apps, desktop apps, and some client-side frameworks. It differs from MVC in that there is a bidirectional interaction between the view and the view model. The view model tells the view what to display, but the view can also trigger changes directly on the view model. It's often used with two-way data binding where a view model is bound to a view.
>
> Some people consider the Razor Pages `PageModel` to be filling this role, but I'm not convinced. Razor Pages definitely seems based on the MVC pattern to me (it's based on the ASP.NET Core MVC framework after all!), and it doesn't have the same two-way binding that I would expect with MVVM.

As you've seen in previous chapters, ASP.NET Core implements Razor Page endpoints using a combination of `RoutingMiddleware` and `EndpointMiddleware`, as shown in figure 13.8. When a request has been processed by earlier middleware (and assuming that

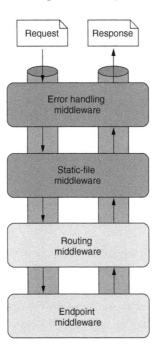

The request passes through each middleware in the pipeline.

Each middleware gets an opportunity to handle the request.

The routing middleware attempts to find an endpoint that will handle the request.

The endpoint middleware is the last in the pipeline. The MVC pattern is implemented entirely by individual Razor Page endpoints.

Figure 13.8   The middleware pipeline for a typical ASP.NET Core application. The request is processed by middleware in sequence. If the request reaches the routing middleware, the middleware selects an endpoint, such as a Razor Page, to execute. The endpoint middleware executes the selected endpoint.

none has handled the request and short-circuited the pipeline), the routing middleware selects which Razor Page handler should be executed, and the endpoint middleware executes the page handler.

As you've seen in earlier chapters, middleware often handles cross-cutting concerns or narrowly defined requests, such as requests for files. For requirements that fall outside these functions or that have many external dependencies, a more robust framework is required. Razor Pages (and/or ASP.NET Core MVC) can provide this framework, allowing interaction with your application's core business logic and the generation of a UI. It handles everything from mapping the request to an appropriate page handler (or controller action method) to generating the HTML response.

In the traditional description of the MVC design pattern, there's only a single type of model, which holds all the non-UI data and behavior. The controller updates this model as appropriate and then passes it to the view, which uses it to generate a UI.

One of the problems when discussing MVC is the vague and ambiguous terms that it uses, such as *controller* and *model*. *Model* in particular is such an overloaded term that it's often difficult to be sure exactly what it refers to; is it an object, a collection of objects, or an abstract concept? Even ASP.NET Core uses the word *model* to describe several related but different components, as you'll see later in this chapter.

13.4.1 Directing a request to a Razor Page and building a binding model

The first step when your app receives a request is routing the request to an appropriate Razor Page handler in the routing middleware. Let's think again about the category to-do list page in listing 13.5. On that page, you're displaying a list of items that have a given category label. If you're looking at the list of items with a category of Simple, you'd make a request to the /category/Simple path.

Routing maps a request URL, /category/Simple, against the route patterns registered with your application. You've seen how this process works for minimal APIs, and it's the same for Razor Pages; each route template corresponds to a Razor Page endpoint. You'll learn more about routing with Razor Pages in chapter 14.

> **TIP** I'm using the term *Razor Page* to refer to the combination of the Razor view and the PageModel that includes the page handler. Note that PageModel class is *not* the model we're referring to when describing the MVC pattern. It fulfills other roles, as you'll see later in this section.

When a page handler is selected in the routing middleware, the request continues down the middleware pipeline until it reaches the endpoint middleware, where the Razor Page executes.

First, the *binding model* (if applicable) is generated. This model is built from the incoming request, based on the properties of the PageModel marked for binding and the method parameters required by the page handler, as shown in figure 13.9. A binding model is normally one or more standard C# objects and works similarly to the way it works in minimal APIs, as you saw in chapter 6. We'll look at Razor Page binding models in detail in chapter 16.

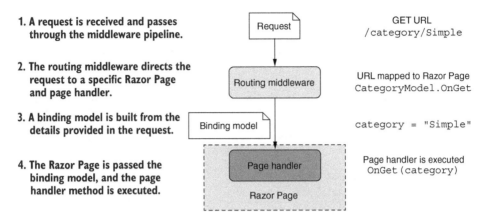

1. A request is received and passes through the middleware pipeline.

GET URL
`/category/Simple`

2. The routing middleware directs the request to a specific Razor Page and page handler.

URL mapped to Razor Page
`CategoryModel.OnGet`

3. A binding model is built from the details provided in the request.

`category = "Simple"`

4. The Razor Page is passed the binding model, and the page handler method is executed.

Page handler is executed
`OnGet(category)`

Figure 13.9 **Routing a request to a Razor Page and building a binding model. A request to the /category/Simple URL results in the execution of the CategoryModel.OnGet page handler, passing in a populated binding model, category.**

> **DEFINITION** A *binding model* is one or more objects that act as a container for the data provided in a request—data that's required by a page handler.

In this case, the binding model is a simple string, `category`, that's bound to the `"Simple"` value. This value is provided in the request URL's path. A more complex binding model could have been used, with multiple properties populated with values from the route template, the query string, and the request body.

> **NOTE** The binding model for Razor Pages is conceptually equivalent to all the parameters you pass in to a minimal API endpoint that are populated from the request.

The binding model in this case corresponds to the method parameter of the `OnGet` page handler. An instance of the Razor Page is created using its constructor, and the binding model is passed to the page handler when it executes, so it can be used to decide how to respond. For this example, the page handler uses it to decide which to-do items to display on the page.

13.4.2 *Executing a handler using the application model*

The role of the page handler as the controller in the MVC pattern is to coordinate the generation of a response to the request it's handling. That means it should perform only a limited number of actions. In particular, it should

- Validate that the data contained in the binding model is valid for the request.
- Invoke the appropriate actions on the application model using services.
- Select an appropriate response to generate based on the response from the application model.

Figure 13.10 shows the page handler invoking an appropriate method on the application model. Here, you can see that the application model is a somewhat-abstract concept that encapsulates the remaining non-UI parts of your application. It contains the *domain model*, several services, and the database interaction.

1. The page handler uses the category provided in the binding model to determine which method to invoke in the application model.

2. The page handler method calls into services that make up the application model. This might use the domain model to determine whether to include completed ToDo items, for example.

3. The services load the details of the ToDo items from the database and return them to the action method.

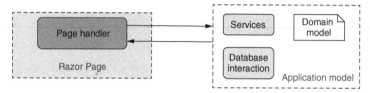

Figure 13.10   **When executed, an action invokes the appropriate methods in the application model.**

> **DEFINITION**   The *domain model* encapsulates complex business logic in a series of classes that don't depend on any infrastructure and are easy to test.

The page handler typically calls into a single point in the application model. In our example of viewing a to-do list category, the application model might use a variety of services to check whether the current user is allowed to view certain items, to search for items in the given category, to load the details from the database, or to load a picture associated with an item from a file. Assuming that the request is valid, the application model returns the required details to the page handler. Then it's up to the page handler to choose a response to generate.

13.4.3 *Building HTML using the view model*

When the page handler has called out to the application model that contains the application business logic, it's time to generate a response. A *view model* captures the details necessary for the view to generate a response.

> **DEFINITION**   A *view model* in the MVC pattern is all the data required by the view to render a UI. It's typically some transformation of the data contained in the application model, plus extra information required to render the page, such as the page's title.

The term *view model* is used extensively in ASP.NET Core MVC, where it typically refers to a single object that is passed to the Razor view to render. With Razor Pages, however, the Razor view can access the Razor Page's page model class directly. Therefore, the Razor Page `PageModel` typically acts as the view model in Razor Pages, with the data required by the Razor view exposed via properties, as you saw in listing 13.5.

NOTE Razor Pages use the `PageModel` class itself as the view model for the Razor view by exposing the required data as properties.

The Razor view uses the data exposed in the page model to generate the final HTML response. Finally, this data is sent back through the middleware pipeline and out to the user's browser, as shown in figure 13.11.

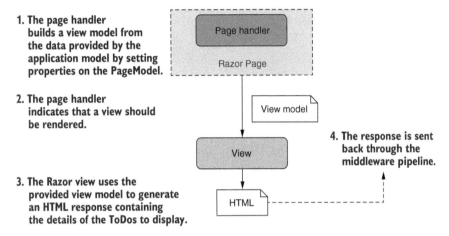

1. The page handler builds a view model from the data provided by the application model by setting properties on the PageModel.

2. The page handler indicates that a view should be rendered.

3. The Razor view uses the provided view model to generate an HTML response containing the details of the ToDos to display.

4. The response is sent back through the middleware pipeline.

Page handler

Razor Page

View model

View

HTML

Figure 13.11 The page handler builds a view model by setting properties on the `PageModel`. It's the view that generates the response.

It's important to note that although the page handler selects whether to execute the view and the data to use, it doesn't control what HTML is generated. The view itself decides what the content of the response will be.

13.4.4 *Putting it all together: A complete Razor Page request*

Now that you've seen the steps that go into handling a request in ASP.NET Core using Razor Pages, let's put them together from request to response. Figure 13.12 shows how the steps combine to handle the request to display the list of to-do items for the Simple category. The traditional MVC pattern is still visible in Razor Pages, made up of the page handler (controller), the view, and the application model.

By now, you may be thinking this whole process seems rather convoluted. So many steps to display some HTML! Why not allow the application model to create the view directly, rather than have to go on a dance back and forth with the page handler method? The key benefit throughout this process is the *separation of concerns:*

- The view is responsible only for taking some data and generating HTML.
- The application model is responsible only for executing the required business logic.
- The page handler (controller) is responsible only for validating the incoming request and selecting which response is required, based on the output of the application model.

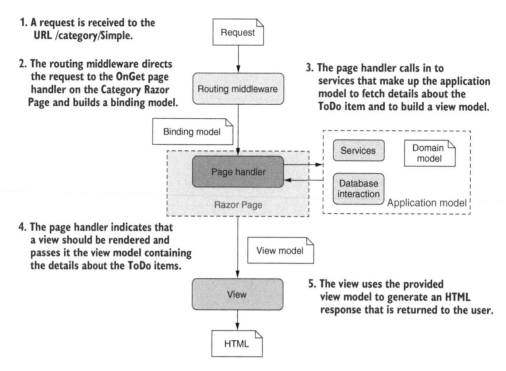

1. A request is received to the URL /category/Simple.

2. The routing middleware directs the request to the OnGet page handler on the Category Razor Page and builds a binding model.

3. The page handler calls in to services that make up the application model to fetch details about the ToDo item and to build a view model.

4. The page handler indicates that a view should be rendered and passes it the view model containing the details about the ToDo items.

5. The view uses the provided view model to generate an HTML response that is returned to the user.

Figure 13.12   A complete Razor Pages request for the list of to-dos in the Simple category

By having clearly defined boundaries, it's easier to update and test each of the components without depending on any of the others. If your UI logic changes, you won't necessarily have to modify any of your business logic classes, so you're less likely to introduce errors in unexpected places.

The dangers of tight coupling

it's generally a good idea to reduce coupling between logically separate parts of your application as much as possible. This makes it easier to update your application without causing adverse effects or requiring modifications in seemingly unrelated areas. Applying the MVC pattern is one way to help with this goal.

As an example of when coupling rears its head, I remember a case a few years ago when I was working on a small web app. In our haste, we hadn't decoupled our business logic from our HTML generation code properly, but initially there were no obvious problems. The code worked, so we shipped it!

A few months later, someone new started working on the app and immediately "helped" by renaming an innocuous spelling error in a class in the business layer. Unfortunately, the names of those classes had been used to generate our HTML code, so renaming the class caused the whole website to break in users' browsers! Suffice it to say that we made a concerted effort to apply the MVC pattern thereafter and ensure that we had a proper separation of concerns.

The examples shown in this chapter demonstrate the bulk of the Razor Pages functionality. It has additional features, such as the filter pipeline, which I cover in chapters 21 and 22, and I discuss binding models in greater depth in chapter 16, but the overall behavior of the system is the same.

Similarly, in chapter 19 I look at MVC controllers and explain why I don't recommend them over Razor Pages for server-rendered applications. By contrast, in chapter 20 I discuss how you can use the MVC design pattern when you're generating machine-readable responses using Web API controllers. The process is for all intents and purposes identical to the MVC pattern you've already seen.

I hope that by this point, you're sold on Razor Pages and their overall design using the MVC pattern. The page handler methods on a Razor Page are invoked in response to a request and select the type of response to generate by returning an `IActionResult`.

An aspect I've touched on only vaguely is how the `RoutingMiddleware` decides which Razor Page and handler to invoke for a given request. You don't want to have a Razor Page for every URL in an app. It would be difficult to have, for example, a different page per product in an e-shop; every product would need its own Razor Page! In chapter 14 you'll see how to define routes for your Razor Pages, how to add constraints to your routes, and how they deconstruct URLs to match a single handler.

Summary

- Razor Pages are located in the Pages folder of a project and by default are named according to the URL path they handle. Privacy.cshtml, for example, handles the path `/Privacy`. This convention makes it easy to quickly add new pages.
- Razor Pages must contain the `@page` directive as the first line of the .cshtml file. Without this directive, ASP.NET Core won't recognize it as a Razor Page, and it won't appear as an endpoint in your app.
- Page models derive from the `PageModel` base class and contain page handlers. Page handlers are methods named using conventions that indicate the HTTP verb they handle. `OnGet`, for example, handles the GET verb. Page handlers are equivalent to minimal API endpoint handlers; they run in response to a given request.
- Razor templates can contain standalone C#, standalone HTML, and dynamic HTML generated from C# values. By combining all three, you can build highly dynamic applications.
- The MVC design pattern allows for a separation of concerns between the business logic of your application, the data that's passed around, and the display of data in a response. This reduces coupling between the different layers of your application.
- Razor Pages should inherit from the `PageModel` base class and contain *page handlers*. The routing middleware selects a page handler based on the incoming request's URL, the HTTP verb, and the request's query string.

- Page handlers generally should delegate to services to handle the business logic required by a request instead of performing the changes themselves. This ensures a clean separation of concerns that aids testing and improves application structure.

Mapping URLs to Razor Pages using routing

This chapter covers

- Routing requests to Razor Pages
- Customizing Razor Page route templates
- Generating URLs for Razor Pages

In chapter 13 you learned about the Model-View-Controller (MVC) design pattern and how ASP.NET Core uses it to generate the UI for an application using Razor Pages. Razor Pages contain page handlers that act as mini controllers for a request. The page handler calls the application model to retrieve or save data. Then the handler passes data from the application model to the Razor view, which generates an HTML response.

Although not part of the MVC design pattern per se, one crucial part of Razor Pages is selecting which Razor Page to invoke in response to a given request. Razor Pages use the same routing system as minimal APIs (introduced in chapter 6); this chapter focuses on how routing works with Razor Pages.

I start this chapter with a brief reminder about how routing works in ASP.NET Core. I'll touch on the two pieces of middleware that are crucial to endpoint routing in .NET 7 and the approach Razor Pages uses of mixing conventions with explicit route templates.

In section 14.3 we look at the default routing behavior of Razor Pages, and in section 14.4 you'll learn how to customize the behavior by adding or changing route templates. Razor Pages have access to the same route template features that you learned about in chapter 6, and in section 14.4 you'll learn how to them.

In section 14.5 I describe how to use the routing system to generate URLs for Razor Pages. Razor Pages provide some helper methods to simplify URL generation compared with minimal APIs, so I compare the two approaches and discuss the benefits of each.

Finally, in section 14.6 I describe how to customize the conventions Razor Pages uses, giving you complete control of the URLs in your application. You'll see how to change the built-in conventions, such as using lowercase for your URLs, as well as how to write your own convention and apply it globally to your application.

By the end of this chapter you should have a much clearer understanding of how an ASP.NET Core application works. You can think of routing as the glue that ties the middleware pipeline to Razor Pages and the MVC framework. With middleware, Razor Pages, and routing under your belt, you'll be writing web apps in no time!

14.1 *Routing in ASP.NET Core*

In chapter 6 we looked in detail at routing and some of the benefits it brings, such as the ability to have multiple URLs pointing to the same endpoint and extracting segments from the URL. You also learned how it's implemented in ASP.NET Core apps, using two pieces of middleware:

- `EndpointMiddleware`—You use this middleware to register the endpoints in the routing system when you start your application. The middleware executes one of the endpoints at runtime.
- `RoutingMiddleware`—This middleware chooses which of the endpoints registered by the `EndpointMiddleware` should execute for a given request at runtime.

The `EndpointMiddleware` is where you register all the endpoints in your app, including minimal APIs, Razor Pages, and MVC controllers. It's easy to register all the Razor Pages in your application using the `MapRazorPages()` extension method, as shown in the following listing.

Listing 14.1   **Registering Razor Pages in** `Startup.Configure`

```
WebApplicationBuilder builder = WebApplication.CreateBuilder(args);

builder.Services.AddRazorPages();        Adds the required Razor Pages
                                         services to dependency injection
var app = builder.Build();
```

```
app.UseStaticFiles();
app.UseRouting();            ◁        Adds the RoutingMiddleware
app.UseAuthorization();               to the middleware pipeline

app.MapRazorPages();         ◁        Registers all the Razor Pages in the
                                      application with the EndpointMiddleware
app.Run();
```

Each endpoint, whether it's a Razor Page or a minimal API, has an associated *route template* that defines which URLs the endpoint should match. The EndpointMiddleware stores these route templates and endpoints in a dictionary, which it shares with the RoutingMiddleware. At runtime the RoutingMiddleware compares the incoming request with the routes in the dictionary and selects the matching endpoint. When the request reaches the EndpointMiddleware, the middleware checks to see which endpoint was selected and executes it, as shown in figure 14.1.

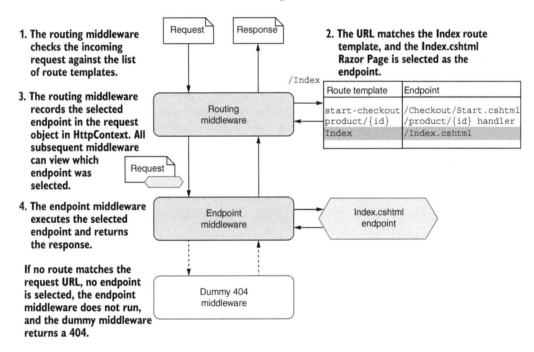

1. The routing middleware checks the incoming request against the list of route templates.

2. The URL matches the Index route template, and the Index.cshtml Razor Page is selected as the endpoint.

3. The routing middleware records the selected endpoint in the request object in HttpContext. All subsequent middleware can view which endpoint was selected.

4. The endpoint middleware executes the selected endpoint and returns the response.

If no route matches the request URL, no endpoint is selected, the endpoint middleware does not run, and the dummy middleware returns a 404.

Route template	Endpoint
`start-checkout`	`/Checkout/Start.cshtml`
`product/{id}`	`/product/{id} handler`
`Index`	`/Index.cshtml`

Figure 14.1 Endpoint routing uses a two-step process. The RoutingMiddleware **selects which endpoint to execute, and the** EndpointMiddleware **executes it. If the request URL doesn't match a route template, the endpoint middleware will not generate a response.**

As discussed in chapter 6, the advantage of having two separate pieces of middleware to handle this process is that any middleware placed after the RoutingMiddleware can see which endpoint is going to be executed before it is. You'll see this benefit in action when we look at authorization in chapter 24.

Routing in ASP.NET Core uses the same infrastructure and middleware whether you're building minimal APIs, Razor Pages, or MVC controllers, but there are some differences in how you define the mapping between your route templates and your handlers in each case. In section 14.2 you'll learn the different approaches each paradigm takes.

14.2 *Convention-based routing vs. explicit routing*

Routing is a key part of ASP.NET Core, as it maps the incoming request's URL to a specific endpoint to execute. You have two ways to define these URL-endpoint mappings in your application:

- Using global, convention-based routing
- Using explicit routing, where each endpoint is mapped with a single route template

Which approach you use typically depends on whether you're using minimal APIs, Razor Pages, or MVC controllers and whether you're building an API or a website (using HTML). These days I lean heavily toward explicit routing, as you'll see.

Convention-based routing is defined globally for your application. You can use convention-based routes to map endpoints (MVC controller actions specifically) to URLs, but those MVC controllers must adhere strictly to the conventions you define. Traditionally, applications using MVC controllers to generate HTML tend to use this approach to routing. The downside of this approach is that customizing URLs for a subset of controllers and actions is tricky.

Alternatively, you can use explicit routing to tie a given URL to a specific endpoint. You've seen this approach with minimal APIs, where each endpoint is directly associated with a route template. You can also use explicit routing with MVC controllers by placing [Route] attributes on the action methods themselves, hence explicit-routing is also often called *attribute-routing*.

Explicit routing provides more flexibility than convention-based based routing, as you can explicitly define the route template for every action method. Explicit routing is generally more verbose than the convention-based approach, as it requires applying attributes to *every* action method in your application. Despite this, the extra flexibility can be useful, especially when building APIs.

Somewhat confusingly, Razor Pages use *conventions* to generate *explicit routes*! In many ways this combination gives you the best of both worlds: the predictability and terseness of convention-based routing with the easy customization of explicit routing. There are tradeoffs to each of the approaches, as shown in table 14.1.

So which approach should you use? I believe that convention-based routing is not worth the effort in 99 percent of cases and that you should stick to explicit routing. If you're following my advice to use Razor Pages for server-rendered applications, you're already using explicit routing under the covers. Also, if you're creating APIs using minimal APIs or MVC controllers, explicit routing is the best option and the recommended approach.

Table 14.1   The advantages and disadvantages of the routing styles available in ASP.NET Core

Routing style	Typical use	Advantages	Disadvantages
Convention-based routes	HTML-generating MVC controllers	Terse definition in one location in your application. Forces a consistent layout of MVC controllers.	Routes are defined in a different place from your controllers. Overriding the route conventions can be tricky and error-prone. Adds an extra layer of indirection when routing a request.
Explicit routes	Minimal API endpoints Web API MVC controllers	Gives complete control of route templates for every endpoint. Routes are defined next to the endpoint they execute.	Verbose compared with convention-based routing. Can be easy to overcustomize route templates. Route templates may be scattered throughout your application rather than defined in one location.
Convention-based generation of explicit routes	Razor Pages	Encourages consistent set of exposed URLs. Terse when you stick to the conventions. Easily override the route template for a single page. Customize conventions globally to change exposed URLs.	Possible to overcustomize route templates. You must calculate what the route template for a page is, rather than its being explicitly defined in your app.

The only scenario where convention-based routing is used traditionally is if you're using MVC controllers to generate HTML. But if you're following my advice from chapter 13, you'll be using Razor Pages for HTML-generating applications and falling back to MVC controllers only when necessary, as I discuss in more detail in chapter 19. For consistency, I would often stick with explicit routing with attributes in that scenario too.

> **NOTE**   For the reasons above, this book focuses on explicit/attribute routing. For details on convention-based routing, see Microsoft's "Routing to controller actions in ASP.NET Core" documentation at http://mng.bz/ZP0O.

You learned about routing and route templates in chapter 6 in the context of minimal APIs. The good news is that exactly the same patterns and features are available with Razor Pages. The main difference with minimal APIs is that Razor Pages use conventions to generate the route template for a page, though you can easily change the template on a page-by-page basis. In section 14.3 we look at the default conventions and how routing maps a request's URL to a Razor Page in detail.

14.3   *Routing requests to Razor Pages*

As I mentioned in section 14.2, Razor Pages use explicit routing by creating route templates based on conventions. ASP.NET Core creates a route template for every Razor Page in your app during app startup, when you call `MapRazorPages()` in Program.cs:

```
app.endpoints.MapRazorPages();
```

For every Razor Page in your application, the framework uses the path of the Razor Page file relative to the Razor Pages root directory (`Pages/`), excluding the file extension (.cshtml). If you have a Razor Page located at the path `Pages/Products/View.cshtml`, the framework creates a route template with the value `"Products/View"`, as shown in figure 14.2.

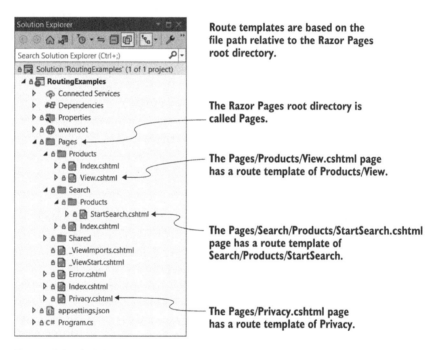

Figure 14.2   By default, route templates are generated for Razor Pages based on the path of the file relative to the root directory, Pages.

Requests to the URL `/products/view` match the route template `"Products/View"`, which in turn corresponds to the View.cshtml Razor Page in the Pages/Products folder. The `RoutingMiddleware` selects the View.cshtml Razor Page as the endpoint for the request, and the `EndpointMiddleware` executes the page's handler when the request reaches it in the middleware pipeline.

> **NOTE**   Remember that routing is not case-sensitive, so the request URL will match even if it has a different URL casing from the route template.

In chapter 13 you learned that Razor Page handlers are the methods that are invoked on a Razor Page, such as `OnGet`. When we say "a Razor Page is executed," we really mean "an instance of the Razor Page's `PageModel` is created, and a page handler on the model is invoked." Razor Pages can have multiple page handlers, so once the `RoutingMiddleware` selects a Razor Page, the `EndpointMiddleware` still needs to choose which handler to execute. You'll learn how the framework selects which page handler to invoke in chapter 15.

By default, each Razor Page creates a single route template based on its file path. The exception to this rule is for Razor Pages that are called Index.cshtml. Index.cshtml pages create two route templates, one ending with `"Index"` and the other without this suffix. If you have a Razor Page at the path `Pages/ToDo/Index.cshtml`, you have two route templates that point to the same page:

- `"ToDo"`
- `"ToDo/Index"`

When either of these routes is matched, the same Index.cshtml Razor Page is selected. If your application is running at the URL https://example.org, you can view the page by executing https://example.org/ToDo or https://example.org/ToDo/Index.

> **WARNING** You must watch out for overlapping routes when using Index.cshtml pages. For example, if you add the Pages/ToDo/Index.cshtml page in the above example you must *not* add a Pages/ToDo.cshtml page, as you'll get an exception at runtime when you navigate to /todo, as you'll see in section 14.6.

As a final example, consider the Razor Pages created by default when you create a Razor Pages application by using Visual Studio or running `dotnet new razor` using the .NET command-line interface (CLI), as we did in chapter 13. The standard template includes three Razor Pages in the Pages directory:

- `Pages/Error.cshtml`
- `Pages/Index.cshtml`
- `Pages/Privacy.cshtml`

That creates a collection of four routes for the application, defined by the following templates:

- `""` maps to Index.cshtml.
- `"Index"` maps to Index.cshtml.
- `"Error"` maps to Error.cshtml.
- `"Privacy"` maps to Privacy.cshtml.

At this point, Razor Page routing probably feels laughably trivial, but this is the basics that you get for free with the default Razor Pages conventions, which are often sufficient for a large portion of any website. At some point, though, you'll find you need something more dynamic, such as using route parameters to include an ID in the URL. This is where the ability to customize your Razor Page route templates becomes useful.

14.4 Customizing Razor Page route templates

The route templates for a Razor Page are based on the file path by default, but you're also able to customize or replace the final template for each page. In this section I show how to customize the route templates for individual pages so you can customize your application's URLs and map multiple URLs to a single Razor Page.

You may remember from chapter 6 that route templates consist of both literal segments and route parameters, as shown in figure 14.3. By default, Razor Pages have URLs consisting of a series of literal segments, such as `"ToDo/Index"`.

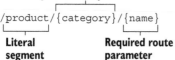

Required route parameter

```
/product/{category}/{name}
```

Literal segment | Required route parameter | **Figure 14.3   A simple route template showing a literal segment and two required route parameters**

Literal segments and route parameters are the two cornerstones of ASP.NET Core route templates, but how can you customize a Razor Page to use one of these patterns? In section 14.4.1 you'll see how to add a segment to the end of a Razor Page's route template, and in section 14.4.2 you'll see how to replace the route template completely.

14.4.1 Adding a segment to a Razor Page route template

To customize the Razor Page route template, you update the @page directive at the top of the Razor Page's .cshtml file. This directive must be the first thing in the Razor Page file for the page to be registered correctly.

To add an extra segment to a Razor Page's route template, add a space followed by the extra route template segment, after the @page statement. To add `"Extra"` to a Razor Page's route template, for example, use

```
@page "Extra"
```

This appends the provided route template to the default template generated for the Razor Page. The default route template for the Razor Page at `Pages/Privacy.html`, for example, is `"Privacy"`. With the preceding directive, the new route template for the page would be `"Privacy/Extra"`.

The most common reason for customizing a Razor Page's route template like this is to add a route parameter. You could have a single Razor Page for displaying the products in an e-commerce site at the path `Pages/Products.cshtml` and use a route parameter in the @page directive

```
@page "{category}/{name}"
```

This would give a final route template of `Products/{category}/{name}`, which would match all the following URLs:

- `/products/bags/white-rucksack`
- `/products/shoes/black-size9`
- `/Products/phones/iPhoneX`

> **NOTE** You can use the same routing features you learned about in chapter 6 with Razor Pages, including optional parameters, default parameters, and constraints.

It's common to add route segments to the Razor Page template like this, but what if that's not enough? Maybe you don't want to have the `/products` segment at the start of the preceding URLs, or you want to use a completely custom URL for a page. Luckily, that's just as easy to achieve.

14.4.2 *Replacing a Razor Page route template completely*

You'll be most productive working with Razor Pages if you can stick to the default routing conventions where possible, adding extra segments for route parameters where necessary. But sometimes you need more control. That's often the case for important pages in your application, such as the checkout page for an e-commerce application or even product pages, as you saw in the previous section.

To specify a custom route for a Razor Page, prefix the route with / in the `@page` directive. To remove the `"product/"` prefix from the route templates in section 14.4.1, use this directive:

```
@page "/{category}/{name}"
```

Note that this directive includes the `"/"` at the start of the route, indicating that this is a *custom* route template, instead of an *addition*. The route template for this page will be `"{category}/{name}"` no matter which Razor Page it is applied to.

Similarly, you can create a static custom template for a page by starting the template with a `"/"` and using only literal segments:

```
@page "/checkout"
```

Wherever you place your checkout Razor Page within the Pages folder, using this directive ensures that it always has the route template `"checkout"`, so it always matches the request URL `/checkout`.

> **TIP** You can also think of custom route templates that start with "/" as *absolute* route templates, whereas other route templates are *relative* to their location in the file hierarchy.

It's important to note that when you customize the route template for a Razor Page, both when appending to the default and when replacing it with a custom route, the *default template is no longer valid*. If you use the `"checkout"` route template above on a Razor Page located at `Pages/Payment.cshtml`, you can access it only by using the URL `/checkout`; the URL `/Payment` is no longer valid and won't execute the Razor Page.

> **TIP** Customizing the route template for a Razor Page using the @page directive replaces the default route template for the page. In section 14.6 I show how you can add extra routes while preserving the default route template.

In this section you learned how to customize the route template for a Razor Page. For the most part, routing to Razor Pages works like minimal APIs, the main difference being that the route templates are created using conventions. When it comes to the other half of routing—generating URLs—Razor Pages and minimal APIs are also similar, but Razor Pages gives you some nice helpers.

14.5 Generating URLs for Razor Pages

In this section you'll learn how to generate URLs for your Razor Pages using the IUrlHelper that's part of the Razor Pages PageModel type. You'll also learn to use the LinkGenerator service you saw in chapter 6 for generating URLs with minimal APIs.

One of the benefits of using convention-based routing in Razor Pages is that your URLs can be somewhat fluid. If you rename a Razor Page, the URL associated with that page also changes. Renaming the Pages/Cart.cshtml page to Pages/Basket/View.cshtml, for example, causes the URL you use to access the page to change from /Cart to /Basket/View.

To track these changes (and to avoid broken links), you can use the routing infrastructure to generate the URLs that you output in your Razor Page HTML and that you include in your HTTP responses. In chapter 6 you saw how to generate URLs for your minimal API endpoints, and in this section, you'll see how to do the same for your Razor Pages. I also describe how to generate URLs for MVC controllers, as the mechanism is virtually identical to that used by Razor Pages.

14.5.1 Generating URLs for a Razor Page

You'll need to generate URLs in various places in your application, and one common location is in your Razor Pages and MVC controllers. The following listing shows how you could generate a link to the Pages/Currency/View.cshtml Razor Page, using the Url helper from the PageModel base class.

Listing 14.2   **Generating a URL using IUrlHelper and the Razor Page name**

```
public class IndexModel : PageModel          ◁——   Deriving from PageModel gives
{                                                   access to the Url property.
    public void OnGet()
    {
        var url = Url.Page("Currency/View", new { code = "USD" });   ◁————
    }
}                                            You provide the relative path to the Razor
                                             Page, along with any additional route values.
```

The Url property is an instance of IUrlHelper that allows you to easily generate URLs for your application by referencing other Razor Pages by their file path.

NOTE IUrlHelper is a wrapper around the LinkGenerator class you learned about in chapter 6. IUrlHelper adds some shortcuts for generating URLs based on the current request.

IUrlHelper exposes a Page() method to which you pass the name of the Razor Page and any additional route data as an anonymous object. Then the helper generates a URL based on the referenced page's route template.

TIP You can provide the *relative* file path to the Razor Page, as shown in listing 14.2. Alternatively, you can provide the *absolute* file path (relative to the Pages folder) by starting the path with a "/", such as "/Currency/View".

IUrlHelper has several different overloads of the Page() method. Some of these methods allow you to specify a specific page handler, others let you generate an absolute URL instead of a relative URL, and some let you pass in additional route values.

In listing 14.2, as well as providing the file path I passed in an anonymous object, new { code = "USD" }. This object provides additional route values when generating the URL, in this case setting the code parameter to "USD", as you did when generating URLs for minimal APIs with LinkGenerator in chapter 6. As before, the code value is used in the URL directly if it corresponds to a route parameter. Otherwise, it's appended as additional data in the query string.

Generating URLs based on the page you want to execute is convenient, and it's the usual approach taken in most cases. If you're using MVC controllers for your APIs, the process is much the same as for Razor Pages, though the methods are slightly different.

14.5.2   Generating URLs for an MVC controller

Generating URLs for MVC controllers is similar to Razor Pages. The main difference is that you use the Action method on the IUrlHelper, and you provide an MVC controller name and action name instead of a page path.

NOTE I've covered MVC controllers only in passing, as I generally don't recommend them over Razor Pages or minimal APIs, so don't worry too much about them. We'll come back to MVC controllers in chapters 19 and 20; the main reason for mentioning them here is to point out how similar MVC controllers are to Razor Pages.

The following listing shows an MVC controller generating a link from one action method to another, using the Url helper from the Controller base class.

Listing 14.3   Generating a URL using IUrlHelper and the action name

```
public class CurrencyController : Controller      ◁──┐  Deriving from Controller gives
{                                                     │  access to the Url property.
    [HttpGet("currency/index")]      ◁──┐
    public IActionResult Index()         │  Explicit route templates using attributes
    {                                    │
```

```
                   var url = Url.Action("View", "Currency",
                       new { code = "USD" });
                   return Content($"The URL is {url}");
               }


               [HttpGet("currency/view/{code}")]
               public IActionResult View(string code)
               {
                   /* method implementation*/
               }
           }
```

The URL generated a route to this action method.

You provide the action and controller name to generate, along with any additional route values.

Returns "The URL is /Currency/View/USD"

You can call the `Action` and `Page` methods on `IUrlHelper` from both Razor Pages and MVC controllers, so you can generate links back and forth between them if you need to. The important question is, what is the destination of the URL? If the URL you need refers to a Razor Page, use the `Page()` method. If the destination is an MVC action, use the `Action()` method.

> **TIP** Instead of using strings for the name of the action method, use the C# 6 `nameof` operator to make the value refactor-safe, such as `nameof(View)`.

If you're routing to an action in the same controller, you can use a different overload of `Action()` that omits the controller name when generating the URL. The `IUrlHelper` uses *ambient values* from the current request and overrides them with any specific values you provide.

> **DEFINITION** *Ambient values* are the route values for the current request. They include `Controller` and `Action` when called from an MVC controller and `Page` when called from a Razor Page. Ambient values can also include additional route values that were set when the action or Razor Page was initially located using routing. See Microsoft's "Routing in ASP.NET Core" documentation for further details: http://mng.bz/OxoE.

`IUrlHelper` can make it simpler to generate URLs by reusing ambient values from the current request, though it also adds a layer of complexity, as the same method arguments can give a different generated URL depending on the page the method is called from.

If you need to generate URLs from parts of your application outside the Razor Page or MVC infrastructure, you won't be able to use the `IUrlHelper` helper. Instead, you can use the `LinkGenerator` class.

14.5.3 *Generating URLs with LinkGenerator*

In chapter 6 I described how to generate links to minimal API endpoints using the `LinkGenerator` class. By contrast with `IUrlHelper`, `LinkGenerator` requires that you always provide sufficient arguments to uniquely define the URL to generate. This makes it more verbose but also more consistent and has the advantage that it can be used anywhere in your application. This differs from `IUrlHelper`, which should be used only inside the context of a request.

If you're writing your Razor Pages and MVC controllers following the advice from chapter 13, you should be trying to keep your Razor Pages relatively simple. That requires you to execute your application's business and domain logic in separate classes and services.

For the most part, the URLs your application uses shouldn't be part of your domain logic. That makes it easier for your application to evolve over time or even to change completely. You may want to create a mobile application that reuses the business logic from an ASP.NET Core app, for example. In that case, using URLs in the business logic wouldn't make sense, as they wouldn't be correct when the logic is called from the mobile app!

> **TIP** Where possible, try to keep knowledge of the frontend application design out of your business logic. This pattern is known generally as the Dependency Inversion principle.

Unfortunately, sometimes that separation is not possible, or it makes things significantly more complicated. One example might be when you're creating emails in a background service; it's likely you'll need to include a link to your application in the email. The LinkGenerator class lets you generate that URL so that it updates automatically if the routes in your application change.

As you saw in chapter 6, the LinkGenerator class is available everywhere in your application, so you can use it inside middleware, minimal API endpoints, or any other services. You can use it from Razor Pages and MVC too, if you want, though the IUrl-Helper is often more convenient and hides some details of using the LinkGenerator.

You've already seen how to generate links to minimal API endpoints with Link-Generator using methods like GetPathByName() and GetUriByName(). LinkGenerator has various analogous methods for generating URLs for Razor Pages and MVC actions, such as GetPathByPage(), GetPathByAction(), and GetUriByPage(), as shown in the following listing.

Listing 14.4   Generating URLs using the `LinkGeneratorClass`

```
public class CurrencyModel : PageModel
{
    private readonly LinkGenerator _link;              ◁── LinkGenerator can
    public CurrencyModel(LinkGenerator linkGenerator)      be accessed using
    {                                                       dependency
        _link = linkGenerator;                              injection.
    }

    public void OnGet ()
    {
        var url1 = Url.Page("Currency/View", new { id = 5 });
        var url3 = _link.GetPathByPage(              ◁── GetPathByPage is equivalent
            HttpContext,                                 to Url.Page and generates a
            "/Currency/View",                            relative URL.
            values: new { id = 5 });
```

You can generate relative paths using Url.Page. You can use relative or absolute Page paths.

```
        var url2 = _link.GetPathByPage(
                "/Currency/View",
                values: new { id = 5 });
        var url4 = _link.GetUriByPage(
                page: "/Currency/View",
                handler: null,
                values: new { id = 5 },
                scheme: "https",
                host: new HostString("example.com"));
    }
}
```

Other overloads don't require an HttpContext.

GetUriByPage generates an absolute URL instead of a relative URL.

> **WARNING** As always, you need to be careful when generating URLs, whether
> you're using `IUrlHelper` or `LinkGenerator`. If you get anything wrong—use the
> wrong path or don't provide a required route parameter—the URL gener-
> ated will be `null`.

At this point we've covered mapping request URLs to Razor Pages and generating
URLs, but most of the URLs we've used have been kind of ugly. If seeing capital letters
in your URLs bothers you, the next section is for you. In section 14.6 we customize the
conventions your application uses to calculate route templates.

14.6   *Customizing conventions with Razor Pages*

Razor Pages is built on a series of conventions that are designed to reduce the amount
of boilerplate code you need to write. In this section you'll see some of the ways you
can customize those conventions. By customizing the conventions Razor Pages uses in
your application, you get full control of your application's URLs without having to customize every Razor Page's route template manually.

By default, ASP.NET Core generates URLs that match the filenames of your Razor
Pages very closely. The Razor Page located at the path `Pages/Products/ProductDetails`
`.cshtml`, for example, corresponds to the route template `Products/ProductDetails`.

These days, it's not common to see capital letters in URLs. Similarly, words in URLs
are usually separated using kebab-case rather than PascalCase—`product-details`
instead of `ProductDetails`. Finally, it's also common to ensure that your URLs always
end with a slash, for example—`/product-details/` instead of `/product-details`. Razor
Pages gives you complete control of the conventions your application uses to generate
route templates, but these are some of the common changes I often make.

You saw how to make some of these changes in chapter 6, by customizing the
`RouteOptions` for your application. You can make your URLs lowercase and ensure that
they already have a trailing slash as shown in the following listing.

> **Listing 14.5   Configuring routing conventions using `RouteOptions` in Program.cs**

```
WebApplicationBuilder builder = WebApplication.CreateBuilder(args);
builder.Services.AddRazorPages();
```

```
builder.Services.Configure<RouteOptions>(o =>
{
    o.LowercaseUrls = true;
    o.LowercaseQueryStrings = true;
    o.AppendTrailingSlash = true;
});
```

Changes the conventions used to generate URLs. By default, these properties are false.

```
WebApplication app = builder.Build();

app.MapRazorPages();

app.Run();
```

To use kebab-case for your application, annoyingly you must create a custom parameter transformer. This is a somewhat advanced topic, but it's relatively simple to implement in this case. The following listing shows how you can create a parameter transformer that uses a regular expression to replace PascalCase values in a generated URL with kebab-case.

Listing 14.6   Creating a kebab-case parameter transformer

```
public class KebabCaseParameterTransformer
    : IOutboundParameterTransformer
{
    public string TransformOutbound(object? value)
    {
        if (value is null) return null;

        return Regex.Replace(value.ToString(),
            "([a-z])([A-Z])", "$1-$2").ToLower();
    }
}
```

Creates a class that implements the parameter transformer interface

Guards against null values to prevent runtime exceptions

The regular expression replaces PascalCase patterns with kebab-case.

Source generators in .NET 7

One of the exciting features introduced in C# 9 was source generators. Source generators are a compiler feature that let you inspect code as it's compiled and generate new C# files on the fly, which are included in the compilation. Source generators have the potential to dramatically reduce the boilerplate required for some features and to improve performance by relying on compile-time analysis instead of runtime reflection.

.NET 6 introduced several source generator implementations, such as a high-performance logging API, which I discuss in this post: http://mng.bz/Y1GA. Even the Razor compiler used to compile .cshtml files was rewritten to use source generators!

In .NET 7, many new source generators were added. One such generator is the regular-expression generator, which can improve performance of your `Regex` instances, such as the one in listing 14.6. In fact, if you're using an IDE like Visual Studio, you should see a code fix suggesting that you use the new pattern. After you apply the code fix, listing 14.6 should look like the following instead, which is functionally identical but will likely be faster:

```
(continued)
partial class KebabCaseParameterTransformer : IOutboundParameterTransformer
{
    public string? TransformOutbound(object? value)
    {
        if (value is null) return null;

        return MyRegex().Replace(value.ToString(), "$1-$2").ToLower();
    }

    [GeneratedRegex("([a-z])([A-Z])")]
    private static partial Regex MyRegex();
}
```

If you'd like to know more about how this source generator works and how it can improve performance, see this post at http://mng.bz/GyEO. If you'd like to learn more about source generators, or even write your own, see my series on the process at http://mng.bz/zX4Q.

You can register the parameter transformer in your application with the AddRazorPages-Options() extension method in Program.cs. This method is chained after the Add-RazorPages() method and can be used to customize the conventions used by Razor Pages. The following listing shows how to register the kebab-case transformer. It also shows how to add an extra page route convention for a given Razor Page.

Listing 14.7   Registering a parameter transformer using `RazorPagesOptions`

```
WebApplicationBuilder builder = WebApplication.CreateBuilder(args);
builder.Services.AddRazorPages()            AddRazorPagesOptions can be used to
    .AddRazorPagesOptions(opts =>    ◁───   customize the conventions used by Razor Pages.
    {
        opts.Conventions.Add(                          Registers the parameter
            new PageRouteTransformerConvention(        transformer as a convention
                new KebabCaseParameterTransformer()));  used by all Razor Pages
        opts.Conventions.AddPageRoute(
            "/Search/Products/StartSearch", "/search-products");
    });
                                        AddPageRoute adds a route template to
WebApplication app = builder.Build();   Pages/Search/Products/StartSearch.cshtml.

app.MapRazorPages();

app.Run();
```

The AddPageRoute() convention adds an alternative way to execute a single Razor Page. Unlike when you customize the route template for a Razor Page using the @page directive, using AddPageRoute() adds an extra route template to the page instead of replacing the default. That means there are two route templates that can access the page.

> **TIP**   Even the name of the Pages root folder is a convention that you can cus-
> tomize! You can customize it by setting the RootDirectory property inside the
> AddRazorPageOptions() configuration lambda.

If you want even more control of your Razor Pages route templates, you can implement a custom convention by implementing the IPageRouteModelConvention interface
and registering it as a custom convention. IPageRouteModelConvention is one of three
powerful Razor Pages interfaces which let you customize how your Razor Pages app
works:

- IPageRouteModelConvention—Used to customize the route templates for all the
  Razor Pages in your app.
- IPageApplicationModelConvention—Used to customize how the Razor Page is
  processed, such as to add filters to your Razor Page automatically. You'll learn
  about filters in Razor Pages in chapters 21 and 22.
- IPageHandlerModelConvention—Used to customize how page handlers are discovered and selected.

These interfaces are powerful, as they give you access to all the internals of your Razor
Page conventions and configuration. You can use the IPageRouteModelConvention, for
example, to rewrite all the route templates for your Razor Pages or to add routes automatically. This is particularly useful if you need to localize an application so that you
can use URLs in multiple languages, all of which map to the same Razor Page.

Listing 14.8 shows a simple example of an IPageRouteModelConvention that adds a
fixed prefix, "page", to all the routes in your application. If you have a Razor Page at
Pages/Privacy.cshtml, with a default route template of "Privacy", after adding the following convention it would also have the route template "page/Privacy".

Listing 14.8   Creating a custom IPageRouteModelConvention

```
public class PrefixingPageRouteModelConvention          The convention implements
    : IpageRouteModelConvention              ◁────────  IPageRouteModelConvention.
{
    public void Apply(PageRouteModel model)  ◁───       ASP.NET Core calls
    {                                                   Apply on app startup.
        var selectors = model.Selectors
            .Select(selector => new SelectorModel
            {
                AttributeRouteModel = new AttributeRouteModel
                {
                    Template = AttributeRouteModel.CombineTemplates(
                        "page",
                        selector.AttributeRouteModel!.Template),
                }
            })
            .ToList();

        foreach(var newSelector in selectors)
        {
```

Adds the new selector to the page's route template collection

Creates a new SelectorModel, defining a new route template for the page

```
        model.Selectors.Add(newSelector);
      }
    }
}
```

You can add the convention to your application inside the call to `AddRazorPages-Options()`. The following applies the contention to all pages:

```
builder.Services.AddRazorPages().AddRazorPagesOptions(opts =>
{
    opts.Conventions.Add(new PrefixingPageRouteModelConvention());
});
```

There are many ways you can customize the conventions in your Razor Page applications, but a lot of the time that's not necessary. If you do find you need to customize all the pages in your application in some way, Microsoft's "Razor Pages route and app conventions in ASP.NET Core" documentation contains further details on everything that's available: http://mng.bz/A0BK.

Conventions are a key feature of Razor Pages, and you should lean on them whenever you can. Although you can override the route templates for individual Razor Pages manually, as you've seen in previous sections, I advise against it where possible. In particular,

- *Avoid* replacing the route template with an absolute path in a page's @page directive.
- *Avoid* adding literal segments to the @page directive. Rely on the file hierarchy instead.
- *Avoid* adding additional route templates to a Razor Page with the `AddPageRoute()` convention. Having multiple URLs to access a page can often be confusing.
- *Do* add route parameters to the @page directive to make your routes dynamic, as in @page "{name}".
- *Do* consider using global conventions when you want to change the route templates for all your Razor Pages, such as using kebab-case, as you saw earlier.

In a nutshell, these rules say "Stick to the conventions." The danger, if you don't, is that you may accidentally create two Razor Pages that have overlapping route templates. Unfortunately, if you end up in that situation, you *won't* get an error at compile time. Instead, you'll get an exception at runtime when your application receives a request that matches multiple route templates, as shown in figure 14.4.

We've covered pretty much everything about routing to Razor Pages now. For the most part, routing to Razor Pages works like minimal APIs, the main difference being that the route templates are created using conventions. When it comes to the other half of routing—generating URLs—Razor Pages and minimal APIs are also similar, but Razor Pages gives you some nice helpers.

Congratulations—you've made it all the way through this detailed discussion on Razor Page routing! I hope you weren't too fazed by the differences from minimal API

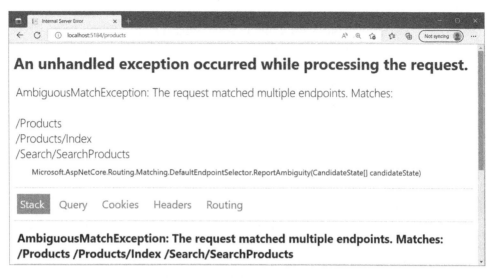

Figure 14.4 If multiple Razor Pages are registered with overlapping route templates, you'll get an exception at runtime when the router can't work out which one to select.

routing. We'll revisit routing again when I describe how to create Web APIs in chapter 20, but rest assured that we've already covered all the tricky details in this chapter!

Routing controls how incoming requests are bound to your Razor Page, but we haven't seen where page handlers come into it. In chapter 15 you'll learn all about page handlers—how they're selected, how they generate responses, and how to handle error responses gracefully.

Summary

- Routing is the process of mapping an incoming request URL to an endpoint that will execute to generate a response. Each Razor Page is an endpoint, and a single page handler executes for each request.
- You can define the mapping between URLs and endpoint in your application using either convention-based routing or explicit routing. Minimal APIs use explicit routing, where each endpoint has a corresponding route template. MVC controllers often use conventional routing in which a single pattern matches multiple controllers but may also use explicit/attribute routing. Razor Pages lies in between; it uses conventions to generate explicit route templates for each page.
- By default, each Razor Page has a single route template that matches its path inside the Pages folder, so the Razor Page Pages/Products/View.cshtml has route template `Products/View`. These file-based defaults make it easy to visualize the URLs your application exposes.
- Index.cshtml Razor Pages have two route templates, one with an `/Index` suffix and one without. Pages/Products/Index.cshtml, for example, has two route

templates: `Products/Index` and `Products`. This is in keeping with the common behavior of index.html files in traditional HTML applications.

- You can add segments to a Razor Page's template by appending it to the `@page` directive, as in `@page "{id}"`. Any extra segments are appended to the Razor Page's default route template. You can include both literal and route template segments, which can be used to make your Razor Pages dynamic. You can replace the route template for a Razor Page by starting the template with a `"/"`, as in `@page "/contact"`.

- You can use `IUrlHelper` to generate URLs as a string based on an action name or Razor Page. `IUrlHelper` can be used only in the context of a request and uses ambient routing values from the current request. This makes it easier to generate links for Razor Pages in the same folder as the currently executing request but also adds inconsistency, as the same method call generates different URLs depending on where it's called.

- The `LinkGenerator` can be used to generate URLs from other services in your application, where you don't have access to an `HttpContext` object. The `Link-Generator` methods are more verbose than the equivalents on `IUrlHelper`, but they are unambiguous as they don't use ambient values from the current request.

- You can control the routing conventions used by ASP.NET Core by configuring the `RouteOptions` object, such as to force all URLs to be lowercase or to always append a trailing slash.

- You can add extra routing conventions for Razor Pages by calling `AddRazor-PagesOptions()` after `AddRazorPages()` in Program.cs. These conventions can control how route parameters are displayed and can add extra route templates for specific Razor Pages.

15

Generating responses with page handlers in Razor Pages

This chapter covers

- Selecting which page handler in a Razor Page to invoke for a request
- Returning an IActionResult from a page handler
- Handling status code errors with StatusCodePagesMiddleware

In chapter 14 you learned how the routing system selects a Razor Page to execute based on its associated route template and the request URL, but each Razor Page can have multiple page handlers. In this chapter you'll learn all about page handlers, their responsibilities, and how a single Razor Page selects which handler to execute for a request.

In section 15.3 we look at some of the ways of retrieving values from an HTTP request in a page handler. Much like minimal APIs, page handlers can accept method arguments that are bound to values in the HTTP request, but Razor Pages can also bind the request to properties on the PageModel.

In section 15.4 you'll learn how to return `IActionResult` objects from page handlers. Then you look at some of the common `IActionResult` types that you'll return from page handlers for generating HTML and redirect responses.

Finally, in section 15.5 you'll learn how to use the `StatusCodePagesMiddleware` to improve the error status code responses in your middleware pipeline. This middleware intercepts error responses such as basic `404` responses and reexecutes the middleware pipeline to generate a pretty HTML response for the error. This gives users a much nicer experience when they encounter an error browsing your Razor Pages app.

We'll start by taking a quick look at the responsibilities of a page handler before we move on to see how the Razor Page infrastructure selects which page handler to execute.

15.1 *Razor Pages and page handlers*

In chapter 13 I described the Model-View-Controller (MVC) design pattern and showed how it relates to ASP.NET Core. In this design pattern, the "controller" receives a request and is the entry point for UI generation. For Razor Pages, the entry point is the page handler that resides in a Razor Page's `PageModel`. A *page handler* is a method that runs in response to a request.

The responsibility of a page handler is generally threefold:

- Confirm that the incoming request is valid.
- Invoke the appropriate business logic corresponding to the incoming request.
- Choose the appropriate kind of response to return.

A page handler doesn't need to perform all these actions, but at the very least it must choose the kind of response to return. Page handlers typically return one of three things:

- *A* `PageResult` *object*—This causes the associated Razor view to generate an HTML response.
- *Nothing (the handler returns* `void` *or* `Task`*)*—This is the same as the previous case, causing the Razor view to generate an HTML response.
- *A* `RedirectToPageResult`—This indicates that the user should be redirected to a different page in your application.

These are the most common results for Razor Pages, but I describe some additional options in section 15.4.

It's important to realize that a page handler doesn't generate a response directly; it selects the type of response and prepares the data for it. For example, returning a `PageResult` doesn't generate any HTML at that point; it merely indicates that a view should be rendered. This is in keeping with the MVC design pattern in which it's the *view* that generates the response, not the *controller*.

> **TIP** The page handler is responsible for choosing what sort of response to send; the *view engine* in the MVC framework uses the result to generate the response.

It's also worth bearing in mind that page handlers generally shouldn't be performing business logic directly. Instead, they should call appropriate services in the application model to handle requests. If a page handler receives a request to add a product to a user's cart, it shouldn't manipulate the database or recalculate cart totals directly, for example. Instead, it should make a call to another class to handle the details. This approach of separating concerns ensures that your code stays testable and maintainable as it grows.

15.2   Selecting a page handler to invoke

In chapter 14 I said routing is about mapping URLs to an endpoint, which for Razor Pages means a page handler. But I've mentioned several times that Razor Pages can contain multiple page handlers. In this section you'll learn how the `EndpointMiddleware` selects which page handler to invoke when it executes a Razor Page.

As you saw in chapter 14, the path of a Razor Page on disk controls the default route template for a Razor Page. For example, the Razor Page at the path `Pages/Products/Search.cshtml` has a default route template of `Products/Search`. When a request is received with the URL `/products/search`, the `RoutingMiddleware` selects this Razor Page, and the request passes through the middleware pipeline to the `EndpointMiddleware`. At this point, the `EndpointMiddleware` must choose which page handler to execute, as shown in figure 15.1.

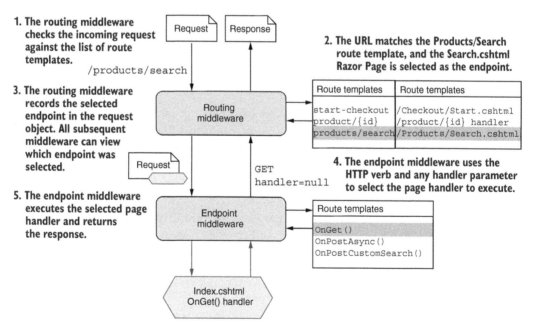

Figure 15.1   The routing middleware selects the Razor Page to execute based on the incoming request URL. Then the endpoint middleware selects the endpoint to execute based on the HTTP verb of the request and the presence (or lack) of a `handler` route value.

Consider the Razor Page `SearchModel` shown in listing 15.1. This Razor Page has three handlers: `OnGet`, `OnPostAsync`, and `OnPostCustomSearch`. The bodies of the handler methods aren't shown, as we're interested only in how the EndpointMiddleware chooses which handler to invoke.

Listing 15.1 Razor Page with multiple page handlers

```
public class SearchModel : PageModel
{
    public void OnGet()  ⟵──── Handles GET requests
    {
        // Handler implementation
    }
    public Task OnPostAsync()  ⟵─┐
    {
        // Handler implementation
    }
    public void OnPostCustomSearch()  ⟵─┐
    {
        // Handler implementation
    }
}
```

Handles POST requests. The async suffix is optional and is ignored for routing purposes.

Handles POST requests where the handler route value has the value CustomSearch

---

Razor Pages can contain any number of page handlers, but only one runs in response to a given request. When the EndpointMiddleware executes a selected Razor Page, it selects a page handler to invoke based on two variables:

- The HTTP verb used in the request (such as GET, POST, or DELETE)
- The value of the handler route value

The handler route value typically comes from a query string value in the request URL, such as /Search?handler=CustomSearch. If you don't like the look of query strings (I don't!), you can include the {handler} route parameter in your Razor Page's route template. For the Search page model in listing 15.2, you could update the page's directive to

```
@page "{handler?}"
```

This would give a complete route template something like "Search/{handler?}", which would match URLs such as /Search and /Search/CustomSearch.

The EndpointMiddleware uses the handler route value and the HTTP verb together with a standard naming convention to identify which page handler to execute, as shown in figure 15.2. The handler parameter is optional and is typically provided as part of the request's query string or as a route parameter, as described earlier. The async suffix is also optional and is often used when the handler uses asynchronous programming constructs such as Task or async/await.

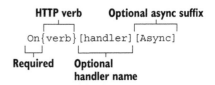

Figure 15.2 Razor Page handlers are matched to a request based on the HTTP verb and the optional handler parameter.

> **NOTE** The async suffix naming convention is suggested by Microsoft, though it is unpopular with some developers. NServiceBus provides a reasoned argument against it here (along with Microsoft's advice): http://mng.bz/e59P.

Based on this convention, we can now identify what type of request each page handler in listing 15.1 corresponds to:

- `OnGet`—Invoked for `GET` requests that don't specify a `handler` value
- `OnPostAsync`—Invoked for `POST` requests that don't specify a `handler` value; returns a `Task`, so it uses the `Async` suffix, which is ignored for routing purposes
- `OnPostCustomSearch`—Invoked for `POST` requests that specify a `handler` value of `"CustomSearch"`

The Razor Page in listing 15.1 specifies three handlers, so it can handle only three verb-handler pairs. But what happens if you get a request that doesn't match these, such as a request using the `DELETE` verb, a `GET` request with a nonblank `handler` value, or a `POST` request with an unrecognized `handler` value?

For all these cases, the `EndpointMiddleware` executes an implicit page handler instead. *Implicit* page handlers contain no logic; they simply render the Razor view. For example, if you sent a `DELETE` request to the Razor Page in listing 15.1, the `Endpoint-Middleware` would execute an implicit handler. The implicit page handler is equivalent to the following handler code:

```
public void OnDelete() { }
```

> **DEFINITION** If a page handler does not match a request's HTTP verb and handler value, an *implicit* page handler is executed that renders the associated Razor view. Implicit page handlers take part in model binding and use page filters but execute no logic.

There's one exception to the implicit page handler rule: if a request uses the `HEAD` verb, and there is no corresponding `OnHead` handler, the `EndpointMiddleware` executes the `OnGet` handler instead (if it exists).

> **NOTE** `HEAD` requests are typically sent automatically by the browser and don't return a response body. They're often used for security purposes, as you'll see in chapter 28.

Now that you know how a page handler is selected, you can think about how it's executed.

15.3 Accepting parameters to page handlers

In chapter 7 you learned about the intricacies of model binding in minimal API endpoint handlers. Like minimal APIs, Razor Page page handlers can use model binding to easily extract values from the request. You'll learn the details of Razor Page model binding in chapter 16; in this section you'll learn about the basic mechanics of Razor Page model binding and the basic options available.

When working with Razor Pages, you'll often want to extract values from an incoming request. If the request is for a search page, the request might contain the search term and the page number in the query string. If the request is POSTing a form to your application, such as a user logging in with their username and password, those values may be encoded in the request body. In other cases, there will be no values, such as when a user requests the home page for your application.

> **DEFINITION** The process of extracting values from a request and converting them to .NET types is called *model binding*. I discuss model binding for Razor Pages in detail in chapter 16.

ASP.NET Core can bind two different targets in Razor Pages:

- *Method arguments*—If a page handler has method parameters, the arguments are bound and created from values in the request.
- *Properties marked with a* [BindProperty] *attribute*—Any properties on the PageModel marked with this attribute are bound to the request. By default, this attribute does nothing for GET requests.

Model-bound values can be simple types, such as strings and integers, or they can be complex types, as shown in the following listing. If any of the values provided in the request are not bound to a property or page handler argument, the additional values will go unused.

Listing 15.2 Example Razor Page handlers

```
public class SearchModel : PageModel
{
    private readonly SearchService _searchService;
    public SearchModel(SearchService searchService)      The SearchService is
    {                                                     injected from DI for
        _searchService = searchService;                  use in page handlers.
    }

    [BindProperty]                                        Properties decorated with the
    public BindingModel Input { get; set; }               [BindProperty] attribute are model-bound.
    public List<Product> Results { get; set; }     ◁

    public void OnGet()                                   Undecorated properties
    {                                                     are not model-bound.
    }
                                                          The page handler doesn't need to check if the
    public IActionResult OnPost(int max)                  model is valid. Returning void renders the view.
    {
        if (ModelState.IsValid)
        {
            Results = _searchService.Search(Input.SearchTerm, max);
            return Page();
        }
        return RedirectToPage("./Index");
    }
}
```

The max parameter is model-bound using values in the request.

If the request was not valid, the method indicates the user should be redirected to the Index page.

In this example, the OnGet handler doesn't require any parameters, and the method is simple: it returns void, which means the associated Razor view will be rendered. It could also have returned a PageResult; the effect would have been the same. Note that this handler is for HTTP GET requests, so the Input property decorated with [BindProperty] is not bound.

> **TIP** To bind properties for GET requests too, use the SupportsGet property of the attribute, as in [BindProperty(SupportsGet = true)].

The OnPost handler, conversely, accepts a parameter max as an argument. In this case it's a simple type, int, but it could also be a complex object. Additionally, as this handler corresponds to an HTTP POST request, the Input property is also model-bound to the request.

> **NOTE** Unlike most .NET classes, you can't use method overloading to have multiple page handlers on a Razor Page with the same name.

When a page handler uses model-bound properties or parameters, it should always check that the provided model is valid using ModelState.IsValid. The ModelState property is exposed as a property on the base PageModel class and can be used to check that all the bound properties and parameters are valid. You'll see how the process works in chapter 16 when you learn about validation.

Once a page handler establishes that the arguments provided to a page handler method are valid, it can execute the appropriate business logic and handle the request. In the case of the OnPost handler, this involves calling the injected SearchService and setting the result on the Results property. Finally, the handler returns a PageResult by calling the helper method on the PageModel base class:

```
return Page();
```

If the model isn't valid, as indicated by ModelState.IsValid, you don't have any results to display! In this example, the action returns a RedirectToPageResult using the RedirectToPage() helper method. When executed, this result sends a 302 Redirect response to the user, which will cause their browser to navigate to the Index Razor Page.

Note that the OnGet method returns void in the method signature, whereas the OnPost method returns an IActionResult. This is required in the OnPost method to allow the C# to compile (as the Page() and RedirectToPage() helper methods return different types), but it doesn't change the final behavior of the methods. You could easily have called Page() in the OnGet method and returned an IActionResult, and the behavior would be identical.

> **TIP** If you're returning more than one type of result from a page handler, you'll need to ensure that your method returns an IActionResult.

In listing 15.2 I used `Page()` and `RedirectToPage()` methods to generate the return value. `IActionResult` instances can be created and returned using the normal `new` syntax of C#:

```
return new PageResult()
```

However, the Razor Pages `PageModel` base class also provides several helper methods for generating responses, which are thin wrappers around the `new` syntax. It's common to use the `Page()` method to generate an appropriate `PageResult`, the `RedirectToPage()` method to generate a `RedirectToPageResult`, or the `NotFound()` method to generate a `NotFoundResult`.

> **TIP** Most `IActionResult` implementations have a helper method on the base `PageModel` class. They're typically named `Type`, and the result generated is called `TypeResult`. For example, the `StatusCode()` method returns a `Status-CodeResult` instance.

In the next section we'll look in more depth at some of the common `IActionResult` types.

15.4   *Returning IActionResult responses*

In the previous section, I emphasized that page handlers decide what type of response to return, but they don't generate the response themselves. It's the `IActionResult` returned by a page handler that, when executed by the Razor Pages infrastructure using the view engine, generates the response.

> **WARNING** Note that the interface type is `IActionResult` *not* `IResult`. `IResult` is used in minimal APIs and should generally be avoided in Razor Pages (and MVC controllers). In .NET 7, `IResult` types returned from Razor Pages or MVC controllers execute as expected, but they don't have all the same features as `IActionResult`, so you should favor `IActionResult` in Razor Pages.

`IActionResult`s are a key part of the MVC design pattern. They separate the decision of what sort of response to send from the generation of the response. This allows you to test your action method logic to confirm that the right sort of response is sent for a given input. You can then separately test that a given `IActionResult` generates the expected HTML, for example.

ASP.NET Core has many types of `IActionResult`, such as

- `PageResult`—Generates an HTML view for the associated page in Razor Pages and returns a `200` HTTP response.
- `ViewResult`—Generates an HTML view for a given Razor view when using MVC controllers and returns a `200` HTTP response.
- `PartialViewResult`—Renders part of an HTML page using a given Razor view and returns a `200` HTTP result; typically used with MVC controllers and AJAX requests.

- `RedirectToPageResult`—Sends a `302` HTTP redirect response to automatically send a user to another page.
- `RedirectResult`—Sends a `302` HTTP redirect response to automatically send a user to a specified URL (doesn't have to be a Razor Page).
- `FileResult`—Returns a file as the response. This is a base class with several derived types:
  - `FileContentResult`—Returns a `byte[]` as a file response to the browser
  - `FileStreamResult`—Returns the contents of a `Stream` as a file response to the browser
  - `PhysicalFileResult`—Returns the contents of a file on disk as a file response to the browser
- `ContentResult`—Returns a provided string as the response.
- `StatusCodeResult`—Sends a raw HTTP status code as the response, optionally with associated response body content.
- `NotFoundResult`—Sends a raw `404` HTTP status code as the response.

Each of these, when executed by Razor Pages, generates a response to send back through the middleware pipeline and out to the user.

> **TIP** When you're using Razor Pages, you generally won't use some of these action results, such as `ContentResult` and `StatusCodeResult`. It's good to be aware of them, though, as you will likely use them if you are building Web APIs with MVC controllers, as you'll see in chapter 20.

In sections 15.4.1–15.4.3 I give a brief description of the most common `IActionResult` types that you'll use with Razor Pages.

15.4.1 PageResult and RedirectToPageResult

When you're building a traditional web application with Razor Pages, usually you'll be using `PageResult`, which generates an HTML response from the Razor Page's associated Razor view. We'll look at how this happens in detail in chapter 17.

You'll also commonly use the various redirect-based results to send the user to a new web page. For example, when you place an order on an e-commerce website, you typically navigate through multiple pages, as shown in figure 15.3. The web application sends HTTP redirects whenever it needs you to move to a different page, such as when a user submits a form. Your browser automatically follows the redirect requests, creating a seamless flow through the checkout process.

In this flow, whenever you return HTML you use a `PageResult`; when you redirect to a new page, you use a `RedirectToPageResult`.

> **TIP** Razor Pages are generally designed to be stateless, so if you want to persist data between multiple pages, you need to place it in a database or similar store. If you want to store data for a single request, you may be able to use `TempData`, which stores small amounts of data in cookies for a single request. See the documentation for details: http://mng.bz/XdXp.

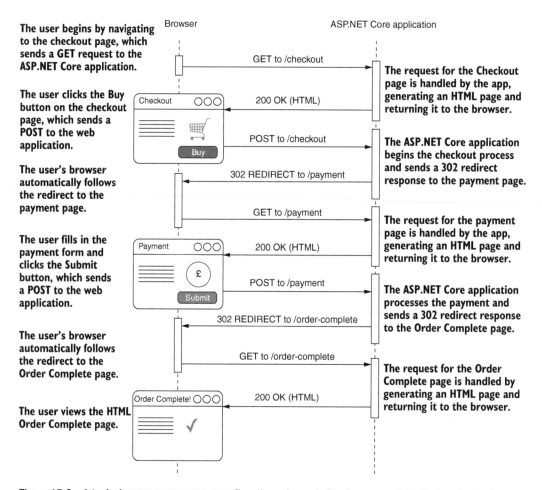

Figure 15.3   A typical POST, REDIRECT, GET flow through a website. A user sends their shopping basket to a checkout page, which validates its contents and redirects to a payment page without the user's having to change the URL manually.

15.4.2   *NotFoundResult and StatusCodeResult*

As well as sending HTML and redirect responses, you'll occasionally need to send specific HTTP status codes. If you request a page for viewing a product on an e-commerce application, and that product doesn't exist, a 404 HTTP status code is returned to the browser, and you'll typically see a "Not found" web page. Razor Pages can achieve this behavior by returning a NotFoundResult, which returns a raw 404 HTTP status code. You could achieve a similar result using StatusCodeResult and setting the status code returned explicitly to 404.

Note that NotFoundResult doesn't generate any HTML; it only generates a raw 404 status code and returns it through the middleware pipeline. This generally isn't a great user experience, as the browser typically displays a default page, such as that shown in figure 15.4.

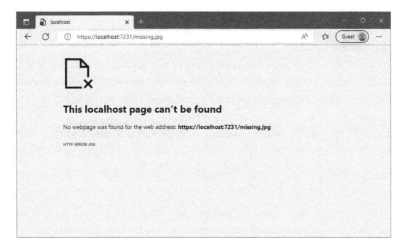

Figure 15.4   If you return a raw `404` **status code without any HTML, the browser will render a generic default page instead. The message is of limited utility to users and may leave many of them confused or thinking that your web application is broken.**

Returning raw status codes is fine when you're building an API, but for a Razor Pages application, this is rarely good enough. In section 15.5 you'll learn how you can intercept this raw `404` status code after it's been generated and provide a user-friendly HTML response for it instead.

15.5 *Handler status codes with StatusCodePagesMiddleware*

In chapter 4 we discussed error handling middleware, which is designed to catch exceptions generated anywhere in your middleware pipeline, catch them, and generate a user-friendly response. In this section you'll learn about an analogous piece of middleware that intercepts error HTTP status codes: `StatusCodePagesMiddleware`.

Your Razor Pages application can return a wide range of HTTP status codes that indicate some sort of error state. You've seen previously that a `500` "server error" is sent when an exception occurs and isn't handled and that a `404` "file not found" error is sent when you return a `NotFoundResult` from a page handler. `404` errors are particularly common, often occurring when a user enters an invalid URL.

> **TIP**   `404` errors are often used to indicate that a specific requested object was not found. For example, a request for the details of a product with an ID of `23` might return a `404` if no such product exists. They're also generated automatically if no endpoint in your application matches the request URL.

Returning "raw" status codes without additional content is generally OK if you're building a minimal API or web API application. But as mentioned before, for apps consumed directly by users such as Razor Pages apps, this can result in a poor user experience. If you don't handle these status codes, users will see a generic error page, as you saw in figure 15.4, which may leave many confused users thinking your application is broken. A better approach is to handle these error codes and return an error page that's in keeping with the rest of your application or at least doesn't make your application look broken.

Microsoft provides StatusCodePagesMiddleware for handling this use case. As with all error handling middleware, you should add it early in your middleware pipeline, as it will handle only errors generated by later middleware components.

You can use the middleware several ways in your application. The simplest approach is to add the middleware to your pipeline without any additional configuration, using

```
app.UseStatusCodePages();
```

With this method, the middleware intercepts any response that has an HTTP status code that starts with 4xx or 5xx and has no response body. For the simplest case, where you don't provide any additional configuration, the middleware adds a plain-text response body, indicating the type and name of the response, as shown in figure 15.5. This is arguably worse than the default message at this point, but it is a starting point for providing a more consistent experience to users.

Figure 15.5   Status code error page for a 404 error. You generally won't use this version of the middleware in production, as it doesn't provide a great user experience, but it demonstrates that the error codes are being intercepted correctly.

A more typical approach to using StatusCodePagesMiddleware in production is to reexecute the pipeline when an error is captured, using a similar technique to the ExceptionHandlerMiddleware. This allows you to have dynamic error pages that fit with the rest of your application. To use this technique, replace the call to UseStatusCodePages with the following extension method:

```
app.UseStatusCodePagesWithReExecute("/{0}");
```

This extension method configures StatusCodePagesMiddleware to reexecute the pipeline whenever a 4xx or 5xx response code is found, using the provided error handling path. This is similar to the way ExceptionHandlerMiddleware reexecutes the pipeline, as shown in figure 15.6.

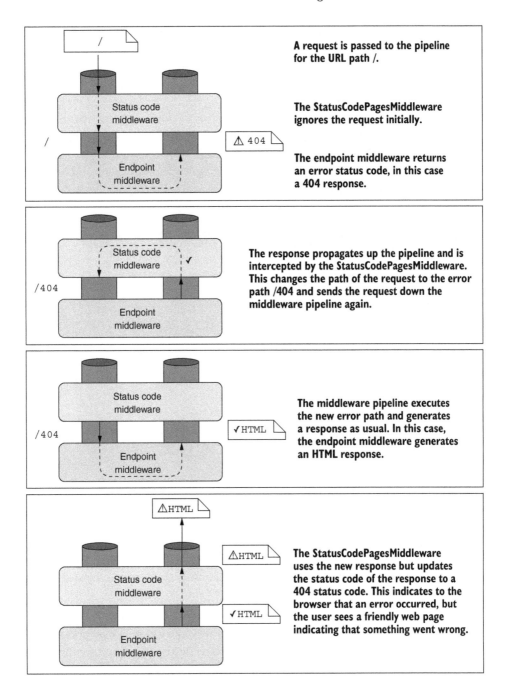

Figure 15.6 `StatusCodePagesMiddleware` reexecuting the pipeline to generate an HTML body for a `404` response. A request to the `/` path returns a `404` response, which is handled by the status code middleware. The pipeline is reexecuted using the `/404` path to generate the HTML response.

Note that the error handling path `"/{0}"` contains a format string token, `{0}`. When the path is reexecuted, the middleware replaces this token with the status code number. For example, a `404` error would reexecute the `/404` path. The handler for the path (typically a Razor Page, but it can be any endpoint) has access to the status code and can optionally tailor the response, depending on the status code. You can choose any error handling path as long as your application knows how to handle it.

With this approach in place, you can create different error pages for different error codes, such as the `404`-specific error page shown in figure 15.7. This technique ensures that your error pages are consistent with the rest of your application, including any dynamically generated content, while also allowing you to tailor the message for common errors.

Figure 15.7   An error status code page for a missing file. When an error code is detected (in this case, a `404` error), the middleware pipeline is reexecuted to generate the response. This allows dynamic portions of your web page to remain consistent on error pages.

> **WARNING**   As I mentioned in chapter 4, if your error handling path generates an error, the user will see a generic browser error. To mitigate this, it's often better to use a static error page that will always work rather than a dynamic page that risks throwing more errors.

The `UseStatusCodePagesWithReExecute()` method is great for returning a friendly error page when something goes wrong in a request, but there's a second way to use the `StatusCodePagesMiddleware`. Instead of reexecuting the pipeline to generate the error response, you can redirect the browser to the error page instead, by calling

```
app.UseStatusCodePagesWithRedirects("/{0}");
```

As for the reexecute version, this method takes a format string that defines the URL to generate the response. However, whereas the reexecute version generates the error response for the original request, the redirect version returns a `302` response initially, directing the browser to send a second request, this time for the error URL, as shown in figure 15.8. This second request generates the error page response, returning it with a 200 status code.

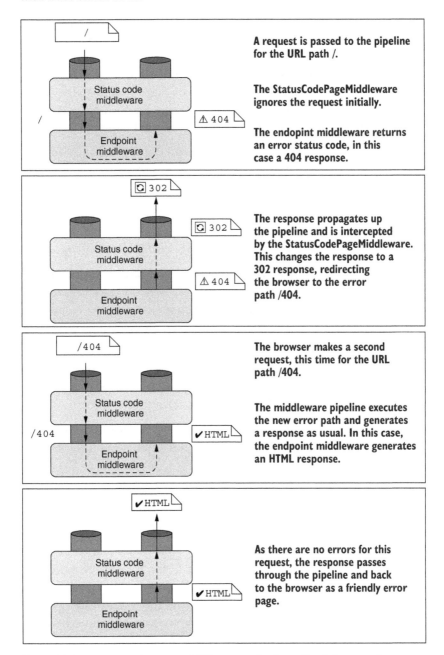

Figure 15.8 StatusCodePagesMiddleware **returning redirects to generate error pages. A request to the** / **path returns a** 404 **response, which is intercepted by the status code middleware and converted to a** 302 **response. The browser makes a second request using the** /404 **path to generate the HTML response.**

Whether you use the reexecute or redirect method, the browser ultimately receives essentially the same HTML. However, there are some important differences:

- With the reexecute approach, the original status code (such as a 404) is preserved. The browser sees the error page HTML as the response to the original request. If the user refreshes the page, the browser makes a second request for the original path.
- With the redirect approach, the original status code is lost. The browser treats the redirect and second request as two separate requests and doesn't "know" about the error. If the user refreshes the page, the browser makes a request for the same error path; it doesn't resend the original request.

In most cases, I find the reexecute approach to be more useful, as it preserves the original error and typically has the behavior that users expect. There may be some cases where the redirect approach is useful, however, such as when an entirely different application generates the error page.

> **TIP**   Favor using UseStatusCodePagesWithReExecute over the redirect approach when the same app is generating the error page HTML for your app.

You can use StatusCodePagesMiddleware in combination with other exception handling middleware by adding both to the pipeline. StatusCodePagesMiddleware modifies the response only if no response body has been written. So if another component, such as ExceptionHandlerMiddleware, returns a message body along with an error code, it won't be modified.

> **NOTE**   StatusCodePagesMiddleware has additional overloads that let you execute custom middleware when an error occurs instead of reexecuting the middleware pipeline. You can read about this approach at http://mng.bz/0K66.

Error handling is essential when developing any web application; errors happen, and you need to handle them gracefully. The StatusCodePagesMiddleware is practically a must-have for any production Razor Pages app.

In chapter 16 we'll dive into model binding. You'll see how the route values generated during routing are bound to your page handler parameters, and perhaps more important, how to validate the values you're provided.

Summary

- A Razor Page page handler is the method in the Razor Page PageModel class that is executed when a Razor Page handles a request.
- Page handlers should ensure that the incoming request is valid, call in to the appropriate domain services to handle the request, and then choose the kind of response to return. They typically don't generate the response directly; instead, they describe how to generate the response.

- Page handlers should generally delegate to services to handle the business logic required by a request instead of performing the changes themselves. This ensures a clean separation of concerns that aids testing and improves application structure.

- When a Razor Page is executed, a single page handler is invoked based on the HTTP verb of the request and the value of the `handler` route value. If no page handler is found, an "implicit" handler is used instead, simply rendering the content of the Razor Page.

- Page handlers can have parameters whose values are taken from properties of the incoming request in a process called *model binding*. Properties decorated with `[BindProperty]` can also be bound to the request. These are the canonical ways of reading values from the HTTP request inside your Razor Page.

- By default, properties decorated with `[BindProperty]` are not bound for GET requests. To enable binding, use `[BindProperty(SupportsGet = true)]`.

- Page handlers can return a `PageResult` or `void` to generate an HTML response. The Razor Page infrastructure uses the associated Razor view to generate the HTML and returns a `200 OK` response.

- You can send users to a different Razor Page using a `RedirectToPageResult`. It's common to send users to a new page as part of the POST-REDIRECT-GET flow for handling user input via forms

- The `PageModel` base class exposes many helper methods for creating an `IActionResult`, such as `Page()` which creates a `PageResult`, and `RedirectToPage()` which creates a `RedirectToPageResult`. These methods are simple wrappers around calling `new` on the corresponding `IActionResult` type.

- `StatusCodePagesMiddleware` lets you provide user-friendly custom error handling messages when the pipeline returns a raw error response status code. This is important for providing a consistent user experience when status code errors are returned, such as `404` errors when a URL is not matched to an endpoint.

Binding and validating requests with Razor Pages

This chapter covers

- Using request values to create binding models
- Customizing the model-binding process
- Validating user input using DataAnnotations attributes

In chapter 7 we looked at the process of model binding and validation in minimal APIs. In this chapter we look at the Razor Pages equivalent: extracting values from a request using model binding and validating user input.

In the first half of this chapter, we look at using binding models to retrieve those parameters from the request so that you can use them in your Razor Pages by creating C# objects. These objects are passed to your Razor Page handlers as method parameters or are set as properties on your Razor Page `PageModel`.

Once your code is executing in a page handler method, you can't simply use the binding model without any further thought. Any time you're using data provided by a user, you need to validate it! The second half of the chapter focuses on how to validate your binding models with Razor Pages.

We covered model binding and validation for minimal APIs in chapter 7, and conceptually, binding and validation are the same for Razor Pages. However, the details and mechanics of both binding and validation are quite different for Razor Pages.

The binding models populated by the Razor Pages infrastructure are passed to page handlers when they execute. Once the page handler has run, you're all set up to use the output models in ASP.NET Core's implementation of Model-View-Controller (MVC): the view models and API models. These are used to generate a response to the user's request. We'll cover them in chapters 19 and 20.

Before we go any further, let's recap the MVC design pattern and how binding models fit into ASP.NET Core.

16.1   Understanding the models in Razor Pages and MVC

In this section I describe how binding models fit into the MVC design pattern we covered in chapter 13. I describe the difference between binding models and the other "model" concepts in the MVC pattern and how they're each used in ASP.NET Core.

MVC is all about the separation of concerns. The premise is that isolating each aspect of your application to focus on a single responsibility reduces the interdependencies in your system. This separation makes it easier to make changes without affecting other parts of your application.

The classic MVC design pattern has three independent components:

- *Model*—The data to display and the methods for updating this data
- *View*—Displays a representation of data that makes up the model
- *Controller*—Calls methods on the model and selects a view

In this representation, there's only one model, the application model, which represents all the business logic for the application as well as how to update and modify its internal state. ASP.NET Core has multiple models, which takes the single-responsibility principle (SRP) one step further than some views of MVC.

In chapter 13 we looked at an example of a to-do list application that can show all the to-do items for a given category and username. With this application, you make a request to a URL that's routed using `todo/listcategory/{category}/{username}`. This returns a response showing all the relevant to-do items, as shown in figure 16.1.

The application uses the same MVC constructs you've already seen, such as routing to a Razor Page handler, as well as various models. Figure 16.2 shows how a request to this application maps to the MVC design pattern and how it generates the final response, including additional details around the model binding and validation of the request.

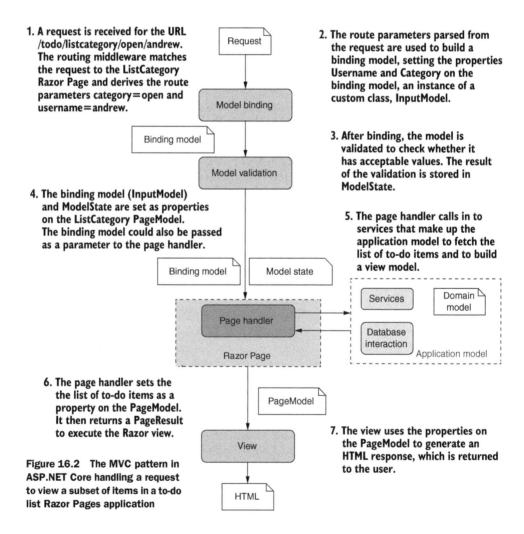

The category and username are provided in the URL.

The category and username are used to filter the list of to-do task items.

The category and username can also be shown in the view model.

Figure 16.1   A basic to-do list application that displays to-do list items. A user can filter the list of items by changing the `category` **and** `username` **parameters in the URL.**

1. A request is received for the URL /todo/listcategory/open/andrew. The routing middleware matches the request to the ListCategory Razor Page and derives the route parameters category=open and username=andrew.

2. The route parameters parsed from the request are used to build a binding model, setting the properties Username and Category on the binding model, an instance of a custom class, InputModel.

3. After binding, the model is validated to check whether it has acceptable values. The result of the validation is stored in ModelState.

4. The binding model (InputModel) and ModelState are set as properties on the ListCategory PageModel. The binding model could also be passed as a parameter to the page handler.

5. The page handler calls in to services that make up the application model to fetch the list of to-do items and to build a view model.

6. The page handler sets the the list of to-do items as a property on the PageModel. It then returns a PageResult to execute the Razor view.

7. The view uses the properties on the PageModel to generate an HTML response, which is returned to the user.

Figure 16.2   The MVC pattern in ASP.NET Core handling a request to view a subset of items in a to-do list Razor Pages application

ASP.NET Core Razor Pages uses several models, most of which are plain old CLR objects (POCOs), and the application model, which is more of a concept around a collection of services. Each of the models in ASP.NET Core is responsible for handling a different aspect of the overall request:

- *Binding model*—The *binding model* is all the information that's provided by the user when making a request, as well as additional contextual data. This includes things like route parameters parsed from the URL, the query string, and form or JavaScript Object Notation (JSON) data in the request body. The binding model itself is one or more POCO objects that you define. Binding models in Razor Pages are typically defined by creating a public property on the page's PageModel and decorating it with the [BindProperty] attribute. They can also be passed to a page handler as parameters.

  For this example, the binding model would include the name of the category, open, and the username, andrew. The Razor Pages infrastructure inspects the binding model before the page handler executes to check whether the provided values are valid, though the page handler executes even if they're not, as you'll see when we discuss validation in section 16.3.

- *Application model*—The application model isn't really an ASP.NET Core model at all. It's typically a whole group of different services and classes and is more of a concept—anything needed to perform some sort of business action in your application. It may include the domain model (which represents the thing your app is trying to describe) and database models (which represent the data stored in a database), as well as any other, additional services.

  In the to-do list application, the application model would contain the complete list of to-do items, probably stored in a database, and would know how to find only those to-do items in the open category assigned to andrew.

- *Page model*—The PageModel of a Razor Page serves two main functions: it acts as the controller for the application by exposing page handler methods, and it acts as the view model for a Razor view. All the data required for the view to generate a response is exposed on the PageModel, such as the list of to-dos in the open category assigned to andrew.

  The PageModel base class that you derive your Razor Pages from contains various helper properties and methods. One of these, the ModelState property, contains the result of the model validation as a series of key-value pairs. You'll learn more about validation and the ModelState property in section 16.3.

These models make up the bulk of any Razor Pages application, handling the input, business logic, and output of each page handler. Imagine you have an e-commerce application that allows users to search for clothes by sending requests to the /search/{query} URL, where {query} holds their search term:

- *Binding model*—This would take the {query} route parameter from the URL and any values posted in the request body (maybe a sort order, or the number of items to show), and bind them to a C# class, which typically acts as a throwaway data transport class. This would be set as a property on the PageModel when the page handler is invoked.
- *Application model*—This is the services and classes that perform the logic. When invoked by the page handler, this model would load all the clothes that match the query, applying the necessary sorting and filters, and return the results to the controller.
- *Page model*—The values provided by the application model would be set as properties on the Razor Page's PageModel, along with other metadata, such as the total number of items available or whether the user can currently check out. The Razor view would use this data to render the Razor view to HTML.

The important point about all these models is that their responsibilities are well defined and distinct. Keeping them separate and avoiding reuse helps ensure that your application stays agile and easy to update.

The obvious exception to this separation is the PageModel, as it is where the binding models and page handlers are defined, and it also holds the data required for rendering the view. Some people may consider the apparent lack of separation to be sacrilege, but it's not generally a problem. The lines of demarcation are pretty apparent. So long as you don't try to, for example, invoke a page handler from inside a Razor view, you shouldn't run into any problems!

Now that you've been properly introduced to the various models in ASP.NET Core, it's time to focus on how to use them. This chapter looks at the binding models that are built from incoming requests—how are they created, and where do the values come from?

16.2   *From request to binding model: Making the request useful*

In this section you will learn

- How ASP.NET Core creates binding models from a request
- How to bind simple types, like int and string, as well as complex classes
- How to choose which parts of a request are used in the binding model

By now, you should be familiar with how ASP.NET Core handles a request by executing a page handler on a Razor Page. Page handlers are normal C# methods, so the ASP.NET Core framework needs to be able to call them in the usual way. The process of extracting values from the request and creating C# objects from them is called *model binding*.

Any publicly settable properties on your Razor Page's PageModel (in the .cshtml.cs file for your Razor Page), that are decorated with the [BindProperty] attribute are created from the incoming request using model binding, as shown in listing 16.1.

Similarly, if your page handler method has any parameters, these are also created using model binding.

> **WARNING** Properties decorated with [BindProperty] must have a public setter; otherwise, binding will silently fail.

Listing 16.1   Model binding requests to properties in a Razor Page

```
public class IndexModel: PageModel
{
    [BindProperty]
    public string Category { get; set; }          Properties decorated with [BindProperty]
                                                   take part in model binding.

    [BindProperty(SupportsGet = true)]
    public string Username { get; set; }           Properties are not model-bound for GET
                                                    requests unless you use SupportsGet.

    public void OnGet()
    {
    }                                                     Parameters to page handlers
                                                          are also model-bound when
    public void OnPost(ProductModel model)    ◁──────┘    that handler is selected.
    {
    }
}
```

As described in chapter 15 and shown in the preceding listing, PageModel properties are *not* model-bound for GET requests, even if you add the [BindProperty] attribute. For security reasons, only requests using verbs like POST and PUT are bound. If you *do* want to bind GET requests, you can set the SupportsGet property on the [BindProperty] attribute to opt in to model binding.

Which part is the binding model?

Listing 16.1 shows a Razor Page that uses multiple binding models: the Category property, the Username property, and the ProductModel parameter (in the OnPost handler) are all model-bound.

Using multiple models in this way is fine, but I prefer to use an approach that keeps all the model binding in a single, nested class, which I often call InputModel. With this approach, the Razor Page in listing 16.1 could be written as follows:

```
public class IndexModel: PageModel
{
    [BindProperty]
    public InputModel Input { get; set; }
    public void OnGet()
    {
    }

    public class InputModel
```

(continued)
```
{
        public string Category { get; set; }
        public string Username { get; set; }
        public ProductModel Model { get; set; }
    }
}
```

This approach has some organizational benefits that you'll learn more about in section 16.4.

ASP.NET Core automatically populates your binding models for you using properties of the request, such as the request URL, any headers sent in the HTTP request, any data explicitly POSTed in the request body, and so on.

> **NOTE** In this chapter I describe how to bind your models to an incoming request, but I don't show how Razor Pages uses your binding models to help *generate* that request using HTML forms. In chapter 17 you'll learn about Razor syntax, which renders HTML, and in chapter 18 you'll learn about Razor Tag Helpers, which generate form fields based on your binding model.

By default, ASP.NET Core uses three different *binding sources* when creating your binding models in Razor Pages. It looks through each of these in order and takes the first value it finds (if any) that matches the name of the binding model:

- *Form values*—Sent in the body of an HTTP request when a form is sent to the server using a POST
- *Route values*—Obtained from URL segments or through default values after matching a route, as you saw in chapter 14
- *Query string values*—Passed at the end of the URL, not used during routing

> **WARNING** Even though conceptually similar, the Razor Page binding process works quite differently from the approach used by minimal APIs.

The model binding process for Razor Pages is shown in figure 16.3. The model binder checks each binding source to see whether it contains a value that could be set on the model. Alternatively, the model can choose the specific source the value should come from, as you'll see in section 16.2.3. Once each property is bound, the model is validated and is set as a property on the PageModel or passed as a parameter to the page handler. You'll learn about the validation process in the second half of this chapter.

> **NOTE** In Razor Pages, different properties of a complex model can be model-bound to different sources. This differs from minimal APIs, where the whole object would be bound from a single source, and "partial" binding is not possible. Razor Pages also bind to form bodies by default, while minimal APIs cannot. These differences are partly for historical reasons and partly because minimal APIs opts for performance over convenience in this respect.

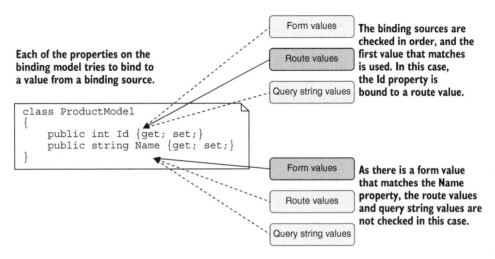

Figure 16.3   Model binding involves mapping values from binding sources, which correspond to different parts of a request.

PageModel properties or page handler parameters?

There are three ways to use model binding in Razor Pages:

- Decorate properties on your `PageModel` with the `[BindProperty]` attribute.
- Add parameters to your page handler method.
- Decorate the whole `PageModel` with `[BindProperties]`.

Which of these approaches should you choose?

The answer to this question is largely a matter of taste. Setting properties on the `Page-Model` and marking them with `[BindProperty]` is the approach you'll see most often in examples. If you use this approach, you'll be able to access the binding model when the view is rendered, as you'll see in chapters 17 and 18.

The second approach, adding parameters to page handler methods, provides more separation between the different MVC stages, because you won't be able to access the parameters outside the page handler. On the downside, if you *do* need to display those values in the Razor view, you'll have to copy the parameters across manually to properties that can be accessed in the view.

I avoid the final approach, decorating the `PageModel` itself with `[BindProperties]`. With this approach, *every* property on your `PageModel` takes part in model binding. I don't like the indirection this gives and the risk of accidentally binding properties I didn't want to be model-bound.

The approach I choose tends to depend on the specific Razor Page I'm building. If I'm creating a form, I will favor the `[BindProperty]` approach, as I typically need access to the request values inside the Razor view. For simple pages, where the binding model is a product ID, for example, I tend to favor the page handler parameter approach for its simplicity, especially if the handler is for a GET request. I give some more specific advice on my approach in section 16.4.

Figure 16.4 shows an example of a request creating the `ProductModel` method argument using model binding for the example shown at the start of this section:

```
public void OnPost(ProductModel product)
```

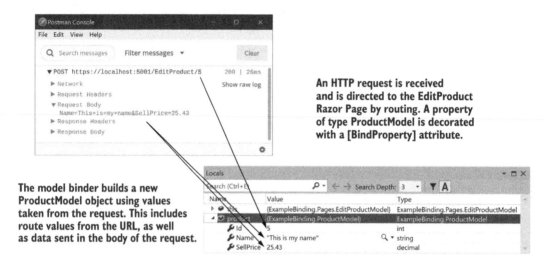

An HTTP request is received and is directed to the EditProduct Razor Page by routing. A property of type ProductModel is decorated with a [BindProperty] attribute.

The model binder builds a new ProductModel object using values taken from the request. This includes route values from the URL, as well as data sent in the body of the request.

Figure 16.4   Using model binding to create an instance of a model that's used to execute a Razor Page

The `Id` property has been bound from a URL route parameter, but the `Name` and `Sell-Price` properties have been bound from the request body. The big advantage of using model binding is that you don't have to write the code to parse requests and map the data yourself. This sort of code is typically repetitive and error-prone, so using the built-in conventional approach lets you focus on the important aspects of your application: the business requirements.

> **TIP**   Model binding is great for reducing repetitive code. Take advantage of it whenever possible, and you'll rarely find yourself having to access the `Request` object directly.

If you need to, the capabilities are there to let you completely customize the way model binding works, but it's relatively rare that you'll find yourself needing to dig too deep into this. For the majority of cases, it works as is, as you'll see in the remainder of this section.

16.2.1 *Binding simple types*

We'll start our journey into model binding by considering a simple Razor Page handler. The next listing shows a simple Razor Page that takes one number as a method parameter and squares it by multiplying the number by itself.

Listing 16.2 A Razor Page accepting a simple parameter

```
public class CalculateSquareModel : PageModel
{
    public void OnGet(int number)
    {
        Square = number * number;
    }

    public int Square { get; set; }
}
```

The method parameter is the binding model.

A more complex example would do this work in an external service, in the application model.

The result is exposed as a property and is used by the view to generate a response.

In chapters 6 and 14, you learned about routing and how it selects a Razor Page to execute. You can update the route template for the Razor Page to be `"CalculateSquare/{number}"` by adding a {number} segment to the Razor Page's @page directive in the .cshtml file:

```
@page "{number}"
```

When a client requests the URL /CalculateSquare/5, the Razor Page framework uses routing to parse it for route parameters. This produces the route value pair

```
number=5
```

The Razor Page's OnGet page handler contains a single parameter—an integer called number—which is your binding model. When ASP.NET Core executes this page handler method, it will spot the expected parameter, flick through the route values associated with the request, and find the number=5 pair. Then it can bind the number parameter to this route value and execute the method. The page handler method itself doesn't care where this value came from; it goes along its merry way, calculating the square of the value and setting it on the Square property.

The key thing to appreciate is that you didn't have to write any extra code to try to extract the number from the URL when the method executed. All you needed to do was create a method parameter (or public property) with the right name and let model binding do its magic.

Route values aren't the only values the Razor Pages model binder can use to create your binding models. As you saw previously, the framework will look through three default binding sources to find a match for your binding models:

- Form values
- Route values
- Query string values

Each of these binding sources store values as name-value pairs. If none of the binding sources contains the required value, the binding model is set to a new, default instance of the type instead. The exact value the binding model will have in this case depends on the type of the variable:

- For value types, the value will be default(T). For an int parameter this would be 0, and for a bool it would be false.
- For reference types, the type is created using the default (parameterless) constructor. For custom types like ProductModel, that will create a new object. For nullable types like int? or bool?, the value will be null.
- For string types, the value will be null.

WARNING It's important to consider the behavior of your page handler when model binding fails to bind your method parameters. If none of the binding sources contains the value, the value passed to the method could be null or could unexpectedly have a default value (for value types).

Listing 16.2 showed how to bind a single method parameter. Let's take the next logical step and look at how you'd bind multiple method parameters.

Let's say you're building a currency converter application. As the first step you need to create a method in which the user provides a value in one currency, and you must convert it to another. You first create a Razor Page called Convert.cshtml and then customize the route template for the page using the @page directive to use an absolute path containing two route values:

```
@page "/{currencyIn}/{currencyOut}"
```

Then you create a page handler that accepts the three values you need, as shown in the following listing.

Listing 16.3 A Razor Page handler accepting multiple binding parameters

```
public class ConvertModel : PageModel
{
    public void OnGet(
        string currencyIn,
        string currencyOut,
        int qty
)
    {
        /* method implementation */
    }
}
```

As you can see, there are three different parameters to bind. The question is, where will the values come from and what will they be set to? The answer is, it depends! Table 16.1 shows a whole variety of possibilities. All these examples use the same route template and page handler, but depending on the data sent, different values will be bound. The actual values might differ from what you expect, as the available binding sources offer conflicting values!

Table 16.1 Binding request data to page handler parameters from multiple binding sources

URL (route values)	HTTP body data (form values)	Parameter values bound
`/GBP/USD`		`currencyIn=GBP` `currencyOut=USD qty=0`
`/GBP/USD?currencyIn=CAD`	`QTY=50`	`currencyIn=GBP` `currencyOut=USD qty=50`
`/GBP/USD?qty=100`	`qty=50`	`currencyIn=GBP` `currencyOut=USD qty=50`
`/GBP/USD?qty=100`	`currencyIn=CAD&` `currencyOut=EUR&qty=50`	`currencyIn=CAD` `currencyOut=EUR qty=50`

For each example, be sure you understand *why* the bound values have the values that they do. In the first example, the `qty` value isn't found in the form data, in the route values, or in the query string, so it has the default value of `0`. In each of the other examples, the request contains one or more duplicated values; in these cases, it's important to bear in mind the order in which the model binder consults the binding sources. By default, form values will take precedence over other binding sources, including route values!

> **NOTE** The default model binder isn't case-sensitive, so a binding value of `QTY=50` will happily bind to the `qty` parameter.

Although this may seem a little overwhelming, it's relatively unusual to be binding from all these different sources at once. It's more common to have your values all come from the request body as form values, maybe with an ID from URL route values. This scenario serves as more of a cautionary tale about the knots you can twist yourself into if you're not sure how things work under the hood.

In these examples, you happily bound the `qty` integer property to incoming values, but as I mentioned earlier, the values stored in binding sources are all strings. What types can you convert a string to?

The model binder will convert pretty much any primitive .NET type such as `int`, `float`, `decimal` (and `string` obviously), any custom type that has a `TryParse` method (like minimal APIs, as you saw in chapter 7) plus anything that has a `TypeConverter`.

> **NOTE** `TypeConverter`s can be found in the System.ComponentModel.Type-Converter package. You can read more about them in Microsoft's "Type conversion in .NET" documentation: http://mng.bz/A0GK.

There are a few other special cases that can be converted from a string, such as `Type`, but thinking of it as built-in types only will get you a long way there!

16.2.2 Binding complex types

If it seems like only being able to bind simple built-in types is a bit limiting, you're right! Luckily, that's not the case for the model binder. Although it can only convert `strings` directly to those simple types, it's also able to bind complex types by traversing any properties your binding models expose, binding each of those properties to `strings` instead.

If this doesn't make you happy straight off the bat, let's look at how you'd have to build your page handlers if simple types were your only option. Imagine a user of your currency converter application has reached a checkout page and is going to exchange some currency. Great! All you need now is to collect their name, email address, and phone number. Unfortunately, your page handler method would have to look something like this:

```
public IActionResult OnPost(
    string firstName, string lastName,
    string phoneNumber, string email)
```

Yuck! Four parameters might not seem that bad right now, but what happens when the requirements change and you need to collect other details? The method signature will keep growing. The model binder will bind the values quite happily, but it's not exactly clean code. Using the `[BindProperty]` approach doesn't really help either; you still have to clutter your `PageModel` with lots of properties and attributes!

SIMPLIFYING METHOD PARAMETERS BY BINDING TO COMPLEX OBJECTS

A common pattern for any C# code when you have many method parameters is to extract a class that encapsulates the data the method requires. If extra parameters need to be added, you can add a new property to this class. This class becomes your binding model, and it might look something like the following listing.

> Listing 16.4 A binding model for capturing a user's details

```
public class UserBindingModel
{
    public string FirstName { get; set; }
    public string LastName { get; set; }
    public string Email { get; set; }
    public string PhoneNumber { get; set; }
}
```

> **NOTE** In this book I primarily use `class` instead of `record` for my binding models, but you can use `record` if you prefer. I find the terseness that the `record` positional syntax provides is lost if you want to add attributes to properties, such as to add validation attributes, as you'll see in section 16.3. You can see the required syntax for positional property attributes in the documentation at http://mng.bz/Kex0.

With this model, you can update your page handler's method signature to

```
public IActionResult OnPost(UserBindingModel user)
```

Alternatively, using the [BindProperty] approach, create a property on the PageModel:

```
[BindProperty]
public UserBindingModel User { get; set; }
```

Now you can simplify the page handler signature even further:

```
public IActionResult OnPost()
```

Functionally, the model binder treats this new complex type a little differently. Rather than look for parameters with a value that matches the parameter name (user, or User for the property), the model binder creates a new instance of the model using new UserBindingModel().

> **NOTE** You don't have to use custom classes for your methods; it depends on your requirements. If your page handler needs only a single integer, it makes more sense to bind to the simple parameter.

Next, the model binder loops through all the properties your binding model has, such as FirstName and LastName in listing 16.4. For each of these properties, it consults the collection of binding sources and attempts to find a name-value pair that matches. If it finds one, it sets the value on the property and moves on to the next.

> **TIP** Although the name of the model isn't necessary in this example, the model binder will also look for properties prefixed with the name of the property, such as user.FirstName and user.LastName for a property called User. You can use this approach when you have multiple complex parameters to a page handler or multiple complex [BindProperty] properties. In general, for simplicity, you should avoid this situation if possible. As for all model binding, the casing of the prefix does not matter.

Once all the properties that can be bound on the binding model are set, the model is passed to the page handler (or the [BindProperty] property is set), and the handler is executed as usual. The behavior from this point on is identical to when you have lots of individual parameters—you'll end up with the same values set on your binding model—but the code is cleaner and easier to work with.

> **TIP** For a class to be model-bound, it must have a default public constructor. You can bind only properties that are public and settable.

With this technique you can bind complex hierarchical models whose properties are themselves complex models. As long as each property exposes a type that can be model-bound, the binder can traverse it with ease.

BINDING COLLECTIONS AND DICTIONARIES

As well as binding to ordinary custom classes and primitives, you can bind to collections, lists, and dictionaries. Imagine you had a page in which a user selected all the currencies they were interested in; you'd display the rates for all those selected, as shown in figure 16.5.

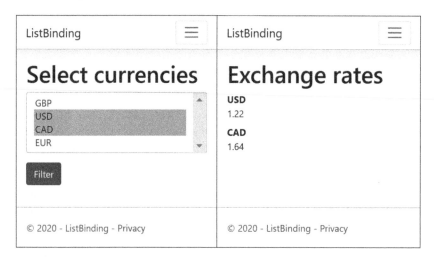

Figure 16.5   The select list in the currency converter application sends a list of selected currencies to the application. Model binding binds the selected currencies and customizes the view for the user to show the equivalent cost in the selected currencies.

To achieve this, you could create a page handler that accepts a `List<string>` type, such as

```
public void OnPost(List<string> currencies);
```

You could then POST data to this method by providing values in several different formats:

- `currencies[index]`—Where `currencies` is the name of the parameter to bind and `index` is the index of the item to bind, such as `currencies[0]=GBP&currencies[1]=USD`.
- `[index]`—If you're binding to a single list (as in this example), you can omit the name of the parameter, such as `[0]=GBP&[1]=USD`.
- `currencies`—Alternatively, you can omit the `index` and send `currencies` as the key for every value, such as `currencies=GBP&currencies=USD`.

The key values can come from route values and query values, but it's far more common to POST them in a form. Dictionaries can use similar binding, where the dictionary key replaces the index both when the parameter is named and when it's omitted.

> **TIP**   In the previous example I showed a collection using the built-in `string` type, but you can also bind collections of complex type, such as a `List<UserBindingModel>`.

If this all seems a bit confusing, don't feel too alarmed. If you're building a traditional web application and using Razor views to generate HTML, the framework will take care of generating the correct names for you. As you'll see in chapter 18, the Razor view ensures that any form data you POST is generated in the correct format.

BINDING FILE UPLOADS WITH IFORMFILE

Razor Pages supports users uploading files by exposing the IFormFile and IFormFile-Collection interfaces. You can use these interfaces as your binding model, either as a method parameter to your page handler or using the [BindProperty] approach, and they will be populated with the details of the file upload:

```
public void OnPost(IFormFile file);
```

If you need to accept multiple files, you can use IFormFileCollection, IEnumerable <IFormFile>, or List<IFormFile>:

```
public void OnPost(IEnumerable<IFormFile> file);
```

You already learned how to use IFormFile in chapter 7 when you looked at minimal API binding. The process is the same for Razor Pages. I'll reiterate one point here: if you don't need users to upload files, great! There are so many potential threats to consider when handling files—from malicious attacks, to accidental denial-of-service vulnerabilities—that I avoid them whenever possible.

For the vast majority of Razor Pages, the default configuration of model binding for simple and complex types works perfectly well, but you may find some situations where you need to take a bit more control. Luckily, that's perfectly possible, and you can completely override the process if necessary by replacing the ModelBinders used in the guts of the framework.

However, it's rare to need that level of customization. I've found it's more common to want to specify which binding source to use for a page's binding instead.

16.2.3 Choosing a binding source

As you've already seen, by default the ASP.NET Core model binder attempts to bind your binding models from three binding sources: form data, route data, and the query string.

Occasionally, you may find it necessary to specifically declare which binding source to bind to. In other cases, these three sources won't be sufficient at all. The most common scenarios are when you want to bind a method parameter to a request header value or when the body of a request contains JSON-formatted data that you want to bind to a parameter. In these cases, you can decorate your binding models with attributes that say where to bind from, as shown in the following listing.

Listing 16.5   Choosing a binding source for model binding

```
public class PhotosModel: PageModel
{
    public void OnPost(
        [FromHeader] string userId,
        [FromBody] List<Photo> photos)
    {
        /* method implementation */
    }
}
```

> The userId is bound from an HTTP header in the request.

> The list of photo objects is bound to the body of the request, typically in JSON format.

In this example, a page handler updates a collection of photos with a user ID. There are method parameters for the ID of the user to be tagged in the photos, userId, and a list of Photo objects to tag, photos.

Rather than binding these method parameters using the standard binding sources, I've added attributes to each parameter, indicating the binding source to use. The [FromHeader] attribute has been applied to the userId parameter. This tells the model binder to bind the value to an HTTP request header value called userId.

We're also binding a list of photos to the body of the HTTP request by using the [FromBody] attribute. This tells the binder to read JSON from the body of the request and bind it to the List<Photo> method parameter.

> **WARNING**   Developers coming from .NET Framework and the legacy version of ASP.NET should take note that the [FromBody] attribute is explicitly required when binding to JSON requests in Razor Pages. This differs from the legacy ASP.NET behavior, in which no attribute was required.

You aren't limited to binding JSON data from the request body. You can use other formats too, depending on which InputFormatters you configure the framework to use. By default, only a JSON input formatter is configured. You'll see how to add an XML formatter in chapter 20, when I discuss web APIs.

> **TIP**   Automatic binding of multiple formats from the request body is one of the features specific to Razor Pages and MVC controllers, which is missing from minimal APIs.

You can use a few different attributes to override the defaults and to specify a binding source for each binding model (or each property on the binding model). These are the same attributes you used in chapter 7 with minimal APIs:

- [FromHeader]—Bind to a header value.
- [FromQuery]—Bind to a query string value.
- [FromRoute]—Bind to route parameters.
- [FromForm]—Bind to form data posted in the body of the request. This attribute is not available in minimal APIs.
- [FromBody]—Bind to the request's body content.

You can apply each of these to any number of handler method parameters or properties, as you saw in listing 16.5, with the exception of the [FromBody] attribute. Only one value may be decorated with the [FromBody] attribute. Also, as form data is sent in the body of a request, the [FromBody] and [FromForm] attributes are effectively mutually exclusive.

> **TIP** Only one parameter may use the [FromBody] attribute. This attribute consumes the incoming request as HTTP request bodies can be safely read only once.

As well as these attributes for specifying binding sources, there are a few attributes for customizing the binding process even further:

- [BindNever]—The model binder will skip this parameter completely. You can use this attribute to prevent mass assignment, as discussed in these two posts on my blog: http://mng.bz/QvfG and http://mng.bz/Vd90.
- [BindRequired]—If the parameter was not provided or was empty, the binder will add a validation error.
- [FromServices]—This is used to indicate the parameter should be provided using dependency injection (DI). This attribute isn't required in most cases, as .NET 7 is smart enough to know that a parameter is a service registered in DI, but you can be explicit if you prefer.

In addition, you have the [ModelBinder] attribute, which puts you into "God mode" with respect to model binding. With this attribute, you can specify the exact binding source, override the name of the parameter to bind to, and specify the type of binding to perform. It'll be rare that you need this one, but when you do, at least it's there!

By combining all these attributes, you should find you're able to configure the model binder to bind to pretty much any request data your page handler wants to use. In general, though, you'll probably find you rarely need to use them; the defaults should work well for you in most cases.

That brings us to the end of this section on model binding. At the end of the model binding process, your page handler should have access to a populated binding model, and it's ready to execute its logic. But before you use that user input for anything, you must always *validate* your data, which is the focus of the second half of this chapter. Razor Pages automatically does validation for you out-of-the-box, but you have to actually check the results.

16.3 Validating binding models

In this section I discuss how validation works in Razor Pages. You already learned how important it is to validate user input in chapter 7, as well as how you can use DataAnnotation attributes to declaratively describe your validation requirements of a model. In this section you'll learn how to reuse this knowledge to validate your Razor Page binding models. The good news is that validation is built into the Razor Pages framework.

16.3.1 Validation in Razor Pages

In chapter 7 you learned that validation is an essential part of any web application. Nevertheless, minimal APIs don't have any direct support for validation in the framework; you have to layer it on top using filters and additional packages.

In Razor Pages, validation is built in. Validation occurs automatically after model binding but before the page handler executes, as you saw in figure 16.2. Figure 16.6 shows a more compact view of where model validation fits in this process, demonstrating how a request to a checkout page that requests a user's personal details is bound and validated.

1. A request is received for the URL /checkout/saveuser, and the routing middleware selects the SaveUser Razor Page endpoint in the Checkout folder.

2. The framework builds a UserBindingModel from the details provided in the request.

3. The UserBindingModel is validated according to the DataAnnotation attributes on its properties.

4. The UserBindingModel and validation ModelState are set on the SaveUser Razor Page, and the page handler is executed.

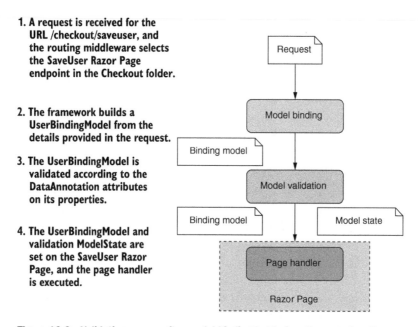

Figure 16.6   Validation occurs after model binding but before the page handler executes. The page handler executes whether or not validation is successful.

As discussed in chapter 7, validation isn't only about protecting against security threats, it's also about ensuring that

- *Data is formatted correctly.* (Email fields have a valid email format.)
- *Numbers are in a particular range.* (You can't buy -1 copies of a product.)
- *Required values are provided while others are optional.* (Name may be required, but phone number is optional.)
- *Values conform to your business requirements.* (You can't convert a currency to itself, it needs to be converted to a different currency.)

It might seem like some of these can be dealt with easily enough in the browser. For example, if a user is selecting a currency to convert to, don't let them pick the same currency; and we've all seen the "please enter a valid email address" messages.

Unfortunately, although this *client-side validation* is useful for users, as it gives them instant feedback, you can never rely on it, as it will always be possible to bypass these browser protections. It's always necessary to validate the data as it arrives at your web application using *server-side validation*.

WARNING Always validate user input on the server side of your application.

If that feels a little redundant, like you'll be duplicating logic and code between your client and server applications, I'm afraid you're right. It's one of the unfortunate aspects of web development; the duplication is a necessary evil. Fortunately, ASP.NET Core provides several features to try to reduce this burden.

TIP Blazor, the new C# single-page application (SPA) framework, promises to solve some of these problems. For details, see http://mng.bz/9D51 and *Blazor in Action*, by Chris Sainty (Manning, 2021).

If you had to write this validation code fresh for every app, it would be tedious and likely error-prone. Luckily, you can use `DataAnnotations` attributes to declaratively describe the validation requirements for your binding models. The following listing, first shown in chapter 7, shows how you can decorate a binding model with various validation attributes. This expands on the example you saw earlier in listing 16.4.

Listing 16.6   Adding `DataAnnotations` to a binding model to provide metadata

```
public class UserBindingModel          Values marked Required must be provided.
{
    [Required]          ◁                The StringLengthAttribute sets the
    [StringLength(100)]      ◁           maximum length for the property.
    [Display(Name = "Your name")]   ◁
    public string FirstName { get; set; }        Customizes the name used
                                                 to describe the property
    [Required]
    [StringLength(100)]
    [Display(Name = "Last name")]
    public string LastName { get; set; }

    [Required]                                Validates that the value of
    [EmailAddress]          ◁                 Email is a valid email address
    public string Email { get; set; }

    [Phone]          ◁                        Validates that the value of
    [Display(Name = "Phone number")]          PhoneNumber has a valid
    public string PhoneNumber { get; set; }   telephone format
}
```

For validation requirements that don't lend themselves to attributes, such as when the validity of one property depends on the value of another, you can implement IValidatableObject, as described in chapter 7. Alternatively, you can use a different validation framework, such as FluentValidation, as you'll see in chapter 32.

Whichever validation approach you use, it's important to remember that these techniques don't protect your application by themselves. The Razor Pages framework automatically executes the validation code after model binding, but it doesn't do anything different if validation fails! In the next section we'll look at how to check the validation result on the server and handle the case where validation has failed.

16.3.2 *Validating on the server for safety*

Validation of the binding model occurs before the page handler executes, but note that the handler always executes, whether the validation failed or succeeded. It's the responsibility of the page handler to check the result of the validation.

> **NOTE** Validation happens automatically, but handling validation failures is the responsibility of the page handler.

The Razor Pages framework stores the output of the validation attempt in a property on the PageModel called ModelState. This property is a ModelStateDictionary object, which contains a list of all the validation errors that occurred after model binding, as well as some utility properties for working with it.

As an example, listing 16.7 shows the OnPost page handler for the Checkout.cshtml Razor Page. The Input property is marked for binding and uses the UserBindingModel type shown previously in listing 16.6. This page handler doesn't do anything with the data currently, but the pattern of checking ModelState early in the method is the key takeaway here.

Listing 16.7   Checking model state to view the validation result

```
public class CheckoutModel : PageModel        ◁—⎯ The ModelState property is available
{                                                    on the PageModel base class.

    [BindProperty]
    public UserBindingModel Input { get; set; }   ⊢ The Input property contains
                                                      the model-bound data.

    public IActionResult OnPost()        ◁—⎯
    {                                            The binding model is validated before
        if (!ModelState.IsValid)                 the page handler is executed.
        {
            return Page();    ◁—⎯ Validation failed, so redisplay the form
        }                           with errors and finish the method early.

        /* Save to the database, update user, return success */   ◁—⎯⎯

        return RedirectToPage("Success");            Validation passed, so
    }                                                it's safe to use the data
}                                                    provided in the model.
```

If there were validation errors, IsValid will be false.

If the `ModelState` property indicates that an error occurred, the method immediately calls the `Page()` helper method. This returns a `PageResult` that ultimately generates HTML to return to the user, as you saw in chapter 15. The view uses the (invalid) values provided in the `Input` property to repopulate the form when it's displayed, as shown in figure 16.7. Also, helpful messages for the user are added automatically, using the validation errors in the `ModelState` property.

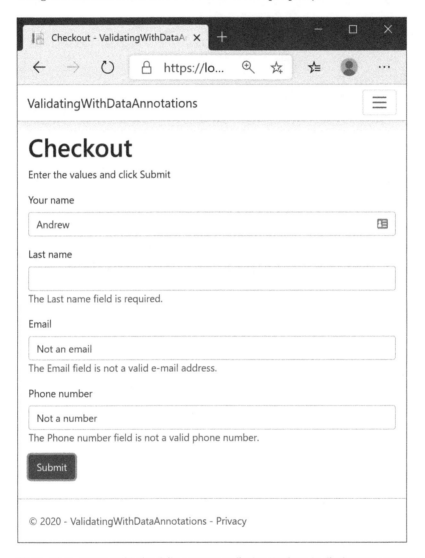

Figure 16.7   When validation fails, you can redisplay the form to display `ModelState` validation errors to the user. Note that the Your Name field has no associated validation errors, unlike the other fields.

> **NOTE** The error messages displayed on the form are the default values for each validation attribute. You can customize the message by setting the Error-Message property on any of the validation attributes. For example, you could customize a [Required] attribute using [Required(ErrorMessage="Required")].

If the request is successful, the page handler returns a RedirectToPageResult (using the RedirectToPage() helper method) that redirects the user to the Success.cshtml Razor Page. This pattern of returning a redirect response after a successful POST is called the POST-REDIRECT-GET pattern.

POST-REDIRECT-GET

The POST-REDIRECT-GET design pattern is a web development pattern that prevents users from accidentally submitting the same form multiple times. Users typically submit a form using the standard browser POST mechanism, sending data to the server. This is the normal way by which you might take a payment, for example.

If a server takes the naive approach and responds with a 200 OK response and some HTML to display, the user will still be on the same URL. If the user refreshes their browser, they will be making an *additional* POST to the server, potentially making *another* payment! Browsers have some mechanisms to prevent this, such as in the following figure, but the user experience isn't desirable.

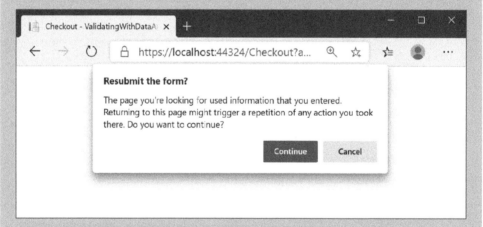

Refreshing a browser window after a POST causes a warning message to be shown to the user

The POST-REDIRECT-GET pattern says that in response to a successful POST, you should return a REDIRECT response to a new URL, which will be followed by the browser making a GET to the new URL. If the user refreshes their browser now, they'll be refreshing the final GET call to the new URL. No additional POST is made, so no additional payments or side effects should occur.

This pattern is easy to achieve in ASP.NET Core applications using the pattern shown in listing 16.7. By returning a RedirectToPageResult after a successful POST, your application will be safe if the user refreshes the page in their browser.

You might be wondering why ASP.NET Core doesn't handle invalid requests for you automatically; if validation has failed, and you have the result, why does the page handler get executed at all? Isn't there a risk that you might forget to check the validation result?

This is true, and in some cases the best thing to do is to make the generation of the validation check and response automatic. In fact, this is exactly the approach we will use for web APIs using MVC controllers with the [ApiController] attribute when we cover them in chapter 20.

For Razor Pages apps, however, you typically still want to generate an HTML response, even when validation failed. This allows the user to see the problem and potentially correct it. This is much harder to make automatic.

For example, you might find you need to load additional data before you can redisplay the Razor Page, such as loading a list of available currencies. That becomes simpler and more explicit with the ModelState.IsValid pattern. Trying to do that automatically would likely end up with you fighting against edge cases and workarounds.

Also, by including the IsValid check explicitly in your page handlers, it's easier to control what happens when additional validation checks fail. For example, if the user tries to update a product, the DataAnnotation validation won't know whether a product with the requested ID exists, only whether the ID has the correct format. By moving the validation to the handler method, you can treat data and business rule validation failures in the same way.

> **TIP** You can also add extra validation errors to the collection, such as business rule validation errors that come from a different system. You can add errors to ModelState by calling AddModelError(), which will be displayed to users on the form alongside the DataAnnotation attribute errors.

I hope I've hammered home how important it is to validate user input in ASP.NET Core, but just in case: VALIDATE! There, we're good. Having said that, performing validation only on the server can leave users with a slightly poor experience. How many times have you filled out a form online, submitted it, gone to get a snack, and come back to find out you mistyped something and have to redo it? Wouldn't it be nicer to have that feedback immediately?

16.3.3 *Validating on the client for user experience*

You can add client-side validation to your application in a few different ways. HTML5 has several built-in validation behaviors that many browsers use. If you display an email address field on a page and use the "email" HTML input type, the browser automatically stops you from submitting an invalid format, as shown in figure 16.8. Your application doesn't control this validation; it's built into modern HTML5 browsers.

> **NOTE** HTML5 constraint validation support varies by browser. For details on the available constraints, see the Mozilla documentation (http://mng.bz/daX3) and http://mng.bz/XNo1.

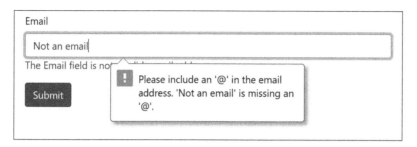

Figure 16.8   By default, modern browsers automatically validate fields of the `email` type before a form is submitted.

The alternative approach to validation is to perform client-side validation by running JavaScript on the page and checking the values the user entered before submitting the form. This is the most common approach used in Razor Pages.

I'll go into detail on how to generate the client-side validation helpers in chapter 18, where you'll see the `DataAnnotation` attributes come to the fore once again. By decorating a view model with these attributes, you provide the necessary metadata to the Razor engine for it to generate the appropriate validation HTML.

With this approach, the user sees any errors with their form immediately, even before the request is sent to the server, as shown in figure 16.9. This gives a much shorter feedback cycle, providing a better user experience.

If you're building an SPA, the onus is on the client-side framework to validate the data on the client side before posting it to the API. The API must still validate the data when it arrives at the server, but the client-side framework is responsible for providing the smooth user experience.

When you use Razor Pages to generate your HTML, you get much of this validation code for free. Razor Pages automatically configures client-side validation for most of the built-in attributes without requiring additional work, as you'll see in chapter 18.

Unfortunately, if you've used custom `ValidationAttributes`, these will run only on the server by default; you need to do some additional wiring up of the attribute to make it work on the client side too. Despite this, custom validation attributes can be useful for handling common validation scenarios in your application, as you'll see in chapter 31.

The model binding framework in ASP.NET Core gives you a lot of options on how to organize your Razor Pages: page handler parameters or `PageModel` properties; one binding model or multiple; options for where to define your binding model classes. In the next section I give some advice on how *I* like to organize my Razor Pages.

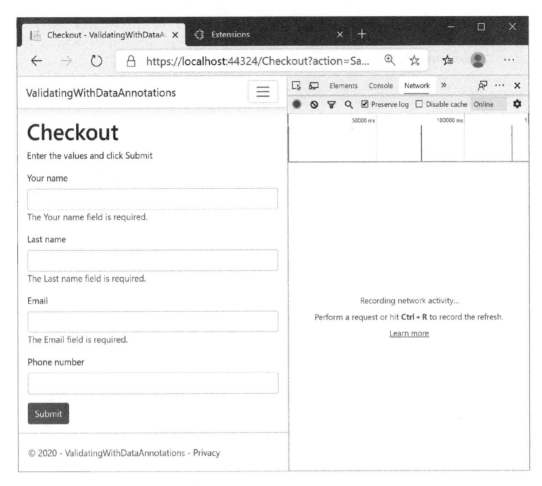

Figure 16.9   With client-side validation, clicking Submit triggers validation to be shown in the browser before the request is sent to the server. As shown in the right pane, no request is sent.

16.4   *Organizing your binding models in Razor Pages*

In this section I give some general advice on how I like to configure the binding models in my Razor Pages. If you follow the patterns in this section, your Razor Pages will follow a consistent layout, making it easier for others to understand how each Razor Page in your app works.

> **NOTE**   This advice is just personal preference, so feel free to adapt it if there are aspects you don't agree with. The important thing is to understand why I make each suggestion, and to take that on board. Where appropriate, I deviate from these guidelines too!

Model binding in ASP.NET Core has a lot of equivalent approaches to take, so there is no "correct" way to do it. Listing 16.8 shows an example of how I would design a simple

Razor Page. This Razor Page displays a form for a product with a given ID and allows you to edit the details using a POST request. It's a much longer sample than we've looked at so far, but I highlight the important points.

Listing 16.8   Designing an edit product Razor Page

```
public class EditProductModel : PageModel
{
    private readonly ProductService _productService;
    public EditProductModel(ProductService productService)
    {
        _productService = productService;
    }

    [BindProperty]
    public InputModel Input { get; set; }

    public IActionResult OnGet(int id)
    {
        var product = _productService.GetProduct(id);

        Input = new InputModel
        {
            Name = product.ProductName,
            Price = product.SellPrice,
        };
        return Page();
    }
    public IActionResult OnPost(int id)
    {
        if (!ModelState.IsValid)
        {
            return Page();
        }

        _productService.UpdateProduct(id, Input.Name, Input.Price);

        return RedirectToPage("Index");
    }

    public class InputModel
    {
        [Required]
        public string Name { get; set; }

        [Range(0, int.MaxValue)]
        public decimal Price { get; set; }
    }
}
```

The ProductService is injected using DI and provides access to the application model.

A single property is marked with BindProperty.

The id parameter is model-bound from the route template for both OnGet and OnPost handlers.

Loads the product details from the application model

Builds an instance of the InputModel for editing in the form from the existing product's details

The id parameter is model-bound from the route template for both OnGet and OnPost handlers.

Updates the product in the application model using the ProductService

If the request was not valid, redisplays the form without saving

Redirects to a new page using the POST-REDIRECT-GET pattern

Defines the InputModel as a nested class in the Razor Page

This page shows the `PageModel` for a typical "edit form." These are common in many line-of-business applications, among others, and it's a scenario that Razor Pages works well for. You'll see how to create the HTML side of forms in chapter 18.

> **NOTE** The purpose of this example is to highlight the model-binding approach. The code is overly simple from a logic point of view. For example, it doesn't check that the product with the provided ID exists or include any error handling.

This form shows several patterns related to model binding that I try to adhere to when building Razor Pages:

- *Bind only a single property with* `[BindProperty]`. I favor having a single property decorated with `[BindProperty]` for model binding in general. When more than one value needs to be bound, I create a separate class, `InputModel`, to hold the values, and I decorate that single property with `[BindProperty]`. Decorating a single property like this makes it harder to forget to add the attribute, and it means all your Razor Pages use the same pattern.
- *Define your binding model as a nested class.* I define the `InputModel` as a nested class inside my Razor Page. The binding model is normally highly specific to that single page, so doing this keeps everything you're working on together. Additionally, I normally use that exact class name, `InputModel`, for all my pages. Again, this adds consistency to your Razor Pages.
- *Don't use* `[BindProperties]`. In addition to the `[BindProperty]` attribute, there is a `[BindProperties]` attribute (note the different spelling) that can be applied to the Razor Page `PageModel` directly. This will cause all properties in your model to be model-bound, which can leave you open to overposting attacks if you're not careful. I suggest you don't use the `[BindProperties]` attribute and stick to binding a *single* property with `[BindProperty]` instead.
- *Accept route parameters in the page handler.* For simple route parameters, such as the `id` passed into the `OnGet` and `OnPost` handlers in listing 16.8, I add parameters to the page handler method itself. This avoids the clunky `SupportsGet=true` syntax for `GET` requests.
- *Always validate before using data.* I said it before, so I'll say it again: validate user input!

That concludes this look at model binding in Razor Pages. You saw how the ASP.NET Core framework uses model binding to simplify the process of extracting values from a request and turning them into normal .NET objects you can work with quickly. The most important aspect of this chapter is the focus on validation. This is a common concern for all web applications, and the use of `DataAnnotations` can make it easy to add validation to your models.

In the next chapter we'll continue our journey through Razor Pages by looking at how to create views. In particular, you'll learn how to generate HTML in response to a request using the Razor templating engine.

Summary

- Razor Pages uses three distinct models, each responsible for a different aspect of a request. The binding model encapsulates data sent as part of a request. The application model represents the state of the application. The `PageModel` is the backing class for the Razor Page, and it exposes the data used by the Razor view to generate a response.

- Model binding extracts values from a request and uses them to create .NET objects the page handler can use when they execute. Any properties on the `PageModel` marked with the `[BindProperty]` attribute and method parameters of the page handlers will take part in model binding.

- By default, there are three binding sources for Razor Pages: POSTed form values, route values, and the query string. The binder will interrogate these sources in order when trying to bind your binding models.

- When binding values to models, the names of the parameters and properties aren't case-sensitive.

- You can bind to simple types or to the properties of complex types. Simple types must be convertible from strings to be bound automatically, such as numbers, dates, Boolean values, and custom types with a `TryParse` method.

- To bind complex types, the types must have a default constructor and public, settable properties. The Razor Pages model binder binds each property of a complex type using values from the binding sources.

- You can bind collections and dictionaries using the `[index]=value` and `[key]=value` syntax, respectively.

- You can customize the binding source for a binding model using `[From*]` attributes applied to the method, such as `[FromHeader]` and `[FromBody]`. These can be used to bind to nondefault binding sources, such as headers or JSON body content. The `[FromBody]` attribute is always required when binding to a JSON body.

- Validation is necessary to check for security threats. Check that data is formatted correctly and confirm that it conforms to expected values and that it meets your business rules.

- Validation in Razor Pages occurs automatically after model binding, but you must manually check the result of the validation and act accordingly in your page handler by interrogating the `ModelState.IsValid` property.

- Client-side validation provides a better user experience than server-side validation alone, but you should always use server-side validation. Client-side validation typically uses JavaScript and attributes applied to your HTML elements to validate form values.

Rendering HTML using Razor views

This chapter covers

- Creating Razor views to display HTML to a user
- Using C# and the Razor markup syntax to generate HTML dynamically
- Reusing common code with layouts and partial views

It's easy to get confused between the terms involved in Razor Pages—`PageModel`, page handlers, Razor views—especially as some of the terms describe concrete features, and others describe patterns and concepts. We've touched on all these terms in detail in previous chapters, but it's important to get them straight in your mind:

- *Razor Pages*—Razor Pages generally refers to the page-based paradigm that combines routing, model binding, and HTML generation using Razor views.
- *Razor Page*—A single Razor Page represents a single page or endpoint. It typically consists of two files: a .cshtml file containing the Razor view and a .cshtml.cs file containing the page's `PageModel`.

- PageModel—The PageModel for a Razor Page is where most of the action happens. It's where you define the binding models for a page, which extracts data from the incoming request. It's also where you define the page's page handlers.
- *Page handler*—Each Razor Page typically handles a single route, but it can handle multiple HTTP verbs such as GET and POST. Each page handler typically handles a single HTTP verb.
- *Razor view*—Razor views (also called Razor templates) are used to generate HTML. They are typically used in the final stage of a Razor Page to generate the HTML response to send back to the user.

In the previous four chapters, I covered a whole cross section of Razor Pages, including the Model-View-Controller (MVC) design pattern, the Razor Page PageModel, page handlers, routing, and binding models. This chapter covers the last part of the MVC pattern: using a view to generate the HTML that's delivered to the user's browser.

In ASP.NET Core, views are normally created using the *Razor* markup syntax (sometimes described as a templating language), which uses a mixture of HTML and C# to generate the final HTML. This chapter covers some of the features of Razor and how to use it to build the view templates for your application. Generally speaking, users will have two sorts of interactions with your app: they'll read data that your app displays, and they'll send data or commands back to it. The Razor language contains several constructs that make it simple to build both types of applications.

When displaying data, you can use the Razor language to easily combine static HTML with values from your PageModel. Razor can use C# as a control mechanism, so adding conditional elements and loops is simple—something you couldn't achieve with HTML alone.

The normal approach to sending data to web applications is with HTML forms. Virtually every dynamic app you build will use forms; some applications will be pretty much nothing *but* forms! ASP.NET Core and the Razor templating language include *Tag Helpers* that make generating HTML forms easy.

> **NOTE** You'll get a brief glimpse of Tag Helpers in section 17.1, but I explore them in detail in chapter 18.

In this chapter we'll be focusing primarily on displaying data and generating HTML using Razor rather than creating forms. You'll see how to render values from your PageModel to the HTML, and how to use C# to control the generated output. Finally, you'll learn how to extract the common elements of your views into subviews called *layouts* and *partial views*, and how to compose them to create the final HTML page.

17.1 Views: Rendering the user interface

In this section I provide a quick introduction to rendering HTML using Razor views. We'll recap the MVC design pattern used by Razor Pages and where the view fits in. Then I'll show how Razor syntax allows you to mix C# and HTML to generate dynamic UIs.

As you know from earlier chapters on the MVC design pattern, it's the job of the Razor Page's page handler to choose what to return to the client. For example, if you're developing a to-do list application, imagine a request to view a particular to-do item, as shown in figure 17.1.

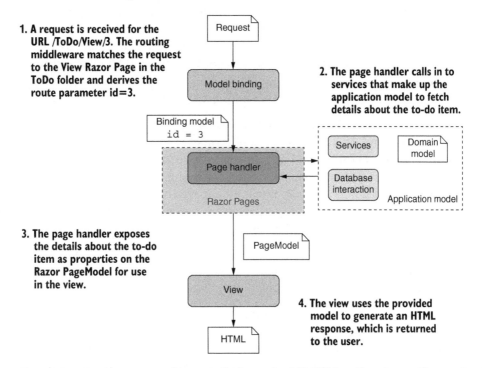

1. A request is received for the URL /ToDo/View/3. The routing middleware matches the request to the View Razor Page in the ToDo folder and derives the route parameter id=3.

2. The page handler calls in to services that make up the application model to fetch details about the to-do item.

3. The page handler exposes the details about the to-do item as properties on the Razor PageModel for use in the view.

4. The view uses the provided model to generate an HTML response, which is returned to the user.

Figure 17.1   Handling a request for a to-do list item using ASP.NET Core Razor Pages. The page handler builds the data required by the view and exposes it as properties on the `PageModel`. **The view generates HTML based only on the data provided; it doesn't need to know where that data comes from.**

A typical request follows the steps shown in figure 17.1:

- The middleware pipeline receives the request, and the routing middleware determines the endpoint to invoke—in this case, the View Razor Page in the ToDo folder.
- The model binder (part of the Razor Pages framework) uses the request to build the binding models for the page, as you saw in chapter 16. The binding models are set as properties on the Razor Page or are passed to the page handler method as arguments when the handler is executed. The page handler checks that you passed a valid id for the to-do item and marks the ModelState as valid if so.
- If the request is valid, the page handler calls out to the various services that make up the application model. This might load the details about the to-do from a database or from the filesystem, returning them to the handler. As part

of this process, either the application model or the page handler itself generates values to pass to the view and sets them as properties on the Razor Page
PageModel.

Once the page handler has executed, the PageModel should contain all the
data required to render a view. In this example, it contains details about the to-
do itself, but it might also contain other data, such as how many to-dos you have
left, whether you have any to-dos scheduled for today, your username, and so
on—anything that controls how to generate the end UI for the request.

- The Razor view template uses the PageModel to generate the final response and
  returns it to the user via the middleware pipeline.

A common thread throughout this discussion of MVC is the separation of concerns
MVC brings, and it's no different when it comes to your views. It would be easy enough
to generate the HTML directly in your application model or in your controller actions,
but instead you delegate that responsibility to a single component: the view.

But even more than that, you separate the *data* required to build the view from the
process of building it by using properties on the PageModel. These properties should
contain all the dynamic data the view needs to generate the final output.

> **TIP** Views shouldn't call methods on the PageModel. The view should gener-
> ally only be accessing data that has already been collected and exposed as
> properties.

Razor Page handlers indicate that the Razor view should be rendered by returning a
PageResult (or by returning void), as you saw in chapter 15. The Razor Pages infrastructure executes the Razor view associated with a given Razor Page to generate the
final response. The use of C# in the Razor template means you can dynamically generate the final HTML sent to the browser. This allows you to, for example, display the
name of the current user in the page, hide links the current user doesn't have access
to, or render a button for every item in a list.

Imagine your boss asks you to add a page to your application that displays a list of
the application's users. You should also be able to view a user from the page or create
a new one, as shown in figure 17.2.

The PageModel contains the data
you wish to display on the page.

Form elements can be used
to send values back to the
application.

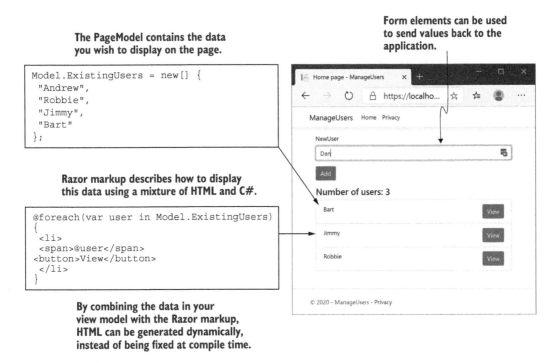

```
Model.ExistingUsers = new[] {
  "Andrew",
  "Robbie",
  "Jimmy",
  "Bart"
};
```

Razor markup describes how to display
this data using a mixture of HTML and C#.

```
@foreach(var user in Model.ExistingUsers)
{
  <li>
  <span>@user</span>
<button>View</button>
  </li>
}
```

By combining the data in your
view model with the Razor markup,
HTML can be generated dynamically,
instead of being fixed at compile time.

Figure 17.2 The use of C# in Razor lets you easily generate dynamic HTML that varies at runtime. In this example, using a `foreach` **loop inside the Razor view dramatically reduces the duplication in the HTML that you would otherwise have to write.**

With Razor templates, generating this sort of dynamic content is simple. Listing 17.1 shows a template that could be used to generate the interface in figure 17.2. It combines standard HTML with C# statements and uses Tag Helpers to generate the form elements.

> **Listing 17.1 A Razor template to list users and a form for adding a new user**

```
@page
@model IndexViewModel
<div class="row">              Normal HTML is sent to
<div class="col-md-6">         the browser unchanged.
<form method="post">
    <div class="form-group">
        <label asp-for="NewUser"></label>
        <input class="form-control" asp-for="NewUser" />     Tag Helpers attach to HTML
        <span asp-validation-for="NewUser"></span>           elements to create forms.
    </div>
    <div class="form-group">
        <button type="submit"
          class="btn btn-success">Add</button>
    </div>
</form>
</div>
```

```
</div>

<h4>Number of users: @Model.ExistingUsers.Count</h4>      ◁─┤  Values can be written
<div class="row">                                                from C# objects to
<div class="col-md-6">                                            the HTML.
<ul class="list-group">
@foreach (var user in Model.ExistingUsers)     ◁──┤  C# constructs such as for
{                                                     loops can be used in Razor.
<li class="list-group-item d-flex justify-content-between">
    <span>@user</span>
    <a class="btn btn-info"
        asp-page="ViewUser"
        asp-route-userName="@user">View</a>      │  Tag Helpers can also be used outside
</li>                                                forms to help in other HTML generation.
}
</ul>
</div>
</div>
```

This example demonstrates a variety of Razor features. There's a mixture of HTML that's written unmodified to the response output, and there are various C# constructs used to generate HTML dynamically. In addition, you can see several Tag Helpers. These look like normal HTML attributes that start with asp-, but they're part of the Razor language. They can customize the HTML element they're attached to, changing how it's rendered. They make building HTML forms much simpler than they would be otherwise. Don't worry if this template is a bit overwhelming at the moment; we'll break it all down as you progress through this chapter and the next.

Razor Pages are compiled when you build your application. Behind the scenes, they become another C# class in your application. It's also possible to enable runtime compilation of your Razor Pages. This allows you to modify your Razor Pages while your app is running without having to explicitly stop and rebuild. This can be handy when developing locally, but it's best avoided when you deploy to production. You can read how to enable this at http://mng.bz/jP2P.

> **NOTE**   As with most things in ASP.NET Core, it's possible to swap out the Razor templating engine and replace it with your own server-side rendering engine. You can't replace Razor with a client-side framework like Angular or React. If you want to take this approach, you'd use minimal APIs or web API controllers instead and a separate client-side framework.

In the next section we'll look in more detail at how Razor views fit into the Razor Pages framework and how you can pass data from your Razor Page handlers to the Razor view to help build the HTML response.

17.2   Creating Razor views

In this section we'll look at how Razor views fit into the Razor Pages framework. You'll learn how to pass data from your page handlers to your Razor views and how you can use that data to generate dynamic HTML.

With ASP.NET Core, whenever you need to display an HTML response to the user, you should use a view to generate it. Although it's possible to directly generate a `string` from your page handlers, which will be rendered as HTML in the browser, this approach doesn't adhere to the MVC separation of concerns and will quickly leave you tearing your hair out.

> **NOTE** Some middleware, such as the `WelcomePageMiddleware` you saw in chapter 4, may generate HTML responses without using a view, which can make sense in some situations. But your Razor Page and MVC controllers should always generate HTML using views.

Instead, by relying on Razor views to generate the response, you get access to a wide variety of features, as well as editor tooling to help. This section serves as a gentle introduction to Razor views, the things you can do with them, and the various ways you can pass data to them.

17.2.1 Razor views and code-behind

In this book you've already seen that Razor Pages typically consist of two files:

- The .cshtml file, commonly called the *Razor view*
- The .cshtml.cs file, commonly called the *code-behind*, which contains the `PageModel`

The Razor view contains the `@page` *directive*, which makes it a Razor Page, as you've seen previously. Without this directive, the Razor Pages framework will not route requests to the page, and the file is ignored for most purposes.

> **DEFINITION** A *directive* is a statement in a Razor file that changes the way the template is parsed or compiled. Another common directive is the `@using newNamespace` directive, which makes objects in the `newNamespace` namespace available.

The code-behind .cshtml.cs file contains the `PageModel` for an associated Razor Page. It contains the page handlers that respond to requests, and it is where the Razor Page typically interacts with other parts of your application.

Even though the .cshtml and .cshtml.cs files have the same name, such as ToDoItem.cshtml and ToDoItem.cshtml.cs, it's not the filename that's linking them. But if it's not by filename, how does the Razor Pages framework know which `PageModel` is associated with a given Razor Page view file?

At the top of each Razor Page, after the `@page` directive, is the `@model` directive with a `Type`, indicating which `PageModel` is associated with the Razor view. The following directives indicate that the `ToDoItemModel` is the `PageModel` associated with the Razor Page:

```
@page
@model ToDoItemModel
```

Once a request is routed to a Razor Page, as covered in chapter 14, the framework looks for the @model directive to decide which PageModel to use. Based on the PageModel selected, it then binds to any properties in the PageModel marked with the [BindProperty] attribute (as we covered in chapter 16) and executes the appropriate page handler (based on the request's HTTP verb, as described in chapter 15).

> **NOTE**   Technically, the PageModel and @model directive are optional. If you don't specify a PageModel, the framework executes an implicit page handler, as you saw in chapter 15, and renders the view directly. It's also possible to combine the .cshtml and .cshtml.cs files into a single .cshtml file. You can read more about this approach in *Razor Pages in Action*, by Mike Brind (Manning, 2022).

In addition to the @page and @model directives, the Razor view file contains the Razor template that is executed to generate the HTML response.

17.2.2 *Introducing Razor templates*

Razor view templates contain a mixture of HTML and C# code interspersed with one another. The HTML markup lets you easily describe exactly what should be sent to the browser, whereas the C# code can be used to dynamically change what is rendered. The following listing shows an example of Razor rendering a list of strings representing to-do items.

> **Listing 17.2   Razor template for rendering a list of strings**

```
@page
@{
    var tasks = new List<string>
      { "Buy milk", "Buy eggs", "Buy bread" };
}
<h1>Tasks to complete</h1>
<ul>
@for(var i=0; i< tasks.Count; i++)
{
  var task = tasks[i];
  <li>@i - @task</li>
}
</ul>
```

Arbitrary C# can be executed in a template. Variables remain in scope throughout the page.

Standard HTML markup will be rendered to the output unchanged.

Mixing C# and HTML allows you to create HTML dynamically at runtime.

The pure HTML sections in this template are in the angle brackets. The Razor engine copies this HTML directly to the output, unchanged, as though you were writing a normal HTML file.

> **NOTE**   The ability of Razor syntax to know when you are switching between HTML and C# can be both uncanny and infuriating at times. I discuss how to control this transition in section 17.3.

As well as HTML, you can see several C# statements in there. The advantage of being able to, for example, use a for loop rather than having to explicitly write out each <li>

element should be self-evident. I'll dive a little deeper into more of the C# features of Razor in the next section. When rendered, the template in listing 17.2 produces the following HTML.

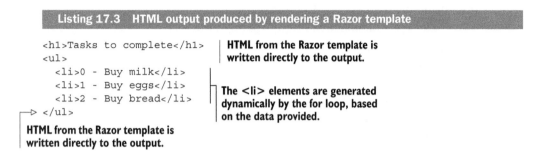

Listing 17.3 HTML output produced by rendering a Razor template

```
<h1>Tasks to complete</h1>
<ul>
    <li>0 - Buy milk</li>
    <li>1 - Buy eggs</li>
    <li>2 - Buy bread</li>
</ul>
```

HTML from the Razor template is written directly to the output.

The <li> elements are generated dynamically by the for loop, based on the data provided.

HTML from the Razor template is written directly to the output.

As you can see, the final output of a Razor template after it's rendered is simple HTML. There's nothing complicated left, only straight HTML markup that can be sent to the browser and rendered. Figure 17.3 shows how a browser would render it.

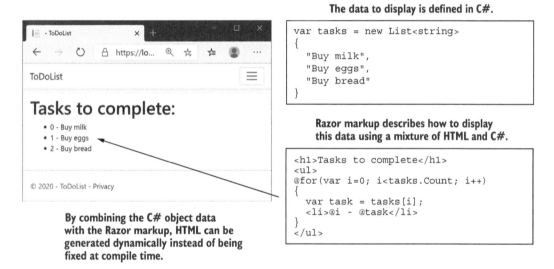

The data to display is defined in C#.

```
var tasks = new List<string>
{
    "Buy milk",
    "Buy eggs",
    "Buy bread"
}
```

Razor markup describes how to display this data using a mixture of HTML and C#.

```
<h1>Tasks to complete</h1>
<ul>
@for(var i=0; i<tasks.Count; i++)
{
    var task = tasks[i];
    <li>@i - @task</li>
}
</ul>
```

By combining the C# object data with the Razor markup, HTML can be generated dynamically instead of being fixed at compile time.

Figure 17.3 Razor templates can be used to generate the HTML dynamically at runtime from C# objects. In this case, a `for` loop is used to create repetitive HTML `<li>` elements.

In this example, I hardcoded the list values for simplicity; no dynamic data was provided. This is often the case on simple Razor Pages, like those you might have on your home page; you need to display an almost static page. For the rest of your application, it will be far more common to have some sort of data you need to display, typically exposed as properties on your `PageModel`.

17.2.3 *Passing data to views*

In ASP.NET Core, you have several ways of passing data from a page handler in a Razor Page to its view. Which approach is best depends on the data you're trying to pass through, but in general you should use the mechanisms in the following order:

- `PageModel` *properties*—You should generally expose any data that needs to be displayed as properties on your `PageModel`. Any data that is specific to the associated Razor view should be exposed this way. The `PageModel` object is available in the view when it's rendered, as you'll see shortly.

- `ViewData`—This is a dictionary of objects with `string` keys that can be used to pass arbitrary data from the page handler to the view. In addition, it allows you to pass data to *layout* files, as you'll see in section 17.4. Layout files are the main reason for using `ViewData` instead of setting properties on the `PageModel`.

- `TempData`—`TempData` is a dictionary of objects with `string` keys, similar to `ViewData`, that is stored until it's read in a different request. This is commonly used to temporarily persist data when using the POST-REDIRECT-GET pattern. By default `TempData` stores the data in an encrypted cookie, but other storage options are available, as described in the documentation at http://mng.bz/Wzx1.

- `HttpContext`—Technically, the `HttpContext` object is available in both the page handler and Razor view, so you could use it to transfer data between them. But don't—there's no need for it with the other methods available to you.

- `@inject` *services*—You can use dependency injection (DI) to make services available in your views, though this should normally be used sparingly. Using the directive `@inject Service myService` injects a variable called `myService` of type `Service` from the DI container, which you can use in your Razor view.

Far and away the best approach for passing data from a page handler to a view is to use properties on the `PageModel`. There's nothing special about the properties themselves; you can store anything there to hold the data you require.

> **NOTE** Many frameworks have the concept of a data context for binding UI components. The `PageModel` is a similar concept, in that it contains values to display in the UI, but the binding is one-directional; the `PageModel` provides values to the UI, and once the UI is built and sent as a response, the `PageModel` is destroyed.

As I described in section 17.2.1, the `@model` directive at the top of your Razor view describes which `Type` of `PageModel` is associated with a given Razor Page. The `PageModel` associated with a Razor Page contains one or more page handlers and exposes data as properties for use in the Razor view, as shown in the following listing.

Listing 17.4 Exposing data as properties on a `PageModel`

```
public class ToDoItemModel : PageModel    ◁──┤ The PageModel is passed to the
{                                             Razor view when it executes.
```

```
public List<string> Tasks { get; set; }        The public properties can be
public string Title { get; set; }               accessed from the Razor view.

public void OnGet(int id)
{
    Title = "Tasks for today";
    Tasks = new List<string>                    Building the required data:
    {                                           this would normally call out
        "Get fuel",                             to a service or database to
        "Check oil",                            load the data.
        "Check tyre pressure"
    };
}
}
```

You can access the PageModel instance itself from the Razor view using the Model property. For example, to display the Title property of the ToDoItemModel in the Razor view, you'd use `<h1>@Model.Title</h1>`. This would render the string provided in the ToDoItemModel.Title property, producing the `<h1>Tasks for today</h1>` HTML.

> **TIP** Note that the @model directive should be at the top of your view, immediately after the @page directive, and it has a lowercase m. The Model property can be accessed anywhere in the view and has an uppercase M.

In most cases, using public properties on your PageModel is the way to go; it's the standard mechanism for passing data between the page handler and the view. But in some circumstances, properties on your PageModel might not be the best fit. This is often the case when you want to pass data between view layouts. You'll see how this works in section 17.4.

A common example is the title of the page. You need to provide a title for every page in your application, so you could create a base class with a Title property and make every PageModel inherit from it. But that's cumbersome, so a common approach for this situation is to use the ViewData collection to pass data around.

In fact, the standard Razor Page templates use this approach by default, by setting values on the ViewData dictionary from within the view itself:

```
@{
    ViewData["Title"] = "Home Page";
}
<h2>@ViewData["Title"].</h2>
```

This template sets the value of the "Title" key in the ViewData dictionary to "Home Page" and then fetches the key to render in the template. This set and immediate fetch might seem superfluous, but as the ViewData dictionary is shared throughout the request, it makes the title of the page available in layouts, as you'll see later. When rendered, the preceding template would produce the following output:

```
<h2>Home Page.</h2>
```

You can also set values in the `ViewData` dictionary from your page handlers in two different ways, as shown in the following listing.

Listing 17.5   Setting `ViewData` values using an attribute

```
public class IndexModel: PageModel          Properties marked with the
{                                           [ViewData] attribute are set
    [ViewData]              ◁───────        in the ViewData.
    public string Title { get; set; }
                                            The value of ViewData["Title"]
    public void OnGet()                     will be set to "Home Page".
    {
        Title = "Home Page";    ◁───────    You can set keys in the
        ViewData["Subtitle"] = "Welcome";  ◁─── ViewData dictionary directly.
    }
}
```

You can display the values in the template in the same way as before:

```
<h1>@ViewData["Title"]</h3>
<h2>@ViewData["Subtitle"]</h3>
```

> **TIP**   I don't find the `[ViewData]` attribute especially useful, but it's another feature to look out for. Instead, I create a set of global, static constants for any `ViewData` keys, and I reference those instead of typing `"Title"` repeatedly. You'll get IntelliSense for the values, they're refactor-safe, and you'll avoid hard-to-spot typos.

As I mentioned previously, there are mechanisms besides `PageModel` properties and `ViewData` that you can use to pass data around, but these two are the only ones I use personally, as you can do everything you need with them. As a reminder, always use `PageModel` properties where possible, as you benefit from strong typing and IntelliSense. Only fall back to `ViewData` for values that need to be accessed *outside* of your Razor view.

You've had a small taste of the power available to you in Razor templates, but in the next section we'll dive a little deeper into some of the available C# capabilities.

17.3   *Creating dynamic web pages with Razor*

You might be glad to know that pretty much anything you can do in C# is possible in Razor syntax. Under the covers, the .cshtml files are compiled into normal C# code (with `string` for the raw HTML sections), so whatever weird and wonderful behavior you need can be created!

Having said that, just because you *can* do something doesn't mean you *should*. You'll find it much easier to work with, and maintain, your files if you keep them as simple as possible. This is true of pretty much all programming, but I find it to be especially so with Razor templates.

This section covers some of the more common C# constructs you can use. If you find you need to achieve something a bit more exotic, refer to the Razor syntax documentation at http://mng.bz/8rMw.

17.3.1 Using C# in Razor templates

One of the most common requirements when working with Razor templates is to render a value you've calculated in C# to the HTML. For example, you might want to print the current year to use with a copyright statement in your HTML, to give this result:

```
<p>Copyright 2022 ©</p>
```

Or you might want to print the result of a calculation:

```
<p>The sum of 1 and 2 is <i>3</i><p>
```

You can do this in two ways, depending on the exact C# code you need to execute. If the code is a single statement, you can use the @ symbol to indicate you want to write the result to the HTML output, as shown in figure 17.4. You've already seen this used to write out values from the `PageModel` or from `ViewData`.

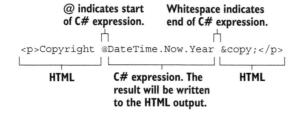

Figure 17.4   Writing the result of a C# expression to HTML. The @ symbol indicates where the C# code begins, and the expression ends at the end of the statement, in this case at the space.

If the C# you want to execute is something that needs a space, you need to use parentheses to demarcate the C#, as shown in figure 17.5.

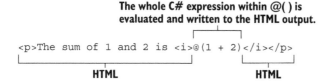

Figure 17.5   When a C# expression contains whitespace, you must wrap it in parentheses using @() so the Razor engine knows where the C# stops and HTML begins.

These two approaches, in which C# is evaluated and written directly to the HTML output, are called *Razor expressions*.

> **TIP**   If you want to write a literal @ character rather than a C# expression, use a second @ character: @@.

Sometimes you'll want to execute some C#, but you don't need to output the values. We used this technique when we were setting values in `ViewData`:

```
@{
    ViewData["Title"] = "Home Page";
}
```

This example demonstrates a *Razor code block*, which is normal C# code, identified by the `@{}` structure. Nothing is written to the HTML output here; it's all compiled as though you'd written it in any other normal C# file.

> **TIP** When you execute code within code blocks, it must be valid C#, so you need to add semicolons. Conversely, when you're writing values directly to the response using Razor expressions, you don't need them. If your output HTML breaks unexpectedly, keep an eye out for missing or rogue extra semicolons.

Razor expressions are one of the most common ways of writing data from your `PageModel` to the HTML output. You'll see the other approach, using Tag Helpers, in the next chapter. Razor's capabilities extend far further than this, however, as you'll see in section 17.3.2, where you'll learn how to include traditional C# structures in your templates.

17.3.2 Adding loops and conditionals to Razor templates

One of the biggest advantages of using Razor templates over static HTML is the ability to generate the output dynamically. Being able to write values from your `PageModel` to the HTML using Razor expressions is a key part of that, but another common use is loops and conditionals. With these, you can hide sections of the UI, or produce HTML for every item in a list, for example.

Loops and conditionals include constructs such as `if` and `for` loops. Using them in Razor templates is almost identical to C#, but you need to prefix their usage with the `@` symbol. In case you're not getting the hang of Razor yet, when in doubt, throw in another `@`!

One of the big advantages of Razor in the context of ASP.NET Core is that it uses languages you're already familiar with: C# and HTML. There's no need to learn a whole new set of primitives for some other templating language: it's the same `if`, `foreach`, and `while` constructs you already know. And when you don't need them, you're writing raw HTML, so you can see exactly what the user is getting in their browser.

In listing 17.6, I've applied a few of these techniques in a template to display a to-do item. The `PageModel` has a `bool IsComplete` property, as well as a `List<string>` property called `Tasks`, which contains any outstanding tasks.

Listing 17.6   Razor template for rendering a `ToDoItemViewModel`

```
@page
@model ToDoItemModel      ⟵── The @model directive indicates
<div>                          the type of PageModel in Model.
```

```
@if (Model.IsComplete)
{
    <strong>Well done, you're all done!</strong>
}
else
{
    <strong>The following tasks remain:</strong>
    <ul>
        @foreach (var task in Model.Tasks)
        {
            <li>@task</li>
        }
    </ul>
}
</div>
```

> The **if** control structure checks the value of the PageModel's **IsComplete** property at runtime.

> The **foreach** structure will generate the **<li>** elements once for each task in **Model.Tasks**.

> A Razor expression is used to write the task to the HTML output.

This code definitely lives up to the promise of mixing C# and HTML! There are traditional C# control structures, such as `if` and `foreach`, that you'd expect in any normal C# program, interspersed with the HTML markup that you want to send to the browser. As you can see, the @ symbol is used to indicate when you're starting a control statement, but you generally let the Razor template infer when you're switching back and forth between HTML and C#.

The template shows how to generate dynamic HTML at runtime, depending on the exact data provided. If the model has outstanding `Tasks`, the HTML generates a list item for each task, producing output something like that shown in figure 17.6.

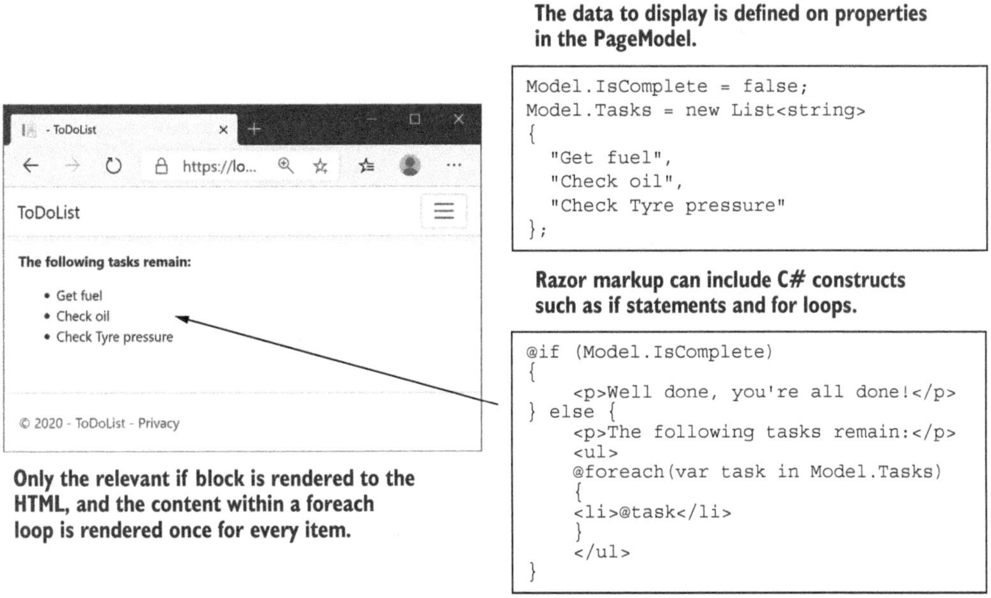

The data to display is defined on properties in the PageModel.

```
Model.IsComplete = false;
Model.Tasks = new List<string>
{
    "Get fuel",
    "Check oil",
    "Check Tyre pressure"
};
```

Razor markup can include C# constructs such as if statements and for loops.

```
@if (Model.IsComplete)
{
    <p>Well done, you're all done!</p>
} else {
    <p>The following tasks remain:</p>
    <ul>
    @foreach(var task in Model.Tasks)
    {
    <li>@task</li>
    }
    </ul>
}
```

Only the relevant if block is rendered to the HTML, and the content within a foreach loop is rendered once for every item.

Figure 17.6 The Razor template generates a `<li>` item for each remaining task, depending on the data passed to the view at runtime. You can use an `if` block to render completely different HTML depending on the values in your model.

IntelliSense and tooling support

The mixture of C# and HTML might seem hard to read in the book, and that's a reasonable complaint. It's also another valid argument for trying to keep your Razor templates as simple as possible.

Luckily, if you're using an editor like Visual Studio or Visual Studio Code, the tooling can help somewhat. Visual Studio highlights the transition between the C# portions of the code and the surrounding HTML, though this is less pronounced in recent versions of Visual Studio.

```
1     @page "{id}"
2     @model ToDoList.Pages.ViewToDoModel
3
4     <p>
5         @if (Model.ToDo.IsComplete)
6         {
7             <strong>Well done, you're all done!</strong>
8         }
9         else
10        {
11            <strong>The following tasks remain:</strong>
12            <ul>
13                @foreach (var task in Model.ToDo.Tasks)
14                {
15                    <li>@task</li>
16                }
17            </ul>
18        }
19    </p>
20
```

Visual Studio highlights the @ symbols where C# transitions to HTML and uses C# syntax coloring for C# code. This makes the Razor templates somewhat easier to read that than the pure plain text.

Although the ability to use loops and conditionals is powerful—they're one of the advantages of Razor over static HTML—they also add to the complexity of your view. Try to limit the amount of logic in your views to make them as easy to understand and maintain as possible.

A common trope of the ASP.NET Core team is that they try to ensure you "fall into the pit of success" when building an application. This refers to the idea that by default, the *easiest* way to do something should be the *correct* way of doing it. This is a great philosophy, as it means you shouldn't get burned by, for example, security problems if you follow the standard approaches. Occasionally, however, you may need to step beyond the safety rails; a common use case is when you need to render some HTML contained in a C# object to the output, as you'll see in the next section

17.3.3 Rendering HTML with Raw

In the previous example, we rendered the list of tasks to HTML by writing the `string` `task` using the `@task` Razor expression. But what if the `task` variable contains HTML you want to display, so instead of `"Check oil"` it contains `"<strong>Check oil</strong>"`? If you use a Razor expression to output this as you did previously, you might hope to get this:

```
<li><strong>Check oil</strong></li>
```

But that's not the case. The HTML generated comes out like this:

```
<li>&lt;strong&gt;Check oil&lt;/strong&gt;</li>
```

Hmm, looks odd, right? What's happened here? Why did the template not write your variable to the HTML, like it has in previous examples? If you look at how a browser displays this HTML, like in figure 17.7, I hope that it makes more sense.

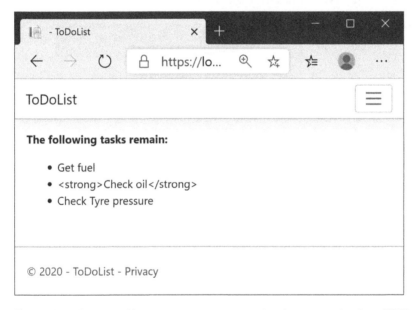

Figure 17.7 The second item, `"<strong>Check oil</strong>"` has been HTML-encoded, so the `<strong>` elements are visible to the user as part of the task. This prevents any security problems, as users can't inject malicious scripts into your HTML.

Razor templates HTML-encode C# expressions before they're written to the output stream. This is primarily for security reasons; writing out arbitrary strings to your HTML could allow users to inject malicious data and JavaScript into your website. Consequently, the C# variables you print in your Razor template get written as HTML-encoded values.

NOTE   Razor also renders non-ASCII Unicode characters, such as ó and è, as HTML entities: `&#243;` and `&egrave;`. You can customize this behavior using `WebEncoderOptions` in Program.cs, as in this example: `builder.Services .Configure<WebEncoderOptions>(o => o.AllowCharacter('ó'))`.

In some cases, you might need to directly write out HTML contained in a `string` to the response. If you find yourself in this situation, first, stop. Do you *really* need to do this? If the values you're writing have been entered by a user, or were created based on values provided by users, there's a serious risk of creating a security hole in your website.

If you really need to write the variable out to the HTML stream, you can do so using the `Html` property on the view page and calling the `Raw` method:

```
<li>@Html.Raw(task)</li>
```

With this approach, the string in `task` is directly written to the output stream, without encoding, producing the HTML you originally wanted, `<li><strong>Check oil</strong></li>`, which renders as shown in figure 17.8.

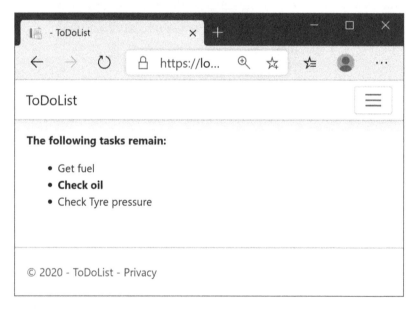

Figure 17.8   The second item, "`<strong>Check oil<strong>`" has been output using `Html.Raw()`, so it hasn't been HTML-encoded. The `<strong>` elements result in the second item being shown in bold instead. Using `Html.Raw()` in this way should be avoided where possible, as it is a security risk.

WARNING   Using `Html.Raw` on user input creates a security risk that users could use to inject malicious code into your website. Avoid using `Html.Raw` if possible.

The C# constructs shown in this section can be useful, but they can make your templates harder to read. It's generally easier to understand the intention of Razor templates that are predominantly HTML markup rather than C#.

In the previous version of ASP.NET, these constructs, and in particular the `Html` helper property, were the standard way to generate dynamic markup. You can still use this approach in ASP.NET Core by using the various `HtmlHelper` methods on the `Html` property, but these have largely been superseded by a cleaner technique: Tag Helpers.

> **NOTE** I discuss Tag Helpers and how to use them to build HTML forms in chapter 18. `HtmlHelper` is essentially obsolete, though it's still available if you prefer to use it.

Tag Helpers are a useful feature that's new to Razor in ASP.NET Core, but many other features have been carried through from the legacy (.NET Framework) ASP.NET. In the next section of this chapter, you'll see how you can create nested Razor templates and use partial views to reduce the amount of duplication in your views.

17.4 Layouts, partial views, and _ViewStart

In this section you'll learn about layouts and partial views, which allow you to extract common code to reduce duplication. These files make it easier to make changes to your HTML that affect multiple pages at once. You'll also learn how to run common code for every Razor Page using _ViewStart and _ViewImports, and how to include optional sections in your pages.

Every HTML document has a certain number of elements that are required: `<html>`, `<head>`, and `<body>`. As well, there are often common sections that are repeated on every page of your application, such as the header and footer, as shown in figure 17.9. Also, each page in your application will probably reference the same CSS and JavaScript files.

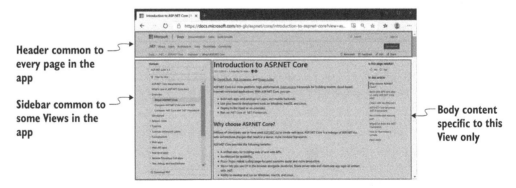

Figure 17.9   A typical web application has a block-based layout, where some blocks are common to every page of your application. The header block will likely be identical across your whole application, but the sidebar may be identical only for the pages in one section. The body content will differ for every page in your application.

All these different elements add up to a maintenance nightmare. If you had to include these manually in every view, making any changes would be a laborious, error-prone process involving editing every page. Instead, Razor lets you extract these common elements into *layouts*.

> **DEFINITION** A *layout* in Razor is a template that includes common code. It can't be rendered directly, but it can be rendered in conjunction with normal Razor views.

By extracting your common markup into layouts, you can reduce the duplication in your app. This makes changes easier, makes your views easier to manage and maintain, and is generally good practice!

17.4.1 *Using layouts for shared markup*

Layout files are, for the most part, normal Razor templates that contain markup common to more than one page. An ASP.NET Core app can have multiple layouts, and layouts can reference other layouts. A common use for this is to have different layouts for different sections of your application. For example, an e-commerce website might use a three-column view for most pages but a single-column layout when you come to the checkout pages, as shown in figure 17.10.

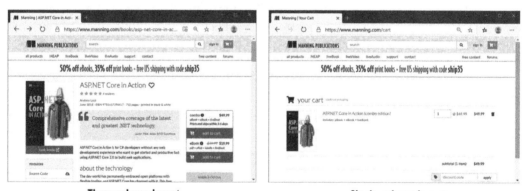

Three-column layout   Single-column layout

Figure 17.10   The https://manning.com website uses different layouts for different parts of the web application. The product pages use a three-column layout, but the cart page uses a single-column layout.

You'll often use layouts across many different Razor Pages, so they're typically placed in the Pages/Shared folder. You can name them anything you like, but there's a common convention to use _Layout.cshtml as the filename for the base layout in your application. This is the default name used by the Razor Page templates in Visual Studio and the .NET CLI.

TIP A common convention is to prefix your layout files with an underscore (_) to distinguish them from standard Razor templates in your Pages folder. Placing them in Pages/Shared means you can refer to them by the short name, such as "_Layout", without having to specify the full path to the layout file.

A layout file looks similar to a normal Razor template, with one exception: every layout must call the @RenderBody() function. This tells the templating engine where to insert the content from the child views. A simple layout is shown in listing 17.7. Typically, your application references all your CSS and JavaScript files in the layout and includes all the common elements, such as headers and footers, but this example includes pretty much the bare minimum HTML.

Listing 17.7　A basic _Layout.cshtml file calling `RenderBody`

```
<!DOCTYPE html>
<html>
<head>
    <meta charset="utf-8" />
    <title>@ViewData["Title"]</title>    ⤚
    <link rel="stylesheet" href="~/css/site.css" />    ⬅
</head>
<body>
    @RenderBody()    ⬅
</body>
</html>
```

ViewData is the standard mechanism for passing data to a layout from a view.

Elements common to every page, such as your CSS, are typically found in the layout.

Tells the templating engine where to insert the child view's content

As you can see, the layout file includes the required elements, such as `<html>` and `<head>`, as well as elements you need on every page, such as `<title>` and `<link>`. This example also shows the benefit of storing the page title in `ViewData`; the layout can render it in the `<title>` element so that it shows in the browser's tab, as shown in figure 17.11.

Figure 17.11　The content of the `<title>` element is used to name the tab in the user's browser, in this case Home Page.

NOTE Layout files are not standalone Razor Pages and do not take part in routing, so they do not start with the @page directive.

Views can specify a layout file to use by setting the `Layout` property inside a Razor code block, as shown in the following listing.

Listing 17.8　Setting the `Layout` property from a view

```
@{
    Layout = "_Layout";    ⬅
```

Sets the layout for the page to _Layout.cshtml

```
        ViewData["Title"] = "Home Page";
    }
    <h1>@ViewData["Title"]</h1>
    <p>This is the home page</p>
```

> ViewData is a convenient way of passing data from a Razor view to the layout.

The content in the Razor view to render inside the layout

Any contents in the view are be rendered inside the layout, where the call to @Render-Body() occurs. Combining the two previous listings generates the following HTML.

Listing 17.9   Rendered output from combining a view with its layout

```
<!DOCTYPE html>
<html>
<head>
    <meta charset="utf-8" />
    <title>Home Page</title>
    <link rel="stylesheet" href="/css/site.css" />
</head>
<body>
    <h1>Home Page</h1>
    <p>This is the home page</p>
</body>
<html>
```

> ViewData set in the view is used to render the layout.

> The RenderBody call renders the contents of the view.

Judicious use of layouts can be extremely useful in reducing the duplication between pages. By default, layouts provide only a single location where you can render content from the view, at the call to @RenderBody. In cases where this is too restrictive, you can render content using *sections*.

17.4.2   *Overriding parent layouts using sections*

A common requirement when you start using multiple layouts in your application is to be able to render content from child views in more than one place in your layout. Consider the case of a layout that uses two columns. The view needs a mechanism for saying "render *this* content in the *left* column" and "render this *other* content in the *right* column." This is achieved using *sections*.

> **NOTE**   Remember, all the features outlined in this chapter are specific to Razor, which is a server-side rendering engine. If you're using a client-side single-page application (SPA) framework to build your application, you'll likely handle these requirements in other ways, within the client.

Sections provide a way of organizing where view elements should be placed within a layout. They're defined in the view using an @section definition, as shown in the following listing, which defines the HTML content for a sidebar separate from the main content, in a section called Sidebar. The @section can be placed anywhere in the file, top or bottom, wherever is convenient.

Listing 17.10 Defining a section in a view template

```
@{
    Layout = "_TwoColumn";
}
@section Sidebar {
    <p>This is the sidebar content</p>
}
<p>This is the main content </p>
```

All content inside the braces is part of the Sidebar section, not the main body content.

Any content not inside an @section will be rendered by the @RenderBody call.

The section is rendered in the parent layout with a call to `@RenderSection()`. This renders the content contained in the child section into the layout. Sections can be either required or optional. If they're required, a view must declare the given `@section`; if they're optional, they can be omitted, and the layout will skip them. Skipped sections won't appear in the rendered HTML. The following listing shows a layout that has a required section called `Sidebar` and an optional section called `Scripts`.

Listing 17.11 Rendering a section in a layout file, _TwoColumn.cshtml

```
@{
    Layout = "_Layout";
}
<div class="main-content">
    @RenderBody()
</div>
<div class="side-bar">
    @RenderSection("Sidebar", required: true)
</div>
@RenderSection("Scripts", required: false)
```

This layout is nested inside a layout itself.

Renders all the content from a view that isn't part of a section

Renders the Sidebar section; if the Sidebar section isn't defined in the view, throws an error

Renders the Scripts section; if the Scripts section isn't defined in the view, ignores it

> **TIP** It's common to have an optional section called `Scripts` in your layout pages. This can be used to render additional JavaScript that's required by some views but isn't needed on every view. A common example is the jQuery Unobtrusive Validation scripts for client-side validation. If a view requires the scripts, it adds the appropriate `@section Scripts` to the Razor markup.

You may notice that the previous listing defines a `Layout` property, even though it's a layout itself, not a view. This is perfectly acceptable and lets you create nested hierarchies of layouts, as shown in figure 17.12.

> **TIP** Most websites these days need to be responsive, so they work on a wide variety of devices. You generally shouldn't use layouts for this. Don't serve different layouts for a single page based on the device making the request. Instead, serve the same HTML to all devices, and use CSS on the client side to adapt the display of your web page as required.

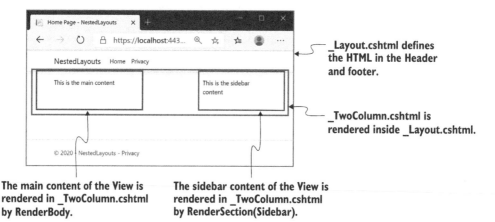

The main content of the View is rendered in _TwoColumn.cshtml by RenderBody.

The sidebar content of the View is rendered in _TwoColumn.cshtml by RenderSection(Sidebar).

Figure 17.12   Multiple layouts can be nested to create complex hierarchies. This allows you to keep the elements common to all views in your base layout and extract layout common to multiple views into sub-layouts.

As well as the simple optional/required flags for sections, Razor Pages have several other messages that you can use for flow control in your layout pages:

- `IsSectionDefined(string section)`—Returns `true` if a Razor Page has defined the named section.
- `IgnoreSection(string section)`—Ignores an unrendered section. If a section is defined in a page but not rendered, the Razor Page throws an exception unless the section is ignored.
- `IgnoreBody()`—Ignores the unrendered body of the Razor Page. Layouts must call either `RenderBody()` or `IgnoreBody()`; otherwise, they will throw an `InvalidOperationException`.

Layout files and sections provide a lot of flexibility for building sophisticated UIs, but one of their most important uses is in reducing the duplication of code in your application. They're perfect for avoiding duplication of content that you'd need to write for every view. But what about those times when you find you want to reuse part of a view somewhere else? For those cases, you have partial views.

17.4.3 *Using partial views to encapsulate markup*

Partial views are exactly what they sound like: part of a view. They provide a means of breaking up a larger view into smaller, reusable chunks. This can be useful for both reducing the complexity in a large view by splitting it into multiple partial views or for allowing you to reuse part of a view inside another.

Most web frameworks that use server-side rendering have this capability. Ruby on Rails has partial views, Django has inclusion tags, and Zend has partials. These all work in the same way, extracting common code into small, reusable templates. Even client-side templating engines such as Mustache and Handlebars, used by client-side frameworks like Angular and Ember, have similar "partial view" concepts.

Consider a to-do list application again. You might find you have a Razor Page called ViewToDo.cshtml that displays a single to-do with a given id. Later, you create a new Razor Page, RecentToDos.cshtml, that displays the five most recent to-do items. Instead of copying and pasting the code from one page to the other, you could create a partial view, called _ToDo.cshtml, as in the following listing.

Listing 17.12 Partial view _ToDo.cshtml for displaying a `ToDoItemViewModel`

```
@model ToDoItemViewModel                    ◁——————    Partial views can bind to data in the Model
<h2>@Model.Title</h2>                                   property, like a normal Razor Page uses a
<ul>                                                    PageModel.
    @foreach (var task in Model.Tasks)      ┐  The content of the partial
    {                                       │  view, which previously existed
        <li>@task</li>                      │  in the ViewToDo.cshtml file
    }                                       ┘
</ul>
```

Partial views are a bit like Razor Pages without the `PageModel` and handlers. Partial views are purely about rendering small sections of HTML rather than handling requests, model binding, and validation, and calling the application model. They are great for encapsulating small usable bits of HTML that you need to generate on multiple Razor Pages.

Both the ViewToDo.cshtml and RecentToDos.cshtml Razor Pages can render the _ToDo.cshtml partial view, which handles generating the HTML for a single class. Partial views are rendered using the `<partial />` Tag Helper, providing the name of the partial view to render and the data (the model) to render. For example, the RecentToDos .cshtml view could achieve this as shown in the following listing.

Listing 17.13 Rendering a partial view from a Razor Page

```
    @page                           ◁———————  This is a Razor Page, so it uses the @page
┌─▷ @model RecentToDoListModel                directive. Partial views do not use @page.
│
│   @foreach(var todo in Model.RecentItems)   ◁———  Loops through the recent items. todo is
│   {                                               a ToDoItemViewModel, as required by
│       <partial name="_ToDo" model="todo" />  ◁─┐  the partial view.
│   }                                            │
│                                                Uses the partial tag helper to render the
│   The PageModel contains the                   _ToDo partial view, passing in the model
│   list of recent items to render.              to render
```

When you render a partial view without providing an absolute path or file extension, such as _ToDo in listing 17.13, the framework tries to locate the view by searching the Pages folder, starting from the Razor Page that invoked it. For example, if your Razor Page is located at `Pages/Agenda/ToDos/RecentToDos.chstml`, the framework would look in the following places for a file called _ToDo.chstml:

- Pages/Agenda/ToDos/ (the current Razor Page's folder)
- Pages/Agenda/
- Pages/
- Pages/Shared/
- Views/Shared/

The first location that contains a file called _ToDo.cshtml will be selected. If you include the .cshtml file extension when you reference the partial view, the framework will look only in the current Razor Page's folder. Also, if you provide an absolute path to the partial, such as /Pages/Agenda/ToDo.cshtml, that's the only place the framework will look.

> **TIP** As with most of Razor Pages, the search locations are conventions that you can customize. If you find the need, you can customize the paths as shown here: http://mng.bz/nM9e.

The Razor code contained in a partial view is almost identical to a standard view. The main difference is the fact that partial views are called only from other views. The other difference is that partial views don't run _ViewStart.cshtml when they execute. You'll learn about _ViewStart.cshtml shortly in section 17.4.4.

> **NOTE**   Like layouts, partial views are typically named with a leading underscore.

Child actions in ASP.NET Core

In the legacy .NET Framework version of ASP.NET, there was the concept of a *child action*. This was an MVC controller action method that could be invoked from *inside* a view. This was the main mechanism for rendering discrete sections of a complex layout that had nothing to do with the main action method. For example, a child action method might render the shopping cart in the corner of every page on an e-commerce site.

This approach meant you didn't have to pollute every page's view model with the view model items required to render the shopping cart, but it fundamentally broke the MVC design pattern by referencing controllers from a view.

In ASP.NET Core, child actions are no more. *View components* have replaced them. These are conceptually quite similar in that they allow both the execution of arbitrary code and the rendering of HTML, but they don't directly invoke controller actions. You can think of them as a more powerful partial view that you should use anywhere a partial view needs to contain significant code or business logic. You'll see how to build a small view component in chapter 32.

Partial views aren't the only way to reduce duplication in your view templates. Razor also allows you to put common elements such as namespace declarations and layout configuration in centralized files. In the next section you'll see how to wield these files to clean up your templates.

17.4.4 Running code on every view with _ViewStart and _ViewImports

Due to the nature of views, you'll inevitably find yourself writing certain things repeatedly. If all your views use the same layout, adding the following code to the top of every page feels a little redundant:

```
@{
    Layout = "_Layout";
}
```

Similarly, if you find you need to reference objects from a different namespace in your Razor views, then having to add `@using WebApplication1.Models` to the top of every page can get to be a chore. Fortunately, ASP.NET Core includes two mechanisms for handling these common tasks: _ViewImports.cshtml and _ViewStart.cshtml.

IMPORTING COMMON DIRECTIVES WITH _VIEWIMPORTS

The _ViewImports.cshtml file contains directives that are inserted at the top of every Razor view. This can include things like the `@using` and `@model` statements that you've already seen—basically any Razor directive. For example, to avoid adding a `@using` statement to every view, you can include it in _ViewImports.cshtml instead of in your Razor Pages, as shown in the following listing.

> Listing 17.14 A typical _ViewImports.cshtml file importing additional namespaces

```
@using WebApplication1              The default namespace of your
@using WebApplication1.Pages        application and the Pages folder        Adds this directive to avoid
@using WebApplication1.Models                                           ◁   placing it in every view
@addTagHelper *, Microsoft.AspNetCore.Mvc.TagHelpers
```

**Makes Tag Helpers available in
your views, added by default**

The _ViewImports.cshtml file can be placed in any folder, and it will apply to all views and subfolders in that folder. Typically, it's placed in the root Pages folder so that it applies to every Razor Page and partial view in your app.

It's important to note that you should only put Razor directives in _ViewImports .cshtml; you can't put any old C# in there. As you can see in the previous listing, this is limited to things like `@using` or the `@addTagHelper` directive that you'll learn about in chapter 18. If you want to run some arbitrary C# at the start of every view in your application, such as to set the `Layout` property, you should use the _ViewStart.cshtml file instead.

RUNNING CODE FOR EVERY VIEW WITH _VIEWSTART

You can easily run common code at the start of every Razor Page by adding a _ViewStart.cshtml file to the Pages folder in your application. This file can contain any Razor code, but it's typically used to set the `Layout` for all the pages in your application, as shown in the following listing. Then you can omit the `Layout` statement from all pages that use the default layout. If a view needs to use a nondefault layout, you can override it by setting the value in the Razor Page itself.

Listing 17.15   A typical _ViewStart.cshtml file setting the default layout

```
@{
    Layout = "_Layout";
}
```

Any code in the _ViewStart.cshtml file runs before the view executes. Note that _ViewStart .cshtml runs only for Razor Page views; it doesn't run for layouts or partial views. Also note that the names for these special Razor files are enforced and can't be changed by conventions.

> **WARNING** You must use the names _ViewStart.cshtml and _ViewImports.cshtml for the Razor engine to locate and execute them correctly. To apply them to all your app's pages, add them to the root of the Pages folder, not to the Shared subfolder.

You can specify additional _ViewStart.cshtml or _ViewImports.cshtml files to run for a subset of your views by including them in a subfolder in Pages. The files in the subfolders run after the files in the root Pages folder.

Partial views, layouts, and AJAX

This chapter describes using Razor to render full HTML pages server-side, which are then sent to the user's browser in traditional web apps. A common alternative approach when building web apps is to use a JavaScript client-side framework to build an SPA, which renders the HTML client-side in the browser.

One of the technologies SPAs typically use is AJAX (Asynchronous JavaScript and XML), in which the browser sends requests to your ASP.NET Core app without reloading a whole new page. It's also possible to use AJAX requests with apps that use server-side rendering. To do so, you'd use JavaScript to request an update for part of a page.

If you want to use AJAX with an app that uses Razor, you should consider making extensive use of partial views. Then you can expose these via additional Razor Page handlers, as shown in this article: http://mng.bz/vzB1. Using AJAX can reduce the overall amount of data that needs to be sent back and forth between the browser and your app, and it can make your app feel smoother and more responsive, as it requires fewer full-page loads. But using AJAX with Razor can add complexity, especially for larger apps. If you foresee yourself making extensive use of AJAX to build a highly dynamic web app, you might want to consider using minimal APIs or web API controllers with a client-side framework, or consider using Blazor instead.

That concludes our first look at rendering HTML using the Razor templating engine. In the next chapter you'll learn about Tag Helpers and how to use them to build

HTML forms, a staple of modern web applications. Tag Helpers are one of the biggest improvements to Razor in ASP.NET Core over legacy ASP.NET, so getting to grips with them will make editing your views an overall more pleasant experience!

Summary

- Razor is a templating language that allows you to generate dynamic HTML using a mixture of HTML and C#. This provides the power of C# without your having to build up an HTML response manually using strings.
- Razor Pages can pass strongly typed data to a Razor view by setting public properties on the `PageModel`. To access the properties on the view model, the view should declare the model type using the `@model` directive.
- Page handlers can pass key-value pairs to the view using the `ViewData` dictionary. This is useful for implicitly passing shared data to layouts and partial views.
- Razor expressions render C# values to the HTML output using `@` or `@()`. You don't need to include a semicolon after the statement when using Razor expressions.
- Razor code blocks, defined using `@{}`, execute C# without outputting HTML. The C# in Razor code blocks must be complete statements, so it must include semicolons.
- Loops and conditionals can be used to easily generate dynamic HTML in templates, but it's a good idea to limit the number of `if` statements in particular, to keep your views easy to read.
- If you need to render a `string` as raw HTML you can use `Html.Raw`, but do so sparingly; rendering raw user input can create a security vulnerability in your application.
- Tag Helpers allow you to bind your data model to HTML elements, making it easier to generate dynamic HTML while staying editor-friendly.
- You can place HTML common to multiple views in a layout to reduce duplication. The layout will render any content from the child view at the location `@RenderBody` is called.
- Encapsulate commonly used snippets of Razor code in a partial view. A partial view can be rendered using the `<partial />` tag.
- _ViewImports.cshtml can be used to include common directives, such as `@using` statements, in every view.
- _ViewStart.cshtml is called before the execution of each Razor Page and can be used to execute code common to all Razor Pages, such as setting a default layout page. It doesn't execute for layouts or partial views.
- _ViewImports.cshtml and _ViewStart.cshtml are hierarchical. Files in the root folder execute first, followed by files in controller-specific view folders.

18

Building forms with Tag Helpers

This chapter covers

- Building forms easily with Tag Helpers
- Generating URLs with the Anchor Tag Helper
- Using Tag Helpers to add functionality to Razor

In chapter 17 you learned about Razor templates and how to use them to generate the views for your application. By mixing HTML and C#, you can create dynamic applications that can display different data based on the request, the logged-in user, or any other data you can access.

Displaying dynamic data is an important aspect of many web applications, but it's typically only half of the story. As well as needing to display data to the user, you often need the user to be able to submit data back to your application. You can use data to customize the view or to update the application model by saving it to a database, for example. For traditional web applications, this data is usually submitted using an HTML form.

In chapter 16 you learned about model binding, which is how you *accept* the data sent by a user in a request and convert it to C# objects that you can use in your Razor

Pages. You also learned about validation and how important it is to validate the data sent in a request. You used `DataAnnotations` attributes to define the rules associated with your models, as well as associated metadata like the display name for a property.

The final aspect we haven't yet looked at is how to build the HTML forms that users use to send this data in a request. Forms are one of the key ways users will interact with your application in the browser, so it's important they're both correctly defined for your application and user-friendly. ASP.NET Core provides a feature to achieve this, called Tag Helpers.

Tag Helpers are additions to Razor syntax that you use to customize the HTML generated in your templates. Tag Helpers can be added to an otherwise-standard HTML element, such as an `<input>`, to customize its attributes based on your C# model, saving you from having to write boilerplate code. Tag Helpers can also be standalone elements and can be used to generate completely customized HTML.

> **NOTE** Remember that Razor, and therefore Tag Helpers, are for server-side HTML rendering. You can't use Tag Helpers directly in frontend frameworks like Angular and React.

If you've used legacy (.NET Framework) ASP.NET before, Tag Helpers may sound reminiscent of HTML Helpers, which could also be used to generate HTML based on your C# classes. Tag Helpers are the logical successor to HTML Helpers, as they provide a more streamlined syntax than the previous, C#-focused helpers. HTML Helpers are still available in ASP.NET Core, so if you're converting some old templates to ASP.NET Core, you can still use them. But if you're writing new Razor templates, I recommend using only Tag Helpers, as they should cover everything you need. I don't cover HTML Helpers in this book.

In this chapter you'll primarily learn how to use Tag Helpers when building forms. They simplify the process of generating correct element names and IDs so that model binding can occur seamlessly when the form is sent back to your application. To put them into context, you're going to carry on building the currency converter application that you've seen in previous chapters. You'll add the ability to submit currency exchange requests to it, validate the data, and redisplay errors on the form using Tag Helpers to do the legwork for you, as shown in figure 18.1.

As you develop the application, you'll meet the most common Tag Helpers you'll encounter when working with forms. You'll also see how you can use Tag Helpers to simplify other common tasks, such as generating links, conditionally displaying data in your application, and ensuring that users see the latest version of an image file when they refresh their browser.

To start, I'll talk a little about why you need Tag Helpers when Razor can already generate any HTML you like by combining C# and HTML in a file.

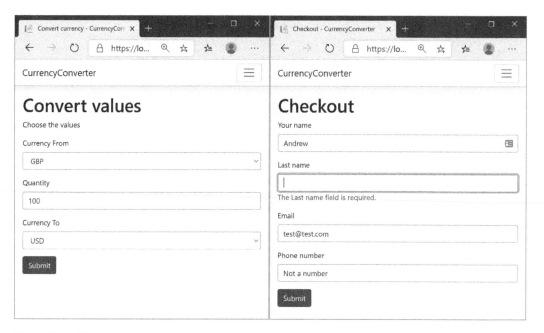

Figure 18.1   The currency converter application forms, built using Tag Helpers. The labels, drop-down lists, input elements, and validation messages are all generated using Tag Helpers.

18.1   *Catering to editors with Tag Helpers*

One of the common complaints about the mixture of C# and HTML in Razor templates is that you can't easily use standard HTML editing tools with them; all the @ and {} symbols in the C# code tend to confuse the editors. Reading the templates can be similarly difficult for people; switching paradigms between C# and HTML can be a bit jarring sometimes.

This arguably wasn't such a problem when Visual Studio was the only supported way to build ASP.NET websites, as it could obviously understand the templates without any problems and helpfully colorize the editor. But with ASP.NET Core going cross-platform, the desire to play nicely with other editors reared its head again.

This was one of the big motivations for Tag Helpers. They integrate seamlessly into the standard HTML syntax by adding what look to be attributes, typically starting with asp-*. They're most often used to generate HTML forms, as shown in the following listing. This listing shows a view from the first iteration of the currency converter application, in which you choose the currencies and quantity to convert.

Listing 18.1   User registration form using Tag Helpers

```
@page
@model ConvertModel
<form method="post">
```
**This is the view for the Razor Page Convert.cshtml.
The Model type is ConvertModel.**

```
<div class="form-group">
    <label asp-for="CurrencyFrom"></label>
    <input class="form-control" asp-for="CurrencyFrom" />
    <span asp-validation-for="CurrencyFrom"></span>
</div>
<div class="form-group">
    <label asp-for="Quantity"></label>
    <input class="form-control" asp-for="Quantity" />
    <span asp-validation-for="Quantity"></span>
</div>
<div class="form-group">
    <label asp-for="CurrencyTo"></label>
    <input class="form-control" asp-for="CurrencyTo" />
    <span asp-validation-for="CurrencyTo"></span>
</div>
<button type="submit" class="btn btn-primary">Submit</button>
</form>
```

Validation messages are written to a span using Tag Helpers.

asp-for on Labels generates the caption for labels based on the view model.

asp-for on Inputs generates the correct type, value, name, and validation attributes for the model.

At first glance, you might not even spot the Tag Helpers, they blend in so well with the HTML! This makes it easy to edit the files with any standard HTML text editor. But don't be concerned that you've sacrificed readability in Visual Studio. As you can see in figure 18.2, elements with Tag Helpers are distinguishable from the standard HTML `<div>` element and the standard HTML `class` attribute on the `<input>` element. The C# properties of the view model being referenced (`CurrencyFrom`, in this case) are also displayed differently from "normal" HTML attributes. And of course you get IntelliSense, as you'd expect. Most other integrated development environments (IDEs) also include syntax highlighting and IntelliSense support.

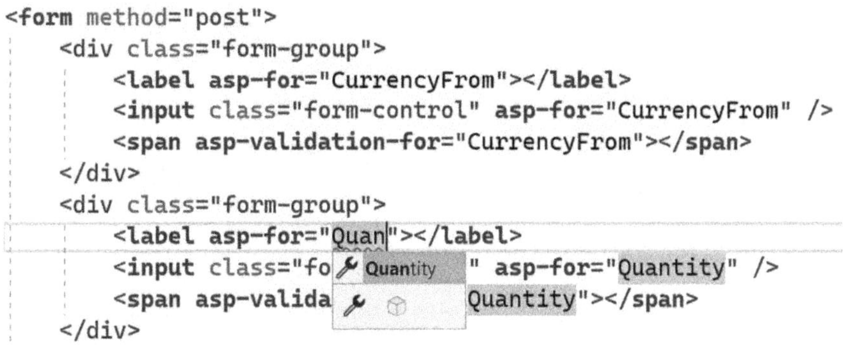

```
<form method="post">
    <div class="form-group">
        <label asp-for="CurrencyFrom"></label>
        <input class="form-control" asp-for="CurrencyFrom" />
        <span asp-validation-for="CurrencyFrom"></span>
    </div>
    <div class="form-group">
        <label asp-for="Quan"></label>
        <input class="fo  🔧 Quantity    " asp-for="Quantity" />
        <span asp-valida  🔧  ⬡      Quantity"></span>
    </div>
```

Figure 18.2 In Visual Studio, Tag Helpers are distinguishable from normal elements by being bold and a different color from standard HTML elements and attributes.

Tag Helpers are extra attributes on standard HTML elements (or new elements entirely) that work by modifying the HTML element they're attached to. They let you easily integrate your server-side values, such as those exposed on your `PageModel`, with the generated HTML.

Notice that listing 18.1 doesn't specify the captions to display in the labels. Instead, you declaratively use `asp-for="CurrencyFrom"` to say "For this `<label>`, use the `CurrencyFrom` property to work out what caption to use." Similarly, for the `<input>` elements, Tag Helpers are used to

- Automatically populate the value from the `PageModel` property.
- Choose the correct `id` and `name`, so that when the form is POSTed back to the Razor Page, the property model-binds correctly.
- Choose the correct input type to display (for example, a `number` input for the `Quantity` property).
- Display any validation errors, as shown in figure 18.3.

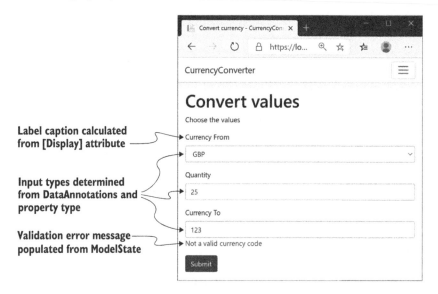

Figure 18.3   Tag Helpers hook into the metadata provided by `DataAnnotations` attributes, as well as the property types themselves. The Validation Tag Helper can even populate error messages based on the `ModelState`, as you saw in chapter 16.

Tag Helpers can perform a variety of functions by modifying the HTML elements they're applied to. This chapter introduces several common Tag Helpers and how to use them, but it's not an exhaustive list. I don't cover all the helpers that come out of the box in ASP.NET Core (there are more coming with every release!), and you can easily create your own, as you'll see in chapter 32. Alternatively, you could use those published by others on NuGet or GitHub.

WebForms flashbacks

For those who used ASP.NET back in the day of WebForms, before the advent of the Model-View-Controller (MVC) pattern for web development, Tag Helpers may be triggering bad memories. Although the `asp-` prefix is somewhat reminiscent of ASP.NET Web Server control definitions, never fear; the two are completely different beasts.

Web Server controls were added directly to a page's backing C# class and had a broad scope that could modify seemingly unrelated parts of the page. Coupled with that, they had a complex life cycle that was hard to understand and debug when things weren't working. The perils of trying to work with that level of complexity haven't been forgotten, and Tag Helpers aren't the same.

Tag Helpers don't have a life cycle; they participate in the rendering of the element to which they're attached, and that's it. They can modify the HTML element they're attached to, but they can't modify anything else on your page, making them conceptually much simpler. An additional capability they bring is the ability to have multiple Tag Helpers acting on a single element—something Web Server controls couldn't easily achieve.

Overall, if you're writing Razor templates, you'll have a much more enjoyable experience if you embrace Tag Helpers as integral to its syntax. They bring a lot of benefits without obvious downsides, and your cross-platform-editor friends will thank you!

18.2   Creating forms using Tag Helpers

In this section you'll learn how to use some of the most useful Tag Helpers: Tag Helpers that work with forms. You'll learn how to use them to generate HTML markup based on properties of your `PageModel`, creating the correct `id` and `name` attributes, and setting the `value` of the element to the model property's value (among other things). This capability significantly reduces the amount of markup you need to write manually.

Imagine you're building the checkout page for the currency converter application, and you need to capture the user's details on the checkout page. In chapter 16 you built a `UserBindingModel` model (shown in listing 18.2), added `DataAnnotations` attributes for validation, and saw how to model-bind it in a POST to a Razor Page. In this chapter you'll see how to create the view for it by exposing the `UserBindingModel` as a property on your `PageModel`.

> **WARNING**   With Razor Pages, you often expose the same object in your view that you use for model binding. When you do this, you must be careful to not include sensitive values (that shouldn't be edited) in the binding model, to prevent mass-assignment attacks on your app. You can read more about these attacks on my blog at http://mng.bz/RXw0.

Listing 18.2   `UserBindingModel` **for creating a user on a checkout page**

```
public class UserBindingModel
{
    [Required]
    [StringLength(100, ErrorMessage = "Maximum length is {1}")]
    [Display(Name = "Your name")]
    public string FirstName { get; set; }

    [Required]
    [StringLength(100, ErrorMessage = "Maximum length is {1}")]
    [Display(Name = "Last name")]
    public string LastName { get; set; }

    [Required]
    [EmailAddress]
    public string Email { get; set; }

    [Phone(ErrorMessage = "Not a valid phone number.")]
    [Display(Name = "Phone number")]
    public string PhoneNumber { get; set; }
}
```

The `UserBindingModel` is decorated with various `DataAnnotations` attributes. In chapter 16 you saw that these attributes are used during model validation when the model is bound to a request, before the page handler is executed. These attributes are also used by the Razor templating language to provide the metadata required to generate the correct HTML when you use Tag Helpers.

You can use the pattern I described in chapter 16, exposing a `UserBindindModel` as an `Input` property of your `PageModel`, to use the model for both model binding and in your Razor view:

```
public class CheckoutModel: PageModel
{
    [BindProperty]
    public UserBindingModel Input { get; set; }
}
```

With the help of the `UserBindingModel` property, Tag Helpers, and a little HTML, you can create a Razor view that lets the user enter their details, as shown in figure 18.4.

The Razor template to generate this page is shown in listing 18.3. This code uses a variety of tag helpers, including

- A Form Tag Helper on the `<form>` element
- Label Tag Helpers on the `<label>`
- Input Tag Helpers on the `<input>`
- Validation Message Tag Helpers on `<span>` validation elements for each property in the `UserBindingModel`

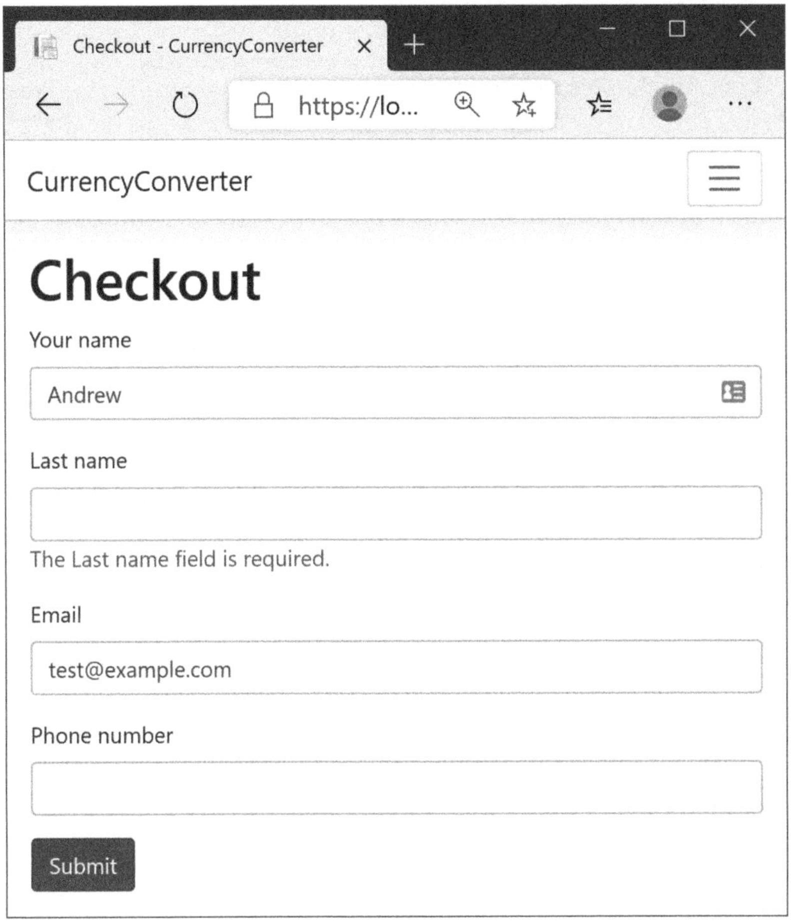

Figure 18.4 The checkout page for an application. The HTML is generated based on a UserBindingModel, using Tag Helpers to render the required element values, input types, and validation messages.

Listing 18.3 Razor template for binding to UserBindingModel on the checkout page

```
@page
@model CheckoutModel
@{
    ViewData["Title"] = "Checkout";
}
<h1>@ViewData["Title"]</h1>
<form asp-page="Checkout">
    <div class="form-group">
        <label asp-for="Input.FirstName"></label>
        <input class="form-control" asp-for="Input.FirstName" />
        <span asp-validation-for="Input.FirstName"></span>
    </div>
```

The CheckoutModel is the PageModel, which exposes a UserBindingModel on the Input property.

Form Tag Helpers use routing to determine the URL the form will be posted to.

The Label Tag Helper uses DataAnnotations on a property to determine the caption to display.

```
    <div class="form-group">
        <label asp-for="Input.LastName"></label>
        <input class="form-control" asp-for="Input.LastName" />
        <span asp-validation-for="Input.LastName"></span>
    </div>
    <div class="form-group">
        <label asp-for="Input.Email"></label>
        <input class="form-control" asp-for="Input.Email" />
        <span asp-validation-for="Input.Email"></span>
    </div>
    <div class="form-group">
        <label asp-for="Input.PhoneNumber"></label>
        <input class="form-control" asp-for="Input.PhoneNumber" />
        <span asp-validation-for="Input.PhoneNumber"></span>
    </div>
    <button type="submit" class="btn btn-primary">Submit</button>
</form>
```

The Input Tag Helper uses DataAnnotations to determine the type of input to generate.

The Validation Tag Helper displays error messages associated with the given property.

You can see the HTML markup that this template produces in listing 18.4, which renders in the browser as you saw in figure 18.4. You can see that each of the HTML elements with a Tag Helper has been customized in the output: the `<form>` element has an `action` attribute, the `<input>` elements have an `id` and `name` based on the name of the referenced property, and both the `<input>` and `<span>` have `data-*` attributes for validation.

Listing 18.4   HTML generated by the Razor template on the checkout page

```
<form action="/Checkout" method="post">
  <div class="form-group">
    <label for="Input_FirstName">Your name</label>
    <input class="form-control" type="text"
      data-val="true" data-val-length="Maximum length is 100"
      id="Input_FirstName" data-val-length-max="100"
      data-val-required="The Your name field is required."
      Maxlength="100" name="Input.FirstName" value="" />
    <span data-valmsg-for="Input.FirstName"
      class="field-validation-valid" data-valmsg-replace="true"></span>
  </div>
  <div class="form-group">
    <label for="Input_LastName">Your name</label>
    <input class="form-control" type="text"
      data-val="true" data-val-length="Maximum length is 100"
      id="Input_LastName" data-val-length-max="100"
      data-val-required="The Your name field is required."
      Maxlength="100" name="Input.LastName" value="" />
    <span data-valmsg-for="Input.LastName"
      class="field-validation-valid" data-valmsg-replace="true"></span>
  </div>
  <div class="form-group">
    <label for="Input_Email">Email</label>
    <input class="form-control" type="email" data-val="true"
      data-val-email="The Email field is not a valid e-mail address."
```

```
      Data-val-required="The Email field is required."
      Id="Input_Email" name="Input.Email" value="" />
    <span class="text-danger field-validation-valid"
      data-valmsg-for="Input.Email" data-valmsg-replace="true"></span>
    </div>
  <div class="form-group">
    <label for="Input_PhoneNumber">Phone number</label>
    <input class="form-control" type="tel" data-val="true"
      data-val-phone="Not a valid phone number." Id="Input_PhoneNumber"
      name="Input.PhoneNumber" value="" />
    <span data-valmsg-for="Input.PhoneNumber"
      class="text-danger field-validation-valid"
      data-valmsg-replace="true"></span>
  </div>
  <button type="submit" class="btn btn-primary">Submit</button>
  <input name="__RequestVerificationToken" type="hidden"
    value="CfDJ8PkYhAINFx1JmYUVIDWbpPyy_TRUNCATED" />
</form>
```

Wow, that's a lot of markup! If you're new to working with HTML, this might all seem a little overwhelming, but the important thing to notice is that you didn't have to write most of it! The Tag Helpers took care of most of the plumbing for you. That's basically Tag Helpers in a nutshell; they simplify the fiddly mechanics of building HTML forms, leaving you to concentrate on the overall design of your application instead of writing boilerplate markup.

> **NOTE** If you're using Razor to build your views, Tag Helpers will make your life easier, but they're entirely optional. You're free to write raw HTML without them or to use the legacy HTML Helpers.

Tag Helpers simplify and abstract the process of HTML generation, but they generally try to do so without getting in your way. If you need the final generated HTML to have a particular attribute, you can add it to your markup. You can see that in the previous listings where class attributes are defined on `<input>` elements, such as `<input class="form-control" asp-for="Input.FirstName" />`. They pass untouched from Razor to the HTML output.

> **TIP** This is different from the way HTML Helpers worked in legacy ASP.NET; HTML helpers often require jumping through hoops to set attributes in the generated markup.

Even better, you can also override attributes that are normally generated by a Tag Helper, like the `type` attribute on an `<input>` element. For example, if the `Favorite-Color` property on your `PageModel` was a `string`, by default Tag Helpers would generate an `<input>` element with `type="text"`. Updating your markup to use the HTML5 `color` picker type is trivial; set the `type` explicitly in your Razor view:

```
<input type="color" asp-for="FavoriteColor" />
```

> **TIP** HTML5 adds a huge number of features, including lots of form elements that you may not have come across before, such as `range` inputs and `color` pickers. You can read about them on the Mozilla Developer Network website at http://mng.bz/qOc1.

For the remainder of section 18.2, you'll build the currency converter Razor templates from scratch, adding Tag Helpers as you find you need them. You'll probably find you use most of the common form Tag Helpers in every application you build, even if it's on a simple login page.

18.2.1   *The Form Tag Helper*

The first thing you need to start building your HTML form is, unsurprisingly, the `<form>` element. In listing 18.3 the `<form>` element was augmented with an `asp-page` Tag Helper attribute:

```
<form asp-page="Checkout">
```

The Tag Helper adds `action` and `method` attributes to the final HTML, indicating which URL the form should be sent to when it's submitted and the HTTP verb to use:

```
<form action="/Checkout" method="post">
```

Setting the `asp-page` attribute allows you to specify a different Razor Page in your application that the form will be posted to when it's submitted. If you omit the `asp-page` attribute, the form will post back to the same URL it was served from. This is common with Razor Pages. You normally handle the result of a form post in the same Razor Page that is used to display it.

> **WARNING** If you omit the `asp-page` attribute, you must add the `method="post"` attribute manually. It's important to add this attribute so the form is sent using the `POST` verb instead of the default `GET` verb. Using `GET` for forms can be a security risk.

The `asp-page` attribute is added by a `FormTagHelper`. This Tag Helper uses the value provided to generate a URL for the `action` attribute, using the URL generation features of routing that I described in chapters 5 and 14.

> **NOTE** Tag Helpers can make multiple attributes available on an element. Think of them like properties on a Tag Helper configuration object. Adding a single `asp-` attribute activates the Tag Helper on the element. Adding more attributes lets you override further default values of its implementation.

The Form Tag Helper makes several other attributes available on the `<form>` element that you can use to customize the generated URL. I hope you'll remember that you can set route values when generating URLs. For example, if you have a Razor Page called Product.cshtml that uses the directive

```
@page "{id}"
```

the full route template for the page would be `"Product/{id}"`. To generate the URL for this page correctly, you must provide the {id} route value. How can you set that value using the Form Tag Helper?

The Form Tag Helper defines an `asp-route-*` wildcard attribute that you can use to set arbitrary route parameters. Set the `*` in the attribute to the route parameter name. For example, to set the `id` route parameter, you'd set the `asp-route-id` value. If the `ProductId` property of your `PageModel` contains the `id` value you require, you could use

```
<form asp-page="Product" asp-route-id="@Model.ProductId">
```

Based on the route template of the Product.cshtml Razor Page (and assuming `ProductId=5` in this example), this would generate the following markup:

```
<form action="/Product/5" method="post">
```

You can add as many `asp-route-*` attributes as necessary to your `<form>` to generate the correct `action` URL. You can also set the Razor Page handler to use the `asp-page-handler` attribute. This ensures that the form POST will be handled by the handler you specify.

> **NOTE** The Form Tag Helper has many additional attributes, such as `asp-action` and `asp-controller`, that you generally won't use with Razor Pages. Those are useful only if you're using MVC controllers with views. In particular, look out for the `asp-route` attribute—this is *not* the same as the `asp-route-*` attribute. The former is used to specify a named route (such as a named minimal API endpoint), and the latter is used to specify the route *values* to use during URL generation.

The main job of the Form Tag Helper is to generate the `action` attribute, but it performs one additional important function: generating a hidden `<input>` field needed to prevent *cross-site request forgery* (CSRF) attacks.

> **DEFINITION** *Cross-site request forgery* (CSRF) attacks are a website exploit that can allow actions to be executed on your website by an unrelated malicious website. You'll learn about them in detail in chapter 29.

You can see the generated hidden `<input>` at the bottom of the `<form>` in listing 18.4; it's named `__RequestVerificationToken` and contains a seemingly random string of characters. This field won't protect you on its own, but I'll describe in chapter 29 how it's used to protect your website. The Form Tag Helper generates it by default, so you generally won't need to worry about it, but if you need to disable it, you can do so by adding `asp-antiforgery="false"` to your `<form>` element.

The Form Tag Helper is obviously useful for generating the `action` URL, but it's time to move on to more interesting elements—those that you can see in your browser!

18.2.2 *The Label Tag Helper*

Every <input> field in your currency converter application needs to have an associated label so the user knows what the <input> is for. You could easily create those yourself, manually typing the name of the field and setting the for attribute as appropriate, but luckily there's a Tag Helper to do that for you.

The Label Tag Helper is used to generate the caption (the visible text) and the for attribute for a <label> element, based on the properties in the PageModel. It's used by providing the name of the property in the asp-for attribute:

```
<label asp-for="FirstName"></label>
```

The Label Tag Helper uses the [Display] DataAnnotations attribute that you saw in chapter 16 to determine the appropriate value to display. If the property you're generating a label for doesn't have a [Display] attribute, the Label Tag Helper uses the name of the property instead. Consider this model in which the FirstName property has a [Display] attribute, but the Email property doesn't:

```
public class UserModel
{
    [Display(Name = "Your name")]
    public string FirstName { get; set; }
    public string Email { get; set; }
}
```

The following Razor

```
<label asp-for="FirstName"></label>
<label asp-for="Email"></label>
```

would generate this HTML:

```
<label for="FirstName">Your name</label>
<label for="Email">Email</label>
```

The inner text inside the <label> element uses the value set in the [Display] attribute, or the property name in the case of the Email property. Also note that the for attribute has been generated with the name of the property. This is a key bonus of using Tag Helpers; it hooks in with the element IDs generated by other Tag Helpers, as you'll see shortly.

> **NOTE**   The for attribute is important for accessibility. It specifies the ID of the element to which the label refers. This is important for users who are using a screen reader, for example, as they can tell what property a form field relates to.

As well as properties on the PageModel, you can also reference sub-properties on child objects. For example, as I described in chapter 16, it's common to create a nested class in a Razor Page, expose that as a property, and decorate it with the `[BindProperty]` attribute:

```
public class CheckoutModel: PageModel
{
    [BindProperty]
    public UserBindingModel Input { get; set; }
}
```

You can reference the `FirstName` property of the `UserBindingModel` by "dotting" into the property as you would in any other C# code. Listing 18.3 shows more examples of this.

```
<label asp-for="Input.FirstName"></label>
<label asp-for="Input.Email"></label>
```

As is typical with Tag Helpers, the Label Tag Helper won't override values that you set yourself. If, for example, you don't want to use the caption generated by the helper, you could insert your own manually. The code

```
<label asp-for="Email">Please enter your Email</label>
```

would generate this HTML:

```
<label for="Email">Please enter your Email</label>
```

As ever, you'll generally have an easier time with maintenance if you stick to the standard conventions and don't override values like this, but the option is there. Next up is a biggie: the Input and Textarea Tag Helpers.

18.2.3 *The Input and Textarea Tag Helpers*

Now you're getting into the meat of your form: the `<input>` elements that handle user input. Given that there's such a wide array of possible input types, there's a variety of ways they can be displayed in the browser. For example, Boolean values are typically represented by a `checkbox` type `<input>` element, whereas integer values would use a `number` type `<input>` element, and a date would use the `date` type, as shown in figure 18.5.

To handle this diversity, the Input Tag Helper is one of the most powerful Tag Helpers. It uses information based on both the type of the property (`bool`, `string`, `int`, and so on) and any `DataAnnotations` attributes applied to it (`[EmailAddress]` and `[Phone]`, among others) to determine the type of the `input` element to generate. The `DataAnnotations` are also used to add `data-val-*` client-side validation attributes to the generated HTML.

Consider the `Email` property from listing 18.2 that was decorated with the `[EmailAddress]` attribute. Adding an `<input>` is as simple as using the `asp-for` attribute:

```
<input asp-for="Input.Email" />
```

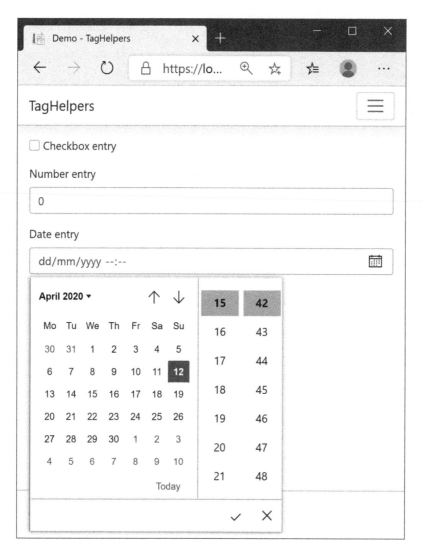

Figure 18.5   Various input element types. The exact way in which each type is displayed varies by browser.

The property is a `string`, so ordinarily the Input Tag Helper would generate an `<input>` with `type="text"`. But the addition of the `[EmailAddress]` attribute provides additional metadata about the property. Consequently, the Tag Helper generates an HTML5 `<input>` with `type="email"`:

```
<input type="email" id="Input_Email" name="Input.Email"
    value="test@example.com" data-val="true"
    data-val-email="The Email Address field is not a valid e-mail address."
    Data-val-required="The Email Address field is required."
    />
```

You can take a whole host of things away from this example. First, the `id` and `name` attributes of the HTML element have been generated from the name of the property. The value of the `id` attribute matches the value generated by the Label Tag Helper in its `for` attribute, `Input_Email`. The value of the `name` attribute preserves the "dot" notation, `Input.Email`, so that model binding works correctly when the field is POSTed to the Razor Page.

Also, the initial `value` of the field has been set to the value currently stored in the property (`"test@example.com"`, in this case). The `type` of the element has also been set to the HTML5 `email` type, instead of using the default `text` type.

Perhaps the most striking addition is the swath of `data-val-*` attributes. These can be used by client-side JavaScript libraries such as jQuery to provide client-side validation of your `DataAnnotations` constraints. Client-side validation provides instant feedback to users when the values they enter are invalid, providing a smoother user experience than can be achieved with server-side validation alone, as I described in chapter 16.

Client-side validation

To enable client-side validation in your application, you need to add some jQuery libraries to your HTML pages. In particular, you need to include the jQuery, jQuery-validation, and jQuery-validation-unobtrusive JavaScript libraries. You can do this in several ways, but the simplest is to include the script files at the bottom of your view using

```
<script src="~/lib/jquery-validation/dist/jquery.validate.min.js"></script>
<script src="~/lib/jquery-validation-unobtrusive/
➥   jquery.validate.unobtrusive.min.js"></script>
```

The default templates include these scripts for you in a handy partial template that you can add to your page in a `Scripts` section. If you're using the default layout and need to add client-side validation to your view, add the following section somewhere on your view:

```
@section Scripts{
    @Html.Partial("_ValidationScriptsPartial")
}
```

This partial view references files in your wwwroot folder. The default layout template includes jQuery itself. If you don't need to use jQuery in your application, you may want to consider a small alternative validation library called *aspnet-client-validation*. I describe why you might consider this library and how to use it in this blog post: http://mng.bz/V1pX.

You can also load these files, whether you're using jQuery or aspnet-client-validation, from a content delivery network (CDN). If you want to take this approach, you should consider scenarios where the CDN is unavailable or compromised, as I discuss in this blog post: http://mng.bz/2e6d.

The Input Tag Helper tries to pick the most appropriate template for a given property based on `DataAnnotations` attributes or the type of the property. Whether this generates the exact `<input>` type you need may depend, to an extent, on your application. As always, you can override the generated type by adding your own type attribute to the element in your Razor template. Table 18.1 shows how some of the common data types are mapped to <input> types and how the data types themselves can be specified.

Table 18.1   Common data types, how to specify them, and the input element type they map to

Data type	How it's specified	Input element type
byte, int, short, long, uint	Property type	number
decimal, double, float	Property type	text
bool	Property type	checkbox
string	Property type, [DataType(DataType.Text)] attribute	text
HiddenInput	[HiddenInput] attribute	hidden
Password	[Password] attribute	password
Phone	[Phone] attribute	tel
EmailAddress	[EmailAddress] attribute	email
Url	[Url] attribute	url
Date	DateTime property type, [DataType(DataType.Date)] attribute	datetime-local

The Input Tag Helper has one additional attribute that can be used to customize the way data is displayed: asp-format. HTML forms are entirely string-based, so when the value of an <input> is set, the Input Tag Helper must take the value stored in the property and convert it to a string. Under the covers, this performs a string.Format() on the property's value, passing in the format string.

The Input Tag Helper uses a default format string for each different data type, but with the asp-format attribute, you can set the specific format string to use. For example, you could ensure that a decimal property, Dec, is formatted to three decimal places with the following code:

```
<input asp-for="Dec" asp-format="{0:0.000}" />
```

If the Dec property had a value of 1.2, this would generate HTML similar to

```
<input type="text" id="Dec" name="Dec" value="1.200">
```

Alternatively, you can define the format to use by adding the [DisplayFormat] attribute to the model property:

```
[DisplayFormat("{0:0.000}")]
public decimal Dec { get; set; }
```

NOTE You may be surprised that `decimal` and `double` types are rendered as `text` fields and not as `number` fields. This is due to several technical reasons, predominantly related to the way different cultures render decimal points and number group separators. Rendering as text avoids errors that would appear only in certain browser-culture combinations.

In addition to the Input Tag Helper, ASP.NET Core provides the Textarea Tag Helper. This works in a similar way, using the `asp-for` attribute, but it's attached to a `<textarea>` element instead:

```
<textarea asp-for="BigtextValue"></textarea>
```

This generates HTML similar to the following. Note that the property value is rendered inside the element, and `data-val-*` validation elements are attached as usual:

```
<textarea data-val="true" id="BigtextValue" name="BigtextValue"
    data-val-length="Maximum length 200." data-val-length-max="200"
    data-val-required="The Multiline field is required." >This is some text,
I'm going to display it
in a text area</textarea>
```

I hope that this section has hammered home how much typing Tag Helpers can cut down on, especially when using them in conjunction with `DataAnnotations` for generating validation attributes. But this is more than reducing the number of keystrokes required; Tag Helpers ensure that the markup generated is correct and has the correct `name`, `id`, and format to automatically bind your binding models when they're sent to the server.

With `<form>`, `<label>`, and `<input>` under your belt, you're able to build most of your currency converter forms. Before we look at displaying validation messages, there's one more element to look at: the `<select>`, or drop-down, input.

18.2.4 *The Select Tag Helper*

As well as `<input>` fields, a common element you'll see on web forms is the `<select>` element, or drop-down lists and list boxes. Your currency converter application, for example, could use a `<select>` element to let you pick which currency to convert from a list.

By default, this element shows a list of items and lets you select one, but there are several variations, as shown in figure 18.6. As well as the normal drop-down list, you could show a list box, add multiselection, or display your list items in groups.

To use `<select>` elements in your Razor code, you'll need to include two properties in your `PageModel`: one property for the list of options to display and one to hold the value (or values) selected. For example, listing 18.5 shows the properties on the `PageModel`

Figure 18.6   Some of the many ways to display `<select>` elements using the Select Tag Helper.

used to create the three leftmost select lists shown in figure 18.6. Displaying groups requires a slightly different setup, as you'll see shortly.

Listing 18.5   View model for displaying select element drop-down lists and list boxes

```
public class SelectListsModel: PageModel
{
    [BindProperty]
    public class InputModel Input { get; set; }

    public IEnumerable<SelectListItem> Items { get; set; }
        = new List<SelectListItem>
    {
        new SelectListItem{Value = "csharp", Text="C#"},
        new SelectListItem{Value = "python", Text= "Python"},
        new SelectListItem{Value = "cpp", Text="C++"},
        new SelectListItem{Value = "java", Text="Java"},
        new SelectListItem{Value = "js", Text="JavaScript"},
        new SelectListItem{Value = "ruby", Text="Ruby"},
    };

    public class InputModel
    {
        public string SelectedValue1 { get; set; }
        public string SelectedValue2 { get; set; }
        public IEnumerable<string> MultiValues { get; set; }
    }
}
```

The InputModel for binding the user's selections to the select boxes

The list of items to display in the select boxes

These properties will hold the values selected by the single-selection select boxes.

To create a multiselect list box, use an IEnumerable<>.

This listing demonstrates several aspects of working with `<select>` lists:

- `SelectedValue1`/`SelectedValue2`—Used to hold the value selected by the user. They're model-bound to the value selected from the drop-down list/list box and used to preselect the correct item when rendering the form.
- `MultiValues`—Used to hold the selected values for a multiselect list. It's an `IEnumerable`, so it can hold more than one selection per `<select>` element.
- `Items`—Provides the list of options to display in the `<select>` elements. Note that the element type must be `SelectListItem`, which exposes the `Value` and `Text` properties, to work with the Select Tag Helper. This isn't part of the `InputModel`, as we don't want to model-bind these items to the request; they would normally be loaded directly from the application model or hardcoded. The order of the values in the `Items` property controls the order of items in the `<select>` list.

NOTE The Select Tag Helper works only with `SelectListItem` elements. That means you'll normally have to convert from an application-specific list set of items (for example, a `List<string>` or `List<MyClass>`) to the UI-centric `List<SelectListItem>`.

The Select Tag Helper exposes the `asp-for` and `asp-items` attributes that you can add to `<select>` elements. As for the Input Tag Helper, the `asp-for` attribute specifies the property in your `PageModel` to bind to. The `asp-items` attribute provides the `IEnumerable <SelectListItem>` to display the available `<option>` elements.

TIP It's common to want to display a list of `enum` options in a `<select>` list. This is so common that ASP.NET Core ships with a helper for generating a `SelectListItem` for any `enum`. If you have an `enum` of the `TEnum` type, you can generate the available options in your view using `asp-items="Html .GetEnumSelectList<TEnum>()"`.

The following listing shows how to display a drop-down list, a single-selection list box, and a multiselection list box. It uses the `PageModel` from the previous listing, binding each `<select>` list value to a different property but reusing the same `Items` list for all of them.

Listing 18.6 Razor template to display a select element in three ways

```
@page
@model SelectListsModel
<select asp-for="Input.SelectedValue1"
    asp-items="Model.Items"></select>
<select asp-for="Input.SelectedValue2"
    asp-items="Model.Items" size="4"></select>
<select asp-for="Input.MultiValues"
    asp-items="Model.Items"></select>
```

Creates a standard drop-down select list by binding to a standard property in asp-for

Creates a single-select list box of height 4 by providing the standard HTML size attribute

Creates a multiselect list box by binding to an IEnumerable property in asp-for

I hope you can see that the Razor for generating a drop-down `<select>` list is almost identical to the Razor for generating a multiselect `<select>` list. The Select Tag Helper takes care of adding the `multiple` HTML attribute to the generated output if the property it's binding to is an `IEnumerable`.

> **WARNING** The `asp-for` attribute *must not* include the `Model.` prefix. The `asp-items` attribute, on the other hand, *must* include it if referencing a property on the `PageModel`. The `asp-items` attribute can also reference other C# items, such as objects stored in `ViewData`, but using a `PageModel` property is the best approach.

You've seen how to bind three types of select lists so far, but the one I haven't yet covered from figure 18.6 is how to display groups in your list boxes using `<optgroup>` elements. Luckily, nothing needs to change in your Razor code; you have to update only how you define your `SelectListItem`s.

The `SelectListItem` object defines a `Group` property that specifies the `SelectListGroup` the item belongs to. The following listing shows how you could create two groups and assign each list item to a "dynamic" or "static" group, using a `PageModel` similar to that shown in listing 18.5. The final list item, C#, isn't assigned to a group, so it will be displayed as normal, without an `<optgroup>`.

Listing 18.7 Adding `Groups` to `SelectListItems` to create `optgroup` elements

```
public class SelectListsModel: PageModel          Holds the selected
{                                                 values where
    [BindProperty]                                multiple selections
    public IEnumerable<string> SelectedValues { get; set; }  ◁──  are allowed
    public IEnumerable<SelectListItem> Items { get; set; }

    public SelectListsModel()     ◁────  Initializes the list items in the constructor
    {
        var dynamic = new SelectListGroup { Name = "Dynamic" };
        var @static = new SelectListGroup { Name = "Static" };     Creates a single
        Items = new List<SelectListItem>                           instance of each
        {                                                          group to pass to
            new SelectListItem {                                   SelectListItems
                Value= "js",
                Text="Javascript",
                Group = dynamic      ◁─┐
            },
            new SelectListItem {
                Value= "cpp",          Sets the
                Text="C++",            appropriate
                Group = @static   ◁─   group for each
            },                         SelectListItem
            new SelectListItem {
                Value= "python",
                Text="Python",
                Group = dynamic    ◁─┘
            },
```

```
            new SelectListItem {
                Value= "csharp",
                Text="C#",
            }
        };
    }
}
```

> **If a SelectListItem doesn't have a Group, it won't be added to an `<optgroup>`.**

With this in place, the Select Tag Helper generates `<optgroup>` elements as necessary when rendering the Razor to HTML. The Razor template

```
@page
@model SelectListsModel
<select asp-for="SelectedValues" asp-items="Model.Items"></select>
```

would be rendered to HTML as follows:

```
<select id="SelectedValues" name="SelectedValues" multiple="multiple">
    <optgroup label="Dynamic">
        <option value="js">JavaScript</option>
        <option value="python">Python</option>
    </optgroup>
    <optgroup label="Static">
        <option value="cpp">C++</option>
    </optgroup>
    <option value="csharp">C#</option>
</select>
```

Another common requirement when working with `<select>` elements is to include an option in the list that indicates that no value has been selected, as shown in figure 18.7. Without this extra option, the default `<select>` drop-down will always have a value, and it will default to the first item in the list.

You can achieve this in one of two ways: you could add the "not selected" option to the available `SelectListItems`, or you could add the option to the Razor manually, such as by using

```
<select asp-for="SelectedValue" asp-items="Model.Items">
    <option Value="">**Not selected**</option>
</select>
```

This will add an extra `<option>` at the top of your `<select>` element, with a blank `Value` attribute, allowing you to provide a "no selection" option for the user.

> **TIP** Adding a "no selection" option to a `<select>` element is so common that you might want to create a partial view to encapsulate this logic.

With the Input Tag Helper and Select Tag Helper under your belt, you should be able to create most of the forms that you'll need. You have all the pieces you need to create the currency converter application now, with one exception.

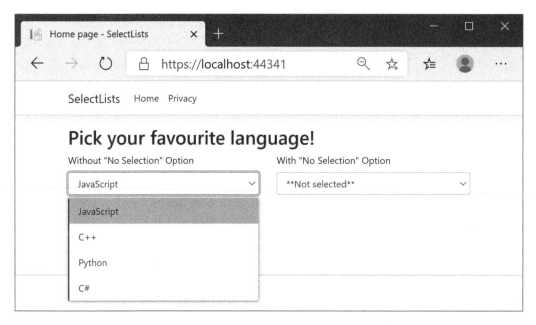

Figure 18.7   Without a "not selected" option, the `<select>` element will always have a value. This may not be the behavior you desire if you don't want an `<option>` to be selected by default.

Remember that whenever you accept input from a user, you should always validate the data. The Validation Tag Helpers provide a way for you to display model validation errors to the user on your form without having to write a lot of boilerplate markup.

18.2.5   *The Validation Message and Validation Summary Tag Helpers*

In section 18.2.3 you saw that the Input Tag Helper generates the necessary `data-val-*` validation attributes on form input elements themselves. But you also need somewhere to display the validation messages. This can be achieved for each property in your view model using the Validation Message Tag Helper applied to a `<span>` by using the `asp-validation-for` attribute:

```
<span asp-validation-for="Email"></span>
```

When an error occurs during client-side validation, the appropriate error message for the referenced property is displayed in the `<span>`, as shown in figure 18.8. This `<span>` element is also used to show appropriate validation messages if server-side validation fails when the form is redisplayed.

Email

The Email field is required.

Figure 18.8   Validation messages can be shown in an associated `<span>` by using the Validation Message Tag Helper.

Any errors associated with the `Email` property stored in `ModelState` are rendered in the element body, and the appropriate attributes to hook into jQuery validation are added:

```
<span class="field-validation-valid" data-valmsg-for="Email"
  data-valmsg-replace="true">The Email Address field is required.</span>
```

The validation error shown in the element is removed or replaced when the user updates the `Email` `<input>` field and client-side validation is performed.

NOTE For more details on `ModelState` and server-side validation, see chapter 16.

As well as display validation messages for individual properties, you can display a summary of all the validation messages in a `<div>` with the Validation Summary Tag Helper, shown in figure 18.9. This renders a `<ul>` containing a list of the `ModelState` errors.

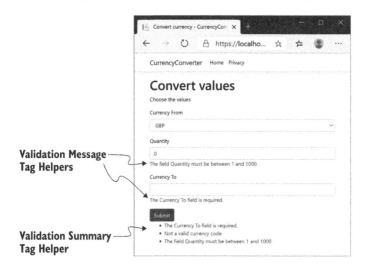

Figure 18.9 Form showing validation errors. The Validation Message Tag Helper is applied to `<span>`, close to the associated input. The Validation Summary Tag Helper is applied to a `<div>`, normally at the top or bottom of the form.

The Validation Summary Tag Helper is applied to a `<div>` using the `asp-validation-summary` attribute and providing a `ValidationSummary` enum value, such as

```
<div asp-validation-summary="All"></div>
```

The `ValidationSummary` enum controls which values are displayed, and it has three possible values:

- `None`—Don't display a summary. (I don't know why you'd use this.)
- `ModelOnly`—Display only errors that are not associated with a property.
- `All`—Display errors associated with either a property or the model.

The Validation Summary Tag Helper is particularly useful if you have errors associated with your page that aren't specific to a single property. These can be added to the model state by using a blank key, as shown in listing 18.8. In this example, the property validation passed, but we provide additional model-level validation to check that we aren't trying to convert a currency to itself.

Listing 18.8   Adding model-level validation errors to the `ModelState`

```
public class ConvertModel : PageModel
{
    [BindProperty]
    public InputModel Input { get; set; }

    [HttpPost]
    public IActionResult OnPost()
    {
        if(Input.CurrencyFrom == Input.CurrencyTo)        ⟵──  Can't convert
        {                                                       currency to itself
            ModelState.AddModelError(                           Adds model-level error, not
                string.Empty,                                   tied to a specific property,
                "Cannot convert currency to itself");           by using empty key
        }
        if (!ModelState.IsValid)
        {                                       If there are any property-level or
            return Page();                      model-level errors, displays them
        }

        //store the valid values somewhere etc
        return RedirectToPage("Checkout");
    }
}
```

Without the Validation Summary Tag Helper, the model-level error would still be added if the user used the same currency twice, and the form would be redisplayed. Unfortunately, there would have been no visual cue to the user indicating why the form did not submit. Obviously, that's a problem! By adding the Validation Summary Tag Helper, the model-level errors are shown to the user so they can correct the problem, as shown in figure 18.10.

> **NOTE** For simplicity, I added the validation check to the page handler. An alternative approach would be to create a custom validation attribute or use `IValidatableObject` (described in chapter 7). That way, your handler stays lean and sticks to the single- responsibility principle (SRP). You'll see how to create a custom validation attribute in chapter 32.

This section covered most of the common Tag Helpers available for working with forms, including all the pieces you need to build the currency converter forms. They should give you everything you need to get started building forms in your own applications. But forms aren't the only area in which Tag Helpers are useful; they're generally applicable any time you need to mix server-side logic with HTML generation.

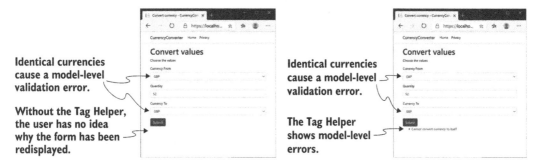

Figure 18.10   Model-level errors are only displayed by the Validation Summary Tag Helper. Without one, users won't have any indication that there were errors on the form and so won't be able to correct them.

One such example is generating links to other pages in your application using routing-based URL generation. Given that routing is designed to be fluid as you refactor your application, keeping track of the exact URLs the links should point to would be a bit of a maintenance nightmare if you had to do it by hand. As you might expect, there's a Tag Helper for that: the Anchor Tag Helper.

18.3   Generating links with the Anchor Tag Helper

In chapters 6 and 15, I showed how you could generate URLs for links to other pages in your application using `LinkGenerator` and `IUrlHelper`. Views are another common place where you need to generate links, normally by way of an `<a>` element with an `href` attribute pointing to the appropriate URL.

In this section I show how you can use the Anchor Tag Helper to generate the URL for a given Razor Page using routing. Conceptually, this is almost identical to the way the Form Tag Helper generates the `action` URL, as you saw in section 18.2.1. For the most part, using the Anchor Tag Helper is identical too; you provide `asp-page` and `asp-page-handler` attributes, along with `asp-route-*` attributes as necessary. The default Razor Page templates use the Anchor Tag Helper to generate the links shown in the navigation bar using the code in the following listing.

Listing 18.9   Using the Anchor Tag Helper to generate URLs in _Layout.cshtml

```
<ul class="navbar-nav flex-grow-1">
    <li class="nav-item">
        <a class="nav-link text-dark"
            asp-area="" asp-page="/Index">Home</a>
    </li>
    <li class="nav-item">
        <a class="nav-link text-dark"
            asp-area="" asp-page="/Privacy">Privacy</a>
    </li>
</ul>
```

As you can see, each `<a>` element has an `asp-page` attribute. This Tag Helper uses the routing system to generate an appropriate URL for the `<a>`, resulting in the following markup:

```
<ul class="nav navbar-nav">
    <li class="nav-item">
        <a class="nav-link text-dark" href="/">Home</a>
    </li>
    <li class="nav-item">
        <a class="nav-link text-dark" href="/Privacy">Privacy</a>
    </li>t
</ul>
```

The URLs use default values where possible, so the `Index` Razor Page generates the simple `"/"` URL instead of `"/Index"`.

If you need more control over the URL generated, the Anchor Tag Helper exposes several additional properties you can set, which are used during URL generation. The attributes most often used with Razor Pages are

- `asp-page`—Sets the Razor Page to execute.
- `asp-page-handler`—Sets the Razor Page handler to execute.
- `asp-area`—Sets the area route parameter to use. Areas can be used to provide an additional layer of organization to your application.[1]
- `asp-host`—If set, the generated link points to the provided host and generates an absolute URL instead of a relative URL.
- `asp-protocol`—Sets whether to generate an http or https link. If set, it generates an absolute URL instead of a relative URL.
- `asp-route-*`—Sets the route parameters to use during generation. Can be added multiple times for different route parameters.

By using the Anchor Tag Helper and its attributes, you generate your URLs using the routing system, as described in chapters 5 and 14. This reduces the duplication in your code by removing the hardcoded URLs you'd otherwise need to embed in all your views.

If you find yourself writing repetitive code in your markup, chances are someone has written a Tag Helper to help with it. The Append Version Tag Helper in the following section is a great example of using Tag Helpers to reduce the amount of fiddly code required.

18.4   *Cache-busting with the Append Version Tag Helper*

A common problem with web development, both when developing and when an application goes into production, is ensuring that browsers are all using the latest files. For performance reasons, browsers often cache files locally and reuse them for subsequent requests rather than calling your application every time a file is requested.

---

[1] I don't cover areas in detail in this book. They're an optional aspect of MVC that are often only used on large projects. You can read about them here: http://mng.bz/3X64.

Normally, this is great. Most of the static assets in your site rarely change, so caching them significantly reduces the burden on your server. Think of an image of your company logo. How often does that change? If every page shows your logo, caching the image in the browser makes a lot of sense.

But what happens if it *does* change? You want to make sure users get the updated assets as soon as they're available. A more critical requirement might be if the JavaScript files associated with your site change. If users end up using cached versions of your JavaScript, they might see strange errors, or your application might appear broken to them.

This conundrum is a common one in web development, and one of the most common ways for handling it is to use a cache-busting query string.

> **DEFINITION**   A *cache-busting query string* adds a query parameter to a URL, such as ?v=1. Browsers will cache the response and use it for subsequent requests to the URL. When the resource changes, the query string is also changed, such as to ?v=2. Browsers will see this as a request for a new resource and make a fresh request.

The biggest problem with this approach is that it requires you to update a URL every time an image, CSS, or JavaScript file changes. This is a manual step that requires updating every place the resource is referenced, so it's inevitable that mistakes are made. Tag Helpers to the rescue! When you add a `<script>`, `<img>`, or `<link>` element to your application, you can use Tag Helpers to automatically generate a cache-busting query string:

```
<script src="~/js/site.js" asp-append-version="true"></script>
```

The `asp-append-version` attribute will load the file being referenced and generate a unique hash based on its contents. This is then appended as a unique query string to the resource URL:

```
<script src="/js/site.js?v=EWaMeWsJBYWmL2g_KkgXZQ5nPe"></script>
```

As this value is a hash of the file contents, it remains unchanged as long as the file isn't modified, so the file will be cached in users' browsers. But if the file *is* modified, the hash of the contents changes and so does the query string. This ensures that browsers are always served the most up-to-date files for your application without your having to worry about updating every URL manually whenever you change a file.

So far in this chapter you've seen how to use Tag Helpers for forms, link generation, and cache busting. You can also use Tag Helpers to conditionally render different markup depending on the current environment. This uses a technique you haven't seen yet, where the Tag Helper is declared as a completely separate element.

18.5   *Using conditional markup with the Environment Tag Helper*

In many cases, you want to render different HTML in your Razor templates depending on whether your website is running in a development or production environment. For example, in development you typically want your JavaScript and CSS assets to be verbose and easy to read, but in production you'd process these files to make them as small as possible. Another example might be the desire to apply a banner to the application when it's running in a testing environment, which is removed when you move to production, as shown in figure 18.11.

Figure 18.11   The warning banner will be shown whenever you're running in a testing environment, to make it easy to distinguish from production.

You've already seen how to use C# to add if statements to your markup, so it would be perfectly possible to use this technique to add an extra div to your markup when the current environment has a given value. If we assume that the env variable contains the current environment, you could use something like this:

```
@if(env == "Testing" || env == "Staging")
{
    <div class="warning">You are currently on a testing environment</div>
}
```

There's nothing wrong with this, but a better approach would be to use the Tag Helper paradigm to keep your markup clean and easy to read. Luckily, ASP.NET Core comes with the EnvironmentTagHelper, which can be used to achieve the same result in a slightly clearer way:

```
<environment include="Testing,Staging">
    <div class="warning">You are currently on a testing environment</div>
</environment>
```

This Tag Helper is a little different from the others you've seen before. Instead of augmenting an existing HTML element using an asp- attribute, the *whole element* is the Tag Helper. This Tag Helper is completely responsible for generating the markup, and it uses an attribute to configure it.

Functionally, this Tag Helper is identical to the C# markup (where the env variable contains the hosting environment, as described in chapter 10), but it's more declarative in its function than the C# alternative. You're obviously free to use either approach, but personally I like the HTML-like nature of Tag Helpers.

We've reached the end of this chapter on Tag Helpers, and with it, we've finished our main look at building traditional web applications that display HTML to users. In the last part of the book, we'll revisit Razor templates when you learn how to build custom components like custom Tag Helpers and view components. For now, you have everything you need to build complex Razor layouts; the custom components can help tidy up your code down the line.

Part 3 of this book has been a whistle-stop tour of how to build Razor Page applications with ASP.NET Core. You now have the basic building blocks to start making server-rendered ASP.NET Core applications. Before we move on to discussing security in part 4 of this book, I'll take a couple of chapters to discuss building apps with MVC controllers.

I've talked about MVC controllers a lot in passing, but in chapter 19 you'll learn why I recommend Razor Pages over MVC controllers for server-rendered apps. Nevertheless, there are some situations for which MVC controllers make sense.

Summary

- With Tag Helpers, you can bind your data model to HTML elements, making it easier to generate dynamic HTML while remaining editor friendly.

- As with Razor in general, Tag Helpers are for server-side rendering of HTML only. You can't use them directly in frontend frameworks, such as Angular or React.

- Tag Helpers can be standalone elements or can attach to existing HTML using attributes. This lets you both customize HTML elements and add entirely new elements.

- Tag Helpers can customize the elements they're attached to, add additional attributes, and customize how they're rendered to HTML. This can greatly reduce the amount of markup you need to write.

- Tag Helpers can expose multiple attributes on a single element. This makes it easier to configure the Tag Helper, as you can set multiple, separate values.

- You can add the asp-page and asp-page-handler attributes to the <form> element to set the action URL using the URL generation feature of Razor Pages.

- You specify route values to use during routing with the Form Tag Helper using asp-route-* attributes. These values are used to build the final URL or are passed as query data.

- The Form Tag Helper also generates a hidden field that you can use to prevent CSRF attacks. This is added automatically and is an important security measure.

- You can attach the Label Tag Helper to a `<label>` using `asp-for`. It generates an appropriate `for` attribute and caption based on the `[Display]` DataAnnotation attribute and the `PageModel` property name.

- The Input Tag Helper sets the `type` attribute of an `<input>` element to the appropriate value based on a bound property's `Type` and any DataAnnotation attributes applied to it. It also generates the `data-val-*` attributes required for client-side validation. This significantly reduces the amount of HTML code you need to write.

- To enable client-side validation, you must add the necessary JavaScript files to your view for jQuery validation and unobtrusive validation.

- The Select Tag Helper can generate drop-down `<select>` elements as well as list boxes, using the `asp-for` and `asp-items` attributes. To generate a multiselect `<select>` element, bind the element to an `IEnumerable` property on the view model. You can use these approaches to generate several different styles of select box.

- The items supplied in `asp-for` must be an `IEnumerable<SelectListItem>`. If you try to bind another type, you'll get a compile-time error in your Razor view.

- You can generate an `IEnumerable<SelectListItem>` for an enum `TEnum` using the `Html.GetEnumSelectList<TEnum>()` helper method. This saves you having to write the mapping code yourself.

- The Select Tag Helper generates `<optgroup>` elements if the items supplied in `asp-for` have an associated `SelectListGroup` on the `Group` property. Groups can be used to separate items in select lists.

- Any extra additional `<option>` elements added to the Razor markup are passed through to the final HTML unchanged. You can use these additional elements to easily add a "no selection" option to the `<select>` element.

- The Validation Message Tag Helper is used to render the client- and server-side validation error messages for a given property. This gives important feedback to your users when elements have errors. Use the `asp-validation-for` attribute to attach the Validation Message Tag Helper to a `<span>`.

- The Validation Summary Tag Helper displays validation errors for the model, as well as for individual properties. You can use model-level properties to display additional validation that doesn't apply to just one property. Use the `asp-validation-summary` attribute to attach the Validation Summary Tag Helper to a `<div>`.

- You can generate `<a>` URLs using the Anchor Tag Helper. This helper uses routing to generate the `href` URL using `asp-page`, `asp-page-handler`, and `asp-route-*` attributes, giving you the full power of routing.

- You can add the `asp-append-version` attribute to `<link>`, `<script>`, and `<img>` elements to provide cache-busting capabilities based on the file's contents. This ensures users cache files for performance reasons, yet still always get the latest version of files.
- You can use the Environment Tag Helper to conditionally render different HTML based on the app's current execution environment. You can use this to render completely different HTML in different environments if you wish.

Creating a website
with MVC controllers

This chapter covers

- Creating a Model-View-Controller (MVC) application
- Choosing between Razor Pages and MVC controllers
- Returning Razor views from MVC controllers

In this book I've focused on Razor Pages over MVC controllers for server-rendered HTML apps, as I consider Razor Pages to be the preferable paradigm in most cases. In this chapter we dig a bit more into exactly why I consider Razor Pages to be the right choice and take a brief look at the alternative.

In section 19.2 you'll create a default MVC application using a template so you can familiarize yourself with the general project layout of an MVC application. We'll look at some of the differences between an MVC application and a Razor Pages app, as well as the many similarities.

Next, I'll dig into why I find Razor Pages to be a preferable application model compared with MVC controllers. You'll learn about the improved developer ergonomics of Razor Pages compared with MVC controllers, as well as the cases in which MVC controllers are nevertheless the right choice.

In section 19.4 you'll learn about rendering Razor views using MVC controllers. You'll learn how the MVC framework relies on conventions to locate view files and how to override these by selecting a specific Razor view template to render. Finally, you'll see the full view selection algorithm in all its glory.

19.1   Razor Pages vs. MVC in ASP.NET Core

In this book I focus on Razor Pages, but I have also mentioned that Razor Pages use the ASP.NET Core MVC framework behind the scenes and that you can choose to use the MVC framework directly if you wish. Additionally, if you're creating an API for working with mobile or client-side apps, and you don't want to (or can't) use minimal APIs, you may well use the MVC framework directly by creating web API controllers.

> **NOTE**   I look at how to build web APIs with the MVC framework in chapter 20.

So what are the differences between Razor Pages and the MVC framework, and when should you choose one or the other?

If you're new to ASP.NET Core, the answer is pretty simple: use Razor Pages for server-side rendered applications, and use minimal APIs (or web API controllers) for building APIs. There are nuances to this advice, which I discuss in section 19.5, but that distinction will serve you well for now.

> **Naming is hard, again**
>
> Microsoft have a long history of creating a framework and naming it after a generic concept: MVC, Web Forms, Web Pages, Multi-platform App UI, and so on. It's frankly incredible that Blazor survived! Web API is no different.
>
> In legacy ASP.NET, Microsoft created a web API framework, which was similar in *design* to the existing MVC framework, but also was not interoperable. You therefore had *MVC controllers*, which were controller classes used with the MVC framework to generate HTML, and *web API controllers*, which were controller classes used with the web API framework, to generate JavaScript Object Notation (JSON) or Extensible Markup Language (XML).
>
> In ASP.NET Core, Microsoft merged these two parallel stacks into a single ASP.NET Core MVC framework. Controllers in ASP.NET Core can generate both HTML and JSON/XML; there is no separation. Nevertheless, it's common for a controller to be dedicated to either HTML generation *or* JSON/XML. For that reason, the names *MVC controller* and *web API controller* are often used to refer to the two general types of controller: MVC for HTML and web API for JSON/XML.
>
> In this book when I refer to web API controllers, I'm talking about standard ASP.NET Core controllers that are generating API responses. This may be described elsewhere as a web API application using MVC controllers or as a web API application. All three cases refer to the same concept: an HTTP API built using ASP.NET Core controllers.

Before we can get to comparisons, though, we should take a brief look at the ASP.NET Core MVC framework itself. Understanding the similarities and differences between MVC controllers and Razor Pages can be useful, as you'll likely find a use for MVC controllers at some point, even if you use Razor Pages most of the time.

19.2   *Your first MVC web application*

In this section you'll learn how to create your first MVC web application, which server-renders HTML pages using MVC controllers and Razor views. We use a template to create the app and compare the generated code to see how it differs from a Razor Pages application.

We'll again use a template to get an application up and running quickly. This time we'll use the ASP.NET Core Web App (Model-View-Controller) template. To create the application in Visual Studio, follow these steps:

1 Choose **File** > **New**.
2 In the **Create a new project** dialog box, select the **ASP.NET Core Web App (Model-View-Controller)** template.
3 In the **Configure your new project** dialog box, enter your project name and review the **Additional information** box, shown in figure 19.1.
4 Choose **Create**. If you're using the command-line interface (CLI), you can create a similar template using dotnet new mvc.

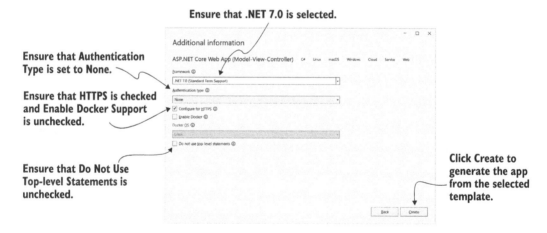

Figure 19.1   The Additional information screen for the MVC template. This screen follows on from the Configure your new project dialog box and lets you customize the template that generates your application.

The MVC template configures the ASP.NET Core project to use MVC controllers with Razor views. As always, you configure your app to use MVC controllers in Program.cs, as shown in listing 19.1. If you compare this template with your Razor Pages projects, you'll see that the web API project uses AddControllersWithViews() instead of AddRazorPages(). The MVC controllers are mapped as endpoints by calling MapControllerRoute(). This method maps all the controllers in your app and configures a default conventional route for them. We discussed conventional routing in chapter 14, and I will discuss it again shortly.

Listing 19.1 Program.cs for the default MVC project

```
WebApplicationBuilder builder = WebApplication.CreateBuilder(args);

builder.Services.AddControllersWithViews();

WebApplication app = builder.Build();

if (!app.Environment.IsDevelopment())
{
    app.UseExceptionHandler("/Home/Error");
    app.UseHsts();
}

app.UseHttpsRedirection();
app.UseStaticFiles();
app.UseRouting();
app.UseAuthorization();

app.MapControllerRoute(
    name: "default",
    pattern: "{controller=Home}/{action=Index}/{id?}");

app.Run();
```

> **AddControllersWithViews adds the services for MVC controllers with Razor Views.**

> **The exception handler path differs from the default Razor Pages path of /Error.**

> **Adds all MVC controllers in your application using conventional routing**

> **Defines the default conventional route pattern**

Much of the configuration for an MVC application is the same as for Razor Pages. The middleware configuration is essentially identical, which isn't that surprising considering that MVC and Razor Pages are the same type of application: a server-rendered app returning HTML. The main difference, as you'll see in section 19.3, is in the project structure.

Before we go any further, run the MVC application by pressing F5 in Visual Studio or by running `dotnet run` in the project folder. The application should look remarkably familiar; it's essentially identical to the Razor Pages version of the application you created in chapter 13, as shown in figure 19.2.

The output of the MVC app is identical to the default Razor Pages app, but the infrastructure used to generate the response differs. Instead of a Razor Page `PageModel` and page handler, MVC uses the concept of *controllers* and *action methods*. The following listing shows the `HomeController` class from the default application. Each nonabstract, public method is an action that runs in response to a request.

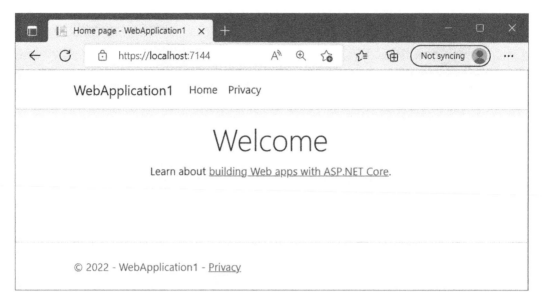

Figure 19.2   The default MVC application. The resulting application is identical to the Razor Pages equivalent created in chapter 13.

You can ensure that a candidate method is not treated as an action method by decorating it with the [NonAction] attribute.

Listing 19.2   The HomeController for the default MVC app

```
public class HomeController : Controller                    ◁──────┐  MVC Controllers
{                                                                  │  often inherit from the
    private readonly ILogger<HomeController> _logger;             │  Controller base class.
    public HomeController(Ilogger<HomeController> logger)
    {
        _logger = logger;
    }
                                          Action methods are the endpoints
    public IActionResult Index()     ◁───┘ that run in response to requests.
    {
        return View();          ◁───── Returning View()
    }                                  renders a Razor view.

    public IActionResult Privacy()
    {
        return View();
    }                                    You can apply filters to actions, as
                                         you'll learn in chapters 21 and 22.
    [ResponseCache(Duration = 0, Location = ResponseCacheLocation.None,
        NoStore = true)]
    public IActionResult Error()
    {
        return View(new ErrorViewModel    Any object returned with View is passed
        {                                 ↓ to the Razor view as a view model.
```

```
            RequestId = Activity.Current?.Id
                ?? HttpContext.TraceIdentifier
        });
    }
}
```

> Any object returned with View is passed to the Razor view as a view model.

DEFINITION An *action* (or *action method*) is a method that runs in response to a request. An *MVC controller* is a class that contains one or more logically grouped action methods.

Each of the three action methods calls `View()` and returns the result. This returns a `ViewResult`, which instructs the MVC framework to render a Razor view for the action. You'll learn more about this process in section 19.4. The `Error` action method also sets an object in the call to `View()`. This is the view model, which is passed to the Razor view when it's rendered.

> **NOTE** MVC controllers use explicit *view model*s to pass data to a Razor view rather than expose the data as properties on themselves (as Razor Pages do with page models). This provides a clearer separation between the various "models" than in Razor Pages, though both cases use the same general MVC design pattern.

Another big difference between Razor Pages and MVC controllers is that MVC controllers typically use conventional routing, as opposed to the explicit routing used by Razor Pages. I touched on conventional routing and how it differs from explicit routing in chapter 14, but you can see it in action in this MVC application.

Conventional routing defines one or more route template patterns, which are used for all the MVC controllers in your app. The default route template, shown in listing 19.1, consists of three optional segments:

```
"{controller=Home}/{action=Index}/{id?}"
```

Conventional routes must describe which controller and action should run for any given request, so they must include `controller` and `action` route parameters at a minimum. When a request is received, ASP.NET Core matches the route template and from that calculates which MVC controller and action method to use. For example, the default route would match all the following URLs:

- `/Home/Privacy`–Executes the `HomeController.Privacy()` action
- `/Home`–Executes the `HomeController.Index()` action
- `/customer/list`–Executes the `CustomerController.List()` action
- `/products/view/123`–Executes the `ProductsController.View()` action, with the route parameter id=123

With conventional routing, a single route template maps to multiple endpoints, whereas in explicit routing, one or more route templates typically map to a single endpoint. There are subtleties in both cases, but in general conventional routing is terser, and explicit routing is more expressive.

NOTE   As I mentioned in chapter 14, I won't discuss conventional routing any further in this book. It is often used only with MVC controllers, but even then, I generally prefer to use explicit routing with attributes. I describe how to use attribute routing in chapter 20 when I discuss web API controllers.

Once you've familiarized yourself with a basic MVC application you will likely have spotted many of the similarities and differences between the MVC framework and Razor Pages. In the next section we look at one aspect of this: MVC controllers and their Razor Page PageModel equivalent.

19.3   *Comparing an MVC controller with a Razor Page PageModel*

In chapter 13 we looked at the MVC design pattern, and at how it applies to Razor Pages in ASP.NET Core. Perhaps unsurprisingly, you can use MVC controllers with the MVC design pattern in almost exactly the same way.

As mentioned in section 19.2, MVC controllers and actions are analogous to their Razor Pages counterparts of `PageModel` and page handlers. Figure 19.3 makes this clearer; it is the MVC controller equivalent of the Razor Pages version from chapter 13.

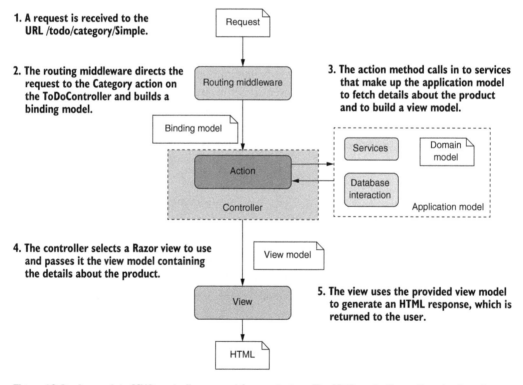

1. A request is received to the URL /todo/category/Simple.

2. The routing middleware directs the request to the Category action on the ToDoController and builds a binding model.

3. The action method calls in to services that make up the application model to fetch details about the product and to build a view model.

4. The controller selects a Razor view to use and passes it the view model containing the details about the product.

5. The view uses the provided view model to generate an HTML response, which is returned to the user.

Figure 19.3   A complete MVC controller request for a category. The MVC controller pattern is almost identical to that of Razor Pages, which was shown in figure 13.12. The controller is equivalent to a Razor Page, and the action is equivalent to a page handler.

In chapter 13 I showed a simple Razor Page `PageModel` for displaying all the to-do items in a given category in a to-do list application. The following listing reproduces that Razor Pages code from listing 13.5 for your convenience.

Listing 19.3   A Razor Page for viewing all to-do items in a given category

```
public class CategoryModel : PageModel
{
    private readonly ToDoService _service;
    public CategoryModel(ToDoService service)
    {
        _service = service;
    }

    public ActionResult OnGet(string category)
    {
        Items = _service.GetItemsForCategory(category);
        return Page();
    }

    public List<ToDoListModel> Items { get; set; }
}
```

The MVC equivalent of this Razor Page is shown in listing 19.4. In the MVC framework, controllers are often used to aggregate similar actions, so the controller in this case is called `ToDoController`, as it would typically contain additional action methods for working with to-do items, such as actions to view a specific item or to create a new one.

Listing 19.4   An MVC controller for viewing all to-do items in a given category

```
public class ToDoController : Controller
{
    private readonly ToDoService _service;
    public ToDoController(ToDoService service)
    {
        _service = service;
    }

    public ActionResult Category(string id)
    {
        var items = _service.GetItemsForCategory(id);
        return View(items);
    }

    public ActionResult Create(ToDoListModel model)
    {
        // ...
    }
}
```

The ToDoService is provided in the controller constructor using dependency injection.

The Category action method takes a parameter, id.

The action method calls out to the ToDoService to retrieve data and build a view model.

Returns a ViewResult indicating the Razor view should be rendered, passing in the view model

MVC controllers often contain multiple action methods that respond to different requests.

Aside from some naming differences, the ToDoController looks similar to the Razor Page equivalent from listing 19.3:

- They both use dependency injection to access services.
- Both handlers (page handler and action method) accept parameters created using model binding in exactly the same way.
- Both interact with the application model in the same way to handle the request.
- They both create a view model for rendering the Razor view.

One of the main differences between Razor Pages and MVC controllers is in the final step: rendering the Razor view. In the next section you'll see how to render Razor views from your MVC controller actions, how the views differ from the Razor views you've seen with Razor Pages, and how the framework locates the correct Razor view to render.

19.4 *Selecting a view from an MVC controller*

This section covers

- How MVC controllers use ViewResults to render Razor views
- How to create a new Razor view
- How the framework locates a Razor view to render

One of the major differences between MVC controllers and Razor Pages is how the page handler or action method chooses a Razor view to render. For Razor Pages, it's easy; the page renders the Razor view associated with the page. For MVC controllers it's more complicated, so it's important to understand how you choose which view to render once an action method has executed. Figure 19.4 shows a zoomed-in view of this process, right after the action has invoked the application model and received some data back.

Some of this figure should be familiar; it's the bottom half of figure 19.3 (with a couple of additions). It shows that the MVC controller action method uses a View-Result object to indicate that a Razor view should be rendered. This ViewResult contains the name of the Razor view template to render and a view model, an arbitrary plain old CLR object (POCO) class containing the data to render.

> **NOTE** ViewResult is the MVC equivalent of a Razor Page's PageResult. The main difference is that a ViewResult includes a view name to render and a model to pass to the view template, while a PageResult always renders the Razor Page's associated view and always passes the PageModel to the view template.

After returning a ViewResult from an action method, the control flow passes back to the MVC framework, which uses a series of heuristics to locate the view, based on the template name provided.

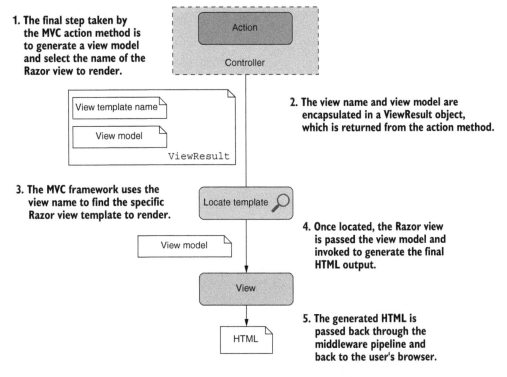

1. The final step taken by the MVC action method is to generate a view model and select the name of the Razor view to render.

2. The view name and view model are encapsulated in a ViewResult object, which is returned from the action method.

3. The MVC framework uses the view name to find the specific Razor view template to render.

4. Once located, the Razor view is passed the view model and invoked to generate the final HTML output.

5. The generated HTML is passed back through the middleware pipeline and back to the user's browser.

Figure 19.4   The process of generating HTML from an MVC controller using a `ViewResult`. This is similar to the process for a Razor Page. The main difference is that for Razor Pages, the view is an integral part of the Razor Page; for MVC controllers, the view must be located at runtime.

Once it locates the Razor view template, the Razor engine passes the view model from the `ViewResult` to the view and executes the template to generate the final HTML. This final step, rendering the HTML, is essentially the same process as for Razor Pages.

You can add a new Razor view template to your application in Visual Studio by right-clicking the folder you wish to add the view to in Solution Explorer. Choose **Add > New Item** and then select **Razor View - Empty** from the dialog, as shown in figure 19.5. If you aren't using Visual Studio, create a blank new file in the Views folder with the file extension .cshtml.

Razor view files are almost identical to the Razor Page .cshtml files you saw in chapter 17. The only difference is that Razor view files must not specify a @page directive at the top of the file. Aside from that, they're identical; you can use the same syntax, partial views, layouts, and view models as you can with Razor Pages.

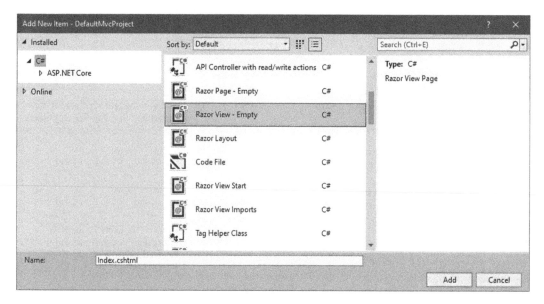

Figure 19.5   The Add New Item dialog box. Choosing Razor View - Empty adds a new Razor view template file to your application.

The following listing, for example, shows part of the Error.cshtml Razor view for the default MVC template. This is all recognizable as standard Razor syntax.

Listing 19.5   A Razor view

```
@model ErrorViewModel      ◁——— Razor views may specify a view model.
@{
    ViewData["Title"] = "Error";   ◁——┐ You can access ViewData, and
}                                       │ execute arbitrary C# statements.

<h1 class="text-danger">Error.</h1>     ◁───┐
<h2 class="text-danger">An error occurred while    │ Standard HTML is written
    processing your request.</h2>               │ directly to the output.

@if (Model.ShowRequestId)   ◁──┐ You can use standard Razor control statements
{                               │ and can access the view model using Model.
    <p>
        <strong>Request ID:</strong> <code>@Model.RequestId</code>    ◁──┐
    </p>                                                                  │
}                       You can write C# expressions using @. │
```

With your view template created, you now need to execute it. In most cases you won't create a `ViewResult` directly in your action methods. Instead, you'll use one of the `View()` helper methods on the `Controller` base class. These helper methods simplify passing in a view model and selecting a view template, but there's nothing magic about them; all they do is create `ViewResult` objects.

In the simplest case you can call the `View` method without any arguments, as shown in the following listing, taken from the default MVC application. The `View()` helper method returns a `ViewResult` that uses conventions to find the view template to render and does not supply a view model when executing the view.

Listing 19.6   Returning `ViewResult` from an action method using default conventions

```
public class HomeController : Controller     ◁───┐   Inheriting from the Controller base class
{                                                │   makes the View helper methods available.
    public IActionResult Index()
    {
        return View();   ◁────── The View helper method returns a ViewResult.
    }
}
```

In this example, the `View` helper method returns a `ViewResult` without specifying the name of the template to run. Instead, the name of the template to use is based on the name of the controller and the name of the action method. Given that the controller is called `HomeController` and the method is called `Index`, by default the Razor template engine looks for a template at the Views/Home/Index.cshtml location, as shown in figure 19.6.

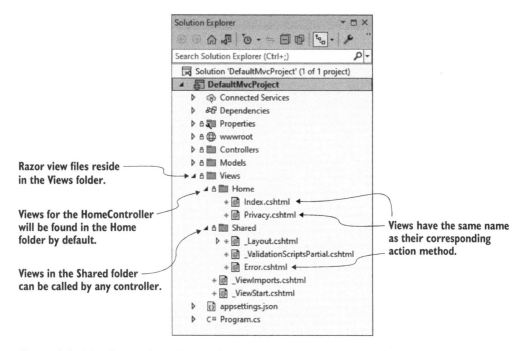

Figure 19.6   View files are located at runtime based on naming conventions. Razor view files reside in a folder based on the name of the associated MVC controller and are named with the name of the action method that requested them. Views in the Shared folder can be used by any controller.

This is another case of using conventions in MVC to reduce the amount of boilerplate you have to write. As always, the conventions are optional. You can also explicitly pass the name of the template to run as a `string` to the `View` method. For example, if the `Index` method in listing 19.6 instead returned `View("ListView")`, the templating engine would look for a template called ListView.cshtml instead. You can even specify the complete path to the view file, relative to your application's root folder, such as `View("Views/global.cshtml")`, which would look for the template at the Views/global .chtml location.

> **NOTE** When specifying the absolute path to a view, you must include both the top-level Views folder and the .cshtml file extension in the path. This is similar to the rules for locating partial view templates.

The process of locating an MVC Razor view is similar to the process of locating a partial view to render, which you learned about in chapter 17. The framework searches in multiple locations to find the requested view. The difference is that for Razor Pages the search process happens only for partial view rendering, as the main Razor view to render is already known; it's the Razor Page's view template.

Figure 19.7 shows the complete process used by the MVC framework to locate the correct View template to execute when a `ViewResult` is returned from an MVC controller. It's possible for more than one template to be eligible, such as if an Index.chtml file exists in both the Home and Shared folders. Similar to the rules for locating partial views, the engine uses the first template it finds.

> **TIP** You can modify all these conventions, including the algorithm shown in figure 19.8, during initial configuration. In fact, you can replace the whole Razor templating engine if you really want to!

You may find it tempting to explicitly provide the name of the view file you want to render in your controller; if so, I'd encourage you to fight that urge. You'll have a much simpler time if you embrace the conventions as they are and go with the flow. That extends to anyone else who looks at your code; if you stick to the standard conventions, there'll be a comforting familiarity when they look at your app. That can only be a good thing!

As well as providing a view template name, you can also pass an object to act as the view model for the Razor view. This object should match the type specified in the view's `@model` directive, and it's accessed in exactly the same way as for Razor Pages; using the `Model` property.

> **TIP** All the other ways of passing data to the view I described in chapter 17 are available in MVC controllers too. You should generally favor the view model where possible, but you can also use `ViewData`, `TempData`, or `@inject` services, for example.

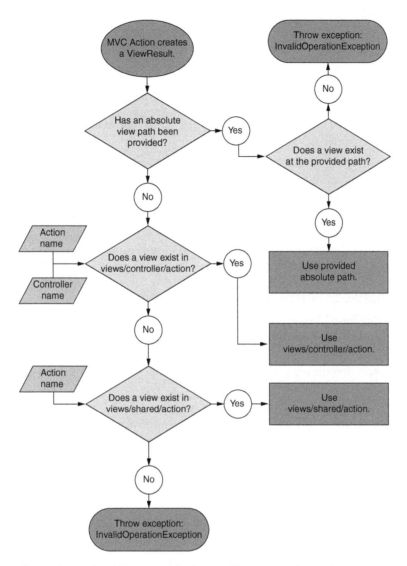

Figure 19.7   A flow chart describing how the Razor templating engine locates the correct view template to execute. Avoiding the complexity of this diagram is one of the reasons I recommend using Razor Pages wherever possible!

The following listing shows two examples of passing a view model to a view.

Listing 19.7   Returning `ViewResult` from an action method using default conventions

```
public class ToDoController : Controller
{
    public IActionResult Index()
    {
        var listViewModel = new ToDoListModel();
```

Creates an instance of the view model to pass to the Razor view

```
        return View(listViewModel);
    }
    public IActionResult View(int id)
    {
        var viewModel = new ViewToDoModel();
        return View("ViewToDo", viewModel);
    }
}
```

The view model is passed as an argument to View.

You can provide the view template name at the same time as the view model.

Once the Razor view template has been located, the view is rendered using the Razor syntax you learned about in chapters 17 and 18. You can use all the features you've already seen—layouts, partial views, _ViewImports, and _ViewStart, for example. From the point of view of the Razor view, there's no difference between a Razor Pages view and an MVC Razor view.

Now you've had a brief overview of an MVC application, we can look in more depth about when to choose MVC controllers over Razor Pages.

19.5 Choosing between Razor Pages and MVC controllers

Throughout this book, I have said that you should generally choose Razor Pages for server-rendered applications instead of using MVC controllers. In this section I show the difference between Razor Pages and MVC controllers from a project structure point of view and defend my reasoning. I also describe the cases where MVC controllers are a good choice.

If you're familiar with legacy .NET Framework ASP.NET or earlier versions of ASP.NET Core, you may already be familiar and comfortable with MVC controllers. If you're unsure whether to stick to what you know or switch to Razor Pages, this section should help you choose. Developers coming from those backgrounds often have misconceptions about Razor Pages initially (as I did!), incorrectly equating them with Web Forms and overlooking their underlying basis of the MVC framework. This section attempts to set the record straight.

Indeed, architecturally, Razor Pages and MVC are essentially equivalent, as they both use the MVC design pattern. The most obvious differences relate to where the files are placed in your project, as I discuss in the next section.

19.5.1 The benefits of Razor Pages

In section 19.5 I showed that the code for an MVC controller looks similar to the code for a Razor Page `PageModel`. If that's the case, what benefit is there to using Razor Pages? In this section I discuss some of the pain points of MVC controllers and how Razor Pages attempts to address them.

In MVC, a single controller can have multiple action methods. Each action handles a different request and generates a different response. The grouping of multiple actions in a controller is somewhat arbitrary, but it's typically used to group actions related to a specific entity or resource: to-do list items in this case. A more complete

Razor Pages are not Web Forms

A common argument I hear from existing ASP.NET developers against Razor Pages is "Oh, they're just Web Forms." That sentiment misses the mark in many ways, but it's common enough that it's worth addressing directly.

Web Forms was a web-programming model that was released as part of .NET Framework 1.0 in 2002. It attempted to provide a highly productive experience for developers moving from desktop development to the web for the first time.

Web Forms are much maligned now, but their weaknesses only became apparent later. Web Forms attempted to hide the complexities of the web from you, to give you the impression of developing a desktop app. That often resulted in apps that were slow, with lots of interdependencies, and that were hard to maintain.

Web Forms provided a page-based programming model, which is why Razor Pages sometimes gets associated with them. However, as you've seen, Razor Pages is based on the MVC design pattern, and it exposes the intrinsic features of the web without trying to hide them from you.

Razor Pages optimizes certain flows using conventions, but it's not trying to build a *stateful* application model over the top of a *stateless* web application, in the way that Web Forms did.

If you were a fan of Web Forms' stateful application model, you should consider Blazor Server, which uses a similar paradigm but embraces the web instead of fighting against it. You can read more about the similarities at http://mng.bz/7Dy9.

version of the `ToDoController` in listing 19.4 might include action methods for listing all to-do items, for creating new items, and for deleting items, for example. Unfortunately, you can often find that your controllers become large and bloated, with many dependencies.[1]

> **NOTE** You don't have to make your controllers very large like this. It's just a common pattern. You could, for example, create a separate controller for every action instead.

Another pitfall of MVC controllers is the way they're typically organized in your project. Most action methods in a controller need an associated Razor view, for generating the HTML, and a view model for passing data to the view. The MVC approach in .NET traditionally groups classes by type (controller, view, view model), while the Razor Page approach groups by function; everything related to a specific page is co-located.

Figure 19.8 compares the file layout for a simple Razor Pages project with the MVC equivalent. Using Razor Pages means much less scrolling up and down between the controller, views, and view model folders whenever you're working on a particular page. Everything you need is found in two files, the .cshtml Razor view and the (nested) .cshtml.cs `PageModel` file.

---

[1] Before moving to Razor Pages, the ASP.NET Core template that includes user login functionality contained two such controllers, each containing more than 20 action methods and more than 500 lines of code!

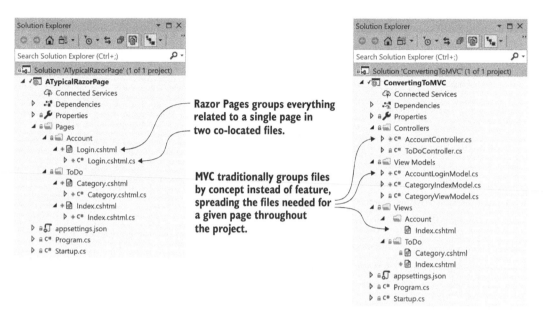

Figure 19.8   Comparing the folder structure for an MVC project with the folder structure for a Razor Pages project

There are additional differences between MVC and Razor Pages, which I have highlighted throughout the book, but this layout difference is really the biggest win. Razor Pages embraces the fact that you're building a page-based application and optimizes your workflow by keeping everything related to a single page together.

TIP You can think of each Razor Page as a mini controller focused on a single page. Page handlers are functionally equivalent to MVC controller action methods.

This layout also has the benefit of making each page a separate class. This contrasts with the MVC approach of making each page an action on a given controller. Each Razor Page is cohesive for a particular feature, such as displaying a to-do item. MVC controllers contain action methods that handle multiple different features for a more abstract concept, such as all the features related to to-do items.

NOTE ASP.NET Core is eminently customizable, so you don't have to group your MVC applications by type; it's simply the default state and the easy path. In fact, if you do choose to use MVC controllers, I strongly suggest grouping using feature folders instead. This MSDN article provides a good introduction: http://mng.bz/mVOr.

Another important point is that Razor Pages doesn't lose any of the separation of concerns that MVC has. The view part of Razor Pages is still concerned only with rendering HTML, and the handler is the coordinator that calls out to the application model. The only real difference is the lack of the explicit view model that you have in MVC, but it's perfectly possible to emulate this in Razor Pages if that's a deal-breaker for you.

The benefits of using Razor Pages are particularly noticeable when you have content websites, such as marketing websites, where you're mostly displaying static data and there's no real logic. In that case, MVC adds complexity without any real benefits, as there's not really any logic in the controllers at all. Another great use case is when you're creating forms for users to submit data. Razor Pages is especially optimized for this scenario, as you saw in previous chapters.

Clearly, I'm a fan of Razor Pages, but that's not to say they're perfect for every situation. In the next section I discuss some of the cases when you might choose to use MVC controllers in your application. Bear in mind it's not an either-or choice; it's possible to use MVC controllers, Razor Pages, and even minimal APIs in the same application, and in many cases that may be the best option.

19.5.2 *When to choose MVC controllers over Razor Pages*

Razor Pages are great for building page-based server-side rendered applications. But not all applications fit that mold, and even some applications that *do* fall in that category might be best developed using MVC controllers instead of Razor Pages. These are a few such scenarios:

- *When you don't want to render views*—Razor Pages are best for page-based applications, where you're rendering a view for the user. If you're building an HTTP API, you should use minimal APIs or MVC (web API) controllers instead. You'll learn about web API controllers in chapter 20.
- *When you're converting an existing MVC application to ASP.NET Core*—If you already have a legacy ASP.NET application that you're converting to ASP.NET Core or an app using an early version of ASP.NET Core that you're updating, you're likely using MVC controllers. It's probably not worth converting your existing MVC controllers to Razor Pages in this case. It makes more sense to keep your existing code and consider whether to do *new* development in the application with Razor Pages.
- *When you're doing a lot of partial page updates*—It's possible to use JavaScript in an MVC application to avoid doing full page navigations by updating only part of the page at a time. This approach, halfway between fully server-side rendered and a client-side application, may be easier to achieve with MVC controllers than Razor Pages. On the other hand, you can easily mix Razor Pages and MVC controllers, using Razor Pages where appropriate and MVC controllers for the partial view results.

I hope that by this point you're sold on Razor Pages and their overall design using the MVC pattern. Nevertheless, using MVC controllers makes sense in some situations, so it's worth bearing that in mind. Another important point to remember is that you can include both MVC controllers and Razor Pages in the same application if you need them.

> **When not to use Razor Pages or MVC controllers**
>
> Typically, you'll use either Razor Pages or MVC controllers to write most of the UI logic for an app. You'll use it to define the APIs and pages in your application and to define how they interface with your business logic. Razor Pages and MVC provide an extensive framework and include a great deal of functionality to help build your apps quickly and efficiently. But they're not suited to *every* app.
>
> Providing so much functionality necessarily comes with a certain degree of performance overhead. For typical line-of-business apps, the productivity gains from using MVC or Razor Pages often outweighs any performance effect. But if you're building a JSON API you will likely want to consider minimal APIs for the performance improvements. For server-to-server APIs or nonbrowser clients, an alternative protocol like gRPC (https://docs.microsoft.com/aspnet/core/grpc) may be a good fit. You might also consider protocols like GraphQL, as discussed in *Building Web APIs in ASP.NET Core*, by Valerio De Sanctis (Manning, 2023).
>
> Alternatively, if you're building an app with real-time functionality, you'll probably want to consider using WebSockets instead of traditional HTTP requests. ASP.NET Core SignalR can be used to add real-time functionality to your app by providing an abstraction over WebSockets. SignalR also provides simple transport fallbacks and a remote procedure call (RPC) app model. For details, see the documentation at https://docs.microsoft.com/aspnet/core/signalr.
>
> Another option available in ASP.NET Core 7 is Blazor. This framework allows you to build interactive client-side web applications by using the WebAssembly standard to run .NET code directly in your browser or by using a stateful model with SignalR. See *Blazor in Action*, by Chris Sainty (Manning, 2022), for more details.

You've learned about MVC controllers as an alternative to Razor Pages, and in part 1 of this book you learned about using minimal APIs to build JSON APIs. Web API controllers sit somewhere in between; they use MVC controllers but generate JSON and other machine-friendly format data, not HTML. In chapter 20 you'll learn why you might choose to use web API controllers over minimal APIs and how to build a web API application.

Summary

- An action (or action method) is a method that runs in response to a request. An MVC controller is a class that contains one or more logically grouped action methods.
- To use MVC controllers in an ASP.NET Core application, call `AddControllers-WithViews()` on your `WebApplicationBuilder`. This adds all the required services for MVC controllers and Razor view rendering to the dependency injection container.
- MVC controllers typically use conventional routing to select an MVC controller and action method. Instead of associating a route template with each action method in your application, conventional routing specifies one or more route

template patterns that map to multiple endpoints. Conventional routes must define a `controller` and `action` route parameter to determine the action to execute.

- You can return `IActionResult` instances from MVC controllers and they are executed in the same way as for Razor Pages. The most commonly returned type is `ViewResult`, using the `View()` helper method, which instructs the framework to render a Razor view.

- `ViewResult` may contain the name of the view to render and optionally a view model object to use when rendering the view. If the view name is not provided, a view is chosen using conventions.

- By convention, MVC Razor views are named the same as the action method that invokes them. They reside either in a folder with the same name as the action method's controller or in the Shared folder.

- MVC controllers contain multiple action methods, typically grouped around a high-level entity or resource. In contrast, Razor Pages groups all the page handlers for a single page in one place, grouping around a page/feature instead of an entity. This gives improved developer ergonomics when working on an endpoint.

- MVC controllers may make sense over Razor Pages if you are upgrading an application that already uses MVC controllers or if your application is using a lot of partial page updates.

Creating an HTTP API using web API controllers

This chapter covers

- Creating a web API controller to return JavaScript Object Notation (JSON) to clients
- Using attribute routing to customize your URLs
- Generating a response using content negotiation
- Applying common conventions with the [ApiController] attribute

In chapters 13 through 19 you worked through each layer of a server-side rendered ASP.NET Core application, using Razor Pages and Model-View-Controller (MVC) controllers to render HTML to the browser. In part 1 of this book you saw a different type of ASP.NET Core application, using minimal APIs to serve JSON for client-side SPAs or mobile apps. In this chapter you'll learn about web API controllers, which fit somewhere in between!

You can apply much of what you've already learned to web API controllers; they use the same routing system as minimal APIs and the same MVC design pattern, model binding, and validation as Razor Pages and MVC controllers.

In this chapter you'll learn how to define web API controllers and actions, and see how similar they are to the Razor Pages and controllers you already know. You'll learn how to create an API model to return data and HTTP status codes in response to a request, in a way that client apps can understand.

After exploring how the MVC design pattern applies to web API controllers, you'll see how a related topic works with web APIs: routing. We'll look at how explicit attribute routing works with action methods, touching on many of the same concepts we covered in chapters 6 and 14.

One of the big features added in ASP.NET Core 2.1 was the `[ApiController]` attribute. This attribute applies several common conventions used in web APIs, reducing the amount of code you must write yourself. In section 20.5 you'll learn how automatic `400 Bad Requests` for invalid requests, model-binding parameter inference, and `ProblemDetails` support make building APIs easier and more consistent.

You'll also learn how to format the API models returned by your action methods using content negotiation, to ensure that you generate a response that the calling client can understand. As part of this, you'll learn how to add support for additional format types, such as Extensible Markup Language (XML), so that you can generate XML responses if the client requests it.

Finally, I discuss some of the differences between API controllers and minimal API applications, and when you should choose one over the other. Before we get to that, we look at how to get started. In section 20.1 you'll see how to create a web API project and add your first API controller.

20.1   Creating your first web API project

In this section you'll learn how to create an ASP.NET Core web API project and create your first web API controllers. You'll see how to use controller action methods to handle HTTP requests and how to use `ActionResults` to generate a response.

> **NOTE** As I mentioned previously, a web API project is a standard ASP.NET Core project, which uses the MVC framework and web API controllers.

Some people think of the MVC design pattern as applying only to applications that render their UI directly, like the Razor views you've seen in previous chapters or MVC controllers with Razor views. However, in ASP.NET Core, I feel the MVC pattern applies equally well when building a web API. For web APIs, the *view* part of the MVC pattern involves generating a *machine*-friendly response rather than a *user*-friendly response.

As a parallel to this, you create web API controllers in ASP.NET Core in the same way you create traditional MVC controllers. The only thing that differentiates them from a code perspective is the type of data they return. MVC controllers typically return a `ViewResult`; web API controllers generally return raw .NET objects from their action methods, or an `IActionResult` instance such as `StatusCodeResult`, as you saw in chapter 15.

You can create a new web API project in Visual Studio using the same process you've seen previously in Visual Studio. Choose **File > New**, and in the **Create a new project** dialog box, select the **ASP.NET Core Web API** template. Enter your project name in the **Configure your new project** dialog box, and review the **Additional Information** box, shown in figure 20.1, before choosing **Create**. If you're using the command-line interface (CLI), you can create a similar template using dotnet new webapi.

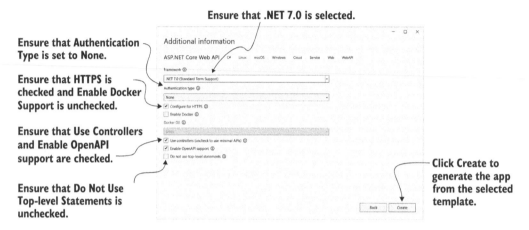

Figure 20.1   The Additional information screen. This screen follows on from the Configure your new project dialog box and lets you customize the template that generates your application.

The web API template configures the ASP.NET Core project for web API controllers only in Program.cs, as shown in listing 20.1. If you compare this template with the MVC controller project in chapter 19, you'll see that the web API project uses AddControllers() instead of AddControllersWithViews(). This adds only the services needed for controllers but omits the services for rendering Razor views. Also, the API controllers are added using MapControllers() instead of MapControllerRoute(), as web API controller typically use explicit routing instead of conventional routing. The default web API template also adds the OpenAPI services and endpoints required by the Swagger UI, as you saw in chapter 11.

Listing 20.1   Program.cs for the default web API project

```
WebApplicationBuilder builder = WebApplication.CreateBuilder(args);

builder.Services.AddControllers();

builder.Services.AddEndpointsApiExplorer();
builder.Services.AddSwaggerGen();

WebApplication app = builder.Build();

if (app.Environment.IsDevelopment())
```

AddControllers adds the necessary services for web API controllers to your application.

Adds services required to generate the Swagger/OpenAPI specification document

```
{
    app.UseSwagger();
    app.UseSwaggerUI();
}
```
Adds Swagger UI middleware for exploring your web API endpoints

```
app.UseHttpsRedirection();
app.UseAuthorization();

app.MapControllers();
```
MapControllers configures the web API controller actions in your app as endpoints.

```
app.Run();
```

The program in listing 20.1 instructs your application to find all the web API controllers in your application and configure them in the `EndpointMiddleware`. Each action method becomes an endpoint and can receive requests when the `RoutingMiddleware` maps an incoming URL to the action method.

NOTE Technically, you can include Razor Pages, minimal APIs, and web API controllers in the same app, but I prefer to keep them separate where possible. There are certain aspects (such as error handling and authentication) that are made easier by keeping them separate. Of course, running two separate applications has its own difficulties!

You can add a web API controller to your project by creating a new .cs file anywhere in your project. Traditionally, this file is placed in a folder called Controllers, but that's not a technical requirement.

TIP *Vertical slice* architecture and feature folders are (fortunately) becoming more popular in .NET circles. With these approaches, you organize your project based on features instead of technical concepts like controllers and models.

Listing 20.2 shows an example of a simple controller, with a single endpoint, that returns an `IEnumerable<string>` when executed. This example highlights the similarity with traditional MVC controllers (using action methods and a base class) and minimal APIs (returning the response object directly to be serialized later).

Listing 20.2   A simple web API controller

The [ApiController] attribute opts in to common conventions.

The ControllerBase class provides helper functions.

```
[ApiController]
public class FruitController : ControllerBase
{
    List<string> _fruit = new List<string>
    {
        "Pear",
        "Lemon",
        "Peach"
    };
    [HttpGet("fruit")]
    public IEnumerable<string> Index()
```

This would typically come from a dependency injection (DI) injected service instead.

The [HttpGet] attribute defines the route template used to call the action.

The name of the action method, Index, isn't used for routing. It can be anything you like.

```
    {
        return _fruit;
    }
}
```
The controller exposes a single action method that returns the list of fruit.

When invoked, this endpoint returns the list of strings serialized to JSON, as shown in figure 20.2.

Figure 20.2   Testing the web API in listing 20.2 by accessing the URL in the browser. A GET request is made to the /fruit URL, which returns a List<string> that is serialized to JSON.

Web API controllers typically use the [ApiController] attribute (introduced in .NET Core 2.1) and derive from the ControllerBase class. The base class provides several helper methods for generating results, and the [ApiController] attribute automatically applies some common conventions, as you'll see in section 20.5.

> **TIP**   The Controller base class is typically used when you use MVC controllers with Razor views. You don't need to return Razor views with web API controllers, so ControllerBase is the better option.

In listing 20.2 you can see that the action method, Index, returns a list of strings directly from the action method. When you return data from an action like this, you're providing the API model for the request. The client will receive this data. It's formatted into an appropriate response, a JSON representation of the list in the case of figure 20.2, and sent back to the browser with a 200 OK status code.

> **TIP**   Web API controllers format data as JSON by default. You'll see how to format the returned data in other ways in section 20.6. Minimal API endpoints that return data directly (rather than via an IResult) will format data only as JSON; there are no other options.

The URL at which a web API controller action is exposed is handled in the same way as for traditional MVC controllers and Razor Pages: using routing. The [Http-Get("fruit")] attribute applied to the Index method indicates that the method should use the route template "fruit" and should respond to HTTP GET requests. You'll learn more about attribute routing in section 20.4, but it's similar to the minimal API routing that you're already familiar with.

In listing 20.2 data is returned directly from the action method, but you don't *have* to do that. You're free to return an IActionResult instead, and often this is required.

Depending on the desired behavior of your API, you sometimes want to return data, and other times you may want to return a raw HTTP status code, indicating whether the request was successful. For example, if an API call is made requesting details of a product that does not exist, you might want to return a 404 Not Found status code.

> **NOTE** This is similar to the patterns you used in minimal APIs. But remember, minimal APIs use IResult, web API controllers, MVC controllers, and Razor Pages use IActionResult.

Listing 20.3 shows an example of where you must return an IActionResult. It shows another action on the same FruitController as before. This method exposes a way for clients to fetch a specific fruit by an id, which we'll assume for this example is an index into the list of _fruit you defined in the previous listing. Model binding is used to set the value of the id parameter from the request.

> **NOTE** API controllers use the same model binding infrastructure as Razor Pages to bind action method parameters to the incoming request. Model binding and validation work the same way you saw in chapter 16: you can bind the request to simple primitives, as well as to complex C# objects. The only difference is that there isn't a PageModel with [BindProperty] properties; you can bind only to action method parameters.

Listing 20.3 A web API action returning IActionResult to handle error conditions

```
[HttpGet("fruit/{id}")]          ◁───  Defines the route template
public ActionResult<string> View(int id)   ◁─ for the action method
{
    if (id >= 0 && id < _fruit.Count)   ◁─
    {
        return _fruit[id];   ◁─
    }
    return NotFound();
}
```

Defines the route template for the action method

The action method returns an ActionResult<string>, so it can return a string or an IActionResult.

An element can be returned only if the id value is a valid _fruit element index.

Returning the data directly returns the data with a 200 status code.

NotFound returns a NotFoundResult, which sends a 404 status code.

In the successful path for the action method, the id parameter has a value greater than 0 and less than the number of elements in _fruit. When that's true, the value of the element is returned to the caller. As in listing 20.2, this is achieved by simply returning the data directly, which generates a 200 status code and returns the element in the response body, as shown in figure 20.3. You could also have returned the data using an OkResult, by returning Ok(_fruit[id]), using the Ok helper method on the ControllerBase class; under the hood, the result is identical.

NOTE Some people get uneasy when they see the phrase *helper method,* but there's nothing magic about the ControllerBase helpers; they're shorthand for creating a new IActionResult of a given type. You don't have to take my word for it, though. You can always view the source code for the base class on GitHub at http://mng.bz/5wQB.

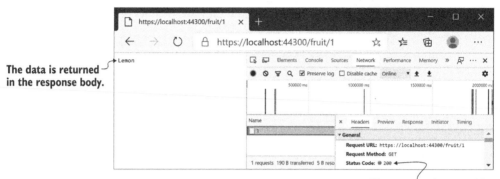

The data is returned in the response body.

The response is sent with a 200 OK status code.

Figure 20.3   Data returned from an action method is serialized into the response body, and it generates a response with status code 200 OK.

If the id is outside the bounds of the _fruit list, the method calls NotFound() to create a NotFoundResult. When executed, this method generates a 404 Not Found status code response. The [ApiController] attribute automatically converts the response into a standard ProblemDetails instance, as shown in figure 20.4.

The [ApiResponse] attribute generates a Problem Details JSON as the response body.

The response is sent with a 404 Not Found status code.

Figure 20.4   The [ApiController] attribute converts error responses (in this case a 404 response) into the standard ProblemDetails format.

One aspect you might find confusing from listing 20.3 is that for the successful case, we return a string, but the method signature of View says we return an Action-Result<string>. How is that possible? Why isn't there a compiler error?

The generic `ActionResult<T>` uses some fancy C# gymnastics with implicit conversions to make this possible. Using `ActionResult<T>` has two benefits:

- You can return either an instance of `T` *or* an `ActionResult` implementation like `NotFoundResult` from the same method. This can be convenient, as in listing 20.3.
- It enables better integration with ASP.NET Core's OpenAPI support.

You're free to return any type of `ActionResult` from your web API controllers, but you'll commonly return `StatusCodeResult` instances, which set the response to a specific status code, with or without associated data. `NotFoundResult` and `OkResult` both derive from `StatusCodeResult`, for example. Another commonly used status code is `400 Bad Request`, which is normally returned when the data provided in the request fails validation. You can generate this using a `BadRequestResult`, but in many cases the `[ApiController]` attribute can automatically generate `400` responses for you, as you'll see in section 20.5.

> **TIP** You learned about various `ActionResults` in chapter 15. `BadRequest-Result`, `OkResult`, and `NotFoundResult` all inherit from `StatusCodeResult` and set the appropriate status code for their type (`400`, `200`, and `404`, respectively). Using these wrapper classes makes the intention of your code clearer than relying on other developers to understand the significance of the various status code numbers.

Once you've returned an `ActionResult` (or other object) from your controller, it's serialized to an appropriate response. This works in several ways, depending on

- The formatters that your app supports
- The data you return from your method
- The data formats the requesting client can handle

You'll learn more about formatters and serializing data in section 20.6, but before we go any further, it's worth zooming out a little and exploring the parallels between traditional server-side rendered applications and web API endpoints. The two are similar, so it's important to establish the patterns that they share and where they differ.

20.2 Applying the MVC design pattern to a web API

In ASP.NET Core, the same underlying framework is used in conjunction with web API controllers, Razor Pages, and MVC controllers with views. You've already seen this yourself; the web API `FruitController` you created in section 20.2 looks similar to the MVC controllers you saw in chapter 19.

Consequently, even if you're building an application that consists entirely of web APIs, using no server-side rendering of HTML, the MVC design pattern still applies. Whether you're building traditional web applications or web APIs, you can structure your application virtually identically.

By now I hope you're nicely familiar with how ASP.NET Core handles a request. But in case you're not, figure 20.5 shows how the framework handles a typical Razor Pages

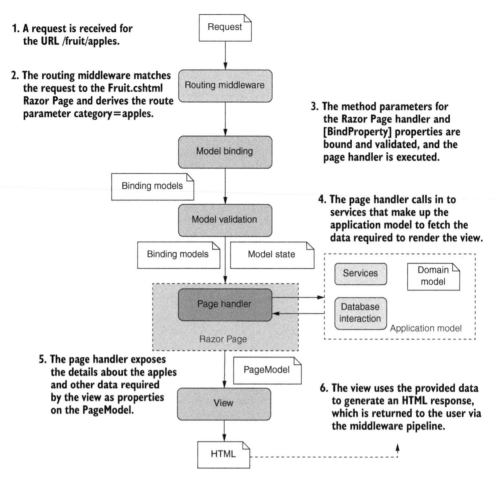

1. A request is received for the URL /fruit/apples.

2. The routing middleware matches the request to the Fruit.cshtml Razor Page and derives the route parameter category=apples.

3. The method parameters for the Razor Page handler and [BindProperty] properties are bound and validated, and the page handler is executed.

4. The page handler calls in to services that make up the application model to fetch the data required to render the view.

5. The page handler exposes the details about the apples and other data required by the view as properties on the PageModel.

6. The view uses the provided data to generate an HTML response, which is returned to the user via the middleware pipeline.

Figure 20.5   Handling a request to a traditional Razor Pages application, in which the view generates an HTML response that's sent back to the user. This diagram should be familiar by now!

request after it passes through the middleware pipeline. This example shows how a request to view the available fruit on a traditional grocery store website might look.

The RoutingMiddleware routes the request to view all the fruit listed in the apples category to the Fruit.cshtml Razor Page. The EndpointMiddleware then constructs a binding model, validates it, sets it as a property on the Razor Page's PageModel, and sets the ModelState property on the PageModel base class with details of any validation errors. The page handler interacts with the application model by calling into services, talking to a database, and fetching any necessary data.

Finally, the Razor Page executes its Razor view using the PageModel to generate the HTML response. The response returns through the middleware pipeline and out to the user's browser.

How would this change if the request came from a client-side or mobile application? If you want to serve machine-readable JSON instead of HTML, what is different for web API controllers? As shown in figure 20.6, the answer is "very little." The main changes are related to switching from Razor Pages to controllers and actions, but as you saw in chapter 19, both approaches use the same general paradigms.

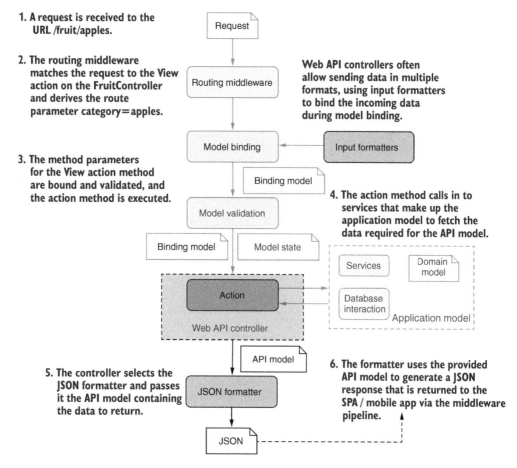

1. A request is received to the URL /fruit/apples.

2. The routing middleware matches the request to the View action on the FruitController and derives the route parameter category=apples.

Web API controllers often allow sending data in multiple formats, using input formatters to bind the incoming data during model binding.

3. The method parameters for the View action method are bound and validated, and the action method is executed.

4. The action method calls in to services that make up the application model to fetch the data required for the API model.

5. The controller selects the JSON formatter and passes it the API model containing the data to return.

6. The formatter uses the provided API model to generate a JSON response that is returned to the SPA / mobile app via the middleware pipeline.

Figure 20.6 A call to a web API endpoint in an e-commerce ASP.NET Core web application. The ghosted portion of the diagram is identical to figure 20.5.

As before, the routing middleware selects an endpoint to invoke based on the incoming URL. For API controllers this is a controller and action instead of a Razor Page.

After routing comes model-binding, in which the binder creates a binding model and populates it with values from the request. Web API controllers often accept data in more formats than Razor Pages, such as XML, but otherwise the model-binding process is the same as for the Razor Pages request. Validation also occurs in the same way, and the `ModelState` property on the `ControllerBase` base class is populated with any validation errors.

> **NOTE**   Web APIs use *input formatters* to accept data sent to them in a variety of formats. Commonly these formats are JSON or XML, but you can create input formatters for any sort of type, such as CSV. I show how to enable the XML input formatter in section 20.6. You can see how to create a custom input formatter at http://mng.bz/e5gG.

The action method is the equivalent of the Razor Page handler; it interacts with the application model in the same way. This is an important point; by separating the behavior of your app into an application model instead of incorporating it into your pages and controllers themselves, you're able to reuse the business logic of your application with multiple UI paradigms.

> **TIP**   Where possible, keep your page handlers and controllers as simple as practicable. Move all your business logic decisions into the services that make up your application model, and keep your Razor Pages and API controllers focused on the mechanics of interacting with a user or client.

After the application model has returned the data necessary to service the request—the fruit objects in the `apples` category—you see the first significant difference between API controllers and Razor Pages. Instead of adding values to the `PageModel` to be used in a Razor view, the action method creates an *API model*. This is analogous to the `PageModel`, but rather than containing data used to generate an HTML view, it contains the data that will be sent back in the response.

> **DEFINITION**   *View models* and `PageModels` contain both the *data* required to build a response and *metadata* about *how* to build the response. API models typically contain only the data to be returned in the response.

When we looked at the Razor Pages app, we used the `PageModel` in conjunction with a Razor view template to build the final response. With the web API app, we use the API model in conjunction with an output formatter. An *output formatter*, as the name suggests, serializes the API model into a machine-readable response, such as JSON or XML. The output formatter forms the V in the web API version of MVC by choosing an appropriate representation of the data to return.

Finally, as for the Razor Pages app, the generated response is sent back through the middleware pipeline, passing through each of the configured middleware components, and back to the original caller.

I hope the parallels between Razor Pages and web APIs are clear. The majority of the behavior is identical; only the response varies. Everything from when the request arrives to the interaction with the application model is similar between the paradigms.

Most of the differences between Razor Pages and web APIs have less to do with the way the framework works under the hood and are instead related to how the different paradigms are used. For example, in the next section you'll learn how the routing constructs you learned about in chapters 6 and 15 are used with web APIs, using attribute routing.

20.3   Attribute routing: Linking action methods to URLs

In this section you'll learn about attribute routing: the mechanism for associating web API controller actions with a given route template. You'll see how to associate controller actions with specific HTTP verbs like GET and POST and how to avoid duplication in your templates.

We covered route templates in depth in chapter 6 in the context of minimal APIs, and again in chapter 14 with Razor Pages, and you'll be pleased to know that you use exactly the same route templates with API controllers. The only difference is how you specify the templates. With Razor Pages you use the @page directive, and with minimal APIs you use MapGet() or MapPost(), whereas with API controllers you use routing attributes.

> **NOTE**   All three paradigms use *explicit routing* under the hood. The alternative, *conventional* routing, is typically used with traditional MVC controllers and views, as described in chapter 19. As I've mentioned, I don't recommend using that approach generally, so I don't cover conventional routing in this book.

With attribute routing, you decorate each action method in an API controller with an attribute and provide the associated route template for the action method, as shown in the following listing.

Listing 20.4   Attribute routing example

```
public class HomeController: Controller
{                                             The Index action will be executed
    [Route("")]          ◁─────────────────── when the / URL is requested.
    public IActionResult Index()
    {
        /* method implementation*/
    }
                                              The Contact action will be executed
    [Route("contact")]   ◁─────────────────── when the /contact URL is requested.
    public IActionResult Contact()
    {
        /* method implementation*/
    }
}
```

Each [Route] attribute defines a route template that should be associated with the action method. In the example provided, the / URL maps directly to the Index method and the /contact URL maps to the Contact method.

Attribute routing maps URLs to a specific action method, but a single action method can still have multiple route templates and hence can correspond to multiple

URLs. Each template must be declared with its own RouteAttribute, as shown in this listing, which shows the skeleton of a web API for a car-racing game.

> **Listing 20.5   Attribute routing with multiple attributes**

```
public class CarController
{
    [Route("car/start")]          ┐   The Start method will be executed when
    [Route("car/ignition")]       │   any of these route templates is matched.
    [Route("start-car")]
    public IActionResult Start()  ◄──┐   The name of the action method has
    {                                │   no effect on the route template.
        /* method implementation*/
    }

    [Route("car/speed/{speed}")]     ┐   The RouteAttribute template can contain
    [Route("set-speed/{speed}")]     │   route parameters, in this case {speed}.
    public IActionResult SetCarSpeed(int speed)
    {
        /* method implementation*/
    }
}
```

The listing shows two different action methods, both of which can be accessed from multiple URLs. For example, the Start method will be executed when any of the following URLs is requested:

- /car/start
- /car/ignition
- /start-car

These URLs are completely independent of the controller and action method names; only the value in the RouteAttribute matters.

> **NOTE** By default, the controller and action name have no bearing on the URLs or route templates when RouteAttributes are used.

The templates used in route attributes are standard route templates, the same as you used in chapter 6. You can use literal segments, and you're free to define route parameters that will extract values from the URL, as shown by the SetCarSpeed method in listing 20.5. That method defines two route templates, both of which define a route parameter, {speed}.

> **TIP** I've used multiple [Route] attributes on each action in this example, but it's best practice to expose your action at a single URL. This will make your API easier to understand and for other applications to consume.

As in all parts of ASP.NET Core, route parameters represent a segment of the URL that can vary. As with minimal APIs, and Razor Pages, the route parameters in your RouteAttribute templates can

- Be optional
- Have default values
- Use route constraints

For example, you could update the `SetCarSpeed` method in the previous listing to constrain `{speed}` to an integer and to default to `20` like so:

```
[Route("car/speed/{speed=20:int}")]
[Route("set-speed/{speed=20:int}")]
public IActionResult SetCarSpeed(int speed)
```

> **NOTE** As discussed in chapter 6, don't use route constraints for validation. For example, if you call the preceding `"set-speed/{speed=20:int}"` route with an invalid value for speed, `/set-speed/oops`, you will get a `404 Not Found` response, as the route does not match. Without the `int` constraint, you would receive the more sensible `400 Bad Request` response.

If you managed to get your head around routing in chapter 6, routing with web API controllers shouldn't hold any surprises for you. One thing you might begin noticing when you start using attribute routing with web API controllers is the amount you repeat yourself. Minimal APIs use route groups to reduce duplication, and Razor Pages removes a lot of the repetition by using conventions to calculate route templates based on the Razor Page's filename. So what can we use with web API controllers?

20.3.1 Combining route attributes to keep your route templates DRY

Adding route attributes to all of your web API controllers can get a bit tedious, especially if you're mostly following conventions where your routes have a standard prefix, such as `"api"` or the controller name. Generally, you'll want to ensure that you don't repeat yourself (DRY) when it comes to these strings. The following listing shows two action methods with several `[Route]` attributes. (This is for demonstration purposes only. Stick to one per action if you can!)

Listing 20.6 Duplication in `RouteAttribute` templates

```
public class CarController
{
    [Route("api/car/start")]
    [Route("api/car/ignition")]
    [Route("start-car")]
    public IActionResult Start()
    {
        /* method implementation*/
    }

    [Route("api/car/speed/{speed}")]
    [Route("set-speed/{speed}")]
    public IActionResult SetCarSpeed(int speed)
    {
```

Multiple route templates use the same "api/car" prefix.

```
            /* method implementation*/
    }
}
```

There's quite a lot of duplication here; you're adding `"api/car"` to most of your routes. Presumably, if you decided to change this to `"api/vehicles"`, you'd have to go through each attribute and update it. Code like that is asking for a typo to creep in!

To alleviate this pain, it's possible to apply `RouteAttributes` to controllers, in addition to action methods. When a controller and an action method both have a route attribute, the overall route template for the method is calculated by combining the two templates.

Listing 20.7   Combining `RouteAttribute` templates

```
[Route("api/car")]
public class CarController
{
    [Route("start")]          ◄──────┐  Combines to give "api/car/start"
    [Route("ignition")]          ◄────── Combines to give "api/car/ignition"
    [Route("/start-car")]     ◄───┐
    public IActionResult Start()  │   Does not combine because it starts
    {                             │   with /; gives the "start-car" template
        /* method implementation*/
    }
                              ┌─ Combines to give "api/car/speed/{speed}"
    [Route("speed/{speed}")]  ◄┘
    [Route("/set-speed/{speed}")]     ◄──┐
    public IActionResult SetCarSpeed(int speed)   Does not combine because it starts
    {                                    │        with /; gives the "set-speed/{speed}"
        /* method implementation*/       │        template
    }
}
```

Combining attributes in this way can reduce some of the duplication in your route templates and makes it easier to add or change the prefixes (such as switching `"car"` to `"vehicle"`) for multiple action methods. To ignore the `RouteAttribute` on the controller and create an absolute route template, start your action method route template with a slash (`/`). Using a controller `RouteAttribute` reduces a lot of the duplication, but you can go one better by using token replacement.

20.3.2   *Using token replacement to reduce duplication in attribute routing*

The ability to combine attribute routes is handy, but you're still left with some duplication if you're prefixing your routes with the name of the controller, or if your route templates always use the action name. If you wish, you can simplify even further!

Attribute routes support the automatic replacement of [action] and [controller] tokens in your attribute routes. These will be replaced with the name of the action and the controller (without the "Controller" suffix), respectively. The tokens are replaced after all attributes have been combined, which can be useful when you have controller inheritance hierarchies. This listing shows how you can create a Base-Controller class that applies a consistent route template prefix to *all* the web API controllers in your application.

Listing 20.8   Token replacement in RouteAttributes

You can apply attributes to a base class, and derived classes will inherit them.

```
[Route("api/[controller]")]
public abstract class BaseController { }

public class CarController : BaseController
{
    [Route("[action]")]
    [Route("ignition")]
    [Route("/start-car")]
    public IActionResult Start()
    {
        /* method implementation*/
    }
}
```

Token replacement happens last, so [controller] is replaced with "car" not "base".

Combines and replaces tokens to give the "api/car/start" template

Combines and replaces tokens to give the "api/car/ignition" template

Does not combine with base attributes because it starts with /, so it remains as "start-car"

> **WARNING**   If you use token replacement for [controller] or [action], remember that renaming classes and methods will change your public API. If that worries you, you can stick to using static strings like "car" instead.

When combined with everything you learned in chapter 6, we've covered pretty much everything there is to know about attribute routing. There's just one more thing to consider: handling different HTTP request types like GET and POST.

20.3.3   *Handling HTTP verbs with attribute routing*

In Razor Pages, the HTTP verb, such as GET or POST, isn't part of the routing process. The RoutingMiddleware determines which Razor Page to execute based solely on the route template associated with the Razor Page. It's only when a Razor Page is about to be executed that the HTTP verb is used to decide which page handler to execute: OnGet for the GET verb, or OnPost for the POST verb, for example.

Web API controllers work like minimal API endpoints: the HTTP verb takes part in the routing process itself. So a GET request may be routed to one action, and a POST request may be routed to a different action, even if the request used the same URL.

The [Route] attribute we've used so far responds to *all* HTTP verbs. Instead, an action should typically only handle a single verb. Instead of the [Route] attribute, you can use

- [HttpPost] to handle POST requests
- [HttpGet] to handle GET requests
- [HttpPut] to handle PUT requests

There are similar attributes for all the standard HTTP verbs, like DELETE and OPTIONS. You can use these attributes instead of the [Route] attribute to specify that an action method should correspond to a single verb, as shown in the following listing.

Listing 20.9   Using HTTP verb attributes with attribute routing

```
public class AppointmentController
{
    [HttpGet("/appointments")]
    public IActionResult ListAppointments()
    {
        /* method implementation */
    }

    [HttpPost("/appointments")]
    public IActionResult CreateAppointment()
    {
        /* method implementation */
    }
}
```

Executed only in response to GET /appointments

Executed only in response to POST /appointments

If your application receives a request that matches the route template of an action method but doesn't match the required HTTP verb, you'll get a 405 Method not allowed error response. For example, if you send a DELETE request to the /appointments URL in the previous listing, you'll get a 405 error response.

When you're building web API controllers, there is some code that you'll find yourself writing repeatedly. The [ApiController] attribute is designed to handle some of this for you and reduce the amount of boilerplate you need.

20.4   *Using common conventions with [ApiController]*

In this section you'll learn about the [ApiController] attribute and how it can reduce the amount of code you need to write to create consistent web API controllers. You'll learn about the conventions it applies, why they're useful, and how to turn them off if you need to.

The [ApiController] attribute was introduced in .NET Core 2.1 to simplify the process of creating web API controllers. To understand what it does, it's useful to look at an example of how you might write a web API controller *without* the [ApiController] attribute and compare that with the code required to achieve the same thing with the attribute.

Listing 20.10   Creating a web API controller without the [ApiController] attribute

```
public class FruitController : ControllerBase
{
    List<string> _fruit = new List<string>
    {
        "Pear", "Lemon", "Peach"
    };
```

The list of strings serves as the application model in this example.

```
                  [HttpPost("fruit")]                          ◄──────────   Web APIs use attribute
                  public ActionResult Update([FromBody] UpdateModel model)   routing to define the
                  {                                                          route templates.
                      if (!ModelState.IsValid)
The [FromBody]        {                                                      You need to check
attribute indicates       return BadRequest(                                if model validation
that the parameter            new ValidationProblemDetails(ModelState));    succeeded and return a
should be bound       }                                                     400 response if it failed.
to the request
body.                 if (model.Id < 0 || model.Id > _fruit.Count)
                      {
                          return NotFound(new ProblemDetails()
                          {                                                  If the data sent
                              Status = 404,                                  does not contain a
                              Title = "Not Found",                          valid ID, returns a
                              Type = "https://tools.ietf.org/html/rfc7231"   404 ProblemDetails
                                   + "#section-6.5.4",                      response
                          });
                      }
                      _fruit[model.Id] = model.Name;    Updates the model and
                      return Ok();                      returns a 200 Response
                  }

                  public class UpdateModel
                  {
                      public int Id { get; set; }        UpdateModel is valid only if the
                                                         Name value is provided, as set
                      [Required]                         by the [Required] attribute.
                      public string Name { get; set; }
                  }
              }
```

This example demonstrates many common features and patterns used with web API controllers:

- Web API controllers read data from the body of a request, typically sent as JSON. To ensure the body is read as JSON and not as form values, you have to apply the [FromBody] attribute to the method parameters to ensure it is model-bound correctly.
- As discussed in chapter 16, after model binding, the model is validated, but it's up to you to act on the validation results. You should return a 400 Bad Request response if the values provided failed validation. You typically want to provide details of *why* the request was invalid: this is done in listing 20.10 by returning a ValidationProblemDetails object in the response body, built from the ModelState.
- Whenever you return an error status, such as a 404 Not Found, where possible you should return details of the problem that will allow the caller to diagnose the issue. The ProblemDetails class is the recommended way of doing that in ASP.NET Core.

The code in listing 20.10 is representative of what you might see in an ASP.NET Core API controller before .NET Core 2.1. The introduction of the [ApiController] attribute in .NET Core 2.1 (and subsequent refinement in later versions) makes this same code much simpler, as shown in the following listing.

Listing 20.11   Creating a web API controller with the [ApiController] attribute

```
[ApiController]                              ◄────────────┐   Adding the [ApiController] attribute
public class FruitController : ControllerBase            │   applies several conventions common
{                                                         │   to API controllers.
    List<string> _fruit = new List<string>
    {
        "Pear", "Lemon", "Peach"
    };                                                        The [FromBody] attribute
                                                              is assumed for complex
    [HttpPost("fruit")]                                       action method parameters.
    public ActionResult Update(UpdateModel model)   ◄─────┘
    {                                               ◄──────┐   The model validation is
        if (model.Id < 0 || model.Id > _fruit.Count)      │   automatically checked,
        {                                                  │   and if invalid, returns a
            return NotFound();                             │   400 response.
        }

        _fruit[model.Id] = model.Name;

        return Ok();
    }

    public class UpdateModel
    {
        public int Id { get; set; }

        [Required]
        public string Name { get; set; }
    }
}
```

Error status codes are automatically converted to a ProblemDetails object. (pointing to `return NotFound();`)

If you compare listing 20.10 with listing 20.11, you'll see that all the bold code in listing 20.10 can be removed and replaced with the [ApiController] attribute in listing 20.11. The [ApiController] attribute automatically applies several conventions to your controllers:

- *Attribute routing*—You must use attribute routing with your controllers; you can't use conventional routing—not that you would, as we've discussed this approach only for API controllers anyway.
- *Automatic 400 responses*—I said in chapter 16 that you should always check the value of ModelState.IsValid in your Razor Page handlers and MVC actions, but the [ApiController] attribute does this for you by adding a filter, as we did with minimal APIs in chapter 7. We'll cover MVC filters in detail in chapters 21 and 22.

- *Model binding source inference*—Without the `[ApiController]` attribute, complex types are assumed to be passed as form values in the request body. For web APIs, it's much more common to pass data as JSON, which ordinarily requires adding the `[FromBody]` attribute. The `[ApiController]` attribute takes care of that for you.
- `ProblemDetails` *for error codes*—You often want to return a consistent set of data when an error occurs in your API. The `[ApiController]` attribute intercepts any error status codes returned by your controller (for example, a `404 Not Found` response), and converts them to `ProblemDetails` responses.

When it was introduced, a key feature of the `[ApiController]` attribute was the Problem Details support, but as I described in chapter 5, the same automatic conversion to Problem Details is now supported by the default `ExceptionHandlerMiddleware` and `StatusCodePagesMiddleware`. Nevertheless, the `[ApiController]` conventions can significantly reduce the amount of boilerplate code you have to write and ensure that validation failures are handled automatically, for example.

As is common in ASP.NET Core, you will be most productive if you follow the conventions rather than trying to fight them. However, if you don't like some of the conventions introduced by `[ApiController]`, or want to customize them, you can easily do so.

You can customize the web API controller conventions your application uses by calling `ConfigureApiBehaviorOptions()` on the `IMvcBuilder` object returned from the `AddControllers()` method in your Program.cs file. For example, you could disable the automatic 400 responses on validation failure, as shown in the following listing.

Listing 20.12 Customizing `[ApiAttribute]` behaviors

```
WebApplicationBuilder builder = WebApplication.CreateBuilder(args);

builder.Services.AddControllers();            Controls which conventions are applied
    .ConfigureApiBehaviorOptions(options =>   by providing a configuration lambda
    {
        options.SuppressModelStateInvalidFilter = true;   This would disable the
    });                                                   automatic 400 responses
                                                          for invalid requests.
// ...
```

TIP You can disable all the automatic features enabled by the `[ApiController]` attribute, but I encourage you to stick to the defaults unless you really need to change them. You can read more about disabling features in the documentation at https://docs.microsoft.com/aspnet/core/web-api.

The ability to customize each aspect of your web API controllers is one of the key differentiators with minimal APIs. In the next section you'll learn how to control the format of the data returned by your web API controllers—whether that's JSON, XML, or a different, custom format.

20.5   *Generating a response from a model*

This brings us to the final topic in this chapter: formatting a response. It's common for API controllers to return JSON these days, but that's not always the case. In this section you'll learn about content negotiation and how to enable additional output formats such as XML.

Consider this scenario: you've created a web API action method for returning a list of cars, as in the following listing. It invokes a method on your application model, which hands back the list of data to the controller. Now you need to format the response and return it to the caller.

Listing 20.13   A web API controller to return a list of cars

```
[ApiController]
public class CarsController : Controller
{
    [HttpGet("api/cars")]
    public IEnumerable<string> ListCars()
    {
        return new string[]
            { "Nissan Micra", "Ford Focus" };
    }
}
```

The action is executed with a request to GET /api/cars.

The API model containing the data is an IEnumerable<string>.

This data would normally be fetched from the application model.

You saw in section 20.2 that it's possible to return data directly from an action method, in which case the middleware formats it and returns the formatted data to the caller. But how does the middleware know which format to use? After all, you could serialize it as JSON, as XML, or even with a simple ToString() call.

> **WARNING** Remember that in this chapter I'm talking only about web API controller responses. Minimal APIs support only automatic serialization to JSON, nothing else.

The process of determining the format of data to send to clients is known generally as *content negotiation* (conneg). At a high level, the client sends a header indicating the types of content it can understand—the Accept header—and the server picks one of these, formats the response, and sends a Content-Type header in the response, indicating which type it chose.

You're not forced into sending only a Content-Type the client expects, and in some cases, you may not even be able to handle the types it requests. What if a request stipulates that it can accept only Microsoft Excel spreadsheets? It's unlikely you'd support that, even if that's the only Accept type the request contains.

When you return an API model from an action method, whether directly (as in listing 20.13) or via an OkResult or other StatusCodeResult, ASP.NET Core always returns something in the response. If it can't honor any of the types stipulated in the Accept header, it will fall back to returning JSON by default. Figure 20.7 shows that even though XML was requested, the API controller formatted the response as JSON.

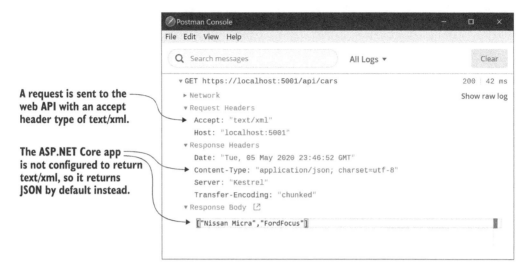

A request is sent to the web API with an accept header type of text/xml.

The ASP.NET Core app is not configured to return text/xml, so it returns JSON by default instead.

Figure 20.7   Even though the request was made with an `Accept` header of `text/xml`, the response returned was JSON, as the server was not configured to return XML.

The `Accept` and `Content-Type` headers

The `Accept` header is sent by a client as part of a request to indicate the type of content that the client can handle. It consists of a number of MIME types, with optional weightings (from 0 to 1) to indicate which type would be preferred. For example, the `application/json,text/xml;q=0.9,text/plain;q=0.6` header indicates that the client can accept JSON, XML, and plain text, with weightings of 1.0, 0.9, and 0.6, respectively. JSON has a weighting of 1.0, as no explicit weighting was provided. The weightings can be used during content negotiation to choose an optimal representation for both parties.

The `Content-Type` header describes the data sent in a request or response. It contains the MIME type of the data, with an optional character encoding. For example, the `application/json; charset=utf-8` header would indicate that the body of the request or response is JSON, encoded using UTF-8.

For more on MIME types, see the Mozilla documentation: http://mng.bz/gop8. You can find the RFC for content negotiation at http://mng.bz/6DXo.

WARNING   In legacy ASP.NET, objects were serialized to JSON using Pascal-Case, where properties start with a capital letter. In ASP.NET Core, objects are serialized using camelCase by default, where properties start with a lower-case letter.

However the data is sent, it's serialized by an `IOutputFormatter` implementation. ASP.NET Core ships with a limited number of output formatters out of the box, but as always, it's easy to add additional ones or change the way the defaults work.

20.5.1 *Customizing the default formatters: Adding XML support*

As with most of ASP.NET Core, the Web API formatters are completely customizable. By default, only formatters for plain text (text/plain), HTML (text/html), and JSON (application/json) are configured. Given the common use case of single-page application (SPAs) and mobile applications, this will get you a long way. But sometimes you need to be able to return data in a different format, such as XML.

> ### Newtonsoft.Json vs. System.Text.Json
>
> Newtonsoft.Json, also known as Json.NET, has for a long time been the canonical way to work with JSON in .NET. It's compatible with every version of .NET under the sun, and it will no doubt be familiar to virtually all .NET developers. Its reach was so great that even ASP.NET Core took a dependency on it!
>
> That all changed with the introduction of a new library in ASP.NET Core 3.0, System.Text.Json, which focuses on performance. In .NET Core 3.0 onward, ASP.NET Core uses System.Text.Json by default instead of Newtonsoft.Json.
>
> The main difference between the libraries is that System.Text.Json is picky about its JSON. It will generally only deserialize JSON that matches its expectations. For example, System.Text.Json won't deserialize JSON that uses single quotes around strings; you have to use double quotes.
>
> If you're creating a new application, this is generally not a problem; you quickly learn to generate the correct JSON. But if you're converting an application to ASP.NET Core or are sending JSON to a third party you don't control, these limitations can be real stumbling blocks.
>
> Luckily, you can easily switch back to the Newtonsoft.Json library instead. Install the Microsoft.AspNetCore.Mvc.NewtonsoftJson package into your project and update the AddControllers() method in Program.cs to the following:
>
> ```
> builder.Services.AddControllers()
>     .AddNewtonsoftJson();
> ```
>
> This will switch ASP.NET Core's formatters to use Newtonsoft.Json behind the scenes, instead of System.Text.Json. For more details on the differences between the libraries, see Microsoft's article "Compare Newtonsoft.Json to System.Text.Json, and migrate to System.Text.Json": http://mng.bz/OmRJ. For more advice on when to switch to the Newtonsoft.Json formatter, see the section "Add Newtonsoft.Json-based JSON format support" in Microsoft's "Format response data in ASP.NET Core Web API" documentation: http://mng.bz/zx11.

You can add XML output to your application by adding an output formatter. You configure your application's formatters in Program.cs by customizing the IMvcBuilder object returned from AddControllers(). To add the XML output formatter, use the following:

```
services.AddControllers()
    .AddXmlSerializerFormatters();
```

NOTE Technically, this also adds an XML input formatter, which means your application can now receive XML in requests too. Previously, sending a request with XML in the body would respond with a `415 Unsupported Media Type` response. For a detailed look at formatters, including creating a custom formatter, see the documentation at http://mng.bz/e5gG.

With this simple change, your API controllers can now format responses as XML as well as JSON. Running the same request as shown in figure 20.7 with XML support enabled means the app will respect the `text/xml` accept header. The formatter serializes the `string` array to XML as requested instead of defaulting to JSON, as shown in figure 20.8.

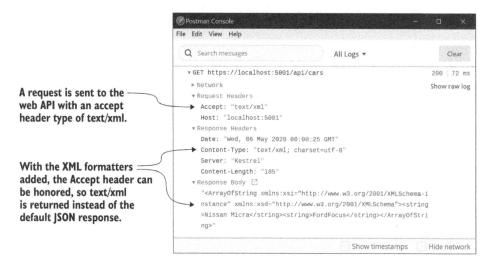

A request is sent to the web API with an accept header type of text/xml.

With the XML formatters added, the Accept header can be honored, so text/xml is returned instead of the default JSON response.

Figure 20.8 With the XML output formatters added, the `Accept` header's `text/xml` value is respected, and the response is serialized to XML.

This is an example of content negotiation, where the client has specified which formats it can handle and the server selects one of those, based on what it can produce. This approach is part of the HTTP protocol, but there are some quirks to be aware of when relying on it in ASP.NET Core. You won't often run into these, but if you're not aware of them when they hit you, they could have you scratching your head for hours!

20.5.2 Choosing a response format with content negotiation

Content negotiation is where a client says which types of data it can accept using the `Accept` header and the server picks the best one it can handle. Generally speaking, this works as you'd hope: the server formats the data using a type the client can understand.

The ASP.NET Core implementation has some special cases that are worth bearing in mind:

- By default, ASP.NET Core returns only `application/json`, `text/plain`, and `text/html` MIME types. You can add `IOutputFormatters` to make other types available, as you saw in the previous section for `text/xml`.

- By default, if you return `null` as your API model, whether from an action method or by passing `null` in a `StatusCodeResult`, the middleware returns a `204 No Content` response.

- When you return a `string` as your API model, if no `Accept` header is set, ASP.NET Core formats the response as `text/plain`.

- When you use any other class as your API model, and there's no `Accept` header or none of the supported formats was requested, the first formatter that can generate a response is used (typically JSON by default).

- If the middleware detects that the request is probably from a browser (the `Accept` header contains `*/*`), it will *not* use conneg. Instead, it formats the response as though an `Accept` header was not provided, using the default formatter (typically JSON).

These defaults are relatively sane, but they can certainly bite you if you're not aware of them. That last point in particular, where the response to a request from a browser is virtually always formatted as JSON, has certainly caught me out when trying to test XML requests locally!

As you should expect by now, all these rules are configurable; you can easily change the default behavior in your application if it doesn't fit your requirements. For example, the following listing, shows how you can force the middleware to respect the browser's `Accept` header and remove the `text/plain` formatter for `strings`.

Listing 20.14   Customizing MVC to respect the browser's `Accept` header in web APIs

```
WebApplicationBuilder builder = WebApplication.CreateBuilder(args);

builder.Services.AddControllers(options =>          AddControllers has an overload
{                                                   that takes a lambda function.
    options.RespectBrowserAcceptHeader = true;
    options.OutputFormatters.RemoveType<StringOutputFormatter>();      Removes the output formatter
});                                                                    that formats strings as text/plain
                                              
False by default; several other properties
are also available to be set.
```

In most cases, conneg should work well for you out of the box, whether you're building an SPA or a mobile application. In some cases, you may find you need to bypass the usual conneg mechanisms for specific action methods, and there are various ways to achieve this, but I won't cover them in this book as I've found I rarely need to use them. For details, see Microsoft's "Format response data in ASP.NET Core Web API" documentation: http://mng.bz/zx11.

At this point we've covered the main points of using API controllers, but you probably still have one major question: why would I use web API controllers over minimal APIs? That's a great question, and one we'll look at in section 20.6.

20.6 Choosing between web API controllers and minimal APIs

In part 1 of this book you learned all about using minimal APIs to build a JSON API. Minimal APIs are the new kid on the block, being introduced in .NET 6, but they are growing up quickly. With all the new features introduced in .NET 7 (discussed in chapter 5), minimal APIs are emerging as a great way to build HTTP APIs in modern .NET.

By contrast, web API controllers have been around since day one. They were introduced in their current form in ASP.NET Core 1.0 and were heavily inspired by the web API framework from legacy ASP.NET. The designs, patterns, and concepts used by web API controllers haven't changed much since then, so if you've ever used web API controllers, they should look familiar in .NET 7.

The difficult question in .NET 7 is if you need to build an API, which should you use, minimal APIs or web API controllers? Both have their pros and cons, and a large part of the decision will be personal preference, but to help your decision, you should ask yourself several questions:

1 Do you need to return data in multiple formats using content negotiation?
2 Is performance critical to your application?
3 Do you have complex filtering requirements?
4 Is this a new project?
5 Do you already have experience with web API controllers?
6 Do you prefer convention over configuration?

Questions 1-3 in this list are focused on technical differences between minimal APIs and web API controllers. Web API controllers support conneg, which allows clients to request data be returned in a particular format: JSON, XML, or CSV, for example, as you learned in section 20.5. Web API controllers support this feature out of the box, so if it's crucial for your application, it may be better to choose web API controllers over minimal APIs.

> **TIP** If you want to use conneg with minimal APIs, it's possible but not built in. I show how to add conneg to minimal APIs using the open-source library Carter on my blog: http://mng.bz/o12d.

Question 2 is about performance. Everyone wants the most performant app, but there's a real question of how important it is. Are you going to be regularly benchmarking your application and looking for any regressions? If so, minimal APIs are probably going to be a better choice, as they're often more performant than web API controllers.

The MVC framework that web API controllers use relies on a lot of conventions and reflection for discovering your controllers and a complex filter pipeline. These are obviously highly optimized, but if you're writing an application where you need to squeeze out every little bit of throughput, minimal APIs will likely help get you there more easily. For most applications, the overhead of the MVC framework will be negligible when compared with any database or network access in your app, so this is worth worrying about only for performance-sensitive apps.

Question 3 focuses on filtering. You learned about filtering with minimal APIs in chapter 5: filters allow you to attach a processing pipeline to your minimal API endpoints and can be used to do things like automatic validation. Web API controllers (as well as MVC controllers and Razor Pages) also have a filter pipeline, but it's *much* more complex than the simple pipeline used by minimal APIs, as you'll see in chapters 21 and 22.

In most cases the filtering provided by minimal APIs will be perfectly adequate for your needs. The main cases where minimal API filtering will fall down will be when you already have an application that uses web API controllers and want to reuse some complex filters. In these cases, there may be no way to translate your existing web API filters to minimal API filters. If the filtering is important, then you may need to stick with web API controllers.

This leads to question 4: are you building a new application or working on an existing application? If this is a new application, I would be strongly in favor of using minimal APIs. Minimal APIs are conceptually simpler than web API controllers, are faster because of this, and are receiving a lot of improvements from the ASP.NET Core team. If there's no other compelling reason to choose web API controllers in your new project, I suggest defaulting to minimal APIs.

On the other hand, if you have an existing web API controller application, I would be strongly inclined to stick with web API controllers. While it's perfectly possible to mix minimal APIs and web API controllers in the same application, I would favor consistency over using the new hotness.

Question 5 considers how familiar you already are with web API controllers. If you're coming from legacy ASP.NET or have already used web API controllers in ASP.NET Core and need to be productive quickly, you might decide to stick with web API controllers.

I consider this one of the weaker arguments, as minimal APIs are conceptually simpler than web API controllers; if you already know web API controllers, you will likely pick up minimal APIs easily. That said, the differences in the model binding approaches can be a little confusing, and you may decide it's not worth the investment or frustration if things don't work as you expect.

The final question comes down entirely to taste and preference: do you like minimal APIs? Web API controllers heavily follow the "convention over configuration" paradigm (though not to the extent of MVC controllers and Razor Pages). By contrast, you must be far more explicit with minimal APIs. Minimal APIs also don't enforce any particular grouping, unlike web API controllers, which all follow the "action methods in a controller class" pattern.

Different people prefer different approaches. Web API controllers mean less manual wiring up of components, but this necessarily means more magic and more rigidity around how you structure your applications.

By contrast, minimal API endpoints must be explicitly added to the WebApplication instance, but this also means you have more flexibility around how to group your endpoints. You can put all your endpoints in Program.cs, create natural groupings for them in separate classes, or create a file per endpoint or any pattern you choose.

> **TIP** You can also more easily layer on helper frameworks to minimal APIs, such as Carter (https://github.com/CarterCommunity/Carter), which can provide some structure and support functionality if you want it.

Overall, the choice is up to you whether web API controllers or minimal APIs are better for your application. Table 20.1 summarizes the questions and where you should favor one approach over the other, but the final choice is up to you!

Table 20.1 Choosing between minimal APIs with web API controllers

Question	Minimal APIs	Web API controllers
1. Do you need conneg?	Can't use conneg out of the box	Built-in and extensible
2. How critical is performance?	More performant than web API controllers	Less performant than minimal APIs
3. Complex filtering?	Have a simple, extensible filter pipeline	Have a complex, nonlinear, filter pipeline
4. Is this a new project?	Minimal APIs are getting many new features and are a focus of the ASP.NET Core team.	The MVC framework is receiving small new features, but is less of a focus.
5. Do you have experience with web API controllers?	Minimal APIs share many of the same concepts, but have subtle differences in model binding.	Web API controllers may be familiar to users of legacy ASP.NET or older ASP.NET Core versions.
6. Do you prefer convention over configuration?	Requires a lot of explicit configuration	Convention- and discovery-based, which can appear more magical when you're unfamiliar

That brings us to the end of this chapter on web APIs. In the next chapter we'll look at one of more advanced topics of MVC and Razor Pages: the filter pipeline and how you can use it to reduce duplication in your code. The good news is that it's similar to minimal API filters in principle. The bad news is that it's far more complicated!

Summary

- Web API action methods can return data directly or can use ActionResult<T> to generate an arbitrary response. If you return more than one type of result from an action method, the method signature must return ActionResult<T>.

- The data returned by a web API action is sometimes called an API model. It contains the data that will be serialized and send back to the client. This differs from view models and PageModels, which contain both data and metadata about how to generate the response.

- Web APIs are associated with route templates by applying RouteAttributes to your action methods. These give you complete control over the URLs that make up your application's API.

- Route attributes applied to a controller combine with the attributes on action methods to form the final template. These are also combined with attributes on inherited base classes. You can use inherited attributes to reduce the amount of duplication in the attributes, such as where you're using a common prefix on your routes.

- By default, the controller and action name have no bearing on the URLs or route templates when you use attribute routing. However, you can use the "[controller]" and "[action]" tokens in your route templates to reduce repetition. They'll be replaced with the current controller and action name.

- The [HttpPost] and [HttpGet] attributes allow you to choose between actions based on the request's HTTP verb when two actions correspond to the same URL. This is a common pattern in RESTful applications.

- The [ApiController] attribute applies several common conventions to your controllers. Controllers decorated with the attribute automatically bind to a request's body instead of using form values, automatically generate a 400 Bad Request response for invalid requests, and return ProblemDetails objects for status code errors. This can dramatically reduce the amount of boilerplate code you must write.

- You can control which of the conventions to apply by using the ConfigureApi-BehaviorOptions() method and providing a configuration lambda. This is useful if you need to fit your API to an existing specification, for example.

- By default, ASP.NET Core formats the API model returned from a web API controller as JSON. In contrast to legacy ASP.NET, JSON data is serialized using camelCase rather than PascalCase. You should consider this change if you get errors or missing values when using data from your API.

- ASP.NET Core 3.0 onwards uses System.Text.Json, which is a strict, high performance library for JSON serialization and deserialization. You can replace this serializer with the common Newtonsoft.Json formatter by calling AddNewtonsoft-Json() on the return value from services.AddControllers().

- Content negotiation occurs when the client specifies the type of data it can handle and the server chooses a return format based on this. It allows multiple clients to call your API and receive data in a format they can understand.

- By default, ASP.NET Core can return text/plain, text/html, and application/json, but you can add formatters if you need to support other formats.

- You can add XML formatters by calling `AddXmlSerializerFormatters()` on the return value from `services.AddControllers()` in your `Startup` class. These can format the response as XML, as well as receive XML in a request body.
- Content negotiation isn't used when the `Accept` header contains `*/*`, such as in most browsers. Instead, your application uses the default formatter, JSON. You can disable this option by setting the `RespectBrowserAcceptHeader` option to `true` when adding your controller services in Program.cs.
- You can mix web API Controllers and minimal API endpoints in the same application, but you may find it easier to use one or the other.
- Choose web API controllers when you need content negotiation, when you have complex filtering requirements, when you have experience with web controllers, or when you prefer convention over configuration for your apps.
- Choose minimal API endpoints when performance is critical, when you prefer explicit configuration over automatic conventions, or when you're starting a new app.

The MVC and Razor Pages filter pipeline

21

This chapter covers

- The filter pipeline and how it differs from middleware
- The different types of filters
- Filter ordering

Part 3 of this book has covered the Model-View-Controller (MVC) and Razor Pages frameworks of ASP.NET Core in some detail. You learned how routing is used to select a Razor Page or action to execute. You also saw model binding, validation, and how to generate a response by returning an `IActionResult` from your actions and page handlers. In this chapter I'm going to head deeper into the MVC/Razor Pages frameworks and look at the *filter pipeline*, sometimes called the *action invocation pipeline*, which is analogous to the minimal API endpoint filter pipeline you learned about in chapter 5.

MVC and Razor Pages use several built-in filters to handle cross-cutting concerns, such as authorization (controlling which users can access which action methods and pages in your application). Any application that has the concept of users will use authorization filters as a minimum, but filters are much more powerful than this single use case. In sections 21.1 and 21.2 you'll learn about all the different types of filters and how they combine to create the MVC filter pipeline for a request that reaches the MVC or Razor Pages framework.

Think of the MVC filter pipeline as a mini middleware pipeline running inside the MVC and Razor Pages frameworks, like the minimal API endpoint filter pipeline. Like the middleware pipeline in ASP.NET Core, the MVC filter pipeline consists of a series of components connected as a pipe, so the output of one filter feeds into the input of the next. In section 21.3 we'll look at the similarities and differences between these two pipelines, and when you should choose one over the other.

In section 21.4 you'll see how to create a simple custom filter. Rather than focus on the functionality of the filter itself, you'll learn how to apply it to multiple endpoints in section 21.5. In section 21.6 you'll see how the choice of *where* you apply your attributes affects the order in which your filters execute.

The filter pipeline is a complex topic, but it can enable some advanced behaviors in your app and potentially reduce overall complexity. In this chapter you'll learn the basics of the pipeline and how it works. In chapter 22 we dig into practical examples of filters, looking at the filters that come out of the box in ASP.NET Core, as well as building custom filters to extract common code from your controllers and Razor Pages.

Before we can start writing code, we should get to grips with the basics of the filter pipeline. The first section of this chapter explains what the pipeline is, why you might want to use it, and how it differs from the middleware pipeline.

21.1 Understanding the MVC filter pipeline

In this section you'll learn all about the MVC filter pipeline. You'll see where it fits in the life cycle of a typical request and the roles of the six types of filters available.

The filter pipeline is a relatively simple concept in that it provides *hooks* into the normal MVC request, as shown in figure 21.1. For example, say you wanted to ensure that users can create or edit products on an e-commerce app only if they're logged in. The app would redirect anonymous users to a login page instead of executing the action.

Without filters, you'd need to include the same code to check for a logged-in user at the start of each specific action method. With this approach, the MVC framework would still execute the model binding and validation, even if the user were not logged in.

With filters, you can use the *hooks* in the MVC request to run common code across all requests or a subset of requests. This way you can do a wide range of things, such as

- Ensure that a user is logged in before an action method, model binding, or validation runs.
- Customize the output format of particular action methods.
- Handle model validation failures before an action method is invoked.
- Catch exceptions from an action method and handle them in a special way.

1. **A request is received for the URL /api/product/1.**

2. **The routing middleware matches the request to the Get action on the ProductController and sets id=1.**

3. **A variety of different filters runs as part of the execution in the endpoint middleware.**

4. **Filters run before model binding, before the action method runs, and before and after the IActionResult is executed.**

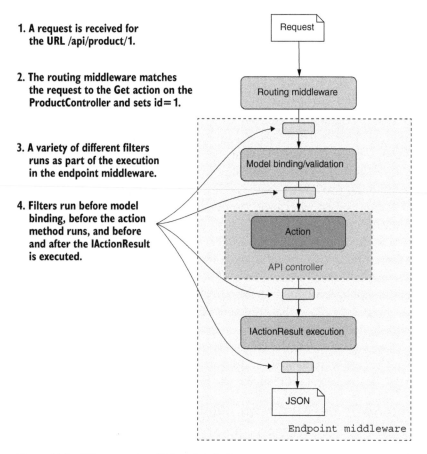

Figure 21.1   Filters run at multiple points in the EndpointMiddleware as part of the normal handling of an MVC request. A similar pipeline exists for Razor Page requests.

In many ways, the MVC filter pipeline is like an extra middleware pipeline, restricted to MVC and Razor Pages requests only. Like middleware, filters are good for handling cross-cutting concerns for your application and are useful tools for reducing code duplication in many cases.

The linear view of an MVC request and the filter pipeline that I've used so far doesn't *quite* match up with how these filters execute. There are five types of filters that apply to MVC requests, each of which runs at a different stage in the MVC framework, as shown in figure 21.2.

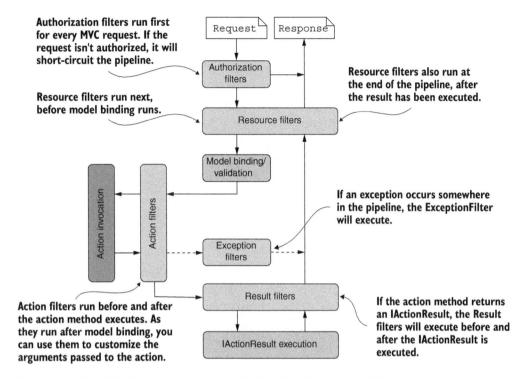

Figure 21.2 The MVC filter pipeline, including the five filter stages. Some filter stages (resource, action, and result) run twice, before and after the remainder of the pipeline.

Each filter stage lends itself to a particular use case, thanks to its specific location in the pipeline, with respect to model binding, action execution, and result execution:

- *Authorization filters*—These run first in the pipeline, so they're useful for protecting your APIs and action methods. If an authorization filter deems the request unauthorized, it short-circuits the request, preventing the rest of the filter pipeline (or action) from running.
- *Resource filters*—After authorization, resource filters are the next filters to run in the pipeline. They can also execute at the *end* of the pipeline, in much the same way that middleware components can handle both the incoming request and the outgoing response. Alternatively, resource filters can completely short-circuit the request pipeline and return a response directly.

  Thanks to their early position in the pipeline, resource filters can have a variety of uses. You could add metrics to an action method; prevent an action method from executing if an unsupported content type is requested; or, as they run before model binding, control the way model binding works for that request.

- *Action filters*—Action filters run immediately before and after an action method is executed. As model binding has already happened, action filters let you manipulate the arguments to the method—before it executes—or they can short-circuit the action completely and return a different IActionResult. Because they also run after the action executes, they can optionally customize an IActionResult returned by the action before the action result is executed.
- *Exception filters*—Exception filters catch exceptions that occur in the filter pipeline and handle them appropriately. You can use exception filters to write custom, MVC-specific error-handling code, which can be useful in some situations. For example, you could catch exceptions in API actions and format them differently from exceptions in your Razor Pages.
- *Result filters*—Result filters run before and after an action method's IActionResult is executed. You can use result filters to control the execution of the result or even to short-circuit the execution of the result.

Exactly which filter you pick to implement will depend on the functionality you're trying to introduce. Want to short-circuit a request as early as possible? Resource filters are a good fit. Need access to the action method parameters? Use an action filter.

Think of the filter pipeline as a small middleware pipeline that lives by itself in the MVC framework. Alternatively, you could think of filters as hooks into the MVC action invocation process that let you run code at a particular point in a request's life cycle.

> **NOTE** The design of the MVC filter pipeline is quite different from the minimal API endpoint filter pipeline you saw in chapter 5. The endpoint filter pipeline is linear and doesn't have multiple types of filters.

This section described how the filter pipeline works for MVC and Web API controllers; Razor Pages use an almost-identical filter pipeline.

21.2 *The Razor Pages filter pipeline*

The Razor Pages framework uses the same underlying architecture as MVC and Web API controllers, so it's perhaps not surprising that the filter pipeline is virtually identical. The only difference between the pipelines is that Razor Pages do not use action filters. Instead, they use *page filters*, as shown in figure 21.3.

The authorization, resource, exception, and result filters are exactly the same filters you saw for the MVC pipeline. They execute in the same way, serve the same purposes, and can be short-circuited in the same way.

> **NOTE** These filters are literally the same classes shared between the Razor Pages and MVC frameworks.

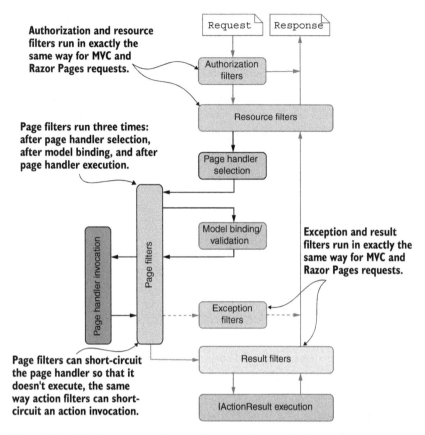

Authorization and resource filters run in exactly the same way for MVC and Razor Pages requests.

Page filters run three times: after page handler selection, after model binding, and after page handler execution.

Exception and result filters run in exactly the same way for MVC and Razor Pages requests.

Page filters can short-circuit the page handler so that it doesn't execute, the same way action filters can short-circuit an action invocation.

Figure 21.3 The Razor Pages filter pipeline, including the five filter stages. Authorization, resource, exception, and result filters execute in exactly the same way as for the MVC pipeline. Page filters are specific to Razor Pages and execute in three places: after page hander selection, after model binding and validation, and after page handler execution.

The difference with the Razor Pages filter pipeline is that it uses page filters instead of action filters. By contrast with other filter types, page filters run three times in the filter pipeline:

- *After page handler selection*—After the resource filters have executed, a page handler is selected, based on the request's HTTP verb and the {handler} route value, as you learned in chapter 15. After page handler selection, a page filter method executes for the first time. You can't short-circuit the pipeline at this stage, and model binding and validation have not yet executed.
- *After model binding*—After the first page filter execution, the request is model-bound to the Razor Page's binding models and is validated. This execution is highly analogous to the action filter execution for API controllers. At this point you could manipulate the model-bound data or short-circuit the page handler execution completely by returning a different IActionResult.

■ *After page handler execution*—If you don't short-circuit the page handler execution, the page filter runs a third and final time after the page handler has executed. At this point you could customize the IActionResult returned by the page handler before the result is executed.

The triple execution of page filters makes it a bit harder to visualize the pipeline, but you can generally think of them as beefed-up action filters. Everything you can do with an action filter, you can do with a page filter, and you can hook in after page handler selection if necessary.

> **TIP**   Each execution of a filter executes a different method of the appropriate interface, so it's easy to know where you are in the pipeline and to execute a filter in only one of its possible locations if you wish.

One of the main questions I hear when people learn about filters in ASP.NET Core is "Why do we need them?" If the filter pipeline is like a mini middleware pipeline, why not use a middleware component directly, instead of introducing the filter concept? That's an excellent point, which I'll tackle in the next section.

21.3   *Filters or middleware: Which should you choose?*

The filter pipeline is similar to the middleware pipeline in many ways, but there are several subtle differences that you should consider when deciding which approach to use. The considerations are essentially the same as those for the minimal API endpoint filter I discussed in chapter 5. MVC filters and middleware are similar in three ways:

■ Requests pass through a middleware component on the way "in," and responses pass through again on the way "out." Resource, action, and result filters are also two-way, though authorization and exception filters run only once for a request, and page filters run three times.

■ Middleware can short-circuit a request by returning a response instead of passing it on to later middleware. MVC and page filters can also short-circuit the filter pipeline by returning a response.

■ Middleware is often used for cross-cutting application concerns, such as logging, performance profiling, and exception handling. Filters also lend themselves to cross-cutting concerns.

Filters and middleware also differ primarily in three ways:

■ Middleware can run for all requests; filters run only for requests that reach the EndpointMiddleware and execute a controller action or Razor Page handler.

■ Filters have access to MVC constructs such as ModelState and IActionResults. Middleware in general is independent from MVC and Razor Pages and works at a lower level, so it can't use these concepts.

■ Filters can be easily applied to a subset of requests, such as all actions on a single controller or a single Razor Page. Middleware generally applies to all requests that reach a given point in the middleware pipeline.

As for the endpoint filter pipeline, I like to think of middleware versus MVC filters as a question of specificity. Middleware is the more general concept, so it has the wider reach. But if you need to access to MVC constructs or want to behave differently for some MVC actions or Razor Pages, you should consider using a filter.

The middleware-versus-filters argument is a subtle one, and it doesn't matter which you choose as long as it works for you. You can even use middleware components inside the MVC filter pipeline, effectively turning a middleware component into a filter!

> **TIP**   The middleware-as-filters feature was introduced in ASP.NET Core 1.1 and is also available in later versions. The canonical use case is for localizing requests to multiple languages. I have a blog series on how to use the feature here: http://mng.bz/RXa0.

Filters can be a little abstract in isolation, so in the next section we'll look at some code and learn how to write a custom MVC filter in ASP.NET Core.

21.4   *Creating a simple filter*

In this section, I show you how to create your first filters; in section 21.5 you'll see how to apply them to MVC controllers and actions. We'll start small, creating filters that only write to the console, but in chapter 22 we look at some more practical examples and discuss some of their nuances.

You implement a filter for a given stage by implementing one of a pair of interfaces, one synchronous (sync) and one asynchronous (async):

- *Authorization filters*—IAuthorizationFilter or IAsyncAuthorizationFilter
- *Resource filters*—IResourceFilter or IAsyncResourceFilter
- *Action filters*—IActionFilter or IAsyncActionFilter
- *Page filters*—IPageFilter or IAsyncPageFilter
- *Exception filters*—IExceptionFilter or IAsyncExceptionFilter
- *Result filters*—IResultFilter or IAsyncResultFilter

You can use any plain old CLR object (POCO) class to implement a filter, but you'll typically implement them as C# attributes, which you can use to decorate your controllers, actions, and Razor Pages, as you'll see in section 21.5. You can achieve the same results with either the sync or async interface, so which you choose should depend on whether any services you call in the filter require async support.

> **NOTE**   You should implement either the sync interface or the async interface, not both. If you implement both, only the async interface will be used.

Listing 21.1 shows a resource filter that implements IResourceFilter and writes to the console when it executes. The OnResourceExecuting method is called when a request first reaches the resource filter stage of the filter pipeline. By contrast, the OnResource-Executed method is called after the rest of the pipeline has executed: after model binding, action execution, result execution, and all intermediate filters have run.

Listing 21.1   Example resource filter implementing `IResourceFilter`

```
public class LogResourceFilter : Attribute, IResourceFilter
{
    public void OnResourceExecuting(
        ResourceExecutingContext context)
    {
        Console.WriteLine("Executing!");
    }

    public void OnResourceExecuted(
        ResourceExecutedContext context)
    {
        Console.WriteLine("Executed");
    }
}
```

Executed at the start of the pipeline, after authorization filters

The context contains the HttpContext, routing details, and information about the current action.

Executed after model binding, action execution, and result execution

Contains additional context information, such as the IActionResult returned by the action

The interface methods are simple and are similar for each stage in the filter pipeline, passing a context object as a method parameter. Each of the two-method sync filters has an *Executing and an *Executed method. The type of the argument is different for each filter, but it contains all the details for the filter pipeline.

For example, the ResourceExecutingContext passed to the resource filter contains the HttpContext object itself, details about the route that selected this action, details about the action itself, and so on. Contexts for later filters contain additional details, such as the action method arguments for an action filter and the ModelState.

The context object for the ResourceExecutedContext method is similar, but it also contains details about how the rest of the pipeline executed. You can check whether an unhandled exception occurred, you can see if another filter from the same stage short-circuited the pipeline, or you can see the IActionResult used to generate the response.

These context objects are powerful and are the key to advanced filter behaviors like short-circuiting the pipeline and handling exceptions. We'll make use of them in chapter 22 when we create more complex filter examples.

The async version of the resource filter requires implementing a single method, as shown in listing 21.2. As for the sync version, you're passed a ResourceExecuting-Context object as an argument, and you're passed a delegate representing the remainder of the filter pipeline. You must call this delegate (asynchronously) to execute the remainder of the pipeline, which returns an instance of ResourceExecutedContext.

Listing 21.2   Example resource filter implementing `IAsyncResourceFilter`

```
public class LogAsyncResourceFilter : Attribute, IAsyncResourceFilter
{
    public async Task OnResourceExecutionAsync(
        ResourceExecutingContext context,
        ResourceExecutionDelegate next)
    {
        Console.WriteLine("Executing async!");
```

Called before the rest of the pipeline executes

Executed at the start of the pipeline, after authorization filters

You're provided a delegate, which encapsulates the remainder of the filter pipeline.

```
        ResourceExecutedContext executedContext = await next();
        Console.WriteLine("Executed async!");
    }
}
```

Executes the rest of the pipeline and obtains a ResourceExecutedContext

Called after the rest of the pipeline executes

The sync and async filter implementations have subtle differences, but for most purposes they're identical. I recommend implementing the sync version for simplicity, falling back to the async version only if you need to.

You've created a couple of filters now, so we should look at how to use them in the application. In the next section we'll tackle two specific issues: how to control which requests execute your new filters and how to control the order in which they execute.

21.5 Adding filters to your actions and Razor Pages

In section 21.3 I discussed the similarities and differences between middleware and filters. One of those differences is that filters can be scoped to specific actions or controllers so that they run only for certain requests. Alternatively, you can apply a filter globally so that it runs for every MVC action and Razor Page.

By adding filters in different ways, you can achieve several different results. Imagine you have a filter that forces you to log in to execute an action. How you add the filter to your app will significantly change your app's behavior:

- *Apply the filter to a single action or Razor Page.* Anonymous users could browse the app as normal, but if they tried to access the protected action or Razor Page, they would be forced to log in.
- *Apply the filter to a controller.* Anonymous users could access actions from other controllers, but accessing any action on the protected controller would force them to log in.
- *Apply the filter globally.* Users couldn't use the app without logging in. Any attempt to access an action or Razor Page would redirect the user to the login page.

NOTE ASP.NET Core comes with such a filter out of the box: Authorize-Filter. I discuss this filter in chapter 22, and you'll be seeing a lot more of it in chapter 24.

As I described in the previous section, you normally create filters as attributes, and for good reason: it makes it easy for you to apply them to MVC controllers, actions, and Razor Pages. In this section you'll see how to apply LogResourceFilter from listing 21.1 to an action, a controller, a Razor Page, and globally. The level at which the filter applies is called its *scope*.

DEFINITION The *scope* of a filter refers to how many different actions it applies to. A filter can be scoped to the action method, to the controller, to a Razor Page, or globally.

You'll start at the most specific scope: applying filters to a single action. The following listing shows an example of an MVC controller that has two action methods, one with `LogResourceFilter` and one without.

Listing 21.3   Applying filters to an action method

```
public class RecipeController : ControllerBase
{
    [LogResourceFilter]
    public IActionResult Index()
    {
        return Ok();
    }
    public IActionResult View()
    {
        return OK();
    }
}
```

LogResourceFilter runs as part of the pipeline when executing this action.

This action method has no filters at the action level.

Alternatively, if you want to apply the same filter to every action method, you could add the attribute at the controller scope, as in the next listing. Every action method in the controller uses `LogResourceFilter` without having to specifically decorate each method.

Listing 21.4   Applying filters to a controller

```
[LogResourceFilter]
public class RecipeController : ControllerBase
{
    public IActionResult Index ()
    {
        return Ok();
    }
    public IActionResult View()
    {
        return Ok();
    }
}
```

The LogResourceFilter is added to every action on the controller.

Every action in the controller is decorated with the filter.

For Razor Pages, you can apply attributes to your `PageModel`, as shown in the following listing. The filter applies to all page handlers in the Razor Page. It's not possible to apply filters to a single page handler; you must apply them at the page level.

Listing 21.5   Applying filters to a Razor Page

```
[LogResourceFilter]
public class IndexModel : PageModel
{
    public void OnGet()
    {
```

The LogResourceFilter is added to the Razor Page's PageModel.

The filter applies to every page handler in the page.

```
        }
        public void OnPost()
        {
        }
    }
}
```

The filter applies to every
page handler in the page.

Filters you apply as attributes to controllers, actions, and Razor Pages are automatically discovered by the framework when your application starts up. For common attributes, you can go one step further and apply filters globally without having to decorate individual classes.

You add global filters in a different way from controller- or action-scoped filters—by adding a filter directly to the MVC services when configuring your controllers and Razor Pages. The next listing shows three equivalent ways to add a globally scoped filter.

Listing 21.6   Applying filters globally to an application

```
WebApplicationBuilder builder = WebApplication.CreateBuilder(args);

builder.Services.AddControllers(options =>      ◁——— Adds filters using the MvcOptions object
{
    options.Filters.Add(new LogResourceFilter());     ◁———┐  You can pass an instance
    options.Filters.Add(typeof(LogResourceFilter));   ◁———┤  of the filter directly. . .
    options.Filters.Add<LogResourceFilter>();
});
```

. . . or pass in the Type of the
filter and let the framework
create it.

Alternatively, the framework can create a
global filter using a generic type parameter.

You can configure the `MvcOptions` by using the `AddControllers()` overload. When you configure filters globally, they apply both to controllers *and* to any Razor Pages in your application. If you wish to configure a global filter for a Razor Pages application, there isn't an overload for configuring the `MvcOptions`. Instead, you need to use the `AddMvcOptions()` extension method to configure the filters, as shown in the following listing.

Listing 21.7   Applying filters globally to a Razor Pages application

```
WebApplicationBuilder builder = WebApplication.CreateBuilder(args);

builder.Services.RazorPages()
    .AddMvcOptions(options =>      ◁——
    {
        options.Filters.Add(new LogResourceFilter());
        options.Filters.Add(typeof(LogResourceFilter));
        options.Filters.Add<LogResourceFilter>();
    });
```

You must use an extension
method to add the filters
to the MvcOptions object.

This method
doesn't let
you pass a
lambda to
configure the
MvcOptions.

You can configure the
filters in any of the ways
shown previously.

With potentially three different scopes in play, you'll often find action methods that have multiple filters applied to them, some applied directly to the action method and others inherited from the controller or globally. Then the question becomes which filter runs first.

21.6 Understanding the order of filter execution

You've seen that the filter pipeline contains five stages, one for each type of filter. These stages always run in the fixed order I described in sections 21.1 and 21.2. But within each stage, you can also have multiple filters of the same type (for example, multiple resource filters) that are part of a single action method's pipeline. These could all have multiple scopes, depending on how you added them, as you saw in the preceding section.

In this section we're thinking about the order of filters within a given stage and how scope affects this. We'll start by looking at the default order and then move on to ways to customize the order to your own requirements.

21.6.1 The default scope execution order

When thinking about filter ordering, it's important to remember that resource, action, and result filters implement two methods: an *Executing before method and an *Executed after method. On top of that, page filters implement three methods! The order in which each method executes depends on the scope of the filter, as shown in figure 21.4 for the resource filter stage.

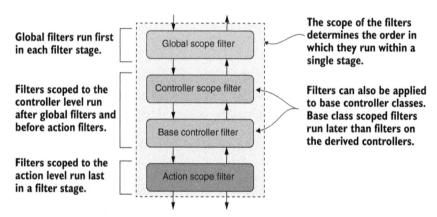

Global filters run first in each filter stage.

Filters scoped to the controller level run after global filters and before action filters.

Filters scoped to the action level run last in a filter stage.

The scope of the filters determines the order in which they run within a single stage.

Filters can also be applied to base controller classes. Base class scoped filters run later than filters on the derived controllers.

Global scope filter

Controller scope filter

Base controller filter

Action scope filter

Figure 21.4   The default filter ordering within a given stage, based on the scope of the filters. For the *Executing method, globally scoped filters run first, followed by controller-scoped, and finally action-scoped filters. For the *Executed method, the filters run in reverse order.

By default, filters execute from the broadest scope (global) to the narrowest (action) when running the *Executing method for each stage. The filters' *Executed methods run in reverse order, from the narrowest scope (action) to the broadest (global).

The ordering for Razor Pages is somewhat simpler, given that you have only two scopes: global scope filters and Razor Page scope filters. For Razor Pages, global scope filters run the *Executing and PageHandlerSelected methods first, followed by the page scope filters. For the *Executed methods, the filters run in reverse order.

You'll sometimes find you need a bit more control over this order, especially if you have, for example, multiple action filters applied at the same scope. The filter pipeline caters to this requirement by way of the IOrderedFilter interface.

21.6.2 Overriding the default order of filter execution with IOrderedFilter

Filters are great for extracting cross-cutting concerns from your controller actions and Razor Page, but if you have multiple filters applied to an action, you'll sometimes need to control the precise order in which they execute.

Scope can get you some of the way, but for those other cases, you can implement IOrderedFilter. This interface consists of a single property, Order:

```
public interface IOrderedFilter
{
    int Order { get; }
}
```

You can implement this property in your filters to set the order in which they execute. The filter pipeline orders the filters in each stage based on the Order property first, from lowest to highest, and uses the default scope order to handle ties, as shown in figure 21.5.

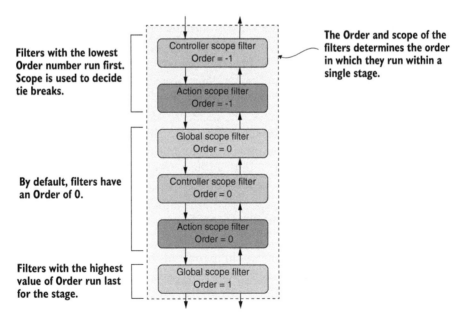

Figure 21.5 Controlling the filter order for a stage using the IOrderedFilter interface. Filters are ordered by the Order property first, and then by scope.

The filters for Order = -1 execute first, as they have the lowest Order value. The controller filter executes first because it has a broader scope than the action-scope filter. The filters with Order = 0 execute next, in the default scope order, as shown in figure 21.5. Finally, the filter with Order = 1 executes.

By default, if a filter doesn't implement IOrderedFilter, it's assumed to have Order = 0. All the filters that ship as part of ASP.NET Core have Order = 0, so you can implement your own filters relative to these.

> **NOTE** You can completely customize how the filter pipeline is built by customizing the MVC framework's *application model* conventions. These control everything about how controllers and Razor Pages are discovered, how they're added to the pipeline, and how filters are discovered. This is an advanced concept, that you won't often need, but it may occasionally come in handy. You can read about the MVC application model in the documentation at http://mng.bz/nWNa.

This chapter has provided a lot of background on the MVC filter pipeline, and we covered most of the technical details you need to use filters and create custom implementations for your own application. In chapter 22 you'll see some of the built-in filters provided by ASP.NET Core, as well as some practical examples of filters you might want to use in your own applications.

Summary

- The filter pipeline provides hooks into an MVC request so you can run functions at various points within an MVC request. With filters you can run code at specific points in the MVC process across all requests or a subset of requests. This is particularly useful for handling cross-cutting concerns that are specific to MVC.

- The filter pipeline executes as part of the MVC or Razor Pages execution. It consists of authorization filters, resource filters, action filters, page filters, exception filters, and result filters. Each filter type is grouped in a stage and can be used to achieve effects specific to that stage.

- Resource, action, and result filters run twice in the pipeline: an *Executing method on the way in and an *Executed method on the way out. Page filters run three times: after page handler selection, and before and after page handler execution.

- Authorization and exception filters run only once as part of the pipeline; they don't run after a response has been generated.

- Each type of filter has both a sync and an async version. For example, resource filters can implement either the IResourceFilter interface or the IAsyncResourceFilter interface. You should use the synchronous interface unless your filter needs to use asynchronous method calls.

- You can add filters globally, at the controller level, at the Razor Page level, or at the action level. This is called the *scope* of the filter. Which scope you should choose depends on how broadly you want to apply the filter.
- Within a given stage, global-scoped filters run first, then controller-scoped, and finally action-scoped. You can also override the default order by implementing the `IOrderedFilter` interface. Filters run from lowest to highest `Order` and use scope to break ties.

Creating custom MVC and Razor Page filters

This chapter covers

- Creating custom filters to refactor complex action methods
- Using authorization filters to protect your action methods and Razor Pages
- Short-circuiting the filter pipeline to bypass action and page handler execution
- Injecting dependencies into filters

In chapter 21 I introduced the Model-View-Controller (MVC) and Razor Pages filter pipeline and showed where it fits into the life cycle of a request. You learned how to apply filters to your action method, controllers, and Razor Pages, and the effect of scope on the filter execution order.

In this chapter you'll take that knowledge and apply it to a concrete example. You'll learn to create custom filters that you can use in your own apps and how to use them to reduce duplicate code in your action methods.

In section 22.1 I take you through the filter types in detail, how they fit into the MVC pipeline, and what to use them for. For each one, I'll provide example implementations that you might use in your own application and describe the built-in options available.

A key feature of filters is the ability to short-circuit a request by generating a response and halting progression through the filter pipeline. This is similar to the way short-circuiting works in middleware, but there are subtle differences for MVC filters. On top of that, the exact behavior is slightly different for each filter, and I cover that in section 22.2.

You typically add MVC filters to the pipeline by implementing them as attributes added to your controller classes, action methods, and Razor Pages. Unfortunately, you can't easily use dependency injection (DI) with attributes due to the limitations of C#. In section 22.3 I show you how to use the `ServiceFilterAttribute` and `TypeFilterAttribute` base classes to enable DI in your filters.

We covered all the background for filters in chapter 21, so in the next section we jump straight into the code and start creating custom MVC filters.

22.1 Creating custom filters for your application

ASP.NET Core includes several filters that you can use out of the box, but often the most useful filters are the custom ones that are specific to your own apps. In this section we'll work through each of the six types of filters I covered in chapter 21. I'll explain in more detail what they're for and when you should use them. I'll point out examples of these filters that are part of ASP.NET Core itself, and you'll see how to create custom filters for an example application.

To give you something realistic to work with, we'll start with a web API controller for accessing the recipe application from chapter 12. This controller contains two actions: one for fetching a `RecipeDetailViewModel` and another for updating a `Recipe` with new values. The following listing shows your starting point for this chapter, including both action methods.

Listing 22.1 **Recipe web API controller before refactoring to use filters**

```
[Route("api/recipe")]
public class RecipeApiController : ControllerBase          This field would be passed in
{                                                          as configuration and is used
    private readonly bool IsEnabled = true;     ◁───────   to control access to actions.
    public RecipeService _service;
    public RecipeApiController(RecipeService service)
    {
        _service = service;
    }

    [HttpGet("{id}")]
    public IActionResult Get(int id)
    {                                                       If the API isn't enabled,
        if (!IsEnabled) { return BadRequest(); }  ◁─────   blocks further execution
        try
        {
```

```
                            if (!_service.DoesRecipeExist(id))
    Sets the                {
  Last-Modified                 return NotFound();
 response header             }
 to the value in            var detail = _service.GetRecipeDetail(id);
    the model               Response.GetTypedHeaders().LastModified =
                                detail.LastModified;
                            return Ok(detail);
  Returns the           }
  view model         catch (Exception ex)
  with a 200         {
    response             return GetErrorResponse(ex);
                     }
                 }

        [HttpPost("{id}")]
        public IActionResult Edit(
            int id, [FromBody] UpdateRecipeCommand command)
        {
            if (!IsEnabled) { return BadRequest(); }
            try
            {
                if (!ModelState.IsValid)
                {
                    return BadRequest(ModelState);
                }
                if (!_service.DoesRecipeExist(id))
                {
                    return NotFound();
                }
                _service.UpdateRecipe(command);
                return Ok();
            }
            catch (Exception ex)
            {
                return GetErrorResponse(ex);
            }
        }

        private static IActionResult GetErrorResponse(Exception ex)
        {
            var error = new ProblemDetails
            {
                Title = "An error occurred",
                Detail = context.Exception.Message,
                Status = 500,
                Type = "https://httpstatuses.com/500"
            };

            return new ObjectResult(error)
            {
                StatusCode = 500
            };
        }
    }
}
```

If the requested Recipe doesn't exist, returns a 404 response

Fetches RecipeDetailViewModel

If an exception occurs, catches it and returns the error in an expected format, as a 500 error

If the API isn't enabled, blocks further execution

Validates the binding model and returns a 400 response if there are errors

If the requested Recipe doesn't exist, returns a 404 response

Updates the Recipe from the command and returns a 200 response

If an exception occurs, catches it and returns the error in an expected format, as a 500 error

These action methods currently have a lot of code to them, which hides the intent of each action. There's also quite a lot of duplication between the methods, such as checking that the `Recipe` entity exists and formatting exceptions.

In this section you're going to refactor this controller to use filters for all the code in the methods that's unrelated to the intent of each action. By the end of the chapter you'll have a much simpler controller that's far easier to understand, as shown here.

Listing 22.2   Recipe web API controller after refactoring to use filters

```
[Route("api/recipe")]
[ValidateModel]
[HandleException]                        The filters encapsulate the majority of logic
[FeatureEnabled(IsEnabled = true)]       common to multiple action methods.
public class RecipeApiController : ControllerBase
{
    public RecipeService _service;
    public RecipeApiController(RecipeService service)
    {
        _service = service;
    }

                                 Placing filters at the action
    [HttpGet("{id}")]            level limits them to a single
    [EnsureRecipeExists]         action.
    [AddLastModifiedHeader]
    public IActionResult Get(int id)              The intent of the action,
    {                                             return a Recipe view
        var detail = _service.GetRecipeDetail(id);    model, is much clearer.
        return Ok(detail);
    }
                                 Placing filters at the action
    [HttpPost("{id}")]           level can control the order
    [EnsureRecipeExists]    ◄────  in which they execute.
    public IActionResult Edit(
        int id, [FromBody] UpdateRecipeCommand command)
    {
        _service.UpdateRecipe(command);      The intent of the action, update
        return Ok();                         a Recipe, is much clearer.
    }
}
```

I think you'll have to agree that the controller in listing 22.2 is much easier to read! In this section you'll refactor the controller bit by bit, removing cross-cutting code to get to something more manageable. All the filters we'll create in this section will use the sync filter interfaces. I'll leave it to you, as an exercise, to create their async counterparts. We'll start by looking at authorization filters and how they relate to security in ASP.NET Core.

22.1.1 Authorization filters: Protecting your APIs

Authentication and *authorization* are related, fundamental concepts in security that we'll be looking at in detail in chapters 23 and 24.

DEFINITION   *Authentication* is concerned with determining who made a request. *Authorization* is concerned with what a user is allowed to access.

Authorization filters run first in the MVC filter pipeline, before any other filters. They control access to the action method by immediately short-circuiting the pipeline when a request doesn't meet the necessary requirements.

ASP.NET Core has a built-in authorization framework that you should use when you need to protect your MVC application or your web APIs. You can configure this framework with custom policies that let you finely control access to your actions.

TIP   It's possible to write your own authorization filters by implementing `IAuthorizationFilter` or `IAsyncAuthorizationFilter`, but I strongly advise against it. The ASP.NET Core authorization framework is highly configurable and should meet all your needs.

At the heart of MVC authorization is an authorization filter, `AuthorizeFilter`, which you can add to the filter pipeline by decorating your actions or controllers with the `[Authorize]` attribute. In its simplest form, adding the `[Authorize]` attribute to an action, as in the following listing, means that the request must be made by an authenticated user to be allowed to continue. If you're not logged in, it will short-circuit the pipeline, returning a `401 Unauthorized` response to the browser.

Listing 22.3   Adding `[Authorize]` to an action method

```
public class RecipeApiController : ControllerBase       The Get method has no [Authorize]
{                                                        attribute, so it can be executed by
    public IActionResult Get(int id)     ◄──────         anyone.
    {
        // method body
    }                          Adds the AuthorizeFilter to the
                               filter pipeline using [Authorize]         The Edit method can be
    [Authorize]     ◄───────                                             executed only if you're
    public IActionResult Edit(                                           logged in.
        int id, [FromBody] UpdateRecipeCommand command)
    {
        // method body
    }
}
```

As with all filters, you can apply the `[Authorize]` attribute at the controller level to protect all the actions on a controller, to a Razor Page to protect all the page handler methods in a page, or even globally to protect every endpoint in your app.

NOTE   We'll explore authorization in detail in chapter 24, including how to add more detailed requirements so that only specific sets of users can execute an action.

The next filters in the pipeline are resource filters. In the next section you'll extract some of the common code from `RecipeApiController` and see how easy it is to create a short-circuiting filter.

22.1.2 Resource filters: Short-circuiting your action methods

Resource filters are the first general-purpose filters in the MVC filter pipeline. In chapter 21 you saw minimal examples of both sync and async resource filters, which logged to the console. In your own apps, you can use resource filters for a wide range of purposes, thanks to the fact that they execute so early (and late) in the filter pipeline.

The ASP.NET Core framework includes a few implementations of resource filters you can use in your apps:

- `ConsumesAttribute`—Can be used to restrict the allowed formats an action method can accept. If your action is decorated with `[Consumes("application/json")]`, but the client sends the request as Extensible Markup Language (XML), the resource filter will short-circuit the pipeline and return a `415 Unsupported Media Type` response.
- `SkipStatusCodePagesAttribute`—This filter prevents the `StatusCodePages-Middleware` from running for the response. This can be useful if, for example, you have both web API controllers and Razor Pages in the same application. You can apply this attribute to the controllers to ensure that API error responses are passed untouched, but all error responses from Razor Pages are handled by the middleware.

Resource filters are useful when you want to ensure that the filter runs early in the pipeline, before model binding. They provide an early hook into the pipeline for your logic so you can quickly short-circuit the request if you need to.

Look back at listing 22.1 and see whether you can refactor any of the code into a resource filter. One candidate line appears at the start of both the `Get` and `Edit` methods:

```
if (!IsEnabled) { return BadRequest(); }
```

This line of code is a *feature toggle* that you can use to disable the availability of the whole API, based on the `IsEnabled` field. In practice, you'd probably load the `IsEnabled` field from a database or configuration file so you could control the availability dynamically at runtime, but for this example I'm using a hardcoded value.

> **TIP** To read more about using feature toggles in your applications, see my series "Adding feature flags to an ASP.NET Core app" at http://mng.bz/2e40.

This piece of code is self-contained cross-cutting logic, which is somewhat orthogonal to the main intent of each action method—a perfect candidate for a filter. You want to execute the feature toggle early in the pipeline, before any other logic, so a resource filter makes sense.

> **TIP** Technically, you could also use an authorization filter for this example, but I'm following my own advice of "Don't write your own authorization filters!"

The next listing shows an implementation of `FeatureEnabledAttribute`, which extracts the logic from the action methods and moves it into the filter. I've also exposed the `IsEnabled` field as a property on the filter.

> **Listing 22.4   The `FeatureEnabledAttribute` resource filter**

```
public class FeatureEnabledAttribute : Attribute, IResourceFilter
{
    public bool IsEnabled { get; set; }
    public void OnResourceExecuting(
        ResourceExecutingContext context)
    {
        if (!IsEnabled)
        {
            context.Result = new BadRequestResult();
        }
    }
    public void OnResourceExecuted(
        ResourceExecutedContext context) { }
}
```

Defines whether the feature is enabled → `public bool IsEnabled { get; set; }`

Executes before model binding, early in the filter pipeline

If the feature isn't enabled, short-circuits the pipeline by setting the context.Result property

Must be implemented to satisfy IResourceFilter, but not needed in this case

This simple resource filter demonstrates a few important concepts, which are applicable to most filter types:

- The filter is an attribute as well as a filter. This lets you decorate your controller, action methods, and Razor Pages with it using `[FeatureEnabled(IsEnabled = true)]`.
- The filter interface consists of two methods: `*Executing`, which runs before model binding, and `*Executed`, which runs after the result has executed. You must implement both, even if you only need one for your use case.
- The filter execution methods provide a `context` object. This provides access to, among other things, the `HttpContext` for the request and metadata about the action method or Razor Page that was selected.
- To short-circuit the pipeline, set the `context.Result` property to an `IActionResult` instance. The framework will execute this result to generate the response, bypassing any remaining filters in the pipeline and skipping the action method (or page handler) entirely. In this example, if the feature isn't enabled, you bypass the pipeline by returning `BadRequestResult`, which returns a `400` error to the client.

By moving this logic into the resource filter, you can remove it from your action methods and instead decorate the whole API controller with a simple attribute:

```
[FeatureEnabled(IsEnabled = true)]
[Route("api/recipe")]
public class RecipeApiController : ControllerBase
```

You've extracted only two lines of code from your action methods so far, but you're on the right track. In the next section we'll move on to action filters and extract two more filters from the action method code.

22.1.3 *Action filters: Customizing model binding and action results*

Action filters run just after model binding, before the action method executes. Thanks to this positioning, action filters can access all the arguments that will be used to execute the action method, which makes them a powerful way of extracting common logic out of your actions.

On top of this, they run after the action method has executed and can completely change or replace the IActionResult returned by the action if you want. They can even handle exceptions thrown in the action.

> **NOTE** Action filters don't execute for Razor Pages. Similarly, page filters don't execute for action methods.

The ASP.NET Core framework includes several action filters out of the box. One of these commonly used filters is ResponseCacheFilter, which sets HTTP caching headers on your action-method responses.

> **NOTE** I have described filters as being attributes, but that's not always the case. For example, the action filter is called ResponseCacheFilter, but this type is internal to the ASP.NET Core framework. To apply the filter, you use the public [ResponseCache] attribute instead, and the framework automatically configures the ResponseCacheFilter as appropriate. This separation between attribute and filter is largely an artifact of the internal design, but it can be useful, as you'll see in section 22.3.

Response caching vs. output caching

Caching is a broad topic that aims to improve the performance of an application over the naive approach. But caching can also make debugging issues difficult and may even be undesirable in some situations. Consequently, I often apply ResponseCache-Filter to my action methods to set HTTP caching headers that disable caching! You can read about this and other approaches to caching in Microsoft's "Response caching in ASP.NET Core" documentation at http://mng.bz/2eGd.

Note that the ResponseCacheFilter applies cache control headers only to your outgoing responses; it doesn't cache the response on the server. These headers tell the client (such as a browser) whether it can skip sending a request and reuse the response. If you have relatively static endpoints, this can massively reduce the load on your app.

This is different from output caching, introduced in .NET 7. Output caching involves storing a generated response on the server and reusing it for subsequent requests. In the simplest case, the response is stored in memory and reused for appropriate requests, but you can configure ASP.NET Core to store the output elsewhere, such as a database.

> **(continued)**
> Output caching is generally more configurable than response caching, as you can choose exactly what to cache and when to invalidate it, but it is also much more resource-heavy. For details on how to enable output caching for an endpoint, see the documentation at http://mng.bz/Bmlv.

The real power of action filters comes when you build filters tailored to your own apps by extracting common code from your action methods. To demonstrate, I'm going to create two custom filters for `RecipeApiController`:

- `ValidateModelAttribute`—This will return `BadRequestResult` if the model state indicates that the binding model is invalid and will short-circuit the action execution. This attribute used to be a staple of my web API applications, but the `[ApiController]` attribute now handles this (and more) for you. Nevertheless, I think it's useful to understand what's going on behind the scenes.

- `EnsureRecipeExistsAttribute`—This uses each action method's `id` argument to validate that the requested `Recipe` entity exists before the action method runs. If the `Recipe` doesn't exist, the filter returns `NotFoundResult` and short-circuits the pipeline.

As you saw in chapter 16, the MVC framework automatically validates your binding models before executing your actions and Razor Page handlers, but it's up to you to decide what to do about it. For web API controllers, it's common to return a `400 Bad Request` response containing a list of the errors, as shown in figure 22.1.

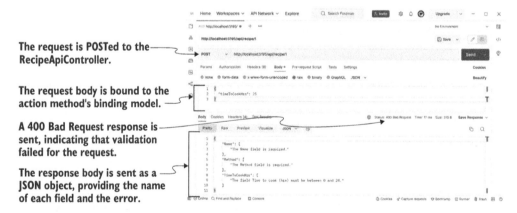

The request is POSTed to the RecipeApiController.

The request body is bound to the action method's binding model.

A 400 Bad Request response is sent, indicating that validation failed for the request.

The response body is sent as a JSON object, providing the name of each field and the error.

Figure 22.1   Posting data to a web API using Postman. The data is bound to the action method's binding model and validated. If validation fails, it's common to return a `400 Bad Request` response with a list of the validation errors.

You should ordinarily use the `[ApiController]` attribute on your web API controllers, which gives you this behavior (and uses Problem Details responses) automatically. But if you can't or don't want to use that attribute, you can create a custom action filter instead. The following listing shows a basic implementation that is similar to the behavior you get with the `[ApiController]` attribute.

Listing 22.5   The action filter for validating `ModelState`

```
public class ValidateModelAttribute : ActionFilterAttribute
{
    public override void OnActionExecuting(
        ActionExecutingContext context)
    {
        if (!context.ModelState.IsValid)
        {
            context.Result =
                new BadRequestObjectResult(context.ModelState);
        }
    }
}
```

Overrides the Executing method to run the filter before the Action executes

For convenience, you derive from the ActionFilterAttribute base class.

Model binding and validation have already run at this point, so you can check the state.

If the model isn't valid, sets the Result property, which short-circuits the action execution

This attribute is self-explanatory and follows a similar pattern to the resource filter in section 22.1.2, but with a few interesting points:

- I have derived from the abstract `ActionFilterAttribute`. This class implements `IActionFilter` and `IResultFilter`, as well as their async counterparts, so you can override the methods you need as appropriate. This prevents needing to add an unused `OnActionExecuted()` method, but using the base class is entirely optional and a matter of preference.
- Action filters run after model binding has taken place, so `context.ModelState` contains the validation errors if validation failed.
- Setting the `Result` property on `context` short-circuits the pipeline. But due to the position of the action filter stage, only the action method execution and later action filters are bypassed; all the other stages of the pipeline run as though the action executed as normal.

If you apply this action filter to your `RecipeApiController`, you can remove this code from the start of both the action methods, as it will run automatically in the filter pipeline:

```
if (!ModelState.IsValid)
{
    return BadRequest(ModelState);
}
```

You'll use a similar approach to remove the duplicate code that checks whether the id provided as an argument to the action methods corresponds to an existing Recipe entity.

The following listing shows the `EnsureRecipeExistsAttribute` action filter. This uses an instance of `RecipeService` to check whether the `Recipe` exists and returns a `404 Not Found` if it doesn't.

Listing 22.6   An action filter to check whether a `Recipe` exists

```
public class EnsureRecipeExistsAtribute : ActionFilterAttribute
{
    public override void OnActionExecuting(
        ActionExecutingContext context)
    {
        var service = context.HttpContext.RequestServices
            .GetService<RecipeService>();
        var recipeId = (int) context.ActionArguments["id"];
        if (!service.DoesRecipeExist(recipeId))
        {
            context.Result = new NotFoundResult();
        }
    }
}
```

Fetches an instance of RecipeService from the DI container

Retrieves the id parameter that will be passed to the action method when it executes

Checks whether a Recipe entity with the given RecipeId exists

If it doesn't exist, returns a 404 Not Found result and short-circuits the pipeline

---

As before, you've derived from `ActionFilterAttribute` for simplicity and overridden the `OnActionExecuting` method. The main functionality of the filter relies on the `Does-RecipeExist()` method of `RecipeService`, so the first step is to obtain an instance of `RecipeService`. The `context` parameter provides access to the `HttpContext` for the request, which in turn lets you access the DI container and use `RequestServices.GetService()` to return an instance of `RecipeService`.

> **WARNING**   This technique for obtaining dependencies is known as *service location* and is generally considered to be an antipattern. In section 22.3 I'll show you a better way to use the DI container to inject dependencies into your filters.

As well as `RecipeService`, the other piece of information you need is the `id` argument of the `Get` and `Edit` action methods. In action filters, model binding has already occurred, so the arguments that the framework will use to execute the action method are already known and are exposed on `context.ActionArguments`.

The action arguments are exposed as `Dictionary<string, object>`, so you can obtain the `id` parameter using the `"id"` string key. Remember to cast the object to the correct type.

> **TIP**   Whenever I see magic strings like this, I always try to replace them by using the `nameof` operator. Unfortunately, `nameof` often won't work for method arguments like this, so be careful when refactoring your code. I suggest explicitly applying the action filter to the action method (instead of globally, or to a controller) to remind you about that implicit coupling.

With `RecipeService` and `id` in place, it's a case of checking whether the identifier corresponds to an existing `Recipe` entity and if not, setting `context.Result` to `NotFoundResult`. This short-circuits the pipeline and bypasses the action method altogether.

> **NOTE** Remember that you can have multiple action filters running in a single stage. Short-circuiting the pipeline by setting `context.Result` prevents later filters in the stage from running and bypasses the action method execution.

Before we move on, it's worth mentioning a special case for action filters. The `ControllerBase` base class implements `IActionFilter` and `IAsyncActionFilter` itself. If you find yourself creating an action filter for a single controller and want to apply it to every action in that controller, you can override the appropriate methods on your controller instead, as in the following listing.

Listing 22.7 Overriding action filter methods directly on `ControllerBase`

```
public class HomeController : ControllerBase    ⟵── Derives from the ControllerBase class
{
    public override void OnActionExecuting(       Runs before any other action filters
        ActionExecutingContext context)           for every action in the controller
    { }
    public override void OnActionExecuted(        Runs after all other action filters
        ActionExecutedContext context)            for every action in the controller
    { }
}
```

If you override these methods on your controller, they'll run in the action filter stage of the filter pipeline for every action on the controller. The `OnActionExecuting` method runs before any other action filters, regardless of ordering or scope, and the `OnAction-Executed` method runs after all other action filters.

> **TIP** The controller implementation can be useful in some cases, but you can't control the ordering related to other filters. Personally, I generally prefer to break logic into explicit, declarative filter attributes, but it depends on the situation, and as always, the choice is yours.

With the resource and action filters complete, your controller is looking much tidier, but there's one aspect in particular that would be nice to remove: the exception handling. In the next section we'll look at how to create a custom exception filter for your controller and why you might want to do this instead of using exception handling middleware.

22.1.4 Exception filters: Custom exception handling for your action methods

In chapter 4 I went into some depth about types of error-handling middleware you can add to your apps. These let you catch exceptions thrown from any later middleware and handle them appropriately. If you're using exception handling middleware, you may be wondering why we need exception filters at all.

The answer to this is pretty much the same as I outlined in chapter 21: filters are great for cross-cutting concerns, when you need behavior that's specific to MVC or that should only apply to certain routes.

Both of these can apply in exception handling. Exception filters are part of the MVC framework, so they have access to the context in which the error occurred, such as the action or Razor Page that was executing. This can be useful for logging additional details when errors occur, such as the action parameters that caused the error.

> **WARNING**   If you use exception filters to record action method arguments, make sure you're not storing sensitive data in your logs, such as passwords or credit card details.

You can also use exception filters to handle errors from different routes in different ways. Imagine you have both Razor Pages and web API controllers in your app, as we do in the recipe app. What happens when an exception is thrown by a Razor Page?

As you saw in chapter 4, the exception travels back up the middleware pipeline and is caught by exception handler middleware. The exception handler middleware reexecutes the pipeline and generates an HTML error page.

That's great for your Razor Pages, but what about exceptions in your web API controllers? If your API throws an exception and consequently returns HTML generated by the exception handler middleware, that's going to break a client that called the API expecting a JavaScript Object Notation (JSON) response!

> **TIP**   The added complexity introduced by having to handle these two very different clients is the reason I prefer to create separate applications for APIs and server-rendered apps.

Instead, exception filters let you handle the exception in the filter pipeline and generate an appropriate response body for API clients. The exception handler middleware intercepts only errors without a body, so it will let the modified web API response pass untouched.

> **NOTE**   The [ApiController] attribute converts error StatusCodeResults to a ProblemDetails object, but it doesn't catch exceptions.

Exception filters can catch exceptions from more than your action methods and page handlers. They'll run if an exception occurs at these times:

- During model binding or validation
- When the action method or page handler is executing
- When an action filter or page filter is executing

You should note that exception filters won't catch exceptions thrown in any filters other than action and page filters, so it's important that your resource and result filters don't throw exceptions. Similarly, they won't catch exceptions thrown when executing an IActionResult, such as when rendering a Razor view to HTML.

Now that you know why you might want an exception filter, go ahead and implement one for `RecipeApiController`, as shown next. This lets you safely remove the `try-catch` block from your action methods, knowing that your filter will catch any errors.

Listing 22.8   The `HandleExceptionAttribute` exception filter

> **ExceptionFilterAttribute is an abstract base class that implements IExceptionFilter.**

```
public class HandleExceptionAttribute : ExceptionFilterAttribute   ◁
{
    public override void OnException(ExceptionContext context)
    {
        var error = new ProblemDetails                                Building a
        {                                                             problem details
            Title = "An error occurred",                             object to return
            Detail = context.Exception.Message,                       in the response
            Status = 500,
            Type = " https://httpwg.org/specs/rfc9110.html#status.500"
        };

        context.Result = new ObjectResult(error)      Creates an ObjectResult to serialize
        {                                             the ProblemDetails and to set the
            StatusCode = 500                          response status code
        };
        context.ExceptionHandled = true;   ◁
    }                                          Marks the exception as handled to prevent it
}                                              propagating into the middleware pipeline
```

> **There's only a single method to override for IExceptionFilter.**

It's quite common to have an exception filter in your application if you are mixing API controllers and Razor Pages in your application, but they're not always necessary. If you can handle all the exceptions in your application with a single piece of middleware, ditch the exception filters and go with that instead.

You're almost done refactoring your `RecipeApiController`. You have one more filter type to add: result filters. Custom result filters tend to be relatively rare in the apps I've written, but they have their uses, as you'll see.

22.1.5   *Result filters: Customizing action results before they execute*

If everything runs successfully in the pipeline, and there's no short-circuiting, the next stage of the pipeline after action filters is result filters. These run before and after the `IActionResult` returned by the action method (or action filters) is executed.

> **WARNING**   If the pipeline is short-circuited by setting `context.Result`, the result filter stage won't run, but the `IActionResult` will still be executed to generate the response. The exceptions to this rule are action and page filters, which only short-circuit the action execution, as you saw in chapter 21. Result filters run as normal, as though the action or page handler itself generated the response.

Result filters run immediately after action filters, so many of their use cases are similar, but you typically use result filters to customize the way the `IActionResult` executes. For example, ASP.NET Core has several result filters built into its framework:

- `ProducesAttribute`—This forces a web API result to be serialized to a specific output format. For example, decorating your action method with `[Produces ("application/xml")]` forces the formatters to try to format the response as XML, even if the client doesn't list XML in its `Accept` header.

- `FormatFilterAttribute`—Decorating an action method with this filter tells the formatter to look for a route value or query string parameter called `format` and to use that to determine the output format. For example, you could call `/api/recipe/11?format=json` and `FormatFilter` will format the response as JSON or call `api/recipe/11?format=xml` and get the response as XML.

NOTE Remember that you need to explicitly configure the XML formatters if you want to serialize to XML, as described in chapter 20. For details on formatting results based on the URL, see my blog entry on the topic: http://mng.bz/1rYV.

As well as controlling the output formatters, you can use result filters to make any last-minute adjustments before `IActionResult` is executed and the response is generated.

As an example of the kind of flexibility available, in the following listing I demonstrate setting the `LastModified` header, based on the object returned from the action. This is a somewhat contrived example—it's specific enough to a single action that it likely doesn't warrant being moved to a result filter—but I hope you get the idea.

Listing 22.9 Setting a response header in a result filter

> **ResultFilterAttribute provides a useful base class you can override.**

```
public class AddLastModifedHeaderAttribute : ResultFilterAttribute    ◁
{
    public override void OnResultExecuting(
        ResultExecutingContext context)
    {
        if (context.Result is OkObjectResult result
            && result.Value is RecipeDetailViewModel detail)    ◁
        {
            var viewModelDate = detail.LastModified;
            context.HttpContext.Response
              .GetTypedHeaders().LastModified = viewModelDate;
        }
    }
}
```

Checks whether the action result returned a 200 Ok result with a view model.

> **You could also override the Executed method, but the response would already be sent by then.**

> **Checks whether the view model type is RecipeDetailViewModel . . .**

. . . and if it is, fetches the LastModified property and sets the Last-Modified header in the response

I've used another helper base class here, `ResultFilterAttribute`, so you need to override only a single method to implement the filter. Fetch the current `IActionResult`, exposed on `context.Result`, and check that it's an `OkObjectResult` instance with a `RecipeDetailViewModel` value. If it is, fetch the `LastModified` field from the view model and add a `Last-Modified` header to the response.

> **TIP**   `GetTypedHeaders()` is an extension method that provides strongly typed access to request and response headers. It takes care of parsing and formatting the values for you. You can find it in the `Microsoft.AspNetCore.Http` namespace.

As with resource and action filters, result filters can implement a method that runs *after* the result has executed: `OnResultExecuted`. You can use this method, for example, to inspect exceptions that happened during the execution of `IActionResult`.

> **WARNING**   Generally, you can't modify the response in the `OnResultExecuted` method, as you may have already started streaming the response to the client.

We've finished simplifying the `RecipeApiController` now. By extracting various pieces of functionality to filters, the original controller in listing 22.1 has been simplified to the version in listing 22.2. This is obviously a somewhat extreme and contrived demonstration, and I'm not advocating that filters should always be your go-to option.

> **TIP**   Filters should be a last resort in most cases. Where possible, it is often preferable to use a simple private method in a controller, or to push functionality into the domain instead of using filters. Filters should generally be used to extract repetitive, HTTP-related, or common cross-cutting code from your controllers.

There's still one more filter we haven't looked at yet, because it applies only to Razor Pages: page filters.

22.1.6   Page filters: Customizing model binding for Razor Pages

As already discussed, action filters apply only to controllers and actions; they have no effect on Razor Pages. Similarly, page filters have no effect on controllers and actions. Nevertheless, page filters and action filters fulfill similar roles.

As is the case for action filters, the ASP.NET Core framework includes several page filters out of the box. One of these is the Razor Page equivalent of the caching action filter, `ResponseCacheFilter`, called `PageResponseCacheFilter`. This works identically to the action-filter equivalent I described in section 22.1.3, setting HTTP caching headers on your Razor Page responses.

Page filters are somewhat unusual, as they implement three methods, as discussed in section 22.1.2. In practice, I've rarely seen a page filter that implements all three. It's unusual to need to run code immediately after page handler selection and before model validation. It's far more common to perform a role directly analogous to action filters. The following listing shows a page filter equivalent to the `EnsureRecipeExists-Attribute` action filter.

Listing 22.10 A page filter to check whether a `Recipe` exists

*Implements IPageFilter and as an attribute so
you can decorate the Razor Page PageModel*

```
public class PageEnsureRecipeExistsAttribute : Attribute, IPageFilter
{
    public void OnPageHandlerSelected(
        PageHandlerSelectedContext context)
    {}

    public void OnPageHandlerExecuting(
        PageHandlerExecutingContext context)
    {
        var service = context.HttpContext.RequestServices
            .GetService<RecipeService>();
        var recipeId = (int) context.HandlerArguments["id"];
        if (!service.DoesRecipeExist(recipeId))
        {
            context.Result = new NotFoundResult();
        }
    }

    public void OnPageHandlerExecuted(
        PageHandlerExecutedContext context)
    {}
}
```

*Executed after handler selection and before
model binding—not used in this example*

*Retrieves the
id parameter
that will be
passed to the
page handler
method when
it executes*

*Executed after model binding and validation,
and before page handler execution*

*Fetches an
instance of
RecipeService
from the DI
container*

*Checks
whether a
Recipe entity
with the given
RecipeId
exists . . .*

*. . . and if it doesn't exist,
returns a 404 Not Found result
and short-circuits the pipeline*

*Executed after page handler execution (or
short-circuiting)—not used in this example*

The page filter is similar to the action filter equivalent. The most obvious difference is the need to implement three methods to satisfy the `IPageFilter` interface. You'll commonly want to implement the `OnPageHandlerExecuting` method, which runs after model binding and validation, and before the page handler executes.

A subtle difference between the action filter code and the page filter code is that the action filter accesses the model-bound action arguments using `context` `.ActionArguments`. The page filter uses `context.HandlerArguments` in the example, but there's also another option.

Remember from chapter 16 that Razor Pages often bind to public properties on the `PageModel` using the `[BindProperty]` attribute. You can access those properties directly instead of using magic strings by casting a `HandlerInstance` property to the correct `PageModel` type and accessing the property directly, as in this example:

```
var recipeId = ((ViewRecipePageModel)context.HandlerInstance).Id
```

This is similar to the way the `ControllerBase` class implements `IActionFilter` and `PageModel` implements `IPageFilter` and `IAsyncPageFilter`. If you want to create an action filter for a single Razor Page, you could save yourself the trouble of creating a separate page filter and override these methods directly in your Razor Page.

> **TIP** I generally find it's not worth the hassle of using page filters unless you have a common requirement. The extra level of indirection that page filters add, coupled with the typically bespoke nature of individual Razor Pages, means that I normally find they aren't worth using. Your mileage may vary, of course, but don't jump to them as a first option.

That brings us to the end of this detailed look at each of the filters in the MVC pipeline. Looking back and comparing listings 22.1 and 22.2, you can see filters allowed us to refactor the controllers and make the intent of each action method much clearer. Writing your code in this way makes it easier to reason about, as each filter and action has a single responsibility.

In the next section we'll take a slight detour into exactly what happens when you short-circuit a filter. I've described *how* to do this, by setting the `context.Result` property on a filter, but I haven't described exactly what happens. For example, what if there are multiple filters in the stage when it's short-circuited? Do those still run?

22.2 Understanding pipeline short-circuiting

In this short section you'll learn about the details of filter-pipeline short-circuiting. You'll see what happens to the other filters in a stage when the pipeline is short-circuited and how to short-circuit each type of filter.

A brief warning: the topic of filter short-circuiting can be a little confusing. Unlike middleware short-circuiting, which is cut-and-dried, the filter pipeline is a bit more nuanced. Luckily, you won't often need to dig into it, but when you do, you'll be glad for the detail.

You short-circuit the authorization, resource, action, page, and result filters by setting `context.Result` to `IActionResult`. Setting an action result in this way causes some or all of the remaining pipeline to be bypassed. But the filter pipeline isn't entirely linear, as you saw in chapter 21, so short-circuiting doesn't always do an about-face back down the pipeline. For example, short-circuited action filters bypass only action method execution; the result filters and result execution stages still run.

The other difficulty is what happens if you have more than one filter in a stage. Let's say you have three resource filters executing in a pipeline. What happens if the second filter causes a short circuit? Any remaining filters are bypassed, but the first resource filter has already run its `*Executing` command, as shown in figure 22.2. This earlier filter gets to run its `*Executed` command too, with `context.Cancelled = true`, indicating that a filter in that stage (the resource filter stage) short-circuited the pipeline.

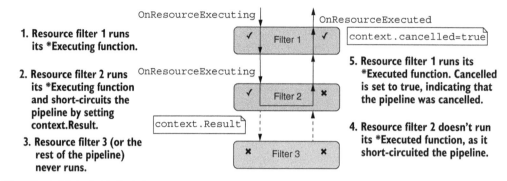

1. Resource filter 1 runs its *Executing function.

2. Resource filter 2 runs its *Executing function and short-circuits the pipeline by setting context.Result.

3. Resource filter 3 (or the rest of the pipeline) never runs.

5. Resource filter 1 runs its *Executed function. Cancelled is set to true, indicating that the pipeline was cancelled.

4. Resource filter 2 doesn't run its *Executed function, as it short-circuited the pipeline.

Figure 22.2 **The effect of short-circuiting a resource filter on other resource filters in that stage. Later filters in the stage won't run at all, but earlier filters run their** OnResourceExecuted **function.**

Running result filters after short-circuits with IAlwaysRunResultFilter

Result filters are designed to wrap the execution of an IActionResult returned by an action method or action filter so that you can customize how the action result is executed. However, this customization doesn't apply to the IActionResult set when you short-circuit the filter pipeline by setting context.Result in an authorization filter, resource filter, or exception filter.

That's often not a problem, as many result filters are designed to handle "happy path" transformations. But sometimes you want to make sure that a transformation is always applied to an IActionResult, regardless of whether it was returned by an action method or a short-circuiting filter.

For those cases, you can implement IAlwaysRunResultFilter or IAsyncAlwaysRunResultFilter. These interfaces extend (and are identical) to the standard result filter interfaces, so they run like normal result filters in the filter pipeline. But these interfaces mark the filter to also run after an authorization filter, resource filter, or exception filter short-circuits the pipeline, where standard result filters *won't* run.

You can use IAlwaysRunResultFilter to ensure that certain action results are always updated. For example, the documentation shows how to use an IAlwaysRunResultFilter to convert a 415 StatusCodeResult to a 422 StatusCodeResult, regardless of the source of the action result. See the "IAlwaysRunResultFilter and IAsyncAlwaysRunResultFilter" section of Microsoft's "Filters in ASP.NET Core" documentation: http://mng.bz/JDoO.

Understanding which other filters run when you short-circuit a filter can be somewhat of a chore, but I've summarized each filter in table 22.1. You'll also find it useful to refer to the pipeline diagrams in chapter 21 to visualize the shape of the pipeline when thinking about short circuits.

Table 22.1   The effect of short-circuiting filters on filter-pipeline execution

Filter type	How to short-circuit?	What else runs?
Authorization filters	Set `context.Result`.	Runs only `IAlwaysRunResultFilters`.
Resource filters	Set `context.Result`.	Resource-filter `*Executed` functions from earlier filters run with `context.Cancelled = true`. Runs `IAlwaysRunResultFilters` before executing the `IActionResult`.
Action filters	Set `context.Result`.	Bypasses only action method execution. Action filters earlier in the pipeline run their `*Executed` methods with `context.Cancelled = true`, then result filters, result execution, and resource filters' `*Executed` methods all run as normal.
Page filters	Set `context.Result` in `OnPageHandlerSelected`.	Bypasses only page handler execution. Page filters earlier in the pipeline run their `*Executed` methods with `context.Cancelled = true`, then result filters, result execution, and resource filters' `*Executed` methods all run as normal.
Exception filters	Set `context.Result` and `Exception.Handled = true`.	All resource-filter `*Executed` functions run. Runs `IAlwaysRunResultFilters` before executing the `IActionResult`.
Result filters	Set `context.Cancelled = true`.	Result filters earlier in the pipeline run their `*Executed` functions with `context.Cancelled = true`. All resource-filter `*Executed` functions run as normal.

The most interesting point here is that short-circuiting an action filter (or a page filter) doesn't short-circuit much of the pipeline at all. In fact, it bypasses only later action filters and the action method execution itself. By building primarily action filters, you can ensure that other filters, such as result filters that define the output format, run as usual, even when your action filters short-circuit.

The last thing I'd like to talk about in this chapter is how to use DI with your filters. You saw in chapters 8 and 9 that DI is integral to ASP.NET Core, and in the next section you'll see how to design your filters so that the framework can inject service dependencies into them for you.

22.3   *Using dependency injection with filter attributes*

In this section you'll learn how to inject services into your filters so you can take advantage of the simplicity of DI in your filters. You'll learn to use two helper filters to achieve this, `TypeFilterAttribute` and `ServiceFilterAttribute`, and you'll see how they can be used to simplify the action filter you defined in section 22.1.3.

The filters we've created so far have been created as attributes. This is useful for applying filters to action methods and controllers, but it means you can't use DI to inject services into the constructor. C# attributes don't let you pass dependencies into their constructors (other than constant values), and they're created as singletons, so there's only a single instance of an attribute for the lifetime of your app. So what happens if you need to access a transient or scoped service from inside the singleton attribute?

Listing 22.6 showed one way of doing this, using a pseudo-service locator pattern to reach into the DI container and pluck out `RecipeService` at runtime. This works but is generally frowned upon as a pattern in favor of proper DI. So how can you add DI to your filters?

The key is to split the filter in two. Instead of creating a class that's both an attribute and a filter, create a filter class that contains the functionality and an attribute that tells the framework when and where to use the filter.

Let's apply this to the action filter from listing 22.6. Previously, I derived from `ActionFilterAttribute` and obtained an instance of `RecipeService` from the context passed to the method. In the following listing I show two classes, `EnsureRecipeExists-Filter` and `EnsureRecipeExistsAttribute`. The filter class is responsible for the functionality and takes in `RecipeService` as a constructor dependency.

Listing 22.11 Using DI in a filter by not deriving from `Attribute`

```
public class EnsureRecipeExistsFilter : IActionFilter        ◁——  Doesn't derive from
{                                                                  an Attribute class
    private readonly RecipeService _service;
    public EnsureRecipeExistsFilter(RecipeService service)         RecipeService is
    {                                                              injected into the
        _service = service;                                        constructor.
    }
    public void OnActionExecuting(ActionExecutingContext context)
    {
        var recipeId = (int) context.ActionArguments["id"];        The rest of
        if (!_service.DoesRecipeExist(recipeId))                   the method
        {                                                          remains the
            context.Result = new NotFoundResult();                 same.
        }
    }

    public void OnActionExecuted(ActionExecutedContext context) { }
}
```

You must implement the Executed action to satisfy the interface.

```
public class EnsureRecipeExistsAttribute : TypeFilterAttribute    ◁——
{
    public EnsureRecipeExistsAttribute()                          Derives from
        : base(typeof(EnsureRecipeExistsFilter)) {}               TypeFilter, which
}                                                                 is used to fill
                                                                  dependencies using
                                                                  the DI container
```

Passes the type EnsureRecipeExistsFilter as an argument to the base TypeFilter constructor

---

`EnsureRecipeExistsFilter` is a valid filter; you could use it on its own by adding it as a global filter (as global filters don't need to be attributes). But you can't use it directly by decorating controller classes and action methods, as it's not an attribute. That's where EnsureRecipeExistsAttribute comes in.

You can decorate your methods with EnsureRecipeExistsAttribute instead. This attribute inherits from TypeFilterAttribute and passes the Type of filter to create as an argument to the base constructor. This attribute acts as a *factory* for EnsureRecipe-ExistsFilter by implementing IFilterFactory.

When ASP.NET Core initially loads your app, it scans your actions and controllers, looking for filters and filter factories. It uses these to form a filter pipeline for every action in your app, as shown in figure 22.3.

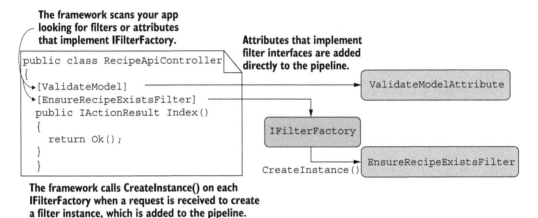

The framework scans your app looking for filters or attributes that implement IFilterFactory.

Attributes that implement filter interfaces are added directly to the pipeline.

```
public class RecipeApiController
{
    [ValidateModel]
    [EnsureRecipeExistsFilter]
    public IActionResult Index()
    {
        return Ok();
    }
}
```

ValidateModelAttribute

IFilterFactory

EnsureRecipeExistsFilter

CreateInstance()

The framework calls CreateInstance() on each IFilterFactory when a request is received to create a filter instance, which is added to the pipeline.

Figure 22.3   The framework scans your app on startup to find both filters and attributes that implement IFilterFactory. At runtime, the framework calls CreateInstance() to get an instance of the filter.

When an action decorated with EnsureRecipeExistsAttribute is called, the framework calls CreateInstance() on the IFilterFactory attribute. This creates a new instance of EnsureRecipeExistsFilter and uses the DI container to populate its dependencies (RecipeService).

By using this IFilterFactory approach, you get the best of both worlds: you can decorate your controllers and actions with attributes, and you can use DI in your filters. Out of the box, two similar classes provide this functionality, which have slightly different behaviors:

- TypeFilterAttribute—Loads all the filter's dependencies from the DI container and uses them to create a new instance of the filter.
- ServiceFilterAttribute—Loads the filter *itself* from the DI container. The DI container takes care of the service lifetime and building the dependency graph. Unfortunately, you must also explicitly register your filter with the DI container:

```
builder.Services.AddTransient<EnsureRecipeExistsFilter>();
```

> **TIP** You can register your services with any lifetime you choose. If your service is registered as a singleton, you can consider setting the IsReusable flag, as described in the documentation: http://mng.bz/d1JD.

If you choose to use ServiceFilterAttribute instead of TypeFilterAttribute, and register the EnsureRecipeExistsFilter as a service in the DI container, you can apply the ServiceFilterAttribute directly to an action method:

```
[ServiceFilter(typeof(EnsureRecipeExistsFilter))]
public IActionResult Index() => Ok();
```

Whether you choose to use TypeFilterAttribute or ServiceFilterAttribute is somewhat a matter of preference, and you can always implement a custom IFilterFactory if you need to. The key takeaway is that you can now use DI in your filters. If you don't need to use DI for a filter, implement it as an attribute directly, for simplicity.

> **TIP** I like to create my filters as a nested class of the attribute class when using this pattern. This keeps all the code nicely contained in a single file and indicates the relationship between the classes.

That brings us to the end of this chapter on the filter pipeline. Filters are a somewhat advanced topic, in that they aren't strictly necessary for building basic apps, but I find them extremely useful for ensuring that my controller and action methods are simple and easy to understand.

In the next chapter we'll take our first look at securing your app. We'll discuss the difference between authentication and authorization, the concept of identity in ASP.NET Core, and how you can use the ASP.NET Core Identity system to let users register and log in to your app.

Summary

- The filter pipeline executes as part of the MVC or Razor Pages execution. It consists of authorization filters, resource filters, action filters, page filters, exception filters, and result filters.
- ASP.NET Core includes many built-in filters, but you can also create custom filters tailored to your application. You can use custom filters to extract common cross-cutting functionality out of your MVC controllers and Razor Pages, reducing duplication and ensuring consistency across your endpoints.
- Authorization filters run first in the pipeline and control access to APIs. ASP.NET Core includes an [Authorization] attribute that you can apply to action methods so that only logged-in users can execute the action.
- Resource filters run after authorization filters and again after an IActionResult has been executed. They can be used to short-circuit the pipeline so that an action method is never executed. They can also be used to customize the model-binding process for an action method.

- Action filters run after model binding has occurred and before an action method executes. They also run after the action method has executed. They can be used to extract common code out of an action method to prevent duplication. They don't execute for Razor Pages, only for MVC controllers.

- The `ControllerBase` base class also implements `IActionFilter` and `IAsyncActionFilter`. They run at the start and end of the action filter pipeline, regardless of the ordering or scope of other action filters. They can be used to create action filters that are specific to one controller.

- Page filters run three times: after page handler selection, after model binding, and after the page handler method executes. You can use page filters for similar purposes as action filters. Page filters execute only for Razor Pages; they don't run for MVC controllers.

- Razor Page `PageModels` implement `IPageFilter` and `IAsyncPageFilter`, so they can be used to implement page-specific page filters. These are rarely used, as you can typically achieve similar results with simple private methods.

- Exception filters execute after action and page filters, when an action method or page handler has thrown an exception. They can be used to provide custom error handling specific to the action executed.

- Generally, you should handle exceptions at the middleware level, but you can use exception filters to customize how you handle exceptions for specific actions, controllers, or Razor Pages.

- Result filters run before and after an `IActionResult` is executed. You can use them to control how the action result is executed or to completely change the action result that will be executed.

- All filters can short-circuit the pipeline by setting a response. This generally prevents the request progressing further in the filter pipeline, but the exact behavior varies with the type of filter that is short-circuited.

- Result filters aren't executed when you short-circuit the pipeline using authorization, resource, or exception filters. You can ensure that result filters also run for these short-circuit cases by implementing a result filter as `IAlwaysRunResultFilter` or `IAsyncAlwaysRunResultFilter`.

- You can use `ServiceFilterAttribute` and `TypeFilterAttribute` to allow dependency injection in your custom filters. `ServiceFilterAttribute` requires that you register your filter and all its dependencies with the DI container, whereas `TypeFilterAttribute` requires only that the filter's dependencies have been registered

Part 4

Securing and deploying your applications

So far in the book you've learned how to use minimal APIs, Razor Pages, and Model-View-Controller (MVC) controllers to build both server-rendered applications and APIs. You know how to dynamically generate JavaScript Object Notation (JSON) and HTML code based on incoming requests, and how to use configuration and dependency injection to customize your app's behavior at runtime. In part 4 you'll learn how to add users and profiles to your app and how to publish and secure your apps.

In chapters 23 through 25 you'll learn how to protect your applications with authentication and authorization. In chapter 23 you'll see how you can add ASP.NET Core Identity to your apps so that users can log in and enjoy a customized experience. You'll learn how to protect your Razor Pages apps using authorization in chapter 24 so that only some users can access certain pages in your app. In chapter 25 you'll learn how to apply the same protections to your minimal API and web API applications.

Adding logging to your application is one of those activities that's often left until after you discover a problem in production. Adding sensible logging from the get-go will help you quickly diagnose and fix errors as they arise. Chapter 26 introduces the logging framework built into ASP.NET Core. You'll see how you can use it to write log messages to a wide variety of locations, whether it's the console, a file, or a third-party remote-logging service.

By this point you'll have all the fundamentals to build a production application with ASP.NET Core. In chapter 27 I cover the steps required to make your app live, including how to publish an app to Internet Information Services (IIS) and how to configure the URLs your app listens on.

Before you expose your application to the world, an important part of web development is securing your app correctly. Even if you don't feel you have any sensitive data in your application, you must make sure to protect your users from attacks by adhering to security best practices. You'll learn how to configure HTTPS for your application in chapter 28 and why this is a vital step for modern web development. Similarly, in chapter 29 I describe some common security vulnerabilities, how attackers can exploit them, and what you can do to protect your applications.

Authentication: Adding users to your application with Identity

This chapter covers

- Seeing how authentication works in web apps in ASP.NET Core
- Creating a project using the ASP.NET Core Identity system
- Adding user functionality to an existing web app
- Customizing the default ASP.NET Core Identity UI

One of the selling points of a web framework like ASP.NET Core is the ability to provide a dynamic app, customized to individual users. Many apps have the concept of an "account" with the service, which you can "sign in" to and get a different experience.

Depending on the service, an account gives you varying things. On some apps you may have to sign in to get access to additional features, and on others you might see suggested articles. On an e-commerce app, you'd be able to place orders and view your past orders; on Stack Overflow you can post questions and answers; on a news site you might get a customized experience based on previous articles you've viewed.

When you think about adding users to your application, you typically have two aspects to consider:

- *Authentication*—The process of creating users and letting them log in to your app
- *Authorization*—Customizing the experience and controlling what users can do, based on the current logged-in user

In this chapter I'm going to be discussing the first of these points, authentication and membership. In the next chapter I'll tackle the second point, authorization. In section 23.1 I discuss the difference between authentication and authorization, how authentication works in a traditional ASP.NET Core web app, and ways you can architect your system to provide sign-in functionality. I don't discuss API applications in detail in this chapter, though many of the authentication principles apply to both styles of app. I discuss API applications in chapter 25.

In section 23.2 I introduce a user-management system called ASP.NET Core Identity (Identity for short). Identity integrates with Entity Framework Core (EF Core) and provides services for creating and managing users, storing and validating passwords, and signing users in and out of your app.

In section 23.3 you'll create an app using a default template that includes ASP.NET Core Identity out of the box. This gives you an app to explore and see the features Identity provides, as well as everything it doesn't.

Creating an app is great for seeing how the pieces fit together, but you'll often need to add users and authentication to an existing app. In section 23.4 you'll see the steps required to add ASP.NET Core Identity to an existing app.

In sections 23.5 and 23.6 you'll learn how to replace pages from the default Identity UI by scaffolding individual pages. In section 23.5 you'll see how to customize the Razor templates to generate different HTML on the user registration page, and in section 23.6 you'll learn how to customize the logic associated with a Razor Page. You'll see how to store additional information about a user (such as their name or date of birth) and how to provide them permissions that you can later use to customize the app's behavior (if the user is a VIP, for example).

Before we look at the ASP.NET Core Identity system specifically, let's take a look at authentication and authorization in ASP.NET Core—what's happening when you sign in to a website and how you can design your apps to provide this functionality.

23.1 *Introducing authentication and authorization*

When you add sign-in functionality to your app and control access to certain functions based on the currently signed-in user, you're using two distinct aspects of security:

- *Authentication*—The process of determining who you are
- *Authorization*—The process of determining what you're allowed to do

Generally you need to know *who* the user is before you can determine *what* they're allowed to do, so authentication always comes first, followed by authorization. In this chapter we're looking only at authentication; we'll cover authorization in chapter 24.

In this section I start by discussing how ASP.NET Core thinks about users, and I cover some of the terminology and concepts that are central to authentication. I found this to be the hardest part to grasp when *I* learned about authentication, so I'll take it slow.

Next, we'll look at what it means to sign in to a traditional web app. After all, you only provide your password and sign into an app on a single page; how does the app know the request came from you for subsequent requests?

23.1.1 Understanding users and claims in ASP.NET Core

The concept of a user is baked into ASP.NET Core. In chapter 3 you learned that the HTTP server, Kestrel, creates an `HttpContext` object for every request it receives. This object is responsible for storing all the details related to that request, such as the request URL, any headers sent, and the body of the request.

The `HttpContext` object also exposes the current *principal* for a request as the `User` property. This is ASP.NET Core's view of which user made the request. Any time your app needs to know who the current user is or what they're allowed to do, it can look at the `HttpContext.User` principal.

DEFINITION You can think of the *principal* as the user of your app.

In ASP.NET Core, principals are implemented using the `ClaimsPrincipal` class, which has a collection of *claims* associated with it, as shown in figure 23.1.

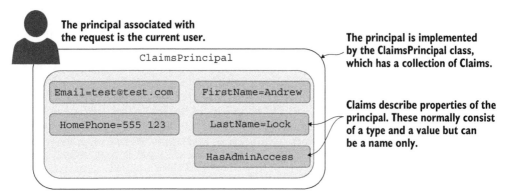

Figure 23.1 The principal is the current user, implemented as `ClaimsPrincipal`. It contains a collection of `Claims` that describe the user.

You can think about claims as properties of the current user. For example, you could have claims for things like email, name, and date of birth.

>   **DEFINITION**   A claim is a single piece of information about a principal; it consists of a *claim type* and an optional *value.*

Claims can also be indirectly related to permissions and authorization, so you could have a claim called `HasAdminAccess` or `IsVipCustomer`. These would be stored in the same way—as claims associated with the user principal.

>   **NOTE**   Earlier versions of ASP.NET used a role-based approach to security rather than a claims-based approach. The `ClaimsPrincipal` used in ASP.NET Core is compatible with this approach for legacy reasons, but you should use the claims-based approach for new apps.

Kestrel assigns a user principal to every request that arrives at your app. Initially, that principal is a generic, anonymous, unauthenticated principal with no claims. How do you log in, and how does ASP.NET Core know that you've logged in on subsequent requests?

In the next section we'll look at how authentication works in a traditional web app using ASP.NET Core and the process of signing into a user account.

23.1.2 *Authentication in ASP.NET Core: Services and middleware*

Adding authentication to any web app involves a few moving parts. The same general process applies whether you're building a traditional web app or a client-side app (though there are often differences in the latter, as I discuss in chapter 25):

1   The client sends an identifier and a secret to the app to identify the current user. For example, you could send an email address (identifier) and a password (secret).
2   The app verifies that the identifier corresponds to a user known by the app and that the corresponding secret is correct.
3   If the identifier and secret are valid, the app can set the principal for the current request, but it also needs a way of storing these details for subsequent requests. For traditional web apps, this is typically achieved by storing an encrypted version of the user principal in a cookie.

This is the typical flow for most web apps, but in this section I'm going to look at how it works in ASP.NET Core. The overall process is the same, but it's good to see how this pattern fits into the services, middleware, and Model-View-Controller (MVC) aspects of an ASP.NET Core application. We'll step through the various pieces at play in a typical app when you sign in as a user, what that means, and how you can make subsequent requests as that user.

SIGNING IN TO AN ASP.NET CORE APPLICATION

When you first arrive on a site and sign in to a traditional web app, the app will send you to a sign-in page and ask you to enter your username and password. After you submit the form to the server, the app redirects you to a new page, and you're magically logged in! Figure 23.2 shows what's happening behind the scenes in an ASP.NET Core app when you submit the form.

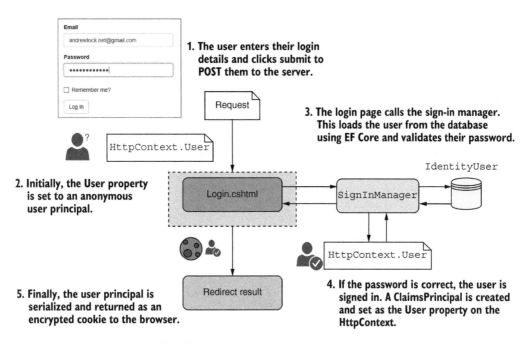

1. The user enters their login details and clicks submit to POST them to the server.

3. The login page calls the sign-in manager. This loads the user from the database using EF Core and validates their password.

2. Initially, the User property is set to an anonymous user principal.

5. Finally, the user principal is serialized and returned as an encrypted cookie to the browser.

4. If the password is correct, the user is signed in. A ClaimsPrincipal is created and set as the User property on the HttpContext.

Figure 23.2   Signing in to an ASP.NET Core application. `SignInManager` **is responsible for setting** `HttpContext.User` **to the new principal and serializing the principal to the encrypted cookie.**

This figure shows the series of steps from the moment you submit the login form on a Razor Page to the point the redirect is returned to the browser. When the request first arrives, Kestrel creates an anonymous user principal and assigns it to the `HttpContext .User` property. The request is then routed to the Login.cshtml Razor Page, which reads the email and password from the request using model binding.

The meaty work happens inside the `SignInManager` service. This is responsible for loading a user entity with the provided username from the database and validating that the password they provided is correct.

> **WARNING** Never store passwords in the database directly. They should be *hashed* using a strong one-way algorithm. The ASP.NET Core Identity system does this for you, but it's always wise to reiterate this point!

If the password is correct, `SignInManager` creates a new `ClaimsPrincipal` from the user entity it loaded from the database and adds the appropriate claims, such as the email address. It then replaces the old, anonymous `HttpContext.User` principal with the new, authenticated principal.

Finally, `SignInManager` serializes the principal, encrypts it, and stores it as a cookie. A *cookie* is a small piece of text that's sent back and forth between the browser and your app along with each request, consisting of a name and a value.

This authentication process explains how you can set the user for a request when they first log in to your app, but what about subsequent requests? You send your password only when you first log in to an app, so how does the app know that it's the same user making the request?

AUTHENTICATING USERS FOR SUBSEQUENT REQUESTS

The key to persisting your identity across multiple requests lies in the final step of figure 23.2, where you serialized the principal in a cookie. Browsers automatically send this cookie with all requests made to your app, so you don't need to provide your password with every request.

ASP.NET Core uses the authentication cookie sent with the requests to rehydrate a `ClaimsPrincipal` and set the `HttpContext.User` principal for the request, as shown in figure 23.3. The important thing to note is when this process happens—in the `AuthenticationMiddleware`.

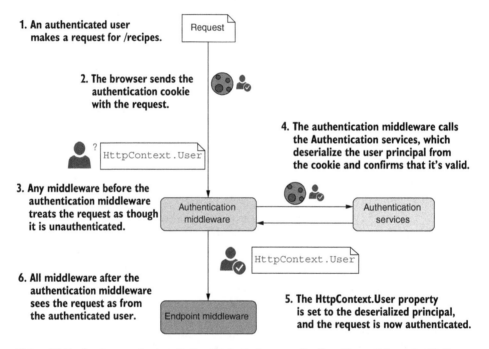

Figure 23.3   A subsequent request after signing in to an application. The cookie sent with the request contains the user principal, which is validated and used to authenticate the request.

When a request containing the authentication cookie is received, Kestrel creates the default, unauthenticated, anonymous principal and assigns it to the `HttpContext.User` principal. Any middleware that runs before the `AuthenticationMiddleware` sees the request as unauthenticated, even if there's a valid cookie.

> **TIP**   If it looks like your authentication system isn't working, double-check your middleware pipeline. Only middleware that runs after `Authentication-Middleware` will see the request as authenticated.

The `AuthenticationMiddleware` is responsible for setting the current user for a request. The middleware calls the authentication services, which reads the cookie from the request, decrypts it, and deserializes it to obtain the `ClaimsPrincipal` created when the user logged in.

The `AuthenticationMiddleware` sets the `HttpContext.User` principal to the new, authenticated principal. All subsequent middleware now knows the user principal for the request and can adjust its behavior accordingly (for example, displaying the user's name on the home page or restricting access to some areas of the app).

> **NOTE** The `AuthenticationMiddleware` is responsible only for authenticating incoming requests and setting the `ClaimsPrincipal` if the request contains an authentication cookie. It is not responsible for redirecting unauthenticated requests to the login page or rejecting unauthorized requests; that is handled by the `AuthorizationMiddleware`, as you'll see in chapter 24.

The process described so far, in which a single app authenticates the user when they log in and sets a cookie that's read on subsequent requests, is common with traditional web apps, but it isn't the only possibility. In chapter 25 we'll take a look at authentication for web API applications, used by client-side and mobile apps and at how the authentication system changes for those scenarios.

Another thing to consider is where you store the authentication details for users of your app. In figure 23.2 I showed the authentication services loading the user authentication details from your app's database, but that's only one option.

Another option is to delegate the authentication responsibilities to a third-party identity provider, such as Okta, Auth0, Azure Active Directory B2B/B2C, or even Facebook. These manage users for you, so user information and passwords are stored in their database rather than your own. The biggest advantage of this approach is that you don't have to worry about making sure your customer data is safe; you can be pretty sure that a third party will protect it, as it's their whole business.

> **TIP** Wherever possible, I recommend this approach, as it delegates security responsibilities to someone else. You can't lose your users' details if you never had them! Make sure to understand the differences in providers, however. With a provider like Auth0, *you* would own the profiles created, whereas with a provider like Facebook, you don't!

Each provider has instructions on how to integrate with their identity services, ideally using the OpenID Connect (OIDC) specification. This typically involves configuring some authentication services in your application, adding some configuration, and delegating the authentication process itself to the external provider. These providers can be used with your API apps too, as I discuss in chapter 25.

> **NOTE** Hooking up your apps and APIs to use an identity provider can require a fair amount of tedious configuration, both in the app and the identity provider, but if you follow the provider's documentation you should have

plain sailing. For example, you can follow the documentation for adding authentication to a traditional web app using Microsoft's Identity Platform here: http://mng.bz/4D9w.

While I recommend using an external identity provider where possible, sometimes you really want to store all the authentication details of your users directly in your app. That's the approach I describe in this chapter.

ASP.NET Core Identity (sometimes shortened to Identity) is a system that simplifies building the user-management aspect of your app. It handles all the boilerplate for saving and loading users to a database, as well as best practices for security, such as user lockout, password hashing, and *multifactor authentication*.

> **DEFINITION**   *Multifactor authentication* (MFA), and the subset *two-factor authentication* (2FA) require both a password and an extra piece of information to sign in. This could involve sending a code to a user's phone by Short Message Service (SMS) or using a mobile app to generate a code, for example.

In the next section I'm going to talk about the ASP.NET Core Identity system, the problems it solves, when you'd want to use it, and when you might not want to use it. In section 23.3 we take a look at some code and see ASP.NET Core Identity in action.

23.2   *What is ASP.NET Core Identity?*

Whenever you need to add nontrivial behaviors to your application, you typically need to add users and authentication. That means you'll need a way of persisting details about your users, such as their usernames and passwords.

This might seem like a relatively simple requirement, but given that this is related to security and people's personal details, it's important you get it right. As well as storing the claims for each user, it's important to store passwords using a strong hashing algorithm, to allow users to use MFA where possible, and to protect against brute-force attacks, to name a few of the many requirements. Although it's perfectly possible to write all the code to do this manually and to build your own authentication and membership system, I highly recommend you don't.

I've already mentioned third-party identity providers such as Auth0 and Azure Active Directory. These Software as a Service (SaaS) solutions take care of the user-management and authentication aspects of your app for you. If you're in the process of moving apps to the cloud generally, solutions like these can make a lot of sense.

If you can't or don't want to use these third-party solutions, I recommend you consider using the ASP.NET Core Identity system to store and manage user details in your database. ASP.NET Core Identity takes care of most of the boilerplate associated with authentication, but it remains flexible and lets you control the login process for users if you need to.

> **NOTE**   ASP.NET *Core* Identity is an evolution of the legacy .NET Framework ASP.NET Identity system, with some design improvements and update to work with ASP.NET Core.

By default, ASP.NET Core Identity uses EF Core to store user details in the database. If you're already using EF Core in your project, this is a perfect fit. Alternatively, it's possible to write your own stores for loading and saving user details in another way.

Identity takes care of the low-level parts of user management, as shown in table 23.1. As you can see from this list, Identity gives you a lot, but not everything—by a long shot!

Table 23.1   Which services are and aren't handled by ASP.NET Core IdentityCH23.fm

Managed by ASP.NET Core Identity	Requires implementing by the developer
Database schema for storing users and claims	UI for logging in, creating, and managing users (Razor Pages or controllers); included in an optional package that provides a default UI
Creating a user in the database	Sending email messages
Password validation and rules	Customizing claims for users (adding new claims)
Handling user account lockout (to prevent brute-force attacks)	Configuring third-party identity providers
Managing and generating MFA/2FA codes	Integration into MFA such as sending SMS messages, time-based one-time password (TOTP) authenticator apps, or hardware keys
Generating password-reset tokens	
Saving additional claims to the database	
Managing third-party identity providers (for example, Facebook, Google, and Twitter)	

The biggest missing piece is the fact that you need to provide all the UI for the application, as well as tying all the individual Identity services together to create a functioning sign-in process. That's a big missing piece, but it makes the Identity system extremely flexible.

Luckily, ASP.NET Core includes a helper NuGet library, Microsoft.AspNet-Core.Identity.UI, that gives you the whole of the UI boilerplate for free. That's over 30 Razor Pages with functionality for logging in, registering users, using 2FA, and using external login providers, among other features. You can still customize these pages if you need to, but having a whole login process working out of the box, with no code required on your part, is a huge win. We'll look at this library and how you use it in sections 23.3 and 23.4.

For that reason, I strongly recommend using the default UI as a starting point, whether you're creating an app or adding user management to an existing app. But the question remains as to when you should use Identity and when you should consider rolling your own.

I'm a big fan of Identity when you need to store your own users, so I tend to suggest it in most situations, as it handles a lot of security-related things for you that are easy to mess up. I've heard several arguments against it, some valid and others less so:

- *I already have user authentication in my app.* Great! In that case, you're probably right, Identity may not be necessary. But does your custom implementation use MFA? Do you have account lockout? If not, and if you need to add them, considering Identity may be worthwhile.

- *I don't want to use EF Core.* That's a reasonable stance. You could be using Dapper, some other object-relational mapper (ORM), or even a document database for your database access. Luckily, the database integration in Identity is pluggable, so you could swap out the EF Core integration and use your own database integration libraries instead.

- *My use case is too complex for Identity.* Identity provides lower-level services for authentication, so you can compose the pieces however you like. It's also extensible, so if you need to, for example, transform claims before creating a principal, you can.

- *I don't like the default Razor Pages UI.* The default UI for Identity is entirely optional. You can still use the Identity services and user management but provide your own UI for logging in and registering users. However, be aware that although doing this gives you a lot of flexibility, it's also easy to introduce a security flaw in your user-management system—the last place you want security flaws!

- *I'm not using Bootstrap to style my application.* The default Identity UI uses Bootstrap as a styling framework, the same as the default ASP.NET Core templates. Unfortunately, you can't easily change that, so if you're using a different framework or need to customize the HTML generated, you can still use Identity, but you'll need to provide your own UI.

- *I don't want to build my own identity system.* I'm glad to hear it. Using an external identity provider like Azure Active Directory or Auth0 is a great way of shifting the responsibility and risk associated with storing users' personal information to a third party.

Any time you're considering adding user management to your ASP.NET Core application, I'd recommend looking at Identity as a great option for doing so. In the next section I'll demonstrate what Identity provides by creating a new Razor Pages application using the default Identity UI. In section 23.4 we'll take that template and apply it to an existing app instead, and in sections 23.5 and 23.6 you'll see how to override the default pages.

23.3   *Creating a project that uses ASP.NET Core Identity*

I've covered authentication and Identity in general terms, but the best way to get a feel for it is to see some working code. In this section we're going to look at the default code generated by the ASP.NET Core templates with Identity, how the project works, and where Identity fits in.

23.3.1 *Creating the project from a template*

You'll start by using the Visual Studio templates to generate a simple Razor Pages application that uses Identity for storing individual user accounts in a database.

> **TIP** You can create a similar project using the .NET CLI by running `dotnet new webapp -au Individual`. The Visual Studio template uses a LocalDB database, but the `dotnet new` template uses SQLite by default. To use LocalDB instead, run `dotnet new webapp -au Individual --use-local-db`.

To create the template using Visual Studio, you must be using the 2022 version or later and have the .NET 7 software development kit (SDK) installed. Follow these steps:

1. Choose **File** > **New** > **Project** or choose **Create a New Project** on the splash screen.
2. From the list of templates, choose **ASP.NET Core Web Application**, ensuring that you select the C# language template.
3. On the next screen, enter a project name, location, and a solution name, and choose **Create**.
4. On the **Additional Information** screen, change the **Authentication Type** to **Individual Accounts**, as shown in figure 23.4. Leave the other settings at their defaults, and choose **Create** to create the application.

   Visual Studio automatically runs `dotnet restore` to restore all the necessary NuGet packages for the project.

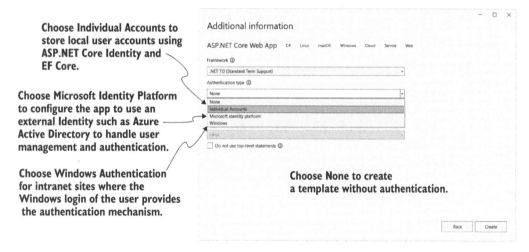

Figure 23.4   Choosing the authentication mode of the new ASP.NET Core application template in VS 2022

5. Run the application to see the default app, as shown in figure 23.5.

> **NOTE**   The Visual Studio template configures the application to use LocalDB and includes EF Core migrations for SQL Server. If you want to use a different database provider, you can replace the configuration and migrations with your database of choice, as described in chapter 12.

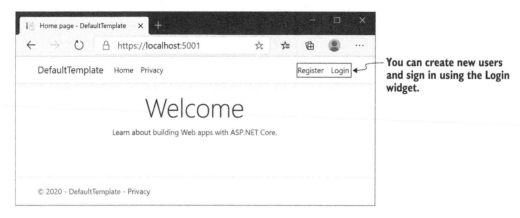

You can create new users and sign in using the Login widget.

Figure 23.5   The default template with individual account authentication looks similar to the no authentication template, with the addition of a Login widget at the top right of the page.

This template should look familiar, with one twist: you now have Register and Login buttons! Feel free to play with the template—creating a user, logging in and out—to get a feel for the app. Once you're happy, look at the code generated by the template and the boilerplate it saved you from writing.

> **TIP**   Don't forget to run the included EF Core migrations before trying to create users. Run `dotnet ef database update` from the project folder.

23.3.2 Exploring the template in Solution Explorer

The project generated by the template, shown in figure 23.6, is similar to the default no-authentication template. That's largely due to the default UI library, which brings in a big chunk of functionality without exposing you to the nitty-gritty details.

The biggest addition is the Areas folder in the root of your project, which contains an Identity subfolder. Areas are sometimes used for organizing sections of functionality. Each area can contain its own Pages folder, which is analogous to the main Pages folder in your application.

> **DEFINITION**   *Areas* are used to group Razor Pages into separate hierarchies for organizational purposes. I rarely use areas and prefer to create subfolders in the main Pages folder instead. The one exception is the Identity UI, which uses a separate Identity area by default. For more details on areas, see Microsoft's "Areas in ASP.NET Core" documentation: http://mng.bz/7Vw9.

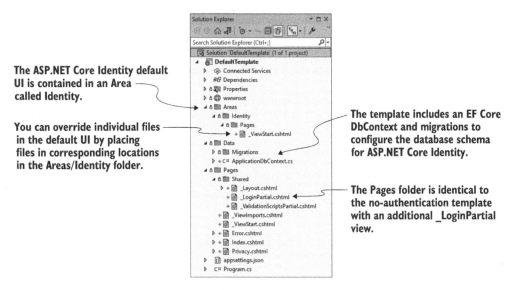

Figure 23.6 The project layout of the default template with individual authentication

The Microsoft.AspNetCore.Identity.UI package creates Razor Pages in the Identity area. You can override any page in this default UI by creating a corresponding page in the Areas/Identity/Pages folder in your application. In figure 23.6, the default template adds a _ViewStart.cshtml file that overrides the template that is included as part of the default UI. This file contains the following code, which sets the default Identity UI Razor Pages to use your project's default _Layout.cshtml file:

```
@{
    Layout = "/Pages/Shared/_Layout.cshtml";
}
```

Some obvious questions at this point are "How do you know what's included in the default UI?" and "Which files can you override?" You'll see the answers to both in section 23.5, but in general you should try to avoid overriding files where possible. After all, the goal with the default UI is to reduce the amount of code you have to write!

The Data folder in your new project template contains your application's EF Core DbContext, called ApplicationDbContext, and the migrations for configuring the database schema to use Identity. I'll discuss this schema in more detail in section 23.3.3.

The final additional file included in this template compared with the no-authentication version is the partial Razor view Pages/Shared/_LoginPartial.cshtml. This provides the Register and Login links you saw in figure 23.5, and it's rendered in the default Razor layout, _Layout.cshtml.

If you look inside _LoginPartial.cshtml, you can see how routing works with areas by combining the Razor Page path with an {area} route parameter using Tag Helpers.

For example, the Login link specifies that the Razor Page `/Account/Login` is in the Identity area using the `asp-area` attribute:

```
<a asp-area="Identity" asp-page="/Account/Login">Login</a>
```

> **TIP** You can reference Razor Pages in the `Identity` area by setting the `area` route value to `Identity`. You can use the `asp-area` attribute in Tag Helpers that generate links.

In addition to viewing the new files included thanks to ASP.NET Core Identity, open Program.cs and look at the changes there. The most obvious change is the additional configuration, which adds all the services Identity requires, as shown in the following listing.

Listing 23.1   Adding ASP.NET Core Identity services to `ConfigureServices`

ASP.NET Core Identity uses EF Core, so it includes the standard EF Core configuration.

```
WebApplicationBuilder builder = WebApplication.CreateBuilder(args);

string connectionString = builder.Configuration
    .GetConnectionString("DefaultConnection");
builder.Services.AddDbContext<ApplicationDbContext>(options =>
    options.UseSqlServer(connectionString));

builder.Services.AddDatabaseDeveloperPageExceptionFilter();
```
Adds optional database services to enhance the DeveloperExceptionPage

```
builder.Services.AddDefaultIdentity<IdentityUser>(options =>
    options.SignIn.RequireConfirmedAccount = true)
        .AddEntityFrameworkStores<ApplicationDbContext>();
builder.Services.AddRazorPages();

// remaining configuration not show
```
Adds the Identity system, including the default UI, and configures the user type as IdentityUser

Configures Identity to store its data in EF Core

Requires users to confirm their accounts (typically by email) before they log in

---

The `AddDefaultIdentity()` extension method does several things:

- Adds the core ASP.NET Core Identity services.
- Configures the application user type to be `IdentityUser`. This is the entity model that is stored in the database and represents a "user" in your application. You can extend this type if you need to, but that's not always necessary, as you'll see in section 23.6.
- Adds the default UI Razor Pages for registering, logging in, and managing users.
- Configures token providers for generating MFA and email confirmation tokens.

Now that you've got an overview of the additions made by Identity, we'll look in a bit more detail at the database schema and how Identity stores users in the database.

> **Where is the authentication middleware?**
>
> If you're already familiar with previous versions of ASP.NET Core, you might be surprised to notice the lack of any authentication middleware in the default template. Given everything you've learned about how authentication works, that *should* be surprising!
>
> The answer to this riddle is that the authentication middleware *is* in the pipeline, even though you can't see it. As I discussed in chapter 4, WebApplication automatically adds many middleware components to the pipeline for you, including the routing middleware, the endpoint middleware, and—yes—the authentication middleware. So the reason you don't see it in the pipeline is that it's already been added.
>
> In fact, WebApplication also automatically adds the *authorization* middleware to the pipeline, but in this case the template still calls UseAuthorization(). Why? For the same reason that the template also calls UseRouting(): to control exactly where in the pipeline the middleware is added.
>
> As I mentioned in chapter 4, you can override the automatically added middleware by adding it yourself manually. It's crucial that the authorization middleware be placed *after* the routing middleware, and as mentioned in chapter 4, you typically want to place your routing middleware after the static file middleware. As the routing middleware needs to move, so does the authorization middleware!
>
> Traditionally, the authentication middleware is also placed after the routing middleware, before the authorization middleware, but this isn't crucial. The only requirement is that it's placed before any middleware that requires an authenticated user, such as the authorization middleware.
>
> If you wish, you can move the location of the authentication middleware by calling UseAuthentication() at the appropriate point. I prefer to be explicit where possible, so I typically take this approach, moving it between the call to UseRouting() and UseAuthorization():
>
> ```
> app.UseRouting();
> app.UseAuthentication();
> app.UseAuthorization();
> app.MapRazorPages();
> app.Run();
> ```
>
> If you don't place the authentication middleware at the correct point in the pipeline, you can run into strange bugs where users aren't authenticated correctly or authorization policies aren't applied correctly. The templates work out of the box, but you need to take care if you're working with an existing application or moving middleware around.

23.3.3 *The ASP.NET Core Identity data model*

Out of the box, and in the default templates, Identity uses EF Core to store user accounts. It provides a base DbContext that you can inherit from, called IdentityDbContext, which uses an IdentityUser as the user entity for your application.

In the template, the app's DbContext is called ApplicationDbContext. If you open this file, you'll see it's sparse; it inherits from the IdentityDbContext base class I described earlier, and that's it. What does this base class give you? The easiest way to see is to update a database with the migrations and take a look.

Applying the migrations is the same process as in chapter 12. Ensure that the connection string points to where you want to create the database, open a command prompt in your project folder, and run this command to update the database with the migrations:

```
dotnet ef database update
```

> **TIP** If you see an error after running the `dotnet ef` command, ensure that you have the .NET tool installed by following the instructions provided in section 12.3.1. Also make sure that you run the command from the project folder, not the solution folder.

If the database doesn't exist, the command-line interface (CLI) creates it. Figure 23.7 shows what the database looks like for the default template.

> **TIP** If you're using MS SQL Server (or LocalDB), you can use the SQL Server Object Explorer in Visual Studio to browse tables and objects in your database. See Microsoft's "How to: Connect to a Database and Browse Existing Objects" article for details: http://mng.bz/mg8r.

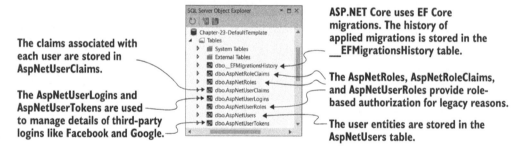

The claims associated with each user are stored in AspNetUserClaims.

The AspNetUserLogins and AspNetUserTokens are used to manage details of third-party logins like Facebook and Google.

ASP.NET Core uses EF Core migrations. The history of applied migrations is stored in the __EFMigrationsHistory table.

The AspNetRoles, AspNetRoleClaims, and AspNetUserRoles provide role-based authorization for legacy reasons.

The user entities are stored in the AspNetUsers table.

Figure 23.7   The database schema used by ASP.NET Core Identity

That's a lot of tables! You shouldn't need to interact with these tables directly (Identity handles that for you), but it doesn't hurt to have a basic grasp of what they're for:

- *__EFMigrationsHistory*—The standard EF Core migrations table that records which migrations have been applied.
- *AspNetUsers*—The user profile table itself. This is where `IdentityUser` is serialized to. We'll take a closer look at this table shortly.
- *AspNetUserClaims*—The claims associated with a given user. A user can have many claims, so it's modeled as a many-to-one relationship.
- *AspNetUserLogins and AspNetUserTokens*—These are related to third-party logins. When configured, these let users sign in with a Google or Facebook account (for example) instead of creating a password on your app.

- *AspNetUserRoles, AspNetRoles, and AspNetRoleClaims*—These tables let you define roles that multiple users can belong to. Each role can be assigned multiple claims. These claims are effectively inherited by a user principal when they are assigned that role.

You can explore these tables yourself, but the most interesting of them is the AspNet-Users table, shown in figure 23.8.

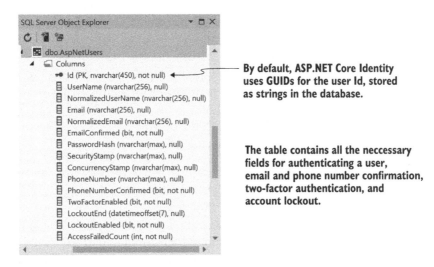

By default, ASP.NET Core Identity uses GUIDs for the user Id, stored as strings in the database.

The table contains all the neccessary fields for authenticating a user, email and phone number confirmation, two-factor authentication, and account lockout.

Figure 23.8 **The AspNetUsers table is used to store all the details required to authenticate a user.**

Most of the columns in the AspNetUsers table are security-related—the user's email, password hash, whether they have confirmed their email, whether they have MFA enabled, and so on. By default, there are no columns for additional information, like the user's name.

> **NOTE** You can see from figure 23.8 that the primary key Id is stored as a string column. By default, Identity uses Guid for the identifier. To customize the data type, see the "Change the primary key type" section of Microsoft's "Identity model customization in ASP.NET Core" documentation: http://mng.bz/5jdB.

Any additional properties of the user are stored as claims in the AspNetUserClaims table associated with that user. This lets you add arbitrary additional information without having to change the database schema to accommodate it. Want to store the user's date of birth? You could add a claim to that user; there's no need to change the database schema. You'll see this in action in section 23.6, when you add a Name claim to every new user.

> **NOTE** Adding claims is often the easiest way to extend the default `IdentityU-ser`, but you can add properties to the `IdentityUser` directly. This requires database changes but is nevertheless useful in many situations. You can read how to add custom data using this approach here: http://mng.bz/Xd61.

It's important to understand the difference between the `IdentityUser` entity (stored in the AspNetUsers table) and the `ClaimsPrincipal`, which is exposed on `HttpContext.User`. When a user first logs in, an `IdentityUser` is loaded from the database. This entity is combined with additional claims for the user from the AspNetUserClaims table to create a `ClaimsPrincipal`. It's this `ClaimsPrincipal` that is used for authentication and is serialized to the authentication cookie, not the `IdentityUser`.

It's useful to have a mental model of the underlying database schema Identity uses, but in day-to-day work, you shouldn't have to interact with it directly. That's what Identity is for, after all! In the next section we'll look at the other end of the scale: the UI of the app and what you get out of the box with the default UI.

23.3.4 *Interacting with ASP.NET Core Identity*

You'll want to explore the default UI yourself to get a feel for how the pieces fit together, but in this section I'll highlight what you get out of the box, as well as areas that typically require additional attention right away.

The entry point to the default UI is the user registration page of the application, shown in figure 23.9. The register page enables users to sign up to your application by creating a new `IdentityUser` with an email and a password. After creating an account, users are redirected to a screen indicating that they should confirm their email. No email service is enabled by default, as this is dependent on your configuring an external email service. You can read how to enable email sending in Microsoft's "Account confirmation and password recovery in ASP.NET Core" documentation at http://mng.bz/6gBo. Once you configure this, users will automatically receive an email with a link to confirm their account.

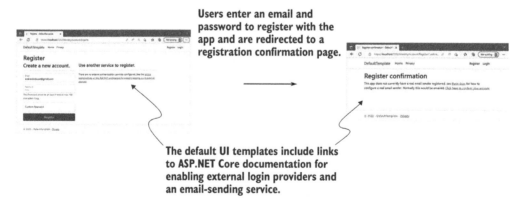

Users enter an email and password to register with the app and are redirected to a registration confirmation page.

The default UI templates include links to ASP.NET Core documentation for enabling external login providers and an email-sending service.

Figure 23.9 The registration flow for users using the default Identity UI. Users enter an email and password and are redirected to a "confirm your email" page. This is a placeholder page by default, but if you enable email confirmation, this page will update appropriately.

By default, user emails must be unique (you can't have two users with the same email), and the password must meet various length and complexity requirements. You can customize these options and more in the configuration lambda of the call to `Add-DefaultIdentity()` in Program.cs, as shown in the following listing.

Listing 23.2 Customizing Identity settings in `ConfigureServices` in Startup.cs

```
builder.Services.AddDefaultIdentity<IdentityUser>(options =>
{
    options.SignIn.RequireConfirmedAccount = true;
    options.Lockout.AllowedForNewUsers = true;
    options.Password.RequiredLength = 12;
    options.Password.RequireNonAlphanumeric = false;
    options.Password.RequireDigit = false;
})
.AddEntityFrameworkStores<AppDbContext>();
```

> Requires users to confirm their account by email before they can log in

> Updates password requirements. Current guidance is to require long passwords.

Enables user lockout, to prevent brute-force attacks against user passwords

After a user has registered with your application, they need to log in, as shown in figure 23.10. On the right side of the login page, the default UI templates describe how you, the developer, can configure external login providers, such as Facebook and Google. This is useful information for you, but it's one of the reasons you may need to customize the default UI templates, as you'll see in section 23.5.

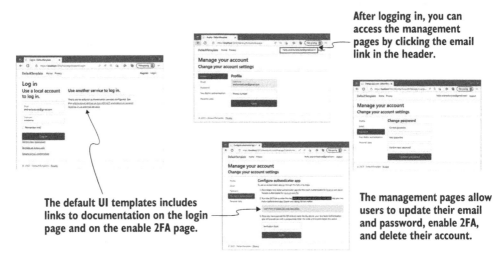

After logging in, you can access the management pages by clicking the email link in the header.

The default UI templates includes links to documentation on the login page and on the enable 2FA page.

The management pages allow users to update their email and password, enable 2FA, and delete their account.

Figure 23.10 Logging in with an existing user and managing the user account. The Login page describes how to configure external login providers, such as Facebook and Google. The user-management pages allow users to change their email and password and to configure MFA.

Once a user has signed in, they can access the management pages of the identity UI. These allow users to change their email, change their password, configure MFA with an authenticator app, or delete all their personal data. Most of these functions work without any effort on your part, assuming that you've already configured an email-sending service.

That covers everything you get in the default UI templates. It may seem somewhat minimal, but it covers a lot of the requirements that are common to almost all apps. Nevertheless, there are a few things you'll nearly always want to customize:

- Configure an email-sending service, to enable account confirmation and password recovery, as described in Microsoft's "Account confirmation and password recovery in ASP.NET Core" documentation: http://mng.bz/vzy7.
- Add a QR code generator for the enable MFA page, as described in Microsoft's "Enable QR Code generation for TOTP authenticator apps in ASP.NET Core" documentation: http://mng.bz/4Zmw.
- Customize the register and login pages to remove the documentation link for enabling external services. You'll see how to do this in section 23.5. Alternatively, you may want to disable user registration entirely, as described in Microsoft's "Scaffold Identity in ASP.NET Core projects" documentation: http://mng.bz/QmMG.
- Collect additional information about users on the registration page. You'll see how to do this in section 23.6.

There are many more ways you can extend or update the Identity system and lots of options available, so I encourage you to explore Microsoft's "Overview of ASP.NET Core authentication" at http://mng.bz/XdGv to see your options. In the next section you'll see how to achieve another common requirement: adding users to an existing application.

23.4   Adding ASP.NET Core Identity to an existing project

In this section we're going to add users to an existing application. The initial app is a Razor Pages app, based on the recipe application from chapter 12. This is a working app that you want to add user functionality to. In chapter 24 we'll extend this work to restrict control regarding who's allowed to edit recipes on the app.

By the end of this section, you'll have an application with a registration page, a login screen, and a manage account screen, like the default templates. You'll also have a persistent widget in the top right of the screen showing the login status of the current user, as shown in figure 23.11.

As in section 23.3, I'm not going to customize any of the defaults at this point, so we won't set up external login providers, email confirmation, or MFA. I'm concerned only with adding ASP.NET Core Identity to an existing app that's already using EF Core.

The Login widget shows the current signed-in user's email and a link for them to log out.

Figure 23.11   The recipe app after adding authentication, showing the Login widget

TIP It's worth making sure you're comfortable with the new project templates before you go about adding Identity to an existing project. Create a test app, and consider setting up an external login provider, configuring an email provider, and enabling MFA. This will take a bit of time, but it'll be invaluable for deciphering errors when you come to adding Identity to existing apps.

To add Identity to your app, you'll need to do the following:

1 Add the ASP.NET Core Identity NuGet packages.
2 Add the required Identity services to the dependency injection (DI) container.
3 Update the EF Core data model with the Identity entities.
4 Update your Razor Pages and layouts to provide links to the Identity UI.

This section tackles each of these steps in turn. At the end of section 23.4 you'll have successfully added user accounts to the recipe app.

23.4.1 Configuring the ASP.NET Core Identity services

You can add ASP.NET Core Identity with the default UI to an existing app by referencing two NuGet packages:

- *Microsoft.AspNetCore.Identity.EntityFrameworkCore*—Provides all the core Identity services and integration with EF Core
- *Microsoft.AspNetCore.Identity.UI*—Provides the default UI Razor Pages

Update your project .csproj file to include these two packages:

```
<PackageReference
    Include="Microsoft.AspNetCore.Identity.EntityFrameworkCore"
    Version="7.0.0" />
<PackageReference
    Include="Microsoft.AspNetCore.Identity.UI" Version="7.0.0" />
```

These packages bring in all the additional required dependencies you need to add Identity with the default UI. Be sure to run `dotnet restore` after adding them to your project.

Once you've added the Identity packages, you can update your Program.cs file to include the Identity services, as shown in the following listing. This is similar to the default template setup you saw in listing 23.1, but make sure to reference your existing `AppDbContext`.

Listing 23.3   Adding ASP.NET Core Identity services to the recipe app

```
WebApplicationBuilder builder = WebApplication.CreateBuilder(args);

builder.Services.AddDbContext<AppDbContext>(options =>
    options.UseSqlite(builder.Configuration
        .GetConnectionString("DefaultConnection")!));
```
The existing service configuration is unchanged.

```
builder.Services.AddDefaultIdentity<ApplicationUser>(options =>
        options.SignIn.RequireConfirmedAccount = true)
    .AddEntityFrameworkStores<AppDbContext>();

builder.Services.AddRazorPages();
builder.Services.AddScoped<RecipeService>();
```
Adds the Identity services to the DI container and uses a custom user type, ApplicationUser

Makes sure you use the name of your existing DbContext app

This adds all the necessary services and configures Identity to use EF Core. I've introduced a new type here, `ApplicationUser`, which we'll use to customize our user entity later. You'll see how to add this type in section 23.4.2.

The next step is optional: add the `AuthenticationMiddleware` after the call to `UseRouting()` on `WebApplication`, as shown in the following listing. As I mentioned previously, the authentication middleware is added automatically by `WebApplication`, so this step is optional.

Listing 23.4   Adding `AuthenticationMiddleware` to the recipe app

```
app.UseStaticFiles();

app.UseRouting();

app.UseAuthentication();
app.UseAuthorization();

app.MapRazorPages();
app.Run
```
StaticFileMiddleware will never see requests as authenticated, even after you sign in.

Adds AuthenticationMiddleware after UseRouting() and before UseAuthorization

Middleware after AuthenticationMiddleware can read the user principal from HttpContext.User.

You've configured your app to use Identity, so the next step is updating EF Core's data model. You're already using EF Core in this app, so you need to update your database schema to include the tables that Identity requires.

23.4.2 Updating the EF Core data model to support Identity

The code in listing 23.3 won't compile, as it references the `ApplicationUser` type, which doesn't yet exist. Create the `ApplicationUser` in the Data folder, using the following line:

```
public class ApplicationUser : IdentityUser { }
```

It's not strictly necessary to create a custom user type in this case (for example, the default templates use the raw `IdentityUser`), but I find it's easier to add the derived type now rather than try to retrofit it later if you need to add extra properties to your user type.

In section 23.3.3 you saw that Identity provides a `DbContext` called `IdentityDbContext`, which you can inherit from. The `IdentityDbContext` base class includes the necessary `DbSet<T>` to store your user entities using EF Core.

Updating an existing `DbContext` for Identity is simple: update your app's `DbContext` to inherit from `IdentityDbContext` (which itself inherits from `DbContext`), as shown in the following listing. We're using the generic version of the base Identity context in this case and providing the `ApplicationUser` type.

> **Listing 23.5 Updating `AppDbContext` to use `IdentityDbContext`**
>
> Updates to inherit from the **Identity context**
> instead of directly from **DbContext**
>
> ```
> public class AppDbContext : IdentityDbContext<ApplicationUser>    ◁
> {
>     public AppDbContext(DbContextOptions<AppDbContext> options)
>         : base(options)
>     { }
>
>     public DbSet<Recipe> Recipes { get; set; }
> }
> ```
>
> The remainder of
> the class remains
> the same.

Effectively, by updating the base class of your context in this way, you've added a whole load of new entities to EF Core's data model. As you saw in chapter 12, whenever EF Core's data model changes, you need to create a new migration and apply those changes to the database.

At this point, your app should compile, so you can add a new migration called `AddIdentitySchema` using

```
dotnet ef migrations add AddIdentitySchema
```

The final step is updating your application's Razor Pages and layouts to reference the default identity UI. Normally, adding 30 new Razor Pages to your application would be a lot of work, but using the default Identity UI makes it a breeze.

23.4.3 *Updating the Razor views to link to the Identity UI*

Technically, you don't have to update your Razor Pages to reference the pages included in the default UI, but you probably want to add the login widget to your app's layout at a minimum. You'll also want to make sure that your Identity Razor Pages use the same base Layout.cshtml as the rest of your application.

We'll start by fixing the layout for your Identity pages. Create a file at the "magic" path `Areas/Identity/Pages/_ViewStart.cshtml`, and add the following contents:

```
@{ Layout = "/Pages/Shared/_Layout.cshtml"; }
```

This sets the default layout for your Identity pages to your application's default layout. Next, add a _LoginPartial.cshtml file in Pages/Shared to define the login widget, as shown in the following listing. This is pretty much identical to the template generated by the default template, but it uses our custom `ApplicationUser` instead of the default `IdentityUser`.

Listing 23.6 Adding a _LoginPartial.cshtml to an existing app

```
@using Microsoft.AspNetCore.Identity              Updates to your project's namespace
@using RecipeApplication.Data;          ◁────────  that contains ApplicationUser
@inject SignInManager<ApplicationUser> SignInManager
@inject UserManager<ApplicationUser> UserManager        The default template uses
                                                        IdentityUser. Update to use
<ul class="navbar-nav">                                 ApplicationUser instead.
@if (SignInManager.IsSignedIn(User))
{
  <li class="nav-item">
    <a  class="nav-link text-dark" asp-area="Identity"
    asp-page="/Account/Manage/Index" title="Manage">
       Hello @User.Identity.Name!</a>
  </li>
    <li class="nav-item">
      <form class="form-inline" asp-page="/Account/Logout"
      asp-route-returnUrl="@Url.Page("/", new { area = "" })"
      asp-area="Identity" method="post" >
        <button  class="nav-link btn btn-link text-dark"
          type="submit">Logout</button>
        </form>
    </li>
}
else
{
  <li class="nav-item">
    <a class="nav-link text-dark" asp-area="Identity"
      asp-page="/Account/Register">Register</a>
  </li>
  <li class="nav-item">
    <a class="nav-link text-dark" asp-area="Identity"
      asp-page="/Account/Login">Login</a>
  </li>
}
</ul>
```

This partial shows the current login status of the user and provides links to register or sign in. All that remains is to render the partial by calling

```
<partial name="_LoginPartial" />
```

in the main layout file of your app, _Layout.cshtml.

And there you have it: you've added Identity to an existing application. The default UI makes doing this relatively simple, and you can be sure you haven't introduced any security holes by building your own UI!

As I described in section 23.3.4, there are some features that the default UI doesn't provide and you need to implement yourself, such as email confirmation and MFA QR code generation. It's also common to find that you want to update a single page here and there. In the next section I'll show how you can replace a page in the default UI, without having to rebuild the entire UI yourself.

23.5 Customizing a page in ASP.NET Core Identity's default UI

In this section you'll learn how to use scaffolding to replace individual pages in the default Identity UI. You'll learn to scaffold a page so that it overrides the default UI, allowing you to customize both the Razor template and the `PageModel` page handlers.

Having Identity provide the whole UI for your application is great in theory, but in practice there are a few wrinkles, as you saw in section 23.3.4. The default UI provides as much as it can, but there are some things you may want to tweak. For example, both the login and register pages describe how to configure external login providers for your ASP.NET Core applications, as you saw in figures 23.12 and 23.13. That's useful information for you as a developer, but it's not something you want to be showing to your users. Another often-cited requirement is the desire to change the look and feel of one or more pages.

Luckily, the default Identity UI is designed to be incrementally replaceable, so you can override a single page without having to rebuild the entire UI yourself. On top of that, both Visual Studio and the .NET CLI have functions that allow you to scaffold any (or all) of the pages in the default UI so that you don't have to start from scratch when you want to tweak a page.

> **DEFINITION** *Scaffolding* is the process of generating files in your project that serve as the basis for customization. The Identity scaffolder adds Razor Pages in the correct locations so they override equivalent pages with the default UI. Initially, the code in the scaffolded pages matches that in the default Identity UI, but you are free to customize it.

As an example of the changes you can easily make, we'll scaffold the registration page and remove the additional information section about external providers. The following steps describe how to scaffold the Register.cshtml page in Visual Studio:

1 Add the Microsoft.VisualStudio.Web.CodeGeneration.Design and Microsoft
.EntityFrameworkCore.Tools NuGet packages to your project file, if they're not
already added. Visual Studio uses these packages to scaffold your application
correctly, and without them you may get an error running the scaffolder:

```
<PackageReference Version="7.0.0"
    Include="Microsoft.VisualStudio.Web.CodeGeneration.Design" />
<PackageReference Version="7.0.0"
    Include="Microsoft.EntityFrameworkCore.Tools" />
```

2 Ensure that your project builds. If it doesn't build, the scaffolder will fail before
adding your new pages.

3 Right-click your project, and choose **Add** > **New Scaffolded Item** from the contextual menu.

4 In the selection dialog box, choose **Identity** from the category, and choose **Add**.

5 In the **Add Identity** dialog box, select the **Account/Register** page, and select
your application's AppDbContext as the Data context class, as shown in figure
23.12. Choose **Add** to scaffold the page.

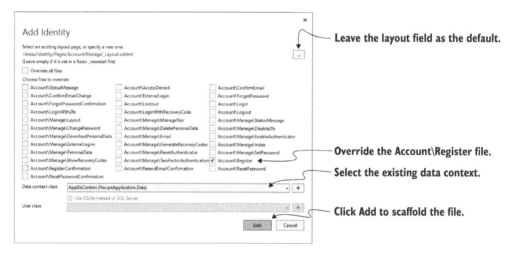

**Figure 23.12   Using Visual Studio to scaffold Identity pages. The generated Razor Pages will override the
versions provided by the default UI.**

TIP To scaffold the registration page using the .NET CLI, install the required
tools and packages as described in Microsoft's "Scaffold Identity in ASP.NET
Core projects" documentation: http://mng.bz/QPRv. Then run dotnet
aspnet-codegenerator identity -dc RecipeApplication.Data.AppDbContext
--files "Account.Register".

Visual Studio builds your application and then generates the Register.cshtml page for
you, placing it in the Areas/Identity/Pages/Account folder. It also generates several

supporting files, as shown in figure 23.13. These are required mostly to ensure that your new Register.cshtml page can reference the remaining pages in the default Identity UI.

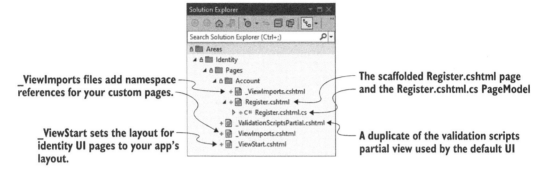

Figure 23.13   The scaffolder generates the Register.cshtml Razor Page, along with supporting files required to integrate with the remainder of the default Identity UI.

We're interested in the Register.cshtml page, as we want to customize the UI on the Register page, but if we look inside the code-behind page, Register.cshtml.cs, we see how much complexity the default Identity UI is hiding from us. It's not insurmountable (we'll customize the page handler in section 23.6), but it's always good to avoid writing code if we can help it.

Now that you have the Razor template in your application, you can customize it to your heart's content. The downside is that you're now maintaining more code than you were with the default UI. You didn't have to write it, but you may still have to update it when a new version of ASP.NET Core is released.

I like to use a bit of a trick when it comes to overriding the default Identity UI like this. In many cases, you don't want to change the *page handlers* for the Razor Page—only the Razor *view*. You can achieve this by deleting the Register.cshtml.cs PageModel file, and pointing your newly scaffolded .cshtml file at the *original* PageModel, which is part of the default UI NuGet package.

The other benefit of this approach is that you can delete some of the other files that were autoscaffolded. In total, you can make the following changes:

- Update the @model directive in Register.cshtml to point to the default UI PageModel:

```
@model
➥ Microsoft.AspNetCore.Identity.UI.V5.Pages.Account.Internal.RegisterModel
```

- Update Areas/Identity/Pages/_ViewImports.cshtml to the following:

```
@addTagHelper *, Microsoft.AspNetCore.Mvc.TagHelpers
```

- Delete Areas/Identity/Pages/_ValidationScriptsPartial.cshtml.

- Delete Areas/Identity/Pages/Account/Register.cshtml.cs.
- Delete Areas/Identity/Pages/Account/_ViewImports.cshtml.

After making all these changes, you'll have the best of both worlds: you can update the default UI Razor Pages HTML without taking on the responsibility of maintaining the default UI code-behind.

> **TIP**   In the source code for the book, you can see these changes in action, where the Register view has been customized to remove the references to external identity providers.

Unfortunately, it's not always possible to use the default UI PageModel. Sometimes you *need* to update the page handlers, such as when you want to change the functionality of your Identity area rather than only the look and feel. A common requirement is needing to store additional information about a user, as you'll see in the next section.

23.6   *Managing users: Adding custom data to users*

In this section you'll see how to customize the ClaimsPrincipal assigned to your users by adding claims to the AspNetUserClaims table when the user is created. You'll also see how to access these claims in your Razor Pages and templates.

Often, the next step after adding Identity to an application is customizing it. The default templates require only an email and password to register. What if you need more details, like a friendly name for the user? Also, I've mentioned that we use claims for security, so what if you want to add a claim called IsAdmin to certain users?

You know that every user principal has a collection of claims, so conceptually, adding any claim requires adding it to the user's collection. There are two main times that you would want to grant a claim to a user:

- *For every user, when they register on the app*—For example, you might want to add a Name field to the Register form and add that as a claim to the user when they register.
- *Manually, after the user has registered*—This is common for claims used as permissions, where an existing user might want to add an IsAdmin claim to a specific user after they have registered on the app.

In this section I'll show you the first approach, automatically adding new claims to a user when they're created. The latter approach is more flexible and ultimately is the approach many apps will need, especially line-of-business apps. Luckily, there's nothing conceptually difficult to it; it requires a simple UI that lets you view users and add a claim through the same mechanism I'll show here.

> **TIP**   Another common approach is to customize the IdentityUser entity, by adding a Name property, for example. This approach is sometimes easier to work with if you want to give users the ability to edit that property. Microsoft's "Add, download, and delete custom user data to Identity in an ASP.NET Core project" documentation describes the steps required to achieve that: http://mng.bz/aoe7.

Let's say you want to add a new `Claim` to a user, called `FullName`. A typical approach would be as follows:

1. Scaffold the Register.cshtml Razor Page, as you did in section 23.5.
2. Add a Name field to the `InputModel` in the Register.cshtml.cs `PageModel`.
3. Add a Name input field to the Register.cshtml Razor view template.
4. Create the new `ApplicationUser` entity as before in the `OnPost()` page handler by calling `CreateAsync` on `UserManager<ApplicationUser>`.
5. Add a new `Claim` to the user by calling `UserManager.AddClaimAsync()`.
6. Continue the method as before, sending a confirmation email or signing the user in if email confirmation is not required.

Steps 1–3 are fairly self-explanatory and require only updating the existing templates with the new field. Steps 4–6 take place in Register.cshtml.cs in the `OnPostAsync()` page handler, which is summarized in the following listing. In practice, the page handler has more error checking, boilerplate, extra features, and abstraction. I've simplified the code in listing 23.7 to focus on the additional lines that add the extra `Claim` to the `ApplicationUser`; you can find the full code in the sample code for this chapter.

Listing 23.7 Adding a custom claim to a new user in the Register.cshtml.cs page

```csharp
public async Task<IActionResult> OnPostAsync(string returnUrl = null)
{
    if (ModelState.IsValid)
    {
        var user = new ApplicationUser {
            UserName = Input.Email, Email = Input.Email };
        var result = await _userManager.CreateAsync(
            user, Input.Password);
        if (result.Succeeded)
        {
            var claim = new Claim("FullName", Input.Name);
            await _userManager.AddClaimAsync(user, claim);
            var code = await _userManager
                .GenerateEmailConfirmationTokenAsync(user);
            await _emailSender.SendEmailAsync(
                Input.Email, "Confirm your email", code );
            await _signInManager.SignInAsync(user);
            return LocalRedirect(returnUrl);
        }
        foreach (var error in result.Errors)
        {
            ModelState.AddModelError(
                string.Empty, error.Description);
        }
    }
    return Page();
}
```

Annotations:
- Creates an instance of the ApplicationUser entity
- Validates that the provided password meets requirements, and creates the user in the database
- Adds the new claim to the ApplicationUser's collection
- Creates a claim, with a string name of "FullName" and the provided value
- Sends a confirmation email to the user, if you have configured the email sender
- Signs the user in by setting the HttpContext.User; the principal will include the custom claim
- There was a problem creating the user. Adds the errors to the ModelState and redisplays the page.

TIP   Listing 23.7 shows how you can add extra claims at registration time, but you will often need to add more data later, such as permission-related claims or other information. You will need to create additional endpoints and pages for adding this data, securing the pages as appropriate (so that users can't update their own permissions, for example).

This is all that's required to *add* the new claim, but you're not using it anywhere currently. What if you want to display it? Well, you've added a claim to the ClaimsPrincipal, which was assigned to the HttpContext.User property when you called SignInAsync. That means you can retrieve the claims anywhere you have access to the ClaimsPrincipal—including in your page handlers and in view templates. For example, you could display the user's FullName claim anywhere in a Razor template with the following statement:

```
@User.Claims.FirstOrDefault(x=>x.Type == "FullName")?.Value
```

This finds the first claim on the current user principal with a Type of "FullName" and prints the assigned value (or, if the claim is not found, prints nothing). The Identity system even includes a handy extension method that tidies up this LINQ expression (found in the System.Security.Claims namespace):

```
@User.FindFirstValue("FullName")
```

With that last tidbit, we've reached the end of this chapter on ASP.NET Core Identity. I hope you've come to appreciate the amount of effort using Identity can save you, especially when you make use of the default Identity UI package.

Adding user accounts and authentication to an app is typically the first step in customizing your app further. Once you have authentication, you can have authorization, which lets you lock down certain actions in your app, based on the current user. In the next chapter you'll learn about the ASP.NET Core authorization system and how you can use it to customize your apps; in particular, the recipe application, which is coming along nicely!

Summary

- Authentication is the process of determining who you are, and authorization is the process of determining what you're allowed to do. You need to authenticate users before you can apply authorization.
- Every request in ASP.NET Core is associated with a user, also known as a principal. By default, without authentication, this is an anonymous user. You can use the claims principal to behave differently depending on who made a request.
- The current principal for a request is exposed on HttpContext.User. You can access this value from your Razor Pages and views to find out properties of the user such as their, ID, name, or email.
- Every user has a collection of claims. These claims are single pieces of information about the user. Claims could be properties of the physical user, such as Name

and `Email`, or they could be related to things the user has, such as `HasAdmin-Access` or `IsVipCustomer`.

- Legacy versions of ASP.NET used roles instead of claims. You can still use roles if you need to, but you should typically use claims where possible.

- Authentication in ASP.NET Core is provided by `AuthenticationMiddleware` and a number of authentication services. These services are responsible for setting the current principal when a user logs in, saving it to a cookie, and loading the principal from the cookie on subsequent requests.

- The `AuthenticationMiddleware` is added automatically by `WebApplication`. You can ensure that it's inserted at a specific point in the middleware pipeline by calling `UseAuthentication()`. It must be placed before any middleware that requires authentication, such as `UseAuthorization()`.

- ASP.NET Core Identity handles low-level services needed for storing users in a database, ensuring that their passwords are stored safely, and for logging users in and out. You must provide the UI for the functionality yourself and wire it up to the Identity subsystem.

- The Microsoft.AspNetCore.Identity.UI package provides a default UI for the Identity system and includes email confirmation, MFA, and external login provider support. You need to do some additional configuration to enable these features.

- The default template for Web Application with Individual Account Authentication uses ASP.NET Core Identity to store users in the database with EF Core. It includes all the boilerplate code required to wire the UI up to the Identity system.

- You can use the `UserManager<T>` class to create new user accounts, load them from the database, and change their passwords. `SignInManager<T>` is used to sign a user in and out by assigning the principal for the request and by setting an authentication cookie. The default UI uses these classes for you, to facilitate user registration and login.

- You can update an EF Core `DbContext` to support Identity by deriving from `IdentityDbContext<TUser>`, where `TUser` is a class that derives from `IdentityUser`.

- You can add additional claims to a user using the `UserManager<TUser>` `.AddClaimAsync(TUser user, Claim claim)` method. These claims are added to the `HttpContext.User` object when the user logs in to your app.

- Claims consist of a type and a value. Both values are strings. You can use standard values for types exposed on the `ClaimTypes` class, such as `ClaimTypes` `.GivenName` and `ClaimTypes.FirstName`, or you can use a custom string, such as `"FullName"`.

Authorization: Securing your application

This chapter covers

- Using authorization to control who can use your app
- Using claims-based authorization with policies
- Creating custom policies to handle complex requirements
- Authorizing a request depending upon the resource being accessed
- Hiding elements from a Razor template that the user is unauthorized to access

In chapter 23 I showed you how to add users to an ASP.NET Core application by adding authentication. With authentication, users can register and log in to your app using an email address and password. Whenever you add authentication to an app, you inevitably find you want to be able to restrict what some users can do. The process of determining whether a user can perform a given action on your app is called *authorization*.

On an e-commerce site, for example, you may have admin users who are allowed to add new products and change prices, sales users who are allowed to view completed orders, and customer users who are allowed only to place orders and buy products.

In this chapter I show how to use authorization in an app to control what your users can do. In section 24.1 I introduce authorization and put it in the context of a real-life scenario you've probably experienced: an airport. I describe the sequence of events, from checking in, to passing through security, to entering an airport lounge, and you'll see how these relate to the authorization concepts in this chapter.

In section 24.2 I show how authorization fits into an ASP.NET Core web application and how it relates to the `ClaimsPrincipal` class you saw in the previous chapter. You'll see how to enforce the simplest level of authorization in an ASP.NET Core app, ensuring that only authenticated users can execute a Razor Page or MVC action. This chapter focuses on authorization in Razor Pages and Model-View-Controller (MVC) controllers; in chapter 25 you'll learn how the same principles apply to minimal API applications.

We'll extend that approach in section 24.3 by adding the concept of *policies*. These let you set specific requirements for a given authenticated user, requiring that they have specific pieces of information to execute an action or Razor Page.

You'll use policies extensively in the ASP.NET Core authorization system, so in section 24.4 we'll explore how to handle more complex scenarios. You'll learn about authorization requirements and handlers, and how you can combine them to create specific policies that you can apply to your Razor Pages and actions.

Sometimes whether a user is authorized depends on which resource or document they're attempting to access. A resource is anything that you're trying to protect, so it could be a document or a post in a social media app. For example, you may allow users to create documents or to read documents from other users, but to edit only documents that they created themselves. This type of authorization, where you need the details of the document to determine if the user is authorized, is called *resource-based authorization*, and it's the focus of section 24.5.

In the final section of this chapter I show how you can extend the resource-based authorization approach to your Razor view templates. This lets you modify the UI to hide elements that users aren't authorized to interact with. In particular, you'll see how to hide the Edit button when a user isn't authorized to edit the entity.

We'll start by looking more closely at the concept of authorization, how it differs from authentication, and how it relates to real-life concepts you might see in an airport.

24.1 Introduction to authorization

In this section I provide an introduction to authorization and discuss how it compares with authentication. I use the real-life example of an airport as a case study to illustrate how claims-based authorization works.

For people who are new to web apps and security, authentication and authorization can be a little daunting. It certainly doesn't help that the words look so similar! The two concepts are often used together, but they're definitely distinct:

- *Authentication*—The process of determining who made a request
- *Authorization*—The process of determining whether the requested action is allowed

Typically, authentication occurs first so that you know who is making a request to your app. For traditional web apps, your app authenticates a request by checking the encrypted cookie that was set when the user logged in (as you saw in chapter 23). API applications typically use a header instead of a cookie for authentication, but the overall process is the same, as you'll see in chapter 25.

Once a request is authenticated and you know who is making the request, you can determine whether they're allowed to execute an action on your server. This process is called *authorization* and is the focus of this chapter.

Before we dive into code and start looking at authorization in ASP.NET Core, I'll put these concepts into a real-life scenario that I hope you're familiar with: checking in at an airport. To enter an airport and board a plane, you must pass through several steps: an initial step to prove who you are (authentication) and subsequent steps that check whether you're allowed to proceed (authorization). In simplified form, these might look like this:

1 Show your passport at the check-in desk. Receive a boarding pass.
2 Show your boarding pass to enter security. Pass through security.
3 Show your frequent-flyer card to enter the airline lounge. Enter the lounge.
4 Show your boarding pass to board the flight. Enter the airplane.

Obviously, these steps, also shown in figure 24.1, will vary somewhat in real life (I don't have a frequent-flyer card!), but we'll go with them for now. Let's explore each step a little further.

When you arrive at the airport, the first thing you do is go to the check-in counter. Here, you can purchase a plane ticket, but to do so, you need to prove who you are by providing a passport; you *authenticate* yourself. If you've forgotten your passport, you can't authenticate, and you can't go any further.

Once you've purchased your ticket, you're issued a boarding pass, which says which flight you're on. We'll assume that it also includes a `BoardingPassNumber`. You can think of this number as an additional claim associated with your identity.

> **DEFINITION** A *claim* is a piece of information about a user that consists of a type and an optional value.

The next step is security. The security guards ask you to present your boarding pass for inspection, which they use to check that you have a flight and so are allowed deeper into the airport. This is an authorization process: you must have the required claim (a `BoardingPassNumber`) to proceed.

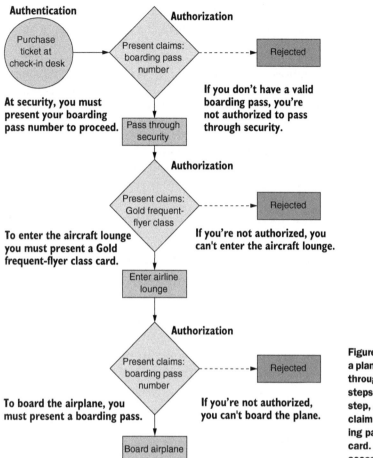

Figure 24.1   When boarding a plane at an airport, you pass through several authorization steps. At each authorization step, you must present a claim in the form of a boarding pass or a frequent-flyer card. If you're not authorized, access is denied.

If you don't have a valid `BoardingPassNumber`, there are two possibilities for what happens next:

- *If you haven't yet purchased a ticket*—You'll be directed back to the check-in desk, where you can authenticate and purchase a ticket. At that point, you can try to enter security again.
- *If you have an invalid ticket*—You won't be allowed through security, and there's nothing else you can do. If, for example, you show up with a boarding pass a week late for your flight, they probably won't let you through. (Ask me how I know!)

Once you're through security, you need to wait for your flight to start boarding, but unfortunately, there aren't any seats free. Typical! Luckily, you're a regular flyer, and you've notched up enough miles to achieve Gold frequent-flyer status, so you can use the airline lounge.

You head to the lounge, where you're asked to present your Gold frequent-flyer card to the attendant, and they let you in. This is another example of authorization. You must have a FrequentFlyerClass claim with a value of Gold to proceed.

> **NOTE** You've used authorization twice so far in this scenario. Each time, you presented a claim to proceed. In the first case, the presence of any Boarding-PassNumber was sufficient, whereas for the FrequentFlyerClass claim, you needed the specific value of Gold.

When you're boarding the airplane, you have one final authorization step, in which you must present the BoardingPassNumber claim again. You presented this claim earlier, but boarding the aircraft is a distinct action from entering security, so you have to present it again.

This whole scenario has lots of parallels with requests to a web app:

- Both processes start with authentication.
- You must prove who you are to retrieve the claims you need for authorization.
- You use authorization to protect sensitive actions like entering security and the airline lounge.

I'll reuse this airport scenario throughout the chapter to build a simple web application that simulates the steps you take in an airport. We've covered the concept of authorization in general, so in the next section we'll look at how authorization works in ASP.NET Core. We'll start with the most basic level of authorization, ensuring that only authenticated users can execute an action, and look at what happens when you try to execute such an action.

24.2   *Authorization in ASP.NET Core*

In this section you'll see how the authorization principles described in the previous section apply to an ASP.NET Core application. You'll learn about the role of the [Authorize] attribute and AuthorizationMiddleware in authorizing requests to Razor Pages and MVC actions. Finally, you'll learn about the process of preventing unauthenticated users from executing endpoints and what happens when users are unauthorized.

The ASP.NET Core framework has authorization built in, so you can use it anywhere in your app, but it's most common to apply authorization via the Authorization-Middleware. The AuthorizationMiddleware should be placed after both the routing middleware and the authentication middleware but before the endpoint middleware, as shown in figure 24.2.

> **NOTE** Remember that in ASP.NET Core, an *endpoint* refers to the handler selected by the routing middleware, which generates a response when executed. It is typically a Razor Page, a web API controller action method, or a minimal API endpoint handler.

With this configuration, the RoutingMiddleware selects an endpoint to execute based on the request's URL, such as a Razor Page, as you saw in chapter 14. Metadata about

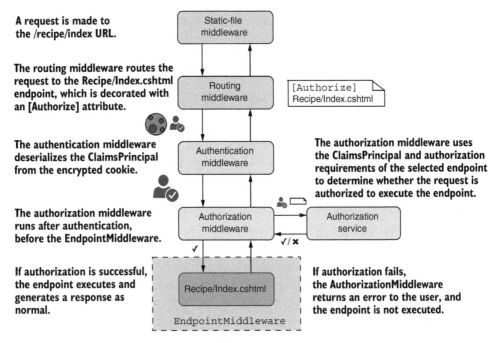

Figure 24.2 Authorization occurs after an endpoint has been selected and after the request is authenticated, but before the action method or Razor Page endpoint is executed.

the selected endpoint is available to all middleware that occurs after the routing middleware. This metadata includes details about any authorization requirements for the endpoint, and it's typically attached by decorating an action or Razor Page with an [Authorize] attribute.

The AuthenticationMiddleware deserializes the encrypted cookie (or bearer token for APIs) associated with the request to create a ClaimsPrincipal. This object is set as the HttpContext.User for the request, so all subsequent middleware can access this value. It contains all the Claims that were added to the cookie when the user authenticated.

> **NOTE** Remember that the authentication middleware may be placed before the routing middleware when the authentication process is the same for all endpoints. Nevertheless, I prefer to place it as shown in figure 24.2, after the routing middleware, and always before the authorization middleware.

Now we come to the AuthorizationMiddleware. This middleware checks whether the selected endpoint has any authorization requirements, based on the metadata provided by the RoutingMiddleware. If the endpoint has authorization requirements, the AuthorizationMiddleware uses the HttpContext.User to determine whether the current request is authorized to execute the endpoint.

If the request is authorized, the next middleware in the pipeline executes as normal. If the request is not authorized, the AuthorizationMiddleware short-circuits the middleware pipeline, and the endpoint middleware is never executed.

> **NOTE**   The call to UseAuthorization() must always be placed after UseRouting() and UseAuthentication(), but before UseEndpoints(). WebApplication automatically adds all this middleware in the correct order, but if you override the position in the pipeline, such as by calling UseRouting(), you must make sure to maintain this overall order.

The AuthorizationMiddleware is responsible for applying authorization requirements and ensuring that only authorized users can execute protected endpoints. In section 24.2.1 you'll learn how to apply the simplest authorization requirement to an endpoint, and in section 24.2.2 you'll see how the framework responds when a user is not authorized to execute an endpoint.

24.2.1   *Preventing anonymous users from accessing your application*

When you think about authorization, you typically think about checking whether a particular user has permission to execute an endpoint. In ASP.NET Core you normally achieve this by checking whether a user has a given claim.

There's an even more basic level of authorization we haven't considered yet: allowing only authenticated users to execute an endpoint. This is even simpler than the claims scenario (which we'll come to later), as there are only two possibilities:

- *The user is authenticated*—The action executes as normal.
- *The user is unauthenticated*—The user can't execute the endpoint.

You can achieve this basic level of authorization by using the [Authorize] attribute, which you saw in chapter 22 when we discussed authorization filters. You can apply this attribute to your actions and Razor Pages, as shown in the following listing, to restrict them to authenticated (logged-in) users only. If an unauthenticated user tries to execute an action or Razor Page protected with the [Authorize] attribute, they'll be redirected to the login page.

Listing 24.1   Applying [Authorize] to an action

```
public class RecipeApiController : ControllerBase
{
    public IActionResult List()          ⟵──┐ This action can be executed by
    {                                        │ anyone, even when not logged in.
        return Ok();
    }
                                          ┌── Applies [Authorize] to individual actions,
    [Authorize]              ⟵────────────┘   whole controllers, or Razor Pages
    public IActionResult View()  ⟵
    {                                     This action can be executed
        return Ok();                      only by authenticated users.
    }
}
```

Applying the [Authorize] attribute to an endpoint attaches metadata to it, indicating that only authenticated users may access the endpoint. As you saw in figure 24.2, this metadata is made available to the `AuthorizationMiddleware` when an endpoint is selected by the `RoutingMiddleware`.

You can apply the `[Authorize]` attribute at the action scope, controller scope, Razor Page scope, or globally, as you saw in chapter 21. Any action or Razor Page that has the `[Authorize]` attribute applied in this way can be executed only by an authenticated user. Unauthenticated users will be redirected to the login page.

> **TIP** There are several ways to apply the `[Authorize]` attribute globally. You can read about the options and when to choose which option on my blog: http://mng.bz/opQp.

Sometimes, especially when you apply the `[Authorize]` attribute globally, you might need to poke holes in this authorization requirement. If you apply the `[Authorize]` attribute globally, any unauthenticated requests are redirected to the login page for your app. But if the `[Authorize]` attribute is *global*, when the login page tries to load, you'll be unauthenticated and redirected to the login page again. And now you're stuck in an infinite redirect loop.

To get around this, you can direct specific endpoints to ignore the `[Authorize]` attribute by applying the `[AllowAnonymous]` attribute to an action or Razor Page, as shown in the next listing. This allows unauthenticated users to execute the action, so you can avoid the redirect loop that would otherwise result.

Listing 24.2 Applying `[AllowAnonymous]` to allow unauthenticated access

```
[Authorize]                                    ◁──────  Applied at the controller scope, so
public class AccountController : ControllerBase          the user must be authenticated for
{                                                        all actions on the controller

    public IActionResult ManageAccount()  ◁──┐
    {                                         Only authenticated users may
        return Ok();                          execute ManageAccount.
    }
    [AllowAnonymous]                   ◁──┐   [AllowAnonymous] overrides [Authorize]
    public IActionResult Login()  ◁──┐        to allow unauthenticated users.
    {
        return Ok();                   Login can be executed
    }                                  by anonymous users.
}
```

> **WARNING** If you apply the `[Authorize]` attribute globally, be sure to add the `[AllowAnonymous]` attribute to your login actions, error actions, password reset actions, and any other actions that you need unauthenticated users to execute. If you're using the default Identity UI described in chapter 23, this is already configured for you.

If an unauthenticated user attempts to execute an action protected by the `[Authorize]` attribute, traditional web apps redirect them to the login page. But what about APIs that don't have a user interface? And what about more complex scenarios, where a user is logged in but doesn't have the necessary claims to execute an action? In section 24.2.2 we'll look at how the ASP.NET Core authentication services handle all this for you.

24.2.2 *Handling unauthorized requests*

In the previous section you saw how to apply the [Authorize] attribute to an action to ensure that only authenticated users can execute it. In section 24.3 we'll look at more complex examples that require you to also have a specific claim. In both cases, you must meet one or more authorization requirements (for example, you must be authenticated) to execute the action.

If the user meets the authorization requirements, the request passes unimpeded through the AuthorizationMiddleware, and the endpoint is executed in the Endpoint-Middleware. If they don't meet the requirements for the selected endpoint, the AuthorizationMiddleware will short-circuit the request. Depending on why the request failed authorization, the AuthorizationMiddleware generates one of two different types of responses, as shown in figure 24.3:

- *Challenge*—This response indicates that the user was not authorized to execute the action because they weren't yet logged in.
- *Forbid*—This response indicates that the user was logged in but didn't meet the requirements to execute the action. They didn't have a required claim, for example.

NOTE   If you apply the [Authorize] attribute in basic form, as you did in section 24.2.1, you will generate only challenge responses. In this case, a challenge response will be generated for unauthenticated users, but authenticated users will always be authorized.

The exact HTTP response generated by a challenge or forbid response typically depends on the type of application you're building and so the type of authentication your application uses: a traditional web application with Razor Pages, or an API application.

For traditional web apps using cookie authentication, such as when you use ASP.NET Core Identity, as in chapter 23, the challenge and forbid responses generate an HTTP redirect to a page in your application. A challenge response indicates the user isn't yet authenticated, so they're redirected to the login page for the app. After logging in, they can attempt to execute the protected resource again. A forbid response means the request was from a user that *already* logged in, but they're still not allowed to execute the action. Consequently, the user is redirected to a "forbidden" or "access denied" web page, as shown in figure 24.4, which informs them they can't execute the action or Razor Page.

The preceding behavior is standard for traditional web apps, but API apps typically use a different approach to authentication, as you'll see in chapter 25. Instead of logging in and using the API directly, you'd typically log in to a third-party application that provides a token to the client-side single-page application (SPA) or mobile app. The client-side app sends this token when it makes a request to your API.

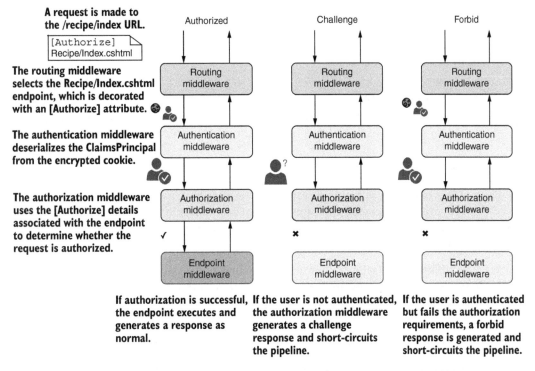

A request is made to the /recipe/index URL.

[Authorize]
Recipe/Index.cshtml

The routing middleware selects the Recipe/Index.cshtml endpoint, which is decorated with an [Authorize] attribute.

The authentication middleware deserializes the ClaimsPrincipal from the encrypted cookie.

The authorization middleware uses the [Authorize] details associated with the endpoint to determine whether the request is authorized.

If authorization is successful, the endpoint executes and generates a response as normal.

If the user is not authenticated, the authorization middleware generates a challenge response and short-circuits the pipeline.

If the user is authenticated but fails the authorization requirements, a forbid response is generated and short-circuits the pipeline.

Figure 24.3   The three types of response to an authorization attempt. In the left example, the request contains an authentication cookie, so the user is authenticated in the `AuthenticationMiddleware`. The `AuthorizationMiddleware` confirms that the authenticated user can access the selected endpoint, so the endpoint is executed. In the center example, the request is not authenticated, so the `Authorization-Middleware` generates a challenge response. In the right example, the request is authenticated, but the user does not have permission to execute the endpoint, so a forbid response is generated.

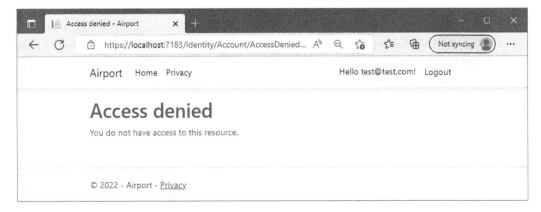

Figure 24.4   A forbid response in traditional web apps using cookie authentication. If you don't have permission to execute a Razor Page and you're already logged in, you'll be redirected to an "access denied" page.

Authenticating a request for an API app is essentially identical to a traditional web app that uses cookies, as you'll see in chapter 25; AuthenticationMiddleware deserializes the credentials to create the ClaimsPrincipal. The difference is in how an API handles authorization failures.

When an API app generates a challenge response, it returns a 401 Unauthorized error response to the caller. Similarly, when the app generates a forbid response, it returns a 403 Forbidden response. The traditional web app essentially handled these errors by automatically redirecting unauthorized users to the login or "access denied" page, but the API app doesn't do this. It's up to the client-side SPA or mobile app to detect these errors and handle them as appropriate.

> **TIP** This difference in authorization behavior is one of the reasons I generally recommend creating separate apps for your APIs and Razor pages apps; it's possible to have both in the same app, but the configuration is often more complex.

The different behavior between traditional web apps and SPAs can be confusing initially, but you generally don't need to worry about that too much in practice. Whether you're building an API app or a traditional MVC web app, the authorization code in your app looks the same in both cases. Apply [Authorize] attributes to your endpoints, and let the framework take care of the differences for you.

> **NOTE** In chapter 23 you saw how to configure ASP.NET Core Identity in a Razor Pages app. This chapter assumes that you're building a Razor Pages app too, but the chapter is equally applicable if you're building an API, as you'll see in chapter 25. Authorization policies are applied in the same way, whichever style of app you're building. Only the final response of unauthorized requests differs.

You've seen how to apply the most basic authorization requirement—restricting an endpoint to authenticated users—but most apps need something more subtle than this all-or-nothing approach. Consider the airport scenario from section 24.1. Being authenticated (having a passport) isn't enough to get you through security. Instead, you also need a specific claim: BoardingPassNumber. In the next section we'll look at how you can implement a similar requirement in ASP.NET Core.

24.3 *Using policies for claims-based authorization*

In the previous section, you saw how to require that users be logged in to access an endpoint. In this section you'll see how to apply additional requirements. You'll learn to use authorization policies to perform claims-based authorization to require that a logged-in user have the required claims to execute a given endpoint.

In chapter 23 you saw that authentication in ASP.NET Core centers on a ClaimsPrincipal object, which represents the user. This object has a collection of claims that contain pieces of information about the user, such as their name, email, and date of birth.

You can use this information to customize the app for each user, by displaying a welcome message addressing the user by name, for example, but you can also use claims for authorization. For example, you might authorize a user only if they have a specific claim (such as `BoardingPassNumber`) or if a claim has a specific value (`Frequent-FlyerClass` claim with the value `Gold`).

In ASP.NET Core the rules that define whether a user is authorized are encapsulated in a *policy*.

> **DEFINITION** A *policy* defines the requirements you must meet for a request to be authorized.

Policies can be applied to an endpoint using the `[Authorize]` attribute, similar to the way you saw in section 24.2.1. This listing shows a Razor Page `PageModel` that represents the first authorization step in the airport scenario. The AirportSecurity.cshtml Razor Page is protected by an `[Authorize]` attribute, but you've also provided a policy name, `"CanEnterSecurity"`, as shown in the following listing.

Listing 24.3 Applying an authorization policy to a Razor Page

```
[Authorize("CanEnterSecurity")]                  ◁       Applying the "CanEnterSecurity"
public class AirportSecurityModel : PageModel            policy using [Authorize]
{
    public void OnGet()   ◁        Only users that satisfy the
    {                              "CanEnterSecurity" policy
                                   can execute the Razor Page.
    }
}
```

If a user attempts to execute the AirportSecurity.cshtml Razor Page, the authorization middleware verifies whether the user satisfies the policy's requirements (we'll look at the policy itself shortly). This gives one of three possible outcomes:

- *The user satisfies the policy*—The middleware pipeline continues, and the `EndpointMiddleware` executes the Razor Page as normal.
- *The user is unauthenticated*—The user is redirected to the login page.
- *The user is authenticated but doesn't satisfy the policy*—The user is redirected to a "forbidden" or "access denied" page.

These three outcomes correlate with real-life outcomes you might expect when trying to pass through security at the airport:

- *You have a valid boarding pass*—You can enter security as normal.
- *You don't have a boarding pass*—You're redirected to purchase a ticket.
- *Your boarding pass is invalid (you turned up a day late, for example)*—You're blocked from entering.

Listing 24.3 shows how you can apply a policy to a Razor Page using the `[Authorize]` attribute, but you still need to define the `CanEnterSecurity` policy.

You add policies to an ASP.NET Core application in Program.cs, as shown in listing 24.4. First, you add the authorization services and return an `AuthorizationBuilder` object using `AddAuthorizationBuilder()`. You can then add policies to the builder by calling `AddPolicy()`. You define the policy itself by calling methods in a lambda method on a `AuthorizationPolicyBuilder` (called `policyBuilder` here).

> **Listing 24.4 Adding an authorization policy using `AuthorizationPolicyBuilder`**

```
WebApplicationBuilder builder = WebApplication.CreateBuilder(args);

builder.Services.AddAuthorizationBuilder()          ← Calls AddAuthorizationBuilder to add
    .AddPolicy(              ←                         the required authorization services
        "CanEnterSecurity",          | Adds a new policy
        policyBuilder => policyBuilder
            .RequireClaim("BoardingPassNumber"));     | Defines the policy
});                                                     requirements using
// Additional configuration                            AuthorizationPolicyBuilder
```

Provides a name for the policy

When you call `AddPolicy` you provide a name for the policy, which should match the value you use in your `[Authorize]` attributes, and you define the requirements of the policy. In this example, you have a single simple requirement: the user must have a claim of type `BoardingPassNumber`. If a user has this claim, whatever its value, the policy is satisfied, and the user will be authorized.

> **NOTE** A *claim* is information about the user, as a key-value pair. A *policy* defines the requirements for successful authorization. A policy may require that a user have a given claim, or it may specify more complex requirements, as you'll see shortly.

`AuthorizationPolicyBuilder` contains several methods for creating simple policies like this, as shown in table 24.1. For example, an overload of the `RequireClaim()` method lets you specify a specific value that a claim must have. The following would let you create a policy where the `"BoardingPassNumber"` claim must have a value of `"A1234"`:

```
policyBuilder => policyBuilder.RequireClaim("BoardingPassNumber", "A1234");
```

Table 24.1 Simple policy builder methods on `AuthorizationPolicyBuilder`

Method	Policy behavior
`RequireAuthenticatedUser()`	The required user must be authenticated. Creates a policy similar to the default `[Authorize]` attribute, where you don't set a policy.
`RequireClaim(claim, values)`	The user must have the specified claim. If provided, the claim must be one of the specified values.
`RequireUsername(username)`	The user must have the specified username.

Table 24.1   Simple policy builder methods on `AuthorizationPolicyBuilder` *(continued)*

Method	Policy behavior
`RequireAssertion(function)`	Executes the provided lambda function, which returns a `bool`, indicating whether the policy was satisfied.

Role-based authorization vs. claims-based authorization

If you look at all of the methods available on the `AuthorizationPolicyBuilder` type using IntelliSense, you might notice that there's a method I didn't mention in table 24.1: `RequireRole()`. This is a remnant of the role-based approach to authorization used in previous versions of ASP.NET, and I don't recommend using it.

Before Microsoft adopted the claims-based authorization used by ASP.NET, role-based authorization was the norm. Users were assigned to one or more roles, such as `Administrator` or `Manager`, and authorization involved checking whether the current user was in the required role.

This role-based approach to authorization is possible in ASP.NET Core, but it's used primarily for legacy compatibility reasons. Claims-based authorization is the suggested approach. Unless you're porting a legacy app that uses roles, I suggest that you embrace claims-based authorization and leave those roles behind.

Note that the fact that you're using claims-based permissions doesn't mean you need to get rid of roles entirely, but you should use roles as a basis for assigning claims to a user rather than authorize that a user belongs to one or more roles.

You can use these methods to build simple policies that can handle basic situations, but often you'll need something more complicated. What if you want to create a policy that enforces that only users over the age of 18 can execute an endpoint?

The `DateOfBirth` claim provides the information you need, but there's no *single* correct value, so you couldn't use the `RequireClaim()` method. You *could* use the `Require-Assertion()` method and provide a function that calculates the age from the `DateOfBirth` claim, but that could get messy pretty quickly.

For more complex policies that can't be easily defined using the `RequireClaim()` method, I recommend that you take a different approach and create a custom policy, as you'll see in the following section.

24.4   Creating custom policies for authorization

You've already seen how to create a policy by requiring a specific claim or requiring a specific claim with a specific value, but often the requirements will be more complex than that. In this section you'll learn how to create custom authorization requirements and handlers. You'll also see how to configure authorization requirements where there are multiple ways to satisfy a policy, any of which are valid.

Let's return to the airport example. You've already configured the policy for passing through security, and now you're going to configure the policy that controls whether you're authorized to enter the airline lounge.

As you saw in figure 24.1, you're allowed to enter the lounge if you have a FrequentFlyerClass claim with a value of Gold. If this was the only requirement, you could use AuthorizationPolicyBuilder to create a policy like this:

```
options.AddPolicy("CanAccessLounge", policyBuilder =>
    policyBuilder.RequireClaim("FrequentFlyerClass", "Gold");
```

But what if the requirements are more complicated? For example, suppose you can enter the lounge if you're at least 18 years old (as calculated from the DateOfBirth claim) and you're one of the following:

- You're a Gold-class frequent flyer (have a FrequentFlyerClass claim with value "Gold")
- You're an employee of the airline (have an EmployeeNumber claim).

If you've ever been banned from the lounge (you have an IsBannedFromLounge claim), you won't be allowed in, even if you satisfy the other requirements.

There's no way of achieving this complex set of requirements with the basic use of AuthorizationPolicyBuilder you've seen so far. Luckily, these methods are a wrapper around a set of building blocks that you can combine to achieve the desired policy.

24.4.1 *Requirements and handlers: The building blocks of a policy*

Every policy in ASP.NET Core consists of one or more *requirements*, and every requirement can have one or more *handlers*. For the airport lounge example, you have a single policy ("CanAccessLounge"), two requirements (MinimumAgeRequirement and AllowedInLoungeRequirement), and several handlers, as shown in figure 24.5.

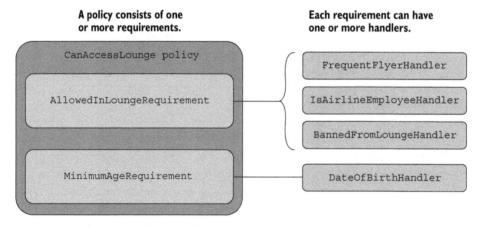

Figure 24.5   A policy can have many requirements, and every requirement can have many handlers. By combining multiple requirements in a policy and providing multiple handler implementations, you can create complex authorization policies that meet any of your business requirements.

For a policy to be satisfied, a user must fulfill all the requirements. If the user fails any of the requirements, the authorize middleware won't allow the protected endpoint to be executed. In this example, a user must be allowed to access the lounge *and* must be over 18 years old.

Each requirement can have one or more handlers, which will confirm that the requirement has been satisfied. For example, as shown in figure 24.5, `AllowedInLounge-Requirement` has two handlers that can satisfy the requirement:

- `FrequentFlyerHandler`
- `IsAirlineEmployeeHandler`

If the user satisfies either of these handlers, `AllowedInLoungeRequirement` is satisfied. You don't need all handlers for a requirement to be satisfied; you need only one.

> **NOTE** Figure 24.5 shows a third handler, `BannedFromLoungeHandler`, which I'll cover in section 24.4.2. It's slightly different in that it can fail a requirement but not satisfy it.

You can use requirements and handlers to achieve most any combination of behavior you need for a policy. By combining handlers for a requirement, you can validate conditions using a logical OR: if any of the handlers is satisfied, the requirement is satisfied. By combining requirements, you create a logical AND: all the requirements must be satisfied for the policy to be satisfied, as shown in figure 24.6.

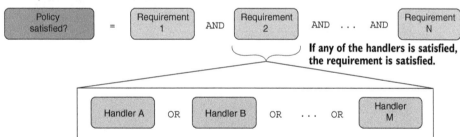

Figure 24.6 For a policy to be satisfied, every requirement must be satisfied. A requirement is satisfied if any of the handlers is satisfied.

> **TIP** You can add multiple policies to a Razor Page or action method by applying the `[Authorize]` attribute multiple times, as in `[Authorize("Policy1"), Authorize("Policy2")]`. All policies must be satisfied for the request to be authorized.

I've highlighted requirements and handlers that will make up your `"CanAccessLounge"` policy, so in the next section you'll build each of the components and apply them to the airport sample app.

24.4.2 *Creating a policy with a custom requirement and handler*

You've seen all the pieces that make up a custom authorization policy, so in this section we'll explore the implementation of the `"CanAccessLounge"` policy.

CREATING AN IAUTHORIZATIONREQUIREMENT TO REPRESENT A REQUIREMENT

As you've seen, a custom policy can have multiple requirements, but what is a requirement in code terms? Authorization requirements in ASP.NET Core are any class that implements the `IAuthorizationRequirement` interface. This is a blank marker interface, which you can apply to any class to indicate that it represents a requirement.

If the interface doesn't have any members, you might be wondering what the requirement class needs to look like. Typically, they're simple plain old CLR object (POCO) classes. The following listing shows `AllowedInLoungeRequirement`, which is about as simple as a requirement can get. It has no properties or methods; it implements the required `IAuthorizationRequirement` interface.

Listing 24.5 `AllowedInLoungeRequirement`

```
public class AllowedInLoungeRequirement
    : IAuthorizationRequirement { }  ◁────
```
The interface identifies the class as an authorization requirement.

This is the simplest form of requirement, but it's also common to have one or two properties that make the requirement more generalized. For example, instead of creating the highly specific `MustBe18YearsOldRequirement`, you could create a parameterized `MinimumAgeRequirement`, as shown in the following listing. By providing the minimum age as a parameter to the requirement, you can reuse the requirement for other policies with different minimum-age requirements.

Listing 24.6 The parameterized `MinimumAgeRequirement`

```
public class MinimumAgeRequirement : IAuthorizationRequirement  ◁──
{
    public MinimumAgeRequirement(int minimumAge)  ◁──
    {
        MinimumAge = minimumAge;
    }
    public int MinimumAge { get; }
}
```
The interface identifies the class as an authorization requirement.

The minimum age is provided when the requirement is created.

Handlers can use the exposed minimum age to determine whether the requirement is satisfied.

The requirements are the easy part. They represent each of the components of the policy that must be satisfied for the policy to be satisfied overall. Note that requirements are meant to be lightweight objects that can be created "manually." So while you can have constructor parameters, as shown in listing 24.6, you can't use dependency injection (DI) here. That's not as limiting as it sounds, because your handlers *can* use DI.

CREATING A POLICY WITH MULTIPLE REQUIREMENTS

You've created the two requirements, so now you can configure the `"CanAccessLounge"` policy to use them. You configure your policies as you did before, in Program.cs. Listing 24.7 shows how to do this by creating an instance of each requirement and passing them to `AuthorizationPolicyBuilder`. The authorization handlers use these requirement objects when attempting to authorize the policy.

Listing 24.7   Creating an authorization policy with multiple requirements

```
WebApplicationBuilder builder = WebApplication.CreateBuilder(args);

builder.services.AddAuthorization(options =>
{
    options.AddPolicy(                                   Adds the previous simple
        "CanEnterSecurity",                              policy for passing through
        policyBuilder => policyBuilder                   security
            .RequireClaim(Claims.BoardingPassNumber));
    options.AddPolicy(
        "CanAccessLounge",
        policyBuilder => policyBuilder.AddRequirements(  Adds an instance of each
        new MinimumAgeRequirement(18),                   IAuthorizationRequirement
        new AllowedInLoungeRequirement()                 object
    ));
});
// Additional configuration
```
Adds a new policy for the airport lounge, called CanAccessLounge

---

You now have a policy called `"CanAccessLounge"` with two requirements, so you can apply it to a Razor Page or action method using the `[Authorize]` attribute, in exactly the same way you did for the `"CanEnterSecurity"` policy:

```
[Authorize("CanAccessLounge")]
public class AirportLoungeModel : PageModel
{
    public void OnGet() { }
}
```

When a request is routed to the AirportLounge.cshtml Razor Page, the authorize middleware executes the authorization policy and each of the requirements is inspected. But you saw earlier that the requirements are purely data; they indicate what needs to be fulfilled, but they don't describe how that has to happen. For that, you need to write some handlers.

CREATING AUTHORIZATION HANDLERS TO SATISFY YOUR REQUIREMENTS

Authorization handlers contain the logic of how a specific `IAuthorizationRequirement` can be satisfied. When executed, a handler can do one of three things:

- Mark the requirement handling as a success.
- Do nothing.
- Explicitly fail the requirement.

Handlers should implement `AuthorizationHandler<T>`, where `T` is the type of requirement they handle. For example, the following listing shows a handler for `AllowedIn-LoungeRequirement` that checks whether the user has a claim called `FrequentFlyerClass` with a value of `Gold`.

> **Listing 24.8 `FrequentFlyerHandler` for `AllowedInLoungeRequirement`**

```
public class FrequentFlyerHandler :                          The handler implements
    AuthorizationHandler<AllowedInLoungeRequirement>  ◁───┤  AuthorizationHandler<T>.
{
    protected override Task HandleRequirementAsync(  ◁───┤  You must override the abstract
        AuthorizationHandlerContext context,  ◁───┤         HandleRequirementAsync method.
        AllowedInLoungeRequirement requirement)      The context contains details such
    {                                                as the ClaimsPrincipal user object.
        if(context.User.HasClaim("FrequentFlyerClass", "Gold"))  ◁───┐
        {                                               Checks whether the user
            context.Succeed(requirement); ◁───┐         has the Frequent-FlyerClass
        }                                               claim with the Gold value
        return Task.CompletedTask;
    }                                                If the user had the necessary claim,
                                                     marks the requirement as satisfied
}                                                    by calling Succeed
```

The requirement instance to handle

If the requirement wasn't satisfied, does nothing

This handler is functionally equivalent to the simple `RequireClaim()` handler you saw at the start of section 24.4, but using the requirement and handler approach instead.

When a request is routed to the AirportLounge.cshtml Razor Page, the authorization middleware sees the `[Authorize]` attribute on the endpoint with the `"CanAccess-Lounge"` policy. It loops through all the requirements in the policy and all the handlers for each requirement, calling the `HandleRequirementAsync` method for each.

The authorization middleware passes the current `AuthorizationHandlerContext` and the requirement to be checked to each handler. The current `ClaimsPrincipal` being authorized is exposed on the context as the `User` property. In listing 24.8, `Frequent-FlyerHandler` uses the context to check for a claim called `FrequentFlyerClass` with the `Gold` value, and if it exists, indicates that the user is allowed to enter the airline lounge by calling `Succeed()`.

> **NOTE** Handlers mark a requirement as being satisfied by calling `context`
> `.Succeed()` and passing the requirement as an argument.

It's important to note the behavior when the user doesn't have the claim. `Frequent-FlyerHandler` doesn't do anything in this case; it returns a completed `Task` to satisfy the method signature.

> **NOTE** Remember that if any of the handlers associated with a requirement
> passes, the requirement is a success. Only one of the handlers must succeed
> for the requirement to be satisfied.

This behavior, whereby you either call `context.Succeed()` or do nothing, is typical for authorization handlers. The following listing shows the implementation of IsAirline-EmployeeHandler, which uses a similar claim check to determine whether the requirement is satisfied.

Listing 24.9   `IsAirlineEmployeeHandler`

```
public class IsAirlineEmployeeHandler :                      The handler implements
    AuthorizationHandler<AllowedInLoungeRequirement>         AuthorizationHandler<T>.
{
    protected override Task HandleRequirementAsync(          You must override the abstract
        AuthorizationHandlerContext context,                HandleRequirementAsync method.
        AllowedInLoungeRequirement requirement)
    {
        if(context.User.HasClaim(c => c.Type == "EmployeeNumber"))
        {
            context.Succeed(requirement);                   If the user has the necessary claim,
        }                                                   marks the requirement as satisfied
        return Task.CompletedTask;                          by calling Succeed
    }
}
```

Checks whether the user has the EmployeeNumber claim

If the requirement wasn't satisfied, does nothing

I've left the implementation of MinimumAgeHandler for MinimumAgeRequirement as an exercise for the reader, as it's similar to the handlers you have already seen. You can find an example implementation in the code samples for the chapter.

> **TIP**   It's possible to write generic handlers that can be used with multiple requirements, but I suggest sticking to handling a single requirement. If you need to extract some common functionality, move it to an external service, and call that from both handlers.

This pattern of authorization handler is common, but in some cases, instead of checking for a *success* condition, you might want to check for a failure condition. In the airport example, you don't want to authorize someone who was previously banned from the lounge, even if they would otherwise be allowed to enter.

You can handle this scenario by using the `context.Fail()` method exposed on the context, as shown in the following listing. Calling `Fail()` in a handler always causes the requirement, and hence the whole policy, to fail. You should use it only when you want to guarantee failure, even if other handlers indicate success.

Listing 24.10   Calling `context.Fail()` in a handler to fail the requirement

```
public class BannedFromLoungeHandler :                       The handler implements
    AuthorizationHandler<AllowedInLoungeRequirement>         AuthorizationHandler<T>.
{
    protected override Task HandleRequirementAsync(          You must override the abstract
        AuthorizationHandlerContext context,                HandleRequirementAsync method.
        AllowedInLoungeRequirement requirement)
```

```
        {
            if(context.User.HasClaim(c => c.Type == "IsBannedFromLounge"))
            {
                context.Fail();
            }
            return Task.CompletedTask;
        }
    }
```

If the claim wasn't found, does nothing → `return Task.CompletedTask;`

Checks whether the user has the IsBannedFromLounge claim → `if(context.User.HasClaim(c => c.Type == "IsBannedFromLounge"))`

If the user has the claim, fails the requirement by calling Fail. The whole policy fails. → `context.Fail();`

In most cases, your handlers will either call Succeed() or will do nothing, but the Fail() method is useful when you need a kill switch to guarantee that a requirement won't be satisfied.

> **NOTE** Whether a handler calls Succeed(), Fail(), or neither, the authorization system always executes all the handlers for a requirement and all the requirements for a policy, so you can be sure your handlers will always be called.

The final step to complete your authorization implementation for the app is to register the authorization handlers with the DI container, as shown in the following listing.

Listing 24.11 Registering the authorization handlers with the DI container

```
WebApplicationBuilder builder = WebApplication.CreateBuilder(args);

builder.Services.AddAuthorization(options =>

    options.AddPolicy(
        "CanEnterSecurity",
        policyBuilder => policyBuilder
            .RequireClaim(Claims.BoardingPassNumber));
    options.AddPolicy(
        "CanAccessLounge",
        policyBuilder => policyBuilder.AddRequirements(
            new MinimumAgeRequirement(18),
            new AllowedInLoungeRequirement()
        ));
});

services.AddSingleton<IAuthorizationHandler, MinimumAgeHandler>();
services.AddSingleton<IAuthorizationHandler, FrequentFlyerHandler>();
services.AddSingleton<IAuthorizationHandler, BannedFromLoungeHandler>();
services.AddSingleton<IAuthorizationHandler, IsAirlineEmployeeHandler>();
// Additional configuration
```

For this app, the handlers don't have any constructor dependencies, so I've registered them as singletons with the container. If your handlers have scoped or transient dependencies (the EF Core DbContext, for example), you might want to register them as scoped instead, as appropriate.

NOTE Services are registered with a lifetime of transient, scoped, or singleton, as discussed in chapter 9.

You can combine the concepts of policies, requirements, and handlers in many ways to achieve your goals for authorization in your application. The example in this section, although contrived, demonstrates the components you need to apply authorization declaratively at the action method or Razor Page level by creating policies and applying the [Authorize] attribute as appropriate.

As well as applying the [Authorize] attribute explicitly to actions and Razor Pages, you can configure it globally, so that a policy is applied to every endpoint in your application. Additionally, for Razor Pages you can apply different authorization policies to different folders. You can read more about applying authorization policies using conventions in Microsoft's "Razor Pages authorization conventions in ASP.NET Core" documentation: http://mng.bz/nMm2.

There's one area, however, where the [Authorize] attribute falls short: resource-based authorization. The [Authorize] attribute attaches metadata to an endpoint, so the authorization middleware can authorize the user before an endpoint is executed. But what if you need to authorize the action from within the endpoint?

This is common when you're applying authorization at the document or resource level. If users are allowed to edit only documents they created, you need to load the document before you can tell whether they're allowed to edit it! This isn't easy with the declarative [Authorize] attribute approach, so you must often use an alternative, imperative approach. In the next section you'll see how to apply this resource-based authorization in a Razor Page handler.

24.5 Controlling access with resource-based authorization

In this section you'll learn about resource-based authorization. This is used when you need to know details about the resource being protected to determine whether a user is authorized. You'll learn how to apply authorization policies manually using the IAuthorizationService and how to create resource-based AuthorizationHandlers.

Resource-based authorization is a common problem for applications, especially when you have users who can create or edit some sort of document. Consider the recipe application you worked on in chapter 23. This app lets users create, view, and edit recipes.

Up to this point, everyone can create new recipes, and anyone can edit any recipe, even if they haven't logged in. Now you want to add some additional behavior:

- Only authenticated users should be able to create new recipes.
- You can edit only the recipes you created.

You've already seen how to achieve the first of these requirements: decorate the Create .cshtml Razor Page with an [Authorize] attribute and don't specify a policy, as shown in the following listing. This will force the user to authenticate before they can create a new recipe.

Listing 24.12   Adding `AuthorizeAttribute` to the Create.cshtml Razor Page

```
[Authorize]                          ◄──────────┐  Users must be authenticated
public class CreateModel : PageModel            │  to execute the Create.cshtml
{                                               │  Razor Page.
    [BindProperty]
    public CreateRecipeCommand Input { get; set; }

    public void OnGet()
    {
        Input = new CreateRecipeCommand();
    }                                                   All page handlers are
                                                        protected. You can apply
    public async Task<IActionResult> OnPost()           [Authorize] only to the
    {                                                   PageModel, not handlers.
        // Method body not shown for brevity
    }
}
```

TIP   As with all filters, you can apply the `[Authorize]` attribute only to the Razor Page, not to individual page handlers. The attribute applies to all page handlers in the Razor Page.

Adding the `[Authorize]` attribute fulfills your first requirement, but unfortunately, with the techniques you've seen so far, you have no way to fulfill the second. You could apply a policy that either permits or denies a user the ability to edit all recipes, but there's currently no easy way to restrict this so that a user can only edit their own recipes.

To find out who created the `Recipe`, you must first load it from the database. Only then can you attempt to authorize the user, taking the specific recipe (resource) into account. The following listing shows a partially implemented page handler for how this might look, where authorization occurs partway through the method, after the `Recipe` object has been loaded.

Listing 24.13   The Edit.cshtml page must load the `Recipe`

```
          ┌──► public IActionResult OnGet(int id)        You must load the Recipe from
          │    {                                          the database before you know
          │        var recipe = _service.GetRecipe(id);   who created it.
The id of │        var createdById = recipe.CreatedById;
the recipe│        // Authorize user based on createdById  ◄──────
to edit is│        if(isAuthorized)                                You must authorize the current
provided  │        {                  The action method can       user to verify that they're allowed
by model  │            return View(recipe);  continue only if the  to edit this specific Recipe.
binding.  │        }                     user was authorized.
          │    }
```

You need access to the resource (in this case, the `Recipe` entity) to perform the authorization, so the declarative `[Authorize]` attribute can't help you. In section 24.5.1 you'll see the approach you need to take to handle these situations and to apply authorization inside your endpoints.

> **WARNING** Be careful when exposing the integer ID of your entities in the URL, as in listing 24.13. Users will be able to edit every entity by modifying the ID in the URL to access a different entity. Be sure to apply authorization checks, or you could expose a security vulnerability called *insecure direct object reference* (IDOR). You can read more about IDOR at http://mng.bz/QPnG.

24.5.1 Manually authorizing requests with IAuthorizationService

All of the approaches to authorization so far have been *declarative*. You apply the [Authorize] attribute, with or without a policy name, and you let the framework take care of performing the authorization itself.

For this recipe-editing example, you need to use *imperative* authorization, so you can authorize the user after you've loaded the Recipe from the database. Instead of applying a marker saying "Authorize this method," you need to write some of the authorization code yourself.

> **DEFINITION** *Declarative* and *imperative* are two different styles of programming. *Declarative programming* describes what you're trying to achieve and lets the framework figure out how to achieve it. *Imperative programming* describes how to achieve something by providing each of the steps needed.

ASP.NET Core exposes IAuthorizationService, which you can inject into any of your services or endpoints for imperative authorization. The following listing shows how you could update the Edit.cshtml Razor Page (shown partially in listing 24.13) to use the IAuthorizationService to verify whether the action is allowed to continue execution.

Listing 24.14 Using `IAuthorizationService` for resource-based authorization

```
[Authorize]                                        Only authenticated users should
public class EditModel : PageModel                 be allowed to edit recipes.
{
    [BindProperty]
    public Recipe Recipe { get; set; }

    private readonly RecipeService _service;
    private readonly IAuthorizationService _authService;

    public EditModel(                                     IAuthorizationService is
        RecipeService service,                            injected into the class
        IAuthorizationService authService)                constructor using DI.
    {
        _service = service;
        _authService = authService;
    }
                                            Calls IAuthorizationService,
    public async Task<IActionResult> OnGet(int id)    providing ClaimsPrinicipal,
    {                                                   resource, and the policy
        Recipe = _service.GetRecipe(id);                            name
        AuthorizationResult authResult = await _authService
            .AuthorizeAsync(User, Recipe, "CanManageRecipe");
```

Loads the Recipe from the database

```
        if (!authResult.Succeeded)
        {                                          If authorization failed,
            return new ForbidResult();             returns a Forbidden result
        }

        return Page();    ←┐   If authorization was successful,
    }                      └── continues displaying the Razor Page
}
```

IAuthorizationService exposes an AuthorizeAsync method, which requires three things to authorize the request:

- The ClaimsPrincipal user object, exposed on the PageModel as User
- The resource being authorized: Recipe
- The policy to evaluate: "CanManageRecipe"

The authorization attempt returns an AuthorizationResult object, which indicates whether the attempt was successful via the Succeeded property. If the attempt wasn't successful, you should return a new ForbidResult, which is converted to an HTTP 403 Forbidden response or redirects the user to the "access denied" page, depending on whether you're building a traditional web app or an API app.

> **NOTE** As mentioned in section 24.2.2, which type of response is generated depends on which authentication services are configured. The default Identity configuration, used by Razor Pages, generates redirects. API apps typically generate HTTP 401 and 403 responses instead.

You've configured the imperative authorization in the Edit.cshtml Razor Page itself, but you still need to define the "CanManageRecipe" policy that you use to authorize the user. This is the same process as for declarative authorization, so you have to do the following:

- Create a policy in Program.cs by calling AddAuthorization().
- Define one or more *requirements* for the policy.
- Define one or more *handlers* for each requirement.
- Register the handlers in the DI container.

With the exception of the handler, these steps are identical to the declarative authorization approach with the [Authorize] attribute, so I run through them only briefly here.

First, you can create a simple IAuthorizationRequirement. As with many requirements, this contains no data and simply implements the marker interface:

```
public class IsRecipeOwnerRequirement : IAuthorizationRequirement { }
```

Defining the policy in Program.cs is similarly simple, as you have only a single requirement. Note that there's nothing resource-specific in any of this code so far:

```
builder.Services.AddAuthorization(options => {
    options.AddPolicy("CanManageRecipe", policyBuilder =>
        policyBuilder.AddRequirements(new IsRecipeOwnerRequirement()));
});
```

You're halfway there. All you need to do now is create an authorization handler for `IsRecipeOwnerRequirement` and register it with the DI container.

24.5.2 Creating a resource-based AuthorizationHandler

Resource-based authorization handlers are essentially the same as the authorization handler implementations you saw in section 24.4.2. The only difference is that the handler also has access to the resource being authorized.

To create a resource-based handler, you should derive from the `Authorization-Handler<TRequirement, TResource>` base class, where `TRequirement` is the type of requirement to handle and `TResource` is the type of resource that you provide when calling `IAuthorizationService`. Compare this with the `AuthorizationHandler<T>` class you implemented previously, where you specified only the requirement.

The next listing shows the handler implementation for your recipe application. You can see that you've specified the requirement as `IsRecipeOwnerRequirement` and the resource as `Recipe`, and you have implemented the `HandleRequirementAsync` method.

Listing 24.15 `IsRecipeOwnerHandler` for resource-based authorization

```
public class IsRecipeOwnerHandler :
        AuthorizationHandler<IsRecipeOwnerRequirement, Recipe>
    {
    private readonly UserManager<ApplicationUser> _userManager;
    public IsRecipeOwnerHandler(
        UserManager<ApplicationUser> userManager)
    {
        _userManager = userManager;
    }
    protected override async Task HandleRequirementAsync(
        AuthorizationHandlerContext context,
        IsRecipeOwnerRequirement requirement,
        Recipe resource)
    {
        var appUser = await _userManager.GetUserAsync(context.User);
        if(appUser == null)
        {
            return;
        }
        if(resource.CreatedById == appUser.Id)
        {
            context.Succeed(requirement);
        }
    }
}
```

Implements the necessary base class, specifying the requirement and resource type

Injects an instance of the UserManager<T> class using DI

As well as the context and requirement, you're provided the resource instance.

If you aren't authenticated, appUser will be null.

Checks whether the current user created the Recipe by checking the CreatedById property

If the user created the document, Succeeds the requirement; otherwise, does nothing

This handler is slightly more complicated than the examples you've seen previously, primarily because you're using an additional service, UserManager<>, to load the ApplicationUser entity based on ClaimsPrincipal from the request.

> **NOTE** In practice, the ClaimsPrincipal will likely already have the Id added as a claim, making the extra step unnecessary in this case. This example shows the general pattern if you need to use dependency-injected services.

The other significant difference is that the HandleRequirementAsync method has provided the Recipe resource as a method argument. This is the same object you provided when calling AuthorizeAsync on IAuthorizationService. You can use this resource to verify whether the current user created it. If so, you Succeed() the requirement; otherwise, you do nothing.

The final task is adding IsRecipeOwnerHandler to the DI container. Your handler uses an additional dependency, UserManager<>, that uses EF Core, so you should register the handler as a scoped service:

```
services.AddScoped<IAuthorizationHandler, IsRecipeOwnerHandler>();
```

> **TIP** If you're wondering how to know whether you register a handler as scoped or a singleton, think back to chapter 9. Essentially, if you have scoped dependencies, you must register the handler as scoped; otherwise, singleton is fine.

With everything hooked up, you can take the application for a spin. If you try to edit a recipe you didn't create by clicking the Edit button on the recipe, you'll either be redirected to the login page (if you hadn't yet authenticated) or see an "access denied" page, as shown in figure 24.7.

By using resource-based authorization, you're able to enact more fine-grained authorization requirements that you can apply at the level of an individual document or resource. Instead of being able to authorize only that a user can edit *any* recipe, you can authorize whether a user can edit *this* recipe.

All the authorization techniques you've seen so far have focused on server-side checks. Both the [Authorize] attribute and resource-based authorization approaches focus on stopping users from executing a protected endpoint on the server. This is important from a security point of view, but there's another aspect you should consider: the user experience when they don't have permission.

You've protected the code executing on the server, but arguably the Edit button should never have been visible to the user if they weren't going to be allowed to edit the recipe! In the next section we'll look at how you can conditionally hide the Edit button by using resource-based authorization in your view models.

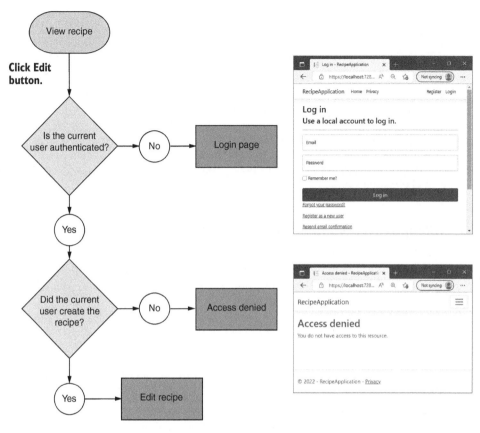

Figure 24.7   If you're logged in but not authorized to edit a recipe, you'll be redirected to an "Access Denied" page. If you're not logged in, you'll be redirected to the Login page.

Resource-based authorization versus business-logic checks

The value proposition of using the ASP.NET Core framework's resource-based authorization approach isn't always clear compared with using simple, manual, business-logic based checks (as in listing 24.13). Using IAuthorizationService and the authorization infrastructure adds an explicit dependency on the ASP.NET Core framework that you may not want to use if you're performing authorization checks in your domain model services.

This is a valid concern without an easy answer. I tend to favor simple business-logic checks inside the domain, without relying on the framework's authorization infrastructure, to make my domain easier to test and framework-independent. But doing so loses some of the benefits of such a framework:

- The IAuthorizationService uses declarative policies, even though you are calling the authorization framework imperatively.
- You can decouple the need to authorize an action from the actual requirements.
- You can easily rely on peripheral services and properties of the request, which may be harder (or undesirable) with business logic checks.

(continued)

You can achieve these benefits in business-logic checks, but that typically requires creating a lot of infrastructure too, so you lose a lot of the benefits of keeping things simple. Which approach is best will depend on the specifics of your application design, and there may well be cases for using both.

For example, one possible approach is to use the basic [Authorize] attribute as described in section 24.2.1 to prevent anonymous access to your APIs, potentially with simple, coarse policies applied to your APIs. You would then rely on "manual" business-logic checks against the ClaimsPrincipal in your domain as required. This may reduce a lot of the complexity and indirection associated with the ASP.NET Core authorization system.

24.6   *Hiding HTML elements from unauthorized users*

All the authorization code you've seen so far has revolved around protecting endpoints on the server side, rather than modifying the UI for users. This is important and should be the starting point whenever you add authorization to an app.

> **WARNING**   Malicious users can easily circumvent your UI, so it's important to always authorize your endpoints on the server, never on the client alone.

From a user-experience point of view, however, it's not friendly to have buttons or links that look like they're available but present an "access denied" page when they're clicked. A better experience would be for the links to be disabled or not visible at all.

You can achieve this in several ways in your own Razor templates. In this section I'm going to show you how to add an additional property to the PageModel, called CanEditRecipe, which the Razor view template will use to change the rendered HTML.

> **TIP**   An alternative approach would be to inject IAuthorizationService directly into the view template using the @inject directive, as you saw in chapter 9, but you should generally prefer to keep logic like this in the page handler.

When you're finished, the rendered HTML looks unchanged for recipes you created, but the Edit button will be hidden when viewing a recipe someone else created, as shown in figure 24.8.

Listing 24.16 shows the PageModel for the View.cshtml Razor Page, which is used to render the recipe page shown in figure 24.8. As you've already seen for resource-based authorization, you can use the IAuthorizationService to determine whether the current user has permission to edit the Recipe by calling AuthorizeAsync.

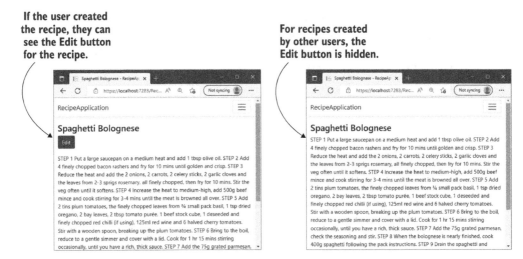

If the user created the recipe, they can see the Edit button for the recipe.

For recipes created by other users, the Edit button is hidden.

Figure 24.8 Although the HTML will appear unchanged for recipes you created, the Edit button is hidden when you view recipes created by a different user.

You can then set this value as an additional property on the `PageModel`, called `CanEditRecipe`.

Listing 24.16 Setting the `CanEditRecipe` property in the View.cshtml Razor Page

```
public class ViewModel : PageModel
{
    public Recipe Recipe { get; set; }
    public bool CanEditRecipe { get; set; }

    private readonly RecipeService _service;
    private readonly IAuthorizationService _authService;
    public ViewModel(
        RecipeService service,
        IAuthorizationService authService)
    {
        _service = service;
        _authService = authService;
    }

    public async Task<IActionResult> OnGetAsync(int id)
    {
        Recipe = _service.GetRecipe(id);
        AuthorizationResult isAuthorised = await _authService
            .AuthorizeAsync(User, recipe, "CanManageRecipe");
        CanEditRecipe = isAuthorised.Succeeded;
        return Page();
    }
}
```

The CanEditRecipe property will be used to control whether the Edit button is rendered.

Loads the Recipe resource for use with IAuthorizationService

Verifies whether the user is authorized to edit the Recipe

Sets the CanEditRecipe property on the PageModel as appropriate

Instead of blocking execution of the Razor Page (as you did previously in the Edit.cshtml page handler), use the result of the call to `AuthorizeAsync` to set the `CanEditRecipe` value on the `PageModel`. You can then make a simple change to the View.chstml Razor template, adding an `if` clause around the rendering of the Edit link:

```
@if(Model.CanEditRecipe)
{
    <a asp-page="Edit" asp-route-id="@Model.Id"
        class="btn btn-primary">Edit</a>
}
```

This ensures that only users who will be able to execute the Edit.cshtml Razor Page can see the link to that page.

> **WARNING**   The `if` clause means that the Edit link will not be displayed unless the current user created the recipe, but you should never rely on client-side security alone. It's important to keep the server-side authorization check in your Edit.cshtml page handler to protect against any direct access attempts. Even if a malicious user circumvents your UI, the server-side authorization ensures that your application is secure.

With that final change, you've finished adding authorization to the recipe application. Anonymous users can browse the recipes created by others, but they must log in to create new recipes. Additionally, authenticated users can edit only the recipes that they created, and they won't see an Edit link for other people's recipes.

Authorization is a key aspect of most apps, so it's important to bear it in mind from an early point. Although it's possible to add authorization later, as you did with the recipe app, it's normally preferable to consider authorization sooner rather than later in the app's development.

In chapters 23 and 24 we focused on authentication and authorization for traditional web applications using Razor. In chapter 25 we'll look at API applications, how authentication works with tokens, and how to add authorization policies to minimal APIs.

Summary

- Authentication is the process of determining who a user is. It's distinct from authorization, the process of determining what a user can do. Authentication typically occurs before authorization.
- You can use the authorization services in any part of your application, but it's typically applied using the `AuthorizationMiddleware` by calling `UseAuthorization()`. This should be placed after the calls to `UseRouting()` and `UseAuthentication()`, and before the call to `UseEndpoints()` for correct operation.
- You can protect Razor Pages and MVC actions by applying the `[Authorize]` attribute. The routing middleware records the presence of the attribute as metadata

with the selected endpoint. The authorization middleware uses this metadata to determine how to authorize the request.

- The simplest form of authorization requires that a user be authenticated before executing an action. You can achieve this by applying the `[Authorize]` attribute to a Razor Page, action, controller, or globally. You can also apply attributes conventionally to a subset of Razor Pages.

- Claims-based authorization uses the current user's claims to determine whether they're authorized to execute an action. You define the claims needed to execute an action in a policy.

- Policies have a name and are configured in Program.cs as part of the call to `AddAuthorization()` in `ConfigureServices`. You define the policy using `AddPolicy()`, passing in a name and a lambda that defines the claims needed.

- You can apply a policy to an action or Razor Page by specifying the policy in the authorize attribute; for example, `[Authorize("CanAccessLounge")]`. This policy will be used by the `AuthorizationMiddleware` to determine whether the user is allowed to execute the selected endpoint.

- In a Razor Pages app, if an unauthenticated user attempts to execute a protected action, they'll be redirected to the login page for your app. If they're already authenticated but don't have the required claims, they'll be shown an "access denied" page instead.

- For complex authorization policies, you can build a custom policy. A custom policy consists of one or more requirements, and a requirement can have one or more handlers. You can combine requirements and handlers to create policies of arbitrary complexity.

- For a policy to be authorized, every requirement must be satisfied. For a requirement to be satisfied, one or more of the associated handlers must indicate success, and none must indicate explicit failure.

- `AuthorizationHandler<T>` contains the logic that determines whether a requirement is satisfied. For example, if a requirement requires that users be over 18, the handler could look for a `DateOfBirth` claim and calculate the user's age.

- Handlers can mark a requirement as satisfied by calling `context.Succeed(requirement)`. If a handler can't satisfy the requirement, it shouldn't call anything on the context, as a different handler could call `Succeed()` and satisfy the requirement.

- If a handler calls `context.Fail()`, the requirement fails, even if a different handler marked it as a success using `Succeed()`. Use this method only if you want to override any calls to `Succeed()` from other handlers to ensure that the authorization policy will fail authorization.

- Resource-based authorization uses details of the resource being protected to determine whether the current user is authorized. For example, if a user is allowed to edit only their own documents, you need to know the author of the document before you can determine whether they're authorized.

- Resource-based authorization uses the same policy, requirements, and handler system as before. Instead of applying authorization with the `[Authorize]` attribute, you must manually call `IAuthorizationService` and provide the resource you're protecting.
- You can modify the user interface to account for user authorization by adding additional properties to your `PageModel`. If a user isn't authorized to execute an action, you can remove or disable the link to that action method in the UI. You should always authorize on the server, even if you've removed links from the UI.

Authentication and authorization for APIs

This chapter covers

- Seeing how authentication works for APIs in ASP.NET Core
- Using bearer tokens for authentication
- Testing APIs locally with JSON Web Tokens
- Applying authorization policies to minimal APIs

In chapter 23 you learned how authentication works with traditional web apps, such as those you would build with Razor Pages or Model-View-Controller (MVC) controllers. Traditional web apps typically use encrypted cookies to store the identity of a user for a request, which the AuthenticationMiddleware then decodes. In this chapter you'll learn how authentication works for API applications, how it differs from traditional web apps, and what options are available.

We start by taking a high-level look at how authentication works for APIs, both in isolation and when they're part of a larger application or distributed system. You'll learn about some of the protocols involved, such as OAuth 2.0 and OpenID

Connect; patterns you can use to protect your APIs; and the tokens used to control access, typically JSON Web Tokens, called JWTs.

In section 25.3 you'll learn how to put this knowledge into practice, adding authentication to a minimal API application using JWTs. In section 25.4 you'll learn how to use the .NET command-line interface (CLI) to generate JWTs for testing your API locally.

The .NET CLI works well for generating tokens, but you need a way to add this token to a request. Specifically, if you're using OpenAPI definitions and Swagger UI as described in chapter 11, you need a way to tell Swagger about your authentication requirements. In section 25.5 you'll learn about some of the authentication configuration options for your OpenAPI documents and how to use Swagger UI to send authenticated requests to your API.

Finally, in section 25.6 I show how to apply authorization policies to minimal API endpoints to restrict which users can call your APIs. The authorization concepts you learned about in chapter 24 for Razor Pages are the same for APIs, so you're still using claims, requirements, handlers, and polices.

We'll start off by looking at how authentication works when you have an API application. Many of the authentication concepts are similar to traditional apps, but the requirement to support multiple types of users, traditional apps, client-side apps, and mobile apps has led to subtly different solutions.

25.1 Authentication for APIs and distributed applications

In this section you'll learn about the authentication process for API applications, why it typically differs from authentication for traditional web apps, and some of the common patterns and protocols that are involved.

25.1.1 Extending authentication to multiple apps

I outlined the authentication process for traditional web apps in chapter 23. When a user signs in to your application, you set an encrypted cookie. This cookie contains a serialized version of the ClaimsPrincipal of the user, including their ID and any associated claims. When you make a second request, the browser automatically sends this cookie. The AuthenticationMiddleware then decodes the cookie, deserializes the ClaimsPrincipal, and sets the current user for the request, as shown previously in figure 23.3 and reproduced in figure 25.1.

This flow works particularly well when you have a single traditional web app that's doing all the work. The app is responsible for authenticating and managing users, as well as serving your app data and executing business logic, as shown in figure 25.2.

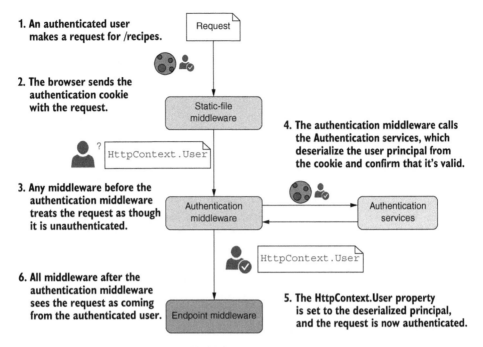

1. An authenticated user makes a request for /recipes.

2. The browser sends the authentication cookie with the request.

3. Any middleware before the authentication middleware treats the request as though it is unauthenticated.

4. The authentication middleware calls the Authentication services, which deserialize the user principal from the cookie and confirm that it's valid.

5. The HttpContext.User property is set to the deserialized principal, and the request is now authenticated.

6. All middleware after the authentication middleware sees the request as coming from the authenticated user.

Figure 25.1 When a user first signs in to an app, the app sets an encrypted cookie containing the `ClaimsPrincipal`. On subsequent requests, the cookie sent with the request contains the user principal, which is deserialized, validated, and used to authenticate the request.

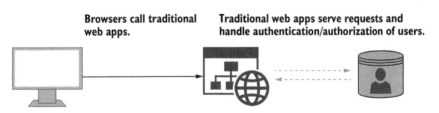

Browsers call traditional web apps.

Traditional web apps serve requests and handle authentication/authorization of users.

Figure 25.2 Traditional apps typically handle all the functionality of an app: the business logic, generating the UI, authentication, and user management.

In addition to traditional web apps, it's common to use ASP.NET Core as an API to serve data for mobile and client-side single-page applications (SPAs). Similarly, even traditional web apps using Razor Pages often need to call API applications behind the scenes, as shown in figure 25.3.

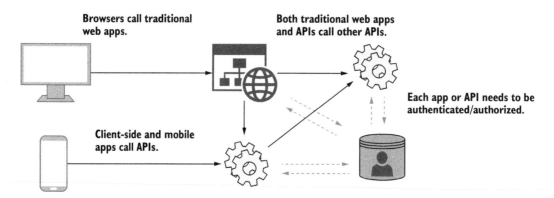

Figure 25.3   Modern applications typically need to expose web APIs for mobile and client-side apps, as well as potentially calling APIs on the backend. When all these services need to authenticate and manage users, this becomes logistically complicated.

In this situation you have multiple apps and APIs, all of which need to understand that the same user is logically making a request across all the apps and APIs. If you keep the same approach as before, where each app manages its own users, things can quickly become unmanageable!

You'd need to duplicate all the sign-in logic between the apps and APIs, as well as have some central database holding the user details. Users would likely need to sign in multiple times to access different parts of the service. On top of that, using cookies becomes problematic for some mobile clients in particular or where you're making requests to multiple domains (as cookies belong to only a single domain). So how can we improve this? By moving the authentication responsibilities to a separate service.

25.1.2   *Centralizing authentication in an identity provider*

Modern systems often have many moving parts, each of which requires some level of authentication and authorization to protect each app from unauthorized use. Instead of embedding authentication responsibilities in each application, a common approach is to extract the code that's common to all the apps and APIs and then move it to an *identity provider*, as shown in figure 25.4.

Instead of signing in to an app directly, the app redirects to an identity provider. The user signs in to this identity provider, which passes *bearer tokens* back to the client (a browser or mobile app, for example) to indicate who the user is and what they're allowed to access. The client can pass these tokens to the APIs to provide information about the logged-in user without needing to reauthenticate or manage users directly in the API.

> **DEFINITION**   *Bearer tokens* are strings that contain authentication details about a user or app. They may or may not be encrypted but are typically signed to avoid tampering. JWTs are the most common format. We'll look more at JWTs in section 25.2.

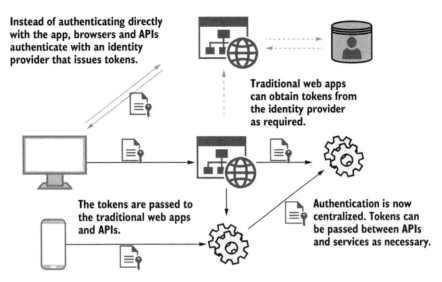

Figure 25.4 An alternative architecture involves using a central identity provider to handle all the authentication and user management for the system. Tokens are passed back and forth among the identity provider, apps, and APIs.

Using a separate identity provider is clearly more complicated on the face of it, as you've thrown a whole new service into the mix, but in the long run this has several advantages:

- *Users can share their identity among multiple services.* As you're logged in to the central identity provider, you're essentially logged in to all apps that use that service. This gives you the single-sign-on experience, where you don't have to keep logging in to multiple services.

- *You don't need to duplicate sign-in logic between multiple services.* All the sign-in logic is encapsulated in the identity provider, so you don't need to add sign-in screens to all your apps.

- *The identity provider has a single responsibility.* The identity provider is responsible only for authentication and managing users. In many cases, this is generic enough that you can (and should!) use a third-party identity service, such as Auth0 or Azure Active Directory, instead of building your own.

- *You can easily add new sign-in mechanisms.* Whether you use the identity provider approach or the traditional approach, it's possible to use external services to handle the authentication of users. You'll have seen this in apps that allow you to "log in using Facebook" or "log in using Google," for example. If you use a centralized identity provider, you can add support for more providers in one place instead of having to configure every app and API explicitly.

Out of the box, ASP.NET Core supports architectures like this and for consuming bearer tokens from identity providers, but .NET 7 doesn't include support for issuing those tokens in the core framework. That means you'll need to use another library or service as the identity provider.

As I mentioned in chapter 23, one excellent option is to use a third-party identity provider, such as Facebook, Google, Okta, Auth0, or Azure Active Directory. These providers take care of storing user passwords, authenticating using modern standards like WebAuthn (https://webauthn.guide), and looking for malicious attempts to impersonate users.

By using an identity provider, you leave the tricky security details to the experts and can focus on the core purpose of your business, whichever domain that is. Not all providers are equal, though: For some providers (such as Auth0) you own the profiles, whereas for others (Facebook or Google) you don't. Make sure to choose a provider that matches your requirements.

> **TIP** Wherever possible, I recommend using a third-party identity provider. Well-respected identity providers have many experts working solely on securing your customers' details, proactively preventing attacks and ensuring that the data is safe. By leaving this tricky job to the experts, you're free to focus on the core business of your app, whatever that may be.

Another common option is to build your *own* identity provider. This may sound like a lot of work (and it is!), but thanks to excellent libraries like OpenIddict (https://github.com/openiddict) and Duende's IdentityServer (https://duendesoftware.com), it's perfectly possible to write your own identity provider to serve bearer tokens that can be consumed by your apps and APIs.

> **WARNING** You should consider carefully whether the effort and risks associated with creating your own identity provider are worthwhile. Bugs are a fact of life, and a bug in your identity provider could easily result in a security vulnerability. Nevertheless, if you have specific identity requirements, creating your own identity provider may be a reasonable or necessary option.

An aspect often overlooked by people getting started with OpenIddict and IdentityServer is that they aren't prefabricated solutions. They consist of a set of services and middleware that you add to a standard ASP.NET Core app, providing an implementation of relevant identity standards, according to the specification. You, as a developer, still need to write the profile management code that knows how to create a new user (normally in a database), load a user's details, validate their password, and manage their associated claims. On top of that, you need to provide all the UI code for the user to log in, manage their passwords, and configure multi-factor authentication (MFA). It's not for the faint of heart!

In many ways, you can think of an identity provider as a traditional web app that has only account management pages. If you want to take on building your own identity provider, ASP.NET Core Identity, described in chapter 23, provides a good basis for the user management side. Adding IdentityServer or OpenIddict gives you the ability to generate tokens for other services, using the OpenID Connect standard, for maximum interoperability with other services.

25.1.3   *OpenID Connect and OAuth 2.0*

OpenID Connect (OIDC) (http://openid.net/connect) is an authentication protocol built on top of the OAuth 2.0 (https://oauth.net/2) specification. It's designed to facilitate the kind of approaches described in section 25.1.2, where you want to leave the responsibility of storing user credentials to someone else (an identity provider). It provides an answer to the question "Which user sent this request?" without your having to manage the user yourself.

> **NOTE** It isn't strictly necessary to understand these protocols to add authentication to your APIs, but I think it's best to have a basic understanding of them so that you understand where your APIs fit into the security landscape. If you want to learn more about OpenID Connect, *OpenID Connect in Action*, by Prabath Siriwardena (Manning, 2023), provides lots more details.

Open ID Connect is built on top of the OAuth 2.0 protocol, so it helps to understand that protocol a little first. OAuth 2.0 is an *authorization* protocol. It allows a user to delegate access of a resource to a different service in a controlled manner without revealing any additional details, such as your identity or any other information.

That's all a bit abstract, so let's consider an example. You want to print some photos of your dog through a photo printing service, dogphotos.com. You sign up to the dogphotos.com service, and they give you two options for uploading your photos:

- Upload from your computer.
- Download directly from Facebook using OAuth 2.0.

As you're using a new laptop, you haven't downloaded all the photos of your dog to your computer, so you choose to use OAuth 2.0 instead, as shown in figure 25.5. This triggers the following sequence:

1. dogphotos.com redirects you to Facebook, where you must sign in (if you haven't already).
2. Once you're authenticated, Facebook shows a consent screen, which describes the data dogphotos.com wants to access, which should be your photos only in this case.
3. When you choose OK, Facebook automatically redirects you to a URL on dog photos.com and includes an authorization code in the URL.
4. dogphotos.com uses this code, in combination with a secret known only by Facebook and dogphotos.com, to retrieve an access token from Facebook.
5. Finally, dogphotos.com uses the token to call the Facebook API and retrieve your dog photos!

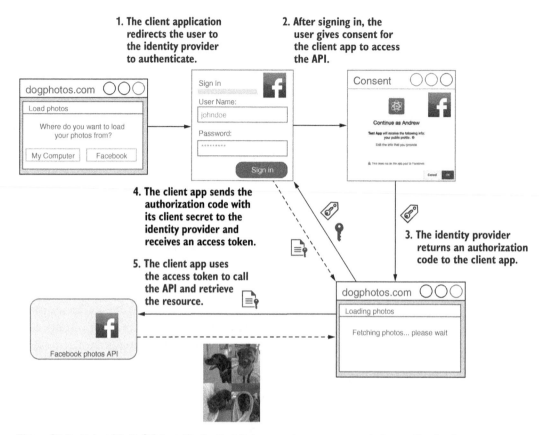

Figure 25.5   Using OAuth 2.0 to authorize dogphotos.com to access your photos on Facebook

There's a lot going on in this example, but it gives some nice benefits:

- You didn't have to give your Facebook credentials to dogphotos.com. You simply signed in to Facebook as normal.
- You had control of which details dogphotos.com could access on your behalf via the Facebook photos API.
- You didn't have to give dogphotos.com any of your identity information (though in practice, this is often requested).

Effectively, you delegated your access of the Facebook photos API to dogphotos.com. This approach is why OAuth 2.0 is described as an authorization protocol, not an authentication protocol. dogphotos.com doesn't know your identity on Facebook; it is authorized only to access the photos API on behalf of someone.

> ## OAuth 2.0 authorization flows and grant types
>
> The OAuth 2.0 example shows in this section uses a common flow or *grant type*, as it's called in OAuth 2.0, for obtaining a token from an identity provider. Oauth 2.0 defines several grant types and extensions, each designed for a different scenario:
>
> - *Authorization code*—This is the flow I described in figure 25.5, in which an application uses the combination of an authorization code and a secret to retrieve a token.
> - *Proof Key for Code Exchange (PKCE)*—This is an extension to the authorization code that you should always favor, if possible, as it provides additional protections against certain attacks, as described in the RFC at https://www.rfc-editor .org/rfc/rfc7636.
> - *Client credentials*—This is used when no user is involved, such as when you have an API talking to another API.
>
> Many more grants are available (see https://oauth.net/2/grant-types), and each grant is suited to a different situation. The examples are the most common types, but if your scenario doesn't match these, it's worth exploring the other OAuth 2.0 grants available before thinking you need to invent your own! And with Oauth 2.1 coming soon (http://mng.bz/XNav), there may well be updated guidance to be aware of.

OAuth 2.0 is great for the scenario I've described so far, in which you want to delegate access to a resource (your photos) to someone else (dogphotos.com). But it's also common for apps to *want* to know your identity in addition to accessing an API. For example, dogphotos.com may want to be able to contact you via Facebook if there's a problem with your photos.

This is where OpenID Connect comes in. OpenID Connect takes the same basic flows as OAuth 2.0 and adds some conventions, discoverability, and authentication. At a high level, OpenID Connect treats your identity (such as an ID or email address) as a resource that is protected in the same way as any other API. You still need to consent to give dogphotos.com access to your identity details, but once you do, it's an extra API call for dogphotos.com to retrieve your identity details, as shown in figure 25.6.

OpenID Connect is a crucial authentication component in many systems, but if you're building the API only (for example, the Facebook photos API from figures 25.5 and 25.6), all you really care about are the tokens in the requests; how that token was obtained is less important from a technical standpoint. In the next section we'll look in detail at these tokens and how they work.

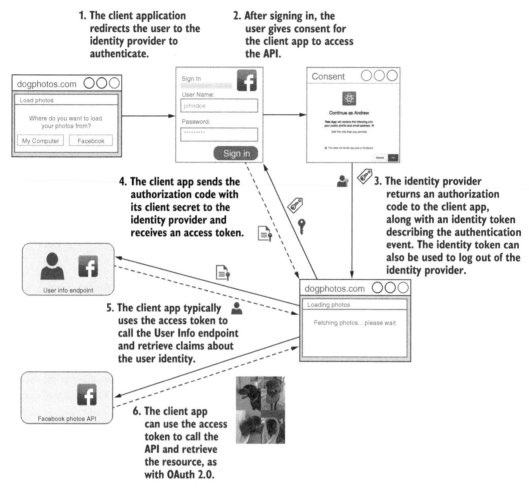

Figure 25.6 Using OpenID Connect to authenticate with Facebook and retrieve identity information. The overall flow is the same as with Oauth 2.0, as shown in figure 25.5, but with an additional identity token describing the authentication event and API call to retrieve the identity details.

25.2 Understanding bearer token authentication

In this section you'll learn about bearer tokens: what they are, how they can be used for security with APIs, and the common JWT format for tokens. You'll learn about some of the limitations of the tokens, approaches to work around these, and some common concepts such as audiences and scopes.

The name *bearer token* consists of two parts that describe its use:

- *Token*—A *security token* is a string that provides access to a protected resource.
- *Bearer*—A *bearer* token is one in which anyone who has the token (the bearer) can use it like anyone else. You don't need to prove that you were the one who received the token originally or have access to any additional key. You can think of a bearer token as being a bit like money: if it's in your possession, you can spend it!

If the second point makes you a little uneasy, that's good. You should think of bearer tokens as being a lot like passwords: you must protect them at all costs! You should avoid including bearer tokens in URL query strings, for example, as these may be automatically logged, exposing the token accidentally.

Everything old is new again: Cookies for APIs

Bearer token authentication is extremely common for APIs, but as with everything in tech, the landscape is constantly evolving. One area that has seen a lot of change is the process of securing SPAs like React, Angular, and Blazor WASM. The advice for some years was to use the Authorization code with PKCE grant (https://www.rfc-editor .org/rfc/rfc8252#section-6), but the big problem with this pattern is that the bearer tokens for calling the API are ultimately stored in the browser.

An alternative pattern has emerged recently: the Backend for Frontend (BFF) pattern. In this approach, you have a traditional ASP.NET Core application (the backend), which hosts the Blazor WASM or other SPA application (the frontend). The main job of the ASP.NET Core application is to handle OpenID Connect authentication, store the bearer tokens securely, and set an authentication cookie, exactly like a traditional web app.

The frontend app in the browser sends requests to the backend app, which automatically includes the cookie. The backend swaps out the authentication cookie for the appropriate bearer token and forwards the request to the real API.

The big advantages of this approach are that no bearer tokens are ever sent to the browser, and much of the frontend code is significantly simplified. The main down side is that you need to run the additional backend service to support the frontend app. Nevertheless, this is quickly becoming the recommended approach. You can read more about the pattern in Duende's documentation at http://mng.bz/yQdB. Alternatively, you can find a project template for the BFF pattern from Damien Bowden at http://mng.bz/MBlW.

Bearer tokens don't have to have any particular value; they could be a completely random string, for example. However, the most common format and the format used by OpenID Connect is a JWT. JWTs (defined in https://www.rfc-editor.org/rfc/rfc7519.html) consist of three parts:

- *A JavaScript Object Notation (JSON) header* describing the token
- *A JSON payload* containing the claims
- *A binary signature* created from the header and the payload

Each part is base64-encoded and concatenated with a ' . ' into a single string that can be safely passed in HTTP headers, for example, as shown in figure 25.7. The signature is created using key material that must be shared by the provider that created the token and any API that consumes it. This ensures that the JWT can't be tampered with, such as to add extra claims to a token.

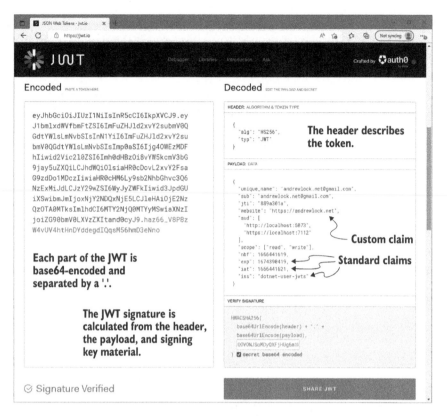

Figure 25.7   An example JWT, decoded using the website https://jwt.io. The JWT consists of three parts: the header, the payload, and the signature. You must always verify the signature of any JWTs you receive.

> **WARNING** Always validate the signature of any JWTs you consume, as described in the JWT Best Current Practices RFC (https://www.rfc-editor.org/rfc/rfc8725). ASP.NET Core does this by default.

Figure 25.7 shows the claims included in the JWT, some of which have cryptic names like iss and iat. These are standard claim names used in OpenID Connect (standing for "Issuer" and "Issued at," respectively). You generally don't need to worry about these, as they're automatically handled by ASP.NET Core when it decodes the token. Nevertheless, it's helpful to understand what some of these claims mean, as it will help when things go wrong:

- sub—The *subject* of the token, the unique identifier of the subject it's describing. This will often be a user, in which case it may be the identity provider's unique ID for the user.
- aud—The *audience* of the token, specifying the domains for which this token was created. When an API validates the token, the API should confirm that the JWT's aud claim contains the domain of the API.

- scope—The *scopes* granted in the token. Scopes define what the user/app consented to (and is allowed to do). Taking the example from section 25.1, dog-photos.com may have requested the `photos.read` and `photos.edit` scopes, but if the user consented only to the `photos.read` scope, the `photos.edit` scope would not be in the JWT it receives for use with the Facebook photos API. It's up to the API itself to interpret what each scope means for the business logic of the request.

- exp—The expiration time of the token, after which it is no longer valid, expressed as the number of seconds since midnight on January 1, 1970 (known as the Unix timestamp).

An important point to realize is that JWTs are not encrypted. That means *anyone* can read the contents of a JWT by default. Another standard, JSON Web Encryption (JWE), can be used to wrap a JWT in an encrypted envelope that can't be read unless you have the key. Many identity providers include support for using JWEs with nested JWTs, and ASP.NET Core includes support for both out of the box, so it's something to consider.

Bearer tokens, access tokens, reference tokens, oh my!

The concept of a bearer token described in this section is a generic idea that can be used in several ways and for different purposes. You've already read about access tokens and identity tokens used in OpenID Connect. These are both bearer tokens; their different names describe the purpose of the token.

The following list describes some of the types of tokens you might read about or run into:

- *Access token*—Access tokens are used to authorize access to a resource. These are the tokens typically referred to when you talk about bearer authentication. They come in two flavors:
  - *Self-contained*—These are the most common tokens, with JWT as the most common format. They contain metadata, claims, and a signature. The strength of self-contained tokens—that they contain all the data and can be validated offline—is also their weakness, as they can't be revoked. Due to this, they typically have a limited valid lifespan. They can also become large if they contain many claims, which increases request sizes.
  - *Reference token*—These don't contain any data and are typically a random string. When a protected API receives a reference token, it must exchange the reference token with the identity provider for the claims (for example, a JWT). This approach ensures more privacy, as the claims are never exposed to the client, and the token can be revoked at the identity provider. However, it requires an extra HTTP round trip every time the API receives a request. This makes reference tokens a good option for high-security environments, where the performance effect is less critical.

(continued)

- *ID token*—This token is used in OpenID Connect (http://mng.bz/a1M7) to describe an authentication event. It may contain additional claims about the authenticated user, but this is not required; if the claims aren't provided in the ID token, they can be retrieved from the identity provider's UserInfo endpoint. The ID token is *always* a JWT, but you should never send it to other APIs; it is not an access token. The ID token can also be used to log out the user at the identity provider.
- *Refresh token*—For security reasons, access tokens typically have relatively short lifetimes, sometimes as low as 5 minutes. After this time, the access token is no longer valid, and you need to retrieve a new one. Making users log in to their identity provider every 5 minutes is clearly a bad experience, so as part of the OAuth or OpenID Connect flow you can also request a *refresh token*.

  When an access token expires, you can send the refresh token to an identity provider, and it returns a new access token without the user's needing to log in again. The power to obtain valid access tokens means that it's critical to protect refresh tokens; should an attacker obtain a refresh token, they effectively have the power to impersonate a user.

In most of your work building and interacting with APIs, you'll likely be using self-contained JWT access tokens. These are what I'm primarily referring to in this chapter whenever I mention bearer tokens or bearer authentication.

Now you know what a token is, as well as how they're issued by identity providers using the OpenID Connect and OAuth 2.0 protocols. Before we get to some code in section 25.3, we'll see what a typical authentication flow looks like for an ASP.NET Core API app using JWT bearer tokens for authentication.

At a high level, authenticating using bearer tokens is identical to authenticating using cookies for a traditional app that has already authenticated, which you saw in figure 25.1. The request to the API contains the bearer token in a header. Any middleware before the authentication middleware sees the request as unauthenticated, exactly the same as for cookie authentication, as shown in figure 25.8.

Things are a bit different in the `AuthenticationMiddleware`. Instead of deserializing a cookie containing the `ClaimsPrincipal`, the middleware decodes the JWT token in the `Authorization` header. It validates the signature using the signing keys from the identity provider, and verifies that the audience has the expected value and that the token has not expired.

If the token is valid, the authentication middleware creates a `ClaimsPrincipal` representing the authenticated request and sets it on `HttpContext.User`. All middleware after the authentication middleware sees the request as authenticated.

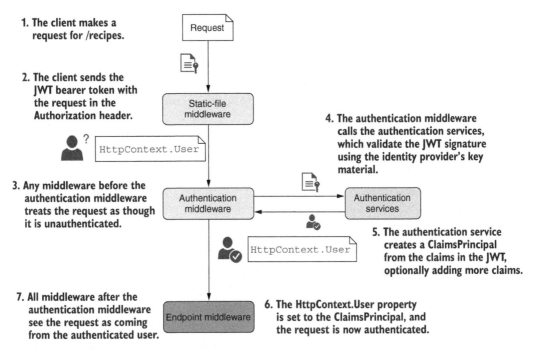

1. The client makes a request for /recipes.

2. The client sends the JWT bearer token with the request in the Authorization header.

3. Any middleware before the authentication middleware treats the request as though it is unauthenticated.

4. The authentication middleware calls the authentication services, which validate the JWT signature using the identity provider's key material.

5. The authentication service creates a ClaimsPrincipal from the claims in the JWT, optionally adding more claims.

6. The HttpContext.User property is set to the ClaimsPrincipal, and the request is now authenticated.

7. All middleware after the authentication middleware see the request as coming from the authenticated user.

Figure 25.8   When an API request contains a bearer token, the token is validated and deserialized by the authentication middleware. The middleware creates a `ClaimsPrincipal` from the token, optionally transforming it with additional claims, and sets the `HttpContext.User` property. Subsequent middleware sees the request as authenticated.

> **TIP** If the claims in the token don't match the key values you're expecting, you can use *claims transformation* to remap claims. This applies to cookie authentication too, but it's particularly common when you're receiving tokens from third-party identity providers, where you don't control the names of claims. You can also use this approach to add extra claims for a user, which weren't in the original token. To learn more about claims transformation, see http://mng.bz/gBJV.

We've covered a lot of theory about JWT tokens in this chapter, so you'll be pleased to hear it's time to look at some code!

25.3 Adding JWT bearer authentication to minimal APIs

In this section you'll learn how to add JWT bearer token authentication to an ASP.NET Core app. I use the minimal API Recipe API application we started in chapter 12 in this chapter, but the process is identical if you're building an API application using web API controllers.

.NET 7 significantly simplified the number of steps you need to get started with JWT authentication by adding some conventions, which we'll discuss shortly. To add

JWT to an existing API application, first install the Microsoft.AspNetCore.Authentication.JwtBearer NuGet package using the .NET CLI

```
dotnet add package Microsoft.AspNetCore.Authentication.JwtBearer
```

or by adding the `<PackageReference>` to your project directly:

```
<PackageReference Include="Microsoft.AspNetCore.Authentication.JwtBearer"
    Version="7.0.0" />
```

Next, add the required services to configure JWT authentication for your application, as shown in listing 25.1. As you may remember, the authentication and authorization middleware are automatically added to your middleware pipeline by `WebApplication`, but if you want to control the position of the middleware, you can override the location, as I do here.

Listing 25.1   Adding JWT bearer authentication to a minimal API application

```
WebApplicationBuilder builder = WebApplication.CreateBuilder(args);

builder.Services.AddAuthentication()      ⟵──│ Adds the core authentication services
    .AddJwtBearer();                      ⟵──── Adds and configures JWT authentication
builder.Services.AddAuthorization();      ⟵──┐
                                             │ Adds the core authorization services
builder.Services.AddScoped<RecipeService>();

WebApplication app = builder.Build();

app.UseAuthentication();      ⟵──│ Adds the authentication middleware
app.UseAuthorization();       ⟵──┐ Adds the authorization middleware
app.MapGet("/recipe", async (RecipeService service) =>
{
    return await service.GetRecipes();    │ Adds an authorization policy
}).RequireAuthorization();    ⟵──────────┘ to the minimal API endpoint

app.Run();
```

As well as configuring the JWT authentication, listing 25.1 adds an authorization policy to the one minimal API endpoint shown in the app. The `RequireAuthorization()` function adds a simple "Is authenticated" authorization policy to the endpoint. This is exactly analogous to when you add an `[Authorize]` attribute to MVC or Web API controllers. Any requests for this endpoint must be authenticated; otherwise, the request is rejected by the authorization middleware with a `401 Unauthorized` reponse, as shown in figure 25.9.

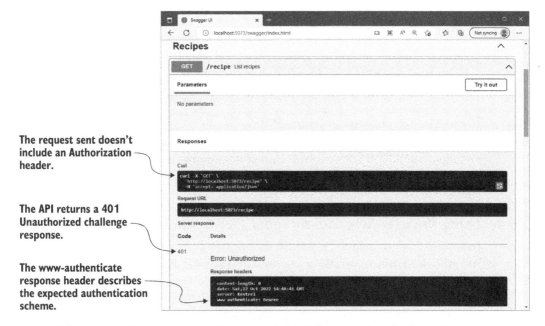

The request sent doesn't include an Authorization header.

The API returns a 401 Unauthorized challenge response.

The www-authenticate response header describes the expected authentication scheme.

Figure 25.9 If you send a request to an API protected with JWT bearer authentication and don't include a token, you'll receive a `401 Unauthorized` challenge response.

Authentication schemes: Choosing between cookies and bearer tokens

One question you may have while reading about bearer authentication is how the authentication middleware knows whether to look for the cookie or a header. The answer is authentication schemes.

An *authentication scheme* in ASP.NET Core has an ID and an associated *authentication handler* that controls how the user is authenticated, as well as how authentication and authorization failures should be handled.

For example, in chapter 23 the cookie authentication scheme was used implicitly by ASP.NET Core Identity. The cookie authentication handler in this case authenticates users by looking for a cookie and redirects users to the login or "access denied" pages for authentication or authorization failures.

In listing 25.1 you registered the JWT Bearer authentication scheme. The JWT bearer authentication handler reads tokens from the `Authorization` header and returns `401` and `403` responses for authentication or authorization failures.

When you register only a single authentication scheme, such as in listing 25.1, ASP.NET Core automatically sets that as the default, but it's possible to register multiple authentication schemes. This is particularly common if you are using OpenID Connect with a traditional web app, for example. In these cases you can choose which scheme is used for authentication events or authentication failures and how the schemes should interact.

(continued)

Using multiple authentication schemes can be confusing, so it's important to follow the documentation closely when configuring authentication for your app. You can read more about authentication schemes at http://mng.bz/5w1a. If you need only a single scheme, you shouldn't have any problems, but otherwise, here be dragons!

Great! The 401 response in figure 25.9 verifies that the app is behaving correctly for unauthenticated requests. The obvious next step is to send a request to your API that includes a valid JWT bearer token. Unfortunately, this is where things traditionally get tricky. How do you generate a valid JWT? Luckily, in .NET 7, the .NET CLI comes with a tool to make creating test tokens easy.

25.4 Using the user-jwts tool for local JWT testing

In section 25.3 you added JWT authentication to your application and protected your API with a basic authorization policy. The problem is that you can't test your API unless you can generate JWT tokens. In production you'll likely have an identity provider such as Auth0, Azure Active Directory, or IdentityServer to generate tokens for you using OpenID Connect. But that can make for cumbersome local testing. In this section you'll learn how to use the .NET CLI to generate JWTs for local testing.

In .NET 7, the .NET CLI includes a tool called user-jwts that you can use to generate tokens. This tool acts as a mini identity provider, meaning that you can generate tokens with any claims you may need, and your API can verify them using signing key material generated by the tool.

> **TIP**   The user-jwts tool is built into the software development kit (SDK), so there's nothing extra to install. You need to enable User Secrets for your project, but user-jwts will do this for you if you haven't already. The user-jwts tool uses User Secrets to store the signing key material used to generate the JWTs, which your app uses to validate the JWT signatures.

Let's look at how to create a JWT with the user-jwts tool and use that to send a request to our application.

25.4.1 Creating JWTs with the user-jwts tool

To create a JWT that you can use in requests to your API, run the following with the user-jwts tool from inside your project folder:

```
dotnet user-jwts create
```

This command does several things:

- *Enables User Secrets in the project* if they're not already configured, as though you had manually run `dotnet user-secrets init`.

- *Adds the signing key material to User Secrets*, which you can view by running `dotnet user-secrets list` as described in chapter 10, which prints out the key material configuration, as in this example:

```
Authentication:Schemes:Bearer:SigningKeys:0:Value =
    rIhUzB3DIbtbUwiIxkgoKfFDkLpY+gIJOB4eaQzczq8=
Authentication:Schemes:Bearer:SigningKeys:0:Length = 32
Authentication:Schemes:Bearer:SigningKeys:0:Issuer = dotnet-user-jwts
Authentication:Schemes:Bearer:SigningKeys:0:Id = c99a872d
```

- *Configures the JWT authentication services* to support tokens generated by the user-jwts tool by adding configuration to appsettings.Development.json, as follows:

```
{
  "Authentication": {
    "Schemes": {
      "Bearer": {
        "ValidAudiences": [
          "http://localhost:5073",
          "https://localhost:7112"
        ],
        "ValidIssuer": "dotnet-user-jwts"
      }
    }
  }
}
```

The user-jwts tool automatically configures the valid audiences based on the profiles in your launchSettings.json file. All the `applicationUrls` listed in launchSettings.json are listed as valid audiences, so it doesn't matter which profile you use to run your app; the generated token should be valid. The JWT bearer authentication service automatically reads this configuration and configures itself to support user-jwts JWTs.

- *Creates a JWT*. By default, the token is created with a `sub` and `unique_claim` set to your operating system's username, with `aud` claims for each of the `application-Urls` in your launchSettings.json and an issuer of `dotnet-user-jwts`. You'll notice that these match the values added to your APIs configuration file.

   After calling `dotnet user-jwts create`, the JWT token is printed to the console, along with the `sub` name used and the ID of the token. I've truncated the tokens throughout this chapter for brevity:

```
New JWT saved with ID 'f2080e51'.
Name: andrewlock

Token: eyJhbGciOiJIUzI1NiIsInR5cCI6IkpXVCJ9.eyJ1bmlxdWVfbmFtZSI6ImFuZHJl…
```

TIP You can visualize exactly what's in the token by copy and pasting it into https://jwt.io, as I showed in figure 25.7.

Now that you have a token, it's time to test it. To use the token, you need to add an `Authorization` header to requests using the following format (where `<token>` is the full token printed by user-jwts):

```
Authorization: Bearer <token>
```

If any part of this header is incorrect—if you misspell `Authorization`, misspell `Bearer`, don't include a space between `Bearer` and your token, or mistype your token—you'll get a `401 Unauthorized` response.

> **TIP**   If you get `401 Unauthorized` responses even after adding an `Authorization` header to your requests, double-check your spelling, and make sure that the token is added correctly with the `"Bearer "` prefix. Typos have a way of creeping in here! You can also increase the logging level in your API to see why failures are happening, as you'll learn in chapter 26.

Once you have added the token you can call your API, which should now return successfully, as shown in figure 25.10.

A request is sent with the Authorization header. The header has the format Bearer <token>.

The request is authenticated correctly, so the API returns a 200 OK response.

Figure 25.10   Sending a request with a bearer token for authorization using Postman. The `Authorization` header must have the format `Bearer <token>`. You can also configure this in the Authorization tab of Postman.

The default token created by the JWT is sufficient to authenticate with your API, but depending on your requirements, you may want to customize the JWT to add or change claims. In the next section you'll learn how.

25.4.2   Customizing your JWTs

By default, the user-jwts tool creates a bare-bones JWT that you can use to call your app. If you need more customization, you can pass extra options to the dotnet user-jwts create command to control the JWT it generates. Some of the most useful options are

- --name sets the sub and unique_name claims for the JWT instead of using the operating system user as the name.
- --claim <key>=<value> adds a claim called <key> with value <value> to the JWT. Use this option multiple times to add claims.
- --scope <value> adds a scope claim called <value> to the JWT. Use this option multiple times to add scopes.

These aren't the only options; you can control essentially everything about the generated JWT. Run dotnet user-jwts create --help to see all the options available. One option that may be useful in certain automated scripts or tests is the --output option. This controls how the JWT is printed to the console after creation. The default value, default, prints a summary of the JWT and the token itself, as you saw previously:

```
New JWT saved with ID 'f2080e51'.
Name: andrewlock

Token: eyJhbGciOiJIUzI1NiIsInR5cCI6IkpXVCJ9.eyJlbmlxdWVfbmFtZSI6ImFuZHJl…
```

This is handy if you're creating tokens ad hoc at the command line, but the alternative output options may be more useful for scripts. For example, running

```
dotnet user-jwts create --output token
```

outputs the token only,

```
eyJhbGciOiJIUzI1NiIsInR5cCI6IkpXVCJ9.eyJlbmlxdWVfbmFtZSI6ImFuZHJl…
```

which is much more convenient if you're trying to parse the output in a script, for example. Alternatively, you can pass --output json, which prints details about the JWT instead, as in this example:

```
{
  "Id": "8bf9b2fd",
  "Scheme": "Bearer",
  "Name": "andrewlock",
  "Audience": " https://localhost:7236, http://localhost:5229",
  "NotBefore": "2022-10-22T17:50:26+00:00",
  "Expires": "2023-01-22T17:50:26+00:00",
  "Issued": "2022-10-22T17:50:26+00:00",
  "Token": "eyJhbGciOiJIUzI1NiIsInR5cCI6IkpXVCJ9.eyJlbmlxdWVfbmFtZSI6Im…",
  "Scopes": [],
  "Roles": [],
  "CustomClaims": {}
}
```

Note that this isn't the payload of the token; it's the configuration details used to create the JWT. The token itself is exposed in the `Token` field. Again, this may be useful if you're generating JWTs using a script and need to parse the output.

25.4.3 *Managing your local JWTs*

When you're generating a JWT, the user-jwts tool automatically saves the JWT configuration (the JSON shown in section 25.4.2) to your hard drive. This is stored next to the secrets.json file that contains the User Secrets, in a location that varies depending on your operating system and the `<UserSecretsId>` in your project file:

- *Windows*—%APPDATA%\Microsoft\UserSecrets\<UserSecretsId>\user-jwts.json
- *Linux and macOS*—~/.microsoft/usersecrets/<UserSecretsId>/user-jwts.json

As for User Secrets, JWTs created by user-jwts aren't encrypted, but they're outside your project directory, so they are a better approach to managing secrets locally. The generated JWTs should be used only for local testing; you should be using a real identity provider for production systems to securely produce JWTs for a logged-in user. This is the reason why the user-jwts tool updates only appsettings.Development.json with the required configuration, not appsettings.json; it stops you from accidentally using user-jwts in production. You should add your production identity provider details in appsettings.json instead.

As well as editing the user-jwts.json file manually, you can use the user-jwts tool to manage the JWTs stored locally. In addition to using `create`, you can call `dotnet user-jwts <command>` from the project folder, where `<command>` is one of the following options:

- `list`—Lists a summary of all the tokens stored in user-jwts.json for the project.
- `clear`—Deletes all the tokens created for a project.
- `remove`—Deletes a single token for the project, using the token ID displayed by the `list` command.
- `print`—Outputs the details of a single JWT, using the token ID, as key value pairs.
- `key`—Can be used to view or reset the signing key material of tokens stored in the User Secrets Manager. Note that resetting the key material renders all previous JWTs generated by the tool invalid.

The user-jwts tool is handy for generating JWTs locally, but you must remember to add it to your local testing tool for all requests. If you're using Postman for testing, you need to add the JWT to your request, as I showed in figure 25.10. However, if you're using Swagger UI as I described in chapter 11, things aren't quite that simple. In the next section you'll learn how to describe your authorization requirements in your OpenAPI document.

25.5 Describing your authentication requirements to OpenAPI

In chapter 11 you learned how to add an OpenAPI document to your ASP.NET Core app that describes your API. This is used to power tooling such as automatic client generation, as well as Swagger UI. In this section you'll learn how to add authentication requirements to your OpenAPI document so you can test your API using Swagger UI with tokens generated by the user-jwts tool.

One of the slightly annoying things about adding authentication and authorization to your APIs is that it makes testing harder. You can't just fire a web request from a browser; you must use a tool like Postman that you can add headers to. Even for command-line aficionados, `curl` commands can become unwieldy once you need to add authorization headers. And tokens expire and are typically harder to generate. The list goes on!

I've seen these difficulties lead people to disable authentication requirements for local testing or to try to add them only late in a product's life cycle. I strongly suggest you don't do this! Trying to add real authentication late in a project is likely to cause headaches and bugs that you could easily have caught if you weren't trying to work around the security complexity.

> **TIP** Add real authentication and authorization to your APIs as soon as you understand the requirements, as you will likely catch more security-related bugs.

The user-jwts tool can help significantly with these challenges, as you can easily generate tokens in a format you need, optionally with a long expiration (so you don't need to keep renewing them) without having to wrestle with an identity provider directly. Nevertheless, you need a way to add these tokens to whichever tool you use for testing, such as Swagger UI.

Swagger UI is based on the OpenAPI definition of your API, so the best (and easiest) way to add support for authentication to Swagger UI is to update the security requirements of your application in your OpenAPI document. This consists of two steps:

- Define the security scheme your API uses, such as OAuth 2.0, OpenID Connect, or simple Bearer authentication.
- Declare which endpoints in your API use the security scheme.

The following listing shows how to configure an OpenAPI document using Swashbuckle for an API that uses JWT bearer authentication. The values defined on `OpenApiSecurityScheme` match the default settings configured by the user-jwts tool when you use `AddJwtBearer()`. `AddSecurityDefinition()` defines a security scheme for your API, and `AddSecurityRequirement()` declares that the whole API is protected using the security scheme.

Listing 25.2   Adding bearer authentication to an OpenAPI document using Swashbuckle

```
WebApplicationBuilder = WebApplication.CreateBuilder(args);

builder.Services.AddAuthentication().AddJwtBearer();
builder.Services.AddAuthorization();

builder.Services.AddEndpointsApiExplorer();
builder.Services.AddSwaggerGen(x =>
{
    x.SwaggerDoc("v1", new OpenApiInfo {
        Title = "Recipe App", Version = "v1" });

    var security = new OpenApiSecurityScheme
    {
        Name = HeaderNames.Authorization,
        Type = SecuritySchemeType.ApiKey,
        In = ParameterLocation.Header,
        Description = "JWT Authorization header",
        Reference = new OpenApiReference
        {
            Id = JwtBearerDefaults.AuthenticationScheme,
            Type = ReferenceType.SecurityScheme
        }
    };

    x.AddSecurityDefinition(security.Reference.Id, security);
    x.AddSecurityRequirement(new OpenApiSecurityRequirement
        {{security, Array.Empty<string>()}});
});

var app = builder.Build();

app.UseSwagger();
app.UseSwaggerUI();

app.UseRouting();
app.UseAuthentication();
app.UseAuthorization();

app.MapGet("/", () => "Hello world!").RequireAuthorization();
app.Run();
```

Annotations:
- Defines the security used by your API
- The type of security; may be OAuth2 or OpenIdConnect if using those (required)
- A friendly description of the scheme, used in the UI
- A unique ID for the scheme. This uses the default JWT scheme name.
- The name of the header to use (required)
- Where the token will be provided (required)
- The type of OpenID object (required)
- Marks the whole API as protected by the security definition
- Adds the security definition to the OpenAPI document

When you run your application after adding the definition to your OpenAPI document, you should see an Authorize button in the top-right corner of Swagger UI, as shown in figure 25.11. Choosing this button opens a dialog box describing your authentication scheme, including a text box to enter your token. You must enter `Bearer <token>` in this box with a space between them. Choose **Authorize**, which saves the value, and then **Close**. Now when you send a request to the API, Swagger UI attaches the token in the `Authorization` header, and the request succeeds.

If you're specifically using OpenID Connect or OAuth 2.0 to protect your APIs, you can configure these in the `OpenApiSecurityScheme` document instead of using bearer authentication. In that case, choosing Authorize in Swagger UI would redirect

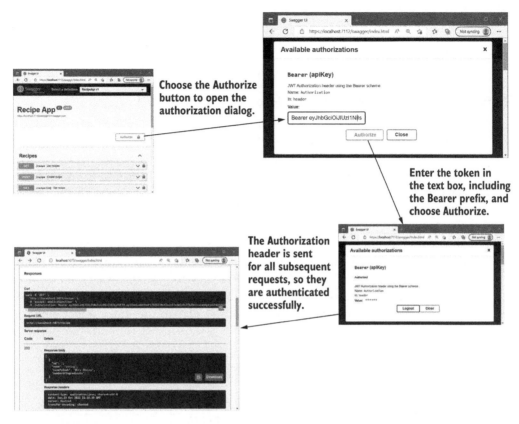

Choose the **Authorize**
button to open the
authorization dialog.

Enter the token in
the text box, including
the **Bearer** prefix, and
choose **Authorize**.

The **Authorization**
header is sent
for all subsequent
requests, so they
are authenticated
successfully.

Figure 25.11   Adding an `Authorization` **header using Swagger UI. When adding the token, ensure that you enter** `Bearer <token>`, **including the** `Bearer` **prefix. Swagger UI then attaches the token to all subsequent requests, so you are authorized to call the API.**

you to your identity provider to sign in and retrieve a token without your having to copy and paste anything. That's extremely useful if you're running an identity provider locally or exposing Swagger UI in production.

The example in listing 25.2 shows the configuration when your whole API is protected by an authorization requirement. That's the most common situation in my experience, but you may want to expose certain endpoints to anonymous users without any authorization requirements. In that case, you can configure Swashbuckle to conditionally apply the requirement to only those endpoints with a requirement.

TIP   See the Swashbuckle documentation to learn how to configure this and many other features related to OpenAPI document generation: http://mng.bz/6D1A. Swashbuckle is highly extensible, but as always, it's worth considering whether the added complexity you introduce to achieve perfect documentation of your API is worth the tradeoff. For publicly exposed OpenAPI documents, this may well be the case, but for local testing or internal APIs, the argument may be harder to make.

In this chapter we've looked in depth at using JWT bearer tokens for authentication and explored the parallels with cookie authentication for traditional apps. In the final section of this chapter we look at authorization and how you can apply different authorization policies to your minimal API endpoints.

25.6 Applying authorization policies to minimal API endpoints

So far in this chapter we've focused on authentication: the process of validating the identity of the request initiator. For APIs, this typically requires decoding and validating a JWT bearer token in the authentication middleware and setting the `Claims-Principal` for the request, as you saw in section 25.2. In this section we look at the next stage in protecting your APIs, authorization, and how you can apply different authorization requirements to your minimal API endpoints.

The good news is that authorization for minimal APIs is essentially identical to the authorization process you learned about in chapter 24 for Razor Pages and MVC controllers. The same concept of authorization policies, requirements, handlers, and claims-based authorization apply in the same way and use the exact same services. Figure 25.12 shows how this looks for a request to a minimal API endpoint protected with bearer authentication, which is remarkably similar to the Razor Pages equivalent in figure 24.2.

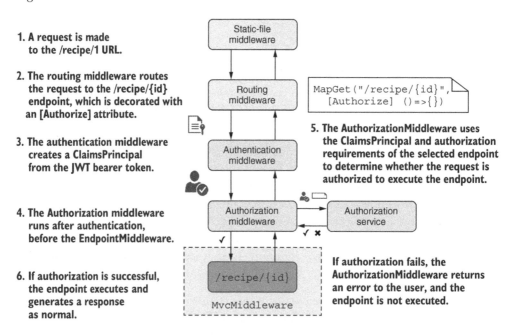

1. A request is made to the /recipe/1 URL.

2. The routing middleware routes the request to the /recipe/{id} endpoint, which is decorated with an [Authorize] attribute.

3. The authentication middleware creates a ClaimsPrincipal from the JWT bearer token.

4. The Authorization middleware runs after authentication, before the EndpointMiddleware.

6. If authorization is successful, the endpoint executes and generates a response as normal.

```
MapGet("/recipe/{id}",
    [Authorize] ()=>{})
```

5. The AuthorizationMiddleware uses the ClaimsPrincipal and authorization requirements of the selected endpoint to determine whether the request is authorized to execute the endpoint.

If authorization fails, the AuthorizationMiddleware returns an error to the user, and the endpoint is not executed.

Figure 25.12 Authorizing a request to a minimal API endpoint. The routing middleware selects an endpoint that is protected by an authorization requirement. The authentication middleware decodes and verifies the bearer token, creating a `ClaimsPrincipal`, which the authorization middleware uses along with the endpoint metadata to determine whether the request is authorized.

You've already seen that you can apply a general authorization requirement by calling `RequireAuthorization()` on an endpoint or a route group. This is directly equivalent to adding the `[Authorize]` attribute to a Razor Page or MVC controller action. In fact, you can use the same `[Authorize]` attribute on an endpoint if you wish, so the following two endpoint definitions are equivalent:

```
app.MapGet("/", () => "Hello world!").RequireAuthorization();
app.MapGet("/", [Authorize] () => "Hello world!");
```

If you want to require a specific policy (the `"CanCreate"` policy, for example), you can pass the policy name to the `RequireAuthorization()` method the same way you would for the `[Authorize]` attribute:

```
app.MapGet("/", () => "Hello world!").RequireAuthorization("CanCreate");
app.MapGet("/", [Authorize("CanCreate")] () => "Hello world!");
```

Similarly, you can exclude endpoints from authentication requirements using the `AllowAnonymous()` function or `[AllowAnonymous]` attribute:

```
app.MapGet("/", () => "Hello world!").AllowAnonymous();
app.MapGet("/", [AllowAnonymous] () => "Hello world!");
```

This is a good start, but as you saw in chapter 24, you often need to perform resource-based authorization. For example, in the context of the recipe API, users should be allowed to edit or delete only recipes that they created; they can't edit someone else's recipe. That means you need to know details about the resource (the recipe) before determining whether a request is authorized.

Resource-based authorization is essentially the same for minimal API endpoints as for Razor Pages or MVC controllers. You must follow several steps, most of which we covered in chapter 24:

1 Create an `AuthorizationHandler<TRequirement, TResource>`, and register it in the DI container, as shown in chapter 24.
2 Inject the `IAuthorizationService` into your endpoint handler.
3 Call `IAuthorizationService.AuthorizeAsync(user, resource, policy)`, passing in the `ClaimsPrincipal` for the request, the resource to authorize access to, and the policy to apply.

The first step is identical to the process shown in chapter 24, so you can reuse the same authorization handlers whether you're using Razor Pages, minimal APIs, or both! You can access the `IAuthorizationService` from a minimal API endpoint using standard dependency injection (DI), which you learned about in chapters 8 and 9.

Listing 25.3 shows an example minimal API endpoint that uses resource-based authorization to protect the "delete" action for a recipe. The `IAuthorizationService` and `HttpContext.User` property are injected into the handler method along with the

RecipeService. The endpoint then retrieves the recipe and calls AuthorizeAsync() to determine whether to continue with the delete or return a 403 Forbidden response.

Listing 25.3   Using resource authorization to protect a minimal API endpoint

```
app.MapDelete("recipe/{id}", async (          Injected to perform resource-based authorization
    int id, RecipeService service,
    IAuthorizationService authService,  ◁───   The HttpContext.User claims
    ClaimsPrincipal user) =>          ◁───     principal for the request
{
                                               Fetches the recipe to access
    var recipe = await service.GetRecipe(id);◁──┘
    var result = await authService.AuthorizeAsync(
        user, recipe, "CanManageRecipe");       Performs resource-based
                                                authorization, passing in the user,
                                                resource, and the policy name
    if (!result.Succeeded)
    {                               If authorization
        return Results.Forbid();    failed, returns
    }                               403 Forbidden

    await service.DeleteRecipe(id);   If authorization succeeded,
    return Results.NoContent();       executes the endpoint as normal
});
```

As is common when you start adding functionality, the logic at the heart of the endpoint has become a bit muddled as the endpoint has grown. There are several possible approaches you could take now:

- *Do nothing.* The logic isn't *that* confusing, and this is only one endpoint. This may be a good approach initially but can become problematic if the logic is duplicated across multiple endpoints.

- *Pull the authorization out into a filter.* As you saw in chapters 5 and 7, endpoint filters can be useful for extracting common cross-cutting concerns, such as validation and authorization. You may find that endpoint filters help reduce the duplication in your endpoint handlers, though this often comes at the expense of additional complexity in the filter itself, as well as a layer of indirection in your handlers. You can see this approach in the source code accompanying this chapter.

- *Push the authorization responsibilities down into the domain.* Instead of performing the resource-based authorization in your endpoint handlers, you could run the checks inside the domain instead, in the RecipeService in this case. This has advantages, in that it often reduces duplication, keeps your endpoints simpler, and ensures that authorization checks are always applied regardless of how you call the domain methods.

  The downside to this approach is that it may cause your domain/application model to depend directly on ASP.NET Core-specific constructs such as IAuthorizationService. You can work around this by creating a wrapper façade around the IAuthorizationService, but this may also add some complexity. Even if you take this approach, you typically want to apply declarative authorization policies to your endpoints as well to ensure that the endpoint executes only for users who could possibly be authorized.

There's no single best answer on which approach to take; it will vary depending on what works best for your application. Authentication and authorization are inevitably tricky subjects, so it's important to consider them early and design your application with security in mind.

Scope-based authorization policies

In section 25.2 I described the role of scopes in the authentication process. When you obtain a bearer token from an identity provider—whether you're using OpenID Connect or OAuth 2.0—you define the scopes that you wish to retrieve. The user can then choose to grant or deny some or all of those requested scopes. Additionally, the identity provider might allow certain client applications access only to specific scopes. The final access token you receive from the identity provider, which is sent to the API, may have some or *none* of the requested scopes.

It's up to the API itself to decide what each scope means and how it should be used to enforce authorization policies. Scopes have no inherent functionality on their own, much like claims, but you can build functionality on top. For example, you can create authorization polices that require a token has the scope `"recipe.edit"` using

```
builder.Services.AddAuthorizationBuilder()
    .AddPolicy("RecipeEditScope", policy =>
        policy.RequireClaim("scope", " recipe.edit "));
```

This policy could then be applied to any endpoints that edit a recipe.

Another common pattern is to require a specific scope for you to be authorized to make *any* requests to a given ASP.NET Core app, such as a `"receipeApi"` scope. This approach can often replace audience validation in bearer token authorization and may be more flexible, as it doesn't require your identity provider to know the domain at which your API app will be hosted.

Alternatively, you can use scopes to partition your APIs into groups that can only be accessed by certain types of clients. For example, you might have one set of APIs that can be accessed only by internal machine-to-machine clients, another set that can be accessed only by admin users, and another set that can be accessed only by nonadmin users.

Duende has many practical examples of approaches to authorization and authentication using OpenID Connect at http://mng.bz/o1Jp. The examples are geared to IdentityServer users but show many best practices and patterns you can use with identity provider services as well.

That brings us to the end of this chapter on authentication and authorization. We're not completely done with security, though; in chapter 27 we look at potential security threats and how to mitigate them. But first, in chapter 26 you'll learn about the logging abstractions in ASP.NET Core and how you can use them to keep tabs on exactly what your app's up to.

Summary

- In large systems with multiple applications or APIs, you can use an identity provider to centralize authentication and user management. This often reduces the authentication responsibilities of apps, reducing duplication and making it easier to add new user management features.

- You should strongly consider using a third-party identity provider service instead of building your own. User management is rarely core to your business, and by delegating responsibility to a third-party you can leave protecting your most vulnerable assets to the experts.

- If you do need to build your own identity provider, you can use the IdentityServer or OpenIddict library. These libraries implement the OpenID Connect protocol, adding token generation to a standard ASP.NET Core application. You must build the user management and UI components yourself.

- OAuth 2.0 is an authorization protocol that allows a user to delegate authorization for accessing a resource to another application. This standard allows applications to interoperate without compromising on security.

- OAuth 2.0 has multiple grant types representing common authorization flows. The authorization code flow with PKCE is the most common interactive grant type when a user initiates an interaction. For machine-only workflows, such as an API calling another API, you can use the client credentials grant type.

- OpenID Connect is built on top of OAuth 2.0. It adds conventions, discoverability, and authentication to OAuth 2.0, making it easier to interact with third-party providers and retrieve identity information about a user.

- JWTs are the most common bearer token format. They consist of a header, a payload, and a signature, and are base64-encoded. When receiving a JWT you must always verify the signature to ensure that it hasn't been tampered with.

- JWTs are not encrypted, so anyone can read them by default. JWE is a standard that wraps the JWT and encrypts it, protecting the contents. Many identity providers support generating JWEs, and ASP.NET Core supports decoding JWEs automatically.

- Bearer token authentication in ASP.NET Core is similar to cookie authentication with traditional web apps. The authentication middleware deserializes the token and validates it. If the token is valid, the middleware creates a `ClaimsPrincipal` and sets `HttpContext.User`.

- Configure JWT bearer authentication by adding the Microsoft.AspNetCore.Authentication.JwtBearer NuGet Package and calling `AddAuthentication()` `.AddJwtBearer()` to add the required services to your app.

- To generate a JWT for local testing, run `dotnet user-jwts create`. This configures your API to support JWTs created by the tool and prints a token to the terminal, which you can use for local testing of your API. Add the token to requests in the `Authorization` header, using the format `"Bearer <token>"`.

- Pass additional options to the `dotnet user-jwts create` command to customize the generated JWT. Add extra claims to the generated JWT using the `--claim` option, change the `sub` claim name using `--name`, or add `scope` claims to the JWT using `--scope`.

- To enable authorization in Swagger UI, you should add a security scheme to your OpenAPI document. Create an `OpenApiSecurityScheme` object, and register it with the OpenAPI document by calling `AddSecurityDefinition()`. Apply it to all the APIs in your app by calling `AddSecurityRequirement()`, passing in the scheme object.

- To add authorization to minimal API endpoints, call `RequireAuthorization()` or add the `[Authorize]` attribute to your endpoint handler. This optionally takes the name of an authorization policy to apply, n the same way as you would apply policies to Razor Pages and MVC controllers. You can call `RequireAuthorization()` on route groups to apply authorization to multiple APIs at the same time.

- Override an authorization requirement on an endpoint by calling `AllowAnonymous()` or by adding the `[AllowAnonymous]` attribute to an endpoint handler. This removes any authentication requirements from the endpoint, so users can call the endpoint without a bearer token in the request.

Monitoring and troubleshooting errors with logging

This chapter covers

- Understanding the components of a log message
- Writing logs to multiple output locations
- Controlling log verbosity in different environments using filtering
- Using structured logging to make logs searchable

Logging is one of those topics that seems unnecessary, right up until you desperately need it! There's nothing more frustrating than finding a problem that you can reproduce only in production and then discovering there are no logs to help you debug it.

Logging is the process of recording events or activities in an app, and it often involves writing a record to a console, a file, the Windows Event Log, or some other system. You can record anything in a log message, though there are generally two different types of messages:

- *Informational messages*—A standard event occurred: a user logged in, a product was placed in a shopping cart, or a new post was created on a blogging app.
- *Warnings and errors*—An error or unexpected condition occurred: a user had a negative total in the shopping cart, or an exception occurred.

Historically, a common problem with logging in larger applications was that each library and framework would generate logs in a slightly different format, if at all. When an error occurred in your app and you were trying to diagnose it, this inconsistency made it harder to connect the dots in your app to get the full picture and understand the problem.

Luckily, ASP.NET Core includes a new generic logging interface that you can plug into. It's used throughout the ASP.NET Core framework code itself, as well as by third-party libraries, and you can easily use it to create logs in your own code. With the ASP.NET Core logging framework, you can control the verbosity of logs coming from each part of your code, including the framework and libraries, and you can write the log output to any destination that plugs into the framework.

In this chapter I cover the .NET logging framework ASP.NET Core uses in detail, and I explain how you can use it to record events and diagnose errors in your own apps. In section 26.1 I'll describe the architecture of the logging framework. You'll learn how dependency injection (DI) makes it easy for both libraries and apps to create log messages, as well as to write those logs to multiple destinations.

In section 26.2 you'll learn how to write your own log messages in your apps with the ILogger interface. We'll break down the anatomy of a typical log record and look at its properties, such as the log level, category, and message.

Writing logs is useful only if you can read them, so in section 26.3 you'll learn how to add logging providers to your application. *Logging providers* control where your app writes your log messages, such as to the console, to a file, or even to an external service.

Logging is an important part of any application, but determining how much logging is enough can be a tricky question. On one hand, you want to provide sufficient information to be able to diagnose any problems. On the other hand, you don't want to fill your logs with data that makes it hard to find the important information when you need it. Even worse, what is sufficient in development might be far too much once you're running in production.

In section 26.4 I'll explain how you can filter log messages from various sections of your app, such as the ASP.NET Core infrastructure libraries, so that your logging providers write only the important messages. This lets you keep that balance between extensive logging in development and writing only important logs in production.

In the final section of this chapter I'll touch on some of the benefits of structured logging, an approach to logging that you can use with some providers for the ASP.NET Core logging framework. *Structured logging* involves attaching data to log messages as key-value pairs to make it easier to search and query logs. You might attach a unique customer ID to every log message generated by your app, for example. Finding all the log messages associated with a user is much simpler with this approach, compared with recording the customer ID in an inconsistent manner as part of the log message.

We'll start this chapter by digging into what logging involves and why your future self will thank you for using logging effectively in your application. Then we'll look at the pieces of the ASP.NET Core logging framework you'll use directly in your apps and how they fit together.

26.1 Using logging effectively in a production app

Imagine you've just deployed a new app to production when a customer calls saying that they're getting an error message using your app. How would you identify what caused the problem? You could ask the customer what steps they were taking and potentially try to re-create the error yourself, but if that doesn't work, you're left trawling through the code, trying to spot errors with nothing else to go on.

Logging can provide the extra context you need to quickly diagnose a problem. Arguably, the most important logs capture the details about the error itself, but the events that led to the error can be equally useful in diagnosing the cause of an error.

There are many reasons for adding logging to an application, but typically, the reasons fall into one of three categories:

- Logging for auditing or analytics reasons, to trace when events have occurred
- Logging errors
- Logging nonerror events to provide a breadcrumb trail of events when an error does occur

The first of these reasons is simple. You may be required to keep a record of every time a user logs in, for example, or you may want to keep track of how many times a particular API method is called. Logging is an easy way to record the behavior of your app by writing a message to the log every time an interesting event occurs.

I find the second and third reasons for logging to be the most common. When an app is working perfectly, logs often go completely untouched. It's when there's a problem and a customer comes calling that logs become invaluable. A good set of logs can help you understand the conditions in your app that caused an error, including the context of the error itself, but also the context in previous requests.

> **TIP** Even with extensive logging in place, you may not realize you have a problem in your app unless you look through your logs regularly. For any medium-size to large app, this becomes impractical, so monitoring services such as Sentry (https://sentry.io) or Datadog (https://www.datadoghq.com) can be invaluable for notifying you of problems quickly.

If this sounds like a lot of work, you're in luck. ASP.NET Core does a ton of the "breadcrumb logging" for you so that you can focus on creating high-quality log messages that provide the most value when diagnosing problems.

26.1.1 *Highlighting problems using custom log messages*

ASP.NET Core uses logging throughout its libraries. Depending on how you configure your app, you'll have access to the details of each request and EF Core query, even without adding logging messages to your own code. In figure 26.1 you can see the log messages created when you view a single recipe in the recipe application.

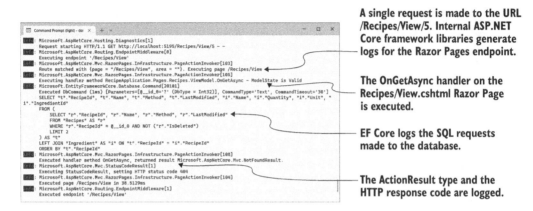

A single request is made to the URL /Recipes/View/5. Internal ASP.NET Core framework libraries generate logs for the Razor Pages endpoint.

The OnGetAsync handler on the Recipes/View.cshtml Razor Page is executed.

EF Core logs the SQL requests made to the database.

The ActionResult type and the HTTP response code are logged.

Figure 26.1   The ASP.NET Core Framework libraries use logging throughout. A single request generates multiple log messages that describe the flow of the request through your application.

This gives you a lot of useful information. You can see which URL was requested, the Razor Page and page handler that were invoked (for a Razor Pages app), the Entity Framework Core (EF Core)database command, the action result executed, and the response. This information can be invaluable when you're trying to isolate a problem, whether it's a bug in a production app or a feature in development when you're working locally.

This infrastructure logging can be useful, but log messages that you create yourself can have even greater value. For example, you may be able to spot the cause of the error from the log messages in figure 26.1; we're attempting to view a recipe with an unknown RecipeId of 5, but it's far from obvious. If you explicitly add a log message to your app when this happens, as in figure 26.2, the problem is much more apparent.

This custom log message easily stands out and clearly states both the problem (the recipe with the requested ID doesn't exist) and the parameters/variables that led to it (the ID value of 5). Adding similar log messages to your own applications will make it easier for you to diagnose problems, track important events, and generally know what your app is doing.

I hope you're now motivated to add logging to your apps, so we'll dig into the details of what that involves. In section 26.1.2 you'll see how to create a log message and how to define where the log messages are written. We'll look in detail at these two aspects in sections 26.2 and 26.3; first, though, we'll look at where they fit in terms of the ASP.NET Core logging framework as a whole.

You can write your own logs from your app's classes, like this log from the View.cshtml Razor Page's PageModel. These are often more useful for diagnosing problems and tracing the behavior of your app.

Figure 26.2   You can write your own logs. These are often more useful for identifying problems and interesting events in your apps.

26.1.2 The ASP.NET Core logging abstractions

The ASP.NET Core logging framework consists of several abstractions (interfaces, implementations, and helper classes), the most important of which are shown in figure 26.3:

- `ILogger`—This is the interface you'll interact with in your code. It has a `Log()` method, which is used to write a log message.

- `ILoggerProvider`—This is used to create a custom instance of an `ILogger`, depending on the provider. A console `ILoggerProvider` would create an `ILogger` that writes to the console, whereas a file `ILoggerProvider` would create an `ILogger` that writes to a file.

- `ILoggerFactory`—This is the glue between the `ILoggerProvider` instances and the `ILogger` you use in your code. You register `ILoggerProvider` instances with an `ILoggerFactory` and call `CreateLogger()` on the `ILoggerFactory` when you need an `ILogger`. The factory creates an `ILogger` that wraps each of the providers, so when you call the `Log()` method, the log is written to every provider.

The design in figure 26.3 makes it easy to add or change where your application writes the log messages without having to change your application code. The following listing shows all the code required to add an `ILoggerProvider` that writes logs to the console.

Listing 26.1   Adding a console log provider in Program.cs

```
WebApplicationBuilder builder = WebApplication.CreateBuilder(args);
builder.Logging.AddConsole()          ◁─────┐
                                            │  Adds a new provider using the Logging
WebApplication app = builder.Build();       │  property on WebApplicationBuilder

app.MapGet("/", () => "Hello World!");

app.Run();
```

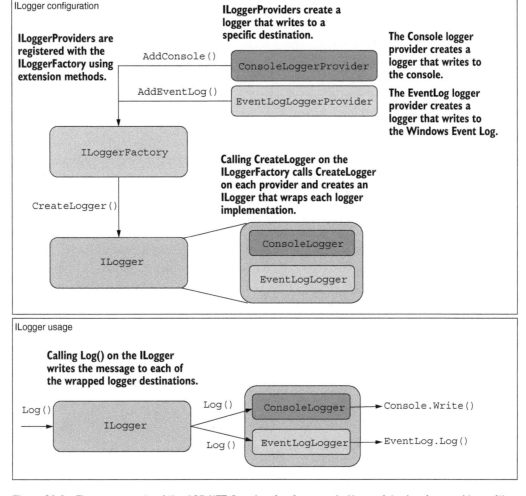

Figure 26.3 The components of the ASP.NET Core logging framework. You register logging providers with an `ILoggerFactory`, which creates implementations of `ILogger`. You write logs to the `ILogger`, which delegates to the `ILogger` implementations that write logs to the console or a file. You can send logs to multiple locations with this design without having to configure the locations when you create a log message.

NOTE The console logger is added by default by `WebApplicationBuilder`, as you'll see in section 26.3.

Other than this configuration on `WebApplicationBuilder`, you don't interact with `ILoggerProvider` instances directly. Instead, you write logs using an instance of `ILogger`, as you'll see in the next section.

26.2 *Adding log messages to your application*

In this section we'll look in detail at how to create log messages in your own application. You'll learn how to create an instance of ILogger, and how to use it to add logging to an existing application. Finally, we'll look at the properties that make up a logging record, what they mean, and what you can use them for.

Logging, like almost everything in ASP.NET Core, is available through DI. To add logging to your own services, you need only inject an instance of ILogger<T>, where T is the type of your service.

> **NOTE**   When you inject ILogger<T>, the DI container indirectly calls ILogger-Factory.CreateLogger<T>() to create the wrapped ILogger of figure 26.3. In section 26.2.2 you'll see how to work directly with ILoggerFactory if you prefer. The ILogger<T> interface also implements the nongeneric ILogger interface but includes additional convenience methods.

You can use the injected ILogger instance to create log messages, which it writes to each configured ILoggerProvider. The following listing shows how to inject an ILogger<> instance into the PageModel of the Index.cshtml Razor Page for the recipe application from previous chapters and how to write a log message indicating how many recipes were found.

Listing 26.2   Injecting `ILogger` into a class and writing a log message

```
public class IndexModel : PageModel
{
    private readonly RecipeService _service;
    private readonly ILogger<IndexModel> _log;

    public ICollection<RecipeSummaryViewModel> Recipes { get; set; }

    public IndexModel(
        RecipeService service,
        ILogger<IndexModel> log)
    {
        _service = service;
        _log = log;
    }

    public void OnGet()
    {
        Recipes = _service.GetRecipes();
        _log.LogInformation(
            "Loaded {RecipeCount} recipes", Recipes.Count);
    }
}
```

Injects the generic ILogger<T> using DI, which implements ILogger → (points to `private readonly ILogger<IndexModel> _log;`, `ILogger<IndexModel> log)`, and `_log = log;`)

Writes an Information-level log. The RecipeCount variable is substituted in the message. (points to the `_log.LogInformation(...)` block)

In this example you're using one of the many extension methods on ILogger to create the log message, LogInformation(). There are many extension methods on ILogger that let you easily specify a LogLevel for the message.

DEFINITION The *log level* of a log is how important it is and is defined by the LogLevel enum. Every log message has a log level.

You can also see that the message you pass to the LogInformation method has a placeholder indicated by braces, {RecipeCount}, and you pass an additional parameter, Recipes .Count, to the logger. The logger replaces the placeholder with the parameter at runtime. Placeholders are matched with parameters by position, so if you include two placeholders, for example, the second placeholder is matched with the second parameter.

TIP You could have used normal string interpolation to create the log message, as in $"Loaded {Recipes.Count} recipes". But I recommend always using placeholders, as they provide additional information for the logger that can be used for structured logging, as you'll see in section 26.5.

When the OnGet page handler in the IndexModel executes, ILogger writes a message to any configured logging providers. The exact format of the log message varies from provider to provider, but figure 26.4 shows how the console provider displays the log message from listing 26.2.

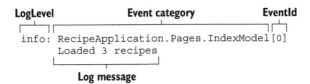

Figure 26.4 An example log message as it's written to the default console provider. The log-level category provides information about how important the message is and where it was generated. The EventId provides a way to identify similar log messages.

The exact presentation of the message will vary depending on where the log is written, but each log record includes up to six common elements:

- *Log level*—The log level of the log is how important it is and is defined by the LogLevel enum.
- *Event category*—The category may be any string value, but it's typically set to the name of the class creating the log. For ILogger<T>, the full name of the type T is the category.
- *Message*—This is the content of the log message. It can be a static string, or it can contain placeholders for variables, as shown in listing 26.2. Placeholders are indicated by braces, {} and are replaced by the provided parameter values.
- *Parameters*—If the message contains placeholders, they're associated with the provided parameters. For the example in listing 26.2, the value of Recipes.Count is assigned to the placeholder called RecipeCount. Some loggers can extract these values and expose them in your logs, as you'll see in section 26.5.

- *Exception*—If an exception occurs, you can pass the exception object to the logging function along with the message and other parameters. The logger records the exception in addition to the message itself.
- *EventId*—This is an optional integer identifier for the error, which can be used to quickly find all similar logs in a series of log messages. You might use an Event-Id of 1000 when a user attempts to load a non-existent recipe and an EventId of 1001 when a user attempts to access a recipe they don't have permission to access. If you don't provide an EventId, the value 0 is used.

High-performance logging with source generators

Source generators are a compiler feature introduced in C# 9. Using this feature, you can automatically generate boilerplate code when your project compiles. .NET 7 includes several built-in source generators, such as the Regex generator I described in chapter 14. There's also a source generator that works with ILogger, which can help you avoid pitfalls such as accidentally using interpolated strings, and makes more advanced and performant logging patterns easy to use.

To use the logging source generator in the OnGet handler from listing 26.2, define a *partial method* in the IndexModel class, decorate it with a [LoggerMessage] attribute, and invoke the method inside the OnGet handler method:

```
[LoggerMessage(10, LogLevel.Information, "Loaded {RecipeCount} recipes")]
partial void LogLoadedRecipes(int recipeCount);

public void OnGet()
{
    Recipes = _service.GetRecipes();
    LogLoadedRecipes(Recipes.Count);
}
```

The [LoggerMessage] attribute defines the event ID, log level, and message the log message uses, and the parameters of the partial method it decorates are substituted into the message at runtime. This pattern also comes with several analyzers to make sure you use it correctly in your code while optimizing the generated code behind the scenes to prevent allocations where possible.

The logging source generator is optional, so it's up to you whether to use it. You can read more about the source generator, the extra configuration options, and how it works on my blog at http://mng.bz/vn14 and in the documentation at http://mng.bz/4D1j.

Not every log message will have all the possible elements. You won't always have an Exception or parameters, for example, and it's common to omit the EventId. There are various overloads to the logging methods that take these elements as additional method parameters. Besides these optional elements, each message has, at very least, a level, category, and message. These are the key features of the log, so we'll look at each in turn.

26.2.1 Log level: How important is the log message?

Whenever you create a log using ILogger, you must specify the *log level*. This indicates how serious or important the log message is, and it's an important factor when it comes to filtering which logs are written by a provider, as well as finding the important log messages after the fact.

You might create an Information level log when a user starts to edit a recipe. This is useful for tracing the application's flow and behavior, but it's not important, because everything is normal. But if an exception is thrown when the user attempts to save the recipe, you might create a Warning or Error level log.

The log level is typically set by using one of several extension methods on the ILogger interface, as shown in listing 26.3. This example creates an Information level log when the View method executes and a Warning level error if the requested recipe isn't found.

Listing 26.3 Specifying the log level using extension methods on ILogger

```
private readonly ILogger _log;          ◁──────────   An ILogger instance is injected into the
public async IActionResult OnGet(int id)             Razor Page using constructor injection.
{
    _log.LogInformation(
        "Loading recipe with id {RecipeId}", id);    ⌐ Writes an Information
                                                       ⌐ level log message
    Recipe = _service.GetRecipeDetail(id);
    if (Recipe is null)
    {
        _log.LogWarning(
            "Could not find recipe with id {RecipeId}", id);
        return NotFound();
    }
    return Page();
}
```

Writes a Warning level log message ⊢ (annotation for the `if (Recipe is null)` block and `_log.LogWarning` call)

The LogInformation and LogWarning extension methods create log messages with a log level of Information and Warning, respectively. There are six log levels to choose among, ordered here from most to least serious:

- Critical—For disastrous failures that may leave the app unable to function correctly, such as out-of-memory exceptions or if the hard drive is out of disk space or the server is on fire.
- Error—For errors and exceptions that you can't handle gracefully, such as exceptions thrown when saving an edited entity in EF Core. The operation failed, but the app can continue to function for other requests and users.
- Warning—For when an unexpected or error condition arises that you can work around. You might log a Warning for handled exceptions or when an entity isn't found, as in listing 26.3.

- Information—For tracking normal application flow, such as logging when a user signs in or when they view a specific page in your app. Typically these log messages provide context when you need to understand the steps leading up to an error message.
- Debug—For tracking detailed information that's particularly useful during development. Generally, this level has only short-term usefulness.
- Trace—For tracking extremely detailed information, which may contain sensitive information like passwords or keys. It's rarely used and not used at all by the framework libraries.

Think of these log levels in terms of a pyramid, as shown in figure 26.5. As you progress down the log levels, the importance of the messages goes down, but the frequency goes up. Typically, you'll find many Debug level log messages in your application, but (I hope) few Critical- or Error-level messages.

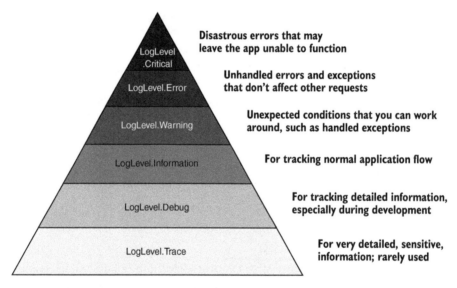

Figure 26.5   The pyramid of log levels. Logs with a level near the base of the pyramid are used more frequently but are less important. Logs with a level near the top should be rare but are important.

This pyramid shape will become more meaningful when we look at filtering in section 26.4. When an app is in production, you typically don't want to record all the Debug-level messages generated by your application. The sheer volume of messages would be overwhelming to sort through and could end up filling your disk with messages that say "Everything's OK!" Additionally, Trace messages shouldn't be enabled in production, as they may leak sensitive data. By filtering out the lower log levels, you can ensure that you generate a sane number of logs in production but have access to all the log levels in development.

In general, higher-level logs are more important than lower-level logs, so a `Warning` log is more important than an `Information` log, but there's another aspect to consider. Where the log came from, or who created the log, is a key piece of information that's recorded with each log message and is called the *category*.

26.2.2 Log category: Which component created the log?

As well as a log level, every log message also has a category. You set the log level independently for every log message, but the category is set when you create the `ILogger` instance. Like log levels, the category is particularly useful for filtering, as you'll see in section 26.4. It's written to every log message, as shown in figure 26.6.

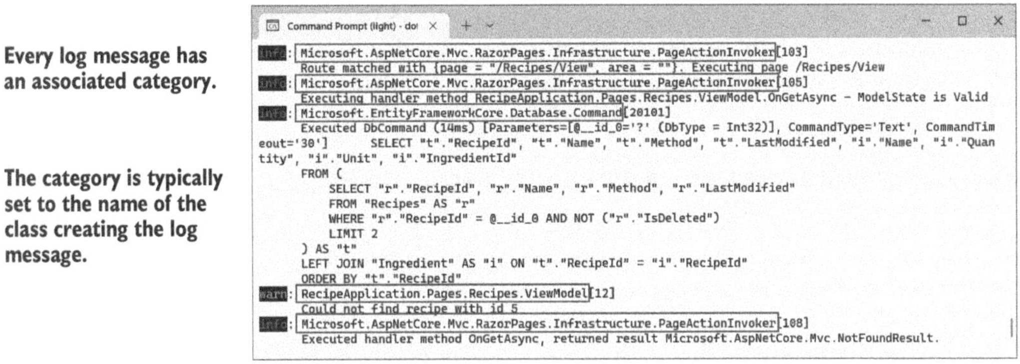

Every log message has an associated category.

The category is typically set to the name of the class creating the log message.

```
Command Prompt (light) - dot   +

info: Microsoft.AspNetCore.Mvc.RazorPages.Infrastructure.PageActionInvoker[103]
      Route matched with {page = "/Recipes/View", area = ""}. Executing page /Recipes/View
info: Microsoft.AspNetCore.Mvc.RazorPages.Infrastructure.PageActionInvoker[105]
      Executing handler method RecipeApplication.Pages.Recipes.ViewModel.OnGetAsync - ModelState is Valid
info: Microsoft.EntityFrameworkCore.Database.Command[20101]
      Executed DbCommand (14ms) [Parameters=[@__id_0='?' (DbType = Int32)], CommandType='Text', CommandTim
      eout='30']      SELECT "t"."RecipeId", "t"."Name", "t"."Method", "t"."LastModified", "i"."Name", "i"."Quan
      tity", "i"."Unit", "i"."IngredientId"
      FROM (
          SELECT "r"."RecipeId", "r"."Name", "r"."Method", "r"."LastModified"
          FROM "Recipes" AS "r"
          WHERE "r"."RecipeId" = @__id_0 AND NOT ("r"."IsDeleted")
          LIMIT 2
      ) AS "t"
      LEFT JOIN "Ingredient" AS "i" ON "t"."RecipeId" = "i"."RecipeId"
      ORDER BY "t"."RecipeId"
warn: RecipeApplication.Pages.Recipes.ViewModel[12]
      Could not find recipe with id 5
info: Microsoft.AspNetCore.Mvc.RazorPages.Infrastructure.PageActionInvoker[108]
      Executed handler method OnGetAsync, returned result Microsoft.AspNetCore.Mvc.NotFoundResult.
```

Figure 26.6 Every log message has an associated category, which is typically the class name of the component creating the log. The default console logging provider outputs the log category for every log.

The category is a `string`, so you can set it to anything, but the convention is to set it to the fully qualified name of the type that's using `ILogger`. In section 26.2 I achieved this by injecting `ILogger<T>` into `RecipeController`; the generic parameter `T` is used to set the category of the `ILogger`.

Alternatively, you can inject `ILoggerFactory` into your methods and pass an explicit category when creating an `ILogger` instance, as shown in the following listing. This lets you change the category to an arbitrary string.

Listing 26.4 Injecting `ILoggerFactory` to use a custom category

```
public class RecipeService
{
    private readonly ILogger _log;
    public RecipeService(ILoggerFactory factory)      ⟵┐ Injects an ILoggerFactory
    {                                                       instead of an ILogger directly
        _log = factory.CreateLogger("RecipeApp.RecipeService");   ⟵─
    }                                                           Passes a category as a string
}                                                               when calling CreateLogger
```

There is also an overload of `CreateLogger()` with a generic parameter that uses the provided class to set the category. If the `RecipeService` in listing 26.4 were in the `RecipeApp` namespace, the `CreateLogger` call could be written equivalently as

```
_log = factory.CreateLogger<RecipeService>();
```

Similarly, the final `ILogger` instance created by this call would be the same as if you'd directly injected `ILogger<RecipeService>` instead of `ILoggerFactory`.

> **TIP** Unless you're using heavily customized categories for some reason, favor injecting `ILogger<T>` into your methods over `ILoggerFactory`.

The final compulsory part of every log entry is fairly obvious: the *log message*. At the simplest level, this can be any string, but it's worth thinking carefully about what information would be useful to record—anything that will help you diagnose problems later on.

26.2.3 *Formatting messages and capturing parameter values*

Whenever you create a log entry, you must provide a message. This can be any string you like, but as you saw in listing 26.2, you can also include placeholders indicated by braces, {}, in the message string:

```
_log.LogInformation("Loaded {RecipeCount} recipes", Recipes.Count);
```

Including a placeholder and a parameter value in your log message effectively creates a key-value pair, which some logging providers can store as additional information associated with the log. The previous log message would assign the value of `Recipes.Count` to a key, `RecipeCount`, and the log message itself is generated by replacing the placeholder with the parameter value, to give the following (where `Recipes.Count=3`):

```
"Loaded 3 recipes"
```

You can include multiple placeholders in a log message, and they're associated with the additional parameters passed to the log method. The order of the placeholders in the format string must match the order of the parameters you provide.

> **WARNING** You must pass at least as many parameters to the log method as there are placeholders in the message. If you don't pass enough parameters, you'll get an exception at runtime.

For example, the log message

```
_log.LogInformation("User {UserId} loaded recipe {RecipeId}", 123, 456)
```

would create the parameters `UserId=123` and `RecipeId=456`. *Structured logging* providers could store these values, in addition to the formatted log message `"User 123 loaded recipe 456"`. This makes it easier to search the logs for a particular `UserId` or `RecipeId`.

> **DEFINITION**   *Structured or semantic logging* attaches additional structure to log messages to make them more easily searchable and filterable. Rather than storing only text, it stores additional contextual information, typically as key-value pairs. JavaScript Object Notation (JSON) is a common format used for structured log messages.

Not all logging providers use semantic logging. The default console logging provider format doesn't, for example; the message is formatted to replace the placeholders, but there's no way of searching the console by key-value.

> **TIP**   You can enable JSON output for the console provider by calling `WebApplicationBuilder.Logging.AddJsonConsole()`. You can further customize the format of the provider, as described in the documentation at http://mng.bz/QP8v.

Even if you're not using structured logging initially, I recommend writing your log messages as though you are, with explicit placeholders and parameters. That way, if you decide to add a structured logging provider later, you'll immediately see the benefits. Additionally, I find that thinking about the parameters that you can log in this way prompts you to record more parameter values instead of only a log message. There's nothing more frustrating than seeing a message like `"Cannot insert record due to duplicate key"` but not having the key value logged!

> **TIP**   Generally speaking, I'm a fan of C#'s interpolated strings, but don't use them for your log messages when a placeholder and parameter would also make sense. Using placeholders instead of interpolated strings gives you the same output message but also creates key-value pairs that can be searched later.

We've looked a lot at how you can create log messages in your app, but we haven't focused on where those logs are written. In the next section we'll look at the built-in ASP.NET Core logging providers, how they're configured, and how you can add a third-party provider.

26.3   Controlling where logs are written using logging providers

In this section you'll learn how to control where your log messages are written by adding `ILoggerProvider`s to your application. As an example, you'll see how to add a simple file logger provider that writes your log messages to a file, in addition to the existing console logger provider.

Up to this point, we've been writing all our log messages to the console. If you've run any ASP.NET Core sample apps locally, you'll probably have seen the log messages written to the console window.

NOTE If you're using Visual Studio and debugging by using the *Internet Information* Services (IIS) Express option, you won't see the console window (though the log messages are written to the Debug Output window instead).

Writing log messages to the console is great when you're debugging, but it's not much use for production. No one's going to be monitoring a console window on a server, and the logs wouldn't be saved anywhere or be searchable. Clearly, you'll need to write your production logs somewhere else.

As you saw in section 26.1, *logging providers* control the destination of your log messages in ASP.NET Core. They take the messages you create using the `ILogger` interface and write them to an output location, which varies depending on the provider.

NOTE This name always gets to me: the log provider effectively consumes the log messages you create and outputs them to a destination. You can probably see the origin of the name from figure 26.3, but I still find it somewhat counterintuitive.

Microsoft has written several first-party log providers for ASP.NET Core that are available out of the box in ASP.NET Core. These providers include

- *Console provider*—Writes messages to the console, as you've already seen
- *Debug provider*—Writes messages to the debug window when you're debugging an app in Visual Studio or Visual Studio Code, for example
- *EventLog provider*—Writes messages to the Windows Event Log and outputs log messages only when running in Windows, as it requires Windows-specific APIs
- *EventSource provider*—Writes messages using Event Tracing for Windows (ETW) or LTTng tracing on Linux

There are also many third-party logging provider implementations, such as an Azure App Service provider, an elmah.io provider, and an Elasticsearch provider. On top of that, there are integrations with other existing logging frameworks like NLog and Serilog. It's always worth looking to see whether your favorite .NET logging library or service has a provider for ASP.NET Core, as most do.

TIP Serilog (https://serilog.net) is my go-to logging framework. It's a mature framework with a huge number of supported destinations for writing logs. See Serilog's ASP.NET Core integration repository for details on how to use Serilog with ASP.NET Core apps: https://github.com/serilog/serilog-aspnetcore.

You configure the logging providers for your app in Program.cs. `WebApplication-Builder` configures the console and debug providers for your application automatically, but it's likely that you'll want to change or add to these.

In this section I show how to add a simple third-party logging provider that writes to a rolling file so our application writes logs to a new file each day. We'll continue to log using the console and debug providers as well, because they're more useful than the file provider when developing locally.

To add a third-party logging provider in ASP.NET Core, follow these steps:

1 Add the logging provider NuGet package to the solution. I'm going to be using a provider called NetEscapades.Extensions.Logging.RollingFile, which is available on NuGet and GitHub. You can add it to your solution using the NuGet Package Manager in Visual Studio or using the .NET command-line interface (CLI) by running

```
dotnet add package NetEscapades.Extensions.Logging.RollingFile
```

from your application's project folder.

NOTE This package is a simple file logging provider, available at http://mng .bz/XN5a. It's based on the Azure App Service logging provider. If you need a more robust package, consider using Serilog's file providers instead.

2 Add the logging provider to `WebApplicationBuilder.Logging`. You can add the file provider by calling `AddFile()`, as shown in the next listing. `AddFile()` is an extension method provided by the logging provider package to simplify adding the provider to your app.

> **Listing 26.5 Adding a third-party logging provider to `WebApplicationBuilder`**

```
WebApplicationBuilder builder = WebApplication.CreateBuilder(args);
builder.Logging.AddFile();

WebApplication app = builder.Build();

app.MapGet("/", () => "Hello world!");

app.Run();
```

The WebApplicationBuilder configures the console and debug providers as normal.

Adds the new file logging provider to the logger factory

NOTE Adding a new provider doesn't replace existing providers. `WebApplicationBuilder` automatically adds the console and debug logging providers in listing 26.5. To remove them, call `builder.Logging.ClearProviders()` before adding the file provider.

With the file logging provider configured, you can run the application and generate logs. Every time your application writes a log using an `ILogger` instance, `ILogger` writes the message to all configured providers, as shown in figure 26.7. The console messages are conveniently available, but you also have a persistent record of the logs stored in a file.

TIP By default, the rolling file provider writes logs to a subdirectory of your application. You can specify additional options such as filenames and file size limits using overloads of `AddFile()`. For production, I recommend using a more established logging provider, such as Serilog.

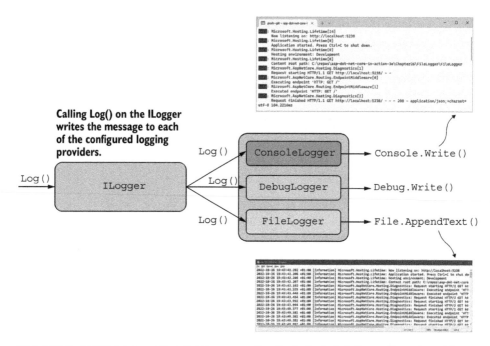

Figure 26.7   Logging a message with `ILogger` writes the log using all the configured providers. This lets you, for example, log a convenient message to the console while also persisting the logs to a file.

The key takeaway from listing 26.5 is that the provider system makes it easy to integrate existing logging frameworks and providers with the ASP.NET Core logging abstractions. Whichever logging provider you choose to use in your application, the principles are the same: add a new logging provider to `WebApplicationBuilder.Logging` using extension methods like `AddConsole()`, or `AddFile()` in this case.

Logging your application messages to a file can be useful in some scenarios, and it's certainly better than logging to a nonexistent console window in production, but it may still not be the best option.

If you discovered a bug in production and needed to look at the logs quickly to see what happened, for example, you'd need to log on to the remote server, find the log files on disk, and trawl through them to find the problem. If you have multiple web servers, you'd have a mammoth job to fetch all the logs before you could even start to tackle the bug—assuming that you even have remote access to the production servers! Not fun. Add to that the possibility of file permission or drive space problems, and file logging seems less attractive.

Instead, it's often better to send your logs to a centralized location, separate from your application. Exactly where this location may be is up to you; the key is that each instance of your app sends its logs to the same location, separate from the app itself.

If you're running your app on Microsoft Azure, you get centralized logging for free because you can collect logs using the Azure App Service provider. Alternatively, you could send your logs to a third-party log aggregator service such as elmah.io (https://elmah.io) or Seq (https://getseq.net). You can find ASP.NET Core logging providers for each of these services on NuGet, so adding them is the same process as adding the file provider you've seen already.

Whichever providers you add, once you start running your apps in production, you'll quickly discover a new problem: the sheer number of log messages your app generates! In the next section you'll learn how to keep this under control without affecting your local development.

26.4 Changing log verbosity with filtering

In this section you'll see how to reduce the number of log messages written to the logger providers. You'll learn how to apply a base level filter, filter out messages from specific namespaces, and use logging provider-specific filters.

If you've been playing around with the logging samples, you'll probably have noticed that you get a lot of log messages, even for a single request like the one in figure 26.2: messages from the Kestrel server and messages from EF Core, not to mention your own custom messages. When you're debugging locally, having access to all that detailed information is extremely useful, but in production you'll be so swamped by noise that picking out the important messages will be difficult.

ASP.NET Core includes the ability to filter out log messages *before* they're written, based on a combination of three things:

- The log level of the message
- The category of the logger (who created the log)
- The logger provider (where the log will be written)

You can create multiple rules using these properties, and for each log that's created, the most specific rule is applied to determine whether the log should be written to the output. You could create the following three rules:

- *The default minimum log level is* Information. If no other rules apply, only logs with a log level of Information or above will be written to providers.
- *For categories that start with* Microsoft, *the minimum log level is* Warning. Any logger created in a namespace that starts with Microsoft will write only logs that have a log level of Warning or above. This would filter out the noisy framework messages you saw in figure 26.6.
- *For the console provider, the minimum log level is* Error. Logs written to the console provider must have a minimum log level of Error. Logs with a lower level won't be written to the console, though they might be written using other providers.

Typically, the goal with log filtering is to reduce the number of logs written to certain providers or from certain namespaces (based on the log category). Figure 26.8 shows a possible set of filtering rules that apply to the console and file logging providers.

In this example, the console logger explicitly restricts logs written in the Microsoft namespace to Warning or above, so the console logger ignores the log message shown.

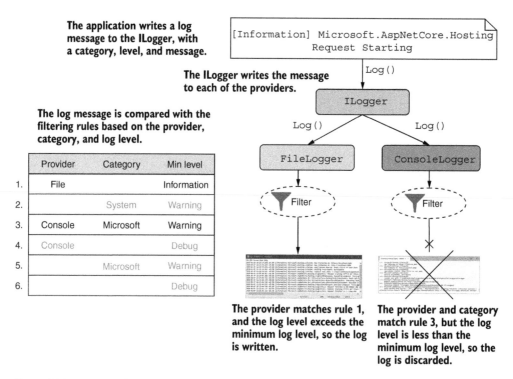

Figure 26.8 Applying filtering rules to a log message to determine whether a log should be written. For each provider, the most specific rule is selected. If the log exceeds the rule's required minimum level, the provider writes the log; otherwise, it discards it.

Conversely, the file logger doesn't have a rule that explicitly restricts the Microsoft namespace, so it uses the configured minimum level of Information and writes the log to the output.

> **TIP** Only a single rule is chosen when deciding whether a log message should be written; rules aren't combined. In figure 26.8, rule 1 is considered to be more specific than rule 5, so the log is written to the file provider, even though technically, both rules could apply.

You typically define your app's set of logging rules using the layered configuration approach discussed in chapter 10, because this lets you easily have different rules when running in development and production.

> **TIP** As you saw in chapter 11, you can load configuration settings from multiple sources, like JSON files and environment variables, and can load them conditionally based on the IHostingEnvironment. A common practice is to include logging settings for your production environment in appsettings.json and overrides for your local development environment in appsettings .Development.json.

WebApplicationBuilder automatically loads configuration rules from the "Logging" section of the IConfiguration object. This happens automatically, and you rarely need to customize it, but listing 26.6 shows how you could also add configuration rules from the "LoggingRules" section using AddConfiguration().

> **NOTE** WebApplicationBuilder always adds the configuration to load from the "Logging" section; you can't remove this. For this reason, it's rarely worth adding configuration yourself; instead, use the default "Logging" configuration section where possible.

Listing 26.6 Loading logging configuration using AddConfiguration()

```
WebApplicationBuilder builder = WebApplication.CreateBuilder(args);
builder.Logging.AddConfiguration(
    builder.Configuration.GetSection("LoggingRules"));    ◁── Loads the log filtering
                                                               configuration from the
var app = builder.Build();                                     LoggingRules section

app.MapGet("/", () => "Hello world!");
app.Run();
```

Assuming that you don't override the configuration section, your appsettings.json will typically contain a "Logging" section, which defines the configuration rules for your app. Listing 26.7 shows how this might look to define all the rules shown in figure 26.8.

Listing 26.7 The log filtering configuration section of appsettings.json

```
{
  "Logging": {
    "LogLevel": {
      "Default": "Debug",            Rules to apply if there
      "System": "Warning",           are no specific rules
      "Microsoft": "Warning"         for a provider
    },
    "File": {
      "LogLevel": {                   Rules to apply to
        "Default": "Information"      the File provider
      }
    },
    "Console": {
      "LogLevel": {                   Rules to apply to the
        "Default": "Debug",           Console provider
        "Microsoft": "Warning"
      }
    }
  }
}
```

When creating your logging rules, the important thing to bear in mind is that if you have *any* provider-specific rules, these will take precedence over the category-based rules defined in the "LogLevel" section. Therefore, for the configuration defined in listing 26.7, if your app uses only the file or console logging providers, the rules in the "LogLevel" section will effectively never apply.

If you find this confusing, don't worry; so do I. Whenever I'm setting up logging, I check the algorithm used to determine which rule applies for a given provider and category, which is as follows:

1 Select all rules for the given provider. If no rules apply, select all rules that don't define a provider (the top "LogLevel" section from listing 26.7).
2 From the selected rules, select rules with the longest matching category prefix. If no selected rules match the category prefix, select the "Default" if present.
3 If multiple rules are selected, use the last one.
4 If no rules are selected, use the global minimum level, "LogLevel:Default" (Debug in listing 26.7).

Each of these steps except the last narrows down the applicable rules for a log message until you're left with a single rule. You saw this in effect for a "Microsoft" category log in figure 26.8. Figure 26.9 shows the process in more detail.

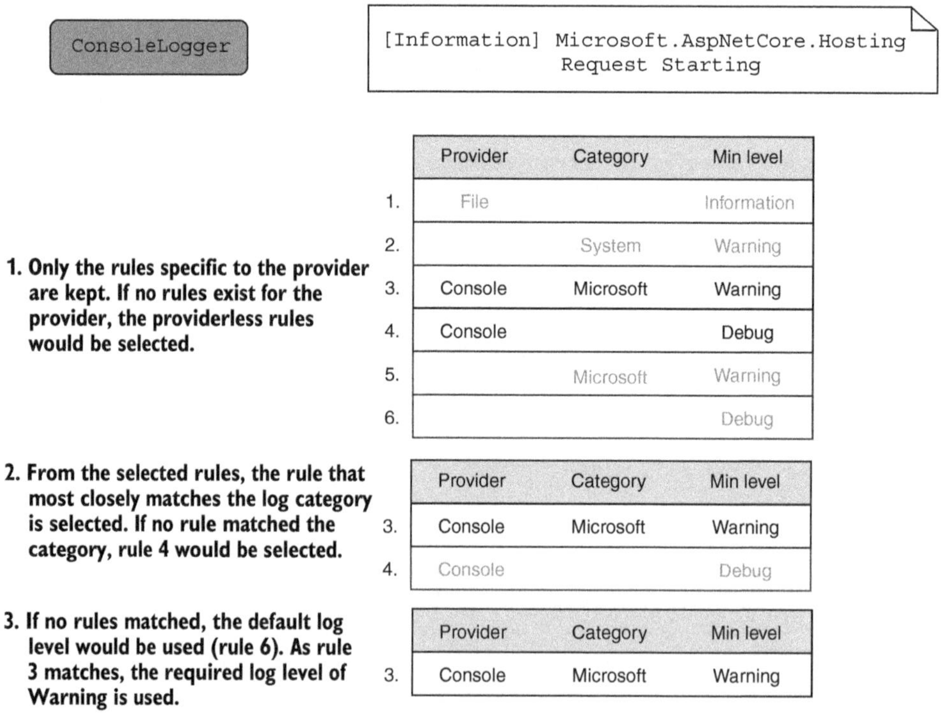

Figure 26.9 Selecting a rule to apply from the available set for the console provider and an Information level log. Each step reduces the number of rules that apply until you're left with only one.

WARNING   Log filtering rules aren't merged; a single rule is selected. Including provider-specific rules will override global category-specific rules, so I tend to stick to category-specific rules where possible to make the overall set of rules easier to understand.

With some effective filtering in place, your production logs should be much more manageable, as shown in figure 26.10. Generally, I find it's best to limit the logs from the ASP.NET Core infrastructure and referenced libraries to Warning or above while keeping logs that my app writes to Debug in development and Information in production.

Only logs of Warning level or above from are written by classes in namespaces that start with Microsoft or System.

Logs of Information level or above are written by the app itself.

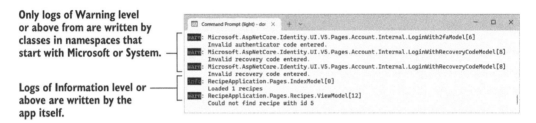

Figure 26.10   Using filtering to reduce the number of logs written. In this example, category filters have been added to the Microsoft and System namespaces, so only logs of Warning and above are recorded. That increases the proportion of logs that are directly relevant to your application.

This is close to the default configuration used in the ASP.NET Core templates. You may find you need to add additional category-specific filters, depending on which NuGet libraries you use and the categories they write to. The best way to find out is generally to run your app and see whether you get flooded with uninteresting log messages.

TIP   Most logging providers listen for configuration changes and update their filters dynamically. That means you should be able to modify your appsettings.json or appsettings.Development.json file and check the effect on the log messages, iterating quickly without restarting your app.

Even with your log verbosity under control, if you stick to the default logging providers like the file or console loggers, you'll probably regret it in the long run. These log providers work perfectly well, but when it comes to finding specific error messages or analyzing your logs, you'll have your work cut out for you. In the next section you'll see how structured logging can help you tackle this problem.

26.5 Structured logging: Creating searchable, useful logs

In this section you'll learn how structured logging makes working with log messages easier. You'll learn to attach key-value pairs to log messages and how to store and query for key values using the structured logging provider Seq. Finally, you'll learn how to use scopes to attach key-value pairs to all log messages within a block.

Let's imagine you've rolled out the recipe application we've been working on to production. You've added logging to the app so that you can keep track of any errors in your application, and you're storing the logs in a file.

One day, a customer calls and says they can't view their recipe. Sure enough, when you look through the log messages, you a see a warning:

```
warn: RecipeApplication.Pages.Recipes.ViewModel [12]
      Could not find recipe with id 3245
```

This piques your interest. Why did this happen? Has it happened before for this *customer*? Has it happened before for this *recipe*? Has it happened for *other* recipes? Does it happen regularly?

How would you go about answering these questions? Given that the logs are stored in a text file, you might start doing basic text searches in your editor of choice, looking for the phrase `"Could not find recipe with id"`. Depending on your notepad-fu skills, you could probably get a fair way in answering your questions, but it would likely be a laborious, error-prone, and painful process.

The limiting factor is that the logs are stored as *unstructured* text, so text processing is the only option available to you. A better approach is to store the logs in a *structured* format so that you can easily query the logs, filter them, and create analytics. Structured logs could be stored in any format, but these days they're typically represented as JSON. A structured version of the same recipe warning log might look something like this:

```
{
  "eventLevel": "Warning",
  "category": "RecipeApplication.Pages.Recipes.ViewModel",
  "eventId": "12",
  "messageTemplate": "Could not find recipe with {recipeId}",
  "message": "Could not find recipe with id 3245",
  "recipeId": "3245"
}
```

This structured log message contains all the same details as the unstructured version, but in a format that would easily let you search for specific log entries. It makes it simple to filter logs by their EventLevel or to show only those logs relating to a specific recipe ID.

> **NOTE** This is only an example of what a structured log could look like. The format used for the logs will vary depending on the logging provider used and could be anything. The main point is that properties of the log are available as key-value pairs.

Adding structured logging to your app requires a logging provider that can create and store structured logs. Elasticsearch is a popular general search and analytics engine that can be used to store and query your logs. One big advantage of using a central store such as Elasticsearch is the ability to aggregate the logs from all your apps in one place and analyze them together. You can add the Elasticsearch.Extensions.Logging provider to your app in the same way as you added the file sink in section 26.3.

> **NOTE** Elasticsearch is a REST-based search engine that's often used for aggregating logs. You can find out more at https://www.elastic.co/elasticsearch.

Elasticsearch is a powerful production-scale engine for storing your logs, but setting it up and running it in production isn't easy. Even after you've got it up and running, there's a somewhat steep learning curve associated with the query syntax. If you're interested in something more user-friendly for your structured logging needs, Seq (https://getseq.net) is a great option. In the next section I'll show you how adding Seq as a structured logging provider makes analyzing your logs that much easier.

26.5.1 Adding a structured logging provider to your app

To demonstrate the advantages of structured logging, in this section you'll configure an app to write logs to Seq. You'll see that the configuration is essentially identical to unstructured providers, but the possibilities afforded by structured logging make considering it a no-brainer.

Seq is installed on a server or your local machine and collects structured log messages over HTTP, providing a web interface for you to view and analyze your logs. It is currently available as a Windows app or a Linux Docker container. You can install a free version for development, which allows you to experiment with structured logging in general.

> **TIP** You can download Seq from https://getseq.net/Download.

From the point of view of your app, the process for adding the Seq provider should be familiar:

1 Install the Seq logging provider using Visual Studio or the .NET CLI with

```
dotnet add package Seq.Extensions.Logging
```

2 Add the Seq logging provider in Program.cs by calling `AddSeq()`:

```
WebApplicationBuilder builder = WebApplication.CreateBuilder(args);
builder.Logging.AddSeq();
```

That's all you need to add Seq to your app. This will send logs to the default local URL when you have Seq installed in your local environment. The `AddSeq()` extension method includes additional overloads to customize Seq when you move to production, but this is all you need to start experimenting locally.

If you haven't already, install Seq on your development machine (or run the Docker container) and navigate to the Seq app at http://localhost:5341. In a different tab, open your app, and start browsing your app and generating logs. Back in Seq, if you refresh the page, you'll see a list of logs, something like figure 26.11. Clicking a log expands it and shows you the structured data recorded for the log.

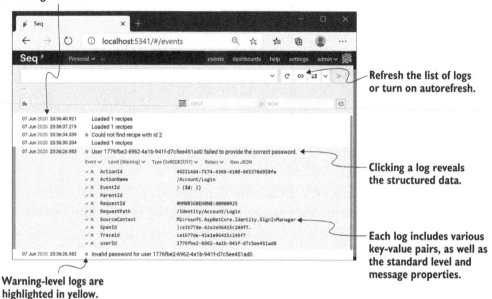

Figure 26.11   The Seq UI. Logs are presented as a list. You can view the structured logging details of individual logs, view analytics for logs in aggregate, and search by log properties.

ASP.NET Core supports structured logging by treating each captured parameter from your message format string as a key-value pair. If you create a log message using the following format string,

```
_log.LogInformation("Loaded {RecipeCount} recipes", Recipes.Count);
```

the Seq logging provider creates a `RecipeCount` parameter with a value of `Recipes` `.Count`. These parameters are added as properties to each structured log, as you can see in figure 26.11.

Structured logs are generally easier to read than your standard-issue console output, but their real power comes when you need to answer a specific question. Consider the problem from before, where you see this error:

```
Could not find recipe with id 3245
```

You want to get a feel for how widespread the problem is. The first step would be to identify how many times this error has occurred and to see whether it's happened to any other recipes. Seq lets you filter your logs, but it also lets you craft SQL queries to analyze your data, so finding the answer to the question takes a matter of seconds, as shown in figure 26.12.

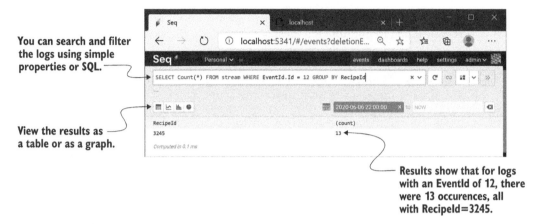

You can search and filter the logs using simple properties or SQL.

View the results as a table or as a graph.

Results show that for logs with an EventId of 12, there were 13 occurences, all with RecipeId=3245.

Figure 26.12   Querying logs in Seq. Structured logging makes log analysis like this example easy.

> **NOTE**   You don't need query languages like SQL for simple queries, but they make digging into the data easier. Other structured logging providers may provide query languages other than SQL, but the principle is the same as in this Seq example.

A quick search shows that you've recorded the log message with `EventId.Id=12` (the `EventId` of the warning we're interested in) 13 times, and every time, the offending `RecipeId` was 3245. This suggests that there may be something wrong with that recipe specifically, which points you in the right direction to find the problem.

More often than not, figuring out errors in production involves logging detective work like this to isolate where the problem occurred. Structured logging makes this process significantly easier, so it's well worth considering, whether you choose Seq, Elasticsearch, or a different provider.

I've already described how you can add structured properties to your log messages using variables and parameters from the message. But as you can see in figure 26.11, there are far more properties visible than exist in the message alone.

Scopes provide a way to add arbitrary data to your log messages. They're available in some unstructured logging providers, but they shine when used with structured logging providers. In the final section of this chapter I'll demonstrate how you can use them to add data to your log messages.

26.5.2   *Using scopes to add properties to your logs*

You'll often find in your apps that you have a group of operations that all use the same data, which would be useful to attach to logs. For example, you might have a series of database operations that all use the same transaction ID, or you might be performing multiple operations with the same user ID or recipe ID. *Logging scopes* provide a way of associating the same data to every log message in such a group.

> **DEFINITION**   *Logging scopes* are used to group multiple operations by adding relevant data to multiple log message.

Logging scopes in ASP.NET Core are created by calling `ILogger.BeginScope<T>(T state)` and providing the `state` data to be logged. You create scopes inside a `using` block; any log messages written inside the scope block will have the associated data, whereas those outside won't.

Listing 26.8   Adding scope properties to log messages with `BeginScope`

```
_logger.LogInformation("No, I don't have scope");
using(_logger.BeginScope("Scope value"))
using(_logger.BeginScope(new Dictionary<string, object>
    {{ "CustomValue1", 12345 } }))
{
    _logger.LogInformation("Yes, I have the scope!");
}
_logger.LogInformation("No, I lost it again");
```

Calling BeginScope starts a scope block, with a scope state of "Scope value".

You can pass anything as the state for a scope.

Log messages written inside the scope block include the scope state.

Log messages written outside the scope block don't include the scope state.

The scope state can be any object at all: an `int`, a `string`, or a `Dictionary`, for example. It's up to each logging provider implementation to decide how to handle the state you provide in the `BeginScope` call, but typically, it is serialized using `ToString()`.

> **TIP**   The most common use for scopes I've found is to attach additional key-value pairs to logs. To achieve this behavior in Seq, you need to pass `Dictionary<string, object>` as the state object. Nicholas Blumhardt, the creator of Serilog and Seq, has examples and the reasoning for this on his blog in the "The semantics of ILogger.BeginScope()" article: http://mng.bz/GxDD.

When the log messages inside the scope block are written, the scope state is captured and written as part of the log, as shown in figure 26.13. The `Dictionary<>` of key-value pairs is added directly to the log message (`CustomValue1`), and the remaining state values are added to the `Scope` property. You will likely find the dictionary approach the more useful of the two, as the added properties are more easily filtered on, as you saw in figure 26.12.

That brings us to the end of this chapter on logging. Whether you use the built-in logging providers or opt to use a third-party provider like Serilog or NLog, ASP.NET Core makes it easy to get detailed logs not only for your app code, but also for the libraries that make up your app's infrastructure, like Kestrel and EF Core. Whichever you choose, I encourage you to add more logs than you think you'll need; you'll thank me when it comes time to track down a problem.

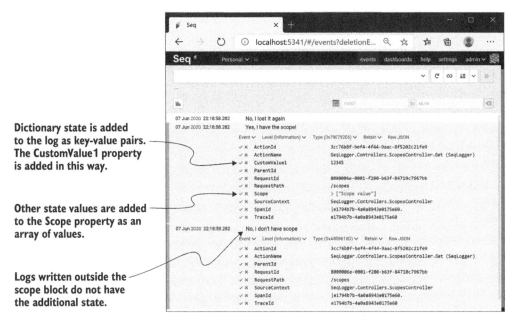

Dictionary state is added to the log as key-value pairs. The CustomValue1 property is added in this way.

Other state values are added to the Scope property as an array of values.

Logs written outside the scope block do not have the additional state.

Figure 26.13 Adding properties to logs using scopes. Any scope state that is added using the dictionary approach is added as structured logging properties, but other state is added to the Scope property. Adding properties makes it easier to associate related logs with one another.

In the next chapter we're going to be looking at your ASP.NET Core application from a different point of view. Instead of focusing on the code and logic behind your app, we're going to look at how you prepare an app for production. You'll see how to specify the URLs your application uses and how to publish an app so that it can be hosted in IIS.

Summary

- Logging is critical for quickly diagnosing errors in production apps. You should always configure logging for your application so that logs are written to a durable location such as a filesystem or other service, not just to the console, where they will be lost if the window closes or the server restarts.

- You can add logging to your own services by injecting ILogger<T>, where T is the name of the service. Alternatively, inject ILoggerFactory and call CreateLogger().

- The log level of a message indicates how important it is and ranges from Trace to Critical. Typically, you'll create many low-importance log messages and a few high-importance log messages.

- You specify the log level of a log by using the appropriate extension method of ILogger to create your log. To write an Information level log, use ILogger.Log-Information(message).

- The log category indicates which component created the log. It is typically set to the fully qualified name of the class creating the log, but you can set it to any string if you wish. `ILogger<T>` will have a log category of `T`.

- You can format messages with placeholder values, similar to the `string.Format` method, but with meaningful names for the parameters. Calling `logger.LogInfo ("Loading Recipe with id {RecipeId}", 1234)` would create a log reading `"Loading Recipe with id 1234"`, but it would also capture the value `RecipeId=1234`. This structured logging makes analyzing log messages much easier.

- ASP.NET Core includes many logging providers out of the box, including the console, debug, EventLog, and EventSource providers. Alternatively, you can add third-party logging providers.

- You can configure multiple `ILoggerProvider` instances in ASP.NET Core, which define where logs are output. `WebApplicationBuilder` adds the console and debug providers, and you can add providers using the `Logging` property.

- You can control logging output verbosity using configuration. `WebApplication-Builder` uses the `"Logging"` configuration section to control output verbosity. You typically filter out more logs in production than when developing your application.

- Only a single log filtering rule is selected for each logging provider when determining whether to output a log message. The most specific rule is selected based on the logging provider and the category of the log message.

- Structured logging involves recording logs so that they can be easily queried and filtered, instead of the default unstructured format that's output to the console. This makes analyzing logs, searching for problems, and identifying patterns easier.

- You can add properties to a structured log by using scope blocks. A scope block is created by calling `ILogger.BeginScope<T>(state)` in a `using` block. The state can be any object and is added to all log messages inside the scope block.

Publishing and deploying your application

This chapter covers

- Publishing an ASP.NET Core application
- Hosting an ASP.NET Core application in IIS
- Customizing the URLs for an ASP.NET Core app

We've covered a vast amount of ground so far in this book. We've gone over the basic mechanics of building an ASP.NET Core application, such as configuring dependency injection (DI), loading app settings, and building a middleware pipeline. We've looked at building APIs using minimal APIs and web API controllers. We've looked at the server-rendered UI side, using Razor templates and layouts to build an HTML response. And we've looked at higher-level abstractions, such as Entity Framework Core (EF Core) and ASP.NET Core Identity, that let you interact with a database and add users to your application. In this chapter we're taking a slightly different route. Instead of looking at ways to build bigger and better applications, we'll focus on what it means to deploy your application so that users can access it.

We'll start by looking again at the ASP.NET Core hosting model in section 27.1 and examining why you might want to host your application behind a reverse proxy instead of exposing your app directly to the internet. I show you the difference between running an ASP.NET Core app in development using `dotnet run` and publishing the app for use on a remote server. Finally, I describe some of the options available when you're deciding how and where to deploy your app.

In section 27.2 I show you how to deploy your app to one such option: a Windows server running Internet Information Services (IIS). This is a typical deployment scenario for many developers who are familiar with the legacy .NET Framework version of ASP.NET, so it acts as a useful case study, but it's certainly not the only possibility. I don't go into all the technical details of configuring the venerable IIS system; instead, I show you the bare minimum required to get it up and running. If your focus is cross-platform development, don't worry, because I don't dwell on IIS for too long.

In section 27.3 I provide an introduction to hosting on Linux. You'll see how it differs from hosting applications on Windows, learn the changes you need to make to your apps, and find out about some gotchas to look out for. I describe how reverse proxies on Linux differ from IIS and point you to some resources you can use to configure your environments rather than give exhaustive instructions in this book.

If you're *not* hosting your application using IIS, you'll likely need to set the URL that your ASP.NET Core app is using when you deploy your application. In section 27.4 I show two approaches: using the special ASPNETCORE_URLS environment variable and using command-line arguments. Although this task generally is not a problem during development, setting the correct URLs for your app is critical when you need to deploy it.

This chapter covers a relatively wide array of topics, all related to deploying your app. But before we get into the nitty-gritty, I'll go over the hosting model for ASP.NET Core so that we're on the same page. This is significantly different from the hosting model of the legacy version of ASP.NET, so if you're coming from that background, it's best to try to forget what you know!

27.1 Understanding the ASP.NET Core hosting model

If you think back to part 1 of this book, you may remember that we discussed the hosting model of ASP.NET Core. ASP.NET Core applications are, essentially, console applications. They have a `static void Main` function that is the entry point for the application, as a standard .NET console app would.

> **NOTE** The entry point for programs using top-level statements is automatically generated by the compiler. It's not called `Main` (it typically has an "invalid" name, such as `<Main>$`), but otherwise it has the same signature as the classic `static void Main` function you would write by hand.

What makes a .NET app an ASP.NET Core app is that it runs a web server, typically Kestrel, inside the console app process. Kestrel provides the HTTP functionality to receive requests and return responses to clients. Kestrel passes any requests it receives to the body of your application and generates a response, as shown in figure 27.1. This

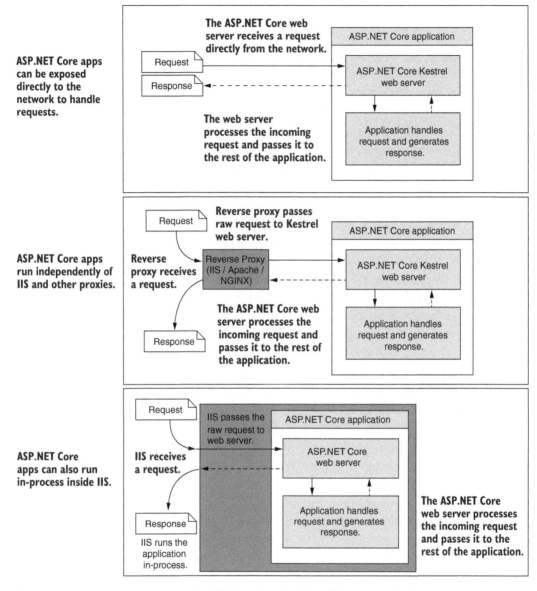

Figure 27.1   The hosting model for ASP.NET Core gives flexibility. The same application can run exposed directly to the network, behind various reverse proxies without modification, and even inside the IIS process.

hosting model decouples the server and reverse proxy from the application itself so that the same application can run unchanged in multiple environments.

In this book we've focused on the "application" part of figure 27.1—the ASP.NET Core application itself—but the reality is that sometimes you'll want to place your ASP.NET Core apps behind a reverse proxy, such as IIS in Windows or NGINX or Apache in Linux. The *reverse proxy* is the program that listens for HTTP requests from the internet and then makes requests to your app as though the request came from the internet directly.

> **DEFINITION**   A *reverse proxy* is software that's responsible for receiving requests and forwarding them to the appropriate web server. The reverse proxy is exposed directly to the internet, whereas the underlying web server is exposed only to the proxy.

If you're running your application using a Platform as a Service (PaaS) offering such as Azure App Service, you're using a reverse proxy there too—one that is managed by Azure. Using a reverse proxy has many benefits:

- *Security*—Reverse proxies are specifically designed to be exposed to malicious internet traffic, so they're typically extremely well-tested and battle-hardened.
- *Performance*—You can configure reverse proxies to provide performance improvements by aggressively caching responses to requests.
- *Process management*—An unfortunate reality is that apps sometimes crash. Some reverse proxies can act as monitors/schedulers to ensure that if an app crashes, the proxy can automatically restart it.
- *Support for multiple apps*—It's common to have multiple apps running on a single server. Using a reverse proxy makes it easier to support this scenario by using the host name of a request to decide which app should receive the request.

I don't want to make it seem like using a reverse proxy is all sunshine and roses. There are some downsides:

- *Complexity*—One of the biggest complaints is how complex reverse proxies can be. If you're managing the proxy yourself (as opposed to relying on a PaaS implementation), there can be lots of proxy-specific pitfalls to look out for.
- *Inter-process communication*—Most reverse proxies require two processes: a reverse proxy and your web app. Communicating between the two is often slower than if you directly exposed your web app to requests from the internet.
- *Restricted features*—Not all reverse proxies support all the same features as an ASP.NET Core app. For example, Kestrel supports HTTP/2, but if your reverse proxy doesn't, you won't see the benefits.

Whether you choose to use a reverse proxy or not, when the time comes to host your app, you can't copy your code files directly to the server. First, you need to *publish* your ASP.NET Core app to optimize it for production. In section 27.1.1 we'll look at building an ASP.NET Core app so that it can be run on your development machine, compared with publishing it so that it can be run on a server.

27.1.1 *Running vs. publishing an ASP.NET Core app*

One of the key changes in ASP.NET Core from previous versions of ASP.NET is making it easy to build apps using your favorite code editors and integrated development environments (IDEs). Previously, Visual Studio was required for ASP.NET development, but with the .NET command-line interface (CLI), you can build apps with the tools you're comfortable with on any platform.

As a result, whether you build using Visual Studio or the .NET CLI, the same tools are being used under the hood. Visual Studio provides an additional graphical user interface (GUI), functionality, and wrappers for building your app, but it (mostly) executes the same commands as the .NET CLI behind the scenes.

As a refresher, you've used four main .NET CLI commands so far to build your apps:

- `dotnet new`—Creates an ASP.NET Core application from a template
- `dotnet restore`—Downloads and installs any referenced NuGet packages for your project
- `dotnet build`—Compiles and builds your project
- `dotnet run`—Executes your app so you can send requests to it

If you've ever built a .NET application, whether it's a legacy ASP.NET app or a .NET Framework console app, you'll know that the output of the build process is written to the bin folder by default. The same is true for ASP.NET Core applications.

If your project compiles successfully when you call `dotnet build`, the .NET CLI writes the artifacts to a bin folder in your project's directory. Inside this bin folder are several files required to run your app, including a .dll file that contains the code for your application. Figure 27.2 shows the output of the bin folder for a basic ASP.NET Core application.

Figure 27.2   The bin folder for an ASP.NET Core app after running `dotnet build`**. The application is compiled into a single .dll file, ExampleApp.dll.**

NOTE   In Windows you also have an executable .exe file, ExampleApp.exe. This is a simple wrapper file for convenience that makes it easier to run the application contained in ExampleApp.dll.

When you call `dotnet run` in your project folder (or run your application using Visual Studio), the .NET CLI uses the .dll to run your application. But this file doesn't contain everything you need to deploy your app.

To host and deploy your app on a server, you first need to *publish* it. You can publish your ASP.NET Core app from the command line using the `dotnet publish` command, which builds and packages everything your app needs to run. The following command packages the app from the current directory and builds it to a subfolder called publish. I've used the `Release` configuration instead of the default `Debug` configuration so that the output will be fully optimized for running in production:

```
dotnet publish --output publish --configuration Release
```

> **TIP** Always use the `Release` configuration when publishing your app for deployment. This ensures that the compiler generates optimized code for your app.

Once the command completes, you'll find your published application in the publish folder, as shown in figure 27.3.

Figure 27.3 The publish folder for the app after running `dotnet publish`. The app is still compiled into a single .dll file, but all the additional files, such as wwwroot, are also copied to the output.

As you can see, the ExampleApp.dll file is still there, along with some additional files. Most notably, the publish process has copied across the wwwroot folder of static files. When running your application locally with `dotnet run`, the .NET CLI uses these files from your application's project folder directly. Running `dotnet publish` copies the files to the output directory, so they're included when you deploy your app to a server.

If your first instinct is to try running the application in the publish folder using the `dotnet run` command you already know and love, you'll be disappointed. Instead of seeing the application starting up, you'll see a somewhat confusing message: `Couldn't find a project to run`.

To run a published application, you need to use a slightly different command. Instead of calling `dotnet run`, you must pass the path to your application's .dll file to the `dotnet` command. If you're running the command from the publish folder, for the example app in figure 27.3, it would look something like

```
dotnet ExampleApp.dll
```

This is the command that your server will run when running your application in production.

> **TIP** You can also use the `dotnet exec` command to achieve the same thing, such as `dotnet exec ExampleApp.dll`. This makes some advanced runtime options available, as described in the docs at http://mng.bz/x4d8.

When you're developing, the `dotnet run` command does a whole load of work to make things easier on you. It makes sure that your application is built, looks for a project file in the current folder, works out where the corresponding .dlls will be (in the bin folder), and finally runs your app.

  In production, you don't need any of this extra work. Your app is already built; it only needs to be run. The `dotnet <dll>` syntax does this alone, so your app starts much faster.

> **NOTE** The `dotnet` command used to run your published application is part of the .NET Runtime. The (identically named) `dotnet` command used to build and run your application during development is part of the .NET software development kit (SDK).

Framework-dependent deployments vs. self-contained deployments

.NET Core applications can be deployed in two ways: runtime-dependent deployments (RDD) and self-contained deployments (SCD).

By default, you'll use an RDD. This relies on the .NET 7 runtime being installed on the target machine that runs your published app, but you can run your app on any platform—Windows, Linux, or macOS—without having to recompile.

By contrast, an SCD contains all the code required to run your app, so the target machine doesn't need to have .NET 7 installed. Instead, publishing your app packages up the .NET 7 runtime with your app's code and libraries.

Each approach has its pros and cons, but in most cases I tend to create RDDs. The final size of RDDs is much smaller, as they contain only your app code instead of the whole .NET 7 framework, which SCDs contain. Also, you can deploy your RDD apps to any platform, whereas SCDs must be compiled specifically for the target machine's operating system, such as Windows 10 64-bit or Red Hat Enterprise Linux 64-bit.

That said, SCDs are excellent for isolating your application from dependencies on the hosting machine. SCDs don't rely on the version of .NET installed on a hosting provider, so you can (for example) use preview versions of .NET in Azure App Service without needing the preview version to be supported.

> **(continued)**
> Another advantage of SCDs is for regulated industries that require certification or procedure to change applications. In RDDs (such as in Azure App Service) the underlying runtime may be patched at any time without your intervention, potentially leading to noncompliance. With SCDs, your app contains a fixed runtime and can be considered an immutable snapshot of your app. Of course, that means you must make sure to patch the runtime of your SCDs manually, performing regular deployments. Patch versions of the .NET runtime are generally released every month, so make sure to plan for at least monthly releases of your SCD apps.
>
> In this book I discuss RDDs only for simplicity, but if you want to create an SCD, provide a runtime identifier (in this case, Windows 10 64-bit) when you publish your app:
>
> ```
> dotnet publish -c Release -r win10-x64 --self-contained -o publish_folder
> ```
>
> The output will contain an .exe file, which is your application, and a ton of .dlls (about 100 MB of .dlls for a default sample app), which are the .NET 7 framework. You need to deploy this whole folder to the target machine to run your app. Note that you need to publish for a specific operating system and architecture. The list of available runtime identifiers is available in the documentation at http://mng.bz/Aolp.
>
> In .NET 7 it's possible to trim these assemblies during the publish process, but this comes with risks in some scenarios. You can also bundle this folder into a single file automatically for easier deployments. For more details, see Microsoft's ".NET application publishing overview" documentation at https://learn.microsoft.com/dotnet/core/deploying.

We've established that publishing your app is important for preparing it to run in production, but how do you go about deploying it? How do you get the files from your computer onto a server so that people can access your app? You have many, many options, so in the next section I'll give you a brief list of approaches to consider.

27.1.2 *Choosing a deployment method for your application*

To deploy any application to production, you generally have two fundamental requirements:

- A server that can run your app
- A means of loading your app onto the server

Historically, putting an app into production was a laborious and error-prone process. For many people, this is still true. If you're working at a company that hasn't changed practices in recent years, you may need to request a server or virtual machine for your app and provide your application to an operations team that will install it for you. If that's the case, you may have your hands tied regarding how you deploy.

For those who have embraced continuous integration (CI) or continuous delivery/deployment (CD), there are many more possibilities. CI/CD is the process of detecting changes in your version control system (for example, Git, SVN, Mercurial, or Team Foundation Version Control) and automatically building, and potentially deploying, your application to a server with little to no human intervention.

> **NOTE** There are important but subtle differences between these terms. Atlassian has a good comparison article, "Continuous integration vs. delivery vs. deployment," at http://mng.bz/vzp4.

There are many CI/CD systems out there—Azure DevOps, GitHub Actions, Jenkins, TeamCity, AppVeyor, Travis, and Octopus Deploy, to name a few. Each can manage some or all of the CI/CD process and can integrate with many systems.

Rather than push any particular system, I suggest trying some of the services available and seeing which works best for you. Some are better suited to open-source projects, and some are better when you're deploying to cloud services; it all depends on your particular situation.

If you're getting started with ASP.NET Core and don't want to have to go through the setup process of getting CI working, you still have lots of options. The easiest way to get started with Visual Studio is to use the built-in deployment options. These are available from Visual Studio via the **Build** > **Publish <AppName>** command, which presents the screen shown in figure 27.4.

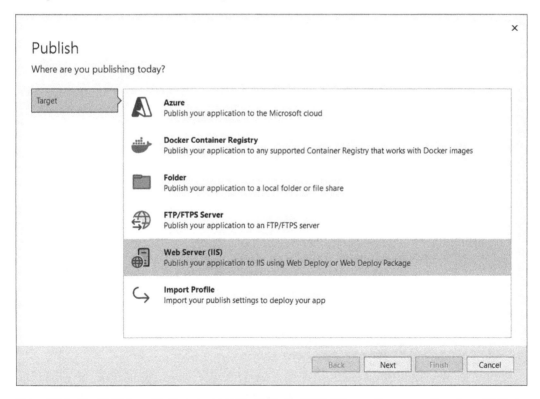

Figure 27.4   The Publish application screen in Visual Studio 2022. This provides easy options for publishing your application directly to Azure App Service, to IIS, to an FTP site, or to a folder on the local machine.

From here, you can publish your application directly from Visual Studio to many locations. This is great when you're getting started, though I recommend looking at a more automated and controlled approach when you have a larger application or a whole team working on a single app.

> **TIP**   For guidance on choosing your Visual Studio publishing options, see Microsoft's "Deploy your app to a folder, IIS, Azure, or another destination" documentation at http://mng.bz/4Z8j.

Given the number of possibilities available in this space and the speed with which these options change, I'm going to focus on one specific scenario in this chapter: you've built an ASP.NET Core application, and you need to deploy it. You have access to a Windows server that's already serving legacy .NET Framework ASP.NET applications using IIS, and you want to run your ASP.NET Core app alongside them.

In the next section you'll see an overview of the steps required to run an ASP.NET Core application in production, using IIS as a reverse proxy. It won't be a master class in configuring IIS (there's so much depth to the 25-year-old product that I wouldn't know where to start!), but I'll cover the basics needed to get your application serving requests.

27.2 *Publishing your app to IIS*

In this section I briefly show you how to publish your first app to IIS. You'll add an application pool and website to IIS and ensure that your app has the necessary configuration to work with IIS as a reverse proxy. The deployment itself will be as simple as copying your published app to IIS's hosting folder.

In section 27.1 you learned about the need to publish an app before you deploy it and the benefits of using a reverse proxy when you run an ASP.NET Core app in production. If you're deploying your application to Windows, IIS will likely be your reverse proxy and will be responsible for managing your application.

IIS is an old and complex beast, and I can't possibly cover everything related to configuring it in this book. Neither would you want me to; that discussion would be tedious! Instead, in this section I'll provide an overview of the basic requirements for running ASP.NET Core behind IIS, along with the changes you may need to make to your application to support IIS.

If you're on Windows and want to try these steps locally, you'll need to enable IIS manually on your development machine. If you've done this with older versions of Windows, nothing much has changed. You can find a step-by-step guide to configuring IIS and troubleshooting tips in the ASP.NET Core documentation at http://mng.bz/6g2R.

27.2.1 *Configuring IIS for ASP.NET Core*

The first step in preparing IIS to host ASP.NET Core applications is installing the ASP.NET Core Windows Hosting Bundle (http://mng.bz/opED). This includes several components needed to run .NET apps:

- *The .NET Runtime*—Runs your .NET 7 application
- *The ASP.NET Core Runtime*—Required to run ASP.NET Core apps
- *The IIS AspNetCore Module*—Provides the link between IIS and your app so that IIS can act as a reverse proxy

If you're going to be running IIS on your development machine, make sure that you install the bundle as well; otherwise, you'll get strange errors from IIS.

> **TIP** The Windows Hosting Bundle provides everything you need for running ASP.NET Core behind IIS in Windows. If you're hosting your application in Linux or Mac, or aren't using IIS in Windows, you need to install only the .NET Runtime and ASP.NET Core Runtime to run runtime-dependent ASP.NET Core apps. Note that you need to install the IIS AspNetCore Module even if you are using SCDs.

Once you've installed the bundle, you need to configure an *application pool* in IIS for your ASP.NET Core apps. Previous versions of ASP.NET would run in a *managed* app pool that used .NET Framework, but for ASP.NET Core you should create a *No Managed Code* pool. The native ASP.NET Core Module runs inside the pool, which boots the .NET 7 Runtime itself.

> **DEFINITION** An *application pool* in IIS represents an application process. You can run each app in IIS in a separate application pool to keep the apps isolated from one another.

To create an unmanaged application pool, right-click **Application Pools** in IIS and choose **Add Application Pool** from the contextual menu. Provide a name for the app pool in the resulting dialog box, such as dotnet7, and set the .NET CLR version to **No Managed Code**, as shown in figure 27.5.

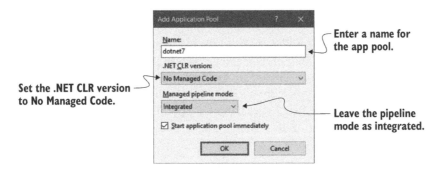

Figure 27.5   Creating an app pool in IIS for your ASP.NET Core app. The .NET CLR version should be set to No Managed Code.

Now that you have an app pool, you can add a new website to IIS. Right-click the **Sites** node, and choose **Add Website** from the contextual menu. In the Add Website dialog box, shown in figure 27.6, you provide a name for the website and the path to the folder where you'll publish your website. I created a folder that I'll use to deploy the Recipe app from previous chapters. It's important to change the Application Pool for the app to the new dotnet7 app pool you created. In production, you'd also provide a hostname for the application, but I've left it blank for now in this example and changed the port to 81 so the application will bind to the URL http://localhost:81.

> **NOTE** When you deploy an application to production, you need to register a hostname with a domain registrar so that your site is accessible by people on the internet. Use that hostname when configuring your application in IIS, as shown in figure 27.6.

Enter the path to the folder where you will publish your app.

Change the app pool to the No Managed Code pool.

In production you will likely leave this as port 80 and must enter a hostname.

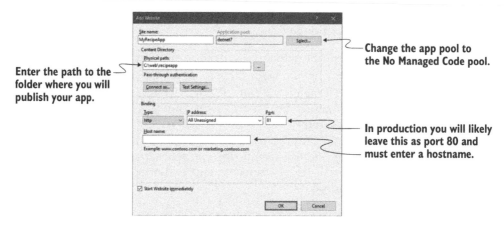

Figure 27.6 Adding a new website to IIS for your app. Be sure to change the Application Pool to the No Managed Code pool created in the previous step. You also provide a name, the path where you'll publish your app files, and the URL that IIS will use for your app.

Once you click OK, IIS creates the application and attempts to start it. But you haven't published your app to the folder, so you won't be able to view it in a browser yet.

You need to carry out one more critical setup step before you can publish and run your app: grant permissions for the dotnet7 app pool to access the path where you'll publish your app. To do this, right-click the folder that will host your app in Windows File Explorer, and choose **Properties** from the contextual menu. In the Properties dialog box, choose **Security > Edit > Add**. Enter IIS AppPool\dotnet7 in the text box, as shown in figure 27.7, where dotnet7 is the name of your app pool; then choose **OK**. Close all the dialog boxes by choosing **OK**, and you're all set.

Out of the box, the ASP.NET Core templates are configured to work seamlessly with IIS, but if you've created an app from scratch, you may need to make a couple of changes. In the next section I'll briefly show the changes you need to make and explain why they're necessary.

Enter IIS AppPool, followed by the name of the No Managed Code app pool— for example, IIS AppPool\dotnet7.

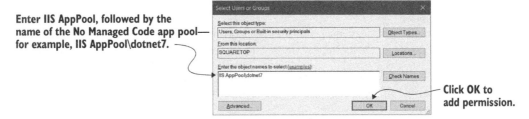

Click OK to add permission.

Figure 27.7 Adding permission for the `dotnet7` app pool to the website's publish folder

27.2.2 *Preparing and publishing your application to IIS*

As I discussed in section 27.1, IIS acts as a reverse proxy for your ASP.NET Core app. That means IIS needs to be able to communicate directly with your app to forward incoming requests to and outgoing responses from your app.

IIS handles this with the ASP.NET Core Module, but a certain degree of negotiation is required between IIS and your app. For this to work correctly, you need to configure your app to use IIS integration.

IIS integration is added automatically when you use `WebApplicationBuilder`, so there's typically nothing more to do. However, in chapter 30 you'll learn about the generic host and how to create custom application builders using `HostBuilder`. If your app uses a customer application builder and you want to use IIS, you need to ensure that you add IIS integration with the `UseIIS()` or `UseIISIntegration()` extension methods:

- `UseIIS()` configures your application to support IIS with an in-process hosting model.
- `UseIISIntegration()` configures your application to support IIS with an out-of-process hosting model.

These methods are automatically called by `WebApplicationBuilder`, but if you're not using your application with IIS, the `UseIIS()` and `UseIISIntegration()` methods will have no effect on your app, so it's safe to include them anyway.

In-process vs. out-of-process hosting in IIS

The common reverse-proxy description assumes that your application is running in a separate process from the reverse proxy itself. That is the case if you're running on Linux and was the default for IIS up until ASP.NET Core 3.0.

In ASP.NET Core 3.0, ASP.NET Core switched to using an in-process hosting model by default for applications deployed to IIS. In this model, IIS hosts your application directly inside the IIS process, reducing interprocess communication and boosting performance.

You can switch to the out-of-process hosting model with IIS if you wish, which can sometimes be useful for troubleshooting problems. Rick Strahl has an excellent post on the differences between the hosting models, how to switch between them, and the advantages of each: "ASP.NET Core In Process Hosting on IIS with ASP.NET Core" at http://mng.bz/QmEv.

(continued)
In general, you shouldn't need to worry about the differences between the hosting models, but it's something to be aware of if you're deploying to IIS. If you choose to use the out-of-process hosting model, you should use the `UseIISIntegration()` extension method. If you use the in-process model, use `UseIIS()`. Alternatively, play it safe and use both; the correct extension method is activated based on the hosting model used in production. Neither extension does anything if you don't use IIS.

When running behind IIS, these extension methods configure your app to pair with IIS so that it can seamlessly accept requests. Among other things, the extensions do the following:

- Define the URL that IIS uses to forward requests to your app and configures your app to listen on this URL
- Configure your app to interpret requests coming from IIS as coming from the client by setting up header forwarding
- Enable Windows authentication if required

Adding the IIS extension methods is the only change you need to make to your application to host in IIS (and even then, only when using a custom application builder). But there's one additional aspect to be aware of when you publish your app. As with legacy .NET Framework ASP.NET, IIS relies on a web.config file to configure the applications it runs. It's important that your application include a web.config file when it's published to IIS; otherwise, you could get broken behavior or even expose files that shouldn't be exposed.

TIP For details on using web.config to customize the IIS AspNetCore Module, see Microsoft's "ASP.NET Core Module" documentation: http://mng.bz/Xdna.

If your ASP.NET Core project already includes a web.config file, the .NET CLI or Visual Studio copies it to the publish directory when you publish your app. If your app doesn't include a web.config file, the `publish` command creates the correct one for you. If you don't need to customize the web.config file, it's generally best not to include one in your project and let the CLI create the correct file for you.

With these changes, you're finally in a position to publish your application to IIS. Publish your ASP.NET Core app to a folder, either from Visual Studio or with the .NET CLI, by running

```
dotnet publish --output publish_folder --configuration Release
```

This will publish your application to the publish_folder folder. You can then copy your application to the path specified in IIS, as shown in figure 27.6. At this point, if all has gone smoothly, you should be able to navigate to the URL you specified for your app (http://localhost:81, in my case) and see it running, as shown in figure 27.8.

The app is served using IIS as a reverse proxy, using the URL specified in the Add Website dialog box.

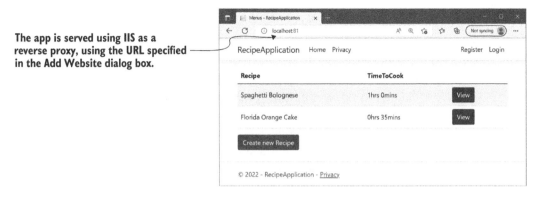

Figure 27.8   The published application, using IIS as a reverse proxy listening at the URL http://localhost:81

And there you have it—your first application running behind a reverse proxy. Even though ASP.NET Core uses a different hosting model from previous versions of ASP.NET, the process of configuring IIS is similar.

As is often the case when it comes to deployment, the success you have is highly dependent on your precise environment and your app itself. If, after following these steps, you find that you can't get your application to start, I highly recommend checking out the documentation at http://mng.bz/Zqom. This contains many troubleshooting steps to get you back on track if IIS decides to throw a hissy fit.

This section was deliberately tailored to deploying to IIS, as it provides a great segue for developers who are used to deploying legacy ASP.NET apps and want to deploy their first ASP.NET Core app. But that's not to say that IIS is the only, or best, place to host your application.

In the next section I provide a brief introduction to hosting your app on Linux, behind a reverse proxy like NGINX or Apache. I won't go into configuration of the reverse proxy itself, but I will provide an overview of things to consider and resources you can use to run your applications on Linux.

27.3   Hosting an application in Linux

One of the great new features in ASP.NET Core is the ability to develop and deploy applications cross-platform, whether on Windows, Linux, or macOS. The ability to run on Linux in particular opens the possibility of cheaper deployments to cloud hosting, deploying to small devices like a Raspberry Pi or to Docker containers.

One of the characteristics of Linux is that it's almost infinitely configurable. Although that's definitely a feature, it can also be extremely daunting, especially if you're coming from the Windows world of wizards and GUIs. This section provides an overview of what it takes to run an application on Linux. It focuses on the broad steps you need to take rather than the details of the configuration itself. Instead, I point to resources you can refer to as necessary.

27.3.1 *Running an ASP.NET Core app behind a reverse proxy in Linux*

You'll be glad to hear that running your application on Linux is largely the same as running your application on Windows with IIS:

1 Publish your app using `dotnet publish`. If you're creating an RDD, the output is the same as you'd use with IIS. For an SCD, you must provide the runtime identifier, as described in section 27.1.1.

2 Install the necessary prerequisites on the server. For an RDD deployment, you must install the .NET 7 Runtime and the necessary prerequisites. You can find details on this in Microsoft's "Install .NET on Linux" documentation at http://mng.bz/Rxlj.

3 Copy your app to the server. You can use any mechanism you like: FTP, USB stick, or whatever you need to get your files onto the server!

4 Configure a reverse proxy, and point it to your app. As you know by now, you may want to run your app behind a reverse proxy, for the reasons described in section 27.1. In Windows you'd use IIS, but in Linux you have more options. NGINX, Apache, and HAProxy are commonly used options. The ASP.NET Core-based YARP is also an option (https://microsoft.github.io/reverse-proxy). Alternatively, go without, and expose your app directly to the network.

5 Configure a process-management tool for your app. In Windows, IIS acts as both a reverse proxy and a process manager, restarting your app if it crashes or stops responding. In Linux, you typically need to configure a separate process manager to handle these duties; the reverse proxies won't do them for you.

The first three steps are generally the same, whether you're running in Windows with IIS or in Linux, but the last two steps are more interesting. By contrast with the monolithic IIS, Linux has a philosophy of small applications, each with a single responsibility.

IIS runs on the same server as your app and takes on multiple duties—proxying traffic from the internet to your app, but also monitoring the app process itself. If your app crashes or stops responding, IIS restarts the process to ensure that you can keep handling requests.

In Linux, the reverse proxy might be running on the same server as your app, but it's also common for it to be running on a different server, as shown in figure 27.9. This is similarly true if you choose to deploy your app to Docker; your app would typically be deployed in a container without a reverse proxy, and a reverse proxy on a server would point to your Docker container.

As the reverse proxies aren't necessarily on the same server as your app, they can't be used to restart your app if it crashes. Instead, you need to use a process manager such as systemd to monitor your app. If you're using Docker, you typically use a container orchestrator such as Kubernetes (https://kubernetes.io) to monitor the health of your containers.

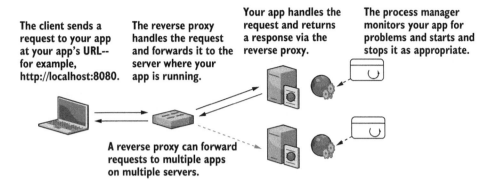

The client sends a request to your app at your app's URL--for example, http://localhost:8080.

The reverse proxy handles the request and forwards it to the server where your app is running.

Your app handles the request and returns a response via the reverse proxy.

The process manager monitors your app for problems and starts and stops it as appropriate.

A reverse proxy can forward requests to multiple apps on multiple servers.

Figure 27.9   In Linux, it's common for a reverse proxy to be on a different server from your app. The reverse proxy forwards incoming requests to your app, while a process manager, such as systemd, monitors your apps for crashes and restarts it as appropriate.

Running ASP.NET Core applications in Docker

Docker is the most commonly used engine for containerizing your applications. A *container* is like a small, lightweight virtual machine, specific to your app. It contains an operating system, your app, and any dependencies for your app. This container can then be run on any machine that runs Docker, and your app will run exactly the same, regardless of the host operating system and what's installed on it. This makes deployments highly repeatable: you can be confident that if the container runs on your machine, it will run on the server too.

All the major cloud vendors have support for running containers, either standalone or as part of an orchestration service. For example, in Azure, you can run containers in Azure App Service, Azure Container Instances, Azure Container Apps, and Azure Kubernetes Service. One advantage of containers is that you can easily use the same container in all these services or even move to a different cloud provider, and your app will run the same.

ASP.NET Core is well suited to container deployments, but moving to Docker involves a big shift in your deployment methodology and may or may not be right for you and your apps. If you're interested in the possibilities afforded by Docker and want to learn more, I suggest checking out the following resources:

- *Docker in Practice*, 2nd ed., by Ian Miell and Aidan Hobson Sayers (Manning, 2019) provides a vast array of practical techniques to help you get the most out of Docker (http://mng.bz/nM8d).
- Even if you're not deploying to Linux, you can use Docker with Docker for Windows. Check out the free e-book *Introduction to Windows Containers*, by John McCabe and Michael Friis (Microsoft Press, 2017), at https://aka.ms/containersebook.
- You can find a lot of details on building and running your ASP.NET Core applications on Docker in the .NET documentation at http://mng.bz/vz5a.
- Steve Gordon has an excellent blog post series on Docker for ASP.NET Core developers at http://mng.bz/2Da8.

Configuring a reverse proxy and process manager on Linux is a laborious task that makes for dry reading, so I won't detail it here. Instead, I recommend checking out the ASP.NET Core docs. They have a guide for NGINX and systemd, "Host ASP.NET Core on Linux with Nginx" (http://mng.bz/yYGd), and a guide for configuring Apache with systemd, "Host ASP.NET Core on Linux with Apache" (http://mng.bz/MXVB).

Both guides cover the basic configuration of the respective reverse proxies and systemd supervisors, but more important, they also show how to configure them securely. The reverse proxy sits between your app and the unfettered internet, so it's important to get it right!

Configuring the reverse proxy and the process manager is typically the most complex part of deploying to Linux, and that isn't specific to .NET development: the same would be true if you were deploying a Node.js web app. But you need to consider a few things inside your application when you're going to be deploying to Linux, as you'll see in the next section.

27.3.2 *Preparing your app for deployment to Linux*

Generally speaking, your app doesn't care which reverse proxy it sits behind, whether it's NGINX, Apache, or IIS; your app receives requests and responds to them without the reverse proxy affecting things. When you're hosting behind IIS, you need `UseIISIntegration()` to tell your app about IIS's configuration; when you're hosting on Linux, you need a similar method.

When a request arrives at the reverse proxy, it contains some information that is lost after the request is forwarded to your app. For example, the original request comes with the IP address of the client/browser connecting to your app; once the request is forwarded from the reverse proxy, the IP address is that of the *reverse proxy*, not the browser. Also, if the reverse proxy is used for SSL/TLS offloading (see chapter 28), then a request that was originally made using HTTPS may arrive at your app as an HTTP request.

The standard solution to these problems is for the reverse proxy to add more headers before forwarding requests to your app. For example, the `X-Forwarded-For` header identifies the original client's IP address, whereas the `X-Forwarded-Proto` header indicates the original scheme of the request (`http` or `https`).

For your app to behave correctly, it needs to look for these headers in incoming requests and modify the request as appropriate. A request to http://localhost with the `X-Forwarded-Proto` header set to `https` should be treated the same as if the request were to https://localhost.

You can use `ForwardedHeadersMiddleware` in your middleware pipeline to achieve this. This middleware overrides `Request.Scheme` and other properties on `HttpContext` to correspond to the forwarded headers. `WebApplicationBuilder` partially handles this for you; the middleware is automatically added to the pipeline in a disabled state. To enable it, set the environment variable `ASPNETCORE_FORWARDEDHEADERS_ENABLED=true`.

If you don't want to use the automatically added middleware for some reason, or if you're using the generic host (which you'll learn about in chapter 30), you can add the middleware to the start of your middleware pipeline manually, as shown in listing 27.1, and configure it with the headers to look for.

> **WARNING**   It's important that `ForwardedHeadersMiddleware` be placed early in the middleware pipeline to correct `Request.Scheme` before any middleware that depends on the scheme runs.

Listing 27.1   Configuring an app to use forwarded headers in Startup.cs

```
WebApplicationBuilder builder = WebApplication.CreateBuilder(args);
WebApplication app = builder.Build();

app.UseForwardedHeaders(new ForwardedHeadersOptions
{
    ForwardedHeaders = ForwardedHeaders.XForwardedFor |
                       ForwardedHeaders.XForwardedProto
});
app.UseHttpsRedirection();
app.UseRouting();
app.MapGet("/", () => "Hello world!");
app.Run();
```

Adds **ForwardedHeadersMiddleware** early in your pipeline

Configures the headers the middleware should look for and use

The forwarded headers middleware must be placed before all other middleware.

> **NOTE**   This behavior isn't specific to reverse proxies on Linux; the `UseIis()` extension adds `ForwardedHeadersMiddleware` under the hood as part of its configuration when your app is running behind IIS.

Aside from considering the forwarded headers, you need to consider a few minor things when deploying your app to Linux that may trip you up if you're used to deploying to Windows alone:

- *Line endings (LF in Linux versus CRLF in Windows)*—Windows and Linux use different character codes in text to indicate the end of a line. This isn't often a problem for ASP.NET Core apps, but if you're writing text files on one platform and reading them on a different platform, it's something to bear in mind.
- *Path directory separator (`"\"` on Windows, `"/"` on Linux)*—This is one of the most common bugs I see when Windows developers move to Linux. Each platform uses a different separator in file paths, so although loading a file using the `"subdir\myfile.json"` path will work fine in Windows, it won't in Linux. Instead, you should use `Path.Combine` to create the appropriate separator for the current platform, such as `Path.Combine("subdir", "myfile.json")`.
- *`":"` in environment variables*—In some Linux distributions, the colon character (`:`) isn't allowed in environment variables. As you saw in chapter 10, this character is typically used to denote different sections in ASP.NET Core configuration,

so you often need to use it in environment variables. Instead, you can use a double underscore in your environment variables (__); ASP.NET Core will treat it the same as though you'd used a colon.

- *Missing time zone and culture data*—Linux distributions don't always come with time zone or culture data, which can cause localization problems and exceptions at runtime. You can install the time zone data using your distribution's package manager.[1] It also may be organized differently. The hierarchy of Norwegian cultures is different in Linux, for example.
- *Different directory structures*—Linux distributions use a different folder structure from Windows, so you need to bear that in mind if your app hardcodes paths. In particular, consider differences in temporary/cache folders.

The preceding list is not exhaustive by any means, but as long as you set up Forwarded-HeadersMiddleware and take care to use cross-platform constructs like Path.Combine, you shouldn't have too many problems running your applications on Linux. But configuring a reverse proxy isn't the simplest of activities, so wherever you're planning on hosting your app, I suggest checking the documentation for guidance at http://mng.bz/1qM1.

27.4   Configuring the URLs for your application

At this point, you've deployed an application, but there's one aspect you haven't configured: the URLs for your application. When you're using IIS as a reverse proxy, you don't have to worry about this inside your app. IIS integration with the ASP.NET Core Module works by dynamically creating a URL that's used to forward requests between IIS and your app. The hostname you configure in IIS (in figure 27.6) is the URL that external users see for your app; the internal URL that IIS uses when forwarding requests is never exposed.

If you're not using IIS as a reverse proxy—maybe you're using NGINX or exposing your app directly to the internet—you may find you need to configure the URLs your application listens to directly.

By default, ASP.NET Core listens for requests on the URL http://localhost:5000. There are lots of ways to set this URL, but in this section I describe two: using environment variables or using command-line arguments. These are the two most common approaches I see (outside of IIS) for controlling which URLs your app uses.

> **TIP**   For further ways to set your application's URL, see my "5 ways to set the URLs for an ASP.NET Core app" blog post: http://mng.bz/go0v.

In chapter 10 you learned about configuration in ASP.NET Core, and in particular about the concept of hosting environments so that you can use different settings when running in development compared with production. You choose the hosting

---

[1] I ran into this problem myself. You can read about it in detail and how I solved it on my blog: http://mng.bz/aoem.

environment by setting an environment variable on your machine called
ASPNETCORE_ENVIRONMENT. The ASP.NET Core framework magically picks up this variable
when your app starts and uses it to set the hosting environment.

You can use a similar special environment variable to specify the URL that your app
uses; this variable is called ASPNETCORE_URLS. When your app starts up, it looks for this
value and uses it as the application's URL. By changing this value, you can change the
default URL used by all ASP.NET Core apps on the machine. For example, you could
set a temporary environment variable in Windows from the command window using

```
set ASPNETCORE_URLS=http://localhost:8000
```

Running a published application using dotnet <app.dll> within the same command
window, as shown in figure 27.10, shows that the app is now listening on the URL provided in the ASPNETCORE_URLS variable.

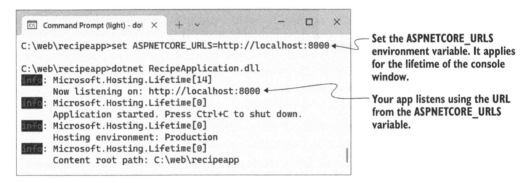

Figure 27.10   Change the ASPNETCORE_URLS **environment variable to change the URL used by ASP.NET Core apps.**

You can instruct an app to listen on multiple URLs by separating them with a semicolon, or you can listen to a specific port without specifying the localhost hostname. If
you set the ASPNETCORE_URLS environment variable to

```
http://localhost:5001;http://*:5002
```

your ASP.NET Core apps will listen for requests sent to the following:

- http://localhost:5001—This address is accessible only on your local computer,
  so it will not accept requests from the wider internet.
- http://*:5002—Any URL on port 5002. External requests from the internet can
  access the app on port 5002, using any URL that maps to your computer.

Note that you can't specify a different hostname, like tastyrecipes.com. ASP.NET Core
listens to all requests on a given port; it doesn't listen for specific domain names. The
exception is the localhost hostname, which allows only requests that came from your
own computer.

> **NOTE** If you find the ASPNETCORE_URLS variable isn't working properly, ensure that you don't have a launchSettings.json file in the directory. When present, the values in this file take precedence. By default, launchSettings.json isn't included in the publish output, so this generally won't be a problem in production.

Setting the URL of an app using a single environment variable works great for some scenarios, most notably when you're running a single application in a virtual machine, or within a Docker container.

> **TIP** ASP.NET Core is well suited to running in containers but working with containers is a separate book in its own right. For details on hosting and publishing apps using Docker, see Microsoft's "Host ASP.NET Core in Docker containers" documentation: http://mng.bz/e5GV.

If you're not using Docker containers or a PaaS offering, chances are that you're hosting multiple apps side-by-side on the same machine. A single environment variable is no good for setting URLs in this case, as it would change the URL of every app.

In chapter 10 you saw that you could set the hosting environment using the ASPNETCORE_ENVIRONMENT variable, but you could also set the environment using the --environment flag when calling dotnet run:

```
dotnet run --no-launch-profile --environment Staging
```

You can set the URLs for your application in a similar way, using the --urls parameter. Using command-line arguments enables you to have multiple ASP.NET Core applications running on the same machine, listening to different ports. For example, the following command would run the recipe application, set it to listen on port 8081, and set the environment to staging (figure 27.11):

```
dotnet RecipeApplication.dll --urls "http://*:8081" --environment Staging
```

The command-line arguments are used to set both the hosting environment and the URLs.

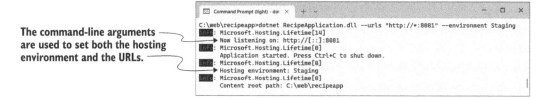

Figure 27.11 Setting the hosting environment and URLs for an application using command-line arguments. The values passed at the command line override values provided from appSettings.json or environment variables.

Remember that you don't need to set your URLs in this way if you're using IIS as a reverse proxy; IIS integration handles this for you. Setting the URLs is necessary only when you're manually configuring the URL your app is listening on, such as if you're using NGINX or are exposing Kestrel directly to clients.

WARNING If you are running your ASP.NET Core application without a reverse proxy, you should use *host filtering* for security reasons to ensure that your app only responds to requests for hostnames you expect. For more details, see my "Adding host filtering to Kestrel in ASP.NET Core" blog entry: http://mng.bz/pVXK.

That brings us to the end of this chapter on publishing your app. This last mile of app development—deploying an application to a server where users can access it—is a notoriously thorny problem. Publishing an ASP.NET Core application is easy enough, but the multitude of hosting options available makes providing concise steps for every situation difficult.

Whichever hosting option you choose, there's one critical topic that you mustn't overlook: security. In the next chapter you'll learn about HTTPS, how to use it when testing locally, and why it's important your production apps all use HTTPS.

Summary

- ASP.NET Core apps are console applications that self-host a web server. In production, you may use a reverse proxy, which handles the initial request and passes it to your app. Reverse proxies can provide additional security, operations, and performance benefits, but they can also add complexity to your deployments.

- .NET has two parts: the .NET SDK (also known as the .NET CLI) and the .NET Runtime. When you're developing an application, you use the .NET CLI to restore, build, and run your application. Visual Studio uses the same .NET CLI commands from the IDE.

- When you want to deploy your app to production, you need to publish your application, using `dotnet publish`. This creates a folder containing your application as a DLL, along with all its dependencies.

- To run a published application, you don't need the .NET CLI because you won't be building the app. You need only the .NET Runtime to run a published app. You can run a published application using the `dotnet app.dll` command, where app.dll is the application .dll created by the `dotnet publish` command.

- To host ASP.NET Core applications in IIS, you must install the ASP.NET Core Module. This allows IIS to act as a reverse proxy for your ASP.NET Core app. You must also install the .NET Runtime and the ASP.NET Core Runtime, which are installed as part of the ASP.NET Core Windows Hosting Bundle.

- IIS can host ASP.NET Core applications using one of two modes: in-process and out-of-process. The out-of-process mode runs your application as a separate process, as is typical for most reverse proxies. The in-process mode runs your application as part of the IIS process. This has performance benefits, as no interprocess communication is required.

- If you are using a custom web application builder with IIS, ensure that you call `UseIISIntegration()` and `UseIIS()` so that IIS forwards the request to your app correctly. If you're using the default `WebApplicationBuilder`, these methods are called automatically for you.

- When you publish your application using the .NET CLI, a web.config file is added to the output folder. It's important that this file be deployed with your application when publishing to IIS, as it defines how your application should run.

- The URL that your app listens on is specified by default using the environment variable `ASPNETCORE_URLS`. Setting this value changes the URL for all the apps on your machine. Alternatively, pass the `--urls` command-line argument when running your app, as in this example: `dotnet app.dll --urls http://localhost:80`.

Adding HTTPS to an application

28

This chapter covers

- Encrypting traffic between clients and your app using HTTPS
- Using the HTTPS development certificate for local development
- Configuring Kestrel with a custom HTTPS certificate
- Enforcing HTTPS for your whole app

Web application security is a hot topic at the moment. Practically every week another breach is reported, or confidential details are leaked. It may seem like the situation is hopeless, but the reality is that the vast majority of breaches could have been prevented with the smallest amount of effort.

In chapter 29 we'll look at a range of common attacks and how to protect against them in your ASP.NET Core app. In this chapter we start by looking at one of the most basic security measures: encrypting the traffic between a client such as a browser and your application.

Without HTTPS encryption, you risk third parties spying on or modifying the requests and responses as they travel over the internet. The risks associated with unencrypted traffic mean that HTTPS is effectively mandatory for production apps these days, and it is heavily encouraged by the makers of modern browsers such as Chrome and Firefox. In section 28.1 you'll learn more about these risks and some of the approaches you can take to protect your application.

In section 28.2 you'll see how to get started with HTTPS locally using the ASP.NET Core development certificate. I describe what it is, how to trust it on your application, and what to do if it's not working as you expect.

The development certificate is great for local work, but in production you'll need to configure a real, production certificate. I don't describe the process of obtaining a certificate in section 28.3, as that will vary by provider; instead, I show how to configure Kestrel to use a custom certificate you've acquired.

In section 28.4 I describe some of the approaches to enforcing HTTPS in your application. Unfortunately, web browsers still expect apps to be available over HTTP by default, so you typically need to expose your application on both HTTP and HTTPS ports. Nevertheless, there are things you can do to push clients toward the HTTPS endpoint, which are considered security best practices these days.

Before we look at HTTPS in ASP.NET Core specifically, we'll start by looking at HTTPS in general and why you should use it in all your applications.

28.1   *Why do I need HTTPS?*

In this section you'll learn about HTTPS: what it is, and why you need to be aware of it for all your production applications. We're not going to go into details about the protocol or how certificates work at this point, instead focusing on why you need to use HTTPS. You'll see two approaches to adding HTTPS to your application: supporting HTTPS directly in your application and using SSL/TLS-offloading with a reverse proxy.

So far in this book, I've shown how the user's browser sends a request across the internet to your app using the HTTP protocol. We haven't looked too much into the details of that protocol other than to establish that it uses *verbs* to describe the type of request (such as GET and POST), that it contains *headers* with metadata about the request, and optionally includes a *body* payload of data.

By default, HTTP requests are unencrypted; they're plain-text files being sent over the internet. Anyone on the same network as a user (such as someone using the same public Wi-Fi in a coffee shop) can read the requests and responses sent back and forth. Attackers can even modify the requests or responses as they're in transit, as shown in figure 28.1.

Using unencrypted web apps in this way presents both a privacy and a security risk to your users. Attackers could read sensitive details such as passwords and personally identifiable information (PII), they could inject malicious code into your responses to attack users, or they could steal authentication cookies and impersonate the user on your app.

To protect your users, your app should encrypt the traffic between the user's browser and your app as it travels over the network by using the HTTPS protocol. This

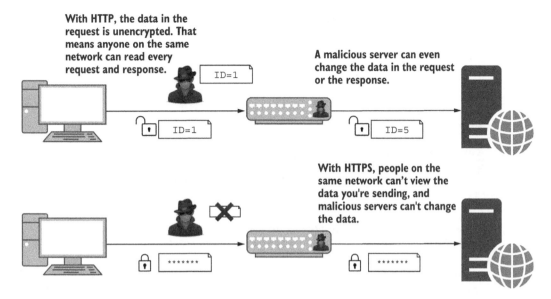

Figure 28.1   Unencrypted HTTP requests can be read by users on the same network. Attackers can even intercept the request and response, reading or changing the data. HTTPS requests can't be read or manipulated by attackers.

is similar to HTTP traffic, but it uses an SSL/TLS certificate to encrypt requests and responses, so attackers cannot read or modify the contents.

> **DEFINITION**   Secure Sockets Layer (SSL) is an older standard that facilitates HTTPS. The SSL protocol has been superseded by Transport Layer Security (TLS), so I'll be using TLS preferentially throughout this chapter. Normally, if you hear someone talking about SSL or SSL certificates, they actually mean TLS. You can find the RFC for the latest version of the TLS protocol at https://www.rfc-editor.org/rfc/rfc8446.

In browsers, you can tell that a site is using HTTPS by the https:// prefix to URLs (notice the s), or sometimes by a padlock, as shown in figure 28.2. Most modern browsers these days deemphasize that a site is using HTTPS, as most sites use HTTPS, and instead highlight when you're on a site that isn't using HTTPS, flagging it as insecure.

The reality is that these days, you should always serve your production websites over HTTPS. The industry is pushing toward HTTPS by default, with most browsers marking HTTP sites as explicitly not secure. Skipping HTTPS will hurt the perception of your app in the long run, so even if you're not interested in the security benefits, it's in your best interest to set up HTTPS.

> **TIP**   You can find a good cheat sheet for HTTPS by OWASP at http://mng.bz/PzxY. ASP.NET Core takes care of most of the points in this list for you, but there are some important ones in the Application section specifically.

**Figure 28.2   Encrypted apps using HTTPS and unencrypted apps using HTTP in Edge.
Using HTTPS protects your application from being viewed or tampered with by attackers.**

Another reason to support HTTPS is that many browser features are available only when your site is served over HTTPS. Some of these features are JavaScript browser APIs, such as location APIs, microphone APIs, and storage APIs. These are available only over HTTPS to protect users from attackers that could modify insecure HTTP requests. Other features apply to server-side apps too, such as Brotli compression and HTTP/2 support.

> **TIP**   For details on how the SSL/TLS protocols work, see chapter 9 of *Real-World Cryptography,* by David Wong (Manning, 2021), http://mng.bz/zxz1.

To enable HTTPS, you need to obtain and configure a TLS certificate for your server. Unfortunately, although that process is a lot easier than it used to be and is now essentially free thanks to Let's Encrypt (https://letsencrypt.org), it's still far from simple in many cases. If you're setting up a production server, I recommend carefully following the tutorials on the Let's Encrypt site. It's easy to get it wrong, so take your time.

> **TIP**   If you're hosting your app in the cloud, most providers will provide one-click TLS certificates so that you don't have to manage certificates yourself. This is extremely useful, and I highly recommend it for everyone. You don't even have to host your application in the cloud to take advantage of this. Cloudflare (https://www.cloudflare.com) provides a CDN service that you can add TLS to. You can even use it for free.

As an ASP.NET Core application developer, you can often get away without directly supporting HTTPS in your app by taking advantage of the reverse-proxy architecture, as shown in figure 28.3, in a process called SSL/TLS offloading/termination. This is generally standard in Platform as a Service (PaaS) cloud services, such as Azure App Service. With SSL/TLS offloading, instead of your application handling requests using HTTPS directly, your app continues to use HTTP. The reverse proxy is responsible for encrypting and decrypting HTTPS traffic to the browser. This often gives you the best

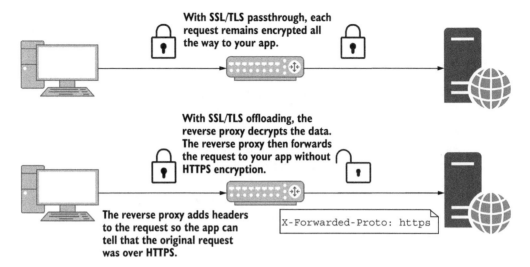

With SSL/TLS passthrough, each request remains encrypted all the way to your app.

With SSL/TLS offloading, the reverse proxy decrypts the data. The reverse proxy then forwards the request to your app without HTTPS encryption.

The reverse proxy adds headers to the request so the app can tell that the original request was over HTTPS.

X-Forwarded-Proto: https

Figure 28.3 You have two options when using HTTPS with a reverse proxy: SSL/TLS passthrough and SSL/TLS offloading. In SSL/TLS passthrough, the data is encrypted all the way to your ASP.NET Core app. For SSL/TLS offloading, the reverse proxy handles decrypting the data, so your app doesn't have to.

of both worlds: data is encrypted between the user's browser and the server, but you don't have to worry about configuring certificates in your application.

> **NOTE** If you're concerned that the traffic is unencrypted between the reverse proxy and your app, I recommend reading Troy Hunt's post "CloudFlare, SSL and unhealthy security absolutism": http://mng.bz/eHCi. It discusses the pros and cons of the problem as it relates to decrypting on the reverse proxy and why you must consider the most likely attacks on your website, in a process called *threat modeling*.

Depending on the specific infrastructure where you're hosting your app, SSL/TLS could be offloaded to a dedicated device on your network, a third-party service like Cloudflare, or a reverse proxy (such as Internet Information Services [IIS], NGINX, or HAProxy) running on the same or a different server. Nevertheless, in some situations, you may need to handle SSL/TLS directly in your app:

- *If you're exposing Kestrel to the internet directly, without a reverse proxy*—This is a supported approach since ASP.NET Core 3.0, and can give high performance. It is also often the case when you're developing your app locally.
- *If having HTTP between the reverse proxy and your app is not acceptable*—While securing traffic inside your network is less critical compared with external traffic, it is undoubtedly more secure to use HTTPS for internal traffic too. This may be a hard requirement for some applications or sectors.
- *If you're using technology that requires HTTPS*—Some newer network protocols, such as gRPC and HTTP/2, generally require an end-to-end HTTPS connection.

In each of these scenarios, you'll need to configure a TLS certificate for your application so Kestrel can receive HTTPS traffic. In section 28.2 you'll see the easiest way to get started with HTTPS when developing locally, using the ASP.NET Core development certificate.

28.2 Using the ASP.NET Core HTTPS development certificates

Working with HTTPS certificates is easier than it used to be, but unfortunately it can still be a confusing topic, especially if you're a newcomer to the web. In this section you'll learn how the .NET software development kit (SDK), Visual Studio, and IIS Express try to improve this experience by handling a lot of the grunt work for you, and what to do when things go wrong.

The first time you run a `dotnet` command using the .NET SDK, the SDK installs an HTTPS development certificate on your machine. Any ASP.NET Core application you create using the default templates (or for which you don't explicitly configure certificates) will use this development certificate to handle HTTPS traffic. However, the development certificate is not trusted by default. If you access a site that's using an untrusted certificate, you'll get a browser warning, as shown in figure 28.4.

The site is served over HTTPS but as the certificate is untrusted, the browser marks it as insecure.

The error code indicates that the certificate authority is invalid.

To access the site, you need to click Advanced and force access (not recommended).

Figure 28.4   The developer certificate is not trusted by default, so apps serving HTTPS traffic using it will be marked as insecure by browsers. Although you can bypass the warnings if necessary, you should instead update the certificate to be trusted.

A brief primer on certificates and signing

HTTPS uses *public key cryptography* as part of the data-encryption process. This uses two keys: a public key that anyone can see and a private key that only your server can see. Anything encrypted with the public key can be decrypted only with the private key. That way, a browser can encrypt something with your server's public key, and only your server can decrypt it. A complete TLS certificate consists of both the public and private parts.

When a browser connects to your app, the server sends the public key part of the TLS certificate. But how does the browser know that it was definitely *your* server that sent the certificate? To achieve this, your TLS certificate contains additional certificates, including one or more certificates from a third party, a certificate authority (CA). At the end of the *certificate chain* is the *root certificate*.

> CAs are special trusted entities, and browsers are hardcoded to trust specific root certificates. For the TLS certificate for your app to be trusted, it must contain (or be signed by) a trusted root certificate. Browsers periodically update their internal list of root certificates and revoke root certificates that can no longer be trusted.
>
> When you use the ASP.NET Core development certificate, or if you create your own self-signed certificate, your site's HTTPS is missing that trusted root certificate. That means browsers won't trust your certificate and won't connect to your server by default. To get around this, you need to tell your development machine to explicitly trust the certificate.
>
> In production, you can't use a development or self-signed certificate, as a user's browser won't trust it. Instead, you need to obtain a signed HTTPS certificate from a service like Let's Encrypt or from a cloud provider like AWS, Azure, or Cloudflare. These certificates are already signed by a trusted CA, so they are automatically trusted by browsers.

To solve these browser warnings, you need to *trust* the certificate. Trusting a certificate is a sensitive operation; it's saying "I know this certificate doesn't look quite right, but ignore that," so it's hard to do automatically. If you're running on Windows or macOS, you can trust the development certificate by running

```
dotnet dev-certs https --trust
```

This command trusts the certificate by registering it in the operating system's certificate store. After you run this command, you should be able to access your websites without seeing any warnings or "not secure" labels, as shown in figure 28.5.

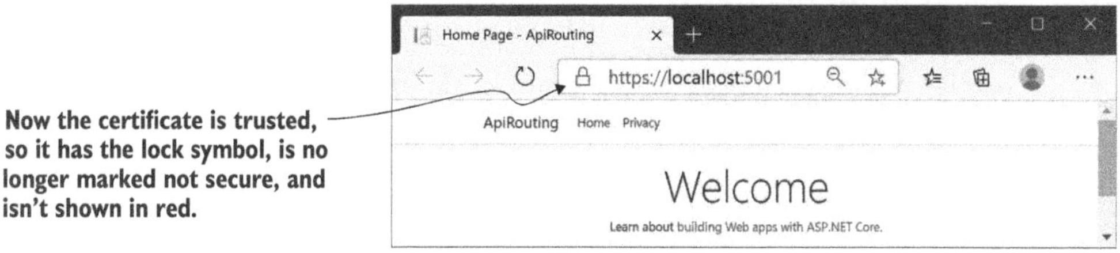

Now the certificate is trusted, so it has the lock symbol, is no longer marked not secure, and isn't shown in red.

Figure 28.5   Once the development certificate is trusted, you will no longer see browser warnings about the connection.

> **TIP** You may need to close your browser after trusting the certificate to clear the browser's cache.

If you're using Windows, Visual Studio, and IIS Express for development, then you might not need to explicitly trust the development certificate. IIS Express acts as a reverse proxy when you're developing locally, so it handles the SSL/TLS setup itself. On top of that, Visual Studio should trust the IIS development certificate as part of installation, so you may never see the browser warnings at all.

> **TIP** In macOS, before .NET 7, you would have to retrust the developer certificate repeatedly for every new app. In .NET 7, the process is a lot smoother, so you shouldn't have to retrust it anything like as often!

Trusting the developer certificate works smoothly in Windows and macOS, in most cases. Unfortunately, trusting the certificate in Linux is a little trickier and depends on the specific flavor of Linux you're using. On top of that, software in Linux often uses its own certificate store, so you'll probably need to add the certificate directly to your favorite browser. If you're using any of the following scenarios, you'll need to do more work:

- Firefox browser in Windows, macOS, or Linux
- Edge or Chrome browsers in Linux
- API-to-API communication in Linux
- An app running in Windows Subsystem for Linux (WSL)
- Running applications in Docker

Each of these scenarios requires a slightly different approach. In many cases it's one or two commands, so I suggest following the documentation for your scenario carefully at http://mng.bz/JglK.

> **TIP** If you've tried trusting the certificate, and your app is still giving errors, try closing all your browser windows and running `dotnet dev-certs https --clean` followed by `dotnet dev-certs https --trust`. Browsers cache certificate trust, so the close and open step is important!

The ASP.NET Core and IIS development certificates make it easy to use Kestrel with HTTPS locally, but those certificates won't help once you move to production. In the next section I show how to configure Kestrel to use a production TLS certificate.

28.3   *Configuring Kestrel with a production HTTPS certificate*

Creating a TLS certificate for production is often a laborious process, as it requires proving to a third-party CA that you own the domain you're creating the certificate for. This is an important step in the trust process and ensures that attackers can't impersonate your servers. The result of the process is one or more files, which is the HTTPS certificate you need to configure for your app.

> **TIP** The specifics of how to obtain a certificate vary by provider and by your OS platform, so follow your provider's documentation carefully. The vagaries and complexities of this process are one of the reasons I strongly favor the SSL/TLS-offloading or "one-click" approaches described previously. Those approaches mean my apps don't need to deal with certificates, and I don't need to use the approaches described in this section; I delegate that responsibility to another piece of the network, or to the underlying platform.

Once you have a certificate, you need to configure Kestrel to use it to serve HTTPS traffic. In chapter 27 you saw how to set the port your application listens on with the `ASPNETCORE_URLS` environment variable or via the command line, and you saw that you could provide an HTTPS URL. As you didn't provide any certificate configuration, Kestrel used the development certificate by default. In production you need to tell Kestrel which certificate to use.

You can configure the certificates Kestrel uses in multiple ways. For a start, you can load the certificate from multiple locations: from a .pfx file, from .pem/.crt and .key files, or from the OS certificate store. You can also use different certificates for different ports, use a different configuration for each URL endpoint you expose, or configure Server Name Indication (SNI). For full details, see the "Replace the default certificate from configuration" section of Microsoft's "Configure endpoints for the ASP.NET Core Kestrel web server" documentation: http://mng.bz/wvv2.

The following listing shows one possible way to set a custom HTTPS certificate for your production app by configuring the default certificate Kestrel uses for HTTPS connections. You can add the `"Kestrel:Certificates:Default"` section to your appsettings.json file (or use any other configuration source, as described in chapter 10) to define the .pfx file of the certificate to use. You must also provide the password for accessing the certificate.

> **Listing 28.1   Configuring the default HTTPS certificate for Kestrel using a .pfx file**

```
{
  "Kestrel": {
    "Certificates": {          Creates a configuration section
      "Default": {             at Kestrel:Certificates:Default
        "Path": "localhost.pfx",      ◁
        "Password": "testpassword"       The relative or absolute
      }                                  path to the certificate
    }
  }
}
```

The password for opening the certificate

The preceding example is the simplest way to replace the HTTPS certificate, as it doesn't require changing any of Kestrel's defaults. You can use a similar approach to load the HTTPS certificate from the OS certificate store (Windows or macOS), as shown in the "Replace the default certificate from configuration" documentation mentioned previously (http://mng.bz/wvv2).

> **WARNING**   Listing 28.1 hardcoded the certificate filename and password for demonstration, but you should never do this in production. Either load these from a configuration store like user-secrets, as you saw in chapter 10, or load the certificate from the local store. Never put production passwords in your appsettings.json files.

All the default ASP.NET Core templates configure your application to serve both HTTP and HTTPS traffic, and with the configuration you've seen so far, you can ensure that your application can handle both HTTP and HTTPS in development and in production.

However, whether you use HTTP or HTTPS may depend on the URL users click when they first browse to your app. For example, imagine you have an app that listens using the default ASP.NET Core URLs: http://localhost:5000 for HTTP traffic and https://localhost:5001 for HTTPS traffic. The HTTPS endpoint is available, but if a user doesn't know that and uses the HTTP URL (the default option in browsers), their traffic is unencrypted. Seeing as you've gone to all the trouble to set up HTTPS, it's probably best that you force users to use it.

28.4   Enforcing HTTPS for your whole app

Enforcing HTTPS across your whole website is practically required these days. Browsers are beginning to explicitly label HTTP pages as insecure. For security reasons, you must use TLS any time you're transmitting sensitive data across the internet. Additionally, thanks to HTTP/2 (and the upcoming HTTP/3), adding TLS can improve your app's performance. In this section you'll learn three techniques for enforcing HTTPS in your application.

> **TIP**   HTTP/2 offers many performance improvements over HTTP/1.x, and all modern browsers require HTTPS to enable it. For a great introduction to HTTP/2, see Google's "Introduction to HTTP/2" at http://mng.bz/9M8j. ASP.NET Core even includes support for HTTP/3, the next version of the protocol! You can read about HTTP/3 at http://mng.bz/qrrJ.

There are multiple approaches to enforcing HTTPS for your application. If you're using a reverse proxy with SSL/TLS-offloading, it might be handled for you anyway, without your having to worry about it within your apps. If that's the case, you may be able to disregard some of the steps in this section.

> **WARNING**   If you're building a web API rather than a Razor Pages app, it's common to reject insecure HTTP requests entirely. You'll see this approach in section 28.4.3.

One approach to improving the security of your app is to use HTTP *security headers*. These are HTTP headers sent as part of your HTTP response that tell the browser how it should behave. There are many headers available, most of which restrict the features your app can use in exchange for increased security. In chapter 30 you'll see how to add your own custom headers to your HTTP responses by creating custom middleware.

> **TIP**   Scott Helme has some great guidance on this and other security headers you can add to your site, such as the Content Security Policy (CSP) header. See "Hardening your HTTP response headers" on his website at http://mng.bz/7DDe.

One of these security headers, the HTTP Strict Transport Security (HSTS) header, can help ensure that browsers use HTTPS where it's available instead of defaulting to HTTP.

28.4.1   Enforcing HTTPS with HTTP Strict Transport Security headers

It's unfortunate, but by default, browsers load apps over HTTP unless otherwise specified. That means your apps must typically support both HTTP and HTTPS, even if you don't want to serve any traffic over HTTP, as shown in figure 28.6. On top of that, if the initial request is over HTTP, the browser may end up sending subsequent requests over HTTP too.

Figure 28.6 When you type in a URL, browsers load the app over HTTP by default. Depending on the links returned by your app or the URLs entered, the browser may make HTTP or HTTPS requests.

One partial mitigation (and a security best practice) is to add HTTP Strict Transport Security headers to your responses.

> **DEFINITION** HTTP Strict Transport Security (HSTS) is a specification (https://www.rfc-editor.org/rfc/rfc6797) for the `Strict-Transport-Security` header that instructs the browser to use HTTPS for all subsequent requests to your application. The HSTS header can be sent only with responses to HTTPS requests. It is also relevant only for requests originating from a browser; it has no effect on server-to-server communication or on mobile apps.

After a browser receives a valid HSTS header, the browser stops sending HTTP requests to your app and uses only HTTPS instead, as shown in figure 28.7. Even if your app has an http:// link or the user enters http:// in the URL bar of the app, the browser automatically replaces the request with an https:// version.

> **TIP** You can achieve a similar upgrading of HTTP to HTTPS requests using the `Upgrade-Insecure-Requests` directive in the `Content-Security-Policy` (CSP) header. This provides fewer protections than the HSTS header but can be used in combination with it. For more details on this directive and CSP in general, see http://mng.bz/mVV4.

HSTS headers are strongly recommended for production apps. You generally don't want to enable them for local development, as that would mean you could never run a non-HTTPS app locally. In a similar fashion, you should use HSTS only on sites for which you *always* intend to use HTTPS, as it's hard (sometimes impossible) to turn off HTTPS once it's enforced with HSTS.

ASP.NET Core comes with built-in middleware for setting HSTS headers, which is included in some of the default templates automatically. Listing 28.2 shows how

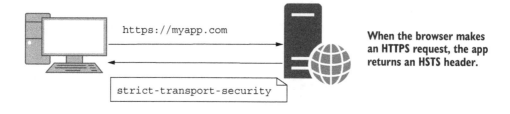

Figure 28.7   After a browser sends an HTTPS request, the app returns an HSTS header, instructing the browser to always send requests over HTTPS. The next time the user attempts to make an http:// request, the browser aborts the request and makes an https:// request instead.

you can configure the HSTS headers for your application using the `HstsMiddleware` in Program.cs.

Listing 28.2   Using `HstsMiddleware` to add HSTS headers to an application

```
WebApplicationBuilder builder = WebApplication.CreateBuilder(args);

builder.Services.AddRazorPages();
builder.Services.AddHsts(options =>
{
    options.MaxAge = TimeSpan.FromHours(1);
});

WebApplication app = builder.Build();

if(app.Environment.IsProduction())
{
    app.UseHsts();
}

app.UseStaticFiles();
app.UseRouting();

app.MapRazorPages();

app.Run();
```

Configures your HSTS header settings and changes the MaxAge from the default of 30 days

You shouldn't use HSTS in local environments.

Adds the HstsMiddleware

The preceding example shows how to change the MaxAge sent in the HSTS header. It's a good idea to start with a small value initially. Once you're sure your app's HTTPS is functioning correctly, you can increase the age for greater security. A typical value for production deployments is one year.

> **WARNING** Once client browsers have received the HSTS header, browsers will default to using HTTPS for all requests to your application. That means you must commit to always using HTTPS for as long as you set MaxAge. If you disable HTTPS, browsers will not revert to using HTTP until this duration has expired, so your application may be inaccessible until then if you aren't listening on HTTPS! You can notify the browser that your app no longer supports HSTS by setting MaxAge to 0.

One limitation with the HSTS header is that you must make an initial request over HTTPS before you can receive the header. If the browser makes only HTTP requests, the app never has a chance to send the HSTS header, so the browser never knows to use HTTPS. One potential solution is called HSTS *preload*.

HSTS preload isn't part of the HSTS specification, but it's supported by all modern browsers. Preload bakes your HSTS header into the browser so that the browser knows it should make only HTTPS requests to your site. That removes the "first request" problem entirely, but be aware that HSTS preload commits you to HTTPS forever, as it can't easily be undone.

Once you're comfortable with your application's HTTPS configuration, you can prepare your app for HSTS preload by configuring an HSTS header that

- Has a MaxAge of at least one year, though two years are recommended
- Has the includeSubDomains directive
- Has the preload directive

Listing 28.3 shows how you can configure these directives in your app. The listing also shows how to exclude the domain never-https.com so that if you host your app at this domain, HSTS headers won't be sent. This can be useful for testing purposes.

Listing 28.3 Configuring the application HSTS header for preload

```
builder.Services.AddHsts(options =>          Sends the includeSubDomains directive
{
    options.Preload = true;                  You must use a max-age
    options.IncludeSubDomains = true;        directive of at least one year.
    options.MaxAge = TimeSpan.FromDays(365);
    options.ExcludedHosts.Add("never-https.com");   Don't send the HSTS header in
});                                                  responses to requests for this
                                                     domain.
```

Sends the preload directive

Once you've prepared your application for HSTS preload, you can submit your app for inclusion in the HSTS preload list that ships with modern browsers. Visit the site https://hstspreload.org, confirm that your application meets the requirements, and submit your domain. If all goes well, your domain will be included in a future release of all modern browsers!

> **TIP** For more details on HSTS and attacks it can mitigate, see Scott Helme's article "HSTS—The missing link in Transport Layer Security," at http://mng.bz/5wwa.

HSTS is a great option for forcing users to use HTTPS on your website, and if you can use HSTS preload, you can ensure that modern clients never send requests over HTTP. Nevertheless, HSTS preload can take months to enforce, and you won't always want to take that approach. In the meantime, if a browser makes an initial request over HTTP, it won't receive the HSTS header and may stay on HTTP! That's unfortunate, but you can mitigate the problem by redirecting insecure requests to HTTPS immediately.

28.4.2 *Redirecting from HTTP to HTTPS with HTTPS redirection middleware*

The HstsMiddleware should always be used in conjunction with middleware that redirects all HTTP requests to HTTPS.

> **TIP** It's possible to apply HTTPS redirection only to specific parts of your application, such as to specific Razor Pages, but I don't recommend that, as it's too easy to open a security hole in your application.

ASP.NET Core comes with HttpsRedirectionMiddleware, which you can use to enforce HTTPS across your whole app. You add it to the middleware pipeline in Program.cs, and it ensures that any requests that pass through it are secure. If an HTTP request reaches the HttpsRedirectionMiddleware, the middleware immediately short-circuits the pipeline with a redirect to the HTTPS version of the request. The browser then repeats the request using HTTPS instead of HTTP, as shown in figure 28.8.

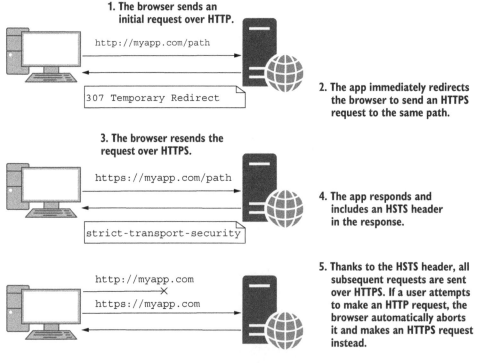

1. The browser sends an initial request over HTTP.

`http://myapp.com/path`

`307 Temporary Redirect`

2. The app immediately redirects the browser to send an HTTPS request to the same path.

3. The browser resends the request over HTTPS.

`https://myapp.com/path`

`strict-transport-security`

4. The app responds and includes an HSTS header in the response.

`http://myapp.com`
`https://myapp.com`

5. Thanks to the HSTS header, all subsequent requests are sent over HTTPS. If a user attempts to make an HTTP request, the browser automatically aborts it and makes an HTTPS request instead.

Figure 28.8 The HttpsRedirectionMiddleware works with the HstsMiddleware to ensure that all requests after the initial request are always sent over HTTPS.

NOTE Even with HSTS and the HTTPS redirection middleware, there is still an inherent weakness: by default, browsers always make an initial insecure request over HTTP to your app. The only way to prevent this is with HSTS preload, which tells browsers to always use HTTPS.

The `HttpsRedirectionMiddleware` is added in some of the default ASP.NET Core templates. It is typically placed after the error handling and `HstsMiddleware`, as shown in the following listing. By default, the middleware redirects all HTTP requests to the secure endpoint, using an HTTP `307 Temporary Redirect` status code.

Listing 28.4   Using `HttpsRedirectionMiddleware`

```
WebApplicationBuilder builder = WebApplication.CreateBuilder(args);

builder.Services.AddRazorPages();
builder.Services.AddHsts(o => options.MaxAge = TimeSpan.FromHours(1));

WebApplication app = builder.Build();

if(app.Environment.IsProduction())
{
    app.UseHsts();
}

app.UseHttpsRedirection();        ◁──  Adds the HttpsRedirectionMiddleware
                                        to the pipeline and redirects all HTTP
                                        requests to HTTPS
app.UseStaticFiles();
app.UseRouting();

app.MapRazorPages();

app.Run();
```

The `HttpsRedirectionMiddleware` automatically redirects HTTP requests to the first configured HTTPS endpoint for your application. If your application isn't configured for HTTPS, the middleware *won't* redirect and instead logs a warning:

```
warn: Microsoft.AspNetCore.HttpsPolicy.HttpsRedirectionMiddleware[3]
      Failed to determine the https port for redirect.
```

If you want the middleware to redirect to a different port than Kestrel knows about, you can configure that by setting the `ASPNETCORE_HTTPS_PORT` environment variable. This is sometimes necessary if you're using a reverse proxy, and it can be set in alternative ways, as described in Microsoft's "Enforce HTTPS in ASP.NET Core" documentation: http://mng.bz/6DDA.

Using the HSTS and HTTPS redirection middleware is best practice when you're building a server-side application such as a Razor Pages app that will always be accessed in the browser. If you're building an API application. however, a better approach is to not listen for insecure HTTP requests at all!

SSL/TLS offloading, header forwarding, and detecting secure requests

At the start of section 28.1 I encouraged you to consider terminating HTTPS requests at a reverse proxy. That way, the user uses HTTPS to talk to the reverse proxy, and the reverse proxy talks to your app using HTTP. With this setup, your users are protected, but your app doesn't have to deal with TLS certificates itself.

For the HttpsRedirectionMiddleware to work correctly, Kestrel needs some way of knowing whether the original request that the reverse proxy received was over HTTP or HTTPS. The reverse proxy communicates to your app over HTTP, so Kestrel can't figure that out without extra help.

The standard approach used by most reverse proxies (such as IIS, NGINX, and HAProxy) is to add headers to the request before forwarding it to your app. Specifically, a header called X-Forwarded-Proto is added, indicating whether the original request protocol was HTTP or HTTPS.

ASP.NET Core includes ForwardedHeadersMiddleware to look for this header (and others) and update the request accordingly, so your app treats a request that was originally secured by HTTPS as secure for all intents and purposes.

If you're using IIS with the UseIisIntegration() extension, the header forwarding is handled for you automatically. If you're using a different reverse proxy, such as NGINX or HAProxy, you can enable the middleware by setting the environment variable ASPNETCORE_FORWARDEDHEADERS_ENABLED=true, as you saw in chapter 27. Alternatively, you can add the middleware to your application manually, as shown in section 27.3.2.

When the reverse proxy forwards a request, the ForwardedHeadersMiddleware looks for the X-Forwarded-Proto header and updates the request details as appropriate. For all subsequent middleware, the request is considered secure. When adding the middleware manually, it's important that you place ForwardedHeadersMiddleware before the call to UseHsts() or UseHttpsRedirection() so that the forwarded headers are read and the request is marked secure, as appropriate.

28.4.3   *Rejecting HTTP requests in API applications*

Browsers have been adding more and more protections, such as the HSTS header, to try to protect users from using insecure HTTP requests. But not all clients are using a web browser. In this section you'll learn why API applications should generally disable HTTP entirely.

If you're building an API application, you often can't rely on requests coming from a browser. Your API application may primarily serve a client-side framework in the browser, but it may also serve mobile applications or provide an API to other backend services. That means you can't rely on the protections built into web browsers to use HTTPS for your API apps.

On top of that, even if you know all your users are using a browser, the only way to prevent sending all requests over HTTP is to use HSTS preload, as you saw in section 28.4.2. Sending even one request over HTTP can compromise a user, so the safest approach is to listen only for HTTPS requests, not HTTP requests. This is the best option for API apps.

NOTE It would be safest to take this same approach for your browser apps, but unfortunately, browsers currently default to the HTTP versions of apps by default.

You can disable HTTP requests for your application by setting the URLs for your app to include only https:// requests, using `ASPNETCORE_URLS` or another approach, as described in chapter 27. Setting

```
ASPNETCORE_URLS=https://*:5001
```

would ensure that your app serves only HTTPS requests on port 5001 and won't handle HTTP connections at all. This protects your clients, as they can't incorrectly make HTTP requests, and it may even make things simpler on your side, as you don't need to add the HTTP redirection middleware.

HTTPS is one of the most basic requirements for adding security to your application these days. It can be tricky to set up initially, but once you're up and running, you can largely forget about it, especially if you're using SSL/TLS termination at a reverse proxy.

Unfortunately, most other security practices require rather more vigilance to ensure that you don't accidentally introduce vulnerabilities into your app as it grows and develops. In the next chapter we'll look at several common attacks, learn how ASP.NET Core protects you, and see a few things you need to watch out for.

Summary

- HTTPS is used to encrypt your app's data as it travels from the server to the browser and back. This encryption prevents third parties from seeing or modifying it.
- HTTPS is virtually mandatory for production apps, as modern browsers like Chrome and Firefox mark non-HTTPS apps as explicitly "not secure."
- In production, you can avoid handling the TLS in your app by using SSL/TLS offloading. This is where a reverse proxy uses HTTPS to talk to the browser, but the traffic is unencrypted between your app and the reverse proxy. The reverse proxy could be on the same or a different server, such as IIS or NGINX, or it could be a third-party service, such as Cloudflare.
- You can use the ASP.NET Core developer certificate or the IIS express developer certificate to enable HTTPS during development. This can't be used for production, but it's sufficient for testing locally. You must run `dotnet dev-certs https --trust` when you first install the .NET SDK to trust the certificate.
- Kestrel is the default web server in ASP.NET Core. It is responsible for reading and writing data from and to the network, parsing the bytes based on the underlying HTTP and network protocols and converting from raw bytes to .NET objects you can use in your apps.

- You can configure an HTTPS certificate for Kestrel in production using the `Kestrel:Certificates:Default` configuration section. This does not require any code changes to your application; Kestrel automatically loads the certificate when your app starts and uses it to serve HTTPS requests.

- You can use the `HstsMiddleware` to set HSTS headers for your application to ensure that the browser always sends HTTPS requests to your app instead of HTTP requests. HSTS can be enforced only when an initial HTTPS request is made to your app, so it's best used in conjunction with HTTP to HTTPS redirection.

- You can enable HSTS preload for your application to ensure that HTTP requests from browsers are never sent and are always upgraded to HTTPS. You must configure your app as shown in listing 28.3, deploy your app with a TLS certificate, and register your app at the URL https://hstspreload.org. This will schedule your app to be included in browsers' built-in list of HTTPS only sites.

- You can enforce HTTPS for your whole app using the `HttpsRedirectionMiddleware`. This will redirect any HTTP requests to the HTTPS version of endpoints.

- If you're building an API application, you should avoid exposing your application over HTTP entirely and use only HTTPS. Mobile and other nonbrowser clients don't have protections such as HSTS, so there's no safe way to support both HTTP and HTTPS. Disable HTTP for your app by listening only on https:// URLs, such as by setting `ASPNETCORE_URLS=https://*:5001`.

Improving your application's security

This chapter covers

- Defending against cross-site scripting attacks
- Protecting from cross-site request forgery attacks
- Allowing calls to your API from other apps using CORS
- Avoiding attach vectors such as SQL injection attacks

In chapter 28 you learned how and why you should use HTTPS in your application: to protect your HTTP requests from attackers. In this chapter we look at more ways to protect your application and your application's users from attackers. Because security is an extremely broad topic that covers lots of avenues, this chapter is by no means an exhaustive guide. It's intended to make you aware of some of the most common threats to your app and how to counteract them, and also to highlight areas where you can inadvertently introduce vulnerabilities if you're not careful.

TIP   I strongly advise exploring additional resources around security after you've read this chapter. The Open Web Application Security Project (OWASP) (www.owasp.org) is an excellent resource. Alternatively, Troy Hunt has some excellent courses and workshops on security, geared toward .NET developers (https://www.troyhunt.com).

In sections 29.1 and 29.2 you'll start by learning about two potential attacks that should be on your radar: cross-site scripting (XSS) and cross-site request forgery (CSRF). We'll explore how the attacks work and how you can prevent them in your apps. ASP.NET Core has built-in protection against both types of attacks, but you have to remember to use the protection correctly and resist the temptation to circumvent it unless you're certain it's safe to do so.

Section 29.3 deals with a common scenario: you have an application that wants to use JavaScript requests to retrieve data from a second app. By default, web browsers block requests to other apps, so you need to enable cross-origin resource sharing (CORS) in your API to achieve this. We'll look at how CORS works, how to create a CORS policy for your app, and how to apply it to specific endpoints.

The final section of this chapter, section 29.4, covers a collection of common threats to your application. Each one represents a potentially critical flaw that an attacker could use to compromise your application. The solutions to each threat are generally relatively simple; the important thing is to recognize where the flaws could exist in your own apps so you can ensure that you don't leave yourself vulnerable.

As I mentioned in chapter 28, you should always start by adding HTTPS to your app to encrypt the traffic between your users' browsers and your app. Without HTTPS, attackers could subvert many of the safeguards you add to your app, so it's an important first step to take.

Unfortunately, most other security practices require rather more vigilance to ensure that you don't accidentally introduce vulnerabilities into your app as it grows and develops. Many attacks are conceptually simple and have been known about for years, yet they're still commonly found in new applications. In the next section we'll look at one such attack and see how to defend against it when building apps using Razor Pages.

29.1   Defending against cross-site scripting (XSS) attacks

In this section I describe XSS attacks and how attackers can use them to compromise your users. I show how the Razor Pages framework protects you from these attacks, how to disable the protections when you need to, and what to look out for. I also discuss the difference between HTML encoding and JavaScript encoding, and the effect of using the wrong encoder.

Attackers can exploit a vulnerability in your app to create XSS attacks that execute code in another user's browser. Commonly, attackers submit content using a legitimate approach, such as an input form, that is later rendered somewhere to the page. By carefully crafting malicious input, the attacker can execute arbitrary JavaScript on a user's browser and so can steal cookies, impersonate the user, and generally do bad things.

> **TIP** For a detailed discussion of XSS attacks, see the "Cross Site Scripting (XSS)" article on the OWASP site: https://owasp.org/www-community/attacks/xss.

Figure 29.1 shows a basic example of an XSS attack. Legitimate users of your app can send their name to your app by submitting a form. The app then adds the name to an internal list and renders the whole list to the page. If the names are not rendered safely, a malicious user can execute JavaScript in the browser of every other user who views the list.

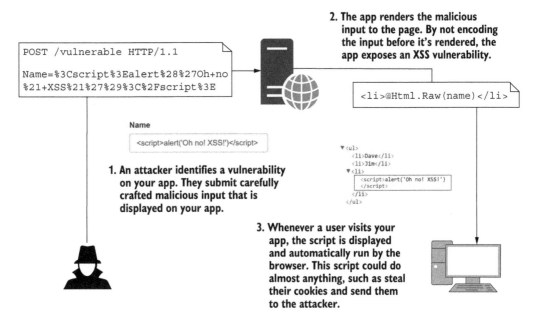

Figure 29.1 How an XSS vulnerability is exploited. An attacker submits malicious content to your app, which is displayed in the browsers of other users. If the app doesn't encode the content when writing to the page, the input becomes part of the HTML of the page and can run arbitrary JavaScript.

In figure 29.1 the user entered a snippet of HTML, such as their name. When users view the list of names, the Razor template renders the names using `@Html.Raw()`, which writes the `<script>` tag directly to the document. The user's input has become part of the page's HTML structure. As soon as the page is loaded in a user's browser, the `<script>` tag executes, and the user is compromised. Once an attacker can execute arbitrary JavaScript on a user's browser, they can do pretty much anything.

TIP You can dramatically limit the control an attacker has even if they exploit an XSS vulnerability using a `Content-Security-Policy` (CSP). You can read about CSP at http://mng.bz/nWW2. I have an open-source library you can use to integrate a CSP into your app available on NuGet at http://mng.bz/vnn4.

The vulnerability here is due to rendering the user input in an unsafe way. If the data isn't encoded to make it safe before it's rendered, you could open your users to attack. By default, Razor protects against XSS attacks by HTML-encoding any data written using Tag Helpers, HTML Helpers, or the @ syntax. So generally you should be safe, as you saw in chapter 17.

Using `@Html.Raw()` is where the danger lies: if the HTML you're rendering contains user input (even indirectly), you could have an XSS vulnerability. By rendering the user input with @ instead, the content is encoded before it's written to the output, as shown in figure 29.2.

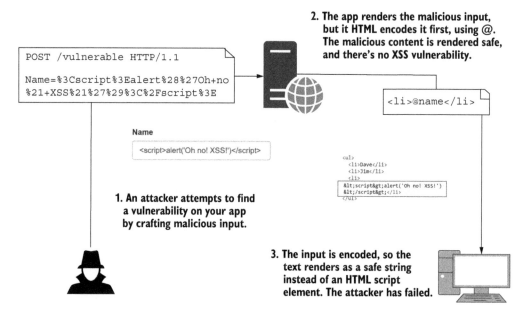

Figure 29.2 Protecting against XSS attacks by HTML-encoding user input using @ in Razor templates. The `<script>` tag is encoded so that it is no longer rendered as HTML and can't be used to compromise your app.

This example demonstrates using HTML encoding to prevent elements being directly added to the HTML Document Object Model (DOM), but it's not the only case you have to think about. If you're passing untrusted data to JavaScript or using untrusted data in URL query values, you must make sure to encode the data correctly.

A common scenario is when you're using JavaScript with Razor Pages, and you want to pass a value from the server to the client. If you use the standard @ symbol to render the data to the page, the output will be HTML-encoded. Unfortunately, if you HTML-encode a string and inject it directly into JavaScript, you probably won't get what you expect.

For example, if you have a variable in your Razor file called `name`, and you want to make it available in JavaScript, you might be tempted to use something like this:

```
<script>var name = '@name'</script>
```

If the name contains special characters, Razor will encode them using HTML encoding, which probably isn't what you want in this JavaScript context. For example, if `name` was `Arnold "Arnie" Schwarzenegger`, rendering it as you did previously would give this:

```
<script>var name = 'Arnold &quot;Arnie&quot; Schwarzenegger';</script>
```

Note that the double quotation marks (`"`) have been HTML-encoded to `&quot;`. If you use this value in JavaScript directly, expecting it to be a safe encoded value, it's going to look wrong, as shown in figure 29.3.

With HTML encoding, the quote marks are displayed incorrectly in JavaScript.

JavaScript encoding gives a safe way to render the user input in the expected format.

Figure 29.3   Comparison of alerts when using JavaScript encoding compared with HTML encoding

Instead, you should encode the variable using JavaScript encoding so that the double-quote character is rendered as a safe Unicode character, `\u0022`. You can achieve this by injecting a `JavaScriptEncoder` into the view and calling `Encode()` on the `name` variable:

```
@inject System.Text.Encodings.Web.JavaScriptEncoder encoder;
<script>var name = '@encoder.Encode(name)'</script>
```

To avoid having to remember to use JavaScript encoding, I recommend that you don't write values into JavaScript like this. Instead, write the value to an HTML element's attributes, and then read that into the JavaScript variable later, as shown in the following listing. That prevents the need for the JavaScript encoder entirely.

Listing 29.1   Passing values to JavaScript by writing them to HTML attributes

```
<div id="data" data-name="@name"></div>        Write the value you want in JavaScript to a
<script>                                        data-* attribute. This HTML-encodes the data.
var ele = document.getElementById('data');
```
Gets a reference to the HTML element

```
var name = ele.getAttribute('data-name'); ◁──┐   Reads the data-* attribute into JavaScript,
</script>                                      │   which converts it to JavaScript encoding
```

XSS attacks are still common, and it's easy to expose yourself to them whenever you allow users to input data. Validation of the incoming data can help sometimes, but it's often a tricky problem. For example, a naive name validator might require that you use only letters, which would prevent most attacks. Unfortunately, that doesn't account for users with hyphens or apostrophes in their name, let alone users with non-Western names. People get (understandably) upset when you tell them that their name is invalid, so be wary of this approach!

Whether or not you use strict validation, you should always encode the data when you render it to the page. Think carefully whenever you find yourself writing @Html.Raw(). Is there any way, no matter how contrived, for a user to get malicious data into that field? If so, you'll need to find another way to display the data.

XSS vulnerabilities allow attackers to execute JavaScript on a user's browser. The next vulnerability we're going to consider lets them make requests to your API as though they're a different logged-in user, even when the user isn't using your app. Scared? I hope so!

29.2 *Protecting from cross-site request forgery (CSRF) attacks*

In this section you'll learn about CSRF attacks, how attackers can use them to impersonate a user on your site, and how to protect against them using antiforgery tokens. Razor Pages protects you from these attacks by default, but you can disable these verifications, so it's important to understand the implications of doing so.

CSRF attacks can be a problem for websites or APIs that use cookies for authentication. A CSRF attack involves a malicious website making an authenticated request to your API on behalf of the user, without the user's initiating the request. In this section we'll explore how these attacks work and how you can mitigate them with antiforgery tokens.

The canonical example of this attack is a bank transfer/withdrawal. Imagine you have a banking application that stores authentication tokens in a cookie, as is common (especially in traditional server-side rendered applications). Browsers automatically send the cookies associated with a domain with every request so the app knows whether a user is authenticated.

Now imagine your application has a page that lets a user transfer funds from their account to another account using a POST request to the Balance Razor Page. You have to be logged in to access the form (you've protected the Razor Page with the [Authorize] attribute or global authorization requirements), but otherwise you post a form that says how much you want to transfer and where you want to transfer it. Seems simple enough?

Suppose that a user visits your site, logs in, and performs a transaction. Then they visit a second website that the attacker has control of. The attacker has embedded a form in their website that performs a POST to your bank's website, identical to the transfer-funds form on your banking website. This form does something malicious, such as transfer all the user's funds to the attacker, as shown in figure 29.4. Browsers automatically send the cookies for the application when the page does a full form post, and the banking app has no way of knowing that this is a malicious request. The unsuspecting user has given all their money to the attacker!

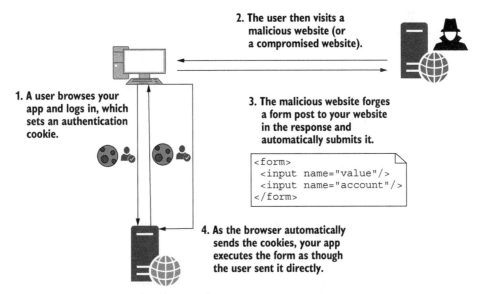

2. The user then visits a malicious website (or a compromised website).

1. A user browses your app and logs in, which sets an authentication cookie.

3. The malicious website forges a form post to your website in the response and automatically submits it.

```
<form>
 <input name="value"/>
 <input name="account"/>
</form>
```

4. As the browser automatically sends the cookies, your app executes the form as though the user sent it directly.

Figure 29.4 A CSRF attack occurs when a logged-in user visits a malicious site. The malicious site crafts a form that matches one on your app and POSTs it to your app. The browser sends the authentication cookie automatically, so your app sees the request as a valid request from the user.

The vulnerability here revolves around the fact that browsers automatically send cookies when a page is requested (using a GET request) or a form is POSTed. There's no difference between a legitimate POST of the form in your banking app and the attacker's malicious POST. Unfortunately, this behavior is baked into the web; it's what allows you to navigate websites seamlessly after initially logging in.

> **TIP** Browsers have additional protections to prevent cookies being sent in this situation, called SameSite cookies. By default, most browsers use SameSite=Lax, which prevents this vulnerable behavior. You can read about SameSite cookies and how to work with them in ASP.NET Core at http://mng.bz/4DDj.

A common solution to this CSRF attack is the *synchronizer token* pattern, which uses user-specific, unique antiforgery tokens to enforce a difference between a legitimate POST and a forged POST from an attacker. One token is stored in a cookie, and another is added to the form you wish to protect. Your app generates the tokens at runtime based on the current logged-in user, so there's no way for an attacker to create one for their forged form.

TIP The "Cross-Site Request Forgery Prevention Cheat Sheet" article on the OWASP site (http://mng.bz/5jRa) has a thorough discussion of the CSRF vulnerability, including the synchronizer token pattern.

When the `Balance` Razor Page receives a form POST, it compares the value in the form with the value in the cookie. If either value is missing or the values don't match, the request is rejected. If an attacker creates a POST, the browser posts the cookie token as usual, but there won't be a token in the form itself or the token won't be valid. The Razor Page rejects the request, protecting from the CSRF attack, as in figure 29.5.

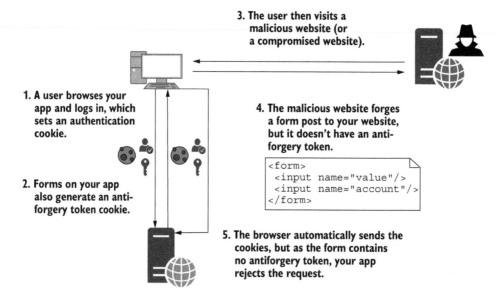

3. The user then visits a malicious website (or a compromised website).

1. A user browses your app and logs in, which sets an authentication cookie.

4. The malicious website forges a form post to your website, but it doesn't have an antiforgery token.

```
<form>
  <input name="value"/>
  <input name="account"/>
</form>
```

2. Forms on your app also generate an antiforgery token cookie.

5. The browser automatically sends the cookies, but as the form contains no antiforgery token, your app rejects the request.

Figure 29.5 Protecting against a CSRF attack using antiforgery tokens. The browser automatically forwards the cookie token, but the malicious site can't read it and so can't include a token in the form. The app rejects the malicious request because the tokens don't match.

The good news is that Razor Pages automatically protects you against CSRF attacks. The Form Tag Helper automatically sets an antiforgery token cookie and renders the token to a hidden field called `__RequestVerificationToken` for every `<form>` element in your app (unless you specifically disable them). For example, take this simple Razor template that posts back to the same Razor Page:

```
<form method="post">
    <label>Amount</label>
    <input type="number" name="amount" />
    <button type="submit">Withdraw funds</button>
</form>
```

When rendered to HTML, the antiforgery token is stored in the hidden field and is posted back with a legitimate request:

```
<form method="post">
    <label>Amount</label>
    <input type="number" name="amount" />
    <button type="submit" >Withdraw funds</button>
    <input name="__RequestVerificationToken" type="hidden"
value="CfDJ8Daz26qb0hBGsw7QCK"/>
</form>
```

ASP.NET Core automatically adds the antiforgery tokens to every form, and Razor Pages automatically validates them. The framework ensures that the antiforgery tokens exist in both the cookie and the form data, ensures that they match, and rejects any requests where they don't.

If you're using Model-View-Controller (MVC) controllers with views instead of Razor Pages, ASP.NET Core still adds the antiforgery tokens to every form. Unfortunately, it *doesn't* validate them for you. Instead, you must decorate your controllers and actions with the [ValidateAntiForgeryToken] attribute. This ensures that the antiforgery tokens exist in both the cookie and the form data, checks that they match, and rejects any requests in which they don't.

> **WARNING** ASP.NET Core doesn't automatically validate antiforgery tokens if you're using MVC controllers with Views. You must make sure to mark all vulnerable methods with [ValidateAntiForgeryToken] attributes instead, as described in the "Prevent Cross-Site Request Forgery (XSRF/CSRF) attacks in ASP.NET Core" documentation: http://mng.bz/QPPv. Note that if you're not using cookies for authentication, you are not vulnerable to CSRF attacks: CSRF attacks arise from attackers exploiting the fact that browsers automatically attach cookies to requests. No cookies, no problem!

Generally, you need to use antiforgery tokens only for POST, DELETE, and other dangerous request types that are used for modifying state. GET requests shouldn't be used for this purpose, so the framework doesn't require valid antiforgery tokens to call them. Razor Pages validates antiforgery tokens for dangerous verbs like POST and ignores safe verbs like GET. As long as you create your app following this pattern (and you should!), the framework does the right thing to keep you safe.

If you need to explicitly ignore antiforgery tokens on a Razor Page for some reason, you can disable the validation by applying the [IgnoreAntiforgeryToken] attribute to a Razor Page's PageModel. This bypasses the framework protections for those cases when you're doing something that you know is safe and doesn't need protecting, but in most cases it's better to play it safe and validate.

CSRF attacks can be a tricky thing to get your head around from a technical point of view, but for the most part everything should work without much effort on your part. Razor adds antiforgery tokens to your forms, and the Razor Pages framework takes care of validation for you.

Things get trickier if you're making a lot of requests to an API using JavaScript, and you're posting JavaScript Object Notation (JSON) objects rather than form data. In these cases, you won't be able to send the verification token as part of a form (because you're sending JSON), so you'll need to add it as a header in the request instead. Microsoft's documentation "Prevent Cross-Site Request Forgery (XSRF/CSRF) attacks in ASP.NET Core" contains an example of adding the header in JavaScript and validating it in your application. See http://mng.bz/XNNa.

> **TIP** If you're not using cookie authentication and instead have a single-page application (SPA) that sends authentication tokens in a header, the good news is that you don't have to worry about CSRF at all! Malicious sites can send only cookies, not headers, to your API, so they can't make authenticated requests.

Generating unique tokens with the data protection APIs

The antiforgery tokens used to prevent CSRF attacks rely on the ability of the framework to use strong symmetric encryption to encrypt and decrypt data. Encryption algorithms typically rely on one or more keys, which are used to initialize the encryption and to make the process reproducible. If you have the key, you can encrypt and decrypt data; without it, the data is secure.

In ASP.NET Core, encryption is handled by the data protection APIs. They're used to create the antiforgery tokens, encrypt authentication cookies, and generate secure tokens in general. Crucially, they also control the management of the key files that are used for encryption. A *key file* is a small XML file that contains the random key value used for encryption in ASP.NET Core apps. It's critical that it's stored securely. If an attacker got hold of it, they could impersonate any user of your app and generally do bad things!

The data protection system stores the keys in a safe location, depending on how and where you host your app:

- *Azure Web App*—In a special synced folder, shared between regions
- *IIS without user profile*—Encrypted in the registry
- *Account with user profile*—In %LOCALAPPDATA%\ASP.NET\DataProtection-Keys on Windows, or ~/.aspnet/DataProtection-Keys on Linux or macOS
- *All other cases*—In memory; when the app restarts, the keys will be lost

So why do you care? For your app to be able to read your users' authentication cookies, it must decrypt them by using the same key that was used to encrypt them. If you're running in a web-farm scenario, by default each server has its own key and won't be able to read cookies encrypted by other servers.

To get around this, you must configure your app to store its data protection keys in a central location. This could be a shared folder on a hard drive, a Redis instance, or an Azure blob storage instance, for example.

Microsoft's documentation on the data protection APIs is extremely detailed, but it can be overwhelming. I recommend reading the section on configuring data protection, ("Configure ASP.NET Core Data Protection," http://mng.bz/d40i) and configuring a key storage provider for use in a web-farm scenario ("Key storage providers in ASP.NET Core," http://mng.bz/5pW6). I also have an introduction to the data protection APIs on my blog at http://mng.bz/yQQd.

It's worth clarifying that the CSRF vulnerability discussed in this section requires that a malicious site does a full form POST to your app. The malicious site can't make the request to your API using client-side-only JavaScript, as browsers block JavaScript requests to your API that are from a different origin.

This is a safety feature, but it can often cause you problems. If you're building a client-side SPA, or even if you have a little JavaScript on an otherwise server-side rendered app, you may need to make such cross-origin requests. In the next section I describe a common scenario you're likely to run into and show how you can modify your apps to work around Pit.

29.3 Calling your web APIs from other domains using CORS

In this section you'll learn about cross-origin resource sharing (CORS), a protocol to allow JavaScript to make requests from one domain to another. CORS is a frequent area of confusion for many developers, so this section describes why it's necessary and how CORS headers work. You'll then learn how to add CORS to both your whole application and specific web API actions, and how to configure multiple CORS policies for your application.

As you've already seen, CSRF attacks can be powerful, but they would be even more dangerous if it weren't for browsers implementing the *same-origin policy*. This policy blocks apps from using JavaScript to call a web API at a different location unless the web API explicitly allows it.

> **DEFINITION** *Origins* are deemed to be the same if they match the scheme (HTTP or HTTPS), domain (example.com), and port (80 by default for HTTP and 443 for HTTPS). If an app attempts to access a resource using JavaScript, and the origins aren't identical, the browser blocks the request.

The same-origin policy is strict. The origins of the two URLs must be identical for the request to be allowed. For example, the following origins are the same:

- http://example.com/home
- http://example.com/site.css

The paths are different for these two URLs (/home and /site.css), but the scheme, domain, and port (80) are identical. So if you were on the home page of your app, you could request the /site.css file using JavaScript without any problems.

By contrast, the origins of the following sites are different, so you couldn't request any of these URLs using JavaScript from the http://example.com origin:

- *https://example.com*—Different scheme (https)
- *http://www.example.com*—Different domain (includes a subdomain)
- *http://example.com:5000*—Different port (default HTTP port is 80)

For simple apps, where you have a single web app handling all your functionality, this limitation might not be a problem, but it's extremely common for an app to make requests to another domain. For example, you might have an e-commerce site hosted at http://shopping.com, and you're attempting to load data from http://api.shop ping.com to display details about the products available for sale. With this configuration, you'll fall foul of the same-origin policy. Any attempt to make a request using JavaScript to the API domain will fail, with an error similar to figure 29.6.

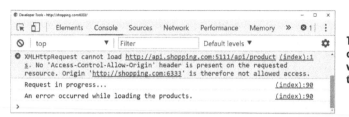

The browser won't allow cross-origin requests by default and will block your app from accessing the response.

Figure 29.6   The console log for a failed cross-origin request. Chrome has blocked a cross-origin request from the app http://shopping.com:6333 to the API at http://api.shopping.com:5111.

The need to make cross-origin requests from JavaScript is increasingly common with the rise of client-side SPAs and the move away from monolithic apps. Luckily, there's a web standard that lets you work around this in a safe way; this standard is CORS. You can use CORS to control which apps can call your API, so you can enable scenarios like this one.

29.3.1 *Understanding CORS and how it works*

CORS is a web standard that allows your web API to make statements about who can make cross-origin requests to it. For example, you could make statements such as these:

- Allow cross-origin requests from https://shopping.com and https://app .shopping.com.
- Allow only GET cross-origin requests.
- Allow returning the Server header in responses to cross-origin requests.
- Allow credentials (such as authentication cookies or authorization headers) to be sent with cross-origin requests.

You can combine these rules into a *policy* and apply different policies to different endpoints of your API. You could apply a policy to your entire application or a different policy to every API action.

CORS works using HTTP headers. When your web API application receives a request, it sets special headers on the response to indicate whether cross-origin requests are allowed, which origins they're allowed from, and which HTTP verbs and headers the request can use—pretty much everything about the request.

In some cases, before sending a real request to your API, the browser sends a *pre-flight* request, a request sent using the OPTIONS verb, which the browser uses to check whether it's allowed to make the real request. If the API sends back the correct headers, the browser sends the true cross-origin request, as shown in figure 29.7.

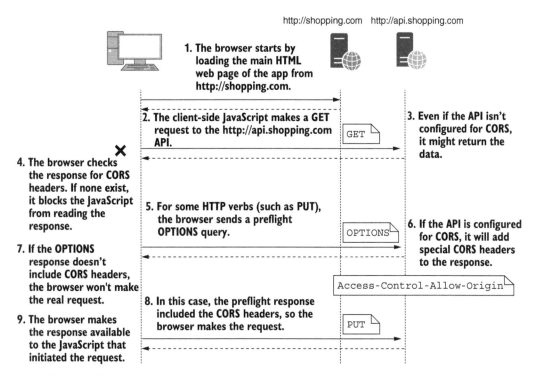

Figure 29.7 Two cross-origin requests. The response to the GET request doesn't contain any CORS headers, so the browser blocks the app from reading it, even though the response may contain data from the server. The second request requires a preflight OPTIONS request to check whether CORS is enabled. As the response contains CORS headers, the browser makes the real request and provides the response to the JavaScript app.

> **TIP** For a more detailed discussion of CORS, see *CORS in Action,* by Monsur Hossain (Manning, 2014), http://mng.bz/aD41.

The CORS specification, which you can find at http://mng.bz/MBBB, is complicated, with a variety of headers, processes, and terminology to contend with. Fortunately, ASP.NET Core handles the details of the specification for you, so your main concern is working out exactly who needs to access your API, and under what circumstances.

29.3.2 Adding a global CORS policy to your whole app

Typically, you shouldn't set up CORS for your APIs until you need it. Browsers block cross-origin communication for a reason: it closes an avenue of attack. They're not being awkward. Wait until you have an API hosted on a different domain to the app that needs to access it.

Adding CORS support to your application requires you to do four things:

- Add the CORS services to your app.
- Configure at least one CORS policy.
- Add the CORS middleware to your middleware pipeline.
- Set a default CORS policy for your entire app or decorate your endpoints with EnableCors metadata to selectively enable CORS for specific endpoints.

To add the CORS services to your application, call `AddCors()` on your `WebApplication-Builder` instance in Program.cs:

```
builder.Services.AddCors();
```

The bulk of your effort in configuring CORS will go into policy configuration. A CORS policy controls how your application responds to cross-origin requests. It defines which origins are allowed, which headers to return, which HTTP methods to allow, and so on. You normally define your policies inline when you add the CORS services to your application.

Consider the previous e-commerce site example. You want your API that is hosted at http://api.shopping.com to be available from the main app via client-side JavaScript, hosted at http://shopping.com. You therefore need to configure the *API* to allow cross-origin requests.

> **NOTE**   Remember, it's the app that will get errors when attempting to make cross-origin requests, but it's the API you're accessing that you need to add CORS to, not the app making the requests.

The following listing shows how to configure a policy called `"AllowShoppingApp"` to enable cross-origin requests from http://shopping.com to the API. Additionally, we explicitly allow any HTTP verb type; without this call, only simple methods (GET, HEAD, and POST) are allowed. The policies are built up using the familiar fluent builder style you've seen throughout this book.

Listing 29.2   Configuring a CORS policy to allow requests from a specific origin

```
public void ConfigureServices(IServiceCollection services)
{
    services.AddCors(options => {
        options.AddPolicy("AllowShoppingApp", policy =>
            policy.WithOrigins("http://shopping.com")
                .AllowAnyMethod());
    });
    // other service configuration
}
```

The AddCors method exposes an Action<CorsOptions> overload.

Every policy has a unique name.

The WithOrigins method specifies which origins are allowed. Note that the URL has no trailing /.

Allows all HTTP verbs to call the API

> **WARNING**   When listing origins in `WithOrigins()`, ensure that they don't have a trailing `"/"`; otherwise, the origin will never match, and your cross-origin requests will fail.

Once you've defined a CORS policy, you can apply it to your application. In the following listing, you apply the `"AllowShoppingApp"` policy to the whole application using `CorsMiddleware` by calling `UseCors()`.

Listing 29.3   Adding the CORS middleware and configuring a default CORS policy

```
var builder = WebApplication.CreateBuilder(args);
builder.Services.AddCors(options => {
    options.AddPolicy("AllowShoppingApp", policy =>
        policy.WithOrigins("http://shopping.com")
            .AllowAnyMethod());
});

var app = builder.Build();
app.UseRouting();
app.UseCors("AllowShoppingApp");       ⟵——┐ Adds the CORS middleware and uses
app.UseAuthentication();                     AllowShoppingApp as the default policy
app.UseAuthorization();

app.MapGet("/api/products", () => new string[] {});

app.Run();
```

> **NOTE**   As with all middleware, the order of the CORS middleware is important.
> You must place the call to UseCors() *after* UseRouting(). The CORS middleware
> needs to intercept cross-origin requests to your web API actions so it can gener-
> ate the correct responses to preflight requests and add the necessary headers. It's
> common to place the CORS middleware before a call to UseAuthentication().

With the CORS middleware in place for the API, the shopping app can now make cross-
origin requests. You can call the API from the http://shopping.com site, and the browser
lets the CORS request through, as shown in figure 29.8. If you make the same request
from a domain other than http://shopping.com, the request continues to be blocked.

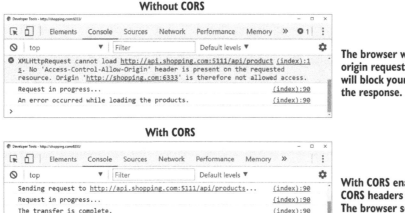

**Figure 29.8   With CORS enabled, as in the bottom image, cross-origin requests can be made, and the
browser will make the response available to the JavaScript. Compare this to the top image, in which the
request was blocked.**

Applying a CORS policy globally to your application in this way may be overkill. If there's only a subset of actions in your API that need to be accessed from other origins, it's prudent to enable CORS only for those specific actions. This can be achieved by adding metadata to your endpoints.

29.3.3 Adding CORS to specific endpoints with EnableCors metadata

Browsers block cross-origin requests by default for good reason: they have the potential to be abused by malicious or compromised sites. Enabling CORS for your entire app may not be worth the risk if you know that only a subset of actions will ever need to be accessed cross-origin.

 If that's the case, it's best to enable a CORS policy only for those specific endpoints. ASP.NET Core provides the `RequireCors()` method, which you can apply to your minimal API endpoints or route groups, and the `[EnableCors]` attribute, which lets you select a policy to apply to a given controller or action method.

> **NOTE** Both these methods add CORS metadata to the endpoint, which is used by the `CorsMiddleware` to determine the policy to apply. This is why the `CorsMiddleware` should be placed after the `RoutingMiddleware`, so that the `CorsMiddleware` knows which endpoint was selected and so which CORS policy to apply.

With the `RequireCors()` method and `[EnableCors]` attribute, you can apply different CORS policies to different endpoints. For example, you could allow GET requests access to your entire API from the http://shopping.com domain but allow other HTTP verbs only for a specific endpoint while allowing anyone to access your product list endpoints.

 You define CORS policies in the call to `AddCors()` by calling `AddPolicy()` and giving the policy a name, as you saw in listing 29.2. If you're using endpoint-specific policies, instead of calling `UseCors("AllowShoppingApp")` as you saw in listing 29.3, you should add the middleware without a default policy by calling `UseCors()` only.

 You can then selectively enable CORS for individual endpoints and specifying the policy to apply. To apply CORS to a minimal API endpoint or route group, call `RequireCors("AllowShoppingApp")`, as shown in the following listing. To apply a policy to a controller or an action method, apply the `[EnableCors("AllowShoppingApp"]` attribute. You can disable cross-origin access for an endpoint by applying the `[DisableCors]` attribute.

Listing 29.4 Applying a CORS policy to minimal API endpoints

```
WebApplicationBuilder builder = WebApplication.CreateBuilder(args);
builder.Services.AddCors(options => { /* Config not shown*/});

var app = builder.Build();      Adds the CorsMiddleware without
app.UseCors();         ◁─────── configuring a default policy
```

```
app.MapGet("/api/products", () => new string[] {})
    .RequireCors("AllowShoppingApp");
```
Applies the AllowShoppingApp CORS policy to the endpoint

```
app.MapGet("/api/products",
    [EnableCors("AllowShoppingApp")] () => new { });
```
You can apply attributes to the lamba or handler method, as well as to MVC action methods.

```
app.MapGroup("/api/categories")
    .RequireCors("AllowAnyOrigin");
```
You can apply CORS policies to whole route groups.

```
app.MapDelete("/api/products",
    [DisableCors] () => Results.NoContent());
```
The DisableCors attribute disables CORS for the endpoint completely.

```
app.Run();
```

If you define a default policy but then also call `RequireCors()` or add an `[EnableCors]` attribute, then both policies are applied. This can get confusing, so I recommend not applying a default CORS policy in the middleware and specifying the policy at the route group or endpoint level. Alternatively, if you do want to apply a policy to your whole app, avoid applying individual policies to endpoints as well.

Whether you choose to use a single default CORS policy or multiple policies, you need to configure the CORS policies for your application in the call to `AddCors`. Many options are available when configuring CORS. In the next section I provide an overview of the possibilities.

29.3.4 Configuring CORS policies

Browsers implement the cross-origin policy for security reasons, so you should carefully consider the implications of relaxing any of the restrictions they impose. Even if you enable cross-origin requests, you can still control what data cross-origin requests can send and what your API returns. For example, you can configure

- The origins that may make a cross-origin request to your API
- The HTTP verbs (such as GET, POST, and DELETE) that can be used
- The headers the browser can send
- The headers the browser can read from your app's response
- Whether the browser will send authentication credentials with the request

You define all these options when creating a CORS policy in your call to `AddCors()` using the `CorsPolicyBuilder`, as you saw in listing 29.2. A policy can set all or none of these options, so you can customize the results to your heart's content. Table 29.1 shows some of the options available and their effects.

Table 29.1 The methods available for configuring a CORS policy and their effect on the policy

CorsPolicyBuilder method example	Result
WithOrigins("http://shopping.com")	Allows cross-origin requests from http://shopping.com
AllowAnyOrigin()	Allows cross-origin requests from any origin. This means any website can make JavaScript requests to your API.

Table 29.1 The methods available for configuring a CORS policy and their effect on the policy *(continued)*

`CorsPolicyBuilder` method example	Result
`WithMethods()`/`AllowAnyMethod()`	Sets the allowed methods (such as `GET`, `POST`, and `DELETE`) that can be made to your API
`WithHeaders()`/`AllowAnyHeader()`	Sets the headers that the browser may send to your API. If you restrict the headers, you must include at least `Accept`, `Content-Type`, and `Origin` to allow valid requests.
`WithExposedHeaders()`	Allows your API to send extra headers to the browser. By default, only the `Cache-Control`, `Content-Language`, `Content-Type`, `Expires`, `Last-Modified`, and `Pragma` headers are sent in the response.
`AllowCredentials()`	By default, the browser won't send authentication details with cross-origin requests unless you explicitly allow it. You must also enable sending credentials client-side in JavaScript when making the request.

One of the first problems in setting up CORS is realizing you have a cross-origin problem at all. Several times I've been stumped trying to figure out why a request won't work, until I realize the request is going cross-domain or from HTTP to HTTPS, for example.

Whenever possible, I recommend avoiding cross-origin requests. You can end up with subtle differences in the way browsers handle them, which can cause more headaches. In particular, avoid HTTP to HTTPS cross-domain problems by running all your applications behind HTTPS. As discussed in chapter 28, that's a best practice anyway, and it'll help prevent a whole class of CORS headaches.

> **TIP** Another (often preferable) option is to configure CORS policies in your reverse proxy or application gateway. You can configure Azure App Service with allowed origins, for example, so that you don't need to modify your application code.

Once I've established that I definitely need a CORS policy, I typically start with the `WithOrigins()` method. Then I expand or restrict the policy further, as need be, to provide cross-origin lockdown of my API while still allowing the required functionality. CORS can be tricky to work around, but remember, the restrictions are there for your safety.

Cross-origin requests are only one of many potential avenues attackers could use to compromise your app. Many of these are trivial to defend against, but you need to be aware of them and know how to mitigate them. In the next section we'll look at common threats and how to avoid them.

29.4 Exploring other attack vectors

So far in this chapter, I've described two potential ways attackers can compromise your apps—XSS and CSRF attacks—and how to prevent them. Both of these vulnerabilities regularly appear in the OWASP top ten list of most critical web app risks, so it's important to be aware of them and to avoid introducing them into your apps.

> **TIP** OWASP publishes the list online, with descriptions of each attack and how to prevent those attacks. There's a cheat sheet for staying safe here: https://cheatsheetseries.owasp.org.

In this section I'll provide an overview of some of the other most common vulnerabilities and how to avoid them in your apps.

29.4.1 Detecting and avoiding open redirect attacks

A common OWASP vulnerability is due to open redirect attacks. An *open redirect attack* occurs when a user clicks a link to an otherwise-safe app and ends up being redirected to a malicious website, such as one that serves malware. The safe app contains no direct links to the malicious website, so how does this happen?

Open redirect attacks occur where the next page is passed as a parameter to an endpoint. The most common example is when you're logging in to an app. Typically, apps remember the page a user is on before redirecting them to a login page by passing the current page as a `returnUrl` query string parameter. After the user logs in, the app redirects the user to the `returnUrl` to carry on where they left off.

Imagine a user is browsing an e-commerce site. They click Buy for a product and are redirected to the login page. The product page they were on is passed as the `returnUrl`, so after they log in, they're redirected to the product page instead of being dumped back to the home screen.

An open redirect attack takes advantage of this common pattern, as shown in figure 29.9. A malicious attacker creates a login URL where the `returnUrl` is set to the website they want to send the user to and convinces the user to click the link to your web app. After the user logs in, a vulnerable app redirects the user to the malicious site.

The simple solution to this attack is to always validate that the `returnUrl` is a local URL that belongs to your app before redirecting users to it. The default Identity UI does this already, so you shouldn't have to worry about the login page if you're using Identity, as described in chapter 23.

If you have redirects in other parts of your app, ASP.NET Core provides a couple of helper methods for staying safe, the most useful of which is `Url.IsLocalUrl()`. Listing 29.5 shows how you could verify that a provided return URL is safe and, if not, redirect to the app's home page.

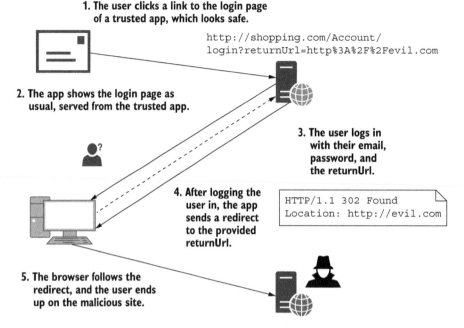

1. The user clicks a link to the login page of a trusted app, which looks safe.

```
http://shopping.com/Account/
login?returnUrl=http%3A%2F%2Fevil.com
```

2. The app shows the login page as usual, served from the trusted app.

3. The user logs in with their email, password, and the returnUrl.

4. After logging the user in, the app sends a redirect to the provided returnUrl.

```
HTTP/1.1 302 Found
Location: http://evil.com
```

5. The browser follows the redirect, and the user ends up on the malicious site.

Figure 29.9 An open redirect makes use of the common return URL pattern. This is typically used for login pages but may be used in other areas of your app too. If your app doesn't verify that the URL is safe before redirecting the user, it could redirect users to malicious sites.

You can also use the `LocalRedirect()` helper method on the `ControllerBase` and Razor Page `PageModel` classes, which throw an exception if the provided URL isn't local.

Listing 29.5 Detecting open redirect attacks by checking for local return URLs

```
[HttpPost]
public async Task<IActionResult> Login(
    LoginViewModel model, string returnUrl = null)
{
    // Verify password, and sign user in

    if (Url.IsLocalUrl(returnUrl))
    {
        return Redirect(returnUrl);
    }
    else
    {
        return RedirectToPage("Index");
    }
}
```

> The return URL is provided as an argument to the action method.

> Returns true if the return URL starts with / or ~/

> The URL is local, so it's safe to redirect to it.

> The URL was not local and could be an open redirect attack, so redirect to the homepage for safety.

This simple pattern protects against open redirect attacks that could otherwise expose your users to malicious content. Whenever you're redirecting to a URL that comes from a query string or other user input, you should use this pattern.

TIP In some authentication flows, such as when authenticating with OpenID Connect, you *can't* redirect to a local URL, so you can't use this pattern. Instead, OpenID Connect requires that you preregister the allowed redirect URLs and redirect only to a registered URL. You should consider using this pattern when you can't enforce a local-only redirect.

Open redirect attacks present a risk to your *users* rather than to your app directly. The next vulnerability represents a critical vulnerability in your app itself.

29.4.2 Avoiding SQL injection attacks with EF Core and parameterization

SQL injection attacks represent one of the most dangerous threats to your application. Attackers craft simple malicious input, which they send to your application as traditional form-based input or by customizing URLs and query strings to execute arbitrary code against your database. An SQL injection vulnerability could expose your entire database to attackers, so it's critical that you spot and remove any such vulnerabilities in your apps.

I hope I've scared you a little with that introduction, so now for the good news: if you're using Entity Framework Core (EF Core) or pretty much any other object-relational mapper (ORM) in a standard way, you should be safe. EF Core has built-in protections against SQL injection, so as long as you're not doing anything funky, you should be fine.

SQL injection vulnerabilities occur when you build SQL statements yourself and include dynamic input that an attacker provides, even indirectly. EF Core provides the ability to create raw SQL queries using the `FromSqlRaw()` method, so you must be careful when using this method.

Imagine your recipe app has a search form that lets you search for a recipe by name. If you write the query using LINQ extension methods (as discussed in chapter 12), you would have no risk of SQL injection attacks. However, if you decide to write your SQL query by hand, you open yourself to such a vulnerability, as shown in the following listing.

Listing 29.6 An SQL injection vulnerability in EF Core due to string concatenation

```
public IList<User> FindRecipe(string search)    ◁──┐ The search parameter comes
{                                                    │ from user input, so it's unsafe.
    return _context.Recipes                    ◁────
        .FromSqlRaw("SELECT * FROM Recipes" +  ◁──┐ The current EF Core DbContext
            "WHERE Name = '" + search + "'")       │ is held in the _context field.
        .ToList();
}                                                    You can write queries by hand using
                                                     the FromSqlRaw extension method.
```

This introduces the vulnerability—including unsafe content directly in an SQL string.

In this listing, the user input held in `search` is included directly in the SQL query. By crafting malicious input, users can potentially perform any operation on your database. Imagine an attacker searches your website using the text

```
'; DROP TABLE Recipes; --
```

Your app assigns this to the `search` parameter, and the SQL query executed against your database becomes

```
SELECT * FROM Recipes WHERE Name = ''; DROP TABLE Recipes; --'
```

Simply by entering text into the search form of your app, the attacker has deleted the entire Recipes table from your app! That's catastrophic, but an SQL injection vulnerability provides more or less unfettered access to your database. Even if you've set up database permissions correctly to prevent this sort of destructive action, attackers will likely be able to read all the data from your database, including your users' details.

The simple way to prevent this from happening is to avoid creating SQL queries by hand this way. If you do need to write your own SQL queries, don't use string concatenation, as in listing 29.6. Instead, use parameterized queries, in which the (potentially unsafe) input data is separate from the query itself, as shown here.

Listing 29.7   Avoiding SQL injection by using parameterization

```
public IList<User> FindRecipe(string search)        The SQL query uses a placeholder
{                                                        {0} for the parameter.
    return _context.Recipes
        .FromSqlRaw( "SELECT * FROM Recipes WHERE Name = '{0}'",    ◄
                search)        ◄
        .ToList();                        The dangerous input is passed as a
}                                         parameter, separate from the query.
```

Parameterized queries are not vulnerable to SQL injection attacks, so the attack presented earlier won't work. If you use EF Core or other ORMs to access data using standard LINQ queries, you won't be vulnerable to injection attacks. EF Core automatically creates all SQL queries using parameterized queries to protect you. Even if you're using the low-level ADO.NET database APIs, stick to parameterized queries!

> **NOTE**   I've talked about SQL injection attacks only in terms of a relational database, but this vulnerability can appear in NoSQL and document databases too. Always use parameterized queries or the equivalent, and don't craft queries by concatenating strings with user input.

Injection attacks have been the number-one vulnerability on the web for more than a decade, so it's crucial to be aware of them and how they arise. Whenever you need to write raw SQL queries, make sure that you always use parameterized queries.

The next vulnerability is also related to attackers accessing data they shouldn't be able to. It's a little subtler than a direct injection attack but is trivial to perform; the only skill the attacker needs is the ability to count.

29.4.3 *Preventing insecure direct object references*

Insecure direct object reference is a bit of a mouthful, but it means users accessing things they shouldn't by noticing patterns in URLs. Let's revisit our old friend the recipe app. As a reminder, the app shows you a list of recipes. You can view any of them, but you can edit only recipes you created yourself. When you view someone else's recipe, there's no Edit button visible.

A user clicks the Edit button on one of their recipes and notices that the URL is /Recipes/Edit/120. That 120 is a dead giveaway as being the underlying database ID of the entity you're editing. A simple attack would be to change that ID to gain access to a different entity, one that you wouldn't normally have access to. The user could try entering /Recipes/Edit/121. If that lets them edit or view a recipe that they shouldn't be able to, you have an insecure direct object reference vulnerability.

The solution to this problem is simple: you should have resource-based authorization in your endpoint handlers. If a user attempts to access an entity they're not allowed to access, they should get a permission-denied error. They shouldn't be able to bypass your authorization by typing a URL directly into the search bar of their browser.

In ASP.NET Core apps, this vulnerability typically arises when you attempt to restrict users by hiding elements from your UI, such as by hiding the Edit button. Instead, you should use resource-based authorization, as discussed in chapter 24.

> **WARNING** You must always use resource-based authorization to restrict which entities a user can access. Hiding or disabling UI elements provides an improved user experience, but it isn't a security measure.

You can sidestep this vulnerability somewhat by avoiding integer IDs for your entities in the URLs, perhaps by using a pseudorandom globally unique identifier (GUID) such as C2E296BA-7EA8-4195-9CA7-C323304CCD12 instead. This makes the process of guessing other entities harder, as you can't simply add 1 to an existing number, but it's masking the problem rather than fixing it. Nevertheless, using GUIDs can be useful when you want to have publicly accessible pages that don't require authentication but don't want their IDs to be easily discoverable.

The final section in this chapter doesn't deal with a single vulnerability. Instead, I discuss a separate but related problem: protecting your users' data.

29.4.4 *Protecting your users' passwords and data*

For many apps, the most sensitive data you'll be storing is the personal data of your users. This could include emails, passwords, address details, or payment information. You should be careful when storing any of this data. As well as presenting an inviting target for attackers, you may have legal obligations for how you handle it, such as data protection laws and Payment Card Industry (PCI) compliance requirements.

The easiest way to protect yourself is to not store data you don't need. If you don't need your user's address, don't ask for it. That way, you can't lose it! Similarly, if you use a third-party identity service to store user details, as described in chapter 23, you won't have to work as hard to protect your users' personal information.

If you store user details in your own app or build your own identity provider, then you need to make sure to follow best practices when handling user information. The new project templates that use ASP.NET Core Identity follow most of these practices by default, so I highly recommend you start from one of these. You need to consider many aspects, too many to go into detail here,[1] but they include the following:

- Never store user passwords anywhere directly. You should store only cryptographic hashes computed using an expensive hashing algorithm, such as BCrypt or PBKDF2.
- Don't store more data than you need. You should never store credit card details.
- Allow users to use multifactor authentication (MFA) to sign in to your site.
- Prevent users from using passwords that are known to be weak or compromised, such as disallowing dictionary words, sequential characters, and so on.
- Mark authentication cookies as `http` (so that they can't be read using JavaScript) and `secure` so they'll be sent only over an HTTPS connection, never over HTTP. Where possible, you should also mark your cookies as `SameSite=strict`. See the documentation for details: http://mng.bz/a11m.
- Don't expose whether a user is already registered with your app. Leaking this information can expose you to enumeration attacks.

TIP You can learn more about website enumeration in this video tutorial by Troy Hunt: http://mng.bz/PAAA.

These guidelines represent the minimum you should be doing to protect your users. The most important thing is to be aware of potential security problems as you're building your app. Trying to bolt on security at the end is always harder than thinking about it from the start, so it's best to think about it earlier rather than later.

This chapter has been a whistle-stop tour of things to look out for. We've touched on most of the big names in security vulnerabilities, but I strongly encourage you to check out the other resources mentioned in this chapter. They provide a more exhaustive list of things to consider, complementing the defenses mentioned in this chapter. On top of that, don't forget about input validation and mass assignment/overposting, as discussed in chapter 16. ASP.NET Core includes basic protections against some of the most common attacks, but you can still shoot yourself in the foot. Make sure it's not your app making headlines for being breached!

---

[1] In 2020 the National Institute of Standards and Technology (NIST) updated its Digital Identity Guidelines on handling user details, which contains some great advice. See http://mng.bz/6gRA.

Summary

- XSS attacks involve malicious users injecting content into your app, typically to run malicious JavaScript when users browse your app. You can prevent XSS injection attacks by always encoding unsafe input before writing it to a page. Razor Pages do this automatically unless you use the @Html.Raw() method, so use it sparingly and carefully.

- CSRF attacks are a problem for apps that use cookie-based authentication, such as ASP.NET Core Identity. These attacks rely on the fact that browsers automatically send cookies to a website. A malicious website could create a form that POSTs to your site, and the browser will send the authentication cookie with the request. This allows malicious websites to send requests as though they're the logged-in user.

- You can mitigate CSRF attacks using antiforgery tokens, which involve writing a hidden field in every form that contains a random string based on the current user. A similar token is stored in a cookie. A legitimate request will have both parts, but a forged request from a malicious website will have only the cookie half; it cannot re-create the hidden field in the form. By validating these tokens, your API can reject forged requests.

- The Razor Pages framework automatically adds antiforgery tokens to any forms you create using Razor and validates the tokens for inbound requests. You can disable the validation check if necessary, using the [IgnoreAntiForgeryToken] attribute.

- Browsers won't allow websites to make JavaScript AJAX requests from one app to others at different origins. To match the origin, the app must have the same scheme, domain, and port. If you wish to make cross-origin requests like this, you must enable CORS in your API.

- CORS uses HTTP headers to communicate with browsers and defines which origins can call your API. In ASP.NET Core, you can define multiple policies, which can be applied globally to your whole app or to specific controllers and actions.

- You can add the CORS middleware by calling UseCors() on WebApplication and optionally providing the name of the default CORS policy to apply. You can also apply CORS to endpoints by calling RequireCors() or adding the [EnableCors] attribute and providing the name of the policy to apply.

- Configure the policies for your application by calling AddCors() on WebApplicationBuilder and adding policies in the lambda using AddPolicy(). A policy defines which origins are allowed to call an endpoint, which HTTP methods they can use, and which headers are allowed.

- Open redirect attacks use the common returnURL mechanism after logging in to redirect users to malicious websites. You can prevent this attack by ensuring that you redirect only to local URLs—URLs that belong to your app.

- Insecure direct object references are a common problem where you expose the ID of database entities in the URL. You should always verify that users have permission to access or change the requested resource by using resource-based authorization in your action methods.
- SQL injection attacks are a common attack vector when you build SQL requests manually. Always use parameterized queries when building requests or use a framework like EF Core, which isn't vulnerable to SQL injection.
- The most sensitive data in your app is often the data of your users. Mitigate this risk by storing only data that you need. Ensure that you store passwords only as a hash, protect against weak or compromised passwords, and provide the option for MFA. ASP.NET Core Identity provides all of this out of the box, so it's a great choice if you need to create an identity provider.

Part 5

Going further with ASP.NET Core

Parts 1 through 4 of this book touched on all the aspects of ASP.NET Core you need to learn to build an HTTP application, whether that's server-rendered applications using Razor Pages or JavaScript Object Notation (JSON) APIs using minimal APIs. In part 5 we look at four topics that build on what you've learned so far: customizing ASP.NET Core to your needs, interacting with third-party HTTP APIs, background services, and testing.

In chapter 30 we start by looking at an alternative way to bootstrap your ASP.NET Core applications, using the generic host instead of the WebApplication approach you've seen so far in the book. The generic host was the standard way to bootstrap apps before .NET 6 (and is the approach you'll find in previous editions of this book), so it's useful to recognize the pattern, but it also comes in handy for building non-HTTP applications, as you'll see in chapter 34.

In part 1 you learned about the middleware pipeline, and you saw how it is fundamental to all ASP.NET Core applications. In chapter 31 you'll learn how to take full advantage of the pipeline, creating branching middleware pipelines, custom middleware, and simple middleware-based endpoints. You'll also learn how to handle some complex chicken-and-egg configuration issues that often arise in real-life applications. Finally, you'll learn how to replace the built-in dependency injection container with a third-party alternative.

In chapter 32 you'll learn how to create custom components for working with Razor Pages and API controllers. You'll learn how to create custom Tag Helpers and validation attributes, and I'll introduce a new component—view components—for encapsulating logic with Razor view rendering. You'll also learn how to replace the attribute-based validation framework used by default in ASP.NET Core with an alternative.

Most apps you build aren't designed to stand on their own. It's common for your app to need to interact with APIs, whether those are APIs for sending emails, taking payments, or interacting with your own internal applications. In chapter 33 you'll learn how to call these APIs using the `IHttpClientFactory` abstraction to simplify configuration, add transient fault handling, and avoid common pitfalls.

This book deals primarily with serving HTTP traffic, both server-rendered web pages using Razor Pages and web APIs commonly used by mobile and single-page applications. However, many apps require long-running background tasks that execute jobs on a schedule or that process items from a queue. In chapter 34 I'll show how you can create these long-running background tasks in your ASP.NET Core applications. I'll also show how to create standalone services that have only background tasks, without any HTTP handling, and how to install them as a Windows Service or as a Linux systemd daemon.

Chapters 35 and 36, the final chapters, cover testing your application. The exact role of testing in application development can lead to philosophical arguments, but in these chapters I stick to the practicalities of testing your app with the xUnit test framework. You'll see how to create unit tests for your apps, test code that's dependent on EF Core using an in-memory database provider, and write integration tests that can test multiple aspects of your application at the same time.

In the fast-paced world of web development there's always more to learn, but by the end of part 5 you should have everything you need to build applications with ASP.NET Core, whether they be server-rendered page-based applications, APIs, or background services.

In the appendices for this book, I provide some background and resources about .NET. Appendix A describes how to prepare your development environment by installing .NET 7 and an IDE or editor. In appendix B you'll find a list of resources I use to learn more about ASP.NET Core and to stay up to date with the latest features.

Building ASP.NET Core apps with the generic host and Startup

This chapter covers
- Using the generic host and a Startup class to bootstrap your ASP.NET Core app
- Understanding how the generic host differs from WebApplication
- Building a custom generic IHostBuilder
- Choosing between the generic host and minimal hosting

Some of the biggest changes introduced in ASP.NET Core in .NET 6 were the minimal hosting APIs, namely the `WebApplication` and `WebApplicationBuilder` types you've seen throughout this book. These were introduced to dramatically reduce the amount of code needed to get started with ASP.NET Core and are now the default way to build ASP.NET Core apps.

Before .NET 6, ASP.NET Core used a different approach to bootstrap your app: the generic host, IHost, IHostBuilder, and a Startup class. Even though this approach is not the default in .NET 7, it's still valid, so it's important that you're aware of it, even if you don't need to use it yourself. In this chapter I introduce the generic host and show how it relates to the minimal hosting APIs you're already familiar with. In chapter 34 you'll learn how to use the generic host approach to build nonweb apps too.

I start by introducing the two main concepts: the generic host components (IHost-Builder and IHost) and the Startup class. These split your app bootstrapping code between two files, Program.cs and Startup.cs, handling different aspects of your app's configuration. You'll learn why this split was introduced, where each component is configured, and how it compares with minimal hosting using WebApplication.

In section 30.4 you'll learn how the helper function Host.CreateDefaultBuilder() works and use this knowledge to customize the IHostBuilder instance. This can give you greater control than minimal hosting, which may be useful in some situations.

In section 30.5 we take a step back and look at some of the drawbacks in the generic host bootstrapping code we've explored, particularly its apparent complexity compared to minimal hosting with WebApplication.

Finally, in section 30.6 I discuss some of the reasons you might nevertheless choose to use the generic host instead of minimal hosting in your .NET 7 app. In most cases I suggest using minimal hosting with WebApplication, but there are valid cases in which the generic host makes sense.

30.1   *Separating concerns between two files*

As you've seen throughout this book, the standard way to create an ASP.NET Core application in .NET 7 is with the WebApplicationBuilder and WebApplication classes inside Program.cs, using top-level statements. Before .NET 6, however, ASP.NET Core used a different approach, which you can still use in .NET 7 if you wish.

This approach typically uses a traditional static void Main() entry point (although top-level statements are supported) and splits its bootstrapping code across two files, as shown in figure 30.1:

- *Program.cs*—This contains the entry point for the application, which bootstraps a host object. This is where you configure the infrastructure of your application, such as Kestrel, integration with Internet Information Services (IIS), and configuration sources.
- *Startup.cs*—The Startup class is where you configure your dependency injection (DI) container, your middleware pipeline, and your application's endpoints.

We'll look at each of these files in turn in section 30.2 and 30.3 to see how they might look for a typical Razor Pages app. I discuss the generic host at the center of this setup and compare the approach with the newer WebApplication APIs you've used so far throughout the book.

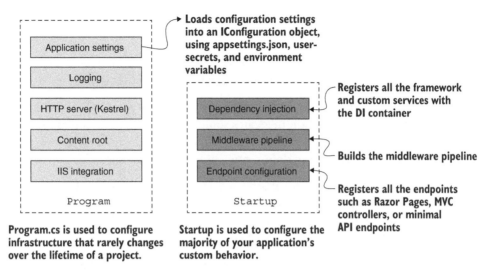

Figure 30.1 The different responsibilities of the `Program` and `Startup` classes in an ASP.NET Core app that uses the generic host instead of `WebApplication`

30.2 The Program class: Building a Web Host

All ASP.NET Core apps are fundamentally console applications. With the `Startup`-based hosting model, the `Main` entry point builds and runs an `IHost` instance, as shown in the following listing, which shows a typical Program.cs file. The `IHost` is the core of your ASP.NET Core application: it contains the HTTP server (Kestrel) for handling requests, along with all the necessary services and configuration to generate responses.

Listing 30.1 The Program.cs file configures and runs an `IHost`

```
public class Program
{
    public static void Main(string[] args)
    {
        CreateHostBuilder(args)          Creates an IHostBuilder using
            .Build()                     the CreateHostBuilder method
            .Run();         Runs the IHost and starts listening for
    }                       requests and generating responses

    public static IHostBuilder CreateHostBuilder(string[] args) =>
        Host.CreateDefaultBuilder(args)
            .ConfigureWebHostDefaults(webBuilder =>
            {
                webBuilder.UseStartup<Startup>();
            });
    }
}
```

Builds and returns an instance of IHost from the IHostBuilder

Creates an IHostBuilder using the default configuration

Configures the application to use Kestrel and listen to HTTP requests

The Startup class defines most of your application's configuration.

The `Main` function contains all the basic initialization code required to create a web server and to start listening for requests. It uses an `IHostBuilder`, created by the call to

CreateDefaultBuilder, to define how the generic IHost is configured, before instantiating the IHost with a call to Build().

> **TIP**   The IHost object represents your built application. The WebApplication type you've used throughout the book also implements IHost.

Much of your app's configuration takes place in the IHostBuilder created by the call to CreateDefaultBuilder, but it delegates some responsibility to a separate class, Startup. The Startup class referenced in the generic UseStartup<> method is where you configure your app's services and define your middleware pipeline.

> **NOTE**   The code to build the IHostBuilder is extracted to a helper method called CreateHostBuilder. The name of this method is historically important, as it was used implicitly by tooling such as the Entity Framework Core (EF Core) tools, as I discuss in section 30.5.

You may be wondering why you need two classes for configuration: Program and Startup. Why not include all your app's configuration in one class or the other? The idea is to separate code that changes often from code that rarely changes.

The Program class for two different ASP.NET Core applications typically look similar, but the Startup classes often differ significantly (though they all follow the same basic pattern, as you'll see in section 30.3). You'll rarely find that you need to modify Program as your application grows, whereas you'll normally update Startup whenever you add additional features. For example, if you add a new NuGet dependency to your project, you'll normally need to update Startup to make use of it.

The Program class is where a lot of app configuration takes place, but this is mostly hidden inside the Host.CreateDefaultBuilder method. CreateDefaultBuilder is a static helper method that simplifies the bootstrapping of your app by creating an IHostBuilder with some common configuration. This is similar to the way you've used WebApplication.CreateDefaultBuilder() throughout the book.

> **NOTE**   You can create custom HostBuilder instances if you want to customize the default setup and create a completely custom IHost instance, as you'll see in section 30.4. This is different from WebApplicationBuilder, which always uses the same defaults.

The other helper method used by default is ConfigureWebHostDefaults. This uses a WebHostBuilder object to configure Kestrel to listen for HTTP requests.

Creating services with the generic host

It might seem strange that you must call ConfigureWebHostDefaults as well as CreateDefaultBuilder. Couldn't we have one method? Isn't handling HTTP requests the whole point of ASP.NET Core?

Well, yes and no! ASP.NET Core 3.0 introduced the concept of a generic host. This allows you to use much of the same framework as ASP.NET Core applications to write non-HTTP applications. These apps can run as console apps or can be installed as Windows services (or as systemd daemons in Linux) to run background tasks or read from message queues, for example.

Kestrel and the web framework of ASP.NET Core build on top of the generic host functionality introduced in ASP.NET Core 3.0. To configure a typical ASP.NET Core app, you configure the generic host features that are common across all apps—features such as configuration, logging, and dependency services. For web applications, you then also configure the services, such as Kestrel, that are necessary to handle web requests. In chapter 34 you'll see how to build applications using the generic host to run scheduled tasks and build background services.

Even in .NET 7, WebApplication and WebApplicationBuilder use the generic host behind the scenes. You can read more about the evolution of ASP.NET Core's bootstrapping code and the relationship between IHost and WebApplication on my blog at http://mng.bz/gBBv.

Once the configuration of the IHostBuilder is complete, the call to Build produces the IHost instance, but the application still isn't handling HTTP requests yet. It's the call to Run() that starts the HTTP server listening. At this point, your application is fully operational and can respond to its first request from a remote browser.

30.3   *The Startup class: Configuring your application*

As you've seen, Program is responsible for configuring a lot of the infrastructure for your app, but you configure some of your app's behavior in Startup. The Startup class is responsible for configuring two main aspects of your application:

- DI container service registration
- Middleware configuration and mapping of endpoints

You configure each of these aspects in its own method in Startup: service registration in ConfigureServices and middleware/endpoint configuration in Configure. A typical outline of Startup is shown in the following listing.

Listing 30.2   An outline of Startup.cs showing how each aspect is configured

```
public class Startup                                   Configures services by registering
{                                                      them with the IServiceCollection
    public void ConfigureServices(IServiceCollection services)    ◁─────────┘
    {
        // method details
    }                                              Configures the middleware
    public void Configure(IApplicationBuilder app)  ◁─ pipeline for handling HTTP
    {                                                  requests
        // method details
    }
}
```

The IHostBuilder created in Program automatically calls ConfigureServices and then Configure, as shown in figure 30.2. Each call configures a different part of your application, making it available for subsequent method calls. Any services registered in the ConfigureServices method are available to the Configure method. Once configuration is complete, you create an IHost by calling Build() on the IHostBuilder.

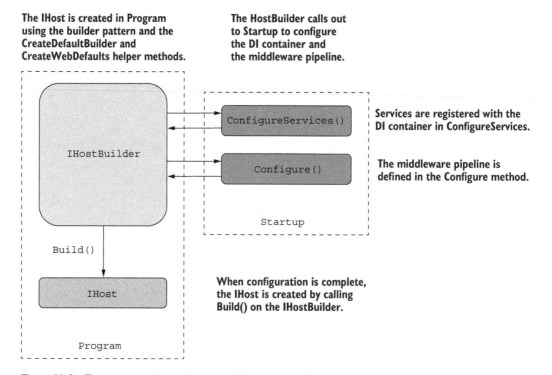

The IHost is created in Program using the builder pattern and the CreateDefaultBuilder and CreateWebDefaults helper methods.

The HostBuilder calls out to Startup to configure the DI container and the middleware pipeline.

IHostBuilder

ConfigureServices()

Services are registered with the DI container in ConfigureServices.

Configure()

The middleware pipeline is defined in the Configure method.

Startup

Build()

IHost

When configuration is complete, the IHost is created by calling Build() on the IHostBuilder.

Program

Figure 30.2   The IHostBuilder is created in Program.cs and calls methods on Startup to configure the application's services and middleware pipeline. Once configuration is complete, the IHost is created by calling Build() on the IHostBuilder.

An interesting point about the Startup class is that it doesn't implement an interface as such. Instead, the methods are invoked by using reflection to find methods with the predefined names of Configure and ConfigureServices. This makes the class more flexible and enables you to modify the signature of the Configure method to inject any services you registered in ConfigureServices using DI.

> **TIP**   If you're not a fan of the flexible reflection approach, you can implement the IStartup interface or derive from the StartupBase class, which provide the method signatures shown previously in listing 30.2. If you take this approach, you won't be able to use DI to inject services into the Configure() method.

ConfigureServices is where you add all your required and custom services to the DI container, exactly as you do with WebApplicationBuilder.Services in a typical .NET 7

ASP.NET Core app. The following listing shows how you might configure all the services for the Razor Pages recipe app you've seen throughout this book. This listing also shows how you can access the IConfiguration for your app: by injecting into the Startup constructor. You'll see how to customize your app's configuration in section 30.4.

Listing 30.3   Registering services with DI in `ConfigureServices`

```
public class Startup
{                                                    The IConfiguration for
    public IConfiguration Configuration { get; }      the app is injected into
    public Startup(IConfiguration configuration)      the constructor.
    {
        Configuration = configuration;                         You must register
    }                                                      your services against the
                                                           provided IServiceCollection.
    public void ConfigureServices(IServiceCollection services)   ◄───────────────
    {
        var conn = Configuration.GetConnectionString("DefaultConnection");

        services.AddDbContext<AppDbContext>(options =>
            options.UseSqlite(conn));                              Registers
        services.AddDefaultIdentity<ApplicationUser>(options =>    all the EF Core
            options.SignIn.RequireConfirmedAccount = true)         and ASP.NET Core
            .AddEntityFrameworkStores<AppDbContext>();             Identity services

        services.AddScoped<RecipeService>();    ◄─┐
        services.AddRazorPages();                 │ Registers the custom
                                                    service implementations
        services.AddScoped<IAuthorizationHandler, IsRecipeOwnerHandler>();
        services.AddAuthorizationBuilder()
            .AddPolicy("CanManageRecipe",
                p => p.AddRequirements(new IsRecipeOwnerRequirement()));
    }

    public void Configure(IApplicationBuilder app) => { /* Not shown */ }
}
```

Registers the framework services → (points to `services.AddRazorPages();`)

After configuring all your services, you need to set up your middleware pipeline and map your endpoints. The process is similar to configuring your middleware pipeline using WebApplication:

- You add middleware to the pipeline by calling Use* extension methods on an IApplicationBuilder instance.
- The order in which you add the middleware to the pipeline is important and defines the final pipeline order.
- You can add middleware conditionally based on the environment.

However, there are some important differences between the WebApplication approach you've seen so far and the Startup approach:

- The IWebHostEnvironment for your app is exposed directly on WebApplication .Environment. To access this information inside Startup, you must inject it into the constructor or the Configure method using DI.
- As you saw in chapter 4, WebApplication automatically adds a lot of middleware to your pipeline, such as routing middleware, endpoint middleware, and the authentication middleware. You must add this middleware manually when using the Startup approach.
- WebApplication implements both IApplicationBuilder and IEndpointRoute- Builder, so you can add endpoints directly to WebApplication, by calling MapGet() or MapRazorPages(), for example. When using the Startup approach, you must call UseEndpoints() and map all your endpoints in a lambda method instead.
- The Configure method is not async, so it's cumbersome to do async tasks. By contrast, when using WebApplication, you're free to use async methods between any of your general bootstrapping code.

Despite these caveats, in many cases your Startup.Configure method will look almost identical to the way you configure the pipeline on WebApplication. The following listing shows how the Configure() method for the Razor Pages recipe app might look.

Listing 30.4 Startup.Configure() for a Razor Pages application

```
public class Startup                        IApplicationBuilder is used to
{                                           build the middleware pipeline.
    public void Configure(
        IApplicationBuilder app,    ◄──┐    Other services can be
        IWebHostEnvironment env)    ◄──┘    accepted as parameters.
    {
        if (env.IsDevelopment())
        {                                   WebApplication adds this
            app.UseDeveloperExceptionPage();  ◄── automatically. You must explicitly
        }                                   add it when using Startup.
        else
        {
            app.UseExceptionHandler("/Error");
            app.UseHsts();
        }

        app.UseHttpsRedirection();
        app.UseStaticFiles();
        app.UseRouting();
                                            Must always be placed between the
        app.UseAuthentication();            call to UseRouting and UseEndpoints
        app.UseAuthorization();    ◄──┘
                                            Adds the endpoint middleware,
        app.UseEndpoints(endpoints =>  ◄──  which executes the endpoints
        {
            endpoints.MapRazorPages();  ◄── Maps the Razor
        });                             Pages endpoints
    }
}
```

Different behavior when in development or production → `if (env.IsDevelopment())`

Similarly, you must explicitly call UseRouting. → `app.UseRouting();`

In this example, the `IWebHostEnvironment` object is injected into the `Configure()` method using DI so that you can configure the middleware pipeline differently in development and production. In this case, we add the `DeveloperExceptionPageMiddleware` to the pipeline when we're running in development.

> **NOTE** Remember that `WebApplication` adds this middleware automatically, but with `Startup` you must add it manually. The same goes for all the other automatically added middleware.

After adding all the middleware to the pipeline, you come to the `UseEndpoints()` call, which adds the `EndpointMiddleware` to the pipeline. When you use `WebApplication`, you rarely need to call this, as `WebApplication` automatically adds it at the end of the pipeline, but when you use `Startup`, you should add it at the end of your pipeline.

Note as well that the call to `UseEndpoints()` is where you define all the endpoints in your application. Whether they're Razor Pages, Model-View-Controller (MVC) controllers, or minimal APIs, you must register them in the `UseEndpoints()` lambda.

> **NOTE** Endpoints must be registered inside the call to `UseEndpoints()` using the `IEndpointRouteBuilder` instance from the lambda method.

Other than the noted differences, moving your service, middleware, and endpoint configuration between a `Startup`-based approach and `WebApplication` should be relatively simple, which may lead you to wonder whether there's any good reason to choose the `Startup` approach over `WebApplication`. As always, the answer is "It depends," but one possible reason is so that you can customize your `IHostBuilder`.

30.4 Creating a custom IHostBuilder

As you saw in section 30.2, the default way to work with a `Startup` class in ASP.NET Core is to use the `Host.CreateDefaultBuilder()` method. This opinionated helper method sets up many defaults for your app. It is analogous to the `WebApplication .CreateBuilder()` method in that way.

However, you don't have to use the `CreateDefaultBuilder` method to create an `IHostBuilder` instance: you can directly create a `HostBuilder` instance and customize it from scratch if you prefer. Before you start doing that, though, it's worth seeing some of the things the `CreateDefaultBuilder` method gives you and what they're used for. You may then consider customizing the default `HostBuilder` instance instead of creating a completely bespoke instance.

> **NOTE** You can use `Host.CreateDefaultBuilder()` in .NET 7 even if you're not using ASP.NET Core by installing the Microsoft.Extensions.Hosting package. You'll learn how to create non-HTTP applications using the generic host in chapter 34.

The defaults chosen by `CreateDefaultBuilder` are ideal when you're initially setting up an app, but as your application grows, you may find you need to break it apart and tinker with some of the internals. The following listing shows a rough overview of the CreateDefaultBuilder method, so you can see how the HostBuilder is constructed. It's not exhaustive or complete, but it should give you an idea of the amount of work the CreateDefaultBuilder method does for you!

Listing 30.5   The Host.CreateDefaultBuilder method

```
public static IHostBuilder CreateDefaultBuilder(string[] args)
{
    var builder = new HostBuilder()          Creates an instance of HostBuilder
        .UseContentRoot(Directory.GetCurrentDirectory())
        .ConfigureHostConfiguration(IConfigurationBuilder config =>    Configures hosting
        {                                                              settings such
            config.AddEnvironmentVariables("DOTNET_");                 as determining
            config.AddCommandLine(args);                               the hosting
        })                                                             environment
        .ConfigureAppConfiguration((hostingContext, config) =>
        {
            IHostEnvironment env = hostingContext.HostingEnvironment;
            config
                .AddJsonFile("appsettings.json")
                .AddJsonFile($"appsettings.{env.EnvironmentName}.json");

            if (env.IsDevelopment())                                   Configures
            {                                                          application
                config.AddUserSecrets();                               settings
            }

            config
                .AddEnvironmentVariables()
                .AddCommandLine();
        })
        .ConfigureLogging((hostingContext, logging) =>
        {
            logging.AddConfiguration(
              hostingContext.Configuration.GetSection("Logging"));
            logging.AddConsole();                                      Sets up the logging
            logging.AddDebug();                                        infrastructure
            logging.AddEventSourceLogger();
            logging.AddEventLog();
        })
        .UseDefaultServiceProvider((context, options) =>
        {
            var isDevelopment = context.HostingEnvironment            Configures the DI
                                .IsDevelopment();                     container, optionally
            options.ValidateScopes = isDevelopment;                   enabling verification
            options.ValidateOnBuild = isDevelopment;                  settings
        });

    return builder;          Returns HostBuilder for further configuration
}                            by calling extra methods before calling Build()
```

The content root defines the directory where configuration files can be found.

The first method called on `HostBuilder` is `UseContentRoot()`. This tells the application in which directory it can find any configuration or Razor files it needs later. This is typically the folder in which the application is running, hence the call to `GetCurrentDirectory`.

> **TIP** Remember that `ContentRoot` is not where you store static files that the browser can access directly. That's the `WebRoot`, typically wwwroot.

The `ConfigureHostingConfiguration()` method is where your application determines which `HostingEnvironment` it's currently running in. The framework looks for environment variables that start with `"DOTNET_"` (such as the `DOTNET_ENVIRONMENT` variable you learned about in chapter 10) and command-line arguments to determine whether it's running in a development or production environment. This is used to populate the `IWebHostEnvironment` object that's used throughout your app.

The `ConfigureAppConfiguration()` method is where you configure the main `IConfiguration` object for your app, populating it from appsettings.json files, environment variables, and User Secrets, for example. The default builder populates the configuration using all the sources shown in listing 30.5, which is similar to the configuration `WebApplicationBuilder` uses.

> **TIP** There are some important differences in how the `IConfiguration` object is built using the default builder and the approach used by `WebApplication-Builder`. You can read about these differences on my blog at http://mng .bz/e11V.

Next up after app configuration comes `ConfigureLogging()`. `ConfigureLogging` is where you specify the logging settings and providers for your application, which you learned about in chapter 26. In addition to setting up the default `ILoggerProviders`, this method sets up log filtering, using the `IConfiguration` prepared in `ConfigureAppConfiguration()`.

The last method call shown in listing 30.5, `UseDefaultServiceProvider`, configures your app to use the built-in DI container. It also sets the `ValidateScopes` and `ValidateOnBuild` options based on the current `HostingEnvironment`. This ensures that when running the application in the development environment, the container automatically checks for captured dependencies, which you learned about in chapter 9.

As you can see, `CreateDefaultBuilder` does a lot for you. In many cases, these defaults are exactly what you need, but if they're not, the default builder is optional. You could call `new HostBuilder()` and start customizing it from there, but you'd need to set up everything that `CreateHostBuilder` does: logging, hosting configuration, and service provider configuration, as well as your app configuration.

An alternative approach is to layer additional configuration on top of the existing defaults. In the following listing, I show how to add a Seq logging provider to the configured providers using `ConfigureLogging()`, as well as how to reconfigure the app configuration to load *only* from the appsettings.json provider by clearing the default providers.

> **Listing 30.6 Customizing the default `HostBuilder`**

```
public class Program
{
    public static void Main(string[] args)
    {
        CreateHostBuilder(args).Build().Run();
    }

    public static IHostBuilder CreateHostBuilder(string[] args) =>
        Host.CreateDefaultBuilder(args)
        .ConfigureLogging(logBuilder => logBuilder.AddSeq())
        .ConfigureAppConfiguration((hostContext, config) =>
        {
            config.Sources.Clear();
            config.AddJsonFile("appsettings.json");

        }
            .ConfigureWebHostDefaults(webBuilder =>
        {
            webBuilder.UseStartup<Startup>();
        });
}
```

Adds the Seq logging provider to the configuration

HostBuilder provides a hosting context and an instance of ConfigurationBuilder.

Adds a JSON configuration provider, providing the filename of the configuration file

Clears the providers configured by default in CreateDefaultBuilder

A new `HostBuilder` is created in `CreateDefaultBuilder()` and executes all the configuration methods you saw in listing 30.5. Next, the `HostBuilder` invokes the extra `ConfigureLogging()` and `ConfigureAppConfiguration()` methods added in listing 30.6. You can call any of the other configuration methods on `HostBuilder` to further customize the instance before calling `Build()`.

> **NOTE** Each call to a `Configure*()` method on `HostBuilder` adds an extra configuration function to the setup code; these calls don't replace existing `Configure*()` calls. The configuration methods are executed in the same order in which they're added to the `HostBuilder`, so they execute after the `CreateDefaultBuilder()` configuration methods.

One of the criticisms of early ASP.NET Core apps was that they were quite complex to understand when you're getting started, and after working your way through this chapter, you might well be able to see why! In the next section we compare the generic host and `Startup` approach with the newer minimal hosting `WebApplication` approach and discuss when you might want to use one over the other.

30.5 *Understanding the complexity of the generic host*

Before .NET 6, all ASP.NET Core apps used the generic host and `Startup` approach. Many people liked the consistent structure this added, but it also has some drawbacks and complexity:

- Configuration is split between two files.
- The separation between Program.cs and `Startup` is somewhat arbitrary.

- The generic `IHostBuilder` exposes newcomers to legacy decisions.
- The lambda-based configuration can be hard to follow and reason about.
- The pattern-based conventions of `Startup` may be hard to discover.
- Tooling historically relies on your defining a `CreateHostBuilder` method in Program.cs.

I'll address each of these problems in turn and afterward discuss how `WebApplication` attempted to improve the situation.

Points 1 and 2 in the preceding list deal with the separation between Program.cs and `Startup`. As you saw in section 30.1, theoretically the intention is that Program.cs defines the host and rarely changes, whereas `Startup` defines the app features (services, middleware, and endpoints). This seems like a reasonable decision, but one inevitable downside is that you need to flick back and forth between at least two files to understand all your bootstrapping code.

On top of that, you don't necessarily need to stick to these conventions. You can register services in Program.cs by calling `HostBuilder.ConfigureServices()`, for example, or register middleware using `WebHostBuilder.Configure()`. This is relatively rare but not entirely unheard-of, further blurring the lines between the files.

Point 3 relates to the fact that you must call `ConfigureWebHostDefaults()` (which uses an `IWebHostBuilder`) to set up Kestrel and register your `Startup` class. This level of indirection (and the introduction of another builder type) is a remnant of decisions harking back to ASP.NET Core 1.0. For people familiar with ASP.NET Core, this pattern is just one of those things, but it adds confusion when you're new to it.

NOTE   For a walk-through of the evolution of ASP.NET Core bootstrapping code, see my blog post at http://mng.bz/pPPK.

Similarly, the lambda-based configuration mentioned in point 4 can be hard for newcomers to ASP.NET Core to follow. If you're new to .NET, lambdas are an extra concept you'll need to understand before you can understand the basics of the code. On top of that, the execution of the lambdas doesn't necessarily happen sequentially; the `HostBuilder` essentially queues the lambda methods so they're executed at the right time. Consider the following snippet:

```
public static IhostBuilder CreateHostBuilder(string[] args) =>
  Host.CreateDefaultBuilder(args)
    .ConfigureLogging(logging => logging.AddSeq())
    .ConfigureAppConfiguration(config => {})
    .ConfigureServices(s => {})
    .ConfigureHostConfiguration(config => {})
    .ConfigureWebHostDefaults(webBuilder =>
    {
        webBuilder.UseStartup<Startup>();
    });
```

The lambdas execute in the following order:

1 `ConfigureWebHostDefaults()`
2 `ConfigureHostConfiguration()`
3 `ConfigureAppConfiguration()`
4 `ConfigureLogging()`
5 `ConfigureServices()`
6 `Startup.ConfigureServices()`
7 `Startup.Configure()`

For the most part, this ordering detail shouldn't matter, but it still adds apparent complexity for those who are new to ASP.NET Core.

Point 5 in the list of challenges relates to the `Startup` class and the default convention/pattern-based approach. Users coming to ASP.NET Core for the first time will likely be familiar with interfaces and base classes, but they may not have experienced the reflection-based approach.

Using conventions instead of an explicit interface adds flexibility but can make things harder for discoverability. There are also various caveats and edge cases to consider. For example, you can inject only `IWebHostEnvironment` and `IConfiguration` into the `Startup` constructor; you can't inject anything into the `ConfigureServices()` method, but you can inject any registered service into `Configure()`. These are implied rules that you discover primarily by breaking them and then having your app shout at you!

> **TIP** The pattern-based approach allows for a lot more than DI into `Configure`. You can also create environment-specific methods, such as `Configure-DevelopmentServices` or `ConfigureProductionServices`, and ASP.NET Core invokes the correct method based on the environment. You can even create a whole `StartupProduction` class if you wish! For more details on these Startup conventions, see the documentation at http://mng.bz/Oxxw.

The `Startup` class isn't the only place where ASP.NET Core relies on opaque conventions. You may remember in section 30.2 I mentioned that Program.cs deliberately extracts the building of the `IHostBuilder` to a method called `CreateHostBuilder`. The name of this method was historically important. Tooling such as the EF Core tools hooked into it so that they could load your application configuration and services when running migrations and other functionality. In earlier versions of ASP.NET Core, renaming this method would break all your tooling!

> **NOTE** As of .NET 6, you don't have to create a `CreateHostBuilder` method; you can create your whole app inside your `Main` function (or using top-level statements), and the EF Core tools will work without error. This was fixed partly to add support for `WebApplication`. If you're interested in the mechanics of how it was fixed, see my blog at http://mng.bz/Y11z.

Once you're experienced with ASP.NET Core, most of these gripes become relatively minor. You quickly get used to the standard patterns and avoid the pitfalls. But for new users of ASP.NET Core, Microsoft wanted a smoother experience, closer to the experience you get in many other languages.

The minimal hosting APIs provided by `WebApplicationBuilder` and `WebApplication` largely address these concerns. Configuration happens all in one file using an imperative style, with far fewer lambda-based configuration methods or implicit convention-based setup. All the relevant objects like configuration and environment are exposed as properties on the `WebApplicationBuilder` or `WebApplication` types, so they're easy to discover.

`WebApplicationBuilder` and `WebApplication` also try to hide much of the complexity and legacy decisions from you. Under the hood, `WebApplication` uses the generic host, but you don't need to know that to use it or be productive. As you've seen throughout the book, `WebApplication` automatically adds various middleware to your pipeline, helping you avoid common pitfalls, such as incorrect middleware ordering.

> **NOTE** If you're interested in how `WebApplicationBuilder` abstracts over the generic host, see my post at http://mng.bz/GyyD.

In most cases, minimal hosting provides an easier bootstrapping experience to the generic host and `Startup`, and Microsoft considers it to be the modern way to create ASP.NET Core apps. But there are cases in which you might want to consider using the generic host instead.

30.6 *Choosing between the generic host and minimal hosting*

The introduction of `WebApplication` and `WebApplicationBuilder` in .NET 6, also known as minimal hosting, was intended to provide a dramatically simpler "getting started" experience for newcomers to .NET and ASP.NET Core. All the built-in ASP.NET Core templates use minimal hosting now, and in most cases there's little reason to look back. In this section I discuss some of the cases in which you might still want to use the generic host approach.

In three main cases, you'll likely want to stick with the generic host instead of using minimal hosting with `WebApplication`:

- When you already have an ASP.NET Core application that uses the generic host
- When you need (or want) fine control of building the `IHost` object
- When you're creating a non-HTTP application

The first use case is relatively obvious: if you already have an ASP.NET Core app that uses the generic host and `Startup`, you don't need to change it. You can still upgrade your app to .NET 7, and you shouldn't need to change any of your startup code. The generic host and `Startup` are fully supported in .NET 7, but they're not the default experience.

> **TIP** In many cases, upgrading an existing project to .NET 7 simply requires updating the framework in the .csproj file and updating some NuGet packages. If you're unlucky, you may find that some APIs have changed. Microsoft publishes upgrade guides for each major version release, so it's worth reading these before upgrading your apps: http://mng.bz/zXX1.

If you're creating a new app, but for some reason you don't like the default options used by `WebApplicationBuilder`, using the generic host may be your best option. I generally wouldn't advise this approach, as it will likely require more maintenance than using `WebApplication`, but it does give you complete control of your bootstrap code if you need or want it.

The final case applies when you're building an ASP.NET Core application that primarily runs background processing services, handling messages from a queue for example, but doesn't handle HTTP requests. The minimal hosting `WebApplication` and `WebApplicationBuilder` are, as their names imply, focused on building web applications, so they don't make sense in this situation.

> **NOTE** You'll learn how to create background tasks and services using the generic host in chapter 34. .NET 8 introduces a non-HTTP version of the `WebApplicationBuilder` called `HostApplicationBuilder` which aims to simplify app bootstrapping for your background services.

If you're not in any of these situations, strongly consider using the minimal hosting `WebApplication` approach and the imperative, scriptlike bootstrapping of top-level statements.

> **NOTE** The fact that you're using `WebApplication` doesn't mean you have to dump all your service and middleware configuration into Program.cs. For alternative approaches, such as using a `Startup` class you invoke manually or local functions to separate your configuration, see my blog post at http://mng.bz/0KKJ.

In this chapter I provided a relatively quick overview of the generic host and Startup-based approach. If you're thinking of moving from the generic host to minimal hosting, or if you're familiar with minimal hosting but need to work with the generic host, you may find yourself looking around for an equivalent feature in the other hosting model. The documentation for migrating from .NET 5 to .NET 6 provides a good description of the differences between the two models, and how each individual feature has changed. You can find it at http://mng.bz/KeeX.

> **TIP** Alternatively, David Fowler from the .NET team has a similar cheat sheet describing the migration. See http://mng.bz/9DDj.

Whether you choose to use the generic host or minimal hosting, all the same ASP.NET Core concepts are there: configuration, middleware, and DI. In the next chapter you'll learn about some more advanced uses of each of these concepts, such as creating branching middleware pipelines and custom DI containers.

Summary

- Before .NET 6, ASP.NET Core apps split configuration between two files: Program.cs and Startup.cs. Program.cs contains the entry point for the app and is used to configure and build a `IHost` object. `Startup` is where you configure the DI container, middleware pipeline, and endpoints for your app.

- The `Program` class typically contains a method called `CreateHostBuilder()`, which creates an `IHostBuilder` instance. The `Main` entry point invokes `CreateHost-Builder()`, calls `IHostBuilder.Build()` to create an instance of `IHost`, and finally runs the app by calling `IHost.Run()`.

- You can create an `IHostBuilder` by calling `Host.CreateDefaultBuilder()`. This creates a `HostBuilder` instance using the default configuration, similar to the configuration used when calling `WebApplication.CreateBuilder()`. The default `HostBuilder` uses default logging and configuration providers, configures the hosting environment based on environment variables and command-line arguments, and configures the DI container settings.

- ASP.NET Core apps using the generic host typically call `ConfigureWebHost-Defaults()`, on the `HostBuilder`, providing a lambda that calls `Use-Startup<Startup>()` on an `IWebHostBuilder` instance. This tells the `HostBuilder` to configure the DI container and middleware pipeline based on the `Startup` class.

- Use the `Startup` class to register services with DI, configure your middleware pipeline, and register your endpoints. It is a conventional class, in that it doesn't have to implement an interface or base class. Instead, the `IHostBuilder` looks for specific named methods to invoke using reflection.

- Register your DI services in the `ConfigureServices(IServiceCollection)` method of `Startup`. You register services using the same `Add*` methods you use to register services on `WebApplicationBuilder.Services` when using minimal hosting.

- If you need to access your app's `IConfiguration` or `IWebHostEnvironment` (exposed as `Configuration` and `Environment`, respectively, on `WebApplication-Builder`), you can inject them into your `Startup` constructor. You can't inject any other services into the `Startup` constructor.

- Register your middleware pipeline in `Startup.Configure(IApplicationBuilder)`. Use the same `Use*` methods you use with `WebApplication` to add middleware to the pipeline. As for `WebApplication`, the order in which you add the middleware defines their order in the pipeline.

- `WebApplication` automatically adds middleware such as the routing middleware and endpoint middleware to the pipeline when you're using minimal hosting. When using `Startup`, you must explicitly add this middleware yourself.

- To register endpoints, call `UseEndpoints(endpoints => {})` and call the appropriate `Map*` functions on the provided `IEndpointRouteBuilder` in the lambda function. This differs significantly from minimal hosting, in which you can call `Map*` directly on the `WebApplication` instance.

- You can customize the IHostBuilder instance by adding configuration methods such as ConfigureLogging() or ConfigureAppConfiguration(). These methods run after any previous invocations, adding extra layers of configuration to the IHostBuilder instance.

- The generic host is flexible but has greater inherent complexity due to its deferred execution style, extensive use of lambda methods, and heavy use of convention. Minimal hosting aimed to simplify the bootstrapping code to make it more imperative, reducing much of the indirection. Minimal hosting enforces more defaults but is generally easier to work with for newcomers to ASP.NET Core.

- If you already have an ASP.NET Core application using Startup and the generic host, there's no need to switch to using WebApplication and minimal hosting; the generic host is fully supported in .NET 7. Additionally, if you're creating a non-HTTP application, the generic host is currently the best option.

- If you're creating a new ASP.NET Core application, minimal hosting will likely provide a smoother experience. You should generally favor it over the generic host for new apps unless you need fine control of the IHostBuilder configuration.

Advanced configuration of ASP.NET Core

This chapter covers

- Building custom middleware
- Using dependency injection (DI) services in IOptions configuration
- Replacing the built-in DI container with a third-party container

---

When you're building apps with ASP.NET Core, most of your creativity and specialization go into the services and models that make up your business logic and the Razor Pages and APIs that expose them. Eventually, however, you're likely to find that you can't quite achieve a desired feature using the components that come out of the box. At that point, you may need to look to more complex uses of the built-in features.

This chapter shows some of the ways you can customize cross-cutting parts of your application, such as your DI container or your middleware pipeline. These approaches are particularly useful if you're coming from a legacy application or are working on an existing project, and you want to continue to use the patterns and libraries you're familiar with.

We'll start by looking at the middleware pipeline. You saw how to build pipelines by piecing together existing middleware in chapter 4, but in this chapter you'll create your own custom middleware. You'll explore the basic middleware constructs of the `Map`, `Use`, and `Run` methods and learn how to create standalone middleware classes. You'll use these to build middleware components that can add headers to all your responses as well as middleware that returns responses. Finally, you'll learn how to turn your custom middleware into a simple endpoint, using endpoint routing.

In chapter 10 you learned about strongly typed configuration using the `IOptions<T>` pattern, and in section 31.2 you'll learn how to take this further. You'll learn how to use the `OptionsBuilder<T>` type to fluently build your `IOptions<T>` object with the builder pattern. You'll also see how to use services from DI when configuring your `IOptions` objects—something that's not possible using the methods you've seen so far.

We stick with DI in section 31.3, where I'll show you how to replace the built-in DI container with a third-party alternative. The built-in container is fine for most small apps, but your `ConfigureServices` function can quickly get bloated as your app grows and you register more services. I'll show you how to integrate the third-party Lamar library into an existing app, so you can use extra features such as automatic service registration by convention.

The components and techniques shown in this chapter are more advanced than most features you've seen so far. You likely won't need them in every ASP.NET Core project, but they're good to have in your back pocket should the need arise!

31.1 *Customizing your middleware pipeline*

In this section you'll learn how to create custom middleware. You'll learn how to use the `Map`, `Run`, and `Use` extension methods to create simple middleware using lambda expressions. You'll then see how to create equivalent middleware components using dedicated classes. You'll also learn how to split the middleware pipeline into branches, and you'll find out when this is useful.

The middleware pipeline is one of the building blocks of ASP.NET Core apps, so we covered it in depth in chapter 4. Every request passes through the middleware pipeline, and each middleware component in turn gets an opportunity to modify the request or to handle it and return a response. ASP.NET Core includes middleware for handling common scenarios out of the box. You'll find middleware for serving static files, handling errors, authentication, and many more tasks.

You'll spend most of your time during development working with Razor Pages, minimal API endpoints, or web API controllers. These are exposed as the endpoints for most of your app's business logic, and they call methods on your app's various business services and models. However, you've also seen middleware like the Swagger middleware and the `WelcomePageMiddleware` that returns a response without using the endpoint routing system. The various improvements to the routing system in .NET 7 mean I rarely find the need to create "terminal" middleware like this, as endpoint routing is easy to work with and extensible. Nevertheless, it may occasionally be preferable to create small, custom, terminal middleware components like these.

At other times, you might have requirements that lie outside the remit of Razor Pages or minimal API endpoints. For example, you might want to ensure that all responses generated by your app include a specific header. This sort of cross-cutting concern is a perfect fit for custom middleware. You could add the custom middleware early in your middleware pipeline to ensure that every response from your app includes the required header, whether it comes from the static-file middleware, the error handling middleware, or a Razor Page.

In this section I show three ways to create custom middleware components, as well as how to create branches in your middleware pipeline where a request can flow down either one branch or another. By combining the methods demonstrated in this section, you'll be able to create custom solutions to handle your specific requirements.

We start by creating a middleware component that returns the current time as plain text whenever the app receives a request. From there we'll look at branching the pipeline, creating general-purpose middleware components, and encapsulating your middleware into standalone classes. Finally, in section 31.1.5 you'll see how to turn your custom middleware component into an endpoint and integrate it with the endpoint routing system.

31.1.1 *Creating simple apps with the Run extension*

As you've seen in previous chapters, you define the middleware pipeline for your app in Program.cs by adding middleware to a WebApplication object, typically using extension methods, as in this example:

```
WebApplicationBuilder builder = WebApplication.CreateBuilder(args);
WebApplication app = builder.Build();
app.UseExceptionHandler();
app.UseStaticFiles();
app.Run();
```

When your app receives a request, the request passes through each middleware component, each of which gets a chance to modify the request or handle it by generating a response. If a middleware component generates a response, it effectively short-circuits the pipeline; no subsequent middleware in the pipeline sees the request. The response passes back through the earlier middleware components on its way back to the browser.

You can use the Run extension method to build a simple middleware component that always generates a response. This extension takes a single lambda function that runs whenever a request reaches the component. The Run extension always generates a response, so no middleware placed after it ever executes. For that reason, you should always place the Run middleware last in a middleware pipeline.

TIP   Remember that middleware components run in the order in which you add them to the pipeline. If a middleware component handles a request and generates a response, later middleware never sees the request.

The Run extension method provides access to the request in the form of the HttpContext object you saw in chapter 4. This contains all the details of the request in the Request property, such as the URL path, the headers, and the body of the request. It also contains a Response property you can use to return a response.

The following listing shows how you could build a simple middleware component that returns the current time. It uses the provided HttpContext context object and the Response property to set the Content-Type header of the response (not strictly necessary in this case, as text/plain is used if an alternative content type is not set) and writes the body of the response using WriteAsync(text).

Listing 31.1   Creating simple middleware using the Run extension

```
app.Run(async (HttpContext context) =>          ◁── Uses the Run extension to create simple
{                                                    middleware that always returns a response
    context.Response.ContentType = "text/plain";  ◁──┐  You should set the content-
    await context.Response.WriteAsync(                │  type of the response you're
        DateTimeOffset.UtcNow.ToString());            │  generating; text/plain is the
});                                                   │  default value.

app.UseStaticFiles();
```

Any middleware added after the
Run extension will never execute.

Returns the time as a string in the
response. The 200 OK status code
is used if not explicitly set.

The Run extension is useful for two different things:

- Creating simple middleware that *always* generates a response
- Creating complex middleware that hijacks the whole request to build an additional framework *on top of* ASP.NET Core

Whether you're using the Run extension to create basic endpoints or a complex extra framework layer, the middleware always generates some sort of response. Therefore, you must always place it at the end of the pipeline, as no middleware placed after it will execute.

TIP   Using the Run extension to unconditionally generate a response is rare these days. The endpoint routing system used by minimal APIs provides many extra niceties such as model binding, routing, integration with other middleware such as authentication and authorization, and so on.

There may be occasional situations where you want to unconditionally generate a response, but a more common scenario is where you want your middleware component to respond only to a specific URL path, such as the way the Swagger UI middleware responds only to the /swagger path. In the next section you'll see how you can combine Run with the Map extension method to create branching middleware pipelines.

31.1.2   Branching middleware pipelines with the Map extension

So far when discussing the middleware pipeline, we've always considered it to be a single pipeline of sequential components. Each request passes through every middleware component until one component generates a response; then the response passes back through the previous middleware.

The Map extension method lets you change that simple pipeline into a branching structure. Each branch of the pipeline is independent; a request passes through one branch or the other but not both, as shown in figure 31.1. The Map extension method looks at the path of the request's URL. If the path starts with the required pattern, the request travels down the branch of the pipeline; otherwise, it remains on the main trunk. This lets you have completely different behavior in different branches of your middleware pipeline.

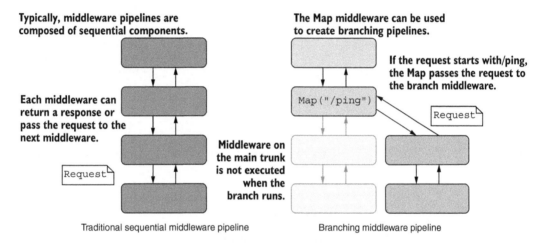

Typically, middleware pipelines are composed of sequential components.

Each middleware can return a response or pass the request to the next middleware.

Traditional sequential middleware pipeline

The Map middleware can be used to create branching pipelines.

If the request starts with/ping, the Map passes the request to the branch middleware.

Map("/ping")

Middleware on the main trunk is not executed when the branch runs.

Branching middleware pipeline

Figure 31.1   A sequential middleware pipeline compared with a branching pipeline created with the Map **extension. In branching middleware, requests pass through only one of the branches at most. Middleware on the other branch never see the request and aren't executed.**

NOTE   The URL-matching used by Map is conceptually similar to the routing you've seen throughout the book, but it is much more basic, with many limitations. For example, it uses a simple string-prefix match, and you can't use route parameters. Generally, you should favor using endpoint routing instead of branching using Map. A similar extension, MapWhen, allows matching based on anything in HttpContext, such as headers or query string parameters.

For example, imagine you want to add a simple health-check endpoint to your existing app. This endpoint is a simple URL you can call that indicates whether your app is running correctly. You could easily create a health-check middleware using the Run extension, as you saw in listing 31.1, but then that's all your app can do. You want the health-check to respond only to a specific URL, /ping. Your Razor Pages should handle all other requests as normal.

> **TIP** The health-check scenario is a simple example for demonstrating the Map method, but ASP.NET Core includes built-in support for health-check endpoints, which integrate into the endpoint routing system. You should use these instead of creating your own. You can learn more about creating health checks in Microsoft's "Health checks in ASP.NET Core" documentation: http://mng.bz/nMA2.

One solution would be to create a branch using the Map extension method and to place the health-check middleware on that branch, as shown in figure 31.1. Only those requests that match the Map pattern /ping will execute the branch; all other requests are handled by the standard routing middleware and Razor Pages on the main trunk instead, as shown in the following listing.

Listing 31.2   Using the Map extension to create branching middleware pipelines

```
app.UseStatusCodePages();              Every request passes
                                       through this middleware.

app.Map("/ping", (IApplicationBuilder branch) =>        The Map extension method
{                                                       branches if a request starts
    branch.UseExceptionHandler();                       with /ping.
    branch.Run(async (HttpContext context) =>
    {                                                   The Run extension always
        context.Response.ContentType = "text/plain";    returns a response, but
        await context.Response.WriteAsync("pong");       only on the /ping branch.
    });
});

app.UseStaticFiles();        The rest of the middleware
app.UseRouting();            pipeline run for requests that
                             don't match the /ping branch.
app.MapRazorPages();
app.Run();
```
This middleware runs only for requests
matching the /ping branch.

The Map middleware creates a completely new IApplicationBuilder (called branch in the listing), which you can customize as you would your main app pipeline. Middleware added to the branch builder are added only to the branch pipeline, not the main trunk pipeline.

> **TIP** The WebApplication object you typically add middleware to implements the IApplicationBuilder interface. Most extension methods for adding middleware use the IApplicationBuilder interface, so you can use the extension methods in branches as well as your main middleware pipeline.

In this example, you add the Run middleware to the branch, so it executes only for requests that start with /ping, such as /ping, /ping/go, and /ping?id=123. Any requests that don't start with /ping are ignored by the Map extension. Those requests stay on the main trunk pipeline and execute the next middleware in the pipeline after Map (in this case, the StaticFilesMiddleware).

> **WARNING**   There are several Map extension method overloads. Some of these are extension methods on IApplicationBuilder and are used to branch the pipeline, as you saw in listing 31.2. Other overloads are extensions on IEndpointRouteBuilder and are used to create minimal endpoints, using the endpoint routing system. If you're struggling to make your app compile, make sure that you're not accidentally using the wrong Map overload!

If you need to, you can create sprawling branched pipelines using Map, where each branch is independent of every other. You could also nest calls to Map so you have branches coming off branches.

The Map extension can be useful, but if you try to get too elaborate, it can quickly get confusing. Remember that you should use middleware for implementing cross-cutting concerns or simple endpoints. The endpoint routing mechanism of minimal APIs and Razor Pages is better suited to more complex routing requirements, so always favor it over Map where possible.

One situation where Map can be useful is when you want to have two independent subapplications but don't want the hassle of multiple deployments. You can use Map to keep these pipelines separate, with separate routing and endpoints inside each branch of the pipeline.

> **TIP**   This approach can be useful, for example, if you're embedding an OpenID Connect server such as IdentityServer in your application. By mapping IdentityServer to a branch, you ensure that the endpoints and controllers in your main app can't interfere with the endpoints exposed by IdentityServer.

Be aware that these branches share configuration and a DI container, so they're independent only from the middleware pipeline's point of view. You must also remember that WebApplication adds lots of middleware to the pipeline by default, so you may need to override these by explicitly calling UseRouting() in all your branches, for example.

> **NOTE** Achieving truly independent branches in the same application requires a lot of effort. See Filip Wojcieszyn's blog post, "Running multiple independent ASP.NET Core pipelines side by side in the same application," for guidance: http://mng.bz/vzA4.

The final point you should be aware of when using the Map extension is that it modifies the effective Path seen by middleware on the branch. When it matches a URL prefix, the Map extension cuts off the matched segment from the path, as shown in figure 31.2. The removed segments are stored on a property of HttpContext called PathBase, so they're still accessible if you need them.

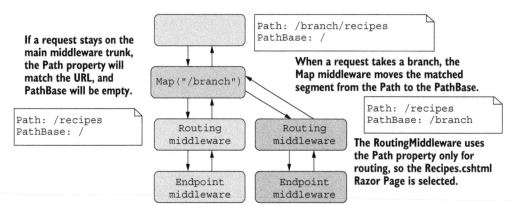

Figure 31.2   When the `Map` extension diverts a request to a branch, it removes the matched segment from the `Path` property and adds it to the `PathBase` property.

> **NOTE** ASP.NET Core's link generator (used in Razor and minimal APIs, as discussed in chapter 6) uses `PathBase` to ensure that it generates URLs that include the `PathBase` as a prefix.

You've seen the `Run` extension, which always returns a response, and the `Map` extension, which creates a branch in the pipeline. The next extension we'll look at is the general-purpose `Use` extension.

31.1.3 *Adding to the pipeline with the Use extension*

You can use the `Use` extension method to add a general-purpose piece of middleware. You can use it to view and modify requests as they arrive, to generate a response, or to pass the request on to subsequent middleware in the pipeline.

As with the `Run` extension, when you add the `Use` extension to your pipeline, you specify a lambda function that runs when a request reaches the middleware. ASP.NET Core passes two parameters to this function:

- *The `HttpContext` representing the current request and response*—You can use this to inspect the request or generate a response, as you saw with the `Run` extension.
- *A pointer to the rest of the pipeline as a `Func<Task>`*—By executing this task, you can execute the rest of the middleware pipeline.

By providing a pointer to the rest of the pipeline, you can use the `Use` extension to control exactly how and when the rest of the pipeline executes, as shown in figure 31.3. If you don't call the provided `Func<Task>` at all, the rest of the pipeline doesn't execute for the request, so you have complete control.

Exposing the rest of the pipeline as a `Func<Task>` makes it easy to conditionally short-circuit the pipeline, which enables many scenarios. Instead of branching the pipeline to implement the health-check middleware with `Map` and `Run`, as you did in

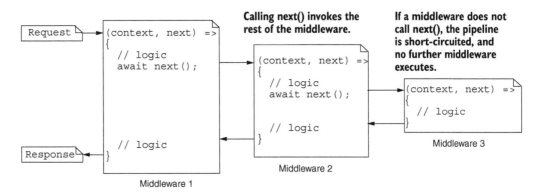

Figure 31.3 Three pieces of middleware, created with the Use extension. Invoking the provided Func<Task> using next() invokes the rest of the pipeline. Each middleware component can run code before and after calling the rest of the pipeline, or it can choose to not call next() to short-circuit the pipeline.

listing 31.2, you could use a single instance of the Use extension, as shown in the following listing. This provides the same required functionality as before but does so without branching the pipeline.

Listing 31.3 Using the Use extension method to create a health-check middleware

```
app.Use(async (HttpContext context, Func<Task> next) =>     ◁──── The Use extension
{                                                                   takes a lambda with
    if (context.Request.Path.StartsWithSegments("/ping"))  ◁────   HttpContext (context)
    {                                                               and Func<Task>
        context.Response.ContentType = "text/plain";               (next) parameters.
        await context.Response.WriteAsync("pong");
    }                                                          The StartsWithSegments
    else                                                       method looks for the
    {                                                          provided segment in
        await next();                                          the current path.
    }
});
```

If the path matches, generates a response and short-circuits the pipeline

```
app.UseStaticFiles();
```

If the path doesn't match, calls the next middleware in the pipeline—in this case UseStaticFiles()

If the incoming request starts with the required path segment (/ping), the middleware responds and doesn't call the rest of the pipeline. If the incoming request doesn't start with /ping, the extension calls the next middleware in the pipeline, with no branching necessary.

With the Use extension, you have control of when and whether you call the rest of the middleware pipeline. But it's important to note that you generally shouldn't modify the Response object after calling next(). Calling next() runs the rest of the middleware pipeline, so subsequent middleware may start streaming the response to the browser. If you try to modify the response after executing the pipeline, you may end up corrupting the response or sending invalid data.

> **WARNING** Don't modify the `Response` object after calling `next()`. Also, don't call `next()` if you've written to the `Response.Body`; writing to this `Stream` can trigger Kestrel to start streaming the response to the browser, and you could cause invalid data to be sent. You can generally read from the `Response` object safely, such as to inspect the final `StatusCode` or `ContentType` of the response.

Another common use for the `Use` extension method is to modify every request or response that passes through it. For example, you should send various HTTP headers with all your applications for security reasons. These headers often disable old, insecure legacy behaviors by browsers or restrict the features enabled by the browser. You learned about the HSTS header in chapter 28, but you can add other headers for additional security.

> **TIP** You can test the security headers for your app at https://securityheaders .com, which also provides information about what headers you should add to your application and why.

Imagine you've been tasked with adding one such header—`X-Content-Type-Options: nosniff`, which provides added protection against cross-site scripting (XSS) attacks—to every response generated by your app. This sort of cross-cutting concern is perfect for middleware. You can use the `Use` extension method to intercept every request, set the response header, and then execute the rest of the middleware pipeline. No matter what response the pipeline generates, whether it's a static file, an error, or a Razor Page, the response will always have the security header.

   Listing 31.4 shows a robust way to achieve this. When the middleware receives a request, it registers a callback that runs before Kestrel starts sending the response back to the browser. It then calls `next()` to run the rest of the middleware pipeline. When the pipeline generates a response, likely in some later middleware, Kestrel executes the callback and adds the header. This approach ensures that the header isn't accidentally removed by other middleware in the pipeline and also ensures that you don't try to modify the headers after the response has started streaming to the browser.

Listing 31.4   Adding headers to a response with the `Use` extension

```
app.Use(async (HttpContext context, Func<Task> next) =>          Sets a function that runs
{                                                                before the response is sent
    context.Response.OnStarting(() =>                            to the browser
    {
        context.Response.Headers["X-Content-Type-Options"] = "nosniff";
        return Task.CompletedTask;
    });
});
```

Adds the middleware at the start of the pipeline

The function passed to OnStarting must return a Task.

Adds the header to the response for added protection against XSS attacks

```
        await next();  ⟵──┐
}                          │
```
Invokes the rest of the middleware pipeline

```
app.UseStaticFiles();
app.UseRouting();

app.MapRazorPages
```
No matter what response is generated, it'll have the security header added.

Simple cross-cutting middleware like the security header example is common, but it can quickly clutter your Program.cs configuration and make it difficult to understand the pipeline at a glance. Instead, it's common to encapsulate your middleware in a class that's functionally equivalent to the Use extension but that can be easily tested and reused.

31.1.4 Building a custom middleware component

Creating middleware with the Use extension, as you did in listings 31.3 and 31.4, is convenient, but it's not easy to test, and you're somewhat limited in what you can do. For example, you can't easily use DI to inject scoped services inside these basic middleware components. Normally, rather than call the Use extension directly, you'll encapsulate your middleware into a class that's functionally equivalent.

Custom middleware components don't have to derive from a specific base class or implement an interface, but they have a certain shape, as shown in listing 31.5. ASP.NET Core uses reflection to execute the method at runtime. Middleware classes should have a constructor that takes a RequestDelegate object, which represents the rest of the middleware pipeline, and they should have an Invoke function with a signature similar to

```
public Task Invoke(HttpContext context);
```

The Invoke() function is equivalent to the lambda function from the Use extension, and it is called when a request is received. The following listing shows how you could convert the headers middleware from listing 31.4 into a standalone middleware class.

Listing 31.5 Adding headers to a Response using a custom middleware component

```
public class HeadersMiddleware
{
    private readonly RequestDelegate _next;
    public HeadersMiddleware(RequestDelegate next)
    {
        _next = next;
    }

    public async Task Invoke(HttpContext context)
    {
        context.Response.OnStarting(() =>
        {
            context.Response.Headers["X-Content-Type-Options"] =
```

The Invoke method is called with HttpContext when a request is received.

The RequestDelegate represents the rest of the middleware pipeline.

Adds the header to the response as before

```
            "nosniff";                          Adds the header
        return Task.CompletedTask;              to the response
    });                                         as before

    await _next(context);                       Invokes the rest of the middleware
}                                               pipeline. Note that you must pass in
}                                               the provided HttpContext.
```

NOTE   Using this shape approach makes the middleware more flexible. In particular, it means you can easily use DI to inject services into the `Invoke` method. This wouldn't be possible if the `Invoke` method were an overridden base class method or an interface. However, if you prefer, you can implement the `IMiddleware` interface, which defines the basic `Invoke` method.

This middleware is effectively identical to the example in listing 31.4, but it's encapsulated in a class called `HeadersMiddleware`. You can add this middleware to your app in `Startup.Configure` by calling

```
app.UseMiddleware<HeadersMiddleware>();
```

A common pattern is to create helper extension methods to make it easy to consume your extension method from Program.cs (so that IntelliSense reveals it as an option on the `WebApplication` instance). The following listing shows how you could create a simple extension method for `HeadersMiddleware`.

Listing 31.6   Creating an extension method to expose `HeadersMiddleware`

```
                                                    By convention, the
                                                    extension method
public static class MiddlewareExtensions            should return an
{                                                   IApplicationBuilder
    public static IApplicationBuilder UseSecurityHeaders(    to allow chaining.
        this IApplicationBuilder app)
    {
        return app.UseMiddleware<HeadersMiddleware>();    Adds the middleware
    }                                                     to the pipeline
}
```

With this extension method, you can now add the headers middleware to your app using

```
app.UseSecurityHeaders();
```

TIP   My SecurityHeaders NuGet package makes it easy to add security headers using middleware without having to write your own. The package provides a fluent interface for adding the recommended security headers to your app. You can find instructions on how to install it at http://mng.bz/JggK.

Listing 31.5 is a simple example, but you can create middleware for many purposes. In some cases you may need to use DI to inject services and use them to handle a request. You can inject singleton services into the constructor of your middleware component, or you can inject services with any lifetime into the `Invoke` method of your middleware, as demonstrated in the following listing.

Listing 31.7   Using DI in middleware components

```
public class ExampleMiddleware
{
    private readonly RequestDelegate _next;
    private readonly ServiceA _a;
    public HeadersMiddleware(RequestDelegate next, ServiceA a)
    {
        _next = next;
        _a = a;
    }
    public async Task Invoke(
        HttpContext context, ServiceB b, ServiceC c)
    {
        // use services a, b, and c
        // and/or call _next.Invoke(context);
    }
}
```

You can inject additional services in the constructor. These must be singletons.

You can inject services into the Invoke method. These may have any lifetime.

WARNING ASP.NET Core creates the middleware only once for the lifetime of your app, so any dependencies injected in the constructor must be singletons. If you need to use scoped or transient dependencies, inject them into the `Invoke` method.

In addition to cross-cutting concerns, a good use for middleware is creating simple handlers with as few dependencies as possible that respond to a fixed URL, similar to the `Use` extension method you learned about in section 31.1.3. These simple handlers can be dropped into multiple applications, regardless of how the app's routing is configured.

So-called *well-known Uniform Resource Identifiers* (URIs) are a good use case for these simple middleware handlers, such as the security.txt well-known URI (https://www .rfc-editor.org/rfc/rfc9116) and the OpenID Connect URIs (http://mng.bz/wvj2). These handlers always respond to a single path, so they can neatly encapsulate all the logic without risk of interfering with any other routing configuration.

Listing 31.8 shows a simple example of a security.txt handler implemented as middleware. It always responds to the well-known path with a fixed value and is easy to add to any application by calling `app.UseMiddleware<SecurityTxtHandler>`.

Listing 31.8   A Security.txt handler implemented as middleware

```
public class SecurityTxtHandler
{
    private readonly RequestDelegate _next;
    public SecurityTxtHandler(RequestDelegate next)
    {
        _next = next;
    }
```

```
public Task Invoke(HttpContext context)
{
    var path = context.Request.Path;
    if(path.StartsWithSegments("/.well-known/security.txt"))
    {
        context.Response.ContentType = "text/plain";
        return context.Response.WriteAsync(
            "Contact: mailto:security@example.com");
    }

    return _next.Invoke(context);
}
}
```

The middleware looks for a fixed, well-known path.

If the path is matched, the middleware returns a response.

If the path didn't match, the next middleware in the pipeline is called.

That covers pretty much everything you need to start building your own middleware components. By encapsulating your middleware in custom classes, you can easily test their behavior or distribute them in NuGet packages, so I strongly recommend taking this approach. Apart from anything else, it will make Program.cs file less cluttered and easier to understand.

31.1.5 *Converting middleware into endpoint routing endpoints*

In this section you'll learn how you can take the custom middleware you created in section 31.1.2 and convert it to a simple middleware endpoint that integrates into the endpoint routing system. Then you can take advantage of features such as routing and authorization.

In section 31.1.2 I described creating a simple ping-pong endpoint, using the Map and Run extension methods, that returns a plain-text pong response whenever a /ping request is received by branching the middleware pipeline. This is fine because it's so simple, but what if you have more complex requirements?

Consider a basic enhancement of this ping-pong example. How would you add authorization to the request? The AuthorizationMiddleware looks for metadata on endpoints like Razor Pages or minimal APIs to see whether there's any authorization metadata, but it doesn't know how to work with the ping-pong Map extension.

Similarly, what if you wanted to use more complex routing? Maybe you want to be able to call /ping/3 and have your ping-pong middleware reply pong-pong-pong. (No, I can't think why you would either!) You now have to try to parse that integer from the URL, make sure it's valid, and so on. That's sounding like a lot more work and seems to be a clear indicator you should have created a minimal API endpoint using endpoint routing!

For our simple ping-pong endpoint, that wouldn't be hard to do, but what if you have a more complex middleware component that you don't want to rewrite completely? Is there some way to convert the middleware to an endpoint?

Let's imagine that you need to apply authorization to the simple ping-pong endpoint you created in section 31.1.2. This is much easier to achieve with endpoint routing than simple middleware branches like Map or Use, but let's imagine you want to stick to using middleware instead of a traditional minimal API endpoint. The first step is creating a standalone middleware component for the functionality, using the approach you saw in section 31.1.4, as shown in the following listing.

Listing 31.9   The `PingPongMiddleware` implemented as a middleware component

```
public class PingPongMiddleware
{
    public PingPongMiddleware(RequestDelegate next)
    {
    }

    public async Task Invoke(HttpContext context)
    {
        context.Response.ContentType = "text/plain";
        await context.Response.WriteAsync("pong");
    }
}
```

Even though it isn't used in this case, you must inject a **RequestDelegate** in the constructor.

Invoke is called to execute the middleware.

The middleware always returns a "pong" response.

Note that this middleware always returns a "pong" response regardless of the request URL; we will configure the "/ping" path later. We can use this class to convert a middleware pipeline from the branching version shown in figure 31.1, to the endpoint version shown in figure 31.4.

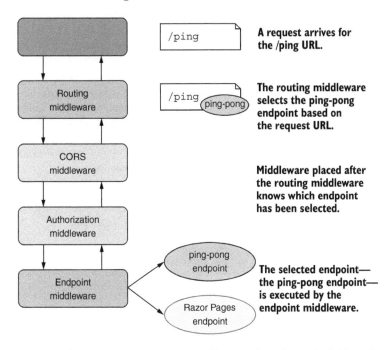

Figure 31.4   Endpoint routing separates the selection of an endpoint from the execution of an endpoint. The routing middleware selects an endpoint based on the incoming request and exposes metadata about the endpoint. Middleware placed before the endpoint middleware can act based on the selected endpoint, such as short-circuiting unauthorized requests. If the request is authorized, the endpoint middleware executes the selected endpoint and generates a response.

Converting the ping-pong middleware to an endpoint doesn't require any changes to the middleware itself. Instead, you need to create a mini middleware pipeline containing only your ping-pong middleware.

TIP Converting response-generating middleware to an endpoint essentially requires converting it to its own mini pipeline, so you can even include additional middleware in the endpoint pipeline if you wish.

To create the mini pipeline, you call `CreateApplicationBuilder()` on `IEndpointRoute-Builder` instance, which creates a new `IApplicationBuilder`. There are two ways to access the `IEndpointRouteBuilder`: call `UseEndpoints(endpoints =>{})` and use the `endpoints` variable or explicitly cast `WebApplication` to `IEndpointRouteBuilder`.

NOTE Although `WebApplication` implements `IEndpointRouteBuilder`, it deliberately hides the advanced `CreateApplicationBuilder()` method from you! This should be a good indication that you're in advanced territory and should probably consider using minimal API endpoints instead.

In the following listing, we create a new `IApplicationBuilder`, add the middleware that makes up the endpoint to it, and then call `Build()` to create the pipeline. Once you have a pipeline, you can associate it with a given route by calling `Map()` on the `IEndpointRouteBuilder` instance and passing in a route template.

Listing 31.10   Mapping the ping-pong endpoint in `UseEndpoints`

```
WebApplicationBuilder builder = WebApplication.CreateBuilder(args);
WebApplication app = builder.Build();

app.UseRouting();
app.UseAuthentication();
app.UseAuthorization();
var endpoint = ((IEndpointRouteBuilder)app)
    .CreateApplicationBuilder()
    .UseMiddleware<PingPongMiddleware>()
    .Build();

app.Map("/ping", endpoint);
app.MapRazorPages();
app.MapHealthChecks("/healthz");
app.Run();
```

> Casts the WebApplication to IEndpointRouteBuilder so you can call CreateApplicationBuilider

> Creates a miniature, standalone IApplicationBuilder to build your endpoint

> Adds the middleware and builds the final endpoint. This is executed when the endpoint is executed.

> Maps the new endpoint with the route template "/ping"

TIP Note that the `Map()` function on `IEndpointRouteBuilder` creates a new endpoint (consisting of your mini-pipeline) with an associated route. Although it has the same name, this is conceptually different from the `Map` function on `IApplicationBuilder` from section 31.1.2, which is used to branch the middleware pipeline. It is analogous to the `MapGet` (and kin) methods you use to create minimal API endpoints.

As is common with ASP.NET Core, you can extract this somewhat-verbose functionality into an extension method to make your endpoint easier to read and discover. The following listing extracts the code to create an endpoint from listing 31.10 into a separate class, taking the route template to use as a method parameter.

Listing 31.11   An extension method for using the `PingPongMiddleware` as an endpoint

```
public static class EndpointRouteBuilderExtensions          Creates an extension
{                                                           method for registering
    public static IEndpointConventionBuilder MapPingPong(   the PingPongMiddleware
        this IEndpointRouteBuilder endpoints,               as an endpoint
        string route)                  ◄─────────
    {                                            Allows the caller to pass in a route
        var pipeline = endpoints                 template for the endpoint
            .CreateApplicationBuilder()
            .UseMiddleware<PingPongMiddleware>()
            .Build();
                                              Adds the new endpoint to the
        return endpoints                      provided endpoint collection,
            .Map(route, pipeline)             using the provide route template
            .RequireAuthorization();  ◄─────
    }                                      You can add additional metadata here directly,
}                                          or the caller can add metadata themselves.
```

Creates the endpoint pipeline labels `.CreateApplicationBuilder()` / `.UseMiddleware<PingPongMiddleware>()` / `.Build();`

Now that you have an extension method, `MapPingPong()`, you can update your mapping code to be simpler and easier to understand:

```
app.MapPingPong("/ping");
app.MapRazorPages();
app.MapHealthChecks("/healthz");
```

Congratulations—you've created your first custom endpoint from middleware! By turning the middleware into an endpoint, you can now add extra metadata, as shown in listing 31.11. Your middleware is hooked into the endpoint routing system and benefits from everything it offers.

The example in listing 31.11 used a basic route template, `"/ping"`, but you can also use templates that contain route parameters, such as `"/ping/{count}"`, as you would with minimal APIs. The big difference is that you don't get the benefits of model binding that you get from minimal APIs, and it clearly takes more effort than using minimal APIs!

> **TIP** For examples of how to access the route data from your middleware, as well as best-practice advice, see my blog entry titled "Accessing route values in endpoint middleware in ASP.NET Core 3.0" at http://mng.bz/4ZRj.

Converting existing middleware like `PingPongMiddleware` to work with endpoint routing can be useful when you have already implemented that middleware, but it's a lot of boilerplate to write if you want to create a new simple endpoint. In almost all cases you should use minimal API endpoints instead. But if you ever find yourself needing to reuse some existing middleware as an endpoint, now you know how!

In the next section we'll move away from the middleware pipeline and look at how to handle a common configuration requirement: using DI services to build a strongly typed IOptions objects.

31.2 *Using DI with OptionsBuilder and IConfigureOptions*

In this section I describe how to handle a common scenario: you want to use services registered in DI to configure IOptions<T> objects. There are several ways to achieve this, but in this section I introduce the OptionsBuilder<T> as one possible approach and highlight some of the other features it enables.

In chapter 10 we discussed the ASP.NET Core configuration system in depth. You saw how an IConfiguration object is built from multiple layers, where subsequent layers can add to or replace configuration values from previous layers. Each layer is added by a configuration provider, which reads values from a file, from environment variables, from User Secrets, or from any number of possible locations.

A common and encouraged practice is to bind your configuration object to strongly typed IOptions<T> objects, as you saw in chapter 10. Typically, you configure this binding in Program.cs by calling builder.Services.Configure<T>() and providing an IConfiguration object or a configuration section to bind.

For example, to bind a strongly typed object called CurrencyOptions to the "Currencies" section of an IConfiguration object, you could use the following:

```
builder.services.Configure<CurrencyOptions>(
    Configuration.GetSection("Currencies"));
```

> **TIP** You can see an example of the CurrencyOptions type and the associated "Currencies" section of appsetttings.json in the source code for this chapter.

This sets the properties of the CurrencyOptions object, based on the values in the "Currencies" section of your IConfiguration object. Simple binding like this is common, but sometimes you might not want to rely on configuring your IOptions<T> objects via the configuration system; you might want to configure them in code instead. The IOptions pattern requires only that you configure a strongly typed object before it's injected into a dependent service; it doesn't mandate that you have to bind it to an IConfiguration section.

> **TIP** Technically, even if you don't configure an IOptions<T> at all, you can still inject it into your services. In that case, the T object is simply created using the default constructor.

The Configure<T>() method has an additional overload that takes a lambda function. The framework executes the lambda function to configure the CurrencyOptions object when it is injected using DI. The following listing shows an example that uses a lambda function to set the `Currencies` property on a configured `CurrencyOptions` object to a fixed array of strings.

> **Listing 31.12   Configuring an `IOptions` object using a lambda function**

```
WebApplicationBuilder builder = WebApplication.CreateBuilder(args);

builder.Services.Configure<CurrencyOptions>(                    │ Configures the IOptions object by
    builder.Configuration.GetSection("Currencies"));           │ binding to an IConfiguration section

builder.services.Configure<CurrencyOptions>(options =>         │ Configures the IOptions object
    options.Currencies = new string[] { "GBP", "USD"});        │ by executing a lambda function

WebApplication app = builder.Build();
app.MapGet("/", (IOptions<CurrencyOptions> opts) => opts.Value);
app.Run();
```

The injected IOptions value is built by first binding to configuration and then applying the lambda.

Each call to `Configure<T>()`, both the binding to `IConfiguration` and the lambda function, adds another configuration step to the `CurrencyOptions` object. When the DI container first requires an instance of `IOptions<CurrencyOptions>`, the steps run in turn, as shown in figure 31.5.

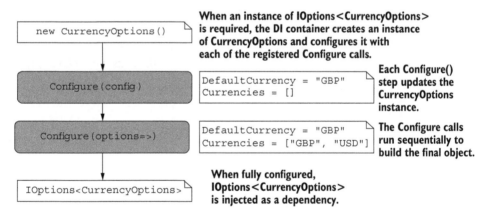

Figure 31.5   Configuring a `CurrencyOptions` object. When the DI container needs an `IOptions<>` instance of a strongly typed object, the container creates the object and then uses each of the registered `Configure()` methods to set the object's properties.

In the previous code snippet, you set the `Currencies` property to a static array of strings in a lambda function. But what if you don't know the correct values ahead of time? You might need to load the available currencies from a database or from some remote service, such as an `ICurrencyProvider`.

This situation, in which you need a configured service to configure your `IOptions<T>`, is potentially hard to resolve. Remember that you declared your

IOptions<T> configuration as part of your app's DI configuration. But if you need to resolve a service from DI to configure the IOptions object, you're stuck with a chicken-and-egg problem: how can you access a service from the DI container before you've finished configuring the DI container?

This circular problem has several potential solutions, but the easiest approach is to use an alternative API for configuring IOptions instances, using the OptionsBuilder<T> type. This type is effectively a wrapper around some of the core IOptions interfaces, but it often results in a terser and more convenient syntax to the approach you've seen so far.

> **TIP** Another helpful feature of OptionsBuilder<T> is adding validation to your IOptions objects. This ensures that your configuration is loaded and bound correctly on app startup so that you don't have any typos in your configuration section names, for example. You can read more about adding validation to your IOptions objects on my blog at http://mng.bz/qrjJ.

The following listing shows the equivalent of listing 31.12 but using OptionsBuilder<T> instead. You create an OptionsBuilder<T> instance by calling AddOptions<T>(), and then chain additional methods such as BindConfiguration() and Configure() to configure your final IOptions<T> object, building up layers of options configuration, as shown previously in figure 31.5.

Listing 31.13   Configuring an IOptions<T> object using OptionsBuilder<T>

```
WebApplicationBuilder builder = WebApplication.CreateBuilder(args);
builder.Services                                        Creates an OptionsBuilder<CurrencyOptions> object
    .AddOptions<CurrencyOptions>()      ◁
    .BindConfiguration("Currencies")    ◁            Binds to the Currencies section of the IConfiguration
    .Configure(opts =>
        opts.Currencies = new string[] { "GBP", "USD"});        Configures the
                                                                IOptions object
WebApplication app = builder.Build();                           by executing a
app.MapGet("/", (IOptions<CurrencyOptions> opts) => opts.Value); lambda function
app.Run();
```

You've seen the builder pattern many times throughout the book, and the pattern in this case is no different. The builder exposes methods that you can chain together fluently. One of the benefits of the builder pattern is that it's easy to discover all the methods it exposes. In this case, if you explore the type in your integrated development environment (IDE), you may notice that OptionsBuilder<T> exposes multiple Configure overloads, such as

- Configure<TDep>(Action<T,TDep> config);
- Configure<TDep1,TDep2>(Action<T, TDep1, TDep2> config);
- Configure<TDep1,TDep2,TDep3>(Action<T,TDep1,TDep2,TDep3> config);

These methods allow you to specify dependencies that are automatically retrieved from the DI container and passed to the config action when the IOptions object is fetched from DI, as shown in figure 31.6. Five overloads for Configure<TDeps> allow you to inject dependencies, allowing you to inject up to five dependencies with these methods.

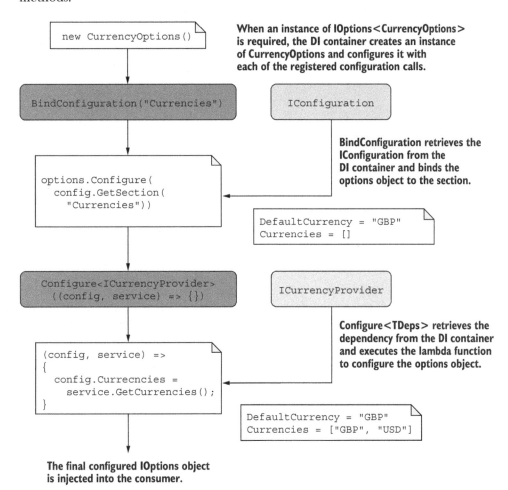

Figure 31.6 **Using** OptionsBuilder **to build an** IOptions **object. Dependencies that are requested via the** Configure<TDeps> **methods are automatically retrieved from the DI container and used to execute the lambda function.**

Using this pattern, we can update the code from listing 31.13 to use the ICurrencyProvider whenever our app needs to create the CurrencyOptions object. We can register the service in the DI container and know that the DI will take care of providing it to the lambda function at runtime, as shown in the following listing.

Listing 31.14   Using a DI service

```
WebApplicationBuilder builder = WebApplication.CreateBuilder(args);

builder.Services
    .AddOptions<CurrencyOptions>()
    .BindConfiguration("Currencies")
    .Configure<ICurrencyProvider>((opts, service) =>
        opts.Currencies = service.GetCurrencies());

builder.Services.AddSingleton<ICurrencyProvider, CurrencyProvider>();

WebApplication app = builder.Build();
app.MapGet("/", (IOptions<CurrencyOptions> opts) => opts.Value);
app.Run();
```

**Configures the Ioptions object
using a service from DI**

**Registers the service
with the DI container**

**Retrieves the IOptions object, which retrieves the
service from DI and runs the lambda method**

With the configuration in listing 31.14, when the `IOptions<CurrencyOptions>` is first injected into the minimal API endpoint, the `IOptions<CurrencyOptions>` object is built as described by the `OptionsBuilder`. First, the `"Currencies"` section of the app `IConfiguration` is bound to a new `CurrencyOptions` object. Then the `ICurrencyProvider` is retrieved from DI and passed to the `Configure<TDep>` lambda, along with the options object. Finally, the `IOptions` object is injected into the endpoint.

> **WARNING** You must inject only singleton services using `Configure<TDeps>` methods. If you try to inject a scoped service, such as a `DbContext`, you will get an error in development warning you about a captive dependency. I describe how to work around this on my blog at http://mng.bz/7Dve.

The `OptionsBuilder<T>` is a convenient way to configure your `IOptions` objects using dependencies, but you can use an alternative approach: implementing the `IConfigureOptions<T>` interface. You implement this interface in a configuration class and use it to configure the `IOptions<T>` object in any way you need, as shown in the following listing. This class can use DI, so you can easily use any other required services.

Listing 31.15   Implementing `IConfigureOptions<T>` to configure an options object

**You can inject services that are available
only after the DI is completely configured.**

```
public class ConfigureCurrencyOptions : IConfigureOptions<CurrencyOptions>
{
    private readonly ICurrencyProvider _currencyProvider;
    public ConfigureCurrencyOptions(ICurrencyProvider currencyProvider)
    {
        _currencyProvider = currencyProvider;
    }

    public void Configure(CurrencyOptions options)
    {
```

**Configure is called when an instance
of IOptions<CurrencyOptions> is
required.**

```
        options.Currencies = _currencyProvider.GetCurrencies();      ◄──────┐
    }
}                                                          Uses the injected service to load the values
```

All that remains is to register the implementation in the DI container. As always, order is important, so if you want `ConfigureCurrencyOptions` to run after binding to configuration, you must add it after configuring your `OptionsBuilder<T>`:

```
builder.Services.AddOptions<CurrencyOptions>()
    .BindConfiguration("Currencies");
builder.AddSingleton
    <IConfigureOptions<CurrencyOptions>, ConfigureCurrencyOptions>();
```

> **TIP** The order in which you configure your options matters. If you want to always run your configuration last, after all other configuration methods, you can use the `PostConfigure()` method on `OptionsBuilder`, or the `IPostConfigure-Options` interface. You can read more about this approach on my blog at http://mng.bz/mVj4.

With this configuration, when `IOptions<CurrencyOptions>` is injected into an endpoint or service, the `CurrencyOptions` object is first bound to the `"Currencies"` section of your `IConfiguration` and then configured by the `ConfigureCurrencyOptions` class.

> **WARNING** The `CurrencyConfigureOptions` object is registered as a singleton, so it will capture any injected services of scoped or transient lifetimes.

Whether you use the `OptionsBuilder<T>` or the `IConfigureOptions<T>` approach, you need to register the `ICurrencyProvider` dependency with the DI container. In the sample code for this chapter, I created a simple `CurrencyProvider` service and registered it with the DI container using

```
builder.Services.AddSingleton<ICurrencyProvider, CurrencyProvider>();
```

As your app grows and you add extra features and services, you'll probably find yourself writing more of these simple DI registrations, where you register a `Service` that implements `IService`. The built-in ASP.NET Core DI container requires you to explicitly register each of these services manually. If you find this requirement frustrating, it may be time to look at third-party DI containers that can take care of some of the boilerplate for you.

31.3 *Using a third-party dependency injection container*

In this section I show you how to replace the default DI container with a third-party alternative, Lamar. Third-party containers often provide additional features compared with the built-in container, such as assembly scanning, automatic service registration, and property injection. Replacing the built-in container can also be useful when you're porting an existing app that uses a third-party DI container to ASP.NET Core.

The .NET community had used DI containers for years before ASP.NET Core decided to include a built-in one. The ASP.NET Core team wanted a way to use DI in their own framework libraries, and they wanted to create a common abstraction[1] that allows you to replace the built-in container with your favorite third-party alternative, such as Autofac, StructureMap/Lamar, Ninject, Simple Injector, or Unity.

The built-in container is intentionally limited in the features it provides, and realistically, it won't be getting many more. By contrast, third-party containers can provide a host of extra features. These are some of the features available in Lamar (https://jasperfx.github.io/lamar/guide/ioc), the spiritual successor to StructureMap (https://structuremap.github.io):

- Assembly scanning for interface/implementation pairs based on conventions
- Automatic concrete class registration
- Property injection and constructor selection
- Automatic `Lazy<T>`/`Func<T>` resolution
- Debugging/testing tools for viewing inside your container

None of these features is a requirement for getting an application up and running, so using the built-in container makes a lot of sense if you're building a small app or are new to DI containers in general. But if at some undefined tipping point, the simplicity of the built-in container becomes too much of a burden, it may be worth replacing.

> **TIP**   A middle-of-the-road approach is to use the Scrutor NuGet package, which adds some features to the built-in DI container without replacing it. For an introduction and examples, see my blog post, "Using Scrutor to automatically register your services with the ASP.NET Core DI container" at http://mng.bz/MX7B.

In this section I show how you can configure an ASP.NET Core app to use Lamar for dependency resolution. It won't be a complex example or an in-depth discussion of Lamar itself. Instead, I'll cover the bare minimum to get you up and running.

Whichever third-party container you choose to install in an existing app, the overall process is pretty much the same:

1 Install the container NuGet package.
2 Register the third-party container with `WebApplicationBuilder` in Program.cs.
3 Configure the third-party container to register your services.

Most of the major .NET DI containers include adapters and extension methods to hook easily into your ASP.NET Core app. For details, it's worth consulting the specific guidance for the container you're using. For Lamar, the process looks like this:

---

[1] Although the promotion of DI as a core practice has been applauded, this abstraction has seen some controversy. This post, titled "What's wrong with the ASP.NET Core DI abstraction?", from one of the maintainers of the SimpleInjector DI library, describes many of the arguments and concerns: http://mng.bz/yYAd. You can also read more about the decisions at http://mng.bz/6DnA.

1   Install the Lamar.Microsoft.DependencyInjection NuGet package using the
    NuGet package manager, by running dotnet add package

```
dotnet add package Lamar.Microsoft.DependencyInjection
```

or by adding a <PackageReference> to your .csproj file:

```
<PackageReference
    Include="Lamar.Microsoft.DependencyInjection" Version="8.1.0" />
```

2   Call UseLamar() on WebApplicationBuilder.Host in Program.cs:

```
WebApplicationBuilder builder = WebApplication.CreateBuilder(args);
builder.Host.UseLamar(services => {})
WebApplication app = builder.Build();
```

3   Configure the Lamar ServiceRegistry in the lambda method passed to
    UseLamar(), as shown in the following listing. This is a basic configuration, but you
    can see a more complex example in the source code for this chapter.

Listing 31.16   Configuring Lamar as a third-party DI container

```
builder.Host.UseLamar(services =>          ◁──┐   Configures your services in UseLamar()
{                                                  instead of on builder.Services
    services.AddAuthorization();
    services.AddControllers()                  ┤
        .AddControllersAsServices();       ──   You can (and should) add ASP.NET Core framework
                                                  services to the ServiceRegistry, as usual.
    services.Scan(_ => {                             Lamar can automatically
        _.AssemblyContainingType(typeof(Program));   scan your assemblies for
        _.WithDefaultConventions();                  services to register.
    });
}
```

**Required so that Lamar is used to
build your web API controllers**

In this example I've used the default conventions to register services. This automatically registers concrete classes and services that are named following expected conventions (for example, Service implements IService). You can change these conventions
or add other registrations in the UseLamar() lambda.

The ServiceRegistry passed into UseLamar() implements IServiceCollection, which
means you can use all the built-in extension methods, such as AddControllers() and
AddAuthorization(), to add framework services to your container.

> **WARNING**   If you're using DI in your Model-View-Controller (MVC) controllers
> (almost certainly!), and you register those dependencies with Lamar rather
> than the built-in container, you may need to call AddControllersAsServices(),
> as shown in listing 31.16. This is due to an implementation detail in the way your

MVC controllers are created by the framework. For details, see my blog entry titled "Controller activation and dependency injection in ASP.NET Core MVC" at http://mng.bz/aogm.

With this configuration in place, whenever your app needs to create a service, it will request it from the Lamar container, which will create the dependency tree for the class and create an instance. This example doesn't show off the power of Lamar, so be sure to check out the documentation (https://jasperfx.github.io/lamar) and the associated source code for this chapter for more examples. Even in modest-size applications, Lamar can greatly simplify your service registration code, but its party trick is showing all the services you have registered and any associated issues.

> **TIP** Third-party containers typically add configuration approaches but don't change any of the fundamentals of how DI works in ASP.NET Core. All the techniques you've seen in this book will work whether you're using the built-in container or a third-party container, so you can use the `IConfigure-Options<T>` approach in section 31.2, for example, regardless of which container you choose.

That brings us to the end of this chapter on advanced configuration. In this chapter I focused on some of the core components of any ASP.NET Core app: middleware, configuration, and DI. In the next chapter you'll learn about more custom components, with a focus on Razor Pages and web API controllers.

Summary

- Use the `Run` extension method to create middleware components that always return a response. You should always place the `Run` extension at the end of a middleware pipeline or branch, as middleware placed after it will never execute.
- You can create branches in the middleware pipeline with the `Map` extension. If an incoming request matches the specified path prefix, the request will execute the pipeline branch; otherwise, it will execute the trunk.
- When the `Map` extension matches a request path segment, it removes the segment from the request's `HttpContext.Path` and moves it to the `PathBase` property. This ensures that routing in branches works correctly.
- You can use the `Use` extension method to create generalized middleware components that can generate a response, modify the request, or pass the request on to subsequent middleware in the pipeline. This is useful for cross-cutting concerns, like adding a header to all responses.
- You can encapsulate middleware in a reusable class. The class should take a `RequestDelegate` object in the constructor and should have a public `Invoke()` method that takes an `HttpContext` and returns a `Task`. To call the next middleware component in the pipeline, invoke the `RequestDelegate` with the provided `HttpContext`.

- To create endpoints that generate a response, build a miniature pipeline containing the response-generating middleware, and call `endpoints.Map(route, pipeline)`. Endpoint routing will be used to map incoming requests to your endpoint.
- You can configure `IOptions<T>` objects using a fluent builder interface. Call `AddOptions<T>()` to create an `OptionsBuilder<T>` instance and then chain configuration calls. `OptionsBuilder<T>` allows easy access to dependencies for configuration, as well as features such as validation.
- You can also use services from the DI container to configure an `IOptions<T>` object by creating a separate class that implements `IConfigureOptions<T>`. This class can use DI in the constructor and is used to lazily build a requested `IOptions<T>` object at runtime.
- You can replace the built-in DI container with a third-party container. Third-party containers often provide additional features, such as convention-based dependency registration, assembly scanning, and property injection.

Building custom MVC and Razor Pages components

This chapter covers

- Creating custom Razor Tag Helpers
- Using view components to create complex Razor views
- Creating a custom DataAnnotations validation attribute
- Replacing the DataAnnotations validation framework with an alternative

In the previous chapter you learned how to customize and extend some of the core systems in ASP.NET Core: configuration, dependency injection (DI), and your middleware pipeline. These components form the basis of all ASP.NET Core apps. In this chapter we're focusing on Razor Pages and Model-View-Controller (MVC)/API controllers. You'll learn how to build custom components that work with Razor views. You'll also learn how to build components that work with the validation framework used by both Razor Pages and API controllers.

We'll start by looking at Tag Helpers. In section 32.1 I show how to create two Tag Helpers: one that generates HTML to describe the current machine and one that lets you write `if` statements in Razor templates without having to use C#. These will give you the details you need to create your own custom Tag Helpers in your own apps if the need arises.

In section 32.2 you'll learn about a new Razor concept: view components. View components are a bit like partial views, but they can contain business logic and database access. For example, on an e-commerce site you might have a shopping cart, a dynamically populated menu, and a login widget all on one page. Each of those sections is independent of the main page content and has its own logic and data-access needs. In an ASP.NET Core app using Razor Pages, you'd implement each of those as a view component.

In section 32.3 I'll show you how to create a custom validation attribute. As you saw in chapter 6, validation is a key responsibility of Razor Page handlers and action methods, and the `DataAnnotations` attributes provide a clean, declarative way of doing so. We previously looked only at the built-in attributes, but you'll often find you need to add attributes tailored to your app's domain. In section 32.3 you'll see how to create a simple validation attribute and how to extend it to use services registered with the DI container.

Throughout this book I've mentioned that you can easily swap out core parts of the ASP.NET Core framework if you wish. In section 32.4 you'll do that by replacing the built-in attribute-based validation framework with a popular alternative, FluentValidation. This open-source library allows you to separate your binding models from the validation rules, which makes building certain validation logic easier. Many people prefer this approach of separating concerns to the declarative approach of `DataAnnotations`.

When you're building pages with Razor Pages, one of the best productivity features is Tag Helpers, and in the next section you'll see how you can create your own.

32.1 *Creating a custom Razor Tag Helper*

In this section you'll learn how to create your own Tag Helpers, which allow you to customize your HTML output. You'll learn how to create Tag Helpers that add new elements to your HTML markup, as well as Tag Helpers that can remove or customize existing markup. You'll also see that your custom Tag Helpers integrate with the tooling of your integrated development environment (IDE) to provide rich IntelliSense in the same way as the built-in Tag Helpers.

In my opinion, Tag Helpers are one of the best additions to the venerable Razor template language in ASP.NET Core. They allow you to write Razor templates that are easier to read, as they require less switching between C# and HTML, and they augment your HTML tags rather than replace them (as opposed to the HTML Helpers used extensively in the legacy version of ASP.NET).

ASP.NET Core comes with a wide variety of Tag Helpers (see chapter 18), which cover many of your day-to-day requirements, especially when it comes to building forms. For example, you can use the Input Tag Helper by adding an `asp-for` attribute to an `<input>` tag and passing a reference to a property on your `PageModel`, in this case `Input.Email`:

```
<input asp-for="Input.Email" />
```

The Tag Helper is activated by the presence of the attribute and gets a chance to augment the `<input>` tag when rendering to HTML. The Input Tag Helper uses the name of the property to set the `<input>` tag's `name` and `id` properties, the value of the model to set the `value` property, and the presence of attributes such as `[Required]` or `[EmailAddress]` to add attributes for validations:

```
<input type="email" id="Input_Email" name="Input.Email"
    value="test@example.com" data-val="true"
    data-val-email="The Email Address field is not a valid e-mail address."
    data-val-required="The Email Address field is required."
    />
```

Tag Helpers help reduce the duplication in your code, or they can simplify common patterns. In this section I show how you can create your own custom Tag Helpers.

In section 32.1.1 you'll create a system information Tag Helper, which prints details about the name and operating system of the server your app is running on. In section 32.1.2 you'll create a Tag Helper that you can use to conditionally show or hide an element based on a C# Boolean property. In section 32.1.3 you'll create a Tag Helper that reads the Razor content written inside the Tag Helper and transforms it.

32.1.1 *Printing environment information with a custom Tag Helper*

A common problem you may run into when you start running your web applications in production, especially if you're using a server-farm setup, is working out which machine rendered the page you're currently looking at. Similarly, when deploying frequently, it can be useful to know which version of the application is running. When I'm developing and testing, I sometimes like to add a little "info dump" at the bottom of my layouts so I can easily work out which server generated the current page, which environment it's running in, and so on.

In this section I'm going to show you how to build a custom Tag Helper to output system information to your layout. You'll be able to toggle the information it displays, but by default it displays the machine name and operating system on which the app is running, as shown in figure 32.1.

You can call this Tag Helper from Razor by creating a `<system-info>` element in your template:

```
<footer>
  <system-info></system-info>
</footer>
```

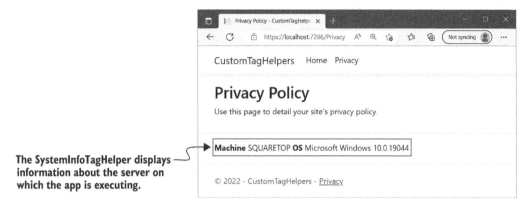

The SystemInfoTagHelper displays
information about the server on
which the app is executing.

Figure 32.1   The `SystemInfoTagHelper` **displays the machine name and operating system on which the application is running. It can be useful for identifying which instance of your app handled the request when running in a web-farm scenario.**

TIP   You might not want to expose this sort of information in production, so you could also wrap it in an `<environment>` Tag Helper, as you saw in chapter 18.

The easiest way to create a custom Tag Helper is to derive from the `TagHelper` base class and override the `Process()` or `ProcessAsync()` function that describes how the class should render itself. The following listing shows your complete custom Tag Helper, `SystemInfoTagHelper`, which renders the system information to a `<div>`. You could easily extend this class if you wanted to display additional fields or add options.

Listing 32.1   `SystemInfoTagHelper` **to render system information to a view**

```
public class SystemInfoTagHelper : TagHelper
{
    private readonly HtmlEncoder _htmlEncoder;
    public SystemInfoTagHelper(HtmlEncoder htmlEncoder)
    {
        _htmlEncoder = htmlEncoder;
    }

    [HtmlAttributeName("add-machine")]
    public bool IncludeMachine { get; set; } = true;

    [HtmlAttributeName("add-os")]
    public bool IncludeOS { get; set; } = true;

    public override void Process(
        TagHelperContext context, TagHelperOutput output)
    {
        output.TagName = "div";
        output.TagMode = TagMode.StartTagAndEndTag;
        var sb = new StringBuilder();
```

Derives
from the
TagHelper
base class

An HtmlEncoder is
necessary when writing
HTML content to the page.

Decorating properties with
HtmlAttributeName allows
you to set their values
from Razor markup.

The main
function
called when
an element
is rendered.

Renders both the
<div> </div>
start and end tag

Replaces the
<system-info>
element with a
<div> element

```
        if (IncludeMachine)
        {
            sb.Append(" <strong>Machine</strong> ");
            sb.Append(_htmlEncoder.Encode(Environment.MachineName));
        }

        if (IncludeOS)
        {
            sb.Append(" <strong>OS</strong> ");
            sb.Append(
                _htmlEncoder.Encode(RuntimeInformation.OSDescription));
        }
        output.Content.SetHtmlContent(sb.ToString());
    }
}
```

If required, adds a <strong> element and the HTML-encoded machine name

If required, adds a <strong> element and the HTML-encoded OS name

Sets the inner content of the <div> tag with the HTML-encoded value stored in the string builder

There's a lot of new code in this example, so we'll work through it line by line. First, the class name of the Tag Helper defines the name of the element you must create in your Razor template, with the suffix removed and converted to kebab-case. As this Tag Helper is called SystemInfoTagHelper, you must create a <system-info> element.

> TIP   If you want to customize the name of the element, for example to <env-info>, but you want to keep the same class name, you can apply [HtmlTargetElement] with the desired name, such as [HtmlTargetElement("Env-Info")]. HTML tags are not case-sensitive, so you could use "Env-Info" or "env-info".

Inject an HtmlEncoder into your Tag Helper so you can HTML-encode any data you write to the page. As you saw in chapter 29, you should always HTML-encode data you write to the page to avoid cross-site scripting (XSS) vulnerabilities and to ensure that the data is displayed correctly.

You've defined two properties on your Tag Helper, IncludeMachine and IncludeOS, which you'll use to control which data is written to the page. These are decorated with a corresponding [HtmlAttributeName], which enables setting the properties from the Razor template. In Visual Studio you'll even get IntelliSense and type-checking for these values, as shown in figure 32.2.

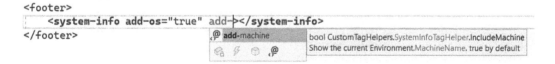

Figure 32.2   In Visual Studio, Tag Helpers are shown in a purple font, and you get IntelliSense for properties decorated with [HtmlAttributeName].

Finally, we come to the Process() method. The Razor engine calls this method to execute the Tag Helper when it identifies the target element in a view template. The Process() method defines the type of tag to render (<div>), whether it should render a start and end tag (or a self-closing tag—it depends on the type of tag you're rendering), and the HTML content of the `<div>`. You set the HTML content to be rendered inside the tag by calling `Content.SetHtmlContent()` on the provided instance of `TagHelperOutput`.

> **WARNING** Always HTML-encode your output before writing to your tag with `SetHtmlContent()`. Alternatively, pass unencoded input to `SetContent()`, and the output will be automatically HTML-encoded for you.

Before you can use your new Tag Helper in a Razor template, you need to register it. You can do this in the _ViewImports.cshtml file, using the `@addTagHelper` directive and specifying the fully qualified name of the Tag Helper and the assembly, as in this example:

```
@addTagHelper CustomTagHelpers.SystemInfoTagHelper, CustomTagHelpers
```

Alternatively, you can add all the Tag Helpers from a given assembly by using the wildcard syntax, `*`, and specifying the assembly name:

```
@addTagHelper *, CustomTagHelpers
```

With your custom Tag Helper created and registered, you're now free to use it in any of your Razor views, partial views, or layouts.

> **TIP** If you're not seeing IntelliSense for your Tag Helper in Visual Studio, and the Tag Helper isn't rendered in the bold font used by Visual Studio, you probably haven't registered your Tag Helpers correctly in _ViewImports .cshtml using `@addTagHelper`.

The `SystemInfoTagHelper` is an example of a Tag Helper that generates content, but you can also use Tag Helpers to control how existing elements are rendered. In the next section you'll create a simple Tag Helper that can control whether an element is rendered based on an HTML attribute.

32.1.2 Creating a custom Tag Helper to conditionally hide elements

If you want to control whether an element is displayed in a Razor template based on some C# variable, you'd typically wrap the element in a C# `if` statement:

```
@{
    var showContent = true;
}
@if(showContent)
{
    <p>The content to show</p>
}
```

Falling back to C# constructs like this can be useful, as it allows you to generate any markup you like. Unfortunately, it can be mentally disruptive having to switch back and forth between C# and HTML, and it makes it harder to use HTML editors that don't understand Razor syntax.

In this section you'll create a simple Tag Helper to avoid the cognitive dissonance problem. You can apply this Tag Helper to existing elements to achieve the same result as shown previously but without having to fall back to C#:

```
@{
    var showContent = true;
}
<p if="showContent" >
    The content to show
</p>
```

When rendered at runtime, this Razor template would return the HTML

```
<p>
    The content to show
</p>
```

Instead of creating a new element, as you did for `SystemInfoTagHelper` (`<system-info>`), you'll create a Tag Helper that you apply as an attribute to existing HTML elements. This Tag Helper does one thing: controls the visibility of the element it's attached to. If the value passed in the `if` attribute is `true`, the element and its content is rendered as normal. If the value passed is `false`, the Tag Helper removes the element and its content from the template. The following listing shows how you could achieve this.

Listing 32.2   Creating an `IfTagHelper` to conditionally render elements

```
[HtmlTargetElement(Attributes = "if")]          ⟵  Setting the Attributes property ensures that
public class IfTagHelper : TagHelper                the Tag Helper is triggered by an if attribute.
{
    [HtmlAttributeName("if")]          ⟵  Binds the value of the if attribute
    public bool RenderContent { get; set; } = true;     to the RenderContent property

    public override void Process(                            The Razor engine calls
        TagHelperContext context, TagHelperOutput output)    Process() to execute
    {                                                        the Tag Helper.
        if(RenderContent == false)          ⟵  If the RenderContent property evaluates
        {                                       to false, removes the element
            output.TagName = null;          ⟵
            output.SuppressOutput();            Sets the element the Tag Helper resides
        }                                       on to null, removing it from the page
    }

    public override int Order => int.MinValue;     ⟵  Ensures that this Tag Helper runs
}                                                      before any others attached to the
                                                       element
```

Doesn't render or evaluate the inner content of the element

Instead of a standalone `<if>` element, the Razor engine executes the `IfTagHelper` whenever it finds an element with an `if` attribute. This can be applied to any HTML element: `<p>`, `<div>`, `<input>`, whatever you need. You should define a Boolean property specifying whether you should render the content, which is bound to the value in the `if` attribute.

The `Process()` function is much simpler here. If `RenderContent` is `false`, it sets the `TagHelperOutput.TagName` to `null`, which removes the element from the page. It also calls `SuppressOutput()`, which prevents any content inside the attributed element from being rendered. If `RenderContent` is `true`, you skip these steps, and the content is rendered as normal.

One other point of note is the overridden `Order` property. This controls the order in which Tag Helpers run when multiple Tag Helpers are applied to an element. By setting `Order` to `int.MinValue`, you ensure that `IfTagHelper` always runs first, removing the element if required, before other Tag Helpers execute. There's generally no point running other Tag Helpers if the element is going to be removed from the page anyway.

> **NOTE** Remember to register your custom Tag Helpers in _ViewImports .cshtml with the `@addTagHelper` directive.

With a simple HTML attribute, you can now conditionally render elements in Razor templates without having to fall back to C#. This Tag Helper can show and hide content without needing to know what the content is. In the next section we'll create a Tag Helper that *does* need to know the content.

32.1.3   Creating a Tag Helper to convert Markdown to HTML

The two Tag Helpers shown so far are agnostic to the content written inside the Tag Helper, but it can also be useful to create Tag Helpers that inspect, retrieve, and modify this content. In this section you'll see an example of one such Tag Helper that converts Markdown content written inside it to HTML.

> **DEFINITION** Markdown is a commonly used text-based markup language that is easy to read but can also be converted to HTML. It is the common format used by README files on GitHub, and I use it to write blog posts, for example. For an introduction to Markdown, see the GitHub guide at http://mng.bz/o1rp.

We'll use the popular Markdig library (https://github.com/xoofx/markdig) to create the Markdown Tag Helper. This library converts a `string` containing Markdown to an HTML `string`. You can install Markdig using Visual Studio by running `dotnet add package Markdig` or by adding a `<PackageReference>` to your .csproj file:

```
<PackageReference Include="Markdig" Version="0.30.4" />
```

The Markdown Tag Helper that we'll create shortly can be used by adding `<markdown>` elements to your Razor Page, as shown in the following listing.

Listing 32.3   Using a Markdown Tag Helper in a Razor Page

```
@page
@model IndexModel
@{
    var showContent = true;          Adds the Markdown Tag Helper using
}                                    the <markdown> element

<markdown>        ◁─────────┐  ┌── Creates titles in Markdown using # to
## This is a markdown title  ◁──┘   denote h1, ## to denote h2, and so on

This is a markdown list:      Markdown converts
                              simple lists to HTML
* Item 1                      <ul> elements.
* Item 2

<div if="showContent">                  Razor content can be nested
  Content is shown when showContent is true   inside other Tag Helpers.
</div>
</markdown>
```

The Markdown Tag Helper renders content with these steps:

1 Render any Razor content inside the Tag Helper. This includes executing any *nested* Tag Helpers and C# code inside the Tag Helper. Listing 32.3 uses the `IfTagHelper`, for example.

2 Convert the resulting `string` to HTML using the Markdig library.

3 Replace the content with the rendered HTML and remove the Tag Helper `<markdown>` element.

The following listing shows a simple approach to implementing a Markdown Tag Helper using Markdig. Markdig supports many additional extensions and features that you could enable, but the overall pattern of the Tag Helper would be the same.

Listing 32.4   Implementing a Markdown Tag Helper using Markdig

```
public class MarkdownTagHelper: TagHelper   ◁─┐ The Markdown Tag Helper will use
{                                             │ the <markdown> element.
    public override async Task ProcessAsync(
        TagHelperContext context, TagHelperOutput output)  ┐ Retrieves the contents
    {                                                      │ of the <markdown>
        TagHelperContent markdownRazorContent = await     ─┘ element
            output.GetChildContentAsync();
        string markdown =
            markdownRazorContent.GetContent();

        string html = Markdig.Markdown.ToHtml(markdown);   ◁─┐ Converts the
                                                              │ Markdown string to
        output.Content.SetHtmlContent(html);  ◁───┐          │ HTML using Markdig
        output.TagName = null;        ◁──────┐    │
    }                                        │    └── Writes the HTML content to the output
}                                            │
          Removes the <markdown>             │
          element from the content           │
```

Renders the Razor contents to a string — bracket beside `TagHelperContent markdownRazorContent = await output.GetChildContentAsync(); string markdown = markdownRazorContent.GetContent();*

When rendered to HTML, the Markdown content in listing 32.3 becomes

```
<h2>This is a markdown title</h2>
<p>This is a markdown list:</p>
<ul>
<li>Item 1</li>
<li>Item 2</li>
</ul>
<div>
  Content is shown when showContent is true
</div>
```

> **NOTE** In listing 32.4 we implemented `ProcessAsync()` instead of `Process()` because we called the async method `GetChildContentAsync()`. You must call async methods only from other async methods; otherwise, you can get problems such as thread starvation. For more details, see Microsoft's "ASP.NET Core Best Practices" at http://mng.bz/KM7X.

The Tag Helpers in this section represent a small sample of possible avenues you could explore, but they cover the two broad categories: Tag Helpers for rendering new content and Tag Helpers for controlling the rendering of other elements.

> **TIP** For further details and examples, see Microsoft's "Author Tag Helpers in ASP.NET Core" documentation at http://mng.bz/Idb0.

Tag Helpers can be useful for providing small pieces of isolated, reusable functionality like this, but they're not designed to provide larger, application-specific sections of an app or to make calls to business-logic services. Instead, you should use view components, as you'll see in the next section.

32.2 View components: Adding logic to partial views

In this section you'll learn about *view components*, which operate independently of the main Razor Page and can be used to encapsulate complex business logic. You can use view components to keep your main Razor Page focused on a single task—rendering the main content—instead of also being responsible for other sections of the page.

If you think about a typical website, you'll notice that it may have multiple independent dynamic sections in addition to the main content. Consider Stack Overflow, shown in figure 32.3. As well as the main body of the page, which shows questions and answers, there's a section showing the current logged-in user, a panel for blog posts and related items, and a section for job suggestions.

Each of these sections is effectively independent of the main content. Each section contains business logic (deciding which posts or ads to show), database access (loading the details of the posts), and rendering logic for how to display the data.

In chapter 7 you saw that you can use layouts and partial views to split the rendering of a view template into similar sections, but partial views aren't a good fit for this example. Partial views let you encapsulate view rendering logic but not business logic

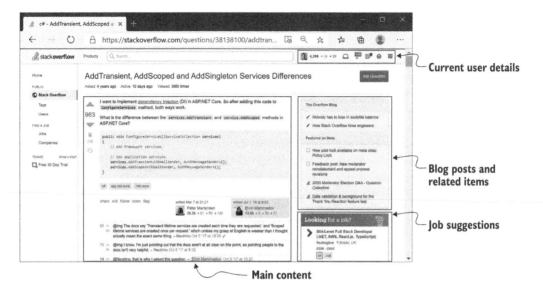

Figure 32.3   The Stack Overflow website has multiple sections that are independent of the main content but contain business logic and complex rendering logic. Each of these sections could be rendered as a view component in ASP.NET Core.

that's independent of the main page content. Instead, view components provide this functionality, encapsulating both the business logic and rendering logic for displaying a small section of the page. You can use DI to provide access to a database context, and you can test view components independently of the view they generate, much like MVC and API controllers. Think of them as being a bit like mini MVC controllers or mini Razor Pages, but you invoke them directly from a Razor view instead of in response to an HTTP request.

> **TIP**   View components are comparable to child actions from the legacy .NET Framework version of ASP.NET, in that they provide similar functionality. Child actions don't exist in ASP.NET Core.

> ## View components vs. Razor Components and Blazor
> In this book I focus on server-side rendered applications using Razor Pages and API applications using minimal APIs and web API controllers. .NET 7 also has a different approach to building ASP.NET Core applications: Blazor. I don't cover Blazor in this book, so I recommend reading *Blazor in Action*, by Chris Sainty (Manning, 2021).
>
> Blazor has two programming models, client-side and server-side, but both approaches use *Blazor components* (confusingly, officially called *Razor components*). Blazor components have a lot of parallels with view components, but they live in a fundamentally different world. Blazor components can interact easily, but you can't use them with Tag Helpers or view components, and it's hard to combine them with Razor Page form posts.

Nevertheless, if you need an island of rich client-side interactivity in a single Razor Page, you can embed a Blazor component in a Razor Page, as shown in the "Render components from a page or view" section of the "Prerender and integrate ASP.NET Core Razor components" documentation at http://mng.bz/PPen. You could also use Blazor components as a way to replace Asynchronous JavaScript and XML (AJAX) calls in your Razor Pages, as I show in my blog entry "Replacing AJAX calls in Razor Pages with Razor Components and Blazor" at http://mng.bz/9MJj.

If you don't need the client-side interactivity of Blazor, view components are still the best option for isolated sections in Razor Pages. They interoperate cleanly with your Razor Pages; have no additional operational overhead; and use familiar concepts like layouts, partial views, and Tag Helpers. For more details on why you should continue to use view components, see my "Don't replace your View Components with Razor Components" blog entry at http://mng.bz/1rKq.

In this section you'll see how to create a custom view component for the recipe app you built in previous chapters, as shown in figure 32.4. If the current user is logged in, the view component displays a panel with a list of links to the user's recently created recipes. For unauthenticated users, the view component displays links to the login and register actions.

When the user is logged in, the view component displays a list of Recipes created by the current user, loaded from the database.

When the user is not logged in, the view component displays links to the Register and Login pages.

Figure 32.4   The view component displays different content based on the currently logged-in user. It includes both business logic (determining which recipes to load from the database) and rendering logic (specifying how to display the data).

This component is a great candidate for a view component, as it contains database access and business logic (choosing which recipes to display) as well as rendering logic (deciding how the panel should be displayed).

> **TIP** Use partial views when you want to encapsulate the rendering of a specific view model or part of view model. Consider using a view component when you have rendering logic that requires business logic or database access or when the section is logically distinct from the main page content.

You invoke view components directly from Razor views and layouts using a Tag Helper-style syntax with a vc: prefix:

```
<vc:my-recipes number-of-recipes="3">
</vc:my-recipes>
```

Custom view components typically derive from the ViewComponent base class and implement an InvokeAsync() method, as shown in listing 32.5. Deriving from this base class allows access to useful helper methods in much the same way that deriving from the ControllerBase class does for API controllers. Unlike with API controllers, the parameters passed to InvokeAsync don't come from model binding. Instead, you pass the parameters to the view component using properties on the Tag Helper element in your Razor view.

Listing 32.5   A custom view component to display the current user's recipes

```
public class MyRecipesViewComponent : ViewComponent        ◁──────  Deriving from the
{                                                                    ViewComponent
    private readonly RecipeService _recipeService;                   base class provides
    private readonly UserManager<ApplicationUser> _userManager;      useful methods like
    public MyRecipesViewComponent(RecipeService recipeService,       View().
        UserManager<ApplicationUser> userManager)
    {
        _recipeService = recipeService;
        _userManager = userManager;               InvokeAsync renders the view
    }                                             component. It should return a
                                                  Task<IViewComponentResult>.
    public async Task<IViewComponentResult> InvokeAsync(   ◁──────
        int numberOfRecipes)
    {                                      Calling View() will
        if(!User.Identity.IsAuthenticated)  render a partial
        {                                    view with the       You can use async
            return View("Unauthenticated");  provided name.      external services,
        }                                ◁──                      allowing you to
                                                                 encapsulate logic
        var userId = _userManager.GetUserId(HttpContext.User);   in your business
        var recipes = await _recipeService.GetRecipesForUser(    domain.
            userId, numberOfRecipes);
                                         You can pass a view model to the
        return View(recipes);   ◁─────  partial view. Default.cshtml is used
    }                                    by default.
}
```

You can use DI in a view component.

You can pass parameters to the component from the view.

This custom view component handles all the logic you need to render a list of recipes when the user is logged in or a different view if the user isn't authenticated. The name of the view component is derived from the class name, like Tag Helpers. Alternatively, you can apply the `[ViewComponent]` attribute to the class and set a different name entirely.

The `InvokeAsync` method must return a `Task<IViewComponentResult>`. This is similar to the way you can return `IActionResult` from an action method or a page handler, but it's more restrictive; view components must render some sort of content, so you can't return status codes or redirects. You'll typically use the `View()` helper method to render a partial view template (as in the previous listing), though you can also return a string directly using the `Content()` helper method, which will HTML-encode the content and render it to the page directly.

You can pass any number of parameters to the `InvokeAsync` method. The name of the parameters (in this case, `numberOfRecipes`) is converted to kebab-case and exposed as a property in the view component's Tag Helper (`<number-of-recipes>`). You can provide these parameters when you invoke the view component from a view, and you'll get IntelliSense support, as shown in figure 32.5.

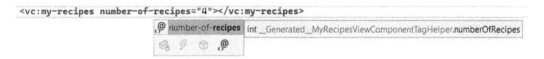

```
<vc:my-recipes number-of-recipes="4"></vc:my-recipes>
```

Figure 32.5 Visual Studio provides IntelliSense support for the method parameters of a view component's `InvokeAsync` method. The parameter name, in this case `numberOfRecipes`, is converted to kebab-case for use as an attribute in the Tag Helper.

View components have access to the current request and `HttpContext`. In listing 32.5 you can see that we're checking whether the current request was from an authenticated user. You can also see that we've used some conditional logic. If the user isn't authenticated, we render the "Unauthenticated" Razor template; if they're authenticated, we render the default Razor template and pass in the view models loaded from the database.

> **NOTE** If you don't specify a specific Razor view template to use in the `View()` function, view components use the template name Default.cshtml.

The partial views for view components work similarly to other Razor partial views that you learned about in chapter 7, but they're stored separately from them. You must create partial views for view components at one of these locations:

- Views/Shared/Components/ComponentName/TemplateName
- Pages/Shared/Components/ComponentName/TemplateName

Both locations work, so for Razor Pages apps I typically use the Pages/ folder. For the view component in listing 32.5, for example, you'd create your view templates at

- `Pages/Shared/Components/MyRecipes/Default.cshtml`
- `Pages/Shared/Components/MyRecipes/Unauthenticated.cshtml`

This was a quick introduction to view components, but it should get you a long way. View components are a simple way to embed pockets of isolated, complex logic in your Razor layouts. Having said that, be mindful of these caveats:

- View component classes must be public, non-nested, and nonabstract classes.
- Although they're similar to MVC controllers, you can't use filters with view components.
- You can use layouts in your view components' views to extract rendering logic common to a specific view component. This layout may contain @sections, as you saw in chapter 7, but these sections are independent of the main Razor view's layout.
- View components are isolated from the Razor Page they're rendered in, so you can't, for example, define a @section in a Razor Page layout and then add that content from a view component; the contexts are completely separate.
- When using the `<vc:my-recipes>` Tag Helper syntax to invoke your view component, you must import it as a custom Tag Helper, as you saw in section 32.1.
- Instead of using the Tag Helper syntax, you may invoke the view component from a view directly by using `IViewComponentHelper Component`, though I don't recommend using this syntax, as in this example:

```
@await Component.InvokeAsync("MyRecipes", new { numberOfRecipes = 3 })
```

We've covered Tag Helpers and view components, which are both features of the Razor engine in ASP.NET Core. In the next section you'll learn about a different but related topic: how to create a custom `DataAnnotations` attribute. If you've used older versions of ASP.NET, this will be familiar, but ASP.NET Core has a couple of tricks up its sleeve to help you out.

32.3 *Building a custom validation attribute*

In this section you'll learn how to create a custom `DataAnnotations` validation attribute that specifies specific values a `string` property may take. You'll then learn how you can expand the functionality to be more generic by delegating to a separate service that is configured in your DI controller. This will allow you to create custom domain-specific validations for your apps.

We looked at model binding in chapter 7, where you saw how to use the built-in `DataAnnotations` attributes in your binding models to validate user input. These provide several built-in validations, such as

- [Required]—The property isn't optional and must be provided.
- [StringLength(min, max)]—The length of the string value must be between min and max characters.
- [EmailAddress]—The value must have a valid email address format.

But what if these attributes don't meet your requirements? Consider the following listing, which shows a binding model from a currency converter application. The model contains three properties: the currency to convert from, the currency to convert to, and the quantity.

Listing 32.6   Currency converter initial binding model

```
public class CurrencyConverterModel
{
    [Required]
    [StringLength(3, MinimumLength = 3)]
    public string CurrencyFrom { get; set; }

    [Required]
    [StringLength(3, MinimumLength = 3)]
    public string CurrencyTo { get; set; }

    [Required]
    [Range(1, 1000)]
    public decimal Quantity { get; set; }
}
```

All the properties are required.

The strings must be exactly three characters.

The quantity can be between 1 and 1000.

There's some basic validation on this model, but during testing you identify a problem: users can enter any three-letter string for the CurrencyFrom and CurrencyTo properties. Users should be able to choose only a valid currency code, like "USD" or "GBP", but someone attacking your application could easily send "XXX" or "£$%".

Assuming that you support a limited set of currencies—say, GBP, USD, EUR, and CAD—you could handle the validation in a few ways. One way would be to validate the CurrencyFrom and CurrencyTo values within the Razor Page handler method, after model binding and attribute validation has already occurred.

Another way would be to use a [RegularExpresssion] attribute to look for the allowed strings. The approach I'm going to take here is to create a custom Validation-Attribute. The goal is to have a custom validation attribute you can apply to the CurrencyFrom and CurrencyTo attributes, to restrict the range of valid values. This will look something like the following example.

Listing 32.7   Applying custom validation attributes to the binding model

```
public class CurrencyConverterModel
{
    [Required]
    [StringLength(3, MinimumLength = 3)]
    [CurrencyCode("GBP", "USD", "CAD", "EUR")]
```

CurrencyCodeAttribute validates that the property has one of the provided values.

```
    public string CurrencyFrom { get; set; }

    [Required]
    [StringLength(3, MinimumLength = 3)]
    [CurrencyCode("GBP", "USD", "CAD", "EUR")]
    public string CurrencyTo { get; set; }

    [Required]
    [Range(1, 1000)]
    public decimal Quantity { get; set; }
}
```

CurrencyCodeAttribute validates that the property has one of the provided values.

Creating a custom validation attribute is simple; you can start with the ValidationAttribute base class, and you have to override only a single method. The next listing shows how you could implement CurrencyCodeAttribute to ensure that the currency codes provided match the expected values.

Listing 32.8 Custom validation attribute for currency codes

```
public class CurrencyCodeAttribute : ValidationAttribute
{
    private readonly string[] _allowedCodes;
    public CurrencyCodeAttribute(params string[] allowedCodes)
    {
        _allowedCodes = allowedCodes;
    }

    protected override ValidationResult IsValid(
        object value, ValidationContext context)
    {
        if(value is not string code
            || !_allowedCodes.Contains(code))
        {
            return new ValidationResult("Not a valid currency code");
        }
        return ValidationResult.Success;
    }
}
```

Derives from ValidationAttribute to ensure that your attribute is used during validation

The attribute takes in an array of allowed currency codes.

The IsValid method is passed the value to validate and a context object.

Tries to cast the value to a string and store it in the code variable

. . .otherwise, returns a success result.

If the value provided isn't a string, is null, or isn't an allowed code, returns an error . . .

As you know from chapter 16, Validation occurs in the filter pipeline after model binding, before the action or Razor Page handler executes. The validation framework calls IsValid() for each instance of ValidationAttribute on the model property being validated. The framework passes in value (the value of the property being validated) and the ValidationContext to each attribute in turn. The context object contains details that you can use to validate the property.

Of particular note is the ObjectInstance property. You can use this to access the top-level model being validated when you validate a subproperty. For example, if the CurrencyFrom property of the CurrencyConvertModel is being validated, you can access the top-level object from the ValidationAttribute as follows:

```
var model = validationContext.ObjectInstance as CurrencyConverterModel;
```

This can be useful if the validity of a property depends on the value of another property of the model. For example, you might want a validation rule that says that GBP is a valid value for `CurrencyTo` except when `CurrencyFrom` is also GBP. `ObjectInstance` makes these sorts of comparison validations easy.

> **NOTE** Although using `ObjectInstance` makes it easy to make model-level comparisons like these, it reduces the portability of your validation attribute. In this case, you would be able to use the attribute only in the application that defines `CurrencyConverterModel`.

Within the `IsValid()` method, you can cast the `value` provided to the required data type (in this case, `string`) and check against the list of allowed codes. If the code isn't allowed, the attribute returns a `ValidationResult` with an error message indicating that there was a problem. If the code *is* allowed, `ValidationResult.Success` is returned, and the validation succeeds.

Putting your attribute to the test in figure 32.6 shows that when `CurrencyTo` is an invalid value (£$%), the validation for the property fails, and an error is added to the `ModelState`. You could do some tidying-up of this attribute to set a custom message, allow nulls, or display the name of the property that's invalid, but all the important features are there.

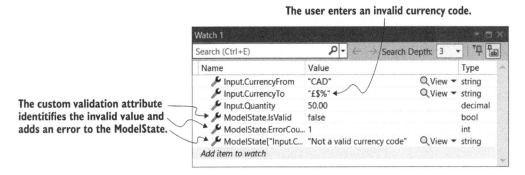

Figure 32.6 The Watch window of Visual Studio showing the result of validation using the custom `ValidationAttribute`. The user has provided an invalid `currencyTo` value, £$%. Consequently, `ModelState` isn't valid and contains a single error with the message "`Not a valid currency code`".

The main feature missing from this custom attribute is client-side validation. You've seen that the attribute works well on the server side, but if the user entered an invalid value, they wouldn't be informed until after the invalid value had been sent to the server. That's safe, and it's as much as you need to do for security and data-consistency purposes, but client-side validation can improve the user experience by providing immediate feedback.

You can implement client-side validation in several ways, but it's heavily dependent on the JavaScript libraries you use to provide the functionality. Currently, ASP.NET Core Razor templates rely on jQuery for client-side validation. See the "Custom client-side validation" section of Microsoft's "Model validation in ASP.NET Core MVC and Razor Pages" documentation for an example of creating a jQuery Validation adapter for your attributes: http://mng.bz/Wd6g.

> **TIP** Instead of using the official jQuery-based validation libraries, you could use the open source aspnet-client-validation library (https://github.com/haacked/aspnet-client-validation) as I describe on my blog at http://mng.bz/AoXe.

Another improvement to your custom validation attribute would be to load the list of currencies from a DI service, such as an `ICurrencyProvider`. Unfortunately, you can't use constructor DI in your `CurrencyCodeAttribute`, as you can pass only constant values to the constructor of an `Attribute` in .NET. In chapter 22 we worked around this limitation for filters by using `[TypeFilter]` or `[ServiceFilter]`, but there's no such solution for `ValidationAttribute`.

Instead, for validation attributes you must use the service locator pattern. As I discussed in chapter 9, this antipattern is best avoided where possible, but unfortunately it's necessary in this case. Instead of declaring an explicit dependency via a constructor, you must ask the DI container directly for an instance of the required service.

Listing 32.9 shows how you could rewrite listing 32.8 to load the allowed currencies from an instance of `ICurrencyProvider` instead of hardcoding the allowed values in the attribute's constructor. The attribute calls the `GetService<T>()` method on `Validation-Context` to resolve an instance of `ICurrencyProvider` from the DI container. Note that `ICurrencyProvider` is a hypothetical service that would need to be registered in your application's `ConfigureServices()` method in Startup.cs.

Listing 32.9 Using the service-locator pattern to access services

```
public class CurrencyCodeAttribute : ValidationAttribute
{
    protected override ValidationResult IsValid(
        object value, ValidationContext context)              ⟵ Retrieves an instance of
    {                                                             ICurrencyProvider directly
        var provider = context                                    from the DI container
            .GetRequiredService<ICurrencyProvider>();
        var allowedCodes = provider.GetCurrencies();    ⟵ Fetches the currency codes using the provider

        if(value is not string code
            || !_allowedCodes.Contains(code))
        {                                                              ⟵ Validates the
            return new ValidationResult("Not a valid currency code");   property as
        }                                                                before
        return ValidationResult.Success;
    }
}
```

TIP The generic `GetRequiredService<T>` method is an extension method available in the `Microsoft.Extensions.DependencyInjection` namespace.

The default `DataAnnotations` validation system can be convenient due to its declarative nature, but this has tradeoffs, as shown by the dependency injection problem above. Luckily, you can replace the validation system your application uses, as shown in the following section.

32.4 Replacing the validation framework with FluentValidation

In this section you'll learn how to replace the `DataAnnotations`-based validation framework that's used by default in Razor Pages and MVC Controllers. You'll see the arguments for why you might want to do this and learn how to use a third-party alternative: FluentValidation. This open-source project allows you to define the validation requirements of your models separately from the models themselves. This separation can make some types of validation easier and ensures that each class in your application has a single responsibility.

Validation is an important part of the model-binding process in ASP.NET Core. In chapter 7 you learned that minimal APIs don't have any validation built in, so you're free to choose whichever framework you like. I demonstrated using `DataAnnotations`, but you could easily choose a different validation framework.

In Razor Pages and MVC, however, the `DataAnnotations` validation framework is built into ASP.NET Core. You can apply `DataAnnotations` attributes to properties of your binding models to define your requirements, and ASP.NET Core automatically validates them. In section 32.3 we even created a custom validation attribute.

But ASP.NET Core is flexible. You can replace whole chunks of the Razor Pages and MVC frameworks if you like. The validation system is one such area that many people choose to replace.

FluentValidation (https://fluentvalidation.net) is a popular alternative validation framework for ASP.NET Core. It is a mature library, with roots going back well before ASP.NET Core was conceived of. With FluentValidation you write your validation code separately from your binding model code. This gives several advantages:

- You're not restricted to the limitations of `Attributes`, such as the dependency injection problem we had to work around in listing 32.9.
- It's much easier to create validation rules that apply to multiple properties, such as to ensure that an `EndDate` property contains a later value than a `StartDate` property. Achieving this with `DataAnnotations` attributes is possible but difficult.
- It's generally easier to test FluentValidation validators than `DataAnnotations` attributes.
- The validation is strongly typed compared with `DataAnnotations` attributes where it's possible to apply attributes in ways that don't make sense, such as applying an `[EmailAddress]` attribute to an `int` property.
- Separating your validation logic from the model itself arguably better conforms to the single-responsibility principle (SRP).

That final point is sometimes given as a reason not to use FluentValidation: FluentValidation separates a binding model from its validation rules. Some people are happy to accept the limitations of DataAnnotations to keep the model and validation rules together.

Before I show how to add FluentValidation to your application, let's see what FluentValidation validators look like.

32.4.1   *Comparing FluentValidation with DataAnnotations attributes*

To better understand the difference between the DataAnnotations approach and FluentValidation, we'll convert the binding models from section 32.3 to use FluentValidation. The following listing shows what the binding model from listing 32.7 would look like when used with FluentValidation. It is structurally identical but has no validation attributes.

Listing 32.10   Currency converter initial binding model for use with FluentValidation

```
public class CurrencyConverterModel
{
    public string CurrencyFrom { get; set; }
    public string CurrencyTo { get; set; }
    public decimal Quantity { get; set; }
}
```

In FluentValidation you define your validation rules in a separate class, with a class per model to be validated. Typically, these rules derive from the AbstractValidator<> base class, which provides a set of extension methods for defining your validation rules.

The following listing shows a validator for the CurrencyConverterModel, which matches the validations added using attributes in listing 32.7. You create a set of validation rules for a property by calling RuleFor() and chaining method calls such as NotEmpty() from it. This style of method chaining is called a *fluent* interface, hence the name.

Listing 32.11   A FluentValidation validator for the currency converter binding model

```
public class CurrencyConverterModelValidator          The validator inherits
    : AbstractValidator<CurrencyConverterModel>       from AbstractValidator.
{
    private readonly string[] _allowedValues          Defines the static list of currency
        = new []{ "GBP", "USD", "CAD", "EUR" };       codes that are supported

    public CurrencyConverterModelValidator()          RuleFor is used to add a new validation rule.
    {                                                 The lambda syntax allows for strong typing.
        RuleFor(x => x.CurrencyFrom)
            .NotEmpty()
            .Length(3)          There are equivalent rules for common
                                DataAnnotations validation attributes.
```

You define validation rules in the validator's constructor.

```
You can easily              .Must(value => _allowedValues.Contains(value))
add custom                  .WithMessage("Not a valid currency code");
validation rules
without having      RuleFor(x => x.CurrencyTo)
to create               .NotEmpty()
separate                .Length(3)
classes.                .Must(value => _allowedValues.Contains(value))
                        .WithMessage("Not a valid currency code");

                    RuleFor(x => x.Quantity)          Thanks to strong typing, the rules
                        .NotNull()                    available depend on the property
                        .InclusiveBetween(1, 1000);  ◁—  being validated.
        }
    }
```

Your first impression of this code might be that it's quite verbose compared with listing 32.7, but remember that listing 32.7 used a custom validation attribute, [Currency-Code]. The validation in listing 32.11 doesn't require anything else. The logic implemented by the [CurrencyCode] attribute is right there in the validator, making it easy to reason about. The Must() method can be used to perform arbitrarily complex validations without having the additional layers of indirection required by custom DataAnnotations attributes.

On top of that, you'll notice that you can define only validation rules that make sense for the property being validated. Previously, there was nothing to stop us from applying the [CurrencyCode] attribute to the Quantity property; that's not possible with FluentValidation.

Of course, just because you can write the custom [CurrencyCode] logic in-line doesn't necessarily mean you have to. If a rule is used in multiple parts of your application, it may make sense to extract it into a helper class. The following listing shows how you could extract the currency code logic into an extension method that can be used in multiple validators.

Listing 32.12   An extension method for currency validation

```
public static class ValidationExtensions          Creates an extension
{                                                 method that can be
    public static IRuleBuilderOptions<T, string>  chained from RuleFor()
        MustBeCurrencyCode<T>(                     for string properties
            this IRuleBuilder<T, string> ruleBuilder)
    {
        return ruleBuilder
            .Must(value => _allowedValues.Contains(value))   Applies the same
            .WithMessage("Not a valid currency code");        validation logic as before
    }

    private static readonly string[] _allowedValues =   The currency code
        new []{ "GBP", "USD", "CAD", "EUR" };            values to allow
}
```

You can then update your `CurrencyConverterModelValidator` to use the new extension method, removing the duplication in your validator and ensuring consistency across country-code fields:

```
RuleFor(x => x.CurrencyTo)
    .NotEmpty()
    .Length(3)
    .MustBeCurrencyCode();
```

Another advantage of the FluentValidation approach of using standalone validation classes is that they are created using DI, so you can inject services into them. As an example, consider the `[CurrencyCode]` validation attribute from listing 32.9, which used a service, `ICurrencyProvider`, from the DI container. This requires using service location to obtain an instance of `ICurrencyProvider` using an injected context object.

With the FluentValidation library, you can inject the `ICurrencyProvider` directly into your validator, as shown in the following listing. This requires fewer gymnastics to get the desired functionality and makes your validator's dependencies explicit.

Listing 32.13   Currency converter validator using dependency injection

```
public class CurrencyConverterModelValidator          Injects the service using standard
    : AbstractValidator<CurrencyConverterModel>       constructor dependency injection
{
    public CurrencyConverterModelValidator(ICurrencyProvider provider)   ◄
    {
        RuleFor(x => x.CurrencyFrom)
            .NotEmpty()
            .Length(3)
            .Must(value => provider          Uses the injected
                .GetCurrencies()             service in a Must() rule
                .Contains(value))
            .WithMessage("Not a valid currency code");

        RuleFor(x => x.CurrencyTo)                                        Uses the injected
            .NotEmpty()                                                   service with an
            .Length(3)                                                    extension method
            .MustBeCurrencyCode(provider.GetCurrencies());   ◄
        
        RuleFor(x => x.Quantity)
            .NotNull()
            .InclusiveBetween(1, 1000);
    }
}
```

The final feature I'll show demonstrates how much easier it is to write validators that span multiple properties with FluentValidation. For example, imagine we want to validate that the value of `CurrencyTo` is different from `CurrencyFrom`. Using FluentValidation, you can implement this with an overload of `Must()`, which provides both the model and the property being validated, as shown in the following listing.

Listing 32.14   Using `Must()` to validate that two properties are different

```
RuleFor(x => x.CurrencyTo)
    .NotEmpty()
    .Length(3)
    .MustBeCurrencyCode()
    .Must((InputModel model, string currencyTo)
        => currencyTo != model.CurrencyFrom)
    .WithMessage("Cannot convert currency to itself");
```

The error message will be associated with the CurrencyTo property.

The Must function passes the top-level model being validated and the current property.

Performs the validation. The currencies must be different.

Uses the provided message as the error message

Creating a validator like this is certainly possible with `DataAnnotations` attributes, but it requires far more ceremony than the FluentValidation equivalent and is generally harder to test. FluentValidation has many more features for making it easier to write and test your validators, too:

- *Complex property validations*—Validators can be applied to complex types as well as to the primitive types like `string` and `int` shown here in this section.
- *Custom property validators*—In addition to simple extension methods, you can create your own property validators for complex validation scenarios.
- *Collection rules*—When types contain collections, such as `List<T>`, you can apply validation to each item in the list, as well as to the overall collection.
- *RuleSets*—You can create multiple collections of rules that can be applied to an object in different circumstances. These can be especially useful if you're using FluentValidation in additional areas of your application.
- *Client-side validation*—FluentValidation is a server-side framework, but it emits the same attributes as `DataAnnotations` attributes to enable client-side validation using jQuery.

There are many more features, so be sure to browse the documentation at https://docs.fluentvalidation.net for details. In the next section you'll see how to add FluentValidation to your ASP.NET Core application.

32.4.2   Adding FluentValidation to your application

Replacing the whole validation system of ASP.NET Core sounds like a big step, but the FluentValidation library makes it easy to add to your application. Simply follow these steps:

1 Install the FluentValidation.AspNetCore NuGet package using Visual Studio's NuGet package manager via the command-line interface (CLI) by running `dotnet add package FluentValidation.AspNetCore` or by adding a `<PackageReference>` to your .csproj file:

```
<PackageReference Include="FluentValidation.AspNetCore" Version="11.2.2" />
```

2   Configure the FluentValidation library for MVC and Razor Pages in Program.cs
    by calling `builder.Services.AddFluentValidationAutoValidation()`. You can fur-
    ther configure the library as shown in listing 32.15.

3   Register your validators (such as the `CurrencyConverterModelValidator` from list-
    ing 32.13) with the DI container. These can be registered manually, using any
    scope you choose:

```
WebApplicationBuilder builder = WebApplication.CreateBuilder(args);
builder.Services.AddRazorPages();
builder.Services.AddFluentValidationAutoValidation();
builder.services.AddScoped<
    IValidator<CurrencyConverterModelValidator>,
    CurrencyConverterModelValidator>();
```

Alternatively, you can allow FluentValidation to automatically register all your
validators using the options shown in listing 32.15.

For such a mature library, FluentValidation has relatively few configuration options to
decipher. The following listing shows some of the options available; in particular, it
shows how to automatically register all the custom validators in your application and
disable `DataAnnotations` validation.

Listing 32.15   Configuring FluentValidation in an ASP.NET Core application

```
var builder = WebApplication.CreateBuilder(args);

builder.Services.AddRazorPages();

builder.Services.AddValidatorsFromAssemblyContaining<Program>();

builder.Services.AddFluentValidationAutoValidation(
  x => x.DisableDataAnnotationsValidation = true)
    .AddFluentValidationClientsideAdapters();

ValidatorOptions.Global.LanguageManager.Enabled = false;
```

Instead of manually registering validators, FluentValidation can autoregister them for you.

Setting to true disables DataAnnotations validation completely for model binding.

Enables integration with client-side validation via data-* attributes

FluentValidation has full localization support, but you can disable it if you don't need it.

It's important to understand that if you don't set `DisableDataAnnotationsValidation` to
`true`, ASP.NET Core will run validation with both `DataAnnotations` and FluentValidation. That may be useful if you're in the process of migrating from one system to the
other, but otherwise, I recommend disabling it. Having your validation split between
both places seems like the worst of both worlds!

One final thing to consider is where to put your validators in your solution. There
are no technical requirements for this; if you've registered your validator with the DI
container, it will be used correctly, so the choice is up to you. I prefer to place validators close to the models they're validating.

For Razor Pages binding-model validators, I create the validator as a nested class of the `PageModel`, in the same place as I create the `InputModel`, as described in chapter 16. That gives a class hierarchy in the Razor Page similar to the following:

```
public class IndexPage : PageModel
{
    public class InputModel { }
    public class InputModelValidator: AbstractValidator<InputModel> { }
}
```

That's my preference. Of course, you're free to adopt another approach if you prefer.

That brings us to the end of this chapter on custom Razor Pages components. When you combine it with the components in the previous chapter, you've got a great base for extending your ASP.NET Core applications to meet your needs. It's a testament to ASP.NET Core's design that you can swap out whole sections like the Validation framework entirely. If you don't like how some part of the framework works, see whether someone has written an alternative!

Summary

- With Tag Helpers, you can bind your data model to HTML elements, making it easier to generate dynamic HTML. Tag Helpers can customize the elements they're attached to, add attributes, and customize how they're rendered to HTML. This can greatly reduce the amount of markup you need to write.
- The name of a Tag Helper class dictates the name of the element in the Razor templates, so the `SystemInfoTagHelper` corresponds to the `<system-info>` element. You can choose a different element name by adding the `[HtmlTargetElement]` attribute to your Tag Helper.
- You can set properties on your Tag Helper object from Razor syntax by decorating the property with an `[HtmlAttributeName("name")]` attribute and providing a name. You can set these properties from Razor using HTML attributes, as in `<system-info name="value">`.
- The `TagHelperOutput` parameter passed to the `Process` or `ProcessAsync` methods control the HTML that's rendered to the page. You can set the element type with the `TagName` property and set the inner content using `Content.SetContent()` or `Content.SetHtmlContent()`.
- You can prevent inner Tag Helper content from being processed by calling `SupressOutput()`, and you can remove the element by setting `TagName=null`. This is useful if you want to conditionally render elements to the response.
- You can retrieve the contents of a Tag Helper by calling `GetChildContentAsync()` on the `TagHelperOutput` parameter. You can then render this content to a `string` by calling `GetContent()`. This will render any Razor expressions and Tag Helpers to HTML, allowing you to manipulate the contents.

- View components are like partial views, but they allow you to use complex business and rendering logic. You can use them for sections of a page, such as the shopping cart, a dynamic navigation menu, or suggested articles.

- Create a view component by deriving from the `ViewComponent` base class and implementing `InvokeAsync()`. You can pass parameters to this function from the Razor view template using HTML attributes, in a similar way to Tag Helpers.

- View components can use DI, access the `HttpContext`, and render partial views. The partial views should be stored in the Pages/Shared/Components/ <Name>/ folder, where Name is the name of the view component. If not specified, view components will look for a default view named Default.cshtml.

- You can create a custom `DataAnnotations` attribute by deriving from `Validation-Attribute` and overriding the `IsValid` method. You can use this to decorate your binding model properties and perform arbitrary validation.

- You can't use constructor DI with custom validation attributes. If the validation attribute needs access to services from the DI container, you must use the Service Locator pattern to load them from the validation context, using the `GetService<T>` method.

- FluentValidation is an alternative validation system that can replace the default `DataAnnotations` validation system. It is not based on attributes, which makes it easier to write custom validations for your validation rules and makes those rules easier to test.

- To create a validator for a model, create a class derived from `AbstractValida-tor<>` and call `RuleFor<>()` in the constructor to add validation rules. You can chain multiple requirements on `RuleFor<>()` in the same way that you could add multiple `DataAnnotations` attributes to a model.

- If you need to create a custom validation rule, you can use the `Must()` method to specify a predicate. If you wish to reuse the validation rule across multiple models, encapsulate the rule as an extension method to reduce duplication.

- To add FluentValidation to your application, install the FluentValidation .AspNetCore NuGet package, call `AddFluentValidationAutoValidation()` in Program.cs, and register your validators with the DI container. This will add Fluent-Validation validations in addition to the built-in `DataAnnotations` system.

- To remove the `DataAnnotations` validation system and use FluentValidation only, set the `DisableDataAnnotationsValidation` option to `true` in your call to `AddFluentValidationAutoValidation()`. Favor this approach where possible to avoid running validation methods from two different systems.

- You can allow FluentValidation to automatically discover and register all the validators in your application by calling `AddValidatorsFromAssemblyContaining<T>()`, where `T` is a type in the assembly to scan. This means you don't have to register each validator in your application with the DI container individually.

Calling remote APIs
with IHttpClientFactory

33

This chapter covers

- Seeing problems caused by using HttpClient
  incorrectly to call HTTP APIs
- Using IHttpClientFactory to manage HttpClient
  lifetimes
- Encapsulating configuration and handling
  transient errors with IHttpClientFactory

So far in this book we've focused on creating web pages and exposing APIs. Whether that's customers browsing a Razor Pages application or client-side SPAs and mobile apps consuming your APIs, we've been writing the APIs for others to consume.

However, it's common for your application to interact with third-party services by consuming their APIs as well as your own API apps. For example, an e-commerce site needs to take payments, send email and Short Message Service (SMS) messages, and retrieve exchange rates from a third-party service. The most common approach for interacting with services is using HTTP. So far in this book we've looked at how you can expose HTTP services, using minimal APIs and API controllers, but we haven't looked at how you can consume HTTP services.

In section 33.1 you'll learn the best way to interact with HTTP services using Http-Client. If you have any experience with C#, it's likely that you've used this class to send HTTP requests, but there are two gotchas to think about; otherwise, your app could run into difficulties.

IHttpClientFactory was introduced in .NET Core 2.1; it makes creating and managing HttpClient instances easier and avoids the common pitfalls. In section 33.2 you'll learn how IHttpClientFactory achieves this by managing the HttpClient handler pipeline. You'll learn how to create named clients to centralize the configuration for calling remote APIs and how to use typed clients to encapsulate the remote service's behavior.

Network glitches are a fact of life when you're working with HTTP APIs, so it's important for you to handle them gracefully. In section 33.3 you'll learn how to use the open-source resilience and fault-tolerance library Polly to handle common transient errors using simple retries, with the possibility for more complex policies.

Finally, in section 33.4 you'll see how you can create your own custom HttpMessage-Handler handlers managed by IHttpClientFactory. You can use custom handlers to implement cross-cutting concerns such as logging, metrics, and authentication, whenever a function needs to execute every time you call an HTTP API. You'll also see how to create a handler that automatically adds an API key to all outgoing requests to an API.

To misquote John Donne, no app is an island, and the most common way of interacting with other apps and services is over HTTP. In .NET, that means using HttpClient.

33.1 *Calling HTTP APIs: The problem with HttpClient*

In this section you'll learn how to use HttpClient to call HTTP APIs. I'll focus on two common pitfalls in using HttpClient—socket exhaustion and DNS rotation problems—and show why they occur. In section 33.2 you'll see how to avoid these problems by using IHttpClientFactory.

It's common for an application to interact with other services to fulfill its duty. Take a typical e-commerce store, for example. In even the most basic version of the application, you will likely need to send emails and take payments using credit cards or other services. You could try to build that functionality yourself, but it probably wouldn't be worth the effort.

Instead, it makes far more sense to delegate those responsibilities to third-party services that specialize in that functionality. Whichever service you use, they will almost certainly expose an HTTP API for interacting with the service. For many services, that will be the *only* way.

In .NET we use the HttpClient class for calling HTTP APIs. You can use it to make HTTP calls to APIs, providing all the headers and body to send in a request, and reading the response headers and data you get back. Unfortunately, it's hard to use correctly, and even when you do, it has limitations.

> ## RESTful HTTP vs. gRPC vs. GraphQL
>
> There are many ways to interact with third-party services, but HTTP RESTful services are still the king, decades after HTTP was first proposed. Every platform and programming language you can think of includes support for making HTTP requests and handling responses. That ubiquity makes it the go-to option for most services.
>
> Despite their ubiquity, RESTful services are not perfect. They are relatively verbose, which means that more data ends up being sent and received than with some other protocols. It can also be difficult to evolve RESTful APIs after you have deployed them. These limitations have spurred interest in two alternative protocols in particular: gRPC and GraphQL.
>
> gRPC is intended to be an efficient mechanism for server-to-server communication. It builds on top of HTTP/2 but typically provides much higher performance than traditional RESTful APIs. gRPC support was added in .NET Core 3.0 and is receiving many performance and feature updates. For a comprehensive view of .NET support, see the documentation at https://learn.microsoft.com/aspnet/core/grpc.
>
> Whereas gRPC works best with server-to-server communication and nonbrowser clients, GraphQL is best used to provide evolvable APIs to mobile and single-page application (SPA) apps. It has become popular among frontend developers, as it can reduce the friction involved in deploying and using new APIs. For details, I recommend *GraphQL in Action*, by Samer Buna (Manning, 2021).
>
> Despite the benefits and improvements gRPC and GraphQL can bring, RESTful HTTP services are here to stay for the foreseeable future, so it's worth making sure that you understand how to use them with `HttpClient`.

The source of the difficulty with `HttpClient` stems partly from the fact that it implements the `IDisposable` interface. In general, when you use a class that implements `IDisposable`, you should wrap the class with a `using` statement whenever you create a new instance to ensure that unmanaged resources used by the type are cleaned up when the class is removed, as in this example:

```
using (var myInstance = new MyDisposableClass())
{
    // use myInstance
}
```

> **TIP** C# also includes a simplified version of the using statement called a *using declaration*, which omits the curly braces, as shown in listing 33.1. You can read more about the syntax at http://mng.bz/nW12.

That might lead you to think that the correct way to create an `HttpClient` is shown in listing 33.1. This listing shows a simple example where a minimal API endpoint calls an external API to fetch the latest currency exchange rates, and returns them as the response.

WARNING   Do not use `HttpClient` as it's shown in listing 33.1. Using it this way could cause your application to become unstable, as you'll see shortly.

Listing 33.1   The incorrect way to use `HttpClient`

```
WebApplicationBuilder builder = WebApplication.CreateBuilder(args);
WebApplication app = builder.Build();
app.MapGet("/", async () =>
{
    using HttpClient client = new HttpClient();
    client.BaseAddress = new Uri("https://example.com/rates/");
    var response = await client.GetAsync("latest");
    response.EnsureSuccessStatusCode();
    return await response.Content.ReadAsStringAsync();
});
app.Run();
```

Wrapping the HttpClient in a using declaration means it is disposed at the end of the scope.

Makes a GET request to the exchange rates API

Configures the base URL used to make requests using the HttpClient

Reads the result as a string and returns it from the action method

Throws an exception if the request was not successful

`HttpClient` is special, and you shouldn't use it like this! The problem is due primarily to the way the underlying protocol implementation works. Whenever your computer needs to send a request to an HTTP server, you must create a connection between your computer and the server. To create a connection, your computer opens a port, which has a random number between 0 and 65,535, and connects to the HTTP server's IP address and port, as shown in figure 33.1. Your computer can then send HTTP requests to the server.

DEFINITION   The combination of IP address and port is called a *socket*.

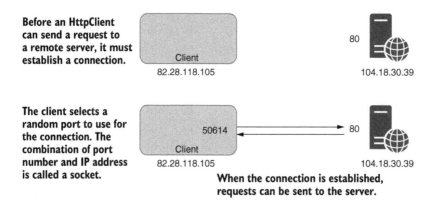

Figure 33.1   To create a connection, a client selects a random port and connects to the HTTP server's port and IP address. The client can then send HTTP requests to the server.

The main problem with the `using` statement/declaration and `HttpClient` is that it can lead to a problem called *socket exhaustion*, illustrated in figure 33.2. This happens when all the ports on your computer have been used up making other HTTP connections, so your computer can't make any more requests. At that point, your application will hang, waiting for a socket to become free—a bad experience!

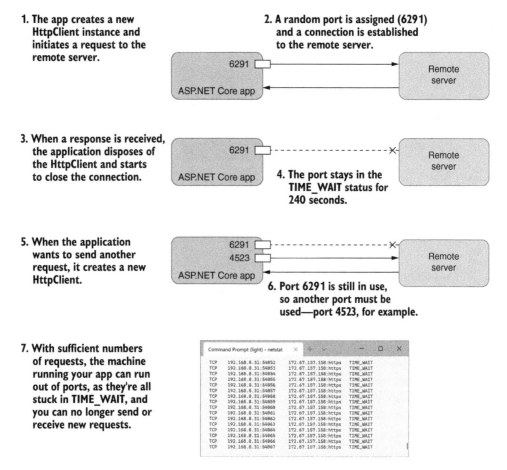

1. The app creates a new HttpClient instance and initiates a request to the remote server.

2. A random port is assigned (6291) and a connection is established to the remote server.

3. When a response is received, the application disposes of the HttpClient and starts to close the connection.

4. The port stays in the TIME_WAIT status for 240 seconds.

5. When the application wants to send another request, it creates a new HttpClient.

6. Port 6291 is still in use, so another port must be used—port 4523, for example.

7. With sufficient numbers of requests, the machine running your app can run out of ports, as they're all stuck in TIME_WAIT, and you can no longer send or receive new requests.

Figure 33.2 Disposing of `HttpClient` **can lead to socket exhaustion. Each new connection requires the operating system to assign a new socket, and closing a socket doesn't make it available until the** `TIME_WAIT` **period of 240 seconds has elapsed. Eventually you can run out of sockets, at which point you can't make any outgoing HTTP requests.**

Given that I said there are 65,536 different port numbers, you might think that's an unlikely situation. It's true that you will likely run into this problem only on a server that is making a lot of connections, but it's not as rare as you might think.

The problem is that when you dispose of an `HttpClient`, *it doesn't close the socket immediately*. The design of the TCP/IP protocol used for HTTP requests means that after trying to close a connection, the connection moves to a state called `TIME_WAIT`. The connection then waits for a specific period (240 seconds in Windows) before closing the socket.

Until the TIME_WAIT period has elapsed, you can't reuse the socket in another Http-Client to make HTTP requests. If you're making a lot of requests, that can quickly lead to socket exhaustion, as shown in figure 33.2.

> **TIP** You can view the state of active ports/sockets in Windows and Linux by running the command netstat from the command line or a terminal window. Be sure to run netstat -n in Windows to skip Domain Name System (DNS) resolution.

Instead of disposing of HttpClient, the general advice (before the introduction of IHttpClientFactory) was to use a single instance of HttpClient, as shown in the following listing.

Listing 33.2 Using a singleton HttpClient to avoid socket exhaustion

```
WebApplicationBuilder builder = WebApplication.CreateBuilder(args);
WebApplication app = builder.Build();

HttpClient client = new HttpClient              ◁── A single instance of
{                                                    HttpClient is created for
    BaseAddress = new Uri("https://example.com/rates/"),   the lifetime of the app.
};

app.MapGet("/", async () =>
{                                                    ◁── Multiple requests use the
    var response = await client.GetAsync("latest");       same instance of HttpClient.

    response.EnsureSuccessStatusCode();
    return await response.Content.ReadAsStringAsync();
});
app.Run();
```

This solves the problem of socket exhaustion. As you're not disposing of the Http-Client, the socket is not disposed of, so you can reuse the same port for multiple requests. No matter how many times you call the API in the preceding example, you will use only a single socket. Problem solved!

Unfortunately, this introduces a different problem, primarily related to DNS. DNS is how the friendly hostnames we use, such as manning.com, are converted to the Internet Protocol (IP) addresses that computers need. When a new connection is required, the HttpClient first checks the DNS record for a host to find the IP address and then makes the connection. For subsequent requests, the connection is already established, so it doesn't make another DNS call.

For singleton HttpClient instances, this can be a problem because the HttpClient won't detect DNS changes. DNS is often used in cloud environments for load balancing to do graceful rollouts of deployments.[1] If the DNS record of a service you're calling changes during the lifetime of your application, a singleton HttpClient will keep calling the old service, as shown in figure 33.3.

---

[1] Azure Traffic Manager, for example, uses DNS to route requests. You can read more about how it works at http://mng.bz/vnP4.

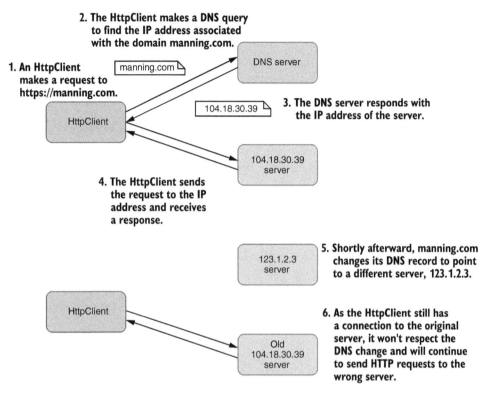

Figure 33.3 `HttpClient` **does a DNS lookup before establishing a connection to determine the IP address associated with a hostname. If the DNS record for a hostname changes, a singleton** `HttpClient` **will not detect it and will continue sending requests to the original server it connected to.**

> **NOTE** `HttpClient` won't respect a DNS change while the original connection exists. If the original connection is closed (for example, if the original server goes offline), it will respect the DNS change, as it must establish a new connection.

It seems that you're damned if you do and damned if you don't! Luckily, `IHttpClient-Factory` can take care of all this for you.

33.2   Creating HttpClients with IHttpClientFactory

In this section you'll learn how you can use `IHttpClientFactory` to avoid the common pitfalls of `HttpClient`. I'll show several patterns you can use to create an `HttpClient`:

- Using `CreateClient()` as a drop-in replacement for `HttpClient`
- Using named clients to centralize the configuration of an `HttpClient` used to call a specific third-party API
- Using typed clients to encapsulate the interaction with a third-party API for easier consumption by your code

IHttpClientFactory makes it easier to create HttpClient instances correctly instead of relying on either of the faulty approaches I discussed in section 33.1. It also makes it easier to configure multiple HttpClients and allows you to create a middleware pipeline for outgoing requests.

Before we look at how IHttpClientFactory achieves all that, we will look at how HttpClient works under the hood.

33.2.1 *Using IHttpClientFactory to manage HttpClientHandler lifetime*

In this section we'll look at the handler pipeline used by HttpClient. You'll see how IHttpClientFactory manages the lifetime of this pipeline and how this enables the factory to avoid both socket exhaustion and DNS problems.

The HttpClient class you typically use to make HTTP requests is responsible for orchestrating requests, but it isn't responsible for making the raw connection itself. Instead, the HttpClient calls into a pipeline of HttpMessageHandler, at the end of which is an HttpClientHandler, which makes the actual connection and sends the HTTP request, as shown in figure 33.4.

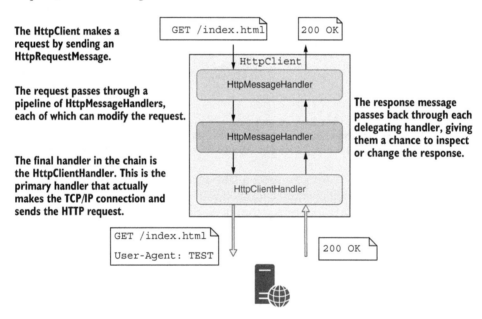

Figure 33.4   Each HttpClient **contains a pipeline of** HttpMessageHandlers. **The final handler is an** HttpClientHandler, **which makes the connection to the remote server and sends the HTTP request. This configuration is similar to the ASP.NET Core middleware pipeline, and it allows you to make cross-cutting adjustments to outgoing requests.**

This configuration is reminiscent of the middleware pipeline used by ASP.NET Core applications, but this is an outbound pipeline. When an HttpClient makes a request, each handler gets a chance to modify the request before the final HttpClientHandler makes the real HTTP request. Each handler in turn then gets a chance to view the response after it's received.

> **TIP** You'll see an example of using this handler pipeline for cross-cutting concerns in section 33.3 when we add a transient error handler.

The problems of socket exhaustion and DNS I described in section 33.1 are related to the disposal of the `HttpClientHandler` at the end of the handler pipeline. By default, when you dispose of an `HttpClient`, you dispose of the handler pipeline too. `IHttpClientFactory` separates the lifetime of the `HttpClient` from the underlying `HttpClientHandler`.

Separating the lifetime of these two components enables the `IHttpClientFactory` to solve the problems of socket exhaustion and DNS rotation. It achieves this in two ways:

- *By creating a pool of available handlers*—Socket exhaustion occurs when you dispose of an `HttpClientHandler`, due to the `TIME_WAIT` problem described previously. `IHttpClientFactory` solves this by creating a pool of handlers.

  `IHttpClientFactory` maintains an active handler that it uses to create all `HttpClients` for two minutes. When the `HttpClient` is disposed of, the underlying handler isn't disposed of, so the connection isn't closed. As a result, socket exhaustion isn't a problem.

- *By periodically disposing of handlers*—Sharing handler pipelines solves the socket exhaustion problem, but it doesn't solve the DNS problem. To work around this, the `IHttpClientFactory` periodically (every two minutes) creates a new active `HttpClientHandler` that it uses for each `HttpClient` created subsequently. As these `HttpClients` are using a new handler, they make a new TCP/IP connection, so DNS changes are respected.

  `IHttpClientFactory` disposes of expired handlers periodically in the background once they are no longer used by an `HttpClient`. This ensures that your application's `HttpClients` use a limited number of connections.

> **TIP** I wrote a blog post that looks in depth at how `IHttpClientFactory` achieves its handler rotation. This is a detailed post, but it may be of interest to those who like to know how things are implemented behind the scenes. See "Exploring the code behind `IHttpClientFactory` in depth" at http://mng.bz/8NRK.

Rotating handlers with `IHttpClientFactory` solves both the problems we've discussed. Another bonus is that it's easy to replace existing uses of `HttpClient` with `IHttpClientFactory`.

`IHttpClientFactory` is included by default in ASP.NET Core. You simply add it to your application's services in Program.cs:

```
builder.Services.AddHttpClient();
```

This registers the `IHttpClientFactory` as a singleton in your application, so you can inject it into any other service. The following listing shows how you can replace the `HttpClient` approach from listing 33.2 with a version that uses `IHttpClientFactory`.

Listing 33.3   Using `IHttpClientFactory` to create an `HttpClient`

```
WebApplicationBuilder builder = WebApplication.CreateBuilder(args);
builder.Services.AddHttpClient();         ◄─┐
                                            │  Registers the IHttpClientFactory
WebApplication app = builder.Build();       │  service in DI
                                                     │  Injects the
app.MapGet("/", async (IHttpClientFactory factory) =>  ◄─┘ IHttpClientFactory using DI
{
    HttpClient client = factory.CreateClient();   ◄─┐
                                                     │  Creates an HttpClient instance
    client.BaseAddress =                             │  with an HttpClientHandler
        new Uri("https://example.com/rates/");       │  managed by the factory

    var response = await client.GetAsync("latest");   ─┐
                                                        │  Uses the HttpClient in
    response.EnsureSuccessStatusCode();                 │  exactly the same way
    return await response.Content.ReadAsStringAsync();  │  you would otherwise
});
app.Run();
```
Configures the HttpClient for calling the API as before

The immediate benefit of using `IHttpClientFactory` in this way is efficient socket and DNS handling. When you create an `HttpClient` using `CreateClient()`, `IHttpClient-Factory` uses a pooled `HttpClientHandler` to create a new instance of an `HttpClient`, pooling and disposing the handlers as necessary to find a balance between the tradeoffs described in section 33.1.

Minimal changes should be required to take advantage of this pattern, as the bulk of your code stays the same. Only the code where you're creating an `HttpClient` instance changes. This makes it a good option if you're refactoring an existing app.

`SocketsHttpHandler` VS. `IHttpClientFactory`

The limitations of `HttpClient` described in section 33.1 apply specifically to the `Http-ClientHandler` at the end of the `HttpClient` handler pipeline in older versions of .NET Core. `IHttpClientFactory` provides a mechanism for managing the lifetime and reuse of `HttpClientHandler` instances.

From .NET 5 onward, the legacy `HttpClientHandler` has been replaced by `Sockets-HttpHandler`. This handler has several advantages, most notably performance benefits and consistency across platforms. The `SocketsHttpHandler` can also be configured to use connection pooling and recycling, like `IHttpClientFactory`.

> So if `HttpClient` can already use connection pooling, is it worth using `IHttpClient-Factory`? In most cases, I would say yes. You must manually configure connection pooling with `SocketsHttpHandler`, and `IHttpClientFactory` has additional features such as named clients and typed clients. In any situations where you're using dependency injection (DI), which is every ASP.NET Core app and most .NET 7 apps, I recommend using `IHttpClientFactory` to take advantage of these benefits.
>
> Nevertheless, if you're working in a non-DI scenario and can't use `IHttpClient-Factory`, be sure to enable the `SocketsHttpHandler` connection pooling as described in this post by Steve Gordon, titled "HttpClient connection pooling in .NET Core": http://mng.bz/E27q.

Managing the socket problem is one big advantage of using `IHttpClientFactory` over `HttpClient`, but it's not the only benefit. You can also use `IHttpClientFactory` to clean up the client configuration, as you'll see in the next section.

33.2.2 *Configuring named clients at registration time*

In this section you'll learn how to use the Named Client pattern with `IHttpClientFactory`. This pattern encapsulates the logic for calling a third-party API in a single location, making it easier to use the `HttpClient` in your consuming code.

> **NOTE** `IHttpClientFactory` uses the same `HttpClient` type you're familiar with if you're coming from .NET Framework. The big difference is that `IHttpClientFactory` solves the DNS and socket exhaustion problem by managing the underlying message handlers.

Using `IHttpClientFactory` solves the technical problems I described in section 33.1, but the code in listing 33.3 is still pretty messy in my eyes, primarily because you must configure the `HttpClient` to point to your service before you use it. If you need to create an `HttpClient` to call the API in more than one place in your application, you must configure it in more than one place too.

`IHttpClientFactory` provides a convenient solution to this problem by allowing you to centrally configure *named clients*, which have a `string` name and a configuration function that runs whenever an instance of the named client is requested. You can define multiple configuration functions that run in sequence to configure your new `HttpClient`.

The following listing shows how to register a named client called `"rates"`. This client is configured with the correct `BaseAddress` and sets default headers that are to be sent with each outbound request. Once you have configured this named client, you can create it from an `IHttpClientFactory` instance using the name of the client, `"rates"`.

Listing 33.4 Using `IHttpClientFactory` to create a named `HttpClient`

```
WebApplicationBuilder builder = WebApplication.CreateBuilder(args);
builder.Services.AddHttpClient("rates", (HttpClient client) =>    ◄──────┐
{
                            Provides a name for the client and a configuration function
```

```
    client.BaseAddress =
        new Uri("https://example.com/rates/");
    client.DefaultRequestHeaders.Add(
        HeaderNames.UserAgent, "ExchangeRateViewer");
})
.ConfigureHttpClient((HttpClient client) => {})
.ConfigureHttpClient(
    (IServiceProvider provider, HttpClient client) => {});

WebApplication app = builder.Build();

app.MapGet("/", async (IHttpClientFactory factory) =>
{
    HttpClient client = factory.CreateClient("rates");

    var response = await client.GetAsync("latest");

    response.EnsureSuccessStatusCode();
    return await response.Content.ReadAsStringAsync();
});
app.Run();
```

The configuration function runs every time the named HttpClient is requested.

You can add more configuration functions for the named client, which run in sequence.

Injects the IHttpClientFactory using DI

Requests the configured named client called "rates"

Uses the HttpClient the same way as before

Additional overloads exist that allow access to the DI container when creating a named client.

> **NOTE**   You can still create unconfigured clients using CreateClient() without a name. Be aware that if you pass an unconfigured name, such as CreateClient ("MyRates"), the client returned will be unconfigured. Take care—client names are case-sensitive, so "rates" is a different client from "Rates".

Named clients help centralize your HttpClient configuration in one place, removing the responsibility for configuring the client from your consuming code. But you're still working with raw HTTP calls at this point, such as providing the relative URL to call ("/latest") and parsing the response. IHttpClientFactory includes a feature that makes it easier to clean up this code.

33.2.3 *Using typed clients to encapsulate HTTP calls*

A common pattern when you need to interact with an API is to encapsulate the mechanics of that interaction in a separate service. You could easily do this with the IHttpClientFactory features you've already seen by extracting the body of the GetRates() function from listing 33.4 into a separate service. But IHttpClientFactory has deeper support for this pattern.

   IHttpClientFactory supports typed clients. A *typed client* is a class that accepts a configured HttpClient in its constructor. It uses the HttpClient to interact with the remote API and exposes a clean interface for consumers to call. All the logic for interacting with the remote API is encapsulated in the typed client, such as which URL paths to call, which HTTP verbs to use, and the types of responses the API returns. This encapsulation makes it easier to call the third-party API from multiple places in your app by using the typed client.

The following listing shows an example typed client for the exchange rates API shown in previous listings. It accepts an `HttpClient` in its constructor and exposes a `GetLatestRates()` method that encapsulates the logic for interacting with the third-party API.

Listing 33.5 Creating a typed client for the exchange rates API

```
public class ExchangeRatesClient                          Injects an HttpClient
{                                                         using DI instead of an
    private readonly HttpClient _client;                 IHttpClientFactory
    public ExchangeRatesClient(HttpClient client)
    {
        _client = client;
    }                                                     The GetLatestRates() logic
                                                          encapsulates the logic for
    public async Task<string> GetLatestRates()    ◁────── interacting with the API.
    {
        var response = await _client.GetAsync("latest");
        response.EnsureSuccessStatusCode();               Uses the HttpClient the
                                                          same way as before
        return await response.Content.ReadAsStringAsync();
    }
}
```

We can then inject this `ExchangeRatesClient` into consuming services, and they don't need to know anything about how to make HTTP requests to the remote service; they need only to interact with the typed client. We can update listing 33.3 to use the typed client as shown in the following listing, at which point the API endpoint method becomes trivial.

Listing 33.6 Consuming a typed client to encapsulate calls to a remote HTTP server

```
app.MapGet("/", async (ExchangeRatesClient ratesClient) =>    ◁─┐
 ┌─▷    await ratesClient.GetLatestRates());                     │  Injects the typed
 │                                                               │  client using DI
Calls the typed client's API. The typed client
handles making the correct HTTP requests.
```

You may be a little confused at this point. I haven't mentioned how `IHttpClientFactory` is involved yet!

The `ExchangeRatesClient` takes an `HttpClient` in its constructor. `IHttpClientFactory` is responsible for creating the `HttpClient`, configuring it to call the remote service and injecting it into a new instance of the typed client.

You can register the `ExchangeRatesClient` as a typed client and configure the `Http-Client` that is injected in `ConfigureServices`, as shown in the following listing. This is similar to configuring a named client, so you can register additional configuration for the `HttpClient` that will be injected into the typed client.

Listing 33.7   Registering a typed client with `HttpClientFactory` in Startup.cs

```
WebApplicationBuilder builder = WebApplication.CreateBuilder(args);
builder.Services.AddHttpClient<ExchangeRatesClient>
        (HttpClient client) =>
    {
        client.BaseAddress =
            new Uri("https://example.com/rates/");
        client.DefaultRequestHeaders.Add(
            HeaderNames.UserAgent, "ExchangeRateViewer");
    })
    .ConfigureHttpClient((HttpClient client) => {});
}
WebApplication app = builder.Build();
app.MapGet("/", async (ExchangeRatesClient ratesClient) =>
    await ratesClient.GetLatestRates());
app.Run();
```

Registers a typed client using the generic AddHttpClient method

You can provide an additional configuration function for the HttpClient that will be injected.

As for named clients, you can provide multiple configuration methods.

Behind the scenes, the call to `AddHttpClient<ExchangeRatesClient>` does several things:

- Registers `HttpClient` as a transient service in DI. That means you can accept an `HttpClient` in the constructor of any service in your app and `IHttpClientFactory` will inject a default pooled instance, which has no additional configuration.
- Registers `ExchangeRatesClient` as a transient service in DI.
- Controls the creation of `ExchangeRatesClient` so that whenever a new instance is required, a pooled `HttpClient` is configured as defined in the `AddHttpClient<T>` lambda method.

TIP   You can think of a typed client as a wrapper around a named client. I'm a big fan of this approach, as it encapsulates all the logic for interacting with a remote service in one place. It also avoids the magic strings that you use with named clients, removing the possibility of typos.

Another option when registering typed clients is to register an interface in addition to the implementation. This is often good practice, as it makes it much easier to test consuming code. If the typed client in listing 33.5 implemented the interface `IExchangeRatesClient`, you could register the interface and typed client implementation using

```
builder.Services.AddHttpClient<IExchangeRatesClient, ExchangeRatesClient>()
```

You could then inject this into consuming code using the interface type

```
app.MapGet("/", async (IExchangeRatesClient ratesClient) =>
    await ratesClient.GetLatestRates());
```

Another common pattern is to not provide any configuration for the typed client in the `AddHttpClient()` call. Instead, you could place that logic in the constructor of your `ExchangeRatesClient` using the injected `HttpClient`:

```
public class ExchangeRatesClient
{
    private readonly HttpClient _client;
    public ExchangeRatesClient(HttpClient client)
    {
        _client = client;
        _client.BaseAddress = new Uri("https://example.com/rates/");
    }
}
```

This is functionally equivalent to the approach shown in listing 33.7. It's a matter of taste where you'd rather put the configuration for your `HttpClient`. If you take this approach, you don't need to provide a configuration lambda in `AddHttpClient()`:

```
builder.Services.AddHttpClient<ExchangeRatesClient>();
```

Named clients and typed clients are convenient for managing and encapsulating `HttpClient` configuration, but `IHttpClientFactory` has another advantage we haven't looked at yet: it's easier to extend the `HttpClient` handler pipeline.

33.3 Handling transient HTTP errors with Polly

In this section you'll learn how to handle a common scenario: transient errors when you make calls to a remote service, caused by an error in the remote server or temporary network problems. You'll see how to use `IHttpClientFactory` to handle cross-cutting concerns like this by adding handlers to the `HttpClient` handler pipeline.

In section 33.2.1 I described `HttpClient` as consisting of a pipeline of handlers. The big advantage of this pipeline, much like the middleware pipeline of your application, is that it allows you to add cross-cutting concerns to all requests. For example, `IHttpClientFactory` automatically adds a handler to each `HttpClient` that logs the status code and duration of each outgoing request.

In addition to logging, another common requirement is to handle transient errors when calling an external API. Transient errors can happen when the network drops out, or if a remote API goes offline temporarily. For transient errors, simply trying the request again can often succeed, but having to write the code to do so manually is cumbersome.

ASP.NET Core includes a library called Microsoft.Extensions.Http.Polly that makes handling transient errors easier. It uses the popular open-source library Polly (https://github.com/App-vNext/Polly) to automatically retry requests that fail due to transient network errors.

Polly is a mature library for handling transient errors that includes a variety of error-handling strategies, such as simple retries, exponential backoff, circuit breaking, and bulkhead isolation. Each strategy is explained in detail at https://github .com/App-vNext/Polly, so be sure to read about the benefits and trade-offs when selecting a strategy.

To provide a taste of what's available, we'll add a simple retry policy to the Exchange-RatesClient shown in section 33.2. If a request fails due to a network problem, such as a timeout or a server error, we'll configure Polly to automatically retry the request as part of the handler pipeline, as shown in figure 33.5.

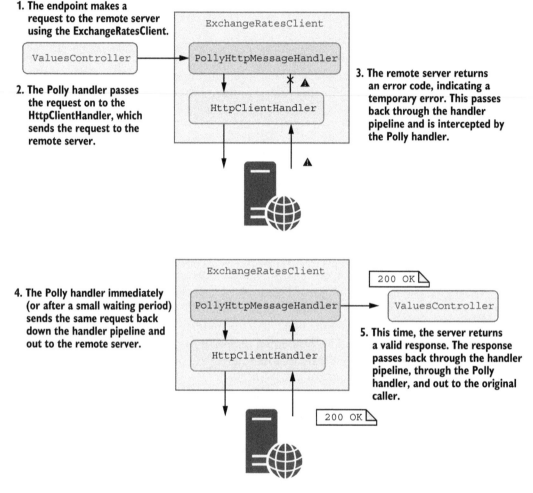

1. **The endpoint makes a request to the remote server using the ExchangeRatesClient.**

2. **The Polly handler passes the request on to the HttpClientHandler, which sends the request to the remote server.**

3. **The remote server returns an error code, indicating a temporary error. This passes back through the handler pipeline and is intercepted by the Polly handler.**

4. **The Polly handler immediately (or after a small waiting period) sends the same request back down the handler pipeline and out to the remote server.**

5. **This time, the server returns a valid response. The response passes back through the handler pipeline, through the Polly handler, and out to the original caller.**

Figure 33.5 Using the `PolicyHttpMessageHandler` to handle transient errors. If an error occurs when calling the remote API, the Polly handler will automatically retry the request. If the request then succeeds, the result is passed back to the caller. The caller didn't have to handle the error, making it simpler to use the `HttpClient` while remaining resilient to transient errors.

To add transient error handling to a named client or HttpClient, follow these steps:

1 Install the Microsoft.Extensions.Http.Polly NuGet package in your project by running `dotnet add package Microsoft.Extensions.Http.Polly`, by using the NuGet explorer in Visual Studio, or by adding a `<PackageReference>` element to your project file as follows:

```
<PackageReference Include="Microsoft.Extensions.Http.Polly"
    Version="7.0.0" />
```

2 Configure a named or typed client as shown in listings 33.4 and 33.7.

3 Configure a transient error-handling policy for your client as shown in listing 33.8.

Listing 33.8   Configuring a transient error-handling policy for a typed client

```
WebApplicationBuilder builder = WebApplication.CreateBuilder(args);
builder.services.AddHttpClient<ExchangeRatesClient>()
    .AddTransientHttpErrorPolicy(policy =>
        policy.WaitAndRetryAsync(new[] {
            TimeSpan.FromMilliseconds(200),
            TimeSpan.FromMilliseconds(500),
            TimeSpan.FromSeconds(1)
        })
    );
```

You can add transient error handlers to named or typed clients.

Uses the extension methods provided by the NuGet package to add transient error handlers

Configures the retry policy used by the handler. There are many types of policies to choose among.

Configures a policy that waits and retries three times if an error occurs

---

In the preceding listing we configure the error handler to catch transient errors and retry three times, waiting an increasing amount of time between requests. If the request fails on the third try, the handler ignores the error and pass it back to the client, as though there was no error handler at all. By default, the handler retries any request that

- Throws an `HttpRequestException`, indicating an error at the protocol level, such as a closed connection
- Returns an HTTP 5xx status code, indicating a server error at the API
- Returns an HTTP 408 status code, indicating a timeout

TIP If you want to handle more cases automatically or to restrict the responses that will be automatically retried, you can customize the selection logic as described in the "Polly and HttpClientFactory" documentation on GitHub: http://mng.bz/NY7E.

Using standard handlers like the transient error handler allows you to apply the same logic across all requests made by a given `HttpClient`. The exact strategy you choose will depend on the characteristics of both the service and the request, but a good retry strategy is a must whenever you interact with potentially unreliable HTTP APIs.

WARNING When designing a policy, be sure to consider the effect of your policy. In some circumstances it may be better to fail quickly instead of retrying a request that is never going to succeed. Polly includes additional policies such as circuit-breakers to create more advanced approaches.

The Polly error handler is an example of an optional `HttpMessageHandler` that you can plug in to your `HttpClient`, but you can also create your own custom handler. In the next section you'll see how to create a handler that adds a header to all outgoing requests.

33.4   *Creating a custom HttpMessageHandler*

Most third-party APIs require some form of authentication when you're calling them. For example, many services require you to attach an API key to an outgoing request, so that the request can be tied to your account. Instead of having to remember to add this header manually for every request to the API, you could configure a custom `Http-MessageHandler` to attach the header automatically for you.

> **NOTE**   More complex APIs may use JSON Web Tokens (JWT) obtained from an identity provider. If that's the case, consider using the open source IdentityModel library (https://identitymodel.readthedocs.io), which provides integration points for ASP.NET Core Identity and `HttpClientFactory`.

You can configure a named or typed client using `IHttpClientFactory` to use your API-key handler as part of the `HttpClient`'s handler pipeline, as shown in figure 33.6. When you use the `HttpClient` to send a message, the `HttpRequestMesssage` is passed through each handler in turn. The API-key handler adds the extra header and passes the request to the next handler in the pipeline. Eventually, the `HttpClientHandler` makes the network request to send the HTTP request. After the response is received, each handler gets a chance to inspect (and potentially modify) the response.

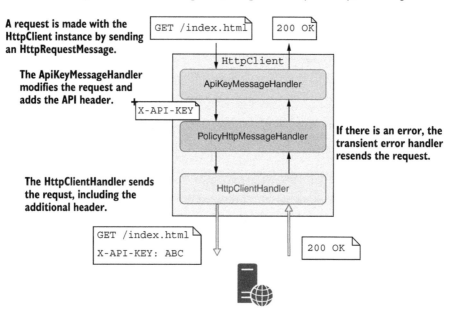

Figure 33.6   You can use a custom `HttpMessageHandler` to modify requests before they're sent to third-party APIs. Every request passes through the custom handler before the final handler (the `HttpClientHandler`) sends the request to the HTTP API. After the response is received, each handler gets a chance to inspect and modify the response.

To create a custom `HttpMessageHandler` and add it to a typed or named client's pipeline, follow these steps:

1 Create a custom handler by deriving from the `DelegatingHandler` base class.
2 Override the `SendAsync()` method to provide your custom behavior. Call `base.SendAsync()` to execute the remainder of the handler pipeline.
3 Register your handler with the DI container. If your handler does not require state, you can register it as a singleton service; otherwise, you should register it as a transient service.
4 Add the handler to one or more of your named or typed clients by calling `AddHttpMessageHandler<T>()` on an `IHttpClientBuilder`, where `T` is your handler type. The order in which you register handlers dictates the order in which they are added to the `HttpClient` handler pipeline. You can add the same handler type more than once in a pipeline if you wish and to multiple typed or named clients.

The following listing shows an example of a custom `HttpMessageHandler` that adds a header to every outgoing request. We use the custom `"API-KEY"` header in this example, but the header you need will vary depending on the third-party API you're calling. This example uses strongly typed configuration to inject the secret API key, as you saw in chapter 10.

Listing 33.9 Creating a custom `HttpMessageHandler`

```
public class ApiKeyMessageHandler : DelegatingHandler    ◁── Custom HttpMessageHandlers should derive from DelegatingHandler.
{
    private readonly ExchangeRateApiSettings _settings;    ◁── Injects the strongly typed configuration values using DI
    public ApiKeyMessageHandler(
        IOptions<ExchangeRateApiSettings> settings)
    {
        _settings = settings.Value;
    }

                                                           Overrides the SendAsync method to implement the custom behavior

    protected override async Task<HttpResponseMessage> SendAsync(
        HttpRequestMessage request,
        CancellationToken cancellationToken)
    {
        request.Headers.Add("API-KEY", _settings.ApiKey);    ◁── Adds the extra header to all outgoing requests

        HttpResponseMessage response =
            await base.SendAsync(request, cancellationToken);    Calls the remainder of the pipeline and receives the response

        return response;    ◁── You could inspect or modify the response before returning it.
    }
}
```

To use the handler, you must register it with the DI container and add it to a named or typed client. In the following listing, we add it to the `ExchangeRatesClient`, along with the transient error handler we registered in listing 33.7. This creates a pipeline similar to that shown in figure 33.6.

> **Listing 33.10   Registering a custom handler in `Startup.ConfigureServices`**

```
WebApplicationBuilder builder = WebApplication.CreateBuilder(args);
builder.Services.AddTransient<ApiKeyMessageHandler>();  ◁─┐
                                                          │ Registers the custom
                                                          │ handler with the DI
builder.Services.AddHttpClient<ExchangeRatesClient>()     │ container
    .AddHttpMessageHandler<ApiKeyMessageHandler>()
    .AddTransientHttpErrorPolicy(policy =>    ◁─┐
        policy.WaitAndRetryAsync(new[] {       │ Adds the transient error
            TimeSpan.FromMilliseconds(200),    │ handler. The order in which the
            TimeSpan.FromMilliseconds(500),    │ handlers are registered dictates
            TimeSpan.FromSeconds(1)            │ their order in the pipeline.
        })
    );
```

Configures the typed client to use the custom handler (annotation pointing to `.AddHttpMessageHandler<ApiKeyMessageHandler>()`)

Whenever you make a request using the typed client `ExchangeRatesClient`, you can be sure that the API key will be added and that transient errors will be handled automatically for you.

That brings us to the end of this chapter on `IHttpClientFactory`. Given the difficulties in using `HttpClient` correctly that I showed in section 33.1, you should always favor `IHttpClientFactory` where possible. As a bonus, `IHttpClientFactory` allows you to easily centralize your API configuration using named clients and to encapsulate your API interactions using typed clients.

Summary

- Use the `HttpClient` class for calling HTTP APIs. You can use it to make HTTP calls to APIs, providing all the headers and body to send in a request, and reading the response headers and data you get back.

- `HttpClient` uses a pipeline of handlers, consisting of multiple `HttpMessageHandlers` connected in a similar way to the middleware pipeline used in ASP.NET Core. The final handler is the `HttpClientHandler`, which is responsible for making the network connection and sending the request.

- `HttpClient` implements `IDisposable`, but typically you shouldn't dispose of it. When the `HttpClientHandler` that makes the TCP/IP connection is disposed of, it keeps a connection open for the `TIME_WAIT` period. Disposing of many `HttpClients` in a short period of time can lead to socket exhaustion, preventing a machine from handling any more requests.

- Before .NET Core 2.1, the advice was to use a single `HttpClient` for the lifetime of your application. Unfortunately, a singleton `HttpClient` will not respect DNS changes, which are commonly used for traffic management in cloud environments.

- `IHttpClientFactory` solves both these problems by managing the lifetime of the `HttpMessageHandler` pipeline. You can create a new `HttpClient` by calling `CreateClient()`, and `IHttpClientFactory` takes care of disposing of the handler pipeline when it is no longer in use.

- You can centralize the configuration of an `HttpClient` in `ConfigureServices()` using named clients by calling `AddHttpClient("test", c => {})`. You can then retrieve a configured instance of the client in your services by calling `IHttpClientFactory.CreateClient("test")`.

- You can create a typed client by injecting an `HttpClient` into a service, `T`, and configuring the client using `AddHttpClient<T>(c => {})`. Typed clients are great for abstracting the HTTP mechanics away from consumers of your client.

- You can use the Microsoft.Extensions.Http.Polly library to add transient HTTP error handling to your `HttpClients`. Call `AddTransientHttpErrorPolicy()` when configuring your `IHttpClientFactory`, and provide a Polly policy to control when errors should be automatically handled and retried.

- It's common to use a simple retry policy to try making a request multiple times before giving up and returning an error. When designing a policy, be sure to consider the effect of your policy; in some circumstances it may be better to fail quickly instead of retrying a request that is never going to succeed. Polly includes additional policies such as circuit-breakers to create more advanced approaches.

- By default, the transient error-handling middleware will handle connection errors, server errors that return a `5xx` error code, and `408` (timeout) errors. You can customize this if you want to handle additional error types but ensure that you retry only requests that are safe to do so.

- You can create a custom `HttpMessageHandler` to modify each request made through a named or typed client. Custom handlers are good for implementing cross-cutting concerns such as logging, metrics, and authentication.

- To create a custom `HttpMessageHandler`, derive from `DelegatingHandler` and override the `SendAsync()` method. Call `base.SendAsync()` to send the request to the next handler in the pipeline and finally to the `HttpClientHandler`, which makes the HTTP request.

- Register your custom handler in the DI container as either a transient or a singleton. Add it to a named or typed client using `AddHttpMessageHandler<T>()`. The order in which you register the handler in the `IHttpClientBuilder` is the order in which the handler will appear in the `HttpClient` handler pipeline.

Building background
tasks and services

This chapter covers

- Creating tasks that run in the background for your application
- Using the generic IHost to create Windows Services and Linux daemons
- Using Quartz.NET to run tasks on a schedule in a clustered environment

We've covered a lot of ground in the book so far. You've learned how to create page-based applications using Razor Pages and how to create APIs for mobile clients and services. You've seen how to add authentication and authorization to your application, use Entity Framework Core (EF Core) for storing state in the database, and create custom components to meet your requirements.

As well as using these UI-focused apps, you may find you need to build background or batch-task services. These services aren't meant to interact with users directly. Rather, they stay running in the background, processing items from a queue or periodically executing a long-running process.

For example, you might want to have a background service that sends email confirmations for e-commerce orders or a batch job that calculates sales and losses for retail stores after the shops close. ASP.NET Core includes support for these background tasks by providing abstractions for running a task in the background when your application starts.

In section 34.1 you'll learn about the background task support provided in ASP.NET Core by the `IHostedService` interface. You'll learn how to use the `Background-Service` helper class to create tasks that run on a timer and how to manage your DI lifetimes correctly in a long-running task.

In section 34.2 we'll take the background service concept one step further to create headless worker services using the generic `IHost`. Worker services don't use Razor Pages, API controllers, or minimal API endpoints; instead, they consist only of `IHostedService` services running tasks in the background. You'll also see how to configure and install a worker service app as a Windows Service or as a Linux daemon.

In section 34.3 I introduce the open-source library Quartz.NET, which provides extensive scheduling capabilities for creating background services. You'll learn how to install Quartz.NET in your applications, create complex schedules for your tasks, and add redundancy to your worker services using clustering.

Before we get to more complex scenarios, we'll start by looking at the built-in support for running background tasks in your apps.

34.1 Running background tasks with IHostedService

In most applications, it's common to create tasks that happen in the background rather than in response to a request. This could be a task to process a queue of emails, handling events published to some sort of a message bus or running a batch process to calculate daily profits. By moving this work to a background task, your user interface can stay responsive. Instead of trying to send an email immediately, for example, you could add the request to a queue and return a response to the user immediately. The background task can consume that queue in the background at its leisure.

In ASP.NET Core, you can use the `IHostedService` interface to run tasks in the background. Classes that implement this interface are started when your application starts, shortly after your application starts handling requests, and they are stopped shortly before your application is stopped. This provides the hooks you need to perform most tasks.

> **NOTE** Even the default ASP.NET Core server, Kestrel, runs as an `IHosted-Service`. In one sense, almost everything in an ASP.NET Core app is a background task.

In this section you'll see how to use the `IHostedService` to create a background task that runs continuously throughout the lifetime of your app. This could be used for many things, but in the next section you'll see how to use it to populate a simple cache. You'll also learn how to use services with a scoped lifetime in your singleton background tasks by managing container scopes yourself.

34.1.1 *Running background tasks on a timer*

In this section you'll learn how to create a background task that runs periodically on a timer throughout the lifetime of your app. Running background tasks can be useful for many reasons, such as scheduling work to be performed later or performing work in advance.

In chapter 33 we used `IHttpClientFactory` and a typed client to call a third-party service to retrieve the current exchange rate between various currencies and returned them in an API endpoint, as shown in the following listing.

Listing 34.1   Using a typed client to return exchange rates from a third-party service

```
app.MapGet("/", async (ExchangeRatesClient ratesClient) =>
    await ratesClient.GetLatestRatesAsync());
```

The typed client is used to retrieve exchange rates from the remote API and returns them.

A typed client created using IHttpClientFactory is injected using dependency injection (DI).

A simple optimization for this code might be to cache the exchange rate values for a period. There are multiple ways you could implement that, but in this section we'll use a simple cache that preemptively fetches the exchange rates in the background, as shown in figure 34.1. The API endpoint simply reads from the cache; it never has to make HTTP calls itself, so it remains fast.

> **NOTE** An alternative approach might add caching to your strongly typed client, `ExchangeRatesClient`. The downside is that when you need to update the rates, you will have to perform the request immediately, making the overall response slower. Using a background service keeps your API endpoint consistently fast.

You can implement a background task using the `IHostedService` interface. This consists of two methods:

```
public interface IHostedService
{
    Task StartAsync(CancellationToken cancellationToken);
    Task StopAsync(CancellationToken cancellationToken);
}
```

There are subtleties to implementing the interface correctly. In particular, the `StartAsync()` method, although asynchronous, runs inline as part of your application startup. Background tasks that are expected to run for the lifetime of your application must return a `Task` immediately and schedule background work on a different thread.

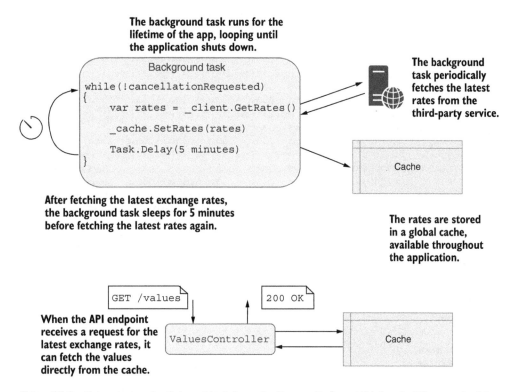

Figure 34.1 You can use a background task to cache the results from a third-party API on a schedule. The API controller can then read directly from the cache instead of calling the third-party API itself. This reduces the latency of requests to your API controller while ensuring that the data remains fresh.

> **WARNING** Calling `await` in the `IHostedService.StartAsync()` method blocks your application from starting until the method completes. This can be useful in some cases, when you don't want the application to start handling requests until the `IHostedService` task has completed, but that's often not the desired behavior for background tasks.

To make it easier to create background services using best-practice patterns, ASP.NET Core provides the abstract base class `BackgroundService`, which implements `IHostedService` and is designed to be used for long-running tasks. To create a background task, you must override a single method of this class, `ExecuteAsync()`. You're free to use `async-await` inside this method, and you can keep running the method for the lifetime of your app.

The following listing shows a background service that fetches the latest interest rates using a typed client and saves them in a cache, as you saw in figure 34.1. The `ExecuteAsync()` method keeps looping and updating the cache until the `Cancellation-Token` passed as an argument indicates that the application is shutting down.

Listing 34.2   Implementing a `BackgroundService` that calls a remote HTTP API

Derives from BackgroundService to create a task that runs for the lifetime of your app

```
public class ExchangeRatesHostedService : BackgroundService
{
    private readonly IServiceProvider _provider;
    private readonly ExchangeRatesCache _cache;
    public ExchangeRatesHostedService(
        IServiceProvider provider, ExchangeRatesCache cache)
    {
        _provider = provider;
        _cache = cache;
    }

    protected override async Task ExecuteAsync(
        CancellationToken stoppingToken)
    {
        while (!stoppingToken.IsCancellationRequested)
        {
            var client = _provider
                .GetRequiredService<ExchangeRatesClient>();

            string rates = await client.GetLatestRatesAsync();
            _cache.SetRates(rates);

            await Task.Delay(TimeSpan.FromMinutes(5), stoppingToken);
        }
    }
}
```

A simple cache for exchange rates

Injects an IServiceProvider so you can create instances of the typed client

You must override ExecuteAsync to set the service's behavior.

The CancellationToken passed as an argument is triggered when the application shuts down.

Keeps looping until the application shuts down

Creates a new instance of the typed client so that the HttpClient is short-lived

Fetches the latest rates from the remote API

Stores the rates in the cache

Waits for 5 minutes (or for the application to shut down) before updating the cache

The `ExchangeRateCache` in listing 34.2 is a simple singleton that stores the latest rates. It must be thread-safe, as it is accessed concurrently by your API endpoint. You can see a simple implementation in the source code for this chapter.

To register your background service with the dependency injection (DI) container, use the `AddHostedService()` extension method in Program.cs, which registers the service using a singleton lifetime, as shown in the following listing.

Listing 34.3   Registering an `IHostedService` with the DI container

```
WebApplicationBuilder builder = WebApplication.CreateBuilder(args);
builder.Services.AddHttpClient<ExchangeRatesClient>();
builder.Services.AddSingleton<ExchangeRatesCache>();
builder.Services.AddHostedService<ExchangeRatesHostedService>();
```

Registers the typed client as before

Registers ExchangeRatesHostedService as an IHostedService

Adds the cache object as a singleton so it is shared throughout your app

By using a background service to fetch the exchange rates, your API endpoint becomes even simpler. Instead of fetching the latest rates itself, it returns the value from the cache, which is kept up to date by the background service:

```
app.MapGet("/", (ExchangeRatesCache cache) =>
    cache.GetLatestRatesAsync());
```

This approach to caching works to simplify the API, but you may have noticed a potential risk: if the API receives a request before the background service has successfully updated the rates, the API will fail to return any rates.

This may be OK, but you could take another approach. As well as updating the rates periodically, you could use the StartAsync method to block app startup until the rates have successfully updated. That way, you guarantee that the rates are available before the app starts handling requests, so the API will always return successfully. Listing 34.4 shows how you could update listing 34.2 to block startup until the rates have been updated while still updating periodically in the background.

Listing 34.4 Implementing `StartAsync` to block startup in an `IHostedService`

```
public class ExchangeRatesHostedService : BackgroundService
{
    private readonly IServiceProvider _provider;
    private readonly ExchangeRatesCache _cache;
    public ExchangeRatesHostedService(
        IServiceProvider provider, ExchangeRatesCache cache)
    {
        _provider = provider;
        _cache = cache;
    }

    public override async Task StartAsync(          ⟵  The StartAsync method runs
        CancellationToken cancellationToken)            on start, before the app starts
    {                                                   handling requests.
        var success = false;
        while(!success && !cancellationToken.IsCancellationRequested)
        {
            success = await TryUpdateRatesAsync();   ⟵  Once the update
        }                                               succeeds, starts
                                                        the background
        await base.StartAsync(cancellationToken);  ⟵┘   process
    }

    protected override async Task ExecuteAsync(
        CancellationToken stoppingToken)
    {
        while (!stoppingToken.IsCancellationRequested)
        {
            await Task.Delay(TimeSpan.FromMinutes(5), stoppingToken);
            await TryUpdateRatesAsync();
        }
    }

    private async Task<bool> TryUpdateRatesAsync()
    {
        try
```

Keeps trying to update the rates until it succeeds

```
    {
        var client = _provider
            .GetRequiredService<ExchangeRatesClient>();
        string rates = await client.GetLatestRatesAsync();
        _cache.SetRates(rates);
        return true;
    }
    catch(Exception ex)
    {
        return false;
    }
}
}
}
```

> **WARNING**   The downside to listing 34.4 is that if there's a problem retrieving the rates, the app won't ever start up and start listening for requests. Whether you consider that a bug or a feature will depend on your deployment process! Many orchestrators, for example, will use rolling updates, which ensure that a new deployment is listening for requests before shutting down the old deployment instances.

One slightly messy aspect of both listings 34.2 and 34.4 is that I used the Service Locator pattern to retrieve the typed client. This isn't ideal, but you shouldn't inject typed clients into background services directly. Typed clients are designed to be short-lived to ensure that you take advantage of the HttpClient handler rotation, as described in chapter 21. By contrast, background services are singletons that live for the lifetime of your application.

> **TIP**   If you wish, you can avoid the Service Locator pattern in listing 34.2 by using the factory pattern described in Steve Gordon's post titled "IHttpClient-Factory Patterns: Using Typed Clients from Singleton Services": http://mng .bz/opDZ.

The need for short-lived services leads to another common question: how can you use scoped services in a background service?

34.1.2   *Using scoped services in background tasks*

Background services that implement IHostedService are created once when your application starts. That means they are by necessity singletons, as there will be only a single instance of the class.

That leads to a problem if you need to use services registered with a scoped lifetime. Any services you inject into the constructor of your singleton IHostedService must themselves be registered as singletons. Does that mean there's no way to use scoped dependencies in a background service?

> **NOTE**   As I discussed in chapter 9, the dependencies of a service must always have a lifetime that's the same as or longer than that of the service itself, to avoid captive dependencies.

Imagine a slight variation on the caching example from section 34.1.1. Instead of storing the exchange rates in a singleton cache object, you want to save the exchange rates to a database so you can look up the historic rates.

Most database providers, including EF Core's DbContext, register their services with scoped lifetimes. That means you need to access the scoped DbContext from inside the singleton ExchangeRatesHostedService, which precludes injecting the DbContext with constructor injection. The solution is to create a new container scope every time you update the exchange rates.

In typical ASP.NET Core applications, the framework creates a new container scope every time a new request is received, immediately before the middleware pipeline executes. All the services that are used in that request are fetched from the scoped container. When the request ends, the scoped container is disposed, along with any of the IDisposable scoped and transient services that were obtained from it. In a background service, however, there *are* no requests, so no container scopes are created. The solution is to create your own.

You can create a new container scope anywhere you have access to an IService-Provider by calling IServiceProvider.CreateScope(). This creates a scoped container, which you can use to safely retrieve scoped and transient services.

> **WARNING** Always make sure to dispose of the IServiceScope returned by CreateScope() when you're finished with it, typically with a using statement. This disposes of any IDisposable services that were created by the scoped container and prevents memory leaks.

The following listing shows a version of the ExchangeRatesHostedService that stores the latest exchange rates as an EF Core entity in the database. It creates a new scope for each iteration of the while loop and retrieves the scoped AppDbContext from the scoped container.

Listing 34.5 Consuming scoped services from an IHostedService

```
public class ExchangeRatesHostedService : BackgroundService
{
    private readonly IServiceProvider _provider;
    public ExchangeRatesHostedService(IServiceProvider provider)
    {
        _provider = provider;
    }

    protected override async Task ExecuteAsync(
        CancellationToken stoppingToken)
    {
        while (!stoppingToken.IsCancellationRequested)
        {
            using(IServiceScope scope = _provider.CreateScope())
            {
                var scopedProvider = scope.ServiceProvider;
```

BackgroundService is registered as a singleton.

The injected IServiceProvider can be used to retrieve singleton services or to create scopes.

The scope exposes an IServiceProvider that can be used to retrieve scoped components.

Creates a new scope using the root IServiceProvider

Retrieves the scoped
services from the container

```
var client = scope.ServiceProvider
    .GetRequiredService<ExchangeRatesClient>();

var context = scope.ServiceProvider
    .GetRequiredService<AppDbContext>();

var rates = await client.GetLatestRatesAsync();

context.Add(rates);
await context.SaveChanges(rates);
```

Disposes
of the
scope with
the using
statement

Fetches the
latest rates,
and saves
using EF
Core

```
await Task.Delay(TimeSpan.FromMinutes(5), stoppingToken);
```

Waits for the next iteration. A new
scope is created on the next iteration.

Creating scopes like this is a general solution whenever you need to access scoped services and you're not running in the context of a request. For example, if you need to access scoped or transient services in Program.cs, you can create a new scope by calling `WebApplication.Services.CreateScope()`. You can then retrieve the services you need, do your work, and dispose the scope to clean up the services.

Another prime example is when you're injecting services into an `OptionsBuilder` instance, as you saw in chapter 31. You can take exactly the same approach—create a new scope—as shown in my blog post titled "The dangers and gotchas of using scoped services in `OptionsBuilder`": http://mng.bz/4D6j.

> **TIP** Using service location in this way always feels a bit convoluted. I typically try to extract the body of the task to a separate class and use service location to retrieve that class only. You can see an example of this approach in the "Consuming a scoped service in a background task" section of Microsoft's "Background tasks with hosted services in ASP.NET Core" documentation: http://mng.bz/4ZER.

`IHostedService` is available in ASP.NET Core, so you can run background tasks in your Razor Pages and minimal API applications. However, sometimes all you want is the background task; you don't need any UI. For those cases, you can use the generic `IHost` abstraction without having to bother with HTTP handling at all.

34.2   *Creating headless worker services using IHost*

In this section you'll learn about worker services, which are ASP.NET Core applications that do not handle HTTP traffic. You'll learn how to create a new worker service from a template and compare the generated code with a traditional ASP.NET Core application. You'll also learn how to install the worker service as a Windows Service or as a systemd daemon in Linux.

In section 34.1 we cached exchange rates based on the assumption that they're being consumed directly by the UI part of your application, such as by Razor Pages or minimal API endpoints. However, in the section 34.1.2 example we saved the rates to a database instead of storing them in-process. That raises the possibility that other applications with access to the database will use the rates too. Taking that one step further, could we create an application which is responsible only for caching these rates and has no UI at all?

Since .NET Core 3.0, ASP.NET Core has been built on top of a generic IHost implementation, as you learned in chapter 30. The IHost implementation provides features such as configuration, logging, and DI. ASP.NET Core adds the middleware pipeline for handling HTTP requests, as well as paradigms such as Razor Pages or Model-View-Controller (MVC) controllers on top of that, as shown in figure 34.2.

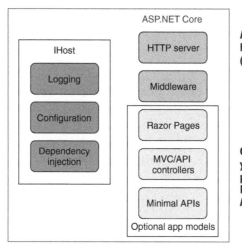

The generic IHost abstraction provides logging, configuration, and dependency injection abstractions.

ASP.NET Core adds HTTP handling using an HTTP server (Kestrel) and middleware.

On top of the middleware basics you can optionally add programming models like Razor Pages, minimal APIs, and API controllers.

Figure 34.2 ASP.NET Core builds on the generic IHost implementation. IHost provides features such as configuration, DI, and configuration. ASP.NET Core adds HTTP handling on top of that by way of the middleware pipeline, Razor Pages, and API controllers. If you don't need HTTP handling, you can use IHost without the additional ASP.NET Core libraries to create a smaller application.

If your application doesn't need to handle HTTP requests, there's no real reason to use ASP.NET Core. You can use the IHost implementation alone to create an application that has a lower memory footprint, faster startup, and less surface area to worry about from a security perspective than a full ASP.NET Core application. .NET applications that use this approach are commonly called *worker services* or *workers*.

> **DEFINITION** A *worker* is a .NET application that uses the generic IHost but doesn't include the ASP.NET Core libraries for handling HTTP requests. They are sometimes called *headless* services, as they don't expose a UI for you to interact with.

Workers are commonly used for running background tasks (IHostedService implementations) that don't require a UI. These tasks could be for running batch jobs, running tasks repeatedly on a schedule, or handling events using some sort of message bus. In the next section we'll create a worker for retrieving the latest exchange rates from a remote API instead of adding the background task to an ASP.NET Core application.

34.2.1 Creating a worker service from a template

In this section you'll see how to create a basic worker service from a template. Visual Studio includes a template for creating worker services: choose **File** > **New** > **Project** > **Worker Service**. You can create a similar template using the .NET command-line interface (CLI) by running `dotnet new worker`. The resulting template consists of two C# files:

- *Worker.cs*—This simple `BackgroundService` implementation writes to the log every second, as shown in listing 34.6. You can replace this class with your own `BackgroundService` implementation, such as the example from listing 34.5.

- *Program.cs*—As in a typical ASP.NET Core application, this contains the entry point for your application, and it's where the `IHost` is built and run. By contrast with a typical .NET 7 ASP.NET Core app, it uses the generic host instead of the minimal hosting `WebApplication` and `WebApplicationBuilder`.

Listing 34.6 Default BackgroundService implementation for worker service template

```
public class Worker : BackgroundService          ⟵  The Worker service derives
{                                                    from BackgroundService.
    private readonly ILogger<Worker> _logger;
    public Worker(ILogger<Worker> logger)
    {
        _logger = logger;
    }
                                                     ExecuteAsync starts the main
                                                     execution loop for the service.
    protected override async Task ExecuteAsync(  ⟵
        CancellationToken stoppingToken)
    {                                                     When the app is
        while (!stoppingToken.IsCancellationRequested)  ⟵ shutting down, the
        {                                                 CancellationToken
            _logger.LogInformation(                       is canceled.
                "Worker running at: {time}", DateTimeOffset.Now);
            await Task.Delay(1000, stoppingToken);  ⟵
        }                                                The service writes a log
    }                                                    message every second
}                                                        until the app shuts down.
```

The most notable difference between the worker service template and an ASP.NET Core template is that Program.cs doesn't use the `WebApplicationBuilder` and `WebApplication` APIs for minimal hosting. Instead, it uses the `Host.CreateDefaultBuilder()` helper method you learned about in chapter 30 to create an `IHostBuilder`.

> **NOTE** .NET 8 will change the worker service template to use a new type, `HostApplicationBuilder`, which is analogous to `WebApplicationBuilder`. `HostApplicationBuilder` brings the familiar script-like setup experience of minimal hosting to worker services, instead of using the callback-based approach of `IHostBuilder`.

You configure your DI services in Program.cs using the `ConfigureServices()` method on `IHostBuilder`, as shown in listing 34.7. This method takes a lambda method, which takes two arguments:

- A `HostBuilderContext` object. This context object exposes the `IConfiguration` for your app as the property `Configuration`, and the `IHostEnvironment` as the property `HostingEnvironment`.
- An `ISeviceCollection` object. You add your services to this collection in the same way you add them to `WebApplicationBuilder.Services` in typical ASP.NET Core apps.

The following listing shows how to configure EF Core, the exchange rates typed client from chapter 33, and the background service that saves exchange rates to the database, as you saw in section 34.1.2. It uses C#'s top-level statements, so no `static void Main` entry point is shown.

Listing 34.7 Program.cs for a worker service that saves exchange rates using EF Core

```
using Microsoft.EntityFrameworkCore;                          Creates an IHostBuilder
                                                              using the default helper
IHost host = Host.CreateDefaultBuilder(args)
    .ConfigureServices((hostContext, services) =>            Configures your DI services
    {
          services.AddHttpClient<ExchangeRatesClient>();          IConfiguration can
Adds      services.AddHostedService<ExchangeRatesHostedService>();  be accessed from the
services to the                                                   HostBuilderContext
IServiceCollection  var connectionString = hostContext.Configuration  parameter.
              .GetConnectionString("SqlLiteConnection"))

          services.AddDbContext<AppDbContext>(options =>          Adds services to the
              options.UseSqlite(connectionString));             IServiceCollection
    })
    .Build();      ◁—— Builds an IHost instance

host.Run();       ◁—— Runs the app and waits for shutdown
```

The changes in Program.cs to use the generic host instead of minimal hosting are the most obvious differences between a worker service and an ASP.NET Core app, but there are some important differences in the .csproj project file too. The following listing shows the project file for a worker service that uses `IHttpClientFactory` and EF Core, and highlights some of the differences with a similar ASP.NET Core application.

Listing 34.8 Project file for a worker service

```
<Project Sdk="Microsoft.NET.Sdk.Worker">          Worker services use a different project
                                                  software development kit (SDK) type
  <PropertyGroup>                                 from ASP.NET Core apps.
    <TargetFramework>net7.0</TargetFramework>
    <Nullable>enable</Nullable>                   The target framework is the
    <ImplicitUsings>enable</ImplicitUsings>       same as for ASP.NET Core apps.
```

If you're using
IHttpClient-
Factory, you'll
need to add
this package
in worker
services.

```
                   <UserSecretsId>5088-4277-B226-DC0A790AB790</UserSecretsId>
                 </PropertyGroup>
                                                        Worker services use configuration so they
                                                        can use User Secrets, like ASP.NET Core apps.
                 <ItemGroup>
                   <PackageReference Include="Microsoft.Extensions.Hosting"
                      Version="7.0.0" />
                   <PackageReference Include="Microsoft.Extensions.Http"
                      Version="7.0.0" />
                   <PackageReference Include="Microsoft.EntityFrameworkCore.Design"
                       Version="7.0.0" PrivateAssets="All" />
                   <PackageReference Include="Microsoft.EntityFrameworkCore.Sqlite"
                       Version="7.0.0" />
                 </ItemGroup>
                 </Project>
```

All worker
services must
explicitly add
this package.
ASP.NET Core
apps add it
implicitly.

**EF Core packages must be explicitly
added, the same as for ASP.NET Core apps.**

Some parts of the project file are the same for both worker services and ASP.NET
Core apps:

- Both types of apps must specify a `<TargetFramework>`, such as `net7.0` for .NET 7.
- Both types of apps use the configuration system, so you can use `<UserSecretsId>`
  to manage secrets in development, as discussed in chapter 10.
- Both types of apps must explicitly add references to the EF Core NuGet packages to use EF Core in the app.

There are also several differences in the project template:

- The `<Project>` element's `Sdk` for a worker service should be `Microsoft.NET`
  `.Sdk.Worker`, whereas for an ASP.NET Core app it is `Microsoft.NET.Sdk.Web`. The
  Web SDK includes implicit references to additional packages that are not generally required in worker services.
- The worker service must include an explicit `PackageReference` for the Microsoft.Extensions.Hosting NuGet package. This package includes the generic
  `IHost` implementation used by worker services.
- You may need to include additional packages to reference the same functionality
  as in an ASP.NET Core app. An example is the Microsoft.Extensions.Http package (which provides `IHttpClientFactory`). This package is referenced implicitly
  in ASP.NET Core apps but must be explicitly referenced in worker services.

Running a worker service is the same as running an ASP.NET Core application: use
`dotnet run` from the command line or press F5 in Visual Studio. A worker service is
essentially a console application (as are ASP.NET Core applications), so they both run
the same way.

You can run worker services in most of the same places you would run an ASP.NET
Core application, though as a worker service doesn't handle HTTP traffic, some
options make more sense than others. In the next section we'll look at two supported
ways of running your application: as a Windows Service or as a Linux systemd daemon.

34.2.2 *Running worker services in production*

In this section you'll learn how to run worker services in production. You'll learn how to install a worker service as a Windows Service so that the operating system monitors and starts your worker service automatically. You'll also see how to prepare your application for installation as a systemd daemon in Linux.

Worker services, like ASP.NET Core applications, are fundamentally .NET console applications. The difference is that they are typically intended to be long-running applications. The common approach for running these types of applications on Windows is to use a Windows Service or to use a systemd daemon in Linux.

> **NOTE** It's also common to run applications in the cloud using Docker containers or dedicated platform services like Azure App Service. The process for deploying a worker service to these managed services is typically identical to deploying an ASP.NET Core application.

Adding support for Windows Services or systemd is easy, thanks to two optional NuGet packages:

- *Microsoft.Extensions.Hosting.Systemd*—Adds support for running the application as a systemd application. To enable systemd integration, call `UseSystemd()` on your `IHostBuilder` in Program.cs.
- *Microsoft.Extensions.Hosting.WindowsServices*—Adds support for running the application as a Windows Service. To enable the integration, call `UseWindows-Service()` on your `IHostBuilder` in Program.cs.

These packages each add a single extension method to `IHostBuilder` that enables the appropriate integration when running as a systemd daemon or as a Windows Service. The following listing shows how to enable Windows Service support.

Listing 34.9 Adding Windows Service support to a worker service

```
IHost host = Host.CreateDefaultBuilder(args)
    .ConfigureServices((hostContext, services) =>        Configures your worker service
    {                                                    as you would normally
        Services.AddHostedService<Worker>();
    })
    .UseWindowsService()    <──┐ Adds support for running
    .Build();                    as a Windows Service.

host.Run();
```

During development, or if you run your application as a console app, `UseWindows-Service()` does nothing; your application runs exactly the same as it would without the method call. However, your application can now be installed as a Windows Service, as your app now has the required integration hooks to work with the Windows Service system. The following basic steps show how to install a worker service app as a Windows Service:

1 Add the Microsoft.Extensions.Hosting.WindowsServices NuGet package to your application using Visual Studio by running `dotnet add package Microsoft .Extensions.Hosting.WindowsServices` in the project folder, or by adding a `<PackageReference>` to your .csproj file:

```
<PackageReference Include="Microsoft.Extensions.Hosting.WindowsServices"
➥ Version="7.0.0" />
```

2 Add a call to `UseWindowsService()` on your `IHostBuilder`, as shown in listing 34.9.

3 Publish your application, as described in chapter 27. From the command line you could run `dotnet publish -c Release` from the project folder.

4 Open a command prompt as Administrator and install the application using the Windows `sc` utility. You need to provide the path to your published project's .exe file and a name to use for the service, such as `My Test Service`:

```
sc create "My Test Service" BinPath="C:\path\to\MyService.exe"
```

5 You can manage the service from the Services control panel in Windows, as shown in figure 34.3. Alternatively, to start the service from the command line run `sc start "My Test Service"`, or to delete the service run `sc delete "My Test Service"`.

After you complete the preceding steps, your worker service will be running as a Windows Service.

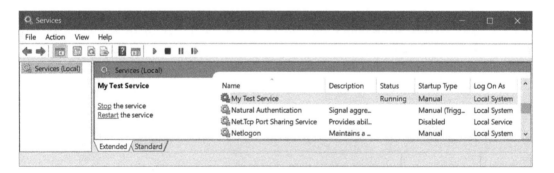

Figure 34.3 The Services control panel in Windows. After installing a worker service as a Windows Service using the `sc` utility, you can manage your worker service from here. This control panel allows you to control when the Windows Service starts and stops, the user account that the application runs under, and how to handle errors.

> **WARNING** These steps are the bare minimum required to install a Windows Service. When running in production, you must consider many security aspects not covered here. For more details, see Microsoft's "Host ASP.NET Core in a Windows Service" documentation: http://mng.bz/Xdy9.

An interesting point of note is that installing as a Windows Service or system daemon isn't limited to worker services; you can install an ASP.NET Core application in the same way. Simply follow the preceding instructions, add the call to `UseWindowsService()`, and install your ASP.NET Core app. You can do this thanks to the fact that the ASP.NET Core functionality is built directly on top of the generic `Host` functionality.

> **NOTE** Hosting an ASP.NET Core app as a Windows Service can be useful if you don't want to (or can't) use Internet Information Services (IIS). Some older versions of IIS don't support gRPC, for example. By hosting as a Windows Service, your application can be restarted automatically if it crashes.

You can follow a similar process to install a worker service as a system daemon by installing the Microsoft.Extensions.Hosting.Systemd package and calling `UseSystemd()` on your `IHostBuilder`. For more details on configuring system, see the "Monitor the app" section of Microsoft's "Host ASP.NET Core on Linux with Nginx" documentation: http://mng.bz/yYDp.

So far in this chapter we've used `IHostedService` and the `BackgroundService` to run tasks that repeat on an interval, and you've seen how to install worker services as long-running applications by installing as a Windows Service.

In the final section of this chapter we'll look at how you can create more advanced schedules for your background tasks, as well as how to add resiliency to your application by running multiple instances of your workers. To achieve that, we'll use a mature third-party library, Quartz.NET.

34.3 *Coordinating background tasks using Quartz.NET*

In this section you'll learn how to use the open-source scheduler library Quartz.NET. You'll learn how to install and configure the library and how to add a background job to run on a schedule. You'll also learn how to enable clustering for your applications so that you can run multiple instances of your worker service and share jobs among them.

All the background tasks you've seen so far in this chapter repeat a task on an interval indefinitely, from the moment the application starts. However, sometimes you want more control of this timing. Maybe you always want to run the application at 15 minutes past each hour. Or maybe you want to run a task only on the second Tuesday of the month at 3 a.m. Additionally, maybe you want to run multiple instances of your application for redundancy but ensure that only one of the services runs a task at any time.

It would certainly be possible to build all this extra functionality into your app yourself, but excellent libraries already provide all this functionality for you. Two of the most well known in the .NET space are Hangfire (https://www.hangfire.io) and Quartz.NET (https://www.quartz-scheduler.net).

Hangfire is an open-source library that also has a Pro subscription option. One of its most popular features is a dashboard UI that shows the state of all your running jobs, each task's history, and any errors that have occurred.

Quartz.NET is completely open-source and essentially offers a beefed-up version of the `BackgroundService` functionality. It has extensive scheduling functionality, as well as support for running in a clustered environment, where multiple instances of your application coordinate to distribute the jobs among themselves.

> **NOTE** Quartz.NET is based on a similar Java library called Quartz Scheduler. When looking for information on Quartz.NET, be sure you're looking at the correct Quartz!

Quartz.NET is based on four main concepts:

- *Jobs*—The background tasks that implement your logic.
- *Triggers*—Control *when* a job runs based on a schedule, such as "every five minutes" or "every second Tuesday." A job can have multiple triggers.
- *Job factory*—Responsible for creating instances of your jobs. Quartz.NET integrates with ASP.NET Core's DI container, so you can use DI in your job classes.
- *Scheduler*—Keeps track of the triggers in your application, creates jobs using the job factory, and runs your jobs. The scheduler typically runs as an `IHostedService` for the lifetime of your app.

Background services vs. cron jobs

It's common to use cron jobs to run tasks on a schedule in Linux, and Windows has similar functionality with Task Scheduler, used to periodically run an application or script file, which is typically a short-lived task.

By contrast, .NET apps using background services are designed to be long-lived, even if they are used only to run tasks on a schedule. This allows your application to do things like adjust its schedule as required or perform optimizations. In addition, being long-lived means your app doesn't only have to run tasks on a schedule. It can respond to ad hoc events, such as events in a message queue.

Of course, if you don't need those capabilities and would rather not have a long-running application, you can use .NET in combination with cron jobs. You could create a simple .NET console app that runs your task and then shuts down, and you could schedule it to execute periodically as a cron job. The choice is yours!

In this section I show you how to install Quartz.NET and configure a background service to run on a schedule. Then I explain how to enable clustering so that you can run multiple instances of your application and distribute the jobs among them.

34.3.1 *Installing Quartz.NET in an ASP.NET Core application*

In this section I show how to install the Quartz.NET scheduler into an ASP.NET Core application. Quartz.NET runs in the background in the same way as the `IHostedService` implementations do. In fact, Quartz.NET uses the `IHostedService` abstractions to schedule and run jobs.

DEFINITION A *job* in Quartz.NET is a task to be executed that implements the IJob interface. It is where you define the logic that your tasks execute.

Quartz.NET can be installed in any .NET 7 application, so in this chapter I show how to install Quartz.NET in a worker service using the generic host rather than an ASP.NET Core app using minimal hosting. You'll install the necessary dependencies and configure the Quartz.NET scheduler to run as a background service. In section 34.3.2 we'll convert the exchange-rate downloader task from section 34.1 to a Quartz.NET IJob and configure triggers to run on a schedule.

NOTE The instructions in this section can be used to install Quartz.NET in either a worker service or a full ASP.NET Core application. The only difference is whether you use the generic host in Program.cs or WebApplicationBuilder.

To install Quartz.NET, follow these steps:

1 Install the Quartz.AspNetCore NuGet package in your project by running dotnet add package Quartz.Extensions.Hosting, by using the NuGet explorer in Visual Studio, or by adding a <PackageReference> element to your project file as follows:

```
<PackageReference Include="Quartz.Extensions.Hosting" Version="3.5.0" />
```

2 Add the Quartz.NET IHostedService scheduler by calling AddQuartzHostedService() on the IServiceCollection in ConfigureServices (or on WebApplicationBuilder.Services) as follows. Set WaitForJobsToComplete=true so that your app will wait for any jobs in progress to finish when shutting down.

```
services.AddQuartzHostedService(q => q.WaitForJobsToComplete = true);
```

3 Configure the required Quartz.NET services. The example in the following listing configures the Quartz.NET job factory to retrieve job implementations from the DI container and adds the required hosted service.

Listing 34.10 Configuring Quartz.NET

```
using Quartz;

IHost host = Host.CreateDefaultBuilder(args)          Adds Quartz.NET in
    .ConfigureServices((hostContext, services) =>      ConfigureServices for
    {                                                  worker services
        services.AddQuartz(q =>          Registers Quartz.NET services
        {                                with the DI container
            q. UseMicrosoftDependencyInjectionJobFactory();
        });

        services.AddQuartzHostedService(          Adds the Quartz.NET IHostedService
            q => q.WaitForJobsToComplete = true);      that runs the Quartz.NET scheduler
    })
    .Build();
host.Run();
```

Configures Quartz.NET to load jobs from the DI container

This configuration registers all Quartz.NET's required components, so you can now run your application using dotnet run or by pressing F5 in Visual Studio. When your app starts, the Quartz.NET IHostedService starts its scheduler, as shown in figure 34.4. We haven't configured any jobs to run yet, so the scheduler doesn't have anything to schedule. The app will sit there, periodically checking whether any jobs have been added.

Quartz.NET uses an in-memory store for tracking jobs and schedules by default.

Quartz.NET runs in nonclustered mode by default, so each running instance of your app is independent.

No jobs or triggers have been configured for this application.

Figure 34.4   The Quartz.NET scheduler starts on app startup and logs its configuration. The default configuration stores the list of jobs and their schedules in memory and runs in a nonclustered state. In this example, you can see that no jobs or triggers have been registered, so the scheduler has nothing to schedule yet.

> **TIP**   Running your application before you've added any jobs is good practice. It lets you check that you have installed and configured Quartz.NET correctly before you get to more advanced configuration.

A job scheduler without any jobs to schedule isn't a lot of use, so in the next section we'll create a job and add a trigger for it to run on a timer.

34.3.2   *Configuring a job to run on a schedule with Quartz.NET*

In section 34.1 we created an IHostedService that downloads exchange rates from a remote service and saves the results to a database using EF Core. In this section you'll see how you can create a similar Quartz.NET IJob and configure it to run on a schedule.

The following listing shows an implementation of IJob that downloads the latest exchange rates from a remote API using a typed client, ExchangeRatesClient. The results are then saved using an EF Core DbContext, AppDbContext.

Listing 34.11   A Quartz.NET IJob for downloading and saving exchange rates

```
public class UpdateExchangeRatesJob : IJob
{
    private readonly ILogger<UpdateExchangeRatesJob> _logger;
    private readonly ExchangeRatesClient _typedClient;
    private readonly AppDbContext _dbContext;
    public UpdateExchangeRatesJob(
```

Quartz.NET jobs must implement the IJob interface.

You can use standard DI to inject any dependencies.

```
            ILogger<UpdateExchangeRatesJob> logger,
            ExchangeRatesClient typedClient,
            AppDbContext dbContext)
        {
            _logger = logger;
            _typedClient = typedClient;
            _dbContext = dbContext;
        }

    public async Task Execute(IJobExecutionContext context)
        {
            _logger.LogInformation("Fetching latest rates");
            var latestRates = await _typedClient.GetLatestRatesAsync();

            _dbContext.Add(latestRates);
            await _dbContext.SaveChangesAsync();

            _logger.LogInformation("Latest rates updated");
        }
    }
```

You can use standard DI to inject any dependencies.

IJob requires you to implement a single asynchronous method, Execute.

Saves the rates to the database

Downloads the rates from the remote API

Functionally, the IJob in listing 34.11 is doing a similar task to the BackgroundService implementation in listing 34.5, with a few notable exceptions:

- *The IJob defines only the task to execute; it doesn't define timing information.* In the BackgroundService implementation, we also had to control how often the task was executed.

- *A new IJob instance is created every time the job is executed.* By contrast, the BackgroundService implementation is created only once, and its Execute method is invoked only once.

- *We can inject scoped dependencies directly into the IJob implementation.* To use scoped dependencies in the IHostedService implementation, we had to create our own scope manually and use service location to load dependencies. Quartz.NET takes care of that for us, allowing us to use pure constructor injection. Every time the job is executed, a new scope is created and used to create a new instance of the IJob.

The IJob defines what to execute, but it doesn't define when to execute it. For that, Quartz.NET uses triggers. *Triggers* can define arbitrarily complex blocks of time during which a job should execute. For example, you can specify start and end times, how many times to repeat, and blocks of time when a job should or shouldn't run (such as only 9 a.m. to 5 p.m. Monday to Friday).

In the following listing, we register the UpdateExchangeRatesJob with the DI container using the AddJob<T>() method, and we provide a unique name to identify the job. We also configure a trigger that fires immediately and then every five minutes until the application shuts down.

Listing 34.12   Configuring a Quartz.NET `IJob` and trigger

```
using Quartz;

IHost host = Host.CreateDefaultBuilder(args)
    .ConfigureServices((hostContext, services) =>
    {
        services.AddQuartz(q =>
        {
            q. UseMicrosoftDependencyInjectionJobFactory();

            var jobKey = new JobKey("Update exchange rates");
            q.AddJob<UpdateExchangeRatesJob>(opts =>
                opts.WithIdentity(jobKey));

            q.AddTrigger(opts => opts
                .ForJob(jobKey)
                .WithIdentity(jobKey.Name + " trigger")
                .StartNow()
                .WithSimpleSchedule(x => x
                    .WithInterval(TimeSpan.FromMinutes(5))
                    .RepeatForever())
            );
        });

        services.AddQuartzHostedService(
            q => q.WaitForJobsToComplete = true);
    })
    .Build();
host.Run();
```

Creates a unique key for the job, used to associate it with a trigger

Adds the IJob to the DI container and associates it with the job key

Provides a unique name for the trigger for use in logging and in clustered scenarios

Registers a trigger for the IJob via the job key

Fires the trigger as soon as the Quartz.NET scheduler runs on app startup

Fires the trigger every 5 minutes until the app shuts down

Simple triggers like the schedule defined here are common, but you can also achieve more complex configurations using other schedules. The following configuration would set a trigger to fire every week on a Friday at 5:30 p.m.:

```
q.AddTrigger(opts => opts
    .ForJob(jobKey)
    .WithIdentity("Update exchange rates trigger")
    .WithSchedule(CronScheduleBuilder
        .WeeklyOnDayAndHourAndMinute(DayOfWeek.Friday, 17, 30)));
```

You can configure a wide array of time- and calendar-based triggers with Quartz.NET. You can also control how Quartz.NET handles missed triggers—that is, triggers that should have fired, but your app wasn't running at the time. For a detailed description of the trigger configuration options and more examples, see the Quartz.NET documentation at https://www.quartz-scheduler.net/documentation.

> **TIP** A common problem people run into with long-running jobs is that Quartz.NET keeps starting new instances of the job when a trigger fires, even though it's already running. To avoid that, tell Quartz.NET to not start another instance by decorating your `IJob` implementation with the `[Disallow-ConcurrentExecution]` attribute.

The ability to configure advanced schedules, the simple use of DI in background tasks, and the separation of jobs from triggers are reasons enough for me to recommend Quartz.NET if you have anything more than the most basic background service needs. However, the real tipping point is when you need to scale your application for redundancy or performance reasons; that's when Quartz.NET's clustering capabilities make it shine.

34.3.3 Using clustering to add redundancy to your background tasks

In this section you'll learn how to configure Quartz.NET to persist its configuration to a database. This is a necessary step in enabling clustering so that multiple instances of your application can coordinate to run your Quartz.NET jobs.

As your applications become more popular, you may need to run more instances of your app to handle the traffic they receive. If you keep your ASP.NET Core applications stateless, the process of scaling is relatively simple: the more applications you have, the more traffic you can handle, everything else being equal.

However, scaling applications that use IHostedService to run background tasks might *not* be as simple. For example, imagine your application includes the BackgroundService that we created in section 34.1.2, which saves exchange rates to the database every five minutes. When you're running a single instance of your app, the task runs every five minutes as expected.

But what happens if you scale your application and run 10 instances of it? Every one of those applications will be running the BackgroundService, and they'll all be updating every five minutes from the time each instance started!

One option would be to move the BackgroundService to a separate worker service app. You could then continue to scale your ASP.NET Core application to handle the traffic as required but deploy a single instance of the worker service. As only a single instance of the BackgroundService would be running, the exchange rates would be updated on the correct schedule again.

> **TIP** Differing scaling requirements, as in this example, are one of the best reasons for splitting bigger apps into smaller microservices. Breaking up an app like this has a maintenance overhead, however, so think about the tradeoffs if you take this route. For more on this tradeoff, I recommend *Microservices in .NET Core*, 2nd ed., by Christian Horsdal Gammelgaard (Manning, 2021).

However, if you take this route, you add a hard limitation that you can have only a single instance of your worker service. If you need to run more instances of your worker service to handle additional load, you'll be stuck.

An alternative option to enforcing a single service is using *clustering*, which allows you to run multiple instances of your application, with tasks distributed among the instances. Quartz.NET achieves clustering by using a database as a backing store. When a trigger indicates that a job needs to execute, the Quartz.NET schedulers in each app attempt to obtain a lock to execute the job, as shown in figure 34.5. Only a single app can be successful, ensuring that a single app handles the trigger for the IJob.

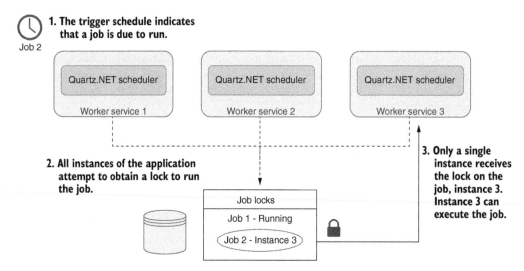

1. The trigger schedule indicates that a job is due to run.

Job 2

Quartz.NET scheduler
Worker service 1

Quartz.NET scheduler
Worker service 2

Quartz.NET scheduler
Worker service 3

2. All instances of the application attempt to obtain a lock to run the job.

3. Only a single instance receives the lock on the job, instance 3. Instance 3 can execute the job.

Job locks

Job 1 - Running

Job 2 - Instance 3

Figure 34.5   Using clustering with Quartz.NET allows horizontal scaling. Quartz.NET uses a database as a backing store, ensuring that only a single instance of the application handles a trigger at a time. This makes it possible to run multiple instances of your application to meet scalability requirements.

Quartz.NET relies on a persistent database for its clustering functionality. Quartz .NET stores descriptions of the jobs and triggers in the database, including when the trigger last fired. The locking features of the database ensure that only a single application can execute a task at a time.

TIP   You can also enable persistence without enabling clustering, allowing the Quartz.NET scheduler to catch up with missed triggers.

Listing 34.13 shows how to enable persistence for Quartz.NET and how to enable clustering. This example stores data in a Microsoft SQL Server (or LocalDB) server, but Quartz.NET supports many other databases. This example uses the recommended values for enabling clustering and persistence as outlined in the documentation.

TIP   The Quartz.NET documentation discusses many configuration setting controls for persistence. See the "Job Stores" documentation at http://mng .bz/PP0R. To use the recommended JSON serializer for persistence, you must also install the Quartz.Serialization.Json NuGet package.

Listing 34.13   Enabling persistence and clustering for Quartz.NET

```
using Quartz;                    Configuration is identical for both
                                 ASP.NET Core apps and worker services.
IHost host = Host.CreateDefaultBuilder(args)
    .ConfigureServices((hostContext, services) =>         Obtains the
    {                                                      connection string
        var connectionString = Configuration              for your database
            .GetConnectionString("DefaultConnection");     from configuration
```

Enables database persistence for the Quartz.NET scheduler data

Enables clustering between multiple instances of your app

Each instance of your app must have a unique SchedulerId. AUTO takes care of this for you.

Stores the scheduler data in a SQL Server (or LocalDb) database

Adds the recommended configuration for job persistence

```
services.AddQuartz(q =>
{
    q.SchedulerId = "AUTO";

    q. UseMicrosoftDependencyInjectionJobFactory();

    q.UsePersistentStore(s =>
    {
        s.UseSqlServer(connectionString);
        s.UseClustering();
        s.UseProperties = true;
        s.UseJsonSerializer();
    });

    var jobKey = new JobKey("Update_exchange_rates");
    q.AddJob<UpdateExchangeRatesJob>(opts =>
        opts.WithIdentity(jobKey));

    q.AddTrigger(opts => opts
        .ForJob(jobKey)
        .WithIdentity(jobKey.Name + " trigger")
        .StartNow()
        .WithSimpleSchedule(x => x
            .WithInterval(TimeSpan.FromMinutes(5))
            .RepeatForever())
    );
});

services.AddQuartzHostedService(
    q => q.WaitForJobsToComplete = true);
})
    .Build();
host.Run();
```

With this configuration, Quartz.NET stores a list of jobs and triggers in the database, and uses database locking to ensure that only a single instance of your app handles a trigger and runs the associated job.

> **WARNING** SQLite doesn't support the database locking primitives required for clustering. You can use SQLite as a persistence store, but you won't be able to use clustering.

Quartz.NET stores data in your database, but it doesn't attempt to create the tables it uses itself. Instead, you must add the required tables manually. Quartz.NET provides SQL scripts on GitHub for all the supported database server types, including SQL Server, SQLite, PostgreSQL, MySQL, and many more; see http://mng.bz/JDeZ.

> **TIP** If you're using EF Core migrations to manage your database, I suggest using them even for ad hoc scripts like these. In the code sample associated with this chapter, you can see a migration that creates the required tables using the Quartz.NET scripts.

Clustering is one of those advanced features that is necessary only as you start to scale your application, but it's an important tool to have in your belt. It gives you the ability to safely scale your services as you add more jobs. There are some important things to bear in mind, however, so I suggest reading the warnings in the Quartz.NET documentation at http://mng.bz/aozj.

That brings us to the end of this chapter on background services. In the final chapters of this book I describe an important aspect of web development that sometimes, despite the best intentions, is left until last: testing. You'll learn how to write simple unit tests for your classes, design for testability, and build integration tests that test your whole app.

Summary

- You can use the IHostedService interface to run tasks in the background of your ASP.NET Core apps. Call AddHostedService<T>() to add an implementation T to the DI container. IHostedService is useful for implementing long-running tasks.

- Typically, you should derive from BackgroundService to create an IHostedService, as this implements best practices required for long-running tasks. You must override a single method, ExecuteAsync, that is called when your app starts. You should run your tasks within this method until the provided CancellationToken indicates that the app is shutting down.

- You can create DI scopes manually using IServiceProvider.CreateScope(). This is useful for accessing scoped lifetime services from within a singleton lifetime component, such as from an IHostedService implementation.

- A worker service is a .NET Core application that uses the generic IHost but doesn't include the ASP.NET Core libraries for handling HTTP requests. It generally has a smaller memory and disk footprint than an ASP.NET Core equivalent.

- Worker services use the same logging, configuration, and DI systems as ASP.NET Core apps. However, they don't use the WebApplicationBuilder minimal hosting APIs, so you must configure your app using the generic host APIs. For example, configure your DI services using IHostBuilder.ConfigureServices().

- To run a worker service or ASP.NET Core app as a Windows Service, add the Microsoft.Extensions.Hosting.WindowsServices NuGet package, and call UseWindowsService() on IHostBuilder. You can install and manage your app with the Windows sc utility.

- To install a Linux systemd daemon, add the Microsoft.Extensions.Hosting.Systemd NuGet package and call AddSystemd() on IHostBuilder. Both the Systemd and Windows Service integration packages do nothing when running the application as a console app, which is great for testing your app. You can even add both packages so that your app can run as a service in both Windows and Linux.

- Quartz.NET runs jobs based on triggers using advanced schedules. It builds on the IHostedService implementation to add extra features and scalability. You can install Quartz by adding the Quartz.AspNetCore NuGet package and calling `AddQuartz()` and `AddQuartzHostedService()` in `ConfigureServices()`.

- You can create a Quartz.NET job by implementing the `IJob` interface. This requires implementing a single method, `Execute`. You can enable DI for the job by calling `UseMicrosoftDependencyInjectionJobFactory` in `AddQuartz()`. This allows you to directly inject scoped (or transient) services into your job without having to create your own scopes.

- You must register your job, `T`, with DI by calling `AddJob<T>()` and providing a `JobKey` name for the job. You can add an associated trigger by calling `AddTrigger()` and providing the `JobKey`. Triggers have a wide variety of schedules available for controlling when a job should be executed.

- By default, triggers spawn new instances of a job as often as necessary. For long-running jobs scheduled with a short interval, that will result in many instances of your job running concurrently. If you want a trigger to execute a job only when an instance is not already running, decorate your job with the `[Disallow-ConcurrentExecution]` attribute.

- Quartz.NET supports database persistence for storing when triggers have executed. To enable persistence, call `UsePersistentStore()` in your `AddQuartz()` configuration method, and configure a database, using `UseSqlServer()` for example. With persistence, Quartz.NET can persist details about jobs and triggers between application restarts.

- Enabling persistence also allows you to use clustering. Clustering enables multiple apps using Quartz.NET to coordinate, so that jobs are spread across multiple schedulers. To enable clustering, first enable database persistence and then call `UseClustering()`. SQLite does not support clustering due to limitations of the database itself.

Testing applications with xUnit

35

This chapter covers

- Testing in ASP.NET Core
- Creating unit test projects with xUnit
- Creating Fact and Theory tests

When I started programming, I didn't understand the benefits of automated testing. It involved writing so much more code. Wouldn't it be more productive to be working on new features instead? It was only when my projects started getting bigger that I appreciated the advantages. Instead of having to run my app and test each scenario manually, I could click Play on a suite of tests and have my code tested for me automatically.

Testing is universally accepted as good practice, but how it fits into your development process can often turn into a religious debate. How many tests do you need? Should you write tests before, during, or after the main code? Is anything less than 100 percent coverage of your code base adequate? What about 80 percent?

This chapter won't address any of those questions. Instead, I focus on the mechanics of creating a test project in .NET. In this chapter I show you how to use isolated unit tests to verify the behavior of your services in isolation. In chapter 36 we build on these basics to create unit tests for an ASP.NET Core application, as well as create integration tests that exercise multiple components of your application at the same time.

> **TIP** For a broader discussion of testing, or if you're brand-new to unit testing, see *The Art of Unit Testing*, 3rd ed., by Roy Osherove (Manning, 2024). If you want to explore unit test best practices using C# examples, see *Unit Testing Principles, Practices, and Patterns*, by Vladimir Khorikov (Manning, 2020). *Effective Software Testing: A Developers Guide*, by Maurício Aniche (Manning, 2022), uses Java examples but covers a broad range of topics and techniques. Alternatively, for an in-depth look at testing with xUnit in .NET Core, see *.NET in Action*, 2nd ed., by Dustin Metzgar (Manning, 2023).

In section 35.1 I introduce the .NET software development kit (SDK) testing framework and show how you can use it to create unit testing apps. I describe the components involved, including the testing SDK and the testing frameworks themselves, like xUnit and MSTest. Finally, I cover some of the terminology I use throughout this chapter and chapter 36.

This chapter focuses on the mechanics of getting started with xUnit. You'll learn how to create unit test projects, reference classes in other projects, and run tests with Visual Studio or the .NET command-line interface (CLI). You'll create a test project and use it to test the behavior of a basic currency-converter service. Finally, you'll write some simple unit tests that check whether the service returns the expected results and throws exceptions when you expect it to.

Let's start by looking at the overall testing landscape for ASP.NET Core, the options available to you, and the components involved.

35.1 An introduction to testing in ASP.NET Core

In this section you'll learn about the basics of testing in ASP.NET Core. You'll learn about the types of tests you can write, such as unit tests and integration tests, and why you should write both types. Finally, you'll see how testing fits into ASP.NET Core.

If you have experience building apps with the full .NET Framework or mobile apps with Xamarin, you might have some experience with unit testing frameworks. If you were building apps in Visual Studio, the steps for creating a test project differed among testing frameworks (such as xUnit, NUnit, and MSTest), and running the tests in Visual Studio often required installing a plugin. Similarly, running tests from the command line varied among frameworks.

With the .NET SDK, testing in ASP.NET Core and .NET Core is a first-class citizen, on a par with building, restoring packages, and running your application. Just as you can run `dotnet build` to build a project, or `dotnet run` to execute it, you can use `dotnet test` to execute the tests in a test project, regardless of the testing framework used.

The `dotnet test` command uses the underlying .NET SDK to execute the tests for a given project. This is the same as when you run your tests using the Visual Studio test runner, so whichever approach you prefer, the results are the same.

Test projects are console apps that contain several tests. A *test* is typically a method that evaluates whether a given class in your app behaves as expected. The test project typically has dependencies on at least three components:

- The .NET Test SDK
- A unit testing framework, such as xUnit, NUnit, Fixie, or MSTest
- A test-runner adapter for your chosen testing framework so that you can execute your tests by calling `dotnet test`

These dependencies are normal NuGet packages that you can add to a project, but they allow you to hook in to the `dotnet test` command and the Visual Studio test runner. You'll see an example .csproj file from a test app in the next section.

Typically, a test consists of a method that runs a small piece of your app in isolation and checks whether it has the desired behavior. If you were testing a `Calculator` class, you might have a test that checks that passing the values 1 and 2 to the `Add()` method returns the expected result, 3.

You can write lots of small, isolated tests like this for your app's classes to verify that each component is working correctly, independent of any other components. Small isolated tests like these are called *unit tests*.

Using the ASP.NET Core framework, you can build apps that you can easily unit-test. You can test some aspects of your API controllers in isolation from your action filters and model binding, for example, because the framework

- Avoids static types
- Uses interfaces instead of concrete implementations
- Has a highly modular architecture, allowing you to test your API controllers in isolation from your action filters and model binding

But the fact that all your components work correctly independently doesn't mean they'll work when you put them together. For that, you need *integration tests*, which test the interaction between multiple components.

The definition of an integration test is another somewhat-contentious problem, but I think of integration tests as testing multiple components together or testing large vertical slices of your app—testing a user manager class that can save values to a database, for example, or testing that a request made to a health-check endpoint returns the expected response. Integration tests don't necessarily include the entire app, but they use more components than unit tests.

> **NOTE** I don't cover UI tests, which (for example) interact with a browser to provide true end-to-end automated testing. Playwright (https://playwright .dev) and Cypress (https://www.cypress.io) are two of the most popular modern tools for UI testing.

ASP.NET Core has a couple of tricks up its sleeve when it comes to integration testing, as you'll see in chapter 36. You can use the Test Host package to run an in-process ASP.NET Core server, which you can send requests to and inspect the responses. This saves you from the orchestration headache of trying to spin up a web server on a different process, making sure ports are available, and so on, but still allows you to exercise your whole app.

At the other end of the scale, the Entity Framework Core (EF Core) SQLite in-memory database provider lets you isolate your tests from the database. Interacting with and configuring a database is often one of the hardest aspects of automating tests, so this provider lets you sidestep the problem. You'll see how to use it in chapter 36.

The easiest way to get to grips with testing is to give it a try, so in the next section you'll create your first test project and use it to write unit tests for a simple custom service.

35.2   Creating your first test project with xUnit

As I described in section 35.1, to create a test project you need to use a testing framework. You have many options, such as NUnit and MSTest, but (anecdotally) the most used test framework with ASP.NET Core is xUnit (https://xunit.net). The ASP.NET Core framework project itself uses xUnit as its testing framework, so it's become somewhat of a convention. If you're familiar with a different testing framework, feel free to use that instead.

Visual Studio includes a template to create a .NET 7 xUnit test project, as shown in figure 35.1. Choose **File** > **New** > **Project**, and choose **xUnit Test Project** in the New Project dialog box. Alternatively, you could choose **MSTest Project** or **NUnit Test Project** if you're more comfortable with those frameworks.

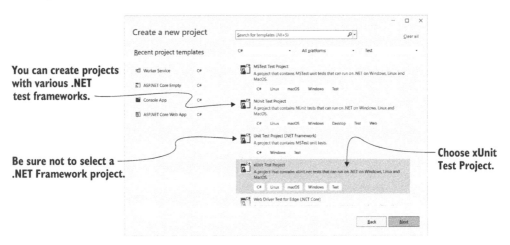

Figure 35.1   The New Project dialog box in Visual Studio. Choose xUnit Test Project to create an xUnit project, or choose Unit Test Project to create an MSTest project.

Alternatively, if you're not using Visual Studio, you can create a similar template using the .NET CLI with

```
dotnet new xunit
```

Whether you use Visual Studio or the .NET CLI, the template creates a console project and adds the required testing NuGet packages to your .csproj file, as shown in the following listing. If you chose to create an MSTest (or other framework) test project, the xUnit and xUnit runner packages would be replaced by packages appropriate to your testing framework of choice.

Listing 35.1   The .csproj file for an xUnit test project

```
<Project Sdk="Microsoft.NET.Sdk">
  <PropertyGroup>
    <TargetFramework>net7.0</TargetFramework>
    <IsPackable>false</IsPackable>
  </PropertyGroup>
  <ItemGroup>
    <PackageReference
       Include="Microsoft.NET.Test.Sdk" Version="17.3.2" />
    <PackageReference Include="xunit" Version="2.4.2" />
    <PackageReference
       Include="xunit.runner.visualstudio" Version="2.4.5" />
    <PackageReference Include="coverlet.collector" Version="3.1.2" />
  </ItemGroup>
</Project>
```

The test project is a standard .NET 7.0 project.

The .NET Test SDK, required by all test projects

The xUnit test adapter for the .NET Test SDK

The xUnit test framework

An optional package that collects metrics about how much of your code base is covered by tests

---

TIP Adding the Microsoft.NET.Test.Sdk package marks the project as a test project by setting the IsTestProject MsBuild property.

In addition to the NuGet packages, the template includes a single example unit test. This doesn't do anything, but it's a valid xUnit test all the same, as shown in the following listing. In xUnit, a test is a method on a public class, decorated with a [Fact] attribute.

Listing 35.2   An example xUnit unit test, created by the default template

```
public class UnitTest1
{
    [Fact]
    public void Test1()
    {
    }
}
```

xUnit tests must be in public classes.

The [Fact] attribute indicates that the method is a test method.

The Fact must be public and have no parameters.

Even though this test doesn't test anything, it highlights some characteristics of xUnit [Fact] tests:

- Tests are denoted by the [Fact] attribute.
- The method should be public, with no method arguments.

- The method is void. It could also be an async method and return Task.
- The method resides inside a public, nonstatic class.

> **NOTE** The [Fact] attribute and these restrictions are specific to the xUnit testing framework. Other frameworks have other ways to denote test classes and different restrictions on the classes and methods themselves.

It's also worth noting that although I said test projects are console apps, there's no Program class or static void Main method. Instead, the app looks more like a class library because the test SDK automatically injects a Program class at build time. It's not something you have to worry about in general, but you may have problems if you try to add your own Program.cs file to your test project.

> **NOTE** This isn't a common thing to do, but I've seen it done occasionally. I describe this problem in detail and how to fix it in my blog post "Fixing the error 'Program has more than one entry point defined' for console apps containing xUnit tests," at http://mng.bz/w9q5.

Before we go any further and create some useful tests, we'll run the test project as it is, using both Visual Studio and the .NET SDK tooling, to see the expected output.

35.3 Running tests with dotnet test

When you create a test app that uses the .NET Test SDK, you can run your tests by using Visual Studio or the .NET CLI. In Visual Studio, you run tests by choosing **Test** > **Run All Tests** or by choosing **Run All** in the Test Explorer window, as shown in figure 35.2.

Click Run All to run all tests in the solution.

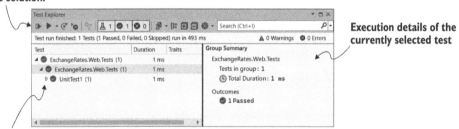

Execution details of the currently selected test

All tests in the solution and their most recent status

Figure 35.2 The Test Explorer window in Visual Studio lists all tests found in the solution and their most recent pass/fail status. Click a test in the left pane to see details about the most recent test run in the right pane.

The Test Explorer window lists all the tests found in your solution and the results of each test. In xUnit, a test passes if it doesn't throw an exception, so UnitTest1.Test1 passed successfully.

NOTE   The Test Explorer in Visual Studio uses the open-source VSTest proto-col (https://github.com/microsoft/vstest) for listing and debugging tests. It's also used by Visual Studio for Mac and Visual Studio Code, for example.

Alternatively, you can run your tests from the command line using the .NET CLI by running

```
dotnet test
```

from the unit-test project's folder, as shown in figure 35.3.

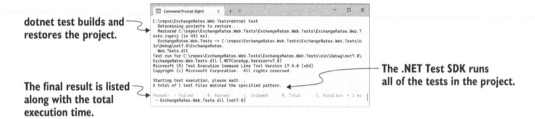

Figure 35.3   You can run tests from the command line using `dotnet test`**. This restores and builds the test project before executing all the tests in the project.**

NOTE   You can also run `dotnet test` from the solution folder. This runs all test projects referenced in the .sln solution file.

Calling `dotnet test` runs a restore and build of your test project and then runs the tests, as you can see from the console output in figure 35.3. Under the hood, the .NET CLI calls in to the same underlying infrastructure that Visual Studio does (the .NET SDK), so you can use whichever approach better suits your development style.

You've seen a successful test run, so it's time to replace that placeholder test with something useful. First things first, though: you need something to test.

35.4   *Referencing your app from your test project*

In test-driven development (TDD), you typically write your unit tests before you write the actual class you're testing, but I'm going to take a more traditional route here and create the class to test first. You'll write the tests for it afterward.

Let's assume you've created an app called ExchangeRates.Web, which exposes an API that converts among different currencies, and you want to add tests for it. You've added a test project to your solution as described in section 35.2.1, so your solution looks like figure 35.4.

For the ExchangeRates.Web.Tests project to test the classes in the Exchange-Rates.Web project, you need to add a reference to the web project from your test project. In Visual Studio, you can do this by right-clicking the **Dependencies** node of your test project and choosing **Add Project Reference** from the contextual menu, as shown

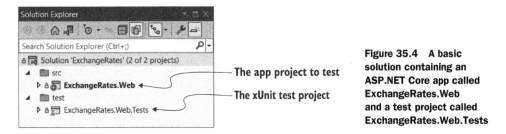

Figure 35.4   A basic solution containing an ASP.NET Core app called ExchangeRates.Web and a test project called ExchangeRates.Web.Tests

in figure 35.5. You can then select the web project in the Reference Manager dialog box. After adding it to your project, it shows up inside the Dependencies node, under Projects.

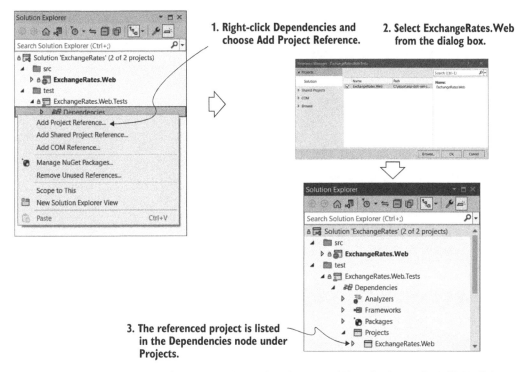

Figure 35.5   To test your app project, you need to add a reference to it from the test project. Right-click the Dependencies node, and choose Add Project Reference from the contextual menu. The app project is referenced inside the Dependencies node, under Projects.

Alternatively, you can edit the .csproj file directly and add a `<ProjectReference>` element inside an `<ItemGroup>` element with the relative path to the referenced project's .csproj file:

```
<ItemGroup>
  <ProjectReference
    Include="..\..\src\ExchangeRates.Web\ExchangeRates.Web.csproj" />
</ItemGroup>
```

Note that the path is the *relative* path. A "`..`" in the path means the parent folder, so the relative path shown correctly traverses the directory structure for the solution, including both the src and test folders shown in Solution Explorer in figure 35.5.

TIP Remember that you can edit the .csproj file directly in Visual Studio by double-clicking the project in Solution Explorer.

Common conventions for project layout

The layout and naming of projects within a solution are completely up to you, but ASP.NET Core projects have generally settled on a couple of conventions that differ slightly from the Visual Studio File > New defaults. These conventions are used by the ASP.NET team on GitHub, as well as by many other open-source C# projects.

The following figure shows an example of these layout conventions. In summary, these are as follows:

- The .sln solution file is in the root directory.
- The main projects are placed in a src subdirectory.
- The test projects are placed in a test or tests subdirectory.
- Each main project has a test project equivalent, named the same as the associated main project with a .Test or .Tests suffix.
- Other folders (such as samples, tools, and docs) contain sample projects, tools for building the project, or documentation.

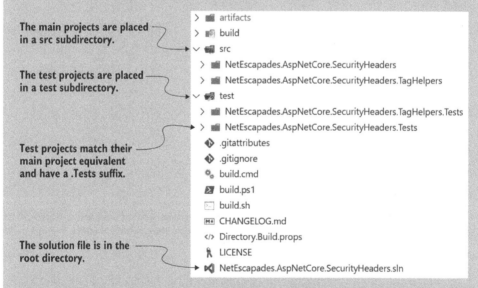

Conventions for project structures have emerged in the ASP.NET Core framework libraries and open-source projects on GitHub. You don't have to follow them for your own project, but it's worth being aware of them.

All these conventions are optional. Whether to follow them is entirely up to you. Either way, it's good to be aware of them so you can easily navigate other projects on GitHub.

Your test project is now referencing your web project, so you can write tests for classes in the web project. You're going to be testing a simple class used for converting among currencies, as shown in the following listing.

Listing 35.3 Example `CurrencyConverter` class to convert currencies to GBP

```
public class CurrencyConverter
{
    public decimal ConvertToGbp(
        decimal value, decimal exchangeRate, int decimalPlaces)
    {
        if (exchangeRate <= 0)
        {
            throw new ArgumentException(
                "Exchange rate must be greater than zero",
                nameof(exchangeRate));
        }
        var valueInGbp = value / exchangeRate;
        return decimal.Round(valueInGbp, decimalPlaces);
    }
}
```

The ConvertToGbp method converts a value using the provided exchange rate and rounds it.

Guard clause, as only positive exchange rates are valid

Converts the value

Rounds the result and returns it

This class has a single method, `ConvertToGbp()`, that converts a `value` from one currency into GBP, given the provided `exchangeRate`. Then it rounds the value to the required number of decimal places and returns it.

> **WARNING** This class is a basic implementation. In practice, you'd need to handle arithmetic overflow/underflow for large or negative values, as well as consider other edge cases. This example is for demonstration purposes only!

Imagine you want to convert 5.27 USD to GBP, and the exchange rate from GBP to USD is 1.31. If you want to round to four decimal places, you'd make this call:

```
converter.ConvertToGbp(value: 5.27, exchangeRate: 1.31, decimalPlaces: 4);
```

You have your sample application, a class to test, and a test project, so it's about time you wrote some tests.

35.5 Adding Fact and Theory unit tests

When I write unit tests, I usually target one of three paths through the method under test:

- *The happy path*—Where typical arguments with expected values are provided
- *The error path*—Where the arguments passed are invalid and tested for
- *Edge cases*—Where the provided arguments are right on the edge of expected values

I realize that this is a broad classification, but it helps me think about the various scenarios I need to consider.

TIP   A completely different approach to testing is property-based testing. This fascinating approach is common in functional programming communities, like F#. You can find a great introduction by Scott Wlaschin in his blog post series "The 'Property Based Testing' Series" at http://mng.bz/o1eZ. That post uses F#, but it is still highly accessible even if you're new to the language.

Let's start with the happy path, writing a unit test that verifies that the ConvertToGbp() method is working as expected with typical input values, as shown in the following listing.

Listing 35.4   Unit test for `ConvertToGbp` using expected arguments

```
[Fact]
public void ConvertToGbp_ConvertsCorrectly()          The [Fact] attribute marks the
{                                                     method as a test method.
    var converter = new CurrencyConverter();
    decimal value = 3;           The parameters of the test that     The class to test,
    decimal rate = 1.5m;         will be passed to ConvertToGbp      commonly called the
    int dp = 4;                                                      "system under test"
    decimal expected = 2;
                                 The result you expect
                                                                     Executes the method
    var actual = converter.ConvertToGbp(value, rate, dp);            and captures the result

    Assert.Equal(expected, actual);      Verifies that the expected and actual values
}                                        match; if they don't, throws an exception
```

You can call the test anything you like.

This is your first proper unit test, which has been configured using Arrange, Act, Assert (AAA) style:

- *Arrange*—Define all the parameters and create an instance of the system (class) under test (SUT).
- *Act*—Execute the method being tested, and capture the result.
- *Assert*—Verify that the result of the Act stage had the expected value.

Most of the code in this test is standard C#, but if you're new to testing, the Assert call will be unfamiliar. This is a helper class provided by xUnit for making assertions about your code. If the parameters provided to Assert.Equal() aren't equal, the Equal() call will throw an exception and fail the test. If you change the expected variable in listing 35.4 to 2.5 instead of 2, for example, and run the test, Test Explorer shows a failure, as you see in figure 35.6.

TIP   Alternative assertion libraries such as Fluent Assertions (https://fluentas sertions.com) and Shouldly (https://github.com/shouldly/shouldly) allow you to write your assertions in a more natural style, such as actual.Should() .Be(expected). These libraries are optional, but I find they make tests more readable and error messages easier to understand.

In listing 35.4 you chose specific values for value, exchangeRate, and decimalPlaces to test the happy path. But this is only one set of values in an infinite number of possibilities,

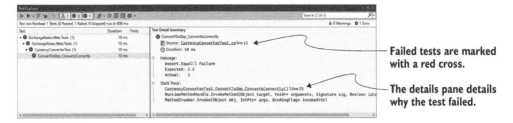

Failed tests are marked with a red cross.

The details pane details why the test failed.

Figure 35.6 When a test fails, it's marked with a red cross in Test Explorer. Clicking the test in the left pane shows the reason for the failure in the right pane. In this case, the expected value was 2.5, **but the actual value was** 2.

so you probably should test at least a few different combinations. One way to achieve this would be to copy and paste the test multiple times, tweak the parameters, and change the test method name to make it unique. xUnit provides an alternative way to achieve the same thing without requiring so much duplication.

> **NOTE** The names of your test class and method are used throughout the test framework to describe your test. You can customize how these are displayed in Visual Studio and in the CLI by configuring an xunit.runner.json file, as described at https://xunit.net/docs/configuration-files.

Instead of creating a [Fact] test method, you can create a [Theory] test method. A theory provides a way of parameterizing your test methods, effectively taking your test method and running it multiple times with different arguments. Each set of arguments is considered a different test.

You could rewrite the [Fact] test in listing 35.4 to be a [Theory] test, as shown in the next listing. Instead of specifying the variables in the method body, pass them as parameters to the method and then decorate the method with three [InlineData] attributes. Each instance of the attribute provides the parameters for a single run of the test.

Listing 35.5 Theory test for `ConvertToGbp` **testing multiple sets of values**

```
[Theory]              ⟵——— Marks the method as a parameterized test
[InlineData(0, 3, 0)]
[InlineData(3, 1.5, 2)]          Each [InlineData] attribute provides all the
[InlineData(3.75, 2.5, 1.5)]     parameters for a single run of the test method.
public void ConvertToGbp_ConvertsCorrectly (
    decimal value, decimal rate, decimal expected)    The method takes parameters, which
{                                                     are provided by the [InlineData]
    var converter = new CurrencyConverter();          attributes.
    int dps = 4;                      ⟵
                                                      The dps variable
    var actual = converter.ConvertToGbp(value, rate, dps);    doesn't change,
                                                             so there's no
                                                             need to include it
    Assert.Equal(expected, actual);    ⟵——— Verifies the result    in [InlineData].
}
```

Executes the SUT

If you run this [Theory] test using dotnet test or Visual Studio, it will show up as three separate tests, one for each set of [InlineData], as shown in figure 35.7.

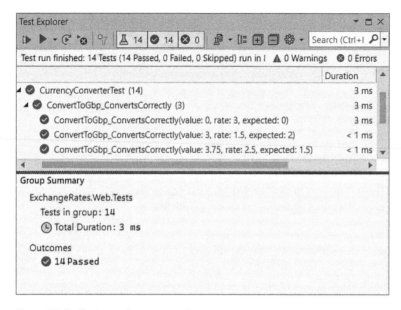

Figure 35.7   Each set of parameters in an [InlineData] attribute for a [Theory] test creates a separate test run. In this example, a single [Theory] has three [InlineData] attributes, so it creates three tests, named according to the method name and the provided parameters.

[InlineData] isn't the only way to provide the parameters for your theory tests, but it's one of the most commonly used. You can also use a static property on your test class with the [MemberData] attribute or a class itself using the [ClassData] attribute.

> **TIP** I describe how you can use the [ClassData] and [MemberData] attributes in my blog post "Creating parameterised tests in xUnit with [InlineData], [ClassData], and [MemberData]": http://mng.bz/8ayP.

You now have some tests for the happy path of the ConvertToGbp() method, and I even sneaked an edge case into listing 35.5 by testing the case where value = 0. The final concept I'll cover is testing error cases, where invalid values are passed to the method under test.

35.6   *Testing failure conditions*

A key part of unit testing is checking whether the system under test handles edge cases and errors correctly. For the CurrencyConverter, that would mean checking how the class handles negative values, small or zero exchange rates, large values and rates, and so on.

Some of these edge cases might be rare but valid cases, whereas other cases might be technically invalid. Calling ConvertToGbp with a negative value is probably valid; the converted result should be negative too. On the other hand, a negative exchange rate doesn't make sense conceptually, so it should be considered an invalid value.

Depending on the design of the method, it's common to throw exceptions when invalid values are passed to a method. In listing 35.3 you saw that we throw an ArgumentException if the exchangeRate parameter is less than or equal to 0.

xUnit includes a variety of helpers on the Assert class for testing whether a method throws an exception of an expected type. You can then make further assertions on the exception, such as to test whether the exception had an expected message.

> **WARNING** Take care not to tie your test methods too closely to the internal implementation of a method. Doing so can make your tests brittle, and trivial changes to a class may break the unit tests.

The following listing shows a [Fact] test to check the behavior of the ConvertToGbp() method when you pass it a 0 exchangeRate. The Assert.Throws method takes a lambda function that describes the action to execute, which should throw an exception when run.

Listing 35.6 Using Assert.Throws<> to test whether a method throws an exception

```
[Fact]
public void ThrowsExceptionIfRateIsZero()
{
    var converter = new CurrencyConverter();
    const decimal value = 1;
    const decimal rate = 0;          // An invalid value
    const int dp = 2;
    var ex = Assert.Throws<ArgumentException>(   // You expect an ArgumentException to be thrown.
        () => converter.ConvertToGbp(value, rate, dp));  // The method to execute, which should throw an exception

    // Further assertions on the exception thrown, ex
}
```

The Assert.Throws method executes the lambda and catches the exception. If the exception thrown matches the expected type, the test passes. If no exception is thrown or the exception thrown isn't of the expected type, the Assert.Throws method throws an exception and fails the test.

That brings us to the end of this brief introduction to unit testing with xUnit. The examples in this section described how to use the new .NET Test SDK, but we didn't cover anything specific to ASP.NET Core. In chapter 36 we'll focus on applying these techniques to testing ASP.NET Core projects specifically.

Summary

- Unit test apps are console apps that have a dependency on the .NET Test SDK, a test framework such as xUnit, MSTest, or NUnit, and a test runner adapter. You can run the tests in a test project by calling `dotnet test` from the command line in your test project or by using Test Explorer in Visual Studio.

- Many testing frameworks are compatible with the .NET Test SDK, but xUnit has emerged as an almost de facto standard for ASP.NET Core projects. The ASP.NET Core team themselves use it to test the framework.

- To create an xUnit test project, choose xUnit Test Project in Visual Studio or use the `dotnet new xunit` CLI command. This creates a test project containing the Microsoft.NET.Test.Sdk, xunit, and xunit.runner.visualstudio NuGet packages.

- xUnit includes two attributes to identify test methods. `[Fact]` methods should be public and parameterless. `[Theory]` methods can contain parameters, so they can be used to run a similar test repeatedly with different parameters. You can provide the data for each `[Theory]` run using the `[InlineData]`, `[ClassData]`, or `[MemberData]` attributes.

- Use assertions in your test methods to verify that the SUT returned an expected value. Assertions exist for most common scenarios, including verifying that a method call raised an exception of a specific type. If your code raises an unhandled exception, the test will fail.

Testing ASP.NET Core applications

This chapter covers

- Writing unit tests for custom middleware, API controllers, and minimal API endpoints
- Using the Test Host package to write integration tests
- Testing your real application's behavior with WebApplicationFactory
- Testing code dependent on Entity Framework Core with the in-memory database provider

In chapter 35 I described how to test .NET 7 applications using the xUnit test project and the .NET Test software development kit (SDK). You learned how to create a test project, add a project reference to your application, and write unit tests for services in your app.

In this chapter we focus on testing ASP.NET Core applications specifically. In sections 36.1 and 36.2 we'll look at how to test common features of your ASP.NET Core apps: custom middleware, API controllers, and minimal API endpoints. I show you how to write isolated unit tests for both, much like you would any other service, and I'll point out the tripping points to watch for.

To ensure that components work correctly, it's important to test them in isolation. But you also need to test that they work correctly in a middleware pipeline. ASP.NET Core provides a handy Test Host package that lets you easily write these integration tests for your components. You can even go one step further with the WebApplication-Factory helper class and test that your app is working correctly. In section 36.3 you'll see how to use WebApplicationFactory to simulate requests to your application and verify that it generates the correct response.

In the final section of this chapter I'll demonstrate how to use the SQLite database provider for Entity Framework Core (EF Core) with an in-memory database. You can use this provider to test services that depend on an EF Core DbContext without having to use a real database. That prevents the pain of having unknown database infrastructure and resetting the database between tests, with different people having slightly different database configurations.

In chapter 35 I showed how to write unit tests for an exchange-rate calculator service, such as you might find in your application's domain model. If well designed, domain services are normally relatively easy to unit-test. But domain services only make up a portion of your application. It can also be useful to test your ASP.NET Core-specific constructs, such as custom middleware, as you'll see in the next section.

36.1 *Unit testing custom middleware*

In this section you'll learn how to test custom middleware in isolation. You'll see how to test whether your middleware handled a request or whether it called the next middleware in the pipeline. You'll also see how to read the response stream for your middleware.

In chapter 31 you saw how to create custom middleware and encapsulate middleware as a class with an Invoke function. In this section you'll create unit tests for a simple health-check middleware component, similar to the one in chapter 31. This is a basic implementation, but it demonstrates the approach you can take for more complex middleware components.

The middleware you'll be testing is shown in listing 36.1. When invoked, this middleware checks that the path starts with /ping and, if it does, returns a plain text "pong" response. If the request doesn't match, it calls the next middleware in the pipeline (the provided RequestDelegate).

Listing 36.1   `StatusMiddleware` to be tested, which returns a "pong" response

```
public class StatusMiddleware
{
    private readonly RequestDelegate _next;
    public StatusMiddleware(RequestDelegate next)
    {
        _next = next;
```

The RequestDelegate representing the rest of the middleware pipeline

```
        }
        public async Task Invoke(HttpContext context)
        {
            if(context.Request.Path.StartsWithSegments("/ping"))
            {
                context.Response.ContentType = "text/plain";
                await context.Response.WriteAsync("pong");
                return;
            }
            await _next(context);
        }
    }
```

Called when the middleware is executed → `public async Task Invoke(HttpContext context)`

If the path starts with "/ping", a "pong" response is returned . . .

`await _next(context);` ← **. . . otherwise, the next middleware in the pipeline is invoked.**

In this section, you're going to test two simple cases:

- When a request is made with a path of `"/ping"`
- When a request is made with a different path

> **WARNING** Where possible, I recommend that you don't directly inspect paths in your middleware like this. A better approach is to use endpoint routing instead, as I discussed in chapter 31. The middleware in this section is for demonstration purposes only.

Middleware is slightly complicated to unit-test because the `HttpContext` object is conceptually a big class. It contains all the details for the request and the response, which can mean there's a lot of surface area for your middleware to interact with. For that reason, I find unit tests tend to be tightly coupled to the middleware implementation, which is generally undesirable.

For the first test, you'll look at the case where the incoming request `Path` doesn't start with `/ping`. In this case, `StatusMiddleware` should leave the `HttpContext` unchanged and call the `RequestDelegate` provided in the constructor, which represents the next middleware in the pipeline.

You could test this behavior in several ways, but in listing 36.2 you test that the `RequestDelegate` (essentially a one-parameter function) is executed by setting a local variable to `true`. In the `Assert` at the end of the method, you verify that the variable was set and therefore that the delegate was invoked. To invoke `StatusMiddleware`, create and pass in a `DefaultHttpContext`, which is an implementation of `HttpContext`.

> **NOTE** The `DefaultHttpContext` derives from `HttpContext` and is part of the base ASP.NET Core framework abstractions. If you're so inclined, you can explore the source code for it on GitHub at http://mng.bz/MB9Q.

Listing 36.2 Unit testing `StatusMiddleware` when a nonmatching path is provided

```
[Fact]
public async Task ForNonMatchingRequest_CallsNextDelegate()
{
    var context = new DefaultHttpContext();
    context.Request.Path = "/somethingelse";
```

Creates a DefaultHttpContext and sets the path for the request

```
          var wasExecuted = false;
          RequestDelegate next = (HttpContext ctx) =>
          {
              wasExecuted = true;
              return Task.CompletedTask;
          };
          var middleware = new StatusMiddleware(next);

          await middleware.Invoke(context);

          Assert.True(wasExecuted);
      }
```

Tracks whether the RequestDelegate was executed

The RequestDelegate representing the next middleware should be invoked in this example.

Creates an instance of the middleware, passing in the next RequestDelegate

Invokes the middleware with the HttpContext; should invoke the RequestDelegate

Verifies that RequestDelegate was invoked

When the middleware is invoked, it checks the provided `Path` and finds that it doesn't match the required value of `/ping`. The middleware therefore calls the next `Request-Delegate` and returns.

The other obvious case to test is when the request `Path` is `"/ping"`; the middleware should generate an appropriate response. You could test several characteristics of the response:

- The response should have a `200 OK` status code.
- The response should have a `Content-Type` of `text/plain`.
- The response body should contain the `"pong"` string.

Each of these characteristics represents a different requirement, so you'd typically codify each as a separate unit test. This makes it easier to tell exactly which requirement hasn't been met when a test fails. For simplicity, in listing 36.3 I show all these assertions in the same test.

The positive case unit test is made more complex by the need to read the response body to confirm it contains `"pong"`. `DefaultHttpContext` uses `Stream.Null` for the `Response.Body` object, which means anything written to `Body` is lost. To capture the response and read it out to verify the contents, you must replace the `Body` with a `MemoryStream`. After the middleware executes, you can use a `StreamReader` to read the contents of the `MemoryStream` into a `string` and verify it.

Listing 36.3   Unit testing `StatusMiddleware` when a matching `Path` is provided

```
[Fact]
public async Task ReturnsPongBodyContent()
{
    var bodyStream = new MemoryStream();
    var context = new DefaultHttpContext();
    context.Response.Body = bodyStream;
    context.Request.Path = "/ping";
    RequestDelegate next = (ctx) => Task.CompletedTask;
    var middleware = new StatusMiddleware(next: next);

    await middleware.Invoke(context);
```

Creates a DefaultHttpContext and initializes the body with a MemoryStream

The path is set to the required value for the StatusMiddleware.

Creates an instance of the middleware and passes in a simple RequestDelegate

Invokes the middleware

```
    string response;
    bodyStream.Seek(0, SeekOrigin.Begin);
    using (var stringReader = new StreamReader(bodyStream))
    {
        response = await stringReader.ReadToEndAsync();
    }
    Assert.Equal("pong", response);
    Assert.Equal("text/plain", context.Response.ContentType);
    Assert.Equal(200, context.Response.StatusCode);
}
```

Rewinds the MemoryStream and reads the response body into a string

Verifies that the response has the correct value

Verifies that the ContentType response is correct

Verifies that the Status Code response is correct

As you can see, unit testing middleware requires a lot of setup. On the positive side, it allows you to test your middleware in isolation, but in some cases, especially for simple middleware without any dependencies on databases or other services, integration testing can (somewhat surprisingly) be easier. In section 36.3 you'll create integration tests for this middleware to see the difference.

Custom middleware is common in ASP.NET Core projects, but far more common are Razor Pages, API controllers, and minimal API endpoints. In the next section you'll see how you can unit test them in isolation from other components.

36.2 *Unit testing API controllers and minimal API endpoints*

In this section you'll learn how to unit-test API controllers and minimal API endpoints. You'll learn about the benefits and difficulties of testing these components in isolation and the situations when it can be useful.

Unit tests are all about isolating behavior; you want to test only the logic contained in the component itself, separate from the behavior of any dependencies. The Razor Pages and MVC/API frameworks use the filter pipeline, routing, and model-binding systems, but these are all external to the controller or `PageModels`. The `PageModels` and controllers themselves are responsible for a limited number of things:

- For invalid requests (that have failed validation, for example), return an appropriate `ActionResult` (API controllers) or redisplay a form (Razor Pages).
- For valid requests, call the required business logic services and return an appropriate `ActionResult` (API controllers), or show or redirect to a success page (Razor Pages).
- Optionally, apply resource-based authorization as required.

Controllers and Razor Pages generally shouldn't contain business logic themselves; instead, they should call out to other services. Think of them more as orchestrators, serving as the intermediary between the HTTP interfaces your app exposes and your business logic services.

If you follow this separation, you'll find it easier to write unit tests for your business logic, and you'll benefit from greater flexibility when you want to change your controllers to meet your needs. With that in mind, there's often a drive to make your controllers and page handlers as thin as possible, to the point where there's not much left to test!

> **TIP** One of my first introductions to this idea was a series of posts by Jimmy Bogard. The following link points to the last post in the series, but it contains links to all the earlier posts too. Bogard is also behind the MediatR library (https://github.com/jbogard/MediatR), which makes creating thin controllers even easier. See "Put your controllers on a diet: POSTs and commands": http://mng.bz/7VNQ.

All that said, controllers and actions are classes and methods, so you can write unit tests for them. The difficulty is deciding what you want to test. As an example, we'll consider the simple API controller in the following listing, which converts a value using a provided exchange rate and returns a response.

Listing 36.4   The API controller under test

```
[Route("api/[controller]")]
public class CurrencyController : ControllerBase
{
    private readonly CurrencyConverter _converter
        = new CurrencyConverter();

    [HttpGet]
    public ActionResult<decimal> Convert(InputModel model)
    {
        if (!ModelState.IsValid)
        {
            return BadRequest(ModelState);
        }

        decimal result = _converter.ConvertToGbp(model)

        return result;
    }
}
```

The CurrencyConverter would normally be injected using DI and is created here for simplicity.

The Convert method returns an Action-Result<T>.

If the input is invalid, returns a 400 Bad Request result, including the ModelState

If the model is valid, calculates the result

Returns the result directly

Let's first consider the happy path, when the controller receives a valid request. The following listing shows that you can create an instance of the API controller, call an action method, and receive an `ActionResult<T>` response.

Listing 36.5   A simple API controller unit test

```
public class CurrencyControllerTest
{
    [Fact]
    public void Convert_ReturnsValue()
    {
```

```
var controller = new CurrencyController();
var model = new InputModel
{                                                    Creates an instance of the
    Value = 1,                                       ConvertController to test and
    ExchangeRate = 3,                                a model to send to the API
    DecimalPlaces = 2,
};

ActionResult<decimal> result = controller.Convert(model);   ◁─────┐
Assert.NotNull(result); ◁──┐                                            │
}                          Asserts that the      Invokes the ConvertToGbp method
}                         IActionResult is not null   and captures the value returned
```

An important point to note here is that you're testing only the return value of the action, the `ActionResult<T>`, not the response that's sent back to the user. The process of serializing the result to the response is handled by the Model-View-Controller (MVC) formatter infrastructure, as you saw in chapter 9, not by the controller.

When you unit-test controllers, you're testing them separately from the MVC infrastructure, such as formatting, model binding, routing, and authentication. This is obviously by design, but as with testing middleware in section 36.1, it can make testing some aspects of your controller somewhat complex.

Consider model validation. As you saw in chapter 6, one of the key responsibilities of action methods and Razor Page handlers is to check the `ModelState.IsValid` property and act accordingly if a binding model is invalid. Testing that your controllers and `Page-Models` handle validation failures correctly seems like a good candidate for a unit test.

Unfortunately, things aren't simple here either. The Razor Page/MVC framework automatically sets the `ModelState` property as part of the model-binding process. In practice, when your action method or page handler is invoked in your running app, you know that the `ModelState` will match the binding model values. But in a unit test, there's no model binding, so you must set the `ModelState` yourself manually.

Imagine you're interested in testing the error path for the controller in listing 36.4, where the model is invalid and the controller should return `BadRequestObjectResult`. In a unit test, you can't rely on the `ModelState` property being correct for the binding model. Instead, you must add a model-binding error to the controller's `ModelState` manually before calling the action, as shown in the following listing.

Listing 36.6 Testing handling of validation errors in MVC controllers

```
[Fact]
public void Convert_ReturnsBadRequestWhenInvalid()
{                                                       Creates an instance of
    var controller = new CurrencyController();  ◁────  the Controller to test
    var model = new ConvertInputModel
    {
        Value = 1,                              Creates an invalid binding
        ExchangeRate = -2,                      model by using a negative
        DecimalPlaces = 2,                      ExchangeRate
    };
```

```
controller.ModelState.AddModelError(
    nameof(model.ExchangeRate),
    "Exchange rate must be greater than zero"
);
```

Manually adds a model error to the Controller's ModelState. This sets ModelState.IsValid to false.

```
ActionResult<decimal> result = controller.Convert(model);
```

Invokes the action method, passing in the binding models

```
    Assert.IsType<BadRequestObjectResult>(result.Result);
}
```

Verifies that the action method returned a BadRequestObjectResult

> **NOTE** In listing 36.6, I passed in an invalid model, but I could just as easily have passed in a valid model or even `null`; the controller doesn't use the binding model if the `ModelState` isn't valid, so the test would still pass. But if you're writing unit tests like this one, I recommend trying to keep your model consistent with your `ModelState`; otherwise, your unit tests won't be testing a situation that occurs in practice.

I tend to shy away from unit testing API controllers directly in this way. As you've seen with model binding, the controllers are somewhat dependent on earlier stages of the MVC framework, which you often need to emulate. Similarly, if your controllers access the `HttpContext` (available on the `ControllerBase` base classes), you may need to perform additional setup.

> **NOTE** You can read more about why I generally don't unit-test my controllers in my blog article "Should you unit-test API/MVC controllers in ASP.NET Core?" at http://mng.bz/YqMo.

So what about minimal API endpoints? There's both good news and bad news here. On one hand, minimal API endpoints are simple lambda functions, so you can unit-test them, but these tests also suffer from many drawbacks:

- You must write your endpoint handlers as static or instance methods on a class, not as lambda methods or local functions, so that you can reference them from the test project.
- You are testing only the execution of the endpoint handler, outside any filters applied to the endpoint or route group that execute in the real app.
- You are not testing model-binding or result serialization—two common sources of errors in practice.
- If your endpoint is simple, as it should be, there's not much to test!

I find unit tests for minimal APIs to be overly restrictive and limited in value, so I avoid them, but you can see an example of a minimal API unit test in the source code for this chapter.

> **NOTE** I haven't discussed Razor Pages much in this section, as they suffer from many of the same problems, in that they are dependent on the supporting infrastructure of the framework. Nevertheless, if you do wish to test your Razor Page `PageModel`, you can read about it in Microsoft's "Razor Pages unit tests in ASP.NET Core" documentation: http://mng.bz/GxmM.

Instead of using unit testing, I try to keep my minimal API endpoints, controllers, and Razor Pages as thin as possible. I push as much of the behavior in these classes into business logic services that can be easily unit-tested, or into middleware and filters, which can be more easily tested independently.

> **NOTE** This is a personal preference. Some people like to get as close to 100 percent test coverage for their code base as possible, but I find testing orchestration classes is often more hassle than it's worth.

Although I tend to forgo unit-testing my ASP.NET Core endpoints, I often write integration tests that test them in the context of a complete application. In the next section, we'll look at ways to write integration tests for your app so you can test its various components in the context of the ASP.NET Core framework as a whole.

36.3 Integration testing: Testing your whole app in-memory

In this section you'll learn how to create integration tests that test component interactions. You'll learn to create a `TestServer` that sends HTTP requests in-memory to test custom middleware components more easily. You'll then learn how to run integration tests for a real application, using your real app's configuration, services, and middleware pipeline. Finally, you'll learn how to use `WebApplicationFactory` to replace services in your app with test versions to avoid depending on third-party APIs in your tests.

If you search the internet for types of testing, you'll find a host of types to choose among. The differences are sometimes subtle, and people don't universally agree on the definitions. I chose not to dwell on that topic in this book. I consider unit tests to be isolated tests of a component and integration tests to be tests that exercise multiple components at the same time.

In this section I'm going to show how you can write integration tests for the `StatusMiddleware` from section 36.1 and the API controller from section 36.2. Instead of isolating the components from the surrounding framework and invoking them directly, you'll specifically test them in a context similar to how you use them in practice.

Integration tests are an important part of confirming that your components function correctly, but they don't remove the need for unit tests. Unit tests are excellent for testing small pieces of logic contained in your components and are typically quick to execute. Integration tests are normally significantly slower, as they require much more configuration and may rely on external infrastructure, such as a database.

Consequently, it's normal to have far more unit tests for an app than integration tests. As you saw in chapter 35, unit tests typically verify the behavior of a component, using valid inputs, edge cases, and invalid inputs to ensure that the component behaves correctly in all cases. Once you have an extensive suite of unit tests, you'll likely need only a few integration tests to be confident your application is working correctly.

You could write many types of integration tests for an application. You could test that a service can write to a database correctly, integrate with a third-party service (for sending emails, for example), or handle HTTP requests made to it.

In this section we're going to focus on the last point: verifying that your app can handle requests made to it, as it would if you were accessing the app from a browser. For this, we're going to use a library provided by the ASP.NET Core team called Microsoft.AspNetCore.TestHost.

36.3.1 *Creating a TestServer using the Test Host package*

Imagine you want to write some integration tests for the StatusMiddleware from section 36.1. You've already written unit tests for it, but you want to have at least one integration test that tests the middleware in the context of the ASP.NET Core infrastructure.

You could go about this in many ways. Perhaps the most complete approach would be to create a separate project and configure StatusMiddleware as the only middleware in the pipeline. You'd then need to run this project, wait for it to start up, send requests to it, and inspect the responses.

This would possibly make for a good test, but it would also require a lot of configuration, and it would be fragile and error-prone. What if the test app can't start because it tries to use an already-taken port? What if the test app doesn't shut down correctly? How long should the integration test wait for the app to start?

The ASP.NET Core Test Host package lets you get close to this setup without having the added complexity of spinning up a separate app. You add the Test Host to your test project by adding the Microsoft.AspNetCore.TestHost NuGet package, using the Visual Studio NuGet GUI, Package Manager Console, or .NET command-line interface (CLI). Alternatively, add the <PackageReference> element directly to your test project's .csproj file:

```
<PackageReference Include="Microsoft.AspNetCore.TestHost" Version="7.0.0"/>
```

In a typical ASP.NET Core app, you create a HostBuilder in your Program class; configure a web server (Kestrel); and define your application's configuration, services, and middleware pipeline (using a Startup file). Finally, you call Build() on the HostBuilder to create an instance of an IHost that can be run and that will listen for requests on a given URL and port.

> **NOTE** All this happens behind the scenes when you use the minimal hosting WebApplicationBuilder and WebApplication APIs. I have an in-depth post exploring the code behind WebApplicationBuilder and how it relates to Host-Builder on my blog at http://mng.bz/a1mj.

The Test Host package uses the same `HostBuilder` to define your test application, but instead of listening for requests at the network level, it creates an `IHost` that uses in-memory request objects, as shown in figure 36.1.

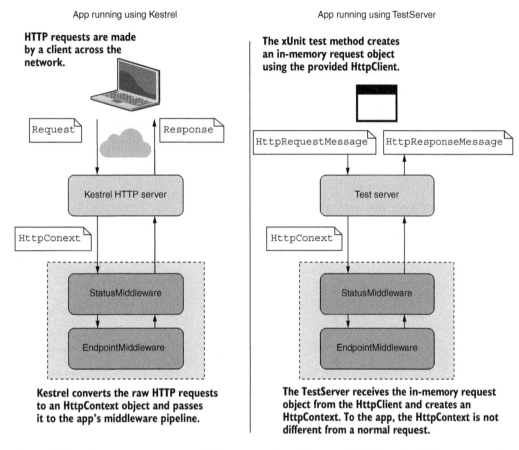

Figure 36.1 **When your app runs normally, it uses the Kestrel server. This listens for HTTP requests and converts the requests to an** `HttpContext`, **which is passed to the middleware pipeline. The** `TestServer` **doesn't listen for requests on the network. Instead, you use an** `HttpClient` **to make in-memory requests. From the point of view of the middleware, there's no difference.**

It even exposes an `HttpClient` that you can use to send requests to the test app. You can interact with the `HttpClient` as though it were sending requests over the network, but in reality, the requests are kept entirely in memory.

Listing 36.7 shows how to use the Test Host package to create a simple integration test for the `StatusMiddleware`. First, create a `HostBuilder`, and call `ConfigureWebHost()` to define your application by adding middleware in the `Configure` method. This is equivalent to the `Startup.Configure()` method you would typically use to configure your application when using the generic host approach.

> **NOTE** You can write a similar test using `WebApplicationBuilder`, but this sets up lots of extra defaults such as configuration, extra dependency injection (DI) services, and automatically added middleware, which can generally slow and add some confusion to simple tests. You can see an example of this approach in `StatusMiddlewareTestHostTests` in the source code for this book, but I recommend using the approach in listing 36.7, using `HostBuilder`, in most cases.

Call the `UseTestServer()` extension method in `ConfigureWebHost()`, which replaces the default Kestrel server with the `TestServer` from the Test Host package. The `TestServer` is the main component in the Test Host package, which makes all the magic possible. After configuring the `HostBuilder`, call `StartAsync()` to build and start the test application. You can then create an `HttpClient` using the extension method `GetTestClient()`. This returns an `HttpClient` configured to make in-memory requests to the `TestServer`, as shown in the following listing.

Listing 36.7   Creating an integration test with `TestServer`

```
public class StatusMiddlewareTests
{
    [Fact]
    public async Task StatusMiddlewareReturnsPong()      Configures a HostBuilder to
    {                                                     define the in-memory test app
        var hostBuilder = new HostBuilder()
            .ConfigureWebHost(webHost =>                         Adds the Status-
            {                                                    Middleware as the
                                                                 only middleware in
                webHost.Configure(app =>                         the pipeline
                    app.UseMiddleware<StatusMiddleware>());
                webHost.UseTestServer();
            });                            Configures the host to use the
                                           TestServer instead of Kestrel
        IHost host = await hostBuilder.StartAsync();
        HttpClient client = host.GetTestClient();          Makes an in-memory
                                                           request, which is handled
        var response = await client.GetAsync("/ping");     by the app as normal

        response.EnsureSuccessStatusCode();
        var content = await response.Content.ReadAsStringAsync();
        Assert.Equal("pong", content);
    }                                          Reads the body content
}                                              and verifies that it
                                               contains "pong"
```

Creates an HttpClient, or you can interact directly with the server object

Builds and starts the host

Verifies that the response was a success (2xx) status code

This test ensures that the test application defined by `HostBuilder` returns the expected value when it receives a request to the /ping path. The request is entirely in-memory, but from the point of view of `StatusMiddleware`, it's the same as if the request came from the network.

The `HostBuilder` configuration in this example is simple. Even though I've called this an integration test, you're specifically testing the `StatusMiddleware` on its own rather than in the context of a real application. I think this setup is preferable for testing custom middleware compared with the "proper" unit tests I showed in section 36.1.

Regardless of what you call it, this test relies on simple configuration for the test app. You may also want to test the middleware in the context of your real application so that the result is representative of your app's real configuration.

If you want to run integration tests based on an existing app, you don't want to have to configure the test HostBuilder manually, as you did in listing 36.7. Instead, you can use another helper package, Microsoft.AspNetCore.Mvc.Testing.

36.3.2 *Testing your application with WebApplicationFactory*

Building up a HostBuilder and using the Test Host package, as you did in section 36.3.1, can be useful when you want to test isolated infrastructure components, such as middleware. However, it's also common to want to test your real app, with the full middleware pipeline configured and all the required services added to DI. This gives you the most confidence that your application is going to work in production.

The TestServer that provides the in-memory server can be used for testing your real app, but in principle, a lot more configuration is required. Your real app likely loads configuration files or static files; it may use Razor Pages and views, as well as using WebApplicationBuilder instead of the generic host. Fortunately, the Microsoft.AspNetCore.Mvc.Testing NuGet package and WebApplicationFactory largely solve these configuration problems for you.

> **NOTE** Don't be put off by the Mvc in the package name; you can use this package for testing ASP.NET Core apps that don't use any MVC or Razor Pages services or components.

You can use the WebApplicationFactory class (provided by the Microsoft.AspNetCore.Mvc.Testing NuGet package) to run an in-memory version of your real application. It uses the TestServer behind the scenes, but it uses your app's real configuration, DI service registration, and middleware pipeline. The following listing shows an example that tests that when your application receives a "/ping" request, it responds with "pong".

Listing 36.8 **Creating an integration test with** WebApplicationFactory

```
public class IntegrationTests:
    IClassFixture<WebApplicationFactory<Program>>
{
    private readonly WebApplicationFactory<Program> _fixture;
    public IntegrationTests(
        WebApplicationFactory<Startup> fixture)
    {
        _fixture = fixture;
    }
```

Implementing the interface
allows sharing an instance
across tests.

Injects an instance of
WebApplicationFactory<T>,
where T is a class in your app

```
[Fact]
public async Task PingRequest_ReturnsPong()
{
    HttpClient client = _fixture.CreateClient();

    var response = await client.GetAsync("/ping");

    response.EnsureSuccessStatusCode();
    var content = await response.Content.ReadAsStringAsync();
    Assert.Equal("pong", content);
}
}
```

Creates an HttpClient that sends requests to the in-memory TestServer

Makes requests and verifies the response as before

One of the advantages of using `WebApplicationFactory` as shown in listing 36.8 is that it requires less manual configuration than using the `TestServer` directly, as shown in listing 36.13, despite performing *more* configuration behind the scenes. The `WebApplication-Factory` tests your app using the configuration defined in your Program.cs and Startup.cs files.

> **NOTE** The generic `WebApplicationFactory<T>` must reference a public class in your app project. It's common to use the `Program` or `Startup` class. If you're using top-level statements for your app (the default in .NET 7), the automatically generated `Program` class is `internal` by default. To make it public and thereby expose it to your test project, add the following partial class definition to your app: `public partial class Program {}`.

Listings 36.8 and 36.7 are conceptually quite different too. Listing 36.7 tests that the `StatusMiddleware` behaves as expected in the context of a dummy ASP.NET Core app; listing 36.7 tests that your app behaves as expected for a given input. It doesn't say anything specific about how that happens. Your app doesn't have to use the `StatusMiddle-ware` for the test in listing 36.7 to pass; it simply has to respond correctly to the given request. That means the test knows less about the internal implementation details of your app and is concerned only with its behavior.

> **DEFINITION** Tests that fail whenever you change your app slightly are called *brittle* or *fragile.* Try to avoid brittle tests by ensuring that they aren't dependent on the implementation details of your app.

To create tests that use `WebApplicationFactory`, follow these steps:

1   Install the Microsoft.AspNetCore.Mvc.Testing NuGet package in your project by running `dotnet add package Microsoft.AspNetCore.Mvc.Testing`, by using the NuGet explorer in Visual Studio, or by adding a `<PackageReference>` element to your project file as follows:

```
<PackageReference Include="Microsoft.AspNetCore.Mvc.Testing"
    Version="7.0.0" />
```

2 Update the `<Project>` element in your test project's .csproj file to the following:

```
<Project Sdk="Microsoft.NET.Sdk.Web">
```

This is required by `WebApplicationFactory` so that it can find your configuration files and static files.

3 Implement `IClassFixture<WebApplicationFactory<T>>` in your xUnit test class, where `T` is a class in your real application's project. By convention, you typically use your application's `Program` class for `T`.
   - `WebApplicationFactory` uses the `T` reference to find the entry point for your application, running the application in memory, and dynamically replacing Kestrel with a `TestServer` for tests.
   - If you're using C# top-level statements and using the `Program` class for `T`, you need to make sure that the `Program` class is accessible from the test project. You can change the visibility of the automatically generated `Program` class by adding `public partial class Program {}` to your app.
   - The `IClassFixture<TFixture>` is an xUnit marker interface that tells xUnit to build an instance of `TFixture` before building the test class and to inject the instance into the test class's constructor. You can read more about fixtures at https://xunit.net/docs/shared-context.

4 Inject an instance of `WebApplicationFactory<T>` in your test class's constructor. You can use this fixture to create an `HttpClient` for sending in-memory requests to the `TestServer`. Those requests emulate your application's production behavior, as your application's real configuration, services, and middleware are all used.

The big advantage of `WebApplicationFactory` is that you can easily test your real app's behavior. That power comes with responsibility: your app will behave as it would in real life, so it will write to a database and send to third-party APIs! Depending on what you're testing, you may want to replace some of your dependencies to avoid this, as well as to make testing easier.

36.3.3 *Replacing dependencies in WebApplicationFactory*

When you use `WebApplicationFactory` to run integration tests on your app, your app will be running in-memory, but other than that, it's as though you're running your application using `dotnet run`. That means any connection strings, secrets, or API keys that can be loaded locally will also be used to run your application.

> **TIP** By default, `WebApplicationFactory` uses the `"Development"` hosting environment, the same as when you run locally.

On the plus side, that means you have a genuine test that your application can start correctly. For example, if you've forgotten to register a required DI dependency that is detected on application startup, any tests that use `WebApplicationFactory` will fail.

On the downside, that means all your tests will be using the same database connection and services as when you run your application locally. It's common to want to replace those with alternative test versions of your services.

As a simple example, imagine the `CurrencyConverter` that you've been testing in this app uses `IHttpClientFactory` to call a third-party API to retrieve the latest exchange rates. You don't want to hit that API repeatedly in your integration tests, so you want to replace the `CurrencyConverter` with your own `StubCurrencyConverter`.

The first step is to ensure that the service `CurrencyConverter` implements an interface—`ICurrencyConverter` for example—and that your app uses this interface throughout, not the implementation. For our simple example, the interface would probably look like the following:

```
public interface ICurrencyConverter
{
    decimal ConvertToGbp(decimal value, decimal rate, int dps);
}
```

You would register your real `CurrencyConverter` service in Program.cs using

```
builder.Services.AddScoped<ICurrencyConverter, CurrencyConverter>();
```

Now that your application depends on `CurrencyConverter` only indirectly, you can provide an alternative implementation in your tests.

> **TIP** Using an interface decouples your application services from a specific implementation, allowing you to substitute alternative implementations. This is a key practice for making classes testable.

We'll create a simple alternative implementation of `ICurrencyConverter` for our tests that always returns the same value, 3. It's obviously not terribly useful as an actual converter, but that's not the point: you have complete control! Create the following class in your test project:

```
public class StubCurrencyConverter : ICurrencyConverter
{
    public decimal ConvertToGbp(decimal value, decimal rate, int dps)
    {
        return 3;
    }
}
```

You now have all the pieces you need to replace the implementation in your tests. To achieve that, we'll use a feature of `WebApplicationFactory` that lets you customize the DI container before starting the test server.

TIP It's important to remember that you want to replace the implementation only when running in the test project. I've seen some people try to configure their real apps to replace live services for fake services when a specific value is set, for example. That is often unnecessary, bloats your apps with test services, and generally adds confusion!

WebApplicationFactory exposes a method, WithWebHostBuilder, that allows you to customize your application before the in-memory TestServer starts. The following listing shows an integration test that uses this builder to replace the default ICurrencyConverter implementation with our test stub.

Listing 36.9 Replacing a dependency in a test using WithWebHostBuilder

```
public class IntegrationTests:                                           Implements
    IClassFixture<WebApplicationFactory<Startup>>                        the required
{                                                                        interface
    private readonly WebApplicationFactory<Startup> _fixture;            and injects
    public IntegrationTests(WebApplicationFactory<Startup> fixture)      it into the
    {                                                                    constructor
        _fixture = fixture;
    }


    [Fact]
    public async Task ConvertReturnsExpectedValue()                 Creates a custom factory
    {                                                              with the additional
        var customFactory = _fixture.WithWebHostBuilder(           configuration
            (IWebHostBuilder hostBuilder) =>
        {                                                          Removes all
            hostBuilder.ConfigureTestServices(services =>          implementations of
            {                                                      ICurrency-Converter
                services.RemoveAll<ICurrencyConverter>();          from the DI container
                services.AddScoped
                    <ICurrencyConverter, StubCurrencyConverter>();
        });                                                        Adds the test
    });                  Calling CreateClient bootstraps the       service as a
                         application and starts the TestServer.    replacement
        HttpClient client = customFactory.CreateClient();

        var response = await client.GetAsync("/api/currency");     Invokes the
                                                                   currency
        response.EnsureSuccessStatusCode();                        converter
        var content = await response.Content.ReadAsStringAsync();  endpoint

        Assert.Equal("3", content);       As the test converter always returns
    }                                     3, so does the API endpoint.
}
```

ConfigureTestServices executes after all other DI services are configured in your real app.

There are a couple of important points to note in this example:

- `WithWebHostBuilder()` returns a *new* WebApplicationFactory instance. The new instance has your custom configuration, and the original injected _fixture instance remains unchanged.
- `ConfigureTestServices()` is called after your real app's `ConfigureServices()` method. That means you can replace services that have been previously registered. You can also use this to override configuration values, as you'll see in section 36.4.

`WithWebHostBuilder()` is handy when you want to replace a service for a single test. But what if you want to replace the `ICurrencyConverter` in every test? All that boilerplate would quickly become cumbersome. Instead, you can create a custom `WebApplicationFactory`.

36.3.4 *Reducing duplication by creating a custom WebApplicationFactory*

If you find yourself writing `WithWebHostBuilder()` a lot in your integration tests, it might be worth creating a custom `WebApplicationFactory` instead. The following listing shows how to centralize the test service we used in listing 36.9 into a custom `WebApplicationFactory`.

Listing 36.10   Creating a custom `WebApplicationFactory` to reduce duplication

```
public class CustomWebApplicationFactory        Derives from
    : WebApplicationFactory<Program>            WebApplicationFactory
{
    protected override void ConfigureWebHost(
        IWebHostBuilder builder)                     There are many functions
    {                                                available to override. This
        builder.ConfigureTestServices(services =>    is equivalent to calling
        {                                            WithWebHostBuilder.
            services.RemoveAll<ICurrencyConverter>();
            services.AddScoped
                <ICurrencyConverter, StubCurrencyConverter>();
        });
    }
}
```

Adds custom configuration for your application

In this example, we override `ConfigureWebHost` and configure the test services for the factory.[1] You can use your custom factory in any test by injecting it as an `IClassFixture`, as you have before. The following listing shows how you would update listing 36.9 to use the custom factory defined in listing 36.10.

---

[1] `WebApplicationFactory` has many other methods you could override for other scenarios. For details, see https://learn.microsoft.com/aspnet/core/test/integration-tests.

Listing 36.11   Using a custom `WebApplicationFactory` in an integration test

```
public class IntegrationTests:                      │  Implements the IClassFixture
    IClassFixture<CustomWebApplicationFactory>      │  interface for the custom factory
{
    private readonly CustomWebApplicationFactory _fixture;
    public IntegrationTests(CustomWebApplicationFactory fixture)
    {
        _fixture = fixture;
    }

    [Fact]                                                    The client
    public async Task ConvertReturnsExpectedValue()           already contains
    {                                                         the test service
        HttpClient client = _fixture.CreateClient();  ◄────┘  configuration.

        var response = await client.GetAsync("/api/currency");

        response.EnsureSuccessStatusCode();
        var content = await response.Content.ReadAsStringAsync();

        Assert.Equal("3", content);   ◄─────┐  The result confirms that
    }                                        │  the test service was used.
}
```

Injects an instance of the factory in the constructor

You can also combine your custom `WebApplicationFactory`, which substitutes services that you always want to replace, with the `WithWebHostBuilder()` method to override additional services on a per-test basis. That combination gives you the best of both worlds: reduced duplication with the custom factory and control with the per-test configuration.

Running integration tests using your real app's configuration provides about the closest thing you'll get to a guarantee that your app is working correctly. The sticking point in that guarantee is nearly always external dependencies, such as third-party APIs and databases.

In the final section of this chapter we'll look at how to use the SQLite provider for EF Core with an in-memory database. You can use this approach to write tests for services that use an EF Core database context without needing access to a real database.

36.4   *Isolating the database with an in-memory EF Core provider*

In this section you'll learn how to write unit tests for code that relies on an EF Core `DbContext`. You'll learn how to create an in-memory database, and you'll see the difference between the EF in-memory provider and the SQLite in-memory provider. Finally, you'll see how to use the in-memory SQLite provider to create fast, isolated tests for code that relies on a `DbContext`.

As you saw in chapter 12, EF Core is an object-relational mapper (ORM) that is used primarily with relational databases. In this section I'm going to discuss one way to test services that depend on an EF Core `DbContext` without having to configure or interact with a real database.

> **NOTE**   To learn more about testing your EF Core code, see *Entity Framework Core in Action*, 2nd ed., by Jon P. Smith (Manning, 2021), http://mng.bz/QPpR.

The following listing shows a highly stripped-down version of the `RecipeService` you created in chapter 12 for the recipe app. It shows a single method to fetch the details of a recipe using an injected EF Core `DbContext`.

Listing 36.12   `RecipeService` to test, which uses EF Core to store and load entities

```
public class RecipeService
{
    readonly AppDbContext _context;
    public RecipeService(AppDbContext context)          An EF Core
    {                                                   DbContext is
        _context = context;                             injected in the
    }                                                   constructor.
    public RecipeViewModel GetRecipe(int id)
    {
        return _context.Recipes          ◀
            .Where(x => x.RecipeId == id)         Uses the DbSet<Recipes>
            .Select(x => new RecipeViewModel      property to load recipes and
            {                                     creates a RecipeViewModel
                Id = x.RecipeId,
                Name = x.Name
            })
            .SingleOrDefault();
    }
}
```

Writing unit tests for this class is a bit of a problem. Unit tests should be fast, repeatable, and isolated from other dependencies, but you have a dependency on your app's `DbContext`. You probably don't want to be writing to a real database in unit tests, as it would make the tests slow, potentially unrepeatable, and highly dependent on the configuration of the database—a failure on all three requirements!

> **NOTE**   Depending on your development environment, you may want to use a real database for your integration tests, despite these drawbacks. Using a database like the one you'll use in production increases the likelihood that you'll detect any problems in your tests. You can find an example of using Docker to achieve this in Microsoft's "Testing ASP.NET Core services and web apps" documentation at http://mng.bz/zxDw.

Luckily, Microsoft ships two in-memory database providers for this scenario. Recall from chapter 12 that when you configure your app's `DbContext` in Program.cs, you configure a specific database provider, such as SQL Server:

```
builder.Services.AddDbContext<AppDbContext>(options =>
    options.UseSqlServer(connectionString);
```

The in-memory database providers are alternative providers designed only for testing. Microsoft includes two in-memory providers in ASP.NET Core:

- *Microsoft.EntityFrameworkCore.InMemory*—This provider doesn't simulate a database. Instead, it stores objects directly in memory. It isn't a relational database as such, so it doesn't have all the features of a normal database. You can't execute SQL against it directly, and it won't enforce constraints, but it's fast. These limitations are large enough that Microsoft generally advise against using it. See http://mng.bz/e1E9.

- *Microsoft.EntityFrameworkCore.Sqlite*—SQLite is a relational database. It's limited in features compared with a database like SQL Server, but it's a true relational database, unlike the in-memory database provider. Normally a SQLite database is written to a file, but the provider includes an in-memory mode, in which the database stays in memory. This makes it much faster and easier to create and use for testing.

  Unfortunately, EF Core migrations are tailored to a specific database, which means you can't run migrations created for SQL Server or PostreSQL against a SQLite database. It's possible to create multiple sets of migrations, as described in the documentation (http://mng.bz/pP15), but this can add a lot of complexity. Consequently, always use `EnsureCreated()` with SQLite tests, which creates the database without running migrations, as you'll see in listing 36.13.

Instead of storing data in a database on disk, both of these providers store data in memory, as shown in figure 36.2. This makes them fast and easy to create and tear down, which allows you to create a new database for every test to ensure that your tests stay isolated from one another.

> **NOTE** In this section I describe how to use the SQLite provider as an in-memory database, as it's more full-featured than the in-memory provider. For details on using the in-memory provider, see Microsoft's "EF Core In-Memory Database Provider" documentation: http://mng.bz/hdIq.

To use the SQLite provider in memory, add the Microsoft.EntityFrameworkCore.Sqlite package to your test project's .csproj file. This adds the `UseSqlite()` extension method, which you'll use to configure the database provider for your unit tests.

Listing 36.13 shows how you could use the in-memory SQLite provider to test the `GetRecipe()` method of `RecipeService`. Start by creating a `SqliteConnection` object and using the `"DataSource=:memory:"` connection string. This tells the provider to store the database in memory and then open the connection. This is typically faster than using a file-based connection-string and means you can easily run multiple tests in parallel, as there's no shared database.

SQL Server database provider

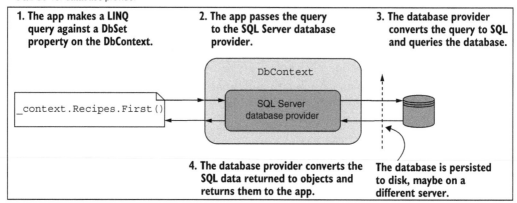

1. **The app makes a LINQ query against a DbSet property on the DbContext.**

2. **The app passes the query to the SQL Server database provider.**

3. **The database provider converts the query to SQL and queries the database.**

`_context.Recipes.First()`

DbContext

SQL Server database provider

4. **The database provider converts the SQL data returned to objects and returns them to the app.**

The database is persisted to disk, maybe on a different server.

SQLite database provider (in-memory)

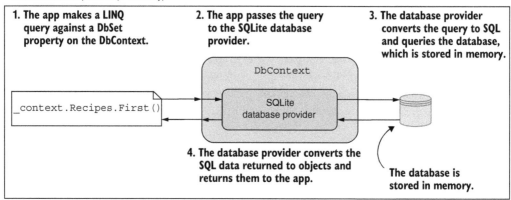

1. **The app makes a LINQ query against a DbSet property on the DbContext.**

2. **The app passes the query to the SQLite database provider.**

3. **The database provider converts the query to SQL and queries the database, which is stored in memory.**

`_context.Recipes.First()`

DbContext

SQLite database provider

4. **The database provider converts the SQL data returned to objects and returns them to the app.**

The database is stored in memory.

In-memory database provider

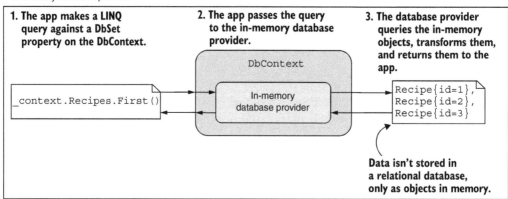

1. **The app makes a LINQ query against a DbSet property on the DbContext.**

2. **The app passes the query to the in-memory database provider.**

3. **The database provider queries the in-memory objects, transforms them, and returns them to the app.**

`_context.Recipes.First()`

DbContext

In-memory database provider

`Recipe{id=1},`
`Recipe{id=2},`
`Recipe{id=3}`

Data isn't stored in a relational database, only as objects in memory.

Figure 36.2   The in-memory database provider and SQLite provider (in-memory mode) compared with the SQL Server database provider. The in-memory database provider doesn't simulate a database as such. Instead, it stores objects in memory and executes LINQ queries against them directly.

WARNING The SQLite in-memory database is destroyed when the connection is closed. If you don't open the connection yourself, EF Core closes the connection to the in-memory database when you dispose of the DbContext. If you want to share an in-memory database between DbContexts, you must explicitly open the connection yourself.

Next, pass the SqliteConnection instance into the DbContextOptionsBuilder<> and call UseSqlite(). This configures the resulting DbContextOptions<> object with the necessary services for the SQLite provider and provides the connection to the in-memory database. Because you're passing this options object in to an instance of AppDbContext, all calls to the DbContext result in calls to the in-memory database provider.

Listing 36.13   Using the in-memory database provider to test an EF Core `DbContext`

```
[Fact]
public void GetRecipeDetails_CanLoadFromContext()                  ← Configures an in-memory SQLite
{                                                                     connection using the special "in-
    var connection = new SqliteConnection("DataSource=:memory:");    memory" connection string
    connection.Open();   ← Opens the connection so EF Core won't close it automatically

    var options = new DbContextOptionsBuilder<AppDbContext>()
        .UseSqlite(connection)                         ← Creates an instance of
        .Options;                                         DbContextOptions<>
                                                          and configures it to use
    using (var context = new AppDbContext(options))       the SQLite connection
    {
        context.Database.EnsureCreated();    ←
        context.Recipes.AddRange(
            new Recipe { RecipeId = 1, Name = "Recipe1" },
            new Recipe { RecipeId = 2, Name = "Recipe2" },
            new Recipe { RecipeId = 3, Name = "Recipe3" });
        context.SaveChanges();
    }
    using (var context = new AppDbContext(options))   ←
    {
        var service = new RecipeService(context);   ←
        var recipe = service.GetRecipe (id: 2);   ←
        Assert.NotNull(recipe);
        Assert.Equal(2, recipe.Id);
        Assert.Equal("Recipe2", recipe.Name);
    }
}
```

- Creates a DbContext and passes in the options
- Adds some recipes to the DbContext
- Saves the changes to the in-memory database
- Ensures that the in-memory database matches EF Core's model (similar to running migrations)
- Creates a fresh DbContext to test that you can retrieve data from the DbContext
- Creates the Recipe-Service to test and pass in the fresh DbContext
- Verifies that you retrieved the recipe correctly from the in-memory database
- Executes the GetRecipe function. This executes the query against the in-memory database.

This example follows the standard format for any time you need to test a class that depends on an EF Core DbContext:

1   Create a SqliteConnection with the "DataSource=:memory:" connection string, and open the connection.

2   Create a DbContextOptionsBuilder<> and call UseSqlite(), passing in the open connection.

3   Retrieve the `DbContextOptions` object from the `Options` property.

4   Pass the options to an instance of your `DbContext` and ensure the database matches EF Core's model by calling `context.Database.EnsureCreated()`. This is similar to running migrations on your database, but it should be used only on test databases. Create and add any required test data to the in-memory database, and call `SaveChanges()` to persist the data.

5   Create a new instance of your `DbContext` and inject it into your test class. All queries will be executed against the in-memory database.

By using a separate `DbContext` for each purpose, you can avoid bugs in your tests due to EF Core caching data without writing it to the database. With this approach, you can be sure that any data read in the second `DbContext` was persisted to the underlying in-memory database provider.

This was a brief introduction to using the SQLite provider as an in-memory database provider and EF Core testing in general, but if you follow the setup shown in listing 36.13, it should take you a long way. The source code for this chapter shows how you can combine this code with a custom `WebApplicationFactory` to use an in-memory database for your integration tests. For more details on testing EF Core, including additional options and strategies, see *Entity Framework Core in Action*, 2nd ed., by Jon P. Smith (Manning, 2021).

Summary

- Use the `DefaultHttpContext` class to unit-test your custom middleware components. If you need access to the response body, you must replace the default `Stream.Null` with a `MemoryStream` instance and read the stream manually after invoking the middleware.

- API controllers, minimal APIs, and Razor Page models can be unit-tested like other classes, but they should generally contain little business logic, so it may not be worth the effort. For example, the API controller is tested independently of routing, model validation, and filters, so you can't easily test logic that depends on any of these aspects.

- Integration tests allow you to test multiple components of your app at the same time, typically within the context of the ASP.NET Core framework itself. The Microsoft.AspNetCore.TestHost package provides a `TestServer` object that you can use to create a simple web host for testing. This creates an in-memory server that you can make requests to and receive responses from. You can use the `TestServer` directly when you wish to create integration tests for custom components like middleware.

- For more extensive integration tests of a real application, you should use the `WebApplicationFactory` class in the Microsoft.AspNetCore.Mvc.Testing package. Implement `IClassFixture<WebApplicationFactory<Program>>` on your test class, and inject an instance of `WebApplicationFactory<Program>` into the constructor.

This creates an in-memory version of your whole app, using the same configuration, DI services, and middleware pipeline. You can send in-memory requests to your app to get the best idea of how your application will behave in production.

- To customize the `WebApplicationFactory`, call `WithWebHostBuilder()` and then call `ConfigureTestServices()`. This method is invoked after your app's standard DI configuration. This enables you to add or remove the default services for your app, such as to replace a class that contacts a third-party API with a stub implementation.

- If you need to customize the services for every test, you can create a custom `WebApplicationFactory` by deriving from it and overriding the `ConfigureWebHost` method. You can place all your configuration in the custom factory and implement `IClassFixture<CustomWebApplicationFactory>` in your test classes instead of calling `WithWebHostBuilder()` in every test method.

- You can use the EF Core SQLite provider as an in-memory database to test code that depends on an EF Core database context. You configure the in-memory provider by creating a `SqliteConnection` with a `"DataSource=:memory:"` connection string. Create a `DbContextOptionsBuilder<>` object and call `UseSqlite()`, passing in the connection. Finally, pass `DbContextOptions<>` into an instance of your app's `DbContext`, and call `context.Database.EnsureCreated()` to prepare the in-memory database for use with EF Core.

- The SQLite in-memory database is maintained as long as there's an open `SqliteConnection`. When you open the connection manually, the database can be used with multiple `DbContexts`. If you don't call `Open()` on the connection, EF Core will close the connection (and delete the in-memory database) when the `DbContext` is disposed of.

appendix A
Preparing your development environment

For .NET developers in a Windows-centric world, Visual Studio was pretty much a developer requirement in the past. But with .NET and ASP.NET Core going cross-platform, that's no longer the case.

All of ASP.NET Core (creating new projects, building, testing, and publishing) can be run from the command line for any supported operating system. All you need is the .NET software development kit (SDK), which provides the .NET command-line interface (CLI). Alternatively, if you're using Windows and not comfortable with the command line, you can choose **File** > **New** > **Project** in Visual Studio to dive straight in. With ASP.NET Core, it's all about choice!

In a similar vein, you can now get a great editing experience outside Visual Studio thanks to the OmniSharp (www.omnisharp.net) project. This is an open-source set of libraries and editor plugins that provide code suggestions and autocomplete (IntelliSense) across a wide range of editors and operating systems. How you set up your environment will likely depend on which operating system you're using and what you're used to.

Remember that for .NET 7, the operating system you choose for development has no bearing on the final systems you can run on. Whether you choose Windows, macOS, or Linux for development, you can deploy to any supported system.

In this appendix I'll show you how to install the .NET SDK so you can build, run, and publish .NET apps. I'll also discuss some of the integrated development environment (IDE) and editor options available for you to build applications.

> **NOTE** In this book I use Visual Studio for most of the examples, but you'll be able to follow along using any of the tools I discuss here. The book assumes that you've successfully installed .NET 7 and an editor on your computer.

A.1   *Installing the .NET SDK*

The most important thing you need for .NET Core and .NET 7 development is the .NET SDK. In this section I describe how to install the .NET SDK and how to check which version you have installed.

To start programming with .NET, you need to install the .NET SDK (also known as the dotnet CLI). This contains the base libraries, tooling, and compiler you need to create .NET applications.

You can download the .NET SDK at https://dotnet.microsoft.com/download. This page contains links to download the latest version of .NET for your operating system. If you're using Windows or macOS, the page contains installer download links; if you're using Linux, the page has instructions for installing .NET using your distribution's package manager, as a Snap package, or as a manual download.

> **WARNING** Make sure that you download the .NET SDK, not the .NET Runtime. The .NET runtime is used to execute .NET applications, but it can't be used to build them. The .NET SDK includes a copy of the runtime, so it can run your applications, but it can also build, test, and publish them. Also make sure to choose the right architecture—x64 or arm64—depending on your processor's architecture.

After installing the .NET SDK, you can run commands with the .NET CLI using the dotnet command. Run dotnet --info to see information about the version of the .NET SDK currently in use, as well as the .NET SDKs and .NET runtimes you have installed, as shown in figure A.1.

The current version of the .NET SDK being used to execute the command

Details about the hardware and operating system

All the versions of the .NET SDK installed on the system

All the versions of the .NET runtime installed on the system

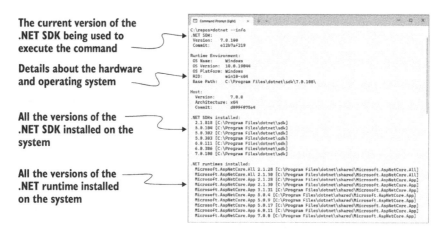

Figure A.1 Use dotnet --info **to check which version of the .NET SDK is currently used and which versions are available. This screenshot shows that I'm currently using the release version of the .NET 7 SDK (version 7.0.100).**

As you can see in figure A.1, I have multiple versions of the .NET SDK installed. This is perfectly fine but not necessary. Newer versions of the .NET SDK can build applications that target older versions of .NET. For example, the .NET 7 SDK can also build .NET 6 apps, .NET 5 apps, .NET Core 3.1 apps, and so on. By contrast, the .NET 6 SDK can't build .NET 7 applications.

> **TIP**   Some IDEs, such as Visual Studio, can automatically install .NET 7 as part of their installation process. There is no problem installing multiple versions of .NET side by side, so you can always install the .NET SDK manually, whether your IDE installs a different version or not.

By default, when you run `dotnet` commands from the command line, you'll be using the latest version of the .NET SDK you have installed. You can control that and use an older version of the SDK by adding a global.json file to the folder. For an introduction to this file, as well as details on how to use it and how to understand .NET's versioning system, see my blog entry "Exploring the new rollForward and allowPrerelease settings in global.json" at http://mng.bz/KMzP.

> **TIP**   If you run into any problems during the install process, the `dotnet` command isn't recognized, or you get an error when running the command, I suggest checking the installation documentation for troubleshooting tips: https://learn.microsoft.com/dotnet/core/install.

Once you have the .NET SDK installed, it's time to choose an IDE or editor. The choices available will depend on which operating system you're using and will largely be driven by personal preference.

A.2   Choosing an IDE or editor

In this section I'll describe a few of the most popular IDEs and editors for .NET development and how to install them. Choosing an IDE is a personal choice, so this section describes only a few of the options. If your favorite IDE isn't listed here, check the documentation to see whether .NET is supported.

A.2.1   Visual Studio (Windows)

For a long time, Windows has been the best system for building .NET applications, and with the availability of Visual Studio that's arguably still the case.

Visual Studio (figure A.2) is a full-featured IDE that provides one of the best all-around experiences for developing ASP.NET Core applications. Luckily, the Visual Studio Community edition is now free for open-source projects, students, and small teams of developers.

Visual Studio comes loaded with a host of templates for building new projects, best-in-class debugging, and publishing; you never need to touch a command prompt. It's especially suitable if you're publishing to Microsoft Azure, as it has many direct hooks to Azure features that make development and deployment easier.

You can install Visual Studio by visiting https://visualstudio.microsoft.com/vs and choosing **Download**. Choose **Community 2022** (unless you have a license for the Professional or Enterprise version) and follow the prompts to install Visual Studio.

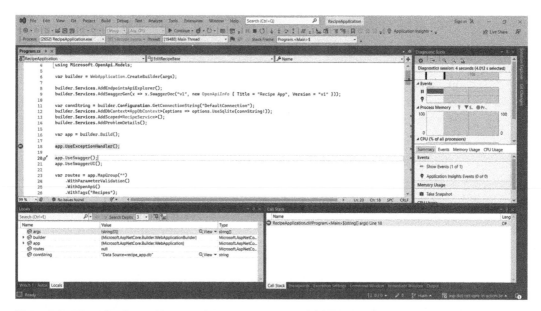

Figure A.2 Visual Studio provides one of the most complete ASP.NET Core development environments for Windows users.

The Visual Studio installer is an application in and of itself. It will ask you to select workloads to install. You can select as many as you like, but for ASP.NET Core development, make sure that you select **ASP.NET and web development** at a minimum.

> **TIP** A lot of workloads and optional components are available in the installer. Don't worry about installing everything now; you can always launch the installer again later to add or remove components.

After selecting your workloads, click Download, and fetch a beverage of your choice. Despite having been on a diet recently, Visual Studio still requires many GB to be downloaded and installed. Once it's finished, you'll be ready to start building ASP.NET Core applications.

A.2.2 *JetBrains Rider (Windows, Linux, macOS)*

Rider (figure A.3), from the company JetBrains, is a cross-platform IDE alternative to Visual Studio. Released in 2017, Rider is another full-featured IDE, based on the venerable ReSharper plugin. If you're used to using Visual Studio with the ReSharper plugin and the multitude of refactorings that this plugin provides, I strongly suggest investigating Rider. Similarly, if you're familiar with JetBrains' IntelliJ products, you will feel at home in Rider.

To install Rider, visit https://www.jetbrains.com/rider, and click **Download**. Rider comes with a 30-day free trial, after which you will need to purchase a license. If you already have a ReSharper license, you may already have a license for Rider. The company also offers discounts and free licenses for various users, such as students and startups, so Rider is worth looking into.

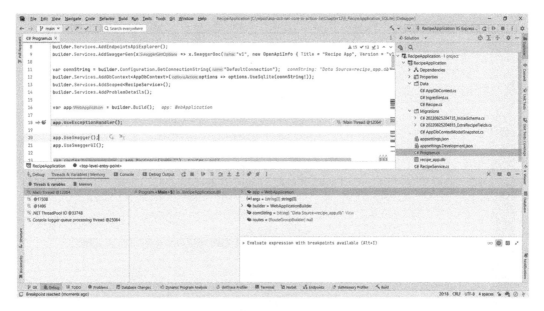

Figure A.3 Rider is a cross-platform .NET IDE from JetBrains. It is based on the ReSharper plugin for Visual Studio, so it includes many of the same refactoring features, as well as a debugger, test runner, and all the other integration features you expect from a full-featured IDE.

A.2.3 Visual Studio for Mac (macOS)

Despite the branding, Visual Studio for Mac is a completely different product from Visual Studio. Rebranded and extended from its Xamarin Studio precursor, Visual Studio for Mac now allows you to build ASP.NET Core applications in macOS. Visual Studio for Mac generally has fewer features than Visual Studio or Rider, but it offers a native experience and is under active development.

To install Visual Studio for Mac, visit https://visualstudio.microsoft.com/vs/mac, choose **Download**, and download and run the installer.

A.2.4 Visual Studio Code (Windows, Linux, macOS)

Sometimes you don't want a full-fledged IDE. Maybe you want to view or edit a file quickly, or you don't like the sometimes-unpredictable performance of Visual Studio. In those cases, a simple editor may be all you want or need, and Visual Studio Code (VS Code) is a great choice. VS Code (figure A.4) is an open-source, lightweight editor that provides editing, IntelliSense, and debugging for a wide range of languages, including C# and ASP.NET Core.

To install VS Code, visit https://code.visualstudio.com, and download and run the installer.

> **NOTE** Make sure to choose the correct download for your operating system and architecture. The download page tries to choose the most appropriate download. You can see all the available options at https://code.visualstudio.com/#alt-downloads.

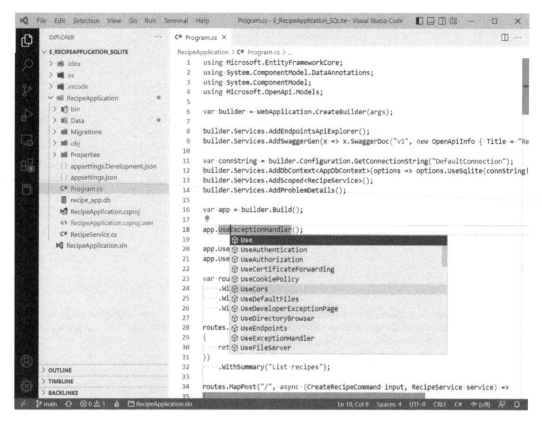

Figure A.4   VS Code provides cross-platform IntelliSense and debugging.

The first time you open a folder containing a C# project or solution file with VS Code, you'll be prompted to install a C# extension, which provides the IntelliSense and integration between VS Code and the .NET SDK.

The extension model of VS Code is one of its biggest assets, as you can add a huge amount of functionality. Whether you're working with Azure, Amazon Web Services (AWS,) or any other technology, be sure to check the extension marketplace at https://marketplace.visualstudio.com/vscode to see what's available. If you search for ".NET", you'll also find a huge array of extensions that can bring VS Code closer to that full-blown IDE experience, if you wish.

appendix B
Useful references

In this appendix I provide many links and references that I've found useful for learning about .NET 7 and ASP.NET Core.

B.1 Relevant books

This book touched on several topics and aspects of the .NET ecosystem that are somewhat peripheral to building ASP.NET Core applications. For a deeper understanding of those topics, I recommend the books in this section. They cover areas that you'll inevitably encounter when building ASP.NET Core applications:

- Vladimir Khorikov, *Unit Testing Principles, Patterns, and Practices* (Manning, 2020), http://mng.bz/E2go. Learn to refine your unit tests using modern best practices in this excellent book that contains examples in C#.
- Dustin Metzgar, *.NET in Action*, 2nd ed. (Manning, 2023), http://mng.bz/OxPK. .NET Core apps are built using .NET 7. This book provides everything you need to know about running on the platform.
- Roy Osherove, *The Art of Unit Testing*, 3rd ed. (Manning, 2024), http://mng.bz/lW5o. In *ASP.NET Core in Action*, I discuss the mechanics of unit testing ASP.NET Core applications. For a deeper discussion of how to create your tests, I recommend *The Art of Unit Testing*.
- Chris Sainty, *Blazor in Action* (Manning, 2021), http://mng.bz/l1P6. Blazor is an exciting new framework that uses the power of industry-standard WebAssembly to run .NET in the browser. With Blazor you can build single-page applications as you would with a JavaScript framework like Angular or React, but using the C# language and tooling that you already know.
- Jon P. Smith, *Entity Framework Core in Action*, 2nd ed. (Manning, 2021), http://mng.bz/BRj0. If you're using EF Core in your apps, I highly recommend *Entity Framework Core in Action*. It covers all the features and pitfalls of EF Core, as well as how to tune your app for performance.

- Steven Van Deursen and Mark Seemann, *Dependency Injection Principles, Practices, and Patterns* (Manning, 2019), http://mng.bz/d4lN. Dependency injection is a core aspect of ASP.NET Core, so *Dependency Injection Principles, Practices, and Patterns* is especially relevant now. It introduces the patterns and antipatterns of dependency injection in the context of .NET and the C# language.

B.2   *Announcement blog posts*

When Microsoft releases a new version of ASP.NET Core or .NET Core, it typically posts an announcement blog. These posts provide a high-level overview of the topic, with many examples of new features. They're a great place to start if you want to get acquainted with a topic quickly:

- Jon Douglas, Jeremy Likness, and Angelos Petropoulos, ".NET 7 is Available Today," *.NET Blog* (Microsoft, November 8, 2022), http://mng.bz/YlRo. Announcement blog post for .NET 7, describing a huge number of the features introduced in .NET 7.
- Richard Lander, "Introducing .NET 5," *.NET Blog* (Microsoft, May 6, 2019), http://mng.bz/Gy9M. The original announcement blog post for .NET 5, describing the One .NET vision for the platform.
- Immo Landwerth, "The future of .NET Standard," *.NET Blog* (Microsoft, September 15, 2020), http://mng.bz/zX0w. A discussion of what .NET 5 means for the future of .NET Standard, including guidance for library authors.
- Immo Landwerth, ".NET Standard—Demystifying .NET Core and .NET Standard," *Microsoft Developer Network* (Microsoft, September 2017), http://mng.bz/0Klp. A long post introducing .NET Core and explaining where .NET Standard fits in the .NET ecosystem.
- Microsoft Docs, ".NET and .NET Core Support Policy," http://mng.bz/Ke9P. Microsoft's official support policy for .NET Core and .NET 7.
- Daniel Roth, "Announcing ASP.NET Core in .NET 7," *ASP.NET Blog* (Microsoft, November 8, 2022), http://mng.bz/gBve. Announcement blog post for ASP.NET Core 7, describing how to upgrade a project from .NET 6 to .NET 7 and providing links to many of the new features introduced in ASP.NET Core 7.
- Mads Torgersen, "Welcome to C# 11," *.NET Blog* (Microsoft, November 8, 2022), http://mng.bz/9DQx. Announcement blog post for C# 11, released alongside .NET 7.

B.3   *Microsoft documentation*

Historically, Microsoft documentation has been poor, but with ASP.NET Core there has been a massive push to ensure that the docs are useful and current. You can find walk-throughs, targeted documentation for specific features, documentation for supported APIs, and even an in-browser C# compiler:

- Microsoft Docs, ".NET API browser," https://learn.microsoft.com/dotnet/api. This is an API browser that can be used to work out which .NET APIs are available on which .NET platforms.
- Microsoft Docs, "ASP.NET documentation," https://learn.microsoft.com/ aspnet/core. This is the official documentation for ASP.NET Core.
- Microsoft Docs, "Cross-platform targeting," http://mng.bz/e1o9. The official guidance on choosing a target framework for your libraries.
- Microsoft Docs, "Entity Framework Core," https://learn.microsoft.com/ef/ core. This is the official documentation for EF Core.

B.4 Security-related links

Security is an important aspect of modern web development. This section contains some of the sites I refer to regularly, which describe some best practices for web development as well as practices to avoid:

- Duende, "Duende IdentityServer v6 Documentation," https://docs.duendesoft ware.com/identityserver/v6. Documentation for Duende's IdentityServer, the OpenID Connect, and OAuth 2.0 framework for ASP.NET Core.
- Dominick Baier, *Dominick Baier on Identity & Access Control* (blog), https:// leastprivilege.com. The personal blog of Dominick Baier, co-author of IdentityServer; a great resource for working with authentication and authorization in ASP.NET Core.
- Scott Helme, *Scott Helme* (blog), https://scotthelme.co.uk. Blog with advice on security standards, especially security headers you can add to your application.
- Scott Helme, "SecurityHeaders.io—Analyse your HTTP response headers," https://securityheaders.com. Test your website's security headers and get advice on why and how you should add them to your app.
- Troy Hunt, *Troy Hunt* (blog), https://www.troyhunt.com. Personal blog of Troy Hunt, with security-related advice for web developers, particularly .NET developers.
- Microsoft Docs, "ASP.NET Core security topics" (Microsoft, March 6, 2022), https://learn.microsoft.com/aspnet/core/security. The home page of the official ASP.NET Core documentation for all things security-related.

B.5 ASP.NET Core GitHub repositories

ASP.NET Core is entirely open-source and developed on GitHub. One of the best ways I've found to learn about the framework is to browse the source code itself. This section contains the main repositories for ASP.NET Core, .NET 7, and EF Core:

- .NET Foundation, "ASP.NET Core," https://github.com/dotnet/aspnetcore. The framework libraries that make up ASP.NET Core.
- .NET Foundation, "Entity Framework Core," https://github.com/dotnet/ efcore. The EF Core library.

- .NET Foundation, ".NET Runtime," https://github.com/dotnet/runtime. The .NET CoreCLR runtime and BCL libraries, as well as extension libraries.
- .NET Foundation, ".NET SDK and CLI," https://github.com/dotnet/sdk. The .NET command-line interface (CLI), assets for building the .NET SDK, and project templates.
- .NET Foundation, "Docker image for .NET," https://github.com/dotnet/dotnet-docker. The Dockerfile definitions for the official .NET Docker images.

B.6   Tooling and services

This section contains links to tools and services you can use to build ASP.NET Core projects:

- .NET SDK—https://dotnet.microsoft.com/download
- Cloudflare, a global content delivery network you can use to add caching and HTTPS to your applications for free—https://www.cloudflare.com
- JetBrains Rider, a fast and powerful cross-platform .NET IDE—https://www.jetbrains.com/rider
- Let's Encrypt, a free, automated, and open certificate authority you can use it to obtain free Secure Sockets Layer (SSL) certificates to secure your application—https://letsencrypt.org
- Muhammed Rehan Saeed's .NET Boxed, a comprehensive collection of templates to get started with ASP.NET Core, preconfigured with many best practices—https://github.com/Dotnet-Boxed/Templates
- Visual Studio, Visual Studio for Mac and Visual Studio Code—https://visualstudio.microsoft.com

B.7   ASP.NET Core blogs

This section contains blogs that focus on ASP.NET Core. Whether you're trying to get an overview of a general topic or trying to solve a specific problem, it can be useful to have multiple viewpoints on a topic:

- Khalid Abuhakmeh, *Abuhakmeh*, https://khalidabuhakmeh.com. A wide variety of posts by Khalid, focused on .NET and software development in general.
- Chris Alcock, *The Morning Brew*, https://blog.cwa.me.uk. A collection of .NET-related blog posts, curated daily.
- Damien Boden, *Software Engineering*, https://damienbod.com. An excellent blog by Microsoft MVP Damien Boden on ASP.NET Core, with lots of posts about ASP.NET Core with Angular.
- Mike Brind, *Mikesdotnetting*, https://www.mikesdotnetting.com. Brind has many posts on ASP.NET Core, especially focused on ASP.NET Core Razor Pages.
- Steve Gordon, *Steve Gordon—Code with Steve*, https://www.stevejgordon.co.uk. Personal blog of Steve Gordon, focused on .NET and often focused on writing high-performance code with .NET.

- Scott Hanselman, *Scott Hanselman*, https://www.hanselman.com/blog. Renowned speaker Scott Hanselman's personal blog, a highly diverse blog focused predominantly on .NET.
- Andrew Lock, *.NET Escapades*, https://andrewlock.net. My personal blog, focused on ASP.NET Core.
- Microsoft .NET Team, *.NET Blog*, https://blogs.msdn.microsoft.com/dotnet. The .NET team's blog, with lots of great links.
- David Pine, *IEvangelist*, https://davidpine.net. Personal blog of David Pine, with lots of posts on ASP.NET Core.
- Muhammed Rehan Saeed, *Muhammed Rehan Saeed*, https://rehansaeed.com. Personal blog of Muhammad Rehan Saeed, Microsoft MVP and author of the .NET Boxed project.
- Rick Strahl, *Rick Strahl's Weblog*, https://weblog.west-wind.com. Excellent blog by Microsoft MVP Rick Strahl covering a wide variety of ASP.NET Core topics.
- Filip W., *StrathWeb*, https://www.strathweb.com. Lots of posts on ASP.NET Core and ASP.NET by Filip, a Microsoft MVP and prolific open-source contributor.

B.8   Video links

If you prefer video for learning a subject, I recommend checking out the links in this section. In particular, the ASP.NET Core community standup provides great insight into the changes you'll see in future ASP.NET Core versions, straight from the team building the framework:

- Microsoft, ".NET Conf 2022," YouTube video playlist (November 15, 2022), http://mng.bz/8r4Z. All the sessions from the .NET Conf 2022 online conference announcing .NET 7.
- .NET Foundation, ".NET Community Standup," https://live.asp.net. Weekly videos with the ASP.NET Core team discussing development of the framework; includes standups with the .NET team, the Xamarin team, and the EF Core team.
- Immo Landwerth, ".NET Standard—Introduction," YouTube video (November 28, 2016), http://mng.bz/Vd0P. The first video in an excellent series on .NET standard.
- Steve Gordon, "Integration Testing ASP.NET Core Applications: Best Practices," Pluralsight course, 3:25 hours (July 15, 2020), http://mng.bz/A09z. One of several courses from Steve Gordon providing guidance and advice on building ASP.NET Core applications.
- Nick Chapsas, "Nick Chapsas", YouTube channel (November 14, 2022), http://mng.bz/pPp5. The YouTube channel of Nick Chapsas, posting many videos about .NET and ASP.NET Core.

index

RELATED MANNING TITLES

Pro ASP.NET Core 7, Tenth Edition
by Adam Freeman

ISBN 9781633437821
1256 pages *(estimated)*, $69.99
August 2023 *(estimated)*

Building Web APIs with ASP.NET Core
by Valerio De Sanctis

ISBN 9781633439481
472 pages, $59.99
April 2023

Essential TypeScript 5, Third Edition
by Adam Freeman

ISBN 9781633437319
550 pages *(estimated)*, $59.99
August 2023 *(estimated)*

.NET MAUI in Action
by Matt Goldman
Foreword by Kym Phillpotts

ISBN 9781633439405
456 pages, $59.99
July 2023

For ordering information go to www.manning.com

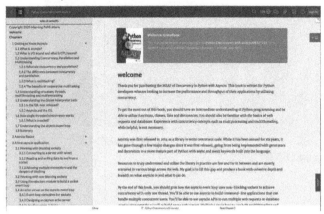

A new online reading experience

liveBook, our online reading platform, adds a new dimension to your Manning books, with features that make reading, learning, and sharing easier than ever. A liveBook version of your book is included FREE with every Manning book.

This next generation book platform is more than an online reader. It's packed with unique features to upgrade and enhance your learning experience.

- Add your own notes and bookmarks
- One-click code copy
- Learn from other readers in the discussion forum
- Audio recordings and interactive exercises
- Read all your purchased Manning content in any browser, anytime, anywhere

As an added bonus, you can search every Manning book and video in liveBook—even ones you don't yet own. Open any liveBook, and you'll be able to browse the content and read anything you like.*

Find out more at www.manning.com/livebook-program.

*Open reading is limited to 10 minutes per book daily